Political Theory

Classic Writings, Contemporary Views

POLITICAL THEORY

Classic Writings, Contemporary Views

Edited by

Joseph Losco
Ball State University

Leonard Williams
Manchester College

St. Martin's Press, New York

Senior editor: Don Reisman
Project management: Omega Publishing Services, Inc.
Cover design: Doug Steele

For information, write:
St. Martin's Press, Inc.
175 Fifth Avenue
New York, NY 10010

ISBN: 0-312-04693-6

For Marcia and Michael
(J.L.)

For Deborah, Christopher, and Jason
(L.W.)

Preface

Like most texts, *Political Theory: Classic Writings, Contemporary Views* was inspired by a perceived need. Until now, political theory instructors could choose among a number of ultimately unsatisfactory options. They could, for example, exclusively use primary readings by the classic political theorists. Doing so meant, however, that students had to purchase as many as a dozen texts in order to cover major theorists. A reader containing abridged selections did not resolve this problem; most have not been sufficiently inclusive to use in a survey course covering a wide array of Western thinkers from antiquity to the present.

Relying on commentaries by contemporary scholars is another option for the teacher of political theory. Commentaries treat a large number of theorists in a short span of time, and they provide students with useful insights about interpreting classic texts. Yet, many teachers of political theory believe that students who read commentaries without encountering the texts themselves are somehow being cheated in their educations. Students should be free to develop firsthand evaluations of the works of political philosophers, no matter how useful commentaries may be in placing those works in social and historical contexts.

One final option has been to structure courses in political theory around topical treatments of the perennial issues in political philosophy. Such treatments introduce students to discussions about the nature of politics or freedom or justice, and then suggest ways in which the classic thinkers have illuminated our understanding of the perennial questions. For the most part, however, this approach provides a very limited analytical framework, a framework usually reflecting only the perspective of the individual instructor or text.

We believe that this volume brings together the best features of each of the above approaches, while minimizing their liabilities. First, it provides extensive excerpts from classic texts for students to confront directly. The thinkers presented extend from Plato to Habermas, allowing instructors to pick and choose from a significant range of political theorists. Second, we have chosen commentaries that present a variety of viewpoints from which to evaluate the tradition of Western political thought. These commentaries, representing a high degree of both scholarship and accessibility, raise important issues for students concerned about the relevance of classic writings to contemporary political problems. Finally, because we know some students will find that this material requires an intellectual stretch, we have provided a few helpful pedagogical tools. **Introductory sections** in each chapter enable students to understand the life and times, as well as major theoretical contributions, of the various political philosophers we treat in the book. These introductions also provide a **short glossary of key words** and a **brief list of recommended readings.**

Our experience in teaching this text (in manuscript form) has confirmed our hunches about the validity of this eclectic approach to teaching political theory. Students genuinely appreciate the introductory sections, which give them a sense of what to look for in both the classic texts and the commentaries. Our students have also found their understanding of the classics to be aided by seeing how contemporary theorists approach those works, by observing how scholars do political theory. With this text, classroom discussions are more informed and useful, and students receive a more well-rounded and balanced view of political theory as an enterprise.

We appreciate the help and encouragement we have received in producing this volume. We would like to thank those instructors who have reviewed this manuscript in various stages of its development. These include Regis J. Amann, Golden Gate University; Christine Di Stefano, University of Washington, Seattle; Eldon J. Eisenach, University of Tulsa; Larry Elowitz, Georgia College; William J. Meyer, University of Michigan, Flint; and Robert O. Schneider, Pembroke State University. Their suggestions were enormously helpful; where possible, we have incorporated their insights in the final manuscript. We would like to thank the authors (and their publishers) who have permitted us to reproduce their work, so that others may learn from them, as we have. Thanks also to the many political theorists who have found the idea of this volume so exciting. We especially want to thank St. Martin's Press; our patient and supportive editor, Don Reisman, and his assistants, Margie Mahrdt and Frances Jones; and Richard Wright of Omega Publishing Services.

Finally, we wish to thank our respective departments at Ball State University and Manchester College. The support staff at these institutions has made the difficult tasks of manuscript development and editing, let alone managing mountains of paper, a great deal easier. Particular thanks go to Sharon Hinkley, Stephanie Thomas, and Ann Sims, at Ball State; and to Pat Weller, Greg Engels, Heather Schilling, Bob Faust, and Mark Neher, at Manchester. Heartfelt thanks also to our many colleagues and friends, teachers and mentors, as well as our families, for their selfless support and nurturance.

Contents

Introduction

This book introduces undergraduate students of political science, philosophy, and other disciplines to the history of Western political thought and the enterprise of political theory. In the last two decades or so, interest in political theory has increased greatly among both undergraduate and graduate students of political science and philosophy.

Read discussions of contemporary developments in any newspaper, watch political events transpire on television, and then think about their meaning. You will quickly see that the questions raised in political theory courses are among the most enduring and compelling issues that any person faces anywhere on the globe. Consider the following questions, for example:

1. What is human nature, and how does it influence political life?
2. What do people mean by such concepts as *freedom, human rights, equality,* and *justice*?
3. Is there a *best* form of government? What are the sources of legitimate political authority?
4. Why, and under what conditions, should citizens obey the state? Is civil disobedience or even revolution ever justified?
5. How can a society's institutions and political life be changed for the better?[1]

Courses in political theory address just such important and perennial concerns. Such courses have always met, and will continue to meet, students' needs for intelligent reflection and guidance as they face the kind of extraordinary political change the world has witnessed in recent years.

---

1. See, for example, Larry Arnhart, *Political Questions: Political Philosophy from Plato to Rawls* (New York: Macmillan, 1987) and Glenn Tinder, *Political Thinking: The Perennial Questions,* fifth edition (New York: HarperCollins, 1991).

Most students will use this book in their only class in political theory. For all, such a class will likely be a new experience. Political science majors, for instance, have studied the structures and processes of American politics, those of other nations, and the complexities of the international political arena. Their education has largely focused on current issues, on institutional structures, or on empirical regularities in political behavior. Philosophy majors have had access to the history of Western (and perhaps Eastern) philosophy, covering the broad spectrum of philosophical thought from aesthetics to epistemology. Unfortunately, given the demands of sampling courses from many academic disciplines, it is likely that many students will find the study of political theory to be little more than an intellectual sideshow in a very busy educational carnival. Nevertheless, it is our hope that by presenting the works of some of the West's most prominent political thinkers, as well as commentaries showing the debates these thinkers continue to generate, most students will come to view political theory as a rich storehouse of ideas for evaluating enduring political concerns.

The Nature of Political Theory

What *is* political theory? What is it that political philosophers do?[2] Two prominent answers to these questions have been given by Leo Strauss and by Sheldon Wolin.[3] Strauss has suggested that political philosophy is essentially an effort devoted to gaining wisdom about the nature of human beings and politics. This effort involves finding one's way amid a conflict between the classics and modernity; between knowledge and opinion. Wolin, on the other hand, has argued that political theory is best conceived as reflective discourse on the meaning of the political. Essentially a perennial dialogue among philosophers, it highlights the relation between continuity and change in political life.

Two more recent views of theory echo and refine the ideas of Strauss and Wolin. Robert Fowler and Jeffrey Orenstein, for instance, suggest that political theory involves reflection on basic political concepts, the analysis of alternative views about human beings and politics, and the pursuit of normative truth about the nature of the best regime.[4] Dante Germino points to the ongoing nature of the theoretical enterprise when he characterizes political philosophy as a "conversation of many voices," a dialogue "between different orientations toward political reality as a whole."[5] Viewed in this way, political philosophy is both a critical and creative activity in which each generation participates in a continuous tradition, uniting present and past.

---

2. Though the term *theory* frequently has been applied to both normative and empirical studies, some political scientists reserve the term *philosophy* for studies of the former sort (e.g., what is the best regime?) and apply theory to the latter sort (e.g., what models best explain voter turnout?). Nonetheless, empirical theorists must make normative assumptions in generating explanatory models, and normative philosophers clearly must take empirical data into account in formulating defensible views. Therefore, for our purposes, we treat the terms *political theory* and *political philosophy* as more or less interchangeable.

3. Leo Strauss, *What is Political Philosophy?*, (Glencoe, Ill.: Free Press, 1959), pp. 10–12. Sheldon Wolin, *Politics and Vision,* (Boston: Little Brown, 1960), pp. 2–5.

4. Robert B. Fowler and Jeffrey Orenstein, *Contemporary Issues in Political Theory,* revised edition (New York: Praeger, 1985), p. 2.

5. Dante Germino, "The Contemporary Relevance of the Classics of Political Philosophy," in Fred Greenstein and Nelson Polsby, eds., *Handbook of Political Science,* vol. 1 (Reading, Mass.: Addison-Wesley, 1975), pp. 229–281.

Efforts to arrive at the essence of political theory (or any other enterprise) are notoriously unproductive. One reason for this is the wide variety of approaches to be found among those who study the history of political thought.[6] For instance, one may choose to study the theorist as a person with unique concerns and motivations (a biographical approach); or, one could approach the theories themselves—locating them in their cultural contexts, accounting for their conceptual development and change, and tracing complex patterns of their influence and impact (an historical approach). Still other approaches have focused on great problems or eternal questions presumed to face political thinkers, without regard to time or place (a perennial-issues approach).

In the face of these many ways of studying political theory, our general approach is to take a problem-solving orientation. We regard political theory as an effort to understand the meaning and significance of political life. Motivated by a given political or philosophical problem, one turns to the history of political theory (including contemporary political thought and political science); shows its importance or relevance to that problem; comments on the ideas offered by various theorists; and thereby, offers a solution to the problem, or at least claims to have illuminated it in some fashion.

We hasten to add, however, that we believe political philosophy is worthy of study in its own right, not merely because it has potential utility. As an enterprise which develops intellectual rigor, adds historical perspective, and provides a sense of identity for the heirs to its traditions, perhaps political philosophy needs no further justification. Moreover, we believe that political theory is not simply a body of authoritative texts (though it includes such authority), but also is the very process of thoughtful reflection about political life itself.

In this vein, John Nelson has offered a useful list of goals for the practice of political theory.[7] He argues that political theory's aims can be summarized as three C's: *comprehend, conserve,* and *criticize. Comprehend* refers to theory's twin goals of explanation and understanding. Theories provide a conceptual vocabulary for describing the important features of political life and their interrelations, as well as for accounting for prevailing forms and behaviors typically found in political practice. Simply put, political theory works to explore political phenomena by placing them in the context of human experience. *Conserve* connotes the role the historical study of political thought plays in preserving cultural tradition and heritage. *Criticize* suggests theory's substance and process. Substantively, theory's ultimate goal is to evaluate and assess both proposed and existing political orders. As a procedure, theory moves by the analysis and criticism of both theoretical arguments and political phenomena.

To Nelson's list, we would add a fourth C: *create.* Theory shapes the way we view politics and gives insights into the problems and opportunities presented by political life. It can either restrict our vision or broaden our horizons. At all times, theorists must be aware that they are not engaging in pure philosophy; not living in a rarefied atmosphere of complete abstraction. As Benjamin Barber has observed,

> politics remains something human beings *do,* not something they possess or use or watch or talk or think about. Those who would do something about it

---

6. Daniel Sabia, "Political Education and the History of Political Thought," *American Political Science Review* 78 (1984), pp. 985–999.

7. John Nelson, "Natures and Futures for Political Theory," in Nelson, ed., *What Should Political Theory Be Now?* (Albany: State University of New York Press, 1983), pp. 3–24.

must do more than philosophize, and philosophy that is politically intelligible must take full political measure of politics as conduct.[8]

Thus, theorists must be attuned to the political world, the world of praxis and action. They should pay attention to the practical implications of theories—the utopian visions which recommend specific political practices, behaviors, or orders.

Consensus on the essential definition of concepts such as *politics,* or of practices such as *political theory,* will likely elude our grasp forever. This does not mean, however, that conceptual definitions or political judgments are wholly subjective matters of whim or taste. Far from it. There are certain criteria good theories ought to meet, standards by which we can evaluate the political theories you will encounter in this book. We have in mind such criteria as logical consistency, breadth or comprehensiveness, clarity of thought and argument, insightfulness, and acceptable implications for political practice. No matter which criterion you choose, though, take the time to argue with the theorists in this book, with your classmates and your instructor, and even with yourself. Question others' assertions and assumptions, and be prepared to justify (offer good reasons for) your own.

Selecting Texts

This book attempts to blend the advantages of reading primary texts with the benefits of reading scholarly commentaries on a political philosopher's work. Thus, each unit contains an introduction to a philosopher (his or her life and major theoretical contributions), selected readings from his or her work, and commentaries illuminating critical aspects of his or her thought. Though our selections are consistent with the type and extent of difficulty encountered in most undergraduate theory courses, some of the readings undoubtedly will require students to stretch themselves intellectually. We have sought to assist this effort by summarizing key arguments and explaining key terms in our introductory essays.

An important question remaining to be addressed concerns how we selected the material presented here. In selecting both philosophers and representative texts, our goal has been to provide a comprehensive *introduction* to political theory, not a compendium of the world's political thought. We chose selections that represent the broad scope of the classics of Western political thought from Plato to the present day. These works are the subject of most of the teaching and commentary done by political theorists and philosophers today. They are works which have made singular contributions to our collective understanding of politics, works to which we return often seeking answers to questions about political life.

As such, this book of readings follows a well-established pattern for textbooks in the history of Western political thought. Frequently, however, textbook authors and editors have attempted to offer a single, overarching vision of the development of political theory. Theorists represented in the accepted canon of classic works are treated from the author's unique perspective. Though we reject the idea that each theorist plays a specific role in a grand drama, we do believe that each has made a distinctive and indispensable contribution to understanding politics.

Clearly, we cannot include the writings of everyone who has had anything of interest to say about politics. Many works of classic or near-classic status simply had

---

8. Benjamin Barber, *The Conquest of Politics: Liberal Philosophy in Democratic Times* (Princeton, N.J.: Princeton University Press, 1988), p. 11.

to be left aside. For instance, we have not felt competent enough to include material expressing the unique insights of Asian, African, or Middle Eastern political thought. Our own philosophical tastes and relative levels of ignorance may result in some taking us to task. However, a more difficult problem with selection emerges from the nature of political theory itself.

Like other theoretical and historical writing, and like political practice, political theory uses largely male terms. Many works of political theory say nothing about women, or if they do, what they have to say is dismissive, derogatory, and sexist. We do not share such sentiments, but have found it difficult to overcome the limitations of political theory both as a scholarly community and and as an intellectual enterprise.[9] The writers that have been accorded classic status are virtually all male; they have all emerged from the conventionally male preserve of politics; and they have all employed non-inclusive language to talk about political life.

Yet, such figures remain the writers to which contemporary theorists of both sexes turn when certain questions (concerning, for example, the nature of politics, the means and ends of power, and the content of rights and duties) are asked. Critics of "the tradition" should learn about it, if only to use what is valuable and jettison what is no longer useful. In doing so, such critics are performing the same critical task political theorists have historically performed for themselves and their societies.

For each of the chosen philosophers, we based our selection of the commentaries on the following considerations: (1) We sought to provide commentaries on some important ideas or controversies associated with the philosopher under study, especially where the concepts advanced are rather murky. So, for example, the commentaries on Jean-Jacques Rousseau explore his views on the "general will" and the role of the "legislator"—two elusive, yet vital elements of his thought. (2) The commentaries (with few exceptions) do not confront each other with differing interpretations of a given political theorist. We have found many of the so-called debates found in some textbooks to be rather artificial and contrived; thus, they frequently shed more heat than light. (3) We believe that the commentaries we have chosen represent significant recent scholarship in political theory. In this way, students may get a sense of the current state of the field. However, when we felt that earlier commentaries were superior in illuminating key ideas or controversies, currency took a back seat. (4) Finally, we tried to include commentaries that would be within the grasp of the average student of political theory.

Thus, the readings we have selected for this volume are a mix of classic writings and contemporary views. We believe this mix will acquaint you with the writings of a representative set of political theorists; provide you with contemporary analyses and interpretations of those works; and raise the major issues, questions, or problems associated with a particular theorist's contributions to understanding the nature and significance of political life. We hope to stimulate your interest so that you will read further in and about the theorists we do present, as well as the many thinkers we have been forced (through limits imposed by convention, space, and time) to omit from this collection.

In short, this book is not a road atlas providing detailed directions to every theoretical city of consequence. Instead, it is a guidebook offering some useful perspectives on places of potential interest to you. Of course, keep in mind that a

---

9. For a discussion of the limits of political theory, see Judith Evans, Jill Hills, Karen Hunt, Elizabeth Meehan, Tessa ten Tusscher, Ursula Vogel, and Georgina Waylen, *Feminism and Political Theory* (London: Sage, 1986), especially chapters 1 and 6.

guidebook is no substitute for going to those places yourself. Treat the selections critically, and use them to blaze your own trails in the forests of political thought.

For Further Reading

Arnhart, L. 1987. *Political Questions: Political Philosophy from Plato to Rawls.* New York: Macmillan.

Fowler, R.B. and J. Orenstein. 1985. *Contemporary Issues in Political Theory,* rev. ed. New York: Praeger.

Gunnell, J. 1983. "Political Theory." In *Political Science: The State of the Discipline,* ed. A. Finifter, pp. 3–45 Washington, D.C.: American Political Science Association.

McDonald, L.C. 1968. *Western Political Theory.* New York: Harcourt Brace Jovanovich.

Nelson, J., ed. 1983. *What Should Political Theory Be Now?* Albany: State University of New York Press.

Redhead, B., ed. 1984. *Political Thought from Plato to NATO.* Chicago: Dorsey Press.

Skinner, Q., ed. 1985. *The Return of Grand Theory in the Human Sciences.* Cambridge: Cambridge University Press.

Spragens, T. 1976. *Understanding Political Theory.* New York: St. Martin's Press.

Plato

If, as Cicero claims, it was Socrates who "called down philosophy from the skies," then it was Plato who summoned humans to respect philosophy as their earthly guide. The name of Plato equates with the onset of political philosophy, for it was Plato, in the West, who advocated the study of politics with the same devotion and rigor used by physicians to investigate the health of the body. While many of Plato's ideas seem anachronistic in modern society, we must remember it was Plato who laid the groundwork for future discussions of politics by pointing to the importance of ideas like justice and prudence, and by generating the very vocabulary of political discourse we use to this day.

Plato was born in Athens in approximately 420 B.C.E.[1] of a wealthy and noble family. While few of the details of his life are certain, we know that he grew up during the final stages of the Peloponnesian War, the great war between the rival factions of Athens and Sparta; that he probably never married; that he traveled widely, especially in Egypt and Sicily; that he founded a school known as the Academy; and, that he was greatly influenced by the teachings of his master, Socrates. Plato died in 347 B.C.E. at about the age of eighty-one.

We know even less about Socrates, since Socrates did not record his own philosophy. Much of what we know of Socrates comes from the works of his pupil,

---

1. Throughout this book, dates before the Common Era will be so marked; unmarked dates can be assumed to be in the Common Era unless clearly established otherwise. This notation seems preferable to the sectarian B.C. and A.D.

whose portrayal no doubt idealizes him, and by some of his critics, like Aristophanes, who ridiculed him. The latter, for example, portrays Socrates in his *Clouds,* as an unwashed vagrant, constantly provoking argument through incessant and useless questioning. A group of itinerant teachers, known as sophists, came to regard Socrates' questioning as particularly bothersome. They argued that terms such as morality and justice were hopelessly subjective and used by leaders merely to attain their own selfish ends. As a result, they specialized in training young well-to-do boys how to use rhetoric in manipulating others. Socrates, on the other hand (at least the Socrates we know through Plato), insisted that objective standards could be set for morality and justice through philosophic reflection, and that neither the good of the city nor the health of the soul could be attained without practicing these virtues. Socrates was eventually accused of impiety, not paying proper respect to the gods, and convicted by a democratic court. Much of Plato's work may be read as a vindication of the Socratic position that philosophy is the highest form of human activity that survives even the death of the philosopher. Plato's school, the Academy, stood as a testament to this truth.

Among the most significant political works of Plato are *The Republic,* the *Statesman,* and the *Laws.* He wrote them in the form of dialogues, partly in an attempt to capture the liveliness of philosophy as practiced by his tutor. This form exemplifies the Socratic dialectic, a manner of argumentation that begins by investigating a commonly held opinion and proceeds to illustrate its flaws and virtues by subjecting it to rigorous questioning. New truths about the original proposition that are realized in this way are then subjected to a new round of questioning, and so on.

While Plato was among the first thinkers to investigate politics in a philosophic manner, the true goal of philosophy, as he saw it, was to understand the good to which a particular political concept such as justice is related as a part to the whole. The Platonic cosmology (one not shared by Socrates) divided the world into two realms, the realm of ideas or forms and the realm of those things that come into being and pass away (what we might today call the material world). For Plato, the realm of ideas was the perfection and cause of those things that the ideas represented. For example, the idea of chair is in some way prior to and "more real" than any particular chair, since the material object is transitory and owes its origin to a thought that must have existed prior to the time any particular worker manufactured chairs. Future thinkers, such as Aristotle, attacked this theory of forms. Nevertheless, Plato held that justice, like the good, was an ideal or form, the content of which could be investigated philosophically, and at least partially realized through the skill of the good ruler in the actual *polis,* or city.

The Republic

The subject of *The Republic* is justice. The format is the dialogue. Socrates agrees to accompany a group of Athenians to the house of Polymarchus where a discussion commences with his host, his host's father, Cephalus, the Sophist Thrasymachus, the young Glaucon and Adeimantus, and several others regarding the proper definition of justice. In the process of discussion, Socrates agrees to "save" the reputation of justice attacked by Thrasymachus and others by showing its true nature. His approach is to make a comparison between the individual soul and a city, arguing that if justice could be identified in the larger unit, the city, it would be easier to find in the soul.

As discussion continues, Socrates engages Glaucon and Adeimantus in the creation of an imaginary utopian city wherein justice might be found. This is a city with three classes: the wise rulers, the courageous warriors or guardians, and the skillful artisans and merchants. The parts of the city are analogous to the parts of the soul. That part of the soul that desires material objects is the counterpart to the moneymaking class; the spirited part that experiences intense passion, such as anger, is the counterpart of the guardian class; and reason corresponds to the city's ruling class. The principle of justice applicable to both city and soul is that justice requires each part to mind its own business; that is, each part must play its own role and not attempt to perform the function of other parts. Just as the wise rulers must lead the other classes in the city, so too must reason lead the other parts of the soul to insure harmony and happiness. The search for justice in the city is complete with the assertion that the good city can only come into being if the truly wise rule. Plato's "allegory of the cave," in which the philosopher comes to recognize that the world of material objects generally thought to be real is only the dim reflection of the sun's rays on the walls of the cave that houses the residents of the *polis,* crystallizes the scope and gravity of this proposal.

We present four passages from *The Republic.* In the first excerpt, taken from Book I, Socrates confronts Thrasymachus' assertion that justice is the advantage of the stronger. In this selection, demonstrating the Socratic dialectic, Socrates maneuvers the argument in a direction that elicits important concessions from Thrasymachus and ultimately undermines the sophist's entire position. The second passage is from Book IV. There, Socrates and his interlocutors search for the virtues in their newly created city, a search that ends with a new definition of justice. In the third selection, from Book V, Socrates makes his boldest proposal for the governance of the good city: rule by the philosopher king. The passage explores some of the reasons why this was considered such an unconventional proposal and sheds light on the nature of philosophy itself. Finally, Socrates summarizes his teaching about the good city in a selection from Book VII. In his "allegory of the cave," Socrates hopes to convince Glaucon and Adeimantus of the necessity of having philosophers rule.

Commentaries

In the following commentaries, Dale Hall attacks the influential interpretation that Plato's Utopian City in *The Republic* is meant to illustrate the "limits of politics" generally, and the impossibility of Plato's perfectly good *polis* in particular. Central to his attack is the contention that the analogy between the soul and the city entertained in *The Republic* is genuine and not meant to be ironic. The philosopher uses reason to harmonize the desirous and spirited part of his own nature and applies these principles in ruling the populace. Allan Bloom responds to Hall's criticism by suggesting that there is irony in Socrates' utopian scheme and that the very suggestion that philosophers rule (i.e., mind the business of others) violates the strict standard of justice (minding one's own business) advanced by Plato. Bloom believes that Plato is really suggesting that the ideal political regime is hopelessly unattainable.

The debate over the proper interpretation of *The Republic* contained in these readings illustrates a broader debate regarding the proper reading of political philosophy. While Bloom calls for strict adherence to textual material, Hall suggests that proper interpretation requires greater attention to historical and social factors as well.

Keywords

Ecclesiazusae. Comedy by Aristophanes about 391 B.C.E. in which Athens is reformed in the direction of extreme democracy.

Eudaimonia. Happiness. Considered as an objective state of well-being.

Kallipolis. The fair or beautiful city. This is the city of speech Socrates builds with Glaucon and Adeimantus.

Paideia. Education.

Phylakes. Guardians; the class of citizens Socrates trains to protect the good city.

Physis. Nature; used in contrast with convention.

Polis. The Greek word for city. *Polis* connotes much more than physical place; it represents a close association of citizens bound by common aims and lifestyles.

Psychai. Souls; the essence of self which Socrates characterizes by a three-part division into rational, spirited, and desirous elements.

Virtue. The excellence of a thing or person. Four virtues that characterized the Athenian citizen were wisdom, moderation, courage, and justice.

For Further Reading

Barker, E. 1918. *Greek Political Theory: Plato and His Predecessors.* London: Methuen.

Bloom, A. 1968. *The Republic Of Plato.* Translated with Notes and An Interpretive Essay. New York: Basic Books.

Hall, R.W. 1981. *Plato.* London: Allen & Unwin.

Hare, R.M. 1982. *Plato.* New York: Oxford University Press.

Strauss, L. 1964. *The City and Man.* Chicago: Rand McNally.

Taylor, A.E. 1960. *The Mind of Plato.* Ann Arbor: University of Michigan Press.

The Republic

Book I

[Socrates:] . . . "As it is, Thrasymachus, you see that—still considering what 345 c
went before—after you had first defined the true doctor, you later thought it
no longer necessary to keep a precise guard over the true shepherd. Rather
you think that he, insofar as he is a shepherd, fattens the sheep, not looking
to what is best for the sheep, but, like a guest who is going to be feasted, to d
good cheer, or in turn, to the sale, like a money-maker and not a shepherd.
The shepherd's art surely cares for nothing but providing the best for what
it has been set over. For that the art's own affairs be in the best possible way
is surely adequately provided for so long as it lacks nothing of being the
shepherd's art. And, similarly, I for my part thought just now that it is
necessary for us to agree that every kind of rule, insofar as it is rule,
considers what is best for nothing other than for what is ruled and cared for, e
both in political and private rule. Do you think that the rulers in the cities,
those who truly rule, rule willingly?"

[Thrasymachus:] "By Zeus, I don't think it," he said. "I know it well."

"But, Thrasymachus," I said, "what about the other kinds of rule? Don't
you notice that no one wishes to rule voluntarily, but they demand wages as
though the benefit from ruling were not for them but for those who are 346 a
ruled? Now tell me this much: don't we, at all events, always say that each
of the arts is different on the basis of having a different capacity? And don't
answer contrary to your opinion, you blessed man, so that we can reach a
conclusion."

"Yes," he said, "this is the way they differ."

"And does each of them provide us with some peculiar benefit and not a
common one, as the medical art furnishes us with health, the pilot's art with
safety in sailing, and so forth with the others?"

"Certainly."

"And does the wage-earner's art furnish wages? For this is its power. Or b
do you call the medical art the same as the pilot's art? Or, if you wish to
make precise distinctions according to the principle you set down, even if a
man who is a pilot becomes healthy because sailing on the sea is advantageous to him, nonetheless you don't for that reason call what he does the
medical art?"

"Surely not," he said.

"Nor do you, I suppose, call the wage-earner's art the medical art, even if 346 b
a man who is earning wages should be healthy?"

"Surely not," he said.

"And, what about this? Do you call the medical art the wage-earner's art,
even if a man practicing medicine should earn wages?"

346 c   He said that he did not.

"And we did agree that the benefit of each art is peculiar?"

"Let it be," he said.

"Then whatever benefit all the craftsmen derive in common is plainly derived from their additional use of some one common thing that is the same for all."

"It seems so," he said.

"And we say that the benefit the craftsmen derive from receiving wages comes to them from their use of the wage-earner's art in addition."

He assented with resistance.

d   "Then this benefit, getting wages, is for each not a result of his own art; but, if it must be considered precisely, the medical art produces health, and the wage-earner's art wages; the housebuilder's art produces a house and the wage-earner's art, following upon it, wages; and so it is with all the others: each accomplishes its own work and benefits that which it has been set over. And if pay were not attached to it, would the craftsman derive benefit from the art?"

e   "It doesn't look like it," he said.

"Does he then produce no benefit when he works for nothing?"

"I suppose he does."

"Therefore, Thrasymachus, it is plain by now that no art or kind of rule provides for its own benefit, but, as we have been saying all along, it provides for and commands the one who is ruled, considering his advantage—that of the weaker—and not that of the stronger. It is for just this reason, my dear Thrasymachus, that I said a moment ago that no one willingly chooses to rule and get mixed up in straightening out other people's troubles; but he

347 a   asks for wages, because the man who is to do anything fine by art never does what is best for himself nor does he command it, insofar as he is commanding by art, but rather what is best for the man who is ruled. It is for just this reason, as it seems, that there must be wages for those who are going to be willing to rule—either money, or honor, or a penalty if he should not rule."

"What do you mean by that, Socrates?" said Glaucon. "The first two kinds of wages I know, but I don't understand what penalty you mean and how you can say it is a kind of wage."

b   "Then you don't understand the wages of the best men," I said, "on account of which the most decent men rule, when they are willing to rule. Or don't you know that love of honor and love of money are said to be, and are, reproaches?"

"I do indeed," he said.

"For this reason, therefore," I said, "the good aren't willing to rule for the sake of money or honor. For they don't wish openly to exact wages for ruling and get called hirelings, nor on their own secretly to take a profit from their ruling and get called thieves. Nor, again, will they rule for the sake of honor.

c   For they are not lovers of honor. Hence, necessity and a penalty must be there in addition for them, if they are going to be willing to rule—it is likely that this is the source of its being held to be shameful to seek to rule and not to await necessity—and the greatest of penalties is being ruled by a worse man if one is not willing to rule oneself. It is because they fear this, in my view, that decent men rule, when they do rule; and at that time they proceed to enter on rule, not as though they were going to something good, or as

though they were going to be well off in it; but they enter on it as a necessity   347 d
and because they have no one better than or like themselves to whom to turn
it over. For it is likely that if a city of good men came to be, there would be
a fight over not ruling, just as there is now over ruling; and there it would
become manifest that a true ruler really does not naturally consider his own
advantage but rather that of the one who is ruled. Thus everyone who knows
would choose to be benefited by another rather than to take the trouble of
benefiting another. So I can in no way agree with Thrasymachus that the just
is the advantage of the stronger. But this we shall consider again at another   e
time. What Thrasymachus now says is in my own opinion a far bigger
thing—he asserts that the life of the unjust man is stronger than that of the
just man. Which do you choose, Glaucon," I said, "and which speech is truer
in your opinion?"

"I for my part choose the life of the just man as more profitable."

"Did you hear," I said, "how many good things Thrasymachus listed a   348 a
moment ago as belonging to the life of the unjust man?"

"I heard," he said, "but I'm not persuaded."

"Then do you want us to persuade him, if we're able to find a way, that
what he says isn't true?"

"How could I not want it?" he said.

"Now," I said, "if we should speak at length against him, setting speech
against speech, telling how many good things belong to being just, and then
he should speak in return, and we again, there'll be need of counting the
good things and measuring how many each of us has in each speech, and   b
then we'll be in need of some sort of judges who will decide. But if we
consider just as we did a moment ago, coming to agreement with one
another, we'll ourselves be both judges and pleaders at once."

"Most certainly," he said.

"Which way do you like?" I said.

"The latter," he said.

"Come now, Thrasymachus," I said, "answer us from the beginning. Do
you assert that perfect injustice is more profitable than justice when it is
perfect?"

"I most certainly do assert it," he said, "and I've said why."   c

"Well, then, how do you speak about them in this respect? Surely you call
one of them virtue and the other vice?"

"Of course."

"Then do you call justice virtue and injustice vice?"

"That's likely, you agreeable man," he said, "when I also say that injustice
is profitable and justice isn't."

"What then?"

"The opposite," he said.

"Is justice then vice?"

"No, but very high-minded innocence."

"Do you call injustice corruption?"   d

"No, rather good counsel."

"Are the unjust in your opinion good as well as prudent, Thrasymachus?"

"Yes, those who can do injustice perfectly," he said "and are able to
subjugate cities and tribes of men to themselves. You, perhaps, suppose I am
speaking of cutpurses. Now, such things, too, are profitable," he said, "when

348 d   one gets away with them; but they aren't worth mentioning compared to those I was just talking about."

e   "As to that," I said, "I'm not unaware of what you want to say. But I wondered about what went before, that you put injustice in the camp of virtue and wisdom, and justice among their opposites?"

"But I do indeed set them down as such."

"That's already something more solid, my comrade," I said, "and it's no longer easy to know what one should say. For if you had set injustice down as profitable but had nevertheless agreed that it is viciousness or shameful, as do some others, we would have something to say, speaking according to customary usage. But as it is, plainly you'll say that injustice is fair and mighty, and, since you also dared to set it down in the camp of virtue and

349 a   wisdom, you'll set down to its account all the other things which we used to set down as belonging to the just."

"Your divination is very true," he said.

"But nonetheless," I said, "one oughtn't to hesitate to pursue the consideration of the argument as long as I understand you to say what you think. For, Thrasymachus, you seem really not to be joking now, but to be speaking the truth as it seems to you."

"And what difference does it make to you," he said, "whether it seems so to me or not, and why don't you refute the argument?"

b   "No difference," I said. "But try to answer this in addition to the other things: in your opinion would the just man want to get the better of the just man in anything?"

"Not at all," he said. "Otherwise he wouldn't be the urbane innocent he actually is."

"And what about this: would he want to get the better of the just action?"

"Not even of the just action," he said.

"And does he claim he deserves to get the better of the unjust man, and believe it to be just, or would he not believe it to be so?"

"He'd believe it to be just," he said, "and he'd claim he deserves to get the better, but he wouldn't be able to."

c   "That," I said, "is not what I am asking, but whether the just man wants, and claims he deserves, to get the better of the unjust and not of the just man?"

"He does," he said.

"And what about the unjust man? Does he claim he deserves to get the better of the just man and the just action?"

"How could it be otherwise," he said, "since he claims he deserves to get the better of everyone?"

"Then will the unjust man also get the better of the unjust human being and action, and will he struggle to take most of all for himself?"

"That's it."

"Let us say it, then, as follows," I said, "the just man does not get the

d   better of what is like but of what is unlike, while the unjust man gets the better of like and unlike?"

"What you said is very good," he said.

"And," I said, "is the unjust man both prudent and good, while the just man is neither?"

"That's good too," he said.

"Then," I said, "is the unjust man also like the prudent and the good,   349 d
while the just man is not like them?"

"How," he said, "could he not be like such men, since he is such as they,
while the other is not like them."

"Fine. Then is each of them such as those to whom he is like?"

"What else could they be?" he said.

"All right, Thrasymachus. Do you say that one man is musical and that   e
another is unmusical?"

"I do."

"Which is prudent and which thoughtless?"

"Surely the musical man is prudent and the unmusical man thoughtless."

"Then, in the things in which he is prudent, is he also good, and in those
in which he is thoughtless, bad?"

"Yes."

"And what about a medical man? Is it not the same with him?"   350 a

"It is the same."

"Then, you best of men, is any musical man who is tuning a lyre in your
opinion willing to get the better of another musical man in tightening and
relaxing the strings, or does he claim he deserves more?"

"Not in my opinion."

"But the better of the unmusical man?"

"Necessarily," he said.

"And what about a medical man? On questions of food and drink, would
he want to get the better of a medical man or a medical action?"

"Surely not."

"But the better of what is not medical?"

"Yes."

"Now, for every kind of knowledge and lack of knowledge, see if in your
opinion any man at all who knows chooses voluntarily to say or do more
than another man who knows, and not the same as the man who is like
himself in the same action."

"Perhaps," he said, "it is necessarily so."   b

"And what about the ignorant man? Would he not get the better of both
the man who knows and the man who does not?"

"Perhaps."

"The man who knows is wise?"

"I say so."

"And the wise man is good?"

"I say so."

"Then the man who is both good and wise will not want to get the better
of the like, but of the unlike and opposite?"

"It seems so," he said.

"But the bad and unlearned will want to get the better of both the like and
the opposite?"

"It looks like it."

"Then, Thrasymachus," I said, "does our unjust man get the better of
both like and unlike? Weren't you saying that?"

"I was," he said.

"And the just man will not get the better of like but of unlike?"   c

"Yes."

350 c   "Then," I said, "the just man is like the wise and good, but the unjust man like the bad and unlearned."

"I'm afraid so."

"But we were also agreed that each is such as the one he is like."

"We were."

"Then the just man has revealed himself to us as good and wise, and the unjust man unlearned and bad."

d   Now, Thrasymachus did not agree to all of this so easily as I tell it now, but he dragged his feet and resisted, and he produced a wonderful quantity of sweat, for it was summer. And then I saw what I had not yet seen before—Thrasymachus blushing. At all events, when we had come to complete agreement about justice being virtue and wisdom, and injustice both vice and lack of learning, I said, "All right, let that be settled for us. . . ."

Book IV

[Socrates:] . . . "So then, son of Ariston," I said, "your city would now be 427 d founded. In the next place, get yourself an adequate light somewhere; and look yourself—and call in your brother and Polemarchus and the others— whether we can somehow see where the justice might be and where the injustice, in what they differ from one another, and which the man who's going to be happy must possess, whether it escapes the notice of all gods and humans or not."

e   "You're talking nonsense," said Glaucon. "You promised you would look for it because it's not holy for you not to bring help to justice in every way in your power."

"What you remind me of is true," I said, "and though I must do so, you too have to join in."

"We'll do so," he said.

"Now, then," I said, "I hope I'll find it in this way. I suppose our city—if, that is, it has been correctly founded—is perfectly good."

"Necessarily," he said.

"Plainly, then, it's wise, courageous, moderate and just."

"Plainly."

"Isn't it the case that whichever of them we happen to find will leave as the remainder what hasn't been found?"

428 a   "Of course."

"Therefore, just as with any other four things, if we were seeking any one of them in something or other and recognized it first, that would be enough for us; but if we recognized the other three first, this would also suffice for the recognition of the thing looked for. For plainly it couldn't be anything but what's left over."

"What you say is correct," he said.

"With these things too, since they happen to be four, mustn't we look for them in the same way?"

"Plainly."

b   "Well, it's wisdom, in my opinion, which first comes plainly to light in it. And something about it looks strange."

"What?" he said.

"The city we described is really wise, in my opinion. That's because it's of   428 b
good counsel, isn't it?"

"Yes."

"And further, this very thing, good counsel, is plainly a kind of knowledge. For it's surely not by lack of learning, but by knowledge, that men
counsel well."

"Plainly."

"But, on the other hand, there's much knowledge of all sorts in the city."

"Of course."

"Then, is it thanks to the carpenters' knowledge that the city must be
called wise and of good counsel?"

"Not at all," he said, "thanks to that it's called skilled in carpentry."   c

"Then, it's not thanks to the knowledge that counsels about how wooden
implements would be best that a city must be called wise."

"Surely not."

"And what about this? Is it thanks to the knowledge of bronze implements or any other knowledge of such things?"

"Not to any knowledge of the sort," he said.

"And not to the knowledge about the production of the crop from the
earth; for that, rather, it is called skilled in farming."

"That's my opinion."

"What about this?" I said. "Is there in the city we just founded a kind of
knowledge belonging to some of the citizens that counsels not about the   d
affairs connected with some particular thing in the city, but about how the
city as a whole would best deal with itself and the other cities?"

"There is indeed."

"What and in whom is it?" I said.

"It's the guardian's skill," he said, "and it's in those rulers whom we just
now named perfect guardians."

"Thanks to this knowledge, what do you call the city?"

"Of good counsel," he said, "and really wise."

"Then, do you suppose," I said, "that there will be more smiths in our city   e
than these true guardians?"

"Far more smiths," he said.

"Among those," I said, "who receive a special name for possessing some
kind of knowledge, wouldn't the guardians be the fewest of all in number?"

"By far."

"It is, therefore, from the smallest group and part of itself and the
knowledge in it, from the supervising and ruling part, that a city founded
according to nature would be wise as a whole. And this class, which prop-   429 a
erly has a share in that knowledge which alone among the various kinds of
knowledge ought to be called wisdom, has, as it seems, the fewest members
by nature."

"What you say," he said, "is very true."

"So we've found—I don't know how—this one of the four, both it and
where its seat in the city is."

"In my opinion, at least," he said, "it has been satisfactorily discovered."

"And, next, courage, both itself as well as where it's situated in the
city—that courage thanks to which the city must be called courageous—isn't
very hard to see."

429 a   "How's that?"

b   "Who," I said, "would say a city is cowardly or courageous while looking to any part other than the one that defends it and takes the field on its behalf?"

"There's no one," he said, "who would look to anything else."

"I don't suppose," I said, "that whether the other men in it are cowardly or courageous would be decisive for its being this or that."

"No, it wouldn't."

c   "So a city is also courageous by a part of itself, thanks to that part's having in it a power that through everything will preserve the opinion about which things are terrible—that they are the same ones and of the same sort as those the lawgiver transmitted in the education. Or don't you call that courage?"

"I didn't quite understand what you said," he said. "Say it again."

"I mean," I said, "that courage is a certain kind of preserving."

"Just what sort of preserving?"

"The preserving of the opinion produced by law through education about what—and what sort of thing—is terrible. And by preserving through d everything I meant preserving that opinion and not casting it out in pains and pleasures and desires and fears. If you wish I'm willing to compare it to what I think it's like."

"But I do wish."

"Don't you know," I said, "that the dyers, when they want to dye wool purple, first choose from all the colors the single nature belonging to white things; then they prepare it beforehand and care for it with no little e preparation so that it will most receive the color; and it is only then that they dye? And if a thing is dyed in this way, it becomes colorfast, and washing either without lyes or with lyes can't take away its color. But those things that are not so dyed—whether one dyes other colors or this one without preparatory care—you know what they become like."

"I do know," he said, "that they're washed out and ridiculous."

"Hence," I said, "take it that we too were, to the extent of our power, do-430 a ing something similar when we selected the soldiers and educated them in music and gymnastic. Don't think we devised all that for any other purpose than that—persuaded by the laws—they should receive them from us in the finest possible way like a dye, so that their opinion about what's terrible and about everything else would be colorfast because they had gotten the proper nature and rearing, and their dye could not be washed out by those lyes so terribly effective at scouring, pleasure—more terribly effective for this than b any Chalestrean soda [1] and alkali; and pain, fear, and desire—worse than any other lye. This kind of power and preservation, through everything, of the right and lawful opinion about what is terrible and what not, I call courage; and so I set it down, unless you say something else."

"But I don't say anything else," he said. "For, in my opinion, you regard the right opinion about these same things that comes to be without education—that found in beasts and slaves—as not at all lawful and call it something other than courage."

---

1. Chalestra was a town on the Thermaic Gulf in Macedonia. In a nearby lake there was carbonate of soda used in washing [Bloom].

"What you say," I said, "is very true."   430 c

"Well, then, I accept this as courage."

"Yes, do accept it, but as political courage," I said, "and you'd be right in accepting it. Later, if you want, we'll give it a still finer treatment. At the moment we weren't looking for it, but for justice. For that search, I suppose, this is sufficient."

"What you say is fine," he said.

"Well, now," I said, "there are still two left that must be seen in the city,   d moderation and that for the sake of which we are making the whole search, justice."

"Most certainly."

"How could we find justice so we won't have to bother about moderation any further?"

"I for my part don't know," he said, "nor would I want it to come to light before, if we aren't going to consider moderation any further. If you want to gratify me, consider this before the other."

"But I do want to," I said, "so as not to do an injustice."   e

"Then consider it," he said.

"It must be considered," I said. "Seen from here, it's more like a kind of accord and harmony than the previous ones."

"How?"

"Moderation," I said, "is surely a certain kind of order and mastery of certain kinds of pleasures and desires, as men say when they use—I don't know in what way—the phrase 'stronger than himself'; and some other phrases of the sort are used that are, as it were, its tracks. Isn't that so?"

"Most surely," he said.

"Isn't the phrase 'stronger than himself' ridiculous though? For, of course, the one who's stronger than himself would also be weaker than himself, and   431 a the weaker stronger. The same 'himself' is referred to in all of them."

"Of course it is."

"But," I said, "this speech looks to me as if it wants to say that, concerning the soul, in the same human being there is something better and something worse. The phrase 'stronger than himself' is used when that which is better by nature is master over that which is worse. At least it's praise. And when, from bad training or some association, the smaller and better part is mastered by the inferior multitude, then this, as though it were   b a reproach, is blamed and the man in this condition is called weaker than himself and licentious."

"Yes," he said, "that's likely."

"Now, then," I said, "take a glance at our young city, and you'll find one of these conditions in it. For you'll say that it's justly designated stronger than itself, if that in which the better rules over the worse must be called moderate and 'stronger than itself.'"

"Well, I am glancing at it," he said, "and what you say is true."

"And, further, one would find many diverse desires, pleasures, and pains,   c especially in children, women, domestics, and in those who are called free among the common many."

"Most certainly."

"But the simple and moderate desires, pleasures and pains, those led by calculation accompanied by intelligence and right opinion, you will come

431 c   upon in few, and those the ones born with the best natures and best educated."

          "True," he said.

d   "Don't you see that all these are in your city too, and that there the desires in the common many are mastered by the desires and the prudence in the more decent few?"

          "I do," he said.

          "If, therefore, any city ought to be designated stronger than pleasures, desires, and itself, then this one must be so called."

          "That's entirely certain," he said.

          "And then moderate in all these respects too?"

          "Very much so," he said.

e   "And, moreover, if there is any city in which the rulers and the ruled have the same opinion about who should rule, then it's this one. Or doesn't it seem so?"

          "Very much so indeed," he said.

          "In which of the citizens will you say the moderation resides, when they are in this condition? In the rulers or the ruled?"

          "In both, surely," he said.

          "You see," I said, "we divined pretty accurately a while ago that moderation is like a kind of harmony."

          "Why so?"

432 a   "Because it's unlike courage and wisdom, each of which resides in a part, the one making the city wise and the other courageous. Moderation doesn't work that way, but actually stretches throughout the whole, from top to bottom of the entire scale, making the weaker, the stronger and those in the middle—whether you wish to view them as such in terms of prudence, or, if you wish, in terms of strength, or multitude, money or anything else whatsoever of the sort—sing the same chant together. So we would quite rightly claim that this unanimity is moderation, an accord of worse and better, according to nature, as to which must rule in the city and in each one."

b   "I am," he said, "very much of the same opinion."

          "All right," I said. "Three of them have been spied out in our city, at least sufficiently to form some opinion. Now what would be the remaining form thanks to which the city would further partake in virtue? For, plainly, this is justice."

          "Plainly."

          "So then, Glaucon, we must, like hunters, now station ourselves in a circle around the thicket and pay attention so that justice doesn't slip

c   through somewhere and disappear into obscurity. Clearly it's somewhere hereabouts. Look to it and make every effort to catch sight of it; you might somehow see it before me and could tell me."

          "If only I could," he said. "However, if you use me as a follower and a man able to see what's shown him, you'll be making quite sensible use of me."

          "Follow," I said, "and pray with me."

          "I'll do that," he said, "just lead."

          "The place really appears to be hard going and steeped in shadows," I said. "At least it's dark and hard to search out. But, all the same, we've got to go on."

d   "Yes," he said, "we've got to go on."

And I caught sight of it and said, "Here! Here! Glaucon. Maybe we've   432 d
come upon a track; and, in my opinion, it will hardly get away from us."

"That's good news you report," he said.

"My, my," I said, "that was a stupid state we were in."

"How's that?"

"It appears, you blessed man, that it's been rolling around at our feet
from the beginning and we couldn't see it after all, but were quite ridiculous.
As men holding something in their hand sometimes seek what they're hold-   e
ing, we too didn't look at it but turned our gaze somewhere far off, which is
also perhaps just the reason it escaped our notice."

"How do you mean?" he said.

"It's this way," I said. "In my opinion, we have been saying and hearing it
all along without learning from ourselves that we were in a way saying it."

"A long prelude," he said, "for one who desires to hear."

"Listen whether after all I make any sense," I said. "That rule we set   433 a
down at the beginning as to what must be done in everything when we were
founding the city—this, or a certain form of it, is, in my opinion, justice.
Surely we set down and often said, if you remember, that each one must
practice one of the functions in the city, that one for which his nature made
him naturally most fit."

"Yes, we were saying that."

"And further, that justice is the minding of one's own business and not
being a busybody, this we have both heard from many others and have often   b
said ourselves."

"Yes, we have."

"Well, then, my friend," I said, "this—the practice of minding one's own
business—when it comes into being in a certain way, is probably justice. Do
you know how I infer this?"

"No," he said, "tell me."

"In my opinion," I said, "after having considered moderation, courage,
and prudence, this is what's left over in the city; it provided the power by
which all these others came into being; and, once having come into being, it
provides them with preservation as long as it's in the city. And yet we were   c
saying that justice would be what's left over from the three if we found
them. . . ."

Book V

[Socrates:] . . . "So, next, as it seems, we must try to seek out and demon-   473 b
strate what is badly done in cities today, and thereby keeps them from being
governed in this way, and with what smallest change—preferably one, if not,
two, and, if not, the fewest in number and the smallest in power—a city
would come to this manner of regime."

[Glaucon:] "That's entirely certain," he said.   c

"Well, then," I said, "with one change—not, however, a small or an easy one,
but possible—we can, in my opinion, show that it would be transformed."

"What change?" he said.

"Well here I am," I said, "coming to what we likened to the biggest wave.
But it shall be said regardless, even if, exactly like a gurgling wave, it's going
to drown me in laughter and ill repute. Consider what I am going to say."

473 c   "Speak," he said.

d   "Unless," I said, "the philosophers rule as kings or those now called kings and chiefs genuinely and adequately philosophize, and political power and philosophy coincide in the same place, while the many natures now making their way to either apart from the other are by necessity excluded, there is no rest from ills for the cities, my dear Glaucon, nor I think for human kind,

e nor will the regime we have now described in speech ever come forth from nature, insofar as possible, and see the light of the sun. This is what for so long was causing my hesitation to speak: seeing how very paradoxical it would be to say. For it is hard to see that in no other city would there be private or public happiness."

And he said, "Socrates, what a phrase and argument you have let burst

474 a out. Now that it's said, you can believe that very many men, and not ordinary ones, will on the spot throw off their clothes, and stripped for action, taking hold of whatever weapon falls under the hand of each, run full speed at you to do wonderful deeds. If you don't defend yourself with speech and get away, you'll really pay the penalty in scorn."

"Isn't it you," I said, "that's responsible for this happening to me?"

"And it's a fine thing I'm doing," he said. "But no, I won't betray you, and I'll defend you with what I can. I can provide good will and encouragement;

b and perhaps I would answer you more suitably than another. And so, with the assurance of such support, try to show the disbelievers that it is as *you* say."

"It must be tried," I said, "especially since you offer so great an alliance. It's necessary, in my opinion, if we are somehow going to get away from the men you speak of, to distinguish for them whom we mean when we dare to assert the philosophers must rule. Thus, when they have come plainly to

c light, one will be able to defend oneself, showing that it is by nature fitting for them both to engage in philosophy and to lead a city, and for the rest not to engage in philosophy and to follow the leader."

"It would be high time," he said, "to distinguish them."

"Come, now, follow me here, if we are somehow or other to set it forth adequately."

"Lead," he said.

"Will you need to be reminded," I said, "or do you remember that when we say a man loves something, if it is rightly said of him, he mustn't show a love for one part of it and not for another, but must cherish all of it?"

d   "I need reminding, as it seems," he said. "For I scarcely understand."

"It was proper for another, Glaucon, to say what you're saying," I said. "But it's not proper for an erotic man to forget that all boys in the bloom of youth in one way or another put their sting in an erotic lover of boys and arouse him; all seem worthy of attention and delight. Or don't you people behave that way with the fair? You praise the boy with a snub nose by calling

e him 'cute'; the hook-nose of another you say is 'kingly'; and the boy between these two is 'well proportioned'; the dark look 'manly'; and the white are 'children of gods.' And as for the 'honey-colored,' do you suppose their very name is the work of anyone other than a lover who renders sallowness endearing and easily puts up with it if it accompanies the bloom of youth? And, in a word, you people take advantage of every excuse and employ any

475 a expression so as to reject none of those who glow with the bloom of youth."

"If you want to point to me while you speak about what erotic men do," 475 a
he said, "I agree for the sake of the argument."

"And what about this?" I said. "Don't you see wine-lovers doing the same
thing? Do they delight in every kind of wine, and on every pretext?"

"Indeed, they do."

"And further, I suppose you see that lovers of honor, if they can't become
generals, are lieutenants, and if they can't be honored by greater and more   b
august men, are content to be honored by lesser and more ordinary men
because they are desirers of honor as a whole."

"That's certainly the case."

"Then affirm this or deny it: when we say a man is a desirer of something,
will we assert that he desires all of that form, or one part of it and not
another?"

"All," he said.

"Won't we also then assert that the philosopher is a desirer of wisdom,
not of one part and not another, but of all of it?"

"True."

"We'll deny, therefore, that the one who's finicky about his learning,   c
especially when he's young and doesn't yet have an account of what's useful
and not, is a lover of learning or a philosopher, just as we say that the man
who's finicky about his food isn't hungry, doesn't desire food, and isn't a
lover of food but a bad eater."

"And we'll be right in denying it."

"But the one who is willing to taste every kind of learning with gusto, and
who approaches learning with delight, and is insatiable, we shall justly
assert to be a philosopher, won't we?"

And Glaucon said, "Then you'll have many strange ones. For all the lovers   d
of sights are in my opinion what they are because they enjoy learning; and
the lovers of hearing would be some of the strangest to include among
philosophers, those who would never be willing to go voluntarily to a
discussion and such occupations but who—just as though they had hired
out their ears for hearing—run around to every chorus at the Dionysia,
missing none in the cities or the villages. We will say that all these men and
other learners of such things and the petty arts are philosophers?"   e

"Not at all," I said, "but they are like philosophers."

"Who do you say are the true ones?" he said.

"The lovers of the sight of the truth," I said.

"And that's right," he said. "But how do you mean it?"

"It wouldn't be at all easy to tell someone else. But you, I suppose, will
grant me this."

"What?"

"Since fair is the opposite of ugly, they are two."

"Of course."   476 a

"Since they are two, isn't each also one?"

"That is so as well."

"The same argument also applies then to justice and injustice, good and
bad, and all the forms; each is itself one, but, by showing themselves
everywhere in a community with actions, bodies, and one another, each
looks like many."

"What you say," he said, "is right."

476a   "Well, now," I said, "this is how I separate them out. On one side I put those of whom you were just speaking, the lovers of sights, the lovers of arts,

b   and the practical men; on the other, those whom the argument concerns, whom alone one could rightly call philosophers."

"How do you mean?" he said.

"The lovers of hearing and the lovers of sights, on the one hand," I said, "surely delight in fair sounds and colors and shapes and all that craft makes from such things, but their thought is unable to see and delight in the nature of the fair itself."

"That," he said, "is certainly so."

"Wouldn't, on the other hand, those who are able to approach the fair itself and see it by itself be rare?"

c   "Indeed they would.". . .

Book VII

514 a   [Socrates:] "Next, then," I said, "make an image of our nature in its education and want of education, likening it to a condition of the following kind. See human beings as though they were in an underground cave-like dwelling with its entrance, a long one, open to the light across the whole width of the cave. They are in it from childhood with their legs and necks in

b   bonds so that they are fixed, seeing only in front of them, unable because of the bond to turn their heads all the way around. Their light is from a fire burning far above and behind them. Between the fire and the prisoners there is a road above, along which see a wall, built like the partitions puppet-handlers set in front of the human beings and over which they show the puppets."

[Glaucon:] "I see," he said.

"Then also see along this wall human beings carrying all sorts of

c   artifacts, which project above the wall, and statues of men and other

515 a   animals wrought from stone, wood, and every kind of material; as is to be expected, some of the carriers utter sounds while others are silent."

"It's a strange image," he said, "and strange prisoners you're telling of."

"They're like us," I said. "For in the first place, do you suppose such men would have seen anything of themselves and one another other than the shadows cast by the fire on the side of the cave facing them?"

b   "How could they," he said, "if they had been compelled to keep their heads motionless throughout life?"

"And what about the things that are carried by? Isn't it the same with them?"

"Of course."

"If they were able to discuss things with one another, don't you believe they would hold that they are naming these things going by before them that they see?"

"Necessarily."

"And what if the prison also had an echo from the side facing them? Whenever one of the men passing by happens to utter a sound, do you suppose they would believe that anything other than the passing shadow was uttering the sound?"

"No, by Zeus," he said. "I don't."   515 b

"Then most certainly," I said, "such men would hold that the truth is   c
nothing other than the shadows of artificial things."

"Most necessarily," he said.

"Now consider," I said, "what their release and healing from bonds and
folly would be like if something of this sort were by nature to happen to
them. Take a man who is released and suddenly compelled to stand up, to
turn his neck around, to walk and look up toward the light; and who,
moreover, in doing all this is in pain and, because he is dazzled, is unable to
make out those things whose shadows he saw before. What do you suppose   d
he'd say if someone were to tell him that before he saw silly nothings, while
now, because he is somewhat nearer to what *is* and more turned toward
beings, he sees more correctly; and, in particular, showing him each of the
things that pass by, were to compel the man to answer his questions about
what they are? Don't you suppose he'd be at a loss and believe that what was
seen before is truer than what is now shown?"

"Yes," he said, "by far."

"And, if he compelled him to look at the light itself, would his eyes hurt   e
and would he flee, turning away to those things that he is able to make out
and hold them to be really clearer than what is being shown?"

"So he would," he said.

"And if," I said, "someone dragged him away from there by force along the
rough, steep, upward way and didn't let him go before he had dragged him
out into the light of the sun, wouldn't he be distressed and annoyed at being   516 a
so dragged? And when he came to the light, wouldn't he have his eyes full of
its beam and be unable to see even one of the things now said to be true?"

"No, he wouldn't," he said, "at least not right away."

"Then I suppose he'd have to get accustomed, if he were going to see
what's up above. At first he'd most easily make out the shadows; and after
that the phantoms of the human beings and the other things in water; and,
later, the things themselves. And from there he could turn to beholding the
things in heaven and heaven itself, more easily at night—looking at the light   b
of the stars and the moon—than by day—looking at the sun and sunlight."

"Of course."

"Then finally I suppose he would be able to make out the sun—not its
appearances in water or some alien place, but the sun itself by itself in its
own region—and see what it's like."

"Necessarily," he said.

"And after that he would already be in a position to conclude about it that
this is the source of the seasons and the years, and is the steward of all   c
things in the visible place, and is in a certain way the cause of all those
things he and his companions had been seeing."

"It's plain," he said, "that this would be his next step."

"What then? When he recalled his first home and the wisdom there, and
his fellow prisoners in that time, don't you suppose he would consider
himself happy for the change and pity the others?"

"Quite so."

"And if in that time there were among them any honors, praises, and
prizes for the man who is sharpest at making out the things that go by, and
most remembers which of them are accustomed to pass before, which after,   d

516 d and which at the same time as others, and who is thereby most able to divine what is going to come, in your opinion would he be desirous of them and envy those who are honored and hold power among these men? Or, rather, would he be affected as Homer says and want very much 'to be on the soil, a serf to another man, to a portionless man,' and to undergo anything whatsoever rather than to opine those things and live that way?"

e "Yes," he said, "I suppose he would prefer to undergo everything rather than live that way."

"Now reflect on this too," I said. "If such a man were to come down again and sit in the same seat, on coming suddenly from the sun wouldn't his eyes get infected with darkness?"

"Very much so," he said.

"And if he once more had to compete with those perpetual prisoners in 517 a forming judgments about those shadows while his vision was still dim, before his eyes had recovered, and if the time needed for getting accustomed were not at all short, wouldn't he be the source of laughter, and wouldn't it be said of him that he went up and came back with his eyes corrupted, and that it's not even worth trying to go up? And if they were somehow able to get their hands on and kill the man who attempts to release and lead up, wouldn't they kill him?"

"No doubt about it," he said.

b "Well, then, my dear Glaucon," I said, "this image as a whole must be connected with what was said before. Liken the domain revealed through sight to the prison home, and the light of the fire in it to the sun's power; and, in applying the going up and the seeing of what's above to the soul's journey up to the intelligible place, you'll not mistake my expectation, since you desire to hear it. A god doubtless knows if it happens to be true. At all events, this is the way the phenomena look to me: in the knowable the last c thing to be seen, and that with considerable effort, is the *idea* of the good; but once seen, it must be concluded that this is in fact the cause of all that is right and fair in everything—in the visible it gave birth to light and its sovereign; in the intelligible, itself sovereign, it provided truth and intelligence—and that the man who is going to act prudently in private or in public must see it."

"I, too, join you in supposing that," he said, "at least in the way I can."

"Come, then," I said, "and join me in supposing this, too, and don't be surprised that the men who get to that point aren't willing to mind the d business of human beings, but rather that their souls are always eager to spend their time above. Surely that's likely, if indeed this, too, follows the image of which I told before."

"Of course it's likely," he said.

"And what about this? Do you suppose it is anything surprising," I said, "if a man, come from acts of divine contemplation to the human things, is graceless and looks quite ridiculous when—with his sight still dim and before he has gotten sufficiently accustomed to the surrounding darkness—he is compelled in courts or elsewhere to contest about the shadows e of the just or the representations of which they are the shadows, and to dispute about the way these things are understood by men who have never seen justice itself?"

"It's not at all surprising," he said.

"But if a man were intelligent," I said, "he would remember that there are two kinds of disturbances of the eyes, stemming from two sources—when they have been transferred from light to darkness and when they have been transferred from darkness to light. And if he held that these same things happen to a soul too, whenever he saw one that is confused and unable to make anything out, he wouldn't laugh without reasoning but would go on to consider whether, come from a brighter life, it is in darkness for want of being accustomed, or whether, going from greater lack of learning to greater brightness, it is dazzled by the greater brilliance. And then he would deem the first soul happy for its condition and its life, while he would pity the second. And, if he wanted to laugh at the second soul, his laughing in this case would make him less ridiculous himself than would his laughing at the soul which has come from above out of the light."

"What you say is quite sensible," he said.

"Then, if this is true," I said, "we must hold the following about these things: education is not what the professions of certain men assert it to be. They presumably assert that they put into the soul knowledge that isn't in it, as though they were putting sight into blind eyes."

"Yes," he said, "they do indeed assert that."

"But the present argument, on the other hand," I said, "indicates that this power is in the soul of each, and that the instrument with which each learns—just as an eye is not able to turn toward the light from the dark without the whole body—must be turned around from that which *is coming into being* together with the whole soul until it is able to endure looking at that which *is* and the brightest part of that which *is*. And we affirm that this is the good, don't we?"

"Yes."

"There would, therefore," I said, "be an art of this turning around, concerned with the way in which this power can most easily and efficiently be turned around, not an art of producing sight in it. Rather, this art takes as given that sight is there, but not rightly turned nor looking at what it ought to look at, and accomplishes this object."

"So it seems," he said.

"Therefore, the other virtues of a soul, as they are called, are probably somewhat close to those of the body. For they are really not there beforehand and are later produced by habits and exercises, while the virtue of exercising prudence is more than anything somehow more divine, it seems; it never loses its power, but according to the way it is turned, it becomes useful and helpful or, again, useless and harmful. Or haven't you yet reflected about the men who are said to be vicious but wise, how shrewdly their petty soul sees and how sharply it distinguishes those things toward which it is turned, showing that it doesn't have poor vision although it is compelled to serve vice; so that the sharper it sees, the more evil it accomplishes?"

"Most certainly," he said.

"However," I said, "if this part of such a nature were trimmed in earliest childhood and its ties of kinship with becoming were cut off—like leaden weights, which eating and such pleasures as well as their refinements naturally attach to the soul and turn its vision downward—if, I say, it were rid of them and turned around toward the true things, this same part of the

518 a

b

c

d

e

519 a

b

519 b   same human beings would also see them most sharply, just as it does those
things toward which it now is turned."

"It's likely," he said.

"And what about this? Isn't it likely," I said, "and necessary, as a
consequence of what was said before, that those who are without education
c   and experience of truth would never be adequate stewards of a city, nor
would those who have been allowed to spend their time in education
continuously to the end—the former because they don't have any single goal
in life at which they must aim in doing everything they do in private or in
public, the latter because they won't be willing to act, believing they have
emigrated to a colony on the Isles of the Blessed[1] while they are still alive?"

"True," he said.

"Then our job as founders," I said, "is to compel the best natures to go to
d   the study which we were saying before is the greatest, to see the good and to
go up that ascent; and, when they have gone up and seen sufficiently, not to
permit them what is now permitted."

"What's that?"

"To remain there," I said, "and not be willing to go down again among
those prisoners or share their labors and honors, whether they be slighter or
more serious."

"What?" he said. "Are we to do them an injustice, and make them live a
worse life when a better is possible for them?"

e   "My friend, you have again forgotten," I said, "that it's not the concern of
law that any one class in the city fare exceptionally well, but it contrives to
bring this about for the whole city, harmonizing the citizens by persuasion
520 a   and compulsion, making them share with one another the benefit that each
class is able to bring to the commonwealth. And it produces such men in the
city not in order to let them turn whichever way each wants, but in order
that it may use them in binding the city together."

"That's true," he said. "I did forget."

"Well, then, Glaucon," I said, "consider that we won't be doing injustice
to the philosophers who come to be among us, but rather that we will say
just things to them while compelling them besides to care for and guard the
b   others. We'll say that when such men come to be in the other cities it is
fitting for them not to participate in the labors of those cities. For they grow
up spontaneously against the will of the regime in each; and a nature that
grows by itself and doesn't owe its rearing to anyone has justice on its side
when it is not eager to pay off the price of rearing to anyone. 'But you we
have begotten for yourselves and for the rest of the city like leaders and
kings in hives; you have been better and more perfectly educated and are
c   more able to participate in both lives. So you must go down, each in his turn,
into the common dwelling of the others and get habituated along with them
to seeing the dark things. And, in getting habituated to it, you will see ten
thousand times better than the men there, and you'll know what each of the
phantoms is, and of what it is a phantom, because you have seen the truth
about fair, just, and good things. And thus, the city will be governed by us
and by you in a state of waking, not in a dream as the many cities nowadays

---

1. A happy place where good men live forever. In some accounts they went there before dying, in
others afterward [Bloom].

are governed by men who fight over shadows with one another and form   520 c
factions for the sake of ruling, as though it were some great good. But the   d
truth is surely this: that city in which those who are going to rule are least
eager to rule is necessarily governed in the way that is best and freest from
faction, while the one that gets the opposite kind of rulers is governed in the
opposite way.'"

"Most certainly," he said.

"Do you suppose our pupils will disobey us when they hear this and be
unwilling to join in the labors of the city, each in his turn, while living the
greater part of the time with one another in the pure region?"

"Impossible," he said. "For surely we shall be laying just injunctions on   e
just men. However, each of them will certainly approach ruling as a
necessary thing—which is the opposite of what is done by those who now
rule in every city."

"That's the way it is, my comrade," I said. "If you discover a life better   521 a
than ruling for those who are going to rule, it is possible that your
well-governed city will come into being. For here alone will the really rich
rule, rich not in gold but in those riches required by the happy man, rich in
a good and prudent life. But if beggars, men hungering for want of private
goods, go to public affairs supposing that in them they must seize the good,
it isn't possible. When ruling becomes a thing fought over, such a war—a
domestic war, one within the family—destroys these men themselves and
the rest of the city as well."

"That's very true," he said.

"Have you," I said, "any other life that despises political offices other   b
than that of true philosophy?"

"No, by Zeus," he said. "I don't."

"But men who aren't lovers of ruling must go to it; otherwise rival lovers
will fight."

"Of course."

"Who else will you compel to go to the guarding of the city than the men
who are most prudent in those things through which a city is best governed,
and who have other honors and a better life than the political life?"

"No one else," he said. . . .

COMMENTARY

The Republic and the "Limits of Politics"
Dale Hall

I

Professors Leo Strauss and Allan Bloom have offered a radical, challenging and new interpretation of Plato's *Republic*.[1] Emphasising the crucial importance of certain passages referring to the philosopher's return to the Cave and reconsidering the general character of Plato's political argument, they question many of our most basic assumptions about Plato's notion of philosophical politics. They turn our attention to the problem of clarifying his overall purpose by offering a startling account of his intentions. They both identify the relation between the *kallipolis* [fair or beautiful city] which Socrates depicts and existing, ordinary *poleis* [cities] as crucial, and they are sure that Plato was preoccupied with the possibility of the good *polis* coming into being. They conclude that Plato is finally pessimistic about the prospects for its realisation, that he presents it as an ideal remote from actual human endeavour. Apparently, the *kallipolis* is unrealisable and unrealistic. They agree that the prospect of philosophical politics is renounced in the *Republic,* and that such a political order is not only impossible but, according to Plato, contrary to nature. Strauss claims that "the *Republic* conveys the broadest and deepest analysis of political idealism ever made."[2] The *Republic's* "claim that the tension between philosophy and the city would be overcome if the philosophers became kings"[3] is only apparent, for, in fact, Plato presents "the most magnificent cure ever devised for every form of political ambition."[4] In this, as in so many other of his conclusions, Bloom is substantially influenced by Strauss. He agrees with Strauss' superlatives: "Political idealism is the most destructive of human passions" and the *Republic* is "the greatest critique of political idealism ever written."[5] He concludes that the "extreme spirit of reform or revolution loses its ground if . . . the infinite longing for justice on earth is merely a dream or a prayer."[6] "The *Republic* serves to moderate the extreme passion for justice by showing the limits of what can be demanded and expected of the city."[7] Instead of an optimistic argument revealing a definitive political order, they find a pessimistic meditation upon the "limits of politics."[8] Plato discloses the "the limits of politics" by revealing, first, that the *kallipolis* is an order contrary to human nature, because it "'abstracts' from the body,"[9] and second, that the philosopher is not naturally a political ruler. We shall examine both claims, but the latter is the more important. According to Strauss and Bloom, because it is contrary to the philosophers' nature that they should rule, the *Republic's* requirement that they be compelled to return to the Cave and rule represents the utmost perversion of nature by art. Apparently, even

Dale Hall, "The Republic and the 'Limits of Politics,'" *Political Theory,* 5:3 pp. 293–313. Copyright © 1977, by Sage Publications, Inc. Reprinted by permission of Sage Publications, Inc.

Authors Note: I am grateful to my colleague, Peter Nicholson, for helpful discussion of issues raised in this paper.

within the *kallipolis* there exists an irreconcilable opposition between the good of the individual and the good of the whole community. Because the individual realises himself most perfectly in philosophy, it is a diminution of his *eudaimonia* [happiness] and contrary to his nature for the philosopher to be compelled to leave the Sunlight and rule for the common good.

Such an account is startling, for we are accustomed to taking Socrates seriously. He does recommend that philosophers should rule; he says that human well-being is achievable only through the union of philosophy and politics; he presents the *kallipolis* as the natural political order and interprets existing, corrupt *poleis* as disordered perversions of the ideal. For Strauss and Bloom the *Republic* must be consummately ironic, as an instance of Socrates appearing to say one thing, in recommending the *kallipolis* as natural, but actually meaning another. Socrates' meaning must be reversed, for the *Republic* is really a "Modest Proposal," proposing ironically a solution to our evils that no rational man would pursue. . . . [A]lthough Strauss and Bloom find Plato ironic in covertly disclosing the unnaturalness of the *politeia* that Socrates appears to advocate, they . . . offer no extended account of his irony. Strauss just says that we should not assume that Socrates is Plato's spokesman, for to speak through the mouth of a man notorious for his irony is "tantamount to not asserting anything."[10] Bloom argues only that to neglect man's physical aspect, "to forget the other side of man—to neglect the irony of Socrates' proposals—is . . . a fatal error. The cosmopolitan communistic society of egalitarian man is a distortion of man and the city which is more terrible than barbarism . . . a society is constituted which satisfies neither body nor soul."[11]

II

To consider their claim that the *Republic* is somehow wholly ironic and discloses the limits of politics we must distinguish three elements in the interpretations of Strauss and Bloom, although they do not separate them clearly. Both of them claim that the earlier parts of Book V have a comic character, that the *kallipolis* of Socrates' construction is unnatural, and that the activity of political ruling is contrary to the philosopher's nature. We shall discuss the first two of these claims briefly here and then concentrate on the third in the next section.

They find Book V comic, particularly in its discussion of communal life and the equality of women. For Strauss, it is "akin to Aristophanes' *Assembly of Women*," and the equality of the sexes is presented as "laughable."[12] For Bloom, Plato's comedy is "more fantastic, more innovative, more comic and more profound than any work of Aristophanes."[13] So both of them relate Book V to the *Ecclesiazusae* [Comedy by Aristophanes, 391 B.C.E.] but neither of them explains or examines the relationship. Quite uncritically they just assume that Plato was trying to outdo Aristophanes in a comic satire of certain radical contemporary ideas, presupposing that Plato's purpose was in common with that of the dramatist. They refer neither to Barker (who is sure that "Plato is seeking to meet the current satire on communism, including that of Aristophanes")[14] nor to the excellent discussion of Adam, who finds that Plato's purpose was far from comic or satiric.[15] Adam writes that Plato was probably dissatisfied with the comedian's travesty of views with which he (Plato) had no little sympathy, and that he touches, with serious purposes, on nearly all the proposals which Aristophanes had tried to make ridiculous.[16] Adam agrees that Plato probably had Aristophanes' satire in mind, but gives no support at all to the speculative claim that Plato's intention was also satiric. Clearly, we should not assimilate Plato's intentions to Aristophanes' just on the basis of certain (superficial) resemblances.[17] Strauss and Bloom neglect that for Aristophanes' satire of such social arrangements to have had point, others must have recommended them quite seriously. They are too ready to interpret the text according to their own responses, forgetting that we are most susceptible mistakenly to call an author comic or ironic when his beliefs and assumptions differ most from our own.[18] They find comic Plato's comparisons with animals, his proposals for selective breeding and for exposure of inferior *phylakes* [guardians], but these ideas were not necessarily unacceptable or ridiculous to a fourth-century Greek.[19] Many Greeks felt that Spartan experience vindicated such arrangements. Similarly, the equality of women and the community of women and children were familiar subjects of speculation and report.[20] There are none of the familiar signs of irony or comedy in Plato's discussion of equality: Socrates does not appeal to absurd premises, nor reason fallaciously, nor contradict himself, and the seriousness of the discussions of Book V is further attested by their coherence with Plato's account of justice in the *Republic*.[21] Clearly, because Strauss and Bloom find the *kallipolis* a fantastic and uncongenial moral and social order, they just assume that Plato could not have meant what he said. Their approach is anachronistic and unhistorical, and it fails to provide any criterion by which we can identify Plato's irony. For example, if they doubt his commitment to the community of women and children, why do they not suspect his seriousness with respect to the theory of forms—for Plato intends the ideal social order to cohere with his psychology and metaphysic?

Strauss has two main grounds for asserting that the *kallipolis* is contrary to nature: first, it disregards the realities of human nature (it "'abstracts' from the body"),[22] and, second, it cannot perfectly embody the form of justice.[23] Like Strauss, Bloom pays most attention to the first of these, also finding an opposition between the *eros* of the body and the requirements and practices of the *kallipolis*. Only through the "depreciation of *eros* can the city come into its own,"[24] for, in abolishing privacy, regulating man's sexual *eros* and allowing women to perform the same functions as men, the *kallipolis* ignores propensities basic to human nature.[25] According to Strauss and Bloom, Plato's regulations impose unnatural arrangements and practices on the *phylakes*.[26] However, they offer no evidence for such conclusions, and they quite neglect all possible historical and anthropological comparisons. For example, Bloom is sure that, "as a political proposal the public nakedness of men and women is nonsense," although men can go naked together, "because it is relatively easy to desexualise their relations."[27] What of Greek homosexuality? And if the regulation of both sexes' public nudity is nonsense, what would Bloom say of Xenophon, who insists that Sparta did just that and avoided licentiousness?[28] Once more, plausible comparisons of Plato's ideas with contemporary practices are ignored, so that, set in an ahistorical limbo, the *kallipolis* appears comic or unnatural. Strauss' subsidiary reason for calling the *kallipolis* unnatural is no more satisfactory. He argues that the just *polis* cannot manifest the form of justice perfectly, for real justice is not capable of coming into being.[29] Because forms are incorporeal, even the most perfect *polis* must fall short of their perfection.[30] Although true, this is more than a little misleading, for there is no suggestion in Plato that the *kallipolis* is *merely* conventional or contrary to nature. Although the just *polis* only approximates the forms, it is the most natural association possible for man. Only in the *kallipolis* do social life and men's *psychai* [souls] manifest the natural order that is well-being. Only there are the forms made immanent; only through philosophic rule does the political order assume its greatest reality and intelligibility. The forms are in nature (*en tei physei*), and so is the *kallipolis* because it is modeled upon them. Strauss' interpretation neglects the relationship of participation between the physical world and the forms, and so he distorts Plato's political argument. On Strauss' reading, human beings are unnatural, for being corporeal.

Socrates is explicit that his *polis is* natural. It is based on no reluctant agreement, but on man's most basic needs; the most primitive relationships represent a division of labour based on *physis* [nature] (370a–c. Cf. 374e); the duality of the dispositions of the *phylakes* is not unnatural (375e), and even the introduction of the rulers complements *physis*, for they are those *phylakes* whose natures are properly harmonized by music and gymnastics (412a). No element of the *kallipolis* is antipathetic to nature, and Socrates reveals that political justice is the natural ordering principle, the division of labour, now more adequately understood to take account of all men's natural differences. In identifying the other excellences, Socrates presupposes that his is the natural *polis* (428e–429a). The same theme continues in Book V, where we are clearly told that all the regulations about women and children are natural (453b, 456b, and 466d). There Socrates introduces the notion of philosophic rule as the precondition for the growth of the only natural political order, for unless philosophy and politics unite, "there is no rest from ills for cities, nor will the regime we have described in speech ever come forth from nature" (473d–e). We learn that the philosopher is he who is fitted by nature both to practice philosophy and to lead the *polis* (474b–c).

III

It is the third aspect of Strauss' and Bloom's case that we must discuss in more detail, namely, their claim that although Plato postulates an harmony of philosophy and politics, his meaning is actually far from straightforward. Properly understood, the *kallipolis* is unnatural, because ruling is an unnatural activity for the philosopher. Their argument depends upon finding two separate senses of justice within the *Republic.* In relation to the individual, there is justice understood as an internal hierarchical harmony of reason, spirit, and appetite within the *psyche,* and there is justice as a quality of actions.[31] It is convenient to refer to the first of these kinds of justice as "platonic justice," a phrase taken from an influential article by Sachs, . . .[32] For Strauss, only the philosopher is platonically just, for only he can perfectly harmonise his *psyche* according to the pattern of the forms.[33] But everyone can be just in the second sense; they can observe what Strauss sometimes calls "civic virtue"[34] and what we shall call (like Sachs) "vulgar justice." Vulgar justice is the quality of our actions realised in service to the *polis* and in our relations with others when we fulfil our obligations and observe the conventional rules of moral conduct. . . . Strauss and Bloom believe that because Plato does not connect vulgar with platonic justice (and so with *eudaimonia*) he fails to show (a) that platonically just men will naturally serve the *polis* and (b) that a life of service to the *polis* (even of fulfilling one's function in the *kallipolis*) constitutes human well-being.[35] Strauss emphasises only the first of these, but Bloom mentions both. He says, "The question is whether . . . devotion to the common good leads to the health of the soul or whether the man with an healthy soul is devoted to the common good."[36] By separating the two senses of justice, . . . Strauss and Bloom infer that men have no good reason for being good citizens; and . . . reason . . . that because the *kallipolis* requires that philosophers serve the common good by accepting the unwelcome burdens of ruling, it follows that even the just *polis* is unnatural.[37]

Although they require that both a and b be satisfied, Strauss and Bloom emphasise a, making b subsidiary. This subordinate aspect of their case, that Plato must show that those who serve the *polis* necessarily enjoy platonic justice, can be dismissed immediately. Contrary to their claim, Plato does not need to show that a life of vulgar justice entails platonic justice. His argument is not impugned by any failure to show that all those whose actions are merely unexceptionable have psychic harmony, for they may be so through fear, or from cynical calculation of likely future advantage. Vulgar justice implies platonic justice only when a man has a settled and sincere disposition to behave justly. In corrupt *poleis* only exceptional men have such dispositions, but in the *kallipolis*, where the philosopher's subjects enjoy the right musical and gymnastic *paideia* [education] such a disposition is characteristic. There the subjects enjoy a measure of psychic harmony, based on right belief, guaranteed by the philosopher's knowledge.[38] Through their participation in the *kallipolis* their spirited and appetitive elements are disciplined and their reason is guided by the ruler's knowledge.

Clearly, then, the crucial question is that referred to as a above, whether the possession of platonic justice will make a man vulgarly just, "whether the man with an healthy soul is devoted to the common good." According to Strauss and Bloom, Plato reveals that the platonically just philosopher does not naturally rule. Apparently, the excellence appropriate to philosophy is distinct from the excellence required for ruling, and the philosopher has no reason to sacrifice his private good, consisting in theoretical contemplation, for the sake of the common good, which consists in his undertaking the practical activity of ruling. They believe that, by emphasizing the opposition of individual and common goods, Plato disclosed the "limits of politics" and revealed the "nature and problems of politics."[39] The central question of the *Republic* is, "Can there be a regime whose laws are such as to serve the common good while allowing each of its members to reach his natural perfection?"[40] When Plato introduces the rulers, Bloom's commentary asks, "Is the wise man, who makes full use of the powers of his reason, the same as the prudent statesman?" And by the end of Book VII, Bloom says, it has become "manifest that the life of reason has a character of its own" and that the *polis* cannot "comprehend the highest activity of man."[41] It cannot "comprehend" the highest theoretical excellence because it demands an inferior practical service, requiring that the philosopher abandon contemplation for ruling. The *kallipolis*' very existence depends upon the most perfect human type sacrificing his excellence and *eudaimonia*.[42] Men can live well in the Cave only if philosophers abandon their odyssey and return from the sunlight to an inferior world and activity. Their reluctance to return, and Socrates' insistence that they must be compelled, intimates the unnatural character of the *kallipolis*, which "abuses and misuses the best men."[43] There is a fundamental opposition between the philosophic *eros*, which aspires to know the forms, and the requirements of any political order.[44] The relation of politics and philosophy is only an "alleged harmony," postulated to reveal an actual opposition.[45] So, instead of recommending that philosophers should rule, Plato reveals that they are not naturally political rulers; instead of approving the *kallipolis*, he discloses that its most fundamental postulate is contrary to nature. And so the *Republic* appears as an indictment of idealism and utopianism, by revealing the "limits of politics."

We shall suggest that this account of the *Republic's* philosophical politics is mistaken, by arguing that (1) Strauss and Bloom misinterpret the reference to the philosophers being compelled to return to the Cave and rule; (2) that they divorce theoretical and practical wisdom in a manner quite foreign to Plato; (3) that the philosopher's well being does not consist exclusively in reflection in the theoretical mode; (4) that the platonically just individual with an harmonious *psyche* will act for the good of others; (5) that the philosopher's goodness is most perfectly realised when he rules politically; (6) that Strauss and Bloom misunderstand Plato's account of "politics" within the *kallipolis*; and (7) that they are unsympathetic to his notion of *eudaimonia*.

1. To maintain their account, Strauss and Bloom must dismiss traditional interpretations of the *Republic*, according to which there exists no opposition between philosophy and politics because the philosopher's excellence is precisely that excellence which qualifies him and equips him to rule. They do dismiss such orthodox interpretations, on the basis of Plato's references to the philosopher's reluctance to rule.[46] Strauss emphasises the important passage (519c–520d) in which Socrates declares that philosophers must be compelled to rule in the *kallipolis*. Socrates insists that:

> Our job as founders is to compel the best natures to go to the study which we were saying before is the greatest, to see the good and to go up that ascent; and, when they have gone up and seen sufficiently, not to permit them . . . to remain there and not be willing to go down again among the prisoners to share their labours. . . . It's not the concern of law that any one class in the city fare exceptionally well, but it contrives to bring this about for the whole city. . . . And it produces such men in the city not in order to let them turn whichever way each wants, but in order that it may use them in binding the city together. . . . We won't be doing injustice to the philosophers who come to be among us. . . . We will say just things to them, while compelling them besides to care for and guard the others. We'll say that . . . "You we have begotten for yourselves and for the rest of the city, like leaders and kings in hives; you have been better and more perfectly educated and are more able to participate in both lives. So you must go down."

Other passages have a similar character, using the language of constraint and necessity (499b–c, 500d 4–5, 539e 2–3, and 540a) or referring to the philosophers' reluctance to rule (520c–521b and 540b), and they are held to support the conclusion that within the *kallipolis* the best men are misused.[47] However, we should not conclude that Plato uses the notion of compulsion (*anagkaxo*) to indicate that the required undertaking is contrary to nature, for there are at least two important instances (one in the passage above) where he refers to compulsion when it is perfectly clear that the relevant action is not unnatural. As founders, Socrates says, they must "compel the best natures" to undertake the study culminating in the apprehension of the Good (519c), at 540a he declares that the philosophers must be compelled to look toward the Good itself, and the Cave suggests that the philosophic odyssey is arduous. Strauss and Bloom do not explain these passages; but, if we were to follow their inference from the language of compulsion, we would conclude that the philosophic education perverts man's natural inclinations! Clearly, in being compelled to undertake the highest studies the philosophers are "forced to be free," and so, although Plato writes of them being compelled to rule, it remains at least possible that political rule is not a perversion, but a completion of the philosophic experience. We should consider seriously the possibility that ruling represents the fulfillment of the philosophic nature because it constitutes, to the greatest degree possible, the natural rule of reason over spirit and appetite. Viewed in this light, ruling provides the philosopher with the opportunity of overcoming his awareness of the disparity between the physical and ideal realms, for the philosopher-ruler models the social order according to the harmony of the forms (501a–c).

2. Bloom, particularly, appears to read Plato through Aristotle, for he finds in the former the latter's separation of theoretical and practical wisdom. He assumes that the exercise of practical wisdom is unrelated to the theoretical wisdom of the forms, and that *eudaimonia* consists exclusively in the practice of theoretical contemplation. . . .[48] These two elements in the interpretation of Strauss and Bloom are distinct, for the distinction between platonic and vulgar justice is compatible with no separation between the two modes of reason. The exercise of practical reason is compatible with either vulgar justice or injustice, and platonic justice cannot be defined simply as the theoretical contemplation of the forms, for it involves the harmony of the whole *psyche*. So we must examine these two distinctions separately, taking first that aspect which is peculiar to Strauss and Bloom.

Strauss and Bloom do not acknowledge that the separation of the practical and theoretical faculties of reason is quite foreign to Plato. Throughout the *Republic* Plato insists on the relation between the intelligible and sensible "worlds," and he does not suggest that the philosopher apprehends an order entirely unrelated to the physical world. Sensible experience is contradictory, uncertain, and impermanent; particulars are poor copies of the forms, and the philosopher is acutely aware of the disparity between the phenomenal and ideal worlds; but the forms are not altogether removed from the particulars of ordinary experience. When perfected, the philosopher's understanding consists not just in contemplating the forms, but in resolving all levels of experience as he recognises the interconnectedness of the intelligible and sensible orders. . . . For Plato, philosophic knowledge is not only a mystic state, but a disciplined recognition that the world is "knowable" and the realisation that all the elements of our experiences are reconcilable in a more complete understanding. The Good is not an object of aesthetic contemplation, or not only that, but the principle of intelligibility by which the philosopher understands how the world is conformed to reason. . . .

Because he asserts the relation of the intelligible and sensible orders, Plato makes no separation of theoretical and practical wisdom. Bloom is reluctant to admit that the knowledge of the forms could authorise practical moral judgements, but that is a most un-Platonic assumption. The belief that the forms are irrelevant to the practical mode might be cogent, given *our* conception of reason, but Plato's conception is distinctive, and to neglect it is to make nonsense of the *Republic's* structure. In terms of the forms and the image of the *kallipolis*, where the nonphilosophers enjoy *arete* based on right belief inculcated by the philosopher-rulers, Plato resolves the Socratic paradoxes that virtue is knowledge and all virtue is one. Knowledge of the forms is the essential qualification for ruling, and when Adeimantus objects that philosophers would be useless (487d), Socrates replies that such is the case only when the public affairs of men are disordered (488a–489c). The forms are the paradigms for the philosopher's ordering of the social world (484c–d, 500d, and 501b). Because Plato sees the physical world as a copy of perfection, there is enough order and goodness in it to sustain the efforts of the philosopher to improve it when once he comes to rule. He does not suggest that philosophizing and ruling are unrelated functions, and he represents the rule of philosophers as the fulfilment of the division of labour principle in the *polis*.

3. However, Strauss and Bloom might allow that Plato separate neither the sensible and intelligible orders nor practical and theoretical wisdom, but still maintain that the philosopher's fullest happiness consists exclusively in reflection in the theoretical mode. . . . Having argued that Plato does not separate the two modes of reason, we must now show that the *Republic's* argument is distorted by the assumption that *eudaimonia* can consist exclusively in theoretical wisdom. Now, Plato's account of reason in the *psyche* should make us question such an interpretation, for reason does its own natural function when it decides what is good and bad for the whole *psyche.* (441e) Reason's function is to order the *psyche,* for the *psyche* is not just, and so is not *eudaimon, only* by virtue of an activity of the reasoning part. When Plato develops his account of reason in man he does not separate its activity of theorising from its role of creating order, and we learn nothing later which contradicts the earlier account that the *psyche* is just and *eudaimon* only when each part does its own with respect to ruling and being ruled (441e–442c, 443b–444a). Plato treats reason's aspiration to know as a kind of desire (589d 6–8), but he does not separate that desire from the inclination to rule. Indeed, each part of the *psyche* seems to possess a natural inclination to impose its own distinctive character on the functioning of the whole *psyche.* Plato does not suggest that it is contrary to the nature of philosophically trained reason to rule in the *psyche,* for reason's inclination is to harmonise it, according to reason's own order. Only reason has the well-being of the whole as its conscious objective, and its function is to promote platonic justice, which is the harmony of the whole *psyche.* In the platonically just man, reason exercises control at such a fundamental level that the other elements are reconciled to their subordination and concur easily.

4. Because Plato interprets the *psyche* as a union of potentially contending elements, the comparison with the *polis* becomes plausible and important. He made no distinction of kind between reason's rule in the *psyche* and its rule in the *polis* through the political preeminence of the philosophers. There is no disjunction between the functioning of reason at the level of the individual *psyche* and its operation politically, for in the two contexts its role is the same: to harmonise spirit and appetite to good functioning under its own rule. It is difficult to see why philosophic reason's rule in the *polis* is unnatural if its role within the individual *psyche* is not so characterised. To defend their case, Strauss and Bloom . . . must distinguish in kind between the "private" and "social" action of reason. Strauss and Bloom attempt this by combining the disjunction between platonic and vulgar justice with their alleged disjunction between theoretical and practical reason. Because they can see no connection between the philosopher's platonic justice and his performing vulgarly just action for the good of others, they assume that he is not naturally a political ruler. Believing that his theoretical activity is unrelated to any practical life and believing that the philosopher's *eudaimonia* consists exclusively in theorising and the possession of an ordered *psyche,* Strauss and Bloom can see no reason to accept that he will be concerned with action for the good of others. Apparently, Plato fails to connect the internal justness of the philosopher with his public role as ruler because platonic justice is a self-centred condition. To answer such a case we must consider whether Plato fails to connect platonic and vulgar justice in general terms before examining the case of the philosopher-ruler in particular.

Plato states explicitly that platonically just men will observe conventional norms (422e–443b), and . . . that the rule of reason in the *psyche* expresses itself in just action. Platonic justice is plausibly understood as the efficient cause of just action, for reason not only apprehends, but aspires to the Good, which includes the form of justice as a universal and not private good. Reason's concern is that the good should be exemplified everywhere. Reason "does its own" only when it makes correct moral judgements, and the platonically just man acts rightly because the sources of his wrongdoing—appetite and spirit—are disciplined and subordinated. The two justices are connected not only because psychic harmony is the efficient cause of just action, but because that harmony is the *telos*, or final cause, of such action. By so understanding platonic justice, Plato introduces a "revisionist" account of ordinary moral conduct: those actions are called just which create and preserve internal harmony, and unjust actions are those which unleash spirit and appetite (443d6–44a2 and 588e–592a). Yet he revises and does not reject altogether ordinary rules of conduct, for their observance contributes to the creation of an harmonious *psyche* (589c–590a). Because that harmony consists in the excellence of the whole *psyche*, it cannot be realised by theoretical reason in isolation. To integrate and harmonise appetite and spirit within a complete life, reason must operate in the practical mode. Obviously, spirit and appetite cannot join with reason in understanding the forms, so they function within the harmony of a whole *psyche* only through the practice of right conduct; like wild beasts, appetite and spirit are disciplined only by being repeatedly trained. Therefore, the philosopher acts naturally for the good of others, perfecting his own nature in so doing.

5. However, Strauss and Bloom might still argue that, although the philosopher will act justly for the good of others, ruling remains an altogether different kind of activity, with a final cause other than the psychic harmony of the philosopher. They might deny that ruling is included within the concept of vulgar justice. To say that a philosopher must act justly is not, it could be argued, the same as saying that a philosopher must rule. The difficulty about such a reply is that it neglects essential aspects of Plato's metaphysic. If we understand his account of reason properly, we shall see that the philosopher's platonically just *psyche* naturally acts justly, and rules, in order to reproduce its own harmony in other subjects. Reason's final cause is the platonic justice of its own and other men's *psychai*, and the philosopher's reason is impartial between its own and their *psychai* as potential spheres of justice. That Plato did consider reason to be impartial in exactly this way is evident from the formal properties that he attributes to its operation in the theoretical mode. In theorising, when it considers the sensible world as an imperfect manifestation of the forms' order, reason is impartial between particulars, as it reflects on the forms in which they share. Certain particulars (say actions) will be better or worse exemplifications of a form (like justice), but the degree of their participation in the form is the only ground for reason's differentiation. For reason there is no "material" difference between particulars, excepting the degrees of their resemblances of the forms. Now, because theoretical and practical reason are the two aspects of the same power or faculty, we can generalize from reason's procedure in the theoretical mode to its operation in the practical. Because in the practical mode reason functions in the same way, it seeks naturally to reproduce platonic justice equally in any of the particular *psychai* that fall within the scope of its action. Just as in the theoretical mode reason's purpose of apprehending the forms is identical in relation to all the particulars of the sensible world, so, in the practical mode, its purpose of recreating the order of the forms is the same in all similar cases. Given the nature of reason, as the element that aspires to the imposition of its own rule and which looks to the good of the whole, and given its manner of operation in the theoretical mode, there is no ground for restricting its natural function of ruling to any one *psyche* rather than another. . . . Because the

philosopher's reason naturally creates the psychic harmony that is based on the forms, its natural role extends potentially to all *psychai* in which order can be created. There is no principle by which the philosopher's reason can be restricted to self-centred operation. Political ruling, then, appears as the natural realisation of reason's function.

6. This conclusion, which arises from Plato's distinctive understanding of reason and the unity of the *psyche*, assumes an enhanced intelligibility if we remember his conception of philosophic rule. Some commentators have found this so singular that they have denied altogether its *political* character.[49] For Wolin, Plato's philosophic rule is nonpolitical because it involves the implementation of a definitive order and the elimination from public life of such features as disagreement, conflict, conciliation, competition, and persuasion—all, or some of which, many modern commentators take as constitutive features of "politics." If politics is so understood, then the activity of ruling can certainly appear foreign to the philosopher's nature. Because Strauss and Bloom implicitly understand politics in such political scientist terms and because they do not recognize how distinctive is Plato's account of political rule, they are inclined to separate sharply the philosopher's contemplation of the forms from his activity of ruling. The harmony of the forms appears so remote from the practices constitutive of politics that philosophical politics appears an unnatural combination, perverting the philosopher's nature. . . .

The *Republic* reveals that competition, conflict, and so on are features of politics only in corrupt *poleis*, which are perversions of the proper political order. Plato does not consider ideal political rule as foreign to the philosopher's nature, because his ruler neither arbitrates nor participates in contingent divisions of opinion. His rulers are not even primarily legislators, but guardians of the right *paideia*, from which so much follows.[50] Their purpose is to preserve those educational arrangements and divisions of social function that make their subjects as far as possible good by developing the harmony of their *psychai*. Their subjects' lives and *psychai* are ordered according to the direction of philosophic reason, which makes each man's *psyche* a unity and combines them all in a further whole that is the *kallipolis*. Benefiting from the right education and observing their social function faithfully, the subjects enjoy a measure of platonic justice. When politics is understood in this way, then there is nothing more appropriate than that philosophers should rule, for that activity consists in modeling the moral and social whole according to the harmony of the forms. Reason realises its own nature most perfectly by creating the natural harmony of appetite, spirit, and reason within the political whole. Ruling is the natural extension of reason's role within the *psyche*.

7. The standpoint just developed makes intelligible Socrates' statement that, for the philosophers, "it is by nature fitting for them both to engage in philosophy and to lead the city" (474c). He is explicit that the philosopher who retires from public life, in corrupt *poleis*, does not realize himself perfectly. In the *kallipolis*, the philosopher "will grow more and save the common things along with the private" (497a). So what of the references to their reluctance to rule? Does Plato imply that ruling is a diminution of their *eudaimonia*? No, for the references mean only that the philosophers see before them, on a larger and more difficult scale in the public world, the task they have already accomplished within their own *psychai*—namely, the ordering of spirit and appetite. That they are individually reluctant to accept the task does not imply that it is not their appropriate role, for Plato presents the rule of reason as the primary and natural imperative. Any refusal to rule would be an artificial restriction upon the sphere of reason and cannot be defended in terms of the philosophers'

personal happiness. Plato, clearly, does not define *eudaimonia* in terms of felt satisfaction, but as the natural harmony of reason, spirit, and appetite, and the *personal* happiness of the philosophers is not his primary desideratum. As we have already maintained, there is no personal identity logically prior to the elements of the *psyche*, which "possesses" them and whose felt happiness varies according to how they are ordered. We misunderstand Plato's notion of *eudaimonia* grossly if we conceive it in terms of the effect of platonic justice on some agent possessing reason, spirit, and appetite. The idea of rational order in the *psyche* is prior to the idea of agent, for the agent's identity consists in that rational order. Within the individual and the moral and social whole, *eudaimonia* consists in the harmony of reason, spirit, and appetite. So the philosophers' reluctance to rule cannot be justified in terms of their private happiness, because *eudaimonia*, when properly understood, is not a personal condition dividing one man from his fellows, but an impersonal or transpersonal rational ordering, in which, ideally, men are combined. Socrates' insistence that he and his interlocutors consider the *eudaimonia* of the whole *polis* is perfectly intelligible, and to reply that a *polis* cannot be *eudaimon* as a man can be betrays a misunderstanding. Socrates leads his listeners away from the notion of happiness as private satisfaction to the idea of *eudaimonia* as transpersonal rational harmony. When the philosophers realise that ultimately there is no incompatibility between their fulfillment and their political role in the *kallipolis*, then, ruling, they combine perfectly with their subjects and achieve their fullest growth.

So the *Republic* does not disclose the "limits of politics" by revealing that the philosopher's life of service to the *polis* is incompatible with his self-realisation. The individual and common goods are not opposed, and, within the *kallipolis*, the philosophic nature is not divorced by its excellence from the rest of the community, for rational order must be realised in both. If they resist the offer to rule, the philosophers act contrary to nature. Quite appropriately, then, Plato says they must be compelled. When we realise that the *Republic* does not disclose the "limits of politics" but represents a truly ideal political order, then we shall understand Plato's intentions more adequately.

Notes

1. L. Strauss, *The City and Man* (Chicago, 1964) and A. Bloom, *The Republic of Plato*, translated, with notes and an "Interpretive Essay," (New York, 1968). Strauss has written about Plato in several works over many years. However, *The City and Man* provides the most developed version of his views and, because we are concerned with the cogency of his interpretation, not with its genesis, and because his account remained stable in essentials, it is to this work that we shall restrict ourselves. Bloom's account derives from that of Strauss. To be sure of being fair to them, our quotations from the *Republic* are taken from Bloom's excellent translation.
2. Strauss, *The City and Man*, p. 127.
3. Ibid., p. 112.
4. Ibid., p. 65.
5. Bloom, *Republic*, p. 410.
6. Ibid., p. 409.
7. Ibid., p. 410. Cf. pp. 343 and 408, and Strauss, *The City and Man*, p. 138.
8. Strauss, *The City and Man*, p. 138, and Bloom, *Republic*, p. 408.
9. Strauss, *The City and Man*, pp. 116–117 and 138, and Bloom, *Republic*, pp. 382–389.
10. Strauss, *The City and Man*, pp. 50–51.

11. Bloom, *Republic*, p. 411.
12. Strauss, *The City and Man*, pp. 61 and 116.
13. Bloom, *Republic*, p. 380.
14. E. Barker, *Greek Political Theory* (reprinted London, 1964), p. 242, n. 1.
15. J. Adam, *The Republic of Plato* (Cambridge, 1902, 2 Vols.), I, pp. 345–355.
16. Ibid., p. 355.
17. Cf. H. D. Rankin, *Plato and the Individual* (London, 1964), p. 93.
18. Cf. W. C. Booth, *A Rhetoric of Irony* (Chicago and London, 1974), p. 81.
19. Cf. Rankin, *Plato and the Individual*, chs. II and V.
20. Cf. E. Barker, *Greek Political Theory*, pp. 252–253 and Rankin, *Plato and the Individual*, p. 92. And see, too, Herodotus, *Histories*, IV, 104, 116, 180.
21. For a discussion of this coherence see Barker, *Greek Political Theory*, pp. 242–276.
22. Strauss, *The City and Man*, pp. 115–117 and 138. Cf. Bloom, *Republic*, pp. 382–389.
23. Ibid., pp. 118–120.
24. Ibid., p. 111.
25. Ibid., pp. 116–117. Cf. Bloom, *Republic*, pp. 364, 375, 382, and 386.
26. Strauss, *The City and Man*, p. 127 and Bloom, *Republic*, p. 411.
27. Bloom, *Republic*, p. 382.
28. Xenophon, *The Constitution of the Lacedaemonians*.
29. Strauss, *The City and Man*, pp. 118–121.
30. Ibid., p. 118.
31. Ibid., pp. 109–110, 115, and cf. Bloom, *Republic*, pp. 374 and 378.
32. D. Sachs, "A Fallacy in Plato's *Republic*," *Philosophical Review*, LXXII (1963), 141–158. Reprinted in A. Sesonske (ed.), *Plato's Republic: Interpretation and Criticism*, pp. 66–81 and in G. Vlastos (ed.), *Plato II: Ethics, Politics and Philosophy* . . .
33. Strauss, *The City and Man*, p. 127.
34. Ibid., p. 97.
35. Ibid., pp. 127–128.
36. Bloom, *Republic*, p. 337 and cf. pp. 373–374 and 378.
37. Ibid., pp. 343–344, 373–374, 378, 380, 407–408, and 411. And cf. Strauss, *The City and Man*, p. 127.
38. Cf. the too-much ignored passage at *Republic* 588b–591a.
39. Bloom, *Republic*, p. 343. Cf. pp. 408 and 410, and the important closing words of Strauss' essay, *The City and Man*, p. 138.
40. Bloom, *Republic*, p. 343 and cf. pp. 373–374.
41. Ibid., pp. 378 and 407–408.
42. Ibid., pp. 380, 407 and 410.
43. Ibid., p. 410. . . .
44. Strauss, *The City and Man*, pp. 111–112, 115, 125, 133, and 138.
45. Bloom, *Republic*, p. 309.
46. Ibid., pp. 407–408 and Strauss, *The City and Man*, pp. 124–125.
47. Bloom, *Republic*, p. 410.
48. Ibid., p. 407.
49. See: S. Wolin, *Politics and Vision* (Boston, 1960), ch. 2. . . .
50. Plato argues this explicitly at 425b–427a. Cf. 412a.

COMMENTARY

Response to Hall
Allan Bloom

[Plato in the Republic] *sought and made a city more to be prayed for than hoped for . . . not such that it can possibly be but one in which it is possible to see the meaning* [ratio] *of political things.*
[*Cicero,* Republic *II 52*]

I am grateful to Professor Hall for a number of reasons, especially for the seriousness with which he has taken my interpretation of the *Republic.* That he disagrees with it is secondary. We do agree on the fundamental thing: it is of utmost importance to understand Plato.

The issues raised by Hall are enormous, and an adequate response to his arguments would require volumes, but what we really disagree about is how to read Plato. He asserts that I read my prejudices into the text. I respond that he does not pay sufficient attention to the text. In looking at a few of his central criticisms, I shall attempt to prove my contention and show the characteristic errors of his approach to the Platonic dialogue.

I

In the first place, Hall presupposes that he knows the Platonic teaching and reads his understanding of it into the text. Arguing against my contention that the best regime of the *Republic* is not a serious proposal, he tells us, "Socrates is explicit that his *polis* is natural." I search in vain for Socrates' statement to that effect. Indeed, I know of no assertion anywhere in the Platonic corpus that the city is natural or that man is by nature a political animal. Whatever the *ideas* may be—and they are the highest and most elusive theme to which we must ascend very carefully and slowly from the commonly sensed particulars—there is not the slightest indication that there is an *idea* of the city or of the best city, as there is said to be an *idea* of the beautiful or an *idea* of the just. What the omission means is debatable, but one must begin by recognizing that it is so. Obviously, from the point of view of the *ideas*, the naturalness of the city must have a status very different from that of, for example, man. The kallipolis cannot participate in an *idea* which is not. While there are many men and an *idea* of man, the city does not exist as a particular or as a universal; it is neither sensed nor intellected.

Careful observation of what the text says about this question of naturalness would have helped Hall. In his discussion of the three waves of paradox in Book V, Socrates

Allan Bloom, "Response to Hall," *Political Theory,* 5:3, pp. 315–330. Copyright © 1977 by Sage Publications, Inc. Reprinted by permission of Sage Publications, Inc.

Author's Note: Hall is quite right in saying that my interpretation of the *Republic* is derivative from that of Leo Strauss. It is the nature of derivative works to be on a lower level than those from which they stem. There is much in Strauss' interpretation that I have understood, but there is also surely much that I have not understood. I cannot speak for him. In what follows I refer only to my essay and leave Strauss' to speak for itself, as he would certainly have wished.

says (a) the same education and way of life for women as for men is possible because it is natural (456b–c); (b) the community of women and children is not against nature (466d)—however, now Socrates shifts the criterion of possibility from naturalness to coming into being (many things which are not natural, and even against nature, can come into being); (c) the coincidence of philosophy and rule is just that, coincidence or chance (473c–d). All the attention is given to the possibility of that highly improbable coincidence. Cities, let alone the best city, do not come into being as do plants and animals. Some men are by nature fit both to philosophize and to rule in the city, but it is not said that it is natural that they do so. If they actually do both, the cause is art, human making, not nature. If I were to use against Hall the methods he uses against me, I would say that, with respect to the naturalness of the city, he has read Aristotle's *Politics*, not Plato's *Republic*. He does not see that the city is more problematic for Plato than for Aristotle.

Just as Hall reads in, he reads out. In trying to argue that for Plato there is no significant distinction between the theoretical and the practical life, he says that Plato "does not suggest that philosophising and ruling are unrelated functions." Compare that to the text: "each of [the philosophers] will go to ruling as a necessary as opposed to a good thing . . . if you discover a life better than ruling for those who are going to rule, it is possible that your well-governed city will come into being. . . . Have you another life that despises political offices other than that of true philosophy? . . . But men who aren't lovers of ruling [they love something other: wisdom] must go to it" (521a–b). The philosophers won't be willing to act [engage in *praxis*] (519c). There could be no more radical distinction made between the practical and theoretical lives than that drawn in Books V–VII and IX of the *Republic* (cf. especially 476a–b). The separateness of the forms is strongly asserted, as are the possibilities of a reason using only forms without admixture of the senses and a life lived in contemplation of the forms purely. This latter life is the best life, the only good life. It is precisely the difference between it and the life of ruling that is the artifice that is supposed to make the city work. Deed and speech are also radically distinguished, and the latter is said to be absolutely superior.[1] I really find it hard to imagine how Hall is able to say the things he does in the face of the evidence to the contrary. I challenge him to find a single statement in the *Republic* that indicates that the philosophic life requires ruling or that the activity of ruling in any way contributes to philosophizing.[2] What is striking about the *Republic* is the distance Socrates puts between the theoretical and practical lives, a distance belied by things he says elsewhere and by his own life. But that is what he does here, and, as Hall says, "we are accustomed to taking Socrates seriously." There is simply not a scintilla of proof that the making, painting, or "creating" activity of the founders of the city is a part of the philosopher's life as such. Hall piles abstraction on abstraction, unrelated to the text, in order to *construct* a case for the sameness of the two lives, but he has no evidence. The most striking aspect of the last half of his paper is its almost entirely personal character and almost total absence of reference to text. It is true, as he says, that the potential philosophers must be compelled to leave the cave as well as return to it. But once out, they recognize how good it is to be out. They never see a reason to go back, and compelling them to go back is said to be good for the city, not the philosophers. If they thought it good to go back, they would not be good rulers. It is only by going out that they became aware that the kallipolis is a cave, nay Hades, and to be in it is as to be a shade (516d; 521c; cf. 386c). In the midst of his complex prestidigitatory activity, Hall announces that it is because I am a modern political scientist that I cannot see that Platonic ruling is really philosophizing. I would like to accept that testimonial to impress some of my colleagues who have their doubts about the genuineness of my credentials as a political scientist, but unfortunately the explanation does not work. Again, one must look at the text. Rulers, in the best city, provide for food, clothing, and shelter, and they lead the soldiers to war. Above all, Hall forgets the reasons the philosophers are invoked: they are primarily matchmakers or eugenicists who have to spend a great deal of time and subtlety on devising "throngs of lies and deceptions" designed to get the right people to have sexual intercourse with one another (458d–460b). Is that a philosophic activity?

Displaying the same tendency to neglect what is really in the text, Hall spins a subtle web of reasonings about a Platonic notion of happiness which is frankly beyond my comprehension, a notion evidently intended to overcome the tensions between philosophy and ruling. In this context he insists that "Plato, clearly, does not define *eudaimonia* in terms of felt satisfaction . . . and the personal happiness of the philosophers is not his primary desideratum." Now, the culmination of the whole dialogue—the judgment concerning the happiness of the unjust man versus that of the just man, which was demanded by Glaucon at the beginning of the dialogue and was its explicit motive—concerns, if I understand what Hall means by *personal* happiness, the personal happiness of the philosopher (576b–588a). The terms of the comparison have been quietly changed during the course of the dialogue from the unjust man versus the just man to the tyrant versus the philosopher. Three tests are made, all three of which are won by the philosopher. The first test is self-sufficiency: the philosopher can get the good things he desires without needing or depending on other men while the tyrant lives in fear and is full of unsatisfiable desires because of his dependency on men. The other two tests prove that the philosopher is the expert *par excellence* in pleasure and that he experiences the purest and most intense pleasures. Socrates calculates that the philosopher's life is 729 times more pleasant than the tyrant's. Is this not "felt satisfaction" of a wholly personal kind? Philosophy is presented as choiceworthy on the ground that it provides permanently accessible pleasures for the individual, and the philosopher here is not presented as ruling or in any way concerned with the city.

In addition to making Plato answer his own questions rather than discovering what Plato's questions are and distorting the phenomena by casting a gray web of abstraction around them rather than letting them come to light in their fullness and complexity, Hall moralizes, not open to the possibility that justice is not preached in the *Republic* but rather questioned and investigated. For example, so sure is he that benefiting one's fellow man is an imperative of Plato's thought that he does not take note of the fact that the city has no concern for other cities and is even willing to harm and stir up factions in them, supporting the inferior elements, solely to keep them from threatening it. Best would be isolation, and next best is crippling one's neighbor; never would it try to improve them (422a–423a). Since the soul is said to be like the city, would not it, too, be concerned only with itself? The vulgar standards of just conduct to which the well-ordered soul is said to conform are all negative—things it does not do, such as stealing, lying, and committing adultery (442e–443a). As was indicated early on, Socrates' just man does no harm; he is not said to do good, to be a benefactor (335d). And the reason why the well-ordered soul does not do harm becomes clear when it is revealed to be the philosophic soul. The philosopher's abstinences are not due to good will, a Kantian "settled and sincere disposition to behave justly," but to a lack of caring for the vulgar things on which the vulgar standards are founded. His passionate love of wisdom makes him indifferent to, for example, money (485d–486b). This is no more praiseworthy than a eunuch's abstinence from rape. There is no "moral" motive involved.[3] It escapes Hall that of the three classes in the city, two have no concern for the common good at all—the artisans are in it for gain or out of fear, and the philosophers are there because they are compelled to be—while the dedicated class, the warriors, are dedicated only because they believe in a lie and are deprived of any possibility of privacy. There is, on the evidence of the *Republic*, no enlightened, nonillusionary love of the common good. The virtues of the warriors are finally said to belong more to the body than to the soul, to be mere habits (518d–e). The only authentic virtue is that of the mind contemplating its proper objects. It is not I who Aristotelianize. The *Republic* is not the *Ethics;* there are no moral virtues in it.

I have chosen to mention these points because they help to illustrate what is required to read a Platonic dialogue; and Plato intended to make the requirements for reading him identical to those for philosophizing; his little world is the preparation for the big world. In fine, what is needed is an openness to things as they appear unaided by the abstractions which so impoverish things that they can no longer cause surprise or wonder and a freedom from a moralism which forbids us to see what in nature defies convention and refuses to console us in our hopes and fears.

II

My difference with Hall can be summarized by saying that he does not take the form of the dialogue seriously, that he does not begin where it fairly cries out for us to begin, with the story or the drama, with those pictures of life on the basis of which we might generalize about life and which are so much more accessible to us than are "Plato's metaphysics" or the *ideas*. If I may be permitted an Aristotelian expression, but one which is of Platonic inspiration, we must begin from the things which are first according to us in order to ascend to the things which are first according to nature. We must talk about shoemakers and pilots and dogs and such things, the Socratic themes so despised by his less wise interlocutors. I can appreciate Hall's opinion that there is something mad in the assertion that a work of political philosophy which argues that philosophers should be kings actually means that philosophers should not be kings. But if we were to suppose for a moment that this is not precisely a book of political philosophy, at least such as we know books of political philosophy to be, but is a drama at one moment of which one of the characters makes an unusual proposal that is designed to affect the action, as are so many speeches in dramas, then the paradoxical character of my interpretation disappears. The tale would go roughly as follows. Socrates visits the Piraeus in the company of a young man whom, according to Xenophon, he is trying to cure of excessive political ambition as a favor to his brother, Plato (Mem. III, vi). There they meet a group of men among whom is a famous intellectual who argues that justice is abiding by laws set down in the interest of the rulers. It is, therefore, in one's interest to be ruler or, put otherwise, to be a tyrant. Glaucon, evidently motivated by more than idle curiosity, asks Socrates to show him that justice (understood as concern for equality or law-abidingness) is a good outweighing all the obvious good things (pleasures and honors) which tyranny (understood as the peak of injustice) can procure. Socrates never precisely shows Glaucon that justice as Glaucon conceives it is good. Rather, in the course of founding a city and, thus, learning the nature of justice, Socrates introduces, as a political necessity, the philosophers. Glaucon learns that to be a ruler in the city he has founded he must be a philosopher. Then, when he is shown what philosophy is, he learns that it is the best life and is essentially independent of political life. From the point of view of philosophy—which Glaucon had not considered and, thus, had not considered as a good thing—the city looks like a cave or a prison. The movement from rulers simply to philosophic rulers is a stage in Glaucon's liberation from the desire to rule. The dialogue has the character of an ascent, like the ascent from the cave to the region of the *ideas*. At the peak of that ascent Socrates reveals himself to be the happy man. He does not persuade Glaucon that he should not pursue his own good. He only makes him aware of goods to which the tyrant cannot attain and the pursuit of which takes away the temptation to meddle in politics and, hence, to be unjust as a tyrant is unjust. At the end of the comparison between the tyrant's and the philosopher's lives, close to the end of his education, Glaucon recognizes that the philosopher's city exists only in speech, and that no longer disturbs him. Socrates tells him it makes no difference whether it exists, for it can exist in the soul and that is enough (592a–b). A man can be happy being a good citizen of the city of philosophy without its existing. Timocrats and timocratic cities exist; democrats and democratic cities exist; tyrants and tyrannical cities exist; but, although there are no philosophical cities, philosophers exist. The tyrannical man who does not rule a city is not fully a tyrant (578b–c); the philosopher is a philosopher whether or not he is a king in a city. And there is, at this final stage, no suggestion that Glaucon should work to establish this city or that he should even long for its establishment. Glaucon has moved from the desire to be a ruler to the desire to be a ruler-philosopher to the desire to be a philosopher. The conceit of philosopher-kings was the crucial stage in his conversion. In the last word of the *Republic*, Odysseus—the archetype of the wise man—cured of love of honor or ambition and, having seen all the human possibilities, chooses the life of a private man who minds his own business. The *Republic*, while demonstrating Socrates' concern for justice, culminates in providing a foundation not for justice but for moderation.

Hall rightly concentrates on the statement that "unless philosophers rule as kings or those now called kings . . . philosophize . . . there is no rest from ills for the cities." That there will be no rest from ills for the cities is the teaching of the *Republic*, and this is what distinguishes ancient from modern philosophical politics. Socrates, moreover, does not suggest that there are ills of philosophy that would be cured by the union of wisdom and politics. The proposal is for the sake of the city, and not the philosopher. The distinction made in the discussion with Thrasymachus between justice as devotion to a community (be it band of thieves), which is only necessary, a means to an end (351c–d; 352c–d), and justice as perfection of the soul, which is good in itself (352d–354a), persists throughout. The philosophers' service to the community is necessary, while their life of contemplation on the Isles of the Blessed is good (540b). The two senses of justice are never resolved into a single coherent one.

Hall's failure to read the dialogue as a dialogue, his unawareness of its movement, causes him to give undue weight to isolated phrases or passages torn from their contexts. His greatest error is to take the discussion of *logismos*—calculation or deliberation—in Book IV as providing a definition of the "natural function" (both words are Hall's, not Plato's) of reason rather than as a provisional statement corresponding to the incomplete stage of the argument and of the interlocutors' awareness. Following the parallel of the rulers in the city, who deliberate about the affairs of the city, reason first comes to light in the *Republic* as the element of the soul which calculates about the desires, deciding which should and which should not be indulged. This description is a consequence of the analogy between city and soul which is being pursued in the discussion. What has first been determined about the city is applied to the soul (although Socrates points out that the discussion is inadequate, 435c–d). What we get in Book IV is a plausible account of reason's activity in the affairs of daily life, an activity akin to that of rulers who deliberate about public affairs, one that supports the view that man and city are in perfect harmony. But after the emergence of philosophy in Book V, a totally different account of the rational part of the soul is given, one which shows that the parallel between city and soul breaks down. The highest reaches of the soul are said to long only to *see* what *is* (437c–487a; 509c–511e; 514a–518b; 532a–534d). Deliberation or calculation (*logismos*), which was the only attribute of the rational part of the soul given in Book IV, is no longer even mentioned. The opposition between desire and calculation which was the defining characteristic of calculation in the earlier passage is overcome and philosophy is described as a form of *eros* (485c; 499b). The contemplative activity of the soul is simply something entirely different from the deliberative activity of a ruling class in a city (533b). Such contemplation is alien to the rulers' ends, and as a body they possess no organ for it. What the soul really is is both a revelation and a surprise in Book V, and its almost accidental discovery changes everything. The philosophic part of the soul has no use for action, and deliberation is not part of its function (527d–528e); it does not calculate. One must look to the difference between *logismos* and *nous* to appreciate the significance of this development. *Logismos* is for action; *nous* is for itself. The rulers of the city are highest because they are most useful to the city and its nonphilosophic ends. Reason in the soul is highest because it is the end of man and should be the end of the city. Unless ones reads the *Republic* as a drama, one does not see that it has a reversal and a discovery, that there is a peripety. Platonic books are closer in form to dramas than to treatises.

III

I have put off until the end discussion of what is only a subsidiary part of Hall's criticism—what he says about Plato's relation to Aristophanes. But this issue seems to me central to our differences. The elusive texture of Platonic thought—so different from our own—can, I believe, only be approached when one becomes aware of its peculiar combination of what we take to be poetry and philosophy. Or, put otherwise, Platonic philosophy is poetic, not merely stylistically but at its intellectual core, not because Plato is not fully dedicated to reason, but because poetry points to problems for reason that unpoetic earlier and later philosophy do not see and because poetic imagination properly understood is part of reason. The Socrates of the *Clouds*—an account of the early Socrates substantially confirmed by the Platonic Socrates (*Phaedo* 96a ff.)—was unpoetic, and this had something to do with his incapacity to understand political things. The Platonic Socrates can in some sense be understood as a response to the Aristophanic Socrates, or, more strongly stated, Socrates may have learned something from Aristophanes. The *Republic*, in one of its guises, is the proof that philosophers are not unpolitical (and it must not be forgotten that, according to all serious testimony, in particular that of Aristotle and Cicero, there was no political philosophy prior to Socrates), that they know the political things best and are most necessary for politics. Socrates, who in the *Clouds* stands aside, is neutral, in the dispute between the just and the unjust speeches, in the *Republic*—in a reference which is clearly to Aristophanes—presents himself as an unconditional partner of the just speech (*Clouds*, 896–7; *Republic*, 368b–c). And in the *Symposium*

Aristophanes is Socrates' only serious competitor in the contest for the best praise of *eros:* only these two have some inkling of what *eros* really is. Socrates the philosopher shows that his valid interlocutor is Aristophanes the comic poet, and that he is Aristophanes' superior in politics and erotics. Until we can take Aristophanes seriously and Plato comically we shall not understand either. It is only our stiff pedantry that causes us to ignore Plato's countless allusions to Aristophanes. For us academics they simply cannot be important. Professor Plato must talk only to his fellow professors. My response is that we must look where Plato tells us to look and not where we think we should look.

Now Hall says he sees nothing funny in Book V. My assertion that there is something ridiculous about the two sexes exercising naked together is tossed off lightly by Hall by reference to a passage in Xenophon which does not exist. Hall really means Plutarch, and a glance at the appropriate passage will prove to him that boys and girls in Sparta did not exercise naked together. He, further, fails to understand me. I know that there was homosexuality in Greece. What I meant is that a legislator can consistently forbid homosexual relations and condemn the attractions connected with them (as did the Athenian and Spartan legislators), but he cannot do the same for heterosexual relations. Socrates explicitly says that those who exercise naked together, because they do so, will be sexually drawn to one another (458c–d). Senses of humor, I am aware, do differ, but imagination suggests that the external signs of those attractions on the playing fields might provide some inspiration for tasteless wits.

Similarly, Hall says that Socrates does not appeal to absurd premises in Book V. I do not think it is just my ethnocentrism which gives me the impression that it is absurd for Socrates to found his argument on the assertion that the difference between male and female is no more to be taken into account than the one between bald men and men with hair.

But, to speak meaningfully about the *Republic's* debt to the *Ecclesiazusae,* we must say a few words about the meaning of that play. . . .

. . . Hall tells us that "for Aristophanes' satire of such social arrangements to have had point, others must have recommended them quite seriously." On the basis of such reasoning we would be forced to say that someone must have seriously proposed that the birds be made gods or that a dung beetle be used to get to heaven and bring back Peace for Aristophanes to have invented such conceits. Why should these schemes not have been among the imaginative poetic novelties on which Aristophanes prided himself? Surely the hilarious schemes which animate every comedy of Aristophanes ridicule, or show the ridiculous aspect of, something important. But the explicit project of the heroes does not reveal the intended object; it must be sought in an understanding of the effect of the play as a whole. In the *Ecclesiazusae,* the point is really quite clear: Aristophanes extends the principle of Athenian democracy to the extreme and shows that it is absurd, and thereby shows the limits, or the problem, of that regime. Athens is ridiculed, not some anonymous political projector. The Athenians want equality or to abolish the distinction between rich and poor, have and have-not. Athens is in trouble, and it is popularly thought that salvation can be achieved only by reforms which realize the goals of its popular regime. New rulers, women, propose communism, the utter destruction of privacy, in order to insure dedication to the common good and allow all to share equally in all good things, in order to make the city one. This will be a city which comprehends everything and satisfies all human longings. Praxagora's reform is subjected to searching criticism in two great scenes: (a) Chremes in good faith gives all his property to the city when it is perfectly clear that other men will not. He appears as a decent fool because the roots of private property go too deep to be torn out. Hence, inequality and selfishness would seem to be necessary concomitants of any political order. (b) A beautiful young man is forced to have sexual intercourse with a succession of ugly old hags. This is the application of the most radical, but also most necessary, reform connected with communism. What seems to be most private and most unequal by nature must become subject to the public sector, or there will be have-nots in the most extreme and important sense, and the young and the beautiful will have profound reservations in their commitment to civil society. This powerful and unsurpassedly ugly scene lays bare the absurdity of trying to make politics total, of trying to make an equal distribution of all that is rare, special, and splendid, of allowing nothing to escape or transcend the political order. It reveals the tension between *physis* and *nomos,* nature and civil society. By hypothesizing a perfect social union, Aristophanes lets his audience see for itself that it would be a hell, that some things must remain private and that men must accept the inconsistencies of a community which leaves much to privacy. The actualization of the Athenian goal is not to be desired.

Socrates adopts the premise of the *Ecclesiazusae:* for there to be a community, everything must be made public; above all there must be a community of women and children. In a passage that is all but a direct quote from the *Ecclesiazusae* (461c–d; *Ecclesiazusae,* 634–9), Glaucon asks how the citizens would recognize their close kin, to which Socrates responds, as did Praxagora, that they will not. Neither of these great reformers is worried about incest, the prohibition against which is most sacred and seems to be the backbone of both family and city. Their reform is far-reaching indeed.

But this defiance of *nomos* in Plato's picture does not turn out to be ugly or ridiculous, and we should therefore conclude that Plato thought Aristophanes to be wrong about the intransigent character of *nomos,* the impossibility of perfect communism and the transpolitical nature of *eros.* Aristophanes' hostility to philosophy made him miss the crucial point: philosophers, those consummate liars, could make it all work. Because he did not understand philosophy, Aristophanes thought the political problem to be insoluble. The focus of the issue for both Praxagora and Socrates is sexual affairs, and Socrates acts as though he can handle them as Praxagora could not. Useless philosophy proves to be most useful. Socrates as the replacement for Praxagora to turn failure into success is the Platonic improvement on Aristophanes' female drama.

Now it must be noted that Socrates is not introducing some grave, ponderous scholar as ruler. Philosophers as types were as yet essentially unknown and hardly respectable. The public model of the philosopher is that silly little fellow in the basket who makes shoes for gnats in the *Clouds.* Socrates dares to say that he is the perfect ruler. The comedy consists partly in Socrates' bringing together two of Aristophanes' plays, the *Clouds* and the *Ecclesiazusae,* using the ridiculous character of the one to solve the ridiculous problem of the other. The philosophers will see to it that the beautiful sleep with the ugly for the public good and do so without disorder or dissatisfaction.

So all is well. But now Socrates adds his scene, akin to those of Aristophanes. We get a glimpse of the relation of the philosopher to the multitude. Socrates follows Aristophanes' procedure. He makes the proposal and then lets his audience see it in action, letting them judge its actualization for themselves. Socrates uses the same language about the philosopher's relation to the multitude that one of the old hags uses to the beautiful young man: their intercourse is a Diomedean necessity (*Ecclesiazusae*, 1028–1029; *Republic*, 493c–494a). The multitude can never know or properly use the beautiful, but it will make the beautiful its slave. Aristophanes' comic scene is repeated on a higher level. The impossible and undesirable thing is the forced intercourse of philosophy and the city. The city, which once looked beautiful, has become ugly, and it compels what has now come to light as the truly beautiful. Hag is to boy as city is to philosopher. The privileged *eros* is philosophic *eros*. The differences between Aristophanes and Socrates have to do with the old war between philosophy and poetry, and here we can do no more than mention it and point out that it is what we must study. They agree about the limits of the city with respect to the highest things. Socrates uses Aristophanes' mad conceits to highlight both of these points. The political result of the inquiry of the *Republic* is revealed in the *Laws*, Plato's discussion of an actualizable regime. There the fundamental compromise is made: private property is accepted. It follows immediately that gentlemen, not philosophers, rule, that women are educated differently and lead very different lives from men, and that the family is retained. . . .

Now, what precedes is nothing but a series of hints. An adequate articulation of the issues involved in Socrates' playful competition with Aristophanes is the work of a lifetime. The real questions will only come to light by looking at the texts in full consciousness that we do not now know what the real questions are, let alone the answers to them. Plato's way is to think about the seemingly trivial or outrageous proposals of a Praxagora. We must imitate that way if we are to understand not only ancient thought but the permanent human problems, problems no longer quite visible to us.

Conclusion

My differences with Hall come down to whether philosopher-king is a compound formula, joining two distinct activities and, thus, violating the rule of justice, one man-one job, as I insist, or whether philosopher and king are two words for the same thing, as Hall insists. I believe Hall produces no evidence for his belief. Socrates' irony, which he claims I invoke as a *deus ex machina*, is to be found in the relation of his speeches to his deeds and his treatment of his various companions. It is present to every eye, and only by looking the other way can the problems I say need explaining be ignored or denied. As I pondered what separates me from Hall, I came to the conclusion that he misunderstands how political I take Socrates to be and how much attention I think he paid to particulars (as opposed to ideas). In other words, he does not pay attention to what I say about the cave or to the cave itself. The philosopher, of course, begins, as do all men, in the cave; and, to go Hall one better, he pays the strictest attention not only to particular or individual things but to their shadows. But the difference between him and other men is that he learns that they are only shadows—shadows which give us access to the truth—whereas they believe the shadows are the real things and are passionately committed to that belief. That is what cave-dwelling means. The cave must always remain cave, so the philosopher is the enemy of the prisoners since he cannot take the nonphilosopher's most cherished beliefs seriously. Similarly, Socrates does care for other men, but only to the extent that they, too, are capable of philosophy, which only a few are. This is an essential and qualitative difference, one that cannot be bridged and that causes fundamental differences of interest. Only they are capable of true virtue (518b–519b). To the extent that the philosopher turns some men to the light, he robs the cave-dwellers of allies. It is not because he lives in the sun, out of the cave, that I say the philosopher is at tension with the city; his problem is due precisely to the fact that he is in it, but in a way different from that of other men. This, however, should be the theme for an ongoing discussion. I only hope that it is clear that Hall's criticism has not settled the issue.

Notes

1. 471e–473b; 475d–480a; 485a–b; 510a–511d; 514a–519c; 532a–b; 540a–b. Plato surely makes a distinction between the practical and theoretical lives. Hall only introduces a red herring when he says I took the distinction from Aristotle. There is a difference between them concerning the distinction between *phronesis* and *sophia*, but that is irrelevant here. Everything I said was based on Plato. Hall, on the other hand, comes dangerously close to saying that knowing is making, a view to be found only in modern thought.
2. The statement at 497a, an intermediary stage in the discussion of philosophy and the city, need mean nothing more than that the philosopher would find more encouragement in such a city than elsewhere. Cf. 528b–c.
3. At 487a justice appears in the list of virtues belonging to the philosopher. By 536a it has dropped out.

Aristotle

Aristotle is probably best known for his assertion that man is the *zoon politikon,* the "political animal." This phrase is especially useful in characterizing Aristotle's work since it represents many facets of his thought. First, it reflects his interest in nature. Aristotle's father was a physician and, no doubt, imparted a love for natural science to his son. Aristotle spent several years away from Athens studying various animal species, especially marine life. This interest in biological studies contributed to Aristotle's reliance on nature as a standard for judging the function and virtue of a thing. We understand the nature of a thing on the basis of the functions it performs when it reaches a mature state. This is the "final factor" or teleological end of which Aristotle often speaks. For example, we might say the *telos* of an acorn is to become a mighty oak. Humans, too, can be understood by virtue of a natural function that, when fully developed, distinguishes us from all other beings. Reason is that function. It is, as Aristotle puts it, the "best thing in us." Reason places humans above all other creatures and provides us with the opportunity to order our own lives and our political communities; but reason can only flourish in political communities where there is time for reflection and opportunity for discourse. Thus, only in the city where politics is a necessary component of life, can man be fully human (i.e., exercise his highest faculty).

Furthermore, the phrase "man is a political animal" reflects Aristotle's interest in the practical. Unlike his tutor, Plato, Aristotle did not believe in the priority of abstract forms. Rather, Aristotle believed the material world provides the objects appropriate for scientific study. Understanding arises from the study of common aspects of particular elements, not from contemplation of abstract ideas. Politics is especially practical since it deals with bringing harmony and order to the city from the actions of diverse individuals. For Aristotle, not all are capable of performing the same functions in the state. As we will see, Aristotle uses differences in capacity to reason to differentiate between the proper function of men and women, masters and slaves. In a practical sense, then, man is political because he apportions political duties on the basis of capacity to reason in the interest of assuring social harmony.

Aristotle was born in 384 B.C.E. in the northern Greek city of Stagira, bordering provinces under Macedonian control. His parents were quite comfortable economically and socially. His father, Nicomachus, was a physician in the service of royalty and, no doubt, inspired his son's interest in biology. Upon the death of his parents when he was still a boy, Aristotle was made a ward of a relative by the name of Proxenus. When he was eighteen, Aristotle entered Plato's Academy where he studied and taught for approximately twenty years until Plato's death. There is still speculation over why Aristotle left Athens at this point. Some say he was disgruntled over not being named Plato's successor at the Academy. For whatever reason, he moved to Assos where he married a woman named Pythias. His wife bore him a daughter but died shortly after their return to Athens. He later entered into a relationship with a woman named Herpyllis and had a son by her, Nicomachus. In 343 B.C.E., Philip of Macedon invited Aristotle to tutor his son. During this period, Aristotle renewed his interest in politics, collecting and studying constitutions from around the world. Little is known about Aristotle's political influence over his pupil, who was to become known as Alexander the Great. Soon after the death of Philip, Aristotle returned to Athens and began his own school, the Lyceum. There he worked productively for twelve or thirteen years, producing most of the works that survive to this day in the form of lecture notes. Aristotle left Athens after the death of Alexander. This was a time when anti-Macedonian feeling swept through Greece and Aristotle, who was associated with the Macedonian ruler, became the subject of attack and unfounded charges, including that of impiety—the same charge that resulted in the death of Socrates. He died in Chalcis one year later at the age of sixty-two or sixty-three. We know from his will that he left his estate to his family. One especially noteworthy item, given his defense of slavery, was that he provided for the gradual emancipation of several of his slaves, an act that clearly set him apart from his contemporaries.

Nicomachean Ethics and The Politics

Aristotle spoke about two kinds of wisdom: theoretical and practical. Theoretical wisdom deals with universal truths and is revealed in studies of philosophy. Practical wisdom deals with those things subject to change; it involves deliberation about means for attaining ends judged to be good. Among the studies belonging to the realm of practical wisdom are ethics and politics. These two subject matters were considered closely related, a contention that is not easily understood in an age of political scandals and corruption. In fact, at the end of the Ethics, Aristotle turns his attention to political constitutions as a way of completing "to the best of our ability our philosophy of human nature." Ethics is a prelude to politics; politics completes the study of ethics.

Aristotle's Nicomachean Ethics (so called after the name of his son, who is supposed to have edited these notes), explores human happiness. According to Aristotle, happiness depends on a number of external factors (including health and some minimal standard of living), and on internal habits or virtues that keep us from pursuing too much or too little of a good thing. Happiness is not a subjective state that differs from individual to individual, but an objective state of personal well-being. For Aristotle, happiness depends on finding the mean in our actions between the extremes of excess and deficiency. For example, he considered courage a mean between the extremes of foolish bravado and cowardice. No citizen can be happy, reasons Aristotle, unless he acquires a level of courage commensurate with his abilities. Justice is one of the virtues Aristotle describes, though it is special in that it exhibits aspects of all the other virtues as applied in our dealings with our neighbors.

Surprisingly, for the modern reader not familiar with Aristotle, we are told that the subject of human happiness is one which political rulers must study since it is their job to create regimes that contribute to the happiness of citizens. The "end" or goal of the city is to lead men to the good life, not mere life. In the selection from Book I, Aristotle explores the notion of happiness and the role political science plays as the "master art" in bringing about happiness in the city.

The *Politics* is a wide-ranging volume containing discussions about the nature and origin of the state, class relationships, various forms of government, a theory of regime change, and a discussion of ideal and actual forms of government. In the first Book, Aristotle speaks of the state as the perfection of earlier forms of association, i.e., the state is the end toward which these earlier associations lead. Not all in the state can perform the same functions, however. In a set of passages which continue to inspire controversy, Aristotle cites the reasons he believes women and slaves must hold lower political status than male citizens.

In the selection from Book III, Aristotle discusses the various forms of government and the place of the multitude within the state. He identifies three pure types of regime and three "perverted" forms, with the distinction between these two categories centering on dedication to the common versus individual good. In the selection from Book IV, Aristotle discusses the broad outlines of the best practicable constitution for most states.

Commentaries

In the first commentary, Wayne Ambler addresses Aristotle's sometimes confusing discussion of the naturalness of the city. Ambler suggests that Aristotle's assertion that the city is natural is not fully supported by Aristotle's own subsequent analysis. In fact, Ambler suggests that Aristotle presents some good evidence against these contentions. Yet, as Ambler concludes, Aristotle does not contend that cities are artificial and that humans come together only out of necessity or contract. Instead, Ambler argues, Aristotle advances the notion of natural sociality as providing a standard at which cities ought to aim—even if humans in a presocietal setting fall short of this goal. In the second commentary, Susan Moller Okin explores Aristotle's treatment of women. She argues that his treatment is based on contemporary standards set by his own male-dominated society and by his hierarchical vision of society in which the role of the many is to provide leisure for the few.

Key Words

Arete. The functional excellence of a person, animal, or thing. For example, the arete of a fine racehorse is speed. In humans, the term refers to those qualities or excellences by which the individual performs well as a member of the political community.

Anthropos. The Greek term for human being or, more generally, the human race.

Logos. Speech, particularly as an element that exhibits human rationality. Sometimes used in denoting reason itself.

Nomos. Law or convention. Often used in contrast with *physis* (nature) to denote an artificial rather than a natural component.

Politeia. Regime or form of government, especially as related to constitutional organization.

Telos. An ultimate end, or function expressing the perfected state of a thing.

For Further Reading

Aristotle. c. 1947. *Introduction to Aristotle,* ed. R. McKeon. New York: Modern Library.

Barker, E. 1959. *The Political Thought of Plato and Aristotle.* New York: Dover Publications.

Lloyd, G.E.R. 1968. *Aristotle: The Growth and Structure of His Thought.* Cambridge: Cambridge University Press.

Lord, C. 1987. "Aristotle." In *History of Political Philosophy,* L. Strauss and J. Cropsey eds. Chicago: University of Chicago Press.

Ross, W.D. 1956. *Aristotle.* London: Methuen.

Strauss, L. 1964. *City and Man.* Chicago: Rand McNally.

Voegelin, E. 1957. *Plato and Aristotle.* Baton Rouge: Louisiana State University Press.

Nicomachean Ethics

Book I

1094^a 1. Every art and every inquiry, and similarly every action and pursuit, is
thought to aim at some good; and for this reason the good has rightly been
declared to be that at which all things aim. But a certain difference is found
among ends; some are activities, others are products apart from the
5 activities that produce them. Where there are ends apart from the actions,
it is the nature of the products to be better than the activities. Now, as there
are many actions, arts, and sciences, their ends also are many; the end of the
medical art is health, that of shipbuilding a vessel, that of strategy victory,
that of economics wealth. But where such arts fall under a single capacity—
10 as bridle-making and the other arts concerned with the equipment of horses
fall under the art of riding, and this and every military action under strategy, in the same way other arts fall under yet others—in all of these the ends
15 of the master arts are to be preferred to all the subordinate ends; for it is for
the sake of the former that the latter are pursued. It makes no difference
whether the activities themselves are the ends of the actions, or something
else apart from the activities, as in the case of the sciences just mentioned.

2. If, then, there is some end of the things we do, which we desire for its
own sake (everything else being desired for the sake of this), and if we do not
20 choose everything for the sake of something else (for at that rate the process
would go on to infinity, so that our desire would be empty and vain), clearly
this must be the good and the chief good. Will not the knowledge of it, then,
have a great influence on life? Shall we not, like archers who have a mark to
25 aim at, be more likely to hit upon what is right? If so, we must try, in outline
at least to determine what it is, and of which of the sciences or capacities it
is the object. It would seem to belong to the most authoritative art and that
which is most truly the master art. And politics appears to be of this nature;
1094^b for it is this that ordains which of the sciences should be studied in a state,
and which each class of citizens should learn and up to what point they
should learn them; and we see even the most highly esteemed of capacities
5 to fall under this, e. g. strategy, economics, rhetoric; now, since politics uses
the rest of the sciences, and since, again, it legislates as to what we are to do
and what we are to abstain from, the end of this science must include those
of the others, so that this end must be the good for man. For even if the end
is the same for a single man and for a state, that of the state seems at all
events something greater and more complete whether to attain or to
preserve; though it is worth while to attain the end merely for one man, it is
10 finer and more godlike to attain it for a nation or for city-states. These, then,
are the ends at which our inquiry aims, since it is political science, in one
sense of that term.

3. Our discussion will be adequate if it has as much clearness as the subject-matter admits of, for precision is not to be sought for alike in all discussions, any more than in all the products of the crafts. Now fine and 15 just actions, which political science investigates, admit of much variety and fluctuation of opinion, so that they may be thought to exist only by convention, and not by nature. And goods also give rise to a similar fluctuation because they bring harm to many people; for before now men have been undone by reason of their wealth, and others by reason of their 20 courage. We must be content, then, in speaking of such subjects and with such premises to indicate the truth roughly and in outline, and in speaking about things which are only for the most part true and with premises of the same kind to reach conclusions that are no better. In the same spirit, therefore, should each type of statement be *received;* for it is the mark of an 25 educated man to look for precision in each class of things just so far as the nature of the subject admits; it is evidently equally foolish to accept probable reasoning from a mathematician and to demand from a rhetorician scientific proofs.

Now each man judges well the things he knows, and of these he is a good judge. And so the man who has been educated in a subject is a good judge 1095ᵃ of that subject, and the man who has received an all-round education is a good judge in general. Hence a young man is not a proper hearer of lectures on political science; for he is inexperienced in the actions that occur in life, but its discussions start from these and are about these; and, further, since he tends to follow his passions, his study will be vain and unprofitable, because the end aimed at is not knowledge but action. And it makes no 5 difference whether he is young in years or youthful in character; the defect does not depend on time, but on his living, and pursuing each successive object, as passion directs. For to such persons, as to the incontinent, knowledge brings no profit; but to those who desire and act in accordance 10 with a rational principle knowledge about such matters will be of great benefit.

These remarks about the student, the sort of treatment to be expected, and the purpose of the inquiry, may be taken as our preface. . . .

7. Let us again return to the good we are seeking, and ask what it can be. 1097ᵃ It seems different in different actions and arts; it is different in medicine, in 15 strategy, and in the other arts likewise. What then is the good of each? Surely that for whose sake everything else is done. In medicine this is 20 health, in strategy victory, in architecture a house, in any other sphere something else, and in every action and pursuit the end; for it is for the sake of this that all men do whatever else they do. Therefore, if there is an end for all that we do, this will be the good achievable by action, and if there are more than one, these will be the goods achievable by action.

So the argument has by a different course reached the same point; but we must try to state this even more clearly. Since there are evidently more than one end, and we choose some of these (e. g. wealth, flutes, and in general 25 instruments) for the sake of something else, clearly not all ends are final ends; but the chief good is evidently something final. Therefore, if there is only one final end, this will be what we are seeking, and if there are more than one, the most final of these will be what we are seeking. Now we call 30 that which is in itself worthy of pursuit more final than that which is worthy of pursuit for the sake of something else, and that which is never desirable for the sake of something else more final than the things that are desirable both in themselves and for the sake of that other thing, and therefore we call final without qualification that which is always desirable in itself and never for the sake of something else.

Now such a thing happiness, above all else, is held to be; for this we choose always for itself and never for the sake of something else, but honour, pleasure, reason, and every virtue we choose indeed for themselves (for if nothing resulted from them we should still choose each of them), but we choose them also for the sake of happiness, judging that by means of them we shall be happy. Happiness, on the other hand, no one chooses for the sake of these, nor, in general, for anything other than itself.

From the point of view of self-sufficiency the same result seems to follow; for the final good is thought to be self-sufficient. Now by self-sufficient we do not mean that which is sufficient for a man by himself, for one who lives a solitary life, but also for parents, children, wife, and in general for his friends and fellow citizens, since man is born for citizenship. But some limit must be set to this; for if we extend our requirement to ancestors and descendants and friends' friends we are in for an infinite series. Let us examine this question, however, on another occasion; the self-sufficient we now define as that which when isolated makes life desirable and lacking in nothing; and such we think happiness to be; and further we think it most desirable of all things, without being counted as one good thing among others—if it were so counted it would clearly be made more desirable by the addition of even the least of goods; for that which is added becomes an excess of goods, and of goods the greater is always more desirable. Happiness, then, is something final and self-sufficient, and is the end of action.

Presumably, however, to say that happiness is the chief good seems a platitude, and a clearer account of what it is is still desired. This might perhaps be given, if we could first ascertain the function of man. For just as for a flute-player, a sculptor, or any artist, and, in general, for all things that have a function or activity, the good and the 'well' is thought to reside in the function, so would it seem to be for man, if he has a function. Have the carpenter, then, and the tanner certain functions or activities, and has man none? Is he born without a function? Or as eye, hand, foot, and in general each of the parts evidently has a function, may one lay it down that man similarly has a function apart from all these? What then can this be? Life seems to be common even to plants, but we are seeking what is peculiar to man. Let us exclude, therefore, the life of nutrition and growth. Next there would be a life of perception, but *it* also seems to be common even to the horse, the ox, and every animal. There remains, then, an active life of the element that has a rational principle; of this, one part has such a principle in the sense of being obedient to one, the other in the sense of possessing one and exercising thought. And, as 'life of the rational element' also has two meanings, we must state that life in the sense of activity is what we mean; for this seems to be the more proper sense of the term. Now if the function of man is an activity of soul which follows or implies a rational principle, and if we say 'a so-and-so' and 'a good so-and-so' have a function which is the same in kind, e. g. a lyre-player and a good lyre-player, and so without

qualification in all cases, eminence in respect of goodness being added to 10
the name of the function (for the function of a lyre-player is to play the lyre,
and that of a good lyre-player is to do so well): if this is the case, [and we
state the function of man to be a certain kind of life, and this to be an activity
or actions of the soul implying a rational principle, and the function of a
good man to be the good and noble performance of these, and if any action
is well performed when it is performed in accordance with the appropriate 15
excellence: if this is the case,] human good turns out to be activity of soul in
accordance with virtue, and if there are more than one virtue, in accordance
with the best and most complete.

But we must add 'in a complete life'. For one swallow does not make a
summer, nor does one day; and so too one day, or a short time, does not make
a man blessed and happy.

Let this serve as an outline of the good; for we must presumably first 20
sketch it roughly, and then later fill in the details. But it would seem that any
one is capable of carrying on and articulating what has once been well
outlined, and that time is a good discoverer or partner in such a work; to
which facts the advances of the arts are due; for any one can add what is
lacking. And we must also remember what has been said before, and not 25
look for precision in all things alike, but in each class of things such
precision as accords with the subject-matter, and so much as is appropriate
to the inquiry. For a carpenter and a geometer investigate the right angle in
different ways; the former does so in so far as the right angle is useful for his 30
work, while the latter inquires what it is or what sort of thing it is; for he is
a spectator of the truth. We must act in the same way, then, in all other
matters as well, that our main task may not be subordinated to minor
questions. Nor must we demand the cause in all matters alike; it is enough
in some cases that the *fact* be well established, as in the case of the first 1098^b
principles; the fact is the primary thing or first principle. Now of first
principles we see some by induction, some by perception, some by a certain
habituation, and others too in other ways. But each set of principles we must
try to investigate in the natural way, and we must take pains to state them 5
definitely, since they have a great influence on what follows. For the
beginning is thought to be more than half of the whole, and many of the
questions we ask are cleared up by it.

Politics

Book I

Every state is a community of some kind, and every community is established with a view to some good; for mankind always act in order to obtain that which they think good. But, if all communities aim at some good, the state or political community, which is the highest of all, and which embraces all the rest, aims at good in a greater degree than any other, and at the highest good.

Some people think that the qualifications of a statesman, king, householder, and master are the same, and that they differ, not in kind, but only in the number of their subjects. For example, the ruler over a few is called a master; over more, the manager of a household; over a still larger number, a statesman or king, as if there were no difference between a great household and a small state. The distinction which is made between the king and the statesman is as follows: When the government is personal, the ruler is a king; when, according to the rules of the political science, the citizens rule and are ruled in turn, then he is called a statesman.

But all this is a mistake; for governments differ in kind, as will be evident to any one who considers the matter according to the method which has hitherto guided us. As in other departments of science, so in politics, the compound should always be resolved into the simple elements or least parts of the whole. We must therefore look at the elements of which the state is composed, in order that we may see in what the different kinds of rule differ from one another, and whether any scientific result can be attained about each one of them.

II. He who thus considers things in their first growth and origin, whether a state or anything else, will obtain the clearest view of them. In the first place there must be a union of those who cannot exist without each other; namely, of male and female, that the race may continue (and this is a union which is formed, not of deliberate purpose, but because, in common with other animals and with plants, mankind have a natural desire to leave behind them an image of themselves), and of natural ruler and subject, that both may be preserved. For that which can foresee by the exercise of mind is by nature intended to be lord and master, and that which can with its body give effect to such foresight is a subject, and by nature a slave; hence master and slave have the same interest. Now nature has distinguished between the female and the slave. For she is not niggardly, like the smith who fashions the Delphian knife for many uses; she makes each thing for a single use, and every instrument is best made when intended for one and not for many uses. But among barbarians no distinction is made between women and slaves, because there is no natural ruler among them: they are a community of slaves, male and female. Wherefore the poets say,

It is meet that Hellenes should rule over barbarians;

as if they thought that the barbarian and the slave were by nature one.

Out of these two relationships between man and woman, master and slave, the first thing to arise is the family, and Hesiod is right when he says,

First house and wife and an ox for the plough,

for the ox is the poor man's slave. The family is the association established by nature for the supply of men's everyday wants, and the members of it are called by Charondas 'companions of the cupboard,' and by Epimenides the Cretan, 'companions of the manager.' But when several families are united, and the association aims at something more than the supply of daily needs, the first society to be formed is the village. And the most natural form of the village appears to be that of a colony from the family, composed of the children and grandchildren, who are said to be suckled 'with the same milk.' And this is the reason why Hellenic states were originally governed by kings; because the Hellenes were under royal rule before they came together, as the barbarians still are. Every family is ruled by the eldest, and therefore in the colonies of the family the kingly form of government prevailed because they were of the same blood. As Homer says:

Each one gives law to his children and to his wives.

For they lived dispersedly, as was the manner in ancient times. Wherefore men say that the Gods have a king, because they themselves either are or were in ancient times under the rule of a king. For they imagine, not only the forms of the Gods, but their ways of life to be like their own.

When several villages are united in a single complete community, large enough to be nearly or quite self-sufficing, the state comes into existence, originating in the bare needs of life, and continuing in existence for the sake of a good life. And therefore, if the earlier forms of society are natural, so is the state, for it is the end of them, and the nature of a thing is its end. For what each thing is when fully developed, we call its nature, whether we are speaking of a man, a horse, or a family. Besides, the final cause and end of a thing is the best, and to be self-sufficing is the end and the best.

Hence it is evident that the state is a creation of nature, and that man is by nature a political animal. And he who by nature and not by mere accident is without a state, is either a bad man or above humanity; he is like the

Tribeless, lawless, heartless one,

whom Homer denounces—the natural outcast is forthwith a lover of war; he may be compared to an isolated piece at draughts.

Now, that man is more of a political animal than bees or any other gregarious animals is evident. Nature, as we often say, makes nothing in vain, and man is the only animal whom she has endowed with the gift of speech. And whereas mere voice is but an indication of pleasure or pain, and is therefore found in other animals (for their nature attains to the perception of pleasure and pain and the intimation of them to one another, and no further), the power of speech is intended to set forth the expedient and inexpedient, and therefore likewise the just and the unjust. And it is a characteristic of man that he alone has any sense of good and evil, of just and unjust, and the like, and the association of living beings who have this sense makes a family and a state.

Further, the state is by nature clearly prior to the family and to the individual, since the whole is of necessity prior to the part; for example, if the whole body be destroyed, there will be no foot or hand, except in an equivocal sense, as we might speak of a stone hand; for when destroyed the hand will be no better than that. But things are defined by their working and power; and we ought not to say that they are the same when they no longer have their proper quality, but only that they have the same name. The proof that the state is a creation of nature and prior to the individual is that the individual, when isolated, is not self-sufficing; and therefore he is like a part in relation to the whole. But he who is unable to live in society, or who has no need because he is sufficient for himself, must be either a beast or a god: he is no part of a state. A social instinct is implanted in all men by nature, and yet he who first founded the state was the greatest of benefactors. For man, when perfected, is the best of animals, but, when separated from law and justice, he is the worst of all; since armed injustice is the more dangerous, and he is equipped at birth with arms, meant to be used by intelligence and virtue, which he may use for the worst ends. Wherefore, if he have not virtue, he is the most unholy and the most savage of animals, and the most full of lust and gluttony. But justice is the bond of men in states, for the administration of justice, which is the determination of what is just, is the principle of order in political society.

III. Seeing then that the state is made up of households, before speaking of the state we must speak of the management of the household. The parts of household management correspond to the persons who compose the household, and a complete household consists of slaves and freemen. Now we should begin by examining everything in its fewest possible elements; and the first and fewest possible parts of a family are master and slave, husband and wife, father and children. We have therefore to consider what each of these three relations is and ought to be: I mean the relation of master and servant, the marriage relation (the conjunction of man and wife has no name of its own), and thirdly, the procreative relation (this also has no proper name). And there is another element of a household, the so-called art of getting wealth, which, according to some, is identical with household management, according to others, a principal part of it; the nature of this art will also have to be considered by us.

Let us first speak of master and slave, looking to the needs of practical life and also seeking to attain some better theory of their relation than exists at present. For some are of opinion that the rule of a master is a science, and that the management of a household, and the mastership of slaves, and the political and royal rule, as I was saying at the outset, are all the same. Others affirm that the rule of a master over slaves is contrary to nature, and that the distinction between slave and freeman exists by law only, and not by nature; and being an interference with nature is therefore unjust.

IV. Property is a part of the household, and the art of acquiring property is a part of the art of managing the household; for no man can live well, or indeed live at all, unless he be provided with necessaries. And as in the arts which have a definite sphere the workers must have their own proper instruments for the accomplishment of their work, so it is in the management of a household. Now instruments are of various sorts; some are living, others lifeless; in the rudder, the pilot of a ship has a lifeless, in the look-out man, a living instrument; for in the arts the servant is a kind of instrument. Thus, too, a possession is an instrument for maintaining life. And so, in the arrangement of the family, a slave is a living possession, and property a number of such instruments; and the servant is himself an instrument which takes precedence of all other instruments. For if every instrument could accomplish its own work, obeying or anticipating the will of others, like the statues of Daedalus, or the tripods of Hephaestus, which, says the poet,

of their own accord entered the assembly of the Gods;

if, in like manner, the shuttle would weave and the plectrum touch the lyre without a hand to guide them, chief workmen would not want servants, nor masters slaves. Here, however, another distinction must be drawn; the instruments commonly so called are instruments of production, whilst a possession is an instrument of action. The shuttle, for example, is not only of use; but something else is made by it, whereas of a garment or of a bed there is only the use. Further, as production and action are different in kind, and both require instruments, the instruments which they employ must likewise differ in kind. But life is action and not production, and therefore the slave is the minister of action. Again, a possession is spoken of as a part is spoken of; for the part is not only a part of something else, but wholly belongs to it; and this is also true of a possession. The master is only the master of the slave; he does not belong to him, whereas the slave is not only the slave of his master, but wholly belongs to him. Hence we see what is the nature and office of a slave; he who is by nature not his own but another's man, is by nature a slave; and he may be said to be another's man who, being a human being, is also a possession. And a possession may be defined as an instrument of action, separable from the possessor.

V. But is there any one thus intended by nature to be a slave, and for whom such a condition is expedient and right, or rather is not all slavery a violation of nature?

There is no difficulty in answering this question, on grounds both of reason and of fact. For that some should rule and others be ruled is a thing not only necessary, but expedient; from the hour of their birth, some are marked out for subjection, others for rule.

And there are many kinds both of rulers and subjects (and that rule is the better which is exercised over better subjects—for example, to rule over men is better than to rule over wild beasts; for the work is better which is executed by better workmen, and where one man rules and another is ruled, they may be said to have a work); for in all things which form a composite whole and which are made up of parts, whether continuous or discrete, a distinction between the ruling and the subject element comes to light. Such a duality exists in living creatures, but not in them only; it originates in the constitution of the universe; even in things which have no life there is a ruling principle, as in a musical mode. But we are wandering from the subject. We will therefore restrict ourselves to the living creature, which, in the first place, consists of soul and body: and of these two, the one is by nature the ruler, and the other the subject. But then we must look for the intentions of nature in things which retain their nature, and not in things which are corrupted. And therefore we must study the man who is in the most perfect state both of body and soul, for in him we shall see the true relation of the two; although in bad or corrupted natures the body will often appear to rule over the soul, because they are in an evil and unnatural condition. At all events we may firstly observe in living creatures both a despotical and a constitutional rule; for the soul rules the body with a despotical rule, whereas the intellect rules the appetites with a constitutional and royal rule. And it is clear that the rule of the soul over the body, and of the mind and the rational element over the passionate, is natural and expedient; whereas the equality of the two or the rule of the inferior is always hurtful. The same holds good of animals in relation to men; for tame animals have a better nature than wild, and all tame animals are better off when they are ruled by man; for then they are preserved. Again, the male is by nature superior, and the female inferior; and the one rules, and the other is ruled; this principle, of necessity, extends to all mankind.

Where then there is such a difference as that between soul and body, or between men and animals (as in the case of those whose business is to use their body, and who can do nothing better), the lower sort are by nature slaves, and it is better for them as for all inferiors that they should be under the rule of a master. For he who can be, and therefore is, another's and he who participates in rational principle enough to apprehend, but not to have, such a principle, is a slave by nature. Whereas the lower animals cannot even apprehend a principle; they obey their instincts. And indeed the use made of slaves and of tame animals is not very different; for both with their bodies minister to the needs of life. Nature would like to distinguish between the bodies of freemen and slaves, making the one strong for servile labor, the other upright, and although useless for such services, useful for political life in the arts both of war and peace. But the opposite often happens—that some have the souls and others have the bodies of freemen. And doubtless if men differed from one another in the mere forms of their bodies as much as the statues of the Gods do from men, all would acknowledge that the inferior class should be slaves of the superior. And if this is true of the body, how much more just that a similar distinction should exist in the soul? But the beauty of the body is seen, whereas the beauty of the soul is not seen. It is clear, then, that some men are by nature free, and others slaves, and that for these latter slavery is both expedient and right.

VI. But that those who take the opposite view have in a certain way right on their side, may be easily seen. For the words slavery and slave are used in two senses. There is a slave or slavery by law as well as by nature. The law of which I speak is a sort of convention—the law by which whatever is taken in war is supposed to belong to the victors. But this right many jurists impeach, as they would an orator who brought forward an unconstitutional measure: they detest the notion that, because one man has the power of doing violence and is superior in brute strength, another shall be his slave and subject. Even among philosophers there is a difference of opinion. The origin of the dispute, and what makes the views invade each other's territory, is as follows: in some sense virtue, when furnished with means, has actually the greatest power of exercising force; and as superior power is only found where there is superior excellence of some kind, power seems to imply virtue, and the dispute to be simply one about justice (for it is due to one party identifying justice with goodwill while the other identifies it with the mere rule of the stronger). If these views are thus set out separately, the other views have no force or plausibility against the view that the superior in virtue ought to rule, or be master. Others, clinging, as they think, simply to a principle of justice (for law and custom are a sort of justice), assume that slavery in accordance with the custom of war is justified by law, but at the same moment they deny this. For what if the cause of the war be unjust? And again, no one would ever say that he is a slave who is unworthy to be a slave. Were this the case, men of the highest rank would be slaves and the children of slaves if they or their parents chance to have been taken captive and sold. Wherefore Hellenes do not like to call Hellenes slaves, but confine the term to barbarians. Yet, in using this language, they really mean the natural slave of whom we spoke at first; for it must be admitted that some are slaves everywhere, others nowhere. The same principle applies to nobility. Hellenes regard themselves as noble everywhere, and not only in their own country, but they deem the barbarians noble only when at home, thereby implying that there are two sorts of nobility and freedom, the one absolute, the other relative. The Helen of Theodectes says:

> Who would presume to call me servant who am on both sides sprung from the stem of the Gods?

What does this mean but that they distinguish freedom and slavery, noble and humble birth, by the two principles of good and evil? They think that as men and animals beget men and animals, so from good men a good man springs. But this is what nature, though she may intend it, cannot always accomplish.

We see then that there is some foundation for this difference of opinion, and that all are not either slaves by nature or freemen by nature, and also that there is in some cases a marked distinction between the two classes, rendering it expedient and right for the one to be slaves and the others to be masters: the one practicing obedience, the others exercising the authority and lordship which nature intended them to have. The abuse of this authority is injurious to both; for the interests of part and whole, of body and soul, are the same, and the slave is a part of the master, a living but separated part of his bodily frame. Hence, where the relation of master and slave between them is natural they are friends and have a common interest, but where it rests merely on law and force the reverse is true. . . .

XII. Of household management we have seen that there are three parts—one is the rule of a master over slaves, which has been discussed already, another of a father, and the third of a husband. A husband and father, we saw, rules over wife and children, both free, but the rule differs, the rule over his children being a royal, over his wife a constitutional rule.

For although there may be exceptions to the order of nature, the male is by nature fitter for command than the female, just as the elder and full-grown is superior to the younger and more immature. But in most constitutional states the citizens rule and are ruled by turns, for the idea of a constitutional state implies that the natures of the citizens are equal, and do not differ at all. Nevertheless, when one rules and the other is ruled we endeavor to create a difference of outward forms and names and titles of respect, which may be illustrated by the saying of Amasis about his foot-pan. The relation of the male to the female is of this kind, but there the inequality is permanent. The rule of a father over his children is royal, for he rules by virtue both of love and of the respect due to age, exercising a kind of royal power. And therefore Homer has appropriately called Zeus 'father of Gods and men,' because he is the king of them all. For a king is the natural superior of his subjects, but he should be of the same kin or kind with them, and such is the relation of elder and younger, of father and son.

XIII. Thus it is clear that household management attends more to men than to the acquisition of inanimate things, and to human excellence more than to the excellence of property which we call wealth, and to the virtue of freemen more than to the virtue of slaves. A question may indeed be raised, whether there is any excellence at all in a slave beyond and higher than merely instrumental and ministerial qualities—whether he can have the virtues of temperance, courage, justice, and the like; or whether slaves possess only bodily and ministerial qualities. And, whichever way we answer the question, a difficulty arises; for, if they have virtue, in what will they differ from freemen? On the other hand, since they are men and share in rational principle, it seems absurd to say that they have no virtue. A similar question may be raised about women and children, whether they too have virtues: ought a woman to be temperate and brave and just, and is a child to be called temperate, and intemperate, or not? So in general we may ask about the natural ruler, and the natural subject, whether they have the same or different virtues. For if a noble nature is equally required in both, why should one of them always rule, and the other always be ruled? Nor can we say that this is a question of degree, for the difference between ruler and subject is a difference of kind, which the difference of more and less never is. Yet how strange is the supposition that the one ought, and that the other ought not, to have virtue! For if the ruler is intemperate and unjust, how can he rule well? If the subject, how can he obey well? If he be licentious and cowardly, he will certainly not do his duty. It is evident, therefore, that both of them must have a share of virtue, but varying as natural subjects also vary among themselves. Here the very constitution of the soul has shown us the way; in it one part naturally rules, and the other is subject, and the virtue of the ruler we maintain to be different from that of the subject; the one being the virtue of the rational, and the other of the irrational part. Now, it is obvious that the same principle applies generally, and therefore almost all things rule and are ruled according to nature. But the kind of rule differs; the freeman rules over the slave after another manner from that in which the male rules over the female, or the man over the child; although the parts of the soul are present in all of them, they are present in different degrees. For the slave has no deliberative faculty at all; the woman has, but it is without authority, and the child has, but it is immature. So it must necessarily be supposed to be with the moral virtues also; all should partake of them, but only in such manner and degree as is required by each for the fulfilment of his duty. Hence the ruler ought to have moral virtue in perfection, for his function, taken absolutely, demands a master artificer, and rational principle is such an artificer; the subjects, on the other hand, require only that measure of virtue which is proper to each of them. Clearly, then, moral virtue belongs to all of them; but the temperance of a man and of a woman, or the courage and justice of a man and of a woman, are not, as Socrates maintained, the same; the courage of a man is shown in commanding, of a woman in obeying. And this holds of all other virtues, as will be more clearly seen if we look at them in detail, for those who say generally that virtue consists in a good disposition of the soul, or in doing rightly, or the like, only deceive themselves. Far better than such definitions is their mode of speaking, who, like Gorgias, enumerate the virtues. All classes must be deemed to have their special attributes; as the poet says of women,

Silence is a woman's glory,

but this is not equally the glory of man. The child is imperfect, and therefore obviously his virtue is not relative to himself alone, but to the perfect man and to his teacher, and in like manner the virtue of the slave is relative to a master. Now we determined that a slave is useful for the wants of life, and therefore he will obviously require only so much virtue as will prevent him from failing in his duty through cowardice or lack of self-control. Some one will ask whether, if what we are saying is true, virtue will not be required also in the artisans, for they often fail in their work through the lack of self-control? But is there not a great difference in the two cases? For the slave shares in his master's life; the artisan is less closely connected with him, and only attains excellence in proportion as he becomes a slave. The meaner sort of mechanic has a special and separate slavery; and whereas the slave exists by nature, not so the shoemaker or other artisan. It is manifest, then, that the master ought to be the source of such excellence in the slave, and not a mere possessor of the art of mastership which trains the slave in his duties. Wherefore they are mistaken who forbid us to converse with slaves and say that we should employ command only, for slaves stand even more in need of admonition than children.

So much for this subject; the relations of husband and wife, parent and child, their several virtues, what in their intercourse with one another is good, and what is evil, and how we may pursue the good and escape the evil, will have to be discussed when we speak of the different forms of government. For, inasmuch as every family is a part of a state, and these relationships are the parts of a family, and the virtue of the part must have regard to the virtue of the whole, women and children must be trained by education with an eye to the constitution, if the virtues of either of them are supposed to make any difference in the virtues of the state. And they must make a difference: for the children grow up to be citizens, and half the free persons in a state are women.

Of these matters, enough has been said; of what remains, let us speak at another time. Regarding, then, our present inquiry as complete, we will make a new beginning. And, first, let us examine the various theories of a perfect state.

Book III

VII. Having determined these points [regarding citizenship and types of rule], we have next to consider how many forms of government there are, and what they are; and in the first place what are the true forms, for when they are determined the perversions of them will at once be apparent. The words constitution and government have the same meaning, and the government, which is the supreme authority in states, must be in the hands of one, or of a few, or of the many. The true forms of government, therefore, are those in which the one, or the few, or the many, govern with a view to the common interest; but governments which rule with a view to the private interest, whether of the one or of the few, or of the many, are perversions. For the members of a state, if they are truly citizens, ought to participate in its advantages. Of forms of government in which one rules, we call that which regards the common interests, kingship or royalty; that in which more than one, but not many, rule, aristocracy; and it is so called, either because the rulers are the best men, or because they have at heart the best interests of the state and of the citizens. But when the citizens at large administer the state for the common interest, the government is called by the generic name—a constitution. And there is a reason for this use of language. One man or a few may excel in virtue; but as the number increases it becomes more difficult for them to attain perfection in every kind of virtue, though they may in military virtue, for this is found in the masses. Hence in a constitutional government the fighting-men have the supreme power, and those who possess arms are the citizens.

Of the above-mentioned forms, the perversions are as follows: of royalty, tyranny; of aristocracy, oligarchy; of constitutional government, democracy. For tyranny is a kind of monarchy which has in view the interest of the monarch only; oligarchy has in view the interest of the wealthy; democracy, of the needy: none of them the common good of all.

VIII. But there are difficulties about these forms of government, and it will therefore be necessary to state a little more at length the nature of each of them. For he who would make a philosophical study of the various sciences, and does not regard practice only, ought not to overlook or omit anything, but to set forth the truth in every particular. Tyranny, as I was saying, is monarchy exercising the rule of a master over the political society; oligarchy is when men of property have the government in their hands; democracy, the opposite, when the indigent, and not the men of property, are the rulers. And here arises the first of our difficulties, and it relates to the distinction just drawn. For democracy is said to be the government of the many. But what if the many are men of property and have the power in their hands? In like manner oligarchy is said to be the government of the few; but what if the poor are fewer than the rich, and have the power in their hands because they are stronger? In these cases the distinction which we have drawn between these different forms of government would no longer hold good.

Suppose, once more, that we add wealth to the few and poverty to the many, and name the governments accordingly—an oligarchy is said to be that in which the few and the wealthy, and a democracy that in which the many and the poor are the rulers—there will still be a difficulty. For, if the only forms of government are the ones already mentioned, how shall we describe those other governments also just mentioned by us, in which the rich are the more numerous and the poor are the fewer, and both govern in their respective states?

The argument seems to show that, whether in oligarchies or in democracies, the number of the governing body, whether the greater number, as in a democracy, or the smaller number, as in an oligarchy, is an accident due to the fact that the rich everywhere are few, and the poor numerous. But if so, there is a misapprehension of the causes of the difference between them. For the real difference between democracy and oligarchy is poverty and wealth. Wherever men rule by reason of their wealth, whether they be few or many, that is an oligarchy, and where the poor rule, that is a democracy. But as a fact the rich are few and the poor many; for few are well-to-do, whereas freedom is enjoyed by all, and wealth and freedom are the grounds on which the oligarchical and democratical parties respectively claim power in the state.

XI. . . . The principle that the multitude ought to be supreme rather than the few best is one that is maintained, and, though not free from difficulty, yet seems to contain an element of truth. For the many, of whom each individual is but an ordinary person, when they meet together may very likely be better than the few good, if regarded not individually but collectively, just as a feast to which many contribute is better than a dinner provided out of a single purse. For each individual among the many has a share of virtue and prudence, and when they meet together, they become in a manner one man, who has many feet, and hands, and senses; that is a figure of their mind and disposition. Hence the many are better judges than a single man of music and poetry; for some understand one part, and some another, and among them they understand the whole. There is a similar combination of qualities in good men, who differ from any individual of the many, as the beautiful are said to differ from those who are not beautiful, and works of art from realities, because in them the scattered elements are combined, although, if taken separately, the eye of one person or some other feature in another person would be fairer than in the picture. Whether this principle can apply to every democracy, and to all bodies of men, is not clear. Or rather, by heaven, in some cases it is impossible of application; for the argument would equally hold about brutes; and wherein, it will be asked, do some men differ from brutes? But there may be bodies of men about whom our statement is nevertheless true. And if so, the difficulty which has been already raised, and also another which is akin to it—viz., what power should be assigned to the mass of freemen and citizens, who are not rich and have no personal merit—are both solved. There is still a danger in allowing them to share the great offices of state, for their folly will lead them into error, and their dishonesty into crime. But there is a danger also in not letting them share, for a state in which many poor men are excluded from office will necessarily be full of enemies. The only way of escape is to assign to them some deliberative and judicial functions. For this reason Solon and certain other legislators give them the power of electing to offices, and of calling the magistrates to account, but they do not allow them to hold office singly. When they meet together their perceptions are quite good enough, and combined with the better class they are useful to the state (just as impure food when mixed with what is pure sometimes makes the entire mass more wholesome than a small quantity of the pure would be), but each individual, left to himself, forms an imperfect judgment. On the other hand, the popular form of government involves certain difficulties. In the first place, it might be objected that he who can judge of the healing of a sick man would be one who could himself heal his disease, and make him whole—that is, in other words, the physician; and so in all professions and arts. As, then, the physician ought to be called to account by physicians, so ought men in general to be called to account by their peers. But physicians are of three kinds: there is the ordinary practitioner, and there is the physician of the higher class, and thirdly the intelligent man who has studied the art: in all arts there is such a class; and we attribute the power of judging to them quite as much as to professors of the art. Secondly, does not the same principle apply to elections? For a right election can only be made by those who have knowledge; those who know geometry, for example, will choose a geometrician rightly, and those who know how to steer, a pilot; and, even if there be some occupations and arts in which private persons share in the ability to choose, they certainly cannot choose better than those who know. So that, according to this argument, neither the election of magistrates, nor the calling of them to account, should be entrusted to the many. Yet possibly these objections are to a great extent met by our old answer, that if the people are not utterly degraded, although individually they may be worse judges than those who have special knowledge—as a body they are as good or better. Moreover, there are some arts whose products are not judged of solely, or best, by the artists themselves, namely those arts whose products are recognized even by those who do not possess the art; for example, the knowledge of the house is not limited to the builder only; the user, or, in other words, the master, of the house will be even a better judge than the builder, just as the pilot will judge better of a rudder than the carpenter, and the guest will judge better of a feast than the cook.

This difficulty seems now to be sufficiently answered, but there is another akin to it. That inferior persons should have authority in greater matters than the good would appear to be a strange thing, yet the election and calling to account of the magistrates is the greatest of all. And these, as I was saying, are functions which in some states are assigned to the people, for the assembly is supreme in all such matters. Yet persons of any age, and having but a small property qualification, sit in the assembly and deliberate and judge, although for the great officers of state, such as treasurers and generals, a high qualification is required. This difficulty may be solved in the same manner as the preceding, and the present practice of democracies may be really defensible. For the power does not reside in the dicast, or senator, or ecclesiast, but in the court, and the senate, and the assembly, of which individual senators, or ecclesiasts, or dicasts, are only parts or members. And for this reason the many may claim to have a higher authority than the few; for the people, and the senate, and the courts consist of many persons, and their property collectively is greater than the property of one or of a few individuals holding great offices. But enough of this.

The discussion of the first question shows nothing so clearly as that laws, when good, should be supreme; and that the magistrate or magistrates should regulate those matters only on which the laws are unable to speak with precision owing to the difficulty of any general principle embracing all particulars. But what are good laws has not yet been clearly explained; the old difficulty remains. The goodness or badness, justice or injustice, of laws varies of necessity with the constitutions of states. This, however, is clear, that the laws must be adapted to the constitutions. But if so, true forms of government will of necessity have just laws, and perverted forms of government will have unjust laws.

Book IV

XI. We have now to inquire what is the best constitution for most states, and the best life for most men, neither assuming a standard of virtue which is above ordinary persons, nor an education which is exceptionally favored by nature and circumstances, nor yet an ideal state which is an aspiration only, but having regard to the life in which the majority are able to share, and to the form of government which states in general can attain. As to those aristocracies, as they are called, of which we were just now speaking, they either lie beyond the possibilities of the greater number of states, or they approximate to the so-called constitutional government, and therefore need no separate discussion. And in fact the conclusion at which we arrive respecting all these forms rests upon the same grounds. For if what was said in the *Ethics* is true, that the happy life is the life according to virtue lived without impediment, and that virtue is a mean, then the life which is in a mean, and in a mean attainable by every one, must be the best. And the same principles of virtue and vice are characteristic of cities and of constitutions; for the constitution is in a figure the life of the city.

Now in all states there are three elements: one class is very rich, another very poor, and a third in a mean. It is admitted that moderation and the mean are best, and therefore it will clearly be best to possess the gifts of fortune in moderation; for in that condition of life men are most ready to follow rational principle. But he who greatly excels in beauty, strength, birth, or wealth, or on the other hand who is very poor, or very weak, or very much disgraced, finds it difficult to follow rational principle. Of these two the one sort grow into violent and great criminals, the others into rogues and petty rascals. And two sorts of offenses correspond to them, the one committed from violence, the other from roguery. Again, the middle class is least likely to shrink from rule, or to be over-ambitious for it; both of which are injuries to the state. Again, those who have too much of the goods of fortune, strength, wealth, friends, and the like, are neither willing nor able to submit to authority. The evil begins at home; for when they are boys, by reason of the luxury in which they are brought up, they never learn, even at school, the habit of obedience. On the other hand, the very poor, who are in the opposite extreme, are too degraded. So that the one class cannot obey, and can only rule despotically; the other knows not how to command and must be ruled like slaves. Thus arises a city, not of freemen, but of masters and slaves, the one despising, the other envying; and nothing can be more fatal to friendship and good fellowship in states than this: for good fellowship springs from friendship; when men are at enmity with one another, they would rather not even share the same path. But a city ought to be composed, as far as possible, of equals and similars; and these are generally the middle classes. Wherefore the city which is composed of middle-class citizens is necessarily best constituted in respect of the elements of which we say the fabric of the state naturally consists. And this is the class of citizens which is most secure in a state, for they do not, like the poor, covet their neighbors' goods; nor do others covet theirs, as the poor covet the goods of the rich; and as they neither plot against others, nor are themselves plotted against, they pass through life safely. Wisely then did Phocylides pray—'Many things are best in the mean; I desire to be of a middle condition in my city.'

Thus it is manifest that the best political community is formed by citizens of the middle class, and that those states are likely to be well-administered, in which the middle class is large, and stronger if possible than both the other classes, or at any rate than either singly; for the addition of the middle class turns the scale, and prevents either of the extremes from being dominant. Great then is the good fortune of a state in which the citizens have a moderate and sufficient property; for where some possess much, and the others nothing, there may arise an extreme democracy, or a pure oligarchy; or a tyranny may grow out of either extreme—either out of the most rampant democracy, or out of an oligarchy; but it is not so likely to arise out of the middle constitutions and those akin to them. I will explain the reason of this hereafter, when I speak of the revolutions of states. The mean condition of states is clearly best, for no other is free from faction; and where the middle class is large, there are least likely to be factions and dissensions. For a similar reason large states are less liable to faction than small ones, because in them the middle class is large; whereas in small states it is easy to divide all the citizens into two classes who are either rich or poor, and to leave nothing in the middle. And democracies are safer and more permanent than oligarchies, because they have a middle class which is more numerous and has a greater share in the government; for when there is no middle class, and the poor greatly exceed in number, troubles arise, and the state soon comes to an end. A proof of the superiority of the middle class is that the best legislators have been of a middle condition; for example, Solon, as his own verses testify; and Lycurgus, for he was not a king; and Charondas, and almost all legislators. . . .

Aristotle's Understanding of the Naturalness of the City
Wayne H. Ambler

It is not at all surprising that Aristotle's political thought should be remembered especially for its teaching that "every city [*polis*] exists by nature."[1] This provocative claim occurs on but the third page of the *Politics,* is twice reaffirmed in short order (1253a2, 25), and appears to be defended to the philosopher's satisfaction in the three pages of book 1, chapter 2. Although modern doctrines on nature and politics have scarcely made it less provocative, unless they have helped to make it simply impossible to take seriously, it must have been striking enough even in Aristotle's own day. Socrates may have held the city ruled by philosopher-kings to be according to nature, but to reserve this distinction for such a city is to deny it to all others; far from maintaining that "*every* city exists by nature," the argument of the *Republic* tacitly rejects the naturalness of actual cities.[2] Of course many of the Sophists were even less indirect than Socrates; these popular intellectuals seem to have made their career by the enticingly radical suggestion that cities are without divine or natural authority over their members.[3] By emphasizing the distinction between nature and law or convention (*physis* and *nomos*), they challenged the city's authority (and enhanced their own), for they traced the origin of law not to the gods but to the self-interested agreements of fearful or greedy men. The opening pages of the *Politics* are thus like a gauntlet thrown in the direction of the Sophists: they affirm the naturalness of every city, and defend the city in terms of a transcendent and beneficent authority. But this discloses a still further aspect of Aristotle's uniqueness, for this higher authority is not the orthodox pantheon but a godlike nature. Aristotle's doctrine is thus neither Platonic, nor sophistic, nor orthodox even if—like the orthodox position—it does appear to defend the authority of existing cities. But to know that Aristotle's position is unique is not yet to understand it. In seeking to understand it, I will argue that Aristotle advances reservations against his "own" doctrine and shows the relationship between nature and the city to be far more complicated than the doctrine itself suggests. In so doing I hope not only to change opinions about the *Politics* but also to shed some light on the problem of political authority as we face it today.

Aristotle's defense of the naturalness of the city may seem so straightforward as not to need a careful study: it is brief; it occurs only once and so takes only one shape; it is typical of what we think we know about Aristotle, for it tries to present both a noble defense of the city and one which grants it generous authority over the individual; and it is often summarized in more or less the same way. But it is for other reasons very much in need of a careful study: upon examination "it" turns out to be at least two different arguments whose relationship is unclear; the very conclusion that "every city exists by nature" is explicitly contingent upon the hypothesis that "the

Wayne H. Ambler, "Aristotle's Understanding of the Naturalness of the City," *The Review of Politics,* Vol. 47:2, pp. 163–185. Copyright © 1985. Reprinted with the permission of the author and the University of Notre Dame Press.

first associations" also be by nature (1252b1); this hypothesis is questionable and is the subject not of one brief chapter but of book 1 in its entirety; and even the place of book 1 in the whole of Aristotle's political teaching is complicated by several factors and especially by its concluding call for a new beginning (allēn archēn, 1260b22; cf. b35–36). In short, to summarize Aristotle's often-summarized argument in defense of the city's naturalness is only to begin to understand his treatment of this issue. A better beginning begins by noting the context of this argument.

The very first sentence of the *Politics* asserts that the city is the supremely authoritative association (hē kuriōtatē koinōnia), that it encompasses all other associations, and that it aims at the most authoritative good. But if Aristotle begins by thus seeming to confirm the city's authority, he immediately proceeds to point out that some deny that the city is truly as authoritative as he has declared (1252a7–16). The seriousness of this denial is partially masked by Aristotle's brevity, indirectness, and reluctance to acknowledge that so worthy an opponent as Socrates was chief among the "some" who advanced it, but chapter 1 ends with a call for a clarification of the issue by means of an investigation into the city's smallest parts (elachista moria, 1252a17–23). It is this investigation which guides and unites the various sections of book 1 (cf. 1253b18–23; 1254b2–6; 1255b16–20; 1258b37–1259a17; 1260a7–17; 1253b12–14, 23–27; 1256a1–3; 1256b26–30, 37–39; 1258a19–25). Albeit the most memorable part, Aristotle's argument that "every city exists by nature" is only one part of this extended and complicated study. Moreover, the very call for such a study suggests the first limit to the city's authority: it is not the city itself but a philosophic investigation which will determine the authority due to that association. If philosophy is introduced as the vindicator of the city, it is also introduced as its superior in certain important respects.

It is of course not an idle matter whether the city should be found to deserve the vast authority which it admittedly exercises, but Aristotle meets this civic danger by seeming to settle in the second chapter the sensitive issue which he had just raised in the first. The three pages of the second chapter present a vigorous defense of the goodness and even nobility of the city and of political life. A review of its major statements will both remind us of its vigor and suggest the magnitude of the interpretive problem it poses. This brief chapter affirms the following: every city exists by nature; the city grows out of earlier associations and is their culmination (telos); it is a better association than they are; indeed, it is a complete (or, "perfect," teleios) association; it is self-sufficient and exists for the sake of the good life; it is especially suited for human beings, for man is by nature a political animal; it is by nature prior to both household and human being; man's relation to the city is that of part to whole; man is completed or perfected in the city; man when separated from law and judgment is the worst of the animals. The brief passage which sets forth these claims must be as welcome to the partisans of political authority as are the Sophists' speeches to its detractors. I know of no other passage in Aristotle so filled with lofty remarks about the city or so uncompromising in its tribute to the city. But Aristotle promised not beautiful claims but a careful analysis (1252a17–23); these claims notwithstanding, he keeps his promise.

It is necessary to see the plan of book 1 before reaching final conclusions about the meaning of any of its parts. At the end of chapter 1, Aristotle indicates that the authority of the city should be investigated by an analytical investigation into its smallest parts. Although chapter 2 is indeed concerned with such parts, it is rather a rapid account of the city's growth than a careful analysis of its parts; and it is only in this account of the city's growth that it is found to be natural.[4] Moreover, the chapters that follow chapter 2 do present themselves as examining the smallest parts of the city. Indeed, chapter 3 both restates the question of chapter 1 and begins the analysis proposed there, as though chapter 2 has not adequately answered this question (1253b18–23). Chapter 2 is thus something of an interlude between the promise of an analytic investigation in chapter one and the fulfillment of this promise in chapters 3 through 13. Perhaps the special character of this interlude is intimated in its opening lines: "If one should look from the beginning at these matters as they grow [ta pragmata phyomena], then, as in other cases, one would behold them in the most noble way [kallista]" (1252a24–26). Aristotle thus suggests that the second chapter's account of the city's growth is the most noble way of seeing the city, whereas he said above that an analysis of its parts would make the issue clear (dēlon, 1252a17). It is left to the reader to determine the extent to which the longer analysis in chapters 3 through 13 supports the noble findings presented in chapter 2.[5]

The structure of book 1 is thus as follows. It opens with an assertion of the authority of the city, only to call it into question; it then seems to resolve this dangerous issue by teaching that the city is natural and that nature is beneficent. The next eleven chapters (and bulk of book 1) go on to discuss not so much the city as the household and, in particular, to examine both slavery and acquisition in terms of their naturalness. It thus might seem that the central issue of the city's naturalness and authority is quickly and easily resolved, while secondary domestic issues become predominant. Nevertheless, these subordinate issues are meant to shed light on the very much unresolved question of the city's naturalness and authority. The discussions of slavery and acquisition are major sections of the analytical investigation called for to determine the city's authority, and the question of the naturalness of the city cannot but be affected by investigations into the naturalness of its institutions or practices. Indeed, the very declaration that "every city exists by nature" was explicitly contingent on the hypothesis, "if indeed the first associations also [exist by nature]" (1252b31). Since slavery in particular and the household in general are among the "first associations" on whose naturalness the naturalness of the city is contingent (1252b9–10, 1257a19–20), the long investigations of slavery and household management have an important bearing on the naturalness of the city. The noble but bold conclusions of chapter 2 must thus be tentative pending the longer and more ambiguous investigations of subsequent chapters. Qualifications regarding the naturalness of slavery and the acquisitive practices of the household must be expected to demand qualifications regarding the naturalness of the city.

My first purpose has been to show how the famous teachings of chapter 2 are linked to their larger context; their interpretation thus depends in part upon an interpretation of this context. . . .

Aristotle's account of the natural genesis of the city traces the city's ancestry to two associations which are said to be formed out of necessity (1252a26–31). The first of these is the association of male and female; the second is that between the "naturally ruling and ruled." What most needs to be stressed about these associations is that neither simply describes the relationship between two human beings. Aristotle emphasizes that the coming together of male and female is hardly unique to human beings; it extends to plants as well as animals (1252a28–30). He does not have in mind only the complex relationship between a man and a woman; he refers in the neuter gender to the simple and even abstract association between "male" and "female" (thēlu men kai arren).

The abstractness of these first two associations is still more clear in the case of the second. Aristotle does not speak of the association between master and slave but of that between "the naturally ruling and ruled" (*archon de physei kai archomenon*). He again uses the neuter gender, that is, and so is not speaking casually, as we do, of "a natural ruler" but in a more precise fashion of "a naturally ruling [element]." A later passage confirms this view (1254a21–33; cf. 1252b6). We learn there that the association between "the naturally ruling and ruled" is detected in the division between soul and body and that it is somehow present even in such inanimate things as musical harmonies. In spite of the widespread occurrence of the ruling-ruled association, then, it is doubtful that the relationship between two human beings can ever be described in such simple terms.

The simplicity and abstractness of the first two associations thus serve this general purpose: they are examples of associations which are natural without qualification. They establish a standard of what a natural association is, or at least of what one kind of natural association is. They invite us to see whether other possibly natural associations can claim to be natural in the manner and extent of their naturalness.

Aristotle himself uses the standard of "the naturally ruling and ruled" to show the unnaturalness of other associations. He does this most directly in the case of the barbarians. The barbarians are said to lack the naturally ruling and to confuse the female with the naturally servile.[6] The barbarian household was successful in bringing the male and the female together for the sake of generation, but it failed of naturalness in its ruling arrangements. Its rule may have been spontaneous, vigorous, and without art, but this is not what Aristotle means by natural rule. A similar but less-direct accusation is made against the household of Greek antiquity. However natural it may have been that men and women came together for the sake of generation, Aristotle is far from suggesting that their association was natural in all of its many aspects. The primitive household was not one of happy anarchy, and the rule which it suffered was not that of "the naturally ruling and ruled." It is thus wrong to identify the primitive with the simply natural and Aristotle's view with the simply conservative. The radical question which he does not yet address, and which he never addresses forthrightly, is whether contemporary households and cities escape the unnatural rule suffered by their predecessors. I shall explain below how Aristotle's discussion of slavery shows that they have not. Aristotle may hold slavery to be a defensible domestic and political institution, but its defense cannot be found in the claim that the naturally ruling rules the naturally ruled.

From the male-female and the mastering-servile comes the first village, and from a multitude of villages comes a city. This is a complete or perfect (*teleios*) association, so there is no growth beyond it (1252b9–28). It is here that we learn that "every city exists by nature." I have already noted the beauty and magnitude of the claims made in support of this contention; let me now sketch out the argument behind them.

The initial argument in support of the view that the city is a natural and a complete association maintains that the city "grows" into being out of villages and households. These first associations are presented as being incomplete, or perhaps "immature," but they seem to point beyond themselves to an end or completion: the mature association which is this end is the city (1252b31–34). The city is thus held to be natural not because it happens to develop from natural associations but because it *grows* from them: they *mature* into it. This point is critical to establish the authority of the city as being superior to that of the household and the village. Maturity and immaturity are both natural, but the former is inherently superior: it completes the incompleteness of the latter. Moreover, to suggest that the city grows naturally out of earlier associations is to deny that a real tension among them is possible. The teaching that the city grows out of earlier associations thus establishes its authority over them while at the same time it implies a harmony among them. Indeed, it would seem to imply a merging of the immature associations into the mature; it does not call our attention to the fact that the household continues to exist even after the city comes into being.[7]

Note that this account of the growth of the city is relatively silent about man's role as cause and beneficiary of this growth.[8] It does not derive the city's naturalness from its contributions to the complete human life. Of course man's needs must lie *behind* the growth of the city, but Aristotle does not yet put them in the forefront. We see an emphasis on the completeness of the city rather than on that of men in the city. The absence of human beings from the forefront of this account enables Aristotle, if only initially, to avoid deriving the authority of the city from its service to human beings. The city is seen at first not as a creature of men's needs but as a natural creature with a life of its own. If man is related to the city as part to whole (1253a19–25), it would seem that the superior and natural being which is the city must guide the lives of the men who are its parts. It would thus be more in keeping with the primary character of this discussion to ask what man can do for the city than to demand of the city what it can do for man.

The account of the growth of the city attempts to see the city as a mature form of earlier associations rather than as a creature of human beings. When this account is complete, however, Aristotle begins to investigate more directly the relationship between city and man (1253a1–39). The now famous thesis of this investigation is that "man [*ho anthropos*] is by nature a political animal" (1253a2–3, 7–8), and its most important suggestion for present purposes is that the city is natural because it completes or perfects man. If it is true that cities cannot exist without human beings, it comes to appear that human beings cannot exist without cities. Only in the city can human beings perform the works which are the defining characteristics of the species (1253a19–25).[9] It thus seems that there are two roughly different kinds of argument in behalf of the naturalness of the city: the first defends the naturalness of the city in its own right, the second defends it as natural for contributing toward the attainment of man's natural end. Although neither argument directly prescribes duties to either city or man, both seem to have implications for how they should act. The first implies that man should serve the city, for it is a superior natural being of which he turns out to be a part, while the second indicates that it is the city's responsibility to bring man to his natural end. The very teaching which thus seems to urge man to serve the city also guides the city to serve man.[10]

Like the famous teaching which affirms the naturalness of the city, however, the famous teaching which holds man to be by nature a political animal lacks the benefit of a simply lucid argument in its behalf. Since the former teaching rests in part upon the latter, it is necessary that we face the complications which beset the argument that man is by nature political.

The present argument concerning man's political nature makes these claims: (1) Man is especially well-endowed by nature to meet the requirements of political life, for man alone can engage in political speech, speech about the just and the unjust (1253a7–18). (2) Man is related to the city as part to whole. This is so because man cannot perform his proper work when taken away from the city, just as a hand detached from the body ceases to be able to do its work (1253a19–29). (3) Man can become complete when in the city; and when he is complete, he is the best of animals. When separated from law and court enforcement and without virtue, however, he is the worst, most unholy, and most savage of the animals (1253a31–39; on becoming virtuous and becoming complete, cf. *Nic. Ethics* 1103a23–26).

Aristotle's brief presentation of these arguments suggests a noble but yet not naive view of man in relation to the city: man is not simply the selfish or possessive individual he seems to be in the seminal works of modern liberalism, nor is his capacity for savage deeds ignored. Man is presented neither as simply rapacious nor as simply social, but as political: he will not acquire virtue in the absence of law and court enforcement, but he can acquire virtue in their presence. If necessary for his safety, political authority is necessary also for man's perfection. Aristotle thus suggests a *via media* between hopes about the withering away of the state and arguments which defend it as a necessary protector of one beast against another.

Though both sober and noble in their implications, Aristotle's arguments here are also perplexing. A chief example of such a perplexing argument is the explanation of why man's unique possession of speech or reason (*logos*) makes him political. Aristotle writes:

> Reason is for making clear the advantageous and the harmful, and thus also the just and the unjust. For in comparison with the other animals, this is peculiar to human beings: the unique possession of a sense of the good, bad, just, and unjust. And the association of these makes a household and a city (1253a15–18).

Rather than draw a clear and direct connection between reason and the city, Aristotle surprisingly concludes that reason "makes" both the city and the household; thus, the uniqueness of the city in at least one respect is being undercut even as it appears that the uniquely political nature of man is being defended. If, in being rational, man is an especially political animal, it would appear from this text that he is also especially domestic. The mention of the household along with the city is especially striking in view of Aristotle's promise to distinguish sharply between these two associations (1252a7–16).

Perhaps the passage at hand suggests that man is political because reason is political in its concerns. It says, "Reason is for making clear the advantageous and the harmful, and thus also the just and the unjust." If reason is concerned especially with such questions, then it would perhaps be sensible to see the rational animal also as an especially political animal. On the other hand, the meaning of the epithet "political animal" would be somewhat different from that usually supposed, for the completely political animal in this sense would be the one which would most "make clear . . . the just and the unjust." If the possession of reason shows man to be political, to be completely political would seem to mean to be rational about politics. To be a political animal would then come to light as to be a political philosopher.

Another reservation against Aristotle's explicit line of argument is that it does not establish that reason is especially political; it treats one use of reason as its exclusive use, for might not reason also be for making clear what is natural and what is not or what is being and what is not? Man's unique possession of reason might thus seem to suggest not that he is the politically philosophic animal but that he is the philosophic animal. Nevertheless, Aristotle does not here explore the relationship between reason and philosophy, or between philosophy and political philosophy.

But perhaps it is not even man's possession of reason which makes him an especially political animal. In fact, the text at hand sees man as unique among the animals in two different ways. Not only does man alone possess reason; man alone possesses a "sense [*aisthēsis*] of the good, bad, just and unjust." Moreover, it is *this* uniqueness of man which Aristotle most closely connects with the "making" of a household and a city. That is, the making of the city seems to follow more immediately from man's "sense" of the good, bad, just, and unjust, than from his ability to explain them in speech (*logos*). Is it man's possibly incorrect "sense" of what is good, rather than his reason, which "makes" the city (and makes him a political animal)? Perhaps this is what Aristotle had in mind when he suggested that every association aims at "some good" and linked this good to "the seeming good" (1252a1–3). If the seeming or perceived good at which a certain city happens to aim is not truly good, then how can we help but to doubt the authority of that city (Cf. 1333b5–35)? And, if it should turn out that the city as such cannot aim at the highest good, then how can we help but to doubt the authority of the city?[11]

Although even the arguments of the second chapter are such as to complicate the attempt to base the authority of the city on its naturalness, it is still more important to see that Aristotle continues to investigate the issue of the city's naturalness and authority far beyond the "conclusions" that man is political, that the city is natural, and that nature is beneficent. As suggested above, Aristotle intends that these conclusions not be accepted as fixed once and for all but that they be examined in the context of his teaching as a whole. I shall support this suggestion further by showing briefly how the remainder of book 1 contributes to our understanding of the issues which seem to have been settled so quickly in chapter 2.

The subjects which receive the longest treatment in book 1 are slavery and acquisition, and they are both studied with a view to the question of whether and how they are natural. The treatment of these subjects thus sheds light both on Aristotle's understanding of nature and on his view of institutions or practices which are at least indirectly political.

Aristotle's discussion of slavery contributes to our understanding of the naturalness of the city in at least two ways. In the first place, it leads us to conclude that the city originated out of, and includes, slavery that is against nature. In the second place, it leads us to wonder whether nature is even an appropriate standard for the investigation of political institutions.

Aristotle's discussion of slavery concludes very clearly that there is such a thing as natural slavery, and it is perhaps the clarity of this conclusion which has led many to see Aristotle as defending the naturalness of such slavery as was practiced in his day. A better reading of this section sees that Aristotle's treatment of natural slavery establishes a standard according to which actual slavery is judged and found to be against nature. Natural slavery is evident in the rule of the soul over the body, but this sort of rule is most unlike that of captors over their captives (or that of the descendants of captors over the descendants of captives), and it is this latter sort of slavery which we find in cities. Actual slavery might be found to be just if it could be established either that it is just for the stronger to rule the weaker or that laws sanctioning slavery are just simply in virtue of their being laws, but Aristotle favors his own view over both of these positions (1255a5–32). Aristotle does succeed in offering a powerful defense of slavery, but the slavery it defends should not be identified with that of actual cities. Thus the very power of Aristotle's defense makes it that much more formidable an indictment.

Nevertheless, Aristotle's treatment of slavery is curious in that its discovery of the discrepancy between natural and actual slavery is not accompanied by a condemnation of the latter; he develops the concept of natural slavery at some length but shrinks from pointing out what seem to be its obvious implications. We might guess that the prudent Aristotle is only trying to help Athens avoid sinning a second time against philosophy, but it becomes clear in Aristotle's account of the best regime that he neither confines himself to natural slavery nor even seeks that his slaves approximate natural slaves as closely as possible. The character of slavery in

Aristotle's best regime thus demands the admission that not even the best city is natural in all respects; more importantly, it makes us wonder whether Aristotle teaches that it should try to be. It is clear that Aristotle teaches that actual slavery is not natural, but it even begins to look as though he doubts that it should be. Is nature, at least as far as slavery is concerned, an appropriate standard by which to guide actual political practices?

The slave is a kind of property, and Aristotle's discussion of slavery gives way to a more general treatment of property and, especially, of how property is acquired (1256a1–3). This section (chaps. 8–11) is like the discussion of slavery in that it too is concerned especially to distinguish between what is natural and what is against nature. It is similar also in emerging as a second indirect way of complicating the city's claim to naturalness. Not only do certain common forms of acquisition come to light as unnatural (which development must qualify the naturalness at least of such cities as employ acquisition of this sort), but the very way of investigating the issue encourages a rethinking of the case of the city. . . .

We have seen that Aristotle's political science begins with the problem of the city's authority and that he purports to solve this problem by defending the city as natural. But what does indeed look like a brief defense turns out to be the prelude to a long investigation: the argument which holds the city to be natural is not only not fully adequate to resolve the issues it raises, it even points the way to its own limitations. Its discussion of the unquestionably natural first associations of male-female and naturally mastering-naturally servile, for example, helps us to see how questionable is the naturalness of actual rule. . . .

The foregoing argues that Aristotle begins the *Politics* by suggesting that the relationship between the city and nature is simple but goes on to show that it is complex; Aristotle stakes out the bold position that "every city exists by nature," but he retreats to a more ambivalent view. This argument thus raises at least these two questions: What is the complex position to which he retreats? And why does Aristotle obscure it with his simple doctrine? A few preliminary thoughts must serve in lieu of settled conclusions.

Aristotle's openness to the use of slavery and acquisition which are against nature might seem to suggest that he abandons nature as an appropriate standard for guiding political practice and that he replaces it with some view of the necessary and the useful. Aristotle's relative silence about nature after the new beginning in book 2 would seem to support the suspicion that nature cannot guide the practices of actual cities; Aristotle's politics are evidently not directly derived from his physics, and after book 1 he pays much more attention to the experiences and opinions of cities and citizens than he does to a study of nature. However tempting it may be to suppose that his reflections on these experiences and opinions are guided by his reflections on nature, so that his rejection of nature in one form would be but a preparation for its adoption in another, it must be admitted that these supposed reflections on nature are well hidden. Nature is very much in the background after book 1, and the relationship between this faint theoretical background and the immediate political foreground is not at all easy to see.

Nevertheless, nature makes an important return to the foreground in support of Aristotle's distinction between the correct (*orthai*) and the deviant (*parekbaseis*) regimes (1287b37–41; cf. 1279a6–16); and the critical importance of this distinction for Aristotle's defense of decent politics may reconfirm the important place of nature in Aristotle's political thought. But even if this should restore the importance of nature in guiding Aristotle's political judgments, its bearing on these judgments would be

+ deviations are options !
the actual options !

different from that implied at the outset of the *Politics.* Nature was originally used in apparent support of every city, and Aristotle did not even acknowledge in this context that cities vary in kind. To note that there are fundamentally different kinds of cities, and especially to note that some regimes are against nature while others are not, is to complicate the claim that every city is natural and supremely authoritative. It may be, then, that from his frontline defense of the naturalness of every city, Aristotle makes a retreat to the position that some regimes are against nature while others are not. Nature would thus come to the aid at least of correct regimes. As it earlier supported the city for its contribution to the good life, it would now support correct cities for their pursuit of the common good. And, if we are troubled that so important a teaching includes but two references to nature, we might suppose that Aristotle is trying to present his philosophic findings in the language of statesmen or gentle-men, or that he fears that too open a reliance on nature might lead to such simplistic and dangerous innovations as those of Socrates or Hippodamus (1261a15–22, 1267b33ff.).[12]

This attractive possibility becomes at least slightly less attractive upon consider-ation, however. In the first place, although Aristotle says that the deviant regimes are against nature (*para physin*), he never says that the correct regimes are in accord with nature (*kata physin*). Nor does he ever say even of his own best regime that it is in accord with nature. (But cf. 1284b25–34; *Nic. Ethics* 1135a5.) Nature may thus help us to distinguish among regimes while at the same time teaching that no regime can be simply according to nature. Perhaps there is an arbitrariness in every regime (*pasai*, 1301a35–36). Further, if even the correct regimes fail of naturalness, actual regimes fail even of being correct: most regimes are deviations and are hence against nature (1296a22–23, 1287b40–41, cf. *nun de* 1279a13–16). The distinction among regimes on the basis of nature thus seems too remote to be immediately useful in guiding actual political choices.

It is thus safe to say at least this much: nature is not the simply conservative principle it seems to be at the very beginning of the *Politics.* The city is not simply natural, and it is dangerous (and ridiculous, 1267b22–30) to demand such natural-ness of it. Certain regimes, or perhaps a certain one regime (1293b22–27, 1290a24–26), may—if the right circumstances obtain (1287b37–41)—be more in accord with nature than others, but even this imperfectly natural regime does not serve as a pattern to be imitated under ordinary circumstances. It is in the nature of ordinary politics that nature is a less appropriate immediate standard for political judgments than what preserves, what moderates, what gives pleasure, what promotes health, what provides for leisure, what promotes virtue, what attaches citizens to their regime. One wonders whether certain Sophists erred so much in seeing most laws as being against nature as in thinking that they could attain natural justice.

We are forced to conclude that Aristotle's opening declaration of the naturalness of the city is made for reasons other than because it is simply true. The first element of the complex truth which underlies it is that various cities are variously authorita-tive, but no city can long endure without claiming that its decisions are most authoritative. Moreover, as Aristotle teaches in his critique of Hippodamus, the attempt to improve cities, and hence to make them more justly authoritative, is beset by extraordinary dangers (1269a12–24). This difficulty, when combined with some sense of the necessity and utility of even the most ordinary of cities, makes it desirable that a general attempt to defend the authority of the city should be made. And, since such attempts will doubtlessly be made in any case, by tyrants such as Creon, for example, it may be useful if they can be guided in one direction or another. . . .

Perhaps the most important consequence of Aristotle's use of nature to defend the city is that it unites philosophy and the city under a single authority, and this promises to be useful to both the city and philosophy. If nature may be said to be the subject and highest authority of philosophy, then to defend the city as natural is to promise a reconciliation between philosophy and the city. Such a defense is clearly a challenge to those Sophists who disparage the city as merely conventional, but it also introduces the subject of philosophy into political discourse. It may thus be intended as much to open patriots to philosophy as to restore the patriotism of intellectuals attracted to sophistry.

Aristotle's political use of nature thus opens the city to the study of nature in a way that appeals to the gods or to the consent of the governed do not, but the appeal to nature has the further advantage of encouraging moderate politics. Nature is, and in the *Politics* becomes, a subject of philosophic investigation, so the assertion of the city's naturalness—even if it appears dogmatic in the first instance—becomes an invitation to study the city philosophically. Such a study, and certainly such a study when conducted by Aristotle, reveals the full force of the city's natural authority, but this means as well that it reveals fully the limitations of its natural authority. Thus the simple claim that the city is natural, when accompanied by a philosophic investigation of nature, is open to the complex truth about the city's authority. The defense of the city in terms of a supernatural theology has no such advantages, and it has the further disadvantage of strengthening the tendency to obtrude religious passions into political deliberations.

But Aristotle's doctrine not only seeks to be useful in its support of the city, moderate in its appeal to nature as disclosed by philosophy, and philosophic in that it points toward the full investigation of nature and the city, it also seeks to ennoble the lives of citizens. In this, the doctrine of the city's naturalness is most unlike modern consent theory. . . .

Notes

I am grateful to the National Endowment for the Humanities for its generous support of my research and writing and to Christopher Bruell for helping me to begin to see the richness of the *Politics*.

1. 1252a30. Bekker numbers will henceforth be cited in the text. References to the books and chapters of Aristotle's works will be based on the *Oxford* edition. Translations are mine. . . .
2. Plato *Republic* 473c6–474c2, 456b12–c2, cf. 497a9–d2, 499a9–c2. . . .
3. For the classic formulations of the view that the city and its laws lack natural status, see Plato *Republic* 358e3–361d3; *Gorgias* 483a7–484c3, 491e5–492c9; cf. *Laws* 889b1–890a9.
4. Chapter 2 declares its intention to watch "matters as they grow" (*ta pragmata phyomena*, 1252a24). Since the word for nature (*physis*) is derived from the word to grow (*phyein*), Aristotle's present choice of "the genetic method" contributes substantially to the conclusion that the city is natural, a conclusion never reached by the analytic method. For an attempt to identify the genetic and the analytic methods, see Ernest Barker, *The Politics of Aristotle* (New York: Oxford University Press, 1962), p. 3n.
5. If Aristotle appears to be following a straightforward method when he promises to address these major issues by an analysis of the city into its parts, the observation that he offers a number of different analyses of the city shows his method to be more complex. Are the parts of the city to be found in its households (1253b1–4), its citizens (1274b39–41), its economic classes (1259b1–3; cf. 1318a30–31), its functional elements (1321a5–7,

1290b37ff.)? If each of these analyses is in some sense correct, then each is also in some sense incomplete. Is not the teaching of chapter 2, which sees human beings as being the parts of the city (1253a19–21), incomplete in failing to note that all cities have ruling arrangements, that different cities have different ruling arrangements, and that different men hold different positions with regard to these ruling arrangements? These differences have a bearing on the city's claim to promote virtue and rule justly. Thus the analysis of book 3 corrects that of book 1.

6. Certainly it is awkward to speak in English of "the naturally servile" (*to physei doulon*), but to say "the natural slave" misleads one into thinking that Aristotle is necessarily thinking of a human being.

7. A partial explanation of the continued existence of the household might be found in Aristotle's discussion of conjugal friendship (*Nic. Ethics* 1162a16–26). This discussion maintains that man is by nature more a conjugal than a political animal. That no such emphasis on conjugal friendship is evident in the account of the city's naturalness contributes to my suspicion that a consciously political account of man's nature is presented in this context.

8. The account of the city's growth is complete by 1253a1. Before this point, the word for "human being" (*anthropos*) was used only once, and this was in a digression (1252b27). The words for woman (*gyne*) and wife (*alochos*) were used once each, but only in quotations from Hesiod and Homer. The remainder of this chapter, on the other hand, uses *anthropos* seven times and has human beings almost always directly in view. It is here that Aristotle calls the first founder "the cause (*aitios*) of the greatest goods" (1253a30–31).

9. Of course the question of the city's contribution not simply to peace and prosperity but especially to virtue is an important theme of the *Politics* as a whole. But that Aristotle is silent for the time being about the frequency with which actual cities neglect and distort virtue is another sign of the civic-minded character of the beginning of the *Politics* (cf. 1336b27–33). . . .

10. I suspect, then, that Aristotle is trying to lead cities to become what they should be rather than simply defending them for what they are. Indeed, if Aristotle's defense of the city should turn out to be a defense only of cities which meet the standard of bringing men to true virtue (cf. 1280b6–8), then it might be less misleading to call it an attack than a defense. In expressing a similar thought, Jaeger remarks that, while appearing to save it, Plato and Aristotle had actually abandoned the ship of state (Werner W. Jaeger, *Paideia: The Ideals of Greek Culture*, trans. Gilbert Highet [Oxford: Oxford University Press, 1968], 1:398–400). While there is much to be said for this view, it does not explain why Aristotle would have created the appearance of supporting actual cities. If they are unworthy of support insofar as their relationship to true virtue is concerned, does Aristotle so simply dismiss their other possible claims on our support?

11. Although Aristotle considers the idea that the best life is identical for city and man, he eventually seems to drop it; perhaps he does so because the city cannot itself philosophize (1323a14–1325b32; *Nic. Ethics* 10. 7–8). Perhaps it is in view of this limitation of the city that Aristotle inverts his earlier statement and implies that the city is a mere part of, or precondition for, the extraordinary man (1288a24–28; cf. 1253a19).

12. When criticizing Socrates' demand that the city be one, Aristotle says that the city is a multitude (*plethos*) in its nature and is hence much less of a unity than is a human being (1261a18–22). Previously, however, and when arguing the city's naturalness, Aristotle had presented the city as a whole (*holos*) and hence analogous to a human being (1253a19–25). This is another of the details which lead me to see the *Politics* as beginning with certain happy exaggerations.

COMMENTARY

Woman's Place and Nature
in a Functionalist World
Susan Moller Okin

... [F]requently stressing that "nature makes nothing in vain," Aristotle argues that plants exist to give subsistence to animals, and animals to give it to men. Since man is clearly at the top of the scale of mortal beings, "all animals must have been made by nature for the sake of men."[1] The vision is not just an anthropocentric one, however. While all human beings are the highest of animals, within the human race, too, the hierarchical ordering is maintained. When Aristotle approaches the study of society, he arrives quickly at some fundamental and very firmly held premises, which are to function as the bases of his ethics and politics. These are that the Greek *polis* is the natural, and therefore best, form of political association, and that the Greek family—with its subordination of wife, children and slaves—is the natural, and therefore best, form of household and family structure. In order to see how he arrives at these beliefs, which of course gain a large part of their strength from the fact that these institutions *were* the Greek world of Aristotle's time, we must examine what he conceives the function of man to be.

Near the beginning of the *Nichomachean Ethics,* Aristotle determines that happiness is the final and self-sufficient end of human activity, and sets out to give an account of what this happiness consists in. "This might perhaps be given," he says, "if we could first ascertain the function of man."[2] Significantly, the function that is peculiar to man, unlike the functions of the lower members on the scale of being, is not found to be some purpose he serves for a being higher on the scale. While man shares some characteristics, such as nutrition, growth and sensation, with the lower animals, Aristotle concludes that what is peculiar to him alone is his reason. Since this is his distinguishing feature, man's highest good is the "active life of the element that has a rational principle."[3] Man's relationship to those above him in the hierarchy is not that of serving some purpose of theirs; though his reasoning power makes him akin to the gods, whose whole existence is spent in rational contemplation, it is clearly for his own sake, not theirs, that he emulates them. His objective is his own happiness, not the fulfillment of the needs of another. In fact, Aristotle is well aware that the gods, anthropomorphic as they are, are the idealization of the highest human virtues, reason and self-sufficiency. The gods are the way they are because man imagines them thus: "We make the lives of the gods in the likeness of our own—as we also make their shapes."[4] It is therefore hardly coincidental that man's highest virtue is also the defining characteristic of the gods, or that the gods are depicted as perpetually engaged in that activity which man has decided on as the most worthwhile for himself.

Thus, whereas most beings serve a function in relation to some higher being, and whereas most activities have an end which lies outside the activity itself and to which it is subordinate, man's proper end is his own happiness, and "the activity of reason, which is contemplative, seems . . . to aim at no end beyond itself, and to have its pleasure proper to itself."[5] The proper activity of man alone among mortals has no end or aim outside of the actor himself.

The word for "man" that Aristotle uses throughout his arguments about the nature of man, and man's highest good, is *anthropos*, the Greek word meaning "human being." It soon becomes very clear, however, that only a small minority of one sex of the human race is to share in what have been characterized as the human virtues and man's highest good and happiness. For "man" requires not only his reason, but also certain essential external goods, if he is to live the good life. He cannot be happy, Aristotle tells us, without assets such as riches, friends, many and good children, leisure, noble birth, and beauty. Some of these clearly depend on the service of other people. Thus, in accordance with his characteristic teleology, Aristotle argues that not only the entire animal kingdom, but the vast majority of humans as well, are intended by nature to be the instruments which supply to the few the necessities and comforts that will enable them to be happy in their contemplative activity. Thus, women, slaves, and artisans and traders are all subsidiary instruments for the achievements of the highest happiness of "man." "In the state," Aristotle asserts, "the conditions which are necessary for the existence of the whole are not organic parts of the whole system which they serve."[6] Human good and human happiness have been defined in such a way that the vast majority of the human race is necessarily excluded from the achievement of either.

From time to time, presumably to make his functionalism appear more palatable, Aristotle argues that the relationships between those whom he perceives as naturally ruling and naturally ruled, such as husband and wife, or master and slave, are good for both parties because the capacities of these are very different. This kind of reasoning forms a substantial part of his argument for slavery. Although the slave is characterized as an instrument or tool, we are told that "the condition of slavery is both beneficial and just" for him, that the relationship between him and his master is "for the preservation of both," and that the two of them "have an identical interest."[7] Moreover, Aristotle argues that in the relationships between soul and body, craftsman and tool, and master and slave, "the latter in each case is benefited by that which uses it."[8] In a parallel manner, he argues, first, that husband and wife have a mutually beneficial relationship—that "they help each other by throwing their peculiar gifts into the common stock," and, second, that it is in fact the woman who is the beneficiary, and the man the benefactor of their relationship.[9]

As we might expect, however, given the hierarchical structure of Aristotle's world, these illusions of mutuality and of benefits accruing to the inferior party are not consistently maintained. With regard to slaves, they very soon disappear. We are told that the relationship is primarily in the interest of the master and only incidentally in that of the slave, "who must be preserved in existence if the rule itself is to remain."[10] In general, moreover, speaking of all such pairs of the ruling and the ruled, Aristotle asserts, "Nor is the good divisible between them but that of both belongs to the one for whose sake they exist."[11] Again, in a context which explicitly includes reference to the rule of men over women, he says that "the ruled may be compared to flute-makers: rulers are like flute-players who use what the flute-makers make."[12]

Aristotle asserts that women are "naturally" inferior to men, and that they are therefore "naturally" ruled by them. However, his use of the word *physis* (nature) and its derivatives is at least as complex and ambiguous as Plato's. Sometimes, clearly, he uses "natural" to refer to innate as opposed to acquired characteristics.[13] At times, again like Plato, he acknowledges that very little clear distinction can be made between the nature of a mature being and the habits it has acquired throughout its life.[14] Aristotle's most usual use of the word "nature," however, is intimately connected with his functionalist approach to the world. I have already pointed out that he considered the "essential character" of a thing to be derived from its function, and the soul of each thing to be its capacity to function. Thus, when he tells us at the beginning of the *Politics* that "what each thing is when its growth is completed we call the nature of that thing, whether it be a man or a horse or a family,"[15] we must not fail to take into account the essential connection which exists in his mind between the way a thing should grow and develop, and its function. It is noteworthy that when he first introduces the three basic relationships that exist within the household, he states his intention to examine "the nature of each and the qualities it ought to possess."[16] It is clear that, in Aristotle's world, these two factors are virtually synonymous. Thus, when he makes the extraordinary statement that "dealing with . . . animate beings, we must fix our attention, in order to discover what nature intends, not on those which are in a corrupt, but on those which are in a natural condition,"[17] it is necessary to perform a substitution of the two equivalents—the nature of a thing, and the goodness pertaining to that thing—in order to give the proposition any content. We must acknowledge Aristotle's normative use of the word "natural," and give the "natural" at the end of his sentence a distinct moral connotation. In order to be meaningfully contrasted with "corrupt," it must mean "well-ordered" or "good," and Aristotle's statement is no longer value free, as it at first appeared. Moreover, as the above discussion of his functionalism indicates, nothing is well-ordered or good unless it can perform and does perform the function ascribed to it within Aristotle's hierarchical world. Thus Aristotle has established a philosophical framework by which he can legitimize the status quo. For the conventional function of any person determines that person's goodness, and a person's nature, or natural condition, is also equated with his or her goodness. Every person, therefore, is naturally suited to his or her existing role and position in society.

Aristotle's arguments about the nature of things and beings, especially of those within the human social realm, are virtually unintelligible unless one continually recognizes his esoteric use of the term. The family exists "by nature"; the *polis* exists "prior in the order of nature to the family and the individual."[18] By saying that the family is natural, Aristotle by no means intends to imply that it has always existed, but rather that its existence is necessary for the well-ordered life of man. The reason that the *polis* is prior in the natural order is, likewise, not that it is more original or basic than the family. It is because, while the family exists "for the satisfaction of daily recurrent needs" and sustains mere life, the *polis* is the only association within which man can enjoy that self-sufficiency which enables him to live the rational life, the highest life to which he can aspire. The *polis* is more natural, in other words, because of the superiority of its aim or object, which makes it a better institution than the family.

Similarly, Aristotle's arguments about the naturalness of slavery are incomprehensible unless one recognizes his totally teleological version of the natural. For his attempts to convince us that some people are by nature slaves are most unpersuasive if we rely on his claims that natural slaves are those men "who differ from others as much as the body differs from the soul, or an animal from a man."[19] It is only if we accept the premises that society is most properly structured when it enables the privileged few to spend their lives in rational activity, and that the functions and therefore the nature of all others must be fixed accordingly, that we can accept Aristotle's justification of slavery as natural.

The same considerations apply to Aristotle's conclusions about the nature and the natural position of women. These can be understood only by reference to the function the female sex is perceived as fulfilling in the stratified society he assumes to be the best for man. At the beginning of his discussion of the household, Aristotle informs his reader that, contrary to what the barbarians think,

> the female and the slave are naturally distinguished from one another. Nature makes nothing in a spirit of stint, as smiths do when they make the Delphic knife to serve a number of purposes: she makes each separate thing for a separate end; and she does so because each instrument has the finest finish when it serves a single purpose and not a variety of purposes.[20]

As the context makes very clear, the slave's function is the provision of the daily needs of subsistence, whereas the female's primary function is reproduction.

On the subject of woman's function, which is on the whole implicit in the *Politics*, we must turn to Aristotle's biological writings for clarification. Reproduction was a subject in which he had an intense interest, since he regarded it as the "most natural" of the operations of mature living beings.[21] In fact, however, compared with the astounding accuracy and originality of his biological findings as a whole, Aristotle's "observations" about sexual reproduction contain a number of serious errors, of which virtually all are attributable to his basic assumption that the male is always and in every way superior to the female.

The reason for the very existence of the sexual form of reproduction in most animals, Aristotle argues, is the superiority of form over matter. His "observations" of sexual reproduction informed him that the male, via his semen, always provides the form or soul of the offspring, while the female, via her menstrual discharge, provides the matter. Since "the Form, is *better* and more divine in its nature than the Matter, it is *better* also that the superior one should be separate from the inferior one. That is why whenever possible and so far as possible the male is separate from the female."[22]

Thus Aristotle explains the need for sexual reproduction in terms of his hierarchical view of the world. Indeed, he argues that it was only the need for this higher form of reproduction that made nature stray from the generic type of each species, which is clearly perceived by him as that embodied in the male. Immediately prior to explaining the appearance of "monstrosities" in nature, he accounts for the "first deviation," which occurs "when a female is formed instead of a male." This deviation from the norm, we are told, "is a necessity required by Nature, since the race . . . has got to be kept in being." Altogether, he concludes, "we should look on the female as being as it were a deformity, though one which occurs in the ordinary course of nature."[23] Even with respect to reproduction, the only reason she exists at all, the female is characterized as inferior and disabled. It is the male who performs the active role, whereas the female merely acts as a passive receptacle for the new life. It is he who provides the new life with its soul, which is after all the raison d'être of the body that she furnishes. "A woman," Aristotle concludes, "is as it were an infertile male," and even in regard to reproduction, "a male is male in virtue of a particular ability, and a female in virtue of a particular inability."[24] In all this, moreover, "what happens is what one would expect to happen," and "in all her workmanship herein Nature acts in every particular as reason would expect."[25]

The proposals made in the *Politics* for the regulation of marriage and breeding clearly reflect these biological beliefs and Aristotle's perception of woman as fundamentally an instrument for breeding men. Marriage is regarded solely as an institution for "the provision of a stock of the healthiest possible bodies (for) the nurseries of our state,"[26] and the age of marriage should therefore be when both partners are at the height of their procreative powers, with the woman in her late teens, and the man in his late thirties. Following the oracle, Aristotle recommends that the citizens "plough not the young fallow"; when mothers are too young they have great difficulty in childbirth. In keeping with his general theory of reproduction, since the mother provides only the matter for the child and the father its rational soul, it is only the father's mental prime that is taken into account, and while the mother is advised to exercise and eat well while pregnant, since the growing foetus draws on her body, her mind should be kept idle, in order that more of her strength be preserved for the child's growth. Since the child is in no way perceived as drawing on the mother's mind, the development of her mind is quite needless.[27]

In spite of her widespread inabilities, then, woman is necessary for the reproduction of man, and this is therefore seen by Aristotle as her natural function. After all, if it were not for the requirements of sexual reproduction, this particular "deformity in nature" would never have existed. Within the well-ordered society, however, reproduction is not woman's only function. Unlike the other animals, man does not couple by chance and temporarily, since he "is not only a political but also a householding animal." For "human beings live together," Aristotle argues, "not only for the sake of reproduction but also for the various purposes of life; for from the start the functions are divided, and those of man and woman are different." While it is the man's function to acquire, it is the woman's "to keep and store."[28] The necessity of all the things and services provided by the household for daily life, taken together with the assumption that all other classes of people are intended by nature to enable the few to pursue their truly human activities, leads Aristotle to regard the entire conventional division of labor between the sexes as strictly in accordance with nature. . . .

Aristotle's assumption that woman is defined by her reproductive function and her other duties within the household permeates everything he has to say about her. Indeed, Aristotle's entire moral philosophy is much affected by the existence of the hierarchy which he considers to be natural because it is necessary for the attainment of the proper objective of human life. First, all the basic relationships discussed in the *Ethics*, such as friendship and justice, are perceived as differing radically in their natures, depending on the relative positions in society occupied by the two or more persons involved. Second, none of the basic moral terms, such as virtue, temperance, or courage, are held to be universally applicable, since a person's position in the human hierarchy, and consequent function, determine the particular type of virtue, temperance, or courage that will be required of him or her. I will discuss each of these two issues in turn.

Because he perceives woman as naturally inferior to man, Aristotle asserts that all relationships between them must acknowledge and, insofar as possible, compensate for this inequality. Political justice, which he regards as the only type that genuinely deserves the name of justice, can exist only between equals, between those who have an equal share in ruling and being ruled, as fellow citizens do. In such a case, it is unjust for equals to be treated in any way other than equally. Where such parity between persons does not exist, however, justice is an entirely different matter, and can only metaphorically be called justice at all. Aristotle seems, however, to have been unsure as to the type of "metaphorical justice" that is properly applied to women. At first, he says that "justice can more truly be manifested toward a wife than toward children and chattels, for the former is household justice; but even this is different from political justice."[29] Subsequently, however, he appears to retract even this concession, comparing justice between husband and wife to that between master and slave (who is certainly a chattel) and to that between the rational and irrational parts of the soul.[30] Since he implies at times that a slave is not a human being at all, and he parallels the relationship between him and his master to that of despot and subject, we are left with the impression that, so far as justice is concerned, Aristotle has relegated woman to an altogether subhuman position.

Like the other moral relations, friendship, too, varies in accordance with the respective status of the friends in Aristotle's social hierarchy. Whereas there can be no friendship at all between a man and a slave *qua* slave (though paradoxically a man can be friends with the same individual *qua* man), the friendships between father and children and between husband and wife are categorized as friendship between benefactor and benefited. "The friendship of man and wife . . . ," Aristotle asserts, "is the same that is found in an aristocracy; for it is in accordance with virtue—the better gets more of what is good, and each gets what befits him; and so, too, with the justice in these relations."[31] The difference between various types of friendship depends both on the respective virtues and functions of the two persons and on the reasons for which they love each other. In all friendships in which the friends are not equal, the love should be proportional to the merit of the two parties, for only if the better is loved more than he loves, will equality be restored.[32] In marriage, the husband is, of course, by virtue of his superiority always the benefactor and the more useful partner. As Aristotle's disciple argues in the *Oeconomica*, one reason that a wife must obey her husband and serve him sedulously is that "he has indeed bought her with a great price—with partnership in his life and the procreation of children; than which things nothing could be greater or more divine."[33] There is no emphasis placed, in such a context, on the fact that the woman's entire life is defined in terms of the function she performs for the man. And thus Aristotle concludes that it would be ludicrous for a wife to expect her affection to be returned in a similar way, just as it would be ludicrous for man to expect the same of God; "for it is the part of a ruler to be loved, not to love, or else to love in another way."[34] Friendship and marriage are no exception to the basic principle that relationships must always reflect the respective merits and functions of those who are party to them.

The second relevant phenomenon of Aristotle's ethics—the variable application of terms and standards—was by no means new at his stage of Greek thought. As A. W. H. Adkins has demonstrated in his illuminating book, *Merit and Responsibility*, the Greeks from the time of Homer to that of Aristotle, with the notable exception of Plato, had no concept of a single standard of human morality or excellence which might be applied to anyone, regardless of his or her role or position in society.[35] Their word of highest praise, *arete* (excellence or virtue), originated in the commendation of an entirely masculine, noble, and leisured way of life, and could only be used of those who had the wherewithal, in terms of both high birth and their command of material goods and other people's services, to pursue such a life. . . . "[W]oman's *arete*" was a relative term, consisting of a set of qualities entirely different from those of men, who alone could achieve absolute excellence. This was the immense weight of custom and opinion that Socrates was combatting, both in the *Meno*, in claiming the irrelevance of sex to *arete*, and in the *Republic*, in implying that sex is no more related to the soul than baldness is. The importance of these passages in the gradual universalizing of ethical values must not be underestimated.

In his ethical and political writings, Aristotle reacts against these heresies of Socrates, and both consolidates and justifies the traditional way of thinking. Having

defined the highest human virtue as reason, he constructs a functionalist rationalization of a society in which this highest virtue can be shared in only by those at the top
of the class- and sex-determined hierarchy. As Adkins asserts, "Thus Aristotle leaves
no hope of establishing any standard for the whole community."[36] Even free males
whose work is considered menial are excluded from the possibility of participation in
the higher things of life, and what is the case for artisans is, of course, even more the
case for slaves, and for women of any class at all. Women's work is clearly regarded
as in no way compatible with the life of excellence.[37]

What Aristotle does, therefore, is to define the goodness of each thing and each
person according to its function; "let it be assumed as to goodness," he says, "that it
is the best disposition or state or faculty of each class of things that have some use or
work."[38] His examples extend from a coat, a ship, and a house, to a soul. While it is
quite easy for us to accept this functional characterization of the excellence of
artefacts, and to agree with Aristotle that "what is healthy or good is different for men
and for fishes," it is jarring to the modern ear to hear the adjectives of commendation
which we are accustomed to think of as constant in their meanings, applied
differently to different classes of human beings. But for Aristotle, human beings have
functions just as much and in the same way as artefacts do, and only those at the very
top of the hierarchy have a function which is defined only in relation to themselves
and not to others. There are two fundamentally different orders of human goodness.
The goodness of the leisured and fully rational men is something absolute, while all
the others can achieve only forms of goodness that are relative and inferior. Their
goodness is determined entirely by their respective functions, and all these functions
are inferior to that of those at the top. Thus, although they cannot attain the higher
form of goodness, "even a woman is 'good' and so is a slave, although it may be said
that a woman is an inferior thing and a slave beneath consideration."[39]

Even in the case of the free male citizen, it is "his good discharge of his function"
which determines his excellence,[40] and in the good *polis* he will have two sorts of
goodness, since because of his constitutional equality with his fellow citizens he must
rule and be ruled in turn. He must therefore have "one sort [of excellence] which fits
him to act as a ruler, and one which fits him to act as a subject."[41] Women, however,
together with all the other persons who are necessary conditions but not parts of the
polis, require only the kind of goodness which fits them to be ruled, since this is their
natural and permanent role.

All the moral standards applied to woman, therefore, are determined by her
function as the bearer of new citizens and the guardian of the household. Since she
has a different function from that of the slave, so must her goodness be different, just
as the slave's differs from that of the artisan. Aristotle asserts:

> They must all share in (moral goodness), but not in the same way—each sharing
> only to the extent required for the discharge of his or her function. The ruler,
> accordingly, must possess moral goodness in its full or perfect form because his
> function . . . demands a master-artificer, and reason is such a master artificer;
> but all other persons need only possess moral goodness to the extent required
> of them. It is thus clear that . . . temperance—and similarly fortitude and
> justice—are not, as Socrates held, the same in a woman as they are in a man.
> Fortitude in the one, for example, is shown in connexion with ruling; in the
> other, it is shown in connexion with serving; and the same is true of the other
> forms of goodness. . . . To speak in general terms, and to maintain that
> goodness consists in "a good condition of the soul," or in "right action," or in

anything of the kind, is to be guilty of self-deception. Far better than such general definitions is the method of simple enumeration of the different forms of goodness. . . .[42]

Accordingly, throughout his works, Aristotle proceeds to apply distinct moral standards to the two sexes, as well as to different classes of men. He says, for example, that Sophocles' statement, "A modest silence is a woman's crown" is "a general truth—but a truth which does not apply to men."[43] Both the bodily and the moral excellences of the two sexes are differently defined. Whereas both require beauty and stature, only the male should have strength and fitness for athletic contests. Whereas both should have self-control, in the male this should be supplemented by courage, but in the female by "industrious habits, free from servility."[44] For what use is courage to one whose occupation must be the care of a house and the provision of food and clothes for her family? Moreover, Aristotle asserts that it is not at all appropriate for a woman to be "manly or clever," and criticizes Euripides for creating a female character with these unsuitable qualities.[45]

The only people who need to possess a full complement of reason, Aristotle argues, are those who rule over others. While practical wisdom is necessary in rulers, only "right opinion" is required in women, slaves, and others who are permanently ruled.[46] Thus, when he ascribes to the various members of the household different amounts of reason, we are not surprised to find that each has just that portion of rationality that is necessary for the performance of his or her function:

It is true that all these persons possess in common the different parts of the soul; but they possess them in different ways. The slave is entirely without the faculty of deliberation; the female indeed possesses it, but in a form which remains inconclusive; and if children also possess it, it is only in an immature form.[47]

Why should nature, who makes nothing in vain, have given woman full rationality, when her function does not require it?

Thus, Aristotle has established the standards of physical, mental and moral excellence in woman according to the functions she performs for man. To be the best of women, she must have many qualities, such as quietness and modesty, that are undesirable in a man. On the other hand, she must *not* have many qualities, such as manliness, strength or cleverness, that are required of a good man. Having prescribed for the two sexes separate and frequently conflicting standards of excellence, however, Aristotle proceeds to weigh perfection in woman against perfection in man, and to conclude that woman, even the best possible woman, falls short.

In the *Eudemian Ethics*, it is asserted that "the state of human character called human goodness is of two kinds." "Let us assume," Aristotle continues, "that man is one of the things that are excellent by nature," and he concludes that man's form of goodness is "good absolutely," while that of the others who are not excellent by nature is good only relatively—"only good for that thing."[48] The two examples chosen to illustrate this are the goodness of a man as compared with that of a woman, and the goodness of a gifted man as compared with that of a dull one. In each case, the latter is clearly an inferior kind of goodness. This same point is repeated several times in the other works—for example, in the *Rhetoric*, when we are told that "virtues and actions are nobler, when they proceed from those who are naturally worthier, for instance, from a man rather than from a woman."[49] What has happened is that Aristotle arrives at the conclusion that woman is inferior to man by a completely circular process of reasoning. Because he perceives woman as an instrument, he has assigned her an entirely separate scale of values, and then he measures her against the scale of male values, and finds her inferior. But the functionalist treatment of women is itself founded on the assumption of the Aristotelian hierarchy, in which woman is "naturally" placed in an inferior position.

Aristotle's view of society as rigidly hierarchical, patriarchal, and functional allows him to "prove" things about its various classes by drawing on assumptions that already presuppose the things he claims to prove. If it were not for his initial assumption that the free and leisured male is the highest of mortal beings, there would be no grounds from which to argue that all other members of the human race are naturally defined by their functions in relation to him. Objectively speaking, there is no more evidence for the proposition that women are intended by nature to reproduce men than that men are intended by nature to beget women (as the Amazons may have argued in their version of the *Politics*).

Aristotle determines that woman is inferior by considering the functions she performs and the relevant qualities she manifests in Athenian society. This was a society, however, in which she was thoroughly disadvantaged and oppressed—a society dominated by men, in which her role and all the qualities valued in her were dictated by men. Aristotle is not interested in the qualities of women apart from this context. Thus, in spite of his expressed beliefs in the power of the environment to shape and alter the human character and abilities, he is no more interested in applying these beliefs to women than in applying them to slaves. Except for the free and leisured man, Aristotle is not interested in the potential of any living being, but only in those "natural" and "naturally inferior" characteristics which enable each person to perform his or her proper function in the social system which has his approval and which he sets out to justify. . . .

Notes

1. *Politics*, trans. Ernest Barker, Oxford, 1946, I, 1256b; cf. also I, 1253a, for an example of nature's "economy."
2. *Nichomachean Ethics*, trans. David Ross, London, 1954, I, 1097b.
3. *Nichomachean Ethics*, I, 1098a.
4. *Politics*, I, 1252b.
5. *Nichomachean Ethics*, X, 1177b.
6. *Politics*, VII, 1328a.
7. *Politics*, I, 1255a, 1252a, 1255b.
8. *Nichomachean Ethics*, VIII, 1161a.
9. *Nichomachean Ethics*, VIII, 1162a; *Eudemian Ethics*, trans. H. Rackham, Loeb Classic Library, 1935, VII, 1238b.
10. *Politics*, III, 1278b.
11. *Eudemian Ethics*, VII, 1242b.
12. *Politics*, III, 1277b. See Jean Bethke Elshtain, "Moral Woman and Immoral Man," *Politics and Society*, Vol. 4, 1974, 453–456, for a discussion of these aspects of Aristotle's functionalism.
13. E.g., *Nichomachean Ethics*, II, 1103a, passim.
14. E.g., *Art of Rhetoric*, trans. John Henry Freese, Loeb Classic Library, 1967, I, 1370a.
15. *Politics*, I, 1252b.
16. *Politics*, I, 1253b.
17. *Politics*, I, 1254a.
18. *Politics*, I, 1253a.
19. *Politics*, I, 1254b.

20. *Politics*, I, 1252b.
21. *De Animo*, trans. K. Foster and S. Humphries, from versions of William of Moerbecke, London, 1951, II, 415a. The reason reproduction is the "most natural" function of living beings is that it is their only means of achieving immortality. As is clear from what follows, however, it is only the male who achieves immortality, since it is he, according to Aristotle, who furnishes the child with its soul.
22. *Generation of Animals*, trans. A. L. Peck, Loeb Classic Library, 1943, II, 732a; cf.I, 727b and II, 738b.
23. *Generation of Animals*, IV, 767b, 775a.
24. *Generation of Animals*, I, 728a, IV, 766a.
25. *Generation of Animals*, I, 729a, 731a.
26. *Politics*, VII, 1334b–1335b.
27. See Barker's note 2, *Politics*, p. 327.
28. *Nichomachean Ethics*, VIII, 1162a; *Politics*, III, 1277b.
29. *Nichomachean Ethics*, V, 1134b.
30. *Nichomachean Ethics*, V, 1138b.
31. *Nichomachean Ethics*, VIII, 1161a.
32. *Nichomachean Ethics*, VIII, 1158b.
33. *Oeconomica*, trans. G. C. Armstrong, Loeb Classic Library, 1933, III, 141.
34. *Eudemian Ethics*, VII, 1238b.
35. A. W. Adkins, *Merit and Responsibility*, Oxford, 1960, especially pp. 30–31 and 341–342.
36. *Merit and Responsibility*, p. 342.
37. *Politics*, V, 1312a, where Aristotle gives, without comment, an example of a monarch who was killed, "from the motive of contempt," by a man who saw him carding wool among women. Oddly enough, it is not so much the actual content of the work done by these subordinate classes of people that Aristotle cites as the reason it is so degrading, but rather the fact that it is done at the behest of other people. See *Politics*, VIII, 1337b.
38. *Eudemian Ethics*, II, 1218b–1219a.
39. *Poetics*, trans. W. H. Fyfe, Loeb Classic Library, 1927, XV, 1454a.
40. *Politics*, III, 1276b.
41. *Politics*, III, 1277b.
42. *Politics*, I, 1260a.
43. *Politics*, I, 1260a.
44. *Art of Rhetoric*, I, 1361a.
45. *Poetics*, XV, 1454a.
46. *Politics*, III, 1277b.
47. *Politics*, I, 1260a.
48. *Eudemian Ethics*, VII, 1237a.
49. *Art of Rhetoric*, I, 1367a.

Saint Augustine

In marked contrast to the claims of American political arguments in the 1980s, Christianity has not always been seen as the pious glue holding society together. Indeed, after the fall of Rome in 410, many authors and politicians alleged that Christianity itself was responsible for undermining the civic virtue of the Roman people, for losing Rome's Mediterranean empire, and for ending its political stability and security. Saint Augustine's major work, *The City of God* (composed from 413 to 425), was written largely to defend the faith from such attacks, and from the urging that Romans return to the old ways of classical philosophy and pagan religions. Augustine sought to do more than parry threats to the faith, he also tried to meld classical philosophy and Christian theology, and to show how these distinctive outlooks complemented each other in various ways.

Augustine's personal and intellectual background clearly prepared him for that task. He was born in Thagaste (now part of Algeria) to a Christian mother and pagan father in the year 354. After moving to Carthage in 370 to finish his education in classical Latin rhetoric, Augustine began teaching in Rome in 383. The next year, he became a professor of rhetoric in Milan, then known as a center of Neoplatonism. After a wild and impetuous young adulthood, Augustine converted to Christianity in 386 and returned to Africa to found an ascetic religious community. By the year 396, Augustine had become the Bishop of Hippo, the city where he died four years later, as the Vandals were conquering North Africa.

We do not find Augustine's political theory in any one treatise devoted specifically to politics. Instead, throughout *The City of God,* he offers political views in the context of discussions of faith. For Augustine, faith involves assenting to something not clearly seen; therefore, faith must always precede any type of authentic understanding. The prime role of reason, therefore, is to guide the individual to the right sort of faith, to direct him or her to the proper authorities.

Both reason and faith led Augustine to view reality as composed of three natures: the divine, the corporeal, and the spiritual. Divine nature, of course, refers to God, whose chief characteristics are immutability, blessedness, and creativity. God is the ultimate ground of existence and understanding, the holder of all ideas, the bestower of all powers, and the highest good. Corporeal nature refers to bodies, which are created by God and are inherently neither blessed nor wretched. Bodies, as creations, are thus subject to change, and to the vicissitudes of time, place, and circumstance. The focus of Augustine's thinking about human beings and society, though, is spiritual nature—the soul. It may change over time, and because it has free will, may change for good or ill. Souls will be wretched if they look toward corporeal nature (e.g., such goods as pleasure, beauty, or strength) and will be blessed if they look toward the divine (e.g., virtue, justice, the good). Having a properly directed will means that one will do what is praiseworthy (or, at least, avoid the blameworthy); true virtue, however, always requires the additional dimension of grace.

Augustine's chief political views find expression in his concept of the "two cities." This concept divides people into two coexistent and intermingled camps: those who live in the earthly city (the City of Man), and those who reside in the heavenly city (the City of God). People in the earthly city live after their corporeal nature and love themselves even to the contempt of God. Most of us fall into this camp, doomed to spend our lives beset by troubles, scarcity, quarrels, and violence. Because we do not love God, an external power (the state) must regulate our unbridled passions; so that conflicts can be submerged, law and order can be achieved, and we can enjoy our share of earthly goods without falling victim to an early, violent death. After the Judgment Day, however, we are condemned to eternal torment.

By contrast, the heavenly city (composed of all those who love God to the contempt of self, who live after the spirit) is an order based on the love of God, ruled by God (after the Last Judgment, by Christ), and characterized by the existence of true justice, peace, harmony, and wisdom. That order only materializes with the Resurrection, however. Until then, the City of God comprises the invisible body of the elect—only some of whom may be found among God's representatives on Earth, the visible Church.

The City of God

The selections from *The City of God* first consider what we now call the problem of theodicy; how God's creations (which must be good, since God made them) could possibly have become evil. Augustine believes that people are evil, neither because the Devil made them so nor because flesh is inherently corrupt. Instead, human beings live wretchedly because their souls freely chose to live by human (rather than divine) standards. Augustine next discusses the origins and ends of the two cities—contrasting their essential natures, their different concepts of peace, and their respective fates at the Last Judgment.

Commentaries

Herbert Deane's *The Political Ideas of St. Augustine* has long been the most frequently cited study of Augustine's political theory. The portion reprinted here suggests that the state may be conceived as, first, a regulatory order maintaining peace as the absence of violence; second, a coercive order, where the fear of pain is the main route to compliance; and finally, a remedial order, to the extent that its rule may be seen as both a punishment and a remedy for sin. Deane also discusses Augustine's famous analogy between kingdoms and gangs of robbers, an analogy resting upon a distinction between ordinary and true justice. Ultimately, for Deane, Augustine presents a political theory marked by a realism that recognizes the ironies of the human condition, and by a political quietism which counsels Christians to endure this world and wait patiently for the next.

Rex Martin further explores Augustine's theory of the state in his article on the two cities. Martin argues that an interpretation of Augustine's thought based on an "identification model," which identifies the state with the earthly city and the church with the heavenly city, cannot be supported. However, those institutions frequently do function as representatives of the two cities in this world.

Key Words

Earthly City.   The invisible community of people who live after the flesh, who love worldly goods and themselves more than God.

Heavenly City.   The invisible community of people (as well as God, Jesus, the angels, and the saints) who live after the spirit and love God.

Commonwealth.   A social and political order whose members share a common-weal, a stake in each others' well-being.

For Further Reading

Chadwick, H. 1986. *Augustine.* Oxford: Oxford University Press.

Markus, R.A. 1970. *Saeculum: History and Society in the Thought of St. Augustine.* Cambridge: Cambridge University Press.

Niebuhr, R. 1953. *Christian Realism and Political Problems.* New York: Scribner's.

Paolucci, H., ed. 1962. *The Political Writings of St. Augustine.* Chicago: Regnery Gateway.

The City of God

Book XIV

Chapter 3

The cause of sin arises in the soul, not in the flesh;
and the corruption resulting from sin is not a sin
but punishment.

Now it may be asserted that the flesh is the cause of every kind of moral failing, on the ground that the bad behaviour of the soul is due to the influence of the flesh. But this contention shows a failure to consider man's nature carefully and in its entirety. For 'the corruptible body weighs down the soul.'[15] Hence also the Apostle, when treating of this corruptible body, first says, 'Our outer man is decaying,'[16] and later goes on thus:

> We know that if the earthly house we inhabit disintegrates, we have a building given by God, a house not made by human hands, eternal, in heaven. For in this body we do indeed sigh—as we long for our heavenly dwelling to be put on over it, hoping that when we have put it on, we shall not find ourselves naked. For we, who are in this present dwelling, feel its weight, and sigh; not that we desire to be stripped of our body; rather we desire to have the other clothing put on over it, so that what is mortal may be absorbed by life.[17]

And so we are weighed down by the corruptible body; and yet we know that the cause of our being weighed down is not the true nature and substance of our body but its corruption; and therefore we do not wish to be stripped of it, but to be clothed with the immortality of the body. For then there will still be a body, but it will not be corruptible, and therefore not a burden. Consequently, in this present life, 'the corruptible body weighs down the soul, and the earthly habitation depresses the mind as it meditates on many questions.' However, those who imagine that all the ills of the soul derive from the body are mistaken.

True, Virgil is apparently expounding Platonic teaching[18] in glorious poetry when he says,

---

15. Wisd. 9, 15.

16. 2 Cor. 4, 16.

17. 2 Cor. 5, 1–4.

18. cf. *Phaedr.*, 245E–250E.

Of those seeds heaven is the source, and fiery
The energy within them, did not bodies
Hamper and thwart them, and these earthly limbs
And dying members dull them.[19]

And he will have it that the body is to be taken as the source of all four of the most familiar emotional disturbances of the mind: desire and fear, joy and grief, which may be called the origins of all sins and moral failings.[20] Thus he adds these lines,

Hence come desire and fear, gladness and sorrow;
They look not up to heaven, but are confined
In darkness, in the sightless dungeon's gloom.

However, our belief is something very different. For the corruption of the body, which weighs down the soul, is not the cause of the first sin, but its punishment. And it was not the corruptible flesh that made the soul sinful; it was the sinful soul that made the flesh corruptible.

No doubt this corruption of the flesh results in some incitements to wrongdoing and in actual vicious longings; yet we must not attribute to the flesh all the faults of a wicked life, which would mean that we absolve the Devil of all those faults, since he has no flesh. Certainly, we cannot accuse the Devil of fornication or drunkenness or any other such wickedness connected with carnal indulgence, although he is the hidden persuader and instigator of such sins. Nevertheless, he is proud and envious in the highest degree; and this moral corruption has so mastered him that he is destined because of it to eternal punishment in the prison of this murky air of ours.

Now those vices, which are predominant in the Devil, are attributed to the flesh by the Apostle, although it is certain that the Devil is without flesh. For St Paul says that enmity, quarrelsomeness, jealousy, animosity, and envy are 'works of the flesh';[21] and the fountain-head of all these evils is pride; and pride reigns in the Devil, although he is without flesh. For who is a greater enemy than he is to the saints? Who is found to quarrel with them more bitterly, to show more animosity, jealousy, and envy towards them? Yet he displays all these faults, without having flesh. So how can they be 'the works of the flesh' except in that they are the works of man, to whom, as I have said, the Apostle applies the term 'flesh'?

It is in fact not by the possession of flesh, which the Devil does not possess, that man has become like the Devil: it is by living by the rule of self, that is by the rule of man. For the Devil chose to live by the rule of self when he did not stand fast in the truth, so that the lie that he told was his own lie, not God's. The Devil is not only a liar; he is 'the father of lies'.[22] He was, as we know, the first to lie, and falsehood, like sin, had its start from him.

---

19. *Aen.*, 6, 730ff.

20. cf. Cic., *Tusc. Disp.*, 3, 11, 24; 4, 6, 11; 12.

21. cf. Gal. 5, 19ff.

22. John 8, 44.

Chapter 4

The meaning of living 'by the standard of man' and 'by the standard of God'

Thus, when man lives 'by the standard of man' and not 'by the standard of God', he is like the Devil; because even an angel should not have lived by the angel's standard, but by God's, so as to stand firm in the truth and speak the truth that comes from God's truth, not the lie that derives from his own falsehood. For the Apostle has this to say about man also, in another passage, 'But if the truth of God has been abundantly displayed through my falsehood'.[23] The point is that the falsehood is ours, but the truth is God's.

So when man lives by the standard of truth he lives not by his own standard, but by God's. For it is God who has said, 'I am the truth.'[24] By contrast, when he lives by his own standard, that is by man's and not by God's standard, then inevitably he lives by the standard of falsehood. Not that man himself is falsehood, since his author and creator is God, who is certainly not the author and creator of falsehood. The fact is that man was created right, on condition that he should live by the standard of his creator, not by his own, carrying out not his own will, but his creator's. Falsehood consists in not living in the way for which he was created.

Man has undoubtedly the will to be happy, even when he pursues happiness by living in a way which makes it impossible of attainment. What could be more of a falsehood than a will like that? Hence we can say with meaning that every sin is a falsehood. For sin only happens by an act of will; and our will is for our own welfare, or for the avoidance of misfortune. And hence the falsehood: we commit sin to promote our welfare, and it results instead in our misfortune; or we sin to increase our welfare, and the result is rather to increase our misfortune. What is the reason for this, except that well-being can only come to man from God, not from himself? And he forsakes God by sinning, and he sins by living by his own standard.

I have already said that two cities, different and mutually opposed, owe their existence to the fact that some men live by the standard of the flesh, others by the standard of the spirit. It can now be seen that we may also put it in this way: that some live by man's standard, others by God's. St Paul puts it very plainly when he says to the Corinthians, 'For since there is jealousy and quarrelling among you, are you not of the flesh, following human standards in your behaviour?'[25] Therefore, to behave according to human standards is the same as to be 'of the flesh', because by 'the flesh', a part of man, man himself is meant.

In fact, St Paul had previously employed the term 'animal' to the same people whom he here calls 'carnal'. This is what he said,

> For what man on earth knows the truth about a man except the spirit of the man which is in him? Similarly, no one knows the truth about God except the Spirit of God. Now we have not received the

---

23. Rom. 3, 7.
24. John 14, 6.
25. 1 Cor. 3, 3.

spirit of this world, but the spirit which is the gift of God, so that we may understand the gifts which God has granted us. We speak of those gifts in words which we have been taught, not by human wisdom, but by the Spirit, interpreting spiritual truths to men possessed by God's Spirit. The 'animal' man does not grasp what belongs to the Spirit of God; it is all folly to him.[26]

It is then to such men, that is, to 'animal' men, that he says, somewhat later, 'Now I, my brothers, could not speak to you as I should to men possessed by the Spirit; I could only speak as to men of the flesh.'[27] Both these terms, 'animal' and 'carnal', are examples of the 'part for whole' figure of speech. For *anima* (the soul) and *caro* (the flesh) are parts of a man, and can stand for man in his entirety. And thus the 'animal' man is not something different from the 'carnal' man: they are identical, that is, man living by human standards. In the same way, the reference is simply to men when we read 'No flesh will be justified as a result of the works of the law',[28] and also when Scripture says, 'Seventy-five souls went down to Egypt with Jacob.'[29] In the first case 'no flesh' means 'no man', and in the second, 'seventy-five souls' means 'seventy-five men'.

Further, in the phrase, 'in words taught not by human wisdom', 'carnal wisdom' could be substituted; and in 'you follow human standards in your behaviour', 'carnal standards' would express the same meaning. This comes out more clearly in the words that follow, 'For when a man says, "I belong to Paul", and another, "I belong to Apollos", are you not merely men?'[30] Paul said earlier, 'You are "animal"', and, 'You are carnal.' Now he makes his meaning plainer by saying, 'You are men.' That is, 'You live by man's standards, not God's. If you lived by his standards, you would be gods.'

Chapter 5

The Platonic theory of body and soul; more tolerable than the Manichean view, but to be rejected because it makes the nature of the flesh responsible for all moral faults

There is no need then, in the matter of our sins and faults, to do our Creator the injustice of laying the blame on the nature of the flesh which is good, in its own kind and on its own level. But it is not good to forsake the good Creator and live by the standard of a created good, whether a man chooses the standard of the flesh, or of the soul, or of the entire man, who consists of soul and flesh and hence can be denoted by either term, soul or flesh, by itself. For anyone who exalts the soul as the Supreme Good, and censures the nature of flesh as something evil, is in fact carnal alike in his cult of the soul and in his revulsion from the flesh, since this attitude is prompted by human folly, not by divine truth.

---

26. 1 Cor. 2, 11ff.
27. 1 Cor. 3, 1.
28. Rom. 3, 20.
29. Gen. 46, 27.
30. 1 Cor. 3, 4.

The Platonists, to be sure, do not show quite the folly of the Manicheans.[31] They do not go so far as to execrate earthly bodies as the natural substance of evil, since all the elements which compose the structure of this visible and tangible world, and their qualities, are attributed by the Platonists to God the artificer. All the same, they hold that souls are so influenced by 'earthly limbs and dying members' that they derive from them their morbid desires and fears, joy and sadness. And those four 'disturbances' (to employ Cicero's word[32]) or 'passions' (which is a literal translation of the Greek, and is the term in common use), cover the whole range of moral failure in human behaviour.[33]

But if this is true, how is it that, in Virgil, when Aeneas is told by his father in the world below that souls will return again to bodies, he is amazed at this notion, and cries out,

Father, can we believe that souls return
To dwell beneath the sky, again to assume
The body's lethargy? Oh, what dread lust
For life under the sun holds them in misery?[34]

Must we really suppose that this 'dread lust', deriving from 'earthly limbs and dying members', still finds a place in that purity of souls which we hear so much about? Does not Virgil assert that souls have been purified from all such 'bodily infections' (as he calls them)? Yet, after that, they begin to feel the desire 'again to assume their bodies'.

Hence, even if it were true (it is in fact an utterly baseless assumption) that souls pass through a ceaseless alternation of cleansing and defilement as they depart and return, we must infer that there can have been no truth in the claim that all their culpable and perverted emotions that arise in them are derived from their earthly bodies. For we see that, on the admission of the Platonists themselves, this 'dread lust', as their renowned spokesman puts it, is so far from deriving from the body that of its own accord it urges the soul towards a bodily existence, even when the soul has been purified from all bodily infection, and has been placed in a situation outside any kind of body. Thus on their own confession, it is not only from the influence of the flesh that the soul experiences desire and fear, joy and distress; it can also be disturbed by those emotions from a source within itself.

Chapter 27

The perversity of sinners does not disturb God's providential design

It follows that the actions of sinners, whether angels or men, cannot obstruct the 'great works of God, carefully designed to fulfil all his decisions',[162] since in his providence and omnipotence he assigns to each his

---

31. Who ascribed the creation of flesh to an evil power, opposed to God, and co-eternal with him (Aug., *De Haer.*, 46); cf. Bk XI, 13n.

32. *Tusc. Disp.*, 4, 6, 11.

33. cf. Bk VIII, 17.

34. *Aen.*, 6, 719ff.

162. Ps. 111, 2.

own gifts and knows how to turn to good account the good and the evil alike. Hence the evil angel had been so condemned and so hardened in evil, as the fitting retribution for his first evil will, that he could no longer have a good will; but nothing prevented God from turning him to good use and allowing him to tempt the first man, who had been created upright, that is, with a good will. For the fact is that man had been so designed that if he had trusted in God's help as a good human being he would have overcome the evil angels, whereas if in pride and self-pleasing he deserted God, his creator and helper, he would be overcome. Thus he would win a good reward with a rightly directed will that was divinely helped, but an evil retribution with a perverted will that deserted God.

Now man could not even trust in the help of God without God's help; but this did not mean that he did not have it in his power to withdraw from the benefits of divine grace by self-pleasing. For just as it is not in our power to live in this physical frame without the support of food, and yet it is in our power not to live in it at all (which is what happens to suicides), so it was not in man's power, even in paradise, to live a good life without the help of God, yet it was in his power to live an evil life; but then his happiness would not continue and a most just punishment would follow. Therefore, since God was well aware that man would fall as he did, was there any reason why he should not have allowed him to be tempted by the malice of the jealous angel? God was perfectly certain that man would be defeated, but he foresaw with equal certainty that this same Devil was to be overcome by the man's seed,[163] helped by God's own grace, to the greater glory of the saints.

Thus it came about that God was not unaware of any event in the future, and yet he did not, by his foreknowledge, compel anyone to sin; and by the consequent experience he showed to angels and men, the rational part of creation, what a difference there was between the individual's own self-confidence and God's divine protection. Who would dare to believe or assert that it was not in God's power to ensure that neither angel nor man should fall? But God preferred not to withdraw this issue from their power, and thus to show the magnitude of their pride's power for evil and of God's grace for good.

Chapter 28

The character of the two cities

We see then that the two cities were created by two kinds of love: the earthly city was created by self-love reaching the point of contempt for God, the Heavenly City by the love of God carried as far as contempt of self. In fact, the earthly city glories in itself, the Heavenly City glories in the Lord.[164] The former looks for glory from men, the latter finds its highest glory in God, the witness of a good conscience. The earthly lifts up its head in its own glory, the Heavenly City says to its God: 'My glory; you lift up my head.'[165] In the former, the lust for domination lords it over its princes as over the nations

---

163. cf. Gen. 3, 15 (the 'Protevangelium').

164. 2 Cor. 10, 17.

165. Ps. 3, 3.

it subjugates; in the other both those put in authority and those subject to them serve one another in love, the rulers by their counsel, the subjects by obedience. The one city loves its own strength shown in its powerful leaders; the other says to its God, 'I will love you, my Lord, my strength.'[166]

Consequently, in the earthly city its wise men who live by men's standards have pursued the goods of the body or of their own mind, or of both. Or those of them who were able to know God 'did not honour him as God, nor did they give thanks to him, but they dwindled into futility in their thoughts, and their senseless heart was darkened: in asserting their wisdom'—that is, exalting themselves in their wisdom, under the domination of pride—'they became foolish, and changed the glory of the imperishable God into an image representing a perishable man, or birds or beasts or reptiles'—for in the adoration of idols of this kind they were either leaders or followers of the general public—'and they worshipped and served created things instead of the Creator, who is blessed for ever.'[167] In the Heavenly City, on the other hand, man's only wisdom is the devotion which rightly worships the true God, and looks for its reward in the fellowship of the saints, not only holy men but also holy angels, 'so that God may be all in all'.[168]

Book XIX

Chapter 12

Peace is the instinctive aim of all creatures, and is even the ultimate purpose of war

Anyone who joins me in an examination, however slight, of human affairs, and the human nature we all share, recognizes that just as there is no man who does not wish for joy, so there is no man who does not wish for peace. Indeed, even when men choose war, their only wish is for victory; which shows that their desire in fighting is for peace with glory. For what is victory but the conquest of the opposing side? And when this is achieved, there will be peace. Even wars, then, are waged with peace as their object, even when they are waged by those who are concerned to exercise their warlike prowess, either in command or in the actual fighting. Hence it is an established fact that peace is the desired end of war. For every man is in quest of peace, even in waging war, whereas no one is in quest of war when making peace. In fact, even when men wish a present state of peace to be disturbed they do so not because they hate peace, but because they desire the present peace to be exchanged for one that suits their wishes. Thus their desire is not that there should not be peace but that it should be the kind of peace they wish for. Even in the extreme case when they have separated themselves from others by sedition, they cannot achieve their aim unless they maintain some sort of semblance of peace with their confederates in conspiracy. Moreover, even robbers, to ensure greater efficiency and security in their assaults on the peace of the rest of mankind, desire to preserve peace with their associates.

---

166. Ps. 18, 1.

167. Rom. 1, 21ff.

168. 1 Cor. 15, 28.

Indeed, one robber may be so unequalled in strength and so wary of having anyone to share his plans that he does not trust any associate, but plots his crimes and achieves his successes by himself, carrying off his booty after overcoming and dispatching such as he can; yet even so he maintains some kind of shadow of peace, at least with those whom he cannot kill, and from whom he wishes to conceal his activities. At the same time, he is anxious, of course, to be at peace in his own home, with his wife and children and any other members of his household; without doubt he is delighted to have them obedient to his beck and call. For if this does not happen, he is indignant; he scolds and punishes; and, if need be, he employs savage measures to impose on his household a peace which, he feels, cannot exist unless all the other elements in the same domestic society are subject to one head; and this head, in his own home, is himself. Thus, if he were offered the servitude of a larger number, of a city, maybe, or a whole nation, on the condition that they should all show the same subservience he had demanded from his household, then he would no longer lurk like a brigand in his hide-out; he would raise himself on high as a king for all to see—although the same greed and malignity would persist in him.

We see, then, that all men desire to be at peace with their own people, while wishing to impose their will upon those people's lives. For even when they wage war on others, their wish is to make those opponents their own people, if they can—to subject them, and to impose on them their own conditions of peace. . . .

It comes to this, then; a man who has learnt to prefer right to wrong and the rightly ordered to the perverted, sees that the peace of the unjust, compared with the peace of the just, is not worthy even of the name of peace. Yet even what is perverted must of necessity be in, or derived from, or associated with—that is, in a sense, at peace with—some part of the order of things among which it has its being or of which it consists. Otherwise it would not exist at all. For instance if anyone were to hang upside-down, this position of the body and arrangement of the limbs is undoubtedly perverted, because what should be on top, according to the dictates of nature, is underneath, and what nature intends to be underneath is on top. This perverted attitude disturbs the peace of the flesh, and causes distress for that reason. For all that, the breath is at peace with its body and is busily engaged for its preservation; that is why there is something to endure the pain. And even if the breath is finally driven from the body by its distresses, still, as long as the framework of the limbs holds together, what remains retains a kind of peace among the bodily parts; hence there is still something to hang there. And in that the earthly body pulls towards the earth, and pulls against the binding rope that holds it suspended, it tends towards the position of its own peace, and by what might be called the appeal of its weight, it demands a place where it may rest. And so even when it is by now lifeless and devoid of all sensation it does not depart from the peace of its natural position, either while possessed of it or while tending towards it. Again, if treatment with embalming fluids is applied to prevent the dissolution and disintegration of the corpse in its present shape, a kind of peace still connects the parts with one another and keeps the whole mass fixed in its earthly condition, an appropriate, and therefore a peaceable state.

On the other hand, if no preservative treatment is given, and the body is left for nature to take its course, there is for a time a kind of tumult in the corpse of exhalations disagreeable and offensive to our senses (for that is what we smell in putrefaction), which lasts until the body unites with the elements of the world as, little by little, and particle by particle, it vanishes into their peace. Nevertheless, nothing is in any way removed, in this process, from the control of the laws of the supreme Creator and Ruler who directs the peace of the whole scheme of things. For although minute animals are produced in the corpse of a larger animal, those little bodies, each and all of them, by the same law of their Creator, are subservient to their little souls in the peace that preserves their lives. And even if the flesh of dead animals is devoured by other animals, in whatever direction it is taken, with whatever substances it is united, into whatever substances it is converted and transformed, it still finds itself subject to the same laws which are diffused throughout the whole of matter for the preservation of every mortal species, establishing peace by a harmony of congruous elements.

Chapter 13

*The peace of the universe maintained through all
disturbances by a law of nature: the individual attains,
by God's ordinance, to the state he has deserved by his
free choice*

The peace of the body, we conclude, is a tempering of the component parts in duly ordered proportion; the peace of the irrational soul is a duly ordered repose of the appetites; the peace of the rational soul is the duly ordered agreement of cognition and action. The peace of body and soul is the duly ordered life and health of a living creature; peace between mortal man and God is an ordered obedience, in faith, in subjection to an everlasting law; peace between men is an ordered agreement of mind with mind; the peace of a home is the ordered agreement among those who live together about giving and obeying orders; the peace of the Heavenly City is a perfectly ordered and perfectly harmonious fellowship in the enjoyment of God, and a mutual fellowship in God; the peace of the whole universe is the tranquillity of order—and order is the arrangement of things equal and unequal in a pattern which assigns to each its proper position.

It follows that the wretched, since, in so far as they are wretched, they are obviously not in a state of peace, lack the tranquillity of order, a state in which there is no disturbance of mind. In spite of that, because their wretchedness is deserved and just, they cannot be outside the scope of order. They are not, indeed, united with the blessed; yet it is by the law of order that they are sundered from them. And when they are free from disturbance of mind, they are adjusted to their situation, with however small a degree of harmony. Thus they have amongst them some tranquillity of order, and therefore some peace. But they are still wretched just because, although they enjoy some degree of serenity and freedom from suffering, they are not in a condition where they have the right to be serene and free from pain. They are yet more wretched, however, if they are not at peace with the law by which the natural order is governed. Now when they suffer, their peace is disturbed in the part where they suffer; and yet peace still continues in the part which feels no burning pain, and where the natural frame is not broken up. Just as there is life, then, without pain, whereas there can be no pain when there is no life, so there is peace without any war, but no war without some degree of peace. This is not a consequence of war as such, but of the fact that war is waged by or within persons who are in some sense natural beings—for they could have no kind of existence without some kind of peace as the condition of their being.

There exists, then, a nature in which there is no evil, in which, indeed, no evil can exist; but there cannot exist a nature in which there is no good. Hence not even the nature of the Devil himself is evil, in so far as it is a nature; it is perversion that makes it evil. And so the Devil did not stand firm in the truth, and yet he did not escape the judgement of the truth. He did not continue in the tranquillity of order; but that did not mean that he escaped from the power of the imposer of order. The good that God imparts, which the Devil has in his nature, does not withdraw him from God's justice by which his punishment is ordained. But God, in punishing, does not chastise the good which he created, but the evil which the Devil has committed. And God does not take away all that he gave to that nature; he takes something, and yet he leaves something, so that there may be some being left to feel pain at the deprivation.

Now this pain is in itself evidence of the good that was taken away and the good that was left. In fact, if no good had been left there could have been no grief for lost good. For a sinner is in a worse state if he rejoices in the loss of righteousness; but a sinner who feels anguish, though he may gain no good from his anguish, is at least grieving at the loss of salvation. And since righteousness and salvation are both good, and the loss of any good calls for grief rather than for joy (assuming that there is no compensation for the loss in the shape of a higher good—for example, righteousness of character is a higher good than health of body), the unrighteous man's grief in his punishment is more appropriate than his rejoicing in sin. Hence, just as delight in the abandonment of good, when a man sins, is evidence of a bad will, so grief at the loss of good, when a man is punished, is evidence of a good nature. For when a man grieves at the loss of the peace of his nature, his grief arises from some remnants of that peace, which ensure that his nature is still on friendly terms with itself. Moreover, it is entirely right that in the last punishment the wicked and ungodly should bewail in their agonies the loss of their 'natural' goods, and realize that he who divested them of these goods with perfect justice is God, whom they despised when with supreme generosity he bestowed them.

God then, created all things in supreme wisdom and ordered them in perfect justice; and in establishing the mortal race of mankind as the greatest ornament of earthly things, he has given to mankind certain good things suitable to this life. These are: temporal peace, in proportion to the short span of a mortal life—the peace that consists in bodily health and soundness, and in fellowship with one's kind; and everything necessary to safeguard or recover this peace—those things, for example, which are appropriate and accessible to our senses: light, speech, air to breathe, water to drink, and whatever is suitable for the feeding and clothing of the body, for the care of the body and the adornment of the person. And all this is granted under the most equitable condition: that every mortal who uses aright such goods, goods designed to serve the peace of mortal men, shall receive goods greater in degree and superior in kind, namely, the peace of immortality, and the glory and honour appropriate to it in a life which is eternal for the enjoyment of God and of one's neighbour in God, whereas he who wrongly uses those mortal goods shall lose them, and shall not receive the blessings of eternal life.

Chapter 14

The order and law, earthly or heavenly, by which government serves the interests of human society

We see, then, that all man's use of temporal things is related to the enjoyment of earthly peace in the earthly city; whereas in the Heavenly City it is related to the enjoyment of eternal peace. Thus, if we were irrational animals, our only aim would be the adjustment of the parts of the body in due proportion, and the quieting of the appetites—only, that is, the repose of the flesh, and an adequate supply of pleasures, so that bodily peace might promote the peace of the soul. For if bodily peace is lacking, the peace of the irrational soul is also hindered, because it cannot achieve the quieting of its appetites. But the two together promote that peace which is a mutual concord between soul and body, the peace of an ordered life and of health. For living creatures show their love of bodily peace by their avoidance of pain, and by their pursuit of pleasure to satisfy the demands of their appetites they demonstrate their love of peace of soul. In just the same way, by shunning death they indicate quite clearly how great is their love of the peace in which soul and body are harmoniously united.

But because there is in man a rational soul, he subordinates to the peace of the rational soul all that part of his nature which he shares with the beasts, so that he may engage in deliberate thought and act in accordance with this thought, so that he may thus exhibit that ordered agreement of cognition and action which we called the peace of the rational soul. For with this end in view he ought to wish to be spared the distress of pain and grief, the disturbances of desire, the dissolution of death, so that he may come to some profitable knowledge and may order his life and his moral standards in accordance with this knowledge. But he needs divine direction, which he may obey with resolution, and divine assistance that he may obey it freely, to prevent him from falling, in his enthusiasm for knowledge, a victim to some fatal error, through the weakness of the human mind. And so long as he is in this mortal body, he is a pilgrim in a foreign land, away from God; therefore he walks by faith, not by sight.[32] That is why he views all peace, of body or of soul, or of both, in relation to that peace which exists between mortal man and immortal God, so that he may exhibit an ordered obedience in faith in subjection to the everlasting Law.

Now God, our master, teaches two chief precepts, love of God and love of neighbour; and in them man finds three objects for his love: God, himself,

---

32. cf. 2 Cor. 5, 6f.

and his neighbour; and a man who loves God is not wrong in loving himself. It follows, therefore, that he will be concerned also that his neighbour should love God, since he is told to love his neighbour as himself; and the same is true of his concern for his wife, his children, for the members of his household, and for all other men, so far as is possible. And, for the same end, he will wish his neighbour to be concerned for him, if he happens to need that concern. For this reason he will be at peace, as far as lies in him, with all men, in that peace among men, that ordered harmony; and the basis of this order is the observance of two rules: first, to do no harm to anyone, and, secondly, to help everyone whenever possible. To begin with, therefore, a man has a responsibility for his own household—obviously, both in the order of nature and in the framework of human society, he has easier and more immediate contact with them; he can exercise his concern for them. That is why the Apostle says, 'Anyone who does not take care of his own people, especially those in his own household, is worse than an unbeliever—he is a renegade.'[33] This is where domestic peace starts, the ordered harmony about giving and obeying orders among those who live in the same house. For the orders are given by those who are concerned for the interests of others; thus the husband gives orders to the wife, parents to children, masters to servants. While those who are the objects of this concern obey orders; for example, wives obey husbands, the children obey their parents, the servants their masters. But in the household of the just man who 'lives on the basis of faith' and who is still on pilgrimage, far from that Heavenly City, even those who give orders are the servants of those whom they appear to command. For they do not give orders because of a lust for domination but from a dutiful concern for the interests of others, not with pride in taking precedence over others, but with compassion in taking care of others.

Chapter 17

The origin of peace between the heavenly society and the earthly city, and of discord between them

But a household of human beings whose life is not based on faith is in pursuit of an earthly peace based on the things belonging to this temporal life, and on its advantages, whereas a household of human beings whose life is based on faith looks forward to the blessings which are promised as eternal in the future, making use of earthly and temporal things like a pilgrim in a foreign land, who does not let himself by taken in by them or distracted from his course towards God, but rather treats them as supports which help him more easily to bear the burdens of 'the corruptible body which weighs heavy on the soul';[42] they must on no account be allowed to increase the load. Thus both kinds of men and both kinds of households alike make use of the things essential for this mortal life; but each has its own very different end in making use of them. So also the earthly city, whose life is not based on faith, aims at an earthly peace, and it limits the harmonious agreement of citizens concerning the giving and obeying of

---

33. 1 Tim. 5, 8.
42. Wisd. 9, 15.

orders to the establishment of a kind of compromise between human wills about the things relevant to mortal life. In contrast, the Heavenly City—or rather that part of it which is on pilgrimage in this condition of mortality, and which lives on the basis of faith—must needs make use of this peace also, until this mortal state, for which this kind of peace is essential, passes away. And therefore, it leads what we may call a life of captivity in this earthly city as in a foreign land, although it has already received the promise of redemption, and the gift of the Spirit as a kind of pledge of it; and yet it does not hesitate to obey the laws of the earthly city by which those things which are designed for the support of this mortal life are regulated; and the purpose of this obedience is that, since this mortal condition is shared by both cities, a harmony may be preserved between them in things that are relevant to this condition.

But this earthly city has had some philosophers belonging to it whose theories are rejected by the teaching inspired by God. Either led astray by their own speculation or deluded by demons, these thinkers reached the belief that there are many gods who must be won over to serve human ends, and also that they have, as it were, different departments with different responsibilities attached. Thus the body is the department of one god, the mind that of another; and within the body itself, one god is in charge of the head, another of the neck and so on with each of the separate members. Similarly, within the mind, one is responsible for natural ability, another for learning, another for anger, another for lust; and in the accessories of life there are separate gods over the departments of flocks, grain, wine, oil, forests, coinage, navigation, war and victory, marriage, birth, fertility, and so on.[43] The Heavenly City, in contrast, knows only one God as the object of worship, and decrees, with faithful devotion, that he only is to be served with that service which the Greeks call *latreia*, which is due to God alone. And the result of this difference has been that the Heavenly City could not have laws of religion common with the earthly city, and in defence of her religious laws she was bound to dissent from those who thought differently and to prove a burdensome nuisance to them. Thus she had to endure their anger and hatred, and the assaults of persecution; until at length that City shattered the morale of her adversaries by the terror inspired by her numbers, and by the help she continually received from God.

While this Heavenly City, therefore, is on pilgrimage in this world, she calls out citizens from all nations and so collects a society of aliens, speaking all languages. She takes no account of any difference in customs, laws, and institutions, by which earthly peace is achieved and preserved—not that she annuls or abolishes any of those, rather, she maintains them and follows them (for whatever divergences there are among the diverse nations, those institutions have one single aim—earthly peace), provided that no hindrance is presented thereby to the religion which teaches that the one supreme and true God is to be worshipped. Thus even the Heavenly City in her pilgrimage here on earth makes use of the earthly peace and defends and seeks the compromise between human wills in respect of the provisions relevant to the mortal nature of man, so far as may be permitted without detriment to true religion and piety. In fact, that City relates the earthly peace to the

---

43. cf. Bks IV, VI, VII.

heavenly peace, which is so truly peaceful that it should be regarded as the only peace deserving the name, at least in respect of the rational creation; for this peace is the perfectly ordered and completely harmonious fellowship in the enjoyment of God, and of each other in God. When we arrive at that state of peace, there will be no longer a life that ends in death, but a life that is life in sure and sober truth; there will be no animal body to 'weigh down the soul' in its process of corruption; there will be a spiritual body with no cravings, a body subdued in every part to the will. This peace the Heavenly City possesses in faith while on its pilgrimage, and it lives a life of righteousness, based on this faith,[44] having the attainment of that peace in view in every good action it performs in relation to God, and in relation to a neighbour, since the life of a city is inevitably a social life.

Chapter 24

An alternative definition of 'people' and 'commonwealth'

If, on the other hand, another definition than this is found for a 'people', for example, if one should say, 'A people is the association of a multitude of rational beings united by a common agreement on the objects of their love', then it follows that to observe the character of a particular people we must examine the objects of its love. And yet, whatever those objects, if it is the association of a multitude not of animals but of rational beings, and is united by a common agreement about the objects of its love, then there is no absurdity in applying to it the title of a 'people'. And, obviously, the better the objects of this agreement, the better the people; the worse the objects of this love, the worse the people. By this definition of ours, the Roman people is a people and its estate is indubitably a commonwealth. But as for the objects of that people's love—both in the earliest times and in subsequent periods—and the morality of that people as it proceeded to bloody strife of parties and then to the social and civil wars, and corrupted and disrupted that very unity which is, as it were, the health of a people—for all this we have the witness of history; and I have had a great deal to say about it in my preceding books. And yet I shall not make that a reason for asserting that a people is not really a people or that a state is not a commonwealth, so long as there remains an association of some kind or other between a multitude of rational beings united by a common agreement on the objects of its love. However, what I have said about the Roman people and the Roman commonwealth I must be understood to have said and felt about those of the Athenians and of any other Greeks, or of that former Babylon of the Assyrians, when they exercised imperial rule, whether on a small or a large scale, in their commonwealths—and indeed about any other nation whatsoever. For God is not the ruler of the city of the impious, because it disobeys his commandment that sacrifice should be offered to himself alone. The purpose of this law was that in that city the soul should rule over the body and reason over the vicious elements, in righteousness and faith. And because God does not rule there the general characteristic of that city is that it is devoid of true justice.

---

44. cf. Hab. 2, 4; Rom. 1, 17 etc.

Chapter 25

True virtues impossible without true religion

The fact is that the soul may appear to rule the body and the reason to govern the vicious elements in the most praiseworthy fashion; and yet if the soul and reason do not serve God as God himself has commanded that he should be served, then they do not in any way exercise the right kind of rule over the body and the vicious propensities. For what kind of a mistress over the body and the vices can a mind be that is ignorant of the true God and is not subjected to his rule, but instead is prostituted to the corrupting influence of vicious demons? Thus the virtues which the mind imagines it possesses, by means of which it rules the body and the vicious elements, are themselves vices rather than virtues, if the mind does not bring them into relation with God in order to achieve anything whatsoever and to maintain that achievement. For although the virtues are reckoned by some people to be genuine and honourable when they are related only to themselves and are sought for no other end, even then they are puffed up and proud, and so are to be accounted vices rather than virtues. For just as it is not something derived from the physical body itself that gives life to that body, but something above it, so it is not something that comes from man, but something above man, that makes his life blessed; and this is true not only of man but of every heavenly dominion and power whatsoever.

Chapter 26

The peace of the people alienated from God is made use of by God's People on their pilgrimage

Thus, as the soul is the life of the physical body, so God is the blessedness of man's life. As the holy Scriptures of the Hebrews say, 'Blessed is the people, whose God is the Lord.'[68] It follows that a people alienated from that God must be wretched. Yet even such a people loves a peace of its own, which is not to be rejected; but it will not possess it in the end, because it does not make good use of it before the end. Meanwhile, however, it is important for us also that this people should possess this peace in this life, since so long as the two cities are intermingled we also make use of the peace of Babylon—although the People of God is by faith set free from Babylon, so that in the meantime they are only pilgrims in the midst of her. That is why the Apostle instructs the Church to pray for kings of that city and those in high positions, adding these words: 'that we may lead a quiet and peaceful life with all devotion and love'.[69] And when the prophet Jeremiah predicted to the ancient People of God the coming captivity, and bade them, by God's inspiration, to go obediently to Babylon, serving God even by their patient endurance, he added his own advice that prayers should be offered for Babylon, 'because in her peace is your peace'[70]—

---

68. Ps. 144, 15.

69. 1 Tim. 2, 2.

70. Jer. 29, 7.

meaning, of course, the temporal peace of the meantime, which is shared by good and bad alike.

Chapter 27

The peace of God's servants, a perfect tranquillity, not experienced in this life

In contrast, the peace which is our special possession is ours even in this life, a peace with God through faith; and it will be ours for ever, a peace with God through open vision.[71] But peace here and now, whether the peace shared by all men or our own special possession, is such that it affords a solace for our wretchedness rather than the joy of blessedness. Our righteousness itself, too, though genuine, in virtue of the genuine Ultimate Good to which it is referred, is nevertheless only such as to consist in the forgiveness of sins rather than in the perfection of virtues. The evidence for this is in the prayer of the whole City of God on pilgrimage in the world, which, as we know, cries out to God through the lips of all its members: 'Forgive us our debts, as we forgive our debtors.'[72] And this prayer is not effective for those whose 'faith, without works, is dead'[73] but only for those whose 'faith is put into action through love'.[74] For such a prayer is needed by righteous men because the reason, though subjected to God, does not have complete command over the vices in this mortal state and in the 'corruptible body which weighs heavy on the soul'.[75] In fact, even though command be exercised over the vices it is assuredly not by any means without a conflict. And even when a man fights well and even gains the mastery by conquering and subduing such foes, still in this situation of weakness something is all too likely to creep in to cause sin, if not in hasty action, at least in a casual remark or a fleeting thought.

For this reason there is no perfect peace so long as command is exercised over the vicious propensities, because the battle is fraught with peril while those vices that resist are being reduced to submission, while those which have been overcome are not yet triumphed over in peaceful security, but are repressed under a rule still troubled by anxieties. Thus we are in the midst of these temptations, about which we find this brief saying amongst the divine oracles: 'Is a man's life on earth anything but temptation?';[76] and who can presume that his life is of such a kind that he has no need to say to God, 'Forgive us our debts', unless he is a man of overwhelming conceit, not a truly great man, but one puffed up and swollen with pride, who is with justice resisted by him who gives grace to the humble, as it says in the Scriptures, 'God resists the proud, but he gives his favour to the humble.'[77] In this life, therefore, justice in each individual exists when God rules and

---

71. cf. 2 Cor. 5, 7.
72. Matt. 6, 12.
73. Jas. 2, 17.
74. Gal. 5, 6.
75. Wisd. 9, 15.
76. Job 7, 1; cf. ch. 8n.
77. Jas. 4, 6; 1 Pet. 5, 5.

man obeys, when the mind rules the body and reason governs the vices even when they rebel, either by subduing them or by resisting them, while from God himself favour is sought for good deeds and pardon for offences, and thanks are duly offered to him for benefits received. But in that ultimate peace, to which this justice should be related, and for the attainment of which this justice is to be maintained, our nature will be healed by immortality and incorruption and will have no perverted elements, and nothing at all, in ourselves or any other, will be in conflict with any one of us. And so reason will not need to rule the vices, since there will be no vices, but God will hold sway over man, and the soul over the body, and in this state our delight and facility in obeying will be matched by our felicity in living and reigning. There, for each and every one, this state will be eternal, and its eternity will be assured; and for that reason the peace of this blessedness, or the blessedness of this peace, will be the Supreme Good.

Chapter 28

The end of the wicked

In contrast with this, however, the wretchedness of those who do not belong to this City of God will be everlasting. This is called also 'the second death', because the soul cannot be said to be alive in that state, when it is separated from the life of God, nor can the body, when it is subjected to eternal torments. And this is precisely the reason why this 'second death' will be harder to bear, because it cannot come to an end in death. But here a question arises; for just as wretchedness is the opposite of blessedness, and death of life, so war is evidently the opposite of peace. And the question is rightly asked: What war, or what kind of war, can be understood to exist in the final state of the wicked, corresponding, by way of contrast, to that peace which is proclaimed with joyful praises in the final state of the good? Now anyone who puts this question should observe what it is that is harmful and destructive in war; and he will see that it is precisely the mutual opposition and conflict of the forces engaged. What war, then, can be imagined more serious and more bitter than a struggle in which the will is so at odds with the feelings and the feelings with the will, that their hostility cannot be ended by the victory of either—a struggle in which the violence of pain is in such conflict with the nature of the body that neither can yield to the other? For in this life, when such a conflict occurs, either pain wins, and death takes away feeling, or nature conquers, and health removes the pain. But in that other life, pain continues to torment, while nature lasts to feel the pain. Neither ceases to exist, lest the punishment also should cease.

These, then, are the final states of good and evil. The first we should seek to attain, the latter we should strive to escape. And since it is through a judgement that the good will pass to the one, and the evil to the other, it is of this judgement that I shall deal, as far as God grants, in the book which follows.

The State: The Return of Order
upon Disorder
Herbert A. Deane

In the last chapter I analyzed Augustine's conceptions of temporal peace and earthly justice as distinguished from "true" or "real" peace and justice, found only in the City of God. We saw that although earthly peace and order are frequently disturbed by conflict, and the justice they provide is often imperfect, they are essential conditions for man's continued existence and must, therefore, be maintained by a political and legal system furnished with powers of coercion. So we come at last to the central theme—Augustine's analysis of the state, its tasks, and its powers. The state operates in this world, and most of its citizens are (and always will be) those sinful men whose characteristics we have already discussed. In any earthly state a small number of the citizens may be men who have been converted by God's grace; since these men have died and been born anew, their loves, their aspirations, and their behavior are completely different from those of the great mass of the unredeemed. However, as long as this world lasts, there will never be a society or a state made up solely or even predominantly of the saved. Since the two cities are inextricably bound together until the Last Judgment, every earthly state will be composed primarily of sinners, with perhaps a scattering of saints living in their midst. The political and legal system must, therefore, be set up and operated on the assumption that it is dealing with fallen men. The motives upon which it relies when it makes laws and imposes penalties must be the drives that impel such men to action, and its expectations should never outrun the characteristics that they can be presumed to possess.

As we have seen, the state, for Augustine, is an external order; the peace that it maintains is external peace—the absence, or at least the diminution, of overt violence. The state is also a coercive order, maintained by the use of force and relying on the fear of pain as its major sanction for compliance to its commands. It has no weapons by which it can mold the thoughts, desires, and wills of its citizens; nor is it really concerned to exert such influence. It does not seek to make men truly good or virtuous. Rather, it is interested in their outward actions, and it attempts, with some success, to restrain its citizens from performing certain kinds of harmful and criminal acts. We have also observed that the state is a non-natural, remedial institution; like private property, slavery, and other forms of domination of man over man, it is a consequence of the Fall. It is both a punishment for sin and a remedy for man's sinful condition; without it anarchy would reign, and self-centered, avaricious, power-hungry, lustful men would destroy one another in a fierce struggle for self-aggrandizement. This external, coercive, repressive, remedial order—and its main virtue is that it *is* an order—is clearly distinguished by Augustine from the order or hierarchy found among the angels and in the whole City of God; the latter is a spontaneous order of love and not an order of coercion or domination.

Herbert A. Deane, *The Political and Social Ideas of St. Augustine.* New York: Columbia University Press, pp. 116–120, 125–129, 136–141, 151–153. Copyright © 1963, Columbia University Press. Reprinted by permission.

The reader of this brief summary of Augustine's doctrine of the state may wonder whether I am talking about Augustine, or about Hobbes or Machiavelli. Certainly, this conception of the state strikes us as essentially "modern," and we may be surprised to find it in a Christian philosopher of the fifth century. Since this formulation of the gist of Augustinian political theory is one to which some of his commentators might take exception, it will be our task to show, by explicit statements from Augustine as well as by deductions from his views of the nature of man, that it is an accurate summary and that it does not do violence to what Augustine himself says throughout the whole corpus of his writings.

Let us turn first to his discussion in *The City of God* of the definitions of a people (*populus*) and of a commonwealth or state (*res publica*) given by Scipio in Cicero's *De Republica*. He first refers to these Scipionic definitions in Book II, where he notes that according to Scipio a people is not "every assemblage or mob, but an assemblage associated by a common acknowledgment of law [i.e., an agreement about right or justice], and by a community of interests . . ." He promises that at a later point he will demonstrate that, according to this definition, there was never a people (*populus*) in Rome, and, consequently, that Rome was never a state or commonwealth (*res publica*), since true justice never had a place in it, and Scipio—and Cicero—has made an agreement about justice (*consensus iuris*) essential to the existence of a people and a state. This, to Augustine, is an absurd conclusion; so he adds, "But accepting the more feasible [i.e., "more probable" (*probabiliores*)] definitions of a republic, I grant there was a republic of a certain kind, and certainly much better administered by the more ancient Romans than by their modern representatives . . ." To make it quite clear that no other earthly state—whether pagan or Christian, ancient or modern— possessed true justice and was therefore a commonwealth according to Scipio's definition, Augustine immediately adds: "But the fact is, true justice has no existence save in that republic whose founder and ruler is Christ . . ."

In Book XIX, Augustine fulfills his promise to return to the consideration of the Scipionic definitions of a "people" and a "commonwealth." Again he notes that, according to Scipio, "a common acknowledgment of right [*consensus iuris*]" is essential to the existence of a people and of a commonwealth; this means

> that a republic cannot be administered without justice. Where, therefore, there is no true justice there can be no right. . . . Thus where there is not true justice there can be no assemblage of men associated by a common acknowledgment of right, and therefore there can be no people, as defined by Scipio or Cicero; and if no people, then no weal of the people [*res populi*], but only of some promiscuous multitude unworthy of the name of people. Consequently . . . most certainly it follows that there is no republic where there is no justice.

After citing the traditional definition of justice as "that virtue which gives every one his due," Augustine proceeds again to show that true justice was never present in the Roman commonwealth, whether we look at its early, heroic period or its later phase of decay and degeneration. "Where, then, is the justice of man, when he deserts the true God and yields himself to impure demons? Is this to give every one his due?" If a man does not serve God,

> what justice can we ascribe to him, since in this case his soul cannot exercise a just control over the body, nor his reason over his vices? And if there is no justice in such an individual, certainly there can be none in a community composed of such persons. Here, therefore, there is not that common acknowledg-

ment of right which makes an assemblage of men a people whose affairs we call a republic.

Once more, Augustine is insisting that true justice can be found only in a community or commonwealth made up of individuals who serve and love God and, *as a result,* possess true justice. However, there is only one such community—the City of God—and it has no earthly representative; so neither the Roman State nor any other state can possibly possess true justice. If, then, in agreement with Scipio, we make justice a constitutive element in the definition of the state, we will be forced to the conclusion that no state or commonwealth has ever existed or will ever exist on this earth. . . .

One of the possible sources of Professor McIlwain's difficulties in dealing with Augustine is the failure to make the distinction, so crucial to understanding his thought, between "true justice" (*vera justitia*), found only in God's kingdom, and the much inferior but still important "image of justice" or "temporal" or "earthly" justice found in all ordered earthly states, whether they are called *res publicae, civitates,* or *regna.* A state or earthly city, for Augustine, can be called "just" only in the sense that it is what he refers to as "well-ordered" (*bene ordinata*) or "well-constituted" (*bene constituta*). It has, that is, a certain harmony and concord among its citizens, and a measure of temporal peace—"what the vulgar call felicity"—is secured in it. Rulers, whether kings or princes, and laws are the major elements in securing this measure of order, peace, and earthly justice, and, therefore, a well-ordered state. "For without these things no people can be well-ordered, not even a people that pursues earthly goods. Even such a people has a measure of beauty of its own." On the other hand, no state or society in this world can be called "just" in the sense of embodying true justice, that is, giving to each his due. For a city or a state would be just only if the men who make up the community—king, court, ministers, and people—were just; for "individual men . . . are, as it were, the elements and seeds of cities."

Since the great majority of the members of any society are men who belong to the earthly city, who place their love in the world and in the things of the world, it necessarily follows that they will be unjust as each strives to outdo the others in the unceasing struggle for material goods, power, and glory.

> For when those things are loved which we can lose against our will, we must needs toil for them most miserably; and to obtain them, amid the straitnesses of earthly cares, whilst each desires to snatch them for himself, and to be beforehand with another, or to wrest it from him, must scheme injustice.

When Augustine speaks of the ungodly or the wicked, he never confines these terms to pagans or to non-Christians, but always insists that many members of the visible Church are included in the ranks of the unredeemed; this will continue to be true as long as this world lasts. Even if the unredeemed have "virtues," such as modesty, continence, or civic virtue, these are not true virtues, and their justice is not true justice, although they may have a certain "uprightness," sufficient to maintain an earthly state.

One of Augustine's most shockingly realistic discussions of earthly states is the famous fourth chapter of Book IV of *The City of God* in which he draws the comparison between kingdoms and robber bands. It is possible to raise questions about the meaning of certain phrases in this passage, but the sense of the chapter as a whole is clear beyond any doubt. A number of different translations and interpretations can be given for the first words of the opening sentence—"And so, justice removed, what are kingdoms but great robber bands? And what are robber bands but small kingdoms?" Does Augustine mean, "If true justice is absent—and it need not be—kingdoms are nothing but large robber bands"? That this cannot be the meaning is clear from what we have said about the impossibility of finding real or true justice in any earthly state. Or is he saying that a kingdom which does not have even earthly or temporal justice—the shadow or image of real justice—is nothing but a great robber band? Or does he perhaps mean that since all kingdoms are unjust they are nothing but great bands of robbers?[1] Perhaps the best course is to set aside the question of the correct meaning of this initial sentence and go on to consider the rest of the paragraph. After the flat statement that robber bands are nothing but small kingdoms, Augustine continues:

> The band itself is made up of men; it is ruled by the authority of a prince; it is knit together by the pact of the confederacy; the booty is divided by the law agreed on. If, by the admittance of abandoned men, this evil increases to such a degree that it holds places, fixes abodes, takes possession of cities, and subdues peoples, it assumes the more plainly the name of a kingdom, because the reality is now manifestly conferred on it, *not by the removal of covetousness [cupiditas], but by the addition of impunity [impunitas].*

At every point there is a parallel between the robber band and the kingdom: both are composed of men, both are ruled by the authority of a leader or prince; both are held together by a *pactum societatis*, a pact of association; in both the spoils are divided in accordance with the rules agreed to by the group. By these means—authority, a fundamental agreement, and operating rules—both maintain a kind of order, harmony, and even "justice." The points of identity are startling enough, but we are even more surprised when Augustine points out the differences between the robber band and the kingdom. Here, if anywhere, we would expect him to tell us that it is the presence of justice that distinguishes the state from the band of robbers. If this is our expectation, we are completely disappointed. The kingdom is larger than the robber band both in numbers and in territory occupied, and it has a fixed abode. As the robber band increases in size and settles down, it assumes the more plainly the name of a kingdom, not because its cupidity has been taken away but because it now possesses the priceless advantage of the "impunity" of a "sovereign state." Kingdoms are no less avaricious than robber bands, but whereas the band of robbers may be punished by the state, there is no super-state or international police force to punish the state for its misdeeds or its depredations.[2] The somber message of the chapter is pointed up by the anecdote that Augustine relates with approval in the final sentences.

> Indeed, that was an apt and true reply which was given to Alexander the Great by a pirate who had been seized. For when that king had asked the man what he meant by keeping hostile possession of the sea, he answered with bold pride, "What thou meanest by seizing the whole earth; but because I do it with a petty ship, I am called a robber, whilst thou who dost it with a great fleet art styled Emperor."

A few pages later Augustine returns to this comparison when he is discussing the wars waged by Ninus, king of the Assyrians, in order to extend his empire. "But to make war on your neighbours, and thence to proceed to others, and through mere lust of dominion to crush and subdue people who do you no harm, what else is this to be called than great robbery?" The similarity between the robber and the king or prince is again pointed out when he says that even the thief and murderer who is unwilling to have any associates or accomplices wants his wife and children to obey his commands, and thus he shows that he desires to have peace in his home.

> And therefore, if a city or nation offered to submit itself to him, to serve him in the same style as he had made his household serve him, he would no longer lurk in a brigand's hiding-places, but lift his head in open day as a king, *though the same covetousness and wickedness should remain in him.* And thus all men desire to have peace with their own circle whom they wish to govern as suits themselves. For even those whom they make war against they wish to make their own, and impose on them the laws of their own peace.

Once more, the point is driven home that the king is distinguished from the robber not by the absence of wickedness or cupidity but rather by his exalted position, his impunity, and his acceptance by the group over which he rules. . . .

It is inescapable dilemmas like these that make it impossible for a state to be truly just, no matter what the character and personality of its rulers may be at any particular moment. The justice that emerges in the well-ordered state is a most imperfect replica or image of true justice, no matter how good the intentions of the rulers may be. Most overt crimes are punished; but some are never detected and others are never solved; sometimes the wrong man is punished, and the guilty go scot free. The rulers and the citizens are only men, fallible, prejudiced, and ignorant of much that they need to know. Even when they do the best that they can, their best is far from true justice; and, often, what they do is far from their best. Rulers are, as St. Paul said, God's ministers, avengers against those that do evil. But a province or a state can only be ruled by instilling fear in those who are ruled, and the fear of punishment can never produce true righteousness or justice. By their fear of the laws and of the punishments attached to them, men can be kept from performing certain injurious actions, but they cannot be made good or righteous by these means. Civil laws do not "bring men to make a good use of their wealth," but "those who make a bad use of it become thereby less injurious." Augustine states the kernel of the problem in one sentence: "But, ruling a province is different from ruling a Church; the former must be governed by instilling fear, the latter is to be made lovable by the use of mildness."

Of course, these dilemmas would not exist and this very imperfect, rough "justice" of the state would be converted into true justice if not only the rulers but all the subjects were truly pious and just men, who obeyed the commandments of Christ, and, as a consequence, preferred common interests to their egoistic, private interests. If this were possible, we could have the "Christian state," the truly just society, based on God's law, that some commentators seem to think that Augustine regarded as feasible or necessary. It is perfectly clear, however, that the conditions *sine qua non* for the existence of such a state can never be realized on this earth. Moreover, if they were to be realized, the result would not be a Christian or truly just state but rather the complete absence of the state as we know it. Since the entire apparatus of law, punishment, coercion, and repression that constitutes the heart of the state would be totally unnecessary, the state would indeed "wither away" and be replaced by the anarchist's paradise—a spontaneous, noncoercive order of love, which would embody true justice, true peace, and true harmony, with no need for armies, courts, policemen, judges, jailers, and hangmen.

In other words, a truly just society would be the City of God brought down from heaven to earth, and that for Augustine is an absolute impossibility. Even when he is defending Christianity against pagan charges that it is incompatible with patriotism and the well-being of the state, he is careful to retain the contrary-to-fact conditional form in speaking of the possibility of a state made up of true Christians.

> Wherefore, let those who say that the doctrine of Christ is incompatible with the State's well-being, give us an army composed of soldiers such as the doctrine of Christ requires them to be; let them give us such subjects, such husbands and wives, such parents and children, such masters and servants, such kings, such judges—in fine, even such taxpayers and tax-gatherers, as *the Christian religion has taught that men should be,* and then let them dare to say that it is adverse to the State's well-being; yea, rather, let them no longer hesitate to confess that *this doctrine, if it were obeyed, would be the salvation of the commonwealth.*

Augustine is perfectly explicit about the purpose of the earthly state and of the coercion and punishment it employs. The heavy hand of the state and its dreadful instruments of repression are necessary because they are the only methods by which sinful men can be restrained; the fear of punishment is the only safeguard of general peace and security. Only by such means can the wicked be kept from destroying one another as their competing egoisms clash, and discouraged from open assaults upon the minority of good and pious men.

> Surely, it is not without purpose that we have the institution of the power of kings, the death penalty of the judge, the barbed hooks of the executioner, the weapons of the soldier, the right of punishment of the overlord [*dominantis*], even the severity of the good father. All those things have their methods, their causes, their reasons, their practical benefits. *While these are feared, the wicked are kept within bounds and the good live more peacefully among the wicked.* However, men are not to be called good because they refrain from wrongdoing through their fear of such things—*no one is good through dread of punishment but through love of righteousness*—even so, it is not without advantage that human recklessness should be confined by fear of the law so that innocence may be safe among evil-doers, and the evil-doers themselves may be cured by calling on God when their freedom of action is held in check by fear of punishment.

By the laws that it enforces the state protects from the encroachments of other men the things that each citizen properly regards as "his"—his body and bodily goods, his liberty (that is, his right as a free man to have no master), his household, his citizenship, and his possessions. The function of the temporal law is to insure that "men may possess the things which may be called 'ours' for a season and which they eagerly covet, on condition that peace and human society be preserved so far as they can be preserved in earthly things." The law determines what the citizen may lawfully possess, and then by its sanctions it secures to each citizen the enjoyment of his proper "possessions." Thereby, it moderates the intensity of the inevitable conflict among earthly men for goods and for glory, and prevents the clash of egoistic interests from totally disrupting the peace and harmony of society. The law operates through the instrument of fear. It has no effect on the men who are subject to it except through the medium of those very goods and possessions that it exists to protect and regulate. In other words, the sanction by means of which the state attempts to insure conformity to the conduct prescribed by the laws consists in the ability to deprive the offender of one or more of these possessions—his property, his liberty, his citizenship, or, in the last resort, his life. Since the men of the earthly city regard these possessions as the highest good, they are afraid of being deprived of any or all of them. Therefore, each man somewhat restrains his unlimited desire to acquire more possessions and more power at the expense of other members of the society, because he feels that the chance of greater gain and satisfaction is outweighed by the deprivations that he will suffer if he is punished for violating the law that protects the property of all.

> It is sufficient to see that the authority of this law in punishing does not go beyond depriving him who is punished of these things or of some of them. It employs fear as an instrument of coercion, and bends to its own ends the minds of the unhappy people to rule whom it is adapted. So long as they fear to lose these earthly goods they observe in using them a certain moderation suited to maintain in being a city such as can be composed of such men. The sin of loving these things is not punished; what is punished is the wrong done to others when their rights are infringed.

Augustine sees that the legal system with its sanctions and punishments does not change, and does not attempt to change, the basic desires and attitudes of the men whose conduct it seeks to regulate. In fact, the system works precisely because these lovers of earthly goods are *not* transformed into lovers of real or eternal goods; unless they continued to place their affections in the things of this world, the law and its punishments would inspire no fear in them and so would have no effect on their behavior. The law can effectively punish only those men who love the possessions that can be taken from them against their will. "You see also that there would be no punishment inflicted on men either by injury done them or by legal sentence if they did not love the things that can be taken from them against their will."

These reflections about the state's purpose—the maintenance of external peace and order—and about the means that it employs to achieve this end—punishment and the deprivation of possessions, liberty, and life—exhibit one of the most characteristic features of Augustine's thoughts about man and his life on earth—his keen awareness of the paradoxes and ironies that mark every aspect of the human condition, and especially of political life. There is a constant danger that men will destroy one another as they seek to accumulate more and more possessions and power by robbing, cheating, or injuring their fellows. They are kept from this mutual injury and annihilation only by being threatened with the loss of the goods that they love and seek to acquire. The very sin of loving earthly goods thus supplies, to some extent, its own corrective and remedy, with the result that human society, which is essential to man's survival, is not completely dissolved and at least a minimum of security and peace is maintained. . . .

The fact that this earth is a land of "dying men," all mortal and all subject to sin, suffering, and misfortune, is at the root of Augustine's political and social quietism. There is little room in his thought for the idea that power may be used to improve the lot of man on earth or to lessen his misery, and certainly no room at all for the view that one form of government should be abolished or a particular ruler replaced so that a better social and political order may be instituted. A relatively peaceful society and good rule are gifts of God to men; social disturbances, cruel and tyrannous rulers, and civil and foreign wars are punishments that He visits upon men when He sees that they require such chastisements. Since everything that takes place, whether "good" or "bad," is part of God's plan for the world and is, therefore, ultimately good, there is little or no impulse toward social or political reconstruction or amelioration. This life is only the anteroom to eternal life, a place of suffering and punishment for sin and a testing-ground for the virtues of the faithful. The institutions of social, economic, and political life have no real positive value. Their essential contribution is that they hold down the dark passions of sinful men and provide a measure of peace and stability. The breakdown of social and political order through disobedience or rebellion is therefore the worst of all possible earthly evils.

As long as the rulers do not force their subjects into impiety or disobedience to God, they should be obeyed quietly and without complaint.

> For, as far as this life of mortals is concerned, which is spent and ended in a few days, *what does it matter under whose government a dying man lives,* if they who govern do not force him to impiety and iniquity?

We should not worry too much about the fact that we may be in bondage to evil rulers, or to evil masters if we are slaves, for both king and subject, master and slave, are on this earth for only a brief period, and the only really important concern is man's eternal salvation. Servitude to the devil and his angels is to be feared far more than temporal—and temporary—servitude to men; the former is servitude of the mind and soul and will last unto all eternity, while the latter is merely servitude of the body in this life. Moreover, no matter how we may be treated by human rulers and masters, we have "inner freedom," freedom of our thoughts and minds and souls.

> Anyone can easily see that under a human lord we are allowed to have our thoughts free. We fear the lordship of demons because it is exercised over the mind in which is found our only means of beholding and grasping the truth. Wherefore, though we be enchained and subjected to all the powers given to men to rule the state, provided we "render unto Caesar the things that are Caesar's and to God the things that are God's," there is no need to fear lest anyone should exact such service after we are dead. The servitude of the soul is one thing, the servitude of the body quite another.

Finally, it should be noted that when Augustine is discussing the relations between rulers and subjects he often expresses a strongly paternalistic view of the position of the ruler. The ruler is not simply a man who occupies an office that is necessary and useful; he is, almost literally, "the father of his people," and it is for him to decide what they should do and how they should do it. He does not ask the people what they want, any more than a father tries to ascertain the desires of his young children before he tells them what they must do. Augustine reveals—perhaps unconsciously—his paternalistic conception of political authority by his frequent use of the analogy between the ruler and the father who regulates and punishes the behavior of his children. The king may be a good and wise father, or a cruel and tyrannous father, but in either case his subjects must not only obey but honor and respect him. Augustine does not conceive of the citizens as mature, rational persons who have a right to be consulted about their wishes. Most of them are willful, passionate children, who must remain permanently under the firm tutelage of a stern master. In one of his letters he argues that

> we confer a benefit upon others, not in every case in which we do what is requested, but when we do that which is not hurtful to our petitioners. *For in most cases we serve others best by not giving, and would injure them by giving, what they desire.* Hence the proverb, "Do not put a sword in a child's hand. . . ." We are convicted of unfaithfulness towards those whom we profess to love, if our only care is lest, by refusing to do what they ask of us, their love towards us be diminished—and what becomes of that virtue which even your

own [i.e., pagan] literature commends, in the ruler of his country who studies not so much the wishes as the welfare of his people?

Notes

1. See the discussion by Christopher Dawson, "St. Augustine and His Age," in M. C. D'Arcy *et al., Saint Augustine* (New York, Meridian Books, 1957), p. 63.
2. Professor McIlwain admits the force of this paragraph, but, as we have seen, he argues that a *regnum* or a *civitas*, which can exist without justice, is essentially different from a *res publica*, which must possess the bond of justice and law which Cicero required (McIlwain, *The Growth of Political Thought*, pp. 155–56). Note the similarity between Augustine's views and those set forth by Cardinal Newman in "Sanctity the Token of the Christian Empire," in *Sermons on Subjects of the Day*, p. 273 (first edition), cited by Dawson, "St. Augustine and His Age."

COMMENTARY

The Two Cities in
Augustine's Political Philosophy
Rex Martin

There has been a surprisingly wide divergence of interpretations of Augustine's conception of the state, especially with respect to the political bearing of his concept of the Two Cities and to his position on the nature and role of justice in the governance of states. In this essay I wish to develop a single, coherent reading of Augustine's theory out of the themes and passages that are generally regarded as the matrix of his conception of the state and, then, to confirm and extend this reading by directing it against some of the major alternative interpretations of his theory.

What are these themes and passages which provide the agreed upon field of interpretation and reinterpretation? There is, first, the concept of the Two Cities and the political interpretation given it. Then, second, there is the well-known passage in the *City of God* (IV. 4, pp. 112–13) where Augustine draws an analogy between a kingdom (*regnum*) and a robber band. Finally, we have Augustine's reflections on, and apparent reworking of, Cicero's definition of a commonwealth (*res publica*).[1] These themes and passages are all of a piece. The political interpretation placed on the idea of the Two Cities will affect the reading one gives to the "robber band" and "commonwealth" passages. The conception that one develops of the state in these passages will be a feature of the way that the idea of the Two Cities is construed. Most commentators appear to regard Augustine's basic position as a consistent one. Differences have come, however, in determining exactly what this position is.

I think the simplest approach to Augustine's position is by way of the Two Cities. According to Augustine, the twofold division of the universe into the "City of God" and the "City of Earth" originated in the prideful revolt of the (now fallen) angels in heaven. As it had been in heaven so it was on earth. Men had primevally lived on earth in peace and comity (joined with one another in natural, familial affection) until the Fall, which brought sin into the world. The two cities on earth had their germ in Cain and Abel. Cain, the fratricide, built the first earthly city, "but Abel, being a sojourner, built none" (XV.1, p. 479). Thus, Augustine can say,

> Accordingly, two cities have been formed by two loves: the earthly by the love of self, even to the contempt of God; the heavenly by the love of God, even to the contempt of self. . . . In the one, the princes and the nations it subdues are ruled by the love of ruling. . . . But in the other city there is no human wisdom, but only godliness, which offers due worship to the true God, and looks for its

1. References to and citations of the text of Augustine's *City of God* will generally occur in the body of the paper and will follow a single style, e.g., IV.4, pp. 112–13, where the numbers denote, respectively, the book (IV), the chapter (4), and the page numbers of the passage in question. The page references are to the Modern Library edition of the *City of God*, trans. by Marcus Dods and others (New York, 1950). For Augustine's discussion of Cicero's definition see, in particular, II.21, pp. 60–63 and XIX.21, 23, 24, pp. 699–701, 706.

reward in the society of the saints, of holy angels as well as holy men, "that God may be all in all" (XIV.28, p. 477).

One model for interpreting Augustine's Two Cities is to *identify* the Earthly City with the state and the City of God with the institutional church. Assuming for the sake of argument that this model is fundamentally sound, we can ask what consequences for the evaluation of political life would follow from the model. As regards the state as such, when taken on its own terms, the consequence would appear to be a radical devaluation of the political side of things and a considerable measure of pessimism respecting the means and ends of man's political condition. On the other hand, the institutional church—at least in the Christian dispensation—would literally be the City of God on earth.

What political implication this would have, however, is not altogether clear. It would seem, though, that if the state could be Christianized through some special relationship with the institutional church, then a fundamentally different evaluation of such a state would be warranted. The basic point here would be to distinguish the state *per se*, on its own principles, from the state as Christianized through some organic relationship with the institutional church.[2] The function of the identification model would be to validate this distinction, to justify this way of looking at politics, and to legitimate the notion of a Christianized state.

The twofold identification which I have described, of the state with the City of Earth and of the church militant with the City of God, could lead to a "clericalist" doctrine of the state. This seems to have happened in the Middle Ages, when there was a strong current of "clericalist" rhetoric in which the identification model was asserted, or at least presupposed.[3] That we should accept this tradition of political rhetoric as an interpretation of Augustine is doubtful. For it may well be that the medieval analysis was about medieval politics rather than about Augustine and, hence, not fundamentally an interpretation of the political doctrine of the *City of God*. In modern times, however, scholarly interpretations have been advanced which lend weight to taking the clericalist doctrine, and the identification model, as a substantially correct account of Augustine's own position. As Figgis says, "Their views are stronger evidence of what Augustine meant, than is the constant use that was made of him by medieval thinkers. The medieval habit of taking tags as text-proofs, apart from the general purpose of the writer, discounts their value as evidence. Besides this there was an immediate polemical interest at stake."[4]

---

2. A variety of possible arrangements could be suggested as suitably satisfying the "organic relationship" in question. Among the alternatives are: (a) some sort of theocracy, (b) Caesaro-papism of the Byzantine sort, (c) a cooperative relationship between church and state within a single polity, as in Charlemagne's conception of the Holy Roman Empire, or (d) a cooperative relationship between two types of authority within a single Christian society, as in the "formula" of Pope Gelasius. It has even been said that the mere establishment of the Christian church or simply the official toleration of Christianity would be sufficient. See J. N. Figgis, *The Political Aspects of St. Augustine's "City of God"* (Gloucester, 1963; originally published in 1921), 60–61.

3. The term "clericalist" is Figgis's (64). A number of medieval thinkers can plausibly be cited as holding the clericalist doctrine on grounds of the identification model: Hildebrand (see Figgis 88–89 for discussion and citation); Engelbert of Admont (Figgis, 85, 97–98); James of Viterbo (C. H. McIlwain, *The Growth of Political Thought in the West* [New York, 1932], 159; McIlwain also cited Hildebrand, 160); the anonymous source cited in the anti-papalist tract *Rex pacificus* (H. A. Deane, *The Political and Social Ideas of St. Augustine* [New York, 1963], 232–33); and Giles of Rome (Deane, 232, 332, n. 25; Giles is also cited by McIlwain, 159n).

4. Figgis, 77. Ritschl, for example, appears to identify the state with the City of Earth (Figgis, 55, 128, n.6 for discussion and citation). Gierke holds a theocratic interpretation of the state based, again, on identifying the City of God with the church (Figgis, 77, 131, n.9). Similar views are held by Dorner and Ritschl (Figgis, 131, nn.8, 10).

Although the identification model would appear to have a certain validity, or at least great historical interest, its acceptability as a substantially correct account of Augustine's position would require the support of Augustine's text, as it bears on the notion of the Two Cities and his analysis of the state. It is my own opinion that the identification model is altogether too simple to fit the salient details of Augustine's own rendering of the Two Cities, as I shall try to make clear in what follows.

Let me begin by elaborating the contention that Augustine had an essentially tripartite conception of the city of God. The first conception is that the city of God is an "eternal city"; as such it is composed of the Trinity, the unfallen or loyal angels, and the eternally predestined-to-grace portion of the human race. The eternal citizenship of the human portion, which is *potentially* eternal "in time" and *actually* eternal "at the end of time" (i.e., in the Heaven of Book XXII), is referred to by Augustine in phrases such as "the eternal life of the saints" (XII.19, p. 402) and "a future eternal priesthood" (XVII.6, p. 583).

The second conception of the city of God is that it is an association (a collective only "in concept" but taken distributively in fact) of individual persons who love God, as distinct from those who love themselves and the things of this earth. By this rubric of "two loves" Augustine divided *all* mankind into two groups, those who live after "the flesh" and those who live after "the Spirit" (XIV.1, p. 441). Members within each group have nothing in common except the peculiar characters of the "love" (or "will") which motivates them. These individuals are not corporately embodied as such in any single institution or set of institutions on earth; yet they are spoken of as forming two "cities." Accordingly, I shall refer to this as the "individualistic" conception of the city of God, for it denotes only individuals and their love.

The third conception of the city of God is that it is a visible and institutional entity. Before Christ, this entity was the Hebrew nation (not state). Christ "took away the kingdom" from Israel, because Israel had become his "enemy" (XVII.7, p. 585), and put it under his own headship in his church, the catholic church. It is especially noteworthy that Augustine used this terminology to describe what he believed to have been an *historical* occurrence, the transfer of God's institutional "kingdom" on earth from the Hebrew nation to the Christian church. . . .

As long as the institutional church is divinely directed to do God's work it *is* the city of God on earth in a most important and indispensable way. Regardless of the general character of its membership and because it always contains the greater portion of the saints on earth, the catholic church (in Augustine's opinion) goes on its pilgrimage, inheritor of the "kingdom" of God from the Hebrews, house of worship, dispenser of the sacraments, and teacher of scripture. It is the peculiar medium through which God's will is worked and is a sharer in God's grace as truly as is the "individualistic" church. Each church, admittedly in its own way and in a nonexclusive and limited sense, is an aspect of the city of God on earth. The conclusion I draw is that Augustine did not treat "City of God on earth" and "institutional church" as identical in meaning. But I have argued that there is a unique relationship here, between the City of God and the visible church, which requires some term to describe it.

Figgis has suggested the notion of a "symbol."[5] While Noah's Ark may be a symbol of the church (by way of analogy), the institutional church is not in that sense a "symbol" of the City of God. For some features of the church are not simply analogous to traits of the City of God but are, rather, actual historical functions of the

---

5. Figgis, 51, 68. Bluhm refers to the "identification," of the city of God with the institutional church, as "only figurative": *Theories of the Political System* (Englewood Cliffs, 1965), 163.

City of God on earth. Perhaps the word to describe the relationship is a stronger one: the institutional church *represents* or is the *agent* of the divine City in certain of the functions the church actually performs, i.e., in worship, sacraments, scripture, and authoritative discipline. Rather than a simple identity there is an identification at certain points and for certain purposes. It is this claim which I would urge against both Figgis and Deane.[6] Although I endorse their contention that Augustine does not identify the City of God on earth with the institutional church, I claim that this fact alone does not require us to withdraw the notion of a Christianized state, since there is still the relationship of special representation.

Deane, however, wants to deny the Christianized state interpretation altogether. To accomplish this, he wants to deny not only the simple identification model but also any notion of special representation. His claim here is quite uncompromising: "No earthly state, city, or association can ever claim to be a part or a representative of the City of God. . . . Even the visible Church, which contains many of the reprobate along with the elect, is not an earthly division of the City of God, although . . . it is more closely related to that City than any earthly state or society can ever be."[7]

One might well agree with Deane, as I do, that the Christianized state is not an Augustinian notion. But I do not think that one can give as his reason that there is *no* basic relationship, either of identity or of representation, between the City of God and the institutional church in Augustine's eyes. It seems to me to run against the grain of Augustine's text to say that the institutional church is "not an earthly division of the City of God" and to suggest that it differs from (other) earthly states or societies only in degree. Rather, I contend that there is a special relationship—representation—and this might provide warrant, although an attenuated one, for retaining the notion of a Christianized state as a possible interpretation of Augustine. Indeed, Sabine has managed to squeeze the whole Christianized state doctrine through the needle's eye of the relationship of representation. He has alleged, though noting that the City of God could not be "identified precisely" with "existing human institutions," including the church, that the Kingdom of Christ was "embodied" in "the church and Christianized empire." This "conception of a Christian commonwealth" is, Sabine says, Augustine's "most characteristic idea" and is based on "a philosophy of history [i.e., the idea of the Two Cities] which presents such a commonwealth as the culmination of man's spiritual development."[8] I would agree with Sabine to this extent: the Christianized state idea must at least be left open as a possibility, given the idea of a partial identification—i.e., in the relationship of agent representation—of the city of God with the Church.

---

6. Both Figgis (51–52, 121) and Deane (24, 34, 121) do, of course, deny the simple identification model. Figgis does it with the qualification "*sans phrase*"; Deane's denial is unqualified: it is "absolutely impossible to identify the City of God . . . with the visible Christian Church in this world" (24).

7. Deane, 29 (see also 28). It is difficult to say here whether Deane is expounding Jesus' opinion or Augustine's. But he is clearly expounding Augustine later, when he says that the City of God "has no earthly representative" (120). If this remark is taken to refer exclusively to *states* I would agree, but if it is meant to include the church militant as well (as it does on 121), I cannot agree.

8. The passages cited are from G. H. Sabine, *History of Political Theory* (3d ed.; New York, 1961), 190–91. It is interesting to note that Sabine presses the Christianized State notion on Augustine, by reference to the Two Cities concept, while specifically asserting that the church "represents" the City of God "even though the latter cannot be identified with the ecclesiastical organization" (190). It is difficult to say exactly what Sabine was referring to with the phrase "Christian commonwealth." I presume that it referred, at least in part, to the "Christianized empire" of the next page. In any case, we do find Sabine endorsing the claim of James Bryce that "the theory of the Holy Roman Empire was built upon Augustine's City of God" and we do find him talking about Augustine's espousal of the notion of "a Christian state" (191–92).

But what about the other basic member of the Two Cities, the City of Earth? Do we have any textual license to *identify* the state *qua* state and the City of Earth? In dealing with this question, I think an *a priori* move might prove helpful: I would suggest that we try to develop a parallel between the institutional church in its relation to the City of God and the state in its relation to the City of Earth. On these *a priori* grounds, we could rule out the relationship of simple identification. Moreover, Figgis' notion of a symbolic relationship would appear warranted—as the text, at a number of points, would confirm. (For example, Cain, who is the first man to be a citizen of the City of Earth, also founded the first city. He was a fratricide, as was Romulus, who founded Rome. [See XV.1, p. 479; XV.8, pp. 488–89; XV.5, pp. 482–83.].) Finally, the idea of some sort of agent representation would, on *a priori* grounds, appear appropriate.

The question is, How would this representation take shape? At what point(s) would the identity hold? For an answer I think we can revert to the passage where Augustine spoke of Two Cities formed by two loves, "the earthly by love of self." There are many forms of self-love, of concern for the things of this life, that could be cited but the one Augustine specifically mentions is the "love of ruling." Obviously, this is a notion relevant to politics. But does it imply that the state as such, through the love of ruling, specifically represents the City of Earth? I do not think it was the state *per se* that Augustine had in mind, for he says, "In the one, the princes and the nations it subdues are ruled by the love of ruling" (XIV.28, p. 477).

It is not the state as such, i.e., any particular state taken at random or all of them taken together, but the *imperial state* that peculiarly represents the City of Earth. The imperial state (e.g., Assyria, Egypt, Rome) plays a role toward the City of Earth analogous to that played by the institutional church towards the City of God. This basic parallelism descends even to details. The translation of empire theme, which we have already noted in relation to the church, is found also in the succession of the great earthly empires (for example, XVIII.21, p.627).

It has been observed by Figgis (p.53) and Deane (p.171), in particular, that Augustine was personally an anti-imperialist. (See, for example, IV.15, p.123.) However, the connection of this attitude to the notion that the imperial state "represents" the City of Earth has not been sufficiently noted. At several points Augustine asserts the essential similarity of all imperial states in their motivation by love of domination and their imposition of rule by war and force, and asserts the connection of this feature of imperial states with what he called the City of Earth, a connection such that we could call these great imperial states the exemplars and institutional representatives of the City of Earth. The earthly city is the city of earthly "loves" or lusts and the master lust is the lust of domination. This lust is a form of pride; it is the pride which apes God himself. This, then, is the principle of the imperial state in its role as the agent representative of the City of Earth: "The earthly city, . . . though it be mistress of the nations, is itself ruled by its lust of rule" (I. preface, p.3; also V.19).

The notion of a basic parallelism within the Two Cities concept is, I think, substantially sound. Sabine puts the institutional aspect of the parallelism well: "Augustine did think of the Kingdom of evil as at least *represented* by the pagan empires, though not exactly identified with them. He also thought of the church as *representing* the City of God, even though the latter cannot be identified with the ecclesiastical organization" (p.190; italics added).

My analysis of Augustine's political philosophy is based on the claim that he does not *identify* either of the Two Cities with institutions on earth. The two cities have a simple corporate character and identity only beyond the Final Judgment, in Heaven and Hell. With respect to this world, the concept of the Two Cities refers primarily to two types or classifications of men. However, I have argued that there are earthly institutions that "represent" and do the work of the two cities in human history: the imperial states are special embodiments of the City of Earth and, after the advent of Christ, the institutional church is the unique and indispensable representative of the City of God.

This conception of the institutional church as the special representative of the City of God allows us neither to dismiss nor to validate the notion of a Christianized state. For it is possible that the church might appropriate some sort of political apparatus for its own purposes just as the Hebrew nation had generated a state, the Hebrew Kingdom. The issue remains open. On the other hand, it is the *imperial* state, and not the state as such, that represents the City of Earth. This fact will allow us to dispense with any identification, whole or partial, of the state *per se* with the "earthly City." In short, the concept of the Two Cities on its own, although it provides the superstructure of Augustine's political doctrines, does not give us all the essential details of Augustine's political philosophy. In particular, the concept does not provide us with sufficient information to determine Augustine's notion of the nature and role of justice in the state, or to establish whether Augustine was advocating the notion of a Christianized state. It does not, in fact, provide us even with Augustine's conception of the state, since any essential link between the state as such and the City of Earth has been broken. . . .

. . . Augustine's basic distinction is drawn between a republic and a "kingdom" of the robber band variety. Now these terms do not denote constitutional entities but, rather, principles of political and social organization. A republic is a matter of "common agreement" (which recalls Cicero's harmony of social classes) but a kingdom or regime (*regnum*) is not organized on the principle of agreement but, rather, on the principle of imposition from above. And this recalls Cicero's notion of tyranny where social harmony was replaced by the dictatorship of one man over all or of one class over the others. The only difference of any apparent importance, and it is really incidental at this point, is that Cicero's notion of popular concurrence referred to a harmony of social classes whereas that same notion in Augustine referred to a harmony of individual persons, without reference to class.

Regimes or kingdoms are structured on the principle of the lust of domination. They are in essence exactly like imperial states, and this is why the word "kingdom" (*regnum*) can be indifferently applied either to imperial states or to "domestic" regimes. The only difference is that imperial states lord it over subject peoples who were once independently organized politically while "domestic" *regna* are juntas that rule over other men in a single state. In either case a *regnum*, be it an imperial state or a regime ruling in a state, is not the property of the people but of their masters. I think Augustine's political philosophy rests on two fundamental distinctions: the one between the heavenly city of God and the "earthly republic"; the other, within the "earthly republic," between a *res publica* and a *regnum*. But the nature of this latter distinction requires further mapping.

The distinction of *regnum/res publica* is drawn by McIlwain (see p.156 where he puts *civitates* and *regna* on one side, over against *res publicae* on the other). McIlwain's point is, I think, fundamental but his way of drawing it is defective. First, he treats it as a terminological distinction which Augustine explicitly drew, whereas I suggest that Augustine's distinction was not drawn at the terminological level at all. Second, he treats the distinction as having to do with *kinds* of states, not so much constitutional kinds as religious kinds (pagan/Christian).[9] But I would assert that Augustine is not contrasting kinds of states but rather, polar political styles, principles of political organization. His distinction is drawn by preference and reflects the grounds on which the preference is based.

If anything is clear, it is that Augustine regards a state organized on the principle of "common agreement" as preferable to one organized on the principle of subjection. This is clear for the simple reason that Augustine endorses the first principle (for it is the principle of organization in Augustine's own definition), and the principle of subjection he condemned (in IV.4) as nothing better than a "grand robbery." I regard the crucial point of difference between these principles, i.e., the difference between agreement and imposition, as the ground of his basic evaluation. And it is a *political* evaluation (for there is here no contrast intended between the divine and the political but, rather, only between the political good and the political bad).

It is also clear from other passages that Augustine took a negative view, morally, of the whole principle of imposition and subjection. He speaks of robbers who "invade the peace of other men" and ultimately would have a city or nation "submit itself" to their brigand's peace in a passage (XIX.12, p.687), recalling his earlier robber band passage (in IV.4). He also speaks of "wicked men [who] wage war to maintain the peace of their own circle, and wish that, if possible, all men belonged to them, that all men and things might serve but one head, and might, either through love or fear, yield themselves to peace with [them]! It is thus that pride in its perversity apes God. It abhors equality with other men under [God]; but, instead of His rule, it seeks to impose a rule of its own upon its equals" (XIX.12, p.689).

We have then, in Augustine's theory, two basic kinds of political values in the organization of states: the community principle, defined by basic social agreement, and the regime principle, defined by an imposed order. However, Augustine's evaluations do not end here, for he recognizes that human freedom (in its political form, i.e., common agreement as to desired political ends) can have a variety of objects. And these objects will themselves vary in moral quality, "higher interests" as opposed to "lower." What Augustine called "true justice" can never be an interest or object of the state (at least, Augustine never allowed that it could). Even strict Ciceronian justice might be unattainable, for Augustine appears to believe that human justice, with or without a proper relationship to God, would always be imperfect, even when judged by internal or human standards, like those of Cicero (XIX.23–27, pp. 705–08). But if a state were to dedicate itself to some attainable "image of justice" (but not to the impossible goal of "true justice") then presumably it would have chosen a "higher interest." Or we might infer that, if a state were to undertake certain tasks in the interest of the church, as, for example, the use of its coercive power in the maintenance of the doctrines and discipline of the church, then that would be a "higher interest." If we interpret the Christianized State notion as meaning, not that a republic can only be a Christian state or that political justice is

---

9. Deane rejects McIlwain's distinction of *regnum/res publica* because he does not see that Augustine uses his terms in the way McIlwain has indicated: Deane, 297, n.28. Even more objectionable is the interpretation McIlwain puts on the distinction once he has drawn it terminologically. He says that all pagan states are *regna*, since they are, as pagan, deprived of justice but that republics would have the quality of justice; and he suggests, but does not say, that a Christianized State would be a republic. Even so, I think the distinction of *regnum/res publica*, if interpreted along the lines I am suggesting, can be used to point to a genuine principle of distinction of Augustine's political thought.

ultimately a theological and ecclesiastical category, but simply that service to the church is a political good (a "higher interest"), then Augustine might be said to hold this notion.

Whether the highest attainable political goal is service to the church or an image of justice, I will not venture to say. But if a commonwealth can have "lower" interests and still remain a commonwealth, then it is clear that virtues like justice (i.e., an "image of justice") or service to the church are not essential to its being a commonwealth, although such virtues may be essential to its merit as a common-wealth. The "image of justice," although it is a high aspiration, is not—perhaps for that very reason—necessary to maintain the conditions for the *existence* of the common-wealth. Justice belongs then (in Reinhold Niebuhr's phrase) "not to the *esse* but to the *bene esse* of the commonwealth."

There may be, however, something other than justice that is essential to the very existence of a commonwealth as defined, and, hence, that belongs of necessity on its agenda. This is, of course, a question of fact. Put in this way, it would seem that Augustine's conclusion is not difficult to fathom. What does belong to its basic agenda, according to him, is peace.

> The earthly city, which does not live by faith, seeks an earthly peace, and the end it proposes, in the well-ordered concord of civil obedience and rule, is the combination of men's wills to attain the things which are helpful to this life. The heavenly city [on earth] makes use of this peace only because it must, until this mortal condition which necessitates it shall pass away. . . . [The heavenly city] makes no scruple to obey the laws of the earthly city, whereby the things necessary for the maintenance of this mortal life are administered; and thus, as this life is common to both cities, so there is a harmony between them in regard to what belongs to [this mortal life] (XIX.17, pp.695–96).

Augustine's notion of peace is complex, but if we take it just in reference to the theme of commonwealth, I think it is clear that he meant it to be more than simply "law and order," the policemen's peace. It does, however, include the suppression of civil commotion and riot; but if this were all, there would be no ultimate distinction between a commonwealth and a regime. Rather what he points to is a "well-ordered concord" in which obedience follows from a rational conception of permanent and mutual interests and not from fear and repression. Augustine says, "The peace of all things is the tranquillity of order. Order is the distribution which allots things equal and unequal, each to its own place" (XIX.13, p.690). At the basis of the Augustinian commonwealth is "order," which requires a rough, pragmatic, but effective "distri-bution." The Augustinian minimum political agenda is *Pax, ordo, lex, societas.*[10] Under his new definition of commonwealth, the necessary condition for one to exist is "the tranquillity of order."

How different, really, is this "tranquillity of order" from Ciceronian justice? Not very. What ultimately divides the two men, after we make the true justice/image of justice distinction, is a fine line. Augustine's "tranquillity of order" can be achieved with a rough and ready justice (i.e., imperfect even by human standards). It does not require an "absolute justice," in Cicero's phrase. If Ciceronian justice (strict fair dealing between men and between classes, giving to each his own) is an "image" of the "true justice," then Augustinian justice (the "order" requisite to tranquillity) is an

---

10. Ernest Barker, "Introduction" to J. Healey's translation of the *City of God* (London, Everyman, 1947) I, xxvii.

image of this image. The degree to which Augustine has moved from Cicero is marked in this proposition: the true test of any state is an appropriate tranquillity.

This marks a difference, a relative devaluation of strict justice in favor of a lesser but more comprehensive good, civil peace. But it is not a rejection of justice as a political category, as Carlyle seemed to think, or of the need for some sort of rough justice; rather, it is a prudential appeal to the strictly necessary conditions for the continuing existence of the "republican" political style.[11]

Augustine's point here is simply a factual one, as was Cicero's, but they differ as to the facts. Cicero thought that a strict justice was required for the existence of a people's state (*res populi*). Augustine believed that a less than strict or perfect justice, i.e., by human standards, was required as a matter of fact. The "tranquillity of order" replaces "absolute" justice on the basic agenda for the commonwealth and this shift is reflected in the difference between Cicero's "definition" of a republic and Augustine's own "more feasible" one.[12]

Augustine's real break with Cicero came, not on the "definition" of the commonwealth (for they agree that it is a matter of popular concurrence in *res populi*) nor on the empirical determination of its necessary conditions (for the difference here is only one of degree and of vocabulary), but on the question of the moral status of politics. Cicero, like the great classical political philosophers Plato and Aristotle, had idealized politics. Politics had as its end the highest human good; the state was, in principle, morally adequate to men. Men could realize their true end in political association: in Aristotle's famous phrase, man is a "political animal." Cicero's emphasis on strict or absolute justice was symptomatic of this basic evaluation just as Augustine's devaluation of justice as a political necessity was symptomatic of a different evaluation.

The point is that Augustine rejected the classical idealization of the state; this is far more central than how he stood on Cicero's definition. There is a gulf of radical discontinuity between Augustine and classical politics. In this sense, Augustine can be said to have written an anti-politics. His program was to put the things of this world, even the best of states, under the things of the next, to commit oneself wholly only to what is absolute, to idealize nothing. Christian political philosophy, like the Christian himself, is a stranger here below; it can be in the world but not of it. The good state, the "republic" with meritorious common interests, can be pointed out, but the state is not a church and the church should not become a state. The church must look beyond, to the heavenly republic. This is the basic truth of the Christian religion, as it must be the constant theme of Christian political philosophy. This is, I think, the political theme of the *City of God*. It is the political meaning of the concept of the Two Cities.

---

11. Carlyle seemed to hold the view that Augustine, in effect, simply got rid of the notion of justice as a political category: A. J. Carlyle, *A History of Medieval Political Theory in the West* (New York, originally published in 1903) I, 170, 174. Carlyle regarded this as quite momentous, out of line with literally centuries of earlier and subsequent political thought (see 169, 221). At the same time Carlyle is bemused that "Augustine seems to take the matter lightly" (166). And he was even led to conclude in another place that Augustine may not have "realized the enormous significance of what he was saying," in F. J. C. Hearnshaw, ed., *Social and Political Ideas of Some Great Medieval Thinkers* (London, 1923), 50. But I would suggest that all this represents too simplistic a reading of Augustine's text.

12. Figgis, of course, recognizes the important role peace plays in Augustine's political thought but he does not see that what Augustine meant by peace (the "tranquillity of order") is essentially continuous with Ciceronian justice (62–64). Deane, on the other hand, tends to *equate* Augustinian peace with what Augustine called the "image" of justice (125, 136). I do not think there is adequate textual warrant for Deane's treatment; moreover, it makes the difference between Augustine's definition and that of Cicero, admittedly more apparent than real, wholly inexplicable. I would suggest that Augustine's "peace" and Cicero's "justice" do differ in name but that they point to the same kind of thing; the only difference between them is one of degree.

Saint Thomas Aquinas

Thomas Aquinas was born near Naples, Italy in 1224 or 1225. The late Medieval period in which he lived was one of great change. It was marked by disintegrating feudal economies, political intrigue within and among city-states and emerging nations, and the continued influence of the powerful Roman church despite challenges posed by pagan thought circulating through Europe in the form of newly discovered classic manuscripts.

Aquinas's parents, minor nobles, prepared Thomas early for the religious life, sending him to study with the Benedictine monks when he was five. At the age of fourteen, Thomas went to the University of Naples for advanced study, but soon after, the Dominican Order of Preachers attracted him. The Dominicans were known for their intellectual pursuits and for their devotion to the poor. This was not the order Thomas's parents had in mind for their son and they sought to dissuade him from serving with them. One tale tells of Thomas being kidnaped by his brothers and held prisoner by the family until he renounced his association with the Dominicans. The family effort was unsuccessful.

Thomas was ordained and went on to study theology in Paris and Cologne. He served as a member of the faculty at the University of Paris from 1257 to 1259 and then returned to Italy where he lectured at various sites for about ten years. During this period, he encountered manuscripts from the works of Aristotle that were entering the country from Moslem Spain. Aquinas began to review the pagan manuscripts and wrote extensive commentaries. Unlike many of his contemporaries, Aquinas believed it was possible to square elements of pagan philosophy with church teaching. Much of his work reads as an attempt to provide a synthesis of classic and theological thought. This effort placed him squarely in the middle of attacks by secular scholars who believed he misrepresented pagan sources and church leaders who were suspicious of mixing pagan ideas with religious dogma. Together with his already rigorous schedule of lectures and studies, the burden of responding to attacks by these groups sapped his strength. He fell into ill health and died near his birthplace in 1274.

According to Aquinas there were two routes to knowledge: one by reason and the other by faith. Reason provided, even for pagans, a means for understanding one's place in the cosmos and a guide to action. Reason was the voice of natural law, the notion that God instilled in man instincts and abilities that, correctly followed, would lead to right action. However, reason alone was fallible. While it could yield knowledge of this world, it revealed little about the next. This was the job of faith, and scripture was the guide. Whether one took the road to knowledge through reason or through faith, both roads subsisted under eternal law, the rule of God. A consequence of this teaching was to demonstrate that there was no inherent conflict between philosophy, the study of those principles that inform the experiential world, and Divine Revelation. This position made safe the study of philosophy and science in a world where the church had a say in such matters.

One of the truths which natural law (as well as divine law) teaches is human sociality. The family and state, according to Aquinas (following Aristotle), are natural. An individual is not sufficient, alone, to provide for his/her well-being. The state is thus the most complete form of sociality. Though maintaining unity among many individuals is difficult, it is the primary responsibility of the ruler to bring unity and peace to the state. These are necessary preconditions if people (under the guide of the church) are to attend to their most important endeavor, the salvation of the soul.

The types of political regime Aquinas acknowledges are those advanced by Aristotle. For Aquinas, there are two answers to the question of the best regime. Ideally, rule by a good monarch is to be preferred over other forms. This is the form that most closely resembles the rule of the universe by one God. However, practical problems with monarchy (including succession) demonstrate the greater resilience of mixed forms in maintaining the unity that defines the good city. Goodness is inherent in the promulgation of human laws that are congruent with the dictates of natural and eternal law. Still, Aquinas's ultimate teachings about government continue to be debated among scholars, partly because his treatment of government is fragmented with portions scattered among his *Summa Contra Gentiles*, his short treatise *On Kingship*, and his more extensive work, *Summa Theologica*.

Summa Theologica and *On Kingship*

The *Summa Theologica* (or *Summa Theologiae*), written by Aquinas between 1256 and 1272, but left unfinished, is considered his most comprehensive attempt to synthesize elements of Christian and pagan thought. The style in which it is written gives testimony to Aquinas's thoroughness and precision as a scholar. Each part of *Summa* is divided into a set of related questions. Each question is addressed in an article. The articles begin by anticipating objections to his proposed thesis. These are followed by a statement of his own position along with authoritative support. He then develops the arguments for his philosophic position and ends each article with a response to the objections raised earlier.

The selections included review Aquinas's teaching on the various types of law he envisioned and illustrate the way in which these laws were interconnected in his cosmology. Aquinas supports his views with references to Classic and Medieval authorities. Two of the more frequent references are to "the philosopher" and "Isidore." The former refers to Aristotle, while the latter is a reference to the seventh century Bishop of Seville who served as a source of important church doctrines.

The selections from *On Kingship* represent a more straightforward prose style. In the selections included here, Aquinas discusses his views on various forms of government, noting the theoretical superiority of rule by one but tempering this assessment with an acknowledgment of the evils brought by tyranny, kingship gone awry.

Commentaries

In the first commentary, Edward A. Goerner advances the controversial position that Aquinas is not to be understood primarily as a natural law theorist, that is one who advances the notion of universal standards for good, enforceable by natural punishment in accord with God's will. Rather, he argues, Aquinas is more like classic natural right theorists, emphasizing virtue as the route to right action and happiness. Goerner argues that Aquinas viewed natural law as a secondary way of inducing good behavior in the special case of one who is evil and incapable of virtuous action. This view clears Aquinas of the often-made charge of inflexibility in his ethical and political teachings. His natural law teaching is shown to apply only to "bad men" and not to those capable of virtue, i.e., those who have no need for rigid codes of conduct.

James Blythe tackles the question of Aquinas's best regime. While noting that some scholars have interpreted Aquinas as preferring monarchy, Blythe says this position rests on a confusion of his use of the terms "regal" and "political." Regal refers to having full power whether vested in one, the few, or the many. Political refers to having power that is constrained by law. Aquinas's best regime, argues Blythe, is clearly a mixed form, for this is the regime that is most practicable and which allows for the type of political rule Aquinas favors.

Key Words

Antinomian. One who holds that faith is the prime requisite for salvation and can even dispense one from moral restraint.

Natural Law. Defined by Aquinas as the participation of the eternal law in the rational creature. Individuals follow this law by habit, fear of punishment, inclination, and most clearly by the exercise of reason. This differs from classic natural right by its reliance on universal standards, under the aegis of one Supreme Being.

Natural Right. A tradition in political thought characterized by seeking standards for moral behavior in nature. In its classic formulation, (e.g., Aristotle) it suggests the search for valid but contingent norms discerned through the proper use of reason. For example, the good person knows that killing is wrong but must weigh this norm against threats on his/her life. In the modern context, (e.g., Hobbes, Locke) natural right theories assert fundamental freedoms as being innate or distinguishing characteristics of human beings.

Propaedeutic. An introduction or preparation for something.

Synderesis. A faculty of the mind allowing one to intuit the principles of right conduct.

For Further Reading

Finnis, J. 1982. *Natural Law and Natural Rights.* Oxford: Clarendon Press.

Fortin, E. 1987. "St. Thomas Aquinas." In (L. Strauss and J. Cropsey, eds.) *History of Political Philosophy.* Chicago: University of Chicago Press.

Gilby, T. 1958. *The Political Thought of St. Thomas Aquinas.* Chicago: University of Chicago Press.

McInerny, R. 1982. *St. Thomas Aquinas.* Notre Dame, Ind.: Notre Dame Press.

Pieper, J. 1962. *A Guide to Thomas Aquinas.* New York: Pantheon.

Summa Theologica

Question 91
Of the Various Kinds of Law

First Article
Whether there is an eternal law?

We proceed thus to the First Article:

Objection 1. It would seem that there is no eternal law. Because every law is imposed on someone. But there was not someone from eternity on whom a law could be imposed, since God alone was from eternity. Therefore no law is eternal.

Obj. 2. Further, promulgation is essential to law. But promulgation could not be from eternity, because there was no one to whom it could be promulgated from eternity. Therefore no law can be eternal.

Obj. 3. Further, a law implies order to an end. But nothing ordained to an end is eternal, for the last end alone is eternal. Therefore no law is eternal.

On the contrary, Augustine says: "That Law which is the Supreme Reason cannot be understood to be otherwise than unchangeable and eternal."[1]

I answer that . . . a law is nothing else but a dictate of practical reason emanating from the ruler who governs a perfect community. Now it is evident, granted that the world is ruled by divine providence, . . . that the whole community of the universe is governed by divine reason. Wherefore the very Idea of the government of things in God the Ruler of the universe has the nature of a law. And since the divine reason's conception of things is not subject to time but is eternal, according to Proverbs viii. 23, therefore it is that this kind of law must be called eternal.

Reply Obj. 1. Those things that are not in themselves exist with God, inasmuch as they are foreknown and preordained by Him, according to Romans iv. 17, "Who calls those things that are not, as those that are." Accordingly the eternal concept of the divine law bears the character of an eternal law in so far as it is ordained by God to the government of things foreknown by Him.

Reply Obj. 2. Promulgation is made by word of mouth or in writing; and in both ways the eternal law is promulgated, because both the divine word and the writing of the Book of Life are eternal. But the promulgation cannot be from eternity on the part of the creature that hears or reads.

Reply Obj. 3. The law implies order to the end actively, in so far as it directs certain things to the end, but not passively—that is to say, the law itself is not ordained to the end—except accidentally, in a governor whose end is extrinsic to him, and to which end his law must needs be ordained. But the end of the divine government is God Himself, and His law is not

---

From *Summa Theologica* in *The Political Ideas of St. Thomas Aquinas*, edited by Dino Bigongiari. 1953. Reprinted with permission of Benziger Publishing Company, Copyright Holder.

1. Augustine, *De libero arbitrio*, i, 6.

distinct from Himself. Wherefore the eternal law is not ordained to another end.

Second Article
Whether there is in us a natural law?

We proceed thus to the Second Article:

Objection 1. It would seem that there is no natural law in us. Because man is governed sufficiently by the eternal law; for Augustine says that "the eternal law is that by which it is right that all things should be most orderly."[2] But nature does not abound in superfluities, as neither does she fail in necessaries. Therefore no law is natural to man.

Obj. 2. Further, by the law man is directed in his acts to the end, as stated above (Q. 90, A. 2). But the directing of human acts to their end is not a function of nature, as is the case in irrational creatures, which act for an end solely by their natural appetite; whereas man acts for an end by his reason and will. Therefore no law is natural to man.

Obj. 3. Further, the more a man is free, the less is he under the law. But man is freer than all the animals, on account of his free will, with which he is endowed above all other animals. Since therefore other animals are not subject to a natural law, neither is man subject to a natural law.

On the contrary, A gloss on Romans ii. 14: "When the Gentiles, who have not the law, do by nature those things that are of the law," comments as follows: "Although they have no written law, yet they have the natural law, whereby each one knows, and is conscious of, what is good and what is evil."

I answer that . . . law, being a rule and measure, can be in a person in two ways: in one way, as in him that rules and measures; in another way, as in that which is ruled and measured, since a thing is ruled and measured in so far as it partakes of the rule or measure. Wherefore, since all things subject to divine providence are ruled and measured by the eternal law, as was stated above (A. 1), it is evident that all things partake somewhat of the eternal law, in so far as, namely, from its being imprinted on them, they derive their respective inclinations to their proper acts and ends. Now among all others the rational creature is subject to divine providence in the most excellent way, in so far as it partakes of a share of providence, by being provident both for itself and for others. Wherefore it has a share of the eternal reason, whereby it has a natural inclination to its proper act and end: and this participation of the eternal law in the rational creature is called the natural law. Hence the Psalmist after saying: "Offer up the sacrifice of justice," as though someone asked what the works of justice are, adds: "Many say, Who showeth us good things?" in answer to which question he says: "The light of Thy countenance, O Lord, is signed upon us";[3] thus implying that the light of natural reason, whereby we discern what is good and what is evil, which is the function of the natural law, is nothing else than an imprint on us of the divine light. It is therefore evident that the natural law is nothing else than the rational creature's participation of the eternal law.

---

2. Augustine, *de libero arbitrio*, i.

3. The Book of Psalms.

Reply Obj. 1. This argument would hold if the natural law were something different from the eternal law, whereas it is nothing but a participation thereof, as stated above.

Reply Obj. 2. Every act of reason and will in us is based on that which is according to nature . . . ; for every act of reasoning is based on principles that are known naturally, and every act of appetite in respect of the means is derived from the natural appetite in respect of the last end. Accordingly the first direction of our acts to their end must needs be in virtue of the natural law.

Reply Obj. 3. Even irrational animals partake in their own way of the eternal reason, just as the rational creature does. But because the rational creature partakes thereof in an intellectual and rational manner, therefore the participation of the eternal law in the rational creature is properly called a law, since a law is something pertaining to reason. . . . Irrational creatures, however, do not partake thereof in a rational manner, wherefore there is no participation of the eternal law in them, except by way of similitude.

Third Article
Whether there is a human law?

We proceed thus to the Third Article:

Objection 1. It would seem that there is not a human law. For the natural law is a participation of the eternal law, as stated above (A. 2). Now through the eternal law "all things are most orderly," as Augustine states.[4] Therefore the natural law suffices for the ordering of all human affairs. Consequently there is no need for a human law.

Obj. 2. Further, a law bears the character of a measure. . . . But human reason is not a measure of things, but vice versa, as stated in *Metaphysics*[5] x. text. 5. Therefore no law can emanate from human reason.

Obj. 3. Further, a measure should be most certain, as stated in *Metaphysics* x. text. 3. But the dictates of human reason in matters of conduct are uncertain, according to Wisdom ix. 14: "The thoughts of mortal men are fearful, and our counsels uncertain." Therefore no law can emanate from human reason.

On the contrary, Augustine distinguishes two kinds of law—the one eternal; the other temporal, which he calls human.[6]

I answer that . . . a law is a dictate of the practical reason. Now it is to be observed that the same procedure takes place in the practical and in the speculative reason, for each proceeds from principles to conclusions. . . . Accordingly we conclude that just as, in the speculative reason, from naturally known indemonstrable principles we draw the conclusions of the various sciences, the knowledge of which is not imparted to us by nature, but acquired by the efforts of reason; so, too, it is from the precepts of the natural law, as from general and indemonstrable principles, that the human reason needs to proceed to the more particular determination of certain

---

4. Augustine, *De libero arbitrio*, i, 6.

5. St. Thomas's Commentaries on Aristotle's *Metaphysics*.

6. Augustine, *De libero arbitrio*, i, 6.

matters. These particular determinations, devised by human reason, are called human laws, provided the other essential conditions of law be observed.... Wherefore Cicero says in his *Rhetoric* that "justice has its source in nature; thence certain things came into custom by reason of their utility; afterward these things which emanated from nature and were approved by custom were sanctioned by fear and reverence for the law."[7]

Reply Obj. 1. The human reason cannot have a full participation of the dictate of the divine reason but according to its own mode, and imperfectly. Consequently, as on the part of the speculative reason, by a natural participation of divine wisdom, there is in us the knowledge of certain general principles, but not proper knowledge of each single truth, such as that contained in the divine wisdom; so, too, on the part of the practical reason man has a natural participation of the eternal law, according to certain general principles, but not as regards the particular determinations of individual cases, which are, however, contained in the eternal law. [Hence the necessity that human reason proceed to certain particular sanctions of law.]

Reply Obj. 2. Human reason is not of itself the rule of things, but the principles impressed on it by nature are general rules and measures of all things relating to human conduct, whereof the natural reason is the rule and measure, although it is not the measure of things that are from nature.

Reply Obj. 3. The practical reason is concerned with practical matters, which are singular and contingent, but not with necessary things, with which the speculative reason is concerned. Wherefore human laws cannot have that inerrancy that belongs to the demonstrated conclusions of sciences. Nor is it necessary for every measure to be altogether unerring and certain, but according as it is possible in its own particular genus.

Fourth Article
Whether there was any need for a divine law?

We proceed thus to the Fourth Article:

Objection 1. It would seem that there was no need for a divine law. Because, as stated above (A. 2), the natural law is a participation in us of the eternal law. But the eternal law is a divine law, as stated above (A. 1). Therefore there is no need for a divine law in addition to the natural law and human laws derived therefrom.

Obj. 2. Further, it is written that "God left man in the hand of his own counsel."[8] Now counsel is an act of reason.... Therefore man was left to the direction of his reason. But a dictate of human reason is a human law, as stated above (A. 3). Therefore there is no need for man to be governed also by a divine law.

Obj. 3. Further, human nature is more self-sufficing than irrational creatures. But irrational creatures have no divine law besides the natural inclination impressed on them. Much less, therefore, should the rational creature have a divine law in addition to the natural law.

---

7. Cicero, *De inventione rhetorica.*

8. *Ecclus*, xv, 14.

On the contrary, David prayed God to set His law before him, saying: "Set before me for a law the way of Thy justifications, O Lord."[9]

I answer that, Besides the natural and the human law it was necessary for the directing of human conduct to have a divine law. And this for four reasons. First, because it is by law that man is directed how to perform his proper acts in view of his last end. And indeed, if man were ordained to no other end than that which is proportionate to his natural faculty, there would be no need for man to have any further direction on the part of his reason besides the natural law and human law which is derived from it. But since man is ordained to an end of eternal happiness which is inproportionate to man's natural faculty . . . therefore it was necessary that, besides the natural and the human law, man should be directed to his end by a law given by God.

Secondly, because, on account of the uncertainty of human judgment, especially on contingent and particular matters, different people form different judgments on human acts; whence also different and contrary laws result. In order, therefore, that man may know without any doubt what he ought to do and what he ought to avoid, it was necessary for man to be directed in his proper acts by a law given by God, for it is certain that such a law cannot err.

Thirdly, because man can make laws in those matters of which he is competent to judge. But man is not competent to judge of interior movements that are hidden, but only of exterior acts which appear; and yet for the perfection of virtue it is necessary for man to conduct himself aright in both kinds of acts. Consequently human law could not sufficiently curb and direct interior acts, and it was necessary for this purpose that a divine law should supervene.

Fourthly, because, as Augustine says, human law cannot punish or forbid all evil deeds; since while aiming at doing away with all evils, it would do away with many good things, and would hinder the advance of the common good, which is necessary for human intercourse.[10] In order, therefore, that no evil might remain unforbidden and unpunished, it was necessary for the divine law to supervene, whereby all sins are forbidden.

And these four causes are touched upon in Psalm cxviii. 8, where it is said: "The law of the Lord is unspotted," i.e., allowing no foulness of sin; "converting souls," because it directs not only exterior but also interior acts; "the testimony of the Lord is faithful," because of the certainty of what is true and right; "giving wisdom to little ones," by directing man to an end supernatural and divine.

Reply Obj. 1. By natural law the eternal law is participated in proportionately to the capacity of human nature. But to his supernatural end man needs to be directed in a yet higher way. Hence the additional law given by God, whereby man shares more perfectly in the eternal law.

Reply Obj. 2. Counsel is a kind of inquiry; hence it must proceed from some principles. Nor is it enough for it to proceed from principles imparted by nature, which are the precepts of the natural law, for the reasons given above; but there is need for certain additional principles, namely, the precepts of the divine law.

9. Psalms, cxviii, 33.

10. Augustine, *De libero arbitrio,* i, 5, 6.

Reply Obj. 3. Irrational creatures are not ordained to an end higher than that which is proportionate to their natural powers; consequently the comparison fails. . . .

Question 94
Of the Natural Law

First Article
Whether the natural law is a habit?

We proceed thus to the First Article:

Objection 1. It would seem that the natural law is a habit. Because, as the Philosopher says, "there are three things in the soul: power, habit, and passion."[11] But the natural law is not one of the soul's powers, nor is it one of the passions, as we may see by going through them one by one. Therefore the natural law is a habit.

Obj. 2. Further, Basil says that the conscience or *"synderesis* is the law of our mind,"[12] which can only apply to the natural law. But the *synderesis* is a habit. . . . Therefore the natural law is a habit.

Obj. 3. Further, the natural law abides in man always. . . . But man's reason, [which is involved in law], does not always think about the natural law. Therefore the natural law is not an act, but a habit.

On the contrary, Augustine says that "a habit is that whereby something is done when necessary."[13] But such is not the natural law, since it is in infants and in the damned who cannot act by it. Therefore the natural law is not a habit.

I answer that, A thing may be called a habit in two ways. First, properly and essentially: and thus the natural law is not a habit. For . . . the natural law is something appointed by reason, just as a proposition is a work of reason. Now that which a man does is not the same as that whereby he does it, for he makes a becoming speech by the habit of grammar. Since, then, a habit is that by which we act, a law cannot be a habit, properly and essentially.

Secondly, the term "habit" may be applied to that which we hold by a habit: thus faith may mean that which we hold by faith. And accordingly, since the precepts of the natural law are sometimes considered by reason actually, while sometimes they are in the reason only habitually, in this way the natural law may be called a habit. Thus, in speculative matters, the indemonstrable principles are not the habit itself whereby we hold those principles, but are the principles the habit of which we possess.

Reply Obj. 1. The Philosopher proposes there to discover the genus of virtue; and since it is evident that virtue is a principle of action, he mentions only those things which are principles of human acts, viz., powers, habits and passions. But there are other things in the soul besides these three: there are acts; thus to will is in the one that wills; again, things known are

---

11. Aristotle, *Ethics,* ii, 5.

12. Damascene, *De fide orthodoxa,* iv, 22.

13. Augustine, *De bono conjugali,* xxi.

in the knower; moreover its own natural properties are in the soul, such as immortality and the like.

Reply Obj. 2. *Synderesis* is said to be the law of our mind, because it is a habit containing the precepts of the natural law, which are the first principles of human actions.

Reply Obj. 3. This argument proves that the natural law is held habitually; and this is granted.

To the argument advanced in the contrary sense we reply that sometimes a man is unable to make use of that which is in him habitually, on account of some impediment: thus, on account of sleep, a man is unable to use the habit of science. In like manner, through the deficiency of his age, a child cannot use the habit of understanding of principles, or the natural law, which is in him habitually.

Second Article
Whether the natural law contains several precepts,
or one only?

We proceed thus to the Second Article:

Objection 1. It would seem that the natural law contains, not several precepts, but one only. For law is a kind of precept.... If therefore there were many precepts of the natural law, it would follow that there are also many natural laws.

Obj. 2. Further, the natural law is consequent to human nature. But human nature, as a whole, is one, though, as to its parts, it is manifold. Therefore, either there is but one precept of the law of nature, on account of the unity of nature as a whole, or there are many, by reason of the number of parts of human nature. The result would be that even things relating to the inclination of the concupiscible faculty belong to the natural law.

Obj. 3. Further, law is something pertaining to reason.... Now reason is but one in man. Therefore there is only one precept of the natural law.

On the contrary, The precepts of the natural law in man stand in relation to practical matters, as the first principles to matters of demonstration. But there are several first indemonstrable principles. Therefore there are also several precepts of the natural law.

I answer that... the precepts of the natural law are to the practical reason what the first principles of demonstrations are to the speculative reason, because both are self-evident principles. Now a thing is said to be self-evident in two ways: first, in itself; secondly, in relation to us. Any proposition is said to be self-evident in itself if its predicate is contained in the notion of the subject, although to one who knows not the definition of the subject it happens that such a proposition is not self-evident. For instance, this proposition, "Man is a rational being," is, in its very nature, self-evident, since who says "man" says "a rational being"; and yet to one who knows not what a man is, this proposition is not self-evident. Hence it is that, as Boethius says, certain axioms or propositions are universally self-evident to all;[14] and such are those propositions whose terms are known to all, as, "Every whole is greater than its part," and, "Things equal to one

---

14. Boethius, *De hebdomadibus.*

and the same are equal to one another." But some propositions are self-evident only to the wise who understand the meaning of the terms of such propositions; thus to one who understands that an angel is not a body, it is self-evident that an angel is not circumspectively in a place; but this is not evident to the unlearned, for they cannot grasp it.

Now a certain order is to be found in those things that are apprehended universally. For that which, before aught else, falls under apprehension, is "being," the notion of which is included in all things whatsoever a man apprehends. Wherefore the first indemonstrable principle is that *the same thing cannot be affirmed and denied at the same time,* which is based on the notion of "being" and "not-being"; and on this principle all others are based, as it is stated in *Metaphysics* iv. text. 9. Now as "being" is the first thing that falls under the apprehension simply, so "good" is the first thing that falls under the apprehension of the practical reason, which is directed to action, since every agent acts for an end under the aspect of good. Consequently the first principle in the practical reason is one founded on the notion of good, viz., that *good is that which all things seek after.* Hence this is the first precept of law, that *good is to be done and ensued, and evil is to be avoided.* All other precepts of the natural law are based upon this, so that whatever the practical reason naturally apprehends as man's good (or evil) belongs to the precepts of the natural law as something to be done or avoided.

Since, however, good has the nature of an end, and evil the nature of a contrary, hence it is that all those things to which man has a natural inclination are naturally apprehended by reason as being good and, consequently, as objects of pursuit, and their contraries as evil and objects of avoidance. Wherefore the order of the precepts of the natural law is according to the order of natural inclinations. Because in man there is first of all an inclination to good in accordance with the nature which he has in common with all substances, inasmuch as every substance seeks the preservation of its own being, according to its nature; and by reason of this inclination, whatever is a means of preserving human life and of warding off its obstacles belongs to the natural law. Secondly, there is in man an inclination to things that pertain to him more specially, according to that nature which he has in common with other animals; and in virtue of this inclination, those things are said to belong to the natural law "which nature has taught to all animals," such as sexual intercourse, education of off-spring, and so forth. Thirdly, there is in man an inclination to good, according to the nature of his reason, which nature is proper to him: thus man has a natural inclination to know the truth about God and to live in society; and in this respect, whatever pertains to this inclination belongs to the natural law, for instance, to shun ignorance, to avoid offending those among whom one has to live, and other such things regarding the above inclination.

Reply Obj. 1. All these precepts of the law of nature have the character of one natural law, inasmuch as they flow from one first precept.

Reply Obj. 2. All the inclinations of any parts whatsoever of human nature, e.g., of the concupiscible and irascible parts, in so far as they are ruled by reason, belong to the natural law and are reduced to one first precept, as stated above, so that the precepts of the natural law are many in themselves, but are based on one common foundation.

Reply Obj. 3. Although reason is one in itself, yet it directs all things regarding man, so that whatever can be ruled by reason is contained under the law of reason. . . .

Question 95
Of Human Law

First Article
Whether it was useful for laws to be framed by men?

We proceed thus to the First Article:

Objection 1. It would seem that it was not useful for laws to be framed by men. Because the purpose of every law is that man be made good thereby. . . . But men are more to be induced to be good willingly, by means of admonitions, than against their will, by means of laws. Therefore there was no need to frame laws.

Obj. 2. Further, as the Philosopher says, "men have recourse to a judge as to animate justice."[15] But animate justice is better than inanimate justice, which is contained in laws. Therefore it would have been better for the execution of justice to be entrusted to the decision of judges than to frame laws in addition.

Obj. 3. Further, every law is framed for the direction of human actions, as is evident from what has been stated above. . . . But since human actions are about singulars, which are infinite in number, matters pertaining to the direction of human actions cannot be taken into sufficient consideration except by a wise man, who looks into each one of them. Therefore it would have been better for human acts to be directed by the judgment of wise men than by the framing of laws. Therefore there was no need of human laws.

On the contrary, Isidore says: "Laws were made that in fear thereof human audacity might be held in check, that innocence might be safeguarded in the midst of wickedness, and that the dread of punishment might prevent the wicked from doing harm."[16] But these things are most necessary to mankind. Therefore it was necessary that human laws should be made.

I answer that, As stated above (Q. 63, A. 1; Q. 94, A. 3), man has a natural aptitude for virtue, but the perfection of virtue must be acquired by man by means of some kind of training. Thus we observe that man is helped by industry in his necessities, for instance, in food and clothing. Certain beginnings of these he has from nature, viz., his reason and his hands, but he has not the full complement, as other animals have to whom nature has given sufficiency of clothing and food. Now it is difficult to see how man could suffice for himself in the matter of this training, since the perfection of virtue consists chiefly in withdrawing man from undue pleasures, to which above all man is inclined, and especially the young, who are more capable of being trained. Consequently a man needs to receive this training from another, whereby to arrive at the perfection of virtue. And as to those young people who are inclined to acts of virtue, by their good natural

---

15. Aristotle, *Ethics*, v. 7.

16. Isidore, *Etymologiae*, v, 20.

disposition, or by custom, or rather by the gift of God, paternal training suffices, which is by admonitions. But since some are found to be depraved and prone to vice, and not easily amenable to words, it was necessary for such to be restrained from evil by force and fear, in order that, at least, they might desist from evil-doing and leave others in peace, and that they themselves, by being habituated in this way, might be brought to do willingly what hitherto they did from fear, and thus become virtuous. Now this kind of training which compels through fear of punishment is the discipline of laws. Therefore, in order that man might have peace and virtue, it was necessary for laws to be framed, for, as the Philosopher says, "as man is the most noble of animals if he be perfect in virtue, so is he the lowest of all if he be severed from law and righteousness";[17] because man can use his reason to devise means of satisfying his lusts and evil passions, which other animals are unable to do.

Reply Obj. 1. Men who are well disposed are led willingly to virtue by being admonished better than by coercion, but men who are evilly disposed are not led to virtue unless they are compelled.

Reply Obj. 2. As the Philosopher says, "It is better that all things be regulated by law than left to be decided by judges";[18] and this for three reasons. First, because it is easier to find a few wise men competent to frame right laws than to find the many who would be necessary to judge aright of each single case. Secondly, because those who make laws consider long beforehand what laws to make, whereas judgment on each single case has to be pronounced as soon as it arises; and it is easier for man to see what is right by taking many instances into consideration than by considering one solitary fact. Thirdly, because lawgivers judge in the abstract and of future events, whereas those who sit in judgment judge of things present, toward which they are affected by love, hatred, or some kind of cupidity; wherefore their judgment is perverted.

Since then the animated justice of the judge is not found in every man, and since it can be deflected, therefore it was necessary, whenever possible, for the law to determine how to judge, and for very few matters to be left to the decision of men.

Reply Obj. 3. Certain individual facts which cannot be covered by the law "have necessarily to be committed to judges," as the Philosopher says in the same passage; for instance, "concerning something that has happened or not happened," and the like.

Second Article
Whether every human law is derived from the
natural law?

We proceed thus to the Second Article:

Objection 1. It would seem that not every human law is derived from the natural law. For the Philosopher says that "the legal just is that which originally was a matter of indifference."[19] But those things which arise

---

17. Aristotle, *Politics*, i, 2.

18. Aristotle, *Rhetoric*, i, I.

19. Aristotle, *Ethics*, v, 7.

from the natural law are not matters of indifference. Therefore the enactments of human laws are not all derived from the natural law.

Obj. 2. Further, positive law is contrasted with natural law, as stated by Isidore[20] and the Philosopher.[21] But those things which flow as conclusions from the general principles of the natural law belong to the natural law. . . . Therefore that which is established by human law does not belong to the natural law.

Obj. 3. Further, the law of nature is the same for all, since the Philosopher says that "the natural just is that which is equally valid everywhere."[22] If, therefore, human laws were derived from the natural law, it would follow that they too are the same for all, which is clearly false.

Obj. 4. Further, it is possible to give a reason for things which are derived from the natural law. But "it is not possible to give the reason for all the legal enactments of the lawgivers," as the Jurist says.[23] Therefore not all human laws are derived from the natural law.

On the contrary, Cicero says: "Things which emanated from nature and were approved by custom were sanctioned by fear and reverence for the laws."[24]

I answer that, As Augustine says, "that which is not just seems to be no law at all";[25] wherefore the force of a law depends on the extent of its justice. Now in human affairs a thing is said to be just from being right according to the rule of reason. But the first rule of reason is the law of nature, as is clear from what has been stated above (Q. 91, A. 2 *ad* 2). Consequently, every human law has just so much of the nature of law as it is derived from the law of nature. But if in any point it deflects from the law of nature, it is no longer a law but a perversion of law.

But it must be noted that something may be derived from the natural law in two ways: first, as a conclusion from premises; secondly, by way of determination of certain generalities. The first way is like to that by which, in the sciences, demonstrated conclusions are drawn from the principles, while the second mode is likened to that whereby, in the arts, general forms are particularized as to details: thus the craftsman needs to determine the general form of a house to some particular shape. Some things are therefore derived from the general principles of the natural law by way of conclusions, e.g., that "one must not kill" may be derived as a conclusion from the principle that "one should do harm to no man"; while some are derived therefrom by way of determination, e.g., the law of nature has it that the evildoer should be punished; but that he be punished in this or that way is not directly by natural law but is a derived determination of it.

Accordingly, both modes of derivation are found in the human law. But those things which are derived in the first way are contained in human law, not as emanating therefrom exclusively, but having some force from the

---

20. Isidore, *Etymologiae*, v, 4.

21. Aristotle, *Ethics*, v, 7.

22. Ibid.

23. *Digest*, i, 3, 5.

24. Cicero, *De rhetorica ad Herennium*, ii.

25. Augustine, *De libero arbitrio*, i, 5.

natural law also. But those things which are derived in the second way have no other force than that of human law.

Reply Obj. 1. The Philosopher is speaking of those enactments which are by way of determination or specification of the precepts of the natural law.

Reply Obj. 2. This argument avails for those things that are derived from the natural law, by way of conclusions.

Reply Obj. 3. The general principles of the natural law cannot be applied to all men in the same way, on account of the great variety of human affairs, and hence arises the diversity of positive laws among various people.

Reply Obj. 4. These words of the Jurist are to be understood as referring to decisions of rulers in determining particular points of the natural law, on which determinations the judgment of expert and prudent men is based as on its principles, in so far, to wit, as they see at once what is the best thing to decide.

Hence the Philosopher says that in such matters "we ought to pay as much attention to the undemonstrated sayings and opinions of persons who surpass us in experience, age, and prudence as to their demonstrations."[26] . . .

Question 96
Of the Power of Human Law

First Article
Whether human law should be framed for the community rather than for the individual?

We proceed thus to the First Article:

Objection 1. It would seem that human law should be framed, not for the community, but rather for the individual. For the Philosopher says that "the legal just . . . includes all particular acts of legislation . . . and all those matters which are the subject of decrees,"[27] which are also individual matters, since decrees are framed about individual actions. Therefore law is framed not only for the community, but also for the individual.

Obj. 2. Further, law is the director of human acts. . . . But human acts are about individual matters. Therefore human laws should be framed, not for the community, but rather for the individual.

Obj. 3. Further, law is a rule and measure of humans acts. . . . But a measure should be most certain, as stated in *Metaphysics* x. Since therefore in human acts no general proposition can be so certain as not to fail in some individual cases, it seems that laws should be framed not in general but for individual cases.

On the contrary, The Jurist says that "laws should be made to suit the majority of instances; and they are not framed according to what may possibly happen in an individual case."[28]

I answer that, Whatever is for an end should be proportionate to that end. Now the end of law is the common good; because, as Isidore says, "law

---

26. Aristotle, *Ethics*, vi, II.

27. Aristotle, *Ethics*, v, 7.

28. *Digest*, i, 3.2.

should be framed, not for any private benefit, but for the common good of all the citizens."[29] Hence human laws should be proportionate to the common good. Now the common good comprises many things. Wherefore law should take account of many things, as to persons, as to [activities], and as to times; because the community of the state is composed of many persons and its good is procured by many actions; nor is it established to endure for only a short time, but to last for all time by the citizens succeeding one another, as Augustine says.[30]

Reply Obj. 1. The Philosopher divides the "legal just," i.e., positive law, into three parts. For some things are laid down simply in a general way: and these are the general laws. Of these he says that "the legal is that which originally was a matter of indifference, but which, when enacted, is so no longer," as the fixing of the ransom of a captive.—Some things affect the community in one respect and individuals in another. These are called "privileges," i.e., "private laws," as it were, because they regard private persons, although their power extends to many matters; and in regard to these, he adds, "and further [any regulations enacted for particular cases."]—Other matters are legal, not through being laws, but through being applications of general laws to particular cases, such are decrees which have the force of law; and in regard to these, he adds "all matters subject to decrees."[31]

Reply Obj. 2. A principle of direction should be applicable to many, wherefore the Philosopher says that all things belonging to one genus are measured by one which is the [first] in that genus.[32] For if there were as many rules or measures as there are things measured or ruled, they would cease to be of use, since their use consists in being applicable to many things. Hence law would be of no use if it did not extend further than to one single act. Because the decrees of prudent men are made for the purpose of directing individual actions, whereas law is a general precept. . . .

Reply Obj. 3. "We must not seek the same degree of certainty in all things."[33] Consequently in contingent matters, such as natural and human things, it is enough for a thing to be certain, as being true in the greater number of instances, though at times and less frequently it fail.

Second Article
Whether it belongs to human law to repress all vices?

We proceed thus to the Second Article:

Objection 1. It would seem that it belongs to human law to repress all vices. For Isidore says that "laws were made in order that, in fear thereof, man's audacity might be held in check."[34] But it would not be held in check sufficiently unless all evils were repressed by law. Therefore human law should repress all evils.

---

29. Isidore, *Etymologiae*, v, 21.

30. Augustine, *De Civitate*, Dei, ii, 21; Xxii, 6.

31. Aristotle, *Ethics*, v, 7.

32. Aristotle, *Metaphysics*, X, text. 4.

33. Aristotle, *Ethics*, i, 3.

34. Isidore, *Etymologiae*, v, 20.

Obj. 2. Further, the intention of the lawgiver is to make the citizens virtuous. But a man cannot be virtuous unless he forbear from all kinds of vice. Therefore it belongs to human law to repress all vices.

Obj. 3. Further, human law is derived from the natural law, as stated above (Q. 95, A. 2). But all vices are contrary to the law of nature. Therefore human law should repress all vices.

On the contrary, We read in *De libero arbitrio* i. 5: "It seems to me that the law which is written for the governing of the people rightly permits these things, and that divine providence punishes them." But divine providence punishes nothing but vices. Therefore human law rightly allows some vices, by not repressing them.

I answer that, As stated above (Q. 90, AA. 1, 2), law is framed as a rule or measure of human acts. Now a measure should be homogeneous with that which it measures, as stated in *Metaphysics* x. text. 3, 4, since different things are measured by different measures. Wherefore laws imposed on men should also be in keeping with their condition, for, as Isidore says,[35] law should be "possible both according to nature, and according to the customs of the country." Now possibility or faculty of action is due to an interior habit or disposition, since the same thing is not possible to one who has not a virtuous habit as is possible to one who has. Thus the same is not possible to a child as to a full-grown man; for which reason the law for children is not the same as for adults, since many things are permitted to children which in an adult are punished by law or at any rate are open to blame. In like manner many things are permissible to men not perfect in virtue which would be intolerable in a virtuous man.

Now human law is framed for a number of human beings, the majority of whom are not perfect in virtue. Wherefore human laws do not forbid all vices from which the virtuous abstain, but only the more grievous vices from which it is possible for the majority to abstain; and chiefly those that are to the hurt of others, without the prohibition of which human society could not be maintained: thus human law prohibits murder, theft, and suchlike.

Reply Obj. 1. Audacity seems to refer to the assailing of others. Consequently it belongs to those sins chiefly whereby one's neighbor is injured; and these sins are forbidden by human law, as stated.

Reply Obj. 2. The purpose of human law is to lead men to virtue, not suddenly, but gradually. Wherefore it does not lay upon the multitude of imperfect men the burdens of those who are already virtuous, viz., that they should abstain from all evil. Otherwise these imperfect ones, being unable to bear such precepts, would break out into yet greater evils; thus it is written: "He that violently bloweth his nose, bringeth out blood";[36] and that if "new wine," i.e., precepts of a perfect life, is "put into old bottles," i.e., into imperfect men, "the bottles break, and the wine runneth out," i.e., the precepts are despised and those men, from contempt, break out into evils worse still.[37]

---

35. Ibid., 21.

36. Book of Proverbs, xxx, 33.

37. Gospel of St. Matthew, IX, 17.

Reply Obj. 3. The natural law is a participation in us of the eternal law, while human law falls short of the eternal law. Now Augustine says: "The law which is framed for the government of states allows and leaves unpunished many things that are punished by divine providence. Nor, if this law does not attempt to do everything, is this a reason why it should be blamed for what it does."[38] Wherefore, too, human law does not prohibit everything that is forbidden by the natural law. . . .

Fourth Article
Whether human law binds a man in conscience?

We proceed thus to the Fourth Article:

Objection 1. It would seem that human law does not bind a man in conscience. For an inferior power has no jurisdiction in a court of higher power. But the power of man which frames human law is beneath the divine power. Therefore human law cannot impose its precept in a divine court, such as is the court of conscience.

Obj. 2. Further, the judgment of conscience depends chiefly on the commandments of God. But sometimes God's commandments are made void by human laws, according to Matthew xv. 6: "You have made void the commandment of God for your tradition." Therefore human law does not bind a man in conscience.

Obj. 3. Further, human laws often bring loss of character and injury on man, according to Isaias x. 1 ff.: "Woe to them that make wicked laws, and when they write, write injustice; to oppress the poor in judgment, and do violence to the cause of the humble of My people." But it is lawful for anyone to avoid oppression and violence. Therefore human laws do not bind man in conscience.

On the contrary, It is written: "This is thanksworthy, if for conscience . . . a man endure sorrows, suffering wrongfully."[39]

I answer that, Laws framed by man are either just or unjust. If they be just, they have the power of binding in conscience, from the eternal law whence they are derived, according to Proverbs viii. 15: "By Me kings reign, and lawgivers decree just things." Now laws are said to be just—from the end, when, to wit, they are ordained to the common good—and from their author, that is to say, when the law that is made does not exceed the power of the lawgiver—and from their form, when, to wit, burdens are laid on the subjects, according to an equality of proportion and with a view to the common good. For, since one man is a part of the community, each man, in all that he is and has, belongs to the community, just as a part, in all that it is, belongs to the whole; wherefore nature inflicts a loss on the part in order to save the whole, so that on this account such laws as these which impose proportionate burdens are just and binding in conscience and are legal laws.

On the other hand, laws may be unjust in two ways: first, by being contrary to human good, through being opposed to the things mentioned above—either in respect of the end, as when an authority imposes on his subjects burdensome laws, conducive, not to the common good, but rather

---

38. Augustine, *De libero arbitrio,* i, 5.

39. Epistle of St. Peter, ii, 19.

to his own cupidity or vainglory; or in respect of the author, as when a man makes a law that goes beyond the power committed to him; or in respect of the form, as when burdens are imposed unequally on the community, although with a view to the common good. The like are acts of violence rather than laws, because, as Augustine says, "A law that is not just, seems to be no law at all."[40] Wherefore such laws do not bind in conscience, except perhaps in order to avoid scandal or disturbance, for which cause a man should even yield his right, according to Matthew v. 40, 41: "If a man . . . take away thy coat, let go thy cloak also unto him; and whosoever will force thee one mile, go with him other two."

Secondly, laws may be unjust through being opposed to the divine good: such are the laws of tyrants inducing to idolatry or to anything else contrary to the divine law; and laws of this kind must nowise be observed because, as stated in Acts v. 29, "we ought to obey God rather than men."

Reply Obj. 1. As the Apostle says, all human power is from God . . . "therefore he that resisteth the power" in matters that are within its scope "resisteth the ordinance of God"; so that he becomes guilty according to his conscience.[41]

Reply Obj. 2. This argument is true of laws that are contrary to the commandments of God, which is beyond the scope of (human) power. Wherefore in such matters human law should not be obeyed.

Reply Obj. 3. This argument is true of a law that inflicts unjust hurt on its subjects. The power that man holds from God does not extend to this, wherefore neither in such matters is man bound to obey the law, provided he avoid giving scandal or inflicting a more grievous hurt.

Fifth Article
Whether all are subject to the law?

We proceed thus to the Fifth Article:

Objection 1. It would seem that not all are subject to the law. For those alone are subject to a law for whom a law is made. But the Apostle says: "The law is not made for the just man."[42] Therefore the just are not subject to the law.

Obj. 2. Further, Pope Urban says: "He that is guided by a private law need not for any reason be bound by the public law."[43] Now all spiritual men are led by the private law of the Holy Ghost, for they are the sons of God, of whom it is said: "Whosoever are led by the Spirit of God, they are the sons of God."[44] Therefore not all men are subject to human law.

Obj. 3. Further, the Jurist says that "the sovereign is exempt from the laws."[45] But he that is exempt from the law is not bound thereby. Therefore not all are subject to the law.

---

40. Augustine, *De libero arbitrio*, i, 5.
41. St. Paul's Epistle to the Romans, xiii, 1, 2.
42. St. Paul's Epistle to Timothy, i, 9.
43. The Decretals of Gregory IX, CAUSA 19, 9u. 2.
44. St. Paul's Epistle to the Romans, viii, 14.
45. *Digest*, i, 3, 31.

On the contrary, The Apostle says: "Let every soul be subject to the higher powers."[46] But subjection to a power seems to imply subjection to the laws framed by that power. Therefore all men should be subject to human law.

I answer that ... the notion of law contains two things: first, that it is a rule of human acts; secondly, that it has coercive power. Wherefore a man may be subject to law in two ways. First, as the regulated is subject to the regulator; and, in this way, whoever is subject to a power is subject to the law framed by that power. But it may happen in two ways that one is not subject to a power. In one way, by being altogether free from its authority; hence the subjects of one city or kingdom are not bound by the laws of the sovereign of another city or kingdom, since they are not subject to his authority. In another way, by being under a yet higher law; thus the subject of a proconsul should be ruled by his command, but not in those matters in which the subject receives his orders from the emperor, for in these matters he is not bound by the mandate of the lower authority, since he is directed by that of a higher. In this way one who is simply subject to a law may not be subject thereto in certain matters in respect of which he is ruled by a higher law.

Secondly, a man is said to be subject to a law as the coerced is subject to the coercer. In this way the virtuous and righteous are not subject to the law, but only the wicked. Because coercion and violence are contrary to the will, but the will of the good is in harmony with the law, whereas the will of the wicked is discordant from it. Wherefore in this sense the good are not subject to the law, but only the wicked.

Reply Obj. 1. This argument is true of subjection by way of coercion, for, in this way, "the law is not made for the just men: because they are a law to themselves," since they "show the work of the law written in their hearts," as the Apostle says.[47] Consequently the law does not enforce itself upon them as it does on the wicked.

Reply Obj. 2. The law of the Holy Ghost is above all law framed by man; and therefore spiritual men, in so far as they are led by the law of the Holy Ghost, are not subject to the law in those matters that are inconsistent with the guidance of the Holy Ghost. Nevertheless the very fact that spiritual men are subject to law is due to the leading of the Holy Ghost, according to I Peter ii. 13: "Be ye subject ... to every human creature for God's sake."

Reply Obj. 3. The sovereign is said to be "exempt from the law," as to its coercive power, since, properly speaking, no man is coerced by himself, and law has no coercive power save from the authority of the sovereign. Thus then is the sovereign said to be exempt from the law, because none is competent to pass sentence on him if he acts against the law. Wherefore on Psalm L. 6: "To Thee only have I sinned," a gloss says that "there is no man who can judge the deeds of a king."—But as to the directive force of law, the sovereign is subject to the law by his own will, according to the statement that "whatever law a man makes for another, he should keep himself."[48]

---

46. St. Paul's Epistle to the Romans, Xiii, 1.

47. Ibid., ii, 14, 15.

48. Decretals of Gregory IX, Book I, tit. 2, c.6.

And a wise authority says: "Obey the law that thou makest thyself."[49] Moreover the Lord reproaches those who "say and do not"; and who "bind heavy burdens and lay them on men's shoulders, but with a finger of their own they will not move them."[50] Hence, in the judgment of God, the sovereign is not exempt from the law as to its directive force, but he should fulfill it of his own free will and not of constraint.—Again the sovereign is above the law in so far as, when it is expedient, he can change the law and dispense in it according to time and place. . . .

---

49. Dionysius Cato, Disticha de Moribus, Bk. I, preface.

50. Gospel of St. Matthew, xxiii, 3, 4.

On Kingship

Chapter 2
Whether it is more expedient for a city or province to be ruled by one man or by many?

[16] Having set forth these preliminary points we must now inquire what is better for a province or a city: whether to be ruled by one man or by many.

[17] This question may be considered first from the viewpoint of the purpose of government. The aim of any ruler should be directed toward securing the welfare of that which he undertakes to rule. The duty of the pilot, for instance, is to preserve his ship amidst the perils of the sea and to bring it unharmed to the port of safety. Now the welfare and safety of a multitude formed into a society lies in the preservation of its unity, which is called peace. If this is removed, the benefit of social life is lost and, moreover, the multitude in its disagreement becomes a burden to itself. The chief concern of the ruler of a multitude, therefore, is to procure the unity of peace. It is not even legitimate for him to deliberate whether he shall establish peace in the multitude subject to him, just as a physician does not deliberate whether he shall heal the sick man encharged to him, for no one should deliberate about an end which he is obliged to seek, but only about the means to attain that end. Wherefore the Apostle, having commended the unity of the faithful people, says: "Be ye careful to keep the unity of the spirit in the bond of peace." Thus, the more efficacious a government is in keeping the unity of peace, the more useful it will be. For we call that more useful which leads more directly to the end. Now it is manifest that what is itself one can more efficaciously bring about unity than several—just as the most efficacious cause of heat is that which is by its nature hot. Therefore the rule of one man is more useful than the rule of many.

[18] Furthermore, it is evident that several persons could by no means preserve the stability of the community if they totally disagreed. For union is necessary among them if they are to rule at all; several men, for instance, could not pull a ship in one direction unless joined together in some fashion. Now several are said to be united according as they come closer to being one. So one man rules better than several who come near being one.

[19] Again, whatever is in accord with nature is best, for in all things nature does what is best. Now every natural governance is governance by one. In the multitude of bodily members there is one which is the principal mover, namely, the heart; and among the powers of the soul one power presides as chief, namely, the reason. Among bees there is one king bee, and in the whole universe there is One God, Maker and Ruler of all things. And there is a reason for this. Every multitude is derived from unity. Wherefore, if artificial things are an imitation of natural things and a work of art is

better according as it attains a closer likeness to what is in nature, it follows that it is best for a human multitude to be ruled by one person.

[20] This is also evident from experience. For provinces or cities which are not ruled by one person are torn with dissensions and tossed about without peace, so that the complaint seems to be fulfilled which the Lord uttered through the Prophet: "Many pastors have destroyed my vineyard." On the other hand, provinces and cities which are ruled under one king enjoy peace, flourish in justice, and delight in prosperity. Hence, the Lord by His prophets promised to His people as a great reward that He will give them one head and that "one Prince will be in the midst of them."

Chapter 3
That the dominion of a tyrant is the worst

[21] Just as the government of a king is the best, so the government of a tyrant is the worst.

[22] For democracy stands in contrary opposition to polity, since both are governments carried on by many persons, as is clear from what has already been said; while oligarchy is the opposite of aristocracy, since both are governments carried on by a few persons; and kingship is the opposite of tyranny, since both are carried on by one person. Now, as has been shown above, monarchy is the best government. If, therefore, "it is the contrary of the best that is worst," it follows that tyranny is the worst kind of government.

[23] Further, a united force is more efficacious in producing its effect than a force which is scattered or divided. Many persons together can pull a load which could not be pulled by each one taking his part separately and acting individually. Therefore, just as it is more useful for a force operating for a good to be more united, in order that it may work good more effectively, so a force operating for evil is more harmful when it is one than when it is divided. Now, the power of one who rules unjustly works to the detriment of the multitude, in that he diverts the common good of the multitude to his own benefit. Therefore, for the same reason that, in a just government, the government is better in proportion as the ruling power is one—thus monarchy is better than aristocracy, and aristocracy better than polity—so the contrary will be true of an unjust government, namely, that the ruling power will be more harmful in proportion as it is more unitary. Consequently, tyranny is more harmful than oligarchy and oligarchy more harmful than democracy.

[24] Moreover, a government becomes unjust by the fact that the ruler, paying no heed to the common good, seeks his own private good. Wherefore the further he departs from the common good the more unjust will his government be. But there is a greater departure from the common good in an oligarchy, in which the advantage of a few is sought, than in a democracy, in which the advantage of many is sought; and there is a still greater departure from the common good in a tyranny, where the advantage of only one man is sought. For a large number is closer to the totality than a small number, and a small number than only one. Thus, the government of a tyrant is the most unjust.

[25] The same conclusion is made clear to those who consider the order of divine providence, which disposes everything in the best way. In all things, good ensues from one perfect cause, i.e., from the totality of the conditions favorable to the production of the effect, while evil results from any one partial defect. There is beauty in a body when all its members are fittingly disposed; ugliness, on the other hand, arises when any one member is not fittingly disposed. Thus ugliness results in different ways from many causes, beauty in one way from one perfect cause. It is thus with all good and evil things, as if God so provided that good, arising from one cause, be stronger, and evil, arising from many causes, be weaker. It is expedient therefore that a just government be that of one man only in order that it may be stronger; however, if the government should turn away from justice, it is more expedient that it be a government by many, so that it may be weaker and the many may mutually hinder one another. Among unjust governments, therefore, democracy is the most tolerable, but the worst is tyranny. . . .

On Thomistic Natural Law: The Bad Man's View of Thomistic Natural Right
E.A. Goerner

The most important thing that can be done for Thomistic studies in ethics and politics is to make clear that neither the notion of law in general nor of natural law in particular is the foundation of his ethical and political teaching. On the contrary, his teaching about virtue is the foundation of his doctrine. Within the teaching about virtue the natural law doctrine plays quite a subordinate role whose character is, furthermore, quite different from what it is commonly presented to be.

This essay presents only the case for the first part of that broad claim. It argues that the treatment of natural law in the *Summa Theologiae,* if carefully read in context, clearly indicates two crucial things that have commonly been overlooked. First, the natural law is only a second-best, imperfect, and supplementary standard for right action according to nature. Second, the primary and perfect standard of naturally right action is to be found in those parts of the *Summa* that deal with virtue. It would take another, and probably longer, essay to explicate Thomas's treatment of that perfect standard.[1] So this essay only takes the first step. It summarizes the main evidence *within the teaching on law* for rejecting the categorization of St. Thomas Aquinas as primarily a natural law thinker. That evidence also suggests the possibility that a careful treatment of Thomas's teaching on virtue would reveal him as a classical natural right, as opposed to natural law, thinker.

With the late Leo Strauss, I take a natural law theorist to be one who holds that the standard of natural morality is a law or laws in the sense of universally valid propositions about what it is right or wrong, by nature, to do or not do. Thus to know whether an act is right or wrong it suffices to know whether it conforms to the law or not. That is how Strauss presents Thomas and it is how modern writers about Thomas have generally presented him, whether they are political philosophers or historians of political thought.[2]

In contrast, the natural right theorist is one who, while agreeing that acts may be right or wrong by nature, does not agree that the standard for such rightness is a law or laws in the sense of universally valid propositions. He holds, with Aristotle for example, that objective rules of right are, at best, generalizations that are not universally valid but are changeable according to circumstances (*Ethics* v. 7. 1134b 17–35). Thus the standard of natural right is the judgement of the virtuous man in particular cases rather than any universally valid law. As Leo Strauss puts it: "There is a universally valid hierarchy of ends, but there are no universally valid rules of action."[3]

From E. A. Goerner, "On Thomistic Natural Law: The Bad Man's View of Thomistic Natural Right," *Political Theory,* 7:1, pp. 101–122. Copyright © 1979 by Sage Publications, Inc. Reprinted by permission of Sage Publications, Inc.

Note: An earlier version of this paper was presented at the Annual convention of the A.P.S.A. in September, 1975 in San Francisco.

What is at stake here is of the greatest importance. Thomistic natural law, as commonly interpreted, "is free from the hesitations and ambiguities characteristic of the teachings" of classical natural right. It surpasses in "definiteness and noble simplicity" the classical natural right teaching. But, in so doing, it considerably restricts the "latitude" of statesmanship. In sum, Thomas's natural law teaching can be said to have failed to avoid "the Scylla of 'absolutism.'" The absolutistic and legalistic cast of teachings about natural law tends to provoke the modern revolt, especially in the form of natural rights doctrines, against classical teachings about natural right.[4]

But if Thomas's doctrine about natural law is not such as it has been commonly interpreted, and if he actually places it in a wholly subordinate position to a doctrine of classical natural right, then Aquinas's relationship to modern natural rights theorizing needs to be drastically rethought. The purpose of this essay is merely to take the first step by summarizing the evidence in the Thomistic teaching about law itself, which suggests that the effort required for so deep a revision of our common conceptions about Thomistic political ethics will be fruitful.

I would like to focus the argument exclusively on the so-called[5] "Treatise on Law" in the *Summa Theologiae*. That is not only the most famous and influential passage in St. Thomas's writings where natural law is mentioned but it is also his most comprehensive and systematic treatment of the subject. . . .

The "Treatise on Law" contains a number of strange arguments that draw the careful reader's attention to issues that do not appear on a superficial reading. Moreover, Thomas himself introduces the whole *Summa Theologiae* with a prologue in which he says that the work is written for beginners. He quotes St. Paul (I. Cor. 3: 1–2) saying: "I gave you milk to drink, not meat." Some of the strange arguments that Thomas makes seem designed precisely to call the attention of the mature reader to the fact that the surface argument is indeed milk rather than meat, good for beginners but not good enough for everyone. Indeed, some of those passages seem designed to tell those who are weaned or ready to be weaned how to find the meat. Thomas also says in the Prologue that the order of the parts of his work has been especially fitted to beginners. That is according to the order of teaching and learning (*ordo disciplinae*) rather than "according to what the order of explication of texts requires or according as the occasion for disputing offers itself." So the mature and careful reader ought to be especially concerned with the order within which Thomas places his discussion of law and ought to ask how that context is especially suitable to the teaching of beginners. Naturally, one may wonder why the meat could not be presented directly to beginners. But that question must wait until the natures of the milk, and of the meat, and of the beginners are clear. So let us begin.

Rule by Law and Rule by the Virtuous

In the "Treatise on Law" St. Thomas does not ask directly whether the full standard of natural morality (as distinguished from supernatural morality) is the natural law or something else. Nevertheless, the question is raised obliquely in question 95, article 1: "Whether it be useful that some laws be laid down by men?"[6] There he specifically raises an objection (obj. 2) to human lawmaking by citing Aristotle (*Eth.* v. 4. 1132a 27) to the effect that "animate justice is better than inanimate which is contained in laws" and that, therefore, justice ought to be done according to the will of the judge rather than according to a law and the will of a judge. This is the middle objection of three. Thomas deals with the other two in a single sentence each, but the reply to this second objection requires two paragraphs and is almost as long as the body of the article itself. The reply has three distinct arguments none of which alone nor all of which together constitute a full reply to the objection.

Since the objection starts with a citation from Aristotle, the reply to it does also. The objection, as noted above, was drawn from the *Nichomachean Ethics*. The context there is that of a general account of the virtue of justice. The reply to the objection, on the other hand, is drawn from the *Rhetoric* (i. 1. 1354a 31–1354b 22) where the issue is the use of rhetoric to sway the passions of judges and how this perversion of the judicial process can be prevented.

So the reply to the objection bases itself on a text from the *Rhetoric* where the relative merits of the animate justice of the judge and the inanimate justice of the law are directly weighed by Aristotle only in a narrow context—a less theoretical context (conceding specific imperfections) than the broad and theoretical context of the passage in the objection itself. One who is looking for meat must ask whether the reply would have gone the same way if the broad, theoretical context of the objection had been accepted. Let us look at the argument of the reply in somewhat greater detail.

St. Thomas simply paraphrases Aristotle's argument in the *Rhetoric*. The first point is that it is easier to find enough wise men to make good laws than to find enough wise men to judge all cases. But notice that this argument does not deny, in principle, the original objection that animate justice is better than inanimate justice. It simply poses a practical difficulty in the way of obtaining the very best justice in most situations and offers a solution for that statistically normal, but morally abnormal, majority of situations.

Second, lawmakers are said to consider, long beforehand, what is best and to consider many cases, whereas judgment on particular cases is under the press of time. But that argument applies only to judges who lack the leisure and inclination to think on such matters before the case. If they lack leisure, it would be hard to see how they had become wise. If they lack the inclination to think on such matters, even though they know that they are to be judges, then they are surely not wise. So the wise judge will be one who has considered many cases over a long time to discover what is usually most just and who adds to that his prudential judgment of the individual case before him, which may have peculiar features requiring a decision unlike the usual one that would be formulated as a law.

Third, he notes that lawgivers judge about universals, and not about particulars and about matters in the future rather than the present. In judging present particulars men are more easily swayed from the course of justice by some personal passion or interest. Again, the argument has great practical force for the general run of situations but does not deal with the objection in principle since it *assumes* judges whose virtue is imperfect.

In a society not addicted to lawsuits one might find enough wise men to act as judges, wise men with the leisure and inclination to meditate on matters of justice, wise men sufficiently mature in virtue not to be deflected by personal passion or interest. In such a society the dictum of the *Rhetoric* that it is better for all to be regulated by law rather than the will of judges is untrue.

But St. Thomas did not set out to answer whether it is *always* useful to have the laws decide as much as possible and the judges as little as possible any more than Aristotle did in the *Rhetoric*. The argument in the *Rhetoric* makes clear that Aristotle is talking about the problems caused by the practice of forensic rhetoric before *popular* law courts and democratic assemblies of the Athenian type, i.e., before a mass of men who do not have the leisure for the study of matters of justice, and who are not preeminent (by definition) in wisdom and virtue. Now medieval judicial practice was not the same as the Athenian but, no more than Aristotle in Athens, could St. Thomas assume that medieval judges and juries were ordinarily wise men in the philosophic sense. The milk-drinkers, the beginning students in theology, are given sound practical advice likely to help the cause of justice in most cases, but those capable of eating meat can see that the matter is not theoretically quite what it seems on the surface.

Our concern here is not with the organization of human judicial systems, but with the divine government of the world by natural law. The primary governor by natural law is not man, according to St. Thomas, but God, in whose eternal law men only participate by what is called natural law (q. 93, a. 6, resp.). So the question at issue here is whether the divine government of the world insofar as it affects human action is *first and foremost* to be spoken of as a government by law or, on the other hand, is first and foremost to be spoken of in analogy with the government of comprehensive kingship or all-kingship, the *omnimodum regnum* or παμβασιλεία of Book III of Aristotle's *Politics* (1276a 8–9). Indeed the last reference to Aristotle in question 95, with which we have been dealing, is to Book III, ch. 7 of the *Politics* where Aristotle sets up his typology of constitutions, including kingship, a subject that Aristotle concludes by the discussion of all-kingship at the end of Book III.

The "Treatise" on law shows God as governing the world by law, i.e., governing as a law-giver and judge rather [than] as an all-king. But the careful reader will notice that none of the reasons why men find it useful to have their wise men be lawgivers rather than kings applies to God. All the arguments that St. Thomas borrows from the *Rhetoric* to establish the superiority of rule by law to rule by men are arguments based on some human defect: (1) there are too few wise men; (2) men find it hard to judge particular cases under pressure of time; (3) men are deflected from doing justice by their passions. But, surely, none of those defects are thought by St. Thomas to be found in God too. So the question arises as to whether God *does* rule men as a law-giver rather than as an all-king and, if so, why?

The first thing to notice is that the treatment of God as governing the world by law is not the first treatment of the divine government of the world in the *Summa*. Earlier, in the First Part, St. Thomas speaks of the divine government as a government by providence. There he makes clear that divine providence is perfect government, and that perfect government is government of individuals as such rather than a government that controls only species or classes as would a law (I, q. 22, art. 1, resp.; I, q. 103, art. 6, resp.). The issue here is a major one, and Thomas calls our attention to the fact that his teaching differs from most of the philosophic tradition. He says his claim, that God governs the universe by a providence that governs each individual being, is at odds not only with Democritus and the Epicureans, who denied all providence, but also with "others," whom he doesn't name, who taught that corruptible substances were not subject to divine government of their individual being but only in their species. The "others" seem to be mainly Aristotle and Averroes (cf. *In I Sent.*, d. xxxix, q.2, a.2).

In short, St. Thomas seems to say two grossly incompatible things about the divine government of the world in the *Summa*. In the First Part he says God governs individuals by providence, i.e., like an all-king rather than a lawgiver. In the "Treatise" on Law he says that God governs the world by the eternal law (of which natural law is the human participation) and that laws treat things in general classes rather than as individuals. How are we to reconcile those arguments? To raise such a question fruitfully requires some attention at first to the overall order or structure of the work, an order to which Thomas explicitly calls attention in the Prologue.

Fear of the Law and the Freedom of Virtue

The *Summa Theologiae* is divided into three main parts of which the first two are of interest to us here. The First Part deals with God and His creative work. The Second Part deals with the principles of human action. One might even speak of the First Part as Thomas's theology, and of the Second Part as his ethics. It is in this theology, i.e., in the First Part, that Thomas goes to great pains to insist upon God's governing the universe by a providence that deals with individuals. It is only in his ethics, i.e., in the Second Part, that he speaks of God governing the world by law.

The ethics, or Second Part, is itself divided into two parts, since ethics can be treated in two ways. The principles of human action can be treated in general terms; that is the burden of the First Part of the Second Part, (cf., I–II, prologue). The principles of action can also be treated in particular, i.e., in terms of particular virtues and vices; that is the burden of the Second Part of the Second Part (cf., II–II prologue). The "Treatise" on Law falls in the First Part of the Second Part. That is to say God is presented as governing the world by the eternal law (in which man participates by natural law) only in that part of the *Summa* that deals with ethics in general. A consideration of the specific order of this First Part of the Second Part and of the place of the "Treatise" on Law within it will help in understanding how the eternal and natural laws are to be understood.

The treatment of ethics in general (i.e. I–II) opens with a discussion of the ultimate end of man as the first principle of human action. It comes to the conclusion that the end of human action is a specific human act, by nature contemplation and by grace the direct vision of the divine essence (qq. 1–5). The question then arises as to how one might be enabled to perform such an act. So there follows a discussion of human action and passion (qq. 6–48). Human acts are said to be led to their proper end by two sorts of principles: intrinsic or interior and extrinsic or exterior.

The intrinsic principles are the human powers as developed in the virtues (qq. 49–70). Insofar as man acts by virtue, intellectual and practical, he realizes in himself the latent image of God; he is, albeit only in a secondary way, an intellectual causal source of order in the created world. However, man is defective in this regard: he sometimes does things badly out of ignorance and sometimes out of sin and vice (qq. 71–89). Now if men always knew everything they were capable of knowing, both as individuals and societies, and never acted maliciously, the order of the world intended by God's government would be realized. But men obviously do not always act virtuously. Thomas thus looks for the means whereby God, who cannot fail of His purposes, achieves His intended universal order in spite of human weakness, i.e., in spite of the fact that men do not of their own inner desire do the works of virtue. That is to say, Thomas looks for external or exterior principles of human acts, causes other than the habitually virtuous human powers.

Here is where the "Treatise" on Law comes in the *Summa Theologiae* (qq. 90–108). Law is the first of two ways by which God, as the extrinsic principle of good human acts, leads men to do good deeds in spite of themselves and their weakness. But law is not a sufficient external corrective for vice. The second way that God achieves the correction of men is grace. The externality of grace is less than that of law, since grace conforms the desire of the soul in such a way that it can even be said to be a quality of the soul (q. 110). Consequently, law, as most external, is discussed first, and then grace. Both discussions constitute a long digression from the discussion of virtue which had to be left off after a general treatment in order to confront the problem of vice and its relation to the ability of God to govern the world. Only after the treatment of God's external correctives (law and grace) for human defect does St. Thomas return to the subject of the virtues, the detailed treatment of which forms the whole of the Second Part of the Second Part.

This, then, is the context within which the "Treatise" on Law must be read. Men are not born perfect in virtue. They are born only with a capacity for virtue from the fulfillment of which they are powerfully distracted by ignorance and malice. The role of law is merely that of a corrective for a defect. Law is "a kind of training (*disciplina*) that compels by fear of punishments" (q. 95, art. I resp.). Law, whether human or divine, habituates men to avoiding evil and doing good *for fear of punishment. Sometimes* they grow to take pleasure in so acting. Then they no longer do the acts of the virtuous out of fear, but out of virtue itself, i.e., of their own will. Of course, some men never come to virtue. For them the law must always be ready with its punishments so that the rest of the community can be left in peace (q. 92, art 2 and q. 95, art 1, resp.). At its worst, law is a kind of barrier to complete social disorder. At its best it is merely a propaedeutic to virtue. Consequently, law, including natural laws, must be understood in relation to that for which it is propaedeutic, namely virtue. Any full understanding of Thomas's ethics and politics, both natural and supernatural, must focus primarily on his treatment of virtue rather than of law.

This point is confirmed by a review of the particular theological problems that Thomas is faced with in writing a book on theology for beginners. On the level of theological ethics, rather than natural ethics, Thomas has to deal with the relationship of the law of Moses, the Old Law as he calls it, to the grace of Christ. There is a special danger that a careful Christian writer on these matters needs to face. There is a considerable danger of antinomianism in the Christian tradition, reflected in both the New Testament and the church fathers. Thus St. Paul says, "Where the spirit of the Lord is, there is liberty" (2 Cor. 3:15) and St. James speaks of the Gospel as "the law of perfect liberty" (Jas. 1:25) and St. Augustine says, ironically, "there is little difference between the Law and the Gospel, fear [*timor*] and love [*amor*]" (*Contra Adimant.,* xvii) all of which St. Thomas cites. But there is not only a permanent *danger* of Christian antinomianism. There was a very serious range of powerful antinomian currents in medieval society. It was not unheard of for milk drinkers to throw off all restraints, claiming the liberty of the Gospel. A whole range of more or less interrelated politico-ecclesiastical movements claimed one sort or another of Spirit-filled perfection that put them above all secular and ecclesiastical authority and the laws of those authorities, natural or divine. This is not the place for a discussion of those movements, but it is important to note that St. Thomas himself draws attention to the problem by devoting article 4 of question 106 precisely to the claim that the New Law of grace (and thus all ecclesiastical law and authority based on it) is to be superseded by an age of the Holy Spirit in which "spiritual men" in a "more perfect state" will rule *(principabuntur).* It is precisely this kind of milleniaristic enthusiasm (represented by the speculations of such men as Abbott Joachim of Fiore) for existence under supposedly Spirit-filled *perfecti* beyond all law, lay and ecclesiastical, that is common enough in the middle ages and that St. Thomas refutes for his theological beginners. The denial of a Third Age of the Spirit is part of St. Thomas's very nuanced treatment of the Gospel as the New Law with which the treatment of law concludes and toward which it is aimed. Having treated the Old Law—the letter, he turns to the Gospel—the Spirit. But he argues for a certain continuity between the law of Moses and the Gospel: even the Gospel is experienced as law, is presented in writing and in dogmas and in required external acts such as sacraments. Consequently, even the Gospel can be called a law, the New Law. That is the case even though the "New Law is principally the grace itself of the Holy Spirit" (q. 106, art. 1 resp.). Only in a secondary way does the Gospel contain such things as rules and external acts that dispose one to the reception of grace. And grace itself is distinct from law (q. 90, prologus). Therefore it is dealt with in the so-called "Treatise" on grace that, following the "Treatise" on law, concludes the First Part of the Second Part.

In short, the careful reader notes that St. Thomas, a theologian who must write to beginning theologians about such heady stuff as the liberty of the Gospel and the supremacy of Spirit over letter, of love over fear and command, is very careful to validate the letter, and constraint, and fear, and command as having a due function in the education and public order of men. And he is very careful to do that before speaking of the heady stuff of grace. And he is careful not to separate them (though he distinguishes them) so that grace itself is accompanied by an appropriate legal propaedeutic. Nevertheless, it is grace, it is love, it is the prompting of the Holy Spirit that is the center and standard of his *Christian* moral teaching.

One other point needs to be made about Thomas's treatment of law and virtue in his theological or supernatural ethics before returning to his natural ethics. First, there is a dynamic of human development, both individually and socially, from innocence to sin, to law, to grace, to virtue. Socially the development in question is the history of innocence and fall into sin, followed by the law given by Moses, then the Gospel announced by Christ followed by the full life of the theological virtues: faith, hope and charity (see e.g., q. 98, arts. 1 and 6).

The case of natural morality is similar. Natural law and natural virtue are the analogues, respectively, of the supernatural Old Law and supernatural virtue. There is even a considerable overlap since the supernatural Old Law is said to contain, among other things, the natural law (q. 98, art. 5, resp.), which had become obscured even for good men by the "exuberance of sin" (q. 98, art. 6, resp.). Note that the implication is that the natural law is known, at least partly, in a social manner—a point that we shall return to.

In any case, the natural law, like all law (cf., q. 92, art. 2, ad 3), is an external constraint effective through fear of punishment whereas natural virtue is an internal principle effective by love of the good. Thus natural law is, at best, propaedeutic to virtue as the Old Law is propaedeutic to supernatural virtue. Consequently, the teachings about virtue must be theoretically prior (even though some of them are temporally subsequent) to the teachings about law, since the perfect is always theoretically prior to the imperfect and the end is theoretically prior to the means. That is to say, a full understanding of Thomas's natural ethics must rest on his teaching about natural virtue rather than about natural law.

But the foregoing argument may be granted and still the objection be raised: all that has been said so far seems to apply only to the motive for which good is done and evil avoided (i.e., fear of punishment vs. pleasure in good deeds) but not to the content of morality. As to content, Thomas may envisage good and evil seen from the perspective of the virtuous man to be identical to the content of the natural law. Then the charge against Thomas's ethics still stands: it is inflexible, unpolitically (even antipolitically) inflexible and, thus, unreasonable.

I have already suggested the broad grounds on which one ought to suspect that such an objection is mistaken, namely Thomas's argument in the First Part that government that touches particulars is superior to government that only reaches classes of things (I, q. 22, art. 2, resp.; I, q. 103, art. 6, resp.). But let us see how he treats the matter in the "Treatise" on Law.

St. Thomas calls attention to the problem in a strange passage in the "Treatise" (q. 91, art. 1, resp.; and cf. art. 2, resp.). He writes:

> Now it is evident, supposing that the world is ruled by divine providence, as is stated in the First Part, that the whole community of the universe is governed by the divine reason. And, therefore, the very idea of the government of things, existing in God as in the principle of the universe, has the nature of law.

St. Thomas calls that law (of Providence) the eternal law *(lex aeterna)*. The natural law *(lex naturalis)* is said, in the next article, to be a human participation in the eternal law, a participation in divine providence. One's surprise at this seeming identification of law and providence is sustained when one notes that Thomas does indeed think that laws do *not* deal with particulars (q. 91, art. 1). This surprising identification of two things that had previously been most clearly distinguished seems designed to encourage the mature and reflective reader to proceed most cautiously.[7]

There is a common element in rule by law and rule by providence: both involve the rule of a community by reason (q. 91, art. 1). The general subject under discussion here is the ruling of the universe by the divine reason. The specific subject under discussion in the ethical part of the *Summa Theologiae* is God's government of the universe through man as a secondary cause who, by virtue of his reason, is endowed with free choice (I, q. 22, art. 2, ad 2). The specific part of that subject under discussion in the "Treatise" on Law is God's manner of governing human affairs so as to achieve His intended universal order in spite of the fact that human beings are not always virtuous. The problem is this: how can God constrain human action to conform to His natural order without destroying the essence of man which is to be a reasonable creature with free choice? Thomas's answer is the natural law.

All of Thomas's discussions of divine government necessarily proceed from its analogy with human experiences of government because one cannot talk directly about God's essence or activity inasmuch as we do not know them (I, q. 12). Consequently, talk about God governing man through the medium of natural law rests on the primary experience of human government by law. Thomas, as we have already seen, lays out the reasons for government by law in response to the question: "whether it was useful for laws to be laid down by men?" (q. 95, art 1). He there argues that there is in man only a natural *aptitude* for virtue, but that aptitude has to be developed to reality by some kind of training. It is important here to note how broad Thomas's notion of human virtue is. It includes the ability to master the means to food and clothing. But all that man has *naturally* for such purposes is "reason and hands." All the rest, in the way of tools and technique, he has to acquire by some training *(disciplina)*. The problem is that discipline or training is not itself pleasant. So the perfecting of virtue "chiefly consists in withdrawing man from undue pleasures, to which men are especially inclined, and most of all the young with respect to whom discipline is more efficacious." So he needs a trainer. Now some young men are inclined to virtue by a naturally good disposition, or by custom, or rather by a divine gift, and they can be trained by paternal discipline which works by admonitions. But there are others, inclined to vice, who cannot easily be moved by words. They "have to be restrained from evil by force and fear" so that they leave others in peace. Sometimes these unruly chaps, from being habituated to act well, come rather to like and to do voluntarily what before they did for fear of punishment "and so they become virtuous men."

Such training could be given by individual virtuous trainers or by human laws. We have already seen Thomas's argument that such discipline is normally the work of human legislation rather than the work of virtuous individuals governing particular cases. I argued there that the lack of virtuous rulers had no direct and obvious analogy in the divine government of the world. But it can now be seen that such a lack does, in fact, have an analogy in the indirect mode of governing the world that Thomas attributes to God in his notion of natural law. Insofar as men have a share in governing the world (a share that Thomas sees as expanding with the development of technique and tools), God governs the world by secondary causes that have reason and free choice. If God retains a control over the actions of those human agents by a natural law it will have to be understood by analogy to the operation of human law. That is to say nature itself had to be structured in such a way that violators of the natural law are punished by nature itself. Furthermore, the natural relationship between the act and its punishment will have to be seen by human reason or the punishment could not have the deterrent and training effects that Thomas attributes to law in general.

Now, how ought such a natural law be envisaged as operating? On the surface, the beginner, the "drinker of milk," will notice Thomas saying that the natural law is unchangeable in its first principles (q. 94, art. 5); and he will notice that the natural law's first and common precepts are known to all whereas only its secondary precepts (which are like proximate conclusions drawn from these principles) are not known to all (q. 94, art. 6, resp.). That seems to sustain, at least in part, the charge that Thomas's natural law teaching is unpolitically and, so, unreasonably inflexible. But one wonders: how general are those first precepts or principles of natural law? Are they as legalistically inflexible as charged? How are they promulgated naturally? How are they made efficacious through fear of punishment?

None of those questions is directly answered in what is surely a marvelously brief treatment by Thomas of so celebrated a subject, a treatment whose surface certainly seems to encourage a certain legalism. Nevertheless, Thomas gives a few striking clues as to how to answer such questions. I should like to follow up one of them in detail.

The Case of the German Robbers

Although the first precepts of natural law are know to all men, according to Thomas, they are evidently of the most general nature, as one gathers from occasional examples. Drawing from Caesar's *de bello gallico* (vi. 23), he remarks that "among the Germans robbery or raiding *(latrocinium)* was not thought to be unjust, although it is expressly against the law of nature" (q. 94, art. 4, resp. and cf. art. 6, resp.). The only other case he mentions of a precept of the natural law being unknown among some men is that of "vices against nature" where the reference to *Romans* 1:24 makes clear that it is a question of sexual preversion. So natural law precepts forbidding robbery and sexual perversion must be only secondary precepts because the primary precepts are known to all. A little reflection on the case of robbery among the Germans can help to clarify both how natural law works, what sort of contents it has, and how it relates to virtue.

Let us assume with Thomas (q. 94, art. 6, resp.) that robbery or raiding or piracy or freebooting is prohibited by one of those secondary precepts of the natural law that are nevertheless very close to the first principles, which are known by all. How is it that they could not have known that robbery was against a precept of the natural law? Moreover, since the Germans knew that precept in Thomas's time and were, one must presume, punished by nature when they broke it, were they not punished by nature in Caesar's time? Or is it that they were punished in Caesar's time but did not know it was a punishment? We cannot assume that they knew they were punished but chose to break the law anyway, because Thomas says they didn't even know robbery was unjust and so could not see any natural consequences as a punishment.

To begin with, Caesar's famous raiding or robbing Germans did not think all robbery was just. They only thought it good if practiced against people outside the community of the raiders, as is clear from the passage in Caesar to which Thomas referred. A society that thought all robbery was good would be a society with no stable property, and, therefore, scarcely any technical mastery of nature.

Insofar as some fairly extensive human artifice is prerequisite to, and contributes to, satisfying the general human inclination to individual self-preservation, to biological and cultural procreation, to the leisure for sociability and learning—all of which men naturally desire (q. 94, a. 2, resp.)—men cannot, without suffering the consequences, either argue or act as if robbery is simply good.

In the context of the very rude economy of the germanic tribes, based on a mixture of hunting, gathering, agriculture and herding, a substantial amount of raiding other groups and being raided by them existed without utterly undermining the economic structure upon which group life rested. Raiding can be viewed as a kind of hunting-gathering activity. It is, furthermore, a more attractive mode of acquiring wealth than farming to a people that have not yet harnessed themselves to the hard discipline of agriculture. Finally, contact with the Roman Empire allowed for a vast expansion of the raiding ethic without immediately disastrous consequences.

For a long time, the Empire maintained a high level of material prosperity rooted in stable property over vast areas west and south of the Rhine. That structure was rich enough to withstand great amounts of raiding over a long period of time during which the Germans did not find it necessary to take any responsibility for maintaining the productivity of the Roman economy, nor did they find that their raids permanently diminished the booty anymore than picking raspberries this year prevents next year's crop. Only when the raiding began to take on the proportions of whole peoples moving through and sacking the Empire did the Roman economy collapse and the seemingly inexhaustible source of booty dry up. Then the invading hordes, conquerors of an indigenous agricultural population, began the long, hard political process of reconstituting an order that suppressed the endemic robbery of the Dark Ages. In order to enjoy what was left of what they had taken from the Romans and in order to raise the defense forces necessary to protect it from the next wave of robbers, the Franks, for example, worked to set up a stable order of property that allowed the slow economic redevelopment of Gaul and parts of Germany. They had learned from nature itself the precept forbidding raiding.

Now laws, according to Thomas, discipline the unvirtuous, training them through fear of punishment. A natural law must punish through consequences that in some way flow naturally from the crime. The kind of training through punishment that the natural law imposes would seem to be just the sort of slow social learning process whereby Germanic, northern Europeans, who liked nothing better than a good raid, had been painfully and imperfectly learning for a millenium that robbery, *as a way of life,* doesn't pay for technically developed societies living together.

The natural law prohibition of robbery, so understood, fits Thomas's definition of law (q. 90, a. 4, resp.). It is a rule of reason, first of all of the reason or intelligible principle in the order of nature itself and secondly of human reason that comes to know it. It is directed at the common good of society rather than the good of some individual. Finally, it is promulgated in the way peculiar to natural law. The rational creature, he says (q. 91, art. 2, resp.), has a share of Providence, by "being provident for itself and others." That "being provident" by men is natural in that man has a natural inclination to his "proper act and end." But the natural law does not promulgate the forms and modalities of property relationships, which necessarily vary according to the economic activities with which they are associated. They have to be worked out by reason in relation to the particular economy of a society. So human law, in the article immediately following that on natural law (i.e., q. 91, art. 3), works out the particulars of such things as property.

But then it necessarily follows that robbery *(lactrocinium)* is only understood in a very general sort of way by natural law since property[8] is itself only defined in its particulars by human law. And the prohibition of robbery by natural law only comes to be effectively promulgated through the slow process by which peoples come to know the relationships between stable property and the relatively high levels of economic development upon which depend high development of the leisured pursuits of sociability and learning, in other words, of civilization. Men are naturally but imperfectly drawn to these last as to their appropriate act and end.

If natural law as a whole is understood analogously to the foregoing treatment of robbery, then it is a kind of crude, rough and external rule of right that comes to be known by discovering the relationship between behavior outside the rule and the natural consequences of that behavior. Then the consequences are seen as punishments for violating the order of nature. And only then do human lawmakers devise new laws with a view to the social reform required by the discovery of this precept of the natural law.

But what kind of wisdom is necessary to legislate against robbery? Is it not possible for a leader, even mad with avarice but disciplined by cunning and calculation, to legislate against robbery for a people who have relished it? Will he not find it useful to urge his less-than-perfectly virtuous people to accept his new laws because, under new circumstances, their (and his) acquisitive desires can be more fully indulged in a system of widespread security of property and its attendant economic expansion? That kind of sagacity seems to be produced by the encounter of reason and the laws of nature, i.e., a law naturally efficacious through fear of the natural consequences of violating it.

In short, natural law is the bad man's view of natural right.[9] It was precisely in terms of controlling even the bad men that Thomas introduced the whole discussion of such external principles controlling human acts as natural law. But such base wisdom is unlikely to be the full standard of naturally right-doing for men. Will the full standard of ethics not have to be that seen by the wise and virtuous, whether individuals or communities?

One could grant all of this and still argue: perhaps the ethical standard of the wise and virtuous might add other things to the standard of the natural law, but still be identical to the latter in matters that it touches, such as robbery. In that case the charge that natural law is unpolitically and, therefore, unreasonably inflexible would still stand. Perhaps a closer look at the case of robbery will provide an answer.

Let us assume that a people of raiders, like the Franks, have come to discover the natural precept against raiding and that raiding has been additionally prohibited by human legislation and rather successfully repressed in fact. Let us further assume that a community of such people is suffering from a most severe famine due to unseasonable floods, while a neighboring community is blessed with such abundance that considerable food rots for lack of demand. Assume that the former have no money to buy the latter's surplus and that the later refuse to give it away. Will the natural law precept against raiding or robbery prohibit the starving from taking by force from the rich the means to subsistence? If it can reasonably be argued that it would prohibit such a raid, then the charge against natural law teaching that it is unreasonably inflexible will be a fair charge.

But recall that the natural law is promulgated to men by way of their reasoned discovery of the good or bad consequences of doing one thing or another, and that it is efficacious by fear of the punishment in the form of bad consequences that naturally flow from doing the prohibited acts. Will the starving men of the first community think that some raiding and its attendant economic disorder is worse, more unjust, or more morally unfitting, than allowing the community to starve to death while food rots among the rich? They will only think such nonsense insofar as they have somehow become captivated by the unnatural and rigid legalism that both the opponents and many of the proponents of natural law ethics have saddled it with.

But, if they undertake raids to get the wherewithal to satisfy their hunger, there are a whole range of important questions left: how much raiding is justified? how many will be killed? how long should the raiding go on? who should do it? if it goes on for a long time, how many young men will be lured by that experience into a love of the vicious, murderous, but exciting life of the freebooter? how can peaceful relations ever be reestablished with the neighbors? how can the wounds be bound up, healed, and cleansed? Those are questions that the crude, rough and ready, external constraint of the natural law does not easily go far to answering.

As Thomas points out, the natural law's precepts, except for its most general platitudes (e.g., do good and avoid evil), may fail to be *right* in some cases even when known (q. 94, art. 4, resp.). That is the case because the natural rightness or wrongness of human acts is ultimately to be understood according to Thomas in terms of the natural end of mankind. That is the reason that he begins the ethical part of the *Summa* with a discussion of the end of human life (I–II, qq. 1–5), which he believes Aristotle has demonstrated to be the happiness of contemplative wisdom (I–II, q. 3 and cf. *SCG*, Bk. III, chs. 37–47).

From the point of view of the roots of universal order, perceived by the contemplative, it is possible to judge intelligently how far a particular moral rule does or does not aid in developing, in realizing, the final end of man. That is the role of the wise man who, knowing and willing the end, by rational necessity wills the means thereto (q. 90, art. 1, ad. 3). But law, as has been shown is precisely for those who do not perfectly know and will the final end. The unwise only will their human happiness imperfectly, perhaps only this or that subordinate part of it or perhaps the whole of it but ill understood (it was in that sense I called them "bad"). So the natural law precepts only tend to converge *toward* the wisdom of the virtuous sage or philosopher.

Consequently, the standard of right in such a difficult case as I asked the reader to assume cannot be the general propositions of the natural law, rules of which even "bad" men can see the wisdom. The full standard of right can only be the judgement of the temperate wisdom of a virtuous man who can choose well because he knows and loves the good rather than the judgment of the intemperate, the unwise, or the vicious who nevertheless refrains from some evils for fear of the consequences. To gain an adequate understanding of Thomas's ethics, one must go primarily to his teaching about virtue which precedes and follows the excursus on law (i.e., to I–II, qq. 1–89 and II–II).

The Rhetorical Problem

If I am right in the foregoing argument that Thomas's natural ethics is fundamentally a natural right teaching rather than one of natural law, the question nevertheless arises: how is it that his natural ethics has been so widely mistaken for an ethics of natural law? There seem to be a number of reasons, at least one of them due to Thomas's editors rather than to Thomas himself.

He himself did not divide the *Summa Theologiae* into "treatises." That seems to be the work of later editors. But, once the work is separated into distinct treatises, the reader interested in political theory is easily led to take the "Treatise" on Law and read it as if it were meant to be taken as a separate work rather than, as I have argued, an integral and theoretically quite subordinate part of a larger and theoretically seamless whole.

Still, it must be said that the format that Thomas adopts for the work surely allows, if it does not actually encourage, just such a misunderstanding and misediting as culminates in the separate publication of sections of the whole work as if they were separate treatises. Thomas writes in the formal question and answer format of the medieval schools. A highly systematic writer, he groups the questions so that the work can be mistaken for a kind of reference encyclopedia to which one has recourse to look up questions that occur at random. Such a practice became easy once editors added schematic tables of contents with the questions grouped under "Treatise" headings.

In any case, Thomas wrote for beginners in theology in an academic system in which a degree did not require some special evidence of saintly sagacity. So just as he found it prudent to emphasize the continuity from supernatural law to grace to virtue, he seems to have found it wise to do analogously with the continuity from natural law to philosophy to virtue for men who, though they had studied philosophy, were not necessarily philosophers in the sense of virtuous sages. In both cases showing the substantial overlap between law and philosophy or grace tends to restrain the newly learned from a certain sophomoric conceit that they are simply beyond any need to consult the law.

Finally, the brevity of Thomas's remarks on natural law (given its minor role in the work as a whole) is such that there is no place for much elaboration of the content of those crucial terms: "primary precepts" (unchangeable) and "secondary precepts" (changeable). But the Western Church has a powerfully legalistic thrust to its morality. Resting on the Roman legal tradition, the Church had developed an elaborate body of canon law and an elaborate system of ecclesiastical courts for dealing with morals. In such an environment it was practically inevitable that there grow up a tradition in which Thomas's teaching on law should be given a role and an interpretation he had not intended. My suspicion is that the unfortunate emphasis on Thomas's natural law teaching is something that develops especially with the split in the western church at the Reformation and Counter-Reformation which tend to reinforce the naturalistic and legalistic strands in Catholicism. Whether that suspicion is true is a matter for careful and extensive historical research. But, however such research may turn out, the time has come for political theorists to return to Thomas's text, as it was written, and to focus on his teaching about virtue rather than on law.

Notes

1. For the main lines of such an investigation see Leon John Ross, *Natural Right and Natural Law in Thomas Aquinas,* Ph.D. dissertation, University of Chicago, 1971.

2. Leo Strauss, *Natural Right and History* (Chicago: Univ. of Chicago Press, 1953), pp. 162–164 and cf., Harry V. Jaffa, *Thomism and Aristotelianism* (Chicago: Univ. of Chicago Press, 1952), pp. 167–188.

   Although the historians of political thought do not commonly make Strauss' distinction between natural law and natural right in so direct a fashion, they are one with Strauss in emphasizing the centrality of the concept of natural law in St. Thomas's ethical and political theory . . .

3. *Natural Right and History,* p. 162.

4. *Ibid.,* pp. 163–164.

5. Thomas's text itself is not separated into parts under "treatise" titles. The practice of assigning titles to groups of questions in the *Summa Theologiae* and calling those sections "treatises" is the work of editors of Thomas rather than of Thomas himself. This fact is of some importance to later parts of my argument.

6. All references to the *Summa Theologiae,* unless otherwise noted, are to the First Part of the Second Part. All translations, unless otherwise noted, are my own.

7. I am here following the Straussian procedure of assuming that, when one encounters a great thinker making what seems to be such a blunder as would shame an intelligent schoolboy, one ought seriously to entertain the possibility that the thinker himself was aware of it—all the more so when he is a writer as systematic as Thomas Aquinas.

8. Perhaps I should remark that the property in question is not necessarily or exclusively private property. It may just as well be communal property.

9. It is not, of course, a question of absolute badness. To begin with, nothing that is is absolutely bad for Thomas since existence itself is good. Furthermore, laws, including natural law, are effective precisely insofar as those subject to them are not utterly bereft of rational judgment in moral matters. They are effective only insofar as bad men are still not so corrupted that they are unable to see precisely that the punishment is worse than the crime. (If they are so mad as to think the punishment good, the law is useless.) That is the minimum kind of human goodness of judgment and will that even bad men have to some degree. Without it human life in a common world would be an utterly unbearable chaos.

The Mixed Constitution and the Distinction between Regal and Political Power in the Work of Thomas Aquinas
James M. Blythe

Thomas Aquinas is possibly the earliest medieval writer to be influenced by Aristotle's *Politics,* and he is certainly the most important for political theory as a whole. He is the giant whom later thinkers will interpret, bend to their own purposes, or, less frequently, refute. It is largely through Aquinas that the ideas of man as a social and political animal, of the citizen as one who participates in government, of the classification of government by the number and quality of its rulers, of the mixed constitution, and many other concepts entered the medieval milieu; and future thought is as much shaped by his peculiar interpretations of these ancient principles as by Aristotle's ideas themselves.

Yet his political theory is sufficiently ambiguous to allow him to be cited by different scholars as an advocate of absolute monarchy, limited monarchy, republicanism, and mixed constitutionalism. As Brian Tierney notes, "We sometimes think of Thomas as a great synthesizer. . . . When one studies his political theory and ecclesiology, the first impression is just the opposite. Thomas seems fascinatingly original but quite incoherent."[1] In many places Thomas exalts kingship and calls it the best government for man.[2] But the king's power, unlike God's, should be "tempered" so as to remove the opportunity to tyrannize.[3] The counsel of the wise is natural and essential, and their authority can even be seen as superior to that of a king.[4] This can be taken as an argument for aristocracy. In other places Thomas suggests that ultimate authority rests with the whole people.[5] So perhaps democracy is the best solution. In a number of places Thomas advocates as best the mixing of all the good simple forms of monarchy, aristocracy, and democracy.[6] Finally, he sometimes suggests that the best form of government is a function of particular peoples, places, and conditions.[7]

Since all these statements were written near the end of what in any case was a relatively short writing career, it is unlikely that the diversity is explainable as the

---

From James M. Blythe, "The Mixed Constitution and the Distinction Between Regal and Political Power in the Work of Thomas Aquinas," *Journal of the History of Ideas,* 47, pp. 547–565. 1986. Reprinted with permission of *Journal of the History of Ideas.*

1. Brian Tierney, "Aristotle, Aquinas, and the Ideal State," *Proceedings of the Patristic, Medieval, and Renaissance Conference,* 4 (1979).

2. E.g., Thomas Aquinas, *De Regimine Principum ad Regem Cypri* (henceforth, *DRP*), ed. Joseph Mathis (Turin, 1971), I.1, I.2, I.q; *Summa Theologiae* (henceforth, *ST*), ed. Petro Caramello (Turin, 1952), I.103.3.

3. *DRP,* I.5.

4. Thomas Aquinas, *Summa Contra Gentiles,* in *Opera Omnia* (Paris, 1889), III.1.81.

5. *ST,* I–II.90.3, and I–II.105.2.

6. *ST,* I–II.105.1, 95.4.ad 3.

7. *ST,* I–II.91.4, 95.4.ad 3.

development over the years of Thomas's own opinion. How, then, can it be explained? Was Thomas simply unable in any coherent manner to fuse the alien and admittedly already somewhat contradictory Greek doctrines with dominant medieval political thought and reality? Was he unsure himself how mankind should best be ruled? Or is there an underlying conception which can unify all these statements? I hope to show that is is possible to find such a conception.[8] I believe that Thomas consistently supported a theory of mixed constitution, but I do not believe that any of the interpretations of modern scholars adequately reflects his thought.

When we consider mixed constitutions, we normally think of mixtures of monarchy, aristocracy, and democracy. This way of thinking occurs also in Thomas, but before discussing it we need to consider another way of classifying regimes which is equally important in his work—the distinction between regal, political, and despotic rule. Aristotle characterized governmental power in several ways, of which the two most important were the six-fold classification of polities (monarchy, aristocracy, polity, tyranny, oligarchy, and democracy) and the four types of rule (regal, political, despotic, and economic). He tended to dwell on the former schema, but the distinction between regal and political rule became of great significance in our period, in part because of an ambiguous translation by Moerbeke* and a consequent misunderstanding by Aquinas.

Aristotle rejects the theory that a household and a city differ only by the number of subjects. At this point he adds: "when one governs it is regal, when one in turn governs and is governed according to the rules of the science, it is political."[9] "Rules" in this context is clearly meant to refer to the regulations and procedures of the polity governing the rotation of offices.

Moerbeke chose to render κατὰ μέρος ("in turn") by secundum partem ("in part") and to translate the whole passage as follows: "when one has precedence, it is regal; when according to the rules of the discipline one is in part both ruler and subject, it is political."[10] It is easy to see the misunderstanding possible: one man seems to be ruler in both regal and political regimes. What, then, are the "rules"? Well, they must be the laws which compel the ruler and make him in part a subject.

This is exactly how Thomas construes the passage:

> For when one man has precedence simply and over all things, it is called a regal regimen. But when according to the rules of such a science he rules in part, that is, according to laws posed through the political discipline, it is a political regimen; as it were he rules in part, as regards those things in his power; and in part he is a subject, as regards those things in which he is subject to law.[11]

It is clear that the definitions Aquinas gives here are to be taken as the proper ones, since a few paragraphs before he said almost exactly the same thing in an unam-

---

8. I will restrict myself to works actually written by Aquinas: ST and the initial portions of the DRP (I.1–II.2.5) and the In Libros Politicorum Aristotelis Expositio (henceforth, LP or Commentary), ed. R. M. Spiazzi (Rome, 1966), I.1–III.5. Two common methodological flaws in the use of the Commentary are the assumptions that all of Thomas's portion represents his own thought and that it is valid to cite even those portions of it not written by him. . . .

*William of Moerbeke, a Flemish friend of Thomas who provided new texts of Aristotle for Thomas' inspection.

9. Aristotle, Politicorum Libri Octo cum vetusta translatione Guilelmi de Moerbeka (henceforth, Politics), ed. Franciscus Susemihl (Leipzig, 1872), I.1.1252a.15f: . . .

10. Aristotle, Politics, I.1.1252a.15: . . .

11. LP, I.1. 15: . . .

biguous context, making it even more apparent that he is referring to one ruler in either case and that the "laws" are the statutes of the polity. Rule in a city, he writes, can be one of two kinds: regal or political. "The regimen is regal when he who rules has full power. It is political when he who rules has power restrained according to some laws of the city." [12]

Aquinas does recognize that political rule at least normally requires the interchange of rulers and ruled, and, strangely, he himself in places glosses the very words *in partem,* misunderstood in I.1, to explain that such an alternation occurs. Aristotle writes: ". . . [in political rule] it is worthy that they rule in part. . . ." [13] Aquinas comments: "Then it seemed worthy that certain ones rule for one part of the time, and others at another time." [14] The basis for this alternation is the fundamental equality of the citizens; if such equality exists it is not just that one should dominate. This is a conviction that Aquinas, following Aristotle, repeats on numerous occasions. [15] In this situation there is no natural difference among the rulers, but only a fortuitous one of the actual time during which each holds an office.

These are two rather disparate conceptions: is it of the essence of political rule that it is limited by law or that the rulers be changed, or must both occur? Aquinas gives two examples, one from human society and the other from nature, in which political rule exists where there is one permanent ruler. The rule of a husband over his wife is political because it is bound by the laws of matrimony; consequently, the husband lacks full power. The relationship, Thomas asserts, is analogous to the situation in which a rector rules according to the statutes of his city. The wife never takes her turn as ruler because the equality necessary for alternation is lacking; the man is naturally and permanently superior, and, as a result, naturally rules. The inequality is so obvious to Aristotle and Aquinas that they sum up the situation by observing that, when rulers change, the new ones take on the honors and appurtenances of rule, but a woman can never become a man.

The other example, again based on natural superiority is more difficult to understand and even more provocative in its formulation. Aristotle states baldly that unlike the soul, which rules despotically over the body, the intellect rules desire by a political and regal principate. Aquinas attempts to clarify this:

> Political and regal principate applies to free men whence they can contradict in some things, and similarly sometimes desire does not follow reason. This diversity results from the fact that the body cannot be moved except by the soul, and therefore it is totally subject to it, but the desire can be moved not only by reason, but even by the sense, and it is not totally subject to reason. [16]

If both political and regal rule are over free men and both allow contradiction to some extent and the rule of one element permanently, then what is the distinction? Why is the rule of reason over desire both political and regal? One explanation suggests itself. "Political" has one of two meanings: either it is a general term for the human government of free men (in which sense all the six non-despotic forms are political), or it is the type of rule distinguished from regal rule by its relation to law.

---

12. *LP,* I.1.13: . . .

13. Aristotle, *Politics,* III.6.1279a10 (Spiazzi, III.5.250) . . .

14. *LP,* III.5.389: . . .

15. *LP,* I.5.90, I.10.154, II.1.183, III.5.389.

16. *LP,* I.3.64: . . .

Thomas is aware of these two meanings; in fact both Aristotle and Thomas introduce the passage under discussion with the comment that both political and despotic rule can be found in the human animal. If this distinction is foremost in Thomas's mind, what he probably means is this: the soul rules the body despotically, but within the soul (which is free and therefore must be ruled by a species of political rule) the reason rules regally over the desire. This reading would eliminate the need to explain a rule both regal and political (in the second sense of "political"). . . .

These two examples show that neither eligibility of a large number of citizens to rule through alternation nor the term of office of the rulers is the essential element of the distinction between political and regal rule, for in both cases political rule exists in a monarchical environment with an unchanging monarch. Political and regal are modes of rule that are not necessarily related to the extent of popular participation, the number of rulers, or the size of the community. These are functions of the actual institutions, which are secondary considerations. Aquinas interprets these terms analogically: regal rule is like that of a king who rules absolutely, political rule like that of a polity in which a king rules according to laws established by the whole community. Aristotle's six-fold schema (which is based on the number of rulers) is simply the list of forms in which the modes of rule can be exercised in a city. Thus, it is quite possible to have political or regal monarchy, aristocracy, or democracy.

Thomas is forced to this abstraction. Aristotle sees things in the light of the Greek polity with wide participation; Aquinas must preserve the terminology but assimilate it to the medieval kingdom. For him a monarchy is a normal state of affairs, and unconsciously he adapts Aristotle's terminology to the situation with which he is familiar. So for him the number or transience of rulers is an accidental quality of rule, although it can be profitable to discuss it in these terms. The essence of the distinction is whether rule is absolute or according to law.

It is to Aquinas's conception of monarchy and its possible limitations in a mixed constitution that we must now turn. In the *Commentary* he paraphrases Aristotle's definition of the six forms of polity without embellishment. With respect to the rule of one man he writes: "He is a king if he is virtuous and upholds the common utility of his subjects. He is a tyrant if he is evil and turns all things to his own convenience, having contempt for the utility of his subjects."[17] Aristotle's hesitation in the Third Book as to whether number is a proper or accidental characteristic of the forms of rule is concerned solely with aristocracy and polity; Thomas never doubts that the rule of one defines and is essential to monarchy.[18] Nor does he ever deny that monarchy is the best form of government. Almost all his arguments for this are derived from metaphysical considerations of the order of the universe, the virtue of unity, and the image of the king as the embodiment of reason.[19] This is at variance with Aristotle who conceded only that monarchy would be best if there existed one of supreme virtue (an unlikely occurrence in his view). Far from making analogies to the natural order of things, he implied that man projected his own predilection for and experience with kingship onto the community of the gods.[20]

17. *LP,* II.7.242: . . .

18. Aristotle, *Politics,* III.8; *LP,* III.6.396–98.

19. The rule of one is inherent in the very nature of both nature and man. In all things ordained to a single end there is some one element which rules the rest (*DRP,* I.1): "Every natural governance is governance by one. In the multitude of bodily members there is one which moves them all, namely the heart; and among the powers of the soul one power presides as chief, namely the reason. Even among bees there is one king and in the whole universe there is one God, maker and rector of all things" (*DRP,* I.2).

20. Artistotle, *Politics,* I.2.1252b.24.

But for the medieval mind this analogy with nature was obvious and decisive. Virtue was a prerequisite for the true king but not the principal justification for the continuance of his office. The principal intention of a ruler (in society or nature) must be the promotion of unity or peace:

> For, it is clear that several cannot be the cause of unity or concord, except so far as they are united. Furthermore, what is in itself one is a more apt and a better cause of unity than several things united. Therefore, a multitude is better governed by one than by several.[21]

Aquinas also gives several practical reasons for monarchy, among them that tyranny is the worst of governments and stems more often from the rule of many than from monarchy, that from experience we know that places ruled by many almost always are torn apart by dissension, but that where there is a king there is peace, and that, since it is more likely that one of many will turn from the common good than one alone, it is more expedient to be ruled by one.[22]

We must next show that his conception of monarchy allows other powers coordinate with or restraining that of the king. Even the *De Regimine Principum*, which consistently praises monarchy, sounds a moderating note. In his discussion of tyranny Thomas suggests three means of avoiding this evil. All presuppose some sort of authority residing in the community.

The first suggests that election of the monarch pertains to at least one segment of the community and can be used to promote to office only those who are of such character as to make tyranny unlikely. Although his example of this shows that this selection may pertain to supernatural agency and not to man (the first Jewish kings), his intention is clearly that in the absence of direct divine intervention the task falls to men.[23]

Another caution is that there should be provision for the situation in which a king is transformed into a tyrant. The method is vague; Thomas warns about the dangers of revolt and advises obedience and restraint in all but the most intolerable situations. In no case should private action be condoned; an attack upon tyranny can be the prerogative only of the "public authority."[24] This phrase is never identified by Thomas with any kind of actual institution. Parliamentary bodies had not yet developed to the point where they were the obvious solution, but Thomas felt that there should be some remedy and that this remedy could not be an individual one as others, such as John of Salisbury,* had suggested.[25] All his emphasis is on legality; he writes not of the best arrangement but of what can be done given the actually existing institutions. If the multitude has the right to choose its king, it has the right to depose him, for the king has broken his pact with his subjects (that is, to govern for the common good). But if a higher authority has the right to provide a king, then it is his responsibility to remove the tyrant.

---

21. *ST,* I.103.3: . . .

22. *DRP,* I.2, I.5.

23. His preference for election over heredity is put forth in several places, for example, *LP,* II.16.334.

24. *DRP,* I.6: . . .

*British Bishop and author of *Policraticus (Statesman's Book),* 1120–80—ed.

25. The examples Thomas gives both pertain to the Roman Empire and show the difference between a free and a subject people. The Roman Senate was able to depose and execute a tyrannical emperor and to revoke his laws, and likewise the emperor could replace a local king under his jurisdiction. In human society, he asserts elsewhere, no man can exercise coercion (which is the essence of law) except through public authority—the prince to whom public power is entrusted must use it within the bounds of justice (*ST,* II–II.66.8).

   This brings us to the third and most important of the means Thomas advocates to avoid tyranny. The proper selection and necessary deposition of kings in no way contradicts the notion of regal rule, although it is perhaps alien to its spirit. It is quite possible to say that the people select their ruler, who then rules by his own will (that is, by the law which he makes) unless he should violate his trust. But Thomas makes the stronger statement that the government of the kingdom should be so arranged that the opportunity to tyrannize is removed and that the king's power should be so tempered that he cannot easily become a tyrant.[26] What can he have meant? The word "tempering" is especially provocative. Certainly something beyond power of deposition or the moral strength of custom is meant. It suggests that the king's power be limited or controlled by other governmental institutions, so that it cannot exceed what is proper. This interpretation is supported by his previous comments on the disposition of the governance of the kingdom. In a number of places Thomas implies that government pertains to a free people as a whole who delegate it or part of it to the monarch—but he always leaves open the possibility of a king representing the interests of the people but not directly responsible to it.[27]

   Thomas is an unswerving champion of the law. He would like to derive this law from the people either as legislator or as the bearer of custom, but because of his misinterpretation of Aristotle's definition of regal and political rule, he feels he must leave the way open for a ruler acting by his own will alone. Even so, he tries to hedge the regal king in with all sorts of restrictions which in fact bring him close to what he calls one who rules politically. Thomas has two choices: he can either reject regal kingship or he can assimilate it to political kingship and try to gloss over the differences. Because of his commitment to monarchy as a principle of the universe he perhaps feels that he cannot reject it in its pure form out of hand (especially since God rules regally if this word has any meaning at all). On the other hand he cannot really eliminate the differences. . . .

   Since the family serves as an exemplar of rule and its most primitive embodiment, it is interesting to see how these ideas apply to it. Since rule of the household (economic rule) encompasses three modes of rule,[28] it would be natural to regard it as a mixed constitution. Perhaps Thomas would agree, but this is not how he puts it. He indicates that since all in the home are ruled by the paterfamilias, economic rule is a type of monarchy. Clearly, it is the number of rulers, not the mode of rule, that is significant in deciding whether a government is a monarchy, since both political and regal rule are here called monarchic. Since the family properly includes monarchy alone of the six basic forms, Thomas may not consider it to be a mixed government. Granted, it is a monarchy exercised in three different modes, but he may well reserve the term "mixed government" for one combining different forms of government, and this the family does only accidentally and temporarily in the absence of a paterfamilias.

   In the *Commentary* Thomas is more explicit about what he means by the word "temper" and confirms our suspicions that he was thinking of a mixed constitution in the recommendations of the *De Regimine Principum* for avoiding tyranny. Thomas

---

26. *DRP,* I.6: . . .

27. The coercive power that is necessary for law is vested in the whole people or in one who has care of the whole people. (*ST,* I–II.90.4). . . .

28. The rule of master over slave is despotic; of father over child, regal; of husband over wife, political. *LP,* I.10.152. The father is not a perfect example of regal rule. He bears a resemblance to the regal ruler but lacks the power of rule that belongs to the king. (*ST,* II–II.50.3).

comments on Aristotle's mention of the "opinion of some" that the best government is a mixture of monarchy, oligarchy, and democracy:

> The reason is because one regimen is tempered from the admixture of another, and less material is given for sedition if all have a part in the rule of the city, namely, if the people rules in something, the powerful in something, and the king in something.[29]

The implication is the same as in the *De Regimine Principum* with respect to the king. The addition of the other coordinate powers ensures that his rule is more temperate; that is, that because of the restraining influence of the others, he will be unable to tyrannize. We find here that the mixture also works the other way: the excesses possible from the rule of the few and the many (extreme oligarchy and democracy) are mutually prevented by the tempering influence of the other powers. We also find that such an arrangement undermines sedition.

These are all practical reasons for the mixed constitution. In two passages of the *Summa Theologiae* Aquinas suggests that it is best in more fundamental ways. In both cases he advances totally original ideas, in one case linking the mixed constitution to the teachings of the Church Fathers, in the other to the Bible and God's will. First, in a discussion of law he implies that it is only in a mixed government that we can speak of law in its proper sense. He notes that human law, being framed by the one who governs, is relative to the form of government. In a monarchy there are constitutions of princes, in an aristocracy *senatusconsulta,* in an oligarchy praetorian law, and in a democracy *plebiscita.* He concludes: "There is a regimen mixed from these, which is the best, and from this form comes *lex,* 'which the elders sanctify together with the plebs,' as Isidore says."[30] In other words in an unmixed state there is the law of this or that group; in a mixed state there is law simply speaking. This is the first time that anyone attempted to assimilate the early medieval ideas of Isidore with the mixed constitution of Aristotle. Isidore presumably meant to refer to the hereditary nobility, that is, the senatorial aristocracy, by the words *maiores natu,* and for him they were a natural element of rule, but he does not mention the mixed constitution at all—this is entirely Thomas's reading.

In his fullest discussion of the best government Thomas makes an even more compelling argument for mixed government: it is the form given by God to his Chosen People. He begins by mentioning two general principles of good government. The first is that "all should have some part in rule, but by this the peace of the people is preserved, and all love such an order and guard it."[31] His reason for giving all a share is practical; each will be content if this is the case. He does not really think that the average person has something to offer, since he is neither (except accidentally) virtuous nor wise. Aquinas never takes up Aristotle's views on the collective wisdom of the whole multitude, and there is no reason to think that he shares them.

Nevertheless, he does insist that all should in some way share in government, and this raises an obvious question. Monarchy, even regal monarchy if a virtuous enough man exists, is a good, even the best form of government (as he himself says in the same question).[32] If one king is to have all power, how can all share? The only

---

29. *LP,* II.7.245: . . . The terms democracy and oligarchy are used rather generally by Aristotle as rule of the people and the few and not as the bad forms of the six-fold classification.

30. *ST,* I–II.95.4.3: . . .

31. *ST,* I–II.105.2: . . .

32. *ST,* I–II.105.2 ad 1.

solution is to consider any political office, of which there must be many in even the most absolute monarchy, to embody a share of rule. In this way there would always be at least a small group of men who could be said to participate in rule. Is it the case, then, that a regal monarchy is in fact a mixed government of monarchy and aristocracy? No, for a distinction can be made between officials performing their duties at the institution of and subject to the king, and those who have an independent right to existence. Even though the mixed constitution cannot preserve in its full purity any of its constituent parts, it cannot be meaningfully mixed unless each part subsists in some way in the mixture.

After saying that all should have a part, Thomas goes on to give another factor which must be considered in setting up a right ordering of society: the form of government:

> Although there are various species of these, as Aristotle reports . . . , the principal ones are the kingdom in which one rules according to virtue; and aristocracy, that is, the power of the best, in which some few rule according to virtue. Whence the best order of princes is in some city or kingdom in which one is placed in authority according to his virtue who precedes all, and under him are some men ruling according to virtue; and nevertheless such rule pertains to all, because they can be chosen from all and they are chosen by all. Such is the best polity, well-mixed from kingdom, insofar as one is over all, and aristocracy, insofar as many rule according to their virtue, and from democracy, that is, from the power of the people, insofar as princes can be chosen from the people, and election of princes pertains to the people.[33]

One cannot ignore the difference between the beginning and end of this passage. There are many forms of government; the best are monarchy and aristocracy; therefore, the best government is a blend of monarchy, aristocracy, and democracy. Both monarchy and aristocracy are based on the principle of virtue; the only difference is the quantitative one of the number of rulers. Why, then, are both desirable? Although the phrasing here (they are the best, therefore their combination is best) suggests that Aquinas also expects that since these are the best forms of government their combination will unite the good qualities of each, it must be repeated that he does not give separate qualities to each and that his primary interest must be in the tempering effect. Buy why democracy at all? Its inclusion is not the result of the second consideration (the forms of government) but of the first (everyone should have a share). There is no necessary virtue connected with the people, but there is something to be gained by making it feel a part of the government. Its role is restricted to the election of the king and aristocrats, so it is excluded from real participation in an Aristotelian sense—that is, in the actual offices of government. Tierney correctly observes that the difference in emphasis is due to the differing forms of political organization in the ancient and medieval worlds. In the Greek city-state the direct involvement of a large body of citizens was possible: the same was not true in a large medieval kingdom. As Tierney puts it: ". . . such an idea does begin to suggest modern constitutional theory where a complex central government derives its authority from the consent of the people."[34]

Thomas then sanctifies the mixed government by identifying it with the form established by God for the Jews:

---

33. *ST*, I–II.105.1: . . .

34. Tierney, "Aristotle," 4.

And this was instituted according to divine law. For Moses and his successors governed the people, ruling the people as it were by themselves, which is a certain species of kingdom. Moreover, they chose seventy-two elders according to virtue, for it is said in Deuteronomy 1: "I took from your tribes wise and noble men and established them as princes," and this was aristocracy. But it was democratic that those were chosen from all the people, for it is said in Exodus 18: "provide from all the people wise men, etc.," and even that the people chose them; whence it is said at Deuteronomy 1: "Give me from your wise men, etc." Whence it is clear that the ordering of princes which the law instituted was the best.[35]

It seems indisputable that Thomas is recommending this form of government as best absolutely, and not just as one suited only to the Jews. It is true that the starting point of this article is the question of whether God correctly ordained the government of His people, and that one conclusion is that God was wise in not at once setting up Jewish kings with full power. But the superiority of the mixed constitution is derived a priori from general principles of what constitutes good government, and the Jews are brought in as an example to demonstrate that what he has deduced by reason is supported by the divine intention. . . .

. . . On the surface there seems to be an insurmountable contradiction: how can the "best" be both regal monarchy and the mixed constitution? First, Thomas makes an implicit distinction (which will become explicit in later writers) between simple forms of government (monarchy, aristocracy, democracy, etc.) and compound forms. This is detectable in the already cited portions of this article: there are several species of rule (*species regiminis*), of which the best are monarchy and aristocracy. The best ordination of rulers (*ordinatio principum*) is the mixed constitution. The mixed constitution is not a species in the sense that monarchy and aristocracy are; rather it is a combination of species. Thus, it is possible to use "best" here for two different forms—monarchy is the best of the simple forms, the mixed government the best form of government.[36]

This observation does not solve our difficulty. Thomas suggests that regal monarchy is the best and that a mixed constitution is best, but a regal monarchy does not seem to be compatible with a mixed constitution. Hence, we must consider yet another distinction of the word "best." Thomas admits that regal kingship is best abstractly but denies that it is best considering the nature of man. When he points to the peculiar traits of the Jews, he implies only that they especially are unsuited to regal government, not that others are suited to it. The perfect virtue needed is almost never found, and he might have added that even if there is such a one, what will happen after his death? Regal monarchy is best only in principle, in the abstract, in a realm of perfection such as the universe. His general principles of government also reflect his concern with man's nature. The reason that all should have a share in power is ultimately that people are unsatisfied and will become rebellious if they cannot participate. This factor would be no less true in the rule of the one of perfect virtue than in any other form, and so Thomas seems to say that regal monarchy is unsuitable even if the proper king could be found. Thus, in any meaningful sense the mixed constitution is the best government for man.

---

35. *ST*, I–II.105.1: . . .

36. One could also argue that his meaning is that monarchy is the best form of government, mixed constitution the best type of monarchy.

Those who have not grasped the distinction between regal and political power and Thomas's support for a political king in a mixed constitution are unable to make complete sense of his position without recourse to strained exegesis. . . . [Thomas] is chiefly concerned with the difference between rule by law and will, and his rejection of absolute rule has to do with the inherent nature of man and not just the situation in this or that place. This is true not only for monarchy but also for the other forms whether in isolation or within a mixed constitution: regal aristocracy or democracy is possible, but it should be rejected in favor of the political rule of law. Far from being a minor and somewhat conflicting classification of rule, it underlies Thomas's whole theory.

Only with a political king is the idea of tempering and balance in a mixed constitution possible. Otherwise the mixed constitution is . . . little different from an absolute monarchy. The monarchic element could be tempered only in the practical sense that the king could not ignore the united voice of the great men and still less the combined demands of them and the people. But there are always great men, the people always exist, and these two groups can always assert themselves against the king. The point would seem to be to give them some institutional machinery for doing this within the law rather than on their own. Thomas wants the three elements of his mixed government to be able to check the excesses of the others and to do this on a regular basis, not just in extreme cases. Because of the political conditions of the time, all the institutional answers were not clear to him, as they would be in a few centuries to the English theorists of the mixed constitution, and so he is not specific as to exact forms. There is simply no way to achieve Thomas's intent in a society governed by a regal king free from the laws and direct restraint of other agencies. This why all of Thomas's effort was directed to deprive the king of his regal prerogatives and to render him a political ruler bound to the laws. Looked at this way, there is no problem in integrating a king into the mixed constitution.

Thomas's choice of the mixed constitution as the best government for men is a result of his conclusion that, in general, it will best serve the common utility. The salient and confirming point is that it denies sovereignty to any one element and in this way avoids the tyranny of either the one, the few, or the many. Thomas may be vague about the institutions through which the power of the community could manifest itself, but he is not at all vague about his purposes. He does not hesitate between alternate sources of authority, since the question of government is not primarily a metaphysical question for him (even though he can demonstrate that his solution accords with the will of God). A political king ruling a people that is represented in government and that can restrain him will most effectively promote the common good, which for Thomas is the most important criterion for rule.

To what degree are these ideas faithful to Aristotle's intent in the *Politics*? Certainly, Aristotle also put emphasis on advancing the common good. And it is easy to understand how someone living among the thirteenth century monarchies could have interpreted Aristotle's comments on regal and political rule as referring to monarchic authority in both modes, especially in light of William of Moerbeke's mistranslation and the fact that Aristotle himself is not very clear in his exposition of monarchy. Aquinas always favors a king, Aristotle only if there exists one of transcendent virtue. This being said, if we equate Thomas's regal king with Aristotle's king, both authors agree with Aristotle's conditions for his rule; and although neither really expects that such a rule is possible, both agree that his superiority would give this king a right to rule and that his rule would be abstractly the best. Failing this, both advocate a mixed constitution; and although it is only Thomas who insists on the inclusion of the three elements of monarchy, aristocracy, and democracy, both stress the importance of law.

But their views of the mixed constitution are quite different. Aristotle's concern is the balancing of the various classes. His mixture itself can be seen as a mixture of classes rather than a formal one of the various constituents. He carries this to the extreme that one of his ideal forms is a mixed constitution in which, in a sense, the various elements disappear and the mixing consists of the assimilation of all citizens to a single class—this is his middle-class polity. All this is of no concern to Thomas, who ignores almost everything to do with class. His concern is not balancing the classes in society but balancing governmental forms to avoid the extremes of any of them. In this, as in his lack of confidence in the wisdom of the people, Thomas is rather closer to Polybius (whom, however, he did not know directly or even indirectly through Cicero, except as the latter was quoted by the Church Fathers). Although the similarity is fortuitous, both stress the checks and balances of one form upon another. When Polybius was rediscovered in the sixteenth century, this affinity aided in the fusion of the Aristotelian and Polybian traditions.

In all these ways and others Thomas created a truly original synthesis of Greek political theory and medieval thought. By distinguishing regal and political power and insisting on a political monarch, Thomas was able to preserve the participation characteristic of Greek society and the unity of rule found, at least in principle, in the medieval kingdom. The generation of scholars that followed Aquinas would take his ideas and develop them in different and sometimes contradictory ways. Some would carry on the theory of the mixed constitution and alter it in subtle ways, apply it to the Church, or reject it altogether for some other favored form. But the idea of a mixed government had reentered the Western World after an absence of some thousand years, and in one form or another it would survive and prosper throughout late medieval and early modern times. From the thirteenth to the sixteenth century the distinction between regal and political power, as this was interpreted by Thomas, remained an important part of this theory.

Niccolo Machiavelli

No name is more synonymous with politics, especially as politics is popularly conceived, than that of Niccolo Machiavelli. Machiavelli's reputation is based largely on the amoral, if not immoral, advice he gave in *The Prince,* written in 1513. Indeed, the book has been so despised that at one time the name "Old Nick" was a synonym for the Devil. Although his works have been somewhat more charitably interpreted in recent years, the view persists that Machiavelli was little more than a "teacher of evil" who urged political rulers to disregard conventional norms and values.

Beyond the appeal of tasting forbidden fruit, however, scholars have found other significant contributions in Machiavelli's work. Offering a rational, empirical analysis of the modern state and politics, his writings (although appearing in the form of practical maxims) are considered a key forerunner of contemporary political science. Moreover, he also advocated a politics of civic republicanism and freedom that continues to shape a number of currents in democratic thought.

The diverse, contradictory character of Machiavelli's writings is, to some extent, mirrored in his life. Born in 1469, Machiavelli spent his early career as a diplomat and administrator for his native city of Florence. Though he never attained the rank of ambassador, he conducted several diplomatic missions and became something of an expert in military affairs. When the Florentine republic fell and was replaced by the rule of the Medici family in 1512, Machiavelli was forced out of office and began a lifetime of study of history and politics. After years of seeking favors from the Medici, Machiavelli returned to public service in 1525, only to be removed with the Medici themselves a year later. Machiavelli died soon afterward, unable to win the trust of Florence's new republican leaders.

Machiavelli believes regimes fall into two types, principalities and republics. In *The Prince,* he offers advice on how to acquire and maintain a principality. To do so, a wise ruler would follow the path set forth by necessity, glory, and the good of the state. Combining machismo, martial spirit, and political sagacity (like the great rulers and heroes of the past), such a ruler should have: (1) the capability to be both good and bad; (2) traits such as boldness, ruthlessness, independence, discipline, and self-control; and, (3) a reputation for generosity, mercy, trustworthiness, and piety. In this way, a ruler can meet the problems of political life head-on, fulfill one's duty to the state, and achieve glory and historical immortality.

By contrast, Machiavelli turns his attention in the *Discourses* (a commentary, published in 1519, on a history of Rome written by Titus Livius) to the creation, maintenance, and renovation of a republican government. There, he suggests that, while the founder or reformer of a state should act alone or even ruthlessly, maintaining a state over the long haul requires a virtuous, democratic rule by the many. Maintenance, it should be noted, does not mean mere persistence; it also connotes the promotion of freedom and political stability, the avoidance of corruption and decadence. For Machiavelli, then, glory (princely or republican) is the definitive political ambition, pursued within limits set by reason, prudence, fortune, and necessity.

The Prince and The Discourses

Machiavelli's *The Prince* is an intriguing little book of advice to any ruler interested in conquering or reforming a state. Though of humble origin, Machiavelli feels he can give such advice not only because of his lengthy study of public affairs, but also because "one needs to be a ruler to understand properly the character of the people, and to be a man of the people to understand properly the character of rulers."[1] From this realistic standpoint, Machiavelli examines the traits for which rulers are praised or blamed. He advises the prince to do whatever is necessary, no matter how apparently vicious, since people are ultimately concerned only with outcomes—that is, with the good of the state. Of course, even a vicious prince must contend with the fickle nature of changing circumstances, the capriciousness of fortune.

The selections from Book One of the *Discourses* illustrate Machiavelli's classical scholarship and his disillusionment with princely rule. Machiavelli begins by outlining a typology of forms of government and the cycle through which governments pass from virtuous to corrupt forms. This leads quite naturally to a general discussion of corrupt peoples and institutions, and the means to renovate and reconstitute political life. Once that reconstitution occurs, Machiavelli (upon comparing the respective virtues and vices of masses and princes) recommends popular rule as the path of stability, security, and glory.

Commentaries

One long-standing dispute among Machiavelli scholars has concerned the extent to which *The Prince* can be reconciled with the *Discourses.* In this context, John

---

1. Niccolo Machiavelli, *The Prince,* edited by Quentin Skinner and Russell Price (Cambridge: Cambridge University Press, 1988), p. 4.

Leonard examines the vocabulary (particularly the concepts of *virtù* and *bontà*) Machiavelli employs in his defense of extraordinary action taken to remedy political and social decadence. In short, no matter whether he is advising princes or peoples, Machiavelli's chief concern is to preserve the public sphere (political life) from the corrupting influences of private interests.

The final piece in this section offers a captivating solution to the problem of reconciling Machiavelli's main political works. Mary Dietz essentially suggests that, his reputation to the contrary, Machiavelli (though undoubtedly a schemer) never really abandoned his basic political stance of civic republicanism. She highlights some representative views of *The Prince,* finds them inadequate in various ways, and then advances the claim that Machiavelli's book is a trap for any ruler foolish enough to heed its ostensible advice.

Key Words

Virtù. The special qualities of an individual or a people that make for success in political life. *Virtù* should be distinguished from both classical humanist (emphasizing dispassionate rationality) and Christian (stressing honesty, charity, and piety) concepts of virtue.

Civic Republicanism. An ideological or philosophical position advocating popular rule and widespread political participation.

For Further Reading

Anglo, S. 1969. *Machiavelli: A Dissection.* New York: Harcourt, Brace & World.

Fleisher, M. ed. 1972. *Machiavelli and the Nature of Political Thought.* New York: Atheneum.

Pitkin, H.F. 1984. *Fortune is a Woman: Gender and Politics in the Thought of Niccolo Machiavelli.* Berkeley: University of California Press.

Pocock, J.G.A. 1975. *The Machiavellian Moment: Florentine Political Thought and the Atlantic Republican Tradition.* Princeton, N.J.: Princeton University Press.

Skinner, Q. 1981. *Machiavelli.* Oxford: Oxford University Press.

The Prince

Chapter XV
The things for which men,
and especially rulers,
are praised or blamed

It remains now to consider in what ways a ruler should act with regard to his subjects and allies.[1] And since I am well aware that many people have written about this subject I fear that I may be thought presumptuous, for what I have to say differs from the precepts offered by others, especially on this matter. But because I want to write what will be useful to anyone who understands, it seems to me better to concentrate on what really happens rather than on theories or speculations. For many have imagined republics and principalities that have never been seen or known to exist.[2] However, how men live is so different from how they should live that a ruler who does not do what is generally done, but persists in doing what ought to be done, will undermine his power rather than maintain it. If a ruler who wants always to act honourably is surrounded by many unscrupulous men his downfall is inevitable. Therefore, a ruler who wishes to maintain his power must be prepared to act immorally when this becomes necessary.

I shall set aside fantasies about rulers, then, and consider what happens in fact. I say that whenever men are discussed, and especially rulers (because they occupy more exalted positions), they are praised or blamed for possessing some of the following qualities. Thus, one man is considered generous, another miserly (I use this Tuscan term because *avaro* in our tongue also signifies someone who is rapacious, whereas we call *misero* someone who is very reluctant to use his own possessions); one is considered a free giver, another rapacious; one cruel, another merciful; one treacherous, another loyal; one effeminate and weak, another indomitable and spirited; one affable, another haughty; one lascivious, another moderate; one upright, another cunning; one inflexible, another easy-going; one serious, another frivolous; one devout, another unbelieving, and so on.

I know that everyone will acknowledge that it would be most praiseworthy for a ruler to have all the above-mentioned qualities that are held to be good. But because it is not possible to have all of them, and because circumstances do not permit living a completely virtuous life, one must be sufficiently prudent to know how to avoid becoming notorious for those vices that would destroy one's power and seek to avoid those vices that are

Reprinted from *The Prince* (edited by Quentin Skinner and Russell Price.) 1988. Cambridge: Cambridge University Press, pp. 54–63, 84–87. Reprinted with permission of Cambridge University Press.

1. A ruler's conduct towards subjects is treated in Chs. XV–XVII, towards allies *(amici)* in Ch. XVIII.

2. M. apparently refers both to some ancient writers (e.g., Plato, in his *Republic*) and to more recent ones who emphasised ideals and the duties of rulers.

not politically dangerous; but if one cannot bring oneself to do this, they can be indulged in with fewer misgivings. Yet one should not be troubled about becoming notorious for those vices without which it is difficult to preserve one's power, because if one considers everything carefully, doing some things that seem virtuous may result in one's ruin, whereas doing other things that seem vicious may strengthen one's position and cause one to flourish.

Chapter XVI
Generosity and meanness

To begin, then, with the first of the above-mentioned qualities, I maintain that it would be desirable to be considered generous; nevertheless, if generosity is practised in such a way that you will be considered generous, it will harm you. If it is practised virtuously, and as it should be, it will not be known about, and you will not avoid acquiring a bad reputation for the opposite vice. Therefore, if one wants to keep up a reputation for being generous, one must spend lavishly and ostentatiously. The inevitable outcome of acting in such ways is that the ruler will consume all his resources in sumptuous display; and if he wants to continue to be thought generous, he will eventually be compelled to become rapacious, to tax the people very heavily, and raise money by all possible means. Thus, he will begin to be hated by his subjects and, because he is impoverished, he will be held in little regard. Since this generosity of his has harmed many people and benefited few, he will feel the effects of any discontent, and the first real threat to his power will involve him in grave difficulties. When he realises this, and changes his ways, he will very soon acquire a bad reputation for being miserly.

Therefore, since a ruler cannot both practise this virtue of generosity and be known to do so without harming himself, he would do well not to worry about being called miserly. For eventually he will come to be considered more generous, when it is realised that, because of his parsimony, his revenues are sufficient to defend himself against any enemies that attack him, and to undertake campaigns without imposing special taxes on the people. Thus he will be acting generously towards the vast majority, whose property he does not touch, and will be acting meanly towards the few to whom he gives nothing.

Those rulers who have achieved great things in our own times have all been considered mean; all the others have failed. Although Pope Julius cultivated a reputation for generosity in order to become pope,[3] he did not seek to maintain it afterwards, because he wanted to be able to wage war. The present King of France[4] has fought many wars without imposing any special taxes on his subjects, because his parsimonious habits have always enabled him to meet the extra expenses. If the present King of Spain[5] had a reputation for generosity, he would not have successfully undertaken so many campaigns.

---

3. I.e., by bribes.

4. Louis XII.

5. Ferdinand the Catholic.

Therefore, a ruler should worry little about being thought miserly: he will not have to rob his subjects; he will be able to defend himself; he will avoid being poor and despised and will not be forced to become rapacious. For meanness is one of those vices that enable him to rule. It may be objected that Caesar obtained power through his open-handedness, and that many others have risen to very high office because they were open-handed and were considered to be so. I would reply that either you are already an established ruler or you are trying to become a ruler. In the first case, open-handedness is harmful; in the second, it is certainly necessary to be thought open-handed. Caesar was one of those who sought power in Rome; but if after gaining power he had survived, and had not moderated his expenditure, he would have undermined his power. And if it should be objected that many rulers who have been considered very generous have had remarkable military successes, I would reply: a ruler spends either what belongs to him or his subjects, or what belongs to others. In the former case, he should be parsimonious; in the latter, he should be as open-handed as possible. A ruler who accompanies his army, supporting it by looting, sacking and extortions, disposes of what belongs to others; he must be open-handed, for if he is not, his soldiers will desert. You can be much more generous with what does not belong to you or to your subjects, as Cyrus, Caesar and Alexander were. This is because giving away what belongs to others in no way damages your reputation; rather, it enhances it. It is only giving away what belongs to yourself that harms you.

There is nothing that is so self-consuming as generosity: the more you practise it, the less you will be able to continue to practise it. You will either become poor and despised or your efforts to avoid poverty will make you rapacious and hated. A ruler must above all guard against being despised and hated; and being generous will lead to both. Therefore, it is shrewder to cultivate a reputation for meanness, which will lead to notoriety but not to hatred. This is better than being forced, through wanting to be considered generous, to incur a reputation for rapacity, which will lead to notoriety and to hatred as well.

Chapter XVII
Cruelty and mercifulness; and whether it is better to be loved or feared

Turning to the other previously mentioned qualities, I maintain that every ruler should want to be thought merciful, not cruel; nevertheless, one should take care not to be merciful in an inappropriate way. Cesare Borgia was considered cruel, yet his harsh measures restored order to the Romagna, unifying it and rendering it peaceful and loyal. If his conduct is properly considered, he will be judged to have been much more merciful than the Florentine people, who let Pistoia be torn apart, in order to avoid acquiring a reputation for cruelty. Therefore, if a ruler can keep his subjects united and loyal, he should not worry about incurring a reputation for cruelty; for by punishing a very few he will really be more merciful than those who over-indulgently permit disorders to develop, with resultant killings and plunderings. For the latter usually harm a whole community, whereas the executions ordered by a ruler harm only specific individuals. And a new ruler, in particular, cannot avoid being considered harsh, since new states are full of dangers. Virgil makes Dido say:

Res dura, et regni novitas me talia cogunt moliri, et late fines custode tueri.[6]

Nevertheless, he should be slow to believe accusations and to act against individuals, and should not be afraid of his own shadow. He should act with due prudence and humanity so that being over-confident will not make him incautious, and being too suspicious will not render him insupportable.

A controversy has arisen about this: whether it is better to be loved than feared, or vice versa. My view is that it is desirable to be both loved and feared; but it is difficult to achieve both and, if one of them has to be lacking, it is much safer to be feared than loved.

For this may be said of men generally: they are ungrateful, fickle, feigners and dissemblers, avoiders of danger, eager for gain. While you benefit them they are all devoted to you: they would shed their blood for you; they offer their possessions, their lives, and their sons, as I said before, when the need to do so is far off. But when you are hard pressed, they turn away. A ruler who has relied completely on their promises, and has neglected to prepare other defences, will be ruined, because friendships that are acquired with money, and not through greatness and nobility of character, are paid for but not secured, and prove unreliable just when they are needed.

Men are less hesitant about offending or harming a ruler who makes himself loved than one who inspires fear. For love is sustained by a bond of gratitude which, because men are excessively self-interested, is broken whenever they see a chance to benefit themselves. But fear is sustained by a dread of punishment that is always effective. Nevertheless, a ruler must make himself feared in such a way that, even if he does not become loved, he does not become hated. For it is perfectly possible to be feared without incurring hatred. And this can always be achieved if he refrains from laying hands on the property of his citizens and subjects, and on their womenfolk. If it is necessary to execute anyone, this should be done only if there is a proper justification and obvious reason. But, above all, he must not touch the property of others, because men forget sooner the killing of a father than the loss of their patrimony. Moreover, there will always be pretexts for seizing property; and someone who begins to live rapaciously will always find pretexts for taking the property of others. On the other hand, reasons or pretexts for taking life are rarer and more fleeting.

However, when a ruler is with his army, and commands a large force, he must not worry about being considered harsh, because armies are never kept united and prepared for military action unless their leader is thought to be harsh. Among the remarkable things recounted about Hannibal is that, although he had a very large army, composed of men from many countries, and fighting in foreign lands, there never arose any dissension, either among themselves or against their leader, whether things were going well or badly.

---

6. Virgil. *Aeneid.* 563–4: 'Harsh necessity and the newness of my kingdom force me to do such things, and to guard all the frontiers.'

This could be accounted for only by his inhuman cruelty which, together with his many good qualities, made him always respected and greatly feared by his troops. And if he had not been so cruel, his other qualities would not have been sufficient to achieve that effect. Thoughtless writers admire this achievement of his, yet condemn the main reason for it.

That his other qualities would not have sufficed is proved by what happened to Scipio, considered a most remarkable man not only in his own times but in all others, whose armies rebelled against him in Spain. The only reason for this was that he was over-indulgent, and permitted his soldiers more freedom than was consistent with maintaining proper military discipline. Fabius Maximus rebuked him for this in the senate, and called him a corrupter of the Roman army. And when Locri was ravaged by one of Scipio's legates, the inhabitants were not avenged by him, and the legate was not punished for his arrogance, all because Scipio was too easy-going. Indeed, a speaker in the senate who wished to excuse him said that there were many men who were better at not committing misdeeds themselves than punishing the misdeeds of others. This character of his would eventually have tarnished his fame and glory, if he had continued his military command unchecked; but since he was controlled by the senate, this harmful quality was not only concealed but contributed to his glory.

Returning to the matter of being feared and loved, then, I conclude that whether men bear affection depends on themselves, but whether they are afraid will depend on what the ruler does. A wise ruler should rely on what is under his own control, not on what is under the control of others; he should contrive only to avoid incurring hatred, as I have said.

Chapter XVIII
How rulers should keep their promises

Everyone knows how praiseworthy it is for a ruler to keep his promises, and live uprightly and not by trickery. Nevertheless, experience shows that in our times the rulers who have done great things are those who have set little store by keeping their word, being skilful rather in cunningly confusing men; they have got the better of those who have relied on being trustworthy.

You should know, then, that there are two ways of contending: one by using laws, the other, force. The first is appropriate for men, the second for animals; but because the former is often ineffective, one must have recourse to the latter. Therefore, a ruler must know well how to imitate beasts as well as employing properly human means. This policy was taught to rulers allegorically by ancient writers: they tell how Achilles and many other ancient rulers were entrusted to Chiron the centaur, to be raised carefully by him. Having a mentor who was half-beast and half-man signifies that a ruler needs to use both natures, and that one without the other is not effective.

Since a ruler, then, must know how to act like a beast, he should imitate both the fox and the lion, for the lion is liable to be trapped, whereas the fox cannot ward off wolves. One needs, then, to be a fox to recognise traps, and a lion to frighten away wolves. Those who rely merely upon a lion's strength do not understand matters.

Therefore, a prudent ruler cannot keep his word, nor should he, when such fidelity would damage him, and when the reasons that made him promise are no longer relevant. This advice would not be sound if all men were upright; but because they are treacherous and would not keep their promises to you, you should not consider yourself bound to keep your promises to them.

Moreover, plausible reasons can always be found for such failure to keep promises. One could give countless modern examples of this, and show how many peace treaties and promises have been rendered null and void by the faithlessness of rulers; and those best able to imitate the fox have succeeded best. But foxiness should be well concealed: one must be a great feigner and dissembler. And men are so naive, and so much dominated by immediate needs, that a skilful deceiver always finds plenty of people who will let themselves be deceived.

I must mention one recent case: Alexander VI was concerned only with deceiving men, and he always found them gullible. No man ever affirmed anything more forcefully or with stronger oaths but kept his word less. Nevertheless, his deceptions were always effective, because he well understood the naivety of men.

A ruler, then, need not actually possess all the above-mentioned qualities, but he must certainly seem to. Indeed, I shall be so bold as to say that having and always cultivating them is harmful, whereas seeming to have them is useful; for instance, to seem merciful, trustworthy, humane, upright and devout, and also to be so. But if it becomes necessary to refrain, you must be prepared to act in the opposite way, and be capable of doing it. And it must be understood that a ruler, and especially a new ruler, cannot always act in ways that are considered good because, in order to maintain his power, he is often forced to act treacherously, ruthlessly or inhumanely, and disregard the precepts of religion. Hence, he must be prepared to vary his conduct as the winds of fortune and changing circumstances constrain him and, as I said before, not deviate from right conduct if possible, but be capable of entering upon the path of wrongdoing when this becomes necessary.

A ruler, then, should be very careful that everything he says is replete with the five above-named qualities: to those who see and hear him, he should seem to be exceptionally merciful, trustworthy, upright, humane and devout. And it is most necessary of all to seem devout. In these matters, most men judge more by their eyes than by their hands. For everyone is capable of seeing you, but few can touch you. Everyone can see what you appear to be, whereas few have direct experience of what you really are, and those few will not dare to challenge the popular view, sustained as it is by the majesty of the ruler's position. With regard to all human actions, and especially those of rulers, who cannot be called to account, men pay attention to the outcome. If a ruler, then, contrives to conquer, and to preserve the state, the means will always be judged to be honourable and be praised by everyone. For the common people are impressed by appearances and results. Everywhere the common people are the vast majority, and the few are isolated when the majority and the government are at one. One present-day ruler, whom it is well to leave unnamed, is always preaching peace and trust, although he is really very hostile to both; and if he had practised them he would have lost either reputation or power several times over.

Chapter XXV
How much power fortune has over human affairs, and how it should be resisted

I am not unaware that many have thought, and many still think, that the affairs of the world are so ruled by fortune and by God that the ability of men cannot control them. Rather, they think that we have no remedy at all; and therefore it could be concluded that it is useless to sweat much over things, but let them be governed by fate. This opinion has been more popular in our own times because of the great changes that have taken place and are still to be seen even now, which could hardly have been predicted. When I think about this, I am sometimes inclined, to some extent, to share this opinion. Nevertheless, so as not to eliminate human freedom, I am disposed to hold that fortune is the arbiter of half our actions, but that it lets us control roughly the other half.

I compare fortune to one of those dangerous rivers that, when they become enraged, flood the plains, destroy trees and buildings, move earth from one place and deposit it in another. Everyone flees before it, everyone gives way to its thrust, without being able to halt it in any way. But this does not mean that, when the river is not in flood, men are unable to take precautions, by means of dykes and dams, so that when it rises next time, it will either not overflow its banks or, if it does, its force will not be so uncontrolled or damaging.

The same happens with fortune, which shows its powers where no force has been organised to resist it, and therefore strikes in the places where it knows that no dykes or dams have been built to restrain it. And if you consider Italy, which has been the seat of these changes, and which has given rise to them, you will see a countryside devoid of any embankments or defences. If it had been protected by proper defences, like Germany, Spain and France, the flood would not have caused such great changes or it would not have occurred at all. But I have said enough in general terms about resisting fortune.

Considering the matter in more detail, I would observe that one sees a ruler flourishing today and ruined tomorrow, without his having changed at all in character or qualities. I believe this is attributable, first, to the cause previously discussed at length, namely, that a ruler who trusts entirely to luck comes to grief when his luck runs out. Moreover, I believe that we are successful when our ways are suited to the times and circumstances, and unsuccessful when they are not. For one sees that, in the things that lead to the end which everyone aims at, that is, glory and riches, men proceed in different ways: one man cautiously, another impetuously; one man forcefully, another cunningly; one man patiently, another impatiently, and each of these different ways of acting can be effective. On the other hand, of two cautious men, one may achieve his aims and the other fail. Again, two men may both succeed, although they have different characters, one acting cautiously and the other impetuously. The reason for these different outcomes is whether their ways of acting conform with the conditions in which they operate. Consequently, as I have said, two men, acting differently, may achieve the same results; and if two men act in the same way, one may succeed and the other fail. From this, again, arise changes in prosperity; because if a man acts cautiously and patiently, and the times and circumstances change in ways for which his methods are appropriate, he will be successful. But if the times and circumstances change again, he will come to grief, because he does not change his methods. And one does not find men who are so prudent that they are capable of being sufficiently flexible: either because our natural inclinations are too strong to permit us to change, or because, having always fared well by acting in a certain way, we do not think it a good idea to change our methods. Therefore, if it is necessary for a cautious man to act expeditiously, he does not know how to do it; this leads to his failure. But if it were possible to change one's character to suit the times and circumstances, one would always be successful.

Pope Julius II always acted impetuously, and found the times and circumstances so suited to his ways that he was always successful. Consider the first expedition he made to Bologna, while messer Giovanni Bentivoglio was still alive. The Venetians were opposed to it, and so was the King of Spain; there were also discussions with the King of France about such an enterprise. Nevertheless, acting with his usual indomitable spirit and impetuosity, he led the expedition personally. This initiative caught the King of Spain and the Venetians off guard and constrained them to be passive spectators, the latter through fear and the former because of his desire to recover the whole of the Kingdom of Naples. On the other hand, Julius involved the King of France: for that King saw the Pope moving and, because he wanted to cultivate the Pope's friendship with a view to reducing the power of Venice, he decided that he could not refuse him troops without offending him very openly. With this swift initiative, then, Julius achieved what no other pope, acting with consummate prudence, could have attained. If he had not left Rome until everything had been agreed and settled, as any other pope would have done, he would never have succeeded. For the King of France would have contrived to find countless excuses, and the others would have produced countless reasons why the Pope should hesitate. I shall not discuss his other actions, which were similar in character, and all turned out well for him. The shortness of his pontificate did not permit him to taste of failure. But if circumstances had changed so that it was imperative to act cautiously, he would have been undone; for he would never have deviated from the methods that were natural to him.

I conclude, then, that since circumstances vary and men when acting lack flexibility, they are successful if their methods match the circumstances and unsuccessful if they do not. I certainly think that it is better to be impetuous than cautious, because fortune is a woman and if you want to control her, it is necessary to treat her roughly. And it is clear that she is more inclined to yield to men who are impetuous than to those who are calculating. Since fortune is a woman, she is always well disposed towards young men, because they are less cautious and more aggressive, and treat her more boldly.

The Discourses

2. How many Kinds of State there are and of what Kind was that of Rome

I propose to dispense with a discussion of cities which from the outset have been subject to another power, and shall speak only of those which have from the outset been far removed from any kind of external servitude, but, instead, have from the start been governed in accordance with their wishes, whether as republics or principalities. As such cities have had diverse origins, so too they have had diverse laws and institutions. For either at the outset, or before very long, to some of them laws have been given by some one person at some one time, as laws were given to the Spartans by Lycurgus; whereas others have acquired them by chance and at different times as occasion arose. This was the case in Rome.

Happy indeed should we call that state which produces a man so prudent that men can live securely under the laws which he prescribes without having to emend them. Sparta, for instance, observed its laws for more than eight hundred years without corrupting them and without any dangerous disturbance. Unhappy, on the other hand, in some degree is that city to be deemed which, not having chanced to meet with a prudent organizer, has to reorganize itself. And, of such, that is the more unhappy which is the more remote from order; and that is the more remote from order whose institutions have missed altogether the straight road which leads it to its perfect and true destiny. For it is almost impossible that states of this type should by any eventuality be set on the right road again; whereas those which, if their order is not perfect, have made a good beginning and are capable of improvement, may become perfect should something happen which provides the opportunity. It should, however, be noted that they will never introduce order without incurring danger, because few men ever welcome new laws setting up a new order in the state unless necessity makes it clear to them that there is need for such laws; and since such a necessity cannot arise without danger, the state may easily be ruined before the new order has been brought to completion. The republic of Florence bears this out, for owing to what happened at Arezzo in '02 it was reconstituted, and owing to what happened at Prato in '12 its constitution was destroyed.

It being now my intention to discuss what were the institutions of the city of Rome and what events conduced to its perfection, I would remark that those who have written about states say that there are to be found in them one of three forms of government, called by them *Principality, Aristocracy* and *Democracy*, and that those who set up a government in any particular state must adopt one of them, as best suits their purpose.

Reprinted from *The Discourses* (edited and with an introduction by Bernard Crick, translated by Leslie J. Walker and revised by Brian Richardson) 1970. London: Penguin, pp. 104–109, 160–164, 252–257. With permission.

Others—and with better judgement many think—say that there are six
types of government of which three are very bad, and three are good in
themselves but easily become corrupt, so that they too must be classed as
pernicious. Those that are good are the three above mentioned. Those that
are bad are the other three, which depend on them, and each of them is so
like the one associated with it that it easily passes from one form to the
other. For *Principality* easily becomes *Tyranny*. From *Aristocracy* the transition to *Oligarchy* is an easy one. *Democracy* is without difficulty converted
into *Anarchy*. So that if anyone who is organizing a commonwealth sets up
one of the three first forms of government, he sets up what will last but for
a while, since there are no means whereby to prevent it passing into its
contrary, on account of the likeness which in such a case virtue has to vice.

These variations of government among men are due to chance. For in the
beginning of the world, when its inhabitants were few, they lived for a time
scattered like the beasts. Then, with the multiplication of their offspring,
they drew together and, in order the better to be able to defend themselves,
began to look about for a man stronger and more courageous than the rest,
made him their head, and obeyed him.

It was thus that men learned how to distinguish what is honest and good
from what is pernicious and wicked, for the sight of someone injuring his
benefactor evoked in them hatred and sympathy and they blamed the
ungrateful and respected those who showed gratitude, well aware that the
same injuries might have been done to themselves. Hence to prevent evil of
this kind they took to making laws and to assigning punishments to those
who contravened them. The notion of justice thus came into being.

In this way it came about that, when later on they had to choose a prince,
they did not have recourse to the boldest as formerly, but to one who
excelled in prudence and justice.

But when at a yet later stage they began to make the prince hereditary
instead of electing him, his heirs soon began to degenerate as compared with
their ancestors, and, forsaking virtuous deeds, considered that princes have
nought else to do but to surpass other men in extravagance, lasciviousness,
and every other form of licentiousness. With the result that the prince came
to be hated, and, since he was hated, came to be afraid, and from fear soon
passed to offensive action, which quickly brought about a tyranny.

From which, before long, was begotten the source of their downfall; for
tyranny gave rise to conspiracies and plots against princes, organized not by
timid and weak men, but by men conspicuous for their liberality, magna-
nimity, wealth and ability, for such men could not stand the dishonourable
life the prince was leading. The masses, therefore, at the instigation of these
powerful leaders, took up arms against the prince, and, when he had been
liquidated, submitted to the authority of those whom they looked upon as
their liberators. Hence the latter, to whom the very term 'sole head' had
become odious, formed themselves into a government. Moreover, in the
beginning, mindful of what they had suffered under a tyranny, they ruled in
accordance with the laws which they had made, subordinated their own
convenience to the common advantage, and, both in private matters and
public affairs, governed and preserved order with the utmost diligence.

But when the administration passed to their descendants who had no
experience of the changeability of fortune, had not been through bad times,

and instead of remaining content with the civic equality then prevailing, reverted to avarice, ambition and to seizing other men's womenfolk, they caused government by an aristocracy to become government by an oligarchy in which civic rights were entirely disregarded; so that in a short time there came to pass in their case the same thing as happened to the tyrant, for the masses, sick of their government, were ready to help anyone who had any sort of plan for attacking their rulers; and so there soon arose someone who with the aid of the masses liquidated them.

Then, since the memory of the prince and of the injuries inflicted by him was still fresh, and since, having got rid of government by the few, they had no desire to return to that of a prince, they turned to a democratic form of government, which they organized in such a way that no sort of authority was vested either in a few powerful men or in a prince.

And, since all forms of government are to some extent respected at the outset, this democratic form of government maintained itself for a while but not for long, especially when the generation that had organized it had passed away. For anarchy quickly supervened, in which no respect was shown either for the individual or for the official, and which was such that, as everyone did what he liked, all sorts of outrages were constantly committed. The outcome was inevitable. Either at the suggestion of some good man or because this anarchy had to be got rid of somehow, principality was once again restored. And from this there was, stage by stage, a return to anarchy, by way of the transitions and for the reasons assigned.

This, then, is the cycle through which all commonwealths pass, whether they govern themselves or are governed. But rarely do they return to the same form of government, for there can scarce be a state of such vitality that it can undergo often such changes and yet remain in being. What usually happens is that, while in a state of commotion in which it lacks both counsel and strength, a state becomes subject to a neighbouring and better organized state. Were it not so, a commonwealth might go on for ever passing through these governmental transitions.

I maintain then, that all the forms of government mentioned above are far from satisfactory, the three good ones because their life is so short, the three bad ones because of their inherent malignity. Hence prudent legislators, aware of their defects, refrained from adopting as such any one of these forms, and chose instead one that shared in them all, since they thought such a government would be stronger and more stable, for if in one and the same state there was principality, aristocracy and democracy each would keep watch over the other. . . .

18. How in Corrupt Cities a Free Government can be maintained where it exists, or be established where it does not exist

It will not, I think, be foreign to my purpose nor contrary to the plan of my previous discourse to consider whether in a corrupt city it is possible to maintain a free government where it exists, and whether, when there has been none, it can be set up. In regard to this question I maintain that in either case it will be a very difficult thing to do. It is, moreover, almost impossible to lay down rules, for the method to be adopted will of necessity depend upon the degree of corruption. None the less, since it is well to take account of all cases, I do not propose to shelve the question. I suppose then an exceedingly corrupt state, whereby the difficulty will clearly be intensified, since in it there will be found neither laws nor institutions which will suffice to check widespread corruption. Because, just as for the maintenance of good customs laws are required, so if laws are to be observed, there is need of good customs. Furthermore, institutions and laws made in the early days of a republic when men were good, no longer serve their purpose when men have become bad. And, if by any chance the laws of the state are changed, there will never, or but rarely, be a change in its institutions. The result is that new laws are ineffectual, because the institutions, which remain constant, corrupt them.

In order to make this point more clear I would point out that in Rome there was a constitution regulating its government, or rather its form of government, and then laws enabling the magistrates to keep the citizens in order. To the constitution determining its form of government pertained the authority vested in the people, the senate, the tribunes, and in the consuls, the method of applying for and of appointing to magisterial posts, and its legislative procedure. These institutions underwent little or no change in the course of events, whereas there were changes in the laws which kept the citizens in order. There was, for instance, the law concerning adultery, the sumptuary law, a law concerning ambition, and many others. These laws were introduced step by step as the citizens became corrupt. But since the institutions determining its form of government remained unchanged and, when corruption had set in, were no longer good, these modifications of the laws did not suffice to keep men good, though they might have helped had the introduction of new laws been accompanied by a modification of the institutions.

That it is true to say that such institutions would not be good in a corrupted state is clearly seen in two important cases, in the appointing of magistrates and in the making of laws. The Roman people had never given the consulate or any other important office in the city except to such as had applied for the post. This institution was at the outset good, because only such citizens applied for posts as judged themselves worthy to fill them, and to be rejected was looked upon as ignominious; so that everybody behaved well in order to be judged worthy. This procedure, when the city became corrupt, was extremely harmful; because not those who had more virtue, but those who had more power, applied for magistracies, and the powerless, though virtuous, refrained from applying through fear. This inconvenience did not come about all at once, but by stages, as is the case with all inconveniences. For when the Romans had conquered Africa and Asia, and had reduced the greater part of Greece to subjection, they had become secure as to their liberty nor had they any more enemies whom there was ground to fear. This sense of security and this weakness on the part of their enemies caused the Roman people in appointing to the consulate to consider not a man's virtue, but his popularity. This drew to that office men who knew better how to get round men, not those who knew better how to conquer enemies. They then turned from those who had more popularity and gave it to those who had more power. Thus owing to the defectiveness of this institution it came about that good men were wholly excluded from consular rank.

Again, a tribune or any other citizen could propose to the people a law, in regard to which every citizen was entitled to speak either in favour of it or against, prior to a decision being reached. This institution was good so long as the citizens were good, because it is always a good thing that anyone anxious to serve the public should be able to propose his plan. It is also a good thing that everyone should be at liberty to express his opinion on it, so that when the people have heard what each has to say they may choose the best plan. But when the citizens had become perverse, this institution became a nuisance; because only the powerful proposed laws, and this for the sake, not of their common liberties, but to augment their own power. And against such projects no one durst speak for fear of such folk; with the result that the people were induced, either by deceit or by force, to adopt measures which spelt their own ruin.

In order to maintain Rome's liberty, therefore, when corruption had set in, it was necessary in the course of its development to introduce new institutions just as there had been made new laws; for different institutions and a different procedure should be prescribed for the governed according as they are good or bad, since similar forms cannot subsist in matter which is disposed in a contrary manner. Now defective institutions must either be renovated all at once as soon as the decline from goodness is noticed, or little by little before they become known to everybody. Neither of which courses is possible, I maintain. For if the renovation is to take place little by little, there is need of someone who shall see the inconvenience coming while yet it is far off and in its infancy. But it may quite easily happen in a state that no such person will ever arise, or, should he arise in point of fact, that he will never be able to persuade others to see things as he does himself; for men accustomed to a certain mode of life are reluctant to change it, especially when they have not themselves noticed the evil in question, but have had their attention called to it by conjectures. While with regard to modifying institutions all at once when everybody realizes that they are no good, I would point out that, though it is easy to recognize their futility, it is not easy to correct it; for, to do this, normal methods will not suffice now that normal methods are bad. Hence it is necessary to resort to extraordinary methods, such as the use of force and an appeal to arms, and, before doing anything, to become a prince in the state, so that one can dispose it as one thinks fit.

But, to reconstitute political life in a state presupposes a good man, whereas to have recourse to violence in order to make oneself prince in a republic supposes a bad man. Hence very rarely will there be found a good man ready to use bad methods in order to make himself prince, though with a good end in view, nor yet a bad man who, having become a prince, is ready to do the right thing and to whose mind it will occur to use well that authority which he has acquired by bad means.

It is on account of all this that it is difficult, or rather impossible, either to maintain a republican form of government in states which have become corrupt or to create such a form afresh. Should a republic simply have to be created or to be maintained, it would be necessary to introduce into it a form of government akin rather to a monarchy than to a democracy, so that those men whose arrogance is such that they cannot be corrected by legal processes, may yet be restrained to some extent by a quasi-regal power. To try to make them become good in any other way would be either a most brutal or an impossible undertaking—the kind of thing that Cleomenes did, as I said above; for that he might rule alone, he killed the ephors, and for the same reasons Romulus killed his brother and Titus Tatius killed the Sabine, and afterwards both of them made good use of their authority. It should, however, be noted that neither the one nor the other had subjects steeped in corruption, which in this chapter we have taken as the basis of our argument; so that both were able to resolve on such steps, and, having done so, to camouflage their plan.

58. The Masses are more Knowing and more Constant than is a Prince

Nothing is more futile and more inconstant than are the masses. So says our author, Titus Livy, and so say all other historians. For in the records of the actions men have performed one often finds the masses condemning someone to death, and then lamenting him and ardently wishing he were alive. The Roman people did this in Manlius Capitolinus's case: first they condemned him to death, then urgently wished him back. Of this our author says that 'soon after he had ceased to be a danger, the desire for him took hold of the people'. And again, when describing the events which happened in Syracuse after the death of Hieronymus, the nephew of Hiero, he says: 'It is of the nature of the masses either servilely to obey or arrogantly to domineer.'

I know not whether the view I am about to adopt will prove so hard to uphold and so full of difficulties that I shall have either shamefully to abandon it or laboriously to maintain it; for I propose to defend a position which all writers attack, as I have said. But, however that may be, I think, and always shall think there can be no harm in defending an opinion by arguments so long as one has no intention of appealing either to authority or force.

I claim, then, that for the failing for which writers blame the masses, any body of men one cares to select may be blamed, and especially princes; for anyone who does not regulate his conduct by laws will make the same mistakes as the masses are guilty of. This is easily seen, for there are and have been any number of princes, but of good and wise ones there have been but few. I am speaking of princes who have succeeded in breaking the bonds which might have held them in check; among which I do not include those kings who were born in Egypt when that most ancient of ancient realms was governed in accordance with the law, nor those born in Sparta, nor those born in France in our own times, for the kingdom of France is better regulated by laws than is any other of which at present we have knowledge. Kings who are born under such conditions are not to be classed among those whose nature we have to consider in each individual case to see whether it resembles that of the masses; for, should there be masses regulated by laws in the same way as they are, there will be found in them the same goodness as we find in kings, and it will be seen that they neither 'arrogantly dominate nor servilely obey'. Such was the Roman populace which, so long as the republic remained uncorrupt, was never servilely obsequious, nor yet did it ever dominate with arrogance: on the contrary, it had its own institutions and magistrates and honourably kept its own place. But when it was necessary to take action against some powerful person, it did so, as is seen in the case of Manlius, of the Ten, and in the case of others who sought to oppress it. Also, when it had to obey dictators or consuls in the public interest, it did so. Nor is it any wonder that the Roman populace wanted Manlius Capitolinus back when he was dead, for what they wanted was his virtues, which had been such that his memory evoked everyone's sympathy, and would have had power to produce the same effect in a prince, for all writers are of opinion that virtue is praised and admired even in one's enemies. Again, had Manlius, in response to this desire, been raised from the dead, the Roman populace would have passed on him the same sentence as it did, have had him arrested and, shortly after, have condemned him to death: though, for that matter, one also finds that reputedly wise princes have put people to death and then wished them alive again; Alexander, for instance, in the case of Cleitus and other of his friends, and Herod in the case of Mariamne. But the truth is that what our historian says of the nature of the masses when disciplined by laws, as were the Romans, but of undisciplined masses, like those of Syracuse, which made the same kind of mistakes as do men when infuriated and undisciplined, just as did Alexander the Great and Herod in the cases cited.

The nature of the masses, then, is no more reprehensible than is the nature of princes, for all do wrong and to the same extent when there is nothing to prevent them doing wrong. Of this there are plenty of examples besides those given, both among the Roman emperors and among other tyrants and princes; and in them we find a degree of inconstancy and changeability in behaviour such as is never found in the masses.

I arrive, then, at a conclusion contrary to the common opinion which asserts that populaces, when in power, are variable, fickle and ungrateful; and affirm that in them these faults are in no wise different from those to be found in certain princes. Were the accusation made against both the masses and princes, it would be true; but, if princes be excepted, it is false. For when the populace is in power and is well-ordered, it will be stable, prudent and grateful, in much the same way, or in a better way, than is a prince, however wise he be thought. And, on the other hand, a prince who contemns the laws, will be more ungrateful, fickle and imprudent than is the populace. Nor is inconstancy of behaviour due to a difference in nature, for they are pretty much the same, or, if one be better than the other, it is the populace: it is due to the greater or less respect which they have for the laws under which both alike are living.

If we consider the Roman populace it will be found that for four hundred years they were enemies to the very name of king and lovers of glory and of the common good of their country. Of both characteristics the Roman populace affords numerous and striking examples. And, should anyone bring up against me the ingratitude the populace displayed towards Scipio, my answer is that I have already discussed this question at length and have there shown the ingratitude of the populace to be less than that of princes. While in the matter of prudence and stability I claim that the populace is more prudent, more stable, and of sounder judgement than the prince. Not without good reason is the voice of the populace likened to that of God; for public opinion is remarkably accurate in its prognostications, so much so that it seems as if the populace by some hidden power discerned the evil and the good that was to befall it. With regard to its judgement, when two speakers of equal skill are heard advocating different alternatives, very rarely does one find the populace failing to adopt the better view or incapable of appreciating the truth of what it hears. While, if in bold actions and such as appear advantageous it errs, as I have said above, so does a prince often err where his passions are involved, and these are much stronger than those of the populace.

It is found, too, that in the election of magistrates the populace makes a far better choice than does the prince; nor can the populace ever be persuaded that it is good to appoint to such an office a man of infamous life or corrupt habits, whereas a prince may easily and in a vast variety of ways be persuaded to do this. Again, one finds that when the populace begins to have a horror of something it remains of the same mind for many centuries; a thing that is never observed in the case of a prince. For both these characteristics I shall content myself with the evidence afforded by the Roman populace, which in the course of so many hundreds of years and so many elections of consuls and tribunes did not make four elections of which it had to repent. So much, too, as I have said, was the title of king hated that no service rendered by one of its citizens who ambitioned it, could render him immune from the penalties prescribed. Besides this, one finds that cities in which the populace is the prince, in a very short time extend vastly their dominions much more than do those which have always been under a prince; as Rome did after the expulsion of the kings, and Athens after it was free of Pisistratus.

This can only be due to one thing: government by the populace is better than government by princes. Nor do I care whether to this opinion of mine all that our historian has said in the aforesaid passage or what others have said, be objected; because if account be taken of all the disorders due to populaces and of all those due to princes, and of all the glories won by populaces and all those won by princes, it will be found that alike in goodness and in glory the populace is far superior. And if princes are superior to populaces in drawing up laws, codes of civic life, statutes and new institutions, the populace is so superior in sustaining what has been instituted, that it indubitably adds to the glory of those who have instituted them.

In short, to bring this topic to a conclusion, I say that, just as princely forms of government have endured for a very long time, so, too, have republican forms of government; and that in both cases it has been essential for them to be regulated by laws. For a prince who does what he likes is a lunatic, and a populace which does what it likes is unwise. If, therefore, it be a question of a prince subservient to the laws and of a populace chained up by laws, more virtue will be found in the populace than in the prince; and if it be a question of either of them loosed from control by the law, there will be found fewer errors in the populace than in the prince, and these of less moment and much easier to put right. For a licentious and turbulent populace, when a good man can obtain a hearing, can easily be brought to behave itself; but there is no one to talk to a bad prince, nor is there any remedy except the sword. From which an inference may be drawn in regard to the importance of their respective maladies; for, if to cure the malady of the populace a word suffices and the sword is needed to cure that of a prince, no one will fail to see that the greater the cure, the greater the fault.

When the populace has thrown off all restraint, it is not the mad things it does that are terrifying, nor is it of present evils that one is afraid, but of what may come of them, for amidst such confusion there may come to be a tyrant. In the case of bad princes it is just the opposite: it is present evils that are terrifying, but for the future there is hope, since men are convinced that the evil ways of a bad prince may make for freedom in the end. Thus one sees the difference between the two cases amounts to the same thing as the difference between what is and what must come to be. The brutalities of the masses are directed against those whom they suspect of conspiring against the common good; the brutalities of a prince against those whom he suspects of conspiring against his own good. The reason why people are prejudiced against the populace is because of the populace anyone may speak ill without fear and openly, even when the populace is ruling. But of princes people speak with the utmost trepidation and the utmost reserve.

Nor does it seem to me foreign to my purpose, since I find the topic attractive, to discuss in the next chapter on which more reliance can be placed, on confederations made by a republic or on confederations formed by a prince.

Public versus Private Claims: Machiavellianism from Another Perspective
John Leonard

Machiavellianism is frequently conceived of as a derivative of the term Machiavellian. The Oxford English Dictionary, beginning with its definition of Machiavellian, reads:

> Of, pertaining to, or characteristic of Machiavelli, or his alleged principles; following the methods recommended by Machiavelli in preferring expediency to morality; practicing duplicity in statecraft or in general conduct; an instance of this.

This derivation of Machiavellianism from Machiavellian has the effect of shifting attention from the foundations of Machiavelli's theory, which are reduced to the principle that expediency should always be placed ahead of morality, and focusing it on various methods and practices consistent with this principle.

The aim of this article is to present a broader interpretation of Machiavelli's theoretical concerns, one which seeks neither to support nor refute the common understanding of Machiavellianism but to go beyond it. To this end the problem of Machiavelli's attitude toward virtue is examined in the context of crucial terms in his conceptual vocabulary, and this examination is used in turn to shed light on other aspects of Machiavelli's thought.

1. Why Virtù Is Never Virtue

The first task in assessing the place of virtue in Machiavelli's political thought is to see if we can locate something that resembles virtue in his writings. The first word to consider, both because Machiavelli uses it frequently and because in appearance it resembles virtue, is *virtù*. *Virtù* is, in fact, a standard equivalent of the English word virtue in contemporary Italian, and because it can be translated as virtue without apparent damage in some of the places Machiavelli uses it, *virtù* is often rendered as virtue in English translations of Machiavelli. This way of finding virtue in Machiavelli's writings is a false trail, but at the same time a promising one.

Virtue involves adherence to some set of moral principles. *Virtù* as Machiavelli uses the term is closer to the Latin *virtus* in its connotation of manly valor and signifies an excellence that manifests itself most clearly in military and political affairs, perhaps because it is associated most prominently with the capacity to act boldly at critical moments. Evidently *virtù* is not the same thing as virtue. A translator sensitive to the diverse contexts in which Machiavelli uses *virtù*, Allan Gilbert, recognizes that there

From John Leonard, "Public versus Private Claims: Machiavellianism from Another Perspective," *Political Theory,* 12:4, pp. 491–501, 504–506. Copyright © 1984 by Sage Publications, Inc. Reprinted by permission of Sage Publications, Inc.

is a problem with translating *virtù* as virtue when he translates *virtù* as ability in contexts in which virtue, with its moral connotations, is obviously out of place, such as Machiavelli's reference in Chapter 17 of *The Prince* to Hannibal's "inhuman cruelty . . . together with his infinite *virtù*." But this method of sometimes translating *virtù* as virtue and sometimes as something else according to context is more misleading than the clumsiness involved in consistently translating *virtù* as virtue, for such clumsiness at least reveals the incompatibility of the terms despite contexts in which they seem compatible at first sight.[1]

Chapter 8 of *The Prince* provides an interesting example of a context in which *virtù* at first sight appears equivalent to virtue. Machiavelli writes.

> Neither can one call it *virtù* to kill one's citizens, to betray one's friends, to be faithless, without pity, without religion; by these means rule may be acquired, but not glory.

Virtue seems a perfectly acceptable substitute for *virtù* in this passage because one certainly cannot call it virtue to kill one's citizens, betray one's friends, etc. But a moment's reflection leads to the realization that this is too obvious to require statement. Either Machiavelli is making an obvious point about what is inconsistent with morality, a proceeding which in the context of *The Prince* as a whole would be distinctly anomalous, or he is making a less obvious but important point about what is inconsistent with *virtù*. It will be necessary to return to this point later. Here it is enough to note that *virtù* turns out not to be equivalent to virtue even in contexts that at first glance suggest such equivalence.

The Prince contains no word equivalent to virtue but it does include a list of moral qualities and a phrase that indicates Machiavelli's view of what it would mean to live in accordance with these qualities. The list appears in Chapter 18 of *The Prince*, in which Machiavelli says a prince should seem to be compassionate, faithful, humane, sincere, and religious. The phrase, which occurs in Chapter 15, is "to make a profession of goodness in all things."[2] To make such a profession would presumably mean to live a life dedicated to the exemplification of the moral qualities listed in Chapter 18. Thus *The Prince* reveals Machiavelli's awareness of what would constitute a high standard of virtue. But Machiavelli does not want the prince to comply with this standard, only to seem to do so. His reasoning on this point helps clarify the incompatibility of virtue and *virtù*.

It is in Chapter 15 of *The Prince* that Machiavelli states his intention of writing for "he who understands" and contrasts this method with that of those who imagine states that have "never been seen nor known to exist in reality." He then proceeds to justify his choice on the grounds that there is such a difference between how men live and how they ought to live that he who departs from what is done for the sake of what should be done will learn his ruin rather than his preservation. The phrase "to make a profession of goodness in all things" occurs in this connection; he who wants to make a profession of goodness in all things, says Machiavelli, must bring about his ruin among the many who are not good.

Machiavelli deduces from this the proposition that a prince must learn how not to be good. He repeats this principle in Chapter 18, in which he advises that the prince should not part from the good without need, but should be able to enter into the bad when to do so is necessary for the maintenance of his position. The words good and bad here take on a moral emphasis deriving from the preceding list of moral qualities, and Machiavelli makes clear what he means by entering into the bad when, referring to these qualities, he says the prince must be able to act, "contrary to faith, contrary to charity, contrary to humanity, contrary to religion." This ability, evidently contrary to virtue, is consistent with *virtù*, as Machiavelli indicates in his treatment of Hannibal's "inhuman cruelty." This cruelty, says Machiavelli, was necessary to maintain order among Hannibal's mixed force of mercenary troops and thus was an essential aspect of Hannibal's excellence as a general, and for this reason Machiavelli includes it among Hannibal's "infinite *virtù*."

That such a quality could be included within *virtù* reveals its difference from virtue. It also raises the question whether *virtù* is defined solely in terms of success in the pursuit of military or political power.

Machiavelli's discussion of what is not *virtù* assumes special significance in this connection. It has been noted that in Chapter 8 of *The Prince* Machiavelli either makes an implausible argument for what is not virtue or some sort of argument for what is not *virtù*. Machiavelli says that it cannot be called *virtù* to kill one's citizens, betray one's friends, and be without honor, piety, and religion because although such methods can lead to rule they cannot lead to the acquisition of glory. If virtue is substituted for *virtù* Machiavelli is doing something very curious, for instead of making the obvious point that such acts and qualities cannot be called virtue because they are directly opposed to it, he is saying that they cannot be called virtue because they cannot lead to glory. Using glory to define virtue in this context makes little sense. But if we read *virtu* as *virtu* the attempt to set a boundary on it through the use of glory makes considerable sense. By limiting the ascription of *virtù* to actions that are consistent with the acquisition of glory Machiavelli can deny *virtù* to actions that involve "entering into the bad" out of choice rather than necessity. At the same time, and unlike virtue, glory is compatible with entering into the bad out of necessity. Thus glory is useful to Machiavelli because it is compatible with the necessities of public life while providing a standard for rejecting its worst excesses.

By employing glory as a critical standard Machiavelli reveals his awareness of the problem posed for political action by the incompatibility of virtue and *virtù*. At its core Machiavellian *virtù* represents pure efficacy unconstrained by any imperative except that of attaining one's end. For *virtù* to play a constructive role in politics such efficacy must be constrained to serve the needs of the public sphere. This is the basis of Machiavelli's appeal to glory. The effectiveness of this appeal will be considered later. At this point it is time to enter the world of the *Discourses* and consider another incompatibility, that of virtue and *bontà*.

2. Why Bontà Is Never Virtue

Machiavelli's *Discourses* differs from *The Prince* alike in its subject matter and its method. *The Prince* is concerned with the exigencies of princely government in the harsh political climate of Machiavelli's Italy. Thus, for example, Machiavelli's reference to states that have never been known to exist is designed to throw into relief the necessities imposed by the political realities of his day. This contrast serves Machiavelli's purposes in *The Prince*, but it also reflects *The Prince* as a whole in leaving no room between the harshness of the reality it describes and the fatuity of utopian thinking for consideration of what a well-ordered state that could exist in reality would look like.

In the *Discourses* Machiavelli opens the way to such consideration by taking as his model a state that actually did exist in an earlier period. This state is the Roman republic as Livy depicts it, and Machiavelli's method is to present the *Discourses* as a commentary on the first ten books of Livy's *History of Rome*. Because Machiavelli represents the Roman republic as a model state in the *Discourses* the role of virtue in public life should reveal itself in this work if it has a place anywhere in Machiavelli's thought.

A careful examination of Machiavelli's comments in the *Discourses* concerning the role of the popular element in Roman society reveals an emphasis on the concept of *bontà*. *Bontà* is worthy of consideration on several grounds. First, it represents Machiavelli's nearest approach to a workable concept of virtue. Second, this little discussed concept is of great importance to Machiavelli, being as important to his well-ordered state as *virtù*.

Chapter 55, Book 1 of the *Discourses* opens with an example of the Roman people's *bontà*. A similar example occurs in Chapter 13 of Book 1, though the word itself does not appear in Chapter 13.[3] Both examples concern oaths that are interpreted by the nobility in a way that threatens the people with the loss of something they desire. In both cases the people have a plausible excuse for evading the obligation created by the oath, and it is their decision not to break the oath outright that makes it possible to come to a workable compromise with the nobility.

In Chapter 13 Machiavelli recounts Livy's story of a feud between the nobles and the people that was interrupted by a slave revolt that succeeded in occupying the Capitol. The nobles called on the people to help put down the revolt whereas the Tribunes argued that no aid should be rendered until the nobles agreed to a proposed law for a committee to devise ways of limiting the power of the Consuls. The people decided to aid in the recapture of the Capitol and swore an oath to obey the Consul's orders. The attack was a success but the Consul was killed. His replacement, seeking to keep the people from renewing their consideration of the disputed law, ordered them out of the city to do battle against a neighboring state. The Tribunes protested that because the oath was made to the previous Consul it was no longer binding, but because the oath did not specify this the people were afraid of breaking it. Thus the Tribunes were forced to compromise with the nobility by promising to drop consideration of the law for a year in exchange for the Consul's promise not to order the people to war during that period.

In Chapter 55 Machiavelli relates how trouble flared up between the people and the nobles when the commander of a victorious Roman army decided to offer a tenth of the spoils of combat to Apollo. The Senate accordingly directed each member of the army to turn over a tenth of his spoils. The common soldiers protested, understandably enough, because they had not participated in the vow and the spoils were their only remuneration for the hardships and dangers of military service. But instead of evading the order individually by cheating, as they could easily have done, and thus invalidating the vow, they chose to protest openly and in a body. This open protest led to a compromise in which the people were released from their obligation and the vow was fulfilled by other means.

The *bontà* of the people in these examples is linked with their fear of breaking oaths. *Bontà* is normally translated as goodness, and inasmuch as the goodness in these examples seems to derive from a form of piety *bontà* appears to have something in common with Christian virtue. But the role of Roman religion with respect to *bontà* is very different from, though just as important as, the role of Christianity with respect to Christian virtue. For although Christianity reinforces admonitions to virtue with warnings of the punishments in store for sinners, it also establishes the principle that true virtue consists in obeying moral precepts out of an inner conviction of their rightness rather than out of fear. Roman religion reinforces *bontà* through fear of the gods, but its purpose in so doing is not to remind men of the wages of sin. The goal of Roman religion is rather to invest the concept of obedience to public authority with a sense of religious awe. It is this use of religious awe or piety to which Machiavelli refers in both his examples of *bontà*. *Bontà* does not lead to the creation of a moral sense in the individual, but it does provide a peaceful means of controlling an armed populace.

That Machiavelli is concerned with *bontà* as an aid in maintaining the public sphere is confirmed by his description of the cause and effect of the loss of religious belief among a people. In Chapter 12, Book 1 of the *Discourses* he says that when religion begins to speak with the voice of the rich and powerful, and this is discovered by the people, "men become unbelievers and disposed to upset every good order." In other words, the loss of religious belief on the part of the people, caused by its shortsighted manipulation by the wealthy and powerful (a manipulation that proves they do not share this belief) leads to the loss of the *bontà* that helps control threats to public order.

Bontà is the closest Machiavelli comes to a workable concept of virtue, but it is a substitute for virtue rather than virtue by another name. In *The Prince* Machiavelli's rejection of virtue had to do with the practical requirements of survival in a disordered political environment. The reason virtue is also absent in Machiavelli's model state and the consequences of its absence remain to be considered.

3. Extraordinary Action and Its Enemy

Machiavelli's analysis of government begins with the institutional structure of political power. A well-ordered state, be it republic or princedom, is in the first instance one in which the structure of political power is well designed to meet the needs of that particular state. But he also shows great sensitivity to the fact that the usefulness of political institutions depends on their authority in the eyes of the citizenry and that a diminution of this authority can lessen the capacity of those institutions to meet the needs of the state.

Machiavelli's discussion of the Roman republic as a model state reveals two of his fundamental political premises. One is that a state that provides an institutional channel for popular participation in public affairs is potentially stronger than a state that makes no such provision. The other is that widespread participation in public affairs requires the highest possible esteem for public authority among all classes of citizens. Any lessening of this esteem signifies the onset of corruption, which manifests itself in inattention to, or self-serving uses of, the laws and religion. The prevention of such corruption requires sanctions against the misuse of the qualities associated with *virtù* as well as the reinforcement of the *bontà*, the almost religious awe with which public authority and its representatives were regarded at the time of the state's founding.

The importance of preventing corruption and various methods of combating it make up the subject matter of Chapter 1, Book 3 of the *Discourses*. The eradication of corruption is linked with a symbolic refounding of a state or religion through the revitalization of its orders. Machiavelli describes three ways by which such a refounding can occur. One is the appearance of danger in the form of a foreign threat so great that it seems capable of destroying the state. Such a threat may serve as a sort of shock therapy that brings the leaders and citizens back to the observance of the principles on which the state was founded. This method is clearly a dangerous one.

A state content to rely on extrinsic accident to combat corruption would not be likely to have a long history.

Machiavelli next turns to a pair of methods that he lists under the category of intrinsic prudence. The first of these methods is legislative. The second is that of personal actions that set a good example for the citizens. Either the *virtù* of a new order created by legislation or the *virtù* exhibited by a citizen at a critical juncture can bring a state back to health. But of these two forms of *virtù* the one embodied in legislation suffers from the defect that it does not inspire men to obedience in itself. Thus Machiavelli concludes his discussion of rejuvenation by means of new orders with the comment: "Those orders need to be brought to life by the *virtù* of a citizen, who boldly agrees to execute them against the power of those who transgress them."

Machiavelli expands on this statement by providing a list of the kind of actions he has in mind. These actions are all taken from Roman history, and most of them are executions. The list begins with the execution of Brutus's sons and continues with the execution of the Ten Citizens, Spurius Melius, Manlius Capitolinus, and the son of Manlius Torquatus. It concludes with several prosecutions that did not result in executions. For Machiavelli the importance of all these actions resides in the fact that, "because they were extreme and noteworthy, whenever one of them occurred it made men retire to their place."

The connection between the extreme and noteworthy quality of these actions and their exemplary effect is revealed in Chapter 3, Book 1 of the *Discourses*. In this chapter Machiavelli notes that Brutus not only voted to condemn his sons to death for treason but actually attended their execution. He refers to this conduct as an example rare in all the records of historical events and claims that the severity exhibited by Brutus on this occasion was not merely useful but necessary to the maintenance of Roman liberty. What makes Brutus's action so extraordinary is the emphatic manner in which he resolved the conflict between the private affection of a father for his sons and the public duty of protecting the orders of the state. By not only condemning his sons to death but witnessing their execution Brutus made a public statement of the citizen's primary duty to maintain the state, a statement that renewed both the respect of the citizens for the state's laws and orders and their fear of transgressing those laws and orders.

A second look at the extraordinary actions listed in Chapter 3, Book 1 of the *Discourses* reveals that the offenses involved are ones that in every case pose threats to the authority of the public sphere. In every case this threat is also enhanced by the existence of a private bond between the transgressors and some or all of their judges that might conduce to leniency. It is in these circumstances that harsh punishments take on the character of extreme and noteworthy actions. This is so because in such circumstances these actions function, to borrow a phrase, by using punishment to make a memory.[4] Extraordinary actions are thus of particular importance in cases in which some obvious threat to public authority conceals the less evident threat of a conflict between personal feelings of affection or obligation and the good of the state.[5] That it is this latter threat to which Machiavelli is particularly sensitive is underscored by his treatment of two actions in which harsh punishment is thwarted by private pleadings.

One of Machiavelli's examples in Chapter 1, Book 3 of the *Discourses* is the prosecution of Papirius Cursor's master of cavalry. This prosecution was extreme and noteworthy because Papirius asked that his master of cavalry be condemned to death for having given battle contrary to orders even though the latter had been victorious. At the end of Chapter 31, Book 1 of the *Discourses* Machiavelli notes that the father of Papirius's master of cavalry argued against this punishment on the grounds that the

Romans did not treat even their defeated commanders in such a fashion. But although earlier in the chapter Machiavelli approves the Roman practice of not punishing their generals for mistakes made in the course of military operations it would be a mistake to construe this as indicating support for the father's plea. For in Chapter 36, Book 3 of the *Discourses* he quotes with approval Livy's account of Papirius's speech in favor of the death penalty. The point of this speech is that an army cannot maintain good order unless discipline is strictly enforced. From this perspective the intervention of his father in the prosecution of the master of cavalry was clearly contrary to the interests of the state.

Another instance of a father interceding for his son is recounted in Chapter 22, Book 1 of the *Discourses*. Horatius, the sole survivor of a combat between three brothers from Rome and three brothers from the neighboring state of Alba, returned home in triumph, but shortly afterward killed his sister when he heard her lament the death of one of the Alban brothers, to whom she had been married. Horatius was put on trial for his life and was acquitted. According to Machiavelli this acquittal owed more to his father's prayers for the life of his last son than Horatius' recent services to the state. Two chapters later Machiavelli returns to this topic and states that although, superficially considered, it might have seemed an act of ingratitude had the Roman people condemned Horatius to death after he had saved Rome, they were actually to blame for having acquitted him. Machiavelli's reasoning is that meritorious actions should never be allowed to mitigate punishment for crimes because examples of such mitigation might encourage men to whom the state owed a debt of gratitude to think they could plot against it with impunity.

Machiavelli's fears that private ties will be used to undermine the state center on leaders and potential leaders, for it is when men of prominence and ability seek the satisfaction of private ends at the expense of the state's laws and orders that the public sphere is most gravely threatened. It is with respect to such threats that the absence of virtue from Machiavelli's theory of politics is revealed as a major problem for what he seeks to accomplish.

Bontà, based as it is on religious credulity, is of considerable importance in controlling the populace but has much less bearing on the control of leaders. Yet the maintenance of *bontà* depends on a state's leaders, for when they become corrupt, religious disillusionment is sure to follow. Thus Machiavelli's fundamental problem is how to keep the most prominent and able members of the state on the path of *virtù* as he defines it: that is, as consistent with glory and, consequently, complementing the needs of the state. This problem is compounded by the ineffectiveness of the image of glory to keep men to the desired standard of conduct. In Chapter 10, Book 1 of the *Discourses* Machiavelli extols both the public and private advantages of actions that strengthen states and religions, including the advantage of a glorious reputation, and emphasizes the disadvantages of actions that harm public institutions. But though he says that given a choice between praiseworthy and blameworthy actions no one would mistake one for the other, he goes on to say that despite this, in practice most men, "deceived by a false good and a false glory," end up in the ranks of those who deserve more blame than praise.

The ineffectiveness of representations of glory to prevail over the urgings of private desire in any but a few cases explains Machiavelli's necessary reliance on extraordinary action. Extraordinary action must fill the gap left by the absence of virtue because the majority of men are incapable of internalizing not only virtue but any code of conduct that requires them to define their own good in terms of a wider good. Thus Machiavelli feels he must rely on a purely external, public form of action that can cow the temptation to break laws and overthrow orders, but which has no roots in the private sphere and no connection with private values. Rather, extraordinary action is a response to a vision of private ties as posing a potential threat to public life. It is important to inquire why this vision should dominate Machiavelli's thinking even in the consideration of his model state. . . .

Conclusion

Machiavellianism is normally understood as the doctrine that no principle or moral scruple should be regarded as binding if it stands in the way of the acquisition or maintenance of political power. On examination, this interpretation stands revealed as a mixture of truth and inaccuracy.

The focus of Machiavelli's political thought is the good of the public sphere. He considers the pursuit of virtue to be incompatible with this good, yet his concern for public life and its fragility makes him highly critical of the means by which power is acquired and maintained. Thus in both *The Prince* and the *Discourses* Machiavelli judges the means by which power is acquired in terms of its effect on the maintenance of the public sphere over time. It is for the purpose of making this connection that Machiavelli attempts to link *virtù* and glory,[6] and the importance he attaches to maintaining *bontà* is likewise related to the needs of the public sphere.

What is troubling in Machiavelli's thought is not an uncritical admiration of power but his view that any conflict between the public and private spheres of life should be resolved in favor of the former. For Machiavelli there seems to be no possibility of mediation between these spheres. The threat posed to the public sphere by private claims and impulses is viewed as insidious, omnipresent, and, insofar as it has its roots in the family, ineradicable.

The consequences of this viewpoint are twofold. First, not only the founding of the public sphere but its continuation must be made dependent on religious credulity and exemplary punishments in the form of extraordinary acts. Second, because the public sphere is represented as the only valid locus of self-assertion, the legitimate expression of private feelings of aggression and ambition is confined to this sphere. This channeling process, although it creates a tremendous dynamism in the public sphere, must also create an agonistic political life that poses a constant threat to the laws and orders established to contain it and give it expression, extraordinary acts notwithstanding.

The absence of virtue in Machiavelli's political thought is not the result of shallow and unprincipled cynicism but of a deeply rooted pessimism concerning the ability of most men to internalize a code of conduct that clashes with immediate self-interest combined with an exaltation of the public sphere as an arena of conflict in which the practice of Christian virtue would amount to self-martyrdom. A theory of politics based on such views is not without problems, but as portrayed by Machiavelli it offers insights and opportunities for thought that are lost to view when Machiavellianism is confused with a version of his thought that is little more than a stalking-horse for moral censure.

Notes

1. For a translation of *The Prince* in which *virtù* is rendered as virtue even in the unlikely context of Machiavelli's reference to Hannibal's cruelty, see the Luigi Ricci/E.R.P. Vincent translation of *The Prince* in the Modern Library College Editions' *The Prince and the*

Discourses (Random House, 1950). Gilbert's translation is included in Volume 1 of *Machiavelli: The Chief Works and Others,* trs. Allan Gilbert (Duke University Press, 1965).

2. To "make a profession" of a quality can either mean to avow it in one's actions or to feign it. Here the term must be understood in the former sense and without any implication of pretence. Otherwise Machiavelli's whole critique of this conduct and his argument in favor of making a false profession of goodness in Chapter 18 are unintelligible. Worth noting is the resemblance of making a profession of goodness in this context to making a profession of religious faith at the risk of martyrdom.

3. As explained below, the importance of religion and honesty in both chapters is the usefulness of these qualities in maintaining respect for public authority and the laws that uphold the public sphere and it is this respect that Machiavelli characterizes as *bontà* in Chapter 55. It is for this reason that he clinches the argument in Chapter 13 concerning the importance of religion with a quotation from Livy in which the latter connects the decline of religion with the interpretation of laws and oaths on the basis of self-interest.

4. The formulation is Nietzsche's and occurs in Section 13 of the second essay of *On the Genealogy of Morals.* The whole of this section and the last paragraph of Section 15 provide insights that can be fruitfully applied to Machiavelli's discussion of the function of extraordinary acts in Chapter 1, Book 3 of the *Discourses.*

5. This same potential conflict and the importance of dealing with it decisively also appear in Machiavelli's accounts of extraordinary acts in his own times. See, for example, his account of Cesare Borgia's execution of a trusted subordinate in Chapter 7 of *The Prince* (an action Machiavelli says is "worthy of notice and imitation by others") and that of Caterina Sforza's renunciation of her children in Chapter 6, Book 3 of the *Discourses.*

6. In Chapters 6 through 9 of *The Prince* Machiavelli discusses different ways of acquiring power in terms of their relation to its maintenance. A ruler who cannot maintain himself once he takes power is of no use to his state. At the same time, a ruler who destroys the public sphere to gain power when he could have achieved power without doing so is subject to censure, as Machiavelli implies in Chapter 8 of *The Prince* and state openly in Chapter 10, Book 1 of the *Discourses,* in which he defines glory and infamy in terms of what is beneficial and harmful to the establishment and maintenance of states and religions. Machiavelli's interest in power has to do not with the maintenance of the ruler per se but with the protection of the public sphere, though admittedly his conflation of ruler and public sphere in the concept of the state (*lo stato*) as he employs it in *The Prince* confuses the issue in that work.

Trapping the Prince: Machiavelli and the Politics of Deception

Mary G. Dietz

[F]or some time I have never said what I believed and never believed what I said, and if I do sometimes happen to say what I think, I always hide it among so many lies that it is hard to recover.

—Machiavelli

Realism is generally considered a necessary first move in the effort to make the study of politics scientific, and when political scientists turn to the history of ideas, they tend to acknowledge Machiavelli as the champion of realism, and *The Prince,* in particular, as the first treatise in political thought to infuse the contemplation of political affairs with a spirit of empiricism, *realpolitik,* and *raison d'état.* By now it has become commonplace for political scientists in fields as diverse as international relations, comparative politics, organization theory, and political psychology to construct explanations about political life and political conduct that rely in part on the "axioms" that evolved from Machiavelli's little treatise. These include the necessities of "naked self-interest," the maintenance of rulership at all costs, the utility of unethical and manipulative behavior, and the centrality of power as an end in and of itself.[1] Accordingly, in many areas of political inquiry Machiavelli has come to be regarded as the theorist of "Machiavellianism," and Machiavellianism itself entails understanding politics primarily in terms of who dominates whom and how successfully.

As far as it goes, this understanding of politics as power is true to Machiavelli's purposes in *The Prince,* but, in the end, I think it does not go far enough. What is missing from the political scientists' rendition of Machiavelli is another vision of politics, a republican one rooted in love of liberty and respect for self-governance, which political theorists have long considered as vital to Machiavelli's thought as power and *realpolitik.*[2] This second vision of politics as participation is one theorists tend to associate with Machiavelli's later works, particularly *The Discourses* and *The History of Florence.* Thus, like political scientists, they too often read *The Prince* in terms of the politics of power and domination.

I suggest that neither political scientists nor political theorists have realized the full force of the Florentine's intentions in *The Prince.* By offering a different perspective on the treatise I hope to show that both groups have underestimated Machiavelli, and in ironic ways—the theorists by not seeing the republican goals that guide the treatise, the political scientists by not recognizing the full force of the "Machiavellian"

From Mary G. Dietz, "Trapping the Prince: Machiavelli and the Politics of Deception," *American Political Science Review,* 80 (September 1986): pp. 777–788, 793–799. Reprinted by permission of the author and The American Political Science Association.

intentions that inform it. My purpose, then, is not only to present a new interpretation of this most famous of Machiavelli's works, but also to encourage a reconsideration of the adjective that bears his name and the vision of politics it represents.

Republicans and *The Prince*

No political thinker was more aware of how crafty assault by deceit could serve as a substitute for brute assault by violence than Niccolò Machiavelli. The theme of deception weaves through all of his work—his drama, his military writings, his history, his political theory. *Mandragola* is a tale of crafty assault practiced by the wily Ligurio, who helps a young rake bed the beautiful wife of a pompous old doctor. *The Art of War* argues that a commander who vanquishes an enemy by stratagem is as praiseworthy as one who gains victory by force. *The History of Florence* tells the story of a city where deceit and guile secure power, while honesty and blind trust ruin it. Nowhere, of course, is Machiavelli's love for the art of deception more vividly unmasked than in *The Prince.* There the subject of crafty assault takes its notorious form in his advice to a ruler on how to play the fox, "confuse men's brains," and employ cunning in the political world. In short, whether the subject is love, war, or politics, Machiavelli recognizes the advantages of crafty assault in any form, be it trickery, stratagem, or artifice.

For those who believe that Machiavelli was a republican and a Florentine patriot, this view of him as the master theorist of deceit poses difficulties. As Hanna Pitkin (1984) reminds us, foxes make poor citizens—their deceit undermines civic *virtù*— and *The Prince* abounds with foxes and advice on deception. Furthermore, in Machiavelli's infamous tract to Lorenzo de Medici we find no defense of the Florentine republic, no call for popular liberty, no praises of republican Rome. Far from denouncing tyranny, as would any bold republican, Machiavelli appears to content himself with forging the absolute and ruthless power of an autocrat. How, then, is it possible to hail him as a defender of liberty, self-government, and civic *virtù*, when these appear to be the very values he teaches his Medici protégé to subvert?

Proponents of the thesis that Machiavelli was a republican, despite his authorship of *The Prince,* fall into two camps. According to the "weak republican" thesis, *The Prince* is an aberration. Despairing of the future of Florence, much less its republican government, Machiavelli saw the Medici as the only alternative to total chaos, and so wrote his advice book in reaction to an impending crisis (Baron, 1961; Hale, 1961; Pocock, 1975). This thesis maintains that after 1513 Machiavelli simply abandoned the idea of the prince as a "political innovator"; he renewed his commitment to republicanism, developed an admiration for antiquity, and refueled his antipathy for the Medici. The result of this renewal was *The Discourses,* complete with its dedication to republican sympathizers and its repudiation of the entire genre of princely advice books. Thus, these scholars view *The Prince* as a tract that reflects both Machiavelli's acceptance (reluctant though it might have been at the time) of Medicean domination and his clear-sighted, if opportunistic, attempt to ingratiate himself with the new rulers of Florence.

Among other things, the weak republican thesis strains credulity. To read *The Prince* as a sudden capitulation to Medici rule, or as a tool to curry favor is, arguably, to underestimate Machiavelli as a citizen and a theorist. Though I find Garrett Mattingly's (1958) ultimate assessment of *The Prince* unconvincing (for reasons I will explain shortly), I think he poses in dramatic terms the correct riposte to the weak republican thesis:

> I suppose it is possible to imagine that a man who has seen his country enslaved, his life's work wrecked and his own career with it, and has, for good measure, been tortured within an inch of his life, should thereupon go home and write a book intended to teach his enemies the proper way to maintain themselves. . . . But it is a little difficult for the ordinary mind to encompass. (1958, p. 485)

The other camp advances a "strong republican" thesis, arguing that even as Machiavelli writes *The Prince,* he remains a defender of republican liberty and an opponent of the Medici (Gentili, 1924; Mattingly, 1958; Rousseau, 1978; Spinoza, 1945; Wolin, 1960). However, if this is indeed the case, and if republican sympathies abound in *The Prince,* then something else must be moving beneath the surface of the text; some drama that the protagonist-prince does not see must be taking shape. This is precisely what the strong republican camp wants to argue, but as is so often the case with Machiavelli, there are differences of opinion on the matter of the subtext of *The Prince.* Three main views emerge.

The first is Rousseau's (1978, p. 88) claim that *The Prince* is a book for republicans. Rousseau argues that the advice book was not intended for the Medici at all, but rather to expose to the people the brutal ruthlessness of princes and lay bare their methods and madness. There is a paradoxical quality to this interpretation of the sort we have come to expect from Rousseau, namely, that even as Machiavelli is fashioning masks for a prince, he is unmasking him. By exposing the prince's stock-in-trade, Machiavelli is arming republicans with all the knowledge they need to avoid being deceived. A simple and telling criticism can, however, be lodged against this Rousseauian opinion: Machiavelli could not be writing a book for republicans, because he never intended that they read it. Interpretative accuracy often hangs on matters of practical political action, not to mention the intention of where to publish and for whom, and in this case we find no evidence that Machiavelli did or attempted to do anything with his treatise but send it to Francesco Vettori, his contact in the Medici Palace.

A second version of Machiavelli as a strong republican hardly takes *The Prince* seriously, for it assumes that the treatise was not intended seriously. Garrett Mattingly (1958) holds that Machiavelli's advice book is nothing more than a joke, a "diabolical burlesque" of the mirror-of-princes literature prevalent in the Renaissance. Nominally agreeing with Rousseau, Mattingly argues that Machiavelli wrote *The Prince* as an alarm, a "tocsin" to the people of Florence. However, this agreement is surely more literary than political, for, unlike Rousseau, Mattingly does not read the treatise as revealing certain truths about princely power that republicans should know. He sees *The Prince* primarily as a fine example of Machiavelli's dramatic temperament, a reflection of his ability simultaneously to shock and amuse his audience. Machiavelli surely intended to shock and perhaps to amuse, and *Mandragola* fully displays his dramatic skills, but this does not suffice to make *The Prince* a burlesque, even if a diabolical one. The most obvious problem with Mattingly's reading is that it fails to take seriously Machiavelli's desire to reconstitute the political world. In *The Prince,* Machiavelli (*P,* p. 56) declares his intention "to write something of use to those who understand."[3] He wishes to *reveal* reality, not ridicule it, and his repeated instruction concerning princely *virtù* sounds less like a satire on the corruption of power than an attempt to determine how those in power might use guile and deceit to mitigate the corruption of the state.

The third strong republican perspective reads *The Prince* literally, as an advice book for a founder. Machiavelli's prince is to be the restorer of order, the man of *virtù* who will lay the foundations from which the republic will emerge. Thus, *The Prince* is "phase one" of a series of events that will lead to liberty and republican government in "phase two." On this account, *The Discourses* takes its point of departure from the (hoped-for) realization of the prince's plans. Put another way, *The Prince* has to do with "heroic" politics, *The Discourses* with mass politics of a republican sort, made possible by the heroism of the virtuoso leader. Thus Sheldon Wolin (1960, p. 231) contends that the prince will "render himself superfluous" and therefore "give way" to the rise of mass politics and the republic. Exactly how the founder renders himself superfluous or how he gives way to the republic, Wolin does not say; the implication, roughly, is that he creates institutions that will subsume and outlive him. Hence the major issue, for Wolin (1960, p. 231), is whether or not the state will be capable of "generating its own momentum" after the founder is dead.[4]

Two problems beset Wolin's attempt to solve the puzzle of the transition from *The Prince* to *The Discourses,* and so to shore up the third version of the strong republican thesis. The first problem is textual: in *The Prince,* Machiavelli gives no specific advice concerning the foundation of republican institutions. Indeed, he does not deal with republics at all. On this score, we should compare *The Prince* with a later work, Machiavelli's advice to Pope Leo X, "On Reforming the State of Florence" (Pansini, 1969, pp. 633–34). There he does offer lengthy and detailed directives on the organization of a republic, and advises, among other things, the reopening of the hall of the Council of the Thousand, the redistribution of offices to the general public, and the return of a gonfalonier. Nothing even remotely similar to this appears in *The Prince,* where Machiavelli seems content to develop Lorenzo's knowledge of historical examples and his appreciation of deceit and violence, rather than his familiarity with republican *ordini.*

The second problem with Wolin's thesis is more political in nature: Would a theorist as cognizant of the vicissitudes of *fortuna* as Machiavelli content himself with the notion that "heroic politics" will somehow "give way" to mass politics, that the death of the prince will lead to the rise of the republic? Moreover, would a Florentine who knew well the personalities of the Medici princes—Giuliano (a man of little ambition, with a lack of aptitude for dealing with Florentine affairs) and Lorenzo (an unapproachable autocrat with Spanish pretensions) (Gilbert, 1984, p. 135; Hale, 1977, p. 99)—truly imagine them fit subjects for heroic politics, much less men great-hearted enough to relinquish their power after creating the conditions for a new republic?

Surely these rhetorical questions answer themselves. The history of the government of Florence, with its unpredictable oscillations between various forms of princely and republican rule, taught Machiavelli at least one lesson: that to wait (as was the Florentine habit) and expect to benefit from circumstances brings disaster. What is necessary is to act and to act boldly to change circumstances. This, in fact, is the very lesson Machiavelli teaches his prince, so it seems odd, to say the least, to assume that Machiavelli himself is willing to wait for the prince's retirement or death and expect that circumstances will, in due course, eventuate in a republic.

These last observations give us the needed purchase, I believe, to understand Machiavelli's strong republican intentions and to solve the puzzle of *The Prince.* Given the Florentine's commitment to boldness and his conviction that successful political action requires the mastery of circumstances, does it not seem plausible that *The Prince* could be read as a political act in itself, a bold attempt to change existing conditions? Despite its main fault, the Rousseauian interpretation is compelling precisely because of this—it approaches *The Prince* as praxis and renders Machiavelli a political actor as well as a political theorist. Again, however, it must be remembered that Machiavelli sent his tract to the prince and not to Piero Soderini, the deposed gonfalonier, or to his republican friends in the castle at Volterra. So the puzzle remains. If we are to be committed to a reading of Machiavelli as a strong republican and of *The Prince* as praxis—as I propose we should—then in what sense is this little book a bold attempt to alter circumstances? How is the author of *The Prince* to be reconciled with the author of *The Discourses*?

These questions can be answered only if we remember Machiavelli's awareness of the advantages of crafty assault, and consider another, arguably more plausible, interpretative possibility: that *The Prince* is not simply about deception, but is itself an act of deception, and that this theorist of deceit is at the same time a practitioner of that very art. In other words, *The Prince* is a tract that in fact aims to restore a republic, though in appearance it dedicates itself to maintaining a princedom. Machiavelli indeed intends this book for the Medici. Thus, his deception resides not in exposing princely tricks to republicans, but in something far more crafty: he intends for a gullible and vainglorious prince to heed the duplicitous advice of *The Prince*, and thereby take actions that will jeopardize his power and bring about his demise. Thus, even as Machiavelli (*P*, p. 65) tells Lorenzo that "one who deceives will always find those who allow themselves to be deceived," he is deceiving Lorenzo. Even as he presses upon the prince the need to establish a relationship to others that is unknown to them, Machiavelli places Lorenzo in exactly this relation to himself. Even as he offers his Medici a "humble testimony of devotion," Machiavelli devises a plot, a series of moves that, if followed, will lead Lorenzo to disaster.

This reasoning presumes, of course, that Machiavelli was a decided enemy of the Medici, and that he intended his advice to be followed to its damning letter. We will turn to that shortly. First we need to consider how, in the course of *The Prince*, this master of political deception sets his trap, disguises his own true aims, and makes Lorenzo his *mannerino*.

Trapping the Prince

Machiavelli's conception of politics in *The Prince* is quite clearly drawn from his understanding of and experience in the art of war. Politics, like warfare, is a vicious struggle to gain control, to dominate and conquer opposing forces, to battle one's way to victory over the enemy. Machiavelli (*P*, p. 53) thus advises his prince to "have no other aim or thought . . . but war and its organization and discipline." That art alone is necessary for glory in politics. The organizer of the Florentine civilian militia also knows that though there is "no comparison" between the armed and the disarmed man, success in war depends upon more than brute assault by sheer force of arms (*P*, p. 54). Machiavelli (1965) recommends another sort of assault in *The Art of War*:

> Where the nature of the terrain is such that you cannot draw the enemy into an ambush easily, you may, however, dig ditches and pitfalls in the plains, cover them over lightly with brushwood and clods and leave areas of solid ground through which you may retire in the heat of battle; if the enemy pursues, he is undone. (1965, p. 118)

Thus, for the general and the prince, the art of war and the art of politics require a knowledge of crafty assault as well as of armed combat. The political actor must be as skilled at setting traps as he is at bold, ferocious attack, for when one is foiled by "terrain" and unable to ambush easily, it may be necessary to deceive.

The political terrain of Florence in 1512 was not advantageous for Machiavelli. No "easy ambush" of the Medici lords was possible, and therefore we might remember Machiavelli's advice to generals in such situations: employ strategy and deception and your enemy will be undone. *The Prince* is Machiavelli's stratagem, an act of assault in the form of deception. As has been recognized for centuries, the text itself provides areas of "solid ground," or firm advice a new prince in a new territory can rely upon to gain and maintain his power. What has been missed, however, is Machiavelli's deceit. Amidst this solid advice he prepares "ditches and pitfalls" in the form of subversive directives for his Medici lord, which he then covers over with promises of power, glory, and popular support. This deceptive advice to Lorenzo concerns three decisive matters for a prince: where to live, how to behave, and whom to arm. If we read Machiavelli's counsel to the prince with historical information at hand, its subversive character begins to appear. If we read it with a complete understanding of Lorenzo de Medici's circumstances in Florence, the conclusion seems obvious: Machiavelli is out to undo this enemy of the republic. Let us consider what he says.

Where to Live

Machiavelli begins *The Prince* by stating that his subject matter concerns monarchies, not republics (*P,* p. 5). This is surely disingenuous, for although his discussion of kinds of principalities and how they are acquired and kept (*P,* pp. 5–41) focuses primarily on princely power and not popular governance, one of his main categories of principality is the former republic. Machiavelli says that of all the new princes, the one who becomes ruler of a once-free city faces the most overwhelming difficulties, and he devotes a short chapter (*P,* pp. 18–19) to explaining princely options in such a situation. We, like Machiavelli, might expect that Lorenzo, a new prince in a former republic, would be particularly interested in this chapter, so we should note what Machiavelli prescribes when he addresses "the way to govern cities or dominions that, previous to being occupied, lived under their own laws" (*P,* p. 18). Machiavelli offers the prince in a formerly free state three choices: he may either despoil, live within, or restore the freedoms of the occupied city. He then discounts the third alternative by appealing to history: The Romans unsuccessfully tried to hold Greece and, at the same time, allow her freedom; hence, their only recourse was to lay waste and despoil the country as they had done in Capua, Carthage, and Numantia. The paradox is not lost on Machiavelli—in order to maintain power in a former republic, one must destroy it. What renders such extreme measures necessary is the character of the citizenry of a subjugated republic: "They do not and cannot cast aside the memory of their ancient liberty," Machiavelli warns, but then he concludes his chapter by offering the second option as another resort. If the prince can neither "lay waste" to the city nor restore its freedoms, then he must reside in it (*P,* p. 19).

Upon first reading, Machiavelli's advice in chapter 5 seems solid. Indeed, he does not even bother to defend it. In chapter 3, on "mixed monarchies," he argues that a prince's residence within his conquered territory renders possession "more secure and durable" (*P,* p. 8) and allows for the immediate remedy of disorder, and in chapter 6, he reiterates that the maintenance of power is facilitated by a prince "being obliged to reside personally in his own territory" (*P,* p. 21). Yet there is something curious, even contradictory, about his advice in chapter 5. Before he counsels residence, Machiavelli unequivocally states that "whoever becomes the ruler of a free city and does not destroy it, can be expected to be destroyed by it." A motive for rebellion against the prince, he argues, can always be found in "the name of liberty," which republican citizens cannot cast aside (*P,* p. 18).

If this is the case, then what should we make of his advice? It seems that a prince who lives within a conquered republic would stand to lose rather than benefit, particularly if the people have not forgotten "the name of liberty." A prince within a city is easier to find and destroy than one who lives in a country villa, as had been the habit of the Medici family; they maintained a palace within Florence but spent much of their time in their villas—Careggi, Cafaggiolo, Castello, Fiesole, Poggio a Caiano—outside the city (Burkhardt, 1958, p. 399; Wackernagel, 1981). Machiavelli's advice seems designed to change the residential practice of the family by strategically placing the prince inside the city's walls. Yet at the same time it seems to run counter to his warning about the vengeful nature of former republicans—why should a prince live in their midst?

Perhaps our perspective is not yet complete. Machiavelli may be determined to assure Lorenzo's power by offering further advice on how to neutralize the "desire for vengeance" and the love of liberty that inflame republican hearts, so that even though the prince resides within the city, he will be secure. Machiavelli does give advice on this score, but what he says is curious indeed.

How to Behave

If any one piece of advice occurs repeatedly in *The Prince,* it is Machiavelli's dictum that the ruler should always strive to gain the favor of the people. In chapter 9, "Of the civic principality," Machiavelli tells Lorenzo to reject the "trite proverb" that, "He who builds on the people builds on mud," for the prince who animates the masses will find "he has laid his foundations well" (*P,* p. 38). Machiavelli reiterates this point in various ways throughout the treatise (*P,* pp. 60, 61, 63, 67, 71, 75, 76, 80). Because the friendship of the people is the prince's "main resource" in times of adversity, he must avoid incurring their hatred in order to insure against conspiracy or ruin; this is "one of the most important matters a prince has to confront" (*P,* p. 67). Machiavelli acknowledges that princes cannot always avoid being hated by someone, but it is best if those who hate him not be the people (*P,* p. 67). In a new age, then, all princes (except the Turk and the Sultan) ought to aim at satisfying the *popolani.* Implicit is a corollary Machiavelli makes explicit in his chapter on civic principalities: be wary of the nobility. The nobles are portrayed as untrustworthy, dishonest, greedy, and dangerous. Machiavelli writes:

> [F]rom hostile nobles [the prince] has to fear not only desertion but their active opposition, and as they are always more far-seeing and more cunning, they are always in time to save themselves and take sides with one who they expect to conquer. (*P,* pp. 36–37)

Hence the wise prince will, when possible, esteem his nobles, but more often he will be suspicious of them. The people provide a far firmer foundation for power.

Before we accept the astuteness of Machiavelli's advice to Lorenzo, we should recall this Medici's situation. As we shall see, the Florentine people were not well inclined toward the new Medici. The mood of the city had changed markedly since the days of *il Magnifico.* The Florentines had become accustomed to a republic; what opposition there was to it came primarily from the aristocracy. It seems, then, that an astute advisor would have told Lorenzo to turn for support to the very class Machiavelli tells him to suspect—the *ottimati*. All the more curious is Machiavelli's own acknowledgement of this elsewhere (though not to Lorenzo in *The Prince*). In his document to Pope Leo X, "On Reforming the State of Florence," Machiavelli tells the Pope what would have to be done if a prince wished to turn the city into a monarchy:

> [I]n Florence where there is a great sense of equality, one would first have to introduce inequality and create nobles with castles and villas, who would join the prince in suppressing the city and the whole province with their armies and factions. A prince alone, without the nobles, cannot bear the weight of a monarchy. (Pansini, 1969, p. 20)

Despite the fact that *The Prince* is (ostensibly) dedicated to a prince who wishes to maintain his power, nowhere in the treatise does Machiavelli offer Lorenzo the advice he gives Pope Leo. In fact, he says exactly the opposite and issues warnings about trusting nobles and alienating the people. Of course, it may be that between 1512 and 1521 Machiavelli simply changed his mind on the subject of whose favor the prince should seek, but before we draw this conclusion we might look at another aspect of his advice on how to behave.

Machiavelli takes up the subject "Of liberality and niggardliness" in chapter 16. In advising the prince on how to behave, he again reminds him of the importance of not being hated by the people, observing that

> one who wishes to obtain the reputation of liberality among men, must not omit every kind of sumptuous display, and to such an extent that a prince of this character will consume by such means all his resources and will be at last compelled, if he wishes to maintain his name for liberality, to impose heavy taxes on his people, become extortionate, and do everything possible to obtain money. This will make his subjects begin to hate him. (*P*, p. 58)

To underscore his warning against liberality *(liberalita)*, Machiavelli concludes the chapter by saying, "of all things that a prince must guard against, the most important are being despicable or hated, and liberality will lead you to one or other of these conditions" (*P*, p. 60). Thus, the prince (who has already noted the danger of alienating the people) will agree to practice "niggardliness" *(parsimonia)*—it is one of the vices that secures his power. However, we have evidence to suggest that Machiavelli's warning against liberality in *The Prince* is more a matter of republican sympathies than helpful advice, for in *The History of Florence* he reveals how the Medici benefitted from liberality.

Book 8 of Machiavelli's *History* relates, among other things, the famous tale of the Pazzi conspiracy against *il Magnifico*, Lorenzo de Medici, in 1478. The details of the attempted but unsuccessful plot against Lorenzo's life need not concern us, but what Machiavelli says about the outcome of the conspiracy is instructive. One of the elements of the plan called for Francesco Pazzi to ride to the gates of the city in the aftermath of Lorenzo's assassination, calling the people to liberty and to arms. However, events took a different turn. Francesco was wounded in the attempt to kill the prince, and it fell to his uncle, Iacopo, to sound the alarm. Machiavelli explains and analyzes the failure of this final effort by the Pazzi in the following way:

> Iacopo rode out with perhaps a hundred men who had been prepared for this job, to make this last trial of their fortune, and he went to the Palace square

calling the people and liberty to his aid. *But the first had been deafened by fortune and the liberality of the Medici* and the second was unknown in Florence, so there was no response. (1970, p. 273, emphasis added)

It is impossible to miss Machiavelli's conclusion—the liberality of the Medici had garnered the people's support. Indeed, the family's practiced munificence and heavy public spending had deafened the Florentines to the *cri de coeur* of the republic—that is, to liberty.

Armed with Machiavelli's analysis of this event, we can now read his advice in chapter 16 of *The Prince* in a different light. His injunction against liberality is intended to deprive Lorenzo of a tactic that had worked exceedingly well for the Medici in the past. As Machiavelli sees it, a liberal prince can spend, then depend on the people's goodwill, a miserly one cannot. It seems, then, that even as he assures Lorenzo that miserliness will win him public support and keep him from being hated, Machiavelli takes steps to guarantee that the name of liberty is not forgotten in Florence—and it is in liberty that citizens of a former republic "can always find a motive for rebellion" (*P*, p. 19). Yet, as Machiavelli knows, rebellion may come to naught unless there are good arms to strengthen it. We must now consider his advice on arms.

Whom to Arm

In chapter 20 of *The Prince,* Machiavelli takes up the matter of "whether fortresses and other things which princes often contrive are useful or injurious." Allan Gilbert (1938, p. 162) has noted this chapter's "un-Machiavellian" advice to the ruler about how to gain the support of the people, but let us take another look. The chapter begins with a review of what princes who want "to hold their possessions securely" have done, and Machiavelli notes that no "definitive judgment" is possible on these matters (*P*, p. 77). Conditions and circumstances vary and require different responses. But, then he issues a most definitive statement:

A new prince has never been known to disarm his subjects, on the contrary, when he has found them disarmed he has always armed them, for by arming them these arms become your own, those that you suspected become faithful and those that were faithful remain so, and from being merely subjects become your partisans. (*P*, p. 77)[5]

As if to leave no further doubt on the matter, Machiavelli goes on to argue that the new prince who disarms his subjects offends them and generates hatred toward himself. As we have seen, he has taken care to prepare the solid ground for this advice by telling the prince that the hatred of the people is precisely what he must avoid; one of his most potent remedies against conspiracy is not being hated by the masses. Therefore, Machiavelli concludes, "a new prince in a new dominion always has his subjects armed. History is full of such examples" (*P*, p. 78). His advice on this score follows from chapter 14, where the prince has been warned of the evils of being disarmed, and from chapter 12, where the prince has been told of the disastrous consequences of hiring mercenary and auxiliary troops.

On the surface, perhaps, Machiavelli's advice on arms seems sound, even "un-Machiavellian," but that impression begins to blur if we consider a seemingly obvious point. Machiavelli's suggestion that the granting of arms inspires loyalty and makes partisans out of subjects, if taken to be sincere, fails to account for the possibility, indeed the probability, that arms may also facilitate plots, incite insurrection, and inspire rebels. The new prince who arms his subjects may just as easily make himself a mark for overthrow by creating the very instrument of his own destruction, namely, a civilian militia. Moreover, earlier in the treatise, when Machiavelli discusses such virtuous new princes as Francesco Sforza in Milan or Cesare Borgia in the Romagna, he makes no mention of their having armed their subjects, doubtless because they did not. His bold claim that "history is full of such examples" is followed by no examples at all, an odd omission for a thinker who is otherwise so willing to present specific historical examples for the prince to emulate.

Most curious of all, however, is Machiavelli's omission of a historical example that would have meant much to Lorenzo. In a letter written to Piero Soderini at the same time he was composing *The Prince,* Machiavelli (1961) makes mention of some causal histories that have led various princes to greatness, and notes that

> Lorenzo de Medici disarmed the people to hold Florence; Messer Giovanni Bentivogli in order to hold Bologna armed them; the Vitelli in Castello and the present Duke of Urbino in his territory destroyed the fortresses in order to retain their states; Count Francesco and many others built them in their territories to make themselves sure of them. (1961, p. 98)

Machiavelli cites the Bentivogli, the Vitelli, and Francesco Sforza in his discussion of the things princes contrive in chapter 20, but he never acknowledges the example of Lorenzo de Medici, a new prince who disarmed his subjects in order to hold them. Surely this is odd, for of all the historical examples for the younger Lorenzo to emulate, his grandfather would have been the best. Not only was *il Magnifico* the most artful *principe* of the Medicean line, he was also the most brilliant secular figure of the age, both loved and feared by the Florentines. But quite clearly, the example of Lorenzo the Magnificent directly contradicts Machiavelli's advice on arming subjects, and Machiavelli appears content to omit this piece of information in his "definitive" advice to the new prince.

The issue here, however, is not simply whether new princes have in the past routinely armed their subjects and, in essence, created civilian militias. At issue is another, more immediately historical matter: is Machiavelli's advice wise counsel for a Medici in Florence? From what we know of the history of the city, the answer to this question can only be no.

In Florence, the idea of liberty was deeply rooted in political tradition. The city's sense of freedom persisted through periods of oligarchical rule, rigged elections, and partisan foreign policies. A proclamation of July 1329, passed by the *pratica* (a citizen assembly), declared that the city would never submit to the autocratic rule of one man, "since liberty is a celestial good which surpasses all the wealth of this world" (Rubinstein, 1968, p. 450). That "celestial good" was what the Florentines believed contributed to their greatness. Coupled with this tradition of republican liberty, the Florentines had a history of strong opposition to the Medici, which grew particularly virulent in the mid-fifteenth century. In an oath sworn in May of 1466, 400 citizens over the age of 14 declared a political program of opposition to Medici rule that demanded, in part, that citizens "be free to debate and judge public and popular government" (Rubinstein, 1968, p. 458). Nor were the Florentines without individual voices raised in defiance of the Medici usurpation of liberty. In his *Laudatio Florentinae Urbis,* Leonardo Bruni declared, "nothing can be achieved by the covetousness of single citizens against the will of so many men," and suggested safeguards against autocratic power (Rubinstein, 1968, p. 446). Alamanno Rinuccini published *De libertate,* a powerful attack on Medici tyranny (Rubinstein, 1968, pp.

461–62), and Girolamo Machiavelli, Niccolo's great-granduncle, was tortured and executed for his part in leading the opposition to Medicean measures instituted under the rule of Cosimo (Machiavelli, 1970, p. 218; Ridolfi, 1963, p. 2).

There is no reason to suspect that this opposition to the Medici or the spirit of Florentine republicanism itself had softened or disappeared by 1512, or that Machiavelli was unaware of it. Without question, the republic was anything but stable and secure; internal struggles between the middle class and the aristocracy were unending, making institutional reform immensely difficult and external affairs precarious. By 1510, Piero Soderini, the gonfalonier, was out of favor; the aristocracy was pressing for his removal from office and for a return to *governo stretto,* though not for an end to the republic. There is, in fact, little evidence to suggest that there was any popular sentiment favoring the return of the Medici, nor is there any indication that the Medici's assumption of power was generated in any major way by forces within the city. No doubt the family had allies among a small number of wealthy families and some younger aristocrats who stood to gain commercially and politically from the decline of the republic (Brucker, 1969), but in the end, the Medici resumed their power with the aid of Spanish bayonets, not the Florentine citizenry (Gilbert, 1984; Hale, 1977; Schevill, 1936). The fact that, once installed in power, the princes kept foreign troops in the city and guards at the palace indicates that they felt some uncertainty about their popularity. Perhaps this is why the younger Lorenzo, unlike his grandfather, *il Magnifico,* rarely ventured into public places to mingle and meet with the citizens. When he did, he was accompanied by armed guards (Gilbert, 1984, p. 108).

With respect to the matter of arms and Florence, let us further consider Machiavelli's advice to Lorenzo on fortresses, for it is as curious as his advice on arming the citizenry. In fact, his injunction against a fortress, when read in light of Florentine republicanism, also seems far more in keeping with the interests of the republic than with those of the Medici.

In chapter 20, Machiavelli tells Lorenzo that "a prince who fears his own people more than foreigners ought to build fortresses, but he who has greater fear of foreigners than of his people ought to do without them" (*P,* pp. 80–81). This is clever strategy, considering that Machiavelli has previously condemned the prince who fears his own people, and has stressed the danger of placing too much trust in foreign powers. Hence, the prince who can read at all cannot help but decide, as Machiavelli would have it, not to build a fortress. More metaphorically, the best fortress is to be found in the "love of the people" (*P,* p. 81).

Militarily, Machiavelli's counsel on fortresses runs counter to the prevailing views in Tuscany in the early Renaissance. Fortresses were considered useful in defending a dominion from outside enemies. In opposition to this, Machiavelli argues that a *fortezza* is useless and cites the example of the Castello Sforzesco, which gave "more trouble to the house of Francesco Sforza than any other disorder in the state" (*P,* p. 81). At best, Machiavelli's military analysis of this matter is exceedingly thin. He seems more interested in the internal, political implications of this strategy, rather than the external military ones. Again, we must examine what such an internal strategy would mean in the context of Florence under a Medici lord.

If the tradition of liberty distinguished Florentine republicanism in a political sense, then the walls of the city marked her republicanism in a strategic one (Hale, 1968, p. 502). The Florentines were notoriously wary of the subject of fortresses within the city. A *fortezza* symbolized the antithesis of republicanism, signaling the demise of popular governance and the emergence of an inner power elite by providing an autocrat with an impregnable stronghold. Observing the circumstances of neighboring city states, the Florentines saw that princes often constructed fortresses in the name of military security, but in fact used them for purposes of domestic oppression. Not surprisingly, then, the Florentines, with their strong republican traditions, viewed the building of a fortress as both a symbolic and a literal danger.

Machiavelli shares this suspicion. In a letter to Guicciardini, written in 1526, he equates the building of a fortress with the enslavement of the Florentines and warns that "the most harmful thing a republic can undertake is to enact something strong or that easily can be made strong within its body" (Machiavelli, 1961, p. 235). He goes on to observe that, if a fortress existed in Florence, "any powerful man" who conquered the city would, upon entering, find it a convenient stronghold, and the Florentines "would become slaves without any protection" (Machiavelli, 1961, p. 235). These observations raise yet another puzzle. If Machiavelli is so convinced of the danger a fortress poses to a free Florence and of the advantages it holds for a prince, then why, when devising a strategy for the Medici, does he not recommend the building of a *fortezza*? Indeed, what would a Medici prince who is backed by Spanish troops in a city under siege stand to gain by not fortifying himself? Yet in the face of such facts, and knowing the problems a fortress would present for republican activity, Machiavelli does not recommend that Lorenzo build one; nor does he recommend any strategies of "containment" other than the "love of the people." How can we account for this puzzling advice on arms and fortresses?

The mystery or oddity of Machiavelli's treatment of arms and fortresses can be explained in only one way. He offers Lorenzo advice on security, with the intention of delivering him into republican hands. Machiavelli has not lost sight of the reality of Florentine politics; he knows full well what the consequences will be if Lorenzo resides in the city, foregoes liberality, arms the people, distrusts the nobles, refuses a fortress, and mingles "from time to time" with the Florentines. In a city where "the desire for vengeance" runs deep and "the memory of ancient liberty" shines bright, an "unarmed prophet" is never fully secure; an unwanted prince who arms his subjects and does not protect himself is even less likely to survive. As his "advice book" proceeds, Machiavelli's warning in chapter 5, "whoever becomes the ruler of a free city and does not destroy it, can be expected to be destroyed by it," (*P*, p. 18) takes on the character of prophecy. Lorenzo will not destroy Florence; that much is clear. His only alternative (if he takes Machiavelli's counsel) is to reside in the city. Once therein, Machiavelli will have him adopt policies that are, in fact, republican snares designed to entrap him. He will be destroyed. These are the "ditches and pitfalls" that lie beneath the seemingly solid ground of Machiavelli's advice to his Medici lords. . . .

The Prince in Perspective

I began by suggesting that Machiavelli's genius resides in his appreciation of crafty assault in all its guises—the lover's trickery, the general's stratagem, the prince's artifice—but in truth, Machiavelli directs his most penetrating attention to the actor/advisor behind the assault, the one who, observing the scene from a distance, controls the lover, the general, the prince. That is, what Machiavelli admires is a kind of Renaissance artistry—a strategic perspective—that allows for a unique conception of space or terrain, and consequently makes possible the manipulation of persons and events. Ligurio employs just such a perspective in *Mandragola*; Fabrizio exhibits it in his topographical advice to generals in *The Art of War.* But *Mandragola* and *The Art of War* are simply later versions—one dramatic, the other military—of the strategic perspective Machiavelli himself practices as advisor to the prince.

We might measure Machiavelli's success as a political advisor who sees things strategically by the labels he has earned—"political realist" and "master of *realpolitik*"—and by the statesmen and politicians, from Metternich to Kissinger, who have adapted his strategic perspective to their own times and circumstances. Yet to stop here, as do so many of the political scientists and political actors who cite him, is to overlook a matter of deepest importance to Machiavelli, namely, the political values—republicanism and liberty—that inform his perspective as advisor to Lorenzo de Medici. When, in the introduction to *The Discourses,* Machiavelli (*D,* p. 101) tells his friends to "[look] rather to the intention of him who gives than to the thing offered," he implicitly underscores the distinction between the apparent meaning of any given work, political counsel, or strategic perspective and its deeper purpose. To put this more broadly, political advising involves more than the capacity to analyze events or to see things as they "really are," for the "reality" that informs the analysis is neither a neutral observation nor a scientific truth, but a perspective colored by the values, purposes, and political commitments of the advisor who offers them. When these are at odds with the interests of those in power, the advisor may choose to retire, to capitulate, to oppose openly, or (as Ligurio puts it) "to pursue deceit to its envisioned dearest goal" (Machiavelli, 1957, p. 38) by painting a particular vision of reality for the ruler whom he or she counsels, with a precise purpose in mind. The latter is Machiavelli's strategy as advisor in *The Prince*; his purpose is the restoration of republican liberty.

I want to argue, then, that there is more involved in Machiavelli's advice in his little treatise than a presentation of *realpolitik,* but at the same time suggest that his deeper purpose—to deceive—is not at odds with reading *The Prince* either in terms of a new science or as a work of Renaissance artistry. By way of clarification, let us consider how Machiavelli himself depicts his perspective in *The Prince* and thereby gain one final interpretative clue to his aims and intentions.

In his dedication to Lorenzo, Machiavelli consciously invokes Renaissance artistry in its most literal sense, and draws an analogy between himself, the advisor to princes, and the landscape painter:

> [F]or in the same way that landscape painters station themselves in the valleys in order to draw mountains or high ground and ascend an eminence in order to get a good view of the plains, so it is necessary to be a prince to know thoroughly the nature of a people and one of the populace to know the nature of princes. (*P,* p. 4)

By inviting us to recall the great innovation of Florentine painting—its attention to accurate representation of pictorial space—Machiavelli also discloses a necessary quality of the political advisor. The intellectual disposition, or, to return to Machiavelli's visual metaphor, the "vantage point" of the advisor, must be fully dimensional and complete. It encompasses the actors and influences that populate and permeate the vast political landscape, and thus avoids the restricted perspectives of the prince or the populace, whose visions are governed solely by their respective relationships to one another. Unlike the actors he observes, the advisor stands "outside" the political canvas and integrates particulars into a sweeping contextual vision of reality. He sees actors not as isolated figures and events not as disconnected instances, but as parts of a richly constituted tapestry, a variegated field of competing interests and ambitions. The advisor's special disposition and imagination are, then, the very opposite of the short-sightedness Machiavelli deplores as the mark of politically ineffectual men, those who cannot control events or see beyond their immediate circumstances.

But, as I have argued, there is more involved in Machiavelli's advice than a detached depiction of political reality, just as there was more involved in the Renaissance art of perspective than the achievement of pictorial veracity. In a literal sense, the discovery of perspective also introduced the art of deception to Renaissance painting. Though the depiction of reality was a central concern for the painter, it did not involve a simple mirroring of the physical universe. Rather, the painter selected particular elements of the visible world, then arranged and conveyed them so as to give the illusion of reality (Brucker, 1969). This act of artistic deception involved more than a dazzling display of technical virtuosity; also vital to it was the relationship the painter forged between the illusion he presented and the person who observed it. Thinking of his canvas as a window through which he viewed the world, the artist sought to convey the illusion as reality, and to stimulate the observer's emotions and sense of possibility (Ackerman, 1969; Brucker, 1958). From "inside" the painting, the artist tantalized his observers with a seductive vista and pulled them toward a point or prospect that seemed attainable. At its most powerful, perspectival art induced the viewers into actually feeling a part of the painting, as though they could step into it and secure the prospect that beckoned them. The artist performed a feat of aesthetic manipulation even as he accomplished an act of pictorial veracity. He used his science to produce a material work of deception, an art.

In much the same way as the art of deception is a distinguishing characteristic of Renaissance perspectival painting, so it is a part of Machiavelli's strategic perspective in The Prince. Just as we can only appreciate the artist's act of aesthetic manipulation if we consider how the painting plays upon the observer's sensory impressions and "tactile values" (Berenson, 1909, p. 11), so we can confirm Machiavelli's act of political manipulation only if we consider how The Prince as text plays upon his reader's—Lorenzo de Medici's—values, desires, and sense of political possibility. Machiavelli will entice Lorenzo with a vision that will overwhelm his every other thought and distort his senses. With this in mind, we might recall the moment in Mandragola where Machiavelli (1957, p. 25) offers a poetic comment on Ligurio's power and on the outrageous gullibility of old Nicia:

> Our doctor here, would not suspect a lie
> If he were told that jackasses can fly;
> He has a heart so set on fatherhood,
> That he's forgotten every other good.

Ligurio can deceive Nicia because of his strategic perspective. He knows how to play upon the old man's desires and to organize his field of choices by advancing some alternatives and concealing others. He makes the prospect of Nicia's fathering a child so palpable that this promise of living on comes to control Nicia's world, his sensibilities, and his every perception. Thus the old doctor is trapped; duped not only by Ligurio's wiles but by his own vanity, his grandiose expectations set the stage for his becoming the cuckold.

If we bring our own strategic perspective to The Prince and look to the relationship Machiavelli establishes between his text and its intended reader, we might see a political version of Ligurian deception at work. Machiavelli offers Lorenzo the promise of a different sort of fatherhood—the fathering of the state of Italy. Machiavelli's strategy is Ligurian—to promise greatness to the Medici lord and thus render him susceptible to the further flatteries that will, in fact, undo him. Nowhere in *The Prince* is the Ligurian strategy as evident as in the famous chapter 26. There Machiavelli paints the prospect of the prince as saviour of Italy, leader of his people, unifier of the fractious city-states, forever immortalized by his power and glory. The passion and spirit of these Machiavellian declamations have long troubled many of his interpreters, who puzzle over the marked contrast between this final chapter and the cold calculation of the rest of *The Prince*. However, the troublesomeness of chapter 26 begins to recede if we remember that technical precision and vivid imagination were no strangers to the Renaissance painter nor, for that matter to Ligurio as he set out to trap his prey. Accordingly, we might read Machiavelli's final call to action as the "bait," or, to return once more to perspectival art, as the "vista" he offers Lorenzo. If the chapter does its work, Lorenzo, like Nicia, will "forget every other good" and so become not only Machiavelli's puppet, but the dupe of his own grandiose expectations of earthly power and political immortality.

Thus, Machiavelli sets out to manipulate the dimensions of Lorenzo's world. After presenting a particular scope of possibilities in *The Prince*, he artfully narrows the field of choices so that, in the end, the prince will live, act, and arm himself in the manner that his advisor recommends. Thus Machiavelli performs a feat of crafty assault, even as he accomplishes an act of political veracity. Lorenzo will be lured into following his advisor's dangerous counsel even as he reads this indeed unprecedented work of *realpolitik*. The beauty of the deception, were it to work, lies in Lorenzo's belief that his acts follow from his own *virtù* and seem perfectly in keeping with his aim to maintain power in life and achieve glory after death, while in reality they work to restore the republic.

Postscript

As a text, *The Prince* succeeded in securing Machiavelli's future fame and in sealing his notoriety. As a trap, it secured nothing. From all we know, Lorenzo never even read it. The republic Machiavelli wanted so passionately to see revived in Florence did indeed come later, but by different means than he envisioned and for but three short years, after which the Medici were installed in the city again. How could Machiavelli's stratagem have come to naught? How could his trap have failed to spring as he had hoped?

The deceiver himself would have a wry and ready answer: *Fortuna,* that mysterious goddess who governs half our actions, thwarted his plans and fouled his chances for success. As the chronicler tells it, on the day Machiavelli presented *The Prince* at the palace, Lorenzo was also given a gift of greyhounds, an unfortunate circumstance indeed, for the Medici lord was more intrigued with his hounds than with princely governance (Barincou, 1961, pp. 76–78). Yet there is more to the turn of fortune's wheel than this. Despite the greyhounds, it is hard to imagine why Lorenzo, a suspicious prince, would have taken this former republican, this *mannerino* of Soderini, into his confidence in the first place. Machiavelli's every attempt to appear to be other than he was in the end was no match for his unblemished reputation as a Florentine republican, and so *The Prince* remained unread and Machiavelli unsummoned, forced to return to the countryside, where he divided his days between the "ancient courts" and his favorite and altogether appropriate pastime—snaring thrushes with his bare hands (Ridolfi, 1963, p. 140).

His misfortune takes yet one more turn, however, and the story is well known. When the republic was restored in 1527, Machiavelli eagerly reapplied for his old job at the Second Chancery. The new republicans, however, were suspicious—at the least they viewed him as an untrustworthy opportunist, at the most as a pro-Medicean. They had, it seems, been more successfully duped by *The Prince* than Lorenzo himself, and they too refused to allow Machiavelli's return to political life. The irony is hard to miss: Machiavelli had, quite simply, outfoxed himself.

Whatever misfortune was dealt this master of deception, however, his designs in *The Prince* now seem clear. We need only to remember circumstances and recall what the chronicler reports on the occasion when the advice book was eclipsed by the hounds. Upon leaving the Medici palace, Machiavelli was said to have muttered that "though he was not a man to plot against princes, his little book would avenge him" (Barincou, 1961, p. 78). Far from avenging him, *The Prince* has for five centuries accused this Florentine patriot. His vindication is long overdue.

Notes

1. In international relations, see Waltz (1954) and Gulick (1955); in comparative politics, see Bluhm (1965); in organization theory, see Pfeffer (1981); in political psychology, see Nardulli, Flemming, and Eisenstein (1984).
2. See, among others, Wolin (1960), Pocock (1975), Shumer (1979), Skinner (1981), Hulliung (1983), and Pitkin (1984).
3. Quotations from Machiavelli's works are cited in the text using the following abbreviations: *P: The Prince* (1950, pp. 3–98); *D: The Discourses* (1950, pp. 101–540).
4. In a related fashion. J.R. Hale (1961, p. 175) suggests that Machiavelli thought "regeneration can be best organized by a prince, but when he feels that civic virtue has been restored, he should retire." Yet surely Machiavelli would not think that a prince would simply "retire" after restoring civic virtue or, for that matter, be interested in restoring the only virtue Machiavelli considers "civic"—republicanism. He knows too much of political rulership and Renaissance Florence to expect that.
5. Machiavelli (*P,* p. 78) offers one exception to this armament rule: the prince who acquires a new state in addition to the old one where his troops are stationed should disarm the former. However, this exception does not apply to the Medici, who were in exile as private citizens before their return to Florence and in control of no "old" state.

References

Ackerman, James. 1969. Concluding Remarks: Science and Art in the Work of Leonardo. In Charles Donald O'Malley, ed., *Leonardo's Legacy.* Berkeley: University of California Press.

Barincou, Edmond. 1961. *Machiavelli.* H. Lane, trans. New York and London: Grove Press and Evergreen Books.

Baron, Hans. 1961. Machiavelli: The Republican Citizen and the Author of *The Prince. English Historical Review,* 299:217–53.

Berenson, Bernhard. 1909. *The Florentine Painters of the Renaissance.* New York: Putnam's Sons.

Bluhm, William. 1965. *Theories of the Political System: Classics of Political Thought and Modern Political Analysis.* Englewood Cliffs: Prentice Hall.

Brucker, Gene. 1969. *Renaissance Florence.* Berkeley: University of California Press.

Burckhardt, Jacob. 1958. *The Civilization of the Renaissance in Italy.* 2 vols. New York: Harper and Row.

Gentili, Alberico. 1924. *De legationibus libri tres* [Three books about legations]. New York: Oxford University Press.

Gilbert, Allan. 1938. *Machiavelli's Prince and Its Forerunners.* Durham, NC: Duke University Press.

Gilbert, Felix. 1977. Machiavelli's *Istorie Fiorentine.* In Myron P. Gilmore, ed., *Studies on Machiavelli.* Florence: G. C. Sansoni.

Gilbert, Felix. 1984. *Machiavelli and Guicciardini: Politics and History in 16th Century Florence.* New York and London: W. W. Norton and Co.

Gulick, Edward Vose. 1955. *Europe's Classical Balance of Power: A Case History of One of the Great Concepts of European Statecraft.* Ithaca: Cornell University Press.

Hale, John Rigby. 1961. *Machiavelli and Renaissance Italy.* London: English University Press.

Hale, John Rigby. 1968. The End of Florentine Liberty: The Fortezza da Basso. In Nicolai Rubinstein, ed., *Florentine Studies: Politics and Society in Renaissance Florence.* London: Farber and Farber.

Hale, John Rigby. 1977. *Florence and the Medici.* London: Thames and Hudson.

Hulliung, Mark. 1983. *Citizen Machiavelli.* Princeton: Princeton University Press.

Machiavelli, Niccolò. 1950. *The Prince and the Discourses.* Luigi Ricci, trans. New York: Modern Library. Pp. 3–98; 101–540, respectively. (Original works published in 1532 and 1531.)

Machiavelli, Niccolò. 1957. *Mandragola.* Anne and Henry Paolucci, trans. New York: Bobbs-Merrill.

Machiavelli, Niccolò. 1961. *Letters.* Allan Gilbert, trans. New York: Capricorn.

Machiavelli, Niccolò. 1965. *The Art of War.* Ellis Farneworth, trans. Indianapolis and New York: Bobbs-Merrill. (Original work published in 1521.)

Machiavelli, Niccolò. 1970. *The History of Florence.* New York: Washington Square Press. (Original work published in 1532.)

Mattingly, Garrett. 1958. Machiavelli's *Prince:* Political Science or Political Satire? *American Scholar,* 27:482–91.

Najemy, John. 1982. Machiavelli and the Medici: The Lessons of Florentine History. *Renaissance Quarterly,* 35:551–76.

Nardulli, Peter, Roy Flemming, and James Eisenstein. 1984. Unraveling the Complexities of Decision Making in Face-to-Face-Groups: A Contextual Analysis of Plea-Bargained Sentences. *American Political Science Review,* 78:912–27.

Pansini, Anthony. 1969. *Niccolo Machiavelli and the United States of America.* Greenvale, NY: Greenvale Press.

Pfeffer, Jeffrey. 1981. *Power in Organizations.* Marshfield, MA: Pitman Press.

Pitkin, Hanna Fenichel. 1984. *Fortune Is a Woman.* Berkeley: University of California Press.

Pocock, J. G. A. 1975. *The Machiavellian Moment.* Princeton: Princeton University Press.

Ridolfi, Roberto. 1963. *The Life of Niccolo Machiavelli.* Chicago: University of Chicago. (Original work published in 1954.)

Rousseau, Jean-Jacques. 1978. *On the Social Contract.* Judith Masters, trans. New York: St. Martin's Press. (Original work published in 1782.)

Rubinstein, Nicolai. 1968. Constitutionalism and Medici Ascendency. In Nicolai Rubinstein, ed., *Florentine Studies.* London: Farber and Farber.

Rubinstein, Nicolai. 1972. Machiavelli and the World of Florentine Politics. In Myron Piper Gilmore, ed., *Studies on Machiavelli.* Florence: G. C. Sansoni.

Schevill, Ferdinand. 1936. *History of Florence from the Founding of the City Through the Renaissance.* New York: Ungar Publishing Company.

Shumer, Sara. 1979. Machiavelli: Republican Politics and Its Corruption. *Political Theory,* 7:5–34.

Skinner, Quentin. 1981. *Machiavelli.* New York: Hill & Wang.

Spinoza, Benedictus de. 1962. *Tractatus politicus* [Political treatise]. T. E. Jessop, trans. Montreal: M. Caselini. (Original work published in 1677.)

Strauss, Leo. 1952. *Persecution and the Art of Writing.* Glencoe, IL: Free Press.

Strauss, Leo. 1958. *Thoughts on Machiavelli.* Chicago: University of Chicago Press.

Wackernagel, Martin. 1981. *The World of the Florentine Renaissance Artist.* Alison Luchs, trans. Princeton: Princeton University Press.

Waltz, Kenneth. 1954. *Man, the State, and War: A Theoretical Analysis.* New York: Columbia University Press.

Wolin, Sheldon. 1960. *Politics and Vision.* Boston: Little, Brown and Co.

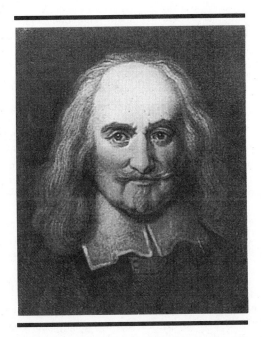

Thomas Hobbes

John Aubrey[1] tells a story of a clergyman who, upon seeing Thomas Hobbes give alms to a beggar, inquired of Hobbes if he was inspired by the commands of Jesus. Hobbes reportedly replied that the commands of Jesus had nothing to do with his act; rather, he had given alms to dismiss the beggar from his sight. While the validity of the tale may be suspect, there is no mistaking the reputation of Hobbes as an ardent advocate for self-interest, which the story conveys.

Hobbes was born at Malmesbury in Wiltshire, England in 1588. His premature birth, at the time when the Spanish Armada was approaching English shores, prompted him to recollect that "fear and I were born twins," a phrase which many believe typifies Hobbes's obsession with death. His father, a preacher, was forced to flee their home as a result of a brawl with a townsman when Thomas was young, leaving the boy to be raised by an uncle. He was educated at Magdalen Hall, Oxford, where he developed a dislike for the classic philosophers and a distrust of academic life. After receiving his Bachelor's degree, he secured the position of tutor for William Cavendish, the future earl of Devonshire. During this period he pursued his own liberal studies and wrote a translation of Thucydides. Hobbes developed an interest in geometry and in the new scientific method sweeping Europe. His tutoring posts allowed him the opportunity to travel, to correspond, and to meet with such Enlightenment notables as Galileo, Rene Descartes, and Francis Bacon.

1. John Aubrey. *Brief Lives.* (Ed. by O. L. Dick) Ann Arbor, Mich.: University of Michigan Press [1957].

Hobbes was particularly taken with the resoluto-compositive method, which he appropriated from Galileo. According to this method, complex phenomena are broken down into their simplest natural motions and components. Once these elements are understood, the workings of complex wholes are easily derived. Hobbes's intent was to develop a systematic study in three parts, starting with simple motions in matter (*De Corpore*), moving to the study of human nature (*De Homine*), and finally to politics (*De Cive*); each based on principles established at a "lower" level of analysis. Political upheavals at home caused him to attend to political writings before the other volumes of his trilogy were completed. He circulated drafts of *The Elements of Law* in 1640 and a limited edition of *De Cive* (On the Citizen) in 1642. In these, he developed the case for absolutism, which made him unpopular with many of his countryment in civil war England. He soon moved to France for fear of his life. There, he served as mathematics tutor to the exiled Prince of Wales, the future King Charles II.

Leviathan appeared in 1651, during the tumultuous period between the execution of Charles I and the naming of Cromwell as Lord Protector. As a result of its bold assertions regarding sovereignty, monarchy, and religion, it received wide attention in political circles. Hobbes returned to England the following year and soon became embroiled in a number of controversies, including one with John Wallis, professor of geometry at Oxford, over Hobbes's mathematical attempt to square the circle. In 1668, he finished a history of the period from 1640 to 1660 entitled *Behemouth*. Charles, his former charge now on the throne, sought to protect Hobbes from his critics by advising against its publication. It was only after Hobbes's death that it was allowed to surface. Hobbes died in 1679 at the age of ninety shortly after completing a translation of Homer's *Iliad* and *Odyssey*.

Leviathan

Leviathan is divided into four parts: Of Man, Of Commonwealth, Of a Christian Commonwealth, and Of the Kingdom of Darkness. While the first two parts are most read by students today, the last two parts were probably of central importance in his own day, when England was torn by religious strife. These parts focus on the power of the Church and the necessity for political control of religion.

The force of Hobbes's political teaching comes from his insistence that human mortality and politics can be understood on the basis of simple units of motion. In the first several chapters of Book I, Hobbes builds a political psychology that advances a view of humans as driven by passions and appetites. Among those passions that create conflict is the desire for the good opinion of others. In a world where there exists no natural standard for the political superiority of any individual, a desire for good opinion leads to conflict and to the "restless desire of power after power that ceaseth only in death." While there are passions that dispose us toward conflict, there also exist those which incline us toward peace; the most important of which is our fear of death. Working with these principles, Hobbes deduces nineteen "laws of nature" that guide human action. Two principal laws include man's "right to everything" and the advisability of laying down this right in the interest of peace and safety, so long as others do the same. These laws lead to the ultimate conclusion that men should unite under a contract for mutual safety and preservation. While those who contract are free to choose the type of enforcement (government) they like, Hobbes clearly favors monarchy as providing the most security with the least possibility of mischief brought by faction.

In the following selections, Hobbes reviews these principles and builds his case for monarchical rule. While Hobbes's absolutist tendencies are anachronistic in an era of democratic change, his discussions of human nature, the roots of obligation, and the nature of contractarian justice continue to provide political scholars with much to ponder regarding the foundation of the nation state.

Commentaries

In an excerpt from his now-classic study of the political foundations of the liberal state, C.B. MacPherson reviews Hobbes's contributions in forging a conceptual framework appropriate for the market economy that was beginning to emerge. While Hobbes may have been mistaken in portraying human nature as universally self-interested, MacPherson claims that Hobbes provided an accurate demonstration of the premises inherent in a competitive market economy. These include the equal subservience of all rational agents to the market as a means of deducing obligations, and the necessity of some type of sovereign power to enforce the "ground rules" upon which a market economy depends. Nevertheless, MacPherson notes that Hobbes's theory is seriously limited by his failure to notice the political significance of unequal social classes likely to develop in a marketplace economy.

In a provocative article, Deborah Baumgold argues that traditional views, portraying Hobbes as an authoritarian without regard for the typical citizen, miss the point that Hobbes was a forceful advocate of good rule. Baumgold reminds us that Hobbes builds enticements for good rule and penalties against abuse into the role of sovereign while providing enough clout to limit the unstabilizing effects of political rivalry. Contrary to popular visions of Hobbes, Baumgold sees in Hobbes the principle that only "lawful, fair rule enhances power."

Key Words

Diffidence. State of distrust. Hobbes believes this passion, along with competition and glory, leads to a state of war of all against all—unless checked by government.

Sovereignty. Ultimate power or authority. While Hobbes acknowledges that political sovereignty may rest in the hands of one, the few, or the many, his strong preference for monarchical supremacy leads him to use this term synonymously with monarchical power.

State of Nature. A philosophic device employed by Hobbes as a means of hypothesizing about human nature in a pre-political state, i.e., a state without external constraints on behavior. As Hobbes indicates, it is not necessary to presume such a state actually existed, only that is captures essential features humans naturally exhibit. The device becomes an important touchstone for many philosophers from this period onward.

For Further Reading

Gauthier, D. 1969. *The Logic of Leviathan: The Moral and Political Theory of Thomas Hobbes.* Oxford: Clarendon Press.

Goldsmith, M. M. 1966. *Hobbes's Science of Politics*. New York: Columbia University Press.

Hobbes, T. [1962.] *Leviathan*. (Ed. by M. Oakeshott with an Introduction by R. S. Peters). London: Collier-Macmillan.

Kavka, G. 1986. *Hobbesian Moral and Political Theory*. Princeton, N.J.: Princeton University Press.

Peters, R. 1956. *Hobbes*. Harmondsworth: Penguin.

Strauss, L. 1963. *The Political Philosophy of Hobbes: Its Basis and its Genesis*. Translated by Elsa Sinclair. Chicago: University of Chicago Press.

Warrender, H. 1957. *The Political Philosophy of Hobbes: His Theory of Obligation*. Oxford: Clarendon.

Leviathan

The First Part Of Man

Chapter 11

Of the Difference of Manners

What is here meant by manners. By manners, I mean not here, decency of behaviour; as how one should salute another, or how a man should wash his mouth, or pick his teeth before company, and such other points of the *small morals;* but those qualities of mankind, that concern their living together in peace, and unity. To which end we are to consider, that the felicity of this life, consisteth not in the repose of a mind satisfied. For there is no such *finis ultimus,* utmost arm, nor *summum bonum,* greatest good, as is spoken of in the books of the old moral philosophers. Nor can a man any more live, whose desires are at an end, than he, whose senses and imaginations are at a stand. Felicity is a continual progress of the desire, from one object to another; the attaining of the former, being still but the way to the latter. The cause whereof is, that the object of man's desire, is not to enjoy once only, and for one instant of time; but to assure for ever, the way of his future desire. And therefore the voluntary actions, and inclinations of all men, tend, not only to the procuring, but also to the assuring of a contented life; and differ only in the way: which ariseth partly from the diversity of passions, in divers men; and partly from the difference of the knowledge, or opinion each one has of the causes, which produce the effect desired.

A restless desire of power in all men. So that in the first place, I put for a general inclination of all mankind, a perpetual and restless desire of power after power, that ceaseth only in death. And the cause of this, is not always that a man hopes for a more intensive delight, than he has already attained to; or that he cannot be content with a moderate power: but because he cannot assure the power and means to live well, which he hath present, without the acquisition of more. And from hence it is, that kings, whose power is greatest, turn their endeavors to the assuring it at home by laws, or abroad by wars: and when that is done, there succeedeth a new desire; in some, of fame from new conquest; in others, of ease and sensual pleasure; in others, of admiration, or being flattered for excellence in some art, or other ability of the mind.

Love of contention from competition. Competition of riches, honour, command, or other power, inclineth to contention, enmity, and war: because the way of one competitor, to the attaining of his desire, is to kill, subdue, supplant, or repel the other. Particularly, competition of praise, inclineth to a reverence of antiquity. For men contend with the living, not with the dead; to these ascribing more than due, that they may obscure the glory of the other.

Civil obedience from love of ease. From fear of death, or wounds. Desire
of ease, and sensual delight, disposeth men to obey a common power:
because by such desires, a man doth abandon the protection that might be
hoped for from his own industry, and labour. Fear of death, and wounds,
disposeth to the same; and for the same reason. On the contrary, needy men,
and hardy, not contented with their present condition; as also, all men that
are ambitious of military command, are inclined to continue the causes of
war; and to stir up trouble and sedition: for there is no honour military but
by war; nor any such hope to mend an ill game, as by causing a new shuffle.

And from love of arts. Desire of knowledge, and arts of peace, inclineth
men to obey a common power: for such desire, containeth a desire of leisure;
and consequently protection from some other power than their own.

Love of virtue from love of praise. Desire of praise, disposeth to laudable
actions, such as please them whose judgment they value; for of those men
whom we contemn, we contemn also the praises. Desire of fame after death
does the same. And though after death, there be no sense of the praise given
us on earth, as being joys, that are either swallowed up in the unspeakable
joys of Heaven, or extinguished in the extreme torments of hell: yet is not
such fame vain; because men have a present delight therein, from the
foresight of it, and of the benefit that may redound thereby to their
posterity; which though they now see not, yet they imagine; and any thing
that is pleasure to the sense, the same also is pleasure in the imagination.

Hate, from difficulty of requiting great benefits. To have received from
one, to whom we think ourselves equal, greater benefits than there is hope
to requite, disposeth to counterfeit love; but really secret hatred; and puts a
man into the estate of a desperate debtor, in that in declining the sight of his
creditor, tacitly wishes him there, where he might never see him more. For
benefits oblige, and obligation is thraldom; and unrequitable obligation
perpetual thraldom; which is to one's equal, hateful. But to have received
benefits from one, whom we acknowledge for superior, inclines to love;
because the obligation is no new depression: and cheerful acceptation,
which men call *gratitude*, is such an honour done to the obliger, as is taken
generally for retribution. Also to receive benefits, though from an equal, or
inferior, as long as there is hope of requital, disposeth to love: for in the
intention of the receiver, the obligation is of aid and service mutual; from
whence proceedeth an emulation of who shall exceed in benefiting; the most
noble and profitable contention possible; wherein the victor is pleased with
his victory, and the other revenged by confessing it. . . .

Vain undertaking from vain-glory. Vain-glorious men, such as without
being conscious to themselves great sufficiency, delight in supposing
themselves gallant men, are inclined only to ostentation; but not to attempt:
because when danger or difficulty appears, they look for nothing but to have
their insufficiency discovered.

Vain-glorious men, such as estimate their sufficiency by the flattery of
other men, or the fortune of some precedent action, without assured ground
of hope from the true knowledge of themselves, are inclined to rash
engaging; and in the approach of danger, or difficulty, to retire if they can:
because not seeing the way of safety, they will rather hazard their honour,
which may be salved with an excuse; than their lives, for which no salve is
sufficient.

Ambition, from opinion of sufficiency. Men that have a strong opinion of their own wisdom in matter of government, are disposed to ambition. Because without public employment in council or magistracy, the honour of their wisdom is lost. And therefore eloquent speakers are inclined to ambition; for eloquence seemeth wisdom, both to themselves and others. . . .

Curiosity to know, from care of future time. Anxiety for the future time, disposeth men to inquire into the causes of things: because the knowledge of them, maketh men the better able to order the present to their best advantage.

Natural religion from the same. . . .

And they that make little, or no inquiry into the natural causes of things, yet from the fear that proceeds from the ignorance itself, of what it is that hath the power to do them much good or harm, are inclined to suppose, and feign themselves, several kinds of powers invisible; and to stand in awe of their own imaginations; and in time of distress to invoke them; as also in the time of an expected good success, to give them thanks; making the creatures of their own fancy, their gods. By which means it hath come to pass, that from the innumerable variety of fancy, men have created in the world innumerable sorts of gods. And this fear of things invisible, is the natural seed of that, which every one in himself calleth religion; and in them that worship, or fear that power otherwise than they do, superstition.

And this seed of religion, having been observed by many; some of those that have observed it, have been inclined thereby to nourish, dress, and form it into laws; and to add to it of their own invention, any opinion of the causes of future events, by which they thought they should be best able to govern others, and make unto themselves the greatest use of their powers.

Chapter 13

Of the Natural Condition of Mankind as concerning their Felicity and Misery

Men by nature equal. Nature hath made men so equal, in the faculties of the body, and mind; as that though there be found one man sometimes manifestly stronger in body, or of quicker mind than another; yet when all is reckoned together, the difference between man, and man, is not so considerable, as that one man can thereupon claim to himself any benefit, to which another may not pretend, as well as he. For as to the strength of body, the weakest has strength enough to kill the strongest, either by secret machination, or by confederacy with others, that are in the same danger with himself.

And as to the faculties of the mind, setting aside the arts grounded upon words, and especially that skill of proceeding upon general, and infallible rules, called science; which very few have, and but in few things; as being not a native faculty, born with us; nor attained, as prudence, while we look after somewhat else, I find yet a greater equality amongst men, than that of strength. For prudence, is but experience; which equal time, equally bestows on all men, in those things they equally apply themselves unto. That which may perhaps make such equality incredible, is but a vain conceit of one's own wisdom, which almost all men think they have in a greater degree, than the vulgar; that is, than all men but themselves, and a few others, whom by fame, or for concurring with themselves, they approve. For such is the nature of men, that howsoever they may acknowledge many others to be more witty, or more eloquent, or more learned; yet they will hardly believe there be many so wise as themselves; for they see their own wit at hand, and other men's at a distance. But this proveth rather that men are in that point equal, than unequal. For there is not ordinarily a greater sign of the equal distribution of any thing, than that every man is contented with his share.

From equality proceeds diffidence. From this equality of ability, ariseth equality of hope in the attaining of our ends. And therefore if any two men desire the same thing, which nevertheless they cannot both enjoy, they become enemies; and in the way to their end, which is principally their own conservation, and sometimes their delectation only, endeavour to destroy, or subdue one another. And from hence it comes to pass, that where an invader hath no more to fear, than another man's single power; if one plant, sow, build, or possess a convenient seat, others may probably be expected to come prepared with forces united, to dispossess, and deprive him, not only of the fruit of his labour, but also of his life, or liberty. And the invader again is in the like danger of another.

From diffidence war. And from this diffidence of one another, there is no way for any man to secure himself, so reasonable, as anticipation; that is, by force, or wiles, to master the persons of all men he can, so long, till he see no other power great enough to endanger him: and this is no more than his own conservation requireth, and is generally allowed. Also because there be some, that taking pleasure in contemplating their own power in the acts of conquest, which they pursue farther than their security requires; if others, that otherwise would be glad to be at ease within modest bounds, should not by invasion increase their power, they would not be able, long time, by standing only on their defence, to subsist. And by consequence, such augmentation of dominion over men being necessary to a man's conservation, it ought to be allowed him.

Again, men have no pleasure, but on the contrary a great deal of grief, in keeping company, where there is no power able to over-awe them all. For every man looketh that his companion should value him, at the same rate he sets upon himself: and upon all signs of contempt, or undervaluing, naturally endeavours, as far as he dares, (which amongst them that have no common power to keep them in quiet, is far enough to make them destroy each other), to extort a greater value from his contemners, by damage; and from others, by the example.

So that in the nature of man, we find three principal causes of quarrel. First, competition; secondly, diffidence; thirdly, glory.

The first, maketh men invade for gain; the second, for safety; and the third, for reputation. The first use violence, to make themselves masters of other men's persons, wives, children, and cattle; the second, to defend them; the third, for trifles, as a word, a smile, a different opinion, and any other sign of undervalue, either direct in their persons, or by reflection in their kindred, their friends, their nation, their profession, or their name.

Out of civil states, there is always war of every one against every one. Hereby it is manifest, that during the time men live without a common power to keep them all in awe, they are in that condition which is called war;

and such a war, as is of every man, against every man. For WAR, consisteth not in battle only, or the act of fighting; but in a tract of time, wherein the will to contend by battle is sufficiently known: and therefore the notion of *time*, is to be considered in the nature of war; as it is in the nature of weather. For as the nature of foul weather, lieth not in a shower or two of rain; but in an inclination thereto of many days together: so the nature of war, consisteth not in actual fighting; but in the known disposition thereto, during all the time there is no assurance to the contrary. All other time is PEACE.

The incommodities of such a war. Whatsoever therefore is consequent to a time of war, where every man is enemy to every man; the same is consequent to the time, wherein men live without other security, than what their own strength, and their own invention shall furnish them withal. In such condition, there is no place for industry; because the fruit thereof is uncertain: and consequently no culture of the earth; no navigation, nor use of the commodities that may be imported by sea; no commodious building; no instruments of moving, and removing, such things as require much force; no knowledge of the face of the earth; no account of time; no arts; no letters; no society; and which is worst of all, continual fear, and danger of violent death; and the life of man, solitary, poor, nasty, brutish, and short.

It may seem strange to some man, that has not well weighed these things; that nature should thus dissociate, and render men apt to invade, and destroy one another: and he may therefore, not trusting to this inference, made from the passions, desire perhaps to have the same confirmed by experience. Let him therefore consider with himself, when taking a journey, he arms himself, and seeks to go well accompanied; when going to sleep, he locks his doors; when even in his house he locks his chests; and this when he knows there be laws, and public officers, armed, to revenge all injuries shall be done him; what opinion he has of his fellow-subjects, when he rides armed; of his fellow citizens, when he locks his doors; and of his children, and servants, when he locks his chests. Does he not there as much accuse mankind by his actions, as I do by my words? But neither of us accuse man's nature in it. The desires, and other passions of man, are in themselves no sin. No more are the actions, that proceed from those passions, till they know a law that forbids them: which till laws be made they cannot know: nor can any law be made, till they have agreed upon the person that shall make it.

It may peradventure be thought, there was never such a time, nor condition of war as this; and I believe it was never generally so, over all the world: but there are many places, where they live so now. For the savage people in many places of America, except the government of small families, the concord whereof dependeth on natural lust, have no government at all; and live at this day in that brutish manner, as I said before. Howsoever, it may be perceived what manner of life there would be, where there were no common power to fear, by the manner of life, which men that have formerly lived under a peaceful government, use to degenerate into, in a civil war.

But though there had never been any time, wherein particular men were in a condition of war one against another; yet in all times, kings, and persons of sovereign authority, because of their independency, are in continual jealousies, and in the state and posture of gladiators; having their weapons pointing, and their eyes fixed on one another; that is, their forts, garrisons, and guns upon the frontiers of their kingdoms; and continual spies upon their neighbours; which is a posture of war. But because they uphold thereby, the industry of their subjects; there does not follow from it, that misery, which accompanies the liberty of particular men.

In such a war nothing is unjust. To this war of every man, against every man, this also is consequent; that nothing can be unjust. The notions of right and wrong, justice and injustice have there no place. Where there is no common power, there is no law: where no law, no injustice. Force, and fraud, are in war the two cardinal virtues. Justice, and injustice are none of the faculties neither of the body, nor mind. If they were, they might be in a man that were alone in the world, as well as his senses, and passions. They are qualities, that relate to men in society, not in solitude. It is consequent also to the same condition, that there be no propriety, no dominion, no *mine* and *thine* distinct; but only that to be every man's, that he can get: and for so long, as he can keep it. And thus much for the ill condition, which man by mere nature is actually placed in; though with a possibility to come out of it, consisting partly in the passions, partly in his reason.

The passions that incline men to peace. The passions that incline men to peace, are fear of death; desire of such things as are necessary to commodious living; and a hope by their industry to obtain them. And reason suggesteth convenient articles of peace, upon which men may be drawn to agreement. These articles, are they, which otherwise are called the Laws of Nature: whereof I shall speak more particularly, in the two following chapters.

Chapter 14

Of the First and Second Natural Laws, and of Contracts

Right of nature what. THE RIGHT OF NATURE, which writers commonly call *jus naturale*, is the liberty each man hath, to use his own power, as he will himself, for the preservation of his own nature; that is to say, of his own life; and consequently, of doing any thing, which in his own judgment, and reason, he shall conceive to be the aptest means thereunto.

Liberty what. By LIBERTY, is understood, according to the proper signification of the word, the absence of external impediments: which impediments, may oft take away part of a man's power to do what he would; but cannot hinder him from using the power left him, according as his judgment, and reason shall dictate to him.

A law of nature what. Difference of right and law. A LAW OF NATURE, *lex naturalis*, is a precept or general rule, found out by reason, by which a man is forbidden to do that, which is destructive of his life, or taketh away the means of preserving the same; and to omit that, by which he thinketh it may be best preserved. For though they that speak of this subject, use to confound *jus*, and *lex*, *right* and *law*: yet they ought to be distinguished; because RIGHT, consisteth in liberty to do, or to forbear: whereas LAW, determineth, and bindeth to one of them: so that law, and right, differ as much, as obligation, and liberty; which in one and the same matter are inconsistent.

Naturally every man has right to every thing. The fundamental law of nature. And because the condition of man, as hath been declared in the precedent chapter, is a condition of war of every one against every one; in which case every one is governed by his own reason; and there is nothing he can make use of, that may not be a help unto him, in preserving his life against his enemies; it followeth, that in such a condition, every man has a right to every thing; even to one another's body. And therefore, as long as this natural right of every man to every thing endureth, there can be no security to any man, how strong or wise soever he be, of living out the time, which nature ordinarily alloweth men to live. And consequently it is a precept, or general rule of reason, *that every man, ought to endeavour peace, as far as he has hope of obtaining it; and when he cannot obtain it, that he may seek, and use, all helps, and advantages of war.* The first branch of which rule, containeth the first, and fundamental law of nature; which is, *to seek peace, and follow it.* The second, the sum of the right of nature; which is, *by all means we can, to defend ourselves.*

The second law of nature. From this fundamental law of nature, by which men are commanded to endeavour peace, is derived this second law; *that a man be willing, when others are so too, as far-forth, as for peace, and defence of himself he shall think it necessary, to lay down this right to all things; and be contented with so much liberty against other men, as he would allow other men against himself.* For as long as every man holdeth this right, of doing any thing he liketh; so long are all men in the condition of war. But if other men will not lay down their right, as well as he; then there is no reason for any one, to divest himself of his: for that were to expose himself to prey, which no man is bound to, rather than to dispose himself to peace. This is that law of the Gospel; *whatsoever you require that others should do to you, that do ye to them.* And that law of all men, *quod tibi fieri non vis, alteri ne feceris.*

What it is to lay down a right. To *lay down* a man's *right* to any thing, is to *divest* himself of the *liberty,* of hindering another of the benefit of his own right to the same. For he that renounceth, or passeth away his right, giveth not to any other man a right which he had not before; because there is nothing to which every man had not right by nature: but only standeth out of his way, that he may enjoy his own original right, without hindrance from him; not without hindrance from another. So that the effect which redoundeth to one man, by another man's defect of right, is but so much diminution of impediments to the use of his own right original.

Renouncing a right, what it is. Transferring right what. Obligation. Duty. Injustice. Right is laid aside, either by simply renouncing it; or by transferring it to another. By *simply* RENOUNCING; when he cares not to whom the benefit thereof redoundeth. By TRANSFERRING; when he intendeth the benefit thereof to some certain person, or persons. And when a man hath in either manner abandoned, or granted away his right; then he is said to be OBLIGED, or BOUND, not to hinder those, to whom such right is granted, or abandoned, from the benefit of it: and that he *ought,* and it is his DUTY, not to make void that voluntary act of his own: and that such hindrance is INJUSTICE, and INJURY, as being *sine jure;* the right being before renounced, or transferred. So that *injury,* or *injustice,* in the controversies of the world, is somewhat like to that, which in the disputations of scholars is called *absurdity.* For as it is there called an absurdity, to contradict what one maintained in the beginning: so in the world, it is called injustice, and injury, voluntarily to undo that, which from the beginning he had voluntarily done. The way by which a man either simply renounceth, or transferreth his right, is a declaration, or signification, by some voluntary and sufficient sign, or signs, that he doth so renounce, or transfer; or hath so renounced, or transferred the same, to him that accepteth it. And these signs are either words only, or actions only; or, as it happeneth most often, both words, and actions. And the same are the BONDS, by which men are bound, and obliged: bonds, that have their strength, not from their own nature, for nothing is more easily broken than a man's word, but from fear of some evil consequence upon the rupture.

Not all rights are alienable. Whensoever a man transferreth his right, or renounceth it; it is either in consideration of some right reciprocally transferred to himself; or for some other good he hopeth for thereby. For it is a voluntary act: and of the voluntary acts of every man, the object is some *good to himself.* And therefore there be some rights, which no man can be understood by any words, or other signs, to have abandoned, or transferred. As first a man cannot lay down the right of resisting them, that assault him by force, to take away his life; because he cannot be understood to aim thereby, at any good to himself. The same may be said of wounds, and chains, and imprisonment; both because there is no benefit consequent to such patience; as there is to the patience of suffering another to be wounded, or imprisoned: as also because a man cannot tell, when he seeth men proceed against him by violence, whether they intend his death or not. And lastly the motive, and end for which this renouncing, and transferring of right is introduced, is nothing else but the security of a man's person, in his life, and in the means of so preserving life, as not to be weary of it. And therefore if a man by words, or other signs, seem to despoil himself of the end, for which those signs were intended; he is not to be understood as if he meant it, or that it was his will; but that he was ignorant of how such words and actions were to be interpreted.

Contract what. The mutual transferring of right, is that which men call CONTRACT.

There is difference between transferring of right to the thing; and transferring, or tradition, that is delivery of the thing itself. For the thing may be delivered together with the translation of the right; as in buying and selling with ready-money; or exchange of goods, or lands: and it may be delivered some time after.

Covenant what. Again, one of the contractors, may deliver the thing contracted for on his part, and leave the other to perform his part at some determinate time after, and in the mean time be trusted; and then the contract on his part, is called PACT, or COVENANT: or both parts may contract now, to perform hereafter: in which cases, he that is to perform in time to come, being trusted, his performance is called *keeping of promise,* or faith; and the failing of performance, if it be voluntary, *violation of faith....*

Covenants how made void. Men are freed of their covenants two ways; by performing; or by being forgiven. For performance, is the natural end of obligation; and forgiveness, the restitution of liberty; as being a retransferring of that right, in which the obligation consisted.

Covenants extorted by fear are valid. Covenants entered into by fear, in the condition of mere nature, are obligatory. For example, if I covenant to pay a ransom, or service for my life, to an enemy; I am bound by it: for it is a contract, wherein one receiveth the benefit of life; the other is to receive money, or service for it; and consequently, where no other law, as in the condition of mere nature, forbiddeth the performance, the covenant is valid. Therefore prisoners of war, if trusted with the payment of their ransom, are obliged to pay it: and if a weaker prince, make a disadvantageous peace with a stronger, for fear; he is bound to keep it; unless, as hath been said before, there ariseth some new, and just cause of fear, to renew the war. And even in commonwealths, if I be forced to redeem myself from a thief by promising him money, I am bound to pay it, till the civil law discharge me. For whatsoever I may lawfully do without obligation, the same I may lawfully covenant to do through fear: and what I lawfully covenant, I cannot lawfully break.

The former covenant to one, makes void the later to another. A former covenant, makes void a later. For a man that hath passed away his right to one man to-day, hath it not to pass to-morrow to another: and therefore the later promise passeth no right, but is null.

A man's covenant not to defend himself is void. A covenant not to defend myself from force, by force, is always void. For, as I have showed before, no man can transfer, or lay down his right to save himself from death, wounds, and imprisonment, the avoiding whereof is the only end of laying down any right; and therefore the promise of not resisting force, in no covenant transferreth any right; nor is obliging. For though a man may covenant thus, *unless I do so, or so, kill me;* he cannot covenant thus, *unless I do so, or so, I will not resist you, when you come to kill me.* For man by nature chooseth the lesser evil, which is danger of death in resisting; rather than the greater, which is certain and present death in not resisting. And this is granted to be true by all men, in that they lead criminals to execution, and prison, with armed men, notwithstanding that such criminals have consented to the law, by which they are condemned. . . .

Chapter 15

Of other Laws of Nature

The third law of nature, justice. From that law of nature, by which we are obliged to transfer to another, such rights, as being retained, hinder the peace of mankind, there followeth a third; which is this, *that men perform their covenants made:* without which, covenants are in vain, and but empty words; and the right of all men to all things remaining, we are still in the condition of war.

Justice and injustice what. And in this law of nature, consisteth the fountain and original of JUSTICE. For where no covenant hath preceded, there hath no right been transferred, and every man has right to every thing; and consequently, no action can be unjust. But when a covenant is made, then to break it is *unjust:* and the definition of INJUSTICE, is no other than *the not performance of covenant.* And whatsoever is not unjust, is *just.*

Justice and propriety begin with the constitution of commonwealth. But because covenants of mutual trust, where there is a fear of not performance on either part, as hath been said in the former chapter, are invalid; though the original of justice be the making of covenants; yet injustice actually there can be none, till the cause of such fear be taken away; which while men are in the natural condition of war, cannot be done. Therefore before the names of just, and unjust can have place, there must be some coercive power, to compel men equally to the performance of their covenants, by the terror of some punishment, greater than the benefit they expect by the breach of their covenant; and to make good that propriety, which by mutual contract men acquire, in recompense of the universal right they abandon: and such power there is none before the erection of a commonwealth. And this is also to be gathered out of the ordinary definition of justice in the Schools: for they say, that *justice is the constant will of giving to every man his own.* And therefore where there is no *own*, that is no propriety, there is no injustice; and where there is no coercive power erected, that is, where there is no commonwealth, there is no propriety; all men having right to all things: therefore where there is no commonwealth, there nothing is unjust. So that the nature of justice, consisteth in keeping of valid covenants: but the validity of covenants begins not but with the constitution of a civil power, sufficient to compel men to keep them: and then it is also that propriety begins.

Justice not contrary to reason. . . .

For the question is not of promises mutual, where there is no security of performance on either side; as when there is no civil power erected over the parties promising; for such promises are no covenants: but either where one of the parties has performed already; or where there is a power to make him perform; there is the question whether it be against reason, that is, against the benefit of the other to perform, or not. And I say it is not against reason. For the manifestation whereof, we are to consider; first, that when a man doth a thing, which notwithstanding any thing can be foreseen, and reckoned on, tendeth to his own destruction, howsoever some accident which he could not expect, arriving may turn it to his benefit; yet such events do not make it reasonably or wisely done. Secondly, that in a condition of war, wherein every man to every man, for want of a common power to keep them all in awe, is an enemy, there is no man who can hope by his own strength, or wit, to defend himself from destruction, without the help of confederates; where every one expects the same defence by the confederation, that any one else does: and therefore he which declares he thinks it reason to deceive those that help him, can in reason expect no other means of safety, than what can be had from his own single power. He therefore that breaketh his covenant, and consequently declareth that he thinks he may with reason do so, cannot be received into any society, that unite themselves for peace and defence, but by the error of them that receive him; nor when he is received, be retained in it, without seeing the danger of their error; which errors a man cannot reasonably reckon upon as the means of his security: and therefore if he be left, or cast out of society, he perisheth; and if he live in society, it is by the errors of other men, which he could not foresee, nor reckon upon; and consequently against the reason of his preservation; and so, as all men that contribute not to his destruction, forbear him only out of ignorance of what is good for themselves.

As for the instance of gaining the secure and perpetual felicity of heaven, by any way; it is frivolous: there being but one way imaginable; and that is not breaking, but keeping of covenant.

And for the other instance of attaining sovereignty by rebellion; it is manifest, that though the event follow, yet because it cannot reasonably be expected, but rather the contrary; and because by gaining it so, others are taught to gain the same in like manner, the attempt thereof is against reason. Justice therefore, that is to say, keeping of covenant, is a rule of reason, by which we are forbidden to do any thing destructive to our life; and consequently a law of nature. . . .

Justice commutative and distributive. Justice of actions, is by writers divided into *commutative,* and *distributive:* and the former they say consisteth in proportion arithmetical; the latter in proportion geometrical. Commutative therefore, they place in the equality of value of the things contracted for; and distributive, in the distribution of equal benefit, to men of equal merit. As if it were injustice to sell dearer than we buy; or to give more to a man than he merits. The value of all things contracted for, is measured by the appetite of the contractors: and therefore the just value, is that which they be contented to give. And merit (besides that which is by covenant, where the performance on one part, meriteth the performance on the other part, and falls under justice commutative, not distributive) is not due to justice; but is rewarded of grace only. And therefore this distinction, in the sense wherein it useth to be expounded, is not right. To speak properly, commutative justice, is the justice, of a contractor; that is, a performance of covenant, in buying, and selling; hiring, and letting to hire; lending, and borrowing; exchanging, bartering, and other acts of contract.

And distributive justice, the justice of an arbitrator; that is to say, the act of defining what is just. Wherein, being trusted by them that make him arbitrator, if he perform his trust, he is said to distribute to every man his own: and this is indeed just distribution, and may be called, though improperly, distributive justice; but more properly equity; which also is a law of nature, as shall be shown in due place. . . .

A rule, by which the laws of nature may easily be examined. And though this may seem too subtle a deduction of the laws of nature, to be taken notice of by all men; whereof the most part are too busy in getting food, and the rest too negligent to understand; yet to leave all men inexcusable, they have been contracted into one easy sum, intelligible even to the meanest capacity; and that is, *Do not that to another, which thou wouldest not have done to thyself;* which sheweth him, that he had no more to do in learning the laws of nature, but, when weighing the actions of other men with his own, they seem too heavy, to put them into the other part of the balance, and his own into their place, that his own passions, and self-love, may add nothing to the weight; and then there is none of these laws of nature that will not appear unto him very reasonable.

The laws of nature oblige in conscience always, but in effect then only when there is security. The laws of nature oblige *in foro interno;* that is to say, they bind to a desire they should take place: but *in foro externo;* this is, to the putting them in act, not always. For he that should be modest, and tractable, and perform all he promises, in such time, and place, where no man else should do so, should but make himself a prey to others, and procure his own certain ruin, contrary to the ground of all laws of nature, which tend to nature's preservation. And again, he that having sufficient security, that others shall observe the same laws towards him, observes them not himself, seeketh not peace, but war; and consequently the destruction of his nature by violence.

And whatsoever laws bind *in foro interno*, may be broken, not only by a fact contrary to the law, but also by a fact according to it, in case a man think it contrary. For though his action in this case, be according to the law; yet his purpose was against the law; which, where the obligation is *in foro interno*, is a breach.

The laws of nature are eternal. The laws of nature are immutable and eternal; for injustice, ingratitude, arrogance, pride, iniquity, acception of persons, and the rest, can never be made lawful. For it can never be that war shall preserve life, and peace destroy it.

And yet easy. The same laws, because they oblige only to a desire, and endeavour, I mean an unfeigned and constant endeavour, are easy to be observed. For in that they require nothing but endeavour, he that endeavoureth their performance, fufilleth them; and he that fulfilleth the law, is just.

The science of these laws, is the true moral philosophy. And the science of them, is the true and only moral philosophy. For moral philosophy is nothing else but the science of what is *good,* and *evil,* in the conversation, and society of mankind. *Good,* and *evil,* are names that signify our appetites, and aversions; which in different tempers, customs, and doctrines of men, are different: and divers men, differ not only in their judgment, on the senses of what is pleasant, and unpleasant to the taste, smell, hearing, touch, and sight; but also of what is conformable, or disagreeable to reason, in the actions of common life. Nay, the same man, in divers times, differs from himself; and one time praiseth, that is, calleth good, what another time he dispraiseth, and calleth evil: from whence arise disputes, controversies, and at last war. And therefore so long as a man is in the condition of mere nature, which is a condition of war, as private appetite is the measure of good, and evil: and consequently all men agree on this, that peace is good, and therefore also the way, or means of peace, which, as I have shewed before, are *justice, gratitude, modesty, equity, mercy,* and the rest of the laws of nature, are good; that is to say; *moral virtues;* and their contrary *vices,* evil. Now the science of virtue and vice, is moral philosophy; and therefore the true doctrine of the laws of nature, is the true moral philosophy. But the writers of moral philosophy, though they acknowledge the same virtues and vices; yet not seeing wherein consisted their goodness; nor that they come to be praised, as the means of peaceable, sociable, and comfortable living, place them in a mediocrity of passions: as if not the cause, but the degree of daring, made fortitude; or not the cause, but the quantity of a gift, made liberality.

These dictates of reason, men used to call by the names of laws, but improperly: for they are but conclusions, or theorems concerning what conduceth to the conservation and defence of themselves; whereas law, properly, is the word of him, that by right hath command over others. But yet if we consider the same theorems, as delivered in the word of God, that by right commandeth all things; then are they properly called laws.

The Second Part Of Commonwealth

Chapter 17

Of the Causes, Generation, and Definition
of a Commonwealth

The end of commonwealth, particularly security. The final cause, end, or design of men, who naturally love liberty, and dominion over others, in the introduction of that restraint upon themselves, in which we see them live in commonwealths, is the foresight of their own preservation, and of a more contented life thereby; that is to say, of getting themselves out from that miserable condition of war, which is necessarily consequent, as hath been shown (chapter 13), to the natural passions of men, when there is no visible power to keep them in awe, and tie them by fear of punishment to the performance of their covenants, and observation of those laws of nature set down in the fourteenth and fifteenth chapters.

Which is not to be had from the law of nature. For the laws of nature, as *justice, equity, modesty, mercy,* and, in sum, *doing to others, as we would be done to,* of themselves, without the terror of some power, to cause them to be observed, are contrary to our natural passions, that carry us to partiality, pride, revenge, and the like. And covenants, without the sword, are but words, and of no strength to secure a man at all. Therefore notwithstanding the laws of nature (which every one hath then kept, when he has the will to keep them, when he can do it safely) if there be no power erected, or not great enough for our security; every man will, and may lawfully rely on his own strength and art, for caution against all other men. And in all places, where men have lived by small families, to rob and spoil one another, has been a trade, and so far from being reputed against the law of nature, that the greater spoils they gained, the greater was their honour; and men observed no other laws therein, but the laws of honour; that is, to abstain from cruelty, leaving to men their lives, and instruments of husbandry. And as small families did then; so now do cities and kingdoms which are but greater families, for their own security, enlarge their dominions, upon all pretences of danger, and fear of invasion, or assistance that may be given to invaders, and endeavour as much as they can, to subdue, or weaken their neighbours, by open force, and secret arts, for want of other caution, justly; and are remembered for it in after ages with honour.

Nor from the conjunction of a few men or families. Nor is it the joining together of a small number of men, that gives them this security; because in small numbers, small additions on the one side or the other, make the advantage of strength so great, as is sufficient to carry the victory; and therefore gives encouragement to an invasion. The multitude sufficient to confide in for our security, is not determined by any certain number, but by comparison with the enemy we fear; and is then sufficient, when the odds of the enemy is not of so visible and conspicuous moment, to determine the event of war, as to move him to attempt.

Nor from a great multitude, unless directed by one judgment. And be there never so great a multitude; yet if their actions be directed according to their particular judgments, and particular appetites, they can expect thereby no defence, nor protection, neither against a common enemy, nor against the injuries of one another. For being distracted in opinions concerning the best use and application of their strength, they do not help but hinder one another; and reduce their strength by mutual opposition to nothing: whereby they are easily, not only subdued by a very few that agree together; but also when there is no common enemy, they make war upon each other, for their particular interests. For if we could suppose a great multitude of men to consent in the observation of justice, and other laws of nature, without a common power to keep them all in awe; we might as well suppose all mankind to do the same; and then there neither would be, nor need to be any civil government, or commonwealth at all; because there would be peace without subjection.

And that continually. Nor is it enough for the security, which men desire should last all the time of their life, that they be governed, and directed by one judgment, for a limited time; as in one battle, or one war. For though they obtain a victory by their unanimous endeavour against a foreign enemy; yet afterwards, when either they have no common enemy, or he that by one part is held for an enemy, is by another part held for a friend, they must needs by the difference of their interests dissolve, and fall again into a war amongst themselves.

Why certain creatures without reason, or speech, do nevertheless live in society, without any coercive power. It is true, that certain living creatures, as bees, and ants, live sociably one with another, which are therefore by Aristotle numbered amongst political creatures; and yet have no other direction, than their particular judgments and appetites; nor speech, whereby one of them can signify to another, what he thinks expedient for the common benefit: and therefore some man may perhaps desire to know, why mankind cannot do the same. To which I answer,

First, that men are continually in competition for honour and dignity, which these creatures are not; and consequently amongst men there ariseth on that ground, envy and hatred, and finally war; but amongst these not so.

Secondly, that amongst these creatures, the common good differeth not from the private; and being by nature inclined to their private, they procure thereby the common benefit. But man, whose joy consisteth in comparing himself with other men, can relish nothing but what is eminent.

Thirdly, that these creatures, having not, as man, the use of reason, do not see, nor think they see any fault, in the administration of their common business; whereas amongst men, there are very many, that think themselves wiser, and abler to govern the public, better than the rest; and these strive to reform and innovate, one this way, another that way; and thereby bring it into distraction and civil war.

Fourthly, that these creatures, though they have some use of voice, in making known to one another their desires, and other affections; yet they want that art of words, by which some men can represent to others, that which is good, in the likeness of evil; and evil, in the likeness of good; and augment, or diminish the apparent greatness of good and evil; discontenting men, and troubling their peace at their pleasure.

Fifthly, irrational creatures cannot distinguish between *injury*, and *damage;* and therefore as long as they be at ease, they are not offended with their fellows: whereas man is then most troublesome, when he is most at ease: for then it is that he loves to shew his wisdom, and control the actions of them that govern the commonwealth.

Lastly, the agreement of these creatures is natural; that of men, is by covenant only, which is artificial: and therefore it is no wonder if there be somewhat else required, besides covenant, to make their agreement constant and lasting; which is a common power, to keep them in awe, and to direct their actions to the common benefit.

The generation of a commonwealth. The definition of a commonwealth. The only way to erect such a common power, as may be able to defend them from the invasion of foreigners, and the injuries of one another, and thereby to secure them in such sort, as that by their own industry, and by the fruits of the earth, they may nourish themselves and live contentedly; is, to confer all their power and strength upon one man, or upon one assembly of men, that may reduce all their wills, by plurality of voices, unto one will: which is as much as to say, to appoint one man, or assembly of men, to bear their person; and every one to own, and acknowledge himself to be author of whatsoever he that so beareth their person, shall act, or cause to be acted, in those things which concern the common peace and safety; and therein to submit their wills, every one to his will, and their judgments, to his judgment. This is more than consent, or concord; it is a real unity of them all, in one and the same person, made by covenant of every man with every man, in such manner, as if every man should say to every man, *I authorize and give up my right of governing myself, to this man, or to this assembly of men, on this condition, that thou give up thy right to him, and authorize all his actions in like manner.* This done, the multitude so united in one person, is called a COMMONWEALTH, in Latin CIVITAS. This is the generation of that great LEVIATHAN, or rather, to speak more reverently, of that *mortal god*, to which we owe under the *immortal God*, our peace and defence. For by this authority, given him by every particular man in the commonwealth, he hath the use of so much power and strength conferred on him, that by terror thereof, he is enabled to form the wills of them all, to peace at home, and mutual aid against their enemies abroad. And in him consisteth the essence of the commonwealth; which, to define it, is *one person, of whose acts a great multitude, by mutual covenants one with another, have made themselves every one the author, to the end he may use the strength and means of them all, as he shall think expedient, for their peace and common defence.*

Sovereign, and subject, what. And he that carrieth this person is called SOVEREIGN, and said to have *sovereign power;* and every one besides, his SUBJECT.

The attaining to this sovereign power, is by two ways. One by natural force; as when a man maketh his children, to submit themselves, and their children to his government, as being able to destroy them if they refuse; or by war subdueth his enemies to his will, giving them their lives on that condition. The other, is when men agree amongst themselves, to submit to some man, or assembly of men, voluntarily, on confidence to be protected by him against all others. This latter, may be called a political commonwealth, or commonwealth by *institution;* and the former, a commonwealth by *acquisition.* And first, I shall speak of a commonwealth by institution.

Chapter 18

Of the Rights of Sovereigns by Institution

The act of instituting a commonwealth, what. A *commonwealth* is said to be *instituted*, when a *multitude* of men do agree, and *covenant, every one, with every one*, that to whatsoever *man*, or *assembly of men*, shall be given by the major part, the *right* to *present* the person of them all, that is to say, to be their *representative;* every one, as well he that *voted for it*, as he that *voted against it*, shall *authorize* all the actions and judgments, of that man, or assembly of men, in the same manner, as if they were his own, to the end, to live peaceably amongst themselves, and be protected against other men.

The consequences to such institutions, are: From this institution of a commonwealth are derived all the *rights*, and *faculties* of him, or them, on whom the sovereign power is conferred by the consent of the people assembled.

1. *The subjects cannot change the form of government.* First, because they covenant, it is to be understood, they are not obliged by former covenant to any thing repugnant hereunto. And consequently they that have already instituted a commonwealth, being thereby bound by covenant, to own the actions, and judgments of one, cannot lawfully make a new covenant, amongst themselves, to be obedient to any other, in any thing whatsoever, without his permission. And therefore, they that are subjects to a monarch, cannot without his leave cast off monarchy, and return to the confusion of a disunited multitude; nor transfer their person from him that beareth it, to another man, or other assembly of men: for they are bound, every man to every man, to own, and be reputed author of all, that he that already is their sovereign, shall do and judge fit to be done: so that any one man dissenting, all the rest should break their covenant made to that man, which is injustice: and they have also every man given the sovereignty to him that beareth their person; and therefore if they depose him, they take from him that which is his own, and so again it is injustice. Besides, if he that attempteth to depose his sovereign, be killed, or punished by him for such attempt, he is author of his own punishment, as being by the institution, author of all his sovereign shall do: and because it is injustice for a man to do any thing, for which he may be punished by his own authority, he is also upon that title, unjust. And whereas some men have pretended for their disobedience to their sovereign, a new covenant, made, not with men, but with God; this also is unjust: for there is no covenant with God, but by mediation of somebody that representeth God's person; which none doth but God's lieutenant, who hath the sovereignty under God. But this pretence of covenant with God, is so evident a lie, even in the pretenders' own consciences, that it is not only an act of an unjust, but also of a vile, and unmanly disposition.

2. *Sovereign power cannot be forfeited.* Secondly, because the right of bearing the person of them all, is given to him they make sovereign, by covenant only of one to another, and not of him to any of them; there can happen no breach of covenant on the part of the sovereign; and consequently none of his subjects, by any pretence of forfeiture, can be freed from his subjection. That he which is made sovereign maketh no covenant with his subjects beforehand, is manifest; because either he must make it with the

whole multitude, as one party to the covenant; or he must make a several covenant with every man. With the whole, as one party, it is impossible; because as yet they are not one person: and if he make so many several covenants as there be men, those covenants after he hath the sovereignty are void; because what act soever can be pretended by any one of them for breach thereof, is the act both of himself, and of all the rest, because done in the person, and by the right of every one of them in particular. Besides, if any one, or more of them, pretend a breach of the covenant made by the sovereign at his institution; and others, or one other of his subjects, or himself alone, pretend there was no such breach, there is in this case, no judge to decide the controversy; it returns therefore to the sword again; and every man recovereth the right of protecting himself by his own strength, contrary to the design they had in the institution. It is therefore in vain to grant sovereignty by way of precedent covenant. The opinion that any monarch receiveth his power by covenant, this is to say, on condition, proceedeth from want of understanding this easy truth, that covenants being but words and breath, have no force to oblige, contain, constrain, or protect any man, but what it has from the public sword; that is, from the untied hands of that man, or assembly of men that hath the sovereignty, and whose actions are avouched by them all, and performed by the strength of them all, in him united. But when an assembly of men is made sovereign; then no man imagineth any such covenant to have passed in the institution; for no man is so dull as to say, for example, the people of Rome made a covenant with the Romans, to hold the sovereignty on such or such conditions; which not performed, the Romans might lawfully depose the Roman people. That men see not the reason to be alike in a monarchy, and in a popular government, proceedeth from the ambition of some, that are kinder to the government of an assembly, whereof they may hope to participate, than of monarchy, which they despair to enjoy.

3. *No man can without injustice protest against the institution of the sovereign declared by the major part.* Thirdly, because the major part hath by consenting voices declared a sovereign; he that dissented must now consent with the rest; that is, be contented to avow all the actions he shall do, or else justly be destroyed by the rest. For if he voluntarily entered into the congregation of them that were assembled, he sufficiently declared thereby his will, and therefore tacitly covenanted, to stand to what the major part should ordain: and therefore if he refuse to stand thereto, or make protestation against any of their decrees, he does contrary to his covenant, and therefore unjustly. And whether he be of the congregation, or not; and whether his consent be asked, or not, he must either submit to their decrees, or be left in the condition of war he was in before; wherein he might without injustice be destroyed by any man whatsoever.

4. *The sovereign's actions cannot be justly accused by the subject.* Fourthly, because every subject is by this institution author of all the actions, and judgments of the sovereign instituted; it follows, that whatsoever he doth, it can be no injury to any of his subjects; nor ought he to be by any of them accused of injustice. For he that doth anything by authority from another, doth therein no injury to him by whose authority he acteth: but by this institution of a commonwealth, every particular man is author of all the sovereign doth: and consequently he that complaineth of injury from

his sovereign, complaineth of that whereof he himself is author; and therefore ought not to accuse any man but himself; no nor himself of injury; because to do injury to one's self, is impossible. It is true that they that have sovereign power may commit iniquity; but not injustice, or injury in the proper signification.

5. *Whatsoever the sovereign doth is unpunishable by the subject.* Fifthly, and consequently to that which was said last, no man that hath sovereign power can justly be put to death, or otherwise in any manner by his subjects punished. For seeing every subject is author of the actions of his sovereign; he punisheth another for the actions committed by himself.

6. *The sovereign is judge of what is necessary for the peace and defence of his subjects.* And because the end of this institution, is the peace and defence of them all; and whosoever has right to the end, has right to the means; it belongeth of right, to whatsoever man, or assembly that hath the sovereignty, to be judge both of the means of peace and defence, and also of the hindrances, and disturbances of the same; and to do whatsoever he shall think necessary to be done, both beforehand, for the preserving of peace and security, by prevention of discord at home, and hostility from abroad; and, when peace and security are lost, for the recovery of the same. And therefore,

And judge of what doctrines are fit to be taught them. Sixthly, it is annexed to the sovereignty, to be judge of what opinions and doctrines are averse, and what conducing to peace; and consequently, on what occasions, how far, and what men are to be trusted withal, in speaking to multitudes of people; and who shall examine the doctrines of all books before they be published. For the actions of men proceed from their opinions; and in the well-governing of opinions, consisteth the well-governing of men's actions, in order to their peace, and concord. And though in matter of doctrine, nothing ought to be regarded but the truth; yet this is not repugnant to regulating the same by peace. For doctrine repugnant to peace, can no more be true, than peace and concord can be against the law of nature. It is true, that in a commonwealth, where by the negligence, or unskilfulness of governors, and teachers, false doctrines are by time generally received; the contrary truths may be generally offensive. Yet the most sudden, and rough busling in of a new truth, that can be, does never break the peace, but only sometimes awake the war. For those men that are so remissly governed, that they dare take up arms to defend, or introduce an opinion, are still in war; and their condition not peace, but only a cessation of arms for fear of one another; and they live, as it were, in the precincts of battle continually. It belongeth therefore to him that hath the sovereign power, to be judge, or constitute all judges of opinions and doctrines, as a thing necessary to peace; thereby to prevent discord and civil war. . . .

9. *And of making war, and peace, as he shall think best.* Ninthly, is annexed to the sovereignty, the right of making war and peace with other nations, and commonwealths; that is to say, of judging when it is for the public good, and how great forces are to be assembled, armed, and paid for that end; and to levy money upon the subjects, to defray the expenses thereof. For the power by which the people are to be defended, consisteth in their armies; and the strength of an army, in the union of their strength under one command; which command the sovereign instituted, therefore

hath; because the command of the *militia,* without other institution, maketh him that hath it sovereign. And therefore whosoever is made general of an army, he that hath the sovereign power is always generalissimo. . . .

Sovereign power not so hurtful as the want of it, and the hurt proceeds for the greatest part from not submitting readily to a less. But a man may here object, that the condition of subjects is very miserable; as being obnoxious to the lusts, and other irregular passions of him, or them that have so unlimited a power in their hands. And commonly they that live under a monarch, think it the fault of monarchy; and they that live under the government of democracy, or other sovereign assembly, attribute all the, inconvenience to that form of commonwealth; whereas the power in all forms, if they be perfect enough to protect them, is the same: not considering that the state of man can never be without some incommodity or other; and that the greatest, that in any form of government can possibly happen to the people in general, is scarce sensible in respect of the miseries, and horrible calamities, that accompany a civil war, or that dissolute condition of masterless men, without subjection to laws, and a coercive power to tie their hands from rapine and revenge: nor considering that the greatest pressure of sovereign governors, proceedeth not from any delight, or profit they can expect in the damage or weakening of their subjects, in whose vigour, consisteth their own strength and glory; but in the restiveness of themselves, that unwillingly contributing to their own defence, make it necessary for their governors to draw from them what they can in time of peace, that they may have means on any emergent occasion, or sudden need, to resist, or take advantage on their enemies. For all men are by nature provided of notable multiplying glasses, that is their passions and self-love, through which, every little payment appeareth a great grievance; but are destitute of those prospective glasses, namely moral and civil science, to see afar off the miseries that hang over them, and cannot without such payments be avoided.

The Political Theory of Possessive Individualism
C.B. MacPherson

Penetration and Limits of Hobbes's Political Theory

i. Historical prerequisites of the deduction

I have argued that the difference between moral and prudential obligation becomes insignificant as soon as reliance on some transcendental will or purpose is rejected; that when it is rejected the significant question is whether any obligation that can be expected to be binding on rational individuals is possible; that such obligation is possible if men see themselves, or can be expected to come to see themselves, as equal in some respect more vital than all their inequalities; that Hobbes grasped this; and that the equal subservience of all men to the determination of the market which he put in his model of society, and which is an attribute of possessive market societies, is a sufficient basis for the deduction of obligation binding on all rational men in that society, so long as possessive market relations prevail and are thought inevitable.

This is a greater measure of validity than is usually allowed Hobbes's system, though it would not have satisfied Hobbes, who thought he had deduced from eternal facts of man's nature the one kind of political obligation that would always be necessary and possible. But if his own claims for his theory were too high, his achievements are still remarkable. He opened a new way in political theory. And he penetrated closer to the nature of modern society than any of his contemporaries and many of his successors. Each of these achievements deserves our notice.

Hobbes's most valid claim is perhaps his most arrogant one: 'Civil Philosophy [is] no older . . . than my own book *De Cive.*'[1] Hobbes was the first political thinker to have seen the possibility of deducing obligation directly from the mundane facts of men's actual relations with each other, including the equality inhering in those relations; having seen this possibility, he was the first to be able to dispense with assumptions of outside purpose or will. The Stoic and Christian natural law traditions had of course asserted the equality of all men, but this was an assertion less of fact than of an aspiration that men should think of themselves as equal by reflecting on their common rationality or common creation. Common rationality is a tenuous and imprecise quality in comparison with the insecurity and subservience to the market which Hobbes found just beneath the surface of everyday life. Perhaps because rationality was so tenuous, divine purpose and will had early been brought in to the natural law tradition to support the postulate of common rationality, and with their introduction the question of getting obligation from the mundane facts no longer arose.

1. *English Works,* (ed. Molesworth) London, 1839; i, p. ix.

It is not surprising that Hobbes was the first political thinker to break away from the traditional reliance on a supposed will or purpose infusing the universe, and base himself on a supposed mundane equality.[2] Before Hobbes, everything had conspired to make political thinkers rely on standards of value and entitlement imported from outside the observed facts. For one thing, market relations had nowhere penetrated all social relations sufficiently to make it conceivable that values could be established by the operation of objective but not supernatural forces. For another, most political thinkers before Hobbes had worked in markedly class-divided societies in which hierarchical order appeared to be the only alternative to political and moral anarchy. In hierarchical societies the danger of slave or peasant revolts or popular equalitarian movements is never entirely absent. As long as such movements are thought to be anarchical, thinkers who are constructing theories of political obligation must assume some functional or moral inequality between classes of men, for hierarchical society requires unequal rights and obligations. And since the merits of hierarchy and an inequalitarian moral code could not be expected to be made rationally evident to a class which might consider itself oppressed, there was an additional reason to deduce a code of obligation from some divine or transcendent order rather than directly from the capacities and needs of men.

Hobbes also lived in a class-divided society. But he did not find it necessary to impute significantly unequal capacities or needs to different classes of men. For on his reading of the facts of seventeenth-century society, social order was no longer dependent on the maintenance of hierarchy. He thought that the objective market had replaced, or could replace, the inequality of ranks, and had at the same time established an equality of insecurity. He did not, of course, rely on the market alone to provide order. A political sovereign was necessary to guarantee order, by enforcing rules which would prevent the peaceful competition of the market turning into, or being supplemented by, open force. But the authority of the sovereign could now be made to rest on a rational transfer of rights agreed upon by men who were equal in a double sense: their value and entitlements were equally governed by the market, and in the face of the market they appeared to be equally insecure. Hobbes, unlike his predecessors, did not need to impose a hierarchy of unequal values on his data, because he did not see any need to read unequal values out again, into his moral and political rules, as unequal rights and obligations. And for the same reason he was able, unlike his predecessors, to dispense with supposed divine or natural purposes: because he did not need to impute inequality, he did not need to assume an unobservable purpose or will into which inequality of value and entitlement could be inserted.

In short, the development of a market society had, by Hobbes's time, provided two necessary conditions for a deduction of political obligation from mundane facts, neither of which conditions had been present earlier. First, it had created, or was visibly creating, an equality before the law of the market, sufficiently compelling to be made the basis of an obligation binding on rational men who saw their real position. The presence of this equality, as I have argued, made the deduction of obligation from fact logically unobjectionable. Secondly, the development of a market society had replaced or was visibly replacing hierarchical order by the objective order of the market, which did not require unequal rights for different ranks.

---

2. The distinction of being the first to have broken away might be claimed for Grotius, who did detach natural law from divine will and purpose. But Grotius relied on a supposed factual quality of sociability which was almost as tenuous as the earlier rationality.

The decline of hierarchical order thus provided, for the first time, at least one of the conditions which would make the deduction of obligation from fact politically unobjectionable. To say that the social conditions which made Hobbes's deduction logically and politically possible were not present before his time is not to belittle his achievement. It is rather to recognize the insight with which he penetrated to the essential relations of his own society, and the skill with which he built on them.

ii. The self-perpetuating sovereign

This assessment of Hobbes's achievement seems strikingly at variance with the actual reception of his doctrine in his own day. If, as I have argued, he grasped the essential relations of his own society and built logically on them, his conclusions should surely have been acceptable at least to the new men of the mid-seventeenth century and later, to those who welcomed the incursion of market relations in English society. Yet we know that Hobbes's doctrine was not accepted by any significant group or movement in England in his own century. Neither royalists nor parliamentarians, neither traditionalists nor radical republicans, neither Whigs nor Tories, could stomach it. Many of his critics, including the most vocal, rejected both his premisses and his conclusions. But even those who substantially accepted Hobbes's analysis of human nature and shared his view of society as a market, among whom we may include Harrington and even Locke, rejected his full conclusions. When we notice what of Hobbes's conclusions they rejected and what they accepted, we shall see more clearly what part of his doctrine is in principle acceptable, and what part unacceptable, in a market society.

Neither Harrington nor Locke objected to sovereign power. Both held that there must be somewhere in any civil society a political power to which every individual must be understood to have resigned all his rights and powers, and which must be unlimited by any conjoint or superior human power. Harrington was perfectly explicit: 'Where the soverain power is not as entire and absolute as in monarchy itself, there can be no government at all.'[3] Locke put sovereign power in the civil society, i.e. in the majority: since they were assumed to will nothing but the public good they could safely have sovereign power, and somebody had to have it.[4] The man or assembly to whom the civil society then entrusted legislative and executive power was, of course, not sovereign; but where this power was given to an elective assembly rather than to a self-perpetuating assembly or a monarch, Locke allowed it to exercise virtually sovereign power.[5] What both Harrington and Locke thought unnecessary, and inconsistent with the only purposes for which individuals could conceivably authorize sovereign power, was that the sovereign power should be put irrevocably in the hands of a person or body of persons with authority to appoint his or their own successors. They objected not to perpetual sovereign power but to a self-perpetuating sovereign person or body.

Yet Hobbes had insisted that the person or persons who held the sovereign power at any given moment should be self-perpetuating. This of course put the holders of sovereign power always beyond the control of the people or of any section of the people; and this, however unfortunate, was in Hobbes's view unavoidable. He considered self-perpetuating power an essential attribute of sovereignty. 'There is no

---

3. *Art of Lawgiving, Oceana and Other Works,* Book III, Preface (London, 1771, p. 404).

4. *Second Treatise,* ed. Peter Laslett, Cambridge, 1960, sects. 89, 95–99.

5. *Second Treatise,* sects. 138, 142.

perfect forme of Government, where the disposing of the Succession is not in the present Soveraign.'[6] A sovereign assembly must have the right to fill vacancies in its membership; a sovereign monarch must have the right to appoint his successor. No one after Hobbes, however much they agreed with Hobbes's estimate of men as self-interested calculating machines and however much they accepted the values of a market society, could agree that this required men to acknowledge the sovereign authority of a self-perpetuating body. Practice also contraverted Hobbes's conclusion. England was governed successfully, at least from 1689 on, by a body, the king in parliament, which was sovereign except in the one power of self-perpetuation: the king could not appoint his successor, nor could the members of a given parliament appoint theirs.

The fact that English society soon came to be adequately governed by a sovereign body without self-perpetuating power shows that Hobbes's full prescription was not necessary for the maintenance of a stable society. It shows also that, in the measure that English society was then a possessive market society, Hobbes's prescription was not necessary for a possessive market society. Yet Hobbes's prescription was a deduction from the necessary behaviour of men in his model of society, which . . . [was] substantially the same as the model of the possessive market society. Where, then, was the error?

The source of the error was . . . that he did not allow for the existence of politically significant unequal classes. He saw society as so necessarily fragmented by the struggle of each for power over others that all were equal in insecurity. He failed to see that the very same characteristic of a society which makes it an incessant competition of each for power over others, makes it also an unequal class-divided society. The characteristic is the all-pervasive market relationship. Only where all men's powers are marketable commodities can there be an incessant competition of each for power over others; and where all men's powers are commodities there is necessarily a division of society into unequal classes.

It was Hobbes's failure to see this that led him to see society as so completely fragmented. And it was from his view of society as so completely fragmented that he deduced the need for a self-perpetuating sovereign person or body. He argued[7] that if the person or persons who hold sovereign power were not acknowledged to have the right to appoint their successors, then whenever any successors had to be chosen, the real power would be thrown back to the fragmented and opposed powers of all the separate members of the society, thus negating the whole purpose for which they had authorized sovereign power.

What Hobbes missed, then, was the possibility of class cohesion offsetting the fragmenting forces in market society. If one assumes no class cohesion, as Hobbes did, there is no way to provide the necessary political power except for all individuals to hand everything over to a self-perpetuating sovereign body. But if there is a cohesive class, its sense of common interest may be strong enough to make its members capable of upholding a sovereign government and of holding it ultimately responsible to themselves by retaining the right of appointing or electing to the sovereign body. Hobbes was not so blind as to have missed the fact that there was a class division in England, as is evident from his remarks in *Behemoth*. He saw, too, that the growth of the market relation had undermined the old values, and that the new men of mercantile wealth had enough cohesion to foment a civil war. But he was apparently more impressed with the divisive effects of the loss of old values, and with the

---

6. *Leviathan,* ed. W. G. Pogson Smith, Oxford, 1929, ch. 19, p. 149.

7. *Leviathan,* ch. 19, p. 149.

contests for power between different groups on the parliamentary side which broke out as soon as the monarchy had been thrown over, than by the cohesion that had enabled the opponents of the old structure to overthrow it. At any rate, he did not put class division into his model. There, the universality of the competitive struggle between individuals is assumed to have dissolved all class inequalities and all class cohesiveness. Hobbes's model failed to correspond, in this one essential, to the model of possessive market society as well as to the actual English society.

This shortcoming in Hobbes's model of society was what misled him to conclude that a self-perpetuating sovereign body was necessary. It made his conclusions inapplicable to the possessive market society, and unacceptable to the proponents of market society in seventeenth-century England. Since he left class division and class cohesion out of his model, there was no place in his conclusions for a sovereign body tied to one class. Yet that is the kind of government most agreeable to the model of a possessive market society. Those who possess substantial property need a sovereign state to sanction the right of possession. They must therefore authorize a sovereign body to do whatever is necessary to maintain the right of possession, and the sovereign body must have the right to decide what is necessary. But the men of property need not give up their right or power to choose the persons who shall from time to time be the members of the sovereign body. And since they need not do so, they cannot, as rational men, do so. They need not do so because, as possessors of substantial property, they are capable of enough cohesion for the recurrent choice of members of the sovereign body to be left to them without all authority being dispersed among myriad conflicting wills every time a choice of members has to be made. The argument on which Hobbes rested the necessity of a self-perpetuating sovereign body is thus without basis in a class-divided society with a cohesive possessing class; and the very fact that a society is so divided tends to give a sufficient degree of cohesion to the possessing class.

iii. Congruence of sovereignty and market society

Although Hobbes was in error in concluding that the men of his society needed or could sustain a self-perpetuating sovereign body, he was right in concluding that they needed and could sustain an irresistible sovereign power. The argument on which he based the need and possibility of every man acknowledging an obligation to a sovereign power remains valid for a possessive market society, even when its class division is taken into account. For even a cohesive possessing class still needs a sovereign power. A sovereign is needed to hold everyone within the limits of peaceful competition. The more nearly the society approximates a possessive market society, subject to the centrifugal forces of opposed competitive self-interests, the more necessary a single centralized sovereign power becomes. In a customary society a network of conditional property rights may be maintained without a single central sovereign. But in a market society, where property becomes an unconditional right to use, to exclude others absolutely from the use of,[8] and to transfer or alienate,[9] land and other goods, a sovereign is necessary to establish and maintain individual property rights. Without a sovereign power, Hobbes said, there can be no property,[10]

---

8. *Philosophic Rudiments Concerning Government and Society* published under the title *De Cive or the Citizen*, ed. S.P. Lamprecht, New York, 1949, ch. 14, sect. 7, p. 160; *Leviathan*, ch. 24, pp. 190–191.

9. Ibid., pp. 192–3.

10. *Leviathan*, ch. 24, pp. 189–90.

and he was right about the kind of property characteristic of a possessive market society.

A sovereign is also needed 'to appoint in what manner, all kinds of contract between Subjects, (as buying, selling, exchanging, borrowing, lending, letting, and taking to hire,) are to bee made; and by what words, and signes they shall be understood for valid'.[11] Hobbes presented this as a need in any society. It is not so in every society, but it is so in a market society. And it is an especially pressing need, requiring a strong sovereign power, when a possessive market society is replacing a customary society, for then customary rights have to be extinguished in favour of contractual rights. A sovereign power is necessary also, especially when market society is not yet firmly established, to instil the motivations or behaviour required in the formative stages of market society. Luxurious consumption must be discouraged, thrift and industry encouraged, the able-bodied 'are to be forced to work; and to avoyd the excuse of not finding employment, there ought to be such Lawes, as may encourage all manner of Arts; as Navigation, Agriculture, Fishing, and all manner of Manifacture that requires labour'.[12]

The need for a sovereign power in a possessive market society, and especially in an emerging one, is thus evident. And it was evident to Hobbes. He held, indeed, that a sovereign power was needed for these purposes in any society. He reached this conclusion because he had put into his model of society as such the essential relations of the possessive market society. If he was at fault in the breadth of his generalization, he was far ahead of any contemporary political thinker in the depth of his insight.

But it is not enough to establish the need for a sovereign power unless at the same time and from the same postulates one can establish the *possibility* of a sovereign power. Can the kind of society which especially needs sovereign power sustain sovereign power? Can the individuals in such a fragmented and competitive society possibly support a political power fully and steadily enough to render it a sovereign power? Here we must distinguish between individuals of the possessing and the non-possessing classes.

The rational man who, in such a society, possesses substantial property, or hopes to acquire it and hold it, is capable of acknowledging obligation to such a sovereign. He is used to long-term contracts, he sees the point of the rule that contracts must be performed. He conducts his affairs by rational calculation of long-run advantage; he does what his rational calculation tells him he should do. He is precisely the kind of man who can see the net advantage of the kind of contractual order which a sovereign power can provide. He is, of course, not a perfect calculator. If he and his fellows were all perfect calculators, steadily seeing the net advantage of staying within the rules of a contractual society, no sovereign would be needed to regulate relations among them (though one might still be needed to regulate relations between them and the non-possessors). Market men are good enough calculators to see the net advantage of everybody sticking to the rules, but each of them cannot be relied on to keep this long-run advantage steadily in his mind alongside the short-run advantage he may see from time to time in breaking the rules. But each is capable of seeing the net advantage to himself of having a sovereign to enforce the rules on everybody. For it is easier to comply with rules so institutionalized; it leaves each man freer to make the day-to-day decisions of net advantage if he does not have to calculate, every time,

---

11. Ibid., p. 193.
12. Ibid., ch. 30, p. 267; cf. *Rudiments*, ch. 13, sect. 14, pp. 150–1.

the probable effect of his breaking the rules on other people's conformity to the rules, or even worse, the probability of others independently breaking the rules and acting in unpredictable ways. Only where there is a sovereign to enforce the rules, is the number of variables in each man's calculation reduced to manageable proportions.

On these grounds, individuals of the possessing class in a market society may well be thought capable of acknowledging obligation to a sovereign who can enforce the rules necessary for the operation of that kind of society. Here again we must credit Hobbes with the essential insight. True, he generalized too widely in attributing this capacity to men in every kind of society. But he got to the heart of the matter. The rational capacity on which he based the need and possibility of men acknowledging a sovereign is precisely the kind and degree of rational calculation that can be expected of the rational man who is making his way in a possessive market society.

What of the man without substantial property or hope of acquiring it? Is the lifelong wage-earner, living at bare subsistence level, capable of acknowledging obligation to a sovereign whose main function is to make and enforce the rules of contract and property, rules which the wage-earner may feel are what have put him and keep him in this precarious position? Yes, so long as he can see no alternative to the possessive market society. If he can see no alternative, he has no rational choice but to acknowledge obligation to a sovereign power which can at least protect his life. Perhaps that is why Hobbes was not at all worried by the objection he foresaw would be made to his doctrine, namely, that 'Common people are not of capacity enough to be made to understand' the principles on which their obligation rests.[13] He thought them perfectly capable of it, more so than 'the Rich, and Potent Subjects of Kingdome, or those that are accounted the most Learned'. The common people, he said, have no interest contrary to their acknowledging a sovereign; a sovereign power does not bridle or diminish them as it does the Potent and the Learned. Rather, 'the Common-peoples minds, unless they be tainted with dependance on the Potent, or scribbled over with the opinions of their Doctors, are like clean paper, fit to receive whatsoever by Publique Authority shall be imprinted in them'. Since they can be brought to acquiesce in religious doctrines which are above reason and against reason, they are capable of accepting this doctrine of obligation to the sovereign 'which is so consonant to Reason'.[14] All that is necessary is that the common people be instructed in it, which Hobbes thought might be done by 'setting a part from their ordinary labour, some certain times, in which they may attend those that are appointed to instruct them'.[15]

In dealing thus with the common people Hobbes shows some awareness of their characteristics as a separate class. He does not say they are capable of this obligation because they see their position is inevitable, but he assumes that in so far as they are made aware of their true position they will see that it is inevitable. In this assumption Hobbes was not far from the mark. The common people, the men of no property, had no alternative to the acceptance of the possessive market society.

I have argued that the society about which Hobbes wrote with such prescience, needed and could support a sovereign power. I have found only two faults with his doctrine. The first is that he mistakenly attributed the characteristics of market society to all societies, and so claimed a wider validity for his conclusions than they can have; this, however, is a fault that does not affect the validity of his conclusions for

---

13. *Leviathan*, ch. 30, p. 260.

14. Ibid.

15. Ibid., p. 262.

possessive market societies. The second is that he failed to see, or to give sufficient weight to, the class division which a possessive market society necessarily generates, and so concluded mistakenly that the sovereign power must and could be in a self-perpetuating person or assembly. When his theory is reduced to historical measure, when it is treated as a theory about possessive market society, only this second fault is, on our analysis, to be alleged against it. This second fault is indeed a serious one, enough by itself to make his full theory untenable for such societies.

But it is still worth while to insist that, apart from this one error, Hobbes's analysis and conclusions are substantially valid for possessive market societies. When his theory is read as a theory about possessive market societies, he makes his case that individuals need, and are capable of acknowledging steady obligation to, an all-powerful sovereign body (though not a self-perpetuating one). That is as much as should be claimed for Hobbes. When no more is claimed, some of the main objections that are generally taken to his theory lose much of their force.

iv. Some objections reconsidered

The most serious and persistent difficulty in Hobbes's theory, when it is taken as a theory about man and society as such, is that men who are moved, as Hobbes has them moved, by unlimited competitive appetites, seem incapable of acknowledging a binding obligation which limits their motion. If all men are so moved that they are necessarily engaged in an incessant competitive struggle for power, how can they admit an obligation which overrides this? If men are necessarily so impelled to invade each other that they need a sovereign, how can they be capable of supporting a sovereign? No very satisfactory answer can be given to these questions when they are posed so generally. But when the questions are asked about men in possessive market societies they can be answered. Such individuals both need a sovereign and can support a sovereign. For in such societies they can incessantly invade each other without destroying each other. They need a sovereign to keep their invasions within non-destructive bounds, and they are capable of sustaining such a sovereign because they can go on invading under the sovereign's rules. They support a sovereign in order to permit themselves to go on invading each other. It is only in possessive market society that all men must invade each other, and only there that all can do so within the rules of the society. They can, therefore, support those rules, and the power necessary to enforce them, without stultifying themselves. One of the central difficulties in Hobbes's theory of obligation thus disappears when the theory is treated as a theory of and for possessive market societies. . . .

There is no mystery about what Hobbes thought. He thought that men now calculate or weigh means and ends less efficiently than they could do; and that they could learn to do it (under Hobbes's tutelage) more efficiently. Men could learn to build better than they do.[16] Educability is one of the assumed elements of human nature. But even if educability is granted, what expectation can there be, except from the accident of Hobbes's publishing his doctrine, that men can now do what they have not yet done? Hobbes relied on a general tendency, supported by historical observation, that when men see some new knowledge to be to their advantage they will use it.

> Time, and Industry, produce every day new knowledge. And as the art of well building, is derived from Principles of Reason, observed by industrious

---

16. *Leviathan*, ch. 20, p. 160.

men, that had long studied the nature of materials, and the divers effects of figure, and proportion, long after mankind began (though poorly) to build: So, long time after men have begun to constitute Commonwealths, imperfect, and apt to relapse into disorder, there may, Principles of Reason be found out, by industrious meditation, to make their constitution (excepting by externall violence) everlasting. And such are those which I have in this discourse set forth. . . .[17]

If it be granted as a law of human nature that men always use new knowledge which they see to be to their advantage, their failure to have acknowledged steady obligation to a sovereign hitherto must be due to one of two reasons: either they had not discovered that it was advantageous, or it had not in fact been as advantageous to them earlier as it was now. Hobbes was satisfied with the first of these reasons. When challenged on the ground that the principles would have been discovered already if they were really so advantageous, he was able to point to the record in the physical sciences, where new principles were being discovered in his century which he thought might as well have been, but which in fact had not been, discovered earlier. The parallel, however, is not exact. For on Hobbes's own analysis of the elements of human nature, the urgency of political science was, and always had been, greater than the urgency of the natural sciences. Natural philosophy produces commodious living, lack of natural philosophy withholds these pleasant commodities; but lack of civil philosophy produces calamity:

> the utility of moral and civil philosophy is to be estimated, not so much by the commodities we have by knowing these sciences, as by the calamities we receive from not knowing them. Now, all such calamities as may be avoided by human industry, arise from war, but chiefly from civil war; for from this proceed slaughter, solitude, and the want of all things.[18]

And the cause of civil war was that men had not learned the rules of civil life sufficiently, the knowledge of which rules was moral philosophy. This being so, and avoidance of violent death being (and always having been) man's greatest need, the slow rate of discovery in natural philosophy can scarcely account for the slow rate in moral and civil philosophy. If men's need for moral and civil philosophy had always been so great, they could reasonably be expected to have made Hobbes's discovery earlier.

It is not a sufficient reply to say that the reason men have not embraced true principles of civil philosophy is that those principles cross their own interests. Hobbes sometimes suggested this, as in his comparison of mathematical and dogmatical learning:

> The former is free from controversies and dispute, because it consisteth in comparing figures and motion only; in which things truth and the interest of men oppose not each other. But in the later there is nothing not disputable, because it compareth men, and meddleth with their right and profit; in which, as oft as reason is against a man, so oft will a man be against reason.[19]

But if true principles of civil philosophy crossed men's interests before, and if men's interests have not changed, the principles must still cross their interests to the same

---

17. Ibid., ch. 30, pp. 259–60.

18. *English Works,* i. 8.

19. *Elements of Law Natural and Politic* (ed. F. Tonnies), Cambridge, 1928. Ep. Ded., p. xvii.

extent. One might conclude from this, as some critics of Hobbes have done, that Hobbes's analysis of human nature was simply incorrect: the reason men had not made and used Hobbes's discovery earlier is that men's nature does not contain the balance of interests or balance of motives that Hobbes said it did. If Hobbes was simply wrong about man's nature, there is no problem about why men have not acted in the way Hobbes said they should act to be consistent with their nature. And if Hobbes was simply wrong about man's nature, the fully rational man need not act in the way Hobbes said he should: Hobbes's whole case collapses.

But it is not necessary to go so far. The reason why men had not hitherto made and used Hobbes's discovery may be neither that he was simply wrong about human nature, nor (as Hobbes alleged) that men hitherto had failed through lack of application or logic to make this advantageous discovery earlier, but that the principle of obligation which Hobbes had discovered had not been as advantageous to men in earlier societies as it now was to men in possessive market society. It may be, in other words, that Hobbes's principle of obligation did cross men's interests (and their capacities) before the arrival of the possessive market society, and does not cross them in that society. A market society needs peace and order to a degree which others do not. War, plunder, and rapine are ordinary and honourable in many non-market societies, but they are inconsistent with market society. They cannot, in possessive market society, be allowed as between citizens of one national community (and it was only the internal relations that Hobbes was dealing with)[20] nor are they needed in a possessive market society to give thrusting men room for their appetitive behaviour. And not only does a market society need internal peace; equally important, men who accept and promote market society can be expected, unlike men in other societies, to see the advantages of it and therefore the advantages of Hobbes's discovery. They need only be shown the logic of their (new) situation; that is all that is needed to render men in the new market society capable, as men were not capable before, of seeing and using Hobbes's doctrine. True, it is only the enterprising men of property who can be expected to see it. But that is enough: the common people need not see it for themselves but can be taught it by authority.

Market men, then, are peculiarly apt learners of Hobbes's doctrine. So if his theory is taken only as a theory of and for possessive market society he is saved in some measure from the reproach of being contradictory about men's capacities. More accurately, he is saved from that reproach if his theory is taken as a theory of and for a possessive market society which is relatively new. So understood, his theory is an attempt to persuade present men, by showing them their actual nature, to behave differently from the way in which men have hitherto behaved, and in which they are now still behaving simply for lack of realizing what is demanded of and permitted to men in possessive market society. Hobbes was addressing men who did not yet think and behave entirely as market men, whose calculation of the kind of political obligation they should acknowledge was still based on less than a full appreciation of what was most to their own interest, most consistent with their true nature as competitive men. He was asking those men to bring their thinking into line with their real needs and capacities as market men. He was so intent on doing this that he presented their real needs and capacities not as new needs and capacities (which they

---

20. Hobbes did not hope to make a commonwealth immune from external violence. He thought that international hostilities were less of an evil than internal warfare. Because sovereigns, by international hostility, 'uphold thereby, the Industry of their Subjects; there does not follow from it, that misery, which accompanies the Liberty of particular men' (*Leviathan*, ch. 13, p. 98).

were) but as the needs and capacities of men of all times and places. In so doing he involved himself in the inconsistency of saying that men's nature requires them to do something they have not been doing. But his fault is less grave than his accusers make it. He could have cleared himself entirely had he claimed less than universal validity for his analysis.

Finally we may notice that when his theory is treated as a theory of and for possessive market society, the main moral objection to his doctrine turns out to be not so much an objection to his doctrine as to the morality of that society. If the real basis of Hobbes's political obligation is, as I have argued, the rational perception of men in possessive market society that they are all irretrievably subject to the determination of the market, then the somewhat inhuman flavour of Hobbes's political obligation is at once explained and justified. The compulsions of the market society do somewhat demean the free rational individual who is usually put at the centre of ethical theory. The morality of the market is not entirely acceptable to the humanist. A theory of obligation built on a recognition and acceptance of the compulsions and morality of the market must seem perverse to the humanist who does not fully accept the values of the possessive market society as the highest, or a sufficient, morality.

Yet Hobbes, in building on the compulsions and morality of the market, penetrated to the heart of the problem of obligation in modern possessive societies. The paradox of Hobbes's individualism, which starts with equal rational individuals and demonstrates that they must submit themselves wholly to a power outside themselves, is a paradox not of his construction but of the market society. The market makes men free; it requires for its effective operation that all men be free and rational; yet the independent rational decisions of each man produce at every moment a configuration of forces which confronts each man compulsively. All men's choices determine, and each man's choice is determined by, the market. Hobbes caught both the freedom and the compulsion of possessive market society.

The English possessing class, however, did not need Hobbes's full prescription. And they had some reason to be displeased with his portrait of themselves: no reader, except the fashionably flippant, could relish such an exposure of himself and his fellows, especially when it was presented as science. Before the end of the century, the men of property had come to terms with the more ambiguous, and more agreeable, doctrine of Locke. . . .

The Art of Government
Deborah Baumgold

As if when Men quitting the State of Nature entered into Society, they agreed that all of them but one, should be under the restraint of Laws, but that he should still retain all the Liberty of the State of Nature, increased with Power, and made licentious by Impunity. This is to think that Men are so foolish that they take care to avoid what Mischiefs may be done them by Pole-Cats, or Foxes, but are content, nay think it Safety, to be devoured by Lions.

John Locke, The Second Treatise of Government, section 93

In popular imagination, Hobbism has come to be identified with arbitrary despotism, even with twentieth-century totalitarianism. To be sure, Hobbes denies in principle the distinction between good and bad government, describing "tyranny" as but the term for monarchy misliked.[1] His formal permission of arbitrary rule inspires images of political horror, like this picture of a mad king. "The citizen of Hobbes's leviathan state is . . . faced with the terrifying absurdity of finding himself totally obligated to obey an insane individual who will not listen to Parliament's advice or seek its assent, and who may be utterly incapable of protecting and governing himself, much less the commonwealth."[2] But more careful readers notice that Hobbes commends fair and lawful government, directed to the common interest. Chapter 30 of *Leviathan,* "Of the OFFICE of the Soveraign Representative," enjoins concern for the people's safety and prosperity, political education, promulgation of good laws, equal justice and taxation, fair execution of punishments and rewards, and the discriminating choice of counselors and military commanders.

Noticing Hobbes's preference for good government is one thing; it is another thing to account this counsel an integral and significant part of the larger theory. The latter view faces several objections. On the supposition that Hobbism is a theory of obligation, which locates the source of state power in a supportive citizenry, his advice regarding the exercise of sovereignty has to be seen as a secondary part of the theory, tangential to the main account of the generation of sovereign power. This first objection merely reflects the familiar bias of orthodox Hobbes studies. Second, there is a common inclination to juxtapose Hobbes's discussion of sovereigns' duties against his account of their rights, and to give the latter much more importance than the former. Mario Cattaneo, for instance, whose commentaries on Hobbes' juridical doctrine emphasize the "liberal" character of this part of the theory, nonetheless concedes there is a "contradiction between the absolute power of the prince and the principle of legality for the protection of the subject."[3] But this is erroneous. Hobbes intended his discussion of rulers' duties to complement the prescription of an absolutist constitution. The enumeration of sovereigns' duties in chapter 30 of *Leviathan* corresponds, as Table 1 shows, to the enumeration of sovereigns' rights in chapter 18.[4] The correspondence is illustrative of an appreciation for the bearing of

Table 1. Sovereigns' rights and duties in *Leviathan*

Chapter 18 "Of the RIGHTS of Soveraignes by Institution"	Chapter 30 "Of the OFFICE of the Soveraign Representative"
1. Foundation of the rights of sovereignty (p. 229) Applications of the principle of unconditional sovereignty (pp. 229–32)	1. Duty to maintain the essential rights of sovereignty (pp. 376–77)
2. Right to "Judge of what Doctrines are fit to be taught them" (p. 233)	2. Duty to teach the people (pp. 377–85): "The Essentiall Rights of Soveraignty" "Not to affect change of Government" "Nor adhere (against the Soveraign) to Popular men" "Nor to Dispute the Soveraign Power" "And to Honour their Parents" "And to avoyd doing of Injury" "And to do all this sincerely from the heart"
3. Right of legislating (p. 234)	3. Duty to make good, i.e., necessary and perspicuous, laws (pp. 387–89)
4. "Right of Judicature" (p. 234)	4. Duty to administer equal justice (p. 385)
5. "Right of making War, and Peace"; of levying money for armies; and of being chief commander (pp. 234–35)	5. Duty to tax equally (pp. 386–87); and to choose good—loyal and popular—army commanders (pp. 393–94)
6. Right of "choosing all Councellours, Ministers, Magistrates, and Officers" (p. 235)	6. Duty "to choose good Counsellours; I mean such" as cannot benefit from evil counsel, and are knowledgeable (pp. 391–93)
7. Power of reward and punishment (p. 235)	7. Duty "to make a right application of Punishments, and Rewards" (pp. 389–91)
8. Right of appointing "Lawes of Honour," e.g., titles (pp. 235–36)	8. Rulers should not show partiality toward "the great," as doing so encourages rebellion (pp. 385–86)

the conduct of government, as well as its constitution, on the possibility of good political order.

The last and strongest objection to taking seriously Hobbes's recommendation of good government is simply that it seems implausible to expect a ruler possessing unconditional authority to heed the counsel. As the duty to govern well cannot be enforced by any human agency, it seems unlikely it would count for much in the calculations of a Hobbesian sovereign. Thus the counsel stands as no more than a pious supplement to a theory that truly licenses tyranny. This is Locke's objection, and Hobbes himself took it seriously. He states the objection in *De Cive:* "If any man had such a Right [of "Absolute Command"], the condition of the Citizens would be miserable: For thus they think, He will take all, spoil all, kill all; and every man counts it his onely happinesse that he is not already spoil'd and kill'd."[5]

There are three Hobbesian replies, the first of which is a negative argument weighing the hazard of wicked rule against the calamity of civil war:

> The Power in all formes [of government], *if they be perfect enough to protect them,* is the same; not considering that the estate of Man can never be without some incommodity or other; and that the greatest, that in any forme of Government can possibly happen to the people in generall, is scarce sensible, in respect of the miseries, and horrible calamities, that accompany a Civill Warre; or that dissolute condition of masterlesse men, without subjection to Lawes, and a coërcive Power to tye their hands from rapine, and revenge.[6]

There is more here than the cynical observation that government per se is a necessary evil in virtue of man's antisocial nature. Hobbes is making a narrower observation about the benefit of an absolutist constitution (i.e., a constitution in which "the [sovereign's] Power . . . is perfect enough to protect them") as a deterrent to civil war. The benefit outweighs the attendant danger of bad government: "He that hath strength enough to protect all, wants not sufficiency to oppress all."[7] In the first instance, then, Hobbes grants that tyranny is a danger inherent to an absolutist constitution, but a risk to be accepted because the constitution deters the greater evil of civil war.

He also thinks, however, that rulers have moral and instrumental reasons for governing well. This is the root issue between Hobbes and constitutionalist thinkers. In the latter's view, legal restraint and popular accountability—the antitheses of unconditional sovereignty—are requisites of good rule. Absolutism is therefore rightly equated with arbitrary government. Hobbes, in this respect typical of royalists in the early Stuart period, distinguishes between the structure of sovereign authority and the conduct of government, "between the *Right,* and the *exercise* of supreme authority."[8] Ruling well is a natural-law duty for which rulers are accountable to God. "And therefore," according to *De Cive,* "there is some security for Subjects in the Oaths which Princes take."[9] But Hobbesian skepticism about the tenets of positive religion precludes attaching strong weight to this consideration. Whereas constitutionalist thinkers favor procedural mechanisms to promote good government, Hobbes counts on sovereigns' interest in ruling well. Duty coheres with interest: "For the duty of a sovereign consisteth in the good government of the people. . . . And as the art and duty of sovereigns consist in the same acts, so also doth their profit."[10]

The argument concerning interest attaches to the role or office of the sovereign, the "politique Person" as opposed to the natural man.[11] Hobbes is therefore only committed to showing that ruling well really is in sovereigns' interest, not to a strong assertion about the propensities of actual rulers. He draws the distinction as between reason and passion, attributing bad rule to "the affections and passions which reign in every one, as well monarch as subject; by which the monarch may be swayed to use that power amiss."[12] In context, which is the comparison of forms of government, this is less than the damaging admission that rationality is unlikely in rulers. Hobbes's immediate point is the greater likelihood of rational rule in a monarchy than in any other form of government. "Where the publique and private interest are most closely united," *Leviathan* claims, "there is the publique most advanced. Now in Monarchy, the private interest is the same with the publique."[13] Why this should be so, regarding hereditary monarchies at least, is suggested in *De Cive.* When the state is rulers' patrimony, there is dynastic reason for identifying personal with state interest:

"We cannot on better condition be subject to any, then one whose interest depends upon our safety, and welfare; and this then comes to passe when we are the inheritance of the Ruler; for every man of his own accord endeavours the preservation of his inheritance."[14]

It improves the motivational plausibility of the role argument that the operative interest is the ubiquitous human passion of desire for power.[15] The secular motive is expressly contrasted, in *A Dialogue . . . of the Common Laws of England,* with the less certain constraint of divine punishment:

> For if, say they, the King may notwithstanding the law do what he please, and nothing to restrain him but the fear of punishment in the world to come, then, in case there come a king that fears no such punishment, he may take away from us, not only our lands, goods, and liberties, but our lives also if he will. And they say true; but they have no reason to think he will, unless it be for his own profit; which cannot be, for he loves his own power; and what becomes of his power when his subjects are destroyed or weakened, by whose multitude and strength he enjoys his power, and every one of his subjects his fortune?[16]

The proposition that Hobbes must establish is that ruling in the public interest and according to law enhances sovereign power. Good government is also powerful government. Right makes might. Contrary to Cattaneo's view, the same desideratum governs Hobbes's consideration of the exercise of power as guides the argument for absolutism. Good rule, in the framework of unified, unconditional sovereign right, provides twin prescriptions for generating coercive authority. Hobbes's "art of government" is the antipode of Machiavellian statecraft. Both are preoccupied with the very real problems for early-modern rulers of consolidating central authority and controlling ambitious rivals. Only Hobbes holds that lawful, fair rule enhances power, while it is Machiavelli who endorses arbitrariness (arguing that for princes it is better to be unpredictable and feared than to be known and loved).[17] They also conceive the problem of good rule differently, Machiavelli focusing on rulers' personal characteristics, their *virtù,* and Hobbes on the incentives of the role.

The Governmental Art

. . . Like the arguments for absolutism, those concerning the exercise of power treat the problem from two sides: on the one hand, the positive prerequisites of power and, on the other, measures deterring challenges to sitting authority. Specifically, Hobbes holds that rulers have a positive interest in their subjects' well-being, and second, that good rule deters elite conflict and rebellion.

"If you be rich I cannot be poor." James I's well-known statement to Parliament is a Hobbesian argument.[18] *Salus populi* is the supreme law and duty of political rule, "by which must be understood, not the mere preservation of their lives, but generally their benefit and good."[19] Caring for the common good, meaning specifically the common wealth, also profits rulers. Hobbes has in mind the dependence of the state, and therefore the sovereign, on social prosperity. "The riches, power, and honour of a Monarch," *Leviathan* observes, "arise onely from the riches, strength and reputation of his Subjects. For no King can be rich, nor glorious, nor secure; whose Subjects are either poore, or contemptible, or too weak through want, or dissention, to maintain a war against their enemies."[20] Taxation, the state's supply, is the pertinent issue. "If therefore," Hobbes explains in *The Elements of Law,* the sovereign provide not so as that particular men may have means, both to preserve themselves, and also to preserve the public; the common or sovereign treasure can be none. And on the other side, if it were not for a common and public treasure belonging to the sovereign power, men's private riches would sooner serve to put them into confusion and war, than to secure or maintain them.[21]

Second, there is much that rulers can do to strengthen their position, and provide for public order, by way of deterring rebellion and elite conflict. The list of rulers' duties, which in *Leviathan* is framed to correspond to the list of sovereigns' rights, appears in the earlier versions of the political theory as a series of remedies to the causes of rebellion, although Hobbes's counsel remains substantially the same throughout.[22] According to *De Cive*, "Many things are required to the conservation of inward Peace, because many things concur (as hath been shewed in the foregoing Chapter) to its perturbation."[23] Specifically, Hobbes lists these "concurring" causes of rebellion: popular discontent, ambitious elites, ideological justification, and political organization.[24] Correspondingly, he commends equal taxation, as an antidote to discontent.[25] Equal justice, or the "constant application of rewards, and punishments," deters the ambitious.[26] Rulers ought also to root out false opinions and attack subversive factions. . . .[27]

Juridical Rule and Coercive Authority

. . . Hobbes's political discussions of juridical rule have two themes, general conditions of social order and, more specifically, the art of deterring ambitious rivals. Under the former heading, he explains why government according to law is preferable to arbitrary rule, and offers standards of good lawmaking. It is in connection with the latter that Hobbes sanctions selective justice, meaning the discriminating—but not capricious—exercise of juridical authority.

"Arbitrary" rule usually refers, in Hobbesian usage, to personal rule and is the opposite of rule according to law (e.g., a punishment is "arbitrary" that has not been defined in law).[28] To start, Hobbes's critique of Coke implies a preference for rule by law. Because men naturally disagree and are therefore in conflict, "it was necessary there should be a common measure of all things that might fall in controversy."[29] For the sovereign's judgments to function as that common measure, a settled standard, they must take the form of codified law. *De Cive* justifies legislative authority as an essential sovereign right in these terms:

Furthermore, since it no lesse, nay it much more conduceth to Peace to prevent brawles from arising, then to appease them being risen; and that all controversies are bred from hence, that the opinions of men differ concerning Meum & Tuum, just and unjust, profitable and unprofitable, good and evill, honest and dishonest, and the like, which every man esteems according to his own judgement; it belongs to the same chiefe power to make some common Rules for all men, and to declare them publiquely, by which every man may know what may be called his, what anothers, what just, what unjust. . . . But those Rules and measures are usually called the civill Lawes, or the Lawes of the City, as being the Commands of him who hath the supreme power in the City.[30]

The explanation of the bearing of law on social order hinges on the deterrence proposition: "It much more conduceth to Peace to prevent brawles from arising, then to appease them being risen." Hobbes has in mind the idea that laws, with appointed punishments, are efficacious in and of themselves in controlling behavior. Action is governed, generally, by expectations and opinions ("the will of doing, or omitting ought, depends on the opinion of the *good* and *evill* of the *reward,* or *punishment,* which a man conceives he shall receive by the act, or omission; so as the actions of all men are ruled by the opinions of each").[31] Under this general psychological principle, juridical rule provides one way of manipulating opinion, and political education is another. Laws, *The Elements* explains, supply a reason for action, distinct from calculations about the utility of an act. Whereas the latter reasoning is appropriate to covenants ("in simple covenants the action to be done, or not done, is first limited and made known, and then followeth the promise to do or not do"),[32] in the case of laws, "the command [itself] is the reason we have of doing the action commanded."[33]

There are two motivations, by Hobbes's account, for obedience to law: the prior promise to obey the legislator (that is, the political covenant) and fear of punishment. The first is the formal ground of the obligation (according to *De Cive,* for example, "the *Law* holds the party obliged by vertue of the universall *Contract* of yeelding obedience");[34] the second supplies a prudential motive for obedience ("the Law . . . compells him to make good his promise, for fear of the punishment appointed by the Law").[35] Thus, unlike John Selden, another member of the Tew Circle, Hobbes does not conflate the obligatoriness of law with the sanction of punishment. In Selden's view, " 'The idea of a law carrying obligation irrespective of any punishment annexed to the violation of it . . . is no more comprehensible to the human mind than the idea of a father without a child'—i.e. [Richard Tuck comments] it is a logical and not contingent connexion."[36]

Still, Hobbes's position is virtually the same as Selden's inasmuch as he holds that it is fear of punishment that makes laws effectual. "Of all Passions, that which enclineth men least to break the Lawes, is Fear. Nay, (excepting some generous natures,) it is the onely thing, (when there is apparence of profit, or pleasure by breaking the Lawes,) that makes men keep them."[37] "Vindicative"—penal—sanctions are therefore an essential part of law. "In vain therefore is the Law, unlesse it contain both parts, that which *forbids* injuries to be done, and that which *punisheth* the doers of them."[38] In addition, the punishments appointed by law must be sufficient to the purpose of deterring crime. "We must therefore provide for our security, not by *Compacts,* but by *Punishments." According to De Cive:*

> And there is then sufficient provision made, when there are so great punishments appointed for every injury, as apparently it prove a greater evill to have done it, then not to have done it: for all men, by a necessity of nature, chuse that which *to them appears to be the lesse evill.*[39]

However, the sanction is not always explicitly included in the law, and is then either "implicit," based on prior instances of punishment, or "arbitrary," dependent on the sovereign's will.[40]

"To the care of the Soveraign, belongeth the making of Good Lawes. But what is a good Law? By a Good Law, I mean not a Just Law: for no Law can be Unjust."[41] From the first proposition, the need for common rules of property and justice, nothing follows about the quality of law. But the accompanying psychological account of the bearing of laws and punishments on expectations, and therefore action, generates criteria for good law and the "right application" of punishment. "A good law is that, which is *Needfull,* for the *Good of the People,* and withall *Perspicuous."*[42] It encourages obedience to limit legislation, as subjects are apt to forget or ignore laws when they are overabundant or otherwise obscure.[43] According to *De Cive*, the policy also encourages private enterprise: "As water inclosed on all hands with banks, stands still and corrupts . . . so subjects, if they might doe nothing without the commands of the Law would grow dull, and unwildly."[44] Brevity is similarly a virtue of good law, aiding understanding and deterring unnecessary litigation.[45] The third criterion falls under the larger claim that rulers have a stake in their subjects' well-being. It cannot be, *Leviathan* explains, that a good law benefits a ruler but not the ruled, "for the good of the Sovereign and People, cannot be separated."[46]

It is further necessary that penal authority be properly exercised because "the fear whereby men are deterred from doing evil, ariseth not from hence, namely, because penalties are set, but because they are executed; for we esteeme the future by what is past, seldome expecting what seldome happens."[47] *Leviathan's* definition of punishment . . . includes the stipulation that punishment should regard the future good (as opposed to the past evil, meaning punishment for revenge).[48] There follow a series of discriminations between acts of punishment and acts of "hostility." All "evil" inflicted without the intention or possibility of encouraging obedience is simply "hostility," including retribution in excess of penalties set by law. Inadequate penalties also fail to qualify, because then the penalty is rather the price for obtaining the benefit of the crime.[49] When a punishment is not specified in law, and is therefore "arbitrary," it should reflect the same policy of encouraging service to the state and deterring disobedience.[50]

Politic justice

Hobbes's preoccupation with discouraging those ambitious of political power enters into his discussion of juridical rule. All three works* recommend the policy of "equal justice" as a means, specifically, "for the keeping under of those, that are disposed to rebellion by ambition."[51] The consistent execution of punishments helps control political ambition: "By constant application of rewards, and punishments, they may so order it, that men may know that the way to honour is, not by contempt of the present government, nor by factions, and the popular ayre, but by the contraries."[52] In reverse, Hobbes warns against rewarding popular and ambitious subjects, seeking to buy their adherence with money or flattery.[53] Partiality toward the "great" encourages insolence, which encourages hatred, which brings rebellion and the ruin of the state.[54]

Going along with this special emphasis on "constant severity in punishing" great and ambitious subjects, Hobbes recognizes and commends a series of politic discriminations in the administration of justice.[55] "Seeing the end of punishing is not revenge, and discharge of choler; but correction, either of the offender, or of others by his example; the severest Punishments are to be inflicted for those Crimes, that are of most Danger to the Publique."[56] The political criterion of punishment has wide-ranging application—to causes, persons, and crimes and their effects. Crimes that proceed from "malice to the Government established" and "contempt of Justice" are worse than "Crimes of Infirmity; such as are those which proceed from great provocation, from great fear, great need, or from ignorance."[57] Prominent persons, who teach and serve as examples to others, bear responsibility for the crimes they encourage, and therefore should be more severely treated:

---

* *Leviathan, De Cive, The Elements of Law.*

> The Punishment of the Leaders, and teachers in a Commotion; not the poore seduced People, when they are punished, can profit the Common-wealth by their example. To be severe to the People, is to punish that ignorance, which may in great part be imputed to the Soveraign, whose fault it was, they were no better instructed.[58]

More generally, crimes by the vainglorious great, those who assume that wit, blood, or riches exempt them from punishment, "are not extenuated, but aggravated by the greatnesse of their persons; because they have least need to commit them."[59] Political crimes, for example, assassination attempts and giving secrets to the enemy, are more serious than crimes against private persons; accepting a bribe to perjure oneself is more serious than simple stealing, as are also robbing the public treasury and counterfeiting.[60] In short, the utilitarian principle applies: "The same fact, when it redounds to the dammage of many, is greater, than when it redounds to the hurt of few."[61] These distinctions technically concern the degree of responsibility for crime, excuses from crime, and extenuating circumstances.[62] But they introduce into Hobbesian theory, under the heading of the administration of justice, a substantive legal policy, a policy with more content than the criteria of good law associated with the general deterrent psychology of juridical rule.

Whereas Hobbesian absolutism and jurisprudence, his formal doctrines of sovereign right, license arbitrary rule and iniquitous law,[63] Hobbes's art of government is a normative account of the exercise of coercive and legislative authority. Rule according to law is preferable to personal rule, however fair, because laws and legally appointed punishments deter disobedience. Substantive criteria for legal policy, absent from Hobbesian jurisprudence, follow from that deterrent psychology and from its extension into a policy of discriminating, politic justice. . . .

Conclusion

Something striking follows from Hobbes's prudential accounts of the bearing of the conduct of government on the reality of political power. He holds rulers responsible for their fate and for their societies' character:

> This same *supreme command,* and *absolute power,* seems so harsh to the greatest part of men, as they hate the very naming of them; which happens chiefly through want of knowledge, what *humane nature,* and the *civill Lawes* are, and *partly also through their default, who when they are invested with so great authority, abuse their power to their own lust.*[64]

Political responsibility, of course, is the topic, as opposed to the formal accountability denied by the absolutist constitution. Still, Hobbes describes rebellion as the "naturall punishment" of negligent government.[65] Furthermore, the "poore seduced People" in a rebellion ought not to be punished severely inasmuch as the sovereign is also at fault for not better instructing them.[66] Short of rebellion, subjects' crimes are extenuated by inconsistent punishment or tacit approval (e.g., duels) on the sovereign's part. In such cases, too, the sovereign "is in part a cause of the transgression"; he "hath his part in the offence."[67] Last, if "the Legislator doth set a lesse penalty on a crime, then will make our feare more considerable with us, then our lust; that excesse of lust above the feare of punishment, whereby sinne is committed, is to be attributed to the Legislator (that is to say) to the supreme";[68] or, as *Leviathan* puts it, such law is an "invitement" to crime.[69]

Assigning responsibility to rulers—to government—is a classic political response to individualistic, moral and psychological, treatments of public goods. The view is articulated by the figure of the "Defaulter" in Colin Strang's dialogue on the principle of universalization (viz., the moral argument that individuals must ask themselves what would happen if everyone acted as they proposed to act):

> If anyone is to blame it is the person whose job it is to circumvent [e.g., tax] evasion. If too few people vote, then it should be made illegal not to vote. If too few people volunteer, then you must introduce conscription. If too many people evade taxes, then you must tighten up your system of enforcement. My answer to your "If everyone did that" is "Then someone had jolly well better see to it that they don't."[70]

Hobbes states the same proposition in *Leviathan's* introductory, metaphorical description of the commonwealth: "*Reward* and *Punishment* (by which fastned to the seate of the Sovereignty, every joynt and member is moved to perform his duty) are the *Nerves*, that do the same in the Body Naturall."[71] From the introduction of conscription in *Leviathan* to furnish an army, through the recommendation of a tax policy that will "least . . . trouble the mind of them that pay," and the recommendation that juridical rule promotes obedience and order, Hobbes translates political and social problems into problems of governmental policy. This of course does not commit him to the strong negative proposition that rulers bear exclusive responsibility.[72] At issue are the relative significance of governmental versus civic virtue in Hobbes's political understanding and the way in which he thinks about subjects' duties. In this chapter . . . , I have argued that Hobbes reflects first on governmental policy—how civic performance can be structured and encouraged by the state—and only secondarily calculates in terms of citizens' virtue and self-interest.

Last, Hobbes supplies good reasons why rulers ought to govern well, and defines good rule, which is different from and lesser than a defense of the proposition that good rule is expectable. The stronger claim, about the benevolence of Hobbesian absolutism, depends on the plausibility of the identification of role and personal interests. Although an interest in coercive authority may be inherent to the office of the sovereign, this does not assure that actual rulers may not desire other goods more than power, or may not perceive some discrepancy between the pursuit of power for themselves and the requisites of a strong state. It is an objection that Hobbes both grants (e.g., "all the acts of *Nero* are not essentiall to Monarchie")[73] and discounts, especially with regard to this relatively best form of government. The problem of translating institutional roles into descriptions of role occupants' intentions is a characteristic problem of structural political analyses.[74] For all that, it is one thing to charge, with Locke, that a benevolent *Leviathan*-state is implausible, and another to dismiss Hobbes's art of government as a trivial part of the political theory.

Notes

1. Thomas Hobbes, *Leviathan*, ed. C. B. MacPherson (Harmondsworth: Penguin, 1968), chapter 19, pp. 239–40 . . .
2. Susan Moller Okin, "'The Sovereign and his Counsellours': Hobbes's Reevaluation of Parliament," *Political Theory* 10 (1982), p. 72.
3. Mario A. Cattaneo, "Hobbes Théoricien de l'Absolutisme Eclairé," in Reinhart Kosselleck and Roman Schnur (eds.), *Hobbes-Forschungen* (Berlin: Duncker & Humblot, 1969), p.

209, translation mine. See also "Hobbes's Theory of Punishment," trans. J. M. Hatwell, in K. C. Brown (ed.), *Hobbes Studies* (Cambridge, Mass.: Harvard University Press, 1965), pp. 275–97, esp. p. 276.

4. Only two duties do not refer to previously specified rights of sovereignty: public charity and policies to deter idleness (*Leviathan* 30, p. 387). . . .

5. Thomas Hobbes, *De Cive: The English Version,* entitled in the first edition, *Philosophical Rudiments Concerning Government and Society,* ed. Howard Warrender (Oxford: Clarendon, 1983), chapter vi, section 13, p. 99 (emphasis omitted) . . .

6. *Leviathan* 18, p. 238 (emphasis mine).

7. *De Cive* vi, 13, p. 99 (emphasis omitted) . . .

8. *De Cive* xiii, 1, p. 156. . . .

9. *De Cive* vi, 13, p. 99 . . . (emphasis omitted).

10. Thomas Hobbes, *The Elements of Law: Natural and Politic,* ed. Ferdinand Tönnies (Cambridge: Cambridge University Press, 1928), Part II, chapter ix, section 1, p. 142. . . .

11. *Leviathan* 19, p. 241.

12. *The Elements of Law* II, v, 4, p. 111. See also *De Cive* x, 4 and 7, pp. 132, 133; and *Leviathan* 19, p. 241.

13. *Leviathan* 19, p. 241.

14. *De Cive* x, 18, p. 140.

15. *Leviathan* 11, p. 161: "I put for a generall inclination of all mankind, a perpetuall and restlesse desire of Power after power, that ceaseth onely in Death."

16. Thomas Hobbes, *A Dialogue between a Philosopher and a Student of the Common Laws of England,* in *The English Works of Thomas Hobbes,* vol. vi, ed. Sir William Molesworth (London: John Bohn, 1840), pp. 33–34.

17. Niccolo Machiavelli, *The Prince,* trans. George Bull (Harmondsworth: Penguin, 1961), chapter 17.

18. The statement is quoted, e.g., in J. A. W. Gunn, *Politics and the Public Interest in the Seventeenth Century* (London: Routledge & Kegan Paul, 1969), p. 68.

19. *The Elements of Law* II, ix, 1, p. 142. . . .

20. *Leviathan* 19, pp. 241–42. . . .

21. *The Elements of Law* II, v, 1, p. 108. . . .

22. Chapters viii and ix in Part II of *The Elements of Law* treat the causes of rebellion and the duties of rulers; they are chapters xii and xiii in *De Cive.*

23. *De Cive* xiii, 9, p. 160. . . .

24. Accurately, there are three Hobbesian categories. *The Elements of Law* (II, viii, 1, p. 133) lists: (1) discontent, encompassing popular fear of punishment and burdensome taxation, as well as political ambition (2–3, pp. 133–35); (2) pretense of right, referring to seditious opinions (4–10, pp. 135–38); and (3) hope of success (11–14, pp. 138–41). Cf. the more abstract categories in *De Cive* (xii, 1, pp. 145–46): (1) "internall disposition," meaning seditious opinions (1–8, pp. 146–52); (2) "externall Agent," or popular and elite discontent (9–10, pp. 152–53); and (3) the "action it selfe," i.e., the organization of a seditious "faction" (11–13, pp. 153–56).

25. *The Elements of Law* II, ix, 5, p. 144; *De Cive* xiii, 10–11, pp. 161–62.

26. *De Cive* xiii, 12, pp. 162–63. See *The Elements of Law* II, ix, 7, p. 145.

27. *The Elements of Law* II, ix, 8, pp. 145–46; *De Cive* xiii, 9 and 13, pp. 160–61, 163–64.

28. *Leviathan* 18, p. 235 (margin note), and 27, pp. 338–39; *De Cive* xiii, 16, p. 166. . . .

29. *The Elements of Law* II, x, 8, p. 150. . . .

30. *De Cive* vi, 9, p. 95 (emphasis omitted). . . .

31. *De Cive* vi, 11, p. 95 (the topic of the paragraph is political education). . . .

32. *The Elements of Law* II, x, 2, p. 147.

33. Ibid. II, viii, 6, p. 136. . . .

34. *De Cive* xiv, 2, p. 169. . . .

35. *De Cive* xiv, 2, p. 170 . . . (emphasis omitted). . . .

36. Richard Tuck, *Natural Rights Theories: Their Origin and Development* (Cambridge: Cambridge University Press, 1979), p. 91, quoting John Selden, *Opera,* I, col. 106. . . .

37. *Leviathan* 27, p. 343.
38. *De Cive* xiv, 7, p. 172. . . .
39. *De Cive* vi, 4, p. 93. . . .
40. *De Cive* xiv, 7, pp. 172–73. . . .
41. *Leviathan* 30, pp. 387–88.
42. *Leviathan* 30, p. 388.
43. *De Cive* xiii, 15, pp. 165–66; *Leviathan* 30, p. 388.
44. *De Cive* xiii, 15, p. 165.
45. *Leviathan* 30, pp. 388–89.
46. Ibid., p. 388.
47. *De Cive* xiii, 17, p. 167. . . .
48. *Leviathan* 28, p. 353. . . .
49. *Leviathan* 28, p. 355. Other distinctions follow from the requirements that punishments be inflicted by public authorities, for the transgression of law. E.g., "private injuries, and revenges," "pain inflicted without publique hearing," or by "Usurped power" are acts of hostility because they are not public acts carried out by public authorities (pp. 354–55). See also *De Cive* xiii, 16, p. 166.
50. *Leviathan* 18, p. 235, and *De Cive* xiii, 16, p. 166.
51. *The Elements of Law* II, ix, 7, p. 145. See *De Cive* xiii, 12, pp. 162–63, and *Leviathan* 30, pp. 385–86.
52. *De Cive* xiii, 12, p. 163; see *Leviathan* 27, pp. 342–43.
53. *Leviathan* 30, pp. 390–91, and 28, pp. 361–62.
54. Ibid. 30, p. 386.
55. Ibid. 27, p. 342.
56. Ibid. 30, p. 389.
57. Ibid., pp. 389–90. Indeed, extreme destitution totally excuses stealing, as necessary for self-preservation (27, p. 346).
58. *Leviathan* 30, p. 390.
59. Ibid., pp. 385–86. See also 27, p. 347.
60. Ibid. 27, pp. 350–51.
61. Ibid., p. 350.
62. Ibid., pp. 344–45: "For though all Crimes doe equally deserve the name of Injustice . . . yet it does not follow that all Crimes are equally unjust, no more than that all crooked lines are equally crooked; which the Stoicks not observing, held it as great a Crime, to kill a Hen, against the Law, as to kill ones Father."
63. Ibid. Review and Conclusion, p. 721: "I have set down for one of the causes of the Dissolutions of Common-wealths, their Imperfect Generation, consisting in the want of an *Absolute and Arbitrary Legislative Power*" (emphasis mine).
64. *De Cive* vi, 17, p. 102 (the latter emphasis—from "partly" to "lust"—is mine).
65. *Leviathan* 31, pp. 406–7.
66. Ibid. 30, p. 390 (the passage is quoted earlier; see text pertaining to note 58).
67. Ibid. 27, pp. 348–49.
68. *De Cive* xiii, 16, p. 166.
69. *Leviathan* 27, p. 339.
70. Colin Strang, "What if Everyone Did That?" In Judith J. Thomson and Gerald Dworkin (eds.), *Ethics* (New York: Harper & Row, 1968), pp. 155–56. In the continuation of the passage, the "Defaulter" announces: The principle of universalization "doesn't impress me as a reason why *I* should [pay, etc.], however many people do or don't." See pp. 159–60 for the argument that responsibility for public goods is shared between ruler and ruled.
71. *Leviathan* Introduction, p. 81.
72. Cf., e.g., *De Cive* vi, 13, p. 99 (annotation to the 1647 edition, emphasis omitted): "Although they, who have the chief Command, doe not all those things they would, and what they know profitable to the City," it is also the case that "Citizens, who busied about their private interest, and carelesse of what tends to the publique, cannot sometimes be drawn to performe their duties without the hazard of the City."

73. *De Cive* x, 7, p. 133.
74. On the importance of the translation, see Maurice Mandelbaum, "Societal Facts," in Alan Ryan (ed.), *The Philosophy of Social Explanation* (Oxford: Oxford University Press, 1973), esp. p. 113.

John Locke

John Locke is often introduced to students of American government as the intellectual ancestor of the U.S. Declaration of Independence and Constitution. There is little doubt that Thomas Jefferson and later, the framers of the U.S. Constitution, took Locke's work very seriously; especially his views on the right to life, liberty and property, the consent of the governed, and the right of resistance. Yet, there is much in Locke's thinking that is at variance with American politics as well. For example, whereas Locke called for separation of government into two distinct branches, legislative and executive, the Founding Fathers, following Montesquieu, added a third branch. Whereas Locke insisted on the supremacy of the legislature, our founders insisted on a more equal division of power, with substantial checks on the legislature. More to the point, however, Locke's views represent not so much a blueprint for government as a combination of prudential political theory, religious belief, and polemic aimed at supporting the parliamentary movement of his day. In considering the combination of these factors we can best appreciate his work. Nevertheless, Locke's work did give inspiration to our framers and continues to inform the democratic liberal tradition that characterizes American politics to this day.

Locke was born in 1632 in Wrington in Somerset, England. His father was an attorney and law clerk who gave John a Puritan upbringing. John studied the classics as a youth at Westminster School and obtained a scholarship to continue his education at Christ Church at Oxford. There he became disenchanted with the Scholastic program of studies and set his sights on more empirical studies. For example, he collaborated for a time with chemist Robert Boyle. He served briefly in the diplomatic corps at Brandenburg where he had the opportunity to study the works of Descartes and he began to rethink his earlier views on religion, which denied toleration to Catholics and others seen as enemies of the state. Upon his father's death, the inheritance left to him allowed him to pursue a degree in medicine. For a time, he worked with the noted physician, Thomas Sydenham.

Ironically, Locke's medical training led him into political intrigues that led to his political writings. Locke's successful operation on the liver of Lord Ashley, earl of Shaftesbury, led to the earl's lifelong gratitude and political tutelage. Shaftesbury was a leader in the parliamentary opposition to the Stuarts. His politics ended in his trial for treason and, though he was acquitted, he thought it best to flee to Holland. Locke, under suspicion because of his association with Shaftesbury, soon followed. During this period of self-exile, Locke penned several of his most important works, including *A Letter on Toleration,* which displayed his newfound toleration for religious practices; *An Essay on Human Understanding,* in which Locke expresses his famous "white paper" theory of human nature; and drafts of his *Two Treatises on Government.* The latter work was written partly as a response to the royalist views of Sir Robert Filmore and partly in support of the opposition movement against Charles II. Locke prudently postponed its publication until 1689.

Events conspired to bring Locke back to England and to accept another political post. The death of Charles II, followed by the ascension of the Catholic James II, brought political turmoil that resulted in a successful plot to seat William of Orange. With the Glorious Revolution of 1688 complete, Locke returned to England where he published his *Two Treatises,* served on the Board of Trade and Plantations, and ended his days in semi-retirement at a country estate at Oates. In his final days, he began to write *The Conduct of the Understanding,* which he never completed.

Second Treatise of Government

Like Hobbes, Locke utilized the convention of the "state of nature" to elucidate his views on human nature and politics. Also like Hobbes, he adopted the contract as the instrument by which societies and governments are founded. Unlike Hobbes, however, Locke's state of nature is relatively peaceful. In it, most humans respect the law of nature, reason, which teaches the folly of pursuing unbridled passions and appetites. Disputes over the ownership of property, however, result in conflict that puts participants in a state of war not unlike the Hobbesian state of nature. Because there is no impartial umpire to settle such disputes in the state of nature, political societies and the governments that regulate them are forged on the basis of consent. Unlike Hobbes, Locke opposed monarchical rule. To give all power to one sovereign in the name of protecting us from one another, as Hobbes suggested, would be like avoiding the mischief done by "Pole Cats or Foxes" only to be "devoured by Lions." There is little doubt that Locke was familiar with Hobbes' work. Yet, he steadfastly denied the connection, perhaps for fear of being too closely associated with the unsavory reputation of his predecessor.

Three major themes Locke emphasizes in the *Second Treatise* are property, consent, and the right of resistance. Locke advanced a labor theory of value in which property arises from the efforts of the individual to make the land and its resources useful. While he insisted that no one has the right to collect resources beyond the use to which they can be put, he recognized that the invention of money allowed for the accumulation of wealth beyond spoilage. With property—and its unequal distribution—came the likelihood of dispute. Civil society and the government which regulates it are created to provide peaceable solutions to disputes that arise primarily over property. Civil society comes into existence on the basis of the consent of all and the governmental form it takes reflects majority rule. Locke staunchly supports the right of members of the commonwealth to resist abuses of power by including a right to dissolve the government, although he did not believe such a remedy would often be employed. He treats these themes within a religious context that some scholars say cannot be ignored. The excerpts below from the *Second Treatise* illustrate Locke's treatment of these themes—property, consent, and resistance.

Commentaries

In the first commentary, Patrick Coby argues that there is more similarity between Locke's vision and the Hobbesian state of nature than is usually admitted. While Locke's rhetoric is less blunt, Coby argues that Locke accepts the proposition that, in the real world, might makes right. Nevertheless, Coby goes on to argue that Locke's departure from Hobbes reminds us of the civilizing possibilities of society.

In the second commentary, Nathan Tarcov reviews Locke's teaching on resistance. He sees it as a radical teaching that alerts rulers of the consequences of the abuse of power. Resistance represents a threat to all of a return to the state of nature; a return which neither ruler nor ruled desires. It is in this light, argues Tarcov, that we can understand Locke's view that the right of resistance is "the best fence against rebellion." Tarcov sees this right as one of the most fundamental elements of Locke's liberal legacy.

Key Words

Federative Power.   The power to make war and to carry on foreign relations. Locke ascribes this power, for pragmatic reasons, to the executive branch.

Legislative Power.   The legislature represents the will of the people and enacts it into law. Locke advocated the political superiority of this function over the executive, unlike the theory of separation of powers that characterizes the American system of government.

Sir Robert F. Refers to Robert Filmer, British author of *Patriarcha* (1680) and spokesman for the doctrine of political absolutism. Locke's *First Treatise* is an attack on Filmer's position.

State of War.   Locke, unlike Hobbes, distinguishes between a state of nature and a state of war. The state of war can break out in the otherwise peaceable state of nature or in civil society. Locke's distinction between these states signals an important difference between Hobbes and Locke as revealed in both the primary source material and commentaries.

For Further Reading

Ashcraft, R. 1987. *Locke's Two Treatises on Government.* London: Allen & Unwin.

Dunn, J. 1984. *John Locke.* Oxford: Clarendon Press.

Cranston, M. 1957. *John Locke: A Biography.* London: Longman, Green.

Locke, J. [1988.] *Two Treatises of Government* (ed. by Peter Laslett). Cambridge: Cambridge University Press.

Pangle, T. 1988. *The Spirit of Modern Republicanism.* Chicago: University of Chicago Press. See especially Part III.

Pocock, J.G.A. 1986. "The Myth of John Locke and the Obsession with Liberalism." In Pocock, J.G.A., and Ashcraft, R. eds. *John Locke.* Los Angeles: Clark Memorial Library.

Seliger, M. 1969. *The Liberal Politics of John Locke.* New York: Praeger.

Tarcov, N. 1984. *Locke's Education for Liberty.* Chicago: University of Chicago Press.

The Second Treatise of Government

An Essay concerning the True Original, Extent, and End of Government

Book II

Chapter 1

1. It having been shewn in the foregoing Discourse,

1°. That *Adam* had not either by natural Right of Fatherhood, or by positive Donation from God, any such Authority over his Children, or Dominion over the World as is pretended.

2°. That if he had, his Heirs, yet, had no Right to it.

3°. That if his Heirs had, there being no Law of Nature nor positive Law of God that determines, which is the Right Heir in all Cases that may arise, the Right of Succession, and consequently of bearing Rule, could not have been certainly determined.

4°. That if even that had been determined, yet the knowledge of which is the Eldest Line of *Adam*'s Posterity, being so long since utterly lost, that in the Races of Mankind and Families of the World, there remains not to one above another, the least pretence to be the Eldest House, and to have the Right of Inheritance.

All these premises having, as I think, been clearly made out, it is impossible that the Rulers now on Earth, should make any benefit, or derive any the least shadow of Authority from that, which is held to be the Fountain of all Power, *Adam's Private Dominion and Paternal Jurisdiction*, so that, he that will not give just occasion, to think that all Government in the World is the product only of Force and Violence, and that Men live together by no other Rules but that of Beasts, where the strongest carries it, and so lay a Foundation for perpetual Disorder and Mischief, Tumult, Sedition and Rebellion, (things that the followers of that Hypothesis so loudly cry out against) must of necessity find out another rise of Government, another Original of Political Power, and another way of designing and knowing the Persons that have it, then what Sir *Robert F.* hath taught us.

2. To this purpose, I think it may not be amiss, to set down what I take to be Political Power. That the Power of a *Magistrate* over a Subject, may be distinguished from that of a *Father* over his Children, a *Master* over his Servant, a *Husband* over his Wife, and a *Lord* over his Slave. All which distinct Powers happening sometimes together in the same Man, if he be considered under these different Relations, it may help us to distinguish these Powers one from another, and shew the difference betwixt a Ruler of a Common-wealth, a Father of a Family, and a Captain of a Galley.

From *Two Treatises of Government* (edited and with an introduction by Peter Laslett.) 1988. New York: Cambridge University Press, pp. 267–282, 285–294, 299–302, 323–328, 330–333, 347–353, 406–416. Reprinted with permission of Cambridge University Press.

3. *Political Power* then I take to be *a Right* of making Laws with Penalties of Death, and consequently all less Penalties, for the Regulating and Preserving of Property, and of employing the force of the Community, in the Execution of such Laws, and in the defence of the Common-wealth from Foreign Injury, and all this only for the Publick Good.

Chapter 2

Of the State of Nature

4. To understand Political Power right, and derive it from its Original, we must consider what State all Men are naturally in, and that is, a *State of perfect Freedom* to order their Actions, and dispose of their Possessions, and Persons as they think fit, within the bounds of the Law of Nature, without asking leave, or depending upon the Will of any other Man.

A *State* also *of Equality*, wherein all the Power and Jurisdiction is reciprocal, no one having more than another: there being nothing more evident, than that Creatures of the same species and rank promiscuously born to all the same advantages of Nature, and the use of the same faculties, should also be equal one amongst another without Subordination or Subjection, unless the Lord and Master of them all, should by any manifest Declaration of his Will set one above another, and confer on him by an evident and clear appointment an undoubted Right to Dominion and Sovereignty. . . .

6. But though this be a *State of Liberty*, yet it is *not a State of Licence*, though Man in that State have an uncontroleable Liberty, to dispose of his Person or Possessions, yet he has not Liberty to destroy himself, or so much as any Creature in his Possession, but where some nobler use, than its bare Preservation calls for it. The *State of Nature* has a Law of Nature to govern it, which obliges every one: And Reason, which is that Law, teaches all Mankind, who will but consult it, that being all equal and independent, no one ought to harm another in his Life, Health, Liberty, or Possessions. For Men being all the Workmanship of one Omnipotent, and infinitely wise Maker; All the Servants of one Sovereign Master, sent into the World by his order and about his business, they are his Property, whose Workmanship they are, made to last during his, not one anothers Pleasure. And being furnished with like Faculties, sharing all in one Community of Nature, there cannot be supposed any such *Subordination* among us, that may Authorize us to destroy one another, as if we were made for one anothers uses, as the inferior ranks of Creatures are for ours. Every one as he is *bound to preserve himself*, and not to quit his Station wilfully; so by the like reason when his own Preservation comes not in competition, ought he, as much as he can, *to preserve the rest of Mankind*, and may not unless it be to do Justice on an Offender, take away, or impair the life, or what tends to the Preservation of the Life, the Liberty, Health, Limb or Goods of another.

7. And that all Men may be restrained from invading others Rights, and from doing hurt to one another, and the Law of Nature be observed, which willeth the Peace and *Preservation of all Mankind*, the *Execution* of the Law of Nature is in that State, put into every Mans hands, whereby every one has a right to punish the transgressors of that Law to such a Degree, as may

hinder its Violation. For the *Law of Nature* would, as all other Laws that concern Men in this World, be in vain, if there were no body that in the State of Nature, had a *Power to Execute* that Law, and thereby preserve the innocent and restrain offenders, and if any one in the State of Nature may punish another, for any evil he has done, every one may do so. For in that *State of perfect Equality*, where naturally there is no superiority or jurisdiction of one, over another, what any may do in Prosecution of that Law, every one must needs have a Right to do.

8. And thus in the State of Nature, *one Man comes by a Power over another*; but yet no Absolute or Arbitrary Power, to use a Criminal when he has got him in his hands, according to the passionate heats, or boundless extravagancy of his own Will, but only to retribute to him, so far as calm reason and conscience dictates, what is proportionate to his Transgression, which is so much as may serve for *Reparation* and *Restraint*. For these two are the only reasons, why one Man may lawfully do harm to another, which is that we call *punishment*. In transgressing the Law of Nature, the Offender declares himself to live by another Rule, than that of *reason* and common Equity, which is that measure God has set to the actions of Men, for their mutual security: and so he becomes dangerous to Mankind, the tye, which is to secure them from injury and violence, being slighted and broken by him. Which being a trespass against the whole Species, and the Peace and Safety of it, provided for by the Law of Nature, every man upon this score, by the Right he hath to preserve Mankind in general, may restrain, or where it is necessary, destroy things noxious to them, and so may bring such evil on any one, who hath transgressed that Law, as may make him repent the doing of it, and thereby deter him, and by his Example others, from doing the like mischief. And in this case, and upon this ground, *every Man hath a Right to punish the Offender, and be Executioner of the Law of Nature*. . . .

11. From these *two distinct Rights*, the one of *Punishing* the Crime *for restraint*, and preventing the like Offence, which right of punishing is in every body; the other of taking *reparation*, which belongs only to the injured party, comes it to pass that the Magistrate, who by being Magistrate, hath the common right of punishing put into his hands, can often, where the publick good demands not the execution of the Law, *remit* the punishment of Criminal Offences by his own Authority, but yet cannot *remit* the satisfaction due to any private Man, for the damage he has received. That, he who has suffered the damage has a Right to demand in his own name, and he alone can *remit*: The damnified Person has this Power of appropriating to himself, the Goods or Service of the Offender, by *Right of Self-preservation*, as every Man has a Power to punish the Crime, to prevent its being committed again, *by the Right he has of Preserving all Mankind*, and doing all reasonable things he can in order to that end: And thus it is, that every Man in the State of Nature, has a Power to kill a Murderer, both to deter others from doing the like Injury, which no Reparation can compensate, by the Example of the punishment that attends it from every body, and also *to secure* Men from the attempts of a Criminal, who having renounced Reason, the common Rule and Measure, God hath given to Mankind, hath by the unjust Violence and Slaughter he hath committed upon one, declared War against all Mankind, and therefore may be destroyed as a *Lyon* or a *Tyger*, one of those wild Savage Beasts, with whom Men can have no Society nor

Security: And upon this is grounded the great Law of Nature, *Who so sheddeth Mans Blood, by Man shall his Blood be shed.* And *Cain* was so fully convinced, that every one had a Right to destroy such a Criminal, that after the Murther of his Brother, he cries out, *Every one that findeth me, shall slay me*; so plain was it writ in the Hearts of all Mankind.

12. By the same reason, may a Man in the State of Nature *punish the lesser breaches* of that Law. It will perhaps be demanded, with death? I answer, Each Transgression may be *punished* to that *degree*, and with so much *Severity* as will suffice to make it an ill bargain to the Offender, give him cause to repent, and terrifie others from doing the like. Every Offence that can be committed in the State of Nature, may in the Sate of Nature be also punished, equally, and as far forth as it may, in a Common-wealth; for though it would be besides my present purpose, to enter here into the particulars of the Law of Nature, or its *measures of punishment*; yet, it is certain there is such a Law, and that too, as intelligible and plain to a rational Creature, and a Studier of that Law, as the positive Laws of Common-wealths, nay possibly plainer; As much as Reason is easier to be understood, than the Phansies and intricate Contrivances of Men, following contrary and hidden interests put into Words; For so truly are a great part of the *Municipal Laws* of Countries, which are only so far right, as they are founded on the Law of Nature, by which they are to be regulated and interpreted.

13. To this strange Doctrine, *viz.* That *in the State of Nature, every one has the Executive Power* of the Law of Nature, I doubt not but it will be objected, That it is unreasonable for Men to be Judges in their own Cases, that Self-love will make Men partial to themselves and their Friends. And on the other side, that Ill Nature, Passion and Revenge will carry them too far in punishing others. And hence nothing but Confusion and Disorder will follow, and that therefore God hath certainly appointed Government to restrain the partiality and violence of Men. I easily grant, that *Civil Government* is the proper Remedy for the Inconveniences of the State of Nature, which must certainly be Great, where Men may be Judges in their own Case, since 'tis easily to be imagined, that he who was so unjust as to do his Brother an Injury, will scarce be so just as to condemn himself for it: But I shall desire those who make this Objection, to remember that *Absolute Monarchs* are but Men, and if Government is to be the Remedy of those Evils, which necessarily follow from Mens being Judges in their own Cases, and the State of Nature is therefore not to be endured, I desire to know what kind of Government that is, and how much better it is than the State of Nature, where one Man commanding a multitude, has the Liberty to be Judge in his own Case, and may do to all his Subjects whatever he pleases, without the least liberty to any one to question or controle those who Execute his Pleasure? And in whatsoever he doth, whether led by Reason, Mistake or Passion, must be submitted to? Much better it is in the State of Nature wherein Men are not bound to submit to the unjust will of another: And if he that judges, judges amiss in his own, or any other Case, he is answerable for it to the rest of Mankind.

14. 'Tis often asked as a mighty Objection, *Where are*, or ever were, there any *Men in such a State of Nature?* To which it may suffice as an answer at present; That since all *Princes* and Rulers of *Independent* Governments all

through the World, are in a State of Nature, 'tis plain the World never was, nor ever will be, without Numbers of Men in that State. I have named all Governors of *Independent* Communities, whether they are, or are not, in League with others: For 'tis not every Compact that puts an end to the State of Nature between Men, but only this one of agreeing together mutually to enter into one Community, and make one Body Politick; other Promises and Compacts, Men may make one with another, and yet still be in the State of Nature. The Promises and Bargains for Truck, *etc.* between the two Men in the Desert Island, mentioned by *Garcilasso De la vega,* in his History of *Peru,* or between a *Swiss* and an *Indian,* in the Woods of *America,* are binding to them, though they are perfectly in a State of Nature, in reference to one another. For Truth and keeping of Faith belongs to Men, as Men, and not as Members of Society. . . .

Chapter 3

Of the State of War

16. The *State of War* is a State of Enmity and Destruction; And therefore declaring by Word or Action, not a passionate and hasty, but a sedate setled Design, upon another Mans Life, *puts him in a State of War* with him against whom he has declared such an Intention, and so has exposed his Life to the others Power to be taken away by him, or any one that joyns with him in his Defence, and espouses his Quarrel: it being reasonable and just I should have a Right to destroy that which threatens me with Destruction. For *by the Fundamental Law of Nature, Man being to be preserved,* as much as possible, when all cannot be preserv'd, the safety of the Innocent is to be preferred: And one may destroy a Man who makes War upon him, or has discovered an Enmity to his being, for the same Reason, that he may kill a *Wolf* or a *Lyon;* because such Men are not under the ties of the Common Law of Reason, have no other Rule, but that of Force and Violence, and so may be treated as Beasts of Prey, those dangerous and noxious Creatures, that will be sure to destroy him, whenever he falls into their Power.

17. And hence it is, that he who attempts to get another Man into his Absolute Power, does thereby *put himself into a State of War* with him; It being to be understood as a Declaration of a Design upon his Life. For I have reason to conclude, that he who would get me into his Power without my consent, would use me as he pleased, when he had got me there, and destroy me too when he had a fancy to it: for no body can desire to *have me in his Absolute Power,* unless it be to compel me by force to that, which is against the Right of my Freedom, *i.e.* make me a Slave. To be free from such force is the only security of my Preservation: and reason bids me look on him, as an Enemy to my Preservation, who would take away that *Freedom,* which is the Fence to it: so that he who makes an *attempt to enslave* me, thereby puts himself into a State of War with me. He that in the State of Nature, *would take away the Freedom,* that belongs to any one in that State, must necessarily be supposed to have a design to take away every thing else, that *Freedom* being the Foundation of all the rest: As he that in the State of Society, would take away the *Freedom* belonging to those of that Society or Common-wealth, must be supposed to design to take away from them every thing else, and so be looked on as *in a State of War.*

18. This makes it Lawful for a Man to *kill a Thief*, who has not in the least hurt him, nor declared any design upon his Life, any farther then by the use of Force, so to get him in his Power, as to take away his Money, or what he pleases from him: because using force, where he has no Right, to get me into his Power, let his pretence be what it will, I have no reason to suppose, that he, who would *take away my Liberty*, would not when he had me in his Power, take away every thing else. And therefore it is Lawful for me to treat him, as one who has put *himself into a State of War* with me, *i.e.* kill him if I can; for to that hazard does he justly expose himself, whoever introduces a State of War, and is *aggressor* in it.

19. And here we have the plain *difference between the State of Nature, and the State of War*, which however some Men have confounded, are as far distant, as a State of Peace, Good Will, Mutual Assistance, and Preservation, and a State of Enmity, Malice, Violence, and Mutual Destruction are one from another. Men living together according to reason, without a common Superior on Earth, with Authority to judge between them, is *properly the State of Nature*. But force, or a declared design of force upon the Person of another, where there is no common Superior on Earth to appeal to for relief, *is the State of War*: And 'tis the want of such an appeal gives a Man the Right of War even against an *aggressor*, though he be in Society and a fellow Subject. Thus a *Thief*, whom I cannot harm but by appeal to the Law, for having stolen all that I am worth, I may kill, when he sets on me to rob me, but of my Horse or Coat: because the Law, which was made for my Preservation, where it cannot interpose to secure my Life from present force, which if lost, is capable of no reparation, permits me my own Defence, and the Right of War, a liberty to kill the aggressor, because the aggressor allows not time to appeal to our common Judge, nor the decision of the Law, for remedy in a Case, where the mischief may be irreparable. *Want of a common Judge with Authority, puts all Men in a State of Nature: Force without Right, upon a Man's Person, makes a State of War,* both where there is, and is not, a common Judge.

20. But when the actual force is over, the *State of War ceases* between those that are in Society, and are equally on both sides Subjected to the fair determination of the Law; because then there lies open the remedy of appeal for the past injury, and to prevent future harm: but where no such appeal is, as in the State of Nature, for want of positive Laws, and Judges with Authority to appeal to, *the State of War once begun, continues*, with a right to the innocent Party, to destroy the other whenever he can, until the aggressor offers Peace, and desires reconciliation on such Terms, as may repair any wrongs he has already done, and secure the innocent for the future: nay where an appeal to the Law, and constituted Judges lies open, but the remedy is deny'd by a manifest perverting of Justice, and a barefaced wresting of the Laws, to protect or indemnifie the violence or injuries of some Men, or Party of Men, *there* it *is* hard to imagine any thing but *a State of War*. For wherever violence is used, and injury done, though by hands appointed to administer Justice, it is still violence and injury, however colour'd with the Name, Pretences, or Forms of Law, the end whereof being to protect and redress the innocent, by an unbiassed application of it, to all who are under it; wherever that is not *bona fide* done, *War is made* upon the Sufferers, who having no appeal on Earth to right them, they are left to the only remedy in such Cases, an appeal to Heaven. . . .

Chapter 5

Of Property

25. Whether we consider natural *Reason*, which tells us, that Men, being once born, have a right to their Preservation, and consequently to Meat and Drink, and such other things, as Nature affords for their Subsistence: Or *Revelation*, which gives us an account of those Grants God made of the World to *Adam*, and to *Noah*, and his Sons, 'tis very clear, that God, as King *David* says, *Psal.* CXV. xvj. *has given the Earth to the Children of Men*, given it to Mankind in common. But this being supposed, it seems to some a very great difficulty, how any one should ever come to have a *Property* in any thing: I will not content my self to answer, That if it be difficult to make out *Property*, upon a supposition, that God gave the World to *Adam* and his Posterity in common; it is impossible that any Man, but one universal Monarch, should have any *Property*, upon a supposition, that God gave the World to *Adam*, and his Heirs in Succession, exclusive of all the rest of his Posterity. But I shall endeavour to shew, how Men might come to have a *property* in several parts of that which God gave to Mankind in common, and that without any express Compact of all the Commoners.

26. God, who hath given the World to Men in common, hath also given them reason to make use of it to the best advantage of Life, and convenience. The Earth, and all that is therein, is given to Men for the Support and Comfort of their being. And though all the Fruits it naturally produces, and Beasts it feeds, belong to Mankind in common, as they are produced by the spontaneous hand of Nature; and no body has originally a private Dominion, exclusive of the rest of Mankind, in any of them, as they are thus in their natural state: yet being given for the use of Men, there must of necessity be a means *to appropriate* them some way or other before they can be of any use, or at all beneficial to any particular Man. The Fruit, or Venison, which nourishes the wild *Indian*, who knows no Inclosure, and is still a Tenant in common, must be his, and so his, *i.e.* a part of him, that another can no longer have any right to it, before it can do him any good for the support of his Life.

27. Though the Earth, and all inferior Creatures be common to all Men, yet every Man has a *Property* in his own *Person*. This no Body has any Right to but himself. The *Labour* of his Body, and the *Work* of his Hands, we may say, are properly his. Whatsoever then he removes out of the State that Nature hath provided, and left it in, he hath mixed his *Labour* with, and joyned to it something that is his own, and thereby makes it his *Property*. It being by him removed from the common state Nature placed it in, it hath by this *labour* something annexed to it, that excludes the common right of other Men. For this *Labour* being the unquestionable Property of the Labourer, no Man but he can have a right to what that is once joyned to, at least where there is enough, and as good left in common for others.

28. He that is nourished by the Acorns he pickt up under an Oak, or the Apples he gathered from the Trees in the Wood, has certainly appropriated them to himself. No Body can deny but the nourishment is his. I ask then, When did they begin to be his? When he digested? Or when he eat? Or when he boiled? Or when he brought them home? Or when he pickt them up? And 'tis plain, if the first gathering made them not his, nothing else could. That *labour* put a distinction between them and common. That added something

to them more than Nature, the common Mother of all, had done; and so they became his private right. And will any one say he had no right to those Acorns or Apples he thus appropriated, because he had not the consent of all Mankind to make them his? Was it a Robbery thus to assume to himself what belonged to all in Common? If such a consent as that was necessary, Man had starved, notwithstanding the Plenty God had given him. We see in *Commons*, which remain so by Compact, that 'tis the taking any part of what is common, and removing it out of the state Nature leaves it in, which *begins the Property*; without which the Common is of no use. And the taking of this or that part, does not depend on the express consent of all the Commoners. Thus the Grass my Horse has bit; the Turfs my Servant has cut; and the Ore I have digg'd in any place where I have a right to them in common with others, become my *Property*, without the assignation or consent of any body. The *labour* that was mine, removing them out of that common state they were in, hath *fixed* my *Property* in them. . . .

31. It will perhaps be objected to this, That if gathering the Acorns, or other Fruits of the Earth, *etc.* makes a right to them, then any one may *ingross* as much as he will. To which I Answer, Not so. The same Law of Nature, that does by this means give us Property, does also *bound* that *Property* too. *God has given us all things richly*, 1 Tim. vi. 17. is the Voice of Reason confirmed by Inspiration. But how far has he given it us? To *enjoy*. As much as any one can make use of to any advantage of life before it spoils; so much he may by his labour fix a Property in. Whatever is beyond this, is more than his share, and belongs to others. Nothing was made by God for Man to spoil or destroy. And thus considering the plenty of natural Provisions there was a long time in the World, and the few spenders, and to how small a part of that provision the industry of one Man could extend it self, and ingross it to the prejudice of others; especially keeping within the *bounds*, set by reason of what might serve for his *use;* there could be then little room for Quarrels or Contentions about Property so establish'd. . . .

37. This is certain, That in the beginning, before the desire of having more than Men needed, had altered the intrinsick value of things, which depends only on their usefulness to the Life of Man; or [Men] had *agreed, that a little piece of yellow Metal*, which would keep without wasting or decay, should be worth a great piece of Flesh, or a whole heap of Corn; though Men had a Right to appropriate, by their Labour, each one to himself, as much of the things of Nature, as he could use: Yet this could not be much, nor to the Prejudice of others, where the same plenty was still left, to those who would use the same Industry. To which let me add, that he who appropriates land to himself by his labour, does not lessen but increase the common stock of mankind. For the provisions serving to the support of humane life, produced by one acre of inclosed and cultivated land, are (to speak much within compasse) ten times more, than those, which are yielded by an acre of Land, of an equal richnesse, lyeing wast in common. And therefor he, that incloses Land and has a greater plenty of the conveniencys of life from ten acres, than he could have from an hundred left to Nature, may truly be said, to give ninety acres to Mankind. For his labour now supplys him with provisions out of ten acres, which were but the product of an hundred lying in common. I have here rated the improved land very low in making its product but as ten to one, when it is much nearer an hundred to one. For I aske whether in the

wild woods and uncultivated wast of America left to Nature, without any improvement, tillage or husbandry, a thousand acres will yield the needy and wretched inhabitants as many conveniencies of life as ten acres of equally fertile land doe in Devonshire where they are well cultivated? . . .

45. Thus *Labour*, in the Beginning, *gave a Right of Property*, where-ever any one was pleased to imploy it, upon what was common, which remained, a long while, the far greater part, and is yet more than Mankind makes use of. Men, at first, for the most part, contented themselves with what un-assisted Nature offered to their Necessities: and though afterwards, in some parts of the World, (where the Increase of People and Stock, with the *Use of Money*) had made Land scarce, and so of some Value, the several *Communities* settled the Bounds of their distinct Territories, and by Laws within themselves, regulated the Properties of the private Men of their Society, and so, *by Compact* and Agreement, *settled the Property* which Labour and Industry began; and the Leagues that have been made between several States and Kingdoms, either expressly or tacitly disowning all Claim and Right to the Land in the others Possession, have, by common Consent, given up their Pretences to their natural common Right, which originally they had to those Countries, and so have, by *positive agreement, settled a Property* amongst themselves, in distinct Parts and parcels of the Earth: yet there are still *great Tracts of Ground* to be found, which (the Inhabitants thereof not having joyned with the rest of Mankind, in the consent of the Use of their common Money) *lie waste*, and are more than the People, who dwell on it, do, or can make use of, and so still lie in common. Tho' this can scarce happen amongst that part of Mankind, that have consented to the Use of Money.

46. The greatest part of *things really useful* to the Life of Man, and such as the necessity of subsisting made the first Commoners of the World look after, as it doth the *Americans* now, *are* generally things *of short duration*; such as, if they are not consumed by use will decay and perish of themselves: Gold, Silver, and Diamonds are things, that Fancy or Agreement hath put the Value on, more then real Use, and the necessary Support of Life. Now of those good things which Nature hath provided in common, every one had a Right (as hath been said) to as much as he could use, and had a Property in all that he could affect with his Labour: all that his Industry could extend to, to alter from the State Nature had put it in, was his. He that *gathered* a Hundred Bushels of Acorns or Apples, had thereby a *Property* in them; they were his Goods as soon as gathered. He was only to look that he used them before they spoiled; else he took more then his share, and robb'd others. And indeed it was a foolish thing, as well as dishonest, to hoard up more than he could make use of. If he gave away a part to any body else, so that it perished not uselesly in his Possession, these he also made use of. And if he also bartered away Plumbs that would have rotted in a Week, for Nuts that would last good for his eating a whole Year, he did no injury; he wasted not the common Stock; destroyed no part of the portion of Goods that belonged to others, so long as nothing perished uselesly in his hands. Again, if he would give his Nuts for a piece of Metal, pleased with its colour; or exchange his Sheep for Shells, or Wool for a sparkling Pebble or a Diamond, and keep those by him all his Life, he invaded not the Right of others, he might heap up as much of these durable things as he pleased; the *exceeding of the bounds of his* just *Property* not lying in the largeness of his Possession, but the perishing of any thing uselesly in it.

47. And thus *came in the use of Money*, some lasting thing that Men might keep without spoiling, and that by mutual consent Men would take in exchange for the truly useful, but perishable Supports of Life.

48. And as different degrees of Industry were apt to give Men Possessions in different Proportions, so this *Invention of Money* gave them the opportunity to continue and enlarge them. For supposing an Island, separate from all possible Commerce with the rest of the World, wherein there were but a hundred Families, but there were Sheep, Horses and Cows, with other useful Animals, wholsome Fruits, and Land enough for Corn for a hundred thousand times as many, but nothing in the Island, either because of its Commonness, or Perishableness, fit to supply the place of *Money*: What reason could any one have there to enlarge his Possessions beyond the use of his Family, and a plentiful supply to its Consumption, either in what their own Industry produced, or they could barter for like perishable, useful Commodities, with others? Where there is not something both lasting and scarce, and so valuable to be hoarded up, there Men will not be apt to enlarge their *Possessions of Land*, were it never so rich, never so free for them to take. For I ask, What would a Man value Ten Thousand, or an Hundred Thousand Acres of excellent *Land*, ready cultivated, and well stocked too with Cattle, in the middle of the in-land Parts of *America*, where he had no hopes of Commerce with other Parts of the World, to draw *Money* to him by the Sale of the Product? It would not be worth the inclosing, and we should see him give up again to the wild Common of Nature, whatever was more than would supply the Conveniencies of Life to be had there for him and his Family.

49. Thus in the beginning all the World was *America*, and more so than that is now; for no such thing as *Money* was any where known. Find out something that hath the *Use and Value of Money* amongst his Neighbours, you shall see the same Man will begin presently to *enlarge* his *Possessions*.

50. But since Gold and Silver, being little useful to the Life of Man in proportion to Food, Rayment, and Carriage, has its *value* only from the consent of Men, whereof Labour yet makes, in great part, *the measure*, it is plain, that Men have agreed to disproportionate and unequal Possession of the Earth, they having by a tacit and voluntary consent found out a way, how a man may fairly possess more land than he himself can use the product of, by receiving in exchange for the overplus, Gold and Silver, which may be hoarded up without injury to any one, these metalls not spoileing or decaying in the hands of the possessor. This partage of things, in an inequality of private possessions men have made practicable out of the bounds of Societie, and without compact, only by putting a value on gold and silver and tacitly agreeing in the use of Money. For in Governments the Laws regulate the right of property, and the possession of land is determined by positive constitutions. . . .

Chapter 7

Of Political or Civil Society

. . . 87. Man being born, as has been proved, with a Title to perfect Freedom, and an uncontrouled enjoyment of all the Rights and Priviledges of the Law of Nature, equally with any other Man, or Number of Men in the World, hath by Nature a Power, not only to preserve his Property, that is, his Life, Liberty and Estate, against the Injuries and Attempts of other Men; but to judge of, and punish the breaches of that Law in others, as he is perswaded the Offence deserves, even with Death it self, in Crimes where the heinousness of the Fact, in his Opinion, requires it. But because no *Political Society* can be, nor subsist without having in it self the Power to preserve the Property, and in order thereunto punish the Offences of all those of that Society; there, and there only is *Political Society*, where every one of the Members hath quitted this natural Power, resign'd it up into the hands of the Community in all cases that exclude him not from appealing for Protection to the Law established by it. And thus all private judgement of every particular Member being excluded, the Community comes to be Umpire, by settled standing Rules, indifferent, and the same to all Parties; and by Men having Authority from the Community, for the execution of those Rules, decides all the differences that may happen between any Members of that Society, concerning any matter of right; and punishes those Offences, which any Member hath committed against the Society, with such Penalties as the Law has established: Whereby it is easie to discern who are, and who are not, in *Political Society* together. Those who are united into one Body, and have a common establish'd Law and Judicature to appeal to, with Authority to decide Controversies between them, and punish Offenders, *are in Civil Society* one with another: but those who have no such common Appeal, I mean on Earth, are still in the state of Nature, each being, where there is no other, Judge for himself, and Executioner; which is, as I have before shew'd it, the perfect *state of Nature*.

88. And thus the Commonwealth comes by a Power to set down, what punishment shall belong to the several transgressions which they think worthy of it, committed amongst the Members of that Society, (which is the *power of making Laws*) as well as it has the power to punish any Injury done unto any of its Members, by any one that is not of it, (which is the *power of War and Peace*;) and all this for the preservation of the property of all the Members of that Society, as far as is possible. But though every Man who has enter'd into civil Society, and is become a member of any Commonwealth, has thereby quitted his power to punish Offences against the Law of Nature, in prosecution of his own private Judgment; yet with the Judgment of Offences which he has given up to the Legislative in all Cases, where he can Appeal to the Magistrate, he has given a right to the Commonwealth to imploy his force, for the Execution of the Judgments of the Commonwealth, whenever he shall be called to it; which indeed are his own Judgments, they being made by himself, or his Representative. And herein we have the original of the *Legislative* and *Executive Power* of Civil Society, which is to judge by standing Laws how far Offences are to be punished, when committed within the Commonwealth; and also to determin, by occasional Judgments founded on the present Circumstances of the Fact, how far Injuries from without are to be vindicated, and in both these to imploy all the force of all the Members when there shall be need.

89. Where-ever therefore any number of Men are so united into one Society, as to quit every one his Executive Power of the Law of Nature, and to resign it to the publick, there and there only is a *Political, or Civil Society*. And this is done where-ever any number of Men, in the state of Nature, enter

into Society to make one People, one Body Politick under one Supreme Government, or else when any one joyns himself to, and incorporates with any Government already made. For hereby he authorizes the Society, or which is all one, the Legislative thereof to make Laws for him as the publick good of the Society shall require; to the Execution whereof, his own assistance (as to his own Decrees) is due. And this *puts Men* out of a State of Nature *into* that of a *Commonwealth*, by setting up a Judge on Earth, with Authority to determine all the Controversies, and redress the Injuries, that may happen to any Member of the Commonwealth; which Judge is the Legislative, or Magistrates appointed by it. And where-ever there are any number of Men, however associated, that have no such decisive power to appeal to, there they are still *in the state of Nature.*

90. Hence it is evident, that *Absolute Monarchy*, which by some Men is counted the only Government in the World, is indeed *inconsistent with Civil Society*, and so can be no Form of Civil Government at all. For the *end of Civil Society*, being to avoid, and remedy those inconveniencies of the State of Nature, which necessarily follow from every Man's being Judge in his own Case, by setting up a known Authority, to which every one of that Society may Appeal upon any Injury received, or Controversie that may arise, and which every one of the Society ought to obey; where-ever any persons are, who have not such an Authority to Appeal to, for the decision of any difference between them, there those persons are still *in the state of Nature*. And so is every *Absolute Prince* in respect of those who are under his *Dominion.* . . .

93. *In Absolute Monarchies* indeed, as well as other Governments of the World, the Subjects have an Appeal to the Law, and Judges to decide any Controversies, and restrain any Violence that may happen betwixt the Subjects themselves, one amongst another. This every one thinks necessary, and believes he deserves to be thought a declared Enemy to Society and Mankind, who should go about to take it away. But whether this be from a true Love of Mankind and Society, and such a Charity as we owe all one to another, there is reason to doubt. For this is no more, than what every Man who loves his own Power, Profit, or Greatness, may, and naturally must do, keep those Animals from hurting or destroying one another who labour and drudge only for his Pleasure and Advantage, and so are taken care of, not out of any Love the Master has for them, but Love of himself, and the Profit they bring him. For if it be asked, what Security, *what Fence* is there in such a State, *against the Violence and Oppression of this Absolute Ruler?* The very Question can scarce be born. They are ready to tell you, that it deserves Death only to ask after Safety. Betwixt Subject and Subject, they will grant, there must be Measures, Laws, and Judges, for their mutual Peace and Security: But as for the *Ruler*, he ought to be *Absolute*, and is above all such Circumstances: because he has Power to do more hurt and wrong, 'tis right when he does it. To ask how you may be guarded from harm, or injury on that side where the strongest hand is to do it, is presently the Voice of Faction and Rebellion. As if when Men quitting the State of Nature entered into Society, they agreed that all of them but one, should be under the restraint of Laws, but that he should still retain all the Liberty of the State of Nature, increased with Power, and made licentious by Impunity. This is to think that Men are so foolish that they take care to avoid what Mischiefs may

be done them by *Pole-Cats*, or *Foxes*, but are content, nay think it Safety, to be devoured by *Lions*. . . .

Chapter 8

Of the Beginning of Political Societies

95. Men being, as has been said, by Nature, all free, equal and independent, no one can be put out of this Estate, and subjected to the Political Power of another, without his own *Consent*. The only way whereby any one devests himself of his Natural Liberty, and *puts on the bonds of Civil Society* is by agreeing with other Men to joyn and unite into a Community, for their comfortable, safe, and peaceable living one amongst another, in a secure Enjoyment of their Properties, and a greater Security against any that are not of it. This any number of Men may do, because it injures not the Freedom of the rest; they are left as they were in the Liberty of the State of Nature. When any number of Men have so *consented to make one Community* or Government, they are thereby presently incorporated, and make *one Body Politick*, wherein the *Majority* have a Right to act and conclude the rest.

96. For when any number of Men have, by the consent of every individual, made a *Community*, they have thereby made that *Community* one Body, with a Power to Act as one Body, which is only by the will and determination of the *majority*. For that which acts any Community, being only the consent of the individuals of it, and it being necessary to that which is one body to move one way; it is necessary the Body should move that way whither the greater force carries it, which is the *consent of the majority*: or else it is impossible it should act or continue one Body, *one Community*, which the consent of every individual that united into it, agreed that it should; and so every one is bound by that consent to be concluded by the *majority*. And therefore we see that in Assemblies impowered to act by positive Laws where no number is set by that positive Law which impowers them, the *act of the Majority* passes for the act of the whole, and of course determines, as having by the Law of Nature and Reason, the power of the whole.

97. And thus every Man, by consenting with others to make one Body Politick under one Government, puts himself under an Obligation to every one of that Society, to submit to the determination of the *majority*, and to be concluded by it; or else this *original Compact*, whereby he with others incorporates into *one Society*, would signifie nothing, and be no Compact, if he be left free, and under no other ties, than he was in before in the State of Nature. For what appearance would there be of any Compact? What new Engagement if he were no farther tied by any Decrees of the Society, than he himself thought fit, and did actually consent to? This would be still as great a liberty, as he himself had before his Compact, or any one else in the State of Nature hath, who may submit himself and consent to any acts of it if he thinks fit.

98. For if *the consent of the majority* shall not in reason, be received, as *the act of the whole*, and conclude every individual; nothing but the consent of every individual can make any thing to be the act of the whole: But such a consent is next impossible ever to be had, if we consider the Infirmities of Health, and Avocations of Business, which in a number, though much less than that of a Common-wealth, will necessarily keep many away from the

publick Assembly. To which if we add the variety of Opinions, and contrariety of Interests, which unavoidably happen in all Collections of Men, the coming into Society upon such terms, would be only like *Cato's* coming into the Theatre, only to go out again. Such a Constitution as this would make the mighty *Leviathan* of a shorter duration, than the feeblest Creatures; and not let it outlast the day it was born in: which cannot be suppos'd, till we can think, that Rational Creatures should desire and constitute Societies only to be dissolved. For where the *majority* cannot conclude the rest, there they cannot act as one Body, and consequently will be immediately dissolved again.

99. Whosoever therefore out of a state of Nature unite into a *Community*, must be understood to give up all the power, necessary to the ends for which they unite into Society, to the *majority* of the Community, unless they expressly agreed in any number greater than the majority. And this is done by barely agreeing to *unite into one Political Society*, which is *all the Compact* that is, or needs be, between the Individuals, that enter into, or make up a *Common-wealth*. And thus that, which begins and actually *constitutes any Political Society*, is nothing but the consent of any number of Freemen capable of a majority to unite and incorporate into such a Society. And this is that, and that only, which did, or could give *beginning* to any *lawful Government* in the World. . . .

119. *Every Man* being, as has been shewed, *naturally free*, and nothing being able to put him into subjection to any Earthly Power, but only his own Consent; it is to be considered, what shall be understood to be *a sufficient Declaration of* a Mans *Consent, to make him subject* to the Laws of any Government. There is a common distinction of an express and a tacit consent, which will concern our present Case. No body doubts but an *express Consent*, of any Man, entring into any Society, makes him a perfect Member of that Society, a Subject of that Government. The difficulty is, what ought to be look'd upon as a *tacit Consent*, and how far it binds, *i.e.* how far any one shall be looked on to have consented, and thereby submitted to any Government, where he has made no Expressions of it at all. And to this I say, that every Man, that hath any Possession, or Enjoyment, of any part of the Dominions of any Government, doth thereby give his *tacit Consent*, and is as far forth obliged to Obedience to the Laws of that Government, during such Enjoyment, as any one under it; whether this his Possession be of Land, to him and his Heirs for ever, or a Lodging only for a Week; or whether it be barely travelling freely on the Highway; and in Effect, it reaches as far as the very being of any one within the Territories of that Government. . . .

122. But submitting to the Laws of any Country, living quietly, and enjoying Priviledges and Protection under them, *makes not a Man a Member of that Society*: This is only a local Protection and Homage due to, and from all those, who, not being in a state of War, come within the Territories belonging to any Government, to all parts whereof the force of its Law extends. But this no more *makes a Man a Member of that Society*, a perpetual Subject of that Commonwealth, than it would make a Man a Subject to another in whose Family he found it convenient to abide for some time; though, whilst he continued in it, he were obliged to comply with the Laws, and submit to the Government he found there. And thus we see, that

Foreigners, by living all their Lives under another Government, and enjoying the Priviledges and Protection of it, though they are bound, even in Conscience, to submit to its Administration, as far forth as any Denison; yet do not thereby come to be *Subjects or Members of that Commonwealth.* Nothing can make any Man so, but his actually entering into it by positive Engagement, and express Promise and Compact. This is that, which I think, concerning the beginning of Political Societies, and that *Consent which makes any one a Member* of any Commonwealth.

Chapter 9

Of the Ends of Political Society and Government

123. If Man in the State of Nature be so free, as has been said; If he be absolute Lord of his own Person and Possessions, equal to the greatest, and subject to no Body, why will he part with his Freedom? Why will he give up this Empire, and subject himself to the Dominion and Controul of any other Power? To which 'tis obvious to Answer, that though in the state of Nature he hath such a right, yet the Enjoyment of it is very uncertain, and constantly exposed to the Invasion of others. For all being Kings as much as he, every Man his Equal, and the greater part no strict Observers of Equity and Justice, the enjoyment of the property he has in this state is very unsafe, very unsecure. This makes him willing to quit this Condition, which however free, is full of fears and continual dangers: And 'tis not without reason, that he seeks out, and is willing to joyn in Society with others who are already united, or have a mind to unite for the mutual *Preservation* of their Lives, Liberties and Estates, which I call by the general Name, *Property.*

124. The great and *chief end* therefore, of Mens uniting into Commonwealths, and putting themselves under Government, *is the Preservation of their Property.* To which in the state of Nature there are many things wanting.

First, There wants an *establish'd,* settled, known *Law,* received and allowed by common consent to be the Standard of Right and Wrong, and the common measure to decide all Controversies between them. For though the Law of Nature be plain and intelligible to all rational Creatures; yet Men being biassed by their Interest, as well as ignorant for want of study of it, are not apt to allow of it as a Law binding to them in the application of it to their particular Cases.

125. *Secondly,* In the State of Nature there wants a *known and indifferent Judge,* with Authority to determine all differences according to the established Law. For every one in that state being both Judge and Executioner of the Law of Nature, Men being partial to themselves, Passion and Revenge is very apt to carry them too far, and with too much heat, in their own Cases; as well as negligence, and unconcernedness, to make them too remiss, in other Mens.

126. *Thirdly,* In the state of Nature there often wants *Power* to back and support the Sentence when right, and to *give* it due *Execution.* They who by any Injustice offended, will seldom fail, where they are able, by force to make good their Injustice: such resistance many times makes the punishment dangerous, and frequently destructive, to those who attempt it.

127. Thus Mankind, notwithstanding all the Priviledges of the state of Nature, being but in an ill condition, while they remain in it, are quickly driven into Society. Hence it comes to pass, that we seldom find any number of Men live any time together in this State. The inconveniencies, that they are therein exposed to, by the irregular and uncertain exercise of the Power every Man has of punishing the transgressions of others, make them take Sanctuary under the establish'd Laws of Government, and therein seek *the preservation of their Property*. 'Tis this makes them so willingly give up every one his single power of punishing to be exercised by such alone as shall be appointed to it amongst them; and by such Rules as the Community, or those authorised by them to that purpose, shall agree on. And in this we have the original *right and rise* of both *the Legislative and Executive Power*, as well as of the Governments and Societies themselves. . . .

131. But though Men when they enter into Society, give up the Equality, Liberty, and Executive Power they had in the State of Nature, into the hands of the Society, to be so far disposed of by the Legislative, as the good of the Society shall require; yet it being only with an intention in every one the better to preserve himself his Liberty and Property; (For no rational Creature can be supposed to change his condition with an intention to be worse) the power of the Society, or *Legislative* constituted by them, *can never be suppos'd to extend farther than the common good*; but is obliged to secure every ones Property by providing against those three defects above-mentioned, that made the State of Nature so unsafe and uneasie. And so whoever has the Legislative or Supream Power of any Common-wealth, is bound to govern by establish'd *standing Laws*, promulgated and known to the People, and not by Extemporary Decrees; by *indifferent* and upright *Judges*, who are to decide Controversies by those Laws; And to imploy the force of the Community at home, *only in the Execution of such Laws*, or abroad to prevent or redress Foreign Injuries, and secure the Community from Inroads and Invasion. And all this to be directed to no other *end*, but the *Peace, Safety*, and *publick good* of the People. . . .

Chapter 19

Of the Dissolution of Government

211. He that will with any clearness speak of the *Dissolution of Government*, ought, in the first place to distinguish between the *Dissolution of the Society*, and the *Dissolution of the Government*. That which makes the Community, and brings Men out of the loose State of Nature, into *one Politick Society*, is the Agreement which every one has with the rest to incorporate, and act as one Body, and so be one distinct Commonwealth. The usual, and almost only way whereby *this Union is dissolved*, is the Inroad of Foreign Force making a Conquest upon them. For in that Case, (not being able to maintain and support themselves, as *one intire* and *independent Body*) the Union belonging to that Body which consisted therein, must necessarily cease, and so every one return to the state he was in before, with a liberty to shift for himself, and provide for his own Safety as he thinks fit in some other Society. Whenever the *Society is dissolved*, 'tis certain the Government of that Society cannot remain. Thus Conquerours Swords often cut up Governments by the Roots, and mangle Societies to pieces, separating the subdued

or scattered Multitude from the Protection of, and Dependence on that Society which ought to have preserved them from violence. The World is too well instructed in, and too forward to allow of this way of dissolving of Governments to need any more to be said of it: and there wants not much Argument to prove, that where the *Society is dissolved*, the Government cannot remain; that being as impossible, as for the Frame of an House to subsist when the Materials of it are scattered, and dissipated by a Whirlwind, or jumbled into a confused heap by an Earthquake.

212. Besides this over-turning from without, *Governments are dissolved from within*,

First, When the *Legislative* is *altered*. Civil Society being a State of Peace, amongst those who are of it, from whom the State of War is excluded by the Umpirage, which they have provided in their Legislative, for the ending all Differences, that may arise amongst any of them, 'tis in their *Legislative*, that the Members of a Commonwealth are united, and combined together into one coherent living Body. This *is the Soul that gives Form, Life, and Unity* to the Commonwealth: From hence the several Members have their mutual Influence, Sympathy, and Connexion: And therefore when the *Legislative* is broken, or *dissolved*, Dissolution and Death follows. For the *Essence and Union of the Society* consisting in having one Will, the Legislative, when once established by the Majority, has the declaring, and as it were keeping of that Will. The *Constitution of the Legislative* is the first and fundamental Act of Society, whereby provision is made for the *Continuation of their Union*, under the Direction of Persons, and Bonds of Laws made by persons authorized thereunto, by the Consent and Appointment of the People, without which no one Man, or number of Men, amongst them, can have Authority of making Laws, that shall be binding to the rest. When any one, or more, shall take upon them to make Laws, whom the People have not appointed so to do, they make Laws without Authority, which the People are not therefore bound to obey; by which means they come again to be out of subjection, and may constitute to themselves a *new Legislative*, as they think best, being in full liberty to resist the force of those, who without Authority would impose any thing upon them. Every one is at the disposure of his own Will, when those who had by the delegation of the Society, the declaring of the publick Will, are excluded from it, and others usurp the place who have no such Authority or Delegation.

213. This being usually brought about by such in the Commonwealth who misuse the Power they have: It is hard to consider it aright, and know at whose door to lay it, without knowing the Form of Government in which it happens. Let us suppose then the Legislative placed in the Concurrence of three distinct Persons.

1. A single hereditary Person having the constant, supream, executive Power, and with it the Power of Convoking and Dissolving the other two within certain Periods of Time.

2. An Assembly of Hereditary Nobility.

3. An Assembly of Representatives chosen *pro tempore*, by the People: Such a Form of Government supposed, it is evident.

214. *First*, That when such a single Person or Prince sets up his own Arbitrary Will in place of the Laws, which are the Will of the Society,

declared by the Legislative, then the *Legislative is changed*. For that being in effect the Legislative whose Rules and Laws are put in execution, and required to be obeyed; when other Laws are set up, and other Rules pretended, and inforced, than what the Legislative, constituted by the Society, have enacted, 'tis plain, that the *Legislative is changed*. Whoever introduces new Laws, not being thereunto authorized by the fundamental Appointment of the Society, or subverts the old, disowns and overturns the Power by which they were made, and so sets up a *new Legislative*.

215. *Secondly*, When the Prince hinders the Legislative from assembling in its due time, or from acting freely, pursuant to those ends, for which it was Constituted, the *Legislative is altered*. For 'tis not a certain number of Men, no, nor their meeting, unless they have also Freedom of debating, and Leisure of perfecting, what is for the good of the Society wherein the Legislative consists: when these are taken away or altered, so as to deprive the Society of the due exercise of their Power, the *Legislative* is truly *altered*. For it is not Names, that Constitute Governments, but the use and exercise of those Powers that were intended to accompany them; so that he who takes away the Freedom, or hinders the acting of the Legislative in its due seasons, in effect *takes away the Legislative*, and *puts an end to the Government*.

216. *Thirdly*, When by the Arbitrary Power of the Prince, the Electors, or ways of Election are altered, without the Consent, and contrary to the common Interest of the People, there also the *Legislative is altered*. For if others, than those whom the Society has authorized thereunto, do chuse, or in another way, than what the Society hath prescribed, those chosen are not the Legislative appointed by the People.

217. *Fourthly*, The delivery also of the People into the subjection of a Foreign Power, either by the Prince, or by the Legislative, is certainly a *change of the Legislative*, and so a *Dissolution of the Government*. For the end why People entered into Society, being to be preserved one intire, free, independent Society, to be governed by its own Laws; this is lost, whenever they are given up into the Power of another. . . .

219. There is one way more whereby such a Government may be dissolved, and that is, when he who has the Supream Executive Power, neglects and abandons that charge, so that the Laws already made can no longer be put in execution. This is demonstratively to reduce all to Anarchy, and so effectually to *dissolve the Government*. For Laws not being made for themselves, but to be by their execution the Bonds of the Society, to keep every part of the Body Politick in its due place and function, when that totally ceases, the *Government* visibly *ceases*, and the People become a confused Multitude, without Order or Connexion. Where there is no longer the administration of Justice, for the securing of Mens Rights, nor any remaining Power within the Community to direct the Force, or provide for the Necessities for the publick, there certainly is *no Government left*. Where the Laws cannot be executed, it is all one as if there were no Laws, and a Government without Laws, is, I suppose, a Mystery in Politicks, unconceivable to humane Capacity, and inconsistent with humane Society.

220. In these and the like Cases, *when the Government is dissolved*, the People are at liberty to provide for themselves, by erecting a new Legislative, differing from the other, by the change of Persons, or Form, or both as they shall find it most for their safety and good. For the *Society* can never, by the

fault of another, lose the Native and Original Right it has to preserve it self, which can only be done by a settled Legislative, and a fair and impartial execution of the Laws made by it. But the state of Mankind is not so miserable that they are not capable of using this Remedy, till it be too late to look for any. To tell *People* they *may provide for themselves*, by erecting a new Legislative, when by Oppression, Artifice, or being delivered over to a Foreign Power, their old one is gone, is only to tell them they may expect Relief, when it is too late, and the evil is past Cure. This is in effect no more than to bid them first be Slaves, and then to take care of their Liberty; and when their Chains are on, tell them, they may act like Freemen. This, if barely so, is rather Mockery than Relief; and Men can never be secure from Tyranny, if there be no means to escape it, till they are perfectly under it: And therefore it is, that they have not only a Right to get out of it but to prevent it. . . .

224. But 'twill be said, this *Hypothesis* lays a *ferment* for frequent *Rebellion*. To which I Answer,

First, No more than any other *Hypothesis*. For when the *People* are made *miserable*, and find themselves *exposed to the ill usage of Arbitrary Power*, cry up their Governours, as much as you will for Sons of *Jupiter*, let them be Sacred and Divine, descended or authoriz'd from Heaven; give them out for whom or what you please, the same will happen. *The People generally ill treated*, and contrary to right, will be ready upon any occasion to ease themselves of a burden that sits heavy upon them. They will wish and seek for the opportunity, which, in the change, weakness, and accidents of humane affairs, seldom delays long to offer it self. He must have lived but a little while in the World, who has not seen Examples of this in his time; and he must have read very little, who cannot produce Examples of it in all sorts of Governments in the World.

225. Secondly, I Answer, such *Revolutions happen* not upon every little mismanagement in publick affairs. *Great mistakes* in the ruling part, many wrong and inconvenient Laws, and all the *slips* of humane frailty will be *born by the People*, without mutiny or murmur. But if a long train of Abuses, Prevarications, and Artifices, all tending the same way, make the design visible to the People, and they cannot but feel, what they lie under, and see, whither they are going; 'tis not to be wonder'd, that they should then rouze themselves, and endeavour to put the rule into such hands, which may secure to them the ends for which Government was at first erected; and without which, ancient Names, and specious Forms, are so far from being better, that they are much worse, than the state of Nature, or pure Anarchy; the inconveniencies being all as great and as near, but the remedy farther off and more difficult.

226. Thirdly, I Answer, That *this Doctrine* of a Power in the People of providing for their safety a-new by a new Legislative, when their Legislators have acted contrary to their trust, by invading their Property, is *the best fence against Rebellion*, and the probablest means to hinder it. For Rebellion being an Opposition, not to Persons, but Authority, which is founded only in the Constitutions and Laws of the Government; those, whoever they be, who by force break through, and by force justifie their violation of them, are truly and properly *Rebels*. For when Men by entering into Society and Civil Government, have excluded force, and introduced Laws for the preservation

of Property, Peace, and Unity amongst themselves; those who set up force again in opposition to the Laws, do *Rebellare*, that is, bring back again the state of War, and are properly Rebels: Which they who are in Power (by the pretence they have to Authority, the temptation of force they have in their hands, and the Flattery of those about them) being likeliest to do; the properest way to prevent the evil, is to shew them the danger and injustice of it, who are under the greatest temptation to run into it. . . .

The Law of Nature in Locke's
Second Treatise:
Is Locke a Hobbesian?
Patrick Coby

Locke scholarship for some thirty years now has fixed itself on the question of Locke's intellectual pedigree—Was the Whig philosopher a sincere Christian and faithful conveyor of the natural law tradition, or was he instead a closet Hobbesian, to say nothing of a bourgeois ideologist? The reason behind such concentrated focus is the recognition by many scholars that Locke is inconsistent, or apparently so, and thus difficult to interpret. A case in point is Locke's description of the state of nature. Locke is at pains to distinguish his account from that of Hobbes *(Second Treatise,* sec. 19), and yet he retains enough Hobbesian features to justify the conclusion that man's life in nature, if not "solitary," is certainly "poor, nasty, brutish, and short." Some scholars explain these problems as changes of mind, perhaps as mere inadvertencies, and are satisfied to say that Locke makes mistakes.[1] Others place Locke in his historical setting, examine thoroughly the debates and vocabulary of the day, and conclude that few if any difficulties really exist, their detection being the consequence of an unhistorical approach.[2] Finally a third group of scholars explain Locke's inconsistencies as a stratagem for concealing his indebtedness to the "justly decried" Hobbes.[3] Those who advance this last interpretation have attempted to show that neither the Bible nor Richard Hooker's *Laws of Ecclesiastical Polity* are authoritative texts for Locke, despite the fact that Locke quotes frequently from both.

I should confess at the outset that my sympathies lie with those scholars of the third group who believe that Locke is a Hobbesian. My intention is to support their position by examining the subject of natural law as presented by Locke in the *Second Treatise.* I might add, however, that while I accept Locke's Hobbesianism, I do not regard him merely as a disciple. There are differences to be observed, and one in particular I will develop in the closing portion of the paper.

Laws of Nature

It is a much remarked fact about Locke that he gives no systematic account of natural law in the *Second Treatise:* "it would be beside my present purpose, to enter here into the particulars of the Law of Nature" (sec. 12).[4] Even so, the work contains an impressive collection of obligations which are called natural laws at some point or

From Patrick Coby, "The Law of Nature in Locke's Second Treatise: Is Locke a Hobbesian?", *The Review of Politics,* Vol. 49:1, pp. 3–28. Copyright © 1987. Reprinted with permission of the author and the University of Notre Dame Press.

Note: This article is a revised and condensed version of a paper presented at the 1985 American Political Science Convention; the original contained a lengthy discussion of the differences between Hobbes and Locke.

another. If Locke's disclaimer is then set aside and a list compiled, one discovers at least thirteen natural laws in total and as many as six functioning in the state of nature. Those which exist prior to and independent of civil society are: (1) self-preservation (secs. 6, 135, 149, 171); (2) the preservation of mankind (secs. 6, 134, 135, 159, 171, 182, 183); (3) private property (secs. 30, 31); (4) restrictions on private acquisition, namely the requirements that nothing appropriated be allowed to spoil (secs. 31, 36, 37, 46, 50) and that there be "enough, and as good left" for others (secs. 27, 33, 34); (5) parents' care of children (secs. 56, 58, 66, 67, 71, 72, 74); and (6) children's care, defense, comfort, and honor of parents (secs. 66, 67, 68, 71, 72, 74). Of the six, the first four mean to regulate the behavior of individuals, while the last two address life in the family.

Once civil society has been established, seven additional laws of nature come into play. They concern the relationship of the commonwealth to its citizens or the commonwealth in its dealings with other states. The first category includes (1) limited government (secs. 135, 137, 138, 140, 141, 142); (2) government by consent (secs. 95, 176, 186, 192); (3) majority rule (sec. 96); (4) legislative supremacy (secs. 149, 150);[5] (5) prerogative power (sec. 159); and (6) the right of revolution (secs. 168, 196). The second sort contains only one law, namely, the law of just conquest, but justice in this regard has the four following specifications:[6] (1) that there be no dominion over former allies (sec. 177); (2) that despotical power extend only to the lives and liberties of the captured enemy (secs. 178, 179, 180); (3) that there be no seizure of enemy property beyond what is needed for reparation (secs. 180–84), and that even this claim be relinquished when the lives of innocent people are at stake (sec. 183); and (4) that there be no governing of conquered territories without the consent of their inhabitants (sec. 192).

Before considering in detail Locke's thirteen laws of nature, we might take note of some apparent departures from the Hobbesian original. First of all, Hobbes does not differentiate, as does Locke, between natural laws appropriate to a state of nature and natural laws appropriate to civil society. He does not because he denies that the state of nature is actually governed by natural law. For Hobbes natural law has the sole function of effecting man's progress from nature to society, which progress is accomplished by socializing an otherwise unsocial creature and by establishing elemental rules of fair treatment (*Elements of Law* I. 4, 10, 15). It is in fact the absence of effective law in nature that leads Hobbes to assert the priority of natural right, defined in *De Cive* as the right "to have all, and to do all" (I. 10). In a Hobbesian state of nature, people enjoy such a degree of license that distinguishing between lawful and lawless conduct is all but impossible. Accordingly, Hobbes's description of the state of nature is pointedly amoral. Locke, on the other hand, presumes a firm demarcation between two types of people, the law-abiding and the criminal. Secondly, Hobbes argues that justice is the keeping of contracts, and that contracts in a state of nature are mostly invalid (*De Cive* II. 11; *Leviathan* xiv. pp. 124–25). Locke, though, believes that any violation of natural law is an injustice, and he identifies six laws in nature that can be violated. Thirdly, Hobbes is convinced that justice is lacking in nature because private property, on which justice depends, is an institution confined to civil society (*De Cive* Dedication). But Locke explains how property is appropriated in nature and how just relations apply in that state.

With respect to civil society, Hobbes and Locke are evidently at opposite poles, with Hobbes using natural law to defend absolutism and Locke using natural law to promote limited government. Hobbes arrives at his conclusion by investigating the various sources of rightful dominion, which sources he claims are three in number:

consent, generation (tacit consent), and conquest. In each case, though, power is absolute and despotical, that is, the ruler rules in his own interest, and the subject submits out of fear. Thus to Hobbes's mind a king and a tyrant are one and the same; likewise a king and a parent-master, for the city is but a large family, and the family a small city (*De Cive* VIII. 1). Hobbes concludes then that the sovereign's legitimacy is a function of strength (either his own [acquired government] or that added to his by the consent of others [instituted government]); and because what the sovereign commands is law, the sovereign's might is the sovereign's right—might makes right.

Locke also differentiates three sources of legitimate power, which happen to be the same three recognized by Hobbes. But these three sources, says Locke, designate three distinct kinds of power: political, parental, and despotical. Only in the case of despotic power is power absolute, political and parental power being strictly limited. Hence there is a difference between kingship and tyranny. There also is a difference between politics and parenting in that parental power is temporary and confined to the liberty of the child. Locke further maintains that those subject to political rule have given their consent freely. Hobbes says much the same, although Hobbes supposes that contracts based on fear (which is how he explains the social contract) are fully valid (*De Cive* II. 16; *Leviathan* xiv. pp. 126–27). Locke insists, however—and rather strenuously—that actions motivated by fear are not to be taken as voluntary. Finally, Locke contends that legitimate political rule derives from the consent of naturally free and equal people. Power is an instrument of government, but it is not the cause of its legitimacy. Thus might does not make right.

In assessing Locke's Hobbesian lineage, a useful place to begin is with the second law of nature, the preservation of mankind, because it is there especially that Locke obliges the individual to interest himself in the well-being of others:

> The *State of Nature* has a Law of Nature to govern it, which obliges every one: And Reason, which is that Law, teaches all Mankind, who will but consult it, that being all equal and independent, no one ought to harm another in his Life, Health, Liberty, or Possessions (sec. 6).

Locke goes on to mention that an additional reason for dutiful behaviour towards others is that all men are the workmanship and property of God:

> For Men being all the Workmanship of one Omnipotent, and infinitely wise Maker; All the Servants of one Sovereign Master, sent into the World by his order and about his business, they are his Property, whose Workmanship they are, made to last during his, not one anothers Pleasure (sec. 6).

Upon reflection this second reason seems more the cause of man's obligations than his species equality.[7] Equality by itself cannot establish duties beyond the single duty to treat fellow human beings equally. The trouble is that human beings are treated as equals if they are equally conceded the natural right "to have all, and to do all." Equality is consistent with, and even supplies the basis for, that absolute license in Hobbes (*Leviathan* xiii. pp. 110–11).[8] Man rather has obligations because he belongs to God—first the obligation to preserve himself, and then the obligation to preserve his equals because they are equally the creatures of God. Self-preservation is therefore the first law of nature, from which is derived the preservation of mankind as the second law of nature. Although we began with the second law of nature, noting that it is other-regarding, we now see that it is tied to the first law of nature, which in an unexpected way is also other-regarding—a regard for God our maker.

Self-preservation, a natural law, is sometimes called by Locke a natural right (secs. 11, 25, 87, 123, 128, 149, 208).[9] Now it would seem to make better sense to treat self-preservation as a natural right, since man is powerfully inclined to preserve himself anyway. Locke speaks openly of this inclination in the *First Treatise* (secs. 56, 86, 87, and 88). Not only is self-preservation the most imperious of man's desires, it is also the seat of his rights (that desire engenders rights is the starting point of Hobbes [*De Cive* I. 71].[10] But if self-preservation is a right rooted in instinct, why is it also a law, a discovery of reason that constricts behavior? Since human beings do not ordinarily line up to destroy themselves, what is there in human conduct to restrain? Two answers seem possible. In the first place it should be noted that Locke's argument here has a rhetorical effect bearing on the second law of nature. Because Locke identifies self-preservation as a duty, this is a consequence of man's creatureliness, it comes as no surprise and is indeed rather obvious that the preservation of mankind is similarly a duty. Locke implies—he does not say directly—that man is obliged to preserve his fellows because he is even less the proprietor of their being than he is the proprietor of himself. Failure to own himself obliges him to preserve himself; failure therefore to own others, who are his equals, obliges that he preserve them as well. But if man in fact is not *obliged* to preserve himself under a law of nature, is rather *inclined* to preserve himself under a right of nature, then no law commanding the preservation of others can be derived from self-preservation. The second law of nature would thus depend on an artful conflation of obligation and inclination as regards the first law-right of nature.

Even though man need hardly be told to preserve himself, still there is a sense in which self-preservation is obligatory. The law of nature is described in its most general terms as reason: *"The State of Nature* has a Law to govern it, which obliges everyone: And Reason, which is that Law . . ."* (sec. 6). Reason can oblige man, not simply to preserve himself—for this is instinctual—but to preserve himself in a way consistent with reason; and rational self-preservation may commonly entail the preservation of others, since to threaten others needlessly is to introduce into one's surroundings the distrust and ill-will that make abandonment of the state of nature and the surrender of natural rights inevitable.[11] Were all men perfectly rational, that is, perfectly obedient to natural law, government would have no cause to exist (sec. 123). But if enlightened utilitarianism is the sense in which self-preservation is a particular precept of natural law and reason the whole of natural law, then Locke's understanding differs in no substantial way from that of Hobbes who says in *Leviathan* that "a law of nature, *lex naturalis,* is a precept or general rule, found out by reason, by which a man is forbidden to do that, which is destructive of his life . . ." (xiv. pp. 116–17).

Man is said to have obligations consequent on his creatureliness. But these obligations are made suspect by Locke's vacillation regarding the matter of suicide. Time and again Locke repeats the prohibition against self-destruction, more often than not for the political purpose of denying government its claim to absolute power. But Locke is not consistent. In section 23 of the *Second Treatise,* he first reiterates the prohibition and then suspends it:

> For a Man, not having the Power of his own Life, *cannot,* by Compact, or his own Consent, *enslave himself* to any one, nor put himself under the Absolute, Arbitrary Power of another, to take away his Life, when he pleases.
> . . . whenever he finds the hardship of his Slavery out-weigh the value of his Life, 'tis in his Power, by resisting the Will of his Master, to draw on himself the Death he desires.

It has been suggested by some that Locke merely acknowledges the power to commit suicide but confers not the right.[12] This argument, however, is less than persuasive since Locke makes no effort in section 23 to distinguish power from right. In the first of the two passages quoted above, the word *power* is used plainly to designate a right (which man is said not to have: "For a Man, not having the Power of his own Life"), and elsewhere in the paragraph *power* is a normative term connoting the rightful or wrongful use of force.[13] It is hardly clear, in this last use of *power*—the slave's power to terminate his life—that the word is devoid of normative connotations. Not only has the slave the capacity to bring on his death (this he shares with others), but he seems also to have the right, for Locke supplies the reasons which impel him to the act.

The slave is understood to have forfeited his right to life, which forfeiture empowers the master to kill the slave at any time and for any cause. To this Locke adds that the slave can precipitate his own execution by defying his master's will. Now it might be argued that Locke concedes here the right to suicide but confines its possession to the slave—having lost the right to life, the slave gains the right to death. The problem is that any right implies an entitlement to some good, in this case the good of death given the hardship of life. But why would a person, who is defined by the absence of rights, come to possess a right that is denied to others? If it is true that under the law of nature only a slave can kill himself, then a person seeking death (perhaps because disease has made his life not worth living) would be in compliance with natural law if before committing suicide, he took steps to become a slave. We can be very artful about this passage, either in defending the prohibition or in devising escapes, but the fact remains that Locke has caused us to question the absoluteness of self-preservation; and given the centrality of this principle to his political teaching (limited government depends directly on the suicide prohibition), it is difficult to believe that Locke could have spoken so casually. Of course Locke has not spoken casually if it is his intention to cast doubt upon the natural law obligation to preserve oneself.

The second law of nature which dictates that no one harm another in his "Life, Health, Liberty, or Possessions" (sec. 6) has its rationale in the theological doctrine that human beings are the creatures of God—"they are his Property" (sec. 6) and thus are forbidden to damage themselves or their neighbors. But elsewhere Locke affirms the very opposite, avowing that man is the owner of himself—"yet every Man has a *Property* in his own *Person*" (sec. 27). The quotation is no incidental remark for it explains why the individual in nature has a right to property—he owns property because he owns his labor, and he owns his labor because he owns his person. The labor theory of ownership founders if Locke sticks by his earlier pronouncement that man is the possession of God, but unless man is the possession of God, the second law of nature cannot oblige solicitous behavior toward others. Thus both laws of nature, the second and the first, seem incompatible with Locke's teaching on property.

Locke explains that man's duty to see to the preservation of his fellows is a contingent duty, operative only when the individual's "own Preservation comes not in competition" (sec. 6). The first law of nature takes priority over the second. On this point it has been noted by others that the second law of nature will effectively oblige only if the individual is not greatly anxious about his existence; that the individual's peace of mind is a direct result of the peace of nature; and that the peace of nature depends on a law of nature that is known and observed by men, and on an economy of abundance that mitigates the competition for necessary goods.[14] It has been further argued that Locke's state of nature satisfies none of these conditions: nature is not bounteous but penurious, requiring human labor to supply the sum of its value (secs. 36, 37); natural law is not apprehended easily and quickly through the medium of conscience but demands study and deliberate consultation (secs. 6, 12, 124, 136); also natural law is not much obeyed, for the greater part of mankind are "no strict Observers of Equity and Justice" (sec. 123); finally nature is more warlike than peaceful because life there is disturbed by "the corruption, and viciousness of degenerate men" (sec. 128) and by passionate, self-interested attempts at enforcing natural law (sec. 136). From these several points it is concluded that man in the state of nature would have ample warrant for neglecting the second law of nature.

An additional point, not so commonly noticed, is the character of this law of nature that stipulates the preservation of mankind. If we hope to find in this law some assurance that man is naturally a moral being with responsibilities to others, we are likely to be disappointed. The second law of nature is not a golden rule commanding that we treat charitably our fellow human beings; nor is it even, in any serious way, a restrictive injunction ordering that we hold back from gratuitous harm. What purpose the second law of nature mainly serves is to supply man in nature with a license to kill, and to explain how political authority comes by the right to inflict punishment on its subjects. The second law of nature is about killing. Consider the scope of operation which Locke concedes to it. The executive power belongs alike to victims and to bystanders. The first class of enforcers is most probably hot for revenge (sec. 125), although they are told to employ "calm reason and conscience" (sec. 8), while the second class are without number—for it becomes everyone and anyone's business to capture, judge, and punish the offender, who, having sinned against the law of nature, is held to be a noxious animal deserving of speedy execution. Nor is it necessary that some hideous crime be committed. Any settled design against the life of another precipitates a state of war (sec. 16). Such a state imparts a general entitlement to take all measures necessary to defend one's life, and also one's liberty, since the slightest threat to liberty is quite possibly the direst threat to life (sec. 17). To be set upon by a robber and forced to hand over one's purse is to be at war and thus empowered by the second law of nature to take the robber's life even when the money lost to him would be of no significant value (sec. 207). More than that, no one but the individual himself is allowed to judge whether a state of war has begun (sec. 21). Hence it is not required that any misdeed be actually done, only that the individual suspect that one is coming. If a person fears his neighbor, whether with cause or without (for only the individual can judge), by this partial and subjective determination the neighbor becomes a wild beast and is lawfully destroyed. But then the neighbor, now the target of attack, might understandably conclude that his assailant is the wild beast (and of this only the neighbor can judge) and so endeavor to execute the law of nature against him. Clearly the state of nature, if not synonymous with the state of war, is harassed by anxieties concerning the outbreak of war and by uncertain identification of the innocent and the guilty. About this moral confusion Locke says:

> For the Law of Nature being unwritten, and so no where to be found but in the minds of Men, they who through Passion or Interest shall mis-cite, or misapply it, cannot so easily be convinced of their mistake where there is no establish'd Judge: And so it serves not, as it ought, to determine the Rights, and fence the Properties of those that live under it, especially where every one is Judge, Interpreter, and Executioner of it too, and that in his own Case (sec. 136).

In the absence of a neutral judge, no one can accurately know whether his cause is right or wrong. Thus everyone is at liberty to believe himself in the right. But this then means that the state of nature will not divide neatly into groups of upright law-abiders and selfish malefactors. Still there are those called "degenerate" by Locke, but they have no conceivable motive to proclaim themselves corrupt; they like everyone will find some grounds for vindicating their behavior—at least to their own satisfaction, which is all that matters. Moreover, because the law of nature "serves not, as it ought, to determine the Rights, and fence the Properties of those that live under it," there cannot be a right to property that is acknowledged and respected by others, for even if labor is the avowed source of property rights, there are other rights, such as self-preservation, that may conflict. Hence no mine and thine is allowed to nature that is unequivocal and unchallenged, and hence no justice in nature that gives to each his own.

Locke, it appears, takes the three fateful steps that in Hobbes lead inexorably to the absolute license of the individual: the right to preserve oneself, the right to adopt the means necessary for preservation, and the right to be the judge of one's own case. These three rights effectively abolish the obligations of natural law, or, more precisely, they abrogate the second law of nature. And even though Locke affirms that nature "is *not a State of License*" (sec. 6) and devotes much space to describing the pain and suffering that await the criminally inclined, nonetheless Locke shows that the actions of men in the state of nature are subject to no real restraint. Locke's "strange doctrine," by which people who are judges in their own case enforce natural law (secs. 9, 13), is little more than Hobbesian natural right dressed up in the splendiferous garb of legal righteousness. Locke thus sides with Hobbes in believing the state of nature to be an amoral condition and in regarding civil society as the true home of justice, for it is only in society that property rights can be defined and protected.

There are other laws of nature that were said before to operate in the state of nature, but they follow much the same pattern as self-preservation and the preservation of mankind and so will be treated more briefly. Private property, or appropriation from the common store, is called a natural law, but like self-preservation it requires nothing that would not be done without it; thus it is better regarded as a natural right (which it is also called). Spoilage is said to be against the law of nature, the reason being that the wastrel invades his neighbor's share (sec. 37). But Locke also maintains that in nature there is more than enough of the materials of wealth to go around,[15] so one wonders how spoilage encroaches upon another's share. Moreover, it is almost comical to hear Locke say that wasting is an offense against nature, when seven times he calls nature a wasteland (secs. 36, 37, 38, 42, 43, 45). Were man not present in nature to appropriate, everything, by Locke's reasoning, would go to waste. In fact Locke implies that the real crime of spoilage is against practical utility and common sense, for it hardly profits a man to heap up apples and plums only to have them rot in his cell (secs. 46, 51). Spoilage is a self-enforcing regulation because wasting is a "foolish thing"; and while it may please Locke to call spoilage "dishonest," nothing is added to the enforcement of the law for his having done so. As for the requirement that there be "enough and as good left" behind, Locke assures us that private appropriation, rather than deplete nature's resources, vastly augments them (secs. 36, 37, 40, 42, 43). He further contends that an exchange economy based on money eliminates the problem of spoilage and so frees the individual to acquire all the property he can (secs. 46, 50). The most Locke offers by way of other-regarding responsibilities is the expectation that free enterprise enlarges the general fund of wealth and that a day laborer under such a system lives better than an Indian chieftain (sec. 41).[16]. . .

The second category of natural laws, those that institute and help govern civil society, are simple utilitarian devices[17]—they effect man's removal from the state of nature for the better preservation of his property. But civil society cannot accomplish its main objective if it does not offer significant relief from what makes the state of nature so threatening. Locke may then agree with Hobbes that in the state of nature "might is right," but seemingly he disputes the claim that civil society is built upon the same principle. Civil society is a fortress erected against the lawlessness of nature. The problem with the Hobbesian sovereign, Locke appears to say, is that he has not come out of the state of nature: his power is absolute; his command is law; his might is right. He is something like a Trojan horse—magnificent from afar but ruinous if let past the city gates. As interpreted by Locke, natural law prohibits his admission.

A second search through Locke's Troy, however, uncovers telltale signs of the horse's presence. One of Locke's natural laws is the right of the majority "when any number of Men have so consented to make one Community or Government, . . . to act and conclude the rest" (sec. 95). Upon joining society, the individual agrees to surrender absolutely and permanently the right to act in his own defense (except when circumstances force him back into the state of nature [secs. 207, 226] or when he chooses to leave one society for another [sec. 121]) and to be judge and executioner of the law of nature (secs. 127, 128). This surrender of right is the origin of society's legislative and executive power (secs. 88, 129, 130). The individual in society is totally under the command of the majority—more immediately of the government—and is expected to believe, in Hobbesian fashion (Leviathan xvii, p. 158), that he authorizes (by his initial consent) all that the government would do, including legislation he directly opposes (secs. 88, 89). Nor does the individual hold on to a residue of rights that are immune to social interference.[18] Locke never quite says that life, liberty, and property are inalienable rights. On the contrary, he explains that it is within society's power, in order to prosecute its wars, to tax an individual's property (sec. 140), to conscript him into service (sec. 130), and to send him to his death (sec. 139)—because there are, as Locke asserts, "nobler" uses than bare preservation (sec. 6). Indeed, once society is created, the first law of nature sanctions society's preservation over and above the preservation of the individuals who comprise it (sec. 135). The individual, in a word, has no guaranteed protections against the power of society and its government.[19] Society's might is society's right.

If Locke then is something less than a champion of individual rights, as he sometimes seems, still he does take up the cause of the majority in its struggles with oppressive government.[20] Locke states that the legislative power is supreme relative to the executive and federative power (secs. 132, 150), but not that it is supreme relative to the people (sec. 149). The people are the final masters and as such have the authority to cashier unwanted governments. But there are no institutional arrangements in Locke for the replacement of one set of rulers by another. What Locke provides instead is the emergency right of revolution. The people have the right to take up arms against their government if through "a long train of abuses" it proves its contempt for the original purposes of society—life, liberty, and property. It should be noted that the right of revolution is not the kind of right which by its self-evidency enjoys the glad deference of others. It does not persuade the opposition of its obligations; it is not calm reasonableness substituting for strength. Rather it is right in the sense of power. Those have the right who have the power to make good their "appeal to heaven," Locke's euphemism for the resort to force. But if people must apply force in order to exercise their right of supremacy, and if the force they apply must prove mightier than that of the government, then the right of revolution, when effectively asserted, is an example of power that is supreme and absolute and a manifestation of the Hobbesian maxim that "might is right."[21] Despite Locke's many precautions and rhetorical denunciations, the Trojan horse of absolute sovereignty (be it popular as in the case of revolution or governmental as in the case of citizen subordination) has slipped into the city.

Justice and the Concealment of Power

Locke is a Hobbesian, I conclude, because he subscribes to the thesis that "might makes right." Even so, I wish now to argue that Hobbes and Locke adopt this principle with varying degrees of satisfaction and that they utilize it in different ways. Hobbes thinks that nothing can better safeguard civil peace than the frank declaration that power is absolute and despotical. Locke thinks that nothing so enhances the prospects for justice and fair dealing than a politic dissembling about the realities of power. Here then is the difference between Hobbes and Locke: Hobbes asks mainly that civil society be the strong guardian of men's lives; Locke asks also that civil society be the fountainhead of justice. It is not then correct, in my estimation, to say that Locke merely perfects the logic of Hobbes, providing the individual with a greater security through the institution of limited government.[22] For it defies demonstration that limited government can actually redeem this promise; it may instead, depending on the times, be the catalyst of civil unrest. Locke does say, and the point is not denied, that the preservation of property—of life, liberty, and estate—is the function of society. But there is another voice in Locke striving to dedicate society to the higher purpose of justice, willing even to take calculated risks with the association's capacity to preserve itself. In Hobbes there is nothing like this concern or this inclination to risk-taking.

Hobbes and Locke both give to civil society the large and general purpose of correcting the deficiencies of the state of nature. Now purposefulness is itself a type of justice—not that justice which looks to the detailed specifics of contractual obligation but the rationale which informs and makes sense of the undertaking. Purposefulness supplies a transcendent standard that allows for the interpretation of ambiguities, the determination of good faith compliance, and the measurement of progress toward the ultimate goal. Any human endeavor that is deliberate and intelligent requires of the participants that they be true to the purpose. Hobbes cannot deny that the purposeful character of the political association carries with it an obligation, and that the obligation applies even to the sovereign. Concerning the sovereign's title to property, Hobbes says:

> For seeing the sovereign, that is to say, the commonwealth, whose person he representeth, is understood to do nothing but in order to the common peace and security, this distribution of lands, is to be understood as done in order to the same: and consequently, whatsoever distribution he shall make in prejudice thereof, is contrary to the will of every subject, that committed his peace, and safety to his discretion, and conscience; and therefore by the will of every one of them, is to be reputed void.

Notice that actions prejudicial to the purpose of the association are "to be reputed void." And yet in the very next sentence, Hobbes denies that the sovereign is under any *binding* obligation whatsoever:

It is true, that a sovereign monarch, or the greater part of a sovereign assembly, may ordain the doing of many things in pursuit of their passions, contrary to their own consciences, which is a breach of trust, and of the law of nature; but this is not enough to authorize any subject, either to make war upon, or so much as to accuse of injustice, or any way to speak evil of their sovereign; because they have authorized all his actions, and in bestowing the sovereign power, made them their own (*Leviathan* xxiv. p. 235).

In order to provide against the consequences of equal power, which characterizes the state of nature and renders it so perilous, there must be instituted a superior power, and the logic of superior power is that it is subject to no obligation. This of course means that society, organized as Leviathan, is compelled to renounce the justice that accompanies faithful attention to society's purposes.

Locke, too, is aware of the logic of power, but he conceals its imperatives behind repeated reminders of why society exists. Unlike Hobbes, Locke rivets the purpose of society foursquare before its rulers, alerting them to the limitations imposed by original intentions.[23] It is as if Locke is trying to strengthen the trusses of rational obligation, recognizing with Hobbes that the sovereign is bound by little else. Rational obligation, says Hobbes in the *Leviathan* (xiv. p. 119),[24] is that predilection of the mind for logical rectitude. Because the mind abhors absurdity, it wants not to contradict itself by saying one thing and then its opposite; likewise it takes offense if a course of action once decided on is later reversed. The mind seeks consistency and endeavors to oblige the will to discharge faithfully its contracts. But the mind is a weak counselor, and so faithful compliance must ultimately rest on fear of punishment (*Leviathan* xvii. pp. 153–54; *De Cive* V. 4). Of course Hobbes would not have his sovereign punished; and although Locke does threaten his supreme power with the specter of revolution, what Locke mainly relies on is the self-restraint of rational obligation brought to full consciousness by exhortation. . . .

As rational creatures men institute society for a purpose, the preservation of property, but their rationality is capable of displaying standards of its own. "Truth and the keeping of Faith belongs to Men, as Men" (Sec. 14). Hence it is an affront to man's nature, an injustice, for promises to be wantonly disregarded. Men are treated as "a Herd of inferior creatures" and as "void of Reason, and brutish" (sec. 163) if their intentions and their welfare are not the guiding star of government. Locke's principal assumption throughout the *Second Treatise* is that men are by nature free, equal, and rational; and the question Locke asks himself is, How would such people behave? Hobbes makes the same assumption, but concludes that two of these features, freedom and equality, are the cause of infinite trouble, and so must be renounced, by the third, reason, which is wholly the servant of fear. Locke permits no renunciation of freedom and equality. To be sure, his main concern lies with safety; men must be accounted free and equal because superior power, in Locke's judgment, is more hazardous than equal power (equal freedom or equal natural right). But a second reason, communicated more by tone than by expressed argument, is that men are no longer men if they allow their freedom and equality to be denied them: they are instead herd animals whose master "keeps them, and works them for his own Pleasure or Profit" (sec. 163).[25] This may help explain why contracts extorted through fear are always invalid—not always are they bad bargains, but always are the insults to human freedom. Locke, as it happens, proffers no rejoinder to Hobbes's contention that fear is a legitimate motive of action and that the social contract is a result of fear. Rather than debate the issue, he appeals to man's intuitive sense of justice:

> Should a Robber break into my House, and with a Dagger at my Throat, make me seal Deeds to convey my Estate to him, would this give him any Title? (sec. 176).

Sealing deeds may save one's life and be the prudent thing to do, but the transaction is void because of the offense it gives to human nature. Justice demands that human beings be treated as free, equal, and rational creatures.

I have attempted to show that Locke remains committed to justice despite having accepted the Hobbesian teaching about power, that "might is right." The question now to be considered is how Locke proposes to make this commitment efficacious, how to find space for justice in a world governed by power. Locke's chapter on conquest provides a clue.

Locke confesses that his remarks treating the subject of just conquest constitute a "strange doctrine" (sec. 180). It might be recalled that Locke proposed another "strange doctrine" earlier in the *Second Treatise,* that one concerning the executive power of punishment. What Locke now calls "strange" is his argument that the victor in a just war has no rightful claim to the property of the vanquished, excepting that portion necessary to make reparations, which reparations he must in turn forego if their payment would jeopardize the lives of innocent people. Both strange doctrines have in common that they specify rules for human behavior in a state of nature; but they differ significantly in the sense in which they are strange. The executive power is strange because it allows an individual to judge in his own case, and so sets loose a cycle of attack and reprisal indistinguishable from Hobbesian natural right. On the other hand, the doctrine of just conquest is strange because it denies the victor the customary spoils of war. One strange doctrine, that governing individuals in a state of nature, prolongs, even perpetuates, the violence (secs. 20, 21); the other strange doctrine, that determining relations among societies, discourages violence by removing a prime incentive to war—no spoils for unjust conquest, and very few where conquest is just. Locke's point, it seems, is that nations are capable of greater restraint and greater justice than are individuals when left to their own resources in a state of nature. Because the individual lacks the barest margin of security, because he has no respite from the burden of defending himself, it is not to be expected that he will take any chances or give any quarter. The people who make up society on the other hand do commonly enjoy the safety of their community; they are spared the worrisome responsibility of preserving themselves; vigilance and combat are not their daily routine. Having been granted the time and the space to build up the habits of peace, they can be put upon, when war comes, to behave more decently and to show their enemies some mercy. Civil society, in a word, civilizes (sec. 299). . . .

. . . Neither the state of nature nor civil society is of itself friendly to virtue. On the contrary, both states are under-girded by the principle that "might makes right." But unlike the state of nature, civil society can civilize, its "strange doctrine" can lessen the inducements to violence, if the dark truth about politics is not fastened upon and propagated. Hobbes counts it among the natural duties of the sovereign to instruct and enlighten his subjects as to the nature of sovereign power; nothing is to be hidden (*Leviathan* xxx. p. 323).[26] Locke chooses instead to write esoterically.[27] He acknowledges and accepts the Hobbesian truth about power, but mainly he looks away from it and has us look away so as to see better a rhetorical surface that teaches justice.[28] Locke therefore is not so honest as Hobbes, but he is more noble in his purposes, and, if I may generalize, more successful, because modern liberal societies have done well by domestic peace without taking Hobbesian precautions to ensure it. In *Elements of*

Law Hobbes anticipates the argument for limited government and refutes it with a series of "what if" objections—what if revenues are needed to defend the state, and the taxing power lies with a refractory parliament (Part II. 1. 13). By dwelling on and making provision for the worst possible case, Hobbes closes the door on justice. By risking justice, at least through the rhetoric of the *Second Treatise* (*e.g.*, sec. 176), Locke helps to produce a society that is less prone to worst-case emergencies.

Notes

1. J. W. Gough, *John Locke's Political Philosophy*, 2nd ed. (Oxford: Clarendon Press, 1973); W. von Leyden, Introduction, *Essays on the Law of Nature* (Oxford: Clarendon Press, 1954); John Plamenatz, *Man and Society*, vol. 1 (New York: McGraw-Hill, 1963).
2. John Dunn, *The Political Thought of John Locke: An Historical Account of the Argument of the 'Two Treatises of Government'* (Cambridge: Cambridge University Press, 1969); Dunn could also be included in the above list, *e.g., ibid.*, p. 164, and "Justice and Locke's Political Theory," *Political Studies* 16 (February 1968): 71; James Tully, *A Discourse on Property: John Locke and His Adversaries* (Cambridge: Cambridge University Press, 1980); Martin Seliger, *The Liberal Politics of John Locke* (New York: Frederick A. Praeger, 1969).
3. Leo Strauss, *Natural Right and History* (Chicago: University of Chicago Press, 1953); Richard Cox, *Locke on War and Peace* (Washington: University Press of America, 1982); Robert Goldwin, "John Locke," in *History of Political Philosophy*, 2nd ed., ed. Leo Strauss and Joseph Cropsey (Chicago: Rand McNally, 1972), pp. 451–86.
4. Locke quotations are from *Two Treatises of Government*, rev. ed., ed. Peter Laslett (New York: New American Library, 1963). Unless otherwise stated, section citations refer to the *Second Treatise*. Hobbes quotations are from *The English Works of Thomas Hobbes of Malmesbury*, ed. Sir William Molesworth (London: John Bohn, 1839–45), vol. 2, *Philosophical Rudiments concerning Government and Society* (but referred to by its more familiar title, *De Cive*), vol. 3, *Leviathan*, and vol. 4, *Elements of Law* (also known as *De Corpore Politico*).
5. Locke never actually says that legislative supremacy is a natural law, but he clearly implies as much. A similar inference would not be warranted in the case of separation of powers, however, since Locke says that "well order'd Commonwealths" divide legislative and executive power, not that all commonwealths do (secs. 143, 159).
6. Locke does not directly explain what a just war is. He takes it for granted that combat can be either just or unjust and proceeds to consider those powers that fall to a *"Conquerour in a Lawful War"* (sec. 177). Cox, however, pieces together a just war theory using both *Treatises* and *A Letter Concerning Toleration*. War is unjust, says Cox, if it is fought for the personal glory of the ruler, if its purpose is imperialistic subjugation of another people, or if it is undertaken in the service of religious belief (*War and Peace*, pp. 154–56).
7. George Windstrup, "Locke on Suicide," *Political Theory* 8 (May 1980): 169.
8. Ramon Lemos, *Hobbes and Locke: Power and Consent* (Athens: University of Georgia Press, 1987), pp. 76–77.
9. In fact nearly all of what Locke calls natural law he also terms natural right. A ready explanation for Locke's seemingly indiscriminate manner is the supposition that every right implies an obligation—one person's entitlement is another person's duty. But this explanation does not hold in the case of self-preservation because the obligatory side of the coin is comprehended under a separate law of nature, the preservation of mankind. Self-preservation is not like care of offspring where the right of the child is simultaneously the duty of the parent.
10. See Cox, *War and Peace*, pp. 85–89; C. B. Macpherson, "Natural Rights in Hobbes and Locke," in *Political Theory and the Rights of Man*, ed. D. B. Raphael (Bloomington: Indiana University Press, 1967), p. 7. . . .

11. Robert Goldwin, "Locke's State of Nature in Political Science," *Western Political Quarterly* 29 (March 1976): 128–31.

12. Dunn has recourse to this explanation, claiming that Locke "did not suppose that a man has a right to do anything which he has a power to do. Indeed the entire *Two Treatises* is specifically concerned to refute such a position . . ." (*Political Thought,* pp. 108–09 n. 5). Dunn accounts for the exception by supposing that a slave is not a moral agent and thus not responsible for anything he might do (pp. 108–10). But could it be Locke's considered opinion, the surface arguments of the *Second Treatise* notwithstanding, that a human being destroys his moral intelligence, becomes in effect an animal, for having once broken some precept of natural law? Dunn himself says otherwise (p. 107). See Windstrup, "Locke on Suicide," pp. 172–73.

13. Seven times in section 23 Locke repeats the word *power*; never does he use the word *right*. Concerning the master and his slave, Locke once says, "when he has him in his Power." *Power* would seem here to mean force, but the larger context is still that of rightful force.

14. Strauss, *Natural Right and History,* pp. 224–31; and Cox, *War and Peace,* pp. 81–94.

15. Lest there be confusion here, nature is potentially wealthy, but actual wealth depends on human labor; and in the absence of human labor nature is penurious.

16. That Locke is a proto-capitalist is the thesis of Macpherson and Strauss. Macpherson, *The Political Theory of Possessive Individualism* (London: Oxford University Press, 1964), pp. 208 ff.; Strauss, *Natural Right and History,* p. 246. See also Cox, "Justice as the Basis of Political Order in Locke," in *Nomos VI: Justice,* pp. 254–61. Cf. Laslett, Introduction, p. 119.

17. Once in force, however, these institutions take on a higher purpose. See below.

18. Wilmoore Kendall, *John Locke and the Doctrine of Majority-Rule* (Urbana: University of Illinois Press, 1965), p. 68.

19. In *A Letter Concerning Toleration* (James Tully, editor, [Indianapolis: Hackett Publishing Company, 1983]) Locke makes an exception for liberty of conscience, suggesting on three occasions that it is an inalienable right (pp. 26, 48, 55) (that it is a natural right he says explicitly [p. 51]). But he later implies that this liberty is inalienable in a Hobbesian sense, *i.e.,* the individual is entitled to exercise it, but if its doctrines are injurious to the public good, the society is also entitled to suppress it (pp. 49–51). Thus there ensues a contest of rights with the stronger prevailing.

20. Kendall, *Majority-Rule,* pp. 103, 112–19; also Lemos, *Hobbes and Locke,* p. 124.

21. This is not to say that revolutionaries *are right* because they prevail, only that because they prevail, they *have a right,* at least one that is effective. If they do not prevail, they may still have a right, but this right avails them little as they are marched to the scaffold or left languishing in prison. See Seliger, *Liberal Politics,* pp. 135–38. On one occasion, however, Locke does suggest that a right may be effective even when disjoined from power. He says that *"the best fence against Rebellion"* is the right of the people to form a new legislature, for when publicly affirmed it can work to deter government from the abuse of its power (sec. 226). If the government practices self-restraint (either out of fear of a multitude made resolute by the doctrine of natural right, or persuaded itself of the injustice of absolute power), then there will be no test of strength and no proving the effectiveness of the right of revolution.

22. This seems to be Strauss's understanding (*Natural Right and History,* p. 231).

23. Because those original intentions—life, liberty, and property—are not merely agreed on, but determined by natural law, it is appropriate to say that Locke is not a strict contractarian. See Patrick Riley, *Will and Political Legitimacy* (Cambridge: Harvard University Press, 1982), pp. 63–74.

24. This expression actually belongs to Michael Oakeshott (Introduction, *Leviathan* [Oxford: Basil Blackwell], p. lix).

25. Kendall, *Majority-Rule,* p. 134.

26. Strauss, *Natural Right and History,* p. 198.

27. Laslett explains in detail how incredibly cautious a man Locke was (Introduction, pp. 58–79; especially pp. 77–79). But Laslett does not draw the conclusion that Locke's caution

might have affected his writing. And when Strauss comes to this conclusion independently, Laslett dismisses it out of hand (p. 119, n. 21). See Kendall, "John Locke Revisited," *The Intercollegiate Review* 2 (January–February 1966): 230–34. Kendall has the distinction of being the only Locke scholar to have changed his mind.

28. Gary Glenn, "Inalienable Rights and Locke's Argument for Limited Government: Political Implications of a Right to Suicide," *Journal of Politics* 46 (February, 1984), esp. pp. 97–102.

Locke's *Second Treatise* and "The Best Fence against Rebellion"
Nathan Tarcov

Locke is at once a traditional and a subversive author for us. As an authority for the American Founders he stands at the source of our tradition. But he was an authority for those revolutionaries because his political teaching culminates in the last chapter of the *Second Treatise*, a defense of the right of resistance. Insofar as we remain a revoluntary or rebellious people (with a particular proclivity to tax rebellions), Locke's political teaching lives in us. But insofar as we have become traditional and taken our revolution for granted, even coming to look at our founding with "sanctimonious reverence" and ascribing to our founders "a wisdom more than human," as Jefferson feared we would,[1] Locke has lost his vitality for us. It is no wonder then that we do not read his defense of the right of resistance with the care it deserves, even as we sometimes see or feel its revolutionary spirit still around us. But careful attention to the structure of Locke's argument for the right of resistance shows that he was more consistent and more radical than is usually supposed.[2]

Locke's defense of the right of resistance has given rise to a number of questions. One question is whether in attributing the right of resistance to the people he was unaware of its usually being exercised by parties, conspiracies, or Whig oligarchs. Another is why he bothers to defend the right of resistance at all since he claims that resistance is inevitable and unaffected by any arguments (224).[3] The related empirical question arises as to whether he expects resistance to be frequent or rare. It has also been asked whether for Locke resistance is a matter of choice or necessity, or whether the people may resist whenever they have a better idea of how to constitute their government or only when certain crimes have been committed.[4]

I will directly consider, however, two other less practical and more technical questions although I hope my answers will indirectly answer those posed above as well. The last and nineteenth chapter of the *Second Treatise* is entitled "Of the Dissolution of Government." Its first sentence reads, "He that will with any clearness speak of the *Dissolution of Government,* ought, in the first place to distinguish

From Nathan Tarcov, "Locke's *Second Treatise* and 'The Best Fence Against Rebellion'," *The Review of Politics,* Vol. 43:2, pp. 198–217. Copyright © 1981. Reprinted with permission of the author and the University of Notre Dame Press.

1. Cf. Jefferson's letter to Samuel Kercheval, 12 July 1816, in Merrill D. Peterson, ed., *The Portable Jefferson* (New York, 1975), pp. 558–59.

2. Since writing this article, I have read Julian H. Franklin, *John Locke and the Theory of Sovereignty: Mixed Monarchy and the Right of Resistance in the Political Thought of the English Revolution* (Cambridge, 1978), which makes clear in other respects how Locke's doctrine of the right of resistance was radical and consistent.

3. Unless otherwise noted, parenthetical references are to Locke's numbered sections in the *Second Treatise* in John Locke, *Two Treatises of Government,* ed. Peter Laslett (New York, 1965).

4. For a subtle and sophisticated consideration of those questions that gives more credit for subtlety and sophistication to Locke than he always receives, cf. Martin Seliger, *The Liberal Politics of John Locke* (New York, 1969), pp. 107–109, 124–38, 294–323. Cf. also Harvey C. Mansfield, Jr., "The Right of Revolution," *Daedalus* (Fall 1976), pp. 151–62.

between the *Dissolution of the Society,* and the Dissolution of the Government" (211). Despite this insistence that clarity requires the distinction between dissolution of government and dissolution of society, Locke seems to have forgotten, muddled, or even obliterated that distinction by the very next paragraph, asserting that the dissolution of government dissolves society (212; cf. also 219). My first question, therefore, is whether Locke contradicts himself in this way.

Locke insists earlier in the *Second Treatise* on distinguishing the state of nature from the state of war (19). Nevertheless in the last chapter he seems to refer to the condition which both antedates and replaces civil society as a state of war (222, 232, 235, 239, 241–42, and especially 226–27). My second question, therefore, is whether Locke contradicts himself in this way.[5]

I understand these two questions to be distinct: to ask whether society can exist without government is not the same as to ask whether the state of nature is peaceful or warlike. Nevertheless, the two questions have in common a bearing on the issue of whether there is a bearable alternative to the government, as there must be for resistance to be prudent. Hobbes had argued that without government there is no society but a state of nature which is a state of war so that resistance is so nearly suicidal as to be prudent only in order to avoid one's own death.[6] To justify resistance, Locke need argue either that society can exist without government or that the state of nature is peaceful, but he need not argue both.

Many writers have failed even to ask these two questions in discussing Locke on the right of resistance, or the right of revolution as it has come to be called (so called, it suggests action to alter government for the better rather than merely to halt its commission of a crime). This policy of benign neglect simply assumes that for Locke society can exist without government and that the state of nature is peaceful; it does not mention the apparently contradictory evidence.[7] A more positive version of this approach assures us that the dissolution of society was "a contingency which Locke never seriously contemplated."[8] A more precise version asserts that only foreign invasion dissolves society.[9] This claim has a basis in the statement in the chapter's first paragraph that "The usual, and almost only way whereby *this Union is dissolved,* is the Inroad of Foreign Force making a Conquest upon them" (211). But it too ignores the apparently contrary passages (212 and 219), which do not concern foreign conquest, as well as the "almost" that Locke uses to qualify his statement that conquest is the only way society is dissolved.

Other writers take note of the apparent contradictions and attribute them to confusion on Locke's part. John Dunn has mitigated this charge by the observation that "Locke's writing here is confused but it is certainly less confused than that of his commentators."[10] If, however, we hope to learn something from Locke, then the verdict of confusion ought to be only our last resort and we had better explore other avenues of interpretation.

5. For a neat statement of our two questions, cf. Laslett's Introduction to Locke, *Two Treatises,* pp. 128–29.

6. Hobbes, *Leviathan,* chaps. 13, 18 end, 21.

7. Cf. e.g., Raymond Polin, *La Politique Morale de John Locke* (Paris, 1960), pp. 225–36.

8. George H. Sabine, *A History of Political Theory* (New York, 1950), p. 538.

9. Charles Bastide, *John Locke: Ses Théories politiques et leur influence en Angleterre* (Geneva, 1970), p. 237; Seliger, *Liberal Politics,* p. 109; John Dunn, *The Political Thought of John Locke: An Historical Account of the Argument of the 'Two Treatises of Government'* (Cambridge, 1969), p. 181, but cf. p. 181 n.2.

10. Dunn, *Political Thought,* p. 181 n.2.

Peter Laslett argues instead that Locke's position on our two questions is "not so inconsistent as it may appear." For he claims that Locke "drew no very rigid distinction between the natural and the political condition" in the first place.[11] This response may suggest to us a conflation of our two questions: if the state of nature is sufficiently peaceful it is almost like having a society without government, just as if it were sufficiently warlike one might think society impossible without government. This response still leaves Locke's argument "rather confused," but it reassures us that "Locke's impreciseness over the dissolution of government has not led to any mis-understanding of his principles. . . . No man, no nation, no exasperated colony about to throw off the insensitive rule of men who had no acceptable policy for them, could ever have sat down to ask whether the state of nature had returned, and if so what it was like."[12] This superb imitation perfectly captures the spirit of Locke's people, who indifferent to political hypotheses, and however amused their understanding, still feel and see and inevitably resist (94, 168, 209, 224–25, and 230). But it is not an accurate account of the arguments we may read in the *Two Treatises*. For Locke attempts to speak with some "clearness" and repeatedly distinguishes the natural and political conditions. Far from saying that the distinction between the dissolutions of society and of government is blurred, Locke begins by stressing its necessity for clarity.

Laslett suggest that there is only a "point of crisis when no one is quite sure" whether or not government exists.[13] His suggestion reminds us of that of Leo Strauss:

Locke teaches, on the one hand, that society can exist without government (*ibid.,* secs. 121 end and 211) and, on the other hand, that society cannot exist without government (*ibid.,* secs. 205 and 219). The contradiction disappears if one considers the fact that society exists, and acts, without government only in the moment of revolution. . . . The revoluntary action thus understood is a kind of majority decision which establishes a new legislative or supreme power in the very moment in which it abolishes the old one.[14]

One might use this suggestion that society exists only momentarily without government to conflate our two questions again. The state of nature is sufficiently peaceful to make it possible for society to exist momentarily without government; it is sufficiently warlike or potentially warlike to make it possible for society to exist *only* momentarily without government. Locke needs the peaceful state of nature to justify the people in resisting tyrants and the warlike state of nature to condemn tyrants for dissolving government.[15] But while the peaceful or only potentially warlike character of the state of nature may help to render plausible the momentary existence of society without government, we shall see that society is not the state of nature. The momentary existence of society without government is compatible with a literal

---

11. Laslett, Introduction, p. 129; cf. pp. 113, 121; cf. also Sheldon Wolin, *Politics and Vision* (Boston, 1960), pp. 305–308.

12. Laslett, Introduction, pp. 129–30; for a discussion of how seriously the American Founders took these questions, at least after winning their victory, and evidence that Madison and a majority understood the issue much as I argue that Locke did, cf. Walter Berns, *The First Amendment and the Future of American Democracy* (New York, 1976), pp. 16–18.

13. Laslett, Introduction, p. 129.

14. Leo Strauss, *Natural Right and History* (Chicago, 1953), p. 232 n. 100; cf. Seliger, *Liberal Politics,* p. 124 n.42.

15. Cf. C.B. Macpherson's immediately retracted suggestion, *The Political Theory of Possessive Individualism: Hobbes to Locke* (London, 1962), p. 241.

reading of the first of Locke's two passages, asserting that when government is dissolved the dissolution of society "follows" (212). It does not take place instantly or by definition, but it "follows" pretty soon. If society remains vestigially for a brief time after the dissolution of government, then we can also understand why the second of Locke's two passages insists that the execution of law must "totally" cease before society is dissolved (219).

Martin Seliger forcefully reminds us that the society that exercises the right of resistance is a political society entirely distinct from the state of nature.[16] This understanding is correct as far as it goes, but it still leaves us puzzled by those passages which return the people to the state of nature rather than to original political society (212 and 219). We must combine the recognition of the momentary character of society without government with the understanding of its political character and find the places of both insights in the structure of Locke's argument.

John Dunn argues that "vicious actions on the part of the ruler do not destroy the moral standing of the entire political community . . . they merely destroy the legal status which the ruler derives from his legal role within it."[17] He denies that there is "a real problem" produced by those passages that suggest society is dissolved by the dissolution of government.[18] Instead he concedes that "the state of nature which is created by the dissolution of government, if such is created, exists between the members of the society, not between them and the sovereign who has entered into a state of war with them." Dunn is unwilling to admit that there is a state of nature between such a "sovereign" and the people, even though Locke explicitly says so in the comparable case of an absolute monarch (90–91 and 93–94), apparently because Dunn believes it is "logically impossible for the state of nature to be a state of war."[19] It remains to be determined whether it is not more accurate to object to this solution that it is logically impossible for the state of nature to be a political community.

I must therefore clarify the relation among the state of nature, the state of war, and civil society, before turning to the right of resistance.[20] In one passage (19), Locke twice explicitly differentiates the states of nature from the state of war:

> Men living together according to reason, without a common Superior on Earth, with Authority to judge between them, is *properly the State of Nature*. But force, or a declared design of force upon the Person of another, where there is no common Superior on Earth to appeal to for relief, *is the State of War:* And 'tis the want of such an appeal gives a Man the Right of War even against an *aggressor,* though he be in Society and a fellow Subject . . . *Want of a common Judge with Authority, puts all Men in a State of Nature: Force without Right, upon a Man's Person, makes a State of War,* both where there is, and is not, a common Judge.

Locke differentiates the state of nature from civil society explicitly when he first introduces civil society:

> Those who are united into one Body, and have a common establish'd Law Judicature to appeal to, with Authority to decide Controversies between them,

16. Seliger, *Liberal Politics,* pp. 107–108, 125–28.

17. Dunn, *Political Thought,* pp. 180–81.

18. *Ibid.,* p. 181 n.2.

19. *Ibid.*

20. I am indebted here to Robert A. Goldwin, "John Locke," in Leo Strauss and Joseph Cropsey, eds., *History of Political Philosophy,* 2nd ed. (Chicago, 1972), pp. 452–60.

and punish Offenders, *are in Civil Society* one with another: but those who have no such common Appeal, I mean on earth, are still in the state of Nature . . . (87; cf. also 89, 90, 91, 94).

Civil society is distinguished from the state of nature by the presence of a common authority; the state of war is distinguished from the state of peace by the presence of force without right. Either the state of war or the state of peace can therefore exist in either the state of nature or civil society, although civil society is generally a state of peace by virtue of possessing an umpire (87, 212, 227). It is logically impossible for the state of nature to be a civil society, but it is not logically impossible for the state of war to be in the state of nature. Accordingly, Locke writes of the state of war in the state of nature (*e.g.,* 20 and 21). Indeed most of Locke's discussion of the state of nature (chapter 2) is about the use of force with right to resist and punish force without right (7–13), that is, the state of war (cf. 16). The chief obstacle to this understanding of the relation of the state of nature and the state of war seems to be the phrase "according to reason" in the first definition quoted above (19). I do not understand it to mean that men in the state of nature always obey reason, as it usually is taken. I understand it to mean rather that men have only their own reason, that is, the law of nature (6), to govern them (4 and 22). They are even less likely to yield constant obedience to the reason that is all they have to govern them in the state of nature than they are to yield constant obedience to the civil law they have to govern them in civil society (cf. 6 to 123–26). Having reason to govern him does not ensure that man always obeys it as the irrational animals obey their instincts (*First Treatise,* 56–58). One might well recall Hobbes's statement that the natural condition of man "is a condition of war of every one against every one; in which case every one is governed by his own reason."[21] Locke's willingness to omit this phrase from the other descriptions of the state of nature shows how little it adds.

One must clarify the relation of the state of nature and the state of war not only definitionally but also empirically. By definition the state of nature may be either a state of war or a state of peace, but which is more likely in fact? Locke answers this question immediately after differentiating between the state of nature and the state of war. He explains that in the state of nature, unlike civil society, "every the least difference is apt to end" in the state of war, which continues even "when the actual force is over," whereas it ceases then in civil society (20–21). The state of nature is not by definition a state of war but it tends in fact to become and remain one, which is why men leave it for civil society (13, 21, 90–91, 93, 94, 123, 127, and 226–27). This fact would seem to make prudent a brief but only a brief return to the state of nature. We can already see the answer to my second question: that the last chapter of the *Second Treatise,* by referring to the state of war as the condition antedating and replacing civil society, does not contradict Locke's earlier presentation of the state of nature.

I must turn now to that last chapter to answer my first question, whether that chapter contradicts its distinction between the dissolutions of government and of society, and to confirm my answer to the second question. I will present an outline of the structure of the argument of the chapter because it is precisely this trivial matter that I believe answers the question. The structure of Locke's argument seems to have been ignored so far in favor of excerpting interesting statements out of context to illustrate Locke's position or his confusion, the usual way of interpreting Locke. I

---

21. Hobbes, *Leviathan,* chap. 14 beg.

might incidentally note that the right of resistance is not the only case in which attention to the structure of Locke's argument corrects the usual confusions and misunderstandings and makes his intention visible.

I have already had occasion to quote the first sentence of the chapter, which insists on the necessity of distinguishing the dissolution of society from that of government. Locke makes clear by the second sentence that the "Society," the dissolution of which he distinguishes from the dissolution of government, is a "Community," a "Politick Society," a "Body," or a "Commonwealth" (211). Locke's distinction therefore ought not to be confused with our contemporary distinction between society and government.[22] Although Locke's political theory has something to do with the modern liberal and social scientific distinction, it is not simply through his use of the two terms in this chapter. When he writes of society here, unlike when he discusses conjugal or domestic society earlier (77–86), he means civil or political society, the community or commonwealth, that condition which is distinguished from the state of nature by having a common authority (cf. 87).

Indeed society, far from being nonpolitical or the state of nature, is a form of government, the original form of government, democracy (95–99 and 132). When Locke first speaks of civil or political society (as distinct from conjugal or domestic society) he speaks of "the Society, or which is all one, the Legislative thereof" (89). Entering into society means entering into a society that has a government or legislative; that is its purpose and its definition. When one enters into society one makes oneself a member of a "community" or "government" or "body politic" of which the majority has the right to conclude the rest (95–99; "community" is the most repeated term). As soon as one enters into society there is already a government or legislative before any other form of government may be chosen. It is the majority, which has the same power as any other form of government does later; "making Laws for the Community from time to time, and Executing those Laws by Officers of their own appointing" (132). When some other later form of government is dissolved, that original democracy, the people, society, community, or majority, resumes power. Society without a distinct government is not something entirely different from government and nonpolitical. It is not the state of nature. It does not require unanimity to act, as is required to establish civil society in the state of nature; it operates by majority rule.

The two chief passages on the right of resistance prior to the last chapter say that the people or the body of the people resists, not that each man uses his individual right of resistance as in the state of nature (168 and 208).

A usurping executive is said to be in "a state of War with the People, who have a right to *reinstate* their *Legislative* . . ." (155). The people therefore are not in a state of nature, let alone a state of war, with each other, for they defend not the individual's right to natural freedom but the people's collective right to their legislature, a right that does not exist in the state of nature. A tyrant is said to put himself "into a State of War with his People, dissolve the Government, and leave them to that defence, which belongs to every one in the State of Nature" (205). This may mean not that society is dissolved, but only that there is a state of war between the people and the tyrant. The people may as a society have "that defence, which belongs to every one in the State of Nature" without everyone's being in the state of nature, for

---

22. Cf. Gordon J. Schochet, *Patriarchalism in Political Thought: The Authoritarian Family and Political Speculation and Attitudes Especially in Seventeenth-Century England* (Oxford, 1975), pp. 54, 255 and n.51, 259 n.60, 264 n.73.

commonwealths have that defense against one another and against aliens (9, 14, 21, 145, 183, 184, and 239).

The right of resistance is an instance of the right of war exercised by a civil society against an enemy with whom it is in the state of nature. For practical purposes it is even the instance for the sake of which the general discussions of the state of nature, the state of war, and civil society are provided.

Locke explains that the "usual, and almost only way" society is dissolved is by foreign conquest (211). This is not the only way; if it were, that might rescue Locke from the charge of contradiction, but such a rescue is not sufficient. For Locke conspicuously insists not that he is merely not going to contradict the distinction between the dissolutions of society and of government, but that this distinction is somehow crucial to the subject of the chapter. If it were only a distinction between foreign conquest and domestic resistance it would hardly be crucial.

Society and government are both dissolved by foreign conquest. It is as impossible for government to remain when society is dissolved "as for the Frame of an House to subsist when the Materials of it are scattered, and dissipated by a Whirl-wind, or jumbled into a confused heap by an Earthquake" (211; cf. also 175). The government is the frame and the society is the house. We may surmise that the whirlwind from without is foreign conquest and the earthquake from below domestic rebellion. Locke does not yet ask whether the house can stand, even briefly, without its frame; so far he has not asked whether society can exist without government.

Governments are dissolved from within as well as from without, the next section begins (212). This beginning might give the impression that in the domestic case, unlike that of foreign conquest, only the government and not the society is dissolved. But here is where the structure of the argument of the chapter begins to be crucial. The domestic dissolution of governments is explicitly divided into two cases. In the *"First,"* beginning here, the dissolution of society "follows" (212) that of government (212–20). In the second case ("secondly," 221), government is dissolved but society remains (221–22). The structure and the point of the chapter rest on the initial distinction that Locke stresses. The right of resistance comes up only in the second case and the peculiar character of Locke's doctrine of the right of resistance depends on that fact.

The first case occurs when "the *Legislative* is *altered*" (212). Locke has left no doubt that society dissolves following the dissolution of government in this case by shifting his metaphor from a house with a frame to a living body with a soul:

> Civil Society being a State of Peace, amongst those who are of it, from whom the State of War is excluded by the Umpirage, which they have provided in their Legislative, for the ending all Differences, that may arise amongst any of them, 'tis in their *Legislative,* that the Members of a Commonwealth are united, and combined together into one coherent living Body. This *is the Soul that gives Form, Life, and Unity* to the Commonwealth: From hence the several Members have their mutual Influence, Sympathy, and Connexion: And therefore when the *Legislative* is broken, or *dissolved,* Dissolution and Death follows. For the *Essence and Union of the Society* consisting in having one Will, the Legislative, when once established by the Majority, has the declaring, and as it were keeping of that Will.

Just as in foreign conquest everyone returns "to the state he was in before, with a liberty to shift for himself" (211), that is, to the state of nature, so in this case "Every one is at the disposure of his own Will" (212). In this case therefore an ongoing society cannot take political action against an enemy; instead individuals out of subjection may constitute a new society.

The crime of altering the legislative is usually committed by those in power (213). Locke does not consider it likely that a private group will succeed in destroying the legislature (but cf. 230.). He supposes a more than hypothetical form of government, consisting in a king, Lords, and Commons, if unlike Locke we can borrow terms from England (213). He enumerates four ways in which the legislative is likely to be altered in such a form. The first is when the king makes laws by himself (214). The second is when the king prevents the legislature from meeting or from enjoying freedom of debate (215).[23] The third is when the king alters the election of the legislature in a way contrary to the common interest (216); if he does it for the common interest it is a public service (158). The fourth way is when either the king or the legislature subjects the people to a foreign power (217; it is not clear whether this includes only such a foreign power as the pope or the king of France or also one such as the European Economic Community which would provide for representation of the people). This way is close to foreign conquest (cf. 239). Locke concludes from this survey that the king is the one who dissolves the government, ignoring the legislative exception in the fourth way (218). One reason why it is the king is that he can "terrifie or suppress Opposers." Such opposers may be the leaders in the second case where the king has not actually succeeded in dissolving society and society can still resist. If anyone else tries to alter the legislature it is "open and visible Rebellion." Just as in this form of government the king is not "visibly" subordinate (152), so he does not visibly rebel. He rebels invisibly. The opposers may make the invisible visible to the people, who only see and feel rather than reason (cf. 94, 168, 209, 224–25, and 230). The other parts of legislature have a duty to "hinder such designs" of the king. Locke presents a theory of opposition as well as of resistance.

The first case also includes one more way the government is dissolved. When the king abandons his charge of executing the laws, "the Bonds of the Society," this is "to reduce all to Anarchy" and turns the people into "a confused Multitude, without Order or Connexion" (219). Locke says a condition is inconsistent with human society.[24]

Locke provides a summary that might seem to contradict my claim that the dissolution of society follows in the first case. He writes:

> In these and the like Cases, *when the Government is dissolved,* the People are at liberty to provide for themselves, by erecting a new Legislative . . . For the *Society* can never, by the fault of another, lose the Native and Original Right it has to preserve itself, which can only be done by a settled Legislative, and a fair and impartial execution of the Laws made by it (220).

This summary might give the impression that in this first case only the government is dissolved while the society remains and can still set up a new government.[25] But the point is rather that society need not wait until the government is so dissolved that the

---

23. Cf. also 222; this is the only context in which Locke defends freedom of speech; in his writings on toleration speech has no greater freedom than conduct.

24. This may be an afterthought of 1689 as Laslett suggests in his note to this passage, but not because it is inconsistent with what Locke says elsewhere about the dissolution of government as opposed to the dissolution of society. It is hard to see how Dunn can read this passage to say that society remains, *Political Thought,* p. 181 n.2.

25. Cf. Dunn, *Political Thought,* p. 181 n.2.

dissolution of society has followed as in the first case. For this very statement indicates that the dissolution of society follows: society can only be preserved by a settled legislative. So that society can preserve itself, it must be possible to say that the government is dissolved before the dissolution of society has followed. For Locke continues:

> But the state of Mankind is not so miserable that they are not capable of using this Remedy, till it be too late to look for any. To tell *People* they *may provide for themselves* by erecting a new Legislative, when by Oppression, Artifice, or being delivered over to a Foreign Power, their old one is gone, is only to tell them they may expect Relief, when it is too late, and the evil is past Cure. . . . And therefore it is, that they have not only a Right to get out of it, but to prevent it (220).

The point is precisely that in this first case, when the legislature is altered ("their old one is gone"), it is "too late." It is too late because society is dissolved and the people are reduced to a confused multitude. The answer is prevention rather than cure.[26]

The second case is therefore introduced immediately after that argument for prevention: "There is therefore, secondly, another way whereby *Governments are dissolved,* and that is; when the Legislative, or the Prince, either of them act contrary to their trust" (221). The crucial term is *therefore. Because* in the first case when the legislative is altered the government is so dissolved that the dissolution of society follows, *therefore* there must be a second case when the legislative is not yet altered but the government can be said to be dissolved before the dissolution of society has followed. Locke enumerates only the *"First"* way whereby this happens: when the legislature tries to gain arbitrary power over the property (life, liberty, or fortunes) of the people (221–22). Locke does not enumerate his discussion of the executive's trying to gain such power (222) or add anything else as the second way, perhaps so as "not to multiply Cases" (239). In this violation of trust by attempt at arbitrary power, the legislators are said to "put themselves into a state of War with the People" (222). There is not a general state of war among the people. Political power "devolves to the People, who have a Right to resume their original Liberty." That is not the original individual liberty of the state of nature, everyone's being "at the disposure of his own Will" as in the first case (212), but the original political power of the original democracy to set up any other form of government (132), as the end of the sentence shows: they "are in Society" (222). They are in the state of nature and the state of war only in the sense that every civil society is with respect to its enemies.

In the first case, that legislative which the people established as a bar to the state of war is without the people's consent directly or in effect taken away or replaced; whereas in the second case, the established legislative remains but itself acts contrary to its trust (221 and 227). This distinction corresponds to that which Locke makes between usurpation, "the exercise of Power, which another hath a right to," and tyranny, *"the exercise of Power beyond Right"* (199; cf. 197), except that the particular usurpation of legislative power by the king substitutes the "Arbitrary Will" of "a single Person" (214) for laws made together with assemblies (213), bringing about absolute monarchy, which is *"inconsistent with Civil Society"* (90; cf. also 91–94). But the two cases differ also in that the legislature or executive is only *trying* to gain arbitrary power in the second ("endeavour" 221; "endeavour" three times, as well as "goes about to" and "attempted" 222; "endeavour" 227; "attempts" 228; "attempts,"

---

26. Cf. Seliger, *Liberal Politics,* p. 126.

"endeavours," and "goes about to" 230; "attempting" 231). That is why the people can *prevent* tyranny in the second case, whereas it is too late in the first. Trying to gain arbitrary power dissolves government because an established government that acts contrary to its trust by so doing ceases to be a lawful government. Yet such a government is not so dissolved that the dissolution of society has followed. Indeed the problem is precisely that such a condition, being only an intention, is not even visible to the people. Intentions ought to be made visible before they are accomplished.

Locke presents a series of hypothetical objections (223–30). These objections are directed against the doctrine of the second case. For it is the doctrine of the second case that is strange, controversial, and in need of defense. Even Hobbes admits that when a society dissolves the people return to the state of nature and can set up a new one.[27] Locke's new doctrine is that instead of waiting until it is too late we can act in the spirit of anticipation of the Hobbesian state of nature or Machiavellian politics.[28] Locke fashions a doctrine of resistance out of Hobbesian or Machiavellian anticipation. Resistance is prevention and not a last resort, as it was traditionally viewed.

The first hypothetical objection is that to lay the foundation of government in the unsteady opinion and uncertain humor of the people is to expose it to certain ruin (223). Locke does not deny that he lays the foundation of government in the opinion and humor of the people; he denies only that their opinion and humor are unsteady and uncertain. The people are slow. Their "slowness," however, has a peculiar character. Using the example of England ("this Kingdom"), Locke reports that "in the many revolutions" the people have always eventually come back to "our old Legislative of King, Lords and Commons" and even to the same royal line. This slowness is not such as to fail to make many revolutions, depositions, and even republican experiments. It fails only to make them so well as not to have to make more. It is a lingering attachment to the "old Forms" or "old Constitutions." It is not simply a testimony to the excellence of the ancient constitution: it is despite "any Original defects, or adventitious ones introduced by time, or corruption," such as even the English constitution may have (233; cf. 156–158, 159, and 165–68). The people may even be attached merely to "ancient Names, and specious Forms" (225; cf. 20 and 215).[29]

The second hypothetical objection accordingly warns of frequent rebellion (224). Locke's first answer to it is that his hypothesis is no more responsible for rebellion than any other, such as that of divine right. The people will always resist when they are *"generally ill treated"* and find the opportunity. This inevitable resistance is compatible with their peculiar slowness: the people feel the faults but do not know how to cure them. One has "seen" examples of such resistance in one's own time and has "read" examples from other times and places (224). The people only *see;* Locke's doctrine has no direct effect on them but only on those who not only see but *read.* Locke's second answer is that the people do not resist over "every little mismanagement" or even "*Great mistakes,*" but only when "a long train of Abuses" (such as the American revolutionaries listed in the Declaration of Independence, we can add) makes "the design visible to the People" (225). "Make the design visible" might well be called the slogan of the chapter. For the second case is characterized by what is still merely a design and by the necessity of making it visible to the people. Locke's third answer is that *"the best fence against Rebellion"* is precisely *"this Doctrine,"* that

---

27. Hobbes, *Leviathan,* chap. 21 end.

28. *Ibid.,* chap. 13; Machiavelli, *The Prince,* chap. 3, *Discourses,* bk. I, chap. 52.

29. Contrast Seliger, *Liberal Politics,* pp. 312–15; cf. Machiavelli, *Discourses,* bk. I, chap. 25.

of the second case, that the government is dissolved when it tries to gain arbitrary power and has not yet actually brought about the dissolution of society (226). Not the people who merely feel, or even those who merely oppose persons, but those in power who oppose the constitutions and laws are likeliest to rebel, "that is, bring back again the state of War." [30] Since they read, Locke may show them "the danger and injustice" of their attempt (226).

Locke redefines rebellion so that those in power rather than those who rightly resist them are guilty of it (contrast 196). He follows up this redefinition by an explanation of how both the first and the second cases exemplify it (227). This digression also serves as a recapitulation articulating the structure I have emphasized. In the first case those who have altered the legislature have taken away the "bar to the state of War" among everyone. In the second case those who have attempted to gain arbitrary power have put "themselves into a state of War" with the people. Only in the first case is the state of war among "everyone," and even there that is not so by definition or at once but only by the removal of the bar to it. For the state of nature is not the state of war but merely has no bar to it (cf. 21 and 212). Only in the second case does society remain as the people at war with the rebels.

We see clearly the answer to our first question: Locke does not contradict himself on the distinction between the dissolutions of society and of government. He discusses two distinct cases, the distinction between which underlies his distinctive doctrine of resistance. Passages used by those who find two contrary views have been excerpted from the two sections treating the two cases.

Locke returns to the second hypothetical objection after the recapitulatory digression. He admits that this objection may mean not that his doctrine leads to rebellions in his sense, but to "Civil Wars, or Intestine Broils," that it is "destructive to the Peace of the World" (228). Locke does not deny, in answering this restated objection, that there will be "disorder or bloodshed" (228; cf. "Blood, Rapine, and Desolation" in 230). But it will not be the fault of the resisters; it will be that of those in power who break their trust. For the "Peace" offered by the alternative, some kind of *"Passive Obedience,"* is only "Violence and Rapine" for "the benefit of Robbers and Oppressors." Such turning of the other cheek does not lead to the wolf and the lamb lying down together, but to the lamb yielding his throat to be torn by the wolf (228). Locke's harsh answer may remind the reader of Machiavelli's attacks against trying to be good among so many who are not, against preferring to suffer rather than to revenge one's beatings, and against not speaking evil of the evil, that is, against Christianity.[31] The model should rather be Ulysses, who as "a prudent Man" did not preach up passive obedience in Polyphemus' den but made the tyrant's design visible to the people and made himself invisible to the tyrant (228). Resistance is better for mankind than tyranny (229).

The final hypothetical objection is that Locke's doctrine lends itself to "a busie head, or turbulent spirit" (230). Such men stir whenever they please, but the people do not "till the mischief be grown general, and the ill designs of the Rulers become visible, or their attempts sensible to the greater part" (230; cf. 168 and 208–209). The people are as little likely to be moved by turbulent malcontents as by a few unfortunate oppressed men (230); earlier Locke argued that they are as little likely to be moved by a few unfortunate oppressed men as by turbulent malcontents (208). The people are not only indifferent to the few but inclined to let themselves suffer, or

---

30. Cf. Hobbes, *Leviathan,* chap.28: "a relapse into the condition of warre, commonly called Rebellion."

31. Machiavelli, *The Prince,* chap. 15. *Discourses,* bk. II, chap. 2; bk. III, chap. 1.

at least not to foresee and forestall their own sufferings. They "can think of things no otherwise than as they find and feel them" (230). Because the people only see and feel (cf. 94, 168, 209, and 225), they are in need of warnings from the few who can foresee whether the oppression of a few is such that "the Precedent, and Consequences seem to threaten all" (209).[32] Locke admits that the people may be used by turbulent private men to cause great disorders or even produce fatal factions, but he suggests that it is the fault of the rulers who incur suspicion (cf. 209). As Machiavelli says, the faults of the people arise from the princes.[33] Private men ought to express their pride and ambition by opposing oppression; rulers ought to be content with their "greater share" (231).

Locke does not argue that there is necessarily less bloodshed his way.[34] It might seem that whereas Hobbes argues that the people should never rebel because it leads to a condition of terrible anarchy, Locke argues that the rulers should not rebel (attempt to gain arbitrary power) because it leads to a condition of terrible anarchy. It seems to be an empirical argument, depending on what one has seen and read. It might seem that, by arguing that in the first case the bar to the state of war is removed while in the second society remains, Locke claims that the second case is always more orderly and less bloody. The contrast between the English Civil War and the Glorious Revolution might confirm such a claim. But Locke's argument is more one of right than an empirical or historical one. The worst may not occur in the first case but the crucial point is that there is no fence against it, that however slow the people may be they are then in right absolved of all duties except those of the state of nature. Similarly, resistance in the second case may lead to civil war or even defeat. Unlike Jephtha, Locke offers justice no divine guarantee of success in battle (cf. 21 and 176).

The antepenultimate part of the chapter invokes Barclay, the champion of divine right monarchy, on behalf of resistance (232–39). It opens with a statement that seems to challenge our understanding that society persists in the second case: he who uses force without right "puts himself into a *state of War* with those, against whom he so uses it, and in that state all former Ties are cancelled, all other Rights cease, and every one has a *Right* to defend himself, and *to resist the Aggressor*" (232). These terms may suggest a general state of nature, but the context indicates that Locke means only the ties between the aggressor and the resisters; "*the State of War* that *levels the Parties*, cancels all former relation of Reverence, Respect, and *Superiority*" (235).[35]

Even Barclay admits that the people may defend their rights against tyrants. Locke does not attack him for denying that a private person may resist. Locke's doctrine permits such resistance as a matter of right if it is worth the trouble and cost, but does not make it prudent unless the majority are persuaded (168, 176, 208). Locke attacks Barclay instead for requiring that resistance be "with Reverence" and without punishment. For Locke, resistance by society is precisely punishing a criminal. The principle behind Locke's ridicule of the necessity of reverent resistance is that the best defense is a good offense, the Machiavellian and Hobbesian principle of anticipation.

---

32. Following Locke's terms, the American Tory "Massachusettensis" denied there was any "oppression that could be either seen or felt," whereas "Novanglus" (John Adams) argued that the people "see and feel" perhaps only "too late" the calamities foreseen "by a few" who perceived the "design" of the Tories, Merrill Jensen, ed., *Tracts of the American Revolution 1763–1776* (Indianapolis, 1967), pp. 283, 299–303.

33. Machiavelli, *Discourses*, bk. III, chap. 29.

34. Contrast Sir Robert Filmer, *Patriarcha*, chap. 19, "Popular Government more Bloody than a Tyranny," in *Patriarcha and Other Political Works of Sir Robert Filmer*, ed. Peter Laslett (Oxford, 1949), pp. 90–93; Hobbes, *Leviathan*, chap. 18 end.

35. Cf. Seliger, *Liberal Politics*, p. 127.

One cannot resist with only a shield and no sword. That is the principle of the chapter and the necessity of the second case.

Barclay admits two cases: when a ruler like Nero literally tries to kill all the people or when a ruler betrays the kingdom to a foreign power. Locke declines to "multiply cases" (cf. 221). It is not specifiable acts that constitute breach of trust but the end or design. One need not wait like Barclay for a Nero who openly declares his intention. According to Locke's reinterpretation of Barclay, "neglect of the publick good is to be taken as an evidence of such a *design,* or at least for a sufficient cause of *resistance*" (239). A sufficient cause for resistance is less than evidence for such a design. The most charming expression of this liberal concern for fences against the worst, and consequent suspicion and vigilance, which has come to seem paranoia to historians of the American Revolution, is Locke's metaphor of the boat to Algiers at the end of the previous chapter, "Of Tyranny" (210). Even if a captain "often" steers away from Algiers one may attribute this to crosswinds and other circumstances and be nonetheless persuaded that he intends to sell one into slavery if he steers that way when he can. Not only may damning evidence be construed into a design, but exculpating evidence may be explained away by circumstances.[36] The part on Barclay concludes with the accusation that the apologists for absolute monarchy "would have all Men born to, what their mean Souls fitted them for, Slavery" (239). This rare neither metaphorical (cf. 212) nor Hookerian (cf. 90n.) use of "soul" suggests that there are slavish souls fit for slavery and liberal ones fit for liberty (cf. *First Treatise,* 1). Resistance may therefore not be as inevitable as Locke made it seem (224); the people must be persuaded by the lovers of liberty likely to embrace Locke's doctrine rather than by the slavish followers of divine right.

The penultimate part of the chapter asks Locke's favorite question: who shall be judge? (240–42; cf. 21 and 168). He answers that the people shall, admitting also that God shall,[37] which means that every man shall, although preferably by appealing to the people. At first it may be only "some of the People" who oppose the prince, but they must make the design visible to "the Body of the *People*" (242). The right of resistance is an instance of the right to execute the law of nature in the state of war in the state of nature. When one does so one is a *judge,* judging not only the wrong committed but the proper time or opportunity for punishment and whether it is worth the trouble and cost (13, 21, 87, 91, 176).

The last chapter concludes with a summary (243) which confirms the importance of the distinction that begins the chapter and underlies the structure I have emphasized. Political power reverts to the individuals when society dissolves and to the people when only the government dissolves.

We have seen that Locke claims that his doctrine of the right of resistance is "the best fence against Rebellion," that is against bringing back the state of war (226).

---

36. This approach was reversed by one American Tory arguing from the last chapter of the *Second Treatise* but apparently also confusing Locke's distinction between the dissolutions of government and of society, Bernard Bailyn, *The Ideological Origins of the American Revolution* (Cambridge, 1967), pp. 149–50.

37. Locke's doctrine of the right of resistance as an "appeal to heaven" is based on Jephtha's appeal "The Lord the Judge be Judge" when taking arms against the Ammonites (21, 176, 241; cf. Judges 11:27). It has been noted that by applying this appeal to heaven, equated with an appeal to arms, not only to relations between nations but also to relations between peoples and governments, Locke was able to oppose "the traditional Christian view which restricted the appeal to heaven of the governed to mere prayer" (Seliger, *Liberal Politics,* pp. 63–64; cf. Strauss, *Natural Right,* pp. 214–15). I would add that the same appeal, "The Lord be Judge," is also invoked in Scripture in a relation between a subject and a ruler, David and Saul, but its meaning is precisely that the subject should *not* take arms against the ruler (1 Samuel 24:12 and 15). Cf. e.g., Martin Luther, *Works,* vol. 46, *The Christian in Society* III, ed. Robert C. Schultz (Philadelphia, 1967), pp. 112–13.

Locke's concern for fences against the worst, rather than for paths to the best or for a balance of good and bad, is not only the basis of the right of resistance and of the principle of anticipation, but the fundamental principle of Locke's liberal politics.[38] At the start of the discussion of the crucial second case in our chapter, Locke justifies both the people's right to choose their representatives and the laws those representatives make as "Fences to the Properties of all the Members of the Society" (222). Absolute monarchies lack a "Fence" against oppression by the ruler (93). The law of nature, similarly, fails to "fence the Properties of those that live under it" (136). Property itself may be considered a sort of fence to preservation (25). On the most fundamental level, liberty is a "Fence" to self-preservation (17; cf. 23). Locke asserts first that "I have reason to conclude" that he who threatens my freedom declares his "design" on my life (17), but that is only because "I have no reason to suppose" he does not (18). Distrust, fear of the worst, and anticipation are not merely psychological characteristics of Lockean rebels but principles built into the theoretical structure of the state of nature and the state of war, of which the crucial practical instance is the right of resistance.

---

38. Cf. Machiavelli's dikes against fortune, *The Prince*, chap. 25.

Jean-Jacques Rousseau

Paradox is a word often associated with Jean-Jacques Rousseau—and with good reason. Paradox abounds in his writings and in his personal life as well. The most famous line from his *Social Contract* illustrates his penchant for paradox: "Man was born free and everywhere he is in chains." Elsewhere in the same work he speaks of the relationship between individual will and the general will of the community, noting that in some cases men must be "forced to be free." His life and writings seem to some a web of inconsistency. Despite his admonition to parents in his treatise on education, *Emile*, to heed parental responsibilities—especially the duty of rearing one's own children—he abandoned his five children in a foundling home. Because Rousseau's prose and lifestyle are so deeply steeped in paradox, his work continues to inspire fierce debate and has led to diametrically opposed characterizations of him as both totalitarian and libertarian. The persistent student of his work will find, however, that Rousseau's use of paradox is intended not to obscure or mislead, but to provide insights that may not adequately be captured in any other manner.

Rousseau's life was both colorful and tragic. His mother died while giving birth to him in Geneva in 1712. His father, a watchmaker, exposed the boy to his own ribald lifestyle and abandoned Jean-Jacques when he was ten. Thereafter, Rousseau drifted through Geneva and France taking odd jobs and making many acquaintances, including some influential friends who helped him through rough times. One of these, Mme de Warens, took Rousseau into her house in Chambéry. He used his time there to study the classics and developed an interest in music. A dispute involving one of his hostess's lovers sent him packing for Paris in 1742. There, he wrote about and composed music, including an opera.

When he was 31, one of his well-placed friends secured for him the post of Secretary to the French Ambassador in Venice. The job did not last long as Rousseau became bored and disenchanted with political life, especially as practiced in the city of canals. It was during this brief political exposure, however, that he became convinced of the centrality of politics for all aspects of life, a theme that informs all of his political writings. When Rousseau returned to Paris, he met Thérèse Levasseur and commenced a relationship, which ended in matrimony only after 25 years of companionship, during which he was involved in several affairs.

In 1749, Rousseau entered a contest, sponsored by the Academy of Dijon, with an essay on the topic: "Has the Restoration of the Sciences and Arts Tended to Purify Morals?" Arguing against the tide of Enlightenment thinking, Rousseau asserted that advances in these disciplines had a corrupting effect on the human personality. Exposure to them was harmful to morals and destructive of natural freedom. Ironically, the publication of the *First Discourse* won for Rousseau the attention of artistic and scientific luminaries in Parisian café society who sought him out for intellectual exchange. These were the same people Rousseau implicitly criticized for corrupting humankind. Rousseau took pleasure in rejecting their lifestyle and went so far as to abandon the typical dress of this circle in favor of peasant garb.

Rousseau submitted *On the Origin and Foundations of Inequality Among Men,* his *Second Discourse,* to the same academy in 1754. Although this discourse won no prize, its influence was substantial. In this work, Rousseau speculated about the origins of society, identifying humans as solitary yet peaceable creatures prior to the onset of society. With the development of speech, reason, and particularly with the advent of private property, the human race began its steady decline to the point where existing governments arose to protect property while subjugating citizens.

In 1756, Rousseau retreated to the country cottage of one of his admirers, Mme d'Épinay. He began working on a number of projects, including a romantic novel, *Julie, ou la Nouvelle Héloïse,* as well as his *Social Contract.* This period was marked by growing disputes between Rousseau and his former café society friends, some of whom he accused of conspiring against him.

In 1762 both the *Social Contract* and *Emile* were published. The latter, a treatise on education in which an unidentified tutor shapes the personality of his student by rejecting book learning in favor of a more "natural," experiential approach, drew wide attention and fire. The section on religion proved politically unpopular for Rousseau: among Enlightenment intellectuals for its reliance on faith, and among French churchgoers for its utilitarian treatment of religion. The Parliament of Paris ordered the volume burned and issued an arrest warrant for Rousseau. The *Social Contract,* an attempt to forge a theory of government upon the premises articulated in the *Second Discourse,* received little attention until after Rousseau's death, particularly by zealots of the French Revolution.

After 1762, Rousseau was a fugitive, darting from one town to another to escape arrest. These years were marked by an increasing paranoia, reflected in his later writings, where he accused old friends like Diderot and Voltaire of being in league with political opponents to ruin him. Rousseau returned to Paris incognito in 1770 where he composed his frank *Confessions,* as well as a series of recollections titled *Reveries of a Solitary Walker.* He and Thérèse retired to Ermonvoille, just outside Paris, where he died in 1778.

Second Discourse and Social Contract

In the *Second Discourse,* or the *Discourse on the Origin and Foundations of Inequality Among Men,* Rousseau speculates about the origin of society and the emergence of government. The first part is an anthropological sketch of life among early humans as Rousseau envisions it might have been (though no claim is made for historical accuracy). In this early state, humans are characterized as equal and free; differences in ability mattered little, and no individual had claim or title over the actions of another. In developing this portrait, Rousseau identified two important characteristics of humans that set them apart from other animals: freedom and perfectibility. Together, these yielded a nature that was malleable, as capable of vice as of virtue, and subject to direction by the type of political community one inhabited. Part Two reveals how natural man was corrupted by the liberation of reason and by claims to private property that, once institutionalized, led to the subservience of the many by the few. This view differs from both classic and modern political accounts. Unlike Aristotle, for example, Rousseau envisions humans as essentially solitary. Unlike Hobbes and other moderns, however, Rousseau paints natural man as innocent, with self-interest tempered by natural, though weak, sympathy for other living beings. Ultimately, Rousseau does not advocate the return to bestial simplicity. Rather, he insists that social man must reorganize political life in such a manner as to affirm his freedom and equality, as far as is practicable, in the context of the political community. The selections from the *Second Discourse* illustrate these themes.

Rousseau states clearly the purpose of the *Social Contract* at the outset: legitimizing the political state to which man has arrived and from which there is no return. What is also clear is the mechanism by which legitimate government is founded. All men must unite by contracting to put themselves and their power under the supreme control of the "general will", and to receive each contracting member as an indivisible part of the whole. By virtue of this contract, each member trades the natural freedom to do what he wishes for the moral freedom to do what the general will determines he must. What is not clear is the nature of some of the arrangements by which this contract is to be executed. For example, the general will is an elusive concept. It is more than a collection of individual wills and resembles what we might call today the common good. The general will becomes known under the skillful leadership of the legislator who resembles a superhuman with the knowledge of human nature but suffering none of its deficiencies. How the general will is made known, and how the legislator leads without manipulating the governed, continue to be sources of debate among Rousseau scholars. While Rousseau is not wholly successful in explicating how his system of government will operate, he does identify the paradoxes faced by the modern nation-state as only he can.

Commentaries

In the first commentary, Asher Horowitz untangles Rousseau's purposes in the *Second Treatise.* Horowitz argues that Rousseau neither attempted to reduce humans to biological function nor to free them entirely from biological constraints. Instead, Rousseau's anthropology demonstrates that evolution predisposed humans to create their own history and that, over time, biological and the social attributes became reciprocally interconnected. Central to Horowitz's thesis is the idea that the necessity of labor gave rise to a host of human attributes, including the need for political society.

Though the general will is an essential component of Rousseau's enterprise to reconstitute political society, its meaning remains elusive. In the second commentary, Andrezej Rapaczynski argues that the general will must be understood within the context of Rousseau's challenge to liberal theory as it emerged in the modern natural right teachings of Hobbes and Locke. While Rousseau agrees with modern theorists that human nature is partly defined by self-interest and free agency, he saw, argues Rapaczynski, that modern society divorced individuals from the community they needed for their own development and identity. The general will expresses Rousseau's attempt (though, perhaps, a failed attempt) to reconcile freedom with community, where community (fraternity) itself is the ultimate goal, rather than a means to some utilitarian end.

Key Words

Amour de soi. The love of self that is, basically, limited and innocent. *Amour de soi* characterizes natural humans in the presocial state, before reason awakens passions and the need for approval by others.

Amour propre. The self-love characterizing social man. This type of love is artificial and creates conflict in society by making individuals seek the good opinion of others. The term is sometimes expressed as vanity.

Natural Right. See definition in section on Aquinas. Rousseau was a critic of modern natural right theory but did not totally abandon some of its tenets.

For Further Reading

Bloom, A. 1987. "Rousseau." In *History of Political Philosophy, Third Edition* (L. Strauss and J. Cropsey, eds.). Chicago: University of Chicago Press.

Hall, J. C. 1973. *Rousseau: An Introduction to his Political Philosophy.* New York: Macmillan.

Masters, R. D. 1968. *The Political Philosophy of Rousseau.* Princeton, N.J.: Princeton University Press.

Rousseau, J. J. [1979.] *Emile,* ed. Allan Bloom. New York: Basic Books.

Shklar, J. 1969. *Men and Citizens.* Cambridge: Cambridge University Press.

Discourse on the Origin and Foundations of Inequality

First Part

...In every animal I see only an ingenious machine to which nature has given senses in order to revitalize itself and guarantee itself, to a certain point, from all that tends to destroy or upset it. I perceive precisely the same things in the human machine, with the difference that nature alone does everything in the operations of a beast, whereas man contributes to his operations by being a free agent. The former chooses or rejects by instinct and the latter by an act of freedom, so that a beast cannot deviate from the rule that is prescribed to it even when it would be advantageous for it to do so, and a man deviates from it often to his detriment. Thus a pigeon would die of hunger near a basin filled with the best meats, and a cat upon heaps of fruits or grain, although each could very well nourish itself on the food it disdains if it made up its mind to try some. Thus dissolute men abandon themselves to excesses which cause them fever and death, because the mind depraves the senses and because the will still speaks when nature is silent.

Every animal has ideas, since it has senses; it even combines its ideas up to a certain point, and in this regard man differs from a beast only in degree. Some philosophers have even suggested that there is more difference between a given man and another than between a given man and a given beast. Therefore it is not so much understanding which constitutes the distinction of man among the animals as it is his being a free agent. Nature commands every animal, and the beast obeys. Man feels the same impetus, but he realizes that he is free to acquiesce or resist; and it is above all in the consciousness of this freedom that the spirituality of his soul is shown. For physics explains in some way the mechanism of the senses and the formation of ideas; but in the power of willing, or rather of choosing, and in the sentiment of this power are found only purely spiritual acts about which the laws of mechanics explain nothing.

But if the difficulties surrounding all these questions should leave some room for dispute on this difference between man and animal, there is another very specific quality that distinguishes them and about which there can be no dispute: the faculty of self-perfection, a faculty which, with the aid of circumstances, successively develops all the others, and resides among us as much in the species as in the individual. By contrast an animal is at the end of a few months what it will be all its life; and its species is at the end of a thousand years what it was the first year of that thousand. Why is man alone subject to becoming imbecile? Is it not that he thereby returns to his primitive state; and that—while the beast, which has acquired nothing and which has, moreover, nothing to lose, always retains its instinct—man, losing again by old age or other accidents all that his *perfectibility* had made him acquire, thus falls back lower than the beast itself? It would be sad for us to be forced to agree that this distinctive and almost unlimited faculty is the source of all man's misfortunes; that it is this faculty which, by dint of time, draws him out of that original condition in which he would pass tranquil and innocent days; that it is this faculty which, bringing to flower over the centuries his enlightenment and his errors, his vices and his virtues, in the long run makes him the tyrant of himself and of nature. It would be horrible to be obliged to praise as a beneficent being the one who first suggested to the inhabitant of the banks of the Orinoco the use of those pieces of wood which he binds on the temples of his children, and which assure them at least a part of their imbecility and original happiness.

Savage man, by nature committed to instinct alone, or rather compensated for the instinct he perhaps lacks by faculties capable of substituting for it at first, and then of raising him far above nature, will therefore begin with purely animal functions. To perceive and feel will be his first state, which he will have in common with all animals. To will and not will, to desire and fear will be the first and almost the only operations of his soul until new circumstances cause new developments in it.

Whatever the moralists may say about it, human understanding owes much to the passions, which by common agreement also owe much to it. It is by their activity that our reason is perfected; we seek to know only because we desire to have pleasure; and it is impossible to conceive why one who had neither desires nor fears would go to the trouble of reasoning. The passions in turn derive their origin from our needs, and their progress from our knowledge. For one can desire or fear things only through the ideas one can have of them or by the simple impulsion of nature; and savage man, deprived of every kind of enlightenment, feels only the passions of this last kind. His desires do not exceed his physical needs, the only goods he knows in the universe are nourishment, a female, and repose; the only evils he fears are pain and hunger. I say pain and not death because an animal will never know what it is to die; and knowledge of death and its terrors is one of the first acquisitions that man has made in moving away from the animal condition. . . .

It seems at first that men in that state [state of nature] not having among themselves any kind of moral relationship or known duties, could be neither good nor evil, and had neither vices nor virtues: unless, taking these words in a physical sense, one calls vices in the individual the qualities that can harm his own preservation, and virtues those that can contribute to it; in which case, it would be necessary to call the most virtuous the one who least resists the simple impulses of nature. But without departing from the ordinary meaning, it is appropriate to suspend the judgment we could make of such a situation and to beware of our prejudices, until one has examined with scale in hand whether there are more virtues than vices among civilized men; or whether their virtues are more advantageous than their vices are deadly; or whether the progress of their knowledge is a sufficient compensation for the harms they do one another as they learn of the good they ought to do; or whether all things considered, they would not be in a happier situation having neither harm to fear nor good to hope for from anyone, rather than subjecting themselves to a universal dependence and obliging themselves to receive everything from those who do not obligate themselves to give them anything.

Above all, let us not conclude with Hobbes that because man has no idea of goodness he is naturally evil; that he is vicious because he does not know virtue; that he always refuses his fellow-men services he does not believe he owes them; nor that, by virtue of the right he reasonably claims to things he needs, he foolishly imagines himself to be the sole proprietor of the whole universe. Hobbes saw very clearly the defect of all modern definitions of natural right; but the consequences he draws from his own definition show that he takes it in a sense which is no less false. Reasoning upon the principles he establishes, this author ought to have said that since the state of nature is that in which care of our self-preservation is the least prejudicial to the self-preservation of others, that state was consequently the best suited to peace and the most appropriate for the human race. He says precisely the opposite, because of having improperly included in the savage man's care of self-preservation the need to satisfy a multitude of passions which are the product of society and which have made laws necessary. The evil man, he says, is a robust child. It remains to be seen whether savage man is a robust child. Should we grant this to him, what would he conclude from it? That if, when he is robust, this man were as dependent on others as when he is weak, there is no kind of excess to which he would not be inclined: that he would beat his mother when she would be too slow in giving him her breast; that he would strangle one of his young brothers when he would be inconvenienced by him; that he would bite another's leg when he was hit or annoyed by it. But to be robust and to be dependent are two contradictory suppositions in the state of nature. Man is weak when he is dependent, and he is emancipated before he is robust. Hobbes did not see that the same cause that prevents savages from using their reason, as our jurists claim, prevents them at the same time from abusing their faculties, as he himself claims. Thus one could say that savages are not evil precisely because they do not know what it is to be good; for it is neither the growth of enlightenment nor the restraint of law, but the calm of passions and the ignorance of vice which prevent them from doing evil: *Tanto plus in illis proficit vitiorum ignoratio, quam in his cognitio virtutis.*[1] There is, besides, another principle which Hobbes did not notice, and which—having been given to man in order to soften, under certain circumstances, the ferocity of his vanity or the desire for self-preservation before the birth of vanity—tempers the ardor he has for his own well-being by an innate repugnance to see his fellowman suffer. I do not believe I have any contradiction to fear in granting man the sole natural virtue that the most excessive detractor of human virtues was forced to recognize. I speak of pity, a disposition that is appropriate to beings as weak and subject to as many ills as we are; a virtue all the more universal and useful to man because it precedes in him the use of all reflection; and so natural that even beasts sometimes give perceptible signs of it. Without speaking of the tenderness of mothers for their young and of the perils they brave to guard them, one observes daily the repugnance of horses to trample a living body underfoot. An animal does not pass near a

---

1. "To such an extent has ignorance of vices been more profitable to them [the Scythians] than the understanding of virtue to these [the Greeks]." Justin, *Histories*, II, ii . . .

dead animal of its species without uneasiness. There are even some animals that give them a kind of sepulcher; and the sad lowing of cattle entering a slaughterhouse announces the impression they receive from the horrible sight that strikes them. One sees with pleasure the author of the *Fable of the Bees*,[2] forced to recognize man as a compassionate and sensitive being, departing from his cold and subtle style in the example he gives in order to offer us the pathetic image of an imprisoned man who sees outside a wild beast tearing a child from his mother's breast, breaking his weak limbs in its murderous teeth, and ripping apart with its claws the palpitating entrails of this child. What horrible agitation must be felt by this witness of an event in which he takes no personal interest! What anguish must he suffer at this sight, unable to bring help to the fainting mother or to the dying child.

Such is the pure movement of nature prior to all reflection. Such is the force of natural pity, which the most depraved morals still have difficulty destroying, since daily in our theaters one sees, moved and crying for the troubles of an unfortunate person, a man who, if he were in the tyrant's place, would aggravate his enemy's torments even more—like bloodthirsty Sulla,[3] so sensitive to ills he had not caused, or like Alexander of Pherae, who did not dare attend the performance of any tragedy lest he be seen moaning with Andromache and Priam, whereas he listened without emotion to the cries of so many citizens murdered daily on his orders.

> Mollissima corda
> Humano generi dare se natura fatetur,
> Quae lacrimas dedit.[4]

Mandeville sensed very well that even with all their ethics men would never have been anything but monsters if nature had not given them pity in support of reason; but he did not see that from this quality alone flow all the social virtues he wants to question in men. In fact, what are generosity, clemency, humanity, if not pity applied to the weak, to the guilty, or to the human species in general? Benevolence and even friendship are, rightly understood, the products of a constant pity fixed on a particular object: for is desiring that someone not suffer anything but desiring that he be happy? Even should it be true that commiseration is only a sentiment that puts us in the position of him who suffers—a sentiment that is obscure and strong in savage man, developed but weak in civilized man—what would this idea matter to the truth of what I say, except to give it more force? In fact, commiseration will be all the more energetic as the observing animal identifies himself more intimately with the suffering animal. Now it is evident that this identification must have been infinitely closer in the state of nature than in the state of reasoning. Reason engenders vanity and reflection fortifies it; reason turns man back upon himself, it separates him from all that bothers and afflicts him. Philosophy isolates him; because of it he says in secret, at the sight of a suffering man: Perish if you will, I am safe.

---

2. Bernard Mandeville [ed.].

3. Lucius Cornelius Sulla, or Sylla, (138–78 B.C.E.), a Roman general and politician who, having been victorious in a civil war, became the dictator of Rome. From this position he proscribed and killed many of those who were opposed to him . . .

4. "Nature, who gave men tears, confesses she gives the human race most tender hearts". . .

No longer can anything except dangers to the entire society trouble the tranquil sleep of the philosopher and tear him from his bed. His fellow-man can be murdered with impunity right under his window; he has only to put his hands over his ears and argue with himself a bit to prevent nature, which revolts within him, from identifying him with the man who is being assassinated. Savage man does not have this admirable talent, and for want of wisdom and reason he is always seen heedlessly yielding to the first sentiment of humanity. In riots or street fights the populace assembles, the prudent man moves away; it is the rabble, the marketwomen, who separate the combatants and prevent honest people from murdering each other.

It is very certain, therefore, that pity is a natural sentiment which, moderating in each individual the activity of love of oneself, contributes to the mutual preservation of the entire species. It carries us without reflection to the aid of those whom we see suffer; in the state of nature, it takes the place of laws, morals, and virtue, with the advantage that no one is tempted to disobey its gentle voice; it will dissuade every robust savage from robbing a weak child or an infirm old man of his hard-won subsistence if he himself hopes to be able to find his own elsewhere. Instead of that sublime maxim of reasoned justice, *Do unto others as you would have them do unto you*, it inspires all men with this other maxim of natural goodness, much less perfect but perhaps more useful than the preceding one: *Do what is good for you with the least possible harm to others*. In a word, it is in this natural sentiment, rather than in subtle arguments, that we must seek the cause of the repugnance every man would feel in doing evil, even independently of the maxims of education. Although it may behoove Socrates and minds of his stamp to acquire virtue through reason, the human race would have perished long ago if its preservation had depended only on the reasonings of its members. . . .

Second Part

The first person who, having fenced off a plot of ground, took it into his head to say *this is mine* and found people simple enough to believe him, was the true founder of civil society. What crimes, wars, murders, what miseries and horrors would the human race have been spared by someone who, uprooting the stakes or filling in the ditch, had shouted to his fellow-men: Beware of listening to this impostor; you are lost if you forget that the fruits belong to all and the earth to no one! But it is very likely that by then things had already come to the point where they could no longer remain as they were. For this idea of property, depending on many prior ideas which could only have arisen successively, was not conceived all at once in the human mind. It was necessary to make much progress, to acquire much industry and enlightenment, and to transmit and augment them from age to age, before arriving at this last stage of the state of nature. Therefore let us start further back in time and attempt to assemble from a single point of view this slow succession of events and knowledge in their most natural order.

Man's first sentiment was that of his existence, his first care that of his preservation. The products of the earth furnished him with all the necessary help; instinct led him to make use of them. Hunger and other appetites making him experience by turns various manners of existing, there was one appetite that invited him to perpetuate his species; and this blind inclination, devoid of any sentiment of the heart, produced only a purely animal act. This need satisfied, the two sexes no longer recognized each other, and even the child no longer meant anything to his mother as soon as he could do without her.

Such was the condition of nascent man; such was the life of an animal limited at first to pure sensations and scarcely profiting from the gifts nature offered him, far from dreaming of wresting anything from it. But difficulties soon arose; it was necessary to learn to conquer them. The height of trees, which prevented him from reaching their fruits, the competition of animals that sought to nourish themselves with these fruits, the ferocity of those animals that wanted to take his very life, all obliged him to apply himself to bodily exercises. It was necessary to become agile, fleet in running, vigorous in combat. Natural arms, which are branches of trees and stones, were soon discovered at hand. He learned to surmount nature's obstacles, combat other animals when necessary, fight for his subsistence even with men, or make up for what had to be yielded to the stronger.

In proportion as the human race spread, difficulties multiplied along with men. Differences of soil, climate, and season could force them to admit differences in their ways of life. Barren years, long and hard winters, and scorching summers which consume everything required of them new industry. Along the sea and rivers they invented the fishing line and hook, and became fishermen and eaters of fish. In forests they made bows and arrows, and became hunters and warriors. In cold countries they covered themselves with the skins of beasts they had killed. Lightning, a volcano, or some happy accident introduced them to fire, a new resource against the rigor of winter. They learned to preserve this element, then to reproduce it, and finally to prepare with it meats they previously devoured raw. . . .

Everything begins to change its appearance. Men who until this time wandered in the woods, having adopted a more fixed settlement, slowly come together, unite into different bands, and finally form in each country a particular nation, unified by customs and character, not by regulations and laws but by the same kind of life and foods and by the common influence of climate. A permanent proximity cannot fail to engender at length some contact between different families. Young people of different sexes live in neighboring huts; the passing intercourse demanded by nature soon leads to another kind no less sweet and more permanent through mutual frequentation. People grow accustomed to consider different objects and to make comparisons; imperceptibly they acquire ideas of merit and beauty which produce sentiments of preference. By dint of seeing one another, they can no longer do without seeing one another again. A tender and gentle sentiment is gradually introduced into the soul and at the least obstacle becomes an impetuous fury. Jealousy awakens with love; discord triumphs, and the gentlest of the passions receives sacrifices of human blood.

In proportion as ideas and sentiments follow upon one another and as mind and heart are trained, the human race continues to be tamed, contacts spread, and bonds are tightened. People grew accustomed to assembling in front of the huts or around a large tree; song and dance, true children of love and leisure, became the amusement or rather the occupation of idle and assembled men and women. Each one began to look at the others and to want to be looked at himself, and public esteem had a value. The one who sang or danced the best, the handsomest, the strongest, the most adroit, or the most eloquent became the most highly considered; and that was the first step toward inequality and, at the same time, toward vice. From these first preferences were born on one hand vanity and contempt, on the other shame and envy; and the fermentation caused by these new leavens eventually produced compounds fatal to happiness and innocence. . . .

In discovering and following thus the forgotten and lost routes that must have led man from the natural state to the civil state; in re-establishing, along with the intermediary positions I have just noted, those that the pressure of time has made me suppress or that imagination has not suggested to me, every attentive reader cannot fail to be struck by the immense space that separates these two states. It is in this slow succession of things that he will see the solution to an infinite number of problems of ethics and politics which the philosophers cannot resolve. He will sense that, the human race of one age not being the human race of another, the reason Diogenes did not find a man was that he sought among his contemporaries the man of a time that no longer existed. Cato, he will say, perished with Rome and freedom because he was out of place in his century; and the greatest of men only astonished the world, which he would have governed five hundred years earlier. In a word, he will explain how the soul and human passions, altering imperceptibly, change their nature so to speak; why our needs and our pleasures change their objects in the long run; why, original man vanishing by degrees, society no longer offers to the eyes of the wise man anything except an assemblage of artificial men and factitious passions which are the work of all these new relations and have no true foundation in nature. . . .

On the Social Contract

Book I

Chapter 1
Subject of This First Book

Man was/is born free, and everywhere he is in chains. One who believes himself the master of others is nonetheless a greater slave than they. How did this change occur? I do not know. What can make it legitimate? I believe I can answer this question.

If I were to consider only force and the effect it produces, I would say that as long as a people is constrained to obey and does so, it does well; as soon as it can shake off the yoke and does so, it does even better. For in recovering its freedom by means of the same right used to steal it, either the people is justified in taking it back, or those who took it away were not justified in doing so. But the social order is a sacred right that serves as a basis for all the others. However, this right does not come from nature; it is therefore based on conventions. The problem is to know what these conventions are. Before coming to that, I should establish what I have just asserted.

Chapter 2
On the First Societies

The most ancient of all societies, and the only natural one, is that of the family. Yet children remain bound to the father only as long as they need him for self-preservation. As soon as this need ceases, the natural bond dissolves. The children, exempt from the obedience they owed the father, and the father, exempt from the care he owed the children, all return equally to independence. If they continue to remain united, it is no longer naturally but voluntarily, and the family itself is maintained only by convention.

This common freedom is a consequence of man's nature. His first law is to attend to his own preservation, his first cares are those he owes himself; and as soon as he has reached the age of reason, as he alone is the judge of the proper means of preserving himself, he thus becomes his own master.

The family is therefore, so to speak, the prototype of political societies. The leader is like the father, the people are like the children; and since all are born equal and free, they only alienate their freedom for their utility. The entire difference is that in the family, the father's love for his children rewards him for the care he provides; whereas in the State, the pleasure of commanding substitutes for this love, which the leader does not have for his people. . . .

Chapter 3
On the Right of the Strongest

The strongest is never strong enough to be the master forever unless he transforms his force into right and obedience into duty. This leads to the right of the strongest, a right that is in appearance taken ironically and in principle really established. But won't anyone ever explain this word to us? Force is a physical power. I do not see what morality can result from its effects. Yielding to force is an act of necessity, not of will. At most, it is an act of prudence. In what sense could it be a duty?

Let us suppose this alleged right for a moment. I say that what comes of it is nothing but inexplicable confusion. For as soon as force makes right, the effect changes along with the cause. Any force that overcomes the first one succeeds to its right. As soon as one can disobey without punishment, one can do so legitimately, and since the strongest is always right, the only thing to do is to make oneself the strongest. But what is a right that perishes when force ceases? If it is necessary to obey by force, one need not obey by duty, and if one is no longer forced to obey, one is no longer obligated to do so. It is apparent, then, that this word right adds nothing to force. It is meaningless here.

Obey those in power. If that means yield to force, the precept is good, but superfluous; I reply that it will never be violated. All power comes from God, I admit, but so does all illness. Does this mean it is forbidden to call the doctor? If a brigand takes me by surprise at the edge of a woods, must I not only give up my purse by force; am I obligated by conscience to give it even if I could keep it away? After all, the pistol he holds is also a power.

Let us agree, therefore, that might does not make right, and that one is only obligated to obey legitimate powers. Thus my original question still remains.

Chapter 4
On Slavery

Since no man has any natural authority over his fellow man, and since force produces no right, there remain only conventions as the basis of all legitimate authority among men.

If a private individual, says Grotius, can alienate his freedom and enslave himself to a master, why can't a whole people alienate its freedom and subject itself to a king? There are many equivocal words in this that need explaining, but let us limit ourselves to the word *alienate*. To alienate is to give or to sell. Now a man who makes himself another's slave does not give himself, he sells himself, at the least for his subsistence. But why does a people sell itself? Far from furnishing the subsistence of his subjects, a king derives his own only from them, and according to Rabelais a king does not live cheaply. Do the subjects give their persons, then, on condition that their goods will be taken too? I do not see what remains for them to preserve.

It will be said that the despot guarantees civil tranquillity to his subjects. Perhaps so, but what have they gained if the wars that his ambition brings on them, if his insatiable greed, if the harassment of his ministers are a greater torment than their dissensions would be? What have they gained, if this tranquillity is one of their miseries? Life is tranquil in jail cells, too. Is that reason enough to like them? The Greeks lived tranquilly shut up in the Cyclop's cave as they awaited their turn to be devoured.

To say that a man gives himself gratuitously is to say something absurd and inconceivable. Such an act is illegitimate and null, if only because he who does so is not in his right mind. To say the same thing about an entire people is to suppose a people of madmen. Madness does not make right.

Even if everyone could alienate himself, he could not alienate his children. They are born men and free. Their freedom belongs to them; no one but themselves has a right to dispose of it. Before they have reached the age of reason, their father can, in their name, stipulate conditions for their preservation, for their well-being; but he cannot give them irrevocably and unconditionally, because such a gift is contrary to the ends of nature and exceeds the rights of paternity. For an arbitrary government to be legitimate, it would therefore be necessary for the people in each generation to be master of its acceptance or rejection. But then this government would no longer be arbitrary.

To renounce one's freedom is to renounce one's status as a man, the rights of humanity and even its duties. There is no possible compensation for anyone who renounces everything. Such a renunciation is incompatible with the nature of man, and taking away all his freedom of will is taking away all morality from his actions. Finally, it is a vain and contradictory convention to stipulate absolute authority on one side and on the other unlimited obedience. Isn't it clear that one is in no way engaged toward a person from whom one has the right to demand everything, and doesn't this condition alone—without equivalent and without exchange—entail the nullification of the act? For what right would my slave have against me, since all he has belongs to me, and his right being mine, my right against myself is a meaningless word?

Grotius and others derive from war another origin of the alleged right of slavery. As the victor has the right to kill the vanquished, according to them, the latter can buy back his life at the cost of his freedom—a convention all the more legitimate in that it is profitable for both of them.

But it is clear that this alleged right to kill the vanquished in no way results from the state of war. Men are not naturally enemies, if only because when living in their original independence, they do not have sufficiently stable relationships among themselves to constitute either the state of peace or the state of war. It is the relationship between things, not between men, that constitutes war; and as the state of war cannot arise from simple, personal relations, but only from proprietary relations, private war between one man and another can exist neither in the state of nature, where there is no stable property, nor in the social state, where everything is under the authority of the laws.

Individual combats, duels, encounters are not acts that constitute a state. And with regard to private wars, authorized by the establishments of King Louis IX of France and suspended by the peace of God, they are abuses of feudal government, an absurd system if there ever was one, contrary to the principles of natural right and to every good polity.

War is not, therefore, a relation between man and man, but between State and State, in which private individuals are enemies only by accident, not as men, nor even as citizens, but as soldiers; not as members of the homeland but as its defenders. Finally, each State can have only other States, and not men, as enemies, since no true relationship can be established between things of differing natures.

This principle even conforms with the established maxims of all ages and with the constant practice of all civilized peoples. Declarations of war are not so much warnings to those in power as to their subjects. The foreigner —whether he be king, private individual, or people—who robs, kills, or imprisons subjects without declaring war on the prince—is not an enemy, but a brigand. Even in the midst of war, a just prince may well seize everything in an enemy country that belongs to the public, but he respects the person and goods of private individuals. He respects rights on which his own are based. The end of war being the destruction of the enemy State, one has the right to kill its defenders as long as they are armed. But as soon as they lay down their arms and surrender, since they cease to be enemies or instruments of the enemy, they become simply men once again, and one no longer has a right to their lives. Sometimes it is possible to kill the State without killing a single one of its members. War confers no right that is not necessary to its end. These principles are not those of Grotius; they are not based on the authority of poets, but are derived from the nature of things, and are based on reason.

With regard to the right of conquest, it has no basis other than the law of the strongest. If war does not give the victor the right to massacre the vanquished peoples, this right he does not have cannot establish the right to enslave them. One only has the right to kill the enemy when he cannot be made a slave. The right to make him a slave does not come, then, from the right to kill him. It is therefore an iniquitous exchange to make him buy his life, over which one has no right, at the cost of his freedom. By establishing the right of life and death on the right of slavery, and the right of slavery on the right of life and death, isn't it clear that one falls into a vicious circle?

Even assuming this terrible right to kill everyone, I say that a man enslaved in war or a conquered people is in no way obligated toward his master, except to obey for as long as he is forced to do so. In taking the equivalent of his life, the victor has not spared it; rather than to kill him purposelessly, he has killed him usefully. Therefore, far from the victor having acquired any authority over him in addition to force, the state of war subsists between them as before; their relation itself is its effect, and the customs of the right of war suppose that there has not been a peace treaty. They made a convention, true; but that convention, far from destroying the state of war, assumes its continuation.

Thus, from every vantage point, the right of slavery is null, not merely because it is illegitimate, but because it is absurd and meaningless. These words *slavery* and *right* are contradictory; they are mutually exclusive. Whether it is said by one man to another or by a man to a people, the following speech will always be equally senseless: *I make a convention with you that is entirely at your expense and entirely for my benefit; that I shall observe for as long as I want, and that you shall observe for as long as I want.*

Chapter 5
That It Is Always Necessary to Go Back
to a First Convention

Even if I were to grant everything I have thus far refuted, the proponents of despotism would be no better off. There will always be a great difference between subjugating a multitude and governing a society. If scattered men, however many there may be, are successively enslaved by one individual, I see only a master and slaves; I do not see a people and its leader. It is an aggregation, if you wish, but not an association. It has neither public good nor body politic. That man, even if he had enslaved half the world, is nothing but a private individual. His interest, separate from that of the others, is still nothing but a private interest. If this same man dies, thereafter his empire is left scattered and without bonds, just as an oak tree disintegrates and falls into a heap of ashes after fire has consumed it.

A people, says Grotius, can give itself to a king. According to Grotius, a people is therefore a people before it gives itself to a king. This gift itself is a civil act; it presupposes a public deliberation. Therefore, before examining the act by which a people elects a king, it would be well to examine the act by which a people becomes a people. For this act, being necessarily prior to the other, is the true basis of society.

Indeed, if there were no prior convention, what would become of the obligation for the minority to submit to the choice of the majority, unless the election were unanimous; and where do one hundred who want a master get the right to vote for ten who do not? The law of majority rule is itself an established convention, and presupposes unanimity at least once.

Chapter 6
On the Social Compact

I assume that men have reached the point where obstacles to their self-preservation in the state of nature prevail by their resistance over the forces each individual can use to maintain himself in that state. Then that primitive state can no longer subsist and the human race would perish if it did not change its way of life.

Now since men cannot engender new forces, but merely unite and direct existing ones, they have no other means of self-preservation except to form, by aggregation, a sum of forces that can prevail over the resistance: set them to work by a single motivation; and make them act in concert.

This sum of forces can arise only from the cooperation of many. But since each man's force and freedom are the primary instruments of his self-preservation, how is he to engage them without harming himself and without neglecting the cares he owes to himself? In the context of my subject, this difficulty can be stated in these terms:

"Find a form of association that defends and protects the person and goods of each associate with all the common force, and by means of which each one, uniting with all, nevertheless obeys only himself and remains as free as before." This is the fundamental problem which is solved by the social contract.

The clauses of this contract are so completely determined by the nature of the act that the slightest modification would render them null and void.

So that although they may never have been formally pronounced, they are everywhere the same, everywhere tacitly accepted and recognized, until the social compact is violated, at which point each man recovers his original rights and resumes his natural freedom, thereby losing the conventional freedom for which he renounced it.

Properly understood, all of these clauses come down to a single one, namely the total alienation of each associate, with all his rights, to the whole community. For first of all, since each one gives his entire self, the condition is equal for everyone, and since the condition is equal for everyone, no one has an interest in making it burdensome for the others.

Furthermore, as the alienation is made without reservation, the union is as perfect as it can be, and no associate has anything further to claim. For if some rights were left to private individuals, there would be no common superior who could judge between them and the public. Each man being his own judge on some point would soon claim to be so on all; the state of nature would subsist and the association would necessarily become tyrannical or ineffectual.

Finally, as each gives himself to all, he gives himself to no one; and since there is no associate over whom one does not acquire the same right one grants him over oneself, one gains the equivalent of everything one loses, and more force to preserve what one has.

If, then, everything that is not of the essence of the social compact is set aside, one will find that it can be reduced to the following terms. *Each of us puts his person and all his power in common under the supreme direction of the general will; and in a body we receive each member as an indivisible part of the whole.*

Instantly, in place of the private person of each contracting party, this act of association produces a moral and collective body, composed of as many members as there are voices in the assembly, which receives from this same act its unity, its common *self*, its life, and its will. This public person, formed thus by the union of all the others, formerly took the name *City*, and now takes that of *Republic* or *body politic*, which its members call *State* when it is passive, *Sovereign* when active, *Power* when comparing it to similar bodies. As for the associates, they collectively take the name *people*; and individually are called *Citizens* as participants in the sovereign authority, and *Subjects* as subject to the laws of the State. But these terms are often mixed up and mistaken for one another. It is enough to know how to distinguish them when they are used with complete precision.

Chapter 7
On the Sovereign

This formula shows that the act of association includes a reciprocal engagement between the public and private individuals, and that each individual, contracting with himself so to speak, finds that he is doubly engaged, namely toward private individuals as a member of the sovereign and toward the sovereign as a member of the State. But the maxim of civil right that no one can be held responsible for engagements toward himself cannot be applied here, because there is a great difference between being obligated to oneself, or to a whole of which one is a part.

It must further be noted that the public deliberation that can obligate all of the subjects to the sovereign—due to the two different relationships in which each of them is considered—cannot for the opposite reason obligate the sovereign toward itself; and that consequently it is contrary to the nature of the body politic for the sovereign to impose on itself a law it cannot break. Since the sovereign can only be considered in a single relationship, it is then in the situation of a private individual contracting with himself. It is apparent from this that there is not, nor can there be, any kind of fundamental law that is obligatory for the body of the people, not even the social contract. This does not mean that this body cannot perfectly well enter an engagement toward another with respect to things that do not violate this contract. For with reference to the foreigner, it becomes a simple being or individual.

But the body politic or the sovereign, deriving its being solely from the sanctity of the contract, can never obligate itself, even toward another, to do anything that violates that original act, such as to alienate some part of itself or to subject itself to another sovereign. To violate the act by which it exists would be to destroy itself, and whatever is nothing, produces nothing.

As soon as this multitude is thus united in a body, one cannot harm one of the members without attacking the body, and it is even less possible to harm the body without the members feeling the effects. Thus duty and interest equally obligate the two contracting parties to mutual assistance, and the same men should seek to combine in this double relationship all the advantages that are dependent on it.

Now the sovereign, formed solely by the private individuals composing it, does not and cannot have any interest contrary to theirs. Consequently, the sovereign power has no need of a guarantee toward the subjects, because it is impossible for the body ever to want to harm all its members, and we shall see later that it cannot harm any one of them as an individual. The sovereign, by the sole fact of being, is always what it ought to be.

But the same is not true of the subjects in relation to the sovereign, which, despite the common interest, would have no guarantee of the subjects' engagements if it did not find ways to be assured of their fidelity.

Indeed, each individual can, as a man, have a private will contrary to or differing from the general will he has as a citizen. His private interest can speak to him quite differently from the common interest. His absolute and naturally independent existence can bring him to view what he owes the common cause as a free contribution, the loss of which will harm others less than its payment burdens him. And considering the moral person of the State as an imaginary being because it is not a man, he might wish to enjoy the rights of the citizen without wanting to fulfill the duties of a subject, an injustice whose spread would cause the ruin of the body public.

Therefore, in order for the social compact not to be an ineffectual formula, it tacitly includes the following engagement, which alone can give force to the others: that whoever refuses to obey the general will shall be constrained to do so by the entire body; which means only that he will be forced to be free. For this is the condition that, by giving each citizen to the homeland, guarantees him against all personal dependence; a condition that creates the ingenuity and functioning of the political machine, and alone gives legitimacy to civil engagements which without it would be absurd, tyrannical, and subject to the most enormous abuses.

Chapter 8
On the Civil State

This passage from the state of nature to the civil state produces a remarkable change in man, by substituting justice for instinct in his behavior and giving his actions the morality they previously lacked. Only then, when the voice of duty replaces physical impulse and right replaces appetite, does man, who until that time only considered himself, find himself forced to act upon other principles and to consult his reason before heeding his inclinations. Although in this state he deprives himself of several advantages given him by nature, he gains such great ones, his faculties are exercised and developed, his ideas broadened, his feelings ennobled, and his whole soul elevated to such a point that if the abuses of this new condition did not often degrade him beneath the condition he left, he ought ceaselessly to bless the happy moment that tore him away from it forever, and that changed him from a stupid, limited animal into an intelligent being and a man.

Let us reduce the pros and cons to easily compared terms. What man loses by the social contract is his natural freedom and an unlimited right to everything that tempts him and that he can get; what he gains is civil freedom and the proprietorship of everything he possesses. In order not to be mistaken about these compensations, one must distinguish carefully between natural freedom, which is limited only by the force of the individual, and civil freedom, which is limited by the general will; and between possession, which is only the effect of force or the right of the first occupant, and property, which can only be based on a positive title.

To the foregoing acquisitions of the civil state could be added moral freedom, which alone makes man truly the master of himself. For the impulse of appetite alone is slavery, and obedience to the law one has prescribed for oneself is freedom. But I have already said too much about this topic, and the philosophic meaning of the word *freedom* is not my subject here.

Chapter 9
On Real Estate

Each member of the community gives himself to it at the moment of its formation, just as he currently is—both himself and all his force, which includes the goods he possesses. It is not that by this act possession, in changing hands, changes its nature and becomes property in the hands of the sovereign. But as the force of the City is incomparably greater than that of a private individual, public possession is by that very fact stronger and more irrevocable, without being more legitimate, at least as far as foreigners are concerned. For with regard to its members, the State is master of all their goods through the social contract, which serves within the State as the basis of all rights. But with regard to other powers, it is master only through the right of the first occupant, which it derives from the private individuals.

The right of the first occupant, although more real than the right of the strongest, becomes a true right only after the establishment of the right of property. Every man naturally has a right to everything he needs; but the positive act that makes him the proprietor of some good excludes him from all the rest. Once his portion is designated, he should limit himself to it, and no longer has any right to the community's goods. That is why the right of the first occupant, so weak in the state of nature, is respectable to every civilized man. In this right, one respects not so much what belongs to others as what does not belong to oneself. . . .

What is extraordinary about this alienation is that far from plundering private individuals of their goods, by accepting them the community thereby only assures them of legitimate possession, changes usurpation into a true right, and use into property. Then, since the possessors are considered as trustees of the public goods, and since their rights are respected by all the members of the State and maintained with all its force against foreigners, through a transfer that is advantageous to the public and even more so to themselves, they have, so to speak, acquired all they have given. This paradox is easily explained by the distinction between the rights of the sovereign and of the proprietor to the same resource, as will be seen hereafter.

It can also happen that men start to unite before possessing anything and that subsequently taking over a piece of land sufficient for all, they use it in common or divide it among themselves, either equally or according to proportions established by the sovereign. However this acquisition is made, the right of each private individual to his own resources is always subordinate to the community's right to all, without which there would be neither solidity in the social bond nor real force in the exercise of sovereignty.

I shall end this chapter and this book with a comment that ought to serve as the basis of the whole social system. It is that rather than destroying natural equality, the fundamental compact on the contrary substitutes a moral and legitimate equality for whatever physical inequality nature may have placed between men, and that although they may be unequal in force or in genius, they all become equal through convention and by right.[1]

Book II

Chapter 1
That Sovereignty Is Inalienable

The first and most important consequence of the principles established above is that the general will alone can guide the forces of the State according to the end for which it was instituted, which is the common good. For if the opposition of private interests made the establishment of societies necessary, it is the agreement of these same interests that made it possible. It is what these different interests have in common that forms the social bond, and if there were not some point at which all the interests are in agreement, no society could exist. Now it is uniquely on the basis of this common interest that society ought to be governed.

---

1. Under bad governments, this equality is only apparent and illusory. It serves merely to maintain the poor man in his misery and the rich in his usurpation. In fact, laws are always useful to those who have possessions and harmful to those who have nothing. It follows from this that the social state is only advantageous to men insofar as they all have something and none of them has anything superfluous.

I say, therefore, that sovereignty, being only the exercise of the general will, can never be alienated, and that the sovereign, which is only a collective being, can only be represented by itself. Power can perfectly well be transferred, but not will.

Indeed, though it is not impossible for a private will to agree with the general will on a given point, it is impossible, at least, for this agreement to be lasting and unchanging. For the private will tends by its nature toward preferences, and the general will toward equality. It is even more impossible for there to be a guarantee of this agreement even should it always exist. It would not be the result of art, but of chance. The sovereign may well say, "I currently want what a particular man wants, or at least what he says he wants." But it cannot say, "What that man will want tomorrow, I shall still want," since it is absurd for the will to tie itself down for the future and since no will can consent to anything that is contrary to the good of the being that wills. Therefore, if the people promises simply to obey, it dissolves itself by that act; it loses the status of a people. The moment there is a master, there is no longer a sovereign, and from then on the body politic is destroyed.

This is not to say that the commands of leaders cannot pass for expressions of the general will, as long as the sovereign, being free to oppose them, does not do so. In such a case, one ought to presume the consent of the people from universal silence. This will be explained at greater length.

Chapter 2
That Sovereignty Is Indivisible

For the same reason that sovereignty is inalienable, it is indivisible. Because either the will is general[2] or it is not. It is the will of the people as a body, or of only a part. In the first case, this declared will is an act of sovereignty and constitutes law. In the second case, it is merely a private will or an act of magistracy; it is at most a decree.

But our political theorists, unable to divide the principle of sovereignty, divide it in its object. They divide it into force and will; into legislative power and executive power; into rights of taxation, justice, and war; into internal administration and power to negotiate with foreigners. Sometimes they mix all these parts together, sometimes they separate them. They turn the sovereign into a fantastic body formed of bits and pieces. It is as though they constructed a man out of several bodies, one of which would have eyes, another arms, another feet, and nothing more. Japanese charlatans are said to cut up a child right in front of the audience; then, tossing all the parts into the air one after another, they make the child come back down alive and in one piece. The juggling acts of our political theorists are about like that. After they have taken the social body apart by a trick worthy of a carnival, they put the pieces back together in some unknown way.

This error comes from not having developed precise concepts of sovereign authority, and from having mistaken for parts of that authority what were merely emanations from it. Thus, for example, the acts of declaring war and making peace have been regarded as acts of sovereignty, which they

---

2. In order for a will to be general, it is not always necessary for it to be unanimous, but it is necessary that all votes be counted. Any formal exclusion destroys the generality.

are not, since each of these acts is not a law but merely an application of the law, a particular act which determines the legal situation, as will be clearly seen when the idea attached to the word *law* is established.

By examining the other divisions in the same way, it would be found that every time it is thought that sovereignty is divided, a mistake has been made, and that the rights that are mistaken for parts of that sovereignty are always subordinate to it and always presuppose supreme wills which these rights merely execute. . . .

Chapter 3
Whether the General Will Can Err

From the foregoing it follows that the general will is always right and always tends toward the public utility. But it does not follow that the people's deliberations always have the same rectitude. One always wants what is good for oneself, but one does not always see it. The people is never corrupted, but it is often fooled, and only then does it appear to want what is bad.

There is often a great difference between the will of all and the general will. The latter considers only the common interest; the former considers private interest, and is only a sum of private wills. But take away from these same wills the pluses and minuses that cancel each other out,[3] and the remaining sum of the differences is the general will.

If, when an adequately informed people deliberates, the citizens were to have no communication among themselves, the general will would always result from the large number of small differences, and the deliberation would always be good. But when factions, partial associations at the expense of the whole, are formed, the will of each of these associations becomes general with reference to its members and particular with reference to the State. One can say, then, that there are no longer as many voters as there are men, but merely as many as there are associations. The differences become less numerous and produce a result that is less general. Finally, when one of these associations is so big that it prevails over all the others, the result is no longer a sum of small differences, but a single difference. Then there is no longer a general will, and the opinion that prevails is merely a private opinion.

In order for the general will to be well expressed, it is therefore important that there be no partial society in the State, and that each citizen give only his own opinion. Such was the unique and sublime system instituted by the great Lycurgus. If there are partial societies, their number must be multiplied and their inequality prevented, as was done by Solon, Numa, and Servius. These precautions are the only valid means of ensuring that the general will is always enlightened and that the people is not deceived.

---

3. *Each interest,* says the Marquis d'Argenson, *has different principles. The agreement of two private interests is formed in opposition to the interest of a third.* He could have added that the agreement of all interests is formed in opposition to the interest of each. If there were no different interests, the common interest, which would never encounter any obstacle, would scarcely be felt. Everything would run smoothly by itself and politics would cease to be an art.

Chapter 4
On the Limits of the Sovereign Power

If the State or the City is only a moral person whose life consists in the union of its members, and if the most important of its concerns is that of its own preservation, it must have a universal, compulsory force to move and arrange each part in the manner best suited to the whole. Just as nature gives each man absolute power over all his members, the social compact gives the body politic absolute power over all its members, and it is this same power, directed by the general will, which as I have said bears the name sovereignty.

But in addition to the public person, we have to consider the private persons who compose it and whose life and freedom are naturally independent of it. It is a matter, then, of making a clear distinction between the respective rights of the citizens and the sovereign,[4] and between the duties that the former have to fulfill as subjects and the natural rights to which they are entitled as men.

It is agreed that each person alienates through the social compact only that part of his power, goods, and freedom whose use matters to the community; but it must also be agreed that the sovereign alone is the judge of what matters.

A citizen owes the State all the services he can render it as soon as the sovereign requests them. But the sovereign, for its part, cannot impose on the subjects any burden that is useless to the community. It cannot even will to do so, for under the law of reason nothing is done without a cause, any more than under the law of nature.

The engagements that bind us to the social body are obligatory only because they are mutual, and their nature is such that in fulfilling them one cannot work for someone else without also working for oneself. Why is the general will always right and why do all constantly want the happiness of each, if not because there is no one who does not apply this word *each* to himself, and does not think of himself as he votes for all? Which proves that the equality of right, and the concept of justice it produces, are derived from each man's preference for himself and consequently from the nature of man; that the general will, to be truly such, should be general in its object as well as in its essence; that it should come from all to apply to all; and that it loses its natural rectitude when it is directed toward any individual, determinate object. Because then, judging what is foreign to us, we have no true principle of equity to guide us.

Indeed, as soon as it is a matter of fact or a particular right concerning a point that has not been regulated by a prior, general convention, the affair is in dispute. It is a lawsuit where the interested private individuals constitute one party and the public the other, but in which I see neither what law must be followed nor what judge should decide. In this case it would be ridiculous to want to turn to an express decision of the general will, which can only be the conclusion of one of the parties and which, for the other

---

4. Attentive readers, please do not be in a hurry to accuse me of inconsistency here. I have been unable to avoid it in my terminology, given the poverty of the language. But wait.

party, is consequently only a foreign, private will, showing injustice on this occasion and subject to error. Thus just as a private will cannot represent the general will, the general will in turn changes its nature when it has a particular object; and as a general will it cannot pass judgment on either a man or a fact. When the people of Athens, for example, appointed or dismissed its leaders, awarded honors to one or imposed penalties on another, and by means of a multitude of particular decrees performed indistinguishably all the acts of government, the people then no longer had a general will properly speaking. It no longer acted as sovereign, but as magistrate. This will appear contrary to commonly held ideas, but you must give me time to present my own.

It should be understood from this that what generalizes the will is not so much the number of votes as the common interest that unites them, because in this institution everyone necessarily subjects himself to the conditions he imposes on others, an admirable agreement between interest and justice which confers on common deliberations a quality of equity that vanishes in the discussion of private matters, for want of a common interest that unites and identifies the rule of the judge with that of the party.

However one traces the principle, one always reaches the same conclusion, namely that the social compact established an equality between the citizens such that they all engage themselves under the same conditions and should all benefit from the same rights. Thus by the very nature of the compact, every act of sovereignty, which is to say every authentic act of the general will, obligates or favors all citizens equally, so that the sovereign knows only the nation as a body and makes no distinctions between any of those who compose it. What really is an act of sovereignty then? It is not a convention between a superior and an inferior, but a convention between the body and each of its members. A convention that is legitimate because it has the social contract as a basis; equitable, because it is common to all; useful, because it can have no other object than the general good; and solid, because it has the public force and the supreme power as guarantee. As long as subjects are subordinated only to such conventions, they do not obey anyone, but solely their own will; and to ask how far the respective rights of the sovereign and of citizens extend is to ask how far the latter can engage themselves to one another, each to all and all to each.

It is apparent from this that the sovereign power, albeit entirely absolute, entirely sacred, and entirely inviolable, does not and cannot exceed the limits of the general conventions, and that every man can fully dispose of the part of his goods and freedom that has been left to him by these conventions. So that the sovereign never has the right to burden one subject more than another, because then the matter becomes individual, and its power is no longer competent.

Once these distinctions are acknowledged, it is so false that the social contract involves any true renunciation on the part of private individuals that their situation, by the effect of this contract, is actually preferable to what it was beforehand; and instead of an alienation, they have only exchanged to their advantage an uncertain, precarious mode of existence for another that is better and safer; natural independence for freedom; the power to harm others for their personal safety; and their force, which others could overcome, for a right which the social union makes invincible. Their life itself, which they have dedicated to the State, is constantly protected by it; and when they risk it for the State's defense, what are they then doing except to give back to the State what they have received from it? What are they doing that they did not do more often and with greater danger in the state of nature, when waging inevitable fights they defend at the risk of their life that which preserves it for them? It is true that everyone has to fight, if need be, for the homeland, but also no one ever has to fight for himself. Don't we still gain by risking, for something that gives us security, a part of what we would have to risk for ourselves as soon as our security is taken away? . . .

Chapter 7
On the Legislator

The discovery of the best rules of society suited to nations would require a superior intelligence, who saw all of men's passions yet experienced none of them; who had no relationship at all to our nature yet knew it thoroughly; whose happiness was independent of us, yet who was nevertheless willing to attend to ours; finally one who, preparing for himself a future glory with the passage of time, could work in one century and enjoy the reward in another. Gods would be needed to give laws to men.

The same reasoning Caligula used with respect to fact was used by Plato with respect to right in defining the civil or royal man he seeks in the *Statesman*. But if it is true that a great prince is a rare man, what about a great legislator? The former only has to follow the model that the latter should propose. The latter is the mechanic who invents the machine; the former is only the workman who puts it together and starts it running. At the birth of societies, says Montesquieu, the leaders of republics create the institutions; thereafter, it is the institutions that form the leaders of republics.

One who dares to undertake the founding of a people should feel that he is capable of changing human nature, so to speak; of transforming each individual, who by himself is a perfect and solitary whole, into a part of a larger whole from which this individual receives, in a sense, his life and his being; of altering man's constitution in order to strengthen it; of substituting a partial and moral existence for the physical and independent existence we have all received from nature. He must, in short, take away man's own forces in order to give him forces that are foreign to him and that he cannot make use of without the help of others. The more these natural forces are dead and destroyed, and the acquired ones great and lasting, the more the institution as well is solid and perfect. So that if each citizen is nothing, and can do nothing, except with all the others, and if the force acquired by the whole is equal or superior to the sum of the natural forces of all the individuals, it may be said that legislation has reached its highest possible point of perfection.

The legislator is an extraordinary man in the State in all respects. If he should be so by his genius, he is no less so by his function. It is not magistracy, it is not sovereignty. This function, which constitutes the republic, does not enter into its constitution. It is a particular and superior activity that has nothing in common with human dominion. For if one who has authority over men should not have authority over laws, one who has authority over laws should also not have authority over men. Otherwise his laws, ministers of his passions, would often only perpetuate his injustices, and he could never avoid having private views alter the sanctity of his work.

When Lycurgus gave his homeland laws, he began by abdicating the throne. It was the custom of most Greek cities to entrust the establishment of their laws to foreigners. The modern republics of Italy often imitated this practice. The republic of Geneva did so too, with good results. During its finest period Rome saw all the crimes of tyranny revived in its midst, and nearly perished as a result of combining legislative authority and sovereign power in the same hands.

However even the Decemvirs never took upon themselves the right to have any law passed solely on their authority. *Nothing that we propose*, they said to the people, *can become law without your consent. Romans, be yourselves the authors of the laws that should create your happiness.*

He who drafts the laws, therefore, does not or should not have any legislative right. And the people itself cannot, even if it wanted to, divest itself of this incommunicable right, because according to the fundamental compact, only the general will obligates private individuals, and one can never be assured that a private will is in conformity with the general will until it has been submitted to the free vote of the people. I have already said this, but it is not useless to repeat it.

Thus one finds combined in the work of legislation two things that seem incompatible: an undertaking beyond human force and, to execute it, an authority that amounts to nothing.

Another difficulty deserves attention. Wise men who want to use their own language, rather than that of the common people, cannot be understood by the people. Now there are a thousand kinds of ideas that are impossible to translate into the language of the people. Overly general views and overly remote objects are equally beyond its grasp. Each individual, appreciating no other aspect of government than the one that relates to his private interest, has difficulty perceiving the advantages he should obtain from the continual deprivations imposed by good laws. In order for an emerging people to appreciate the healthy maxims of politics, and follow the fundamental rules of statecraft, the effect would have to become the cause; the social spirit, which should be the result of the institution, would have to preside over the founding of the institution itself; and men would have to be prior to laws what they ought to become by means of laws. Since the legislator is therefore unable to use either force or reasoning, he must necessarily have recourse to another order of authority, which can win over without violence and persuade without convincing.

This is what has always forced the fathers of nations to have recourse to the intervention of heaven and to attribute their own wisdom to the Gods; so that the peoples, subjected to the laws of the State as to those of nature, and recognizing the same power in the formation of man and of the City, might obey with freedom and bear with docility the yoke of public felicity.

It is this sublime reason, which rises above the grasp of common men, whose decisions the legislator places in the mouth of the immortals in order to convince by divine authority those who cannot be moved by human prudence. But it is not every man who can make the Gods speak or be believed when he declares himself their interpreter. The legislator's great soul is the true miracle that should prove his mission. Any man can engrave stone tablets, buy an oracle, pretend to have a secret relationship with some divinity, train a bird to talk in his ear, or find other crude ways to impress the people. One who knows only that much might even assemble, by chance, a crowd of madmen, but he will never found an empire, and his extravagant work will soon die along with him. False tricks can form a fleeting bond; wisdom alone can make it durable. The Jewish law, which is still in existence, and the law of the son of Ishmael, which has ruled half the world for ten centuries, still bear witness today to the great men who formulated them. And whereas proud philosophy or blind partisan spirit regards them merely as lucky imposters, the true political theorist admires in their institutions that great and powerful genius which presides over lasting establishments.

One must not conclude from all this, as Warburton does, that politics and religion have a common object for us, but rather that at the origin of nations, one serves as an instrument of the other....

Book III

Chapter 1
On Government in General

I warn the reader that this chapter should be read carefully, and that I do not know the art of being clear for those who are not willing to be attentive.

Every free action has two causes that combine to produce it. One is moral, namely the will that determines the act; the other is physical, namely the power that executes it. When I walk toward an object, I must first want to go there, and in the second place my feet must take me there. A paralyzed man who wants to run, or an agile man who does not want to do so, will both remain where they are. The body politic has the same motivating causes; force and will are distinguishable within it in the same sense, the latter under the name *legislative power* and the former under the name *executive power*. Nothing is or should be done there without their cooperation.

We have seen that the legislative power belongs to the people and can belong only to it. It is easy to see, on the contrary, by the principles already established, that the executive power cannot belong to the general public in its legislator's or sovereign capacity, because this power consists solely of particular acts which are not within the jurisdiction of the law, nor consequently of the sovereign, all of whose acts can only be laws.

The public force must therefore have its own agent, which unites it and puts it into operation according to the directions of the general will; which serves as a means of communication between the State and the sovereign; and which does in a sense for the public person what the union of the soul and the body does in man. This is the reason why, in the State, there is government, which has been incorrectly confounded with the sovereign, of which it is only the minister.

What is the government then? An intermediate body established between the subjects and the sovereign for their mutual communication, and charged with the execution of the laws and the maintenance of civil as well as political freedom.

The members of this body are called magistrates or *kings*, that is to say *governors*; and the body as a whole bears the name *prince*. Thus those who claim that the act by which a people subjects itself to leaders is not a contract are entirely right. It is absolutely nothing but a commission, a function in which, as simple officers of the sovereign, they exercise in its name the power that has been entrusted to them by the sovereign, and that the sovereign can limit, modify, and take back whenever it pleases, since the alienation of such a right is incompatible with the nature of the social body and contrary to the goal of the association.

I therefore give the name *government* or supreme administration to the legitimate exercise of the executive power, and Prince or magistrate to the man or the body charged with that administration.

It is in the government that are found the intermediate forces whose relationships compose the relationship of the whole to the whole or of the sovereign to the State. The latter relationship can be represented by the extremes of a continuous proportion, of which the proportional mean is the government. The government receives from the sovereign the orders that it gives to the people; and in order for the State to be in good equilibrium, all things considered, the product or power of the government, taken by itself, must be equal to the product or power of the citizens, who are sovereigns on the one hand and subjects on the other.

Moreover, none of the three terms could be altered without simultaneously destroying the proportion. If the sovereign wants to govern, or if the magistrate wants to make laws, or if the subjects refuse to obey, disorder replaces rule, force and will no longer act in concert, and the dissolved State thereby falls into despotism or anarchy. Finally, since there is only one proportional mean for each relationship, there is no more than one good government possible in a State. But as a thousand events can change the relationships of a people, not only can different governments be suited to various peoples, but also to the same people at different times.

To try to give some idea of the various relationships that can exist between these two extremes, I shall take as an example the number of people, which is a comparatively easy relationship to express.

Let us suppose that the State is composed of ten thousand citizens. The sovereign can only be considered collectively and as a body. But each private individual in his status as a subject is considered as an individual. Thus the sovereign is to the subject as ten thousand is to one. Which is to say that the share of each member of the State is only one ten-thousandth of the sovereign authority, even though he is totally subjected to it. If the people is composed of one hundred thousand men, the condition of the subjects does not change, and each is equally under the whole dominion of the laws, while his vote, reduced to one hundred-thousandth, has ten times less influence on their drafting. Thus since the subject always remains one, the ratio of the sovereign to the subject increases in proportion to the number of citizens. From which it follows that the larger the State grows, the less freedom there is.

When I say that the ratio increases, I mean that it grows further away from equality. Thus the greater the ratio in the geometrician's sense, the less relationship there is in the ordinary sense. In the former, the ratio—

considered in terms of quantity—is measured by the quotient, and in the latter, the relationship—considered in terms of likeness—is estimated by the similarity.

Now the less relationship there is between private wills and the general will, that is between the mores and the laws, the more repressive force should increase. Thus, in order for the government to be good, it ought to be relatively stronger in proportion as the people is more numerous.

On the other hand, as the enlargement of the State gives those entrusted with the public authority more temptations and means to abuse their power, the more force the government should have to restrain the people, the more the sovereign should have in turn to restrain the government. I am not speaking here of absolute force, but of the relative force of the various parts of the State.

It follows from this double relationship that the continuous proportion between the sovereign, the prince, and the people is no arbitrary idea, but rather a necessary consequence of the nature of the body politic. It also follows that since one of the extremes, namely the people as subject, is fixed and represented by unity, whenever the doubled ratio increases or decreases, the simple ratio increases or decreases similarly; and that consequently the middle term is changed. This shows that there is no unique and absolute constitution of government, but that there can be as many governments of different natures as there are States of different sizes.

If in ridiculing this system, it was said that in order to find this proportional mean and form the body of the government, it is only necessary, according to me, to calculate the square root of the number of people, I would reply that I merely use that number here as an example; that the relationships of which I speak are not measured solely by the number of men, but in general by the quantity of action, which is itself the combined result of a multitude of causes; and moreover that if I momentarily borrow the vocabulary of geometry in order to express myself in fewer words, I am nevertheless not unaware that geometric precision does not exist in moral quantities.

The government is on a small scale what the body politic that contains it is on a large scale. It is a moral person, endowed with certain faculties; active like the sovereign, passive like the State; and that can be broken down into other similar relationships from which a new proportion consequently arises, and still another within this one according to the order of tribunals, until an indivisible middle term is reached; that is, a single leader or supreme magistrate, who can be considered, in the middle of this progression, as the unity between the series of fractions and that of whole numbers.

Without becoming involved in this multiplication of terms, let us be satisfied to consider the government as a new body in the State, distinct from both the people and the sovereign, and intermediate between them.

The essential difference between these two bodies is that the State exists by itself, but the government exists only through the sovereign. Thus the dominant will of the prince is not or should not be anything except the general will or the law; his force is only the public force concentrated in him. As soon as he wants to derive from himself some absolute and independent act, the bond tying the whole together begins to loosen. If it finally came about that the prince had a private will more active than that of the sovereign, and that he used some of the public force at his discretion to obey that private will, so that there were, so to speak, two sovereigns—one by right, the other in fact—at that moment the social union would vanish and the body politic would be dissolved.

However, in order for the body of the government to exist, to have a real life that distinguishes it from the body of the State, and for all its members to be able to act in concert and fulfill the purpose for which it is instituted, it must have a separate *self*, a sensibility shared by its members, a force or will of its own that leads to its preservation. This separate existence supposes assemblies, councils, power to deliberate and decide, rights, titles, privileges that belong exclusively to the prince and that make the magistrate's status more honorable in proportion as it is more laborious. The difficulties lie in organizing this subordinate whole within the whole in such a way that it does not change the general constitution by strengthening its own; that it always distinguishes between its separate force intended for its own preservation and the public force intended for the preservation of the State; and in short that it is ever ready to sacrifice the government to the people and not the people to the government.

Besides, although the artificial body of the government is the product of another artificial body and has, in a sense, only a borrowed and subordinate life, this does not prevent it from acting with more or less vigor or speed, or from enjoying a more or less robust state of health, so to speak. Finally, without directly departing from the goal of its institution, it can deviate from that goal to a greater or lesser extent according to the way in which it is constituted.

From all these differences arise the various relationships the government ought to have with the body of the State, according to the accidental and particular relationships that modify a given State. For often the government that is in itself the best will become the worst if its relationships are not modified according to the defects of the body politic to which it belongs.

Chapter 2
On the Principle that Constitutes the Various Forms of the Government

In order to present the general cause of these differences, it is necessary here to distinguish between the prince and the government, as I have already distinguished between the State and the sovereign.

The body of the magistracy can be composed of a larger or smaller number of members. We have said that the ratio of the sovereign to the subjects was greater as the people was more numerous, and by an obvious analogy we can say the same about the government with reference to the magistrates.

Now the total force of the government, being always that of the State, does not vary; from which it follows that the more of this force the government uses on its own members, the less is left for acting upon the entire people.

Therefore, the more numerous the magistrates, the weaker the government. Since this maxim is fundamental, let us try to explain it more clearly.

We can distinguish three essentially different wills in the person of the magistrate. First, the individual's own will, which tends only toward his private advantage. Second, the common will of the magistrates, which relates uniquely to the advantage of the prince; which may be called the corporate will, and is general in relation to the government and private in relation to the State, of which the government is a part. Third, the will of the people or the sovereign will, which is general both in relation to the State considered as the whole and in relation to the government considered as part of that whole.

In perfect legislation, the private or individual will should be null; the corporate will of the government very subordinate; and consequently the general or sovereign will always dominant and the unique rule of all the others.

According to the natural order, on the contrary, these different wills become more active as they are more concentrated. Thus the general will is always the weakest, the corporate will has second place, and the private will is the first of all. So that each member of the government is first himself, and then magistrate, and then citizen—a gradation that is exactly opposite to the one required by the social order.

Given the above, suppose that the entire government is in the hands of one man. Then the private will and the corporate will are perfectly combined, and consequently the latter attains the highest possible degree of intensity. Now as the use of force is dependent on the degree of will, and as the absolute force of the government does not vary, it follows that the most active of governments is that of one man.

On the contrary, let us combine the government with the legislative authority; let us make the prince out of the sovereign and all of the citizens into as many magistrates. Then the corporate will has no more activity than the general will with which it is combined, and leaves to the particular will its full force. Thus the government, always with the same absolute force, will have the minimum relative force or activity.

These relationships are incontestable and are further confirmed by other considerations. It is apparent, for example, that each magistrate is more active in his group than each citizen in his, and consequently that the private will has much more influence on acts of the government than on those of the sovereign. For each magistrate is almost always responsible for some function of the government, whereas each citizen, taken separately, performs no function of sovereignty. Besides, the more the State expands, the more its real force increases, although not in proportion to its size. But if the State stays the same, increasing the number of magistrates is useless; the government does not thereby acquire greater real force, because this force is that of the State, whose size is unchanged. Thus the relative force or the activity of the government diminishes, while its absolute or real force cannot increase.

It is also certain that business is expedited more slowly in proportion as more people are responsible for it; that by overestimating prudence, chance is underestimated, opportunity escapes, and by dint of deliberating, the fruits of deliberation are often lost.

I have just proved that the government becomes slack in proportion as the magistrates multiply, and I have proved earlier that the more numerous the people, the greater the increase in repressive force should be. From which it follows that the ratio of magistrates to government should be the inverse of the ratio of subjects to sovereign, which means that the more the State grows, the more the government should shrink, so that the number of leaders diminishes in proportion to the increase of people.

However, I refer here only to the relative force of the government, and not to its rectitude. For on the contrary, the more numerous the body of magistrates, the closer the corporate will is to the general will, whereas under a unique magistrate, this same corporate will, as I have said, is merely a private will. Thus what can be gained on one side is lost on the other, and the legislator's art is knowing how to find the point at which the government's force and will, always in a reciprocal proportion, are combined in the relationship most advantageous to the State.

Chapter 3
Classification of Governments

In the preceding chapter, we have seen why the various kinds or forms of governments are distinguished by the number of members composing them. It remains to be seen in this chapter how this classification is made.

The sovereign can, in the first place, entrust the government to the entire people or to the majority of people, so that there are more citizens who are magistrates than citizens who are simply private individuals. This form of government is given the name *democracy*.

Or else it can restrict the government to the hands of a small number, so that there are more simple citizens than magistrates; and this form bears the name *aristocracy*.

Finally, it can concentrate the whole government in the hands of a single magistrate from whom all the others derive their power. This third form is the most common, and is called *monarchy* or royal government.

It should be noted that all these forms, or at least the first two, admit different degrees, and even have a rather broad range. For democracy can include all the people, or be restricted to half. In turn, aristocracy can be indeterminately restricted from half the people down to the smallest number. Even royalty admits some division. Sparta constantly had two kings as provided by its constitution; and in the Roman Empire there were as many as eight emperors at a time, yet one couldn't say that the Empire was divided. Thus there is a point at which each form of government is indistinguishable from the next, and it is apparent that under these three names, government really admits as many diverse forms as there are citizens in the State.

Furthermore, since this same government can, in certain respects, be subdivided into other segments, one administered in one way, the other in another, the combination of these three forms can produce a multitude of mixed forms, each of which can be multiplied by all the simple forms.

People have always argued a great deal over the best form of government, without considering that each of them is the best in certain cases, and the worst in others.

If the number of supreme magistrates in different States ought to be in inverse proportion to the number of citizens, it follows that in general democratic government is suited to small States, aristocratic to medium-sized ones, and monarchical to large ones. This rule is derived directly from the principle; but countless circumstances can furnish exceptions. . . .

Book IV

Chapter 1
That the General Will Is Indestructible

As long as several men together consider themselves to be a single body, they have only a single will, which relates to their common preservation and the general welfare. Then all the mechanisms of the State are vigorous and simple, its maxims are clear and luminous, it has no tangled, contradictory interests; the common good is clearly apparent everywhere, and requires only good sense to be perceived. Peace, union, and equality are enemies of political subtleties. Upright and simple men are hard to fool because of their simplicity; traps and refined pretexts do not deceive them. They are not even clever enough to be duped. When, among the happiest people in the world, groups of peasants are seen deciding the affairs of State under an oak tree, and always acting wisely, can one help scorning the refinements of other nations, which make themselves illustrious and miserable with so much art and mystery?

A State governed in this way needs very few laws, and to the degree that it becomes necessary to promulgate new ones, this necessity is universally seen. The first to propose them merely states what everyone has already felt, and there is no question of intrigues nor of eloquence to pass into law what each has already resolved to do as soon as he is sure that others will do likewise.

What misleads reasoners, who only see States that have been badly constituted from the beginning, is that they are struck by the impossibility of maintaining similar order in such States. They laugh when they imagine all the nonsense that a clever swindler or an insinuating talker could put over on the people of Paris or London. They don't know that Cromwell would have been condemned to hard labor by the people of Berne, and the Duc de Beaufort sentenced to the reformatory by the Genevans.

But when the social tie begins to slacken and the State to grow weak; when private interests start to make themselves felt and small societies to influence the large one, the common interest changes and is faced with opponents; unanimity no longer prevails in the votes; the general will is no longer the will of all; contradictions and debates arise and the best advice is not accepted without disputes.

Finally, when the State, close to its ruin, continues to subsist only in an illusory and ineffectual form; when the social bond is broken in all hearts; when the basest interest brazenly adopts the sacred name of the public good, then the general will becomes mute; all—guided by secret motives —are no more citizens in offering their opinions than if the State had never existed, and iniquitous decrees whose only goal is the private interest are falsely passed under the name of laws.

Does it follow from this that the general will is annihilated or corrupted? No, it is always constant, unalterable, and pure. But it is subordinate to others that prevail over it. Each person, detaching his interest from the common interest, sees perfectly well that he cannot completely separate himself from it; but his share of the public misfortune seems like nothing to him compared to the exclusive good that he claims he is getting. With the exception of this private good, he wants the general good in his own interest just as vigorously as anyone else. Even in selling his vote for money, he doesn't extinguish the general will within himself, he evades it. The mistake he makes is to change the state of the question and to answer something other than what he is asked. So that rather than saying through his vote *it is advantageous to the State,* he says *it is advantageous to a given man or to a given party for a given motion to pass.* Thus the law of public order in assemblies is not so much to maintain the general will therein as it is to be sure that it is always questioned and that it always answers.

I could make many comments here about the simple right to vote in every act of sovereignty—a right that nothing can take away from the citizens; and on the right to give an opinion, to make propositions, to analyze, to discuss, which the government is always very careful to allow only to its members. But this important subject would require a separate treatise, and I cannot say everything in this one. . . .

Rousseau, Nature and History
Asher Horowitz

The Presuppositions of Historicity

. . . Rousseau's reconstruction of human history, his version of savage man, is, to be sure, an abstraction. It is, however, meant to be utterly unlike the abstractions performed by Hobbes, Locke, and the natural-law school. Their versions of nature stop with essentially civilized men existing outside political society but embedded in highly developed social relations patterned after the market. Rousseau's savage man is truly solitary and an animal. The device of abstracting from existing social relations has also in his hands a different aim. Rousseau's original man is an abstraction not from an essentially static social condition that can be opposed to an equally static nature but from a dynamic process of development. In order to be able to reconstruct the development process logically, Rousseau requires a starting-point that embodies several presuppositions. . . . [T]hese do not include the assumption of a metaphysical gap between man and animals. Savage man is therefore an animal of a peculiar sort. Like any other he is endowed with drives and desires for the physical necessities of life. He is also equipped with a particular anatomical structure and a sensorium compatible with his self-preservation. Yet in order to assure a human 'species' able to emerge from nature, Rousseau must make further presuppositions. The abstraction that he calls 'l'homme sauvage' is not simply an ideal of freedom and happiness against which the misery and oppression of the social state can be measured. He is also the hypothetically real starting-point of a hypothetically real historical evolution. A further presupposition must follow if savage man, 'dull and stupid,' lazy and self-sufficient, is to be capable of both accomplishing the transition to a historical existence and undergoing the transformation associated with it.

The further presuppositions required are concerned with the biopsychological structure of the human animal. [T]hese peculiarities, which are presuppositions of proto-human and human openness to historical development, also constitute a fateful dimension of the process of real historical development. As we shall see, it is the unique malleability of the human drive that both permits the emergence of a historical existence and constitutes the chief source of the human capacity for psychic misery.

Savage man in *his* mode of existence is, to begin with, virtually indistinguishable from other animals, a variety in whom Rousseau tends to see nothing more than an 'ingenious machine' (*DOI*[1] 169). Animal existence in general is governed by a homeostatic principle. And the equilibrium this principle demands is established through an inherited repertoire of instinctual behaviours. In thus championing the role of instinct in animal behaviour, Rousseau was going against the tendency of sensationalist psychology to make even animals into blank slates, their behaviour

Excerpts from Asher Horowitz, 1987, *Rousseau Nature and History.* Toronto: University of Toronto Press, pp. 67–85. Reprinted with permission of University of Toronto Press.

1. Discourse on the Origin of Inequality in *The Social Contract and Discourses,* trans. by G. D. H. Cole (London: Dent, 1968).

governed by the patterned associations of sensory experience. Animals are endowed with a complex of instincts responsible for the preservation of the individual in the species; this is one of the meanings of *amour-de-soi*. And, to the degree to which they are social, animals are endowed with mechanisms for checking the expression of aggression and facilitating identification with their fellows. Savage man shares this endowment (*DOI* 169). There is thus in every animal, and in the proto-human to begin with, a kind of pre-adaptation of the organism to its environment, a unity of instinct and instinctual aim that underlies the psychological unity of the organism. The proto-human, since he has not dispensed with instinctual forms of self-regulation, can therefore be essentially independent of the other members of his species. At this stage and only at this stage is he truly an atom, and moreover an atom that is fundamentally contented, since the environment offers him immediately (that is, without reflection, labour, co-operation, communication, or the postponement of drive-gratifying behaviour) whatever he is capable of wanting. What he might want is identical to what he is programmed and adapted to pursue. Like all other animals he lives entirely in the here and now: 'His soul, which nothing disturbs, is wholly wrapped up in the feeling of its present existence, without any idea of the future, however near at hand' (*DOI* 172). There is, as it were, no difference between satisfying the demands of reality and pursuing his immediate desires, no distinction between reality principle and pleasure principle, a perfect identity of subject and object, because subject and object do not yet exist.

These qualities, this mode of existence, the proto-human shares with animal life in general. At this stage what separates him from the rest is the degree to which his instincts are 'open' rather than 'closed.'[2] Closed instincts are patterns of behaviour fixed in every detail by genetic programming, so that even an animal reared in total isolation from other members of its species will, in appropriate circumstances, reproduce the complicated behaviours characteristic of that species. Closed instincts are at that end of the continuum of instincts where learning plays no part in development. Learning, for the closed-instinctual structure, is identical with physical maturation. Open instincts, on the other hand, are incompletely determined patterns of behaviour. What is given biologically is a general tendency to certain kinds of behaviour, but a tendency that remains open to various forms of learning dependent on experience. Thus the other animals, which tend to be governed more by closed instinctual patterns, also tend to be fitted more narrowly into a specific ecological niche. In Rousseau's terms:

> hence the brute cannot deviate from the rules prescribed to it, even when it would be advantageous for it to do so; and, on the contrary, man frequently deviates from such rules to his own prejudice. Thus a pigeon would be starved to death by the side of a dish of the choicest meats, and a cat on a heap of fruit or grain, though it is certain that either might find nourishment . . . did it think of trying them. (*DOI* 169-70)

Yet even Rousseau, who, in over-reaction to the sensationalist idea of the blank slate, tends to overplay the role that closed instincts play in animal life, leaves a certain amount of room for animal learning: 'Every animal has ideas since it has senses; it even combines those ideas in a certain degree; and it is only in degree that man differs, in this respect, from the brute' (*DOI* 170).

---

2. See Mary Midgley, *Beast and Man: The Roots of Human Nature,* Ithaca: Cornell University Press, 1978, 51ff.

In the proto-human stage, human free agency is thus severely restricted. It consists, that is, in a greater openness to experience, a capacity to temporarily check the promptings of instinct. At this stage, however, there is little or no occasion or reason for the proto-human animal to rein in the pressure of the biological drives. . . .

. . . Free agency, in its human rather than its proto-human form, can therefore be seen to be as much a result of socio-historical development as is the rest of the complex of processes that constitute 'human nature.' What is confusing, and has also led to a great deal of confusion in treating Rousseau as a spiritualist, is that free agency is both a condition and a result of the historical process. Yet in its beginnings there is nothing supranatural about it. It is used in the second *Discourse* as a concept proper to a philosophical biology and not as a partial or total or final determination of an ahistorical human essence. When Rousseau asserts that this 'power of willing or rather of choosing' is 'inexplicable by the laws of mechanism' (*DOI* 170), he is not asserting the co-existence in human beings of two distinct substances that persist unchanged in the midst of differences in their formation and development. He is simply indicating that biological thought cannot be reduced to the same categories as underlie the physical laws of matter and motion. There are also the important implications that historical and cultural existence has a definite biological ground and that biology therefore cannot be totally neglected in the analysis of particular cultures or phases of historical development, or in the transition from one to another: 'Nature lays her command on every animal, and the brute obeys her voice. Man receives the same impulsion, but at the same time knows himself at liberty to acquiesce or resist, and it is particularly in his *consciousness* of this liberty that the spirituality of his soul is displayed' (*DOI* 170; emphasis added). In its *origins,* however, there is no spirituality since there is no self-consciousness. And self-consciousness is in turn the product of social relations and linguistic communication—it is predicated upon the existence of a symbolic order. It is not spirituality that is the metaphysical ground and origin of conscience and virtue. Rather, spirituality, as the ability and need to delay and modify or negate the 'voice of nature,' is first of all the result of a bio-cultural evolution that, secondly, creates the pre-conditions for the socialization of individuals in such a way as to internalize the laws of the community as conscience. . . .

Both self-consciousness and conscience presuppose a considerable distance from raw biological need. But *l'homme sauvage* is as yet entirely identified with his desire. He is totally at one with his environment; in every sense he is part of nature. If he engages in any action such action expresses no distance from either his environment or his desire. 'Action' is merely an automatic device for the restoration of the state of static equilibrium in which nothing is transformed, neither without nor within him. None of his acts leaves any traces; there is no object (neither thing nor person) in which he can recognize himself. If desire for the satisfaction of some simple physical need should rouse him to some activity, the activity performed is a simple, unitary response, unarticulated into means and end and out of which he immediately falls back into the eternal present, a present in which there is no consciousness of the passage of time or of death. Under these circumstances the I cannot arise out of opposition to the It: 'in the true state of nature, egoism [amour-propre] did not exist; for as each man regarded himself as the only observer of his actions, the only being in the universe who took any interest in him, and the sole judge of his deserts, no feeling arising from comparisons he could not be led to make could take root in his soul' (*DOI* 182). . . . Freedom consists in the biological endowment of a creature with relatively open instincts and therefore possessed of a rudimentary negativity, a rudimentary capacity to oppose himself to things, other 'persons,' to his own drives, to his own past, and to the objectified image of himself he constructs from his interactions with others. . . .

Perfectibility and Labor

At the proto-human stage nature is still an undifferentiated whole, a simple unity in which neither subject nor object can be said to have yet appeared. Any transformations that appear within nature at this stage do not constitute an essential rupture in its fabric. Transformations in the biological realm, when they do appear, appear as the result of organic adaptation and do not constitute a qualitative change in the order of beings, only minor modifications and adjustments. The proto-human, however, is biologically predisposed to be able to acquire a different mode of adaptation than the animal. The rudiments of free agency are the grounds of human perfectibility. But perfectibility *per se* is meaningless in a state of static equilibrium. Perfectibility itself is not an abstract quality, although Rousseau refers to it as a 'specific quality' and a 'faculty' (*DOI* 170). Perfectibility does not mean the capacity to achieve an ideal state but refers to the process of self-transformation that occurs when men at first unconsciously and later consciously set out to transform nature. It encompasses broadly speaking two stages: a first stage during which the biological and psychological foundations of culture are laid (a stage of pre-history, as it were) and a second stage during which adaptation is primarily cultural. . . .

In the state of equilibrium that characterizes savage man, perfectibility along with free agency means little more than that man has a slight advantage over the other animals in a greater capacity for learning. Yet even the mimetic [imitative] form of learning is, like the rest of proto-human activity, essentially a passive relation to the environment. Although proto-men, in the activity of satisfying their desires, take up a position of opposition to their environment, as soon as the pressure of whatever drive they are obeying is reduced, they immediately fall back into a state of rest. Their activity is in essence identical to that of the rest of organic nature. There is no essential opposition to either themselves, external nature, or other 'men.' In keeping with the attempt at a purely naturalistic explanation of human development, Rousseau can only envision the process as in its inception caused by an external interruption of the condition of static equilibrium. The bio-cultural evolution that follows is therefore essentially fortuitous, ungoverned by providence or by the logic inherent in any world-spirit: 'Barren years, long and sharp winters, scorching summers must have demanded *a new industry*' (*DOI* 193; emphasis added). It is worth noting that among the environmental pressures responsible for the process, Rousseau counts relative over-population, a factor of great importance in the Darwinian theory as part of the account of the struggle for existence: 'In proportion as the human race grew more numerous, men's cares increased . . . he learnt to surmount the obstacles of nature, to contend in case of necessity with other animals, and to dispute for the means of subsistence even with other men' (*DOI* 193). At the same time Rousseau recognizes the activity of natural selection as an agency of organic transformation: 'Nature in this case treats them exactly as Sparta treated the children of her citizens: those who come well formed into the world she renders strong and robust, and all the rest she destroys' (*DOI* 164). But all the while that organic evolution continues, it is being supplanted by the inception of a new mode of adaptation—culture. In a sense the physical changes that take place are those necessary for the emergence of culture.

Rousseau has already mentioned erect stature, bipedal locomotion, and implicitly at least the prehensile thumb ('he . . . made use of his hands as we do').

The essential distinction, however, between organic evolution and incipient human-cultural evolution is based on the emergence of labour as a distinct forming and transforming force. When Rousseau alludes to a 'new industry' as being called forth by the physical necessity that ruptures the static equilibrium, this is not meant to indicate a quantitative change in energy expended but the birth of a new mode of existence, qualitatively different from the rest of the animal realm. At this stage, however, the social relations in which men labour and oppose themselves to nature are not as important as the fact of production as such. For it is labour or, more properly, social labour that in Rousseau's eyes constitutes the core of the process of humanization. Human phylogenesis [evolutionary history] is conceived of as impossible without social labour. Society and the *human* being emerge together in a *single* process. The abstract man of the theorists of natural law and the rational subject whose essential expression is the maximization of utilities are therefore concretely demonstrated not to belong to nature but to be the result of a concatenation of social forces in process.

The precise order and logic of the stages of bio-cultural evolution remain 'conditional and hypothetical reasonings.' All we know is that by the time of the 'Golden Age,' the earliest stages of primitive society, 'men' were fully human. The process of bio-cultural evolution is pictured as a long and complex course of interaction among various factors, issuing in a new mode of species existence that can be characterized as historical or cultural evolution. In a real sense perfectibility, which is 'inherent in the species as in the individual' (*DOI* 170), just as much as free agency, is a result more than it is an origin, substantial essence, or end. Human cultural existence, and therefore the possibility of historical development, rest on a number of biological acquisitions, which in turn make possible further biological transformation, and so on. The process in its concrete specificity is not even known to modern anthropology and will certainly always remain largely a matter of informed conjecture. We can only indicate some of the most important factors Rousseau recognizes and some of the relations among them.

One of the most important, if not one of the first of the transformations, is the creation of human language. What is most noteworthy in this connection is that Rousseau establishes a substantial gulf between what he calls 'the first language of mankind' (*DOI* 176)—a combination of auditory signal, 'excited only by a sort of instinct,' gesture, and onomatopoiea—and human language properly so called. Human language is based on the 'articulate sounds of the voice, which, without bearing the same [iconic] relation to any particular ideas, are better calculated to express them all, as conventional signs' (*DOI* 176). The gulf between a naturally given system of signals that recognizes only particular things, events, and states and a system of conventional signs is the gulf between sense-perception and conceptual thought. It is the process of social labour that leads from one to the other. Tool making and co-operative labour, the necessity of an active technical mastery of nature together with others, established both a stable context for meaning and the practice of bringing things into relation. The relation is itself what 'occasions' the concept. Concepts, which in Rousseau's eyes express relations, cannot arise except in the activity of bringing things into relation: 'This repeated relevance of various beings to himself [as a result of the "new industry"], and, one to another, would naturally give rise in the human mind to the perception of certain relations between them. Thus the relations which we denote by the terms great, small, strong, weak, swift, slow . . . and the like, almost insensibly compared at need must have at length produced in him a kind of reflection' (*DOI* 193). Human consciousness that takes the unique form of conceptual thought is therefore from the start a product of social labour. Rousseau even goes on in the *Essay on the Origin of Languages* to suggest that particular historical forms of social existence are 'mirrored' in different forms of language, psychology, and cognition.[3]

One of the ways in which the essential connection of labour with perfectibility can be expressed is as an equation of 'enlightenment' (meaning here the ability for conceptual thought) and industry: 'In proportion as they grew enlightened, they grew industrious' (*DOI* 198). Although Rousseau puts his words to indicate the possible priority of the first quality, the sentence can just as well be reversed. The connection between labour and language capable of embodying conceptual thought receives a further emphasis precisely from the lack of a role assigned to the family in its inception. Both Condillac [eighteenth century philosopher and friend of Rousseau] and the theorists of natural law assumed that the family was natural. But Rousseau opposes the notion that 'language arose in the domestic intercourse between parents and their children' (*DOI* 174). In the first place the two sexes did not remain united long enough for the father even to see the child's birth; in the second place the type of activity relating mother and child could not have been of the proper kind to occasion the growth of any but a language of cries and gestures.

Rousseau goes to some lengths in note 12 to the second *Discourse* to criticize Locke's theory that the naturalness of the family—that is, that men and women are obliged by nature to a longer period of conjugal society—is due to the prolonged dependence of the human infant as a result of neoteny in the human species. Rousseau does recognize the fact of neoteny [maturation] and prolonged dependence. . . . [They] are, as it were, the obverse of educability and of cultural as opposed to biological adaptation. But the fact of prolonged dependence does not follow, as it seems to for Locke, from nature (in this case from the nature of the carnivors). Neoteny too is a result: 'With respect to children, there are many reasons for believing that their forces and their organs develop later on among us than they did in the primitive condition of which I am speaking' (*DI*[4] 217). Although in its functions the family may be beneficial to mankind, there is no reason to assume, as Locke does, that this means that it is natural (*DI* 215–16).

Locke not only believed that the family was natural but that it was instituted by a wise creator to stimulate human industry. In Rousseau's terms this providential reasoning is the most specious of arguments and means that 'Locke's argument therefore falls to the ground, and all the logic of this philosopher has not secured him from the mistake committed by Hobbes and others' (*DOIC*[5] 255). The crucial question is rather why the male and female would remain together, not after the birth of the child but after it was conceived. It is much more likely that after the period of gestation they would not even recognize each other (*DI* 217). The conjugal bond therefore presupposes the development of a peculiarly human form of sexuality.

---

3. Rousseau, Essay on the Origin of Languages in J.H. Moran and Alexander Gode, *On the Origin of Languages* (New York: Ungar, 1966).

4. Discours sur l'inegalité in *Ouvres Complétes de Jean-Jacques Rousseau,* ed. Bernard Gagnebin and Marcel Raymond, vol. 3 (Paris: Gallimard, 1964).

5. Discourse On the Origin of Inequality, in *The Social Contract and Discourse on the Origin of Inequality,* ed. L.G. Crocker (New York: Simon and Schuster, 1967).

Humans are unique in not having, like the other animals, 'their stated times of passion and indifference' (*DOI* 187). But human sexuality is not a simple natural given, for *l'homme sauvage* did not suffer the 'moral ingredients in the feeling of love' (*DOI* 186). Human sexuality is open and malleable sexuality. It depends essentially on these 'moral ingredients' to lend it that 'glowing impetuosity' that arises with society. The frequency of social contacts, which might arise from the necessity of co-operative labour, does not immediately give rise to a malleable sexuality. It rather finds itself the intermediate result of society by way of the moral ingredients that arise with language, conceptual thinking, and imagination. These are in turn dependent upon the emergence of labour, which presupposes and expresses the active, negative stance in relation to nature, the stance that relates all entities and in a very real sense constitutes them as instances of symbolic structures of meaning.

Society is not, then, the creature of the family. If anything, the reverse is true; the family is the creature of society. And the family is conceived of as the creature of society in much more than a juridical sense. The transition to a symbolic mode of existence issues in a gradual alteration of biological desire. In place of a seasonal urge that embodies no meaning for the 'savage,' human sexuality is extended in scope by virtue of its being affected, extended, and transformed by symbolization. Whereas savage man finds that 'every woman equally answers his purpose,' the human cannot choose without expressing ideas of 'beauty and merit.' Human sexuality emerges out of a process (and becomes part of that process) that establishes a decisive change in the human bio-psychological constitution. In place of the earlier identity of relatively open instinct and adaptive behaviour that characterizes savage man, human beings exhibit malleable drives organized and modified by cultural systems of meaning. The consequence of the acquisition of culture is that the biological drives no longer constitute a hermetically distinct sphere. Biological nature is itself now essentially modified by culture. Rousseau puts the distinction in terms of the differentiation in the human of what was previously a purely 'instinctual' organization into a 'physical' (read biological) and a 'moral' (read cultural or symbolic) dimension, a differentiation that applies not only to sexual desire but to 'all the other passions' as well: 'The physical part of love is that *general desire* which urges the sexes to union with each other. The moral part is that which *determines and fixes this desire* exclusively upon one particular object; or at least *gives it a greater degree of energy toward the object* thus preferred' (*DOI* 186; emphasis added). Thus *human* aims and objects are no longer biologically given, although they do have the force of biological desire. What allows the energy of the general desire to be fixed and determined is the acquisition of the symbolic function, which is simultaneously the cause of the desire's generality.

For Rousseau the general energy of desire can be displaced from object to object and from aim to aim through the operation of the imagination, which 'never speaks to the heart of savages' (*DOI* 186). And the faculty of imagination is in turn conditional upon the acquisition of language, the articulation of the world into entities defined by the relations discovered or produced in the course of the social negation of nature. Henceforward the passions cannot be considered to be solely the work of nature but are suffused by the distinctively human form of cognition: 'The human understanding is greatly indebted to the passions, which . . . are also much indebted to the understanding . . . The passions . . . originate in our wants and their progress depends on that of our knowledge; for we cannot desire or fear anything, except from the idea we have of it, or from the simple impulse of nature' (*DOI* 171). And it should be understood that when Rousseau refers to the understanding, he does not include only conceptual thought but also the work of the imagination. Imagination thus ensures both that the human drives are open to the moulding influences of culture and that the drives are in a continual process of transformation. 'Everything is in constant flux on this earth. Nothing keeps the same unchanging shape, and our affections, that are attached to things outside us, necessarily change and pass away as they do' (RW[6] 88). The malleability of the passions is therefore both a result of historical activity (social labour) and a precondition of history properly so called. History includes, in a sense, the course of the vicissitudes of desire under the various social forms of the organization of labour.

From Anthropology to History

Perfectibility, which among other things refers to a biological openness to the acquisition of culture, is not, as it turns out, an abstract quality inhering in a substance by virtue of its essence. Nor does Rousseau use the concept to refer human history back to a supposed origin in a hypostatized abstraction. The concept of perfectibility comprises, in its anthropological sense, a number of interlocking factors describing an open-ended process. To recapitulate, these factors include labour, the acquisition of language, neoteny and its obverse of prolonged infantile dependence, non-seasonal sexuality and the family, and the substitution of culturally malleable drives for the instinctual structure of ecologically restricted animals. If any factor is of primary importance in the inception and continuation of this process it is the necessity that men face to undertake labour in co-operative relations. If there is any preconception, it is that of an animal capable of evolving to the point where cultural and historical development takes the place of organic evolution as the mode of response to environmental change. But human history, although it presupposes an emergence from nature, does not, as Rousseau envisions it, do away with the necessity embodied in nature. Human history as opposed to pre-history will reproduce a blind, quasi-natural necessity in its own sphere. Also, and in a different sense, nature is preserved as desire that cannot be integrated into the cultural order.

The general conception of nature among the thinkers of the Enlightenment and the theorists of classical liberalism was embodied in the idea of phenomena governed by abstract universal laws. This view of nature was also applied to human nature, which was therefore conceived of as static, fixed, sealed off from any essential transformation. This was supposed to be true of human nature whether what was referred to was the sensuous, bodily, affective, desirous dimension, a[s] with the materialists and utilitarians, or the cognitive, rational, moral dimension, as with the theorists of natural law. Even for Locke and those who followed him, the discovery that reason had a history determined by experience did little to shake the belief in its ability to discover universal laws of nature in the ethical domain suited to the needs of a sensuous and desiring creature. Nature itself was taken to be immediately accessible to experience as long as it remained untainted by the inheritance of the artificial, 'metaphysical' contrivances of the old order. The problem of politics was thought to be in principle reducible to the same experientially based knowledge of human nature. The laws of nature when revealed would give the lie to the irrational artifice of the *ancien régime*. The problem of politics *was* the problem of liberating nature.

Rousseau's essential discovery was aimed at transforming the entire program of the Enlightenment. Agreeing that the central problems of politics require an understand-

---

6. *Reveries of the Solitary Walker,* trans. Peter France (Harmondsworth: Penguin, 1979).

ing of human nature, he disagrees with all the rest: the identification on the one hand of human nature with reason, according to which men were endowed with social instincts; the equation on the other of human nature, with abstract and general laws arrived at inductively; and the opposition of nature and artifice. His attempt at 'reducing the question to its proper form' (*DOI* 155) rather collapses the distinction between nature and artifice, upon which the political thought of the epoch rests, into a conception of nature as the history of artifice. In this history man is his own artificer, even to the extent that he creates himself as a species. Human nature, which cannot be identified with the logic of abstract body or abstract thought, or with either biology or culture, is therefore not something fixed or static; nor does it appear whole, either at the origin of the historical process or as an abstract end transcending it. Human nature is, rather, constituted in historical activity, primarily in the social process of labour, as praxis. To understand human nature it is necessary to understand the variety of human social formations, the forms in which men undertake to transform external nature. 'It is in fact easy to see that many of the differences which distinguish men are merely the effect of habit and *the different methods of life men adopt in society'* (*DOI* 188; emphasis added). It is also to understand the vicissitudes that human drives undergo as they are affected by various modes of the social labour process. The inquiry into human nature can therefore not stop with anthropology. Anthropology is the necessary foundation for and propaedeutic to a philosophical inquiry into history. But with the discovery that nature is constituted in historical activity, anthropology must pass over into an examination of the historical process itself.

It does not therefore seem unwarranted to assert that in grasping a historical anthropology as the self-constitution of human nature in the social process of labour, Rousseau surpasses not only the social philosophy of seventeenth- and eigthteenth-century liberalism but even in some respects the historico-philosophical insights of German idealism. Unlike the natural-right thinkers Rousseau succeeds in not establishing society as an abstraction in opposition to the individual. This goes far beyond the views usually attributed to him—either that men are born good and corrupted only by false social institutions, or that there is an inescapable contradiction between individual and society. His aping of the social-contract versions of the inception of civil society has for too long obscured attention to his breakthrough. The genetic analysis of human nature is in reality an analytic description of a process of phylogenetic humanization predicated upon socialization. Society and the human being are constituted in a single process that is only remotely analogous to the association of atomized individuals. For Rousseau, individuals are already social beings. Unlike the German idealists he understands history not as the activity of an absolute subject but as the product of men who are objective, sensuous, suffering beings. These men are not to be equated with the passivity of nature, but in confronting the necessity to labour, they emerge as an independent transforming force. . . .

. . . , Rousseau with his conception of humanity as biologically formed to be the cultural animal (and, obversely, culturally formed to be biologically 'unfinished') transcends both the fundamental biologism of Condillac and the unqualified culturalism of some of the other empiricists. Rousseau's essential modification with respect to Condillac is thus not a reversion to Cartesian spiritualism but the demonstration that the human subject cannot be identified with biology. The drives are modified and transformed in human culture, in the necessity of labour, which drives an immovable wedge between biological need and its expression. With respect to the empiricists, however, Rousseau effectively denies that the human subject is a *tabula rasa*, to be wholly identified with the cultural order. In fact, this can be seen as the main significance of *l'homme sauvage* in the second *Discourse*. Savage man refers not only to the Buffonian [reference to Georges-Louis Leclerc, Comte de Buffon, eighteenth century French naturalist and author] species, of which civilized man is a descendant and a variety, but to a certain biological core in human nature 'which your education and habits may have depraved, but cannot have entirely destroyed' (*DOI* 162). Cultural transformation is therefore limited in the species and in the individual by the dependence of the mind on bodily desire. In the *human* being, the social being, there is an eternal tension between biology and culture, between bodily desire and its modes of expression and satisfaction. Nature is therefore something that lives on in history just as history is the dialectical unfolding of human nature.

COMMENTARY

The Concept of the General Will
Andrezej Rapaczynski

. . . Rousseau's political theory and the broader philosophical justification that it entails should be read in light of the fact that Rousseau was a critic of the natural-right tradition. This point must be constantly kept in mind in interpreting Rousseau's theory of the general will, for he developed the very concept of a general will in response to what he saw as the most fundamental problem of liberalism: the problem of alienation and social atomization. Early liberal political theories (in the broadest sense, which includes Hobbes's philosophy, despite its authoritarian solution to the problem of social cooperation) rest on an investigation of the nature of man. The common element in all these theories is the claim that "life according to nature" does not involve sociability as a fundamental human characteristic. The nominalist background of modern science, which the natural-right theorists use as a foundation of their political theories, inclines them to think of society as an artificial product of men's will and not as an Aristotelian totality within which the very essence of human individuality is constituted. The whole problematic of the contractual origin of society is based on the conviction that men are fully constituted, autonomous, and self-enclosed entities before they come to make any political arrangements among themselves. Before the creation of a political society they are already as much *rational agents* (at least in kind, though not perhaps in degree) as they are ever going to be. They are also as capable of moral agency (although this may not mean much in practice for someone like Hobbes) as they are ever going to become. The *meaning of their lives* may lie in their self-preservation, as in Hobbes; or in their moral self-sufficiency achieved through property ownership, as in Locke; or in the independence from all interpersonal arrangements in their search for a direct relation to God and salvation, as in the Puritan tradition. Yet, no matter what its source, the meaning of men's lives is fully determined before they ever come to institute a political commonwealth. Consequently, social organization is above all a form of cooperation between autonomous agents, according to the natural-right theorists, and not a higher-order totality with its own goals and meaning independent of the realization of individual pursuits. Even if, as in Hobbes, stress is laid on political unity and not a loose form of association, the very essence of the natural-right conception is that political legitimization must ultimately refer to the benefits of society accruing to an individual. When such benefits are sacrificed for the sake of goals that transcend the values of an individual, the natural right of this individual is violated; and even if society can legitimize such a violation in the eyes of other people, the individual in question is no longer bound by any obligation to the community.[1] As a result, the natural-right theorists no longer see active participation in politics as indispensable to a meaningful life: an individual's goals may in some cases be furthered or thwarted

1. Cf., for example, Hobbes's insistence that no man can alienate his right to self-defense, even if he is to use it against the state. *Leviathan,* ed. by C. B. MacPherson (Penguin Books, 1968), p. 70.

by society, but they are not constituted by it. Because the locus of the meaning of human life is to be found elsewhere, politics is no longer a *sine qua non* of one's humanity.

Rousseau's criticism of liberal theory is based . . . on his agreement with the natural-right theorists that man's nature, insofar as it must be understood within the conceptual framework of modern science, leaves no room for sociability. But Rousseau's further reasoning goes in the direction of showing that there is more to man than his nature, and that only on the basis of this "more" can a meaningful theory of society be founded. If this point is overlooked, and if all the features of humanity are reduced to natural phenomena, the ensuing theory of political cooperation will be unable to account for the fundamental aspirations of man and for the expectations he has of a political community. A man expects from his association with other men to overcome his "fallen condition"; he expects to reintegrate his individual activity into a broader context that will take the place of his original unity with nature. He expects that in a community with other men he is going to find the cure for the cosmic solitude to which his *amour propre* has exiled him from the womb of nature. He looks not for the mere security of his own individual existence, but for a moral fraternity that will remedy the insecurity and anxiety so fundamental to the very mode of individual existence that they will persist regardless of whether or not he enters into some forms of cooperation with others. An individual's insecurity is an expression not of his fear of any concrete danger that he could overcome by obtaining other people's cooperation, but of an "existential anxiety" attached to his very human condition. He looks to other people not for help in achieving the goals he has set for himself, but precisely for the sake of life with them, that is, for the sake of society *as such*.

It is easy to dismiss Rousseau as a romantic dreamer and forerunner of totalitarianism if, like J. L. Talmon, one does not see that he strikes an extremely sensitive chord in a man brought up in a liberal society.[2] Rousseau's protest against liberalism is not merely an expression of his inability to think of progress in terms of piecemeal and gradual changes. Neither Talmon nor Burke (Talmon's clear forerunner in the critique of Rousseau) has noticed that Rousseau can sometimes think in very conservative and traditionalist terms.[3] But in his critique of liberalism he is not simply impatient; he demands a revolution in the liberal assumptions concerning the nature of society, because he believes that the very framework of liberal theory leaves no room for a society capable of remedying the isolated, atomistic character of modern life. One may agree or disagree with Rousseau's vision of what society is supposed to be (and I think that his vision cannot be sustained), but it will not suffice to reduce his objections to liberalism to his lack of social pragmatism. With reference to a mere temporal duration of change, Rousseau could be—and sometimes was—a pragmatist. But in his vision of the role of society as such, he consciously attacked the very premise of liberal pragmatism: society, according to him, is not a pragmatic but a moral creation; it is designed not to solve problems essentially preexisting and independent with respect to it, but to respond to an inner need to which it *itself* is the

---

2. J. L. Talmon, *The Origins of Totalitarian Democracy* (New York, 1970), 38–49 passim.

3. See particularly the conservative character of Rousseau's proposals in his *Constitution for Poland* and those parts of *The Social Contract* (Maurice Cranston, trans. [Penguin, 1968]) in which he excuses the institution of slavery in ancient Greece (III, 15). See also the studies devoted to the similarities between Rousseau and Burke: D. Cameron, *The Social Thought of Rousseau and Burke* (London, 1973); A. M. Osborn, *Rousseau and Burke* (London, 1940). See also W. Pickles, "The Notion of Time in Rousseau's Political Thought," in Cranston and Peters, eds., *Hobbes and Rousseau* (New York: Doubleday, 1972), 366–400.

answer. Rousseau may be wrong in his claim that the inner need for a tightly integrated social system is compatible with freedom, but he is not wrong that such a need exists and that a liberal society can never fully satisfy it. The unceasing hold that Rousseau retains over the minds of modern thinkers, the fact that throughout the two centuries since the publication of his work he has been a constant source of inspiration for both leftist and rightist critics of liberalism, the periodic waves of dissatisfaction with what liberal society has to offer, despite its enormous success in emancipating one class and nation after another—these are the best witnesses that Rousseau, with his theory of alienation, touched on the most sensitive weak spot of the liberal system. Unless this problem is dealt with directly, rather than being explained away as a temporary or unreal difficulty, no philosophical defense of liberalism is possible. . . .

Rousseau's critique of the natural-right theory that underlies the contractarianism of Hobbes and Locke makes him only a qualified contractarian himself. As the *Second Discourse* clearly shows, Rousseau does not envisage the origins of society in a contractual agreement. The evolution of the "unnatural man" is from the very first connected with the introduction of social relations. In the state of nature man has only casual encounters with other members of the species,[4] and he establishes no meaningful relations with them. Even family life, according to Rousseau, is a product of civilization, since love, unlike sexual drive, is not a natural feeling.[5] Reason, which distinguishes man from animals, develops only with the introduction of language, and both are immediately connected with a meaningful intercourse with other people brought about as a result of overpopulation. Thus, Rousseau believes that it is impossible to speak about a man's contracting into society, for the development of human agency, which is indispensable for his entering into any kind of obligation, comes about only concurrently with the development of society. It is only a legitimate, political society that has its origin in a contract, whereas social cooperation (or competition) precedes any contractual arrangements. Thus, Rousseau is one of the first thinkers to make a strong distinction between civil society (which he most often calls "civilization" or simply "society") and political institutions. In a somewhat Aristotelian fashion, his objection to liberalism is that what it refers to as the "state" is in reality nothing but a form of civil society: a private association devoid of the truly general character of the state. But unlike Aristotle, Rousseau does not view this prepolitical association as subhuman, on a par with the "society" of ants or bees, but rather as a typically human phenomenon, involving intercourse between rational, self-oriented individuals.

Thus, the problem of an individual's isolation and alienation at the stage of *amour propre* is, despite the seemingly self-sufficient nature of the self, inherently connected with social interaction among many individuals. A political community of equals is already implicit in the self-enclosed world of the civilized man; it is a misperceived ideal norm of his relationships with other men, which an individual unconsciously longs for but consciously defeats. His rationality being *par excellence* a social phenomenon, his egocentric world view is obviously an illusion. The reason an individual is alienated and unhappy under the conditions of civilization is that the self-sufficiency he ascribes to his ego is in fact spurious. Reason involves a relationship to other people, without which it is ineffective. When an individual believes that he can rationally establish his own self-identity, that he can establish

---

4. *Second Discourse,* translated by L. Crocker (New York, 1967), 140, 146–47, 159–60.

5. Ibid., 157–58: *Emile,* translated by B. Foxley (London, 1911), 493–94.

himself as a private moral cosmos, independently of both his subhuman, natural existence and his relationship to other people, reason is deprived of the context on which it thrives. As a result, an individual falls prey to antinomies. The purely formal character of individual rationality is responsible for the emptiness of an individual's moral life, the emptiness that must be filled by particular, *ad hoc* arising passions. These passions, on the other hand, involve man in the endless and meaningless pursuit of gratifications that only remove him further and further from self-sufficiency and from a communion with other agents. Rousseau differs from Aristotle in his insistence that human happiness and self-sufficiency are not fulfillments of a natural order; they are, according to him, results of a consistent realization of an ideal of life of which man himself is the author and which he brings about through his own freedom and spontaneity. Man does not have a nature and is himself the author of what he is. But in *political* terms, Rousseau's critique of liberalism is Aristotelian: the Hobbesian "continual progress of desire" appears to Rousseau a perversion of both nature and reason.

The Political Solution

. . . Entering a political society . . . is not primarily a prudent step designed to assure an individual of his security. Neither is it a matter of compromise in which the satisfaction of certain interests is traded for a renunciation of others. Rather, political association rests on the acceptance of a form of interaction with other men in which no one stands to lose and everyone stands to gain. It is in this light that we must read Rousseau's presentation of his own task and of the "fundamental problem to which the social contract holds the solution": "How to form a form of association . . . under which each individual, while uniting himself with others, obeys no one but himself, and remains as free as before."[6]

It is not very difficult to see how, within the context of the human community, reason acquires, according to Rousseau, the motivational power that it does not have for an isolated individual. To begin with, social relationships developing on the basis of individual pursuits of interest result in an arrangement that virtually all people must see as basically unjust and inhuman. Like Marx after him, though more intuitively than "scientifically," Rousseau viewed the liberal model of society as bringing forth an ever sharper inequality and ever sharper polarization between the haves and the have-nots. Ultimately, the interests of most people are thwarted by the very system that allows their unhampered development. Rousseau is a Hobbesian in this respect, with one significant difference: the Hobbesian state of nature very well describes for Rousseau the state of prepolitical civilization. Rousseau's complete lack of awareness of what Mandeville called the "public benefit of private vices," and of what Adam Smith described as the "invisible hand," may be one of the weakest points in his system.[7] But in any case, once Rousseau has postulated ever increasing social antagonisms within civil society, it is not surprising that he postulated the need for a revolutionary change that would restructure the ends, and not just the means, of social intercourse. The development of social antagonisms, he held, will have to bring an ever increasing realization of the self-defeating character of *amour propre*

---

6. *Social Contract*, I, 6, (360). . . .

7. Surprisingly enough, Smith himself was not always particularly conscious of this difference between himself and Rousseau, and in one of his reviews he compared Rousseau to Mandeville.

and provide a decisive impetus for subjecting passions to reason.[8] Furthermore, once the political order envisaged in *The Social Contract* is established, the power of the sovereign—and here again Rousseau reminds us of Hobbes—will provide a counteracting force to the centrifugal forces of interest. This includes both direct intervention of the state in cases where parties and other private associations are being formed[9] and a long-term educational effort directed at the citizenry (of which the establishment of public religion is only one example).[10]

But the main problem of Rousseau's political philosophy, besides discovering what brings about the harmony between collective policies and individual freedom, is the problem of explaining exactly how the communal context of life will translate the formal principle embodied in Rousseau's [general will] . . . into a system of substantive moral commands. In other words, how will the fact that a citizen votes in an assembly of his compatriots rather than in the solitude of his own mind enable him to fill reason with the content that it previously lacked? . . .

. . . The content that the commands of reason receive upon becoming translated into the commands the general will is fraternity itself. Rousseau thinks of the general will as the moral substance of the community, much as Hegel thinks of his "objective spirit." The requirements to be satisfied in order for the outcome of an assembly vote to represent the general will are: (a) that each individual consider only the public good and not his private interests;[11] and (b) that all the decrees of the assembly have the form of general laws.[12] The problem that remains, of course, is what substantive criteria the citizen is to use when he asks himself what is in the public good. The dilemma becomes apparent when we see that Rousseau believes that "when a law is proposed in the people's assembly, what is asked of them is not precisely whether they approve of the proposition or reject it, but whether it is in conformity with the general will which is theirs."[13] On the face of it, it would seem that as a citizen I am obligated to ignore the content of the law being proposed, second-guess how the others are going to vote, and then cast my vote accordingly. As well as extreme opportunism, such a procedure also implies that the result of the voting will depend on chance alone. Having nothing else to go by, I might assume that the chances of acceptance or rejection of the proposed law are exactly equal. As a rational agent, I would then toss a coin and vote accordingly. But this, of course, is not what Rousseau has in mind. When he says that the question asked of the people is "not *precisely*" whether they accept or reject the proposed law, he does not mean that I cannot take the content of the law into consideration. A citizen has a right—indeed a duty—to be pragmatic and to consider whether the law contributes to the stability of the community and even to its members' interest; in the narrow, materialistic sense. He is prohibited from considering his private interest above the collective interest, so as to avoid the pernicious consequences of the prisoner's-dilemma* type of situation. He is further prohibited from considering the collective interest of all the individuals

---

8. I do not mean to deny that Rousseau was often very pessimistic about the chances of establishing a legitimate state in any of the large European countries of his time. . . .

9. *Social Contract,* II, 3 (371–72).

10. Ibid., IV, 8.

11. Ibid., IV, 1 (438).

12. Ibid., II, 6.

13. Ibid., IV, 2 (440–41).

*A two player game in which each player can either cooperate or defect on the basis of a schedule of rewards or punishments. It is often used to illustrate the social ramifications of individual decisions.—ed.

involved if its increase were to contribute to the demise of the political bond that unites them (for example, a certain decision may greatly contribute to the wealth of the whole community, but at the same time undermine the civic spirit of the citizenry; in this case for *moral* and not merely pragmatic reasons, I should oppose such a decision). Still, pragmatic considerations do in fact determine the content of a citizen's decisions. But his pragmatic or utilitarian calculations are not "precisely" what is asked of him, because the good that he is primarily supposed to aim at is not what accrues to the community from its decisions but the *community* itself. When Rousseau says that the general will is always right,[14] he does not mean that it is pragmatically right, and he is not repeating Aristotle's doubtful claim that among a great number of people the extremes of opinion balance each other out and the remaining mean is most often closest to the truth.[15] On the contrary, Rousseau believes that people are very often wrong in the pragmatic sense[16] and this is why they need a wise legislator to guide them and why even the best states finally disintegrate.[17] But the "right" and "wrong" that apply to political decisions are moral and not pragmatic terms. And this moral rightness consists in the merging of individual wills into one universal will that eliminates the isolation and alienation of each person in the fraternal bond of the community. . . .

. . . The fraternity that Rousseau aims at is not a formal equality of all citizens, but the very *content* of justice and the supreme command of morality. Its sense does not lie in a mere conformity with a universal principle, but in an actual love of one's neighbor. . . .

Rousseau strongly insists that a political law must be universal in character. His point, however, does not concern the merely formal character of the general will. Laws must contain an element of particularity, since they are not empty; they order or prohibit something, and they will always affect some people differently from others. . . . The universality of law that Rousseau has in mind rests in the intention of the assembly, the intention to attend to the public interest in such a way that the bond uniting the people become stronger and not weaker. This is why a law cannot be inimical to any particular citizen, even if his particular interest is being thwarted; it is always designed to integrate him further into the community, which gives him his moral worth. He himself may believe that the result of the law will be the opposite of the one that its authors desire—and he may even be right. For this reason, he is given the opportunity to argue against it in the assembly and to bring it for reconsideration when there is a chance that others may have come to agree with him. But to disobey the law would be to bring about immediately what he claims he wants to avoid, since disobedience to a law amounts to breaking the unity of the general will here and now and not only in the future. It means either that one wants to secede from the state—a form of moral suicide for Rousseau—or that one wants to impose one's will on others and destroy the autonomy of the community. But since the moral quality of the community consists in its autonomy, "the worst of laws is still better than the best master."[18] People have a right to legislate bad laws as much as good ones, and "if they choose to do themselves an injury, who has the right to prevent them

---

14. Ibid., II, 3 (371).

15. *Politics,* 1282a.

16. *Social Contract,* II, 6 (380).

17. Ibid., III, 10–11 (esp. 424).

18. *Lettres écrites de la montagne.* In *Oeuvres Complète* Pléiade edition, vol. III (Paris, 1959–69), 842–43.

from doing so?"[19] They can be advised against, but not forcibly prevented from, harming themselves; for the practical harm that they might cause to themselves could never be greater than the moral damage they would suffer by being deprived of their freedom.

It is with this type of consideration in mind that Rousseau formulates his controversial theory of majority rule. To Locke, for example, majority rule is a pragmatic solution to the problems of legislation, and the limitations of political power in general leave the basic rights of the minority protected by delegitimizing any fundamental encroachments of positive law on the natural rights of individuals. To Rousseau, on the other hand, the problem of majority rule is crucial, since political participation is the main locus of moral life and the power of the sovereign is absolute (in the sense of not being limited by any nonpolitical constraints, such as natural law). Hence no minority is protected *qua* minority; its only consolation is that it is not singled out arbitrarily by the law. There are no doubt dangerous political consequences implied in this state of affairs, and no amount of explaining the famous phrase "on le forcera d'être libre" will eliminate its totalitarian implications.[20] But even if to understand is not to forgive, we should try to understand Rousseau's meaning. A man who enters the social contract—and the original pact requires unanimity—has renounced his individual freedom for the sake of social integration. The structure of the general will thus created is such that in participating in the political process and in obeying the laws of the community, the individual is finally able to live according to reason and not according to the dictates of passion. In one of the less brilliant passages of *The Social Contract,* Rousseau represents the relation of an individual to the general will as a proportion of one to the number of citizens, and he draws the conclusion that "the more the state is enlarged, the more freedom is diminished."[21] If that were indeed to be the case, Rousseau's whole scheme would fall to pieces. Not only would the citizen not be "as free as before,"[22] but in fact he could hardly be said to be free at all. To say that he has 1/10,000th part of the power to decide about his own life (and we are speaking of a small community indeed) is the same as saying that he is 9,999/10,000 unfree, and no tyranny could probably make him more of a slave. But Rousseau makes these naive calculations only in the context of his consideration of the size of the executive authority that a state needs. In the context of his discussion of the social pact itself, he clearly states that in obeying the law a citizen "obeys no one but himself."[23] True autonomy being possible only in a truly communal action, the general will expresses not a collection of wills but one will of the whole community of which I am as much a part as a totality, since my moral agency is realized only in the common decision. I may disagree with the *contingent* content of any particular law, but I cannot disagree with the *necessary* unity of the community. Such a disagreement would amount to a disagreement with myself, that is, a disagreement between my passions, which enslave me, and my reason, which emancipates me. In other words, by being forced to obey my reason I am forced (by the community that embodies *my own* moral agency) to be free.

---

19. *Social Contract,* II, 12.

20. Ibid., I, 7 (364). . . .

21. *Social Contract,* III, 1 (397).

22. Ibid., I, 6 (360).

23. Ibid.

Edmund Burke

Edmund Burke is widely known as the founder and most articulate representative of conservative political ideology. Indeed, some contemporary discussions of what conservatives believe amount to little more than catalogues of Burke's ideas.[1] However, his work offers a version of conservatism largely unfamiliar to Americans. With such notable exceptions as George Will, Russell Kirk, and John C. Calhoun, most American "conservatives" are really classical liberals, whose views have more in common with those of John Locke and Adam Smith than with those of Burke.

Burke was born in Dublin, Ireland, in 1729. His life was that of a "man of letters," writing for political journals and serving as an adviser to politically prominent aristocrats. As a member of the Whig party, Burke entered upon a parliamentary career noteworthy for his defense of the American struggle for political rights and for a theory of representation outlined in his famous "Speech to the Electors of Bristol." By his death in 1797, Burke had left a body of writings addressing the major political issues of his day and expressing a political theory of tradition and stability.

Burke's most famous writings, of course, were critical of the theory and practice of the French Revolution. Unlike the English Revolution of 1688, the French Revolution did not produce a cautious, limited change in constitutional government. Based as it was on rationalist political theories and abstract conceptions of human rights, it destroyed a

---

1. Samuel Huntington, "Conservatism as Ideology," *American Political Science Review* 52 (1958), pp. 454–473; Russell Kirk, "Introduction," in Kirk, ed., *The Portable Conservative Reader* (New York: Penguin, 1982), pp. xi–xl.

long-established social order and led to elitist abuses of power (ending with the Reign of Terror). For Burke, the Enlightenment's influence in public affairs was nothing to celebrate, for it replaced the steady guidance of custom, tradition, and feeling with the cold calculations of reason and the pernicious ideas of "metaphysical scribblers."

As you might expect from someone who spent many years in Parliament, Burke tended not to trace his economic and political views directly to abstract philosophical principles. He believed that sound policy would more likely emerge from pragmatism and prudence than either dogmatism or doctrine. On the whole, what general principles he held can be summarized by the following terms: prescription, prejudice, and presumption. By prescription, Burke meant that political rights or privileges, duties or obligations, as well as property, were truly acquired only through long, patient, and considerate use. By prejudice, he meant not bigotry, but the natural feelings people have which temper reason and guide them through the complexities of life. It is largely a product of the distilled wisdom of the ages found in custom, habit, tradition, and ritual. Finally, by presumption, Burke invoked the idea that long-established practices or institutions are to be seen as beneficial until proven otherwise. They should not be changed, except for good reason, and even then, only in a cautious and gradual manner.

This stance of prudence, of course, is the only acceptable course of action given Burke's conception of society. He viewed society as very much like a living organism, whose parts are shaped by the common life of the whole. Society is not a human artifact, as the model of social contract theory would suggest. It cannot be created at will by a band of radical reformers proclaiming a new, absolute theory of politics. A social order has to grow and develop over many generations; slowly adapt to changing circumstances over a long period of time. Thus, Burke believed that the institutions and ideas that have survived thus far have proved themselves in a historical trial by fire, have shown their adaptability and, having endured, they are worthy of our belief, respect, and support.

Reflections on the Revolution in France

Burke's most celebrated work is the *Reflections on the Revolution in France,* which first appeared in 1790. It takes the form of a lengthy letter to a French friend, commenting upon recent political events and criticizing the Revolution's supporters in England. In the selections reprinted here, Burke attacks the Revolution's claims regarding the natural rights of individuals. He argues against the Lockean view that governments are formed to protect these rights and suggests, instead, that governments aim to provide for human wants largely by restraining our passions. By emphasizing the rational individualism of social contract theory, the Revolution's supporters ultimately deny society's true foundation in religion. They view society more like a business partnership than like an invisible link across the generations —binding people in a sacred commonwealth of established customs and institutions, in a chain of mutual obligations and respected privileges.

Commentaries

Gérard Gengembre's excellent summary of the *Reflections* highlights the key differences Burke found between English and French politics. Ably illustrating Burke's chief concerns regarding the French Revolution, Gengembre focuses on such Burkean concepts as tradition, property, and community. He then sketches Burke's immediate political legacy.

Michael Freeman sees Burke as constructing a useful critique of political radicalism. This critique asserts that radicalism (no matter where or when it appears) is fundamentally flawed, because it presumes a level of knowledge about people and society that is impossible for human beings to have, and because its inevitable results are disorder, fanaticism, and tyranny. For Freeman, the hard questions Burke poses for radicals of any generation, as well as his defense of political pragmatism, make the study of his writings a valuable exercise.

Key Words

"The rights of men." Burke's phrase for the liberal theory of individual rights, derived from such thinkers as Locke and Rousseau and given political expression in the Declaration of the Rights of Man and Citizen.

Prejudice. An established belief or customary practice, supported by training or intuition rather than rational argument. Prejudice (in the form of religious beliefs and political institutions) is a virtue because it binds people together in a common enterprise.

Radicalism. A thoroughgoing hostility to the institutions, practices, and ideas of the status quo, occasionally accompanied by extralegal efforts to achieve political change.

For Further Reading

MacPherson, C.B. 1980. *Burke.* New York: Hill and Wang.

Harbour, W.R. 1982. *The Foundations of Conservative Thought: An Anglo-American Tradition in Retrospect.* Notre Dame, Ind.: University of Notre Dame Press.

Kramnick, I. 1979. *The Rage of Edmund Burke: The Conscience of an Ambivalent Conservative.* New York: Basic Books.

Pocock, J.G.A. 1989. "Burke and the Ancient Constitution: A Problem in the History of Ideas." Pp. 202–232 in his *Politics, Language, and Time.* Chicago: The University of Chicago Press.

Reflections on the Revolution in France

You will observe that from Magna Charta to the Declaration of Right it has been the uniform policy of our constitution to claim and assert our liberties as an *entailed inheritance* derived to us from our forefathers, and to be transmitted to our posterity—as an estate specially belonging to the people of this kingdom, without any reference whatever to any other more general or prior right. By this means our constitution preserves a unity in so great a diversity of its parts. We have an inheritable crown, an inheritable peerage, and a House of Commons and a people inheriting privileges, franchises, and liberties from a long line of ancestors.

This policy appears to me to be the result of profound reflection, or rather the happy effect of following nature, which is wisdom without reflection, and above it. A spirit of innovation is generally the result of a selfish temper and confined views. People will not look forward to posterity, who never look backward to their ancestors. Besides, the people of England well know that the idea of inheritance furnishes a sure principle of conservation and a sure principle of transmission, without at all excluding a principle of improvement. It leaves acquisition free, but it secures what it acquires. Whatever advantages are obtained by a state proceeding on these maxims are locked fast as in a sort of family settlement, grasped as in a kind of mortmain forever. By a constitutional policy, working after the pattern of nature, we receive, we hold, we transmit our government and our privileges in the same manner in which we enjoy and transmit our property and our lives. The institutions of policy, the goods of fortune, the gifts of providence are handed down to us, and from us, in the same course and order. Our political system is placed in a just correspondence and symmetry with the order of the world and with the mode of existence decreed to a permanent body composed of transitory parts, wherein, by the disposition of a stupendous wisdom, molding together the great mysterious incorporation of the human race, the whole, at one time, is never old or middle-aged or young, but, in a condition of unchangeable constancy, moves on through the varied tenor of perpetual decay, fall, renovation, and progression. Thus, by preserving the method of nature in the conduct of the state, in what we improve we are never wholly new; in what we retain we are never wholly obsolete. By adhering in this manner and on those principles to our forefathers, we are guided not by the superstition of antiquarians, but by the spirit of philosophic analogy. In this choice of inheritance we have given to our frame of polity the image of a relation in blood, binding up the constitution of our country with our dearest domestic ties, adopting our fundamental laws into the bosom of our family affections, keeping inseparable and cherishing with

From *Reflections on the Revolution in France* (edited by J.G.A. Pocock). Indianapolis: Hackett, pp. 29–33, 50–56, 79–81, 84–87. Copyright © 1987 by J.G.A. Pocock. With the permission of Hackett Publishing Company, Inc. Indianapolis, IN and Cambridge, MA.

the warmth of all their combined and mutually reflected charities our state, our hearths, our sepulchres, and our altars.

Through the same plan of a conformity to nature in our artificial institutions, and by calling in the aid of her unerring and powerful instincts to fortify the fallible and feeble contrivances of our reason, we have derived several other, and those no small, benefits from considering our liberties in the light of an inheritance. Always acting as if in the presence of canonized forefathers, the spirit of freedom, leading in itself to misrule and excess, is tempered with an awful gravity. This idea of a liberal descent inspires us with a sense of habitual native dignity which prevents that upstart insolence almost inevitably adhering to and disgracing those who are the first acquirers of any distinction. By this means our liberty becomes a noble freedom. It carries an imposing and majestic aspect. It has a pedigree and illustrating ancestors. It has its bearings and its ensigns armorial. It has its gallery of portraits, its monumental inscriptions, its records, evidences, and titles. We procure reverence to our civil institutions on the principle upon which nature teaches us to revere individual men: on account of their age and on account of those from whom they are descended. All your sophisters cannot produce anything better adapted to preserve a rational and manly freedom than the course that we have pursued, who have chosen our nature rather than our speculations, our breasts rather than our inventions, for the great conservatories and magazines of our rights and privileges.

You might, if you pleased, have profited of our example and have given to your recovered freedom a correspondent dignity. Your privileges, though discontinued, were not lost to memory. Your constitution, it is true, whilst you were out of possession, suffered waste and dilapidation; but you possessed in some parts the walls and in all the foundations of a noble and venerable castle. You might have repaired those walls; you might have built on those old foundations. Your constitution was suspended before it was perfected, but you had the elements of a constitution very nearly as good as could be wished. In your old states you possessed that variety of parts corresponding with the various descriptions of which your community was happily composed; you had all that combination and all that opposition of interests; you had that action and counteraction which, in the natural and in the political world, from the reciprocal struggle of discordant powers, draws out the harmony of the universe. These opposed and conflicting interests which you considered as so great a blemish in your old and in our present constitution interpose a salutary check to all precipitate resolutions. They render deliberation a matter, not of choice, but of necessity; they make all change a subject of *compromise*, which naturally begets moderation; they produce *temperaments* preventing the sore evil of harsh, crude, unqualified reformations, and rendering all the headlong exertions of arbitrary power, in the few or in the many, for ever impracticable. Through that diversity of members and interests, general liberty had as many securities as there were separate views in the several orders, whilst, by pressing down the whole by the weight of a real monarchy, the separate parts would have been prevented from warping and starting from their allotted places.

You had all these advantages in your ancient states, but you chose to act as if you had never been molded into civil society and had everything to begin anew. You began ill, because you began by despising everything that belonged to you. You set up your trade without a capital. If the last generations of your country appeared without much luster in your eyes, you might have passed them by and derived your claims from a more early race of ancestors. Under a pious predilection for those ancestors, your imaginations would have realized in them a standard of virtue and wisdom beyond the vulgar practice of the hour; and you would have risen with the example to whose imitation you aspired. Respecting your forefathers, you would have been taught to respect yourselves. You would not have chosen to consider the French as a people of yesterday, as a nation of lowborn servile wretches until the emancipating year of 1789. In order to furnish, at the expense of your honor, an excuse to your apologists here for several enormities of yours, you would not have been content to be represented as a gang of Maroon slaves suddenly broke loose from the house of bondage, and therefore to be pardoned for your abuse of the liberty to which you were not accustomed and ill fitted. Would it not, my worthy friend, have been wiser to have you thought, what I, for one, always thought you, a generous and gallant nation, long misled to your disadvantage by your high and romantic sentiments of fidelity, honor, and loyalty; that events had been unfavorable to you, but that you were not enslaved through any illiberal or servile disposition; that in your most devoted submission you were actuated by a principle of public spirit, and that it was your country you worshiped in the person of your king? Had you made it to be understood that in the delusion of this amiable error you had gone further than your wise ancestors, that you were resolved to resume your ancient privileges, whilst you preserved the spirit of your ancient and your recent loyalty and honor; or if, diffident of yourselves and not clearly discerning the almost obliterated constitution of your ancestors, you had looked to your neighbors in this land who had kept alive the ancient principles and models of the old common law of Europe meliorated and adapted to its present state—by following wise examples you would have given new examples of wisdom to the world. You would have rendered the cause of liberty venerable in the eyes of every worthy mind in every nation. You would have shamed despotism from the earth by showing that freedom was not only reconcilable, but, as when well disciplined it is, auxiliary to law. You would have had an unoppressive but a productive revenue. You would have had a flourishing commerce to feed it. You would have had a free constitution, a potent monarchy, a disciplined army, a reformed and venerated clergy, a mitigated but spirited nobility to lead your virtue, not to overlay it; you would have had a liberal order of commons to emulate and to recruit that nobility; you would have had a protected, satisfied, laborious, and obedient people, taught to seek and to recognize the happiness that is to be found by virtue in all conditions; in which consists the true moral equality of mankind, and not in that monstrous fiction which, by inspiring false ideas and vain expectations into men destined to travel in the obscure walk of laborious life, serves only to aggravate and embitter that real inequality which it never can remove, and which the order of civil life establishes as much for the benefit of those whom it must leave in a humble state as those whom it is able to exalt to a condition more splendid, but not more happy. You had a smooth and easy career of felicity and glory laid open to you, beyond anything recorded in the history of the world, but you have shown that difficulty is good for man. . . .

... It is no wonder, therefore, that with these ideas of everything in their constitution and government at home, either in church or state, as illegitimate and usurped, or at best as a vain mockery, they look abroad with an eager and passionate enthusiasm. Whilst they are possessed by these notions, it is vain to talk to them of the practice of their ancestors, the fundamental laws of their country, the fixed form of a constitution whose merits are confirmed by the solid test of long experience and an increasing public strength and national prosperity. They despise experience as the wisdom of unlettered men; and as for the rest, they have wrought underground a mine that will blow up, at one grand explosion, all examples of antiquity, all precedents, charters, and acts of parliament. They have "the rights of men". Against these there can be no prescription, against these no agreement is binding; these admit no temperament and no compromise; anything withheld from their full demand is so much of fraud and injustice. Against these their rights of men let no government look for security in the length of its continuance, or in the justice and lenity of its administration. The objections of these speculatists, if its forms do not quadrate with their theories, are as valid against such an old and beneficent government as against the most violent tyranny or the greenest usurpation. They are always at issue with governments, not on a question of abuse, but a question of competency and a question of title. I have nothing to say to the clumsy subtilty of their political metaphysics. Let them be their amusement in the schools.—*"Illa se jactet in aula Aeolus, et clauso ventorum carcere regnet"*.[1] —But let them not break prison to burst like a *Levanter*, to sweep the earth with their hurricane and to break up the fountains of the great deep to overwhelm us.

Far am I from denying in theory, full as far is my heart from withholding in practice (if I were of power to give or to withhold) the *real* rights of men. In denying their false claims of right, I do not mean to injure those which are real, and are such as their pretended rights would totally destroy. If civil society be made for the advantage of man, all the advantages for which it is made become his right. It is an institution of beneficence; and law itself is only beneficence acting by a rule. Men have a right to live by that rule; they have a right to do justice, as between their fellows, whether their fellows are in public function or in ordinary occupation. They have a right to the fruits of their industry and to the means of making their industry fruitful. They have a right to the acquisitions of their parents, to the nourishment and improvement of their offspring, to instruction in life, and to consolation in death. Whatever each man can separately do, without trespassing upon others, he has a right to do for himself; and he has a right to a fair portion of all which society, with all its combinations of skill and force, can do in his favor. In this partnership all men have equal rights, but not to equal things. He that has but five shillings in the partnership has as good a right to it as he that has five hundred pounds has to his larger proportion. But he has not a right to an equal dividend in the product of the joint stock; and as to the share of power, authority, and direction which each individual ought to have

---

1. Virgil, *Aenid*, I, 140–41. "Let Aeolus bluster in that hall, and reign in the closed prison of the winds". Aelous was a wind god, and the winds were imagined as shut up until released. A Levanter was a strong gale from the east.

in the management of the state, that I must deny to be amongst the direct original rights of man in civil society; for I have in my contemplation the civil social man, and no other. It is a thing to be settled by convention.

If civil society be the offspring of convention, that convention must be its law. That convention must limit and modify all the descriptions of constitution which are formed under it. Every sort of legislative, judicial, or executory power are its creatures. They can have no being in any other state of things; *and how can any man claim under the conventions of civil society rights which do not so much as suppose its existence—rights which are absolutely repugnant to it?* One of the first motives to civil society, and which becomes one of its fundamental rules, is *that no man should be judge in his own cause.* By this each person has at once divested himself of the first fundamental right of uncovenanted man, that is, to judge for himself and to assert his own cause. He abdicates all right to be his own governor. He inclusively, in a great measure, abandons the right of self-defense, the first law of nature. Men cannot enjoy the rights of an uncivil and of a civil state together. That he may obtain justice, he gives up his right of determining what it is in points the most essential to him. That he may secure some liberty, he makes a surrender in trust of the whole of it.

Government is not made in virtue of natural rights, which may and do exist in total independence of it, and exist in much greater clearness and in a much greater degree of abstract perfection; but their abstract perfection is their practical defect. By having a right to everything they want everything. Government is a contrivance of human wisdom to provide for human *wants.* Men have a right that these wants should be provided for by this wisdom. Among these wants is to be reckoned the want, out of civil society, of a sufficient restraint upon their passions. Society requires not only that the passions of individuals should be subjected, but that even in the mass and body, as well as in the individuals, the inclinations of men should frequently be thwarted, their will controlled, and their passions brought into subjection. This can only be done *by a power out of themselves,* and not, in the exercise of its function, subject to that will and to those passions which it is its office to bridle and subdue. In this sense the restraints on men, as well as their liberties, are to be reckoned among their rights. But as the liberties and the restrictions vary with times and circumstances and admit to infinite modifications, they cannot be settled upon any abstract rule; and nothing is so foolish as to discuss them upon that principle.

The moment you abate anything from the full rights of men, each to govern himself, and suffer any artificial, positive limitation upon those rights, from that moment the whole organization of government becomes a consideration of convenience. This it is which makes the constitution of a state and the due distribution of its powers a matter of the most delicate and complicated skill. It requires a deep knowledge of human nature and human necessities, and of the things which facilitate or obstruct the various ends which are to be pursued by the mechanism of civil institutions. The state is to have recruits to its strength, and remedies to its distempers. What is the use of discussing a man's abstract right to food or medicine? The question is upon the method of procuring and administering them. In that deliberation I shall always advise to call in the aid of the farmer and the physician rather than the professor of metaphysics.

The science of constructing a commonwealth, or renovating it, or reforming it, is, like every other experimental science, not to be taught *a priori*. Nor is it a short experience that can instruct us in that practical science, because the real effects of moral causes are not always immediate; but that which in the first instance is prejudicial may be excellent in its remoter operation, and its excellence may arise even from the ill effects it produces in the beginning. The reverse also happens: and very plausible schemes, with very pleasing commencements, have often shameful and lamentable conclusions. In states there are often some obscure and almost latent causes, things which appear at first view of little moment, on which a very great part of its prosperity or adversity may most essentially depend. The science of government being therefore so practical in itself and intended for such practical purposes—a matter which requires experience, and even more experience than any person can gain in his whole life, however sagacious and observing he may be—it is with infinite caution that any man ought to venture upon pulling down an edifice which has answered in any tolerable degree for ages the common purposes of society, or on building it up again without having models and patterns of approved utility before his eyes.

These metaphysic rights entering into common life, like rays of light which pierce into a dense medium, are by the laws of nature refracted from their straight line. Indeed, in the gross and complicated mass of human passions and concerns the primitive rights of men undergo such a variety of refractions and reflections that it becomes absurd to talk of them as if they continued in the simplicity of their original direction. The nature of man is intricate; the objects of society are of the greatest possible complexity; and, therefore, no simple disposition or direction of power can be suitable either to man's nature or to the quality of his affairs. When I hear the simplicity of contrivance aimed at and boasted of in any new political constitutions, I am at no loss to decide that the artificers are grossly ignorant of their trade or totally negligent of their duty. The simple governments are fundamentally defective, to say no worse of them. If you were to contemplate society in but one point of view, all these simple modes of polity are infinitely captivating. In effect each would answer its single end much more perfectly than the more complex is able to attain all its complex purposes. But it is better that the whole should be imperfectly and anomalously answered than that, while some parts are provided for with great exactness, others might be totally neglected or perhaps materially injured by the over-care of a favorite member.

The pretended rights of these theorists are all extremes; and in proportion as they are metaphysically true, they are morally and politically false. The rights of men are in a sort of *middle*, incapable of definition, but not impossible to be discerned. The rights of men in governments are their advantages; and these are often in balances between differences of good, in compromises sometimes between good and evil, and sometimes between evil and evil. Political reason is a computing principle: adding, subtracting, multiplying, and dividing, morally and not metaphysically or mathematically, true moral denominations.

By these theorists the right of the people is almost always sophistically confounded with their power. The body of the community, whenever it can come to act, can meet with no effectual resistance; but till power and right are the same, the whole body of them has no right inconsistent with virtue, and the first of all virtues, prudence. Men have no right to what is not reasonable and to what is not for their benefit; for though a pleasant writer said, *liceat perire poetis,* when one of them, in cold blood, is said to have leaped into the flames of a volcanic revolution, *ardentem frigidus Aetnam insiluit,*[2] I consider such a frolic rather as an unjustifiable poetic license than as one of the franchises of Parnassus; and whether he was a poet, or divine, or politician that chose to exercise this kind of right, I think that more wise, because more charitable, thoughts would urge me rather to save the man than to preserve his brazen slippers as the monuments of his folly.

The kind of anniversary sermons to which a great part of what I write refers, if men are not shamed out of their present course in commemorating the fact, will cheat many out of the principles, and deprive them of the benefits, of the revolution they commemorate. I confess to you, Sir, I never liked this continual talk of resistance and revolution, or the practice of making the extreme medicine of the constitution its daily bread. It renders the habit of society dangerously valetudinary; it is taking periodical doses of mercury sublimate and swallowing down repeated provocatives of cantharides to our love of liberty.

This distemper of remedy, grown habitual, relaxes and wears out, by a vulgar and prostituted use, the spring of that spirit which is to be exerted on great occasions. It was in the most patient period of Roman servitude that themes of tyrannicide made the ordinary exercise of boys at school—*cum perimit saevos classis numerosa tyrannos.*[3] In the ordinary state of things, it produces in a country like ours the worst effects, even on the cause of that liberty which it abuses with the dissoluteness of an extravagant speculation. Almost all the high-bred republicans of my time have, after a short space, become the most decided, thorough-paced courtiers; they soon left the business of a tedious, moderate, but practical resistance to those of us whom, in the pride and intoxication of their theories, they have slighted as not much better than Tories. Hypocrisy, of course, delights in the most sublime speculations, for, never intending to go beyond speculation, it costs nothing to have it magnificent. But even in cases where rather levity than fraud was to be suspected in these ranting speculations, the issue has been much the same. These professors, finding their extreme principles not applicable to cases which call only for a qualified or, as I may say, civil and legal resistance, in such cases employ no resistance at all. It is with them a war or a revolution, or it is nothing. Finding their schemes of politics not adapted to the state of the world in which they live, they often come to think lightly of all public principle, and are ready, on their part, to abandon for a very trivial interest what they find of very trivial value. Some, indeed, are of more steady and persevering natures, but these are eager politicians out of parliament who have little to tempt them to abandon their favorite projects. They have some change in the church or state, or both, constantly in their view. When that is the case, they are always bad citizens and perfectly unsure connections. For, considering their speculative designs as of infinite

---

2. Horace, *Ars Poetica,* 465–66. "Poets are permitted to perish . . . In cold blood he jumped into burning Etna"; a reference to the suicide of Empedocles, supposed to have thrown himself into a volcano, where his sandals alone survived.

3. Juvenal, *Satires,* VII, 151: "When the numerous class destroys the cruel tyrants".

value, and the actual arrangement of the state as of no estimation, they are at best indifferent about it. They see no merit in the good, and no fault in the vicious, management of public affairs; they rather rejoice in the latter, as more propitious to revolution. They see no merit or demerit in any man, or any action, or any political principle any further than as they may forward or retard their design of change; they therefore take up, one day, the most violent and stretched prerogative, and another time the wildest democratic ideas of freedom, and pass from one to the other without any sort of regard to cause, to person, or to party. . . .

. . . We know, and what is better, we feel inwardly, that religion is the basis of civil society and the source of all good and of all comfort. In England we are so convinced of this, that there is no rust of superstition with which the accumulated absurdity of the human mind might have crusted it over in the course of ages, that ninety-nine in a hundred of the people of England would not prefer to impiety. We shall never be such fools as to call in an enemy to the substance of any system to remove its corruptions, to supply its defects, or to perfect its construction. If our religious tenets should ever want a further elucidation, we shall not call on atheism to explain them. We shall not light up our temple from that unhallowed fire. It will be illuminated with other lights. It will be perfumed with other incense than the infectious stuff which is imported by the smugglers of adulterated metaphysics. If our ecclesiastical establishment should want a revision, it is not avarice or rapacity, public or private, that we shall employ for the audit, or receipt, or application of its consecrated revenue. Violently condemning neither the Greek nor the Armenian, nor, since heats are subsided, the Roman system of religion, we prefer the Protestant, not because we think it has less of the Christian religion in it, but because, in our judgment, it has more. We are Protestants, not from indifference, but from zeal.

We know, and it is our pride to know, that man is by his constitution a religious animal; that atheism is against, not only our reason, but our instincts; and that it cannot prevail long. But if, in the moment of riot and in a drunken delirium from the hot spirit drawn out of the alembic of hell, which in France is now so furiously boiling, we should uncover our nakedness by throwing off that Christian religion which has hitherto been our boast and comfort, and one great source of civilization amongst us and amongst many other nations, we are apprehensive (being well aware that the mind will not endure a void) that some uncouth, pernicious, and degrading superstition might take place of it.

For that reason, before we take from our establishment the natural, human means of estimation and give it up to contempt, as you have done, and in doing it have incurred the penalties you well deserve to suffer, we desire that some other may be presented to us in the place of it. We shall then form our judgment.

On these ideas, instead of quarrelling with establishments, as some do who have made a philosophy and a religion of their hostility to such institutions, we cleave closely to them. We are resolved to keep an established church, an established monarchy, an established aristocracy, and an established democracy, each in the degree it exists, and in no greater. I shall show you presently how much of each of these we possess.

It has been the misfortune (not, as these gentlemen think it, the glory) of this age that everything is to be discussed as if the constitution of our country were to be always a subject rather of altercation than enjoyment. For this reason, as well as for the satisfaction of those among you (if any such you have among you) who may wish to profit of examples, I venture to trouble you with a few thoughts upon each of these establishments. I do not think they were unwise in ancient Rome who, when they wished to new-model their laws; set commissioners to examine the best constituted republics within their reach.

First, I beg leave to speak of our church establishment, which is the first of our prejudices, not a prejudice destitute of reason, but involving in it profound and extensive wisdom. I speak of it first. It is first and last and midst in our minds. For, taking ground on that religious system of which we are now in possession, we continue to act on the early received and uniformly continued sense of mankind. That sense not only, like a wise architect, hath built up the august fabric of states, but, like a provident proprietor, to preserve the structure from profanation and ruin, as a sacred temple purged from all the impurities of fraud and violence and injustice and tyranny, hath solemnly and forever consecrated the commonwealth and all that officiate in it. This consecration is made that all who administer the government of men, in which they stand in the person of God himself, should have high and worthy notions of their function and destination, that their hope should be full of immortality, that they should not look to the paltry pelf of the moment nor to the temporary and transient praise of the vulgar, but to a solid, permanent existence in the permanent part of their nature, and to a permanent fame and glory in the example they leave as a rich inheritance to the world.

Such sublime principles ought to be infused into persons of exalted situations, and religious establishments provided that may continually revive and enforce them. Every sort of moral, every sort of civil, every sort of politic institution, aiding the rational and natural ties that connect the human understanding and affections to the divine, are not more than necessary in order to build up that wonderful structure Man, whose prerogative it is to be in a great degree a creature of his own making, and who, when made as he ought to be made, is destined to hold no trivial place in the creation. But whenever man is put over men, as the better nature ought ever to preside, in that case more particularly, he should as nearly as possible be approximated to his perfection.

The consecration of the state by a state religious establishment is necessary, also, to operate with a wholesome awe upon free citizens, because, in order to secure their freedom, they must enjoy some determinate portion of power. To them, therefore, a religion connected with the state, and with their duty toward it, becomes even more necessary than in such societies where the people, by the terms of their subjection, are confined to private sentiments and the management of their own family concerns. All persons possessing any portion of power ought to be strongly and awfully impressed with an idea that they act in trust, and that they are to account for their conduct in that trust to the one great Master, Author, and Founder of society. . . .

... To avoid, therefore, the evils of inconstancy and versatility, ten thousand times worse than those of obstinacy and the blindest prejudice, we have consecrated the state, that no man should approach to look into its defects or corruptions but with due caution, that he should never dream of beginning its reformation by its subversion, that he should approach to the faults of the state as to the wounds of a father, with pious awe and trembling solicitude. By this wise prejudice we are taught to look with horror on those children of their country who are prompt rashly to hack that aged parent in pieces and put him into the kettle of magicians, in hopes that by their poisonous weeds and wild incantations they may regenerate the paternal constitution and renovate their father's life.

Society is indeed a contract. Subordinate contracts for objects of mere occasional interest may be dissolved at pleasure—but the state ought not to be considered as nothing better than a partnership agreement in a trade of pepper and coffee, calico, or tobacco, or some other such low concern, to be taken up for a little temporary interest, and to be dissolved by the fancy of the parties. It is to be looked on with other reverence, because it is not a partnership in things subservient only to the gross animal existence of a temporary and perishable nature. It is a partnership in all science; a partnership in all art; a partnership in every virtue and in all perfection. As the ends of such a partnership cannot be obtained in many generations, it becomes a partnership not only between those who are living, but between those who are living, those who are dead, and those who are to be born. Each contract of each particular state is but a clause in the great primeval contract of eternal society, linking the lower with the higher natures, connecting the visible and invisible world, according to a fixed compact sanctioned by the inviolable oath which holds all physical and all moral natures, each in their appointed place. This law is not subject to the will of those who by an obligation above them, and infinitely superior, are bound to submit their will to that law. The municipal corporations of that universal kingdom are not morally at liberty at their pleasure, and on their specula- tions of a contingent improvement, wholly to separate and tear asunder the bands of their subordinate community and to dissolve it into an unsocial, uncivil, unconnected chaos of elementary principles. It is the first and supreme necessity only, a necessity that is not chosen but chooses, a necessity paramount to deliberation, that admits no discussion and de- mands no evidence, which alone can justify a resort to anarchy. This necessity is no exception to the rule, because this necessity itself is a part, too, of that moral and physical disposition of things to which man must be obedient by consent or force; but if that which is only submission to necessity should be made the object of choice, the law is broken, nature is disobeyed, and the rebellious are outlawed, cast forth, and exiled from this world of reason, and order, and peace, and virtue, and fruitful penitence, into the antagonist world of madness, discord, vice, confusion, and unavail- ing sorrow.

These, my dear Sir, are, were, and, I think, long will be the sentiments of not the least learned and reflecting part of this kingdom. They who are included in this description form their opinions on such grounds as such persons ought to form them. The less inquiring receive them from an authority which those whom Providence dooms to live on trust need not be ashamed to rely on. These two sorts of men move in the same direction, though in a different place. They both move with the order of the universe. They all know or feel this great ancient truth: *Quod illi principi et praepotenti Deo qui omnem hunc mundum regit, nihil eorum quae quidem fiant in terris acceptius quam concilia et coetus hominum jure sociati quae civitates appellantur.*[4] They take this tenet of the head and heart, not from the great name which it immediately bears, nor from the greater from whence it is derived, but from that which alone can give true weight and sanction to any learned opinion, the common nature and common relation of men. Persuaded that all things ought to be done with reference, and referring all to the point of reference to which all should be directed, they think themselves bound, not only as individuals in the sanctuary of the heart or as congregated in that personal capacity, to renew the memory of their high origin and cast, but also in their corporate character to perform their national homage to the institutor and author and protector of civil society; without which civil society man could not by any possibility arrive at the perfection of which his nature is capable, nor even make a remote and faint approach to it. They conceive that He who gave our nature to be perfected by our virtue willed also the necessary means of its perfection. He willed therefore the state—He willed its connection with the source and original archetype of all perfection. They who are convinced of this His will, which is the law of laws and the sovereign of sovereigns, cannot think it reprehensible that this our corporate fealty and homage, that this our recognition of a seigniory paramount, I had almost said this oblation of the state itself as a worthy offering on the high altar of universal praise, should be performed as all public, solemn acts are performed, in buildings, in music, in decoration, in speech, in the dignity of persons, according to the customs of mankind taught by their nature; that is, with modest splendor and unassuming state, with mild majesty and sober pomp. For those purposes they think some part of the wealth of the country is as usefully employed as it can be in fomenting the luxury of individuals. It is the public ornament. It is the public consolation. It nourishes the public hope. The poorest man finds his own importance and dignity in it, whilst the wealth and pride of individuals at every moment makes the man of humble rank and fortune sensible of his inferiority and degrades and vilifies his condition. It is for the man in humble life, and to raise his nature and to put him in mind of a state in which the privileges of opulence will cease, when he will be equal by nature, and may be more than equal by virtue, that this portion of the general wealth of his country is employed and sanctified.

I assure you I do not aim at singularity. I give you opinions which have been accepted amongst us, from very early times to this moment, with a continued and general approbation, and which indeed are worked into my mind that I am unable to distinguish what I have learned from others from the results of my own meditation.

It is on some such principles that the majority of the people of England, far from thinking a religious national establishment unlawful, hardly think

---

4. Cicero, *De Republica*, VI, 13: "That nothing indeed of the events which occur on earth is more pleasing to that supreme and prepotent God who rules this entire universe than those societies and associations of men, cemented by laws, which are called states".

it lawful to be without one. In France you are wholly mistaken if you do not believe us above all other things attached to it, and beyond all other nations; and when this people has acted unwisely and unjustifiably in its favor (as in some instances they have done most certainly), in their very errors you will at least discover their zeal.

This principle runs through the whole system of their polity. They do not consider their church establishment as convenient, but as essential to their state, not as a thing heterogeneous and separable, something added for accommodation, what they may either keep or lay aside according to their temporary ideas of convenience. They consider it as the foundation of their whole constitution, with which, and with every part of which, it holds an indissoluble union. Church and state are ideas inseparable in their minds, and scarcely is the one ever mentioned without mentioning the other. . . .

COMMENTARY

Burke
Gérard Gengembre

Edmund Burke burst upon the French Revolution on November 29, 1790. Two thousand copies of his just-translated *Reflections on the Revolution in France* were snapped up in Paris in two days. In London, where the work had been published on the first of the month, it had already had the effect of a bombshell. With eleven editions in less than a year, it was one of the era's best-selling books.

The counterrevolution, previously limited to parliamentary maneuvering, court intrigue, rousing of public opinion by a vehement press, and the first signs of an émigré reaction, had suddenly found a persuasive theorist capable of depicting events in the light of a philosophy of history. All Europe seized upon his facts and assimilated his ideas. Nevertheless, French historians from Thiers to Lefebvre have shown little interest in Burke. Only Jaurès attempted to read him closely and refute his arguments in detail. Recently, however, he has found his way back into the good graces of French scholars and publishers and has at last been receiving the kind of attention he deserves.

Little known in France at the time of the Revolution, Burke nevertheless occupied an important place on the English political scene. Born in Ireland in 1729, educated at Trinity College, and thoroughly familiar with Enlightenment thought through the *Annual Register,* a review he founded in 1758, Burke began his career as a man of letters with the publication in 1757 of his authoritative *Philosophical Enquiry into the Origin of Our Ideas of the Sublime and the Beautiful,* and later he entered politics. A Whig member of Parliament from 1766 onward, he was a brilliant speaker well known for his important writings and speeches on the day's burning issues: Ireland, for which he desired religious freedom; America, with which he advocated reconciliation; free trade; and the status of the East India Company. Between 1785 and 1788 he emerged as the rival of men like Fox and Thomas Paine.

His position is paradoxical, for it was as a liberal—albeit a conservative one—that he attacked the Revolution, in opposition to those in England who saw it as a reprise of English history, the eighteenth century being much given to such historical parallels. The full title of his book suggests the urgency of his concern: *Reflections on the Revolution in France and on the Proceedings in Certain Societies in London Relative to the Events, in a Letter Intended to Have Been Sent to a Gentleman in Paris.* His principal domestic adversary was the Revolution Society and its learned spokesman Richard Price, an ardent champion of the Revolution. But Price merely provided Burke with a pretext. The Revolution was a radically new and "astonishing" event, which threatened to alter the course of history. A monster had been born. Like a contagious disease, it threatened to undermine world order, and in particular it posed a menace to English stability and civilization. (Burke's book was therefore an exercise in political exorcism.) Like any abnormality, however, the Revolution was

Reprinted by permission of the publishers from *A Critical Dictionary of the French Revolution* by Francois Furet and Mona Ozouf, Editors, Cambridge, MA: The Belknap Press of Harvard University Press. Copyright © 1989 by the President and Fellows of Harvard College.

also fascinating. It therefore called for a detailed examination. Such close scrutiny, it was hoped, would also yield prophylactic benefits. Burke's diagnosis proved to be extraordinarily perceptive. With a deft style and penetrating insight he issued a prophecy: that this Revolution was unlike any other the world had ever known and, because its view of things was utopian and depraved, it would inevitably prove harmful and evil.

Burke begins by denying the assertion that the new French institutions had been modeled on English ones. Conveniently omitting mention of the 1640s, Burke shows that the Glorious Revolution of 1688 had restored legitimacy to the monarchy and set English history back on the right road of constitutional government. It was a revolution because it violated the rules governing dynastic succession, but in the context of the event those rules were outweighed by a higher national interest. In no way did the revolution of 1688 establish that the English had a right to choose their own king. Even if the people had possessed such a right before, they solemnly abjured it now. The Bill of Rights of 1689, the cornerstone of the English constitution, established an indissoluble tie between the rights and liberties of British subjects and the laws of succession to the throne. Burke's interpretation of the Glorious Revolution differs sharply from that of Locke, for whom the accomplished fact was by definition reasonable: if the government infringed upon natural rights, most notably liberty and property, then the governed had the right to rebel. Thus for Locke the revolution of 1688 was a consequence of natural law. Burke, however, adopted the classical position on legitimate disobedience. The gravity and urgency of the situation justified the use of exceptional means. The whole episode was merely "a small and temporary deviation." In essence, the Whig writer interpreted 1688 as a Tory.

Where the English Revolution had been a sober restoration of the national tradition, the French was a mad attempt to start with a clean slate. Burke saw the French Revolution not as the logical culmination of steadily growing enlightenment but as a dictatorship of reason, in the name of which the precious legacy of generations past was cast aside rather than preserved as every nation must preserve its heritage. From Locke by way of Hume, Burke took the idea that nations must plumb the past in search of sure and definite values to guide their actions. Philosophy leads to skepticism (which Burke had denounced as early as 1756 in *A Vindication of Natural Society*); its conclusions are negative, and with such conclusions it is impossible to formulate positive reforms. The past is a record of man's fundamental experiences; it determines what conventions are legitimate by transmitting them to posterity. Our culture consists of what the past teaches us about our nature. Custom, far from being a "second nature," is nature itself. Hence the "prejudices" reviled by the philosophers are also natural. They are the fund of wealth amassed by the genuine, collective wisdom of the nation, and their effectiveness demonstrates their validity. Burke thus rejects the Rousseauian social contract in the name of a philosophy of nature; for him, the legitimacy of the constitution rests on prescription, not convention. History, the slow, natural evolution of society, has seen society become more complex but without making man more perfect, for man bears the mark of original sin. Man's natural state is to live in society and progress slowly toward civilization. Like Hume, and as Bonald would later argue at great length, Burke held that man is by nature a social being.

Slowly but surely, Burke continues, the English people had built themselves a constitution. That constitution became their heritage, the increase in its value by each new generation illustrating the link between conservation and progress. One improves what one already possesses, ensuring its preservation. The past, always vital and active, continuously molds present and future. To judge where we are going, we must know how we got where we are. The existence of government is legitimate because time has shown that delegation of power by the people to their representatives serves the common interest. Such delegation is a virtue by consensus.

It is often said that Burke, the champion of tradition, was an antirationalist: he identifies reason with experience and invokes the principles of the common law. For him, empiricism is the only law that ought to guide peoples and statesmen. For Burke the question is not "What is to be done?" but "What decision will best reflect the lessons of history and do most to promote the common good?" Politics is then a matter of finding the best compromise with what actually exists in a society composed of individuals guided by self-interest. Conflicts are managed and kept within reasonable limits by the state as prescribed by the constitution. The state is also the guarantor of economic freedom. (That tireless advocate of the free market, the economist Friedrich Hayek, traces his ideological ancestry to Burke.) A legacy of history, the right to property and to free enjoyment of the fruits of one's labor is confirmed by the existence of "corporate bodies," which are veritable institutions, social organs legitimated by time, as opposed to the idealized "people" of the philosophes. The French Revolution, a philosophical construct based on the abstract individual, had done away with all corporate bodies capable of serving as reasonable representative institutions, as necessary intermediaries and buffers between the individual and the state. The primary function of modern government is to ensure the equitable distribution of opportunities; at bottom its only ideology is to be useful. Forgetting this, the Revolution sacrificed the people's genuine interests. By attempting to wipe out their prejudices and misconceptions, it left them with nothing.

Thus, natural law is made concrete by history. At the same time, a divine law is gradually revealed to man through his social practice. Nevertheless, it would be wrong to portray Burke as a theocrat, if only because of the importance he ascribes to parliament and, more generally, because of the autonomy he sees in the political process. He does, however, identify English constitutional order with world order: "Our political system is placed in a just correspondence and symmetry with the order of the world." But the English constitution is England's property alone and not exportable. The common law is compounded of history and tradition, not of abstract theories about the rights of man or myths of universal reason. For Burke the universal and the particular had come together in England in a unique way: the country enjoyed freedom by virtue of its own inalienable and inimitable history and because its laws had gradually been brought into conformity with the laws of nature.

Could France have followed a similar course, one suited to its own genius, to what Herder would have called its *Volksgeist?* Though the comparison should not be carried too far, it is worth noting that Burke, like Herder, viewed a people as a living thing. Evolution was part of his thinking about families and societies, a fact that influenced later naturalistic political philosophies.

The French revolutionaries, feverish to impose their will on society, rent the social fabric by substituting a dictatorship based on abstract principles for sound administration of natural progress. They lost contact with the concrete substance of history. Instead of acknowledging the rights of *men,* rights rooted in reality and therefore worthy of being taken seriously, France's misguided rulers proclaimed the Rights of Man, a dangerously metaphysical notion. They advocated a democratic utopia based on the absurd dogma of equality, according to which individuals were like interchangeable cogs; they severed all ancestral ties and abolished the institutions that integrated men into society. Although men are morally equal, they are in many concrete ways unequal; this is a consequence of the operation of civil society. The levelers, by attacking this factual state of affairs, this necessary evil, wreaked havoc without bringing about equality, which was in fact impossible to achieve. The fatal contradiction between the abstract and the concrete is a constant refrain in Burke's text. It was a theme that would be taken up not only by subsequent counterrevolutionary thinkers but also by adversaries of democracy.

Rationalistic folly had turned reformists into apologists of change for change's sake. Change was necessary, Burke acknowledged, but it must be moderate: "A state without the means of some change is without the means of its conservation." In contrast to counterrevolutionaries who idealized the Ancien Régime, Burke stressed the abuses of absolutism, which he said had interrupted the evolution of French society toward a harmonious equilibrium of liberty and power: "The constitution was suspended before it was perfected." Burke was overly inclined to see France through a liberal's spectacles, in which respect he resembles the royalist Ferrand, who, as a follower of Boulainvilliers before becoming a royalist, alluded in his *Essai d'un citoyen* (1789) to the "unwritten constitution . . . which collects venerable customs . . . [and] imposes specific obligations on the king, limiting his absolute power." Burke states that elements of a French constitution did exist. The Estates General could and should have used them as a basis for establishing a modern French system of government. For example, the *cahiers de doléances* proposed numerous improvements that would have neither overturned nor destroyed existing institutions. The *cahiers* reflected the true principles of the French constitution, and the inability of absolutism to wipe those principles from memory was proof of its fundamental illegitimacy. In France, 1789 should have been what 1688 was in England. But things quickly got out of hand—a theme that was to be endlessly repeated.

According to Burke, the loss of control began politically with the rejection of bicameralism in September, even if it did not manifest itself publicly until the October Days. He cites two scandalous decisions, to revoke the rights of property and to promulgate atheism. He sees a growing conflict in French society between "the landed interest" and "the moneyed interest," a point that interested Jaurès. In England these two interests formed a dynamic combination that promoted economic progress and therefore liberty, but in France conflict between them led to the victory of the moneyed interest, which Burke says was more receptive to innovation. The reasons for this difference between England and France have to do with specific features of French history: ancient customs, the nobles' relation to the land, the extent of inalienable property held by the Crown and the Church. Spurred on by the intrigues of the philosophes—"literary politicians" bent on the destruction of Christianity—the moneyed interest successfully persuaded the Assembly to confiscate the property of the Church. France was transformed: the new oligarchy that was created controlled the circulation of paper money and struck at the heart of religion, the basis of all civilization. No excess, no outrage was too great for revolutionaries hostile to the one institution that bound French society together.

Burke then paints a broad-brushed portrait of revolutionary France, a country with civil and military anarchy for a constitution; an assembly of usurpers, composed of garrulous, obscure country lawyers, simple, inexperienced rural priests, and restless, dissatisfied gentlemen; an arbitrary, abstract division of the territory, a division that threatened to destroy the unity of the nation and give undue power to Paris; streets ruled by screaming, frenzied, brutal mobs; and a passion for that unnatural monstrosity, equality, and for the law of numbers, when in fact the country was ruled by profiteers and stock-jobbers. Such was the France created by the Constituent

Assembly. Generalized law-breaking had produced chaos. The Revolution had de-generated into an orgy of crime and grotesque debauch upon which people looked with a mixture of fascinated horror and astonished disbelief.

Burke was able to predict the outcome of all this chaos, as if he had discerned in it the laws of disorder. No community could be founded by abstract individuals. Hence the nation would have to seek the bond of federation in the abstraction of the state, with all its potential for despotism. The new democratic regime left the citizen directly dependent on the government, with nothing to buffer its power. The only course open to the Revolution led inexorably to tyranny. The Terror and the recourse to military rule were therefore implicit in the premises of 1789. If, moreover, the monarchy should happen to be restored, it would be totally arbitrary, for it would no longer be hampered by the checks to despotism once established by age-old tradition. What prescience! Before he died in 1797, Burke saw part of his prognosis come true, and he advocated all-out war against the perverted nation that the Revolution had engendered.

Such folly, Burke says, was totally unpredictable—and this view is perhaps one weakness of his book. Philosophy, economic and social tensions, and human weakness all bear part of the blame, but even together they cannot account for a disaster of such magnitude. In the end it is impossible to ascribe a cause to the Revolution. To go from the Estates General to the eruption of the democratic ideal required a leap—an astonishing, mystifying leap. What mysterious force can account for a nation's attempting to put a philosophy into practice? A supernatural explanation beckons: it is tempting, Burke says, to think that France, by committing some great crime, drew upon itself the wrath of heaven. Maistre would later take up the theme of the Revolution as punishment. But Burke was not out to create a religious ideology. If time is the fundamental dimension in which all societies exist, the Revolution, a Promethean aberration, committed the supreme error by seeking to establish itself as a new beginning, an origin of historical time. It went astray because it believed implicitly in the nonsensical proposition that freedom can be created out of nothing. By attempting to divinize man, it led only to a dehumanized society.

Burke's book is a veritable breviary of counterrevolution. Its formal structure is loose: without chapter or section titles, it is neither pamphlet nor treatise in political philosophy. It won an audience by its virtues alone: a sure gift for description, rigorous analysis, and powerful polemic. English opinion was divided; while the Tories and some Whigs felt that Burke's book had captured their views, radical Whigs like Mary Wollstonecraft and MacIntosh violently attacked him. Godwin, Bentham, and James Mill joined the battle as well. Above all, Thomas Paine in 1791 published *The Rights of Man*. In the debate between Paine and Burke, Pierre Manent sees an "emblem of subsequent conflicts between 'right' and 'left' that divided liberal societies and societies in search of liberal institutions." Both men accepted the liberal system of representation, but Burke interpreted that system in a conservative light, Paine in a progressive one. Translated into German in 1791, Burke's work influenced Brandes, already known for his *Political Considerations of the French Revolution* (1790), who in 1792 published a staunchly Burkean book entitled *On Some Consequences of the French Revolution Relative to Germany;* Burke's influence is also evident in Rehberg's *Research on the French Revolution* (1792) and in the work of Gentz, his translator, known as the "German Burke."

In France his fortunes were less assured, at least in the decades after the Revolution. Maistre and Bonald read him and praised the power of his work, but they saw no deep affinities between it and their own doctrines: a providentialist reading of history on the one hand, an organicist and essentially reactionary theocracy on the other, both imbued with nostalgia for the Ancien Régime and idealization of absolute monarchy. From Burke they naturally drew arguments to bolster their counterrevolutionary positions, but they were not really influenced by him. As the nineteenth century progressed, Burke's seminal importance gradually became more apparent. Paine, in particular, read Burke as confirming his own political and social naturalism, which he opposed to the abstract idealism and metaphysics of the Revolution and which helped shape his *Origines de la France contemporaine*.

Burke's wholly negative portrait of France troubled even the monarchist right, and early French liberals could not abide his deep-dyed conservatism. Some even denied that Burke was a liberal, as if traditionalism and liberalism were mutually exclusive.

French liberals agreed with Burke, however, that the Revolution had inaugurated a new chapter in French history. The French liberal tradition begins in 1789, and despite their borrowings from England and defense of the English model, Benjamin Constant and Mme. de Staël were well aware of the profound differences between a liberalism that had matured over a long period of time and a liberalism suddenly sprung on a renovated France. In 1798, in a work entitled "On the Present Circumstances Which May End the Revolution and the Principles That Ought to Underlie the French Republic," Staël elaborated a program for government based on the republican party's assuming full powers with the support of the army and for the purpose of achieving not compromise but consensus. Thereafter the government's aim would be to convert the nation gradually to its own ideology, by means of education based on sound morals and self-interest. In other words, the new France should proceed along English lines.

All the various strands of liberalism claimed the legacy of 1789, from the Doctrinaires on the right to the more left-wing Rémusat, who in 1853 published a magisterial article in the *Revue des deux mondes* in which he confidently demolished Burke's counterfactual argument that if the history of France had been different, there need not have been a Revolution. Liberal historians from Guizot to Tocqueville, along with the famous "fatalist school" discussed by Chateaubriand, saw the Revolution, including the pressure to proceed beyond the objectives originally set by the Estates General, as necessary. Burke defended continuity, the French liberals insisted on a radical break with the past, misunderstanding was inevitable. Study of this penetrating foreigner's scrutiny of France remains profitable for anyone who would understand what was truly at stake in a Revolution from which the whole modern French political tradition ultimately derives.

The Critique of Political Radicalism
Michael Freeman

Edmund Burke constructed a classic conservative critique of political radicalism. The chief immediate object of his attack was the radicalism of late eighteenth-century France and England. But he appealed to general principles which, though expressed in the language and with the concepts of his own time, are sufficiently similar to widely-held conservative ideas of today that we may and should assess their value. Today's radicals are not Burke's radicals and vary greatly in their beliefs. But Burke's radicals were never the real radicals of his own time. Nowhere in his works can we find a scrupulous account of the ideas or actions of any particular radical thinker or politician. Burke attacked certain abstract radical ideas by means of certain abstract conservative arguments. These abstract ideas may be held by radicals in different times and places, facing different concrete problems.

To the proposal that we should evaluate Burke's critique of radicalism it may be objected that, since he appealed to 'natural feeling' and rejected systematic argument, he protected himself, many would say illegitimately, from systematic rational criticism. I have shown, however, that he did not reject reason nor the idea that politics should be rational.

Burke not only at times expressed a preference for intuition over ratiocination but also advocated pragmatism against theory. Theory, he said, was speculative, not real. Theory was too broad and too deep. The real problems of society were particular and their remedies must therefore also be particular. A theoretical approach to social problems led to the characteristic defects and dangers of radicalism: solutions too remote from reality and too big for the problems. But, although he did not present his ideas systematically and was far from consistent, he did have a theory of politics and of political radicalism. This political theory was based upon the metaphysical doctrine that nature was order. This doctrine had two meanings. Nature ordained stability: good order is the foundation of all good things. Nature is also regular. Thus politics is governed by discoverable laws. Because stability is natural, revolution is against nature. But, though revolution is (morally) unnatural, it is still governed by nature's laws. These dictate that revolution leads to anarchy, which in turn must lead to tyranny. Thus, for all his pragmatism, Burke proposed a law of revolution for us to assess, a law both general and normative, a law derived from a highly articulated political theory.

Burke's metaphysics is banal and unpersuasive. His epistemology carries much more force. The project of revolution, he argues, presupposes a degree of reliable social knowledge which no individual or faction can reasonably claim. The radical is, not as a matter of contingent psychological fact, but in his essence intellectually arrogant. As a theorist he thinks big. As a radical, he applies his big theories without adequate knowledge of the probable consequences of his actions and with little understanding of the inadequacy of his knowledge. The identification of practical

Michael Freeman. 1980. *Edmund Burke and the Critique of Political Radicalism*. Chicago: The University of Chicago Press, pp. 237–245. Reprinted by permission of the University of Chicago Press and Basil Blackwell.

grievances or real abuses in government is easy. They are always there and plain enough. The cure of grievances and the correction of abuses is often possible and always desirable when possible. But the radical who attempts the reconstruction of society cannot achieve his goal. Where abuses are clear and great, and grievances strongly felt, destruction of old institutions may not be difficult. But building new order out of the chaos of destruction is a formidible task. Tyranny is the short cut. Thus, the necessary relation between radical politics and tyranny is not only metaphysical, it derives from the sociological consequences of acting politically upon weak theories and a poor theory about the practical possibilities of theory.

This is perhaps Burke's strongest argument. Few would deny that social knowledge is highly uncertain. The conclusion that we should change social institutions with caution appears to follow. The radical claims that he has great tasks to perform but he lacks the technique to perform them.

The argument is strong but not conclusive. Burke himself recognized its weak point. His fallibilist case against radicalism, like the very similar case that has been made by conservatives many times, presupposes a certain view of the relation between the radical and his political problems. It sees the radical confronting injustice in society. He theorises the causes and the cures. He concludes that the injustice is not an accident lying on the surface of society, to be removed by a well-aimed reformist blow, but is rooted in the foundations of the existing social form. The remedy, therefore, must be to remove, not merely the injustice, but the social form which necessarily produced it. But this objective, says the conservative, is impossible on the epistemological grounds already given.

But the radical does not always, perhaps does not typically, confront a stable society with an accidental blemish. He faces a society already in disorder, a society whose rulers cannot solve the problems before them. Burke did not believe that revolutions were caused by conspiracies of radical intellectuals. Rather, they were caused by the mistakes, stupidity, arrogance and oppression of rulers, and by the strains produced by social and economic development. In such a situation, radicals might make bad worse. But societies may disintegrate from their internal contradictions. Particular radical solutions may be ill-conceived and lead to new oppression. But in some circumstances no moderate solution may work. Caution may become a speculative ideal, not a practical method.

Because Burke held this view of the causes of revolution, he acknowledged that revolution might be justified by necessity. Whether any particular revolution is justified by necessity can only be answered by analysis of the particular circumstances. But, even when the circumstances have been analyzed, conservatives and radicals will not agree. Where radical action has been taken, the conservative will argue that less ambitious solutions would have produced better results. Not only will the two not have the same idea of 'better', but the conservative case rests upon a counterfactual claim that if conservative solution x had been tried then beneficial result y would have ensued. This claim presupposes precisely the kind of knowledge of social cause and effect which the conservative criticizes the radical for claiming. Thus, the fallibilist case againt radicalism is not conclusive. Conservatives are fallible, too. And the mistakes they make may also be big ones.

Burke held that radicals were doomed not merely to failure but to achieve the opposite of what they intended. If this argument were correct, it would be decisive. As Burke put it himself: 'Proceeding, therefore, as we are obliged to proceed, that is upon an hypothesis that we address rational men, can false political principles be more effectually exposed, than by demonstrating that they lead to consequences directly inconsistent with, and subversive of, the arrangements grounded upon them?' In the case of the French Revolution, he maintained that the revolutionaries proclaimed and then trampled on the rights of man. They promised freedom and happiness but delivered tyranny and misery. This was not due to bad luck nor merely to bad judgement. It was in the nature of things. The promise of radical emancipation from evil is an illusion which, if acted on, necessarily leads to radical evil.

Radical ideals, Burke freely acknowledges, are, in the abstract, extremely appealing. But abstract ideals are not only an inadequate substitute for practical remedies, they often mask vicious intent. Those who seek the support of others to further their own ambitions will state their aims in terms of the interests of those others, not of themselves. Thus, their ideals will appear altruistic and noble. The results may not match the stated aims because the stated aims were never the real aims. To modernize the point: would-be dictators will manipulate popular-democratic symbols to secure popular support for their ambitions.

But this is an argument against fake not genuine radicalism. Burke was concerned to emphasize, however, that the people may easily mistake the one for the other. None the less, his case against radicalism does not rest on the assumption that radicals are insincere. True radicalism is as dangerous as false. Radicals believe that existing society is fundamentally unjust and that the society they aspire to is very fine. Slow and cautious reform seems to them a sort of toleration of the intolerable. Justice demands impatience with injustice. But impatience is not wise. Nor is it just. Impatience imbued with a sense of justice becomes fanaticism. And fanaticism is a tyrant.

Burke was the first of a long line of conservative thinkers who have seen political radicalism as a sort of fanatical secular religion. One of the stigmata of fanaticism is manichaeanism: dividing the world into the just and the unjust, the saved and the damned. This manichaeanism seems reasonable when the just are 'the people', the overwhelming majority, and the unjust their oppressors. But the radical is not humble before the popular will. He has a theory of the popular interest. He has a mission to bring the people happiness. And if the people take a different view of the means to their own happiness, the radical leader, the just man, feels constrained to bring them to a true consciousness of their own interest, by force if necessary.

There was, Burke thought, a deep cause of a difference of view between radicals and the people whose interests they claimed to represent about the sources of general happiness. Radicals wish to change society fundamentally and fast. The majority, even if sorely abused, has a vested interest in society. Society guarantees a certain minimum, however low. Even if it be indeed low, there is a degree of security in it. People adjust to difficult circumstances, even if they wish they were better. They know what to expect and can plan their lives accordingly. The radical promises something much better. But he creates disorder and with disorder not even the minimum is guaranteed, there is no security, and the future is uncertain. Stable societies, even if unjust, provide security, which is an important source of happiness. Radicals offer promises of great benefits and the probability of actual chaos. The people wisely distrust their radical saviours. Radicals trust themselves too much and therefore come to distrust the people it is their mission to help.

Revolutions achieve the opposite of what they intend because what they intend —radical freedom, equality, democracy and perfect justice—cannot be achieved and because they offer the people, in the name of freedom and democracy, what the people prudently decline. Consequently, radicals must force through the impossible and the unpopular. The result can only be the negation of the freedom, equality, democracy and justice that they promised.

There is much truth in all this. The vocation of the radical and that of the democrat are often heard to reconcile. The people are, of course, sometimes radical, so that radical and popular aims coincide. But the alliance is unstable. Theories of 'false consciousness' at best explain why the problem exists, they do not provide a solution. The 'radical' Burke here attacks is an abstraction: an extreme case rather than an ideal type. Not all radicals are fanatics. Some restrain their pursuit of justice when it clashes with democracy and liberty. Respect for the popular will and self-criticism are neither impossible nor unknown among radicals. Nevertheless, such self-restraint is a restraint upon radicalism: the more restrained the seeker after justice, the less radical he is. Except in times of unusual popular radicalism, a certain tension must exist between radical means and radical ends.

Radicalism is not necessarily incompatible with freedom and democracy. Indeed, in any unfree and undemocratic society, freedom and democracy entail a radicalism of ends. But radicalism of means, fundamental change fast, is undoubtedly despotic in tendency.

Burke warns the democratic radical that democratic radicalism of means may well be self-contradictory. The radical may reply, with the argument already canvassed, that, in situations of social disintegration, there may be no non-radical solutions and, even if radicalism be an evil, a choice of the least evil is the best available option. He may also reply that, if radicalism may lead to despotism, conservatism may conserve it.

Burke opposed despotism but saw justifiable political change as the specific remedy of particular grievances and abuses. 'I would not exclude alteration neither; but even when I changed, it should be to preserve. I should be led to my remedy by a great grievance.' Safe politics is slow, cautious and dull. This is not an easy course. The virtue of moderation requires a deep courage to be temperate when the multitude impatiently condemns you. Radicalism is more exciting. Self-restraint is necessary to resist the temptation of political adventure and instant popularity. Hang on to the real good you have and improve it. Resist the blandishments of speculative blessings. Only the real can be good. What the radical promises is not real.

But what if the defect is radical? If moderation is complicity with despotism? If the multitude is impatient because the abuse is indeed intolerable? Reality is then evil, not imperfect good. Radicalism is not adventurism but realism. If radicals are often caught in a contradiction between their aims and their achievements, so was Burke. Time and again, he exposed the British Government as despotic, at home and abroad, but he continued to advocate a piecemeal, patient reform which was hardly adequate to the objectives he set it. Burke's gradualist approach to slavery entailed complicity with despotism. So did his toleration of a society in which the wealthy fed their dogs and horses with the food which should have nourished the children of the poor. Burke acknowledged this difficulty for gradualism. In desperation, he appealed from real misery to abstract laws of nature.

Burke still deserves our attention, therefore, because his arguments can be generalized and, when generalized, put hard, though not unaswerable questions to radicals. I have also sought to show that his understanding of the French Revolution in particular and of revolutionary dynamics in general has been widely misunderstood and, as a consequence, underestimated by scholars. Burke was a much better sociologist of revolution than is usually recognized. He had an implicit general theory of revolution which is superior to many recent theories of revolution in two important respects. Firstly, he had an integrated theory of the causes, processes and consequences of revolution while most modern theory is confined mainly to the causes and has little to say about the consequences. Secondly, he integrated empirical and normative theory while modern theorists tend to separate the two and largely ignore the latter.[1]

Edmund Burke teaches that the business of political radicals—the uprooting of established political and social institutions—may lead to quite unexpected and undesired consequences, involving great human suffering. He excoriated radicals for dogmatism and frivolous adventurism. He called for realism, pragmatism and respect for persons. 'I must see with my own eyes, I must, in a manner, touch with my own hands, not only the fixed, but the momentary circumstances, before I could venture to suggest any political project whatsoever. . . . I must see all the aids, and all the obstacles. I must see the means of correcting the plan, where correctives would be wanted. I must see the things; I must see the men.' 'No man carries further than I do the policy of making government pleasing to the people. But the widest range of this politic complaisance is confined within the limits of justice. . . . I never will act the tyrant for their amusement. If they will mix malice in their sports, I shall never consent to throw them any living, sentient creature whatsoever, no not so much as a kitling, to torment.' He often did not practise what he preached. He was not always humane. He was often dogmatic. He understood less than he thought he did. But he did understand that what appears to be good will may be evil will. He understood that good will may motivate acts with evil consequences. That identifying and damning evil is easy, while making good is hard and usually slow. That our fond desires cannot alter the nature of things, by contending against which what have we got, or shall ever get, but defeat and shame?

Radicals, especially Marxists, often pride themselves on their realism. Conservatives teach that realists are conservatives. Radical projects usually fail and often lead to disaster. Radicals are self-righteous and intellectually arrogant. There seems to me enough truth in this for the theory underlying it to be considered seriously. But, because conservatives hold that radical projects are utopian and dangerous, they are inclined to minimize existing misery or attribute it to necessary laws. The first position belies their claim to realism and the second their critique of abstract dogma. Thus the debate between conservatives and radicals remains inconclusive. Burke is still worth our attention because his is a classic statement of conservatism. It has the classic strengths and weaknesses of that position. He offered eighteenth-century solutions to eighteenth-century problems. But those problems belong to a family whose descendents live still among us. We still do not have very good solutions. We must therefore come to grips with his.

Note

1. See Michael Freeman, 'Edmund Burke and the Theory of Revolution', *Political Theory*, 6, 1978, pp. 277–97, and Ted Robert Gurr, 'Burke and the Modern Theory of Revolution: A Reply to Freeman', *ibid.*, pp. 298 et seq. For very recent, and more convincing theorizing about revolution, see S. N. Eisenstadt, *Revolution and the Transformation of Societies* (London: Collier Macmillan, 1978) and Theda Skocpol, *States and Social Revolutions* (Cambridge: Cambridge University Press, 1979).

Georg Wilhelm Friedrich Hegel

G.W.F. Hegel's thought has undergone a substantial revival in recent years. His ideas have been used to develop a less deterministic brand of Marxism, to criticize liberalism for its excessive individualism, and even to proclaim that history has ended with the fall of Communist regimes in Eastern Europe. Though part of the Hegel revival can be attributed to intellectual fashion, Hegel's widespread influence on many significant philosophical and political traditions cannot be denied. Indeed, his rational syntheses of thought in philosophy, history, and politics provide an excellent starting point for understanding many of today's intellectual trends.

However, the very name of Hegel may send shivers down the spine of almost any political theorist. The complexity of Hegel's work frequently challenges even the most advanced student of political theory, and his verbose, ponderous writing style is quite difficult to comprehend, largely because he speaks in a unique philosophical language. Indeed, a very simple idea can often be hidden by his verbal monsters. Yet, once one has some clues to deciphering the code in which he speaks, Hegel can begin to be more or less understood. Keep in mind that reading Hegel's work for the first time is like beginning an exercise program—the basic rule of thumb is "no pain, no gain."

Hegel was born in 1770 in Stuttgart, Germany. In 1788, he started his study of philosophy and theology at the seminary in Tubingen, and after graduation, served as a private tutor in both Switzerland and Germany. Beginning in 1801, Hegel held positions in philosophy at universities in Jena and Heidelberg. Hegel's philosophical career, and the development of his system of thought, both reached their peak after his appointment to a prestigious professorship at the University of Berlin. Hegel died in 1831.

Hegel's thought can be seen as a philosophical effort to overcome the tensions or oppositions between human beings and nature, between the individual and society, between human beings as they are and as they ought to be, or between finite and infinite spirit. These oppositions cannot be simply undone, for we cannot return to an original state of unity. Instead, Hegel's "aspiration is to retain the fruits of separation, free rational consciousness, while reconciling this with unity, that is, with nature, society, God and fate."[1]

Within this context, Hegel's tool of choice is the dialectic. Though often stereotyped as a sterile formula of Thesis-Antithesis-Synthesis, the dialectic is perhaps best understood as (1) a dynamic unity of opposites, in which the world is seen as a developmental unfolding of partial, yet essential natures; or (2) a method of probing ideas and phenomena for their internal contradictions, in order to deepen understanding and to arrive at comprehensive knowledge of the whole ("Absolute Knowledge"). For Hegel, the dialectic should be seen both as the principle underlying the workings of the universe and as his preferred philosophical method.

Properly understood, the universe is both an expression and an embodiment of *Geist* (Spirit). Hegel's view is that *Geist* creates (i.e., "posits," since the universe and thought work in the same way) the world in order to realize itself, to express and thereby understand the full range of its powers. Since this expression creates a world apart from *Geist,* history thus becomes the story of efforts by human beings (finite spirit—the self-conscious part of the universe) to fully understand themselves and the material world as various forms of *Geist,* thereby restoring the unity of creation and creator. Unity can only be restored when the universe is finally seen as operating by rational necessity; when we understand that the world cannot be other than it is and still be rational. Of course, by then, the story itself will be at an end; Absolute Knowledge, for Hegel, is always retrospective.

The Philosophy of History and The Philosophy of Right

Hegel produced a remarkably consistent philosophical system, whose parts form a seamless web. Of course, for our purposes, we will have to treat his philosophy of history and politics apart from his epistemology and logic. The first selection comes from *The Philosophy of History* (1837), edited notes taken by students from Hegel's lectures in Berlin. In those lectures, Hegel seeks to demonstrate that reason rules the world. He does not mean simply that there is an order to human events, nor does he mean that divine providence rules the world. Instead, Hegel believes that reason (as spirit) can be shown to direct the specific, concrete aspects of history (good and bad, positive and negative) toward an identifiable end. History thus comprises a lengthy process of human development aimed at realizing self-conscious, universal freedom.

Hegel develops his political theory most clearly in the 1821 work, the *Philosophy of Right*. There, Hegel begins by outlining the philosopher's task of comprehending the concrete aspects of political life, of developing a theory of the rational state. After

---

1. Charles Taylor, *Hegel* (Cambridge: Cambridge University Press, 1975), p. 79.

pursuing the idea of Right through the "moments" (dialectical stages of development) of morality and abstract right, Hegel seeks to outline a social order (labelled "ethical life" or *Sittlichkeit*) which would overcome the oppositions between individual and society, between particular and universal wills, and between right and duty. Emerging out of the unreflective unity of the family, a person becomes an individual pursuing his or her unique needs in civil society—the realm of economic activity and private welfare, safeguarded by the structures of civil and criminal law. These structures themselves depend upon the state, organized as a constitutional monarchy and functioning as the rational, overarching unity of particular and universal interests.

Commentaries

The selections from Charles Taylor's excellent interpretive survey analyze the general outlines of both Hegel's philosophy of history and his theory of the state. Taylor first discusses the dialectical unfolding of Spirit through various civilizations. He also shows how Hegel's philosophy of history yields important lessons for political theory, namely, the need for the modern state to consist of a constitutional monarch, a trained bureaucracy, and a people organized into estates or classes. Taylor then summarizes the opening parts of the *Philosophy of Right* and outlines Hegel's views on the family, civil society, and the state.

Steven Smith further explores Hegel's concept of right *(Recht)* as it is embodied in the rational state. Smith argues that Hegel views history as a developmental process by which people are educated in the ways of freedom, and by which people accept the rule of law and a society based on right. (Right and law are two possible English translations of *Recht.*) Hegel's primary concept of right is that of equal concern and respect for persons, a right of recognition. Smith develops three theses about the concept of right; argues that right is the quintessential feature of the modern state; and then, discusses Hegel's thought in the context of contemporary American liberalism.

Key Words

Reason.   The thinking involved in calculation, understanding, scientific inquiry, and philosophical argument. For Hegel, reason (its concepts and processes) not merely discovers facts about the universe, but in many ways creates or posits them.

The Idea or the Concept.   The rational principle essential to the nature and development of a historical phenomenon or social institution. In the case of world history, for example, the Idea is that of freedom.

***Recht* (right).**   Hegel's term for the complex of ideas and practices noted by such concepts as individual freedom, privilege, moral duty, and the rule of law.

***Sittlichkeit* (ethical life).**   The social order whose ethos and mores would overcome the oppositions between individual and society, between particular and universal wills, and between right and duty.

For Further Reading

Avineri, S. 1972. *Hegel's Theory of the Modern State.* Cambridge: Cambridge University Press.

MacIntyre, A., ed. 1972. *Hegel: A Collection of Critical Essays.* Garden City, N.J.: Anchor Books.

Maletz, D. 1983. "History in Hegel's *Philosophy of Right.*" *The Review of Politics.* 47: 209–233.

Marcuse, H. 1960. *Reason and Revolution: Hegel and the Rise of Social Theory.* Boston: Beacon Press.

Smith, S. 1989. *Hegel's Critique of Liberalism: Rights in Context.* Chicago: University of Chicago Press.

The Philosophy of History

Chapter 2
Reason in History

The only thought which philosophy brings with it, in regard to history, is the simple thought of Reason—the thought that Reason rules the world, and that world history has therefore been rational in its course. This conviction and insight is a *presuppostion* in regard to history as such, although it is not a presupposition in philosophy itself.

In philosophy, speculative reflection has shown that Reason is the *substance* as well as the *infinite power;* that Reason is for itself the *infinite material* of all natural and spiritual life, as well as the *infinite form,* and that its actualization of itself is its content. (And we can stand by the term "Reason" here, without examining its relation and connection with "God" more closely.)

Thus Reason is the *substance* [of our historic world] in the sense that it is that whereby and wherein all reality has its being and subsistence. It is the *infinite power,* since Reason is not so powerless as to arrive at nothing more than the ideal, the ought, and to remain outside reality—who knows where —as something peculiar in the heads of a few people. Reason is the *infinite content,* the very stuff of all essence and truth, which it gives to its own *activity* to be worked up. For, unlike finite activity, it does not need such conditions as an external material, or given means from which to get its nourishment and the objects of its activity. It lives on itself, and it is itself the material upon which it works. Just as Reason is its own presupposition and absolute goal, so it is the activation of that goal in world history— bringing it forth from the inner source to external manifestation, not only in the natural universe but also in the spiritual. That this Idea is the True, the Eternal, simply the Power—that it reveals itself in the world, and that nothing else is revealed in the world but that Idea itself, its glory and majesty—this, as we said, is what has been shown in philosophy, and it is here presupposed as already proven.

Those of you who are not yet acquainted with philosophy can at least be expected to come to these lectures on world history with the belief in Reason, with the desire, the thirst to know it. And indeed what must be presupposed as a subjective need in the study of the sciences is the desire for rational insight, for knowledge, not merely for a collection of facts. Thus, even if you do not bring to world history the thought and the knowledge of Reason, you ought at least to have the firm and unconquerable belief that there is Reason in history, together with the belief that the world of intelligence and self-conscious will is not subject to chance, but rather that it must demonstrate itself in the light of the self-conscious Idea.

From *Introduction to the Philosophy of History* (translated by Leo Rauch). Indianapolis: Hackett, pp. 12–14, 16–24. Copyright © 1988 by Leo Rauch. With the permission of Hackett Publishing Company, Inc. Indianapolis, IN and Cambridge, MA.

But in fact I need not require this belief on your part in advance. What I have said so far, and will say again, is not just to be taken as a presupposition of our science, but as a summary of the totality—as the *result* of the discussion upon which we are embarking, a result that is known to *me* because I already know that totality. Thus it is the consideration of world history itself that must reveal its rational process—namely, that it has been the rational, necessary course of the World Spirit, the Spirit whose nature is indeed always one and the same, but which reveals this one nature in the world's reality. As I said, this must be the outcome of the study of history.

Yet we must take history as it is, and proceed historically, i.e., empirically. Among other things, we must not be misled by the professional historians, particularly the Germans, who possess great authority, and do precisely what they accuse philosophers of doing, namely creating *a priori* fabrications in history. For example, there is a widespread fabrication that there existed an original, primeval people, taught directly by God and having complete insight and wisdom, with a penetrating knowledge of all the laws of nature and spiritual truth; or that there were such or such priestly peoples; or, to speak of something more specific, that there was a Roman epic from which the Roman historians drew their earliest history, and so on. Let us leave all such *a priori* constructions to the clever professionals, for whom (in Germany) such constructions are not uncommon.

As the first condition to be observed, we could therefore declare that we must apprehend the historical faithfully. But with such general terms as "apprehend" and "faithfully" there lies an ambiguity. Even the ordinary, average historian, who believes and says that he is merely receptive to his data, is not passive in his thinking; he brings his categories along with him, and sees his data through them. In every treatise that is to be scientific, Reason must not slumber, and reflection must be actively applied. To him who looks at the world rationally, the world looks rational in return. The relation is mutual. But the various kinds of reflection, of possible viewpoints, of judgment even in regard to the mere importance and unimportance of facts (the most basic category in historical judgment)—all this does not concern us here. . . .

. . . In world history, however, we are concerned with "individuals" that are nations, with wholes that are states. Accordingly, we cannot stop at the (so to speak) "retail" version of the belief in providence—still less can we be content with the merely abstract, indefinite belief which goes only so far as the general view that there is a providence, and says nothing of its more definite acts. On the contrary, we must seriously try to recognize the ways of providence, and to connect its means and manifestations in history—relating these to that universal principle.

But in mentioning the possibility of our knowing the plan of divine providence in general, I have touched on a question that has become prominent in our own time: the question about the possibility of our knowing God—or, inasmuch as it has ceased to be a question, there is the doctrine (which has now become a prejudice) that it is impossible to know God. Holy Scripture commands it as our highest duty not only to love God but also to know God. But in direct opposition to this, there now prevails the denial of what is there written: that it is the Spirit that leads us to truth, that the Spirit knows all things and penetrates even to the depths of the Godhead.*

When the Divine Being is placed beyond the reach of our knowing and beyond human affairs altogether, we gain the convenience of indulging in our own imaginings. We are thereby excused from having to give our knowledge some relation to the Divine and the True. On the contrary, the vanity of human knowledge and subjective feeling receives a complete justification for itself. And when pious humility places the knowing of God at a distance, it knows full well what it has thereby gained for its arbitrariness and vain efforts.

I could not avoid mentioning the connection between our thesis (that Reason rules the world and has ruled it) and the question about the possibility of our knowing God, since I did not want to dodge the accusation that philosophy shuns (or must shun) all discussion of religious truths due to a bad conscience about them. On the contrary, in modern times we have come to the point where philosophy has to take up the defense of religious truths against many types of theological doctrine. In the Christian religion God has revealed Himself: that is to say, He has allowed human beings to understand what He is, so that He is no longer hidden and secret. With this possibility of our knowing God, the obligation to know Him is placed upon us. God wants no narrow-minded souls and empty heads for His children. Rather, He wants those who (however poor in spirit) are rich in the knowledge of Him, and who place the highest value in this knowledge of Him. The development of the thinking spirit, which began from this basis in the revelation of the Divine Being, must finally come to the point where what was originally present only to feeling and to the imagining spirit, can now be grasped by thought. And the time must finally come when we comprehend the rich product of creative Reason that is world history.

For some time, it was customary to admire God's wisdom at work in animals, in plants, and in the destinies of individuals. If we grant that providence reveals itself in such objects and materials, then why not also in world history? Here, the material seems too great. Yet the divine wisdom, i.e., Reason, is one and the same on the large scale and on the small, and we must not consider God to be too weak to apply His wisdom on a large scale. In our knowledge, we aim for the insight that whatever was intended by the Eternal Wisdom has come to fulfillment—as in the realm of nature, so in the realm of spirit that is active and actual in the world. To that extent our approach is a theodicy, a justification of the ways of God. Leibniz attempted a theodicy in metaphysical terms, using indefinite abstract categories—so that when once the evil in the world was comprehended in this way, the thinking mind was supposed to be reconciled to it. Nowhere, in fact, is there a greater challenge to such intellectual reconciliation than in world history. This reconciliation can be achieved only through the recognition of that positive aspect, in which the negative disappears as something subordinate and overcome. It is attained (on the one hand) through the awareness of the true end-goal of the world, and (on the other) through the awareness that

---

* See I Corinthians 2:10. "God has revealed these things to us through the Spirit. For the Spirit searches all things, even the depths of God." [Translator's note.]

this end has been actualized in the world and that the evil has not prevailed in it in any ultimate sense.

For this purpose, however, the mere belief in *nous* and providence is still quite inadequate. "Reason"—which is said to rule the world—is just as indefinite a term as "Providence." We hear Reason spoken of, without anyone being able to say just what its definition is, or its content (according to which we could judge whether something is rational or irrational). To grasp Reason in its definition—that is of primary importance. If we merely stick to the bare term, "Reason", throughout, the rest of what we say is just words. With these declarations behind us, we can go on to the second viewpoint we wish to consider in this Introduction.

Chapter 3
Freedom, the Individual, and the State

If we think of Reason in its relation to the world, then the question of the *definition* of Reason in itself coincides with the question about the *final goal* of the world. Implicit in that latter term is the suggestion that the goal is to be realized, made actual. There are two things to be considered here: the content of that goal (i.e., the definition itself, as such), and its actualization.

At the outset we must note that our object—*world history*—takes place in the realm of Spirit. The term "world" includes both physical and mental nature. Physical nature impinges on world history as well, and from the very beginning we shall have to draw attention to the fundamental relations [between the two natures] in the definition. But it is Spirit, and the process of its development, that is the substance of history. Nature in itself, which is likewise a rational system in its particular and characteristic element, is not our concern here, except as related to Spirit.

Spirit is to be observed in the theater of world history, where it has its most concrete reality. In spite of this, however (or rather in order for us to grasp the universal aspect in this mode of Spirit's concrete reality), we must set forth, before all else, some abstract definitions of the *nature of Spirit*. These can, of course, be no more than mere assertions here. This is not the place to go into the Idea of Spirit in a speculative fashion, for what can be said in an introduction is simply to be taken historically—as a presupposition which (as we said) has either been worked out and proven elsewhere, or else is to receive its verification only as the outcome of the science of history itself.

We have therefore to address the following topics:

  I. The abstract characteristics of the nature of Spirit
 II. The means Spirit uses in order to realize its Idea
III. The shape taken on by Spirit in its complete realization in the world—the State.

I. The Nature of Spirit. This can be seen by looking at its complete antithesis—matter. Just as the essence of matter is gravity [that is, in being determined by a force outside it], so the essence of Spirit is its freedom [that is, in its self-determination]. Everyone will immediately agree that Spirit is endowed with freedom, among other characteristics. Philosophy, however, teaches us that all the characteristics of Spirit subsist only by means of freedom; that all of them are only the means to freedom, and that they seek and produce only freedom. This is one of the truths of speculative philosophy: that freedom is the only truth of Spirit.

Matter has weight insofar as it strives toward a central point outside itself. It is essentially composed of parts which are separable. It seeks its unity, which would be its own negation, its opposite. If it were to achieve this, it would no longer be matter but would have perished. It strives toward the ideal, for in unity [i.e., in being self-determining, self-moving], matter is idealized.

Spirit, on the other hand, is that which has its center in itself. Its unity is not outside itself; rather, it has found it within its own self. It is in its own self and alone unto itself. While matter has its "substance" [i.e., its source of support] outside itself, Spirit is autonomous and self-sufficient, a Being-by-itself (Bei-sich-selbst-sein). But this, precisely, is freedom—for when I am dependent, I relate myself to something else, something which I am not; as dependent, I cannot be without something which is external. I am free when I exist independently, all by myself. This self-sufficient being is self-consciousness, the consciousness of self.

Two things must be distinguished in consciousness: first, the fact *that* I know; and second, *what* I know. In self-consciousness, the two—subject and object—coincide. Spirit knows itself: it is the judging of its own nature, and at the same time it is the activity of coming to itself, of producing itself, making itself actually what it is in itself potentially.

According to this abstract definition, we can say of world history that it is the exhibition of the Spirit, the working out of the explicit knowledge of what it is potentially. Just as the germ of the plant carries within itself the entire nature of the tree, even the taste and shape of its fruit, so the first traces of Spirit virtually contain all history.

In the world of the ancient Orient, people do not yet know that the Spirit—the human as such—is free. Because they do not know this, they are not free. They know only that *one* person is free; but for this very reason such freedom is mere arbitrariness, savagery, stupefied passion; or even a softness or tameness of passion, which is itself a mere accident of nature and therefore quite arbitrary. This *one* person is therefore only a despot, not a free man.

It was among the Greeks that the consciousness of freedom first arose, and thanks to that consciousness they were free. But they, and the Romans as well, knew only that *some* persons are free, not the human as such. Even Plato and Aristotle did not know this. Not only did the Greeks have slaves, therefore—and Greek life and their splendid freedom were bound up with this—but their freedom itself was partly a matter of mere chance, a transient and limited flowering, and partly a hard servitude of the human and the humane.

It was first the Germanic peoples, through Christianity, who came to the awareness that *every* human is free by virtue of being human, and that the freedom of spirit comprises our most human nature. This awareness arose first in religion, in the innermost region of Spirit. But to introduce this principle into worldly reality as well: that was a further task, requiring long effort and civilization to bring it into being. For example, slavery did not end immediately with the acceptance of the Christian religion; freedom did not suddenly prevail in Christian states; nor were governments and constitutions organized on a rational basis, or indeed upon the principle of freedom.

This application of the principle of freedom to worldly reality—the dissemination of this principle so that it permeates the worldly situation—this is the long process that makes up history itself. I have already drawn attention to the distinction between a principle as such and its application, its introduction and implementation in the actuality of spirit and life. This distinction is fundamental to our science, and it must be kept in mind. Just as this distinction was noted in a preliminary way with regard to the Christian principle of self-consciousness and freedom, so it has its essential place in regard to the principle of freedom in general. World history is the progress in the consciousness of freedom—a progress that we must come to know in its necessity.

Above, I made a general statement regarding the different levels in the awareness of freedom—namely, that the Orientals knew only that *one* person is free; the Greeks and Romans that *some* are free; while *we* know that *all* humans are implicitly free, *qua* human. At the same time, this statement gives us the division of world history and the basis for our consideration of it. But this is noted merely provisionally and in passing. We must first explain some other concepts.

The *final goal of the world*, we said, is Spirit's consciousness of its freedom, and hence also the actualization of that very freedom. This, then, is what characterizes the spiritual world—and this therefore is the substantially real world, to which the physical world is subordinate (or, to say this in speculative terms, the physical world has no truth as against the spiritual). But this "freedom," as so far described, is itself indefinite and infinitely ambiguous. As the highest of concepts it carries with it infinitely many misunderstandings, confusions and errors, and comprises all possible excesses within it. Never has all this been better known and felt than at the present time. For the time being, however, we must content ourselves with using it in that general sense.

We have also drawn attention to the importance of the infinite difference between the principle, which is as yet merely implicit, and that which is real. But at the same time it is freedom in itself that contains the infinite necessity of bringing itself to consciousness (for in its very concept it is knowledge of itself) and thereby to reality. Freedom is for itself the goal to be achieved, and the only goal of Spirit.

It is the final goal—freedom—toward which all the world's history has been working. It is this goal to which all the sacrifices have been brought upon the broad altar of the earth in the long flow of time. This is the one and only goal that accomplishes itself and fulfills itself—the only constant in the change of events and conditions, and the truly effective thing in them all. It is this goal that is God's will for the world. But God is the absolutely perfect Being, and He can therefore will nothing but Himself, His own will. The nature of His will, however—i.e., His own nature, that is what we are here calling the Idea of freedom (since we are translating the religious image into philosophic thought). The question that now follows immediately, then, can be this: What means does this Idea of freedom use for its realization? This is the second point to be considered.

II. The Means of Spirit. This question—as to the *means* whereby freedom develops itself into a world—leads us into the phenomenon of history itself. While freedom as such is primarily an internal concept, its means are external: namely, the phenomena which present themselves directly before our eyes in history. Our first look at history convinces us that the actions of human beings stem from their needs, their passions, their interests, their characters and talents. And it appears that the only springs of action in this theater of activity, and the mainsprings, are these needs, passions, and interests. Of course, the play also involves universal aims, benevolence, noble patriotism, and so on. But these virtues and their universality are insignificant in their relation to the world and its doings.

We might well see the ideal of Reason realized in these subjective individuals themselves and in their sphere of influence, but individuals are of slight importance compared to the mass of the human race; likewise, the scope of their virtues is relatively restricted in its range. Instead, it is the passions, the aims of particular interests, the satisfaction of selfish desire that are the most forceful things. They get their power from the fact that they observe none of the limits which the law and morality would seek to impose upon them—and from the fact that these forces of nature are closer and more immediate to human beings than the artificial and tedious discipline toward order and moderation, toward law and morality.

When we look at this drama of human passions, and observe the consequences of their violence and of the unreason that is linked not only to them but also (and especially) to good intentions and rightful aims; when we see arising from them all the evil, the wickedness, the decline of the most flourishing nations mankind has produced, we can only be filled with grief for all that has come to nothing. And since this decline and fall is not merely the work of nature but of the will of men, we might well end with moral outrage over such a drama, and with a revolt of our good spirit (if there is a spirit of goodness in us). Without rhetorical exaggeration, we could paint the most fearful picture of the misfortunes suffered by the noblest of nations and states as well as by private virtues—and with that picture we could arouse feelings of the deepest and most helpless sadness, not to be outweighed by any consoling outcome. We can strengthen ourselves against this, or escape it, only by thinking that, well, so it was at one time; it is fate; there is nothing to be done about it now. And finally—in order to cast off the tediousness that this reflection of sadness could produce in us and to return to involvement in our own life, to the present of our own aims and interests—we return to the selfishness of standing on a quiet shore where we can be secure in enjoying the distant sight of confusion and wreckage.

But as we contemplate history as this slaughter-bench, upon which the happiness of nations, the wisdom of states, and the virtues of individuals were sacrificed, the question necessarily comes to mind: What was the ultimate goal for which these monstrous sacrifices were made? And from this there usually follows the question which we made the starting-point of our consideration. And in this perspective the events that present such a grim picture for our troubled feeling and thoughtful reflection have to be seen as the *means* for what we claim is the substantial definition, the absolute end-goal or, equally, the true *result* of world history. . . .

The Philosophy of Right

Preface

. . . It is therefore to be taken as a piece of *luck* for philosophic science—though in actual fact, as I have said, it is the *necessity* of the thing—that this philosophizing which like an exercise in scholasticism might have continued to spin its web in seclusion, has now been put into closer touch and so into open variance with actuality, in which the principles of rights and duties are a serious matter, and which lives in the light of its consciousness of these.

It is just this placing of philosophy in the actual world which meets with misunderstandings, and so I revert to what I have said before, namely that, since philosophy is the exploration of the rational, it is for that very reason the apprehension of the present and the actual, not the erection of a beyond, supposed to exist, God knows where, or rather which exists, and we can perfectly well say where, namely in the error of a one-sided, empty, ratiocination. In the course of this book, I have remarked that even Plato's *Republic*, which passes proverbially as an empty ideal, is in essence nothing but an interpretation of the nature of Greek ethical life. Plato was conscious that there was breaking into that life in his own time a deeper principle which could appear in it directly only as a longing still unsatisfied, and so only as something corruptive. To combat it, he needs must have sought aid from that very longing itself. But this aid had to come from on High and all that Plato could do was to seek it in the first place in a particular external form of that same Greek ethical life. By that means he thought to master this corruptive invader, and thereby he did fatal injury to the deeper impulse which underlay it, namely free infinite personality. Still, his genius is proved by the fact that the principle on which the distinctive character of his Idea of the state turns is precisely the pivot on which the impending world revolution turned at that time.

What is rational is actual and what is actual is rational.[1] On this conviction the plain man like the philosopher takes his stand, and from it philosophy starts in its study of the universe of mind as well as the universe of nature. If reflection, feeling, or whatever form subjective consciousness may take, looks upon the present as something vacuous and looks beyond it with the eyes of superior wisdom, it finds itself in a vacuum, and because it is actual only in the present, it is itself mere vacuity. If on the other hand the Idea passes for 'only an Idea', for something represented in an opinion, philosophy rejects such a view and shows that nothing is actual except the Idea. Once that is granted, the great thing is to apprehend in the show of the temporal and transient the substance which is immanent and the eternal which is present. For since rationality (which is synonymous with the Idea) enters upon external existence simultaneously with its actualization,[2] it

Excerpts from G.W.F. Hegel. 1967. *Hegel's Philosophy of Right* (translated by T.M. Knox). Oxford: Oxford University Press, pp. 9–13, 105–107, 109–110, 122, 124–125, 154–156, 160–161. Reprinted by permission of Oxford University Press.

emerges with an infinite wealth of forms, shapes, and appearances. Around its heart it throws a motley covering with which consciousness is at home to begin with, a covering which the concept has first to penetrate before it can find the inward pulse and feel it still beating in the outward appearances. But the infinite variety of circumstance which is developed in this external-ity by the light of the essence glinting in it—this endless material and its organization—this is not the subject matter of philosophy. To touch this at all would be to meddle with things to which philosophy is unsuited; on such topics it may save itself the trouble of giving good advice. Plato might have omitted his recommendation to nurses to keep on the move with infants and to rock them continually in their arms. And Fichte too need not have carried what has been called the 'construction' of his passport regulations to such a pitch of perfection as to require suspects not merely to sign their passports but to have their likenesses painted on them. Along such tracks all trace of philosophy is lost, and such super-erudition it can the more readily disclaim since its attitude to this infinite multitude of topics should of course be most liberal. In adopting this attitude, philosophic science shows itself to be poles apart from the hatred with which the folly of superior wisdom regards a vast number of affairs and institutions, a hatred in which pettiness takes the greatest delight because only by venting it does it attain a feeling of its self-hood.

This book, then, containing as it does the science of the state, is to be nothing other than the endeavour to apprehend and portray the state as something inherently rational. As a work of philosophy, it must be poles apart from an attempt to construct a state as it ought to be. The instruction which it may contain cannot consist in teaching the state what it ought to be; it can only show how the state, the ethical universe, is to be understood.

'Ιδού 'Ρόδος ἰδού καὶ τὸ πήδημα.
Hic Rhodus, *hic* saltus.[3]

To comprehend what is, this is the task of philosophy, because what is, is reason. Whatever happens, every individual is a child of his time; so philosophy too is its own time apprehended in thoughts. It is just as absurd to fancy that a philosophy can transcend its contemporary world as it is to fancy that an individual can overleap his own age, jump over Rhodes. If his theory really goes beyond the world as it is and builds an ideal one as it ought to be, that world exists indeed, but only in his opinions, an unsub-stantial element where anything you please may, in fancy, be built.

With hardly an alteration, the proverb just quoted would run:

Here is the rose, dance thou here.[4]

What lies between reason as self-conscious mind and reason as an actual world before our eyes, what separates the former from the latter and prevents it from finding satisfaction in the latter, is the fetter of some abstraction or other which has not been liberated [and so transformed] into the concept. To recognize reason as the rose in the cross of the present[5] and thereby to enjoy the present, this is the rational insight which reconciles us to the actual, the reconciliation which philosophy affords to those in whom there has once arisen an inner voice bidding them to comprehend, not only to dwell in what is substantive while still retaining subjective freedom, but also to possess subjective freedom while standing not in anything particular and accidental but in what exists absolutely.[6]

It is this too which constitutes the more concrete meaning of what was described above rather abstractly as the unity of form and content; for form in its most concrete signification is reason as speculative knowing, and content is reason as the substantial essence of actuality, whether ethical or natural. The known identity of these two is the philosophical Idea. It is a sheer obstinacy, the obstinacy which does honour to mankind, to refuse to recognize in conviction anything not ratified by thought. This obstinacy is the characteristic of our epoch, besides being the principle peculiar to Protestantism. What Luther initiated as faith in feeling and in the witness of the spirit, is precisely what spirit, since become more mature, has striven to apprehend in the concept in order to free and so to find itself in the world as it exists to-day. The saying has become famous that 'a half-philosophy leads away from God'—and it is the same half-philosophy that locates knowledge in an 'approximation' to truth—'while true philosophy leads to God'; and the same is true of philosophy and the state. Just as reason is not content with an approximation which, as something 'neither cold nor hot', it will 'spue out of its mouth,' so it is just as little content with the cold despair which submits to the view that in this earthly life things are truly bad or at best only tolerable, though here they cannot be improved and that this is the only reflection which can keep us at peace with the world: There is less chill in the peace with the world which knowledge supplies.

One word more about giving instruction as to what the world ought to be. Philosophy in any case always comes on the scene too late to give it. As the thought of the world, it appears only when actuality is already there cut and dried after its process of formation has been completed. The teaching of the concept, which is also history's inescapable lesson, is that it is only when actuality is mature that the ideal first appears over against the real and that the ideal apprehends this same real world in its substance and builds it up for itself into the shape of an intellectual realm. When philosophy paints its grey in grey, then has a shape of life grown old. By philosophy's grey in grey it cannot be rejuvenated but only understood. The owl of Minerva spreads its wings only with the falling of the dusk.

But it is time to close this preface. After all, as a preface, its only business has been to make some external and subjective remarks about the standpoint of the book it introduces. If a topic is to be discussed philosophically, it spurns any but a scientific and objective treatment, and so too if criticisms of the author take any form other than a scientific discussion of the thing itself, they can count only as a personal epilogue and as capricious assertion, and he must treat them with indifference.

BERLIN, *June 25th*, 1820.

Third Part
Ethical Life

142. Ethical life is the Idea of freedom in that on the one hand it is the good become alive—the good endowed in self-consciousness with knowing and willing and actualized by self-conscious action—while on the other hand self-consciousness has in the ethical realm its absolute foundation and the end which actuates its effort. Thus ethical life is the concept of freedom developed into the existing world and the nature of self-consciousness.

143. Since this unity of the concept of the will with its embodiment—i.e. the particular will—is knowing, consciousness of the distinction between these two moments of the Idea is present, but present in such a way that now each of these moments is in its own eyes the totality of the Idea and has that totality as its foundation and content.

144. (α) The objective ethical order, which comes on the scene in place of good in the abstract, is substance made concrete by subjectivity as infinite form.[7] Hence it posits within itself distinctions whose specific character is thereby determined by the concept, and which endow the ethical order with a stable content independently necessary and subsistent in exaltation above subjective opinion and caprice. These distinctions are absolutely valid laws and institutions.

145. It is the fact that the ethical order is the system of these specific determinations of the Idea which constitutes its rationality. Hence the ethical order is freedom or the absolute will as what is objective, a circle of necessity whose moments are the ethical powers which regulate the life of individuals. To these powers individuals are related as accidents to substance, and it is in individuals that these powers are represented, have the shape of appearance, and become actualized.

146. (β) The substantial order, in the self-consciousness which it has thus actually attained in individuals, knows itself and so is an object of knowledge. This ethical substance and its laws and powers are on the one hand an object over against the subject, and from his point of view they are—'are' in the highest sense of self-subsistent being. This is an absolute authority and power infinitely more firmly established than the being of nature.

The sun, the moon, mountains, rivers, and the natural objects of all kinds by which we are surrounded, *are*. For consciousness they have the authority not only of mere being but also of possessing a particular nature which it accepts and to which it adjusts itself in dealing with them, using them, or in being otherwise concerned with them. The authority of ethical laws is infinitely higher, because natural objects conceal rationality under the cloak of contingency and exhibit it only in their utterly external and disconnected way.

147. On the other hand, they are not something alien to the subject. On the contrary, his spirit bears witness to them as to its own essence, the essence in which he has a feeling of his selfhood, and in which he lives as in his own element which is not distinguished from himself. The subject is thus directly linked to the ethical order by a relation which is more like an identity than even the relation of faith or trust.

Faith and trust emerge along with reflection; they presuppose the power of forming ideas and making distinctions. For example, it is one thing to be a pagan, a different thing to believe in a pagan religion. This relation or rather this absence of relation, this identity in which the ethical order is the actual living soul of self-consciousness, can no doubt pass over into a relation of faith and conviction and into a relation produced by means of further reflection, i.e. into an *insight* due to reasoning starting perhaps from some particular purposes, interests, and considerations, from fear or hope, or from historical conditions. But adequate *knowledge* of this identity depends on thinking in terms of the concept.

148. As substantive in character, these laws and institutions are duties binding on the will of the individual, because as subjective, as inherently undetermined, or determined as particular, he distinguishes himself from them and hence stands related to them as to the substance of his own being.

The 'doctrine of duties' in moral philosophy (I mean the objective doctrine, not that which is supposed to be contained in the empty principle of moral subjectivity, because that principle determines nothing—see Paragraph 134) is therefore comprised in the systematic development of the circle of ethical necessity which follows in this Third Part. The difference between the exposition in this book and the form of a 'doctrine of duties' lies solely in the fact that, in what follows, the specific types of ethical life turn up as necessary relationships; there the exposition ends, without being supplemented in each case by the addition that 'therefore men have a duty to conform to this institution'.

A 'doctrine of duties' which is other than a philosophical science takes its material from existing relationships and shows its connexion with the moralist's personal notions or with principles and thoughts, purposes, impulses, feelings, &c., that are forthcoming everywhere; and as reasons for accepting each duty in turn, it may tack on its further consequences in their bearing on the other ethical relationships or on welfare and opinion. But an immanent and logical 'doctrine of duties' can be nothing except the serial exposition of the relationships which are necessitated by the Idea of freedom and are therefore actual in their entirety, to wit in the state.

149. The bond of duty can appear as a restriction only on indeterminate subjectivity or abstract freedom, and on the impulses either of the natural will or of the moral will which determines its indeterminate good arbitrarily. The truth is, however, that in duty the individual finds his liberation; first, liberation from dependence on mere natural impulse and from the depression which as a particular subject he cannot escape in his moral reflections on what ought to be and what might be; secondly, liberation from the indeterminate subjectivity which, never reaching reality or the objective determinacy of action, remains self-enclosed and devoid of actuality. In duty the individual acquires his substantive freedom. . . .

155. Hence in this identity of the universal will with the particular will, right and duty coalesce, and by being in the ethical order a man has rights in so far as he has duties, and duties in so far as he has rights. In the sphere of abstract right, I have the right and another has the corresponding duty. In the moral sphere, the right of my private judgement and will, as well as of my happiness, has not, but only ought to have, coalesced with duties and become objective.

156. The ethical substance, as containing independent self-consciousness united with its concept, is the actual mind of a family and a nation.

157. The concept of this Idea has being only as mind, as something knowing itself and actual, because it is the objectification of itself, the movement running through the form of its moments. It is therefore

(A) ethical mind in its natural or immediate phase—the *Family*. This substantiality loses its unity, passes over into division, and into the phase of relation, i.e. into

(B) *Civil Society*—an association of members as self-subsistent individuals in a universality which, because of their self-subsistence, is only abstract. Their association is brought about by their needs, by the legal system—the means to security of person and property—and by an external organization for attaining their particular and common interests. This external state

(C) is brought back to and welded into unity in the *Constitution of the State* which is the end and actuality of both the substantial universal order and the public life devoted thereto.

158. The family, as the immediate substantiality of mind, is specifically characterized by love, which is mind's feeling of its own unity. Hence in a family, one's frame of mind is to have self-consciousness of one's individuality within this unity as the absolute essence of oneself, with the result that one is in it not as an independent person but as a member. . . .

181. The family disintegrates (both essentially, through the working of the principle of personality, and also in the course of nature) into a plurality of families, each of which conducts itself as in principle a self-subsistent concrete person and therefore as externally related to its neighbours. In other words, the moments bound together in the unity of the family, since the family is the ethical Idea still in its concept, must be released from the concept to self-subsistent objective reality. This is the stage of difference. This gives us, to use abstract language in the first place, the determination of particularity which is related to universality but in such a way that universality is its basic principle, though still only an inward principle; for that reason, the universal merely shows in the particular as its form.[8] Hence this relation of reflection prima facie portrays the disappearance of ethical life or, since this life as the essence necessarily shows itself, this relation constitutes the world of ethical appearance—civil society. . . .

187. Individuals in their capacity as burghers in this state are private persons whose end is their own interest. This end is *mediated* through the universal which thus *appears* as a *means* to its realization. Consequently, individuals can attain their ends only in so far as they themselves determine their knowing, willing, and acting in a universal way and make themselves links in this chain of social connexions. In these circumstances, the interest of the Idea—an interest of which these members of civil society are as such unconscious—lies in the process whereby their singularity and their natural condition are raised, as a result of the necessities imposed by nature as well as of arbitrary needs, to formal freedom and formal universality of knowing and willing—the process whereby their particularity is educated up to subjectivity. . . .

255. As the family was the first, so the Corporation is the second ethical root of the state, the one planted in civil society. The former contains the moments of subjective particularity and objective universality in a substantial unity. But these moments are sundered in civil society to begin with; on the one side there is the particularity of need and satisfaction, reflected into itself, and on the other side the universality of abstract rights. In the

Corporation these moments are united in an inward fashion, so that in this union particular welfare is present as a right and is actualized.

The sanctity of marriage and the dignity of Corporation membership are the two fixed points round which the unorganized atoms of civil society revolve.

256. The end of the Corporation is restricted and finite, while the public authority was an external organization involving a separation and a merely relative identity of controller and controlled. The end of the former and the externality and relative identity of the latter find their truth in the absolutely universal end and its absolute actuality. Hence the sphere of civil society passes over into the state.

The town is the seat of the civil life of business. There reflection arises, turns in upon itself, and pursues its atomizing task; each man maintains himself in and through his relation to others who, like himself, are persons possessed of rights. The country, on the other hand, is the seat of an ethical life resting on nature and the family. Town and country thus constitute the two moments, still ideal moments, whose true ground is the state, although it is from them that the state springs.

The philosophic proof of the concept of the state is this development of ethical life from its immediate phase through civil society, the phase of division, to the state, which then reveals itself as the true ground of these phases. A proof in philosophic science can only be a development of this kind.

Since the state appears as a result in the advance of the philosophic concept through displaying itself as the true ground [of the earlier phases], that show of mediation is now cancelled and the state has become directly present before us. Actually, therefore, the state as such is not so much the result as the beginning. It is within the state that the family is first developed into civil society, and it is the Idea of the state itself which disrupts itself into these two moments. Through the development of civil society, the substance of ethical life acquires its infinite form, which contains in itself these two moments: (1) infinite differentiation down to the inward experience of independent self-consciousness, and (2) the form of universality involved in education, the form of thought whereby mind is objective and actual to itself as an organic totality in laws and institutions which are its will in terms of thought.

257. The state is the actuality of the ethical Idea. It is ethical mind *qua* the substantial will manifest and revealed to itself, knowing and thinking itself, accomplishing what it knows and in so far as it knows it. The state exists immediately in custom, mediately in individual self-consciousness, knowledge, and activity, while self-consciousness in virtue of its sentiment towards the state finds in the state, as its essence and the end and product of its activity, its substantive freedom.

The *Penates* are inward gods, gods of the underworld; the mind of a nation (Athene for instance) is the divine, knowing and willing itself. Family piety is feeling, ethical behaviour directed by feeling; political virtue is the willing of the absolute end in terms of thought.

258. The state is absolutely rational inasmuch as it is the actuality of the substantial will which it possesses in the particular self-consciousness once that consciousness has been raised to consciousness of its universality. This substantial unity is an absolute unmoved end in itself, in which freedom comes into its supreme right. On the other hand this final end has supreme right against the individual, whose supreme duty is to be a member of the state.

If the state is confused with civil society, and if its specific end is laid down as the security and protection of property and personal freedom, then the interest of the individuals as such becomes the ultimate end of their association, and it follows that membership of the state is something optional. But the state's relation to the individual is quite different from this. Since the state is mind objectified, it is only as one of its members that the individual himself has objectivity, genuine individuality, and an ethical life. Unification pure and simple is the true content and aim of the individual, and the individual's destiny is the living of a universal life. His further particular satisfaction, activity, and mode of conduct have this substantive and universally valid life as their starting point and their result.

Rationality, taken generally and in the abstract, consists in the thorough-going unity of the universal and the single. Rationality, concrete in the state, consists (a) so far as its content is concerned, in the unity of objective freedom (i.e. freedom of the universal or substantial will) and subjective freedom (i.e. freedom of everyone in his knowing and in his volition of particular ends); and consequently, (b) so far as its form is concerned, in self-determining action on laws and principles which are thoughts and so universal. This Idea is the absolutely eternal and necessary being of mind.[9]

But if we ask what is or has been the historical origin of the state in general, still more if we ask about the origin of any particular state, of its rights and institutions, or again if we inquire whether the state originally arose out of patriarchal conditions or out of fear or trust, or out of Corporations, &c., or finally if we ask in what light the basis of the state's rights has been conceived and consciously established, whether this basis has been supposed to be positive divine right, or contract, custom, &c.—all these questions are no concern of the Idea of the state. We are here dealing exclusively with the philosophic science of the state, and from that point of view all these things are mere appearance and therefore matters for history. So far as the authority of any existing state has anything to do with reasons, these reasons are culled from the forms of the law authoritative within it. . . .

260. The state is the actuality of concrete freedom. But concrete freedom consists in this, that personal individuality and its particular interests not only achieve their complete development and gain explicit recognition for their right (as they do in the sphere of the family and civil society) but, for one thing, they also pass over of their own accord into the interest of the universal, and, for another thing, they know and will the universal; they even recognize it as their own substantive mind; they take it as their end and aim and are active in its pursuit. The result is that the universal does not prevail or achieve completion except along with particular interests and through the co-operation of particular knowing and willing; and individuals likewise do not live as private persons for their own ends alone, but in the very act of willing these they will the universal in the light of the universal, and their activity is consciously aimed at none but the universal end. The principle of modern states has prodigious strength and depth because it allows the principle of subjectivity to progress to its culmination in the extreme of self-subsistent personal particularity, and yet at the same time brings it back to the substantive unity and so maintains this unity in the principle of subjectivity itself.

261. In contrast with the spheres of private rights and private welfare (the family and civil society), the state is from one point of view an external necessity and their higher authority; its nature is such that their laws and interests are subordinate to it and dependent on it. On the other hand, however, it is the end immanent within them, and its strength lies in the unity of its own universal end and aim with the particular interest of individuals, in the fact that individuals have duties to the state in proportion as they have rights against it (see Paragraph 155). . . .

Translator's Notes

1. This statement is further explained and defended in *Enc.*, §6. Note that Hegel is not saying that what exists or is 'real' is rational. By 'actuality' (see Translator's Foreword, §3) he means the synthesis of essence and existence. If we say of a statesman who accomplishes nothing that he is not a 'real' statesman, then we mean by 'real' what Hegel calls 'actual'. The statesman exists as a man in office, but he lacks the essence constitutive of what statesmanship ought to be, say effectiveness. Conversely, and in Hegel's view no less important, if effectiveness were never the quality of an existing statesman, then it would not be the rational essence of statesmanship, but a mere ideal or dream. Hegel's philosophy as a whole might be regarded as an attempt to justify his identification of rationality with actuality and vice versa, but his doctrine depends ultimately on his faith in God's Providence, his conviction that history is the working out of His rational purpose. That purpose, as the purpose of the Almighty, is not so impotent as to remain a mere ideal or aspiration, and conversely, what is genuinely actual or effective in the world is simply the working of that purpose.—It follows that Hegel's identification of the actual and the rational is not a plea for conservatism in politics. The actualization of God's purpose is not yet complete. See the Addition to Paragraph 270 and the closing pages of the *Philosophy of History*.

2. Thought at any stage does not attain full actuality until it passes over into existence and embodies itself in something objective. E.g. religious convictions are not genuinely actual until they are objectified in institutions, churches, &c. Similarly, the state, as an objectification in the external world of man's rational will, is that in which alone his freedom, the essence of his will, is fully actualized.

3. The ultimate source of the Greek proverb ('here is Rhodes, here's your jump') is Michael Apostolius viii. 100 (Leutsch: *Paroemiographi Graeci*, Göttingen, 1851, vol. ii). But in its Latin form it is a commonplace of German elementary Latin text-books, and it may have reached them, and Hegel also, from Erasmus, *Adagia*, III. iii. 28. Erasmus quotes the Greek, gives a Latin translation, and continues: 'The proverb will be apt when someone is asked to show on the spot that he can do what he boasts he has done elsewhere.' (Hegel's interpretation seems to have been slightly different.) Cf. Goethe: *Zahme Xenien*, III. ii.

4. Hegel is playing on words. 'Ρόδος means not only the island of Rhodes, but also a rose. *Saltus* means a jump, but *salta* is the imperative of the verb 'to dance'. The rose is the symbol of joy, and the philosopher's task is to find joy in the present by discovering reason within it. In other words, philosophy may 'dance' for joy in this world; it need not postpone its 'dancing' until it builds an ideal world elsewhere.

5. If the actual is rational, then however tragic the actual may seem to be, reason will be able to find joy in it, because it will find itself in it as its essence. Hegel uses the same metaphor in *Philosophy of Religion*, i. 284–5. As he indicates in *Werke*[1], xvii. 227, the metaphor was suggested to him by the Rosicrucians. (See Lasson: *Beiträge zur Hegel-Forschung*, Part 2, Berlin, 1910, pp. 49–50.)

6. Cf. Hegel's criticism of Spinoza in, e.g., *Phenomenology*, p. 80, and *Enc.*, § 151. His point is that Spinoza's view of the universe as substance or necessity needs to be supplemented by the Christian doctrine of subjectivity and subjective freedom. God is substance, but is person or subject as well. Hegel applies this doctrine to the state and holds that although the state is a substance, in modern times it has come to consciousness of itself in its citizens and its monarch, and so has become not a mere external necessity but the embodiment of freedom. Cf. Note 3 to Paragraph 144.

7. We have seen (Note 61 to Paragraph 141) that right and morality were both abstractions; the whole from which they are abstracted is therefore that on which they depend. This whole is a unity of universal and particular, of object and subject. Now 'a thing which has subsistence in itself, a thing that upholdeth that which else would fall' (a phrase of Hobbes, quoted here from Laird: *Hobbes*, London, 1943, pp. 92–3) is a substance. And throughout Hegel's account of ethical life, it is with substance that we are dealing; each type of this life—family, civil society, state—is a substantiality, but it is a substantiality of *mind*, and so one of a special sort. 'In my view', says Hegel (*Phenomenology*, p. 80), 'everything depends on grasping and expressing the ultimate truth not as substance but as subject as well.' (a) The family is a substance (in Hegel's view a single mind—see Paragraph 156) of which its members are accidents, but the substantiality is not external or visible; it depends solely on the consciousness of its members. The family's bond of union, its substance, is love; and love, in Hegel's view, is reason in its immediacy, i.e. an immature form of reason. Here there is no explicit difference between substance and accident; unity is present and the family members are not conscious that their unity is a unity of differences. (b) At the next stage, civil society, difference becomes explicit; the substance (the mind of the nation), 'appears' in particulars and it is their essence even though they may not realize it. They have risen above love to intelligence, but this is concentrated on a private end. (c) The third stage is the synthesis of the first two. The substantial mind of the nation, objectified in the state, rises to consciousness of itself in the minds of the citizens; it particularizes itself into rational laws and institutions. It is concrete because, unlike the family, it is particularized consciously and because, unlike civil society, its particulars are not an 'appearance' of its substantial essence, but the differentiation of that essence. It is concrete again because these laws and institutions, like the state itself as the unity of these, are actual in the minds of the citizens who live under them. They regulate their willing deliberately in accordance with rational ends; the members of the family pursue an ethical end, but only under the influence of feeling; members of civil society are intelligent, but pursue the universal end only under the disguise of the particular. The state, then, has acquired the form of subjectivity, and subjectivity as we have seen, is infinite because self-related. Hegel contrasts his state with an oriental despotism, i.e. with a substance which is an absolute power over individual accidents and alien to them. The essence of his state is that it is not only a substance but one which incorporates individual freedom by means of the parliamentary and other institutions which he later describes.

8. The transition from family to civil society corresponds on a higher level to that from right to morality. In each case the transition is the emergence of the particular; in each case we leave behind an undifferentiated universality and arrive at a realm of appearance, i.e. what is visible and obvious is particularity, though

universality is its underlying essence. . . . Universal and particular, form and content, appear in civil society to fall apart, the Idea appears to be divided, but none the less the pursuit of private ends here turns out to be conditioned by universal laws. These are implicit to start with (as the laws of economics), but they become explicit later as a system of laws and institutions for the protection of private property and as barriers against private selfishness. . . .

9. Hegel's theory of the state has his theory of syllogism for its background. 'The syllogism is the rational and everything rational' (*Enc.*, §181) because it is a concrete unity of explicit differences, and these differences are the three moments of the concept, universality, particularity, and individuality. 'The state is a system of three syllogisms: (i) The individual or person, through his particularity or physical or mental needs . . . is coupled with the universal, i.e. with society, law, right, government. (ii) The will or action of individuals is the intermediating force which procures for these needs satisfaction in society, law, &c., and which gives to society, law, &c., their fulfilment and actualization. (iii) But the universal, i.e. the state, government, and law, is the permanent underlying mean in which the individuals and their satisfaction have and receive their fulfilled reality, intermediation, and persistence. Each of the moments of the concept, as it is brought by intermediation to coalesce with the other extreme, is brought into union with itself and produces itself. . . . It is only by this triad of syllogisms with the same terms that the whole is thoroughly understood in its organization' (*Enc.*, §198). What essentially differentiates the state from civil society and makes it rational, is the parliamentary organization which mediates between particulars on the one hand and the individual monarch on the other (see Paragraphs 302–4). The state is the Idea because it is in this way the unity of universal and particular, form and content, and since in the state this is a conscious unity, it may be described as mind in being, since reason is 'essential and actual truth' and 'truth, aware of what it is, is mind' (*Enc.*, §§438–9).

COMMENTARY

History and Politics
Charles Taylor

Chapter XV Reason and History

2

Let us now look at the main themes of the philosophy of history. The principal drama of the sweep of history is the one which builds towards the major crux of Hegel's philosophy of politics; how to reconcile the freedom of the individual who knows himself as universal rationality with a restored *Sittlichkeit*. The main drama of history is then opened by the breakdown of the perfect unity of *Sittlichkeit* in the Greek world, the birth of the individual with universal consciousness. It then follows the slow development through the succeeding centuries both of the individual (his *Bildung*) and of the institutions embodying *Sittlichkeit,* so that the two can eventually rendez-vous in the rational state.

The version of the history in compressed form which we have in Chapter VI of the *PhG* starts with the Greek world. But the major version contained in the lectures on the philosophy of history starts earlier, takes us through Chinese, Indian, Persian, Phoenician, Egyptian civilizations in the run up to Greek. It also deals with the Jews. There are also differences in the way Hegel cuts into even the areas common to the two versions; as there are between different cycles of the lectures. This reinforces what was said above about the detail of Hegel's philosophy of history.

My aim here will be simply to give the general line of the dialectic of history, as a background to the main political problem mentioned above. In dealing with the pre-Greek civilizations, Hegel discusses their religious consciousness, and there are many elements here which reappear in the philosophy of religion. Their political structures and public life are closely bound up with this religious consciousness. As ever with Hegel the different aspects of a people's life are bound together in its *Geist*. But the religious consciousness for these early peoples offers the most striking expression of the stage they were at, of the way in which they tried to realize the ontological reality, *Geist,* and its relation to the world and subject.

Spirit is struggling to achieve an understanding of itself as spirit, that is, as free subjectivity, and to see this as the absolute. But with the pre-Greek peoples—except for the Jews—the absolute is still less than subject; it is still bound up with external, hence impersonal reality, nature, or the total abstraction of the void (one aspect of Indian religion). The Persians achieve a high form of this in that they see the absolute symbolized in light, which is the most spiritual among natural forms, but they are still not yet at the breakthrough point.

This comes in one form with the Jews. Here we suddenly come to the realization that God is pure subject, spirit. But this realization can only be won at that stage by a radical separation of God as spirit from all contamination with natural, finite reality.

Excerpts from Charles Taylor. 1975. *Hegel*. Cambridge: Cambridge University Press, pp. 393–400, 428–439. Reprinted with permission of the author and Cambridge University Press.

The Jewish spirit, thinks Hegel, is therefore one of separation, radical transcendence. Abraham starts off by leaving his family and home in Ur of the Chaldees to become a wanderer. The Jewish people wage a constant fight against idolatry, which amounts to a mixing of the divine again with the finite. But this solution can only be a stage on the way, for it is radically imperfect. God is spirit, but at the cost of being beyond the world, and above all beyond, above and over finite subjectivity, that of man. Man is not reconciled with God, does not see himself as at one with the absolute, as its vehicle, but rather the absolute is over against him, he is its slave, totally submitted to it. Similarly, the natural world is totally emptied of the divine. It is 'entgöttert', as Hegel puts it; Jewish consciousness sees only a world of finite things, which are to be used by man, not the embodiment of Deity. The world is totally under spirit, at our disposal, even as we are totally under God. Hegel also speaks of this vision of God as of 'pure thought', which in Hegelian terms is closely linked with being pure subject. In this formulation he stresses again that the Jewish concept of the absolute is of something universal, totally without particularization.

The Greek solution is in a sense the opposite of the Jewish one. The Greeks, too, win through to a consciousness of God as subject. But it is not a subjectivity which is frighteningly beyond nature, which negates natural expression in the purity of thought. Rather the Greek gods are perfectly harmonized with their natural expression. But instead of this being something infra-personal, as with the earlier natural religions, the paradigm expression of these Gods is in the form of realized subjectivity, that is, in human form.

But the Greek God, unlike the Jewish, is parochial. And this same parochial nature is what we shall see reflected in the Greek polis, and will be the cause of its downfall. A similar advantage is won at similar cost. On one hand, the Greek concept of the divine is the charter of Greek freedom. It is the sense that the divine is not totally other, that finite subjectivity has its place in it. And this is the sense of freedom, that man is not the slave of the absolute, of something which is utterly foreign to his will. Hence the Greek polity will be the first home of freedom.

It was this which enabled the Greeks to build an embodiment of *Sittlichkeit* for which Hegel's day pined, one in which men were fully at home, in which their whole identity was bound up with the living public reality of their polis. The vision of God in human form was the foundation for a public life woven around this divinity, the God of the city, in which the citizens could fully recognize themselves. This public life was a reality which was fully theirs. Their activity kept it going, and yet it also represented what was of ultimate significance for them, an expression of the divine. Hence their realized public life was their 'substance', the basis of their identity. Their ethic was one of *Sittlichkeit,* where what ought to be also was.

But this was a limited freedom. Only those who were citizens, who were thus members of a certain polis and the servers of its God, were so reflected in public reality. Slaves, and in general outsiders, were not. Each state had its own God, own laws, with which its members were fully reconciled, but these were different from state to state. The reassuring form of the divine was reassuring only for some. It reflected only part of humanity. Hence the Greeks did not have the intuition that man as such is free. Freedom was the appanage of citizens; slaves and barbarians were outside its ban.[1]

---

1. This is, of course, the background to the famous passage in which Hegel resumes the history of freedom (*VG,* 62): The oriental world knew only that one man was free—the king represented the absolute principle, e.g., the Persian despot (but of course in an important sense not even he was free, as a really rational

Correspondingly, the identification with the city on the part of its citizens was not based on universal reflection, but was one of immediate unreflecting adherence. The laws must be obeyed because they are those of our city, *sans plus.*

In this world, democracy (direct democracy) is the most natural form of government. For all men are totally identified with the whole. They only want to live and die for it; they can thus be entrusted with running it. But it is a parochial democracy, it excludes slaves and metics; for the identification is parochial.

Hegel makes clear why in his view ancient democracy is inappropriate as a model for the modern world. Ancient, direct democracy was possible in part because societies were so small; all could really take part and be really present when decisions were taken. But this is not all. One of the essential conditions of Greek democracy was precisely its exclusiveness. All the menial economic tasks were taken over by non-citizens. This not only meant that citizens had in general more leisure than otherwise would be possible to attend the ecclesia and see to affairs of state. It also meant a homogeneity of the population which cannot be attained in a modern polity where all functions are fulfilled by citizens. But heterogeneity makes essential an articulation of the modern state which in Hegel's view excludes democracy.

But there is a third reason why ancient democracy is not an appropriate model for our time. The Greek state could work because men were immediately identified with it. Now while we hope to restore the integrity of *Sittlichkeit,* we can never restore this immediate, unreflecting unity. Modern man will also remain a universal individual. And this individuality will be reflected in the structure of modern society, and we shall see—in the form of civil society. This necessary articulation of the polity to take account of the greater complexity of man requires a balance between institutions which Hegel thinks is incompatible with direct democracy. More of this below.

This beautiful unity of the Greek state is doomed. It is doomed because of its limitations, its parochialness. The world spirit has to march on. Hence once the polis is realized the cunning of reason calls world-historical individuals to look beyond. Such a figure in his own way is Socrates. Socrates turns his allegiance to universal reason. And although he wants to remain obedient to the laws of his polis, he would like to found them on reason. Thus while he maintains his allegiance to Athens to the death, nevertheless his teaching cannot but corrupt the youth, for it undermines that immediate identification with the public life on which the polis rests. Men turn to a universal reason, turn their back on the parochial state and its gods. But this universal reason is not embodied in public life, it is the beyond.

The dissolution of the polity is the birth of the individual with universal consciousness. This is an individual who defines himself as subject of universal reason. But he can find no identification with the public life of his city. He lives in a larger community, the city of men and Gods of the Stoics, but this is unrealized. Hence the new individual is an internal émigré.

But this has the necessary consequence that the life goes out of the public institutions of the polis. It cannot but go under and gives way to the universal empire, a form of dominance from on top which is predicated precisely on there being no such identification. This universal empire is no more than the polis a realization of the universal reason which has now come to consciousness. It is the correlative in the sense that the individual of universal reason must bring about the collapse of the city-state, but it is not at all expression in public life of this reason. On the contrary,

---

subjectivity). The Greek world won through to an intuition of freedom, but saw only that some were free. Only with Christianity do we win through to the intuition that man as such is free.

it is the expression of the fact that this reason is now felt as beyond the world. Thus the individual is cast into an external world which is ruled not by reason but by the arbitrary will of emperors, powerful despots. Internally he defines himself as universal reason, but externally he is a bit of flotsam on the huge flood of events, entirely at the mercy of external power.

In this diremption he goes even more to an inward definition of himself. This is the age in which Stoicism flourishes. But for Hegel, this cannot be a solution, for it is a completely unrealized figure of reason and freedom. Hence the individual cannot but yearn to go beyond this, to find realization. The ground is laid for the unhappy consciousness.

This is the era of the Roman Empire. Thus Roman society is the place of origin of the idea of the Person, an individual defined as a subject of rights in abstraction from his relation to the substance of *Sittlichkeit*. The Person is the bearer of 'abstract' right, right unconnected to social and political role; he is the bearer of right as property. This will be one of the dimensions of the modern state. It has its origins here.

The stage is set for the birth of Christianity. Christianity comes to answer the yearning of the universal individual, who cannot be reconciled with the universal in this political world, that nevertheless the finite subject and the absolute be fully united. And so they become so united once, in the person of Christ. There is no question of this happening many times, as with the avatars of Hindu religion. The absolute is one, and the paradigmatic founding unity can only be realized once. But this unity, as we have seen, must also be overcome in its immediate form. Christ must die. And he must rise again, go to the Father, and return in spirit to animate the community.

But with the birth of Christianity this unity is only realized in principle. It is still not fully realized in the world. The Church which is the external realization of the new community is thus in inner exile at first as well, just like the universal individual. The task of history now is to make this reconciliation externally, politically real; to make the church community in a sense one with the society. And this means a slow transformation of institutions, and a slow making over of men—*Bildung*. This is the task of the next eighteen centuries, and it will be undertaken by a new world-historical people, the Germanic nations.

The German nations Hegel means are the barbarians who swarmed over the Roman empire at its end and founded the new nations of Western Europe. There is no particular chauvinism in this use of the word German. Montesquieu and others also recognized that modern European politics had issued out of these Germanic barbarian kingdoms.

But these Germans were ideally suited to take history to the next stage—the *Weltgeist* always sees to such convergence of material and ends—because they were naturally very conscious of their individual independence from authority. They were only with difficulty, and then precariously, submitted to authority. Hegel pictures the early German as being loosely under leaders who, like Agamemnon, were barely primus inter pares. In this way, they were as it were pre-programmed to build a civilization which would be based on the freedom of the individual. But first this freedom has to be purified, it has to grow into and incorporate the rational inner freedom which was achieved by the ancient word and Christianity. The real, external independence of the German in the woods has to be united to this spiritual freedom, and this freedom given reality. But second, it is essential to this that the wild independent German must learn to accept rational authority, must accept to be integrated into a rational state.

The development of medieval and modern Europe is the working out of these two related processes. The feudal system in which the public realm is shot through with private relationships is the natural form in which these German tribes set up states. But then the process starts by which these loose skeins of private relations are united into the common overarching will which is inseparable from the state. In Europe this comes in the form of the growing power of the monarchy. Charlemagne represents a crucial phase in this process.

We have here the foundation of one of the essential features of a modern state for Hegel. It must be united at the top by a monarchy. Hegel seems to hold that this is essentially linked with the principle of modern individual freedom. The Greek city-state could be a republic since all gave themselves immediately to the state, they had no private will outside it. But the modern universal individual also has a private identity, he cannot be simply a member of the state. In order to be real as a common will, any state must however have this moment of immediate unity in it. At some moment, at some point, the will of the whole must be one with a real existent will. This not just in the sense that in order for the state to act, some men must act in its name. Rather Hegel is making the ontological point that there must be some place in which the immediate unity of concrete and general will is realized. The state cannot be for everybody just one dimension among many of their action and will.

What Hegel is presenting here, and later in the *PR*, is a renewed variant of the medieval idea of the representative individual, that is, an individual who bodies forth a basic principle of the common life. This is 'representation' not in the modern sense of standing in for someone else or being delegated by him, but of bodying forth, of incarnating an underlying common reality to which all show allegiance. The notion of kingly majesty, that the king is the point at which the majesty of the whole is manifest, belongs to this idea. In the ontological dimension of his political thought, where he is concerned to derive the structures of the state from the 'Concept', that is, from the ontological structure of things, Hegel has recourse to an idea of this kind. Different features of the constitution 'represent' in this sense different aspects of ontological reality.

Alongside the powerful monarch, who draws together the unruly subjects, there grow up the institutions known as estates, which in England became Parliament. These are the necessary mediating elements between the sovereign will and the particulars. And hence we have here another essential institution of a modern state, thinks Hegel. It is by the estates that the people as a whole take part in the life of the state. Here again we shall see that Hegel's notion of the participation of the people is not founded on the modern notion of representation, as it is in theories of modern representative government. It is not a matter of legitimating decisions, by leading them back to popular choices, but of establishing some kind of identification.

At the same time the state develops more and more towards impersonality, the dependence on law, and what Weber was later to call rationality. The kingly power becomes less and less a private appanage, and is seen as the public power of government. Service by magnates is replaced over the centuries by a trained bureaucracy. The state becomes more and more founded on general principles, on legal rationality.

As these institutions are developing—to what final fruition we shall discuss further below—the parallel process of spiritualization is going on, purification of the raw, primitive human material, and its formation (Bildung). One of the key stages in this is the Reformation. The Christian Church took over a good part of the task of forming the raw barbarians. But in the process it had to sink to some degree to their level. The higher spiritual truths of Christianity were united with gross external realities. Men tried to find God by the actual physical conquest of the Holy Land, the presence of

God was reified in the host, and so on. This is Hegel's notion of what underlay medieval Catholicism. In order for the spirit to progress, there had to be a recovery of purity, a rediscovery of the spiritual meaning of the presence of the spirit in the world, a setting aside of the gross sensuous meaning this had with Catholicism. This is essential to the development of the modern state; so much so that Catholic countries are incapable of realizing this state integrally.

With the Reformation, and the freeing of spirituality from its imprisonment in gross external things, with the recovery of a sense of the presence of God in the community which was purely spiritual, the way was free for the task of making this presence objective and real in the external world, not in the gross and inadequate way of the external rites and hierarchy of Catholicism, but by building a real earthly community which would realize the universal, reason. The world was ready for a state founded on reason. In other words, the unity of God and man has to be externally realized. But we have to go beyond the primitive, purely external, and hence totally inadequate realization in host, sanctuary, relics, indulgences, etc.; we have to liberate the true spiritual dimension, if we are to achieve the adequate realization in a political community. Thus from the Reformed Europe comes the attempt to realize the rational state, to overcome the opposition of Church and state. The Protestant religion is at the foundation of this state.

The spiritualization process begun by the Reformation, however, carries on and brings about what we call the Enlightenment. More and more aware of themselves as at one with the universal, men come to recognize that they are inwardly free with the freedom of pure thought. The spiritualization brings them back to an understanding of their identity as resting in the freedom of universal thought. But this is not simply a return to the ancients. For these latter found themselves faced with a world which was totally refractory to reason; their sense of their identity as reason was a purely inner one, buffeted by the forces of the world; the world of reason was a beyond. But since then men have come to see that they are at one with the very foundation of things. Christian culture has wrought this. Consequently the modern Enlightenment does not just define man as thought, it is sure that the whole of external reality conforms to thought too. This is Hegel's reading of the new scientific consciousness which strives to understand the world as law-governed order.

In other words, thought and being are one. This is Hegel's rather idiosyncratic reading of the Cogito ergo sum of Descartes. The point is that man is reason, and he is as such one with the principle of things; so he will find reason in the external world if he only looks for it. . . .

Chapter XVI The Realized State

1

PR explores what flows from the notion of rational will concerning human affairs. It goes beyond a simple political theory. It turns out to englobe also what Hegel calls civil society, and the family. But also it discusses the dimension of morality and private rights.[1]

---

1. This scope was not, of course, entirely original. Standard treatises on law or right had to discuss private right and law relating to the family, marriage, inheritance, etc. And Kant in his treatise dealing with law, *Metaphysik der Sitten*, had also dealt with morality or a theory of duties (Pflichtenlehre) as well. What is new is the distinction of civil society and the state, and of course, the whole 'architectonic' of Hegel's system in which these different parts are deduced from the Idea.

Hegel intends to proceed from the most abstract to the most concrete. He will end with a picture of the state, because this is the highest embodiment of *Sittlichkeit*, which is implicit in the notion that man is the vehicle of rational will.

But we start off with the notion of private rights. Man is a bearer of private rights because he is essentially a vehicle of rational will. As such he commands respect. Man is a bodily existence who has to have commerce with the external world in order to live; he has to appropriate things and use them. But this fact becomes a value because man is the essential vehicle of the realization of reason or spirit, which is the same thing as saying that man is endowed with will. Hence man's appropriation is to be seen as in fulfilment of the ontologically grounded purpose. It is something infinitely worthy of respect. Thus the de facto process of appropriation becomes the de jure right to property. Man is a bearer of rights because as a will he is worthy of respect. An attack on his external bodily existence or his property is thus a crime, an attack against the very purpose underlying reality as a whole, including my own existence. The right of appropriation over things comes from the fact that these have no inherent ends; they are given to them by will. Will has the rights (*PR*, §44).

Hegel thus justifies the right to property. He sees this as a right to private property. For this right falls to man in the abstract, as an individual rational will. This is because it is on this immediate, individual level than man is related to things, that he is in interchange with nature.[2] Man is also part of a community of *Sittlichkeit*, but this touches him at another, higher level than this commerce with things. It touches his identification, his spiritual life, that for which he should be ready to give up life and property.

Hence in property we are dealing with the will of man as a single individual, as a person (*PR*, §46). Of course, this very basic consideration of man as a person, bearer of abstract right, although the starting point for the Logic-derived exposition of the *PR*, is not the point of departure, historically speaking. A long development was necessary before man was actually first considered in history as a person, as we saw in our consideration of the philosophy of history above. This occurred in the Roman world.

Hegel then goes on to consider a number of other matters related to rights, particularly property rights; for instance, contract, and crime and punishment. Crime, says Hegel, taking up a theme we saw in the Logic is a negative infinite judgement. It is not just saying, as it were, this particular thing is not mine, which my rival in a civil suit says; it denies the whole category of 'mine' and 'thine'.

Crime is an attack on the very purpose underlying things, the purpose even of the criminal, his will *an sich* (*PR*, §100). Punishment has as goal to undo this rebellion against the purpose of things. This attack has come from a will which has set itself against the very principle of will. The undoing must therefore be a counter-injury against the particular will of the criminal.

> The sole positive existence which the injury possesses is that it is the particular will of the criminal. Hence to injure (or penalize) this particular will as a will determinately existent is to annul the crime, which otherwise would have been held valid, and to restore the right.   (*PR*, §99)

---

2. We can see the important differences from Marx. Although Hegel understood the importance of the division of labour, and was astonishingly prescient about the consequences of its extension in the industrial system, as we shall see, he did not see this necessary interdependence as an integral, conscious expression of ethical substance. The domain of interchange with nature, or civil society, remains that of individual action and goals. The substantial element, which brings men to unity here, is quite unconscious. It is the operation of an 'invisible hand'.

Hegel is therefore quite out of sympathy with the various liberal theories of punishment as preventive, deterrent, reformative, etc. And he opposes the softening of the penal code which springs from this kind of philosophy. In particular, he is opposed to the abolition of capital punishment. In an important sense if the punishment is to undo the crime it has to 'fit the crime'. To let someone off on the grounds that punishment is reformative is not to treat man with the full dignity of a bearer of will, whose will can thus incarnate wrong, and hence cry for punishment. It is treating him 'as a harmful animal who has to be made harmless' (*PR,* § 100). Punishment is a *right* of the criminal. He calls for it with his will *an sich.*

The exploration of what is involved in man's being rational will has led us first to see him as the bearer of rights, as such, as a person, outside of specific political contexts. But now we go farther. As will he not only has rights, but he has the duty to determine himself. He determines himself by giving a content to his will; and this should be a rational, universal content. This is the sphere of morality.

Man is a moral agent because as a bearer of will he ought to conform his will to universal reason. Man as a willing being is first of all a natural being, seeking the fulfilment of his own inclinations, needs, passions. But he has to purify his will and make the rationally conceived good his goal.

But as the subject of morality man still figures as an individual. The demand of morality is that I come to recognize that I am under the obligation of willing universal reason, simply in virtue of being a man. And this means as well that I come to this realization myself, by my own reason. The subject of morality is the universal subjectivity which rose on the ruins of the ancient city.

The demands of morality in other words are inner as well as outer. It is not enough that I do the right thing. If the requirement is that I conform my will to universal reason, then I must not only do what is right, but will the right as the right. In other words I have to do the right because it is the right; and it folllows from this that I have to understand the right myself. This is, of course, what Kant made central to morality, following a hint of Rousseau's: morality consists in the purity of the will, and this is considered by Hegel to be the highest expression of this category. Morality touches our intentions and not just our acts.

But this, of course, is radically incomplete for reasons which are now familiar to us. Morality needs a complement in the external world, a world of public life and practices where it is realized. For without this it remains a pure aspiration, a pure ought to be (Sollen) as Hegel puts it. It remains something purely inner. But there is more than that. The concept of rational will alone, as the will of an individual, is ultimately vacuous, as we saw in Chapter XIV. We cannot derive a content from the notion of duty for duty's sake (*PR,* § 135). It is only as ontological reason, which seeks its own embodiment in a community with a certain necessary structure, that rationality yields a criterion of the good. The content of the rational will is what this community requires of us. This then is our duty. It is not derived from formal reason but from the nature of the community which alone can embody reason.

Hence morality, the individual's search to conform his will to universal reason, refers us beyond itself both in order to complete its own attempt of deriving the right from reason, and in order to realize this right effectively. The demands on man as a bearer of rational will are thus that he live in a community which embodies reason, which is the fulfilled goal of reason. That is, what is implicit in the concept of man as a vehicle of rational will is only fully realized in such a community.

The two earlier stages thus refer us beyond to the concept of *Sittlichkeit* which is the third and major part of *PR.* Right is inadequate because it is simply the external expression of the fact that man is a bearer of will. It has no interiority. Besides it too requires to be defended by political power. By itself it is powerless. Morality shows a dimension of human life which answers one of the lacks of right; it shows human moral life as an inner purification of the will. But it cannot reach its goal of deriving the fullness of human moral duties from reason, nor realize these unless it is completed by a community in which morality is not simply an 'ought', but is realized in the public life. Thus right and morality find their place and are secured as parts of a larger whole.

But one essential feature of morality must be preserved in this community as it arises in its mature form in history. It must not as the earlier city-state have no place for moral man. On the contrary the basic freedom of moral man as man, the freedom to judge in conscience, must be preserved. This is an essential requirement of a *Sittlichkeit* which can incorporate modern man and with which he can identify himself. For the modern state, therefore, conscience is a sanctuary not to be violated (*PR*, §137). Man retains this reflective dimension and this is why he cannot recapture the immediate unity and identity of the citizens with the state characteristic of the polis. But this is not to say that the modern or any state can allow men to decide by conscience alone whether to obey the laws. It means rather that freedom of conscience is an essential right in the modern state.

We thus come to *Sittlichkeit* which is substantial freedom in Hegel's terms. It is realized good. Men identify with it. It becomes their 'second nature' (*PR*, §151), and they are its effective realization in subjectivity.

The *sittlich* is what has to do with a community in which the good is realized in a public or common life. Hence the category englobes more than the state. And Hegel will deal with three forms of common life in this section, which are also placed in an ascending order: the family, civil society and the state.

The first is an immediate unreflecting unity based on feeling. The second is society in so far as it conforms to the vision of the modern atomist theories of contract, a society of individuals who come together out of mutual need. Radically inadequate as a theory of the state, this vision is realized in Hegel's view in the modern bourgeois economy. Civil society is modern society seen as an economy of production and exchange between men considered as subjects of needs. This is at the antipodes of the family, for here there is no immediate unity but maximum consciousness of individuality in which men are bound together by external ties.

The state comes to complete this trio. For it offers once more a deeper unity, an inward unity, like the family. But it will not be just an immediate one based on feeling. Rather unity here is mediated by reason. The state is a community in which universal subjectivities can be bound together while being recognized as such.

First the family is a unity of feeling, of love. Men sense themselves as members within a family, not as persons with rights vis-à-vis each other. When rights enter into it, the family is dissolving. In this section Hegel deals with marriage, family property and the education of children. The main point of the family as *sittlich* is this fact that within it men see themselves as members of something greater, as having identity by their part in a common life.

But of course the family is quite inadequate alone as *Sittlichkeit,* for within it man is not really an individual and the allegiance to the common life is not founded on reason but on feeling only. Hence beyond the family, man is in another community in which he operates purely as an individual. This is what Hegel calls civil society.

Civil society is the society considered as a set of economic relations between individuals. Hegel had read and carefully considered the writings of the British political economists, most notably James Steuart and Adam Smith, whose works had been translated into German. His model of civil society owes a lot to these writers.

Civil society is the level of relations into which men enter not as members of family, nor as members of some ethical community, such as a state or a church, but just as men. It is a sphere in which men are related to each other as persons in Hegel's sense, i.e., as bearers of rights. In this sphere 'a man counts as a man in virtue of his humanity alone, not because he is a Jew, Catholic, Protestant, German, Italian, etc.' (*PR*, § 209 E).

In the level of social relations called civil society, men are thus individuals on their own; their relations to each other are founded on the fact that in fulfilling their needs they require each other. In other words, in this sphere we look at men as the subjects of individual purposes; they become related through these individual purposes whose fulfilment requires social co-operation. . . .

But Hegel now goes on to develop traits of civil society (*PR*, § 201–7) which properly belong to his own ideas. He argues for the necessary articulation of civil society into classes or estates. The necessary division of labour gives rise to groups (allgemeinen Massen, *PR*, § 201) which have not just a different type of work, but also different life-styles and hence values. These are the Hegelian 'estates' (Stände). Hegel uses the older term, rather than class, and it is better to follow him here since these groups are not just differentiated by their relation to the means of production, but by their life-style.

Hegel singles out three: the substantial or agricultural class which lives close to nature and which is generally unreflective, living rather 'an ethical life which is immediate, resting on family relationship and trust' (*PR*, § 203); the reflecting or business class which really lives the life of individuality, that is which has the orientation to the fulfilment of individual needs through rationalized work. This is the class which is most saliently identified with civil society as a system of needs. Thirdly, there is the universal class; this is the class of civil servants which identifies itself with the interests of the community as a whole.

We see here Hegel's notion of the inescapable differentiation of society which underlay his critique of the French Revolutionaries and their attempt to abolish differences in a régime of total participation. Because men in order to fulfil their needs cannot but differentiate themselves in this way, a polity which tries to abstract from this is bound to come to grief. But the differentiation is not simply to be understood as a by-product of the division of labour; we can also see in it by anticipation the structures of rational necessity.

The three classes represent each a dimension which must be present in the modern state. There must be the sense of allegiance to a whole which is above and greater than oneself, the dependence on something bigger; this the substantial class has in an unreflecting way. There must be a sense of the individual as a universal subjectivity; this the business class has. There must finally be a reasoned identification with the universal in a will which embodies this universal; and this the class of civil servants has. These three classes can also be lined up against the three levels of *Sittlichkeit*: family, civil society and state.

One of the crucial points of Hegel's philosophy is his belief that these three cannot be brought to synthesis by being present in all citizens and harmonized in each of them. Rather the synthesis is achieved by a community in which the different dimensions are carried primarily by a specific group; but where these are bound together and live a common allegiance to the whole. A state in which everyone is immediately identified with the principle of common life in the same way, this was possible among the ancients, but not with the more complex moderns. Today, we unite individuality and identification with the state by an articulation into estates where these different dimensions respectively are preponderant, and yet where all have a sense of common life, and recognize that they are part of a larger whole. . . .

This of course sharply differentiates Hegel's 'estate' from those of traditional society. These usually defined a station into which men were born and to which they had to cleave throughout life. But Hegel rejects this immobile society, along with anything approaching a caste system. For this is incompatible with the principle of individual freedom, which is central to the fully realized state. This is generally overlooked by those who want to class Hegel simply as a conservative.[1]

Civil society as a system of needs is naturally forced to develop further beyond the simple set of relations of production and exchange. Since it is the sphere in which men are related as persons, it has to protect and maintain men's rights. Hence it is involved in the administration of justice. But beyond this, the operation of the economy for the good of its members is far from being entirely assured by automatic mechanisms, in spite of the good work of the invisible hand. Lots of things can go wrong; and in the name of the good of individuals public authority has to intervene.

Hegel thus takes us in the second and third sections of civil society beyond the level of economic relations to functions which are judicial and properly political. But we are not yet dealing with the state. The reason is that we are still dealing here with individual men, the subjects of needs, united together for their common interest. What we discover is that the exigency of this common interest takes us beyond relations of production and exchange; and requires as well the administration of justice and a certain amount of regulation of economic activity. But we are not yet at the stage where we are looking on the political community as the substance, that is as constituting itself the end. The goal of all the regulations spoken of in the third section of civil society is still the good of individuals.

Hegel sees the necessary regulation being done partly by public authority, partly by corporations which are representative of various groups and professions and which operate with a publically recognized status. But what is particularly interesting and worth pausing over for a moment is Hegel's insights into the problems of civil society. It is not just that many accidents of economic life, natural disasters, overproduction, etc., can reduce men to poverty and that society thus has to operate some kind of welfare state. It is also that there is an inherent drive in civil society towards dissolution.

If civil society expands in an unimpeded way, it grows indefinitely in GNP and population. This increases greatly the wealth of some. But it also leads to an intensification of the division of labour, the increasing subdivision of jobs, and the growth of a proletariat which is tied to work of this sort. This proletariat is both materially impoverished, and spiritually as well by the narrowness and monotony of its work. But once men are reduced in this way materially and spiritually they lose their sense of self-respect and their identification with the whole community, they cease really to be integrated into it and they become a 'rabble' (Pöbel). The creating of this rabble goes along with the concentration of wealth in a few hands (*PR*, §244). . . .

---

1. But by the same token one cannot but doubt the viability of this system. Is it possible to sustain estates with really different modes of life in a society where there is real mobility, and where men are free to choose their profession? Does not for instance the unreflecting loyalty of the agricultural class presuppose a way of life into which one is born? So that entry could only be free into the other two estates. Generalized mobility is a powerful solvent. It would end up destroying estates altogether. Which is, indeed, what has happened. Although, of course, we benefit from hindsight in second-guessing Hegel on this.

For Hegel civil society is thus to be kept in balance by being incorporated in a deeper community. It cannot govern itself. Its members need allegiance to a higher community to turn them away from infinite self-enrichment as a goal and hence the self-destruction of civil society. Self-management through corporations can be seen as a stage on this road. It makes the individual member of a larger whole, and lifts him, as it were, toward the state. In the corporation he has the respect and dignity which he would otherwise seek, left as a simple individual, in endless self-enrichment (*PR*, §253 E).

2

We come now to the state which is the full realization of the Idea of *Sittlichkeit*, that is a community in which the good is realized in common life. The family and civil society were only partial, non-self subsistent realizations. With the state, we have a full and self-subsistent one. It is the manifestation of substantial will. It is the community in which the fullness of rational will is manifest in public life. The fully realized state reconciles the fully developed individual subjectivity and the universal. It is concrete freedom.

> Concrete freedom consists in this, that personal individuality and its particular interests not only achieve their complete development and gain explicit recognition for their right (as they do in the sphere of the family and civil society) but, for one thing, they also pass of their own accord into the interest of the universal, and, for another thing, they know and will the universal; they even recognize it as their own substantive mind; they take it as their end and aim and are active in its pursuit.
> (*PR*, §260)

This is what is achieved in the modern state.

The state is to be seen as a realization of rational necessity, of the Idea. As such, its articulations are to be understood as self-articulations of the Idea. Hegel speaks of the state as an 'organism'. But it is an organism which is thought of as producing its articulations according to a necessary plan. These articulations are fixed by the Concept (*PR*, §269). They form the constitution of the state.

Hegel here has a note on the relations of Church and state. Religion contains the same truths as the state expresses in reality. True religion should thus support the state; it should cultivate the inner conviction that the state ought to be obeyed, supported, identified with. It is a deviation when religion either retreats into other-worldliness or turns around and sets itself up against the state. The state should afford help and protection to the Church, for religion is a form of spirit's knowledge of itself. But it cannot accept a claim by the Church to be higher, for this would imply that the state was simply an external authority, as association for utility, like civil society, and not itself an embodiment of reason (*PR*, §270 E).

Because the constitution of the state is rational, that is, the state is articulated like an organism into its different members, we cannot think of the division of powers in a spirit of checks and balances. This assumes that the different powers are already self-subsistent and have either to strive against each other or reach a compromise. But this is contrary to the very principle of the state as an organic unity, a unity which articulates itself, and in which a common life flows through all the members. If we have got as far as to engage in the game of checks and balances 'the destruction of the state is forthwith a fait accompli' (*PR*, §272 E).

There is an important general point here which is central to Hegel's philosophy of the state. The state as a community embodying reason has to be lived as an organic whole; it cannot be seen simply as an aggregation of its elements, be these groups or individuals. For in this case it could not be lived by its citizens as the locus of a larger life with which they identify. Hegel argues strenuously against the type of constitution or constitutional provision which is based on this atomistic or composite view of the state. This is the view of men in society as simply 'a heap', as against an articulated unity. If we start with men fractioned into individual atoms, no rational state or indeed common life will be possible. . . .

What Is "Right" in Hegel's *Philosophy of Right?*
Steven B. Smith

The concept of rights has recently undergone a revival in political philosophy. This might seem surprising given that the concept of human or natural rights has until recently been regarded as hopelessly passé, useful perhaps for Fourth of July speeches but outside the bounds of acceptable academic discourses. Indeed, the classic statement affirming the status of rights—"We hold these truths to be self-evident, that all men are created equal, that they are endowed by their Creator with certain unalienable Rights, that among these are Life, Liberty, and the Pursuit of Happiness"—is taken by many to be either meaningless or false. If *self-evident* means true by virtue of the terms involved, it is not difficult to show that by no means have these rights appeared to be self-evident to all (Hart 1979; Oppenheim 1957).

The Right of Recognition

Recently, though, the tide has begun to turn. We have been told to "take rights seriously" and that all human beings are endowed by virtue of their humanity alone to have a set of absolute and inviolable moral claims that take precedence over all competing reasons or policies. While rights claims, to be sure, are not scientifically demonstrable, they are thought to be morally necessary in the sense that without them we would have no grounds on which to attribute to the person an absolute and irreplaceable dignity. Furthermore, we would have no grounds for opposing policies that treat individuals as no more than an expression of impersonal social aggregates to be used in any way that serves the collective ends of society.

It is by no means obvious that a concern for the future of human rights should lead us back to a reconsideration of Hegel. Hegel is better known as a critic of rights than as a defender. In the first place, he attacked natural rights theories for proposing an "atomistic" conception of the self as denuded of all cultural traits and characteristics. Natural rights theorists from Hobbes to Kant (and more recently Rawls) typically claim to discover the most universal features of human beings by means of a kind of thought experiment, hypothetically stripping or peeling away everything we have acquired through the influence of custom, history, and tradition in order to discover the prepolitical state of nature and the natural man lurking behind it. In an early essay on *Natural Law* Hegel even criticized the "antisocialistic" theories of Kant and Fichte for denying the natural sociality of man and for "posit[ing] the being of the individual as the primary and supreme thing" (1975, 70; *Werke* 2:454).

Steven B. Smith, "What is 'Right' in Hegel's *Philosophy of Right?*" *American Political Science Review,* 83 (March 1989): pp. 3–18. Reprinted by permission of the author and the American Political Science Association.

Second, he criticized rights theories as static, lacking any sense of the dynamics of human history and the developmental character of the moral personality. The self as Hegel understands it is not something "given" once and for all but is a being in the making, that is, a creature with a history. Whatever previous theorists might have claimed, rights claims are not static but are themselves part of a long and arduous historical process leading men gradually but inexorably toward an awareness of their own freedom. The idea that history represents a kind of collective *Bildung*—a moral education of the human race—toward a mutual recognition of right, I take to be Hegel's distinctive contribution to political philosophy.

This is not to say that Hegel thought it desirable to dispense with rights claims altogether. Rather he regarded rights as bound up with the dynamic structure of human history and especially the great revolutionary "moments" of the modern age—the Copernican, the French, and the Kantian. These events, he reasoned, were not isolated or discrete happenings but part of a worldwide struggle aimed at the realization of a certain desirable goal, namely, freedom (1956, 23; *Werke* 12: 38). If we look at history as previous historians have, namely by concentrating on particular events (the Peloponnesian War, the rise of Christianity, the reign of Louis XIV), we see nothing more than an interesting sequence of deeds with no connecting threads of rationality. But if we examine history as Hegel recommends, that is, not as a series of localized particulars but as a single process unfolding over time, we shall see in it the emergence of a "collective singular" (Koselleck 1985, 29).

The emergence of this conception of history as a collective singular made it possible to ask for the first time whether there was some point or meaning to history. Instead of regarding history in all of its infinite variety, Hegel conceived it as a struggle of different nations and cultures—Indians, Persians, Greeks, Romans, and modern Europeans—each trying to achieve freedom. Accordingly he believed it possible to divide history into a number of different epochs or states, each based on the degree of freedom that had been achieved (1956, 18–19; *Werke* 12:31–32). Thus in the oriental world, Hegel could write, only one man—the despot—was free. In the Greco-Roman world some were free, the free-born citizens of the various *poleis*. But in the modern world, disciplined by such events as the Protestant Reformation and the French Revolution, freedom is extended to all. Hegelian history, as W. H. Walsh has noted, represents nothing so much as the success story of modern European man (Walsh 1971, 183).

What made Hegel's argument about freedom anathema, especially to liberals, was his tendency to argue that it had been more or less realized in the modern European state. The famous prefatory remark in the *Philosophy of Right* declaring that "what is rational is real and what is real is rational" appeared to many as a blanket justification of the status quo however it stood. Thus hostile critics from Rudolph Haym (1962) to Karl Popper (1963) have argued that for Hegel freedom has been fully and adequately realized in the Prussian state of the 1820s. But this is not what Hegel says at all. Hegel's *Philosophy of Right* is not a justification for the Prussian monarchy but is rather the profoundest piece of philosophical jurisprudence in the modern world.

The state that Hegel has in mind is not identified with any particular or existing state but with the idea of the *Rechtsstaat*, a term for which there is no precise English equivalent but that is perhaps best captured in our phrase "the rule of law" (Oakeshott 1975, 257–63). Only in a state governed by law is freedom possible. By *a state governed by law* Hegel means one that extends the right of recognition (*Anerkennung*) or respect to every one of its members. It means the right to what members of the liberal tradition have taken to calling "equal concern and respect." Without some token of esteem or respect from one's neighbors, Hegel argues, none of the other goods afforded by society will have value. The various "categories" that structure social life, chiefly including civil society and the state, are not just conservative restraints on freedom but the necessary context for persons who mutually seek to acknowledge and enhance one another's right to recognition.

It may be objected that the concept of recognition, while central to Hegel's *Phenomenology of Mind,* is downplayed, perhaps dropped altogether, in the later *Philosophy of Right.* As sober an interpreter as George A. Kelly has remarked that to see the struggle for recognition as a "regulative idea" guiding all of Hegel's thought is to risk "anachronistic overtones of the Marxian class struggle" (Kelly 1978, 31–32). But this is perhaps an overstatement. Hegel's argument is based upon the assumption that human agents are driven by a powerful common interest in rational freedom that is in turn logically tied to the concept of mutual recognition. The word *recognition* need not be literally present for the concept to function. Freedom is, for Hegel, an interactive concept. Human beings are free only when they see themselves expressed in their relations to nature and their social institutions. These two aspects of freedom are not unrelated. The first involves an awareness that we are both separate from and sovereign over nature, which includes not just the external world but our bodily desires and inclinations. The second presupposes the mutual recognition of each person within a framework supplied by law. The right of recognition, I will argue, is intended to provide the basis for a new form of ethical life *(Sittlichkeit)* for the modern world.

The Idea of Right

The subject matter of the *Philosophy of Right* is stated quite simply in the introduction to the text as "the idea of right" (1972, 14; *Werke* 7:29). As the term suggests, Hegel was not simply interested in the historical question of how the right order is brought into being but with such traditional questions as the right or just ordering of political relationships. The book would seem to be intended as an analogue not only to modern works like Hobbes's *Leviathan* and Rousseau's *Social Contract* but also to ancient studies like Plato's *Republic* and Aristotle's *Politics.* Yet the appearance of continuity with the past is at least partially deceptive. The term *right* in the title is ambiguous. The German *Recht* can mean either "right" or "law," and the phrase *philosophy of right* has a peculiar ring to it that *philosophy of law* does not. In its widest sense *Recht* refers to the entire normative structure of a people's way of life, not just their civil rights and liberties but the whole system of ethical norms and values—not to mention religious rules and precepts—informing a culture.

Hegel tends to distinguish *Recht* from *Gesetz,* the term he uses for law in the narrow sense when referring to civil or positive legal codes. Indeed, he makes much of the etymological point that the German word for law, *Gesetz,* is related to the word for posit, *setzen* (1972, 134; *Werke* 7:361; see also Foster 1935, 119). It is preferable, therefore, to continue thinking of his book as philosophical inquiry into *Recht,* where *Recht* roughly means the entire range of practical reason. This is no longer Kant's *reine praktische Vernunft* but a matter of immanent rules proceeding from the rational will embedded in historical circumstances. Hegel himself gives credence to this interpretation when he says, "In speaking of Right ←*Recht*→ . . . we mean not merely what is generally meant by civil law, but also morality, ethical life, and world-history" (1972, 233; *Werke* 7:90–91).

Still, Hegel's meaning is not so much clarified as complicated by a glance at the subtitle of the work, namely, *Natural Right and the Science of the State in Outline* (*Naturrecht und Staatswissenschaft im Grumdrisse*). The term *natural right* is a traditional one that Hegel deems "not altogether correct." In one sense it points backwards to the normative theory of right that has its origins in classical antiquity. The ancients used this term to indicate what is by nature right or just in opposition to the rules or laws laid down by particular communities, which have their basis in arbitrary whim or fiat. On Hegel's view, however, right is crucially misunderstood if it is regarded as an expression of nature. Neither the external physical environment nor the internal sphere of human needs, wants, and desires can serve as an adequate basis for right. The term *natural right* is misleading whether it is understood to mean "something implanted by immediate nature [*unmittelbarer Naturweise*] or something determined by the nature of the thing [*Natur der Sache*]." Right, properly speaking, has its basis in the "free personality alone—on self-determination or autonomy, which is the very contrary of determination by nature." The term *natural right* should consequently be abandoned and replaced by the expression *the philosophical doctrine of right* (*die philosophische Rechtslehre*) (1971a, 248; *Werke* 10: 311–12).

This leads me, then, to my first thesis about right, namely, that it has its ground (*Boden*) in the individual subject or *Wille* (1972, 20; *Werke* 7:46). Hegel's starting point here is the minimal, or "thin," theory of the subject as a will capable of distinguishing itself from the rest of nature. Unlike ancient and medieval writers who sought to infer the proper ordering of human relations from our place within the whole, Hegel follows the lead of Hobbes, Rousseau, and Kant in denying that there are natural ends or purposes there to be discovered. There is no graduated scale of nature where there is a place for everything and everything has its place. Nature in fact provides no clues or evidence for how the moral order should be constructed. It is this fact that ultimately renders the term *natural right* so equivocal, since "nature is not free and therefore is neither just nor unjust" (1972, 44; *Werke* 7:113).

The *Philosophy of Right* takes the form of a phenomenology of the moral will. The will is simply the way the mind functions when it functions practically as opposed to theoretically. The first moment, or "determination" (*bestimmung*) of the will is defined by an abstraction from all content, from everything empirical or merely "given." What is left is the purely "negative will," the pure "I," which is characterized by a capacity for freedom. Hegel tries to explicate the freedom, or self-determination, of the will by an analogy to the sciences of nature:

> Freedom . . . is just as fundamental a character of the will as weight is of bodies. If we say: matter is "heavy" we might mean that this predicate is only contingent; but it is nothing of the kind, for nothing in matter is without weight. Matter is rather weight itself. Heaviness constitutes the body and is the body. The same is the case with freedom and the will, since the free entity is the will. Will without freedom is an empty word, while freedom is actual only as will, the subject. (1972, 226; *Werke* 7:46)

One might infer from this passage that the concept of freedom would result in a kind of nihilism, the condition in which everything goes. Hegel even implies as much when he remarks that "only in destroying something does this negative will possess the feeling of itself as existent." He refers, further, to "the fanaticism of the Hindu pure contemplation" and the "universal equality" pursued by the French revolutionaries as evidence of the nihilistoc goals of this purely negative freedom. It is the freedom identified with arbitrary choice (*Wilkür*) rather than with freedom under law. Thus while negative freedom has produced the "maximum of frightfulness and terror" and as such is a source of contemporary irrationalism, Hegel also maintains that the will has the resources to provide out of itself a new purified order of right and justice (1972, 22, 227–28; *Werke* 7:49–52).

The need for some kind of self-limitation leads to my second thesis about the will's activity. The need for limits is not a contradiction of freedom but essential to it. Freedom, as we shall see in the next section, does not imply a world ungoverned by law but one inhabited by subjects capable of supplying these principles themselves. Willing is not an arbitrary activity but already implies some minimal notion of a meaningful way of life within which willing and choosing can take place. Hegel's point is that willing presupposes a community of wills or rational agents whom we cannot choose to be without. Willing is never an isolated activity but always takes place within the context of a plurality of wills. It is the irreducible plurality of the human condition that makes willing a transaction between subjects, between an "I" and a "we" or, as he put it in the *Phenemenology of Mind,* between an "I that is a we . . . and a we that is an I" (1966, 227; *Werke* 3:145).

The subject of rights is, then, the "rational will" (*vernünftige Wille*), which Hegel characterizes as "self-determining universality" (1972, 25; *Werke* 7:62). So long as we understand the will to mean sheer "arbitrariness," it is not really free. For reasons similar to those of Rousseau and Kant, Hegel believed that such a view of freedom generally meant no more than slavery to natural appetites and desires. The self-determination of the arbitrary will is a "moment" of freedom but not yet developed, rational liberty. The moral will is characterized not just by a capacity for free choice but by deliberation and reflection on ends. While the arbitrary will may be able to pursue various impulses and desires, it has not yet attained control over its impulses and desires. The will understood as mere negative or arbitrary freedom can never be more than the Hobbesian "last appetite in deliberation" (Hobbes 1962, 54). Moral freedom contains, then, the capacity not just to desire but also to reflect evaluatively upon the kinds of things we ought to desire. It contains, in the last instance, the capacity to select and evaluate desires.

Hegel must answer the question of what the particular content of the will is or to what it can attach itself. The idea that right has its ground in the will appears to ignore the social basis of personality—that we are socially constituted in a variety of complex ways. His answer to this question is that in concentrating on the first aspect of the will—its ability to distinguish itself from all content—Hegel's early modern predecessors forgot that willing is also a teleological or purposive activity. To will is not merely to declare one's independence, it is to will something. Hegel here appears to return to an older position that was given its classic formulation by Aristotle, namely, that every human deliberate action is performed for the sake of some end to be brought about in the future. It is in "the nature of mind" (*die Natur des Geistes*)—a phrase with obvious Aristotelian overtones—to express itself in specific institutions and activities (Taylor 1979, 76, n. 2). The will is not something prior to its action, or—to put it differently—a person cannot be totally detached from the kinds of commitments and choices he or she has made. Rather, the will is always embedded in an "objective" world of political and legal institutions that reach their fruition in the idea of the state (1972, 242; *Werke* 7:159).

This leads us to a third thesis about right, that is, that the will achieves its realization, or "substantive end," only in the state. This is the phrase that has so alarmed many of Hegel's critics. Now, to say that the will becomes rational and free only in the state is, to be sure, hard doctrine. Hegel's *etatisme* allegedly identifies freedom with obedience to the police. But what Hegel means by the state need carry none of these sinister implications. The Hegelian state is above all an organization of laws, a *Rechtsstaat.* Law is what purges the state of caprice and makes possible such modern freedoms as contract, property, career choice, religion, and speech. The result is by no means some kind of irrational state worship but the deepening of a recognition and respect for the wishes and ways of life of others, a manner of behavior that could be called "civility" (Oakeshott 1975, 108–84).

The core of the modern state is, then, respect for the person, or "free personality," as such. This is much different, for example, from the ancient world, where, according to Hegel's investigations, the individual had not yet learned to distinguish him- or herself from the environment but lived in an "immediate" condition of trust or faith with his or her surroundings. As Hegel's interpretation of Sophocles' *Antigone* indicates, the Greeks simply did not think of themselves as individual subjects capable of choice and deliberation but as accidents of certain all-powerful substances that had already sealed their fates in advance. It is the exercise of the will—of free critical intelligence—and the desire to be *in* everything we do that most clearly distinguishes modern from ancient freedom. "This 'I will,'" he says, "constitutes the great difference between the ancient world and the modern, and in the great edifice of the state it must therefore have its appropriate objective and existence" (1972, 288; *Werke* 7:449).

The difference, then, between the ancient polis and the modern state is that far from recognizing the individual autonomy of each of its members, the polis was the paradigm of a tutelary community based on a shared moral understanding and directed toward a specific way of life. This conception of a closed homogeneous society was given its profoundest expression in Plato's *Republic,* which Hegel sees as "nothing but an interpretation of the nature of Greek ethical life." Unlike Socrates, whom Hegel interprets as a moral skeptic questioning all traditional values and institutions, Plato sought to close the lid on the Pandora's box opened by his teacher by requiring restraints on marriage, the family, and property. While Hegel commends Plato's "genius" for recognizing that "there was breaking into that life in his own time a deeper principle which could appear in it . . . only as something corruptive," his proposals in the *Republic* "did fatal injury to the deeper impulse which underlay it, namely, free infinite personality" (1972, 10; *Werke* 7:24).

The oppressive character of Plato's *Republic* is typically contrasted by Hegel to the principle of the will, or "infinite personality," that is recognized by the modern state. The person largely responsible for this principle is Rousseau, who in *The Philosophy of Right* is congratulated for "adducing the will as the principle of the state" and "not a principle like gregarious instinct . . . or divine authority" (1972, 156–57; *Werke* 7:400). The reference to Rousseau here is by no means accidental. Hegel frequently singles out Plato and Rousseau as the two thinkers most characteristic of ancient substantialism and modern subjectivity, respectively. What distinguishes modernity is precisely the emphasis on the will and individual consent as the core of right. In Plato's *Republic* "the subjective end simply coincided with the state's will. In modern times . . . we make claims for private conscience" (1972, 280; *Werke* 7:410). And he later remarks that, "In Plato's state, subjective freedom does not count, because people have their occupations assigned to them by the guardians. . . . But subjective freedom, which must be respected, demands that individuals should have free choice in this matter" (1972, 280; *Werke* 7:410).

The Struggle for Right

It is well known that Hegel rejected the state of nature and social contract methodologies of his early modern predecessors. Their "abstract" individualism and lack of attention to the dynamic, developmental aspects of history are their most frequently cited deficiencies. What is less often noted, however, is that Hegel himself used a crypto-state-of-nature teaching to derive his theory of right. The account of "the idea of right" in the *Philosophy* of *Right* presupposes the famous "struggle for recognition" in the opening pages of the chapter on "self-consciousness" in the *Phenomenology* and his later clarification of this theme in the *Encyclopedia* version of the *Philosophy of Mind*. Every bit as much as Hobbes or any other contractarian, Hegel explains the origins of right by reference to a putatively "natural" condition that is one of maximum conflict and insecurity. Political life is not natural to men but required to rectify the inadequacies of nature.

Hegel presents the origin of right as laying in the desire (*Begierde*) of two individuals seeking some sign of recognition from one another. Hegel infers the desire for recognition from the very nature of self-consciousness. The mind that desires to know everything desires first of all to know itself. But how is self-knowledge acquired? Hegel's answer is that we come to know ourselves not by isolated introspection in the manner of a Descartes but through interaction with others. The mind is led to reflect back upon itself only after experiencing those around us. "Self-consciousness," he writes, "exists in and for itself, in that, and by the fact that it exists for another self-consciousness; that is to say, it is only by being recognized (*Anerkanntes*)" (1966, 229; *Werke* 3:145). The view of the self developed here could be called relational insofar as it sees us as parts of complex systems of mutual interaction that determine our identities.

The desire for recognition is, for Hegel, the quintessentially human desire. Hegel presents the will as containing a number of conflicting, even contradictory, desires, for instance, the desires for food, clothing, and shelter, each one of which cries out for satisfaction. But if we acted only to satisfy our biological urges, human existence would never rise above the state of nature. Obviously, the satisfaction of basic animal needs for warmth, food, and protection is a necessary but not a sufficient condition for the fulfillment of our truly human needs. Like Rousseau in the *Second Discourse*, Hegel is impressed by the elasticity of our desires. We are instinctually underdetermined (Rousseau 1964, 114). While the desire for food may be universal, there is a great deal of room left to determine how we should eat, when, where, and with whom. Furthermore, there is virtually nothing that cannot become an object of our desires. To use a vocabulary that is not Hegel's own but that, I hope, does not do violence to his meaning, it is because humans have the capacity to desire not only natural objects but also nonnatural objects or values that they are able to rise above the level of the brutes and become human at all. Our desires are not the product of sheer unmediated instinct but of will and reflection; they are *intentional* desires precisely as elaborated by H. P. Grice (1957, 377–88).

Hegel's concern could be put in the following terms. We begin with some object of immediate desire. Such an object is here conceived as a means to the fulfillment of some specifiable end. It is the kind of desire attributed to all of us all of the time by Hobbes when he wrote that "felicity is a continual progress of the desire, from one object to another, the attaining of the former being still but the way to the latter" (Hobbes 1962, 80).

But unlike Hobbes and later utilitarian writers, for Hegel this is only to state a problem, not to provide a solution. Human beings not only have desires of various kinds; we also have desires to have desires. Our identities are not fixed in stone; we can desire to have identities of a particular sort. We have the capacity, cognitively speaking, to stand back from our desires and ask whether they are the kinds of desires we wish to have. It is this desire to desire, or what Harry Frankfurt has called "second-order desires" (1971, 5–20), that leads us out of the infinite regress implied by Hobbes, where every desire is simply a means to another desire.

The desire for recognition is a desire unlike any other desire. It is not just a means to some specifiable end but a means to the enjoyment of any end whatever. If this sounds odd it is because we have been conditioned to think of desires as a part of our makeup opposed to rationality. But Hegel rejects this modern mind-body dualism in favor of a more complex relationship. Desires, he believes, entail rationality, and rationality involves desire. Our appetites are, so to speak, "shot through" with reason. Reason is not something superimposed on the passions from outside but is more like a principle of organization that works both in and through the passions (1971a, 235–36; Werke 10:296–97). Thus the desire to be recognized is not just another desire that we happen to have; it is the core human desire central to our sense of well-being, of who and what we are. We are beings who are not just constituted by a desire for comfort, safety, and security but who cannot live—or at least cannot live well—if our desires are not respected by those around us. What we desire, above all, is to be treated with a sense of decency and respect. Such treatment is necessary for our basic sense of self-respect.

Hegel's account of the struggle for recognition and the so-called "master-and-slave" relation that grows out of it is too well known to require much exegesis. His main point is that the recognition to which each person believes him- or herself entitled is not immediately forthcoming. Each wants to be recognized without in turn having to grant recognition to others, and this one-sided and unequal state of affairs leads one to enter a life-and-death struggle not unlike the Hobbesian *bellum omnium contra omnes*. It is from this life-and-death struggle, in which humanity's passion for honor and prestige is asserted over its fear and terror at the possibility of violent death, that the all-important relationship between master and slave arises. This arises because in the struggle one of the parties is unwilling to go all the way and risk life for the sake of recognition, thereby submitting to the other, granting recognition without requiring it in turn. In short, the vanquished party subordinates its own desire for esteem to the biologically stronger desire for self-preservation.

Hegel's account of the struggle for recognition seems almost like a satire on Aristotle's account of slavery in book 1 of the *Politics*. For Aristotle slavery was justified because it was the political institution that corresponded most closely to the natural hierarchy, or inequality, between the body and the soul. Just as it is the function of the body to submit to the rule or governance of the soul, so is it the function of the slave to free from a life of drudgery and toil those few capable of engaging in political activity and philosophy. If nature provides a model, or paradigm, for our institutions, slavery has its origins in human nature itself. Aristotle, of course, uses his doctrine of natural slavery to show that not all existing slaves are in fact slaves by nature, as many have been taken as prisoners of war. Yet he elsewhere argues that just as the soul and body can work together to produce a well-functioning, or healthy, individual, so too is there a kind of common interest and even friendship possible between a master and a slave.

Hegel turns Aristotle on his head. The conceptual basis for slavery is the need of one self-conscious mind to be recognized by another. In the ensuing struggle the vanquished grants recognition to the lord by the very fact of being forced to work in the latter's service. The master's enjoyment is predicated upon freedom from work. However, the recognition that the master now enjoys is not that from an equal but from a degraded tool who is merely employed to satisfy the master's material comforts. The master ends up in the same position as Aristotle's "great-souled man" who desires honor and recognition but finds it unworthy once it has been bestowed (*Nicomachean Ethics* 1123b–25a [1975]). The master is somehow greater than any sign of recognition received. Rather than having gained a level of contemplative autonomy and self-sufficiency, the master comes to realize a dependence on the slave to satisfy desires, and this realization serves to undermine the asymmetry of the relationship.

Marxist interpreters have made much of Hegel's account of the origins of society, especially the role of slave labor in the production of culture. They point to the relatively greater importance Hegel assigns to making or fabricating—what the Greeks called *poiesis*—than on acting, or doing, (*praxis*) (Riedel 1969, 29–33). Whatever his later strictures against Hegel's idealism, Marx's own historical materialism was crucially dependent on Hegel as he himself recognized in the *1844 Manuscripts*. "Hegel's standpoint," he says there, "is that of modern political economy. He conceives labor as the essence . . . of man" (Marx 1978, 112).

Nevertheless, this interpretation can be overdone. Unlike his Marxist interpreters, Hegel views labor fundamentally as an intentional activity (Bernstein 1984, 14–39). It is an expression of the will, or free personality, and cannot be reduced to more rudimentary "material" determinants like external pressures or bodily needs. For the Marxist, intentionality is always secondary to material conditions, while for Hegel it is the essence of the human. Thus Hegel explains mastery and slavery as the outcome of a struggle not for self-preservation (a material end) but for recognition (a spiritual one).

Hegel's resolution to the conflict of master and slave seems unduly forced. Nevertheless, it provides a convenient transition from the struggle for recognition to the ethical sphere of "universal self-consciousness." Hegel defines this sphere as "the affirmative awareness of self in an other self," which is "the form of consciousness which lies at the root of all true mental or spiritual life—in family, fatherland, state, and of all virtues, love, friendship, valor, honor, and fame" (1971a, 176; *Werke* 10:226). From the context it is clear that what Hegel calls "universal self-consciousness" is a close approximation of his conception of ethical life, or *Sittlichkeit*. This means something more than the Kantian self-determination of the will. It is something like a common culture consisting of a set of shared ideas, norms, and values. The practices and institutions of ethical life—family life, economic activity, and politics—are not just limitations on the will's activity but the social context within which freedom is possible. Only from within the concrete forms of ethical life is mutual recognition possible.

Recognition and Moral Personality

The point of the foregoing discussion was to show that Hegel's idea of right is not just tautologically posited to make sense of the modern state but historically constructed through a process of labor and struggle. Unlike a contemporary legal philosopher—say, Ronald Dworkin—who lays down a right to equal concern and respect and then goes about describing the kinds of social and political institutions necessary to sustain that right, Hegel regards the concept of right as tied to a distinctive conception of human personality (*Persönlichkeit*). "Personality," he writes, "essentially involves the capacity for rights" (1972, 37; *Werke* 7:95). Being a person means here having a sense of one's self as an autonomous agent with a will and consciousness of one's own.

The idea of right is only possible, then, where there is some universal conception of the self or personhood that is the designated bearer of right. What Hegel calls a "person" is essentially a legal entity entitled to disposition over the objects that have become its property. While property is defined simply as that over which we have acquired legal title, it follows that from the legal point of view it is "a matter of indifference" how much, if any, property a person possesses (1972, 44; *Werke* 7:112–13). All that matters is the individual's abstract capacity to acquire, utilize, and exchange property with other persons. Accordingly, the maxim regulating the behavior of such legal *personnae* is simply, "Be a person and respect others as persons" (1972, 37; *Werke* 7:95). This maxim is by no means idiosyncratic or capricious but is central to much of our legal reasoning. For whenever we think of persons as the law enjoins, we do so not on the basis of their specific accomplishments or character traits but as formally identical entities related only by their capacities to recognize and understand the law.

Hegel traces the legal concept of personhood back to the Roman Empire, when the essentially modern idea of "legal status" came to take precedence over active citizenship. Unlike the modern legal person, who claims rights against the state, the ancient citizen was regarded as a part of a larger ethical whole or totality. This conception of citizenship was given its canonical expression in book 1 of Aristotle's *Politics*, where it is expressly stated that the city is prior to the individual and that a human being is "by nature" a "political animal" capable of realizing faculties only through political participation. Consequently, "a man who is without a city [*apolis*] through nature rather than chance is either a mean sort or a being superior to man" like "the 'clanless, lawless, heartless' man reviled by Homer" (*Politics* 1253a [1977]). Aristotle actually calls the city a *koinonia politike*, a political association or community, to grasp better the nature of the civic tie. A community is a society not just of strangers but of friends or comrades (*heteroi*) whose lives are centered on certain common, corporate goals. The city is, in short, something literally "held in common" (Mulgan 1977, 13–17; Riedel 1969, 140–44).

All of this is quite different from the modern *Rechtsstaat*. Hegel's conception of the emergence of legal status is noteworthy especially because of its place within the various nineteenth- and twentieth-century theories of political modernization and development. Like Henry Maine, whose classic work, *The Ancient Law*, saw the development of the modern state in terms of a shift from status to contract, or Ferdinand Tönnies who characterized the same process as a movement from *Gemeinschaft* to *Gesellschaft*, Hegel sought to account for this as a move from classical citizen to the modern bourgeois or *Bürger* (1972, 124, 127; *Werke* 7:343, 348). Unlike the citizen whose identity stemmed from membership in a particular community, the *Bürger* is defined precisely by freedom from all such parochial attachments and traditions. While a citizen is related to fellows by a shared moral understanding, the *Bürger* is a private individual who engages in competitive struggle with others in the arena of civil society. Thus, underlying the *Bürger's* way of life is a formal equality expressed in a demand for mutual respect. For the *Bürger* "A man counts as a man in virtue of his manhood alone, not because he is a Jew, Catholic, Protestant, German, Italian, and so on" (1972, 134; *Werke* 7:360).

The right to recognition, we might say, is not simply a contingent feature of the modern state; it is its inner soul and purpose. What Hegel calls the right to recognition is not unlike what the liberal tradition has deemed as equal treatment before the law or what has recently come to be called the doctrine of equal concern and respect. Hegel says as much in a passage from the *Encyclopedia*: In the state "man is recognized and treated as a rational being, as free, as a person; and the individual, on his side, makes himself worthy of this recognition by overcoming the natural state of his self-consciousness and obeying a universal, the will that is in essence and actuality will, the law; he behaves, therefore, towards others in a manner that is universally valid, recognizing them—as he wishes others to recognize him—as free, as persons" (1971a, 172–73; *Werke* 10:221–22).

Hegel's defense of the right of recognition could take one of two strategies. The first, adopted variously by Kant, Rawls, and Dworkin argues that human beings are entitled to equal recognition not because of their substantive achievements but because of an underlying skepticism about the human good. Because, it is argued, opinions about the good are ultimately a question of value and thus incorrigible, the most appropriate political response is the construction of a constitutional framework that is neutral to substantive questions about the good. In the language of contemporary Kantian liberalism the right must take precedence over the good. Since there is no single or comprehensive goal for which we all strive, the optimum solution to the plurality of ends is something like the modern liberal state, which professes official indifference or neutrality toward the ways of life of its citizens.

This line of defense fails for two reasons. First, consistent skepticism about the good engenders not respect for persons but the opposite. Rather consistent skepticism of the type advocated by Max Weber promotes an unconstrained struggle between competing values and ways of life. "It is really a question not only of alternatives," Weber wrote, "but of an irreconcilable death struggle like that between 'God' and the 'Devil' (Weber 1949, 17). Only if the parties in question have made a prior commitment not to be skeptical about equal respect will this defense not degenerate into a war of all against all.

The second flaw with skepticism is that on closer inspection it is frequently not skeptical at all. The value that the skeptic frequently elevates above all others is individual liberty. For the skeptic, the greatest political sin is governmental paternalism—the attempt to "legislate morality." Paternalism is ruled out because it violates our sacred right to choose for ourselves how to live. Perhaps the boldest defense of individual autonomy against the claims of governmental paternalism was put forward a generation after Hegel's death by J. S. Mill in his classic, *On Liberty.*

The second line of defense argues for a more positive defense of right. The right of recognition, as Hegel understands it, is not just a watery tolerance of others, adopting a hands-off attitude. It requires a more robust sense of respect for the "free personality" that is at the basis of right. At the basis of personality lies the idea of moral self-realization or self-development so crucial to Hegelian ethics. Here it is important to note that the personality is never something given but is always in the making. What sort of selves we become is always dependent on what sorts of activities we engage in. The specific institutions discussed in the *Philosophy of Right* are intended to provide the necessary categorical framework within which our individual powers and capacities can grow and develop. Without such a categorical framework to provide some kind of moral ballast, our lives would threaten to become rootless, alienated, and anomic.

What I have called Hegel's positive defense of right is indicated in his decision to treat politics as a branch of ethics. Like Plato and Aristotle, he denies the possibility of an independent sphere of morality detached from politics and consequently an independent science of morality detached from political philosophy. Indeed, the Hegelian state is not neutral vis-à-vis the ways of life of its citizens. Its goal is the positive one of promoting a form of *Sittlichkeit* in which all citizens can share. The division of ethical life into family, civil society, and the state is a form of social differentiation that seeks to imbue citizens with some sense of esprit de corps, or common purpose (1972, 133; *Werke* 7:359). In the final analysis, then, Hegel's political program is a form of civic education or *Bildung*.

Many interpreters have seen in Hegel's theory of *Sittlichkeit* an incipient relativism according to which standards of right and wrong can only come from existing conventions and institutions. His well-known claim that "every individual is a child of his time" and that a philosopher can no more transcend his age than "an individual can . . . jump over Rhodes" is often taken as evidence for his relativism (1972, 11; *Werke* 7:26). Likewise, his identification of *Sittlichkeit* with "absolutely valid laws and institutions" and "habitual practice" appears to give it a conservative dimension similar to Burke or any apostle of traditionalism (1972, 105, 108; *Werke* 7:294, 301).

But this is to misunderstand. Hegel's theory of *Sittlichkeit* is not just an empirical, sociological description of what institutions happen to exist; it is a rational reconstruction of what institutions *must* exist if rational freedom is to be possible. Institutions and practices are not in Hegel's philosophy called upon to be the judges in their own case. Rather they are judged by their capacity to further and sustain our mutual desire for freedom. Hegel's idea of freedom is tied to an evolutionary or progressive theory of history, the culmination of which is the modern constitutional state. Only in the institutions of the modern constitutional state does one find the kinds of practices and institutions that embody "the actuality of concrete freedom" (*die Wirklichkeit der konkreten Freiheit*) (1972, 160; *Werke* 7:406). In the rational state, now coming into being, the conflict between philosophy and politics will cease to exist. In such a state institutions will be arranged to express every facet of a developed human intelligence and the "plain man," like the philosopher, will live in a condition of mutual trust and respect.

Conclusion

Two objections stand in the way of an endorsement of Hegel's theory of right today. The first is that whatever undoubted merit Hegel's arguments may have, they are simply outside the U.S. context, where there has never been a strong state-centered tradition as required by Hegel. In Hegelian terms the United States has evinced the power of civil society over the state. U.S. attachment to liberalism, especially in its Lockean forms, has prohibited the development of a more robust sense of "the political," which Hegelian politics seems to require. Accordingly, the creed of unbridled individualism has been virtually the one "self-evident" truth shared by most U.S. citizens. "The reality of atomistic social freedom," Louis Hartz proclaimed in his magisterial *Liberal Tradition in America*," is [as] instinctive to the American mind, as in a sense the concept of the polis was instinctive to Platonic Athens or the concept of the church was to the mind of the middle ages" (Hartz 1955, 62).

Without dwelling on the vexed question of the role of Lockean liberalism in defining U.S. national character or the adequacy of Hartz's depiction of Locke, it is at least arguable that another more "Hegelian" conception of statehood and political development has been at work in our tradition ever since the founding. According to Samuel Beer, the United States is and has been since 1787 not just a collection of semisovereign states united for the limited purposes of security and prosperity but—to use the language of Daniel Webster—a genuinely "national community" where "liberty and union" are "one and inseparable." By a *community* Beer means first of all "an emotional fact: a massive background feeling of 'belongingness' and identi- fication." On such a view "we are joined with a vast national community by a distinctive kind of emotional tie: by *public* joy, grief, pride, anger, envy, fear, hope, and so on" (Beer 1967, 165). Among those who have invoked the national idea have been Alexander Hamilton, Daniel Webster, Abraham Lincoln, and, in our century, Theodore and Franklin Roosevelt. The national idea is one that cuts across party cleavages and unites Federalists, Whigs, Republicans, and Democrats. And in a subsequent article Beer argues that our most important political task today is "to keep alive in our speech and our intention the move toward the consolidation of the union" as opposed to a destructive particularism (Beer 1982, 23–29).

A second and perhaps more formidable objection to Hegel runs as follows. Even granted the persistence of certain consolidating or "Hegelianizing" tendencies in our tradition, it does not follow that the national idea represents some kind of historical absolute as Hegel thought it did—a final reconciliation of reason and reality. It is just this metaphysical interpretation of the state, so this objection runs, that condemns to irrelevance whatever apparent merits Hegel's arguments may have. One could argue, as some of Hegel's defenders do, that Hegel's insights can be saved only by disentangling them from the skeins of his speculative metaphysics and philosophy of history. But to be consistent, one would have to admit that Hegel's depiction of the modern state as the crowning apex of world history is simply wrong.

This objection need not be accorded the last word. In the first place, this objection is often premised on an alleged inconsistency in Hegel's thought. His attempt to portray history as a completed (or completable) process moving toward a final telos is said to betray the dialectical element in his thought with its endless negativity and rebellion against all fixity. The true Hegel is not the conservative idealist but the revolutionary dialectician for whom "overcoming" and "self-transcendence" are all that matter.

The claim that Hegel arbitrarily arrests the dialectic, forcing it to culminate in the present, is flawed. Here I can only say that the distinction often drawn between dialectic and system, methodology and metaphysics, is entirely foreign to Hegel's thought. This was a distinction foisted onto his thought by latter-day disciples seeking to put his dialectic into the service of various radical causes. Hegel's dialectic is more concerned with the "mediation and overcoming" (*Vermittlung und Aufhebung*) of conflicts than their intensification. The crucial role assigned by Hegel to these concepts is lost if we persist in regarding the dialectic simply as the power of the negative and see all societal forms as so many varieties of unfreedom. The Hegelian dialectic is concerned with the resolution of contradiction by means of speculative reason. It is my contention that far from being at odds with his politics, Hegel's dialectical logic is profoundly consistent with the ethical community sketched out in the *Philosophy of Right*.

Second, it would be overly hasty to dismiss Hegel's thesis about an end of history as an antiquated metaphysical prejudice left over from an age of faith. If we understand the end of history to mean a condition characterized by an overall consensus on the ends of life, we can see that it bears an uncanny resemblance to another movement of modern thought, the "end-of-ideology" thesis proclaimed by several prominent U.S. intellectuals in the 1950s and 1960s. The proclamation of an end of ideology assumed that the passions that had generated the political fanaticisms of the past were now spent and that the imperatives of attending to the postwar industrial economy would form the basis for a new consensus. This consensus would not just be another ideology but would be an anti- or counterideology where individuals would agree to resolve their differences in a more pragmatic, piecemeal manner without recourse to grand principles.

I take the end-of-ideology thesis to be self-refuting for the same reason that Hegel's end-of-history thesis is. Far from making an end of history, Hegel's thesis was itself a notable expression of the history of his own time and place. Hegel was not the first—and will certainly not be the last—philosopher to succumb to the temptation of endowing his thought with a permanence and validity that he denied to others. This is not to make the obvious point that Hegel underestimated the peculiar limitations of the time and circumstances in which he wrote. The point is that if Hegel was correct when he said that every philosopher is a child of his time and that philosophy is "its own time apprehended in thoughts," his attempts to insulate his philosophy from the process of historical change that he so brilliantly analyzed could not but meet with failure.

Hegel was, I believe, profoundly correct to see in history a rational process where great and liberating ideas become impediments to the development of future thought and thus unwittingly provoke their own demise. When applied to itself, Hegel's end-of-history thesis could not but become another orthodoxy that in time would generate its own antithesis, namely, an end to the end of history.

Critical theory, deconstruction, and hermeneutics represent but three candidates to succeed Hegel. Postmodern critics like Jacques Derrida and Jean-Francois Lyotard have seen in Hegel's monumental "system" with its periodization of history into distinct phases of spirit nothing but a thinly veiled attempt to gain control over the past and thereby to dominate the future. In place of Hegel's synthesis of reason and history, post-modernism claims to offer no new philosophical system or "grand theory" but rather a "hermeneutics of suspicion," a perpetual watchfulness over the self-professed purveyors of schemes proclaiming emancipation and enlightenment.

The question, then, is what can be retained of Hegel's progressive philosophy of history once it has been submitted to the assaults of postmodern skepticism? One answer could be, a more supple or provisional notion of an end of history. "Every historian" Jürgen Habermas has written, "is in the role of last historian" (Habermas 1977, 350). This is to say that we must regard our own epistemic standards and norms of rationality not as absolute in some transcendent sense but as binding on us at least until something better comes along. Unless we are prepared to give up altogether the idea of gaining a critical purchase on history, we are compelled to judge it from some kind of absolute standpoint. Such a standpoint need not be metaphysically grounded but can perhaps be discovered immanently or pragmatically in the forms of human discourse. There is, as Habermas has suggested, a telos of agreement implicit in our very use of language. In any case I take this to be a worthwhile task for the political philosophy of the future.

References

Aristotle. 1975. *Nicomachean Ethics*. Trans. H. Rackham. Cambridge: Harvard University Press.
Aristotle. 1977. *Politics*. Trans. H. Rackman. Cambridge: Harvard University Press.

Aron, Raymond. 1957. *The Opium of the Intellectuals.* Trans. Terence Kilmartin. New York: Doubleday.

Beer, Samuel. 1967. "Liberalism and the National Idea." In *Left, Right, and Center,* ed. Robert Goldwin. Chicago: Rand McNally.

Beer, Samuel. 1982. "The Idea of the Nation." *New Republic,* 19/26 July.

Bell, Daniel. 1960. *The End of Ideology: On the Exhaustion of Political Ideas in the Fifties.* New York: Free Press.

Bernstein, J. M. 1984. "From Self-Consciousness to Community: Act and Recognition in the Master-Slave Relationship." In *The State and Civil Society,* ed. Z. A. Pelczynski. Cambridge: Cambridge University Press.

Foster, Michael B. 1935. *The Political Philosophies of Plato and Hegel.* Oxford: Clarendon.

Frankfurt, Harry. 1971. "Freedom of the Will and the Concept of a Person." *Journal of Philosophy* 67:5–20.

Grice, H. P. 1957. "Meaning." *Philosophical Review* 66:377–88.

Habermas, Jürgen. 1977. "Review of Gadamer's *Truth and Method."* In *Understanding and Social Inquiry,* ed. Fred R. Dallmayr and Thomas A. McCarthy. Notre Dame: University of Notre Dame Press.

Hart, H. L. A. 1979. "Between Rights and Utility." In *The Idea of Freedom,* ed. Alan Ryan. Oxford: Clarendon.

Hartz, Louis. 1955. *The Liberal Tradition in America.* New York: Harcourt, Brace & World.

Haym, Rudolph. 1962. *Hegel und seine Zeit.* Hildesheim: Olms.

Hegel, G. W. F. 1956. *Philosophy of History.* Trans. J. Sibree. New York: Dover.

Hegel, G. W. F. 1966. *Phenomenology of Mind.* Trans. J. B. Baille. London: George Allen & Unwin.

Hegel, G. W. F. 1971a. *Philosophy of Mind: Being Part Three of the "Encyclopedia of the Philosophical Sciences."* Trans. William Wallace and A. V. Miller. Oxford: Clarendon.

Hegel, G. W. F. 1971b. *Werke in zwanzig Bänden.* Ed. Eva Moldenhauer and Karl M. Michel. Frankfurt: Suhrkamp.

Hegel, G. W. F. 1972. *Philosophy of Right.* Trans. T. M. Knox. Oxford: Clarendon.

Hegel, G. W. F. 1975. *Natural Law.* Trans. T. M. Knox. Philadelphia: University of Pennsylvania Press.

Hinchman, Lewis. 1984. "The Origins of Human Rights: A Hegelian Perspective." *Western Political Quarterly* 37:7–31.

Hobbes, Thomas. 1962. *Leviathan.* Ed. Michael Oakeshott. London: Macmillan.

Kelly, George A. 1978. *Hegel's Retreat from Eleusis.* Princeton: Princeton University Press.

Kojève, Alexandre. 1947. *Introduction à la lecture de Hegel.* Ed. Raymond Queneau. Paris: Gallimard.

Koselleck, Reinhart. 1985. *Futures Past: On the Semantics of Historical Time.* Trans. Keith Tribe. Cambridge: MIT Press.

Lipset, Seymour Martin. 1959. *Political Man.* New York: Doubleday.

Marx, Karl. 1978. "Economic and Philosophic Manuscripts of 1844." In *Marx-Engels Reader,* ed. Robert Tucker. New York: W. W. Norton.

Mulgan, R. G. 1977. *Aristotle's Political Theory.* Oxford: Clarendon.

Nisbet, Robert. 1966. *The Sociological Tradition.* New York: Basic Books.

Oakeshott, Michael. 1975. *On Human Conduct.* Oxford: Clarendon.

Oppenheim, Felix. 1957. "The Natural Law Thesis: Affirmation or Denial?" *American Political Science Review* 51:41–53.

Popper, Karl. 1963. *The Open Society and Its Enemies.* Princeton: Princeton University Press.

Riedel, Manfred. 1969. *Studien zu Hegel's Rechtsphilosophie.* Frankfurt: Suhrkamp.

Riedel, Manfred, ed. 1975. *Materialien zu Hegels Rechtsphilosophie.* Vol. 1. Frankfurt: Suhrkamp.

Rousseau, Jean-Jacques. 1964. *The First and Second Discourses.* Trans. Roger D. and Judith R. Masters. New York: Saint Martin's.

Shklar, Judith. 1971. "Hegel's Phenomenology: An Elegy for Hellas." In *Hegel's Political Philosophy,* ed. Z. A. Pelczynski. Cambridge: Cambridge University Press.

Smith, Steven B. 1986. "Hegel's Critique of Liberalism." *American Political Science Review* 80:121–39.

Steiner, George. 1986. *Antigones*. Oxford: Clarendon.

Stillman, Peter. 1974. "Hegel's Critique of Liberal Theories of Rights." *American Political Science Review* 68:1086–92.

Taylor, Charles. 1979. *Hegel and Modern Society*. Cambridge: Cambridge University Press.

Toews, John E. 1980. *Hegelianism: The Path Toward Dialectical Humanism, 1805–1841*. Cambridge: Cambridge University Press.

Walsh, W. H. 1971. "Principle and Prejudice in Hegel's Philosophy of History." In *Hegel's Political Philosophy*, ed. Z. A. Pelczynski. Cambridge: Cambridge University Press.

Weber, Max. 1949. *The Methodology of the Social Science*. Trans. Edward Shils and Henry Finch. New York: Free Press.

Karl Marx

Karl Marx, widely known as the founder of Communist ideology, was actually a great theorist of capitalism. He believed that capitalism had created a brave new world out of the ashes of feudalism. As Marx and his colleague Friedrich Engels noted in the *Communist Manifesto,* capitalism was a revolutionary force in the modern world. It set loose massive productive forces; scientific discoveries and technological innovations increasingly were put to work in industrial and agricultural production. It created wonders far superior to Egyptian pyramids or Gothic cathedrals, and yielded riches far beyond the wildest dreams of past rulers and conquerors. It developed a social order in perpetual motion and constant upheaval in economics, technology, politics, and culture. Despite capitalism's achievements, brutal exploitation still characterized the life of most people. Under capitalism, "All that is solid melts into air, all that is holy is profaned, and man is at last compelled to face with sober senses, his real conditions of life, and his relations with his kind."[1]

This contradiction spurred Marx to begin a lifetime of study of the origins, development, and operations of capitalism. His studies led him to a wide variety of sources. As Engels once observed, Marx's ideas had their roots in German philosophy, British political economy, and French socialist politics. The circumstances of Marx's life make it easy to see how such a theoretical synthesis might have been possible. Born in Trier, Germany, in 1818, Marx's university years (in Bonn, Berlin, and Jena)

1. Karl Marx and Friedrich Engels, "The Communist Manifesto," in David McLellan, ed., *Karl Marx: Selected Writings* (Oxford: Oxford University Press, 1977), p. 224.

were influenced by the Young Hegelians, liberal intellectuals who adapted Hegel's views and method to a critique of the Prussian political system. After completing his Ph.D. in philosophy in 1841, Marx began a career in journalism as editor of the liberal newspaper, *Rheinische Zeitung*. Expelled from Germany for his radical democratic views, he stayed first in Paris (where he wrote critiques of Hegelianism and began collaborating with Engels), then Brussels (where the *Manifesto* was written), then back to Germany (where he participated in the 1848 revolution), finally settling in London. After devoting his life to extensive research and writing on political economy, as well as working-class political activism, Marx died in London in 1883.

True to the synthetic origins of his study of capitalism, Marx views society as a web of interpersonal relations, an organic whole or totality that undergoes historical evolution, shapes human activities, and constitutes what other theorists call human nature. Though there are a variety of starting points from which to begin a study of social relations (e.g., religion, politics, law, literature, philosophy), production (or, more broadly, economics) becomes the most fruitful for Marx. Though it is not the only path to knowledge about society, production is nevertheless a pervasive light that colors all other aspects of social life. Thus, any specific mode of production (the structures and processes of material life) tends to be associated with a certain social or historical stage of development, with a particular way of life. Although the economic aspect is central, it does not always dominate or directly determine all features of society and culture.

The starting point for Marx, then, is the production of material life, the satisfaction of evolving needs, and the constant renewal of life. Labor is simultaneously the means of satisfying need, of building an external world of artifacts, of renewing life, and of actualizing or realizing oneself. Unlike the work of animals, human labor potentially is a free and conscious activity—labor can be done apart from the demands of instinct or physical necessity, and it can be done according to a plan conceived in the imagination. However, capitalism erects serious obstacles (e.g., alienation and exploitation) to realizing labor's potential; it has become a hindrance to further growth and development.

Because of the specific factors (political conflicts, ideological controversies, and economic crises) that make it an obstacle to progress, capitalism will inevitably fall and give rise to a new mode of production—socialism or communism. Such a fall will not occur without class conflict; without the (spontaneous, yet prepared) revolutionary activity of human beings. Although Marx left few discussions of the nature of communist society (he felt that drawing a blueprint would be utopian and futile), he nevertheless did sketch its major features: an end to private property, the division of labor, and social classes; a radical democratic polity and economic planning; and a genuine community of authentic individuals.

The 1844 Manuscripts, The German Ideology, and Capital

The selections that follow focus on Marx's method, his critique of capitalism, and his vision of communist society. We have left out the political writings, such as the *Communist Manifesto*, partly because they are widely available, and partly because the core of Marx's theory is not so much the details of revolutionary strategy as an analysis of the human condition under capitalism. In the selection from the *Economic and Philosophic Manuscripts* (1844), Marx begins with a Hegelian critique of the categories and explanations of behavior offered by political economy, which essentially hides the fact of alienated labor in capitalist society. Marx then discusses the fourfold nature of this alienation—namely, alienation from one's product, from the activity of production, from fellow human beings, and from one's "species being."

In the selection from *The German Ideology* (written with Engels from 1845 to 1847), Marx identifies the key premises of his approach to social and political theory. In addition to providing a sketch of the history of modes of production, Marx and Engels argue for the materialist thesis that "Life is not determined by consciousness, but consciousness by life."[2] They also discuss, in some vague and poetic passages, the nature of communist society and of the struggles necessary to bring it about.

The final selections come from Marx's last work, the first volume of *Capital* (1867). These selections set forth the labor theory of value as it is discussed in two contexts: (1) the distinction between a commodity's use-value (the utility we get from a thing, its ability to satisfy a particular need we have) and its exchange-value (what we can get in exchange for it); and (2) the concept of surplus value as an indicator of the degree to which workers are exploited by capitalists. Here, Marx shows that "exploitation" is not a moral category, but an economic one. Workers are exploited not because individual capitalists are vicious, but because of the nature of wage labor itself; the fact that one person contracts to work for another for a specified time.

Commentaries

Bertell Ollman (in his significant book on alienation) argues that Marx offers a theory of internal relations, in which the various facets of society (e.g., capital, labor, class, ideology) are constituted by their relations with other parts of the whole. Identifying alienation under capitalism as the opposite of unalienation under communism, Ollman proceeds to analyze in some detail the four broad relations discussed in Marx's theory of alienation.

The absence of alienation, then, is one of the hallmarks of communist society. William James Booth, starting from a famous passage in *The German Ideology,* explores just what the end of alienation might mean for the critique of political economy. In particular, for Marx, communism should result in a society where individuals have considerable self-determination over how they spend their time in the context of a cooperative, self-governing community.

Key Words

Species being. The human potential or essence reflected in free, self-conscious activity (labor), and frustrated by alienation under capitalism.

Division of labor. The apportionment of economic or productive tasks among individuals and classes in a society.

Labor theory of value. The theory that a commodity's value (i.e., exchange value—what a good or service can be exchanged for) is determined by the average amount of time it takes workers to produce that commodity.

---

2. Marx and Engels, "The German Ideology," in McLellan, ed., *Karl Marx: Selected Writings,* p. 164. Compare Marx's formulation of this same idea in the 1859 "Preface to the Critique of Political Economy" (loc. cit., p. 389).

Surplus value. The difference between the value created by a worker during a given workday and the value (his or her wage) necessary to permit the worker to return for another day's work.

For Further Reading

Avineri, S. 1968. *The Social and Political Thought of Karl Marx.* Cambridge: Cambridge University Press.

Ball, T., and J. Farr, eds. 1984. *After Marx.* Cambridge: Cambridge University Press.

Buchanan, A. 1982. *Marx and Justice: The Radical Critique of Liberalism.* Totowa, N.J.: Rowman and Allanheld.

Cohen, G.A. 1978. *Karl Marx's Theory of History: A Defence.* Princeton: Princeton University Press.

Elster, J. 1985. *Making Sense of Marx.* Cambridge: Cambridge University Press.

Economic and Philosophic Manuscripts

Alienated Labour

We started from the presuppositions of political economy. We accepted its vocabulary and its laws. We presupposed private property, the separation of labour, capital, and land, and likewise of wages, profit, and ground rent; also division of labour; competition; the concept of exchange value, etc. Using the very words of political economy we have demonstrated that the worker is degraded to the most miserable sort of commodity; that the misery of the worker is in inverse proportion to the power and size of his production; that the necessary result of competition is the accumulation of capital in a few hands, and thus a more terrible restoration of monopoly; and that finally the distinction between capitalist and landlord, and that between peasant and industrial worker disappears and the whole of society must fall apart into the two classes of the property owners and the propertlyless workers.

Political economy starts with the fact of private property, it does not explain it to us. It conceives of the material process that private property goes through in reality in general abstract formulas which then have for it a value of laws. It does not understand these laws, i.e. it does not demonstrate how they arise from the nature of private property. Political economy does not afford us any explanation of the reason for the separation of labour and capital, of capital and land. When, for example, political economy defines the relationship of wages to profit from capital, the interest of the capitalist is the ultimate court of appeal, that is, it presupposes what should be its result. In the same way competition enters the argument everywhere. It is explained by exterior circumstances. But political economy tells us nothing about how far these exterior, apparently fortuitous circumstances are merely the expression of a necessary development. We have seen how it regards exchange itself as something fortuitous. The only wheels that political economy sets in motion are greed and war among the greedy, competition.

It is just because political economy has not grasped the connections in the movement that new contradictions have arisen in its doctrines, for example, between that of monopoly and that of competition, freedom of craft and corporations, division of landed property and large estates. For competition, free trade, and the division of landed property were only seen as fortuitous circumstances created by will and force, not developed and comprehended as necessary, inevitable, and natural results of monopoly, corporations, and feudal property.

So what we have to understand now is the essential connection of private property, selfishness, the separation of labour, capital, and landed property, of exchange and competition, of the value and degradation of man, of monopoly and competition, etc.—the connection of all this alienation with the money system.

Let us not be like the political economist who, when he wishes to explain something, puts himself in an imaginary original state of affairs. Such an original state of affairs explains nothing. He simply pushes the question back into a grey and nebulous distance. He presupposes as a fact and an event what he ought to be deducing, namely the necessary connection between the two things, for example, between the division of labour and exchange. Similarly, the theologian explains the origin of evil through the fall, i.e. he presupposes as an historical fact what he should be explaining.

We start with a contemporary fact of political economy:

The worker becomes poorer the richer is his production, the more it increases in power and scope. The worker becomes a commodity that is all the cheaper the more commodities he creates. The depreciation of the human world progresses in direct proportion to the increase in value of the world of things. Labour does not only produce commodities; it produces itself and the labourer as a commodity and that to the extent to which it produces commodities in general.

What this fact expresses is merely this: the object that labour produces, its product, confronts it as an alien being, as a power independent of the producer. The product of labour is labour that has solidified itself into an object, made itself into a thing, the objectification of labour. The realization of labour is its objectification. In political economy this realization of labour appears as a loss of reality for the worker, objectification as a loss of the object or slavery to it, and appropriation as alienation, as externalization.

The realization of labour appears as a loss of reality to an extent that the worker loses his reality by dying of starvation. Objectification appears as a loss of the object to such an extent that the worker is robbed not only of the objects necessary for his life but also of the objects of his work. Indeed, labour itself becomes an object he can only have in his power with the greatest of efforts and at irregular intervals. The appropriation of the object appears as alienation to such an extent that the more objects the worker produces, the less he can possess and the more he falls under the domination of his product, capital.

All these consequences follow from the fact that the worker relates to the product of his labour as to an alien object. For it is evident from this presupposition that the more the worker externalizes himself in his work, the more powerful becomes the alien, objective world that he creates opposite himself, the poorer he becomes himself in his inner life and the less he can call his own. It is just the same in religion. The more man puts into God, the less he retains in himself. The worker puts his life into the object and this means that it no longer belongs to him but to the object. So the greater this activity, the more the worker is without an object. What the product of his labour is, that he is not. So the greater this product the less he is himself. The externalization of the worker in his product implies not only that his labour becomes an object, an exterior existence but also that it exists outside him, independent and alien, and becomes a self-sufficient power opposite him, that the life that he has lent to the object affronts him, hostile and alien.

Let us now deal in more detail with objectification, the production of the worker, and the alienation, the loss of the object, his product, which is involved in it.

The worker can create nothing without nature, the sensuous exterior world. It is the matter in which his labour realizes itself, in which it is active, out of which and through which it produces.

But as nature affords the means of life for labour in the sense that labour cannot live without objects on which it exercises itself, so it affords a means of life in the narrower sense, namely the means for the physical subsistence of the worker himself.

Thus the more the worker appropriates the exterior world of sensuous nature by his labour, the more he doubly deprives himself of the means of subsistence, firstly since the exterior sensuous world increasingly ceases to be an object belonging to his work, a means of subsistence for his labour; secondly, since it increasingly ceases to be a means of subsistence in the direct sense, a means for the physical subsistence of the worker.

Thus in these two ways the worker becomes a slave to his object: firstly he receives an object of labour, that is he receives labour, and secondly, he receives the means of subsistence. Thus it is his object that permits him to exist first as a worker and secondly as a physical subject. The climax of this slavery is that only as a worker can he maintain himself as a physical subject and it is only as a physical subject that he is a worker.

(According to the laws of political economy the alienation of the worker in his object is expressed as follows: the more the worker produces the less he has to consume, the more values he creates the more valueless and worthless he becomes, the more formed the product the more deformed the worker, the more civilized the product, the more barbaric the worker, the more powerful the work the more powerless becomes the worker, the more cultured the work the more philistine the worker becomes and more of a slave to nature.)

Political economy hides the alienation in the essence of labour by not considering the immediate relationship between the worker (labour) and production. Labour produces works of wonder for the rich, but nakedness for the worker. It produces palaces, but only hovels for the worker; it produces beauty, but cripples the worker; it replaces labour by machines but throws a part of the workers back to a barbaric labour and turns the other part into machines. It produces culture, but also imbecility and cretinism for the worker.

The immediate relationship of labour to its products is the relationship of the worker to the objects of his production. The relationship of the man of means to the objects of production and to production itself is only a consequence of this first relationship. And it confirms it. We shall examine this other aspect later.

So when we ask the question: what relationship is essential to labour, we are asking about the relationship of the worker to production.

Up to now we have considered only one aspect of the alienation or externalization of the worker, his relationship to the products of his labour. But alienation shows itself not only in the result, but also in the act of production, inside productive activity itself. How would the worker be able to affront the product of his work as an alien being if he did not alienate himself in the act of production itself? For the product is merely the summary of the activity of production. So if the product of labour is externalization, production itself must be active externalization, the externalization of activity, the activity of externalization. The alienation of the object of labour is only the résumé of the alienation, the externalization in the activity of labour itself.

What does the externalization of labour consist of then?

Firstly, that labour is exterior to the worker, that is, it does not belong to his essence. Therefore he does not confirm himself in his work, he denies himself, feels miserable instead of happy, deploys no free physical and intellectual energy, but mortifies his body and ruins his mind. Thus the worker only feels a stranger. He is at home when he is not working and when he works he is not at home. His labour is therefore not voluntary but compulsory, forced labour. It is therefore not the satisfaction of a need but only a means to satisfy needs outside itself. How alien it really is is very evident from the fact that when there is no physical or other compulsion, labour is avoided like the plague. External labour, labour in which man externalizes himself, is a labour of self-sacrifice and mortification. Finally, the external character of labour for the worker shows itself in the fact that it is not his own but someone else's, that it does not belong to him, that he does not belong to himself in his labour but to someone else. As in religion the human imagination's own activity, the activity of man's head and his heart, reacts independently on the individual as an alien activity of gods or devils, so the activity of the worker is not his own spontaneous activity. It belongs to another and is the loss of himself.

The result we arrive at then is that man (the worker) only feels himself freely active in his animal functions of eating, drinking, and procreating, at most also in his dwelling and dress, and feels himself an animal in his human functions.

Eating, drinking, procreating, etc. are indeed truly human functions. But in the abstraction that separates them from the other round of human activity and makes them into final and exclusive ends they become animal.

We have treated the act of alienation of practical human activity, labour, from two aspects. (1) The relationship of the worker to the product of his labour as an alien object that has power over him. This relationship is at the same time the relationship to the sensuous exterior world and to natural objects as to an alien and hostile world opposed to him. (2) The relationship of labour to the act of production inside labour. This relationship is the relationship of the worker to his own activity as something that is alien and does not belong to him; it is activity that is passivity, power that is weakness, procreation that is castration, the worker's own physical and intellectual energy, his personal life (for what is life except activity?) as an activity directed against himself, independent of him and not belonging to him. It is self-alienation, as above it was the alienation of the object.

We now have to draw a third characteristic of alienated labour from the two previous ones.

Man is a species-being not only in that practically and theoretically he makes both his own and other species into his objects, but also, and this is only another way of putting the same thing, he relates to himself as to the present, living species, in that he relates to himself as to a universal and therefore free being.

Both with man and with animals the species-life consists physically in the fact that man (like animals) lives from inorganic nature, and the more universal man is than animals the more more universal is the area of inorganic nature from which he lives. From the theoretical point of view, plants, animals, stones, air, light, etc. form part of human consciousness, partly as objects of natural science, partly as objects of art; they are his intellectual inorganic nature, his intellectual means of subsistence, which he must first prepare before he can enjoy and assimilate them. From the practical point of view, too, they form a part of human life and activity. Physically man lives solely from these products of nature, whether they appear as food, heating, clothing, habitation, etc. The universality of man appears in practice precisely in the universality that makes the whole of nature into his inorganic body in that it is both (i) his immediate means of subsistence and also (ii) the material object and tool of his vital activity. Nature is the inorganic body of a man, that is, in so far as it is not itself a human body. That man lives from nature means that nature is his body with which he must maintain a constant interchange so as not to die. That man's physical and intellectual life depends on nature merely means that nature depends on itself, for man is a part of nature.

While alienated labour alienates (1) nature from man, and (2) man from himself, his own active function, his vital activity, it also alienates the species from man; it turns his species-life into a means towards his individual life. Firstly it alienates species-life and individual life, and secondly in its abstraction it makes the latter into the aim of the former which is also conceived of in its abstract and alien form. For firstly, work, vital activity, and productive life itself appear to man only as a means to the satisfaction of a need, the need to preserve his physical existence. But productive life is species-life. It is life producing life. The whole character of a species, its generic character, is contained in its manner of vital activity, and free conscious activity is the species-characteristic of man. Life itself appears merely as a means to life.

The animal is immediately one with its vital activity. It is not distinct from it. They are identical. Man makes his vital activity itself into an object of his will and consciousness. He has a conscious vital activity. He is not immediately identical to any of his characterizations. Conscious vital activity differentiates man immediately from animal vital activity. It is this and this alone that makes man a species-being. He is only a conscious being, that is, his own life is an object to him, precisely because he is a species-being. This is the only reason for his activity being free activity. Alienated labour reverses the relationship so that, just because he is a conscious being, man makes his vital activity and essence a mere means to his existence.

The practical creation of an objective world, the working-over of inorganic nature, is the confirmation of man as a conscious species-being, that is, as a being that relates to the species as to himself and to himself as to the species. It is true that the animal, too, produces. It builts itself a nest, a dwelling, like the bee, the beaver, the ant, etc. But it only produces what it needs immediately for itself or its offspring; it produces one-sidedly whereas man produces universally; it produces only under the pressure of immediate physical need, whereas man produces freely from physical need and only truly produces when he is thus free; it produces only itself whereas man reproduces the whole of nature. Its product belongs immediately to its physical body whereas man can freely separate himself from his product. The animal only fashions things according to the standards and needs of the species it belongs to, whereas man knows how to produce according to the measure of every species and knows everywhere how to apply its inherent standard to the object; thus man also fashions things according to the laws of beauty.

Thus it is in the working over of the objective world that man first really affirms himself as a species-being. This production is his active species-life. Through it nature appears as his work and his reality. The object of work is therefore the objectification of the species-life of man; for he duplicates himself not only intellectually, in his mind, but also actively in reality and thus can look at his image in a world he has created. Therefore when alienated labour tears from man the object of his production, it also tears from him his species-life, the real objectivity of his species and turns the advantage he has over animals into a disadvantage in that his inorganic body, nature, is torn from him.

Similarly, in that alienated labour degrades man's own free activity to a means, it turns the species-life of man into a means for his physical existence.

Thus consciousness, which man derives from his species, changes itself through alienation so that species-life becomes a means for him.

Therefore alienated labour:

(3) makes the species-being of man, both nature and the intellectual faculties of his species, into a being that is alien to him, into a means for his individual existence. It alienates from man his own body, nature exterior to him, and his intellectual being, his human essence.

(4) An immediate consequence of man's alienation from the product of his work, his vital activity and his species-being, is the alienation of man from man. When man is opposed to himself, it is another man that is opposed to him. What is valid for the relationship of a man to his work, of the product of his work and himself, is also valid for the relationship of man to other men and of their labour and the objects of their labour.

In general, the statement that man is alienated from his species-being, means that one man is alienated from another as each of them is alienated from the human essence.

The alienation of man and in general of every relationship in which man stands to himself is first realized and expressed in the relationship with which man stands to other men.

Thus in the situation of alienated labour each man measures his relationship to other men by the relationship in which he finds himself placed as a worker.

We began with a fact of political economy, the alienation of the worker and his production. We have expressed this fact in conceptual terms: alienated, externalized labour. We have analysed this concept and thus analysed a purely economic fact. . . .

The German Ideology

The Premisses of the Materialist Method

The premisses from which we begin are not arbitrary ones, not dogmas, but real premisses from which abstraction can only be made in the imagination. They are the real individuals, their activity and the material conditions under which they live, both those which they find already existing and those produced by their activity. These premisses can thus be verified in a purely empirical way.

The first premiss of all human history is, of course, the existence of living human individuals. Thus the first fact to be established is the physical organization of these individuals and their consequent relation to the rest of nature. Of course, we cannot here go either into the actual physical nature of man, or into the natural conditions in which man finds himself—geological, oro-hydrographical, climatic, and so on. The writing of history must always set out from these natural bases and their modification in the course of history through the action of men.

Men can be distinguished from animals by consciousness, by religion, or anything else you like. They themselves begin to distinguish themselves from animals as soon as they begin to produce their means of subsistence, a step which is conditioned by their physical organization. By producing their means of subsistence men are indirectly producing their actual material life.

The way in which men produce their means of subsistence depends first of all on the nature of the actual means of subsistence they find in existence and have to reproduce. This mode of production must not be considered simply as being the production of the physical existence of the individuals. Rather it is a definite form of activity of these individuals, a definite form of expressing their life, a definite mode of life on their part. As individuals express their life, so they are. What they are, therefore, coincides with their production, both with *what* they produce and with *how* they produce. The nature of individuals thus depends on the material conditions determining their production.

This production only makes its appearance with the increase of population. In its turn this presupposes the intercourse of individuals with one another. The form of this intercourse is again determined by production.

The relations of different nations among themselves depend upon the extent to which each has developed its productive forces, the division of labour, and internal intercourse. This statement is generally recognized. But not only the relation of one nation to others, but also the whole internal structure of the nation itself depends on the stage of development reached by its production and its internal and external intercourse. How far the productive forces of a nation are developed is shown most manifestly by the degree to which the division of labour has been carried. Each new productive force, in so far as it is not merely a quantitative extension of productive forces already known (for instance the bringing into cultivation of fresh land), causes a further development of the division of labour.

The division of labour inside a nation leads at first to the separation of industrial and commercial from agricultural labour, and hence to the separation of town and country and to the conflict of their interests. Its further development leads to the separation of commercial from industrial labour. At the same time, through the division of labour inside these various branches there develop various divisions among the individuals co-operating in definite kinds of labour. The relative position of these individual groups is determined by the methods employed in agriculture, industry, and commerce (patriarchalism, slavery, estates, classes). These same conditions are to be seen (given a more developed intercourse) in the relations of different nations to one another.

The various stages of development in the division of labour are just so many different forms of ownership, i.e. the existing stage in the division of labour determines also the relations of individuals to one another with reference to the material, instrument, and product of labour.

The first form of ownership is tribal ownership. It corresponds to the undeveloped stage of production, at which a people lives by hunting and fishing, by the rearing of beasts, or, in the highest stage, agriculture. In the latter case it presupposes a great mass of uncultivated stretches of land. The division of labour is at this stage still very elementary and is confined to a further extension of the natural division of labour existing in the family. The social structure is, therefore, limited to an extension of the family; patriarchal family chieftains, below them the members of the tribe, finally slaves. The slavery latent in the family only develops gradually with the increase of population, the growth of wants, and with the extension of external relations, both of war and of barter.

The second form is the ancient communal and State ownership which proceeds especially from the union of several tribes into a city by agreement or by conquest, and which is still accompanied by slavery. Beside communal ownership we already find movable, and later also immovable, private property developing, but as an abnormal form subordinate to communal ownership. The citizens hold power over their labouring slaves only in their community, and on this account alone, therefore, they are bound to the form of communal ownership. It is the communal private property which compels the active citizens to remain in this spontaneously derived form of association over against their slaves. For this reason the whole structure of society based on this communal ownership, and with it the power of the people, decays in the same measure as, in particular, immovable private property evolves. The division of labour is already more developed. We already find the antagonism of town and country; later the antagonism between those states which represent town interests and those which represent country interests, and inside the towns themselves the antagonism between industry and maritime commerce. The class relation between citizens and slaves is now completely developed.

With the development of private property, we find here for the first time the same conditions which we shall find again, only on a more extensive scale, with modern private property. On the one hand, the concentration of private property, which began very early in Rome (as the Licinian agrarian law proves) and proceeded very rapidly from the time of the civil wars and especially under the Emperors; on the other hand, coupled with this, the transformation of the plebeian small peasantry into a proletariat, which, however, owing to its intermediate position between propertied citizens and slaves, never achieved an independent development.

The third form of ownership is feudal or estate property. If antiquity started out from the town and its little territory, the Middle Ages started out from the country. This differing starting-point was determined by the sparseness of the population at that time, which was scattered over a large area and which received no large increase from the conquerors. In contrast to Greece and Rome, feudal development at the outset, therefore, extends over a much wider territory, prepared by the Roman conquests and the spread of agriculture at first associated with it. The last centuries of the declining Roman Empire and its conquest by the barbarians destroyed a number of productive forces; agriculture had declined, industry had decayed for want of a market, trade had died out or been violently suspended, the rural and urban population had decreased. From these conditions and the mode of organization of the conquest determined by them, feudal property developed under the influence of the Germanic military constitution. Like tribal and communal ownership, it is based again on a community; but the directly producing class standing over against it is not, as in the case of the ancient community, the slaves, but the enserfed small peasantry. As soon as feudalism is fully developed, there also arises antagonism towards the towns. The hierarchical structure of landownership, and the armed bodies of retainers associated with it, gave the nobility power over the serfs. This feudal organization was, just as much as the ancient communal ownership, an association against a subjected producing class; but the form of association and the relation to the direct producers were different because of the different conditions of production.

This feudal system of landownership had its counterpart in the towns in the shape of corporative property, the feudal organization of trades. Here property consisted chiefly in the labour of each individual person. The necessity for association against the organized robber barons, the need for communal covered markets in an age when the industrialist was at the same time a merchant, the growing competition of the escaped serfs swarming into the rising towns, the feudal structure of the whole country: these combined to bring about the guilds. The gradually accumulated small capital of individual craftsmen and their stable numbers, as against the growing population, evolved the relation of journeyman and apprentice, which brought into being in the towns a hierarchy similar to that in the country.

Thus the chief form of property during the feudal epoch consisted on the one hand of landed property with serf labour chained to it, and on the other of the labour of the individual with small capital commanding the labour of journeymen. The organization of both was determined by the restricted conditions of production—the small-scale and primitive cultivation of the land and the craft type of industry. There was little division of labour in the heyday of feudalism. Each country bore in itself the antithesis of town and country; the division into estates was certainly strongly marked; but apart from the differentiation of princes, nobility, clergy, and peasants in the country, and masters, journeymen, apprentices, and soon also the rabble of casual labourers in the towns, no division of importance took place. In agriculture it was rendered difficult by the strip-system, beside which the cottage industry of the peasants themselves emerged. In industry there was no division of labour at all in the individual trades themselves, and very little between them. The separation of industry and commerce was found already in existence in older towns; in the newer it only developed later, when the towns entered into mutual relations.

The grouping of larger territories into feudal kingdoms was a necessity for the landed nobility as for the towns. The organization of the ruling class, the nobility, had, therefore, everywhere a monarch at its head.

The fact is, therefore, that definite individuals who are productively active in a definite way enter into these definite social and political relations. Empirical observation must in each separate instance bring out empirically, and without any mystification and speculation, the connection of the social and political structure with production. The social structure and the State are continually evolving out of the life-process of definite individuals, but of individuals, not as they may appear in their own or other people's imagination, but as they really are, i.e. as they operate, produce materially, and hence as they work under definite material limits, presuppositions, and conditions independent of their will.

The production of ideas, of conceptions, of consciousness, is at first directly interwoven with the material activity and the material intercourse of men, the language of real life. Conceiving, thinking, the mental intercourse of men, appear at this stage as the direct efflux of their material behaviour. The same applies to mental production as expressed in the language of politics, laws, morality, religion, metaphysics, etc. of a people. Men are the producers of their conceptions, ideas, etc.—real, active men, as they are conditioned by a definite development of their productive forces and of the intercourse corresponding to these, up to its furthest forms. Consciousness can never be anything else than conscious existence, and the existence of men is their actual life-process. If in all ideology men and their circumstances appear upside-down as in a *camera obscura*, this phenomenon arises just as much from their historical life-process as the inversion of objects on the retina does from their physical life-process.

In direct contrast to German philosophy which descends from heaven to earth, here we ascend from earth to heaven. That is to say, we do not set out from what men say, imagine, conceive, nor from men as narrated, thought of, imagined, conceived, in order to arrive at men in the flesh. We set out from real, active men, and on the basis of their real life-process we demonstrate the development of the ideological reflexes and echoes of this life-process. The phantoms formed in the human brain are also, necessarily, sublimates of their material life-process, which is empirically verifiable and bound to material premises. Morality, religion, metaphysics, all the rest of ideology and their corresponding forms of consciousness, thus no longer retain the semblance of independence. They have no history, no development; but men, developing their material production and their material intercourse, alter, along with this their real existence, their thinking and the products of their thinking. Life is not determined by consciousness, but consciousness by life. In the first method of approach the starting-point is consciousness taken as the living individual; in the second method, which conforms to real life, it is the real living individuals themselves, and consciousness is considered solely as their consciousness.

This method of approach is not devoid of premisses. It starts out from the real premisses and does not abandon them for a moment. Its premisses are men, not in any fantastic isolation and rigidity, but in their actual, empirically perceptible process of development under definite conditions. As soon as this active life-process is described, history ceases to be a collection of dead facts as it is with the empiricists (themselves still abstract), or an imagined activity of imagined subjects, as with the idealists.

Where speculation ends—in real life—there real, positive science begins: the representation of the practical activity, of the practical process of development of men. Empty talk about consciousness ceases, and real knowledge has to take its place. When reality is depicted, philosophy as an independent branch of knowledge loses its medium of existence. At the best its place can only be taken by a summing-up of the most general results, abstractions which arise from the observation of the historical development of men. Viewed apart from real history, these abstractions have in themselves no value whatsoever. They can only serve to facilitate the arrangement of historical material, to indicate the sequence of its separate strata. But they by no means afford a recipe or schema, as does philosophy, for neatly trimming the epochs of history. On the contrary, our difficulties begin only when we set about the observation and the arrangement—the real depiction—of our historical material, whether of a past epoch or of the present. The removal of these difficulties is governed by premisses which it is quite impossible to state here, but which only the study of the actual life-process and the activity of the individuals of each epoch will make evident. We shall select here some of these abstractions, which we use in contradistinction to the ideologists, and shall illustrate them by historical examples.

Since we are dealing with the Germans, who are devoid of premisses, we must begin by stating the first premiss of all human existence and, therefore, of all history, the premiss, namely, that men must be in a position to live in order to be able to 'make history'. But life involves before everything else eating and drinking, a habitation, clothing, and many other things. The first historical act is thus the production of the means to satisfy these needs, the production of material life itself. And indeed this is an historical act, a fundamental condition of all history, which today, as thousands of years ago, must daily and hourly be fulfilled merely in order to sustain human life. Even when the sensuous world is reduced to a minimum, to a stick as with Saint Bruno, it presupposes the action of producing the stick. Therefore in any interpretation of history one has first of all to observe this fundamental fact in all its significance and all its implications and to accord it its due importance. It is well known that the Germans have never done this, and they have never, therefore, had an earthly basis for history and consequently never an historian. The French and the English, even if they have conceived the relation of this fact with so-called history only in an extremely one-sided fashion, particularly as long as they remained in the toils of political ideology, have nevertheless made the first attempts to give the writing of history a materialistic basis by being the first to write histories of civil society, of commerce and industry.

The second point is that the satisfaction of the first need (the action of satisfying, and the instrument of satisfaction which has been acquired) leads to new needs; and this production of new needs is the first historical act. Here we recognize immediately the spiritual ancestry of the great historical wisdom of the Germans who, when they run out of positive material and when they can serve up neither theological nor political nor literary rubbish, assert that this is not history at all, but the 'prehistoric era'. They do not, however, enlighten us as to how we proceed from this nonsensical 'prehistory' to history proper; although, on the other hand, in their historical speculation they seize upon this 'prehistory' with especial eagerness because they imagine themselves safe there from interference on the part of 'crude facts', and, at the same time, because there they can give full rein to their speculative impulse and set up and knock down hypotheses by the thousand.

The third circumstance which, from the very outset, enters into historical development, is that men, who daily remake their own life, begin to make other men, to propagate their kind: the relation between man and woman, parents and children, the family. The family, which to begin with is the only social relationship, becomes later, when increased needs create new social relations and the increased population new needs, a subordinate one (except in Germany), and must then be treated and analysed according to the existing empirical data, not according to 'the concept of the family', as is the custom in Germany. These three aspects of social activity are not of course to be taken as three different stages, but just as three aspects or, to make it clear to the Germans, three 'moments', which have existed simultaneously since the dawn of history and the first men, and which still assert themselves in history today.

The production of life, both of one's own in labour and of fresh life in procreation, now appears as a double relationship: on the one hand as a natural, on the other as a social, relationship. By social we understand the co-operation of several individuals, no matter under what conditions, in what manner, and to what end. It follows from this that a certain mode of production, or industrial stage, is always combined with a certain mode of co-operation, or social stage, and this mode of co-operation is itself a 'productive force'. Further, that the multitude of productive forces accessible to men determines the nature of society, hence, that the 'history of humanity' must always be studied and treated in relation to the history of industry and exchange. But it is also clear how in Germany it is impossible to write this sort of history, because the Germans lack not only the necessary power of comprehension and the material but also the 'evidence of their senses', for across the Rhine you cannot have any experience of these things since history has stopped happening. Thus it is quite obvious from the start that there exists a materialistic connection of men with one another, which is determined by their needs and their mode of production, and which is as old as men themselves. This connection is ever taking on new forms, and thus presents a 'history' independently of the existence of any political or religious nonsense which in addition may hold men together.

Only now, after having considered four moments, four aspects of the primary historical relationships, do we find that man also possesses 'consciousness', but, even so, not inherent, not 'pure' consciousness. From the start the 'spirit' is afflicted with the curse of being 'burdened' with matter, which here makes its appearance in the form of agitated layers of air, sounds, in short, of language. Language is as old as consciousness, language is practical consciousness that exists also for other men, and for that reason alone it really exists for me personally as well; language, like consciousness, only arises from the need, the necessity, of intercourse with other men. Where there exists a relationship, it exists for me: the animal does not enter into 'relations' with anything, it does not enter into any relation at all. For the animal, its relation to others does not exist as a relation. Consciousness is, therefore, from the very beginning a social product, and remains so as long as men exist at all. Consciousness is at first, of course, merely consciousness concerning the immediate sensuous environment and consciousness of the limited connection with other persons and things outside the individual who is growing self-conscious. At the same time it is consciousness of nature, which first appears to men as a completely alien, all-powerful, and unassailable force, with which men's relations are purely animal and by which they are overawed like beasts; it is thus a purely animal consciousness of nature (natural religion) just because nature is as yet hardly modified historically. (We see here immediately that this natural religion or this particular relation of men to nature is determined by the form of society and vice versa. Here, as everywhere, the identity of nature and man appears in such a way that the restricted relation of men to nature determines their restricted relation to one another, and their restricted relation to one another determines men's restricted relation to nature.) On the other hand, man's consciousness of the necessity of associating with the individuals around him is the beginning of the consciousness that he is living in society at all. This beginning is as animal as social life itself at this stage. It is mere herd-consciousness, and at this point man is only distinguished from sheep by the fact that with him consciousness takes the place of instinct or that his instinct is a conscious one. This sheep-like or tribal consciousness receives its further development and extension through increased productivity, the increase of needs, and, what is fundamental to both of these, the increase of population. With these there develops the division of labour, which was originally nothing but the division of labour in the sexual act, then that division of labour which develops spontaneously or 'naturally' by virtue of natural predisposition (e.g. physical strength), needs, accidents, etc. etc. Division of labour only becomes truly such from the moment when a division of material and mental labour appears. (The first form of ideologists, priests, is concurrent.) From this moment onwards consciousness can really flatter itself that it is something other than consciousness of existing practice, that it really represents something without representing something real; from now on consciousness is in a position to emancipate itself from the world and to proceed to the formation of 'pure' theory, theology, philosophy, ethics, etc. But even if this theory, theology, philosophy, ethics, etc. comes into contradiction with the existing relations, this can only occur because existing social relations have come into contradiction with existing forces of production; this, moreover, can also occur in a particular national sphere of relations through the appearance of the contradiction, not within the national orbit, but between this national consciousness and the practice of other nations, i.e. between the national and the general consciousness of a nation (as we see it now in Germany).

Moreover, it is quite immaterial what consciousness starts to do on its own: out of all such muck we get only the one inference that these three moments, the forces of production, the state of society, and consciousness, can and must come into contradiction with one another, because the division of labour implies the possibility, nay the fact, that intellectual and material activity—enjoyment and labour, production and consumption—devolve on different individuals, and that the only possibility of their not coming into contradiction lies in the negation in its turn of the division of labour. It is self-evident, moreover, that 'spectres', 'bonds', 'the higher being', 'concept', 'scruple', are merely the idealistic, spiritual expression, the conception apparently of the isolated individual, the image of very empirical fetters and limitations, within which the mode of production of life and the form of intercourse coupled with it move.

Private Property and Communism

With the division of labour, in which all these contradictions are implicit, and which in its turn is based on the natural division of labour in the family and the separation of society into individual families opposed to one another, is given simultaneously the distribution, and indeed the unequal distribution, both quantitative and qualitative, of labour and its products, hence property: the nucleus, the first form of which lies in the family, where wife and children are the slaves of the husband. This latent slavery in the family, though still very crude, is the first property, but even at this early stage it corresponds perfectly to the definition of modern economists who call it the power of disposing of the labour-power of others. Division of labour and private property are, moreover, identical expressions: in the one the same thing is affirmed with reference to activity as is affirmed in the other with reference to the product of the activity.

Further, the division of labour implies the contradiction between the interest of the separate individual or the individual family and the communal interest of all individuals who have intercourse with one another. And indeed, this communal interest does not exist merely in the imagination, as the 'general interest', but first of all in reality, as the mutual interdependence of the individuals among whom the labour is divided. And finally, the division of labour offers us the first example of how, as long as man remains in natural society, that is, as long as a cleavage exists between the particular and the common interest, as long, therefore, as activity is not voluntarily, but naturally, divided, man's own deed becomes an alien power opposed to him, which enslaves him instead of being controlled by him. For as soon as the distribution of labour comes into being, each man has a particular, exclusive sphere of activity, which is forced upon him and from which he cannot escape. He is a hunter, a fisherman, a shepherd, or a critical critic, and must remain so if he does not want to lose his means of livelihood; while in communist society, where nobody was one exclusive sphere of activity but each can become accomplished in any branch he wishes, society regulates the general production and thus makes it possible for me to do one thing today and another tomorrow, to hunt in the morning, fish in the afternoon, rear cattle in the evening, criticize after dinner, just as I have a mind, without ever becoming hunter, fisherman, cowherd, or critic. This fixation of social activity, this consolidation of what we ourselves produce into an objective power above us, growing out of our control, thwarting our expectations, bringing to naught our calculations, is one of the chief factors in historical development up till now.

And out of this very contradiction between the interest of the individual and that of the community the latter takes an independent form as the state, divorced from the real interests of individual and community, and at the same time as an illusory communal life, always based, however, on the real ties existing in every family and tribal conglomeration—such as flesh and blood, language, division of labour on a larger scale, and other interests —and especially, as we shall enlarge upon later, on the classes, already determined by the division of labour, which in every such mass of men separate out, and of which one dominates all the others. It follows from this that all struggles within the State, the struggle between democracy, aristocracy, and monarchy, the struggle for the franchise, etc. etc. are merely the illusory forms in which the real struggles of the different classes are fought out among one another. Of this the German theoreticians have not the faintest inkling, although they have received a sufficient introduction to the subject in the *Deutsch-französische Jahrbücher* and *Die heilige Familie*. Further, it follows that every class which is struggling for mastery, even when its domination, as is the case with the proletariat, postulates the abolition of the old form of society in its entirety and of domination itself, must first conquer for itself political power in order to represent its interest in turn as the general interest, which immediately it is forced to do. Just because individuals seek only their particular interest, which for them does not coincide with their communal interest, the latter will be imposed on them as an interest 'alien' to them, and 'independent' of them, as in its turn a particular, peculiar 'general' interest; or they themselves must remain within this discord, as in democracy. On the other hand, too, the practical struggle of these particular interests, which constantly really run counter to the communal and illusory communal interests, makes practical intervention and control necessary through the illusory 'general' interest in the form of the State.

The social power, i.e. the multiplied productive force, which arises through the co-operation of different individuals as it is determined by the division of labour, appears to these individuals, since their co-operation is not voluntary but has come about naturally, not as their own united power, but as an alien force existing outside them, of the origin and goal of which they are ignorant, which they thus cannot control, which on the contrary passes through a peculiar series of phases and stages independent of the will and the action of man, nay even being the prime governor of these.

How otherwise could, for instance, property have had a history at all, have taken on different forms, and landed property, for example, according to the different premises given, have proceeded in France from parcellation to centralization in the hands of a few, in England from centralization in the hands of a few to parcellation, as is actually the case today? Or how does it happen that trade, which after all is nothing more than the exchange of products of various individuals and countries, rules the whole world through the relation of supply and demand—a relation which, as an English economist says, hovers over the earth like the Fates of the ancients, and with invisible hand allots fortune and misfortune to men, sets up empires and overthrows empires, causes nations to rise and to disappear—while with the abolition of the basis of private property, with the communistic regulation of production (and, implicit in this, the destruction of the alien relation between men and what they themselves produce), the power of the relation of supply and demand is dissolved into nothing, and men get exchange, production, the mode of their mutual relation, under their own control again?

This 'alienation' (to use a term which will be comprehensible to the philosophers) can, of course, only be abolished given two practical premisses. For it to become an 'intolerable' power, i.e. a power against which men make a revolution, it must necessarily have rendered the great mass of humanity 'propertyless', and produced, at the same time, the contradiction of an existing world of wealth and culture, both of which conditions presuppose a great increase in productive power, a high degree of its development. And, on the other hand, this development of productive forces (which itself implies the actual empirical existence of men in their world-historical, instead of local, being) is an absolutely necessary practical premiss because without it want is merely made general, and with destitution the struggle for necessities and all the old filthy business would necessarily be reproduced; and furthermore, because only with this universal development of productive forces is a universal intercourse between men established, which produces in all nations simultaneously the phenomenon of the 'propertyless' mass (universal competition), makes each nation dependent on the revolutions of the others, and finally has put world-historical, empirically universal individuals in place of local ones. Without this, (1) communism could only exist as a local event; (2) the forces of intercourse themselves could not have developed as universal, hence intolerable powers: they would have remained home-bred conditions surrounded by superstition; and (3) each extension of intercourse would abolish local communism. Empirically, communism is only possible as the act of the dominant peoples 'all at once' and simultaneously, which presupposes the universal development of productive forces and the world intercourse bound up with communism. Moreover, the mass of propertyless workers—the utterly precarious position of labour-power on a mass scale cut off from capital or from even a limited satisfaction and, therefore, no longer merely temporarily deprived of work itself as a secure source of life—presupposes the world market through competition. The proletariat can thus only exist world-historically, just as communism, its activity, can only have a 'world-historical' existence. World-historical existence of individuals means existence of individuals which is directly linked up with world history.

Communism is for us not a state of affairs which is to be established, an ideal to which reality will have to adjust itself. We call communism the real movement which abolishes the present state of things. The conditions of this movement result from the premisses now in existence. . . .

Capital

Commodities: Use-Value and Exchange-Value

The wealth of those societies in which the capitalist mode of production prevails presents itself as 'an immense accumulation of commodities', its unit being a single commodity. Our investigation must therefore begin with the analysis of a commodity.

A commodity is, in the first place, an object outside us, a thing that by its properties satisfies human wants of some sort or another. The nature of such wants, whether, for instance, they spring from the stomach or from fancy, makes no difference. Neither are we here concerned to know how the object satisfies these wants, whether directly as means of subsistence, or indirectly as means of production.

Every useful thing, as iron, paper, etc., may be looked at from the two points of view: of quality and quantity. It is an assemblage of many properties, and may therefore be of use in various ways. To discover the various uses of things is the work of history. So also is the establishment of socially recognized standards of measure for the quantities of these useful objects. The diversity of these measures has its origin partly in the diverse nature of the objects to be measured, partly in convention.

The utility of a thing makes it a use-value. But this utility is not a thing of air. Being limited by the physical properties of the commodity, it has no existence apart from that commodity. A commodity, such as iron, corn, or a diamond, is therefore, so far as it is a material thing, a use-value, something useful. This property of a commodity is independent of the amount of labour required to appropriate its useful qualities. When treating of use-value, we always assume we are dealing with definite quantities, such as dozens of watches, yards of linen, or tons of iron. The use-values of commodities furnish the material for a special study, that of the commercial knowledge of commodities. Use-values become a reality only by use or consumption; they also constitute the substance of all wealth, whatever may be the social form of that wealth. In the form of society we are about to consider, they are, in addition, the material depositories of exchange-value.

Exchange-value, at first sight, presents itself as a quantitative relation, as the proportion in which values in use of one sort are exchanged for those of another sort, a relation constantly changing with time and place. Hence exchange-value appears to be something accidental and purely relative, and consequently an intrinsic value, i.e. an exchange-value that is inseparably connected with, inherent in, commodities, seems a contradiction in terms. Let us consider the matter a little more closely.

A given commodity, e.g, a quarter of wheat is exchanged for x blacking, y silk, or z gold, etc.—in short, for other commodities in the most different proportions. Instead of one exchange-value, the wheat has, therefore, a great many. But since x blacking, y silk, or z gold, etc., each represent the exchange-value of one quarter of wheat, x blacking, y silk, z gold, etc., must, as exchange-values, be replaceable by each other, or equal to each other. Therefore, first: the valid exchange-values of a given commodity express something equal; secondly, exchange-value, generally, is only the mode of expression, the phenomenal form, of something contained in it, yet distinguishable from it.

Let us take two commodities, e.g., corn and iron. The proportions in which they are exchangeable, whatever those proportions may be, can always be represented by an equation in which a given quantity of corn is equated to some quantity of iron: e.g., 1 quarter corn = x cwt. iron. What does this equation tell us? It tells us that in two different things—in 1 quarter of corn and x cwt. of iron, there exists in equal quantities something common to both. The two things must therefore be equal to a third, which in itself is neither the one nor the other. Each of them, so far as it is exchange-value, must therefore be reducible to this third.

A simple geometrical illustration will make this clear. In order to calculate and compare the areas of rectilinear figures, we decompose them into triangles. But the area of the triangle itself is expressed by something totally different from its visible figure, namely, by half the product of the base into the altitude. In the same way the exchange-values of commodities must be capable of being expressed in terms of something common to them all, of which thing they represent a greater or less quantity.

This common 'something' cannot be either a geometrical, a chemical, or any other natural property of commodities. Such properties claim our attention only in so far as they affect the utility of those commodities, make them use-values. But the exchange of commodities is evidently an act characterized by a total abstraction from use-value. Then one use-value is just as good as another, provided only it be present in sufficient quantity. Or, as old Barbon says, 'one sort of wares is as good as another, if the values be equal. There is no difference or distinction in things of equal value. . . . A hundred pounds' worth of lead or iron is of as great value as one hundred pounds' worth of silver or gold.' As use-values, commodities are, above all, of different qualities, but as exchange-values they are merely different quantities, and consequently do not contain an atom of use-value.

If then we leave out of consideration the use-value of commodities, they have only one common property left, that of being products of labour. But even the product of labour itself has undergone a change in our hands. If we make abstraction from its use-value, we make abstraction at the same time from the material elements and shapes that make the product a use-value; we see in it no longer a table, a house, yarn, or any other useful thing. Its existence as a material thing is put out of sight. Neither can it any longer be regarded as the product of the labour of the joiner, the mason, the spinner, or of any other definite kind of productive labour. Along with the useful qualities of the products themselves, we put out of sight both the useful character of the various kinds of labour embodied in them, and the concrete forms of that labour; there is nothing left but what is common to them all; all are reduced to one and the same sort of labour, human labour in the abstract.

Let us now consider the residue of each of these products; it consists of the same unsubstantial reality in each, a mere congelation of homogeneous human labour, of labour power expended without regard to the mode of its expenditure. All that these things now tell us is that human labour power has been expended in their production, that human labour is embodied in them. When looked at as crystals of this social substance, common to them all, they are—Values.

We have seen that when commodities are exchanged, their exchange-value manifests itself as something totally independent of their use-value. But if we abstract from their use-value, there remains their Value as defined above. Therefore, the common substance that manifests itself in the exchange-value of commodities, whenever they are exchanged, is their value. The progress of our investigation will show that exchange-value is the only form in which the value of commodities can manifest itself or be expressed. For the present, however, we have to consider the nature of value independently of this, its form.

A use-value, or useful article, therefore, has value only because human labour in the abstract has been embodied or materialized in it. How, then, is the magnitude of this value to be measured? Plainly, by the quantity of the value-creating substance, the labour, contained in the article. The quantity of labour, however, is measured by its duration, and labour time in its turn finds its standard in weeks, days, and hours.

Some people might think that if the value of a commodity is determined by the quantity of labour spent on it, the more idle and unskilful the labourer, the more valuable would his commodity be, because more time would be required in its production. The labour, however, that forms the substance of value, is homogeneous human labour, expenditure of one uniform labour power. The total labour power of society, which is embodied in the sum total of the values of all commodities produced by that society, counts here as one homogeneous mass of human labour power, composed though it be of innumerable individual units. Each of these units is the same as any other, so far as it has the character of the average labour power of society, and takes effect as such; that is, so far as it requires for producing a commodity no more time than is needed on average, no more than is socially necessary. The labour time socially necessary is that required to produce an article under the normal conditions of production, and with the average degree of skill and intensity prevalent at the time. The introduction of power-looms into England probably reduced by one-half the labour required to weave a given quantity of yarn into cloth. The hand-loom weavers, as a matter of fact, continued to require the same time as before; but for all that, the product of one hour of their labour represented after the change only half an hour's social labour, and consequently fell to one-half its former value.

We see then that that which determines the magnitude of the value of any article is the amount of labour socially necessary, or the labour time socially necessary for its production. Each individual commodity, in this connection, is to be considered as an average sample of its class. Commodities, therefore, in which equal quantities of labour are embodied, or which can be produced in the same time, have the same value. The value of one commodity is to the value of any other, as the labour time necessary for the production of the one is to that necessary for the production of the other. 'As values, all commodities are only definite masses of congealed labour time.'

The value of a commodity would therefore remain constant, if the labour time required for its production also remained constant. But the latter changes with every variation in the productiveness of labour. This productiveness is determined by various circumstances, among others, by the average amount of skill of the workmen, the state of science, and the degree of its practical application, the social organization of production, the extent and capabilities of the means of production, and by physical conditions. For example, the same amount of labour in favourable seasons is embodied in eight bushels of corn, and in unfavourable, only in four. The same labour extracts from rich mines more metal than from poor mines. Diamonds are of very rare occurrence on the earth's surface, and hence their discovery costs, on an average, a great deal of labour time. Consequently much labour is represented in a small compass. Jacob doubts whether gold has ever been paid for at its full value. This applies still more to diamonds. According to Eschwege, the total produce of the Brazilian diamond mines for the eighty years ending in 1823, had not realized the price of one-and-a-half years' average produce of the sugar and coffee plantations of the same country, although the diamonds cost much more labour, and therefore represented more value. With richer mines, the same quantity of labour would embody itself in more diamonds, and their value would fall. If we could succeed, at a small expenditure of labour, in converting carbon into diamonds, their value might fall below that of bricks. In general, the greater the productiveness of labour, the less is the labour time required for the production of an article, the less is the amount of labour crystallized in that article, and the less is its value; and vice versa, the less the productiveness of labour, the greater is the labour time required for the production of an article, and the greater is its value. The value of a commodity, therefore, varies directly as the quantity, and inversely as the productiveness, of the labour incorporated in it.

A thing can be a use-value, without having value. This is the case whenever its utility to man is not due to labour. Such are air, virgin soil, natural meadows, etc. A thing can be useful, and the product of human labour, without being a commodity. Whoever directly satisfies his wants with the produce of his own labour creates, indeed, use-values, but not commodities. In order to produce the latter, he must not only produce use-values, but use-values for others, social use-values. (And not only for others. The medieval peasant produced quit-rent-corn for his feudal lord and tithe-corn for his parson. But neither the quit-rent-corn nor the tithe-corn became commodities by reason of the fact that they had been produced for others. To become a commodity a product must be transferred to another, whom it will serve as a use-value, by means of an exchange.) Lastly, nothing can have value without being an object of utility. If the thing is useless, so is the labour contained in it; the labour does not count as labour, and therefore creates no value. . . .

The Rate of Surplus Value

. . . If we look at the means of production, in their relation to the creation of value, and to the variation in the quantity of value, apart from anything else, they appear simply as the material in which labour power, the value-creator, incorporates itself. Neither the nature, nor the value of this material is of any importance. The only requisite is that there be a sufficient supply to absorb the labour expended in the process of production. That supply once given, the material may rise or fall in value, or even be, as land and the sea, without any value in itself; but this will have no influence on the creation of value or on the variation in the quantity of value.

In the first place then we equate the constant capital to zero. The capital advanced is consequently reduced from c + v to v, and instead of the value of the product (c + v) + s we have now the value produced (v + s). Given the new value produced = £180, which sum consequently represents the whole labour expended during the process, then subtracting from it £90, the value of the variable capital, we have remaining £90, the amount of the surplus value. This sum of £90 or s expresses the absolute quantity of surplus value produced. The relative quantity produced, or the increase per cent of the variable capital, is determined, it is plain, by the ratio of the surplus value to the variable capital, or is expressed by s/v. In our example this ratio is $\frac{90}{90}$, which gives an increase of 140 per cent. This relative increase in the value of the variable capital, or the relative magnitude of the surplus value, I call, 'The rate of surplus value'.

We have seen that the labourer, during one portion of the labour process, produces only the value of his labour power, that is, the value of his means of subsistence. Now since his work forms part of a system, based on the social division of labour, he does not directly produce the actual necessaries which he himself consumes; he produces instead a particular commodity, yarn for example, whose value is equal to the value of those necessaries or of the money with which they can be bought. The portion of his day's labour devoted to this purpose will be greater or less, in proportion to the value of the necessaries that he daily requires on an average, or, what amounts to the same thing, in proportion to the labour time required on an average to produce them. If the value of those necessaries represent on an average the expenditure of six hours' labour, the workman must on an average work for six hours to produce that value. If instead of working for the capitalist, he worked independently on his own account, he would, other things being equal, still be obliged to labour for the same number of hours, in order to produce the value of his labour power, and thereby to gain the means of subsistence necessary for his conservation or continued reproduction. But as we have seen, during that portion of his day's labour in which he produces the value of his labour power, say three shillings, he produces only an equivalent for the value of his labour power already advanced by the capitalist; the new value created only replaces the variable capital advanced. It is owing to this fact, that the production of the new value of three shillings takes the semblance of a mere reproduction. That portion of the working-day, then, during which this reproduction takes place, I call 'necessary' labour time, and the labour expended during that time I call 'necessary' labour. Necessary, as regards the labourer, because independent of the particular social form of his labour; necessary, as regards capital, and the world of capitalists, because on the continued existence of the labourer depends their existence also.

During the second period of the labour process, that in which his labour is no longer necessary labour, the workman, it is true, labours, expends labour power; but his labour, being no longer necessary labour, he creates no value for himself. He creates surplus value which, for the capitalist, has all the charms of a creation out of nothing. This portion of the working-day, I name surplus labour time, and to the labour expended during that time, I give the name of surplus labour. It is every bit as important, for a correct understanding of surplus value, to conceive it as a mere congelation of surplus labour time, as nothing but materialized surplus labour, as it is, for a proper comprehension of value, to conceive it as a mere congelation of so many hours of labour, as nothing but materialized labour. The essential difference between the various economic forms of society, between, for instance, a society based on slave-labour, and one based on wage-labour, lies only in the mode in which this surplus labour is in each case extracted from the actual producer, the labourer.

Since, on the one hand, the values of the variable capital and of the labour power purchased by that capital are equal, and the value of this labour power determines the necessary portion of the working-day; and since, on the other hand, the surplus value is determined by the surplus portion of the working-day, it follows that surplus value bears the same ratio to variable capital, that surplus labour does to necessary labour, or in other words, the rate of surplus value

$$\frac{s}{v} = \frac{\text{surplus labour}}{\text{necessary labour}}.$$

Both ratios,

$$\frac{s}{v} \text{ and } \frac{\text{surplus labour}}{\text{necessary labour}},$$

express the same thing in different ways; in the one case by reference to materialized, incorporated labour, in the other by reference to living, fluent labour.

The rate of surplus value is therefore an exact expression for the degree of exploitation of labour power by capital, or of the labourer by the capitalist. . . .

The Theory of Alienation
Bertell Ollman

Chapter 18 The theory of alienation

The theory of alienation is the intellectual construct in which Marx displays the devastating effect of capitalist production on human beings, on their physical and mental states and on the social processes of which they are a part. Centered on the acting individual, it is Marx's way of seeing his contemporaries and their conditions (a set of forms for comprehending their interaction) as well as what he sees there (the content poured into these forms). Brought under the same rubric are the links between one man, his activity and products, his fellows, inanimate nature and the species. Hence, as a grand summing up, as Marx's conception of man in capitalist society, the theory of alienation could only be set out after its constituent elements had been accounted for.

For purposes of discussing alienation, the following points, made early in Part I and illustrated in subsequent chapters, will serve as my philosophical charter: Marx's subject matter comprises an organic whole; the various factors he treats are facets of this whole; internal relations exist between all such factors; reciprocal effect predominates and has logical priority over causality; laws are concerned with patterns of reciprocal effect; the concepts Marx uses to refer to factors convey their internal relations; this makes it possible to speak of each factor as an 'expression' of the whole (or some large part of it) or as a 'form' of some other factor; finally, Marx's view that factors are internally related, together with his practise of incorporating such relations as part of the meanings of the covering concepts, allows him to transfer qualities which are associated in the popular mind with one factor to another to register some significant alteration in their reciprocal effect. In attempting to construct a coherent account of Marx's theory of alienation within this framework, this framework itself will be put to test.

Perhaps the most significant form into which the theory of alienation is cast—most significant because it chiefly determines the theory's application—is the internal relation it underscores between the present and the future. Alienation can only be grasped as the absence of unalienation, each state serving as a point of reference for the other. And, for Marx, unalienation is the life man leads in communism. Without some knowledge of the future millennium, alienation remains a reproach that can never be clarified. An approach to grasping the 'logical geography' involved may be made by contrasting the expressions 'health' and 'disease': we only know what it is to have a particular disease because we know what it is not to. If we did not have a conception of health, the situation covered by the symptoms would appear 'normal'.[1] Furthermore, when we declare that someone is ill we consider this a statement of 'fact' and not an evaluation based on an outside standard. This is because we

Excerpts from Bertell Ollman. 1976. *Alienation: Marx's Conception of Man in Capitalist Society*, 2nd Edition. Cambridge: Cambridge University Press, pp. 131–152. Reprinted with the permission of the author and Cambridge University Press.

ordinarily conceive of health and disease as internally related, the absence of one being a necessary element in the meaning of the other. Similarly, it is because Marx posits an internal relation between the states of alienation and unalienation that we cannot regard his remarks as evaluations. There is no 'outside' standard from which to judge.

'Alienation', then, is used by Marx to refer to any state of human existence which is 'away from' or 'less than' unalienation, though, admittedly, he generally reserves this reproach for the more extreme instances.[2] It is in this sense and on this scale, however, that Marx refers to alienation as 'a mistake, a defect, which ought not to be'. Both the individual and his way of life can be spoken of as 'alienated', and in the latter case the tag 'realm of estrangement' is applied to the most infected areas.

Moreover, it follows from the acceptance of communism as the relevant measure that all classes are considered alienated in the ways and to the degree that their members fall short of the communist ideal. Accordingly, Marx claims that one of the manifestations of alienation is that 'all is under the sway of inhuman power', and adds, 'this applies also to the capitalist'. The forms of alienation differ for each class because their position and style of life differ, and, as expected, the proletariat's affliction is the most severe. Marx dwells far more, too, on the fate of the producers, and usually has them in mind when he makes general statements about 'man's alienation'. In such cases, other classes are included in the reference in so far as they share with the proletariat the qualities or conditions which are being commented on. I have adopted the same practise in relating Marx's views. By adding a special chapter on the peculiar alienation of capitalists, I hope to dispel whatever confusion this may cause.

The theory of alienation, however, is more than a mere summary of what has already been said regarding Marx's conception of man. It is also a new focal point from which to view human beings and hence to speak of them, one which stresses the fact of segmentation or practical breakdown of the interconnected elements in their definition. All those traits, grasped by Marx as relations, which mark man out from other living creatures have altered, have become something else. In one statement of his task, Marx declares:

> What requires explanation is not the *unity* of living and active human beings with the natural, inorganic conditions of their metabolism, with nature, and therefore their appropriation of nature; nor is this the result of a historical process. What we must explain is the *separation* of these inorganic conditions of human existence from this active existence, a separation which is only fully completed in the relation between wage-labor and capital. (Marx's emphasis.)

Given the particular unity between man and nature with Marx—abetted by his conception of internal relations—grasps as human nature, any significant alteration in these relations which diminishes the individual's role as initiator is seen as rendering them apart. From evident expressions of his distinctive character, the relations between man and the external world have become means to dissimulate this character behind each of the various elements over which he has lost control. The theory of alienation focuses on the presumed independence of these elements.

The distortion in what Marx takes to be human nature is generally referred to in language which suggests that an essential tie has been cut in the middle. Man is spoken of as being separated from his work (he plays no part in deciding what to do or how to do it)—a break between the individual and his life activity. Man is said to be separated from his own products (he has no control over what he makes or what becomes of it afterwards)—a break between the individual and the material world. He is also said to be separated from his fellow men (competition and class hostility has rendered most forms of cooperation impossible)—a break between man and man. In each instance, a relation that distinguishes the human species has disappeared and its constituent elements have been reorganized to appear as something else.

What is left of the individual after all these cleavages have occurred is a mere rump, a lowest common denominator attained by lopping off all those qualities on which is based his claim to recognition as a man. Thus denuded, the alienated person has become an 'abstraction'. As we saw, this is a broader term Marx uses to refer to any factor which appears isolated from the social whole. It is in this sense that estranged labor and capital are spoken of as 'abstractions'. At its simplest, 'abstraction' refers to the type of purity that is achieved in emptiness. Its opposite is a set of meaningful particulars by which people know something to be one of a kind. Given that these particulars involve internal relations with other factors, any factor is recognized as one of kind to the degree that the social whole finds expression in it. It is because we do not grasp the ways in which the social whole is present in any factor (which is to say, the full range of its particular qualities in their internal relations) that this factor seems to be independent of the social whole, that it becomes an 'abstraction'. As an abstraction, what is unique about it (which—again—is the particular ways in which it is linked to others, conceived as part of what it is) is lost sight of behind its superficial similarities with other abstractions. And it is on the basis of these similarities, generalized as classes of one sort or another, that alienated men set out to understand their world. In this manner is intelligence misdirected into classification.

Alienated man is an abstraction because he has lost touch with all human specificity. He has been reduced to performing undifferentiated work on humanly indistinguishable objects among people deprived of their human variety and compassion. There is little that remains of his relations to his activity, product and fellows which enables us to grasp the peculiar qualities of his species. Consequently, Marx feels he can speak of this life as 'the abstract existence of man as a mere workman who may therefore fall from his filled void into the absolute void'. Though Marx clearly overstates his case in calling alienated man a hole in the air, it is in such an extreme notion that the term 'abstraction' is rooted.

At the same time that the individual is degenerating into an abstraction, those parts of his being which have been split off (which are no longer under his control) are undergoing their own transformation. Three end products of this development are property, industry and religion, which Marx calls man's 'alienated life elements'. (This list is by no means complete, but the point does not require further examples.) In each instance, the other half of a severed relation, carried by a social dynamic of its own, progresses through a series of forms in a direction away from its beginning in man. Eventually, it attains an independent life, that is, takes on 'needs' which the individual is then forced to satisfy, and the original connection is all but obliterated. It is this process which largely accounts for the power that money has in capitalist societies, the buying of objects which could never have been sold had they remained integral components of their producer.

What occurs in the real world is reflected in people's minds: essential elements of what it means to be a man are grasped as independent and, in some cases, all powerful entities, whose links with him appear other than what they really are. The ideas which encompass this reality share all its shortcomings. The whole has broken up into numerous parts whose interrelation in whole can no longer be ascertained.

This is the essence of alienation, whether the part under examination is man, his activity, his product or his ideas. The same separation and distortion is evident in each.

If alienation is the splintering of human nature into a number of misbegotten parts, we would expect communism to be presented as a kind of reunification. And this is just what we find. On one occasion, Marx asserts that communism is 'the complete return of man to himself as a social (i.e. human) being—a return become conscious, and accomplished with the entire wealth of previous development'. It is 'the positive transcendence of all estrangement—that is to say, the return of man from religion, family, state, etc., to his human, i.e. social mode of existence'. In communism the breach is healed, and all the elements which constitute a human being for Marx are reunited. Many of the characteristics ascribed to full communism, such as the end of the division of labor (each person is engaged in a variety of tasks) and the erasure of social classes, are clear instances of this unification process at work. In the remainder of this study, I will be mainly concerned to show the evidence of segmentation that required such a remedy.

Chapter 19 Man's relation to his productive activity

In his only organized treatment of the subject, Marx presents alienation as partaking of four broad relations which are so distributed as to cover the whole of human existence. These are man's relations to his productive activity, his product, other men and the species.[3] Productive activity in capitalism is spoken of as 'active alienation, the alienation of activity, the activity of alienation'. Asking 'What, then, constitutes the alienation of labor?', Marx offers the following reply:

> First, the fact that labor is external to the worker, i.e., it does not belong to his essential being; that in his work, therefore, he does not affirm himself but denies himself, does not feel content but unhappy, does not develop freely his physical and mental energy but mortifies his body and ruins his mind. The worker therefore only feels himself outside his work, and in his work feels outside himself. He is at home when he is not working, and when he is working he is not at home. His labor is therefore not voluntary, but coerced; it's forced labor. It is therefore not the satisfaction of a need; it is merely a means to satisfy needs external to it.

In claiming that labor does not belong to man's essential being, that in it he denies rather than affirms himself and that it is not a satisfaction of a need but merely satisfies needs external to it, Marx's point of reference is species man. In asserting that labor in capitalism mortifies man's body and ruins his mind and that in it he is uncomfortable and unhappy, Marx is alluding to the actual appearance of the proletariat. Alienated labor marks the convergence of these two strands of thought.

Before trying to explain Marx's comments on labor from the standpoint of species man, a brief review of what was said about activity in the previous Part is in order. Marx attributes to man certain powers, which he divides into natural and species, and maintains that each of these powers is reflected in one's consciousness by a corresponding need: the individual feels needs for whatever is necessary to realize his powers. The objects of nature, including other men, provide the matter through which these powers are realized and, consequently, for which needs are felt. Realization occurs through the appropriation of objects which accord in kind and level of development with these powers themselves. 'Appropriation' is Marx's most general expression for the fact that man incorporates the nature he comes into contact with into himself. Activity enters this account as the chief means by which man appropriates objects and becomes, therefore, the effective medium between the individual and the outer world. Marx sees such activity in three special relationships to man's powers: first, it is the foremost example of their combined operation; second, it establishes new possibilities for their fulfillment by transforming nature and, hence, all nature imposed limitations; and third, it is the main means by which their own potential, as powers, is developed.

In asserting that labor in capitalism does not belong to man's essential being, that he denies himself in this labor and that he only satisfies needs external to it, Marx is describing a state where the relations between activity and man's powers exist at a very low level of achievement. As we saw earlier, the terms 'essence' and 'essential' are used by Marx to refer to the whole thread of real and potential ties that link man and nature. Capitalist labor does not belong to man's essential being in the sense that it leaves most of the relations that constitute a human being for Marx unaffected. With the development of the division of labor and the highly repetitive character of each productive task, productive activity no longer affords a good example of the operation of all man's powers, or does so only in so far as these powers have become fewer and narrower in their application. As regards the second relationship, by producing slums, wastelands, dirty factories, etc., such labor does as much or more to decrease the possibilities in nature for the fulfillment of man's powers than it does to increase them.

However, it is the third relationship between activity and powers that capitalism almost completely reverses. Instead of developing the potential inherent in man's powers, capitalist labor consumes these powers without replenishing them, burns them up as if they were a fuel, and leaves the individual worker that much poorer. The qualities that mark him as a human being become progressively diminished. I referred to this process on another occasion as the 'retrogression' of man's powers. It is in this sense that Marx refers to labor as 'man lost to himself'. Communist society supplies the proper contrast. Here, man's productive activity engages all his powers and creates ever widening opportunities for their fulfillment. In this manner, work in communism is an affirmation of human nature, while capitalist labor is its denial, withholding from man what in Marx's view belongs to him as a human being.

Marx also conceives of alienated labor, in part, as the actual appearance of people who engage in such activity. What has capitalist labor done to workers on a level where everyone can observe the results? Marx's answer is that it 'mortifies his body and ruins his mind'. *Capital* I is, in at least one very important respect, an attempt to document this thesis. Among the physical distortions described in this work are stunted size, bent backs, overdeveloped and underdeveloped muscles, gnarled fingers, enlarged lungs and death pale complexions. Some of these distortions—Marx singles out the overdevelopment of certain muscles and bone curvatures—may even add to the worker's efficiency in performing his limited and one-sided task, and become in this way an advantage to his employer. Such physical traits are matched by as many industrial diseases. In Marx's words, the worker is a 'mere fragment of his own body', 'a living appendage of the machine', and he looks the part.

The worker's mind, too, has been ruined by the nature of his task and the conditions in which he does it. His delusions, decaying will power, mental inflexibility and particularly his ignorance are all of monumental proportions. Capitalist industry produces in its laborers, according to Marx, 'idiocy' and 'cretinism'. The total contrast between this condition of man and his condition under communism is too obvious to require comment, and, as before, it is the connection Marx presumes between them which allows him to register the one as alienation.

The worker's subjective feelings of being 'at home when he is not working' and 'not at home' when he is working is still another indication of the alienated character of his labor. Marx's concern about workers being discontented and uncomfortable is incomprehensible if we adopt the view that people will always dislike their work, that work is by its very nature an activity that people cannot wait to finish with. Given what he foresaw in communism, Marx did not and could not share this view.

With capitalist labor variously described as a 'torment', a 'sacrifice of life' and 'activity as suffering', it is not to be wondered at that no one in capitalism works unless he is forced. Only circumstances which require that one labor in order to eat drives workers to make such an extraordinary sacrifice. Whenever compulsion disappears, 'labor is shunned like the plague'.

Two other aspects of alienated labor dealt with by Marx are that this labor is the private property of non-workers and that it results in a reversal of man's human and animal functions. As regards the former, Marx says, 'the external character of labor for the worker appears in the fact that it is not his own, but someone else's, that it does not belong to him, that in it he belongs, not to himself, but to another'. If labor is forced, even if its effectiveness lies in the worker's impoverished circumstances, someone must be doing the forcing. According to Marx, 'If his own activity is to him an unfree activity, then he is treating it as activity performed in the service, under the domination, the coercion and the yoke of another man'. This overlord, of course, is the capitalist. And so complete is his control that he determines the form of labor, its intensity, duration, the kind and number of its products, surrounding conditions and—most important of all—whether or not it will even take place. The worker engages in his productive activity only on the sufferance of the capitalist, and when the latter decides he has had enough, that is, that further production will not yield a profit, this activity comes to a halt.

What we called a 'reversal of man's human and animal functions' refers to a state in which the activities man shares with animals appear more human than those activities which mark him out as a man. Marx claims that as a result of his productive activity,

> man (the worker) no longer feels himself to be freely active in any but his animal functions—eating, drinking, procreating, or at most in his dwelling and in dressing-up, etc.; and in his human functions he no longer feels himself to be anything but an animal. What is animal becomes human and what is human becomes animal. Certainly eating, drinking, procreating, etc., are also genuine human functions. But in the abstraction which separates them from the sphere of all other human activity and turns them into sole and ultimate ends, they are animal.

An abstraction, as we saw, is a break in connections, a link in the chain which has set itself off as an independent piece. Eating, drinking and procreating are occasions when all man's powers may be fulfilled together; yet, in capitalism, they only serve their direct and most obvious functions as do their equivalents in the animal kingdom. Despite their depraved state, however, the individual exercises more choice in these activities than he does in those others, work in particular, which distinguish him as a human being. As unsatisfactory as eating and drinking are from a human point of view, the worker feels at least he is doing something he wants to do. The same cannot be said of his productive activity.

All the components of alienated labor are best understood as particular relations which converge to form the Relation, alienated labor. Stated as accurately as possible, the relations of capitalist productive activity to man's species self, to his body and mind, to his subjective feelings when doing labor, to his will to engage in labor, to the capitalist, to his own human and animal functions and to what productive activity will be like under communism equal alienated labor.

It should be apparent that these particular relations are constantly finding their way into one another, but Marx never meant them to be distinct. His practise of seeing the whole in the part links all particular relations together as aspects in the full unfolding of any one of them. Overlapping explanations, therefore, cannot be avoided. This coin has another side: just because a full explanation of each of these relations results in the conception of alienated labor, it does not follow that the latter contains only these parts. In reconstructing alienated labor I have limited myself to the largest and most obvious building blocks given in the few pages devoted to this subject in the *1844 Manuscripts*. Many other relations enter into its structure, and we are about to learn that at least one of them, which has been bypassed to facilitate exposition, is of crucial importance.

Chapter 20 Man's relation to his product

The second of the four broad relations into which Marx divides alienation is the individual's relation to his product. This is, in Marx's words, 'the relation of the worker to the product of labor as an alien object exercising power over him'. Between activity and product the link is clear and direct; man is alienated from his product because the activity which produced it was alienated. According to Marx, 'the product is . . . but the summary of the activity, of production . . . In the estrangement of the object of labor is merely summarized the estrangement, the alienation, in the activity of labor itself.' He asks, 'How would the worker come to face the product of his activity as a stranger, were it not that in the very act of production he was estranging himself from himself?'

Man's alienation in his product can be viewed as one of the particular relations which constitute alienated activity or as a coequal general relation. If taken in the context of alienated activity, product alienation appears as a result alongside the ruination of the worker's own body and mind. However Marx, by treating product alienation on a par with alienated activity, wishes to stress its significance, some might claim its primary significance, for understanding the worker's overall alienation.

The account of product alienation is scattered through Marx's writings. Nevertheless, the pieces can be collected without too much difficulty under the three particular relations that appear in the following statement: 'The alienation of the worker in his product means not only that his labor becomes an object, an external existence, but that it exists outside him, independently, as something alien to him, and that it becomes a power on its own confronting him.' The first relation is brought out more clearly in Marx's claim that 'The product of labor is labor which has been congealed in an object, which has become material: it is the objectification of labor. Labor's realization is its objectification.' As the chief means of expressing the life of the species, productive activity is often referred to as life itself. So it is more than a turn of phrase when Marx says, 'The worker puts his life into the object.'

We can only grasp the full sense of this claim by returning once again to Marx's conception of human nature. Here, man's relation to nature was declared to be intimate, because his powers exist in one real object, himself, and can only be expressed in others equally real. Accordingly, Marx says of man, that 'he is nature', and of objects, that they 'reside in the very nature of his being'. The relation between the two is an internal one. As the chief means by which man's powers interact with nature, productive activity is also the medium through which they become objectified. These powers exist in their products as the amount and type of change which their exercise has brought about. The degree of change is always proportionate to the expenditure of powers, just as its quality is always indicative of their state. Marx, we will recall, refers to industry, by which he means the forces of production as well as its products, as 'the exoteric revelation of man's essential powers'. By transforming the real world to satisfy his needs, man's productive activity leaves its mark, the mark of his species powers at this level of their development, on all he touches. It is in this manner that he 'puts his life' into his objects, the latter expressing in what they are the character of the organic whole to which both they and the living person who made them belong.

Man's productive activity, however, is objectified in his products in all societies. What distinguishes such objectification in capitalism is the presence of two further relations which have their roots in alienated labor. These are that man's product 'exists outside him, independently, as something alien to him, and that it becomes a power on its own confronting him'. What Marx means by the objectification of products that are alien to the worker is elaborated upon when, speaking of alienated labor, he says,

> The worker can create nothing without nature, without the sensuous external world. It is the material on which his labor is manifested, in which it is active, from which and by means of which it produces. But just as nature provides labor with the means of life in the sense that labor cannot live without objects on which to operate, on the other hand, it also provides the means of life in the more restricted sense—i.e., the means for the physical subsistence of the worker himself. Thus the more the worker by his labor appropriates the external world, sensuous nature, the more he deprives himself of the means of life in the double respect: first, that the sensuous external world more and more ceases to be an object belonging to his labor—to be his labor's means of life: and secondly, that it more and more ceases to be means of life in the immediate sense, means for the physical subsistence of the worker.

The worker's products are alien to him in that he cannot use them to keep alive or to engage in further productive activity. Marx claims, 'So much does the labor's realization appear as loss of reality that the worker loses reality to the point of starving to death', and elsewhere that 'the more the worker produces, the less he has to consume'. The worker's needs, no matter how desperate, do not give him a license to lay hands on what these same hands have produced, for all his products are the property of another.

Not only can he not use them, but he does not recognize them as his. It follows, of course, that he has no control over what becomes of his products, nor does he even know what becomes of them. Only indirectly, through spending the wage he receives for his labor, can the worker take possession of part of what this same labor has created.

Like the products the worker requires to live, the products he needs for his work are also beyond his control: 'So much does objectification appear as loss of the object that the worker is robbed of the objects most necessary not only for his life but for his work.' Thus, the forces of production, which are products of yesterday's labor, 'appear as a world for themselves, quite independent of and divorced from the individuals, alongside the individuals'. Although man's species powers can only be fulfilled through his use of the means of production, the means of production which come into existence in capitalism are decidedly hostile to his fulfillment. By transforming nature through alienated labor, man has deprived himself of all that he has transformed. The individual's helplessness before his products must be contrasted with the ready accessibility of nature in communism to grasp the full measure of his alienation in this area.

What remains of the worker after subtracting the products he needs to live and to carry on his work—both internal components of human nature according to Marx—is an abstraction, the 'abstract individual'. Earlier, work in capitalism was labelled 'abstract activity' because of an equally drastic paring down of relationships. This abstract individual is humanly impoverished; he has lost his life in proportion to his having lived it and as much of nature as he has worked upon. His productive potential has been drained off into his product without giving him any return. According to Marx,

> the more the worker spends himself, the more powerful the alien objective world becomes which he creates over-against himself, the poorer he himself— his inner world—becomes, the less belongs to him as his own . . . The worker puts his life into the object; but now his life no longer belongs to him but to the object. Hence, the greater this activity, the greater is the worker's lack of objects. Whatever the product of his labor is, he is not. Therefore the greater is this product, the less is he himself.

The interaction which occurs in all productive activity between man's species powers and their object results, in capitalism, in a one-sided enrichment of the object. The product gains in power the more the worker spends his own and, Marx maintains, even acquires qualities (now suitably altered) that the worker loses. As the embodiment of powers the workers no longer have, products may be spoken of, Marx believes, in ways otherwise reserved for the people who produce them. Essential here is that these products have the ability to enter into certain relationships with one another and with man himself as a result of their production under conditions of capitalism, which ability the workers have lost, likewise as a result of such production.

This displacement of certain relations from the worker to his product is responsible for the illusion that the inanimate object is a living organism with powers and needs of its own: 'In bourgeois society capital is independent and has individuality, while the living person is dependent and has no individuality.' For the most part, the life of the workers' products in capitalist society is the course of events which befall them in the process of exchange, which includes their production for purposes of exchange. People follow the progress of these products in the market place as if they were watching a play enacted by real flesh and blood creatures. In this drama, the part played by individuals 'is that of owners of commodities only. Their mutual relations are those of their commodities.' With men taking themselves and others as appendages of their products, their own social relations will appear in the first instance as relations between things. Thus, an exchange of shoes for cloth, an exchange in which given amounts of these articles are seen to be equivalent, merely masks a relationship between the people involved in their production. In terms of the attention Marx gave it, particularly in *Capital*, this aspect of alienation constitutes one of the major themes in his writings.

The third relation in product alienation has to do with the worker being subservient to what he has lost. His product has become 'a power on its own confronting him'. 'So much', Marx claims, 'does the appropriation of the object appear as estrangement, that the more objects the worker produces the fewer can he possess and the more he falls under the dominion of his product, capital.' For Marx, those things with which the individual is closely related but which he does not control are, in fact, controlling him. He requires his products for consumption and further production, but he has no power to make them available. The worker, further, has no part in deciding what form these needed products will take. Instead, in every situation, he can merely respond to what already exists. His products face him as something given, both as to amount and form. The resulting interaction between the worker and his product, therefore, becomes one of total adjustment on the part of the former to the requirements (and hence the demands) of the latter. It is chiefly in this sense that the products of capitalism control their producers. This is probably the outstanding example of what was referred to above as a 'displaced relation'; whereas man, being a man, has the power to control nature, through exercising this power, his product is now in a position to control him.

This exchange of roles between the worker and his product is equally evident in production and consumption. The former, in particular, is emphasized, as where Marx says:

> It is no longer the laborer that employs the means of production, but the means of production that employ the laborer. Instead of being consumed by him as material elements of his productive activity, they consume him as the ferment necessary to their own life-process . . . Furnaces and workshops that stand idle by night, and absorb no living labor, are 'a mere loss' to the capitalist. Hence, furnaces and workshops constitute lawful claims upon the night-labor of the workpeople. The simple transformation of money into the material factors of the process of production, into means of production transforms the latter into a title and right to the labor and surplus-labor of others.

Marx adds that 'this complete inversion of the relation between dead and living labor' is a 'sophistication, peculiar to and characteristic of capitalist production'.

Articles of consumption, on the other hand, have power over their producers by virtue of the desires which they create. Marx understood how a product could precede the need that people feel for it, how it could actually create this need. Consumption, we are told, 'is furthered by its objects as a moving spring. The want of it which consumption experiences is created by its appreciation of the product. The object of art, as well as any other product, creates an artistic and beauty-enjoying public.' What can we expect, therefore, where consumers have no say in the production of things which they must consume? In this situation, the very character of man is at the mercy of his products, of what they make him want and become in order to get what he wants. These products are responsive to forces outside his control, serving purposes other than his own, generally the greed of some capitalist. Hence, Marx's claim that 'every new product represents a new potency of mutual swindling and mutual plundering'.

Besides manipulating people's needs, the form given to articles of consumption helps determine the prevailing mode of consumption. Every product carries with it a whole set of accepted usages. Taken together they constitute the greater part of what is meant by the way of life of a people. In capitalism, the worker's way of life has degenerated into one drawn out response to the requirements of his own products. Herein lies the inhuman power of man-made matter over man.

Chapter 21 Man's relation to his fellow men

The third broad relation in which Marx exhibits the worker's alienation is his tie with other men. This social alienation is fitted on to activity and product alienation in the following manner:

> If the product of labor does not belong to the worker, if it confronts him as an alien power, this can only be because it belongs to some other man than the worker . . . man's relation to himself only becomes objective and real for him through his relation to other men. Thus, if the product of his labor, his labor objectified, is for him an alien, hostile, powerful object independent of him, then his position towards it is such that someone else is master of this object, someone who is alien, hostile, powerful, and independent of him . . . Every self-estrangement of man from himself and from nature appears in the relation in which he places himself and nature to men other than and differentiated from himself.

The hostility of the worker's product is due to the fact that it is owned by a capitalist, whose interests are directly opposed to those of the worker. The product serves Marx as both the mask and the instrument of the capitalist's power.

If, when describing capitalists, Marx states they are but personal embodiments of capital, he is equally able to assert, when dealing with capital as a product, that it is an expression of the real power of the capitalist. One claim must not be read as being more 'ultimate' than the other, or else we shall forever be turning in circles as Marx's writings abound with claims of both sorts. On the basis of the internal relations Marx posits between the worker, his product and the man who controls it, these otherwise incompatible remarks become complementary characterizations of the same whole. When proceeding from the vantage point of the product, Marx wants to show ways in which the product of alienated labor exercises power over people (including, as we shall see, the capitalist). And when proceeding from the vantage point of the capitalist, he wants to show ways in which this man controls the product. It is with this latter relation that the present chapter deals.

The worker's dwelling provides an excellent example of how his relation to his product is bound up with his relation to the man who owns it. Marx refers to the worker's home as a 'cave' which he occupies 'only precariously, it being for him an alien habitation which can be withdrawn from him any day—a place from which, if he does not pay, he can be thrown out'. Comparing capitalism with primitive society, Marx adds:

> The savage in his cave—a natural element which freely offers itself for his use and protection—feels himself no more a stranger, or rather feels himself to be just as much at home as a fish in water. But the cellar-dwelling of the poor man is a hostile dwelling, 'an alien, restraining power which only gives itself up to him so far as he gives up to it his blood and sweat'—a dwelling which he cannot look upon as his own home where he might at last exclaim, 'here I am at home', but where instead he finds himself in someone else's house, in the

house of a stranger who daily lies in wait for him and throws him out if he does not pay his rent.

As elsewhere in capitalism, the worker's need carries no title to use what his own labor has produced. In his dwelling, man should feel himself 'at home as much as a fish in water'. This really expresses the degree of acceptance and trust in the possession of nature that all men will feel in communism. Under capitalism, however, the worker's relation to his home is one of uncertainty which he manifests through his fear of the landlord.

As with the worker's relation to his product, his alienated relation to the man who owns his product is a necessary result of his productive activity being what it is. Marx maintains:

> through alienated labor man not only engenders his relationship to the object and to the act of production as powers that are alien and hostile to him; he also engenders the relationship in which other men stand to his production and to his product, and the relationship in which he stands to these other men. Just as he begets his own product as a loss, as a product not belonging to him; so he begets the dominion of the one who does not produce over production and over the product. Just as he estranges himself from his own activity, so he confers to the stranger activity which is not his own . . . a man alien to labor and standing outside it . . . the capitalist, or whatever one chooses to call the master of labor.

Each capitalist only retains his pedestal through the repeated acts of workers. Without capitalist production in which the creative force is alienated labor there would be no capitalists. By engaging in totally unfulfilling labor, labor which destroys his mind and body, labor which is forced upon him by his drive to live, labor in which all choice is left to someone else who also controls the finished articles, that is, capitalist labor, the worker is said to produce the degrading social relations that distinguish this period.

Marx is capable, as we know, of approaching the same relation from the other side. He says, for example:

> The estrangement of man, and in fact every relationship in which man stands to himself, is first realized and expressed in the relationship in which a man stands to other men. Hence within the relationship of estranged labor each man views the other in accordance with the standard and the position in which he finds himself as a worker.

By separating out social relations and treating them as primary, Marx has in mind the fact that the worker-capitalist relation is already established when the worker asks for a job. On the other hand, this relation is the product of previous labor, and is reproduced for tomorrow by labor today.

In making the transition from man's relation to his product to his relation to the owner of this product, Marx allows, we will recall, the adjectives applied to the former to stand also for the latter. He claims that 'if the product of his labor . . . is for him an alien, hostile, powerful object independent of him, then his position towards it is such that someone else is master of this object, someone who is alien, hostile, and independent of him'. The worker faces the capitalist with the very same attitudes, but whereas his employer is able to act toward him with the callous and reckless abandon of the strong, the worker shows his weakness only too clearly through sullen and hateful acquiescence. Their social alienation is a two-way street. Pulling in opposite directions, at the command of competing interests, their relations are necessarily antagonistic.

Chapter 22 Man's relation to his species

The last of the four broad relations Marx uses to reconstruct man's alienation in capitalist society is the tie between the individual and his species. Species, as we saw, is the category of the possible, denoting in particular those potentialities which mark man off from other living creatures. In so far as the conditions of communism allow an individual to develop and express all that he is capable of as a human being, communist man and species man are identical. When, therefore, Marx claims that 'estranged human labor estranges the species from man', he is saying that the unique configuration of relations which distinguishes the individual as a human being has been transformed into something quite different by the performance of capitalist labor.

Man's relation to his species differs qualitatively from the other relations that were examined. His relations to his work, product and other men are tangible, both ends of which exist in the present, while the relation between man and his species is removed, in which living people are measured by the standard of what it means to be a man. Perhaps this facet of alienation can be more clearly grasped if we consider it a reformulation of man's alienation in his work, product and other men, viewed now from the angle of the individual's membership in the species. As Marx says:

> In tearing away from man the object of his production . . . estranged labor tears from him his species life, his real species objectivity, and transforms his advantage over animals into the disadvantage that his inorganic body, nature, is taken from him. Similarly, in degrading spontaneous activity, free activity, to a means, estranged labor makes man's species life a means to his physical existence.

The connection between species alienation and social alienation is made explicit elsewhere: 'The proposition that man's species nature is estranged from him means that one man is estranged from the other, as each of them is from man's essential nature.'

Marx makes several comparisons between man and animals in his attempts to clarify what is lost through species alienation. When the capitalist appropriates the product of the worker's labor, Marx declares that the latter's 'advantage over animals' is transformed 'into the disadvantage that his inorganic body, nature, is taken from him'. All living creatures have numerous relationships to the natural objects about them. As a result of his powers and needs being more extensive than any animal's, man enjoys the advantage of having the most complex ties of all. This shows in production where he is able to create things which are not objects of immediate need, a greater range of things, more beautiful things; he can also reproduce the objects he finds in nature.

All man's advantages over animals become disadvantages when the natural objects to which he is related become the property of other men. While animals in the forest take whatever they need from their immediate surroundings, man is restricted in his use of objects to what their owners will allow, which is invariably less than his powers require. If, as Marx says, 'The object of work is . . . the objectification of man's species life,' with the removal of these objects from his control, the human species is deprived of its reality, of what it requires to manifest itself as the human species.

We must be careful here as elsewhere not to substitute our concept of the processes and events which come into the discussion for Marx's own. Thus, though we may consider that people realize their human potential in conditions of private property, Marx does not. And his conception of this potential and of individual control over any part of nature is such that each necessarily excludes the other. This conclusion in no way affects the historical role that Marx attributes to the institution of private property in helping to prepare a time when man—through the abolition of such property—will be able to fully manifest his species powers. Until then, however, the distinctive character of man's complex relationship to nature is lost below the horizon of the animal world through the confiscation of this entire nature by another.

In treating species alienation, Marx gives a favored place, as we might expect, to man's relation to his activity. For Marx, 'the productive life is the life of the species'. Such activity is the chief means through which the individual expresses and develops his powers, and is distinguished from animal activity by its range, adaptability, skill and intensity. In capitalism, however, the worker's labor 'turns for him the life of the species into a means of individual life'. Work has become a means to stay alive rather than life being an opportunity to do work. Living, mere existence, has always been a necessary pre-condition for engaging in productive activity, but in capitalism it becomes the operative motive.

The worker's departure from what it means to be a man is also found in the world of thought. Marx says, 'The consciousness which man has of his species is thus transformed by estrangement in such a way that the species life becomes for him a means.' As a conscious being, the individual is aware of what he is doing and possesses the faculty of being able to choose and to plan. He can also make provisions to acquire the skills and knowledge necessary for his fulfillment. This degree of foresight belongs to him as a member of the human species. In estranged labor, however, 'it is just because man is a conscious being that he makes his life activity, his essential being, a mere means to his existence'. The greater part of man's consciousness in capitalism is used to direct his efforts at staying alive, for he recognizes that such concentration is necessary if he is to be successful.

What is left after the most distinctive qualities which set man apart from other living creatures are erased by the processes of capitalist society? For Marx, the 'rump' of human nature which remains is neither man nor animal, nor is it simply matter. It is, in his terminology, an 'abstraction'. Thus, when he says estranged labor 'makes individual life in its abstract form the purpose of the life of the species, likewise in its abstract form', he is asserting that man's existence, denuded of all human characteristics, has become the purpose of work, likewise denuded of all human characteristics. In this comment, the reversal of his species relations to activity, product and other men has gone the full distance, and man has succeeded in becoming all that he is not.

Notes

1. We see the same 'logical geography' in the whole host of 'double-headed' adjectives with which Marx showered his contemporaries. How can he describe the laborer's plight as 'degradation', 'dehumanization' and 'fragmentation', and the laborer himself as 'stunted', 'thwarted' and 'broken'? Only because he is aware, however imprecisely, of their opposites.

2. That communism is the yardstick by which Marx ascribes alienation in the present emerges clearly from the following: 'the community from which the worker is isolated is a community of quite other dimensions than the political community. The community from which his own labor separates him, is life itself, physical and intellectual life, human morality, human activity, human enjoyment, human essence.' 'Kritische Randglossen', *Werke*, I, 408. 'Human', we will recall, is an adjective that Marx usually reserves for describing communism.

3. The account referred to appears in the *1844 Manuscripts*, pp. 69–80. Most of the material for these chapters on the basic relations of alienation is taken from these pages. As with other relations in Marx's work, the four listed here are aspects of an organic whole. Hence, an explanation of alienation could begin with any one and go naturally on to the others. Marx himself begins with man's alienation in his product, but, for reasons which will soon become apparent, alienated activity offers a better starting point. Also for purposes of facilitating exposition, I have transposed Marx's relations three and four. Thus, what appears in the order—product, activity, species and other men—in Marx's explanation of alienation, appears as—activity, product, other men and species—in my own.

Gone Fishing: Making Sense of Marx's Concept of Communism
William James Booth

Introduction

In a splendid essay entitled "On Being Conservative" Michael Oakeshott writes that certain activities are eminently attractive to those of a conservative disposition. Fishing is one such activity—not fishing in order to supply the immediate sustenance of life, nor fishing as a commercial venture intended to yield a profit. Rather, what Oakeshott is describing is the activity of a trout fisherman by a mountain stream. His casting of the fly into the passing waters is not compulsory, that is, he does not have to catch fish in order to survive. Nor is it directed to any other end, or purpose, for instance, the sale of his catch. It is the activity itself that is enjoyable, the display of skill or "perhaps merely passing the time."[1] In sum, fishing is neither something necessitous (survival) nor externally purposive (market oriented).

Let us now draw a few inferences from Oakeshott's account of the activity of fishing. The person engaged in such an activity is not, as such, a fisherman. A fisherman is one who earns a living by means of this activity: He cannot while away his hours at that mountain stream, because his dinner or his earnings depend upon success. Displays of skill in fishing will matter to him only insofar as they yield the desired consequences, a result external to the activity, for example, nutrition or a paycheck. Time, for him, is indeed money (productivity as yield over time) not something merely to be "passed." His associates in this activity will be cooperants in a production process, helpers in maximizing his yield. And lastly, his activity will be an instrument for him—a means of ensuring his continued survival. Insofar as he must maximize his catch (to feed his community, to make a greater profit, or to win a wage-bonus), he has to make himself an "expert" fisherman, a specialized practitioner of that one set of tasks, or allocate those tasks among his associates. He is, then, an expert, not an amateur, of the activity of fishing.

Another person, someone not a fisherman but merely fishing by the side of the stream, pursues this activity as time spent pleasurably. He passes his time at it and that time is not measured or determined by output. The underlying reason for the free, unbound quality of this time is that the activity that fills it is one neither compelled by natural necessity nor is it one bound to the production of surpluses. Freed from these external pressures, time can merely be passed, the activity savored for itself, not for what it may yield. One's fishing companions are presumably freely chosen friends, people who enjoy each other's company in a shared pursuit. They are not moments of a production process, cooperants in maximizing productivity. Finally, this person is an amateur of fishing; it is not his expertise (however skilled he may be), not something to which he must devote his whole life, but rather a chosen pastime.

William James Booth, "Gone Fishing: Making Sense of Marx's Concept of Communism," *Political Theory,* 17:2, pp. 205–222. Copyright © 1989 by Sage Publications, Inc. Reprinted by permission of Sage Publications, Inc.

In Oakeshott's analysis, the activity of fishing is evidence of a nonutilitarian disposition to enjoy the present as it is, a conservative attitude toward the relations between activity and the world. I have sought to unpack Oakeshott's account of fishing, that is, to show the features that such an activity must have. These are (1) that time can be "whiled away," that is, it is not subject to the compulsion of nature (essential needs) or of the market (productivity). Where time is determined by the latter constraints, output shapes the activity as an external end and transforms it from a pastime into disciplined labor. (2) Skill is valued for itself, not for what it can produce. This is another way of formulating the idea that the activity is not driven by a purpose external to itself. (3) As a corollary of the preceding point, the skill displayed must be that of the amateur, a chosen prowess and not a functionally defined role within a rationalized production process. (4) A group or community of such persons, of the amateurs of fishing, would be voluntary because the association, like the activity, would be one chosen for its intrinsic pleasure and not for its contribution to the meeting of an external end. This analysis goes well beyond Oakeshott's few paragraphs; nevertheless it draws on his central idea and it sets a framework (activity, time, community) for understanding another political philosopher who also wrote about fishing.

Karl Marx's *German Ideology* contains what is perhaps the single most celebrated description of communism: "In communist society, where nobody has one exclusive sphere of activity . . . society regulates production and thus makes it possible for me to do one thing today and another tomorrow, to hunt in the morning, fish in the afternoon, rear cattle in the evening, criticize after dinner, just as I have a mind, without ever becoming hunter, fisherman, shepherd or critic." [2] That this passage contains a tongue-in-cheek, polemical barb directed at Marx's erstwhile philosophical allies is certain; that it suggests important features of his vision of communist society is something that I shall argue for in this essay. The question before Marx's readers is how to interpret this exceedingly elliptical description of communism. Marx himself provides us some guidance: "We do not dogmatically anticipate the world, but only want to find the new world through criticism of the old one." [3] What this says is that the shape of the future can best be seen in the criticism, the exposure of the faults, of the present. In the paragraphs that follow, I wish to draw on the analysis of fishing presented in these opening pages, that is, on the intertwined themes of activity, time, and community in order to sketch central elements of Marx's critique of capitalism and to derive from that critique the sense of his portrait of communism. The traditional approach, what G. A. Cohen has called the Plain Marxist Argument, focuses its normative critique of capitalism on the phenomena of exploitation, domination of society by the bourgeoisie, and domination at the point of production. From that perspective, communist society is the corrective in that it is nonexploitative and classless. What I now wish to do is to cut into these issues from a different angle, to move from a reading of Marx that turns around questions of ownership, surplus extraction, and the rule of one class over society to one whose critical locus is to be found neither in issues of distribution (ownership and exploitation) nor in the rule of some over others but in the idea of domination by an autonomous economic process. The advantage of this reading of Marx over the Plain Argument account is that it allows us to grasp more precisely what Marx considered to be the *differentia specifica* of capitalism in relation to its antecedents and thereby to come to a new appreciation of his critique of capitalism as well as of his vision of communism. More important, perhaps, it sets the stage for the consideration of the profound radicalness of Marx's project in the history of political thought: the move away from the traditional question of justice between persons to the critique of political economy.

I. Being a Fisherman

To be a fisherman is different from going fishing. The latter is the result of choice among possible activities, hunting, rearing cattle, reading philosophy. The former is the consequence of a life determined. To go fishing or whatever just because "I have a mind" to do so is an activity that is the efflux of my will, that is, I set the purpose and make the choice. I am distinct from this activity that I have elected to pursue: It is chosen and therefore can be put aside. In brief, I am not subordinated to fishing; I elect to do it and I can reel in my line, walk away from it, and return to my philosophical books as I see fit.

Being a fisherman is something quite different. It suggests that in some way or other, my activity, a single activity, has come to be what I am simply. I am my function and that function is determined by nature or by an economic process. In precapitalist societies where human productive powers had not yet developed sufficiently to allow society to become the effective master of nature, that function was largely determined by nature and elementary need. Capitalist society, in which people have become perhaps as much as is possible the "sovereigns of nature," also "allocates" functional roles to its members. It is the source of that "allocation" that constitutes the perverse essence of capitalism, the key characteristics that distinguish it from earlier societies.

Under capitalism, according to Marx, the labor process is absorbed into the valorization process. The valorization process is expressed by the general formula, M-C-M', in which M' or surplus value is the self-renewing and unlimited purpose or goal of a circuit that includes both production and circulation. The whole of society's metabolic interaction with nature, that is, the labor process embracing equally the human, or subjective side, and the material instruments of that interaction is subsumed under a process the goal of which is to produce constantly expanding value. This process, that is, the *movement* of the various components of value through their transformation from labor-power and the materials and instruments of production into expanded surplus value is, according to Marx, an *autonomous* process, and its "dominant subject" is not the humans involved in the process but value itself.[4]

Capital, as self-valorizing value, comprises class, Marx writes.[5] The persons who occupy various and functionally different places along capital's circuit of metamorphoses have their behavior and their purposes determined by their particular functional positions. "Real political economy," he adds elsewhere must then treat the capitalist only "as personified capital, M-C-M, agent of production."[6] The capitalist's purpose is, consistent with his or her functional role in the valorization process, to maximize value, that is, to accumulate and not to consume. The capitalist, in sum, is "personified" capital, its mere "functionary." Workers, for their part, are personified labor-time or labor-power.[7] It is thus appropriate, Marx states, that in England workers are called "hands." Proletarian and capitalist are equally subsumed under the valorization process; both are its "slaves."

The functional positions allocated by the valorization process to the various "representatives" along its circuit are duplicated, *mutatis mutandis,* in the smaller world of the factory, the "technological expression" of capital.[8] In the mechanized factory, a whole exists, a process, consisting of the movements of machines. The nature of each individual's work, the worker's physical location, and the work relationship with his or her associates are determined by the structure of the mechanized operations of the factory. The worker's activity is determined through the activity of the whole, of the "iron mechanism"; the worker loses independence and is "appropriated by the process." Similarly, the capitalist's activity of superintendence arises directly from the nature of capitalist factory production itself. Thus just as in the broader circuit of capital individuals are transformed into mere "bearers," "representatives," or "functionaries" of the phases of the valorization process, so too in the microcosm of the factory, activity is determined by the needs of the "iron" process of the mechanized atelier.

What happens in the broader circuit of capital (M-C-M′) as well as in its reflection-in-miniature (the factory) is "deindividualization."[9] The persons involved become the bearers of the functional positions they occupy within the circuit of capital. Their activities are reduced to moments in capital's metamorphosis; moments that are determined by the self-recreating valorization process, that is, are not set by conscious human agency. The naturally imposed necessity of skill or physical prowess is overcome through cooperative, mechanized production; labor becomes the expenditure of homogeneous labor time, that is, contentless work subordinated to the creation of surplus value. In Marx's account, then, being a fisherman, a capitalist, or whatever is to be subsumed under an economic process. It is to be a member of a class, a functionally defined group of persons.

The (postcapitalist) world of those who hunt in the morning and fish in the afternoon is a classless society. Though in Marx's celebrated description, only a single individual is mentioned, we can infer the community's classlessness from the fact that neither the individual nor his or her activities are characterized as functionally related to a production process. The individual is not, as one in bourgeois society is, in a "situation of being assigned."[10] Rather, the individual does what "he has a mind to" and not what the "representative" of capital or labor power must do according to their roles in the metamorphosis of value. One's activities, hunting, philosophizing, and so forth are under the dominion neither of another person nor of a process and hence they are not bound down by some purpose or goal other than that set by the person. The result, then, of the abolition of classes (understood as the abolition of the allocation of functional roles by an economic process beyond human control) is, according to Marx, the individualization of humans in the sense of self-determination just outlined.

II. Whiling away the Hours

Time is the "space" (*Raum*) of human development, the forum of one's "active existence."[11] A person's wealth, Marx adds, does not consist in the objects he or she accumulates, but rather in the time freely available to him or her. That is, wealth is not the sum of embodied past activity, of "dead labor" as Marx calls it, but time yet to be shaped, yet to be filled with hunting, philosophizing, or whatever. Now time can be either bound down or free. Time is bound down when its use is determined not by the agents' own purposes but by forces external to them. While humankind does not have technology sufficient to allow for the mastering of nature, nature is one such force. The cycle of the seasons imposes a labor-rhythm on agrarian communities independent of their wills. Time may also be determined by the class structure of society where the leisure of one segment of society, for example, the housemaid masters of Aristotle's *Politics*, Book I, is purchased at the expense of the time of the laboring population. Capitalist society, in which nature is less a constraint than in any preceding epoch and in which production is not intended to provide leisure and consumption goods for a few but rather aims at an ever increasing surplus for its own sake, also binds time but in a radically different manner.

In his essay on *The Condition of the Working-Class in England,* Engels, describing the time pressure on the workers referred to them as being subject to the "despotic bell." Marx, in his 1861–1863 *Notebooks,* quoted that passage and put the phrase "despotic bell" in italics.[12] We may speculate that what struck Marx in the words "the despotic bell" was the notion of time (under capitalism) as a dominating, alien force rather than as the "space" for the development of human capacities.

Capital has "encroached" upon time; it has "usurped" the time of society, Marx writes. To understand what Marx means by this, it is important to recall that he considers capital to be not simply a bundle of property/appropriation relations, but a process, a "circulatory" movement of value. This movement is temporally measured and it is divided into the various phases of the reproduction and expansion of value. In brief, across the entire spectrum of its economic phenomena, from the most elementary, that is, the commodity as "congealed" labor time, to the most expansive, that is, the creation of a world market, capitalism more than any previous economic order is a process concerned with time.[13] This time, however, is subsumed under the requirements of capital for rapid reproduction (completion of its circuit and recommencement of its next cycle). In all the stages of its metamorphosis, capital seeks to compress time, to "close its pores." In other words, capital attempts to appropriate for its reproductive process all available time while also striving to reduce as far as possible the time necessary for the completion of its circuit. In this broadly formulated description, we can grasp the general import of Marx's reference to the "despotic bell" and we can also see the intimations of why Marx thought capitalism to be a liberating force.

For Marx, the consequence of this is that capitalism's greatest achievement, its historical "justification,"[14] the shortening of necessary labor time, does not in fact lead to a lessening of bound time for the producing population. Quite the contrary, the result of this unprecedented transformation and extension of society's productive powers is the simultaneous lengthening and intensification (closing the pores of production time) of the working day. This outcome does not depend, Marx argues, on the good or bad will of the capitalist; rather, it is determined by the laws of capitalism.

In sum, no previous epoch has seen such great time pressure on the population as is found under capitalism. Overwork, Marx claims, was not a significant problem in antiquity and, to the extent that laws dealt with additional labor, it was to try to compel more of it. It is, however, characteristic of capitalism that laws here are introduced to restrain the economic compulsion to excessive labor.[15] The concern for the reduction of necessary labor time (leaving aside the issue of the reduction of circulation time) is central in a process that seeks constantly to yield increasingly large surpluses (embodied surplus time); but since surplus is its purpose, not free time, the reduction of necessary labor does not alter the character of time for the living bearers of that process, except insofar as still more of their time is absorbed by the process.

We saw in the previous section that Marx observed how appropriate it was that in England laborers were called "hands," the living servants of machines, their activity subsumed under the systematic order and activity of those machines. Marx also commented on the common designation of workers as "full time" or "half time."[16] On the one hand, the worker is thereby shown to be mere personified labor time. On the other hand, time itself—full or half—is revealed as something determined by the valorization circuit of wealth. This, and not the horrors of child labor or overwork in early industrial Britain, is the principal locus of Marx's understanding and critique of capitalism's impact upon time. What capital has done is to provide human beings with that temporal "space" for their development, for the exercise of their free purposiveness, and it has, in the same moment, taken that time (liberated, as it were, from natural necessity) and subordinated it to a nondesigned and, in some ways, perversely purposeful process, M-C-M'.

The recovery of that time (now not from nature but from an economic order) is a part of what is being portrayed in the *German Ideology* passage concerning hunting and fishing. Not only can I *do* what "I have a mind to" (hence the overcoming of functional roles assigned by the circuit), but I can do it *when* I wish to (the overcoming of the circuit's appropriation of surplus or free time). Nor is there a need to rush: the fishing pole lying by my side is no longer fixed capital impatiently demanding valorization, but is rather something for me to use when I choose to. That I can so while away the hours has no other significance than this, that through the subordination of economic processes to the conscious human will time is brought under one's control and not that of an external purposiveness.

III. Fishermen All

Capital has made a world in its own image. It has, Marx argues, transformed human activity from a condition in which skill, physical prowess, age, and sex were the major determinants of one's labor into one in which an equal but contentless activity is in the service of capital generally and, within the factory (capital's portrait-in-miniature), in the service of the system of machines. We have observed, too, how capital has supplanted nature, human and inanimate both, as the force governing time and has subordinated time to its need for increased velocity of reproduction. What is more, capital determines the community, the association of persons, its creators who have also become its valets. It is this question, Marx's concept of the community under capital, that we shall now address. My concern here, then, will be less with the topic so central to Marx's early writings, that is, the illusory community of the state, than with his analysis of the community as it emerges from the mature critique of political economy.

III. A In the Market

What emerges in the capitalist market is the end of relations of personal dependence based on status and of the "natural bonds" of attachment of individuals to their community and their replacement by the interaction and exchanges of commodity owners. It is certain that, in Marx's view, the dissolution of the natural community and bound labor represented a genuine emancipation both of the individual worker and of society from the limits of a community that sought nothing higher than its own survival. Despite his many polemical references to wage-labor as "wage-slavery," Marx's analysis holds that there is a sharp difference between bound labor of all types and the labor power possessed as a commodity by the worker.

The existence of a pervasive labor market also presupposes what Marx calls capital's "original sin," that is, the expropriation of the producers, their separation from the means of production. This original act of expropriation leaves workers with only labor power to sell, and sell it the workers must since they no longer have the means to produce for themselves. However, the person whom one meets in the market, the owner of the means of production, does not stand before one as master over servant or lord over vassal but as a fellow owner of commodities, as an equal.

Marx's purpose in setting out capital's "original sin" is to make clear that the market did not appear *ex nihilo,* that its beginnings are coercive, and, lastly, that they are centered on a fundamental shift of ownership of the means of production away from the direct producers, that is, their expropriation, as well as the dissolution of the old system of personal bonds within the community. In short, Marx wants to take some of the bloom from the rose of the contract theory of the origins of the market and free enterprise. But what is important for our purposes is that from the debris of the now destroyed world of the precapitalist community, there emerges a new type, the one that we encounter in the market, the universe of commodity owners, buyers, and sellers, united by a money relation with each other: the nexus of "cash payment."

In this new world, this community under capital, individuals, according to Marx, appear to be and indeed are freed of ties of personal dependence and distinctions of blood. They exist, in the market expression of their community, in a condition of reciprocal isolation connected only by the need to exchange their commodities. They have been freed of any ties other than exchange and they therefore appear to be free. Marx's account of the genesis of this arrangement suggests force, not choice, as its foundation. But what of their present condition? Recall that the market is only one of the moments of the life cycle of capital, that time in which value realizes itself as money, which in turn reappears in the market, there to buy new labor-power and materials in order to start the circuit anew. The social relations of the market are not relations between individuals, Marx argues, but rather between proletarian and capitalist. They exist for one another as the "representatives" of their commodities, bearers of the metamorphoses of their wares.[17]

Thus the members of this community live in a "bewitched world," one where their relations appear as relations between things. The "social character," the communal nature, of their interchange appears as something independent of them, as a moment in the valorization process.[18] History and their respective functions in that process have assigned them different roles (though formally, in terms of ownership status, equal) in the market. Yet the fact that the market works through voluntary agreement and not direct coercion and that the market as a whole seems to be anarchical, that is, composed of the accidental "collisions" of individuals give it the appearance of the "very Eden of the innate rights of man." What I wish to look more closely at is the notion central to Marx's analysis, that the literal anarchy of the market is not freedom at all but merely a form of external rule, the "silent compulsion" of capital: "It is not individuals who are set free by free competition; it is, rather, capital which is set free."[19]

This argument of Marx's can be construed in two principal, and not necessarily consistent, ways. Here I shall do no more than to sketch them. (1) Buyers and sellers in the market are compelled to act as they do. Free will is not an adequate account of their interaction. They are compelled by the external purposive process, M-C-M', of which they are mere moments, functional bearers of phases or elements of the metabolism of capital. In this version, an all-embracing process is said to express and to be determined by the general, underlying laws of capital. Anarchy is mere appearance, the seeming surface of things. (2) The individual moments of circulation *are* the result of the "conscious will" of individuals. But the totality of the process, the result of their individual collisions, is an "objective" process, that is, something not under their control, an "alien social power" that generates, Marx concludes, their "objective dependency."[20] The idea here is that while wills and individual decisions are attributable to persons, the result of their interactions is a process that, viewed as a whole, takes on an independent existence. This is to be distinguished from the previous version in that the latter asserted an identity (and a causal relation) among the dominant, systemic purpose, accumulation or M-C-M', and the (determined) purpose of the individuals enmeshed in that process. For reasons that I have set out elsewhere, I am inclined to think that argument (1) above represents Marx's preferred position. What is important for the analysis of this article is that the community in one specific moment of the intercourse of its members, that of the market, is determined by the circuit of capital, however the latter is construed. Marx's fundamental point is that relations between individuals, the substance of their communal existence, are determined by the valorization process and not by the community itself. Those various relations are thus functionally and externally allocated by the movement of value through the phases of its life cycle.

III.B In the Factory

Beneath the "haze" of the world of circulation lies another sphere, a second form of the community under capital. This is the production process, the other major moment in value's circuit. The "interconnections of capital," its laws, that are barely visible in the world of the marketplace, that seemingly anarchical environment of competition, buying and selling, are more readily apparent in the production sphere, to which we shall now turn.

The "real subsumption" of labor to capital begins when workers and capitalists meet not only in the labor market but when the production process itself has come under the control of capital. The nature of labor is now altered: It becomes social, directly cooperative labor, that is, the factory. A second community, that of the factory, is thus formed. But this social form of production is not the "offspring of association."[21] What Marx means by this is that the character of their cooperation is not determined by the community, but rather by the needs of the M-C-M' circuit. It is thus a "fate," and not the result of choice. Their combination, the new productive community under capital, appears to them as an "alien" combination, as the "subjectivity" or will of capital.[22] Just as the origin of the free exchanges in the labor market is to be found in the coercive act of expropriation, so here the beginnings of the production community are located in a "will" external to that community, the "will" of a purposive process, the valorization of capital.

In the marketplace, individuals appear indeed as buyers and sellers, representatives of their commodities or capital, but also as juridical persons, as owners equal and free disposing over their commodities. In the production process, they lose even the semblance of autonomy from the capital circuit. Here they become "hands" and "full timers," accessories or servants of the process. This is not merely what has come to be known as domination at the point of production, the direct control of capitalist over worker or, in other words, the "barracks-like discipline" of the factory. More central for Marx, it is that the combination of labor, the community created by capital, stands over against the individual as an alien, controlling force. It is a community that abolishes the independence and individuality of its members.[23]

The association of the factory is not the association or community of its members, it is a "form of existence of capital," an objective association. Marx's analysis of the factory, that is, of the real subsumption of labor under capital, is not merely an account of what transpires within the walls of that institution. Rather, that commentary is one directed to a "form of existence of capital." Marx also uses the factory as a concretization of the entire capital relation in this sense: The subordination of living to objectified labor (man/machines = society/M-C-M') that is the heart of capitalism, that is, the nature of its metabolism (the feeding on and replenishing itself from surplus labor), is in the factory rendered more plainly visible. Marx's account of the market and production moments of the community under capital (exchange and the factory system) is clearly *not* meant to suggest that they be judged against the measure of an arcadian, precapitalist community. The stagnant world of primitive communal ownership, the violence and degradation of the community of slaves and their masters, in general, all the forms of what Marx calls the "natural" community (ones not based on exchange) are inferior stages of humankind's development. Capitalism has broken down national boundaries and prejudices, created a universal community, and unleashed the powers of social labor. It has also subordinated the community that it has called into being to the demands of its autonomous valorization process. This community does not represent the wills of its members but rather the needs of the capital cycle.

In the passage from the *German Ideology* that has set the guiding thread for our discussion, only a single individual is mentioned. Moreover, all of his activities, fishing, hunting, and philosophizing are, given the circumstances in which he conducts them (i.e., not fishing for profit, where cooperation would be necessary or primitive food-hunting where cooperation is for different reasons also required), potentially solitary activities. If this person seeks the company of his fellow human beings it will not be because he is enmeshed in an economic cycle that demands cooperation of him, nor will it be the result of the underdevelopment of his productive powers, a condition that uses humans and their cooperation where machines do not yet exist that could take over a substantial part of the task. He will, we can imagine, associate freely with his fellows. Their combined (social) efforts will not be something imposed on them from the outside; their community will be self-determined and not subject to the laws of the metabolism of capital.

There is clearly something Robinson Crusoe-like about this solitary fisherman/hunter/philosopher and Marx himself provides a corrective in Volumes One and Three of *Capital*.[24] Transpose him, however, to a community of others like himself and the sense of Marx's image (moderated in his later writings) becomes at least somewhat more evident. Such a community would be the expression writ large of our fisherman/hunter/philosopher's relation to his activity. Subordinated neither to nature nor to the dictates of the valorization process, this individual is not "assigned" a functional role in production; he fishes but is not a fisherman and he controls his time, rather than having it determined by capital's need for rapid reproduction. In sum, he does (as far as is possible) what he "has a mind to." So too would his community of the "freely associated" do as it has a mind to.

On one level, the idea of the community as a free association signifies, for Marx, that the cooperation of its members is not something wholly imposed on them from the outside. On a second and related level, it means that the community and its cooperation are not forces that abolish the individual, that is, rob the individual of his or her will (i.e., the community as a coercive, externally imposed power). From this element of Marx's critique, one can infer the outlines of his vision of a communist society. It is a "free association" in the sense that it sets its own ends and, presumably, the continued reduction of necessary labor time would be central among them.[25] It is also free inasmuch as its members are not "assigned" their cooperative situation, nor are they related to one another as bearers of functional moments in the production process. Both of these notions rest on the underlying idea that the *summum malum* of capitalism is domination by the valorization circuit, a circuit that is autonomous in relation to the will of the community that it controls.

Conclusion

The portrait of communist society set out in the passage from the *German Ideology* and the critique of capitalism that underpins it remained a centerpiece of Marx's project. The passage's youthful enthusiasm, especially evident in its implied claim that necessity could be overcome altogether, was in *Capital*, Volume Three, to be reined in by the recognition that material production, the "realm of necessity," would continue to be the foundation even of a postcapitalist society. Nevertheless, on those same pages of *Capital* in which the mature Marx moderated somewhat the wildly hopeful vision of his youth, the heart of that vision is still present: Material production is made as free as can be when "the associated producers govern the human metabolism with nature in a rational way, bringing it under their collective control instead of being dominated by it as a blind power. . . ."[26] This conscious control of the economy, the greatest achievable human autonomy in the productive interaction between human beings and nature, creates the foundation of the "true realm of freedom, the development of human powers as an end in itself. . . ." Here, as in the 1845 passage, the *summum malum* is the promise denied of autonomy, that is, the control over human affairs by forces external to their will, forces that provided humankind with the means to become the sovereign of nature. Communism cannot, in Marx's view, abolish the need for the continued interaction of human beings with nature, but it can deprive that process of its independent law-giving capacity by subordinating it to the community's conscious control.

This core of Marx's critique of capitalism is evident in one rather quiet passage from *Capital*, Volume One, in which he contrasts the legally limited working day to the "pompous catalogue of the 'inalienable rights of man.'"[27] To the reader steeped in the Plain Marxist Argument the importance that Marx here attaches to the limited working day must be perplexing, as also must be (for different reasons) his insistence in Volume Three that the shortening of the working day is a prerequisite of communism. The Ten Hours Act is not praised for its effects on income or asset endowments nor does it alter the fact of exploitation. Rather Marx lauds it as a "social barrier" to capital, that is, as an instance of the subordination of the economy to the purposes of the community rather than to the requirements of the valorization process. The "catalogue of the 'inalienable rights of man,'" Marx seems to suggest, has (to borrow the phrases of the *German Ideology*) freed people from the "violence of men" only to submit them to the "violence of things," that is, the autonomous economic process. In sum, the relation of master and servant, dominator and dominated, must be rethought and supplied with a new idiom. It is that idiom that Marx sought to provide.

The exegetical consequences of this analysis for the reading of Marx can be only briefly stated here. It suggests that the Plain Marxist Argument interpretation, with its emphasis on domination of persons over persons and on exploitation as the great evil of capitalism, is seriously misguided. Domination, class, and exploitation assume a sharply different form in a society (capitalist) in which the economy has become independent of, and legislative over, society. To put the matter rather too starkly, the reading presented in this article suggests that the principal issue for Marx is the relationship between the "blind power" of the autonomous economic process of capital and the community it governs, rather than the relationship between the bourgeoisie and the proletariat, both of which are governed in different ways by laws not of their own making.

Viewed in a broader compass, the interpretation set out here shows, on the one side, Marx's deep indebtedness to preliberal political economy, indeed to classical Greek conceptions of an embedded economy serving the leisure and cultivation of the virtue of citizens. On the other side, in its nonhierarchical, nonorganic concept of the free association of producers, Marxism draws on liberal ideas of the human community. Yet Marx's project seeks to move beyond the tradition of political philosophy, ancient and modern. That move is evident above all in Marx's silence about the central question of the tradition, that is, justice. Various efforts have been made to explain that silence: that Marx really had a theory of justice *malgré lui,* that Marx's historicism prevented him from using ideas of justice for critical purposes, or that his aspiration to a scientific critique led him to shun the normative propositions of his socialist ancestors. The argument of this essay suggests a different answer: Ideas of justice, the regulative norms of affairs among persons, have little to say to society in which the new master is not a person but an economic process become autonomous, a blind power ruling society. It is that understanding of capitalism, present in an inchoate form in Marx's early writings, that leads to the shift away from the question of justice and to the critique of political economy. And it is just that move that constitutes the most radical heart of Marx's challenge.

One of the principal moments of this challenge can be set out in a manner that neither requires of us that we accept the viability of Marx's counterfactual world of communism nor demands that we subscribe to the details of his analysis of capitalism. We might sketch this central point as follows: (1) liberalism grasps one form of unfreedom, coercion, or the arbitrary rule of one will over another, which was the dominant form in precapitalist societies; (2) contractarianism and the language of rights are the correctives to coercive unfreedom—power, private and public, is now made, by and large, to rest on a consensual, nonhierarchical foundation; (3) but the sources of unfreedom are not exhausted by the sea of coercion. There is another form, objective compulsion, the reduction of autonomy of persons not through the arbitrary wills of others but rather as a consequence of the independence of the process of production itself, in other words, of the fact that the economy is autonomous and, beyond the control of individuals who occupy its various stages, it comes to legislate over them. (4) The liberal concept of unfreedom as the state of being coerced is not adequate to an understanding of objective compulsion and, conversely, its idea of autonomy as exclusionary rights against others (that is, as a counter to coercion) is too limited—limitations evident in the coexistence of this autonomy with the most radical restrictions on the power of self-determination brought about by the "silent compulsion," the "cold-blooded inevitability" of economic laws.[28]

Like most painters of worlds to come, Marx was less concerned with the portrait itself than with the questions thereby raised about the present order of things. It is those questions, the center of his critique of liberalism, that remain of interest, however implausible (or impalatable) we may judge his vision of communism to have been and however flawed his arguments were in their details. It is the sense of that critique that I have sought to draw out in this essay.

Notes

1. Michael Oakeshott, "On Being Conservative," *Rationalism and Politics* (New York: Basic Books, 1962), 168–196.
2. Karl Marx and Frederick Engels, *The German Ideology,* in *Karl Marx and Frederick Engels Collected Works* (Vol. 5) (New York: International Publishers, 1976), 47. The *Collected Works* are cited hereafter as MECW plus the volume number. A brief discussion of the irony of this passage is to be found in Frank E. Manuel, "In Memoriam: Critique of the Gotha Program, 1875–1975," *Daedelus* (Fall 1975), 59–77. For an extended analysis of some of the issues raised in this essay, see chapter XI of G.A. Cohen, *Karl Marx's Theory of History: A Defense* (Princeton, NJ: Princeton University Press, 1978).
3. Marx, *Letters from the Deutsch-Franzoesische Jahrbuecher,* in MECW, 3, 142.
4. Marx, *Capital* (Vol. 2), trans. David Fernbach (New York: Vintage Books, 1981), 185–186; Marx, *Capital* (Vol. 1), trans. Ben Fowkes (New York: Vintage Books, 1977), 255. Cited hereafter, respectively, as C2 and C1. For a more detailed analysis of the method of Marx's political economy, see my "Explaining Capitalism: The Method of Marx's Political Economy." *Political Studies* (forthcoming).
5. Marx, C2, 185.
6. Marx, *Theories of Surplus Value* (Part 1), trans. Emile Burns (Moscow: Progress Publishers, 1963), 270.
7. Marx *Zur Kritik der politischen Okonomie,* Manuscript 1861–1863, in *Karl Marx, Friedrich Engels Gesamtausgabe* II 3.6 (Berlin: Dietz Verlag, 1982) 2024. These manuscripts are cited hereafter as MEGA plus the volume number.
8. Marx, MEGA II 3.6, 2058.
9. Marx, MEGA II 3.6, 2024.
10. Marx, *Grundrisse,* trans. Martin Nicolaus (New York: Vintage Books, 1974), 6.
11. Marx, MEGA II 3.6, 2026–2027.
12. Frederick Engels, *The Condition of the Working-Class in England,* MECW: 4, 467; Marx, MEGA II 3.6, 2023. In Engels's original the phrase is not in italics.
13. Marx, MEGA II 3.6, 174–175; Marx, *Grundrisse,* 615.
14. Marx, *Theories of Surplus Value* (Part 2), no translator cited (Moscow: Progress Publishers, 1968), 405. Cited hereafter as TSV2.
15. Marx, C1, 345; Marx, MEGA II 3.1, 203–204.
16. Marx, MEGA II 3.6, 2024.
17. Marx, MEGA II 3.1, 288; Marx, C1, 179.
18. Marx, *Grundrisse,* 157.
19. Marx, *Grundrisse,* 650; Marx, C1, 899.
20. Marx, *Grundrisse,* 164, 196–197.
21. Marx, *Grundrisse,* 158.
22. Marx, MEGA II 3.6, 2013; Marx, *Grundrisse,* 470.
23. Marx, C1: 638; Marx, *Grundrisse,* 700; Marx, MEGA II 3.1, 244–246.
24. Marx, C1: 171–172; Marx, *Capital* (Vol. 3), trans. David Fernbach (New York: Vintage Books, 1981), 958–959.
25. Marx, TSV2: 405; Marx, *Grundrisse,* 172–173.
26. Marx, C3: 958–959.
27. Marx, C1: 416.
28. Marx, C1: 899; Marx, "Moralising Criticism," MECW: 6, 336. See also G. A. Cohen, "The Structure of Proletarian Unfreedom." *Philosophy and Public Affairs* 12, no. 1 (1982): 3–33.

John Stuart Mill

If by the elusive term liberalism one means a philosophy based upon individual rights, a belief that reason can overcome prejudice, and a progressive view of history, then John Stuart Mill is perhaps liberalism's greatest spokesperson. While skeptical about political developments in his own day, Mill believed that a tolerant, democratic majority could be forged, combining stability with individual freedom to think, to be heard, and to live a lifestyle of one's choosing. Mill struggled to develop this view against the Utilitarian philosophy instilled in him by his father. Although John never abandoned the older position, and perhaps never succeeded in meshing his father's brand of utility with his own preferences, he nevertheless gave vent to some of the strongest sentiments associated with the modern liberal state.

John Stuart Mill was born in London in 1806. His father, James, embarked on a great educational experiment with his son, providing him with early and rigorous intellectual training in the home. At three, John learned Greek; at six, Latin. All the while, he was treated to an intensive regimen of mathematics and logic. In 1823, John became a clerk with the East India Company and rose to a prominent position with the company. In 1831, he was introduced to Harriet Taylor, the wife of a wealthy merchant. Mill's platonic affair with Harriet is legendary. They had intense political conversations and Mill credits Harriet with inspiring much of his own thinking and writing. There continues to be debate in scholarly circles whether she penned any of Mill's works. Her husband died in 1849 and three years later Harriet and John married. She died in 1858. Thereafter, John wrote and served a term in Parliament from 1865 to 1868. He died in Avignon in 1873 after a brief illness.

John was introduced to the doctrine associated with his father and his father's associate, Jeremy Bentham. Going under the name of Utilitarianism, the doctrine combined a straightforward view of human nature with a simple prescription for society. Humans, Bentham argued, are "governed by two sovereign masters: pleasure and pain." Each individual tries to maximize the total amount of pleasure while minimizing pain. By rationally ordering individual preferences, government could provide conditions for the achievement of the greatest happiness for the greatest number. According to the elder Mill, this order could be secured by a representative government, though the voting franchise would have to be limited to those who had demonstrated rationality in their private pursuits. James reasoned this would limit the electorate to middle class males.

John was a staunch supporter of his father's creed until about 1826 when he suffered a bout of severe depression. He attributed this condition to the failure in his education to attend to the emotive side of his personality. Turning to the works of poets like Wordsworth and Coleridge, he sought to correct this imbalance. He began as well to alter his view of human nature and politics by seeking to humanize utility theory and to broaden it. Perhaps not all pleasures are equally worthy of advance. Some are more conducive to the innate desire for self-improvement and society must support these efforts by guaranteeing individual expression. Only with such guarantees might society hope to benefit from the insights of the exceptional few.

In *System of Logic,* Mill explored the relation of the various sciences to each other. He advocated the study of human character (ethology as he called it) as a scholarly enterprise that would stand somewhere between the solid principles of human psychology and emerging laws of sociology as gleaned by French scholars like August Comte. He wrote on economics as well, exploring socialistic proposals as perhaps necessary safeguards against the excesses of the free market. Finally, he was one of the first and most ardent exponents of feminism; surely a result of his association with Harriet Taylor.

On Liberty and The Subjection of Women

Perhaps the work for which John Stuart Mill is best known is *On Liberty.* Published in 1859, this is an impassioned plea for social toleration of individual differences and free expression, but still grounded in utilitarian language. According to Mill, the greatest threat to advanced civilizations like his own lay in the tyranny of the majority, expressed through political and social intolerance. Majority rule was a fine principle of self-government. However, majorities had to be made to respect the beliefs and actions of a few, if only because the majority stood to gain by the contributions of the occasional genius. The selection included from Chapter II reviews the reasons Mill advances for freedom of thought and expression.

The Subjection of Women often reads like contemporary feminist literature. In this work, which Mill completed in 1861—three years after Harriet Taylor's death, but not published until 1869—Mill describes the plight of women within a social order they do not control. He argues that women must be granted equal status with males in the family, in the workplace, and in the political arena. It should be clear from reading the excerpts in this chapter why *The Subjection of Women* continues to inspire feminist writers to the present day.

Commentaries

In his essay, Clark Bouton argues that Mill's advocacy of liberty can only be understood in light of his progressive view of history. While liberty opens society to new possibilities, it also can destabilize. Thus, liberty is best attained only in those societies that have managed to guarantee a certain level of stability. Yet, while history is progressive, it does not proceed without fluctuation. While Mill believed the England of his day had attained the degree of stability that could sustain liberty, it was not inevitable that England would always maintain this position. In short, order is the necessary ground upon which liberty flourishes.

In her article, Mary Lyndon Shanley reviews propositions that some critics have advanced against Mill's feminism. While some critics believe Mill did not go far enough in advancing the cause of women, Shanley argues that such attacks fail to acknowledge the significant achievements of Mill's feminism, especially concerning his call for inculcating genuine friendship between the sexes in marriage.

Key Words

Androgynous. Having the characteristics of both sexes. Mill believed the socially ascribed characteristics of gender stifled the development of men and women alike. Equality and reciprocity in ideal marriages would lead to a blending of roles that enriched the lives of both sexes.

Coverture. Shelter. Refers to the protective legal status of women during marriage in the age in which Mill wrote.

Utilitarianism. Political theory associated with the works of Jeremy Bentham and James Mill in which the aim of government is to procure the "greatest good for the greatest number," where good is measured in terms of pleasure or happiness. While John Stuart Mill did not reject this theory, he sought to humanize and broaden it.

For Further Reading

Eisenach, E. 1981. *Two Worlds of Liberalism: Religion and Politics in Hobbes, Locke, and Mill.* Chicago: University of Chicago Press.

Halliday, R. J. 1976. *John Stuart Mill.* London: Allen & Unwin.

Mill, J. S. [1961] *The Essential Works of John Stuart Mill.* (Edited with an Introduction by M. Lerner.) New York: Bantam.

Mill, J.S. and Taylor, H. [1970.] *Essays on Sex Equality.* (Ed. with an Introductory Essay by A. S. Rossi.) Chicago: University of Chicago Press.

Robson, J. 1968. *The Improvement of Mankind: The Social and Political Thought of John Stuart Mill.* Toronto: University of Toronto Press.

Thompson, D. 1976. *John Stuart Mill and Representative Government.* Princeton, N.J.: Princeton University Press.

On Liberty

Chapter II
Of the Liberty of Thought and Discussion

The time, it is to be hoped, is gone by, when any defence would be necessary of the "liberty of the press" as one of the securities against corrupt and tyrannical government. No argument, we may suppose, can now be needed, against permitting a legislature or an executive, not identified in interest with the people, to prescribe opinions to them, and determine what doctrines or what arguments they shall be allowed to hear. This aspect of the question, besides, has been so often and so triumphantly enforced by preceding writers, that it needs not be specially insisted on in this place. Though the law of England, on the subject of the press, is as servile to this day as it was in the time of the Tudors, there is little danger of its being actually put in force against political discussion, except during some temporary panic, when fear of insurrection drives ministers and judges from their pro- priety;[1] and, speaking generally, it is not, in constitutional countries, to be apprehended, that the government, whether completely responsible to the people or not, will often attempt to control the expression of opinion, except when in doing so it makes itself the organ of the general intolerance of the public. Let us suppose, therefore, that the government is entirely at one with the people, and never thinks of exerting any power of coercion unless in agreement with what it conceives to be their voice. But I deny the right of the people to exercise such coercion, either by themselves or by their govern- ment. The power itself is illegitimate. The best government has no more title to it than the worst. It is as noxious, or more noxious, when exerted in

---

Excerpts from John Stuart Mill. 1961. *On Liberty.* In *Essential Works of John Stuart Mill.* (edited by Max Lerner.) New York: Bantam, pp. 17–26, 34–51. Reprinted with permission of Bantam Press.

1. These words had scarcely been written, when, as if to give them an emphatic contradiction, occurred the Government Press Prosecutions of 1858. That ill-judged interference with the liberty of public discussion has not, however, induced me to alter a single word in the text, nor has it at all weakened my conviction that, moments of panic excepted, the era of pains and penalties for political discussion has, in our own country, passed away. For, in the first place, the prosecutions were not persisted in; and, in the second, they were never, properly speaking, political prosecu- tions. The offence charged was not that of criticising institutions, or the acts or persons of rulers, but of circulating what was deemed an immoral doctrine, the lawfulness of Tyrannicide.

If the arguments of the present chapter are of any validity, there ought to exist the fullest liberty of professing and discussing, as a matter of ethical conviction, any doctrine, however immoral it may be considered. It would, therefore, be irrelevant and out of place to examine here, whether the doctrine of Tyrannicide deserves that title. I shall content myself with saying that the subject has been at all times one of the open questions of morals; that the act of a private citizen in striking down a criminal, who, by raising himself above the law, has placed himself beyond the reach of legal punishment or control, has been accounted by whole nations, and by some of the best and wisest of men, not a crime, but an act of exalted virtue; and that, right or wrong, it is not of the nature of assassination, but of civil war. As such, I hold that the instigation to it, in a specific case, may be a proper subject of punishment, but only if an overt act has followed, and at least a probable connection can be established between the act and the instigation. Even then, it is not a foreign government, but the very government assailed, which alone, in the exercise of self-defence, can legitimately punish attacks directed against its own existence.

accordance with public opinion, than when in opposition to it. If all mankind minus one were of one opinion, and only one person were of the contrary opinion, mankind would be no more justified in silencing that one person, than he, if he had the power, would be justified in silencing mankind. Were an opinion a personal possession of no value except to the owner; if to be obstructed in the enjoyment of it were simply a private injury, it would make some difference whether the injury was inflicted only on a few persons or on many. But the peculiar evil of silencing the expression of an opinion is, that it is robbing the human race; posterity as well as the existing generation; those who dissent from the opinion, still more than those who hold it. If the opinion is right, they are deprived of the opportunity of exchanging error for truth: if wrong, they lose, what is almost as great a benefit, the clearer perception and livelier impression of truth, produced by its collision with error.

It is necessary to consider separately these two hypotheses, each of which has a distinct branch of the argument corresponding to it. We can never be sure that the opinion we are endeavouring to stifle is a false opinion; and if we were sure, stifling it would be an evil still.

First: the opinion which it is attempted to suppress by authority may possibly be true. Those who desire to suppress it, of course deny its truth; but they are not infallible. They have no authority to decide the question for all mankind, and exclude every other person from the means of judging. To refuse a hearing to an opinion, because they are sure that it is false, is to assume that *their* certainty is the same thing as *absolute* certainty. All silencing of discussion is an assumption of infallibility. Its condemnation may be allowed to rest on this common argument, not the worse for being common.

Unfortunately for the good sense of mankind, the fact of their fallibility is far from carrying the weight in their practical judgment which is always allowed to it in theory; for while every one well knows himself to be fallible, few think it necessary to take any precautions against their own fallibility, or admit the supposition that any opinion, of which they feel very certain, may be one of the examples of the error to which they acknowledge themselves to be liable. Absolute princes, or others who are accustomed to unlimited deference, usually feel this complete confidence in their own opinions on nearly all subjects. People more happily situated, who sometimes hear their opinions disputed, and are not wholly unused to be set right when they are wrong, place the same unbounded reliance only on such of their opinions as are shared by all who surround them, or to whom they habitually defer; for in proportion to a man's want of confidence in his own solitary judgment, does he usually repose, with implicit trust, on the infallibility of "the world" in general. And the world, to each individual, means the part of it with which he comes in contact; his party, his sect, his church, his class of society; the man may be called, by comparison, almost liberal and large-minded to whom it means anything so comprehensive as his own country or his own age. Nor is his faith in this collective authority at all shaken by his being aware that other ages, countries, sects, churches, classes, and parties have thought, and even now think, the exact reverse. He devolves upon his own world the responsibility of being in the right against the dissentient worlds of other people; and it never troubles him that mere accident has decided which of these numerous worlds is the object of his reliance, and that the same causes which make him a Churchman in London, would have made him a Buddhist or a Confucian in Pekin. Yet it is as evident in itself, as any amount of argument can make it, that ages are no more infallible than individuals; every age having held many opinions which subsequent ages have deemed not only false but absurd; and it is as certain that many opinions now general will be rejected by future ages, as it is that many, once general, are rejected by the present.

The objection likely to be made to this argument would probably take some such form as the following. There is no greater assumption of infallibility in forbidding the propagation of error, than in any other thing which is done by public authority on its own judgment and responsibility. Judgment is given to men that they may use it. Because it may be used erroneously, are men to be told that they ought not to use it at all? To prohibit what they think pernicious, is not claiming exemption from error, but fulfilling the duty incumbent on them, although fallible, of acting on their conscientious conviction. If we were never to act on our opinions, because those opinions may be wrong, we should leave all our interests uncared for, and all our duties unperformed. An objection which applies to all conduct can be no valid objection to any conduct in particular. It is the duty of governments, and of individuals, to form the truest opinions they can; to form carefully, and never impose them upon others unless they are quite sure of being right. But when they are sure (such reasoners may say), it is not conscientiousness but cowardice to shrink from acting on their opinions, and allow doctrines which they honestly think dangerous to the welfare of mankind, either in this life or in another, to be scattered abroad without restraint, because other people, in less enlightened times, have persecuted opinions now believed to be true. Let us take care, it may be said, not to make the same mistake: but governments and nations have made mistakes in other things, which are not denied to be fit subjects for the exercise of authority: they have laid on bad taxes, made unjust wars. Ought we therefore to lay on no taxes, and, under whatever provocation, make no wars? Men and governments, must act to the best of their ability. There is no such thing as absolute certainty, but there is assurance sufficient for the purposes of human life. We may, and must, assume our opinion to be true for the guidance of our own conduct: and it is assuming no more when we forbid bad men to pervert society by the propagation of opinions which we regard as false and pernicious.

I answer, that it is assuming very much more. There is the greatest difference between presuming an opinion to be true, because, with every opportunity for contesting it, it has not been refuted, and assuming its truth for the purpose of not permitting its refutation. Complete liberty of contradicting and disproving our opinion is the very condition which justifies us in assuming its truth for purposes of action; and on no other terms can a being with human faculties have any rational assurance of being right.

When we consider either the history of opinion, or the ordinary conduct of human life, to what is it to be ascribed that the one and the other are no worse than they are? Not certainly to the inherent force of the human understanding; for, on any matter not self-evident, there are ninety-nine persons totally incapable of judging of it for one who is capable; and the capacity of the hundredth person is only comparative; for the majority of the eminent men of every past generation held many opinions now known to be erroneous, and did or approved numerous things which no one will now justify. Why is it, then, that there is on the whole a preponderance among mankind of rational opinions and rational conduct? If there really is this preponderance—which there must be unless human affairs are, and have always been, in an almost desperate state—it is owing to a quality of the human mind, the source of everything respectable in man either as an intellectual or as a moral being, namely, that his errors are corrigible. He is capable of rectifying his mistakes, by discussion and experience. Not by experience alone. There must be discussion, to show how experience is to be interpreted. Wrong opinions and practices gradually yield to fact and argument; but facts and arguments, to produce any effect on the mind, must be brought before it. Very few facts are able to tell their own story, without comments to bring out their meaning. The whole strength and value, then, of human judgment, depending on the one property, that it can be set right when it is wrong, reliance can be placed on it only when the means of setting it right are kept constantly at hand. In the case of any person whose judgment is really deserving of confidence, how has it become so? Because he has kept his mind open to criticism on his opinions and conduct. Because it has been his practice to listen to all that could be said against him; to profit by as much of it as was just, and expound to himself, and upon occasion to others, the fallacy of what was fallacious. Because he has felt, that the only way in which a human being can make some approach to knowing the whole of a subject, is by hearing what can be said about it by persons of every variety of opinion, and studying all modes in which it can be looked at by every character of mind. No wise man ever acquired his wisdom in any mode but this; nor is it in the nature of human intellect to become wise in any other manner. The steady habit of correcting and completing his own opinion by collating it with those of others, so far from causing doubt and hesitation in carrying it into practice, is the only stable foundation for a just reliance on it: for, being cognisant of all that can, at least obviously, be said against him, and having taken up his position against all gainsayers—knowing that he has sought for objections and difficulties, instead of avoiding them, and has shut out no light which can be thrown upon the subject from any quarter—he has a right to think his judgment better than that of any person, or any multitude, who have not gone through a similar process.

It is not too much to require that what the wisest of mankind, those who are best entitled to trust their own judgment, find necessary to warrant their relying on it, should be submitted to by that miscellaneous collection of a few wise and many foolish individuals, called the public. The most intolerant of churches, the Roman Catholic Church, even at the canonisation of a saint, admits, and listens patiently to, a "devil's advocate." The holiest of men, it appears, cannot be admitted to posthumous honours, until all that the devil could say against him is known and weighed. If even the Newtonian philosophy were not permitted to be questioned, mankind could not feel as complete assurance of its truth as they now do. The beliefs which we have most warrant for have no safeguard to rest on, but a standing invitation to the whole world to prove them unfounded. If the challenge is not accepted, or is accepted and the attempt fails, we are far enough from certainty still; but we have done the best that the existing state of human reason admits of;

we have neglected nothing that could give the truth a chance of reaching us: if the lists are kept open, we may hope that if there be a better truth, it will be found when the human mind is capable of receiving it; and in the meantime we may rely on having attained such approach to truth as is possible in our own day. This is the amount of certainty attainable by a fallible being, and this the sole way of attaining it.

Strange it is, that men should admit the validity of the arguments for free discussion, but object to their being "pushed to an extreme"; not seeing that unless the reasons are good for an extreme case, they are not good for any case. Strange that they should imagine that they are not assuming infallibility, when they acknowledge that there should be free discussion on all subjects which can possibly be *doubtful*, but think that some particular principle or doctrine should be forbidden to be questioned because it is so *certain*, that is, because *they are certain* that it is certain. To call any proposition certain, while there is any one who would deny its certainty if permitted, but who is not permitted, is to assume that we ourselves, and those who agree with us, are the judges of certainty, and judges without hearing the other side.

In the present age—which has been described as "destitute of faith, but terrified at scepticism"—in which people feel sure, not so much that their opinions are true, as that they should not know what to do without them —the claims of an opinion to be protected from public attack are rested not so much on its truth, as on its importance to society. There are, it is alleged, certain beliefs so useful, not to say indispensable, to well-being that it is as much the duty of governments to uphold those beliefs, as to protect any other of the interests of society. In a case of such necessity, and so directly in the line of their duty, something less than infallibility may, it is maintained, warrant, and even bind, governments to act on their own opinion, confirmed by the general opinion of mankind. It is also often argued, and still oftener thought, that none but bad men would desire to weaken these salutary beliefs; and there can be nothing wrong, it is thought, in restraining bad men, and prohibiting what only such men would wish to practise. This mode of thinking makes the justification of restraints on discussion not a question of the truth of doctrines, but of their usefulness; and flatters itself by that means to escape the responsibility of claiming to be an infallible judge of opinions. But those who thus satisfy themselves, do not perceive that the assumption of infallibility is merely shifted from one point to another. The usefulness of an opinion is itself matter of opinion: as disputable, as open to discussion, and requiring discussion as much as the opinion itself. There is the same need of an infallible judge of opinions to decide an opinion to be noxious, as to decide it to be false, unless the opinion condemned has full opportunity of defending itself. And it will not do to say that the heretic may be allowed to maintain the utility or harmlessness of his opinion, though forbidden to maintain its truth. The truth of an opinion is part of its utility. If we would know whether or not it is desirable that a proposition should be believed, is it possible to exclude the consideration of whether or not it is true? In the opinion, not of bad men, but of the best men, no belief which is contrary to truth can be really useful: and can you prevent such men from urging that plea, when they are charged with culpability for denying some doctrine which they are told is useful, but which they believe to be false? Those who are on the side of received opinions never fail to take all possible advantage of this plea: you do not find *them* handling the question of utility as if it could be completely abstracted from that of truth: on the contrary, it is, above all, because their doctrine is "the truth," that the knowledge or the belief of it is held to be so indispensable. There can be no fair discussion of the question of usefulness when an argument so vital may be employed on one side, but not on the other. And in point of fact, when law or public feeling do not permit the truth of an opinion to be disputed, they are just as little tolerant of a denial of its usefulness. The utmost they allow is an extenuation of its absolute necessity, or of the positive guilt of rejecting it.

In order more fully to illustrate the mischief of denying a hearing to opinions because we, in our own judgment, have condemned them, it will be desirable to fix down the discussion to a concrete case; and I choose, by preference, the cases which are least favourable to me—in which the argument against freedom of opinion, both on the score of truth and on that of utility, is considered the strongest. Let the opinions impugned be the belief in a God and in a future state, or any of the commonly received doctrines of morality. To fight the battle on such ground gives a great advantage to an unfair antagonist; since he will be sure to say (and many who have no desire to be unfair will say it internally), Are these the doctrines which you do not deem sufficiently certain to be taken under the protection of law? Is the belief in a God one of the opinions to feel sure of which you hold to be assuming infallibility? But I must be permitted to observe, that it is not the feeling sure of a doctrine (be it what it may) which I call an assumption of infallibility. It is the undertaking to decide that question *for others*, without allowing them to hear what can be said on the contrary side. And I denounce and reprobate this pretension not the less, if put forth on the side of my most solemn convictions. However positive any one's persuasion may be, not only of the falsity but of the pernicious consequences—not only of the pernicious consequences, but (to adopt expressions which I altogether condemn) the immorality and impiety of an opinion; yet if, in pursuance of that private judgment, though backed by the public judgment of his country or his cotemporaries, he prevents the opinion from being heard in its defence, he assumes infallibility. And so far from the assumption being less objectionable or less dangerous because the opinion is called immoral or impious, this is the case of all others in which it is most fatal. These are exactly the occasions on which the men of one generation commit those dreadful mistakes which excite the astonishment and horror of posterity. It is among such that we find the instances memorable in history, when the arm of the law has been employed to root out the best men and the noblest doctrines; with deplorable success as to the men, though some of the doctrines have survived to be (as if in mockery) invoked in defence of similar conduct towards those who dissent from *them*, or from their received interpretation.

Mankind can hardly be too often reminded, that there was once a man named Socrates, between whom and the legal authorities and public opinion of his time there took place a memorable collision. Born in an age and country abounding in individual greatness, this man has been handed down to us by those who best knew both him and the age, as the most virtuous man in it; while *we* know him as the head and prototype of all subsequent teachers of virtue, the source equally of the lofty inspiration of Plato and the judicious utilitarianism of Aristotle, *"i maestri di color che sanno,"* [the masters of those who know] the two headsprings of ethical as of all other philosophy. This acknowledged master of all the eminent thinkers who have since lived—whose fame, still growing after more than two thousand years, all but outweighs the whole remainder of the names which make his native city illustrious—was put to death by his countrymen, after a judicial conviction, for impiety and immorality. Impiety, in denying the gods recognised by the State; indeed his accuser asserted (see the "Apologia") that he believed in no gods at all. Immorality, in being, by his doctrines and instructions, a "corruptor of youth." Of these charges the tribunal, there is every ground for believing, honestly found him guilty, and condemned the man who probably of all then born had deserved best of mankind to be put to death as a criminal.

To pass from this to the only other instance of judicial iniquity, the mention of which, after the condemnation of Socrates, would not be an anti-climax: the event which took place on Calvary rather more than eighteen hundred years ago. The man who left on the memory of those who witnessed his life and conversation such an impression of his moral grandeur that eighteen subsequent centuries have done homage to him as the Almighty in person, was ignominiously put to death, as what? As a blasphemer. Men did not merely mistake their benefactor; they mistook him for the exact contrary of what he was, and treated him as that prodigy of impiety which they themselves are now held to be for their treatment of him. The feelings with which mankind now regard these lamentable transactions, especially the later of the two, render them extremely unjust in their judgment of the unhappy actors. These were, to all appearance, not bad men—not worse than men commonly are, but rather the contrary; men who possessed in a full, or somewhat more than a full measure, the religious, moral and patriotic feelings of their time and people: the very kind of men who, in all times, our own included, have every chance of passing through life blameless and respected. The high-priest who rent his garments when the words were pronounced, which, according to all the ideas of his country, constituted the blackest guilt, was in all probability quite as sincere in his horror and indignation at the generality of respectable and pious men now are in the religious and moral sentiments they profess; and most of those who now shudder as his conduct, if they had lived in his time, and been born Jews, would have acted precisely as he did. Orthodox Christians who are tempted to think that those who stoned to death the first martyrs must have been worse men than they themselves are, ought to remember that one of those persecutors was Saint Paul. . . .

Let us now pass to the second division of the argument, and dismissing the supposition that any of the received opinions may be false, let us assume them to be true, and examine into the worth of the manner in which they are likely to be held, when their truth is not freely and openly canvassed. However unwillingly a person who has a strong opinion may admit the possibility that his opinion may be false, he ought to be moved by the consideration that, however true it may be, if it is not fully, frequently, and fearlessly discussed, it will be held as a dead dogma, not a living truth.

There is a class of persons (happily not quite so numerous as formerly) who think it enough if a person assents undoubtingly to what they think true, though he has no knowledge whatever of the grounds of the opinion, and could not make a tenable defence of it against the most superficial objections. Such persons, if they can once get their creed taught from authority, naturally think that no good, and some harm, comes of its being allowed to be questioned. Where their influence prevails, they make it nearly impossible for the received opinion to be rejected wisely and considerately, though it may still be rejected rashly and ignorantly; for to shut out discussion entirely is seldom possible, and when it once gets in, beliefs not grounded on conviction are apt to give way before the slightest semblance of an argument. Waiving, however, this possibility—assuming that the true opinion abides in the mind, but abides as a prejudice, a belief independent of, and proof against, argument—this is not the way in which truth ought to be held by a rational being. This is not knowing the truth. Truth, thus held, is but one superstition the more, accidentally clinging to the words which enunciate a truth.

If the intellect and judgment of mankind ought to be cultivated, a thing which Protestants at least do not deny, on what can these faculties be more appropriately exercised by any one, than on the things which concern him so much that it is considered necessary for him to hold opinions on them? If the cultivation of the understanding consists in one thing more than in another, it is surely in learning the grounds of one's own opinions. Whatever people believe, on subjects on which it is of the first importance to believe rightly, they ought to be able to defend against at least the common objections. But, some one may say, "Let them be *taught* the grounds of their opinions. It does not follow that opinions must be merely parroted because they are never heard controverted. Persons who learn geometry do not simply commit the theorems to memory, but understand and learn likewise the demonstrations; and it would be absurd to say that they remain ignorant of the grounds of geometrical truths, because they never hear any one deny, and attempt to disprove them." Undoubtedly: and such teaching suffices on a subject like mathematics, where there is nothing at all to be said on the wrong side of the question. The peculiarity of the evidence of mathematical truths is that all the argument is on one side. There are no objections, and no answers to objections. But on every subject on which difference of opinion is possible, the truth depends on a balance to be struck between two sets of conflicting reasons. Even in natural philosophy, there is always some other explanation possible of the same facts; some geocentric theory instead of heliocentric, some phlogiston instead of oxygen, and it has to be shown why that other theory cannot be the true one: and until this is shown, and until we know how it is shown, we do not understand the grounds of our opinion. But when we turn to subjects infinitely more complicated, to morals, religion, politics, social relations, and the business of life, three-fourths of the arguments for every disputed opinion consist in dispelling the appearances which favour some opinion different from it. The greatest orator, save one, of antiquity, has left it on record that he always studied his adversary's case with as great, if not still greater, intensity than even his own. What Cicero practised as the means of forensic success requires to be imitated by all who study any subject in order to arrive at the truth. He who knows only his own side of the case, knows little of that. His reasons may be good, and no one may have been able to refute them. But if he is equally unable to refute the reasons on the opposite side; if he does not so much as know what they are, he has no ground for preferring either opinion. The rational position for him would be suspension of judgment, and unless he contents himself with that, he is either led by authority, or adopts, like the generality of the world, the side to which he feels most inclination. Nor is it enough that he should hear the arguments of adversaries from his own teachers, presented as they state them, and accompanied by what they offer as refutations. That is not the way to do justice to the arguments, or bring them into real contact with his own mind. He must be able to hear them from persons who actually believe them; who defend them in earnest, and do their very utmost for them. He must know them in their most plausible and persuasive form; he must feel the whole force of the difficulty which the true view of the subject has to encounter and dispose of; else he will never really possess himself of the portion of truth which meets and removes that difficulty. Ninety-nine in a hundred of what are called educated men are in this condition; even of those who can argue fluently for their opinions. Their conclusion may be true, but it might be false for anything they know: they have never thrown themselves into the mental position of those who think differently from them, and considered what such persons may have to say; and consequently they do not, in any proper sense of the word, know the doctrine which they themselves profess. They do not know those parts of it which explain and justify the remainder; the considerations which show that a fact which seemingly conflicts with another is reconcilable with it, or that, of two apparently strong reasons, one and not the other ought to be preferred. All that part of the truth which turns the scale, and decides the judgment of a completely informed mind, they are strangers to; nor is it ever really known, but to those who have attended equally and impartially to both sides, and endeavoured to see the reasons of both in the strongest light. So essential is this discipline to a real understanding of moral and human subjects, that if opponents of all important truths do not exist, it is indispensible to imagine them, and supply them with the strongest arguments which the most skilful devil's advocate can conjure up.

To abate the force of these considerations, an enemy of free discussion may be supposed to say, that there is no necessity for mankind in general to know and understand all that can be said against or for their opinions by philosophers and theologians. That it is not needful for common men to be able to expose all the misstatements or fallacies of an ingenious opponent. That it is enough if there is always somebody capable of answering them, so that nothing likely to mislead uninstructed persons remains unrefuted. That simple minds, having been taught the obvious grounds of the truths inculcated on them, may trust to authority for the rest, and being aware that they have neither knowledge nor talent to resolve every difficulty which can be raised, may repose in the assurance that all those which have been raised have been or can be answered, by those who are specially trained to the task.

Conceding to this view of the subject the utmost that can be claimed for it by those most easily satisfied with the amount of understanding of truth which ought to accompany the belief of it; even so, the argument for free discussion is no way weakened. For even this doctrine acknowledges that mankind ought to have a rational assurance that all objections have been satisfactorily answered; and how are they to be answered if that which requires to be answered is not spoken? or how can the answers be known to be satisfactory, if the objectors have no opportunity of showing that it is unsatisfactory? If not the public, at least the philosophers and theologians who are to resolve the difficulties, must make themselves familiar with those difficulties in their most puzzling form; and this cannot be accomplished unless they are freely stated, and placed in the most advantageous light which they admit of. The Catholic Church has its own way of dealing with this embarrassing problem. It makes a broad separation between those who can be permitted to receive its doctrines on conviction, and those who must accept them on trust. Neither, indeed, are allowed any choice as to what they will accept; but the clergy, such at least as can be fully confided in, may admissibly and meritoriously make themselves acquainted with the arguments of opponents, in order to answer them, and may, therefore, read heretical books; the laity, not unless by special permission, hard to be obtained. This discipline recognises a knowledge of the enemy's case as beneficial to the teachers, but finds means, consistent with this, of denying it to the rest of the world: thus giving to the *élite* more mental culture, though not more mental freedom, than it allows to the mass. By this device it succeeds in obtaining the kind of mental superiority which its purposes require; for though culture without freedom never made a large and liberal mind, it can make a clever *nisi prius* advocate of a cause. But in countries professing Protestantism, this resource is denied; since Protestants hold, at least in theory, that the responsibility for the choice of a religion must be borne by each for himself, and cannot be thrown off upon teachers. Besides, in the present state of the world, it is practically impossible that writings which are read by the instructed can be kept from the uninstructed. If the teachers of mankind are to be cognisant of all that they ought to know, everything must be free to be written and published without restraint.

If, however, the mischievous operation of the absence of free discussion, when the received opinions are true, were confined to leaving men ignorant of the grounds of those opinions, it might be thought that this, if an intellectual, is no moral evil, and does not affect the worth of the opinions, regarded in their influence on the character. The fact, however, is, that not only the grounds of the opinion are forgotten in the absence of discussion, but too often the meaning of the opinion itself. The words which convey it cease to suggest ideas, or suggest only a small portion of those they were originally employed to communicate. Instead of a vivid conception and a living belief there remain only a few phrases retained by rote; or, if any part, the shell and husk only of the meaning is retained, the finer essence being lost. The great chapter in human history which this fact occupies and fills, cannot be too earnestly studied and meditated on.

It is illustrated in the experience of almost all ethical doctrines and religious creeds. They are all full of meaning and vitality to those who originate them, and to the direct disciples of the originators. Their meaning continues to be felt in undiminished strength, and is perhaps brought out into even fuller consciousness, so long as the struggle lasts to give the doctrine or creed an ascendancy over other creeds. At last it either prevails, and becomes the general opinion, or its progress stops; it keeps possession of the ground it has gained, but ceases to spread further. When either of these results has become apparent, controversy on the subject flags, and gradually dies away. The doctrine has taken its place, if not as a received opinion, as one of the admitted sects or divisions of opinion: those who hold it have generally inherited, not adopted it; and conversion from one of these doctrines to another, being now an exceptional fact, occupies little place in the thoughts of their professors. Instead of being, as at first, constantly on the alert either to defend themselves against the world, or to bring the world over to them, they have subsided into acquiescence, and neither listen, when they can help it, to arguments against their creed, nor trouble dissentients (if there be such) with arguments in its favour. From this time may usually be dated the decline in the living power of the doctrine. We often hear the teachers of all creeds lamenting the difficulty of keeping up in the minds of believers a lively apprehension of the truth which they nominally recognise, so that it may penetrate the feelings, and acquire a real mastery over the conduct. No such difficulty is complained of while the creed is still fighting for its existence: even the weaker combatants then know and feel what they are fighting for, and the difference between it and other doctrines; and in that period of every creed's existence, not a few persons may be found, who have realised its fundamental principles in all the forms of thought, have weighed and considered them in all their important bearings, and have experienced the full effect on the character which belief in that creed ought to produce in a mind thoroughly imbued with it. But when it has come to be an hereditary creed, and to be received passively, not actively—when the mind is no longer compelled, in the same degree as at first, to exercise its vital powers on the questions which its belief presents to it, there is a progressive tendency to forget all of the belief except the formularies, or to give it a dull and torpid assent, as if accepting it on trust dispensed with the necessity of realising it in consciousness, or testing it by personal experience, until it almost ceases to connect itself at all with the inner life of the human being. Then are seen the cases, so frequent in this age of the world as almost to form the majority, in which the creed remains as it were outside the mind, incrusting and petrifying it against all other influences addressed to the higher parts of our nature; manifesting its power by not suffering any fresh and living conviction to get in, but itself doing nothing for the mind or heart, except standing sentinel over them to keep them vacant. . . .

It still remains to speak of one of the principal causes which make diversity of opinion advantageous, and will continue to do so until mankind shall have entered a stage of intellectual advancement which at present seems at an incalculable distance. We have hitherto considered only two possibilities: that the received opinion may be false, and some other opinion, consequently, true; or that the received opinion being true, a conflict with the opposite error is essential to a clear apprehension and deep feeling of its truth. But there is a commoner case than either of these; when the conflicting doctrines, instead of being one true and the other false, share the truth between them; and the nonconforming opinion is needed to supply the remainder of the truth, of which the received doctrine embodies only a part. Popular opinions, on subjects not palpable to sense, are often true, but seldom or never the whole truth. They are a part of the truth; sometimes a greater, sometimes a smaller part, but exaggerated, distorted, and disjointed from the truths by which they ought to be accompanied and limited. Heretical opinions, on the other hand, are generally some of these suppressed and neglected truths, bursting the bonds which kept them down, and either seeking reconciliation with the truth contained in the common opinion, or fronting it as enemies, and setting themselves up, with similar exclusiveness, as the whole truth. The latter case is hitherto the most frequent, as, in the human mind, one-sidedness has always been the rule, and many-sidedness the exception. Hence, even in revolutions of opinion, one part of the truth usually sets while another rises. Even progress, which ought to superadd, for the most part only substitutes, one partial and incomplete truth for another; improvement consisting chiefly in this, that the new fragment of truth is more wanted, more adapted to the needs of the time, than that which it displaces. Such being the partial character of prevailing opinions, even when resting on a true foundation, every opinion which embodies somewhat of the portion of truth which the common opinion omits, ought to be considered precious, with whatever amount of error and confusion that truth may be blended. No sober judge of human affairs will feel bound to be indignant because those who force on our notice truths which we should otherwise have overlooked, overlook some of those which we see. Rather, he will think that so long as popular truth is one-sided, it is more desirable than otherwise that unpopular truth should have one-sided assertors too; such being usually the most energetic, and the most likely to compel reluctant attention to the fragment of wisdom which they proclaim as if it were the whole.

Thus, in the eighteenth century, when nearly all the instructed, and all those of the uninstructed who were led by them, were lost in admiration of what is called civilisation, and of the marvels of modern science, literature, and philosophy, and while greatly overrating the amount of unlikeness between the men of modern and those of ancient times, indulged the belief that the whole of the difference was in their own favour, with what a salutary shock did the paradoxes of Rousseau explode like bombshells in the midst, dislocating the compact mass of one-sided opinion, and forcing its elements to recombine in a better form and with additional ingredients. Not that the current opinions were on the whole farther from the truth than Rousseau's were; on the contrary, they were nearer to it; they contained more of positive truth, and very much less of error. Nevertheless there lay in Rousseau's doctrine, and has floated down the stream of opinion along with it, a considerable amount of exactly those truths which the popular opinion wanted; and these are the deposit which was left behind when the flood subsided. The superior worth of simplicity of life, the enervating and demoralising effect of the trammels and hypocrisies of artificial society, are ideas which have never been entirely absent from cultivated minds since Rousseau wrote; and they will in time produce their due effect, though at present needing to be asserted as much as ever, and to be asserted by deeds, for words, on this subject, have nearly exhausted their power.

In politics, again, it is almost a commonplace, that a party of order or stability, and a party of progress or reform, are both necessary elements of a healthy state of political life; until the one or the other shall have so enlarged its mental grasp as to be a party equally of order and of progress, knowing and distinguishing what is fit to be preserved from what ought to be swept away. Each of these modes of thinking derives its utility from the deficiencies of the other; but it is in a great measure the opposition of the other that keeps each within the limits of reason and sanity. Unless opinions favourable to democracy and to aristocracy, to property and to equality, to co-operation and to competition, to luxury and to abstinence, to sociality and individuality, to liberty and discipline, and all the other standing antagonisms of practical life, are expressed with equal freedom, and enforced and defended with equal talent and energy, there is no chance of both elements obtaining their due; one scale is sure to go up, and the other down. Truth, in the great practical concerns of life, is so much a question of the reconciling and combining of opposites, that very few have minds sufficiently capacious and impartial to make the adjustment with an approach to correctness, and it has to be made by the rough process of a struggle between combatants fighting under hostile banners. On any of the great open questions just enumerated, if either of the two opinions has a better claim than the other, not merely to be tolerated, but to be encouraged and countenanced, it is the one which happens at the particular time and place to be in a minority. That is the opinion which, for the time being, represents the neglected interests, the side of human well-being which is in danger of obtaining less than its share. I am aware that there is not, in this country, any intolerance of differences of opinion on most of these topics. They are adduced to show, by admitted and multiplied examples, the universality of the fact, that only through diversity of opinion is there, in the existing state of human intellect, a chance of fair play to all sides of the truth. When there are persons to be found who form an exception to the apparent unanimity of the world on any subject, even if the world is in the right, it is always probable that dissentients have something worth hearing to say for themselves, and that truth would lose something by their silence. . . .

I do not pretend that the most unlimited use of the freedom of enunciating all possible opinions would put an end to the evils of religious or philosophical sectarianism. Every truth which men of narrow capacity are in earnest about, is sure to be asserted, inculcated, and in many ways even acted on, as if no other truth existed in the world, or at all events none that could limit or qualify the first. I acknowledge that the tendency of all opinions to become sectarian is not cured by the freest discussion, but is often heightened and exacerbated thereby; the truth which ought to have been, but was not, seen, being rejected all the more violently because proclaimed by persons regarded as opponents. But it is not on the impassioned partisan, it is on the calmer and more disinterested bystander, that this collision of opinions works its salutary effect. Not the violent conflict between parts of the truth, but the quiet suppression of half of it, is the formidable evil; there is always hope when people are forced to listen to both sides; it is when they attend only to one that errors harden into prejudices, and truth itself ceases to have the effect of truth, by being exaggerated into falsehood. And since there are few mental attributes more rare than that judicial faculty which can sit in intelligent judgment between two sides of a question, of which only one is represented by an advocate before it, truth has no chance but in proportion as every side of it, every opinion which embodies any fraction of the truth, not only finds advocates, but is so advocated as to be listened to.

We have now recognised the necessity to the mental well-being of man-kind (on which all their other well-being depends) of freedom of opinion, and freedom of the expression of opinion, on four distinct grounds; which we will now briefly recapitulate.

First, if any opinion is compelled to silence, that opinion may, for aught we can certainly know, be true. To deny this is to assume our own infallibility.

Secondly, though the silenced opinion be an error, it may, and very com-monly does, contain a portion of truth; and since the general or prevailing opinion on any subject is rarely or never the whole truth, it is only by the collision of adverse opinions that the remainder of the truth has any chance of being supplied.

Thirdly, even if the received opinion be not only true, but the whole truth; unless it is suffered to be, and actually is, vigorously and earnestly con-tested, it will, by most of those who receive it, be held in the manner of a prejudice, with little comprehension or feeling of its rational grounds. And not only this, but, fourthly, the meaning of the doctrine itself will be in danger of being lost, or enfeebled, and deprived of its vital effect on the char-acter and conduct; the dogma becoming a mere formal profession, ineffica-cious for good, but cumbering the ground, and preventing the growth of any real and heartfelt conviction, from reason or personal experience. . . .

The Subjection of Women

1

The object of this Essay is to explain as clearly as I am able, the grounds of an opinion which I have held from the very earliest period when I had formed any opinions at all on social or political matters, and which, instead of being weakened or modified, has been constantly growing stronger by the progress of reflection and the experience of life: That the principle which regulates the existing social relations between the two sexes—the legal subordination of one sex to the other—is wrong in itself, and now one of the chief hindrances to human improvement; and that it ought to be replaced by a principle of perfect equality, admitting no power or privilege on the one side, nor disability on the other.

The very words necessary to express the task I have undertaken, show how arduous it is. But it would be a mistake to suppose that the difficulty of the case must lie in the insufficiency or obscurity of the grounds of reason on which my conviction rests. The difficulty is that which exists in all cases in which there is a mass of feeling to be contended against. So long as an opinion is strongly rooted in the feelings, it gains rather than loses in stability by having a preponderating weight of argument against it. For if it were accepted as a result of argument, the refutation of the argument might shake the solidity of the conviction; but when it rests solely on feeling, the worse it fares in argumentative contest, the more persuaded its adherents are that their feeling must have some deeper ground, which the arguments do not reach; and while the feeling remains, it is always throwing up fresh intrenchments of argument to repair any breach made in the old. And there are so many causes tending to make the feelings connected with this subject the most intense and most deeply-rooted of all those which gather round and protect old institutions and customs, that we need not wonder to find them as yet less undermined and loosened than any of the rest by the progress of the great modern spiritual and social transition; nor suppose that the barbarisms to which men cling longest must be less barbarisms than those which they earlier shake off. . . .

The generality of a practice is in some cases a strong presumption that it is, or at all events once was, conducive to laudable ends. This is the case, when the practice was first adopted, or afterwards kept up, as a means to such ends, and was grounded on experience of the mode in which they could be most effectually attained. If the authority of men over women, when first established, had been the result of a conscientious comparison between different modes of constituting the government of society; if, after trying various other modes of social organization—the government of women over

Excerpts from John Stuart Mill. 1970. *The Subjection of Women.* In John Stuart Mill and Harriet Taylor Mill's *Essays on Sex Equality,* (edited by Alice Rossi) Chicago: University of Chicago Press, pp. 125–126, 129–131, 155–161, 181–185. Reprinted with permission of the University of Chicago Press.

men, equality between the two, and such mixed and divided modes of government as might be invented—it had been decided, on the testimony of experience, that the mode in which women are wholly under the rule of men, having no share at all in public concerns, and each in private being under the legal obligation of obedience to the man with whom she has associated her destiny, was the arrangement most conducive to the happiness and well being of both; its general adoption might then be fairly thought to be some evidence that, at the time when it was adopted, it was the best: though even then the considerations which recommended it may, like so many other primeval social facts of the greatest importance, have subsequently, in the course of ages, ceased to exist. But the state of the case is in every respect the reverse of this. In the first place, the opinion in favour of the present system, which entirely subordinates the weaker sex to the stronger, rests upon theory only; for there never has been trial made of any other: so that experience, in the sense in which it is vulgarly opposed to theory, cannot be pretended to have pronounced any verdict. And in the second place, the adoption of this system of inequality never was the result of deliberation, or forethought, or any social ideas, or any notion whatever of what conduced to the benefit of humanity or the good order of society. It arose simply from the fact that from the very earliest twilight of human society, every woman (owing to the value attached to her by men, combined with her inferiority in muscular strength) was found in a state of bondage to some man. Laws and systems of polity always begin by recognising the relations they find already existing between individuals. They convert what was a mere physical fact into a legal right, give it the sanction of society, and principally aim at the substitution of public and organized means of asserting and protecting these rights, instead of the irregular and lawless conflict of physical strength. Those who had already been compelled to obedience became in this manner legally bound to it. Slavery, from being a mere affair of force between the master and the slave, became regularized and a matter of compact among the masters, who, binding themselves to one another for common protection, guaranteed by their collective strength the private possessions of each, including his slaves. In early times, the great majority of the male sex were slaves, as well as the whole of the female. And many ages elapsed, some of them ages of high cultivation, before any thinker was bold enough to question the rightfulness, and the absolute social necessity, either of the one slavery or of the other. By degrees such thinkers did arise: and (the general progress of society assisting) the slavery of the male sex has, in all the countries of Christian Europe at least (though, in one of them, only within the last few years) been at length abolished, and that of the female sex has been gradually changed into a milder form of dependence. But this dependence, as it exists at present, is not an original institution, taking a fresh start from considerations of justice and social expediency—it is the primitive state of slavery lasting on, through successive mitigations and modifications occasioned by the same causes which have softened the general manners, and brought all human relations more under the control of justice and the influence of humanity. It has not lost the taint of its brutal origin. No presumption in its favour, therefore, can be drawn from the fact of its existence. The only such presumption which it could be supposed to have, must be grounded on its having lasted till now, when so many other things which came down from the same odious source have been done away with. And this, indeed, is what makes it strange to ordinary ears, to hear it asserted that the inequality of rights between men and women has no other source than the law of the strongest. . . .

The general opinion of men is supposed to be, that the natural vocation of a woman is that of a wife and mother. I say, is supposed to be, because, judging from acts—from the whole of the present constitution of society—one might infer that their opinion was the direct contrary. They might be supposed to think that the alleged natural vocation of women was of all things the most repugnant to their nature; insomuch that if they are free do do anything else—if any other means of living, or occupation of their time and faculties, is open, which has any chance of appearing desirable to them —there will not be enough of them who will be willing to accept the condition said to be natural to them. If this is the real opinion of men in general, it would be well that it should be spoken out. I should like to hear somebody openly enunciating the doctrine (it is already implied in much that is written on the subject)—"It is necessary to society that women should marry and produce children. They will not do so unless they are compelled. Therefore it is necessary to compel them." The merits of the case would then be clearly defined. It would be exactly that of the slaveholders of South Carolina and Louisiana. "It is necessary that cotton and sugar should be grown. White men cannot produce them. Negroes will not, for any wages which we choose to give. *Ergo* they must be compelled." An illustration still closer to the point is that of impressment. Sailors must absolutely be had to defend the country. It often happens that they will not voluntarily enlist. Therefore there must be the power of forcing them. How often has this logic been used! and, but for one flaw in it, without doubt it would have been successful up to this day. But it is open to the retort—First pay the sailors the honest value of their labour. When you have made it as well worth their while to serve you, as to work for other employers, you will have no more difficulty than others have in obtaining their services. To this there is no logical answer except "I will not": and as people are now not only ashamed, but are not desirous, to rob the labourer of his hire, impressment is no longer advocated. Those who attempt to force women into marriage by closing all other doors against them, lay themselves open to a similar retort. If they mean what they say, their opinion must evidently be, that men do not render the married condition so desirable to women, as to induce them to accept it for its own recommendations. It is not a sign of one's thinking the boon one offers very attractive, when one allows only Hobson's choice, "that or none." And here, I believe, is the clue to the feelings of those men, who have a real antipathy to the equal freedom of women. I believe they are afraid, not lest women should be unwilling to marry, for I do not think that any one in reality has that apprehension; but lest they should insist that marriage should be on equal conditions; lest all women of spirit and capacity should prefer doing almost anything else, not in their own eyes degrading, rather than marry, when marrying is giving themselves a master, and a master too of all their earthly possessions. And truly, if this consequence were necessarily incident to marriage, I think that the apprehension would be very well founded. I agree in thinking it probable that few women, capable of anything else, would, unless under an irresistible *entrainement,* rendering them for the time insensible to anything but itself, choose such a lot, when any other means were open to them of filling a conventionally honourable place in life: and if men are determined that the law of marriage shall be a law of despotism, they are quite right, in point of mere policy, in leaving to women only Hobson's choice. But, in that case, all that has been done in the modern world to relax the chain on the minds of women, has been a mistake. They never should have been allowed to receive a literary education. Women who read, much more women who write, are, in the existing constitution of things, a contradiction and a disturbing element: and it was wrong to bring women up with any acquirements but those of an odalisque, or of a domestic servant.

2

It will be well to commence the detailed discussion of the subject by the particular branch of it to which the course of our observations has led us: the conditions which the laws of this and all other countries annex to the marriage contract. Marriage being the destination appointed by society for women, the prospect they are brought up to, and the object which it is intended should be sought by all of them, except those who are too little attractive to be chosen by any man as his companion; one might have supposed that everything would have been done to make this condition as eligible to them as possible, that they might have no cause to regret being denied the option of any other. Society, however, both in this, and, at first, in all other cases, has preferred to attain its object by foul rather than fair means: but this is the only case in which it has substantially persisted in them even to the present day. Originally women were taken by force, or regularly sold by their father to the husband. Until a late period in European history, the father had the power to dispose of his daughter in marriage at his own will and pleasure, without any regard to hers. The Church, indeed, was so far faithful to a better morality as to require a formal "yes" from the woman at the marriage ceremony; but there was nothing to shew that the consent was other than compulsory; and it was practically impossible for the girl to refuse compliance if the father persevered, except perhaps when she might obtain the protection of religion by a determined resolution to take monastic vows. After marriage, the man had anciently (but this was anterior to Christianity) the power of life and death over his wife. She could invoke no law against him; he was her sole tribunal and law. For a long time he could repudiate her, but she had no corresponding power in regard to him. By the old laws of England, the husband was called the *lord* of the wife; he was literally regarded as her sovereign, inasmuch that the murder of a man by his wife was called treason (*petty* as distinguished from *high* treason), and was more cruelly avenged than was usually the case with high treason, for the penalty was burning to death. Because the various enormities have fallen into disuse (for most of them were never formally abolished, or not until they had long ceased to be practised) men suppose that all is now as it should be in regard to the marriage contract; and we are continually told that civilization and Christianity have restored to the woman her just rights. Meanwhile the wife is the actual bond-servant of her husband: no less so, as far as legal obligation goes, than slaves commonly so called. She vows a lifelong obedience to him at the altar, and is held to it all through her life by law. Casuists may say that the obligation of obedience stops short of participation in crime, but it certainly extends to everything else. She can do no act whatever but by his permission, at least tacit. She can acquire no property but for him; the instant it becomes hers, even if by inheritance, it becomes *ipso facto* his. In this respect the wife's position under the common law of England is worse than that of slaves in the laws of many countries: by the Roman law, for example, a slave might have his peculium, which to a certain extent the law guaranteed to him for his exclusive use. The higher classes in this country have given an analogous advantage to their women, through special contracts setting aside the law, by conditions of pin-money, etc.: since parental feeling being stronger with fathers than the class feeling of their own sex, a father generally prefers his own daughter to a son-in-law who is a stranger to him. By means of settlements, the rich usually contrive to withdraw the whole or part of the inherited property of the wife from the absolute control of the husband: but they do not succeed in keeping it under her own control; the utmost they can do only prevents the husband from squandering it, at the same time debarring the rightful owner from its use. The property itself is out of the reach of both; and as to the income derived from it, the form of settlement most favourable to the wife (that called "to her separate use") only precludes the husband from receiving it instead of her: it must pass through her hands, but if he takes it from her by personal violence as soon as she receives it, he can neither be punished, nor compelled to restitution. This is the amount of the protection which, under the laws of this country, the most powerful nobleman can give to his own daughter as respects her husband. In the immense majority of cases there is no settlement: and the absorption of all rights, all property, as well as all freedom of action, is complete. The two are called "one person in law," for the purpose of inferring that whatever is hers is his, but the parallel inference is never drawn that whatever is his is hers; the maxim is not applied against the man, except to make him responsible to third parties for her acts, as a master is for the acts of his slaves or of his cattle. I am far from pretending that wives are in general no better treated than slaves; but no slave is a slave to the same lengths, and in so full a sense of the word, as a wife is. Hardly any slave, except one immediately attached to the master's person, is a slave at all hours and all minutes; in general he has, like a soldier, his fixed task, and when it is done, or when he is off duty, he disposes, within certain limits, of his own time, and has a family life into which the master rarely intrudes. "Uncle Tom" under his first master had his own life in his "cabin," almost as much as any man whose work takes him away from home, is able to have in his own family. But it cannot be so with the wife. Above all, a female slave has (in Christian countries) an admitted right, and is considered under a moral obligation, to refuse to her master the last familiarity. Not so the wife: however brutal a tyrant she may unfortunately be chained to—though she may know that he hates her, though it may be his daily pleasure to torture her, and though she may feel it impossible not to loathe him—he can claim from her and enforce the lowest degradation of a human being, that of being made the instrument of an animal function contrary to her inclinations. While she is held in this worst description of slavery as to her own person, what is her position in regard to the children in whom she and her master have a joint interest? They are by law *his* children. He alone has any legal rights over them. Not one act can she do towards or in relation to them, except by delegation from him. Even after he is dead she is not their legal guardian, unless he by will has made her so. He could even send them away from her, and deprive her of the means of seeing or corresponding with them, until this power was in some degree restricted by Serjeant Talfourd's Act. This is her legal state. And from this state she has no means of withdrawing herself. If she leaves her husband, she can take nothing with her, neither her children nor anything which is rightfully her own. If he chooses, he can compel her to return, by law, or by physical force; or he may content himself with seizing for his own use anything which she may earn, or which may be given to her by her relations. It is only legal separation by a decree of a court of justice, which entitles her to live apart, without being forced back into the custody of an exasperated jailer—or which empowers her to apply any earnings to her own use, without fear that a man whom perhaps she has not seen for twenty years will pounce upon her some day and carry all off. This legal separation, until lately, the courts of justice would only give at an expense which made it inaccessible to any one out of the higher ranks. Even now it is only given in cases of desertion, or of the extreme of cruelty; and yet complaints are made every day that it is granted too easily. Surely, if a woman is denied any lot in life but that of being the personal body-servant of a despot, and is dependent for everything upon the chance of finding one who may be disposed to make a favourite of her instead of merely a drudge, it is a very cruel aggravation of her fate that she should be allowed to try this chance only once. The natural sequel and corollary from this state of things would be, that since her all in life depends upon obtaining a good master, she should be allowed to change again and again until she finds one. I am not saying that she ought to be allowed this privilege. That is a totally different consideration. The question of divorce, in the sense involving liberty of remarriage, is one into which it is foreign to my purpose to enter. All I now say is, that to those to whom nothing but servitude is allowed, the free choice of servitude is the only, though a most insufficient, alleviation. Its refusal completes the assimilation of the wife to the slave—and the slave under not the mildest form of slavery: for in some slave codes the slave could, under certain circumstances of ill usage, legally compel the master to sell him. But no amount of ill usage, without adultery superadded, will in England free a wife from her tormentor. . . .

3

On the other point which is involved in the just equality of women, their admissibility to all the functions and occupations hitherto retained as the monopoly of the stronger sex, I should anticipate no difficulty in convincing any one who has gone with me on the subject of the equality of women in the family. I believe that their disabilities elsewhere are only clung to in order to maintain their subordination in domestic life; because the generality of the male sex cannot yet tolerate the idea of living with an equal. Were it not for that, I think that almost every one, in the existing state of opinion in politics and political economy, would admit the injustice of excluding half the human race from the greater number of lucrative occupations, and from almost all high social functions; ordaining from their birth either that they are not, and cannot by any possibility become, fit for employments which are legally open to the stupidest and basest of the other sex, or else that however fit they may be, those employments shall be interdicted to them, in order to be preserved for the exclusive benefit of males. In the last two centuries, when (which was seldom the case) any reason beyond the mere existence of the fact was thought to be required to justify the disabilities of women, people seldom assigned as a reason their inferior mental capacity; which, in times when there was a real trial of personal faculties (from which all women were not excluded) in the struggles of public life, no one really believed in. The reason given in those days was not women's unfitness, but the interest of society, by which was meant the interest of men; just as the *raison d'état*, meaning the convenience of the government, and the support of existing authority, was deemed a sufficient explanation and excuse for the most flagitious crimes. In the present day, power holds a smoother language, and whomsoever it oppresses, always pretends to do so for their own good: accordingly, when anything is forbidden to women, it is thought necessary to say, and desirable to believe, that they are incapable of doing it, and that they depart from their real path of success and happiness when they aspire to it. But to make this reason plausible (I do not say valid), those by whom it is urged must be prepared to carry it to a much greater length than any one ventures to do in the face of present experience. It is not sufficient to maintain that women on the average are less gifted than men on the average, with certain of the higher mental faculties, or that a smaller number of women than of men are fit for occupations and functions of the highest intellectual character. It is necessary to maintain that no women at all are fit for them, and that the most eminent women are inferior in mental faculties to the most mediocre of the men on whom those functions at present devolve. For if the performance of the function is decided either by competition, or by any mode of choice which secures regard to the public interest, there needs to be no apprehension that any important employments will fall into the hands of women inferior to average men, or to the average of their male competitors. The only result would be that there would be fewer women than men in such employments; a result certain to happen in any case, if only from the preference always likely to be felt by the majority of women for the one vocation in which there is nobody to compete with them. Now, the most determined depreciator of women will not venture to deny, that when we add the experience of recent times to that of ages past, women, and not a few merely, but many women, have proved themselves capable of everything, perhaps without a single exception, which is done by men, and of doing it successfully and creditably. The utmost that can be said is, that there are many things which none of them have succeeded in doing as well as they have been done by some men—many in which they have not reached the very highest rank. But there are extremely few, dependent only on mental faculties, in which they have not attained the rank next to the highest. Is not this enough, and much more than enough, to make it a tyranny to them, and a detriment to society, that they should not be allowed to compete with men for the exercise of these functions? Is it not a mere truism to say, that such functions are often filled by men far less fit for them than numbers of women, and who would be beaten by women in any fair field of competition? What difference does it make that there may be men somewhere, fully employed about other things, who may be still better qualified for the things in question than these women? Does not this take place in all competitions? Is there so great a superfluity of men fit for high duties, that society can afford to reject the service of any competent person? Are we so certain of always finding a man made to our hands for any duty or function of social importance which falls vacant, that we lose nothing by putting a ban upon one-half of mankind, and refusing beforehand to make their faculties available, however distinguished they may be? And even if we could do without them, would it be consistent with justice to refuse to them their fair share of honour and distinction, or to deny to them the equal moral right of all human beings to choose their occupation (short of injury to others) according to their own preferences, at their own risk? Nor is the injustice confined to them: it is shared by those who are in a position to benefit by their services. To ordain that any kind of persons shall not be physicians, or shall not be advocates, or shall not be members of parliament, is to injure not them only, but all who employ physicians or advocates, or elect members of parliament, and who are deprived of the stimulating effect of greater competition on the exertions of the competitors, as well as restricted to a narrower range of individual choice.

It will perhaps be sufficient if I confine myself, in the details of my argument, to functions of a public nature: since, if I am successful as to those, it probably will be readily granted that women should be admissible to all other occupations to which it is at all material whether they are admitted or not. And here let me begin by marking out one function, broadly distinguished from all others, their right to which is entirely independent of any question which can be raised concerning their faculties. I mean the suffrage, both parliamentary and municipal. The right to share in the choice of those who are to exercise a public trust, is altogether a distinct thing from that of competing for the trust itself. If no one could vote for a member of parliament who was not fit to be a candidate, the government would be a narrow oligarchy indeed. To have a voice in choosing those by whom one is to be governed, is a means of self-protection due to every one, though he were to remain for ever excluded from the function of governing: and that women are considered fit to have such a choice, may be presumed from the fact, that the law already gives it to women in the most important of all cases to themselves: for the choice of the man who is to govern a woman to the end of life, is always supposed to be voluntarily made by herself. In the case of election to public trusts, it is the business of constitutional law to surround the right of suffrage with all needful securities and limitations; but whatever securities are sufficient in the case of the male sex, no others need be required in the case of women. Under whatever conditions, and within whatever limits, men are admitted to the suffrage, there is not a shadow of justification for not admitting women under the same. The majority of the women of any class are not likely to differ in political opinion from the majority of the men of the same class, unless the question be one in which the interests of women, as such, are in some way involved; and if they are so, women require the suffrage, as their guarantee of just and equal consideration. This ought to be obvious even to those who coincide in no other of the doctrines for which I contend. Even if every woman were a wife, and if every wife ought to be a slave, all the more would these slaves stand in need of legal protection: and we know what legal protection the slaves have, where the laws are made by their masters.

With regard to the fitness of women, not only to participate in elections, but themselves to hold offices or practise professions involving important public responsibilities; I have already observed that this consideration is not essential to the practical question in dispute: since any woman, who succeeds in an open profession, proves by that very fact that she is qualified for it. And in the case of public offices, if the political system of the country is such as to exclude unfit men, it will equally exclude unfit women: while if it is not, there is no additional evil in the fact that the unfit persons whom it admits may be either women or men. As long therefore as it is acknowledged that even a few women may be fit for these duties, the laws which shut the door on those exceptions cannot be justified by any opinion which can be held respecting the capacities of women in general. But, though this last consideration is not essential, it is far from being irrelevant. An unprejudiced view of it gives additional strength to the arguments against the disabilities of women, and reinforces them by high considerations of practical utility. . . .

John Stuart Mill:
On Liberty and History
Clark W. Bouton

In the current discussions of the problems of liberty, perhaps no other work possesses the authority still maintained by John Stuart Mill's essay, *On Liberty*. Even one of Mill's most uncompromising critics has stated that the grounds on which the liberals argue today "have not varied perceptibly since Mill" and that none of his followers have stated the arguments with Mill's "clarity or vigor of mind."[1] While there is strong disagreement over the validity of Mill's position, there is little disagreement as to what his position was, or as to its importance. The prevalent interpretation, accepted by critics and admirers alike, attributes to Mill a position which may be designated, for lack of a better term, as doctrinaire liberalism. According to this interpretation, Mill espoused a doctrine of complete freedom of thought and speech as a universal and absolute rule for society and thus elevated this freedom to the position of society's highest good. Two different reasons are given for Mill's having adopted such a position. First, he is supposed to have been somehow oblivious to the dangers of unlimited freedom; second, liberty was viewed by him as such an absolute principle that it must be maintained at all costs.

In spite of its popularity, however, this interpretation of Mill's thought cannot be accepted as accurate. There are certainly many passages in *On Liberty* that do seem to express the most doctrinaire liberalism. But one may not accept these passages as a definitive expression of Mill's position while their doctrinairism is contradicted by other passages equally clear in meaning and, indeed, by the entire import of Mill's utilitarian philosophy. There are those who have seen these difficulties and consequently rejected the prevalent interpretation. But while insisting that Mill is not so doctrinaire in regard to liberty as he is generally thought to be, they have not gone beyond this to develop a coherent understanding of his thought, which would explain Mill's frequently doctrinaire statements as well as the qualifications which these seem to require.

The failure to achieve a coherent understanding of Mill's liberalism has in turn been caused by the failure to recognize the central role that a philosophy of history plays in his thought. The task of this article will therefore be to present this philosophy of history as it is developed in various of his writings and to show how his liberalism becomes understandable in terms of this historical thought.

The lack of attention given to Mill's historical thought is surprising when one considers that Mill himself has stated that it was responsible for the most radical change that occurred in his thought.[2] The great defect of the eighteenth-century philosophy (and of his own earlier thought), as Mill came to see it, was its "abstract and

---

Clark W. Bouton. 1965. "John Stuart Mill: On Liberty and History." *Western Political Quarterly*, 18:3, pp. 569–578. Reprinted with permission of the University of Utah, Copyright Holder.

1. Willmore Kendall, "The 'Open Society' and Its Fallacies," *APSR*, 54 (December 1960), 973.

2. *Autobiography* (New York: Holt, 1883), p. 253.

metaphysical" character.[3] On the basis of the new historical thought, Mill rejected their efforts to develop an abstract conception of human nature, free from the changing concrete situations in which man finds himself. Men are always "historical human beings, already shaped, and made what they are, by human society" and "by the accumulated influence of past generations over the present."[4] The changes in man's nature are thus no less great than the changes in society; his nature ranges from a level "very little above the highest of the beasts" to that of the present civilization, and much greater change may be expected in the future.[5]

The belief that history revealed the changing nature of man caused the rejection of "abstract" theories in rejecting the uniformities assumed by these theories. However, history itself suggested new uniformities. History is only change, but within that universal flux, one might discover uniformities of change itself. If history is not simply chaotic, if there is a "determinate course, a certain order" to historical events, then history might itself furnish the meaning and standards that could no longer be found in the concept of nature. At this point, historical thought becomes philosophy of history.

The mere recognition of a direction in history, such as the concept of progress, or of a certain pattern of events, is not in itself sufficient. While "the history of our species, looked at as a comprehensive whole, does exhibit a determinate course, a certain order of development; . . . history alone cannot prove this to be a necessary law, as distinguished from a temporary accident."[6] History provides only empirical generalizations, it does not provide "necessary" laws. To achieve these laws, Mill argued for a fusion of the laws of historical development and the laws of human nature. Human nature was to reveal itself within the laws of historical development; history was to exhibit "the inherent tendencies of the human race."[7] History becomes something more than merely descriptive if its course can be shown to have been "determined more or less precisely by the original constitution of mankind and by the circumstances of the planet on which we live."[8] On the other hand, this "original constitution" is discoverable only through a study of the whole course and order of history. The laws of human nature do not reveal the essential character of man, but only the ways in which the particular character of each age is formed, the ways in which circumstances work to form this character.[9] Political philosophy is thus only possible as philosophy of history.[10]

At any point in history, man's character is the result of the whole previous history of humanity. Each stage of history, being determined by all that preceded it, must have a distinct individuality which sets it off from the past as well as future states; it cannot be understood apart from its place in the historical development. Mill described the historical development in the following manner: "It is my belief indeed that the general tendency is, and will continue to be, saving occasional and temporary ex-

---

3. John Stuart Mill, *Dissertations and Discussions* (London: Longmans, 1867), I, 403.

4. John Stuart Mill, *The Positive Philosophy of Auguste Comte* (New York: Holt, 1887), p. 78. Cf. *A System of Logic* (London: Longmans, 1865), II, 509.

5. *Representative Government* (New York: Dutton, 1951), p. 264. Cf. *Comte,* p. 84; *Dissertations,* p. 232; *Liberty,* pp. 157, 166.

6. *Comte,* p. 79.

7. *Dissertations,* II, 134.

8. *Ibid.,* p. 223. Cf. *Logic,* II, 444.

9. *Logic,* II, 447, 452, 508, 510.

10. *Dissertations,* I, 425; II, 222; *Comte,* p. 78.

ceptions, one of improvement; a tendency towards a better and happier state."[11] A major aspect of this improvement, and the driving force behind it, is the growth of knowledge. Mill accepted Comte's [Nineteenth Century French philosopher sometimes known as the Father of Sociology] division of universal history into three stages, based on the development of knowledge, or the "natural succession" of three modes of thought: the theological, metaphysical, and positive. It is this succession that determines the order and direction of history, and its irreversible course. In the present, mankind has finally rested its knowledge on the solid foundation of positive science and may look forward to a future of increasing knowledge and certainty.

Mill did not, however, anticipate a steady, controlled improvement of knowledge and institutions such as envisaged by Comte. Progress is not achieved by the simple addition of new truths and the improvement of old, but through the opposition of conflicting ideas. As one mode of thought succeeds another, whatever new perception of truth it contains will be exaggerated, and whatever truth possessed by the older conceptions will be undervalued. In turn, the new doctrine will provoke another reaction. The history of thought thus reveals an oscillation between extremes, "improvement consisting only in this, that the oscillation, each time, departs rather less widely from the center."[12]

This conception of intellectual development sees certain conditions as necessary for progress; opposing viewpoints must come into existence, and in a situation where they are able to work out their opposition. This in turn requires "freedom and variety of situations."[13] Intellectual progress is achieved only under certain conditions and in certain periods, interspersed among other ages of stagnate or declining civilization. On this basis, Mill accepts the division of all history into "organic" and "critical" periods. During an organic period, "mankind accepts with firm conviction some positive creed, claiming jurisdiction over all their actions, and containing more or less of truth and adaptions to the needs of humanity."[14] Then they outgrow the creed, and a critical period follows, wherein the old convictions are criticized and rejected, without the acquisition of any new conviction to replace them. Ultimately this critical period is followed by the acceptance of new ideas and common beliefs and the consequent development of a new organic period.

It was within the framework of this theory of history that Mill sought to understand his contemporary period. The most remarkable characteristic of the period was that "all results must more and more be decided by movements of masses."[15] Against this rising power of the masses, the traditional ruling groups are no longer serious contenders for power; the contest is between the middle class and the working class. While recognizing the potential power of the working class, Mill did not believe it capable of effectively exerting this power under contemporary conditions; and as they attained the higher standard of living and education that would make this possible, Mill expected them to be gradually absorbed into the middle class. What Mill saw in the future for Europe was not an impending struggle between classes, but the increasing dominance of the middle class. From this point of view, he expected radical agitation to decline in strength rather than to become more violent, as others

---

11. *Logic,* II, 507.

12. *Dissertations,* I, 403.

13. *Liberty* (New York: Dutton, 1951), pp. 154, 174.

14. *Autobiography,* p. 163.

15. *Dissertations,* I, 163.

predicted. It is the middle class that has become the danger in society; it constitutes the "mass."[16]

Mill's theory of the conditions necessary for progress opposes the preponderance of any one class in society. This preponderance has been attained by the middle class. To combat the unrestrained influence of the middle class was seen by Mill as the first need of society in his time. (Only in respect to this analysis does Mill's bewildering espousal of the most radically democratic as well as the most conservative views become understandable.) The seriousness of the problem of middle-class dominance, and Mill's inability to find a satisfactory solution to the problem, can be seen in comparing his early writings on the subject with a later work such as *On Liberty.* In the earlier works, he saw hope of opposing the middle-class influence with other vigorous classes.[17] He thus saw the remedy for the increase in combinations and the loss of the importance of the individual in a "more perfect combination among individuals,"[18] in a balance of forces in society which would form a protection for unpopular opinions. In *On Liberty,* this hope seems to have disappeared, and his only solution is to insulate the individual from the public opinion of the dominant class.[19]

The middle-class dominance threatened, from Mill's viewpoint, to put an end to the long critical period that was responsible for the enormous progress achieved by modern Europe. If the middle class were to gain complete preponderance, and majority opinion should come to impress on the whole of society its own spirit, there was no doubt in Mill's mind but that there would "commence an era either of stationariness or of decline."[20] It is in the light of this situation that the essay *On Liberty* must be understood. Given his understanding of his age and of the foreseeable future, Mill could demand the maximum of liberty in the strongest terms. This was practical because the greatest dangers were not to be expected from any excess of liberty, but from the increasing conformity of the age.

When, in an earlier essay, "Coleridge," [Eighteenth Century British poet, critic, and philosopher] Mill presented a very different analysis of the contemporary period, his discussion of liberty took on a correspondingly different tone. Mill there argued that the new historical thought of his time revealed "the essential requisites of civil society the Eighteenth Century unfortunately overlooked."[21] Mill regarded three such requisites as fundamental: first, a system of education producing a "restraining discipline"; second, an allegiance to a common principle; third, a feeling of sympathy and common interest.[22] Without these requisites, no stable society was possible.

---

16. *Ibid.,* p. 67.

17. "What is requisite in politics . . . is not that public opinion should not be, what it is, and must be, the ruling power; but that, in order to the formation of the best public opinion, there should exist somewhere a great social support for opinions and sentiments different from these of the mass." *Ibid.,* p. 73. Mill nevertheless recognized in his early writings that this opposition could exist only through the sufferance of the middle class. *Ibid.,* II, 77.

18. *Ibid.,* I, 188.

19. This aspect of the problem is emphasized in *On Liberty* almost to the exclusion of other aspects of Mill's thought. This should not, however, lead one to lose sight of the fact that Mill always continued to regard public opinion as an inevitable and desirable force of constraint in society. Cf. *Liberty,* pp. 90, 152, 177, 180, 181; *Autobiography,* pp. 166, 233; *Dissertations,* I, 201 and IV, 70ff.; *Representative Government,* p. 404. Mill by no means demanded of society or the individual the ethical indifference toward others that is so often attributed to his thought.

20. *Dissertations,* II, 72.

21. *Ibid.,* I, 422.

22. *Ibid.,* pp. 416–21.

Of these, the second is for us the most important: that there be "*something* which is settled, something permanent, and not to be called into question." This something may variously be such things as religion, prerogatives, or laws.

> But in all political societies which have a durable existence, there has been some fixed point; something which men agreed in holding sacred; . . . which . . . was in the common estimation placed beyond discussion. . . . When the questioning of these fundamental principles is (not the occasional disease, or salutary medicine but) the habitual condition of the body politic, and when all the violent animosities are called forth which spring naturally from such a situation, the State is virtually in a position of civil war; and can never long remain free from it in act and fact.[23]

The necessity of holding certain principles beyond dispute applies to the present as well as the past, and to the future, "until mankind are vastly improved."[24] Mill therefore criticizes the eighteenth-century philosophers for "the weakening of all government," in "unsettling everything which was still considered settled, making men doubtful of the few things of which they still felt certain."[25]

In his essay on Coleridge, Mill expressed perhaps more forcefully than any of his own critics the dangers that exist in unrestrained liberty of discussion. The work contrasts most strongly with his *On Liberty,* wherein the plea was made for liberty of discussion in the strongest terms, seemingly oblivious of the dangers involved. The difference between these two works cannot be attributed simply to a change in Mill's opinions. It lies in the difference in his analysis of the contemporary situations surrounding the two works. In the "Coleridge," Mill was most concerned with "the evils characteristic of the transition from a system of opinions which had worn out"[26]; in Carlyle's [Nineteenth Century Scottish historian and philosopher] phrase, an "age of unbelief." In this situation, it was necessary to stress the need for stability, within which progress can take place without destroying the very conditions of progress.

Mill never abandoned the position set forth in his earlier essay.[27] In writing *On Liberty,* however, he saw the age of transition coming to an end and a new organic period, with its excessive forces for conformity, coming into existence. In this situation, it was no longer necessary to stress the need for consensus and stability or the dangers of liberty. Given the contemporary situation, Mill could safely exert his whole power in attempting to keep alive the forces of progress.

---

23. *Ibid.,* p. 419. Cf. *Autobiography,* p. 254.

24. *Dissertations,* I, 418.

25. *Ibid.,* p. 422. Cf. *Ibid.,* p. 424. Mill did not deny the necessity of the changes brought about, but criticized the manner in which it was done.

26. *Autobiography,* pp. 164, 173.

27. The interpretation which sees in "Coleridge" a "reactionary" position, which was soon rejected by Mill, cannot be maintained. When, late in life, Mill came to publish a selection of his essays, *Dissertations and Discussions,* the essay on Coleridge was among that selection. In preparing the essays for republication, Mill took the liberty of "striking out such passages as were no longer in accordance with my opinions." "Coleridge" was retained in its original form. That Mill continued to hold the position stated in that essay can better be seen in the fact that in his *Logic* he quoted the whole section referred to above, as a model of the kind of theorems sociology should develop. Even later, after the publication of *On Liberty,* when Mill returned to the problem of "order and progress," his thought was not essentially different from that of his essay on Coleridge. It is true that, in his *Autobiography,* Mill reappraised his early essay. But while he mentioned some qualifications in regard to the essay, these related to its "appearance" and not to the thought itself. And while Mill said that he overemphasized one side of the problem in "Coleridge" for the purpose of gaining a practical effect on his readers, this raises the interesting question of to what extent the same might be said of *On Liberty.*

We do not mean to suggest that *On Liberty* is therefore unrepresentative of Mill's thought, or that his real position is to be found in another work; this would be to repeat the error we are attempting to correct. *On Liberty* is undoubtedly Mill's most brilliant work in the area of politics, but it does not follow that it is therefore a full statement of his political thought. Only when *On Liberty* is understood in relation to Mill's other writings, does it reveal the breadth and complexity of his thought, and the essential agreement common to all of his writings. Seen in the context of his other works and his general historical thought, Mill's *On Liberty* does not reveal a doctrinaire liberalism, but a teaching related to a certain historical situation and meant to be limited to certain conditions. It is, however, necessary to define more clearly these limits.

Even those who have attributed to Mill the most doctrinaire liberalism have noted the exceptions to it in Mill's discussion of past societies. However, once exceptions are made, the limits to these exceptions must be determined, not on the basis of an absolute principle but, on the basis of the expected consequences (the utility) in any particular situation. The problems posed by these exceptions is thus crucial for an understanding of Mill's liberalism. The rules presented in *On Liberty* are meant only to apply generally to the more advanced Western nations in Mill's own time; the attempt to extend them more broadly must take into account the very different circumstances existing elsewhere. Mill's belief in liberty is only understandable in the same terms as his belief in democracy. There is no doubt in his mind that democracy is the best form of government, but it does not follow that it is the best in all situations.

Mill does not give, in *On Liberty,* a clear indication of the conditions which must exist in a society before liberalism becomes feasible for it. His only specific reference to the limitations on liberalism occurs in the following passage:

> Liberty, as a principle, has no application to any state of things anterior to the time when mankind have become capable of being improved by free and equal discussion. Until then, there is nothing for them but implicit obedience to an Akbar or a Charlemagne, if they are so fortunate as to find one. But as soon as mankind have attained the capacity of being guided to their own improvement by conviction or persuasion (a period long since reached in all nations with whom we need here concern ourselves), compulsion, either in the direct form or in that of pains and penalties for non-compliance, is no longer admissible as a means to their own good, and justifiable only for the security of others.[28]

Mill does not say here to what extent or under what conditions restrictions on freedom are justifiable in advanced societies, but only that they must be for the purpose of security. That Mill accepted extensive restrictions on freedom in advanced societies, under certain conditions, can be shown by another example from *On Liberty.* After speaking of the practice in the ancient republics of "the regulation of every part of private conduct by public authority," Mill concludes that it "may have been admissible in small republics surrounded by powerful enemies, in constant peril of being subverted by foreign attack or internal commotion, and to which even a short interval of relaxed energy and self-command might so easily be fatal that they could not afford to wait for the salutary permanent effects of freedom."[29] The Greek city states cannot be regarded as backward, but their situation made it "admissible" to practice extensive restrictions on freedom.

---

28. *Liberty,* pp. 96–97.
29. *Ibid.,* p. 100.

The common interpretation, according to which Mill naïvely believed that society could only lose by restricting freedom, and was thus always unjustified in doing so, cannot be maintained. Mill is too much concerned with the consequences of actions, and too much aware of the different consequences to be expected under different conditions, to adopt such an absolute position. Those passages in *On Liberty* in which Mill states that society has no right to limit freedom of speech or the private actions of the individual cannot be understood to apply even to all advanced societies. To determine under what conditions they do apply, one must look to Mill's other writings.

In his writings both prior and subsequent to *On Liberty,* Mill argued that progress is dependent upon the existence of a stable society. "Order . . . is not an additional end to be reconciled with Progress, but a part and means of Progress itself."[30] Order in turn rests on those essential requisites already discussed in his essay on Coleridge: education, common principles, and a common interest. It would seem to follow from this that the extent of liberty permissible in a society is directly proportional to the force of these essential requisites.[31] Liberty exerts a progressive, but also disruptive, force on society; it must therefore be balanced by the cohesive forces in society. When such a balance is achieved, society will progress through an internal "systematic opposition," without this opposition becoming destructive.

That this emphasis on the essential cohesive forces in society was fundamental to Mill's understanding of liberty can be seen even in his discussion of the ideal society of the future.[32] The "unchecked liberty of thought" will be possible because of common convictions "engraven on the feelings by early education and general unanimity of sentiment." Education will still in the best society need to provide a "restraining discipline," and increased liberty of thought becomes possible because of the high consensus in the society. This agreement is in turn the result of the progressive discovery of truth, which destroys the multiplicity of conflicting errors and half-truths.[33] This will create the basis for a greater consensus, which will be maintained by education and public opinion; given the force of these cohesive factors, the greatest freedom can be permitted without threat to the society. It is the increased strength of the cohesive factors that make increased liberty possible.

In his own time, Mill saw a consensus in society sufficient to allow the most extensive liberties to the individual. He could not, however, be certain that this would remain true in the future. Even assuming that progress continued, which is "not inevitable," it is not certain that such broad protections for liberty could be maintained. Mill saw the immediate future as the development of a new organic period in history. It is only with this period that the teachings of *On Liberty* "will have their greatest value."[34] However, one would expect from the laws of history that this would in turn lead to a new critical period, under which the liberalism of *On Liberty* might again require some qualification.

This result need not, however, necessarily take place. From Mill's viewpoint, contemporary thought had for the first time come to understand the order and conditions of historical development. The knowledge of these laws itself creates the

---

30. *Representative Government,* p. 255; cf. 251–254.

31. Cf. *Representative Government,* p. 239.

32. See below, p. 541.

33. *Liberty,* p. 187; *Autobiography,* pp. 211–212; *Comte,* pp. 90–91.

34. *Autobiography,* p. 254.

possibility of transcending them. Thus Mill looked forward to "a future which shall combine the best qualities of the critical with the best qualities of the organic periods; unchecked liberty of thought, unbounded freedom of individual action in all modes not hurtful to others; but also, convictions about what is right and wrong, useful and pernicious, deeply engraved on the feelings by early education and general unanimity of sentiment, and so firmly grounded in reason and in the true exigencies of life, that they shall not, like all former and present creeds, religious, ethical and political, require to be periodically thrown off and replaced by others."[35]

Mill believed in the possibility of a society in which the fullest freedom could be permitted without endangering peace and stability, but not because he was somehow oblivious to the dangers of free speech and individual actions. Mill recognized that throughout history it has often been necessary to restrict these freedoms. However, on the basis of his philosophy of history, he was also able to envisage a future in which the laws operating in the past need no longer govern. Mill saw his contemporary period as one in which, because of favorable circumstances, the maximum of liberty could be allowed. He looked to a future in which liberty need not be limited to accidentally favorable circumstances, but be solidly based on an understanding of man and society, on a general intellectual and moral improvement.

Liberty is, however, the cause as well as the effect of this moral and intellectual improvement that Mill so optimistically predicted. As such, liberty possesses the unique value of being "the only unfailing and permanent source of improvement."[36] While Mill placed the highest value on liberty, he did so on the basis of its utility, in relation to a general improvement of man, and not on the basis of a conception of liberty as an abstract ultimate principle. There is indeed no place in Mill's utilitarianism for any principle having an abstract and independent validity. Much of the distortion of Mill's liberalism can be traced to the attempt to discover such a principle, and thus, to the failure to take Mill's utilitarianism quite seriously. Until Mill can be shown to have fallen into self-contradictions of the most fundamental nature, there is no alternative to accepting happiness as, for him, the sole ultimate end of human action and the principle of all ethical judgment. This is not to deny that liberty is both the indispensable means and an essential part of any real happiness. But from this to conclude that Mill elevates liberty to the position of what he would call an "abstract right"—a right which could be independent of, and possibly in opposition to, the criterion of utility—is certainly an error.

Mill's concept of utility, as well as his concept of liberty, is imbued with the essential optimism of his historical thought. Utility is the ultimate ethical standard, "but it must be utility in the largest sense, grounded on the permanent interests of

---

35. *Ibid.,* p. 166.

36. *Liberty,* p. 171. Given Mill's emphasis on "qualitative differences," the improvement of which he speaks is an increase of virtue rather than of mere pleasure. Virtue is itself valued in relation to happiness, but this relationship is by no means fully clear. Virtue has originally value only as a means to happiness and yet is a necessary part of happiness. It becomes, in addition, desirable in itself, apart from its relation to happiness. Virtue would seem to be at once a means, a necessary component of the end, and an end in itself. (*Utilitarianism,* Everyman edition, pp. 11–12, 23, 42–46.) Mill's only explanation of this peculiar relationship is a psychological explanation which accounts only for the origin and development of virtue from a mere means to an end, but does not explain its relation to the supposedly sole ultimate end, happiness, once the psychological development has taken place. (*Utilitarianism,* pp. 48, 50). Mill's attempt to introduce a broader content into the narrow utilitarian framework created similar ambiguities in regard to the value of liberty and its relation to happiness. But, if there is any "higher doctrine" in Mill, it is that of virtue rather than liberty or individuality. Of the three, only virtue is ever referred to by Mill as possessing an ultimate value apart from the extent to which it contributes to happiness.

man as a progressive being."[37] The failure to see the importance of this emphasis on the progressive improvement of man is responsible for the two most common misinterpretations of his thought. On the one hand, Mill is believed to have established the fundamental right of the individual; on the other hand, he is supposed to have been concerned only with the "profit or advantage to society."[38] We have already examined the interpretation of Mill which sees the basis of his liberalism in the right of the individual. This interpretation cannot be maintained. When Mill argues that "society has no right" to restrict certain liberties, he does not mean to imply any contrary right of the individual. He means only that there is no utility in, and thus no justification for, such restrictions in the situation to which he refers. From a recognition of this meaning, the contrary interpretation is drawn: that Mill treats the individual with a "socializing cruelty" which considers only the profit to society. There is undoubtedly some truth to this; the ultimate criterion is the totality of human happiness, not any "right" of the individual. However, the utility in question is not that of the particular society, but the utility of "man as a progressive being." The ultimate criterion is not the happiness of the particular society, but the progress of mankind. Thus the greatest evil of censorship is not in its effect on the individual or the happiness of the society, but "that it is robbing the human race."[39] The criterion is the intellectual and moral improvement of man spoken of in the above paragraphs. While Mill does not come out in support of the sanctity of the individual favored by some liberals, neither is the individual being sacrificed to the mere hedonistic pleasures of the majority.

Understood in the larger framework of Mill's philosophical and historical thought, *On Liberty* reveals a doctrine different from that usually attributed to it. But the essential liberalism of the work remains. While not seen as an abstract and ultimate principle, the value of liberty is scarcely underestimated. While Mill does not present the absolute and unequivocal defense of liberty that has been sought in his writings by liberals struggling for the preservation of freedom in our time, his writings on liberty have not lost their value for the contemporary discussion. Lest one regret the loss of such an absolute defense of liberty as supposedly existed in Mill's writings, it is necessary to add the doubt that the doctrinaire liberalism, which has falsely claimed Mill's support, has in fact been favorable to the realization of liberty. Its unreasonable demands have called forth an equally uncompromising emphasis on "necessity," and, for lack of a sound alternative, this "necessity" with its short-sighted reasonableness has too often won acceptance.

---

37. *Liberty,* p. 97. Cf. pp. 100, 104.

38. Jose Ortega y Gasset, *Toward a Philosophy of History* (New York: Norton, 1941), p. 64.

39. *Liberty,* p. 104.

Marital Slavery and Friendship:
John Stuart Mill's
The Subjection of Women
Mary Lyndon Shanley

John Stuart Mill's essay *The Subjection of Women* was one of the nineteenth century's strongest pleas for opening to women opportunities for suffrage, education, and employment. Some contemporary feminists, however, have denigrated the work, questioning the efficacy of merely striking down legal barriers against women as the way to establish equality between the sexes. These contemporary critics argue that Mill's failure to extend his critique of inequality to the division of labor in the household, and his confidence that most women would choose marriage as a "career," subverted his otherwise egalitarian impulses.[1]

I argue in this essay, however, that such critics have ignored an important aspect of Mill's feminism. *The Subjection of Women* was not solely about equal opportunity for women. It was also, and more fundamentally, about the corruption of male-female relationships and the hope of establishing friendship in marriage. Such friendship was desirable not only for emotional satisfaction, it was crucial if marriage were to become, as Mill desired, a "school of genuine moral sentiment."[2] The fundamental assertion of *The Subjection of Women* was not that equal opportunity would ensure the liberation of women, but that male-female equality, however achieved, was essential to marital friendship and to the progression of human society.

Mill's vision of marriage as a locus of sympathy and understanding between autonomous adults not only reforms our understanding of his feminism, but also draws attention to an often submerged or ignored aspect of liberal political thought. Liberal individualism is attacked by Marxists and neo-conservatives alike as wrongly encouraging the disintegration of affective bonds and replacing them with merely self-interested economic and contractual ties. Mill's essay, however, emphasizes the value of noninstrumental relationships in human life. His depictions of both corrupt and well-ordered marriage traces the relationship of family order to right political order. His vision of marriage as a locus of mutual sympathy and understanding between autonomous adults stands as an unrealized goal for those who believe that the liberation of women requires not only formal equality of opportunity but measures which will enable couples to live in genuine equality, mutuality, and reciprocity.

I. The Perversion of Marriage by the Master-Slave Relationship

Mill's reconstruction of marriage upon the basis of friendship was preceded by one of the most devastating critiques of male domination in marriage in the history of Western philosophy. In *The Subjection of Women* Mill repeatedly used the language

Mary Lyndon Shanley, "Marital Slavery and Friendship: John Stuart Mill's 'The Subjection of Women',"
Political Theory, 9:2, pp 229–247. Copyright © 1981 by Sage Publications, Inc. Reprinted by permission of
Sage Publications, Inc.

of "master and slave" or "master and servant" to describe the relationship between husband and wife. In the first pages of the book, Mill called the dependence of women upon men "the primitive state of slavery lasting on" (1: 130). Later he said that despite the supposed advances of Christian civilization, "the wife is the actual bond-servant of her husband: no less so, as far as legal obligation goes, than slaves commonly so called" (2: 158). Still later he asserted that "there remain no legal slaves, except the mistress of every house" (4: 217). The theme of women's servitude was not confined to *The Subjection of Women.* In his speech on the Reform Bill of 1867, Mill talked of that "obscure feeling" which members of Parliament were "ashamed to express openly" that women had no right to care about anything except "how they may be the most useful and devoted servants of some man."[3] To Auguste Comte he wrote comparing women to "domestic slaves" and noted that women's capacities were spent "seeking happiness not in their own life, but exclusively in the favor and affection of the other sex, which is only given to them on the condition of their dependence."[4]

But what did Mill mean by denouncing the "slavery" of married women? How strongly did he wish to insist upon the analogy between married women and chattel slaves? I believe that he chose the image quite deliberately. For Mill, the position of married women resembled that of slaves in several ways: the social and economic system gave women little alternative except to marry; once married, the legal personality of the woman was subsumed in that of her husband; and the abuses of human dignity permitted by custom and law within marriage were egregious.

In Mill's eyes, women were in a double bind: they were not free within marriage, and they were not truly free not to marry.[5] What could an unmarried woman do? Even if she were of the middle or upper classes, she could not attend any of the English universities, and thus she was barred from a systematic higher education.[6] If somehow she acquired a professional education, the professional associations usually barred her from practicing her trade. "No sooner do women show themselves capable of competing with men in any career, than that career, if it be lucrative or honorable, is closed to them."[7] Mill's depiction of the plight of Elinor Garrett, sister of Millicent Garrett Fawcett, the suffrage leader, is telling:

> A young lady, Miss Garrett, . . . studied the medical profession. Having duly qualified herself, she . . . knocked successively at all the doors through which, by law, access is obtained into the medical profession. Having found all other doors fast shut, she fortunately discovered one which had accidentally been left ajar. The Society of Apothecaries, it seems, had forgotten to shut out those who they never thought would attempt to come in, and through this narrow entrance this young lady found her way into the profession. But so objectionable did it appear to this learned body that women should be the medical attendants even of women, that the narrow wicket through which Miss Garrett entered has been closed after her.[8]

Working-class women were even worse off. In the *Principles of Political Economy,* Mill argued that their low wages were due to the "prejudice" of society which "making almost every woman, socially speaking, an appendage of some man, enables men to take systematically the lion's share of whatever belongs to both." A second cause of low wages for women was the surplus of female labor for unskilled jobs. Law and custom ordained that a woman has "scarcely any means open to her of gaining a livelihood, except as a wife and mother."[9] Marriage was, as Mill put it, a "Hobson's choice" for women, "that or none" (1: 156).[10]

Worse than the social and economic pressure to marry, however, was women's status within marriage. Mill thoroughly understood the stipulations of the English common law which deprived a married woman of a legal personality independent of that of her husband. The doctrine of coverture or spousal unity, as it was called, was based on the Biblical notion that "a man [shall] leave his father and his mother, and shall cleave to his wife, and they shall be one flesh" (Genesis ii, 22–23). If "one flesh," then, as Blackstone put it, "by marriage, the husband and wife are one person in law." And that "person" was represented by the husband. Again Blackstone was most succinct: "The very being or legal existence of the woman is suspended during the marriage, or at least is incorporated and consolidated into that of the husband."[11] One of the most commonly felt injustices of the doctrine of spousal unity was the married woman's lack of ownership of her own earnings. As the matrimonial couple was "one person," the wife's earnings during marriage were owned and controlled by her husband.[12] During his term as a member of Parliament, Mill supported a Married Women's Property Bill, saying that its opponents were men who thought it impossible for "society to exist on a harmonious footing between two persons unless one of them has absolute power over the other," and insisting that England has moved beyond such a "savage state."[13] In *The Subjection of Women* Mill argued that the "wife's position under the common law of England [with respect to property] is worse than that of slaves in the laws of many countries: by the Roman law, for example, a slave might have his peculium, which to a certain extent the law guaranteed to him for his exclusive use" (2: 158–159). Similarly, Mill regarded the husband's exclusive guardianship over the married couple's children as a sign of the woman's dependence on her husband's will (2: 160). She was, in his eyes, denied any role in life except that of being "the personal body-servant of a despot" (2: 161).

The most egregious aspects of both common and statute law, however, were those which sanctioned domestic violence. During the Parliamentary debates on the Representation of the People Bill in 1867, Mill argued that women needed suffrage to enable them to lobby for legislation which would punish domestic assault:

> I should like to have a Return laid before this House of the number of women who are annually beaten to death, or trampled to death by their male protectors; and, in an opposite column, the amount of sentence passed. . . . I should also like to have, in a third column, the amount of property, the wrongful taking of which was . . . thought worthy of the same punishment. We should then have an arithmetical value set by a male legislature and male tribunals on the murder of a woman.[14]

But the two legal stipulations which to Mill most demonstrated "the assimilation of the wife to the slave" were her inability to refuse her master "the last familiarity" and her inability to obtain a legal separation from her husband unless he added desertion or extreme cruelty to his adultery (2: 160–161). Mill was appalled by the notion that no matter how brutal a tyrant a husband might be, and no matter how a woman might loathe him, "he can claim from her and enforce the lowest degradation of a human being," which was to be made the instrument of "an animal function contrary to her inclination" (2: 160). A man and wife being one body, rape was by definition a crime which a married man could not commit against his own wife. By law a wife could not leave her husband on account of this offense without being guilty of desertion, nor could she prosecute him. The most vicious form of male domination of women according to Mill was rape within marriage; it was particularly vicious because it was legal. Mill thus talked not of individual masters and wives as aberrations, but of a legally sanctioned system of domestic slavery which shaped the character of marriage in his day.[15]

Mill's depiction of marriage departed radically from the majority of Victorian portrayals of home and hearth. John Ruskin's praise of the home in *Sesame and Lilies* reflected the feelings and aspirations of many: "This is the true nature of home—it is the place of Peace; the shelter, not only from all injury, but from all terror, doubt, and division. . . . It is a sacred place, a vestal temple, a temple of the hearth watched over by Household Gods."[16] Walter Houghton remarked that the title of Coventry Patmore's poem, *The Angel in the House,* captured "the essential character of Victorian love," and reflected "the exaltation of family life and feminine character" characteristic of the mid-nineteenth century.[17] James Fitzjames Stephen, who wrote that he disagreed with *The Subjection of Women* "from the first sentence to the last," found not only Mill's ideas but his very effort to discuss the dynamics of marriage highly distasteful. "There is something—I hardly know what to call it; indecent is too strong a word, but I may say unpleasant in the direction of indecorum—in prolonged and minute discussions about the relations between men and women, and the character of women as such."[18]

The Subjection of Women challenged much more than Victorian decorum, however; it was a radical challenge to one of the most fundamental and preciously held assumptions about marriage in the modern era, which is that it was a relationship grounded on the consent of the partners to join their lives. Mill argued to the contrary that the presumed consent of women to marry was not, in any real sense, a free promise, but one socially coerced by the lack of meaningful options. Further, the laws of marriage deprived a woman of many of the normal powers of autonomous adults, from controlling her earnings, to entering contracts, to defending her bodily autonomy by resisting unwanted sexual relations. Indeed, the whole notion of a woman "consenting" to the marriage "offer" of a man implied from the outset a hierarchical relationship. Such a one-way offer did not reflect the relationship which should exist between those who were truly equal, among beings who should be able to create together by free discussion and mutual agreement an association to govern their lives together.

In addition, Mill's view of marriage as slavery suggested a significantly more complicated and skeptical view of what constituted a "free choice" in society than did either his own earlier works or those of his liberal predecessors. Hobbes, for example, regarded men as acting "freely" even when moved by fear for their lives. Locke disagreed, but he in turn talked about the individual's free choice to remain a citizen of his father's country, as if emigration were a readily available option for all. In other of his works Mill himself seemed overly sanguine about the amount of real choice enjoyed, for example, by wage laborers in entering a trade. Yet Mill's analysis of marriage demonstrated the great complexity of establishing that any presumed agreement was the result of free volition, and the fatuousness of presuming that initial consent could create perpetual obligation. By implication, the legitimacy of many other relationships, including supposedly free wage and labor agreements and the political obligation of enfranchised and unenfranchised alike, was thrown into question. *The Subjection of Women* exposed the inherent fragility of traditional conceptualizations of free choice, autonomy, and self-determination so important to liberals, showing that economic and social structures were bound to limit and might coerce any person's choice of companions, employment, or citizenship.

Mill did not despair of the possibility that marriages based on true consent would be possible. He believed that some individuals even in his own day established such associations of reciprocity and mutual support. (He counted his own relationship with Harriet Taylor Mill as an example of a marriage between equals.)[19] But there were systemic impediments to marital equality. To create conditions conducive to a marriage of equals rather than one of master and slave, marriage law itself would have to be altered, women would have to be provided equal educational and employment opportunity, and both men and women would have to become capable of sustaining genuinely equal and reciprocal relationships within marriage. The last of these, in Mill's eyes, posed the greatest challenge.

II. The Fear of Equality

Establishing legal equality in marriage and equality of opportunity would require, said Mill, that men sacrifice those political, legal, and economic advantages they enjoyed "simply by being born male." Mill therefore supported such measures as women's suffrage, the Married Women's Property Bills, the Divorce Act of 1857, the repeal of the Contagious Diseases Acts, and the opening of higher education and the professions to women. Suffrage, Mill contended, would both develop women's faculties through participation in civic decisions and enable married women to protect themselves from male-imposed injustices such as lack of rights to child custody and to control of their income. Access to education and jobs would give women alternatives to marriage. It would also provide a woman whose marriage turned out badly some means of self-support if separated or divorced. The Divorce Act of 1857, which established England's first civil divorce courts, would enable women and men to escape from intolerable circumstances (although Mill rightly protested the sexual double standard ensconced in the Act).[20] And for those few women with an income of their own, a Married Women's Property Act would recognize their independent personalities and enable them to meet their husbands more nearly as equals.

However, Mill's analysis went further. He insisted that the subjection of women could not be ended by law alone, but only by law and the reformation of education, of opinion, of social inculcation, of habits, and finally of the conduct of family life itself. This was so because the root of much of men's resistance to women's emancipation was not simply their reluctance to give up their position of material advantage, but many men's fear of living with an equal. It was to retain marriage as "a law of despotism" that men shut all other occupations to women, Mill contended (1: 156). Men who "have a real antipathy to the equal freedom of women" were at bottom afraid "lest [women] should insist that marriage be on equal conditions" (1: 156). One of Mill's startling assertions in *The Subjection of Women* was that "[women's] disabilities [in law] are only clung to in order to maintain their subordination in domestic life: *because the generality of the male sex cannot yet tolerate the idea of living with an equal*" (3: 181; italics added). The public discrimination against women was a manifestation of a disorder rooted in family relationships. The progression of humankind could not take place until the dynamics of the master-slave relationship were eliminated from marriages, and until the family was instead founded on spousal equality.

Mill did not offer any single explanation or account of the origin of men's fear of female equality. Elsewhere, he attributed the general human resistance to equality to the fear of the loss of privilege, and to apprehensions concerning the effect of leveling on political order.[21] But these passages on the fear of spousal equality bring to a twentieth-century mind the psychoanalytic works about human neuroses and the male fear of women caused by the infant boy's relationship to the seemingly all-powerful mother, source of both nurturance and love and of deprivation and punishment.[22] But it is impossible to push Mill's text far in this direction. His account of the fear of equality was not psychoanalytic. He did, however, undertake to depict the consequences of marital inequality both for the individual psyche and for social justice. The rhetorical purpose of *The Subjection of Women* was not only to convice men that their treatment of women in law was unjust, but also that their treatment of women in the home was self-defeating, even self-destructive.

Women were those most obviously affected by the denial of association with men on equal footing. Women's confinement to domestic concerns was a wrongful "forced repression" (1: 148). Mill shared Aristotle's view that participation in civic life was enriching and ennobling activity, but Mill saw that for a woman, no public-spirited dimension to her life was possible. There was no impetus to consider with others the principles which were to govern their common life, no incentive to conform to principles which defined their mutual activity for the common good, no possibility for the self-development which comes from citizen activity.[23] The cost to women was obvious; they were dull, or petty, or unprincipled (2: 168; 4: 238). The cost to men was less apparent but no less real; in seeking a reflection of themselves in the consciousness of these stunted women, men deceived, deluded, and limited themselves.

Mill was convinced that men were corrupted by their dominance over women. The most corrupting element of male domination of women was that men learned to "worship their own will as such a grand thing that it is actually the law for another rational being" (2: 172). Such self-worship arises at a very tender age, and blots out a boy's natural understanding of himself and his relationship to others.

A boy may be "the most frivolous and empty or the most ignorant and stolid of mankind," but "by the mere fact of being born a male" he is encouraged to think that "he is by right the superior of all and every one of an entire half of the human race: including probably some whose real superiority he had daily or hourly occasion to feel" (4: 218). By contrast, women were taught "to live for others" and "to have no life but in their affections," and then further to confine their affections to "the men with whom they are connected, or to the children who constitute an additional indefeasible tie between them and a man" (1: 141). The result of this upbringing was that what women would tell men was not, could not be, wholly true; women's sensibilities were systematically warped by their subjection. Thus the reflections were not accurate and men were deprived of self-knowledge.[24]

The picture which emerged was strikingly similar to that which Hegel described in his passages on the relationship between master and slave in *The Phenomenology of Mind*.[25] The lord who sees himself solely as master, wrote Hegel, cannot obtain an independent self-consciousness. The master thinks he is autonomous, but in fact he relies totally upon his slaves, not only to fulfill his needs and desires, but also for his identity: "Without slaves, he is no master." The master could not acquire the fullest self-consciousness when the "other" in whom he viewed himself was in the reduced human condition of slavery: to be *merely* a master was to fall short of full self-consciousness, and to define himself in terms of the "thing" he owns. So for Mill, men who have propagated the belief that all men are superior to all women have fatally affected the dialectic involved in knowing oneself through the consciousness others have of one. The present relationship between the sexes produced in men that "self-worship" which "all privileged persons, and all privileged classes" have had. That distortion deceives men and other privileged groups as to both their character and their self-worth.[26]

No philosopher prior to Mill had developed such a sustained argument about the corrupting effects on men of their social superiority over and separation from women. Previous philosophers had argued either that the authority of men over women was natural (Aristotle, Grotius), or that while there was no natural dominance of men over women prior to the establishment of families, in any civil society such preeminence was necessary to settle the dispute over who should govern the household (Locke), or the result of women's consent in return for protection (Hobbes), or the consequence of the development of the sentiments of nurturance and love (Rousseau).[27] None had suggested that domestic arrangements might diminish a man's ability to contribute to public debates in the agora or to the rational governing of a democratic republic. Yet Mill was determined to show that the development of the species was held in check by that domestic slavery produced by the fear of equality, by spousal hierarchy, and by a lack of the reciprocity and mutuality of true friendship.

III. The Hope of Friendship

Mill's remedy for the evils generated by the fear of equality was his notion of marital friendship. The topic of the rather visionary fourth chapter of *The Subjection of Women* was friendship, "the ideal of marriage" (4: 233, 235). That ideal was, according to Mill, "a union of thoughts and inclinations" which created a "foundation of solid friendship" between husband and wife (4: 231, 233).

Mill's praise of marital friendship was almost lyrical, and struck resonances with Aristotle's, Cicero's, and Montaigne's similar exaltations of the pleasures as well as the moral enrichment of this form of human intimacy. Mill wrote:

> When each of two persons, instead of being a nothing, is a something; when they are attached to one another, and are not too much unlike to begin with; the constant partaking of the same things, assisted by their sympathy, draws out the latent capacities of each for being interested in the things . . . by a real enriching of the two natures, each acquiring the tastes and capacities of the other in addition to its own [4: 233].

This expansion of human capacities did not, however, exhaust the benefits of friendship. Most importantly, friendship developed what Montaigne praised as the abolition of selfishness, the capacity to regard another human being as fully as worthy as oneself. Therefore friendship of the highest order could only exist between those equal in excellence.[28] And for precisely this reason, philosophers from Aristotle to Hegel had consistently argued that women could not be men's friends, for women lacked the moral capacity for the highest forms of friendship. Indeed, it was common to distinguish the marital bond from friendship not solely on the basis of sexual and procreative activity, but also because women could not be part of the school of moral virtue which was found in friendship at its best.

Mill therefore made a most significant break with the past in adopting the language of friendship in his discussion of marriage. For Mill, no less than for any of his predecessors, "the true virtue of human beings is the fitness to live together as equals." Such equality required that individuals "[claim] nothing for themselves but what they as freely concede to every one else," that they regard command of any kind as "an exceptional necessity," and that they prefer whenever possible "the society of those with whom leading and following can be alternate and reciprocal" (4: 174–175). This picture of reciprocity, of the shifting of leadership according to need, was a remarkable characterization of family life. Virtually all of Mill's liberal contemporaries accepted the notion of the natural and inevitable complimentariness of male and female personalities and roles. Mill, however, as early as 1833 had expressed his belief that "the highest masculine and the highest feminine" characters were without any real distinction.[29] That view of the androgynous personality lent support to Mill's brief for equality within the family.

Mill repeatedly insisted that his society had no general experience of "the marriage relationship as it would exist between equals," and that such marriages would be impossible until men rid themselves of the fear of equality and the will to domination.[30] The liberation of women, in other words, required not just legal reform but a reeducation of the passions. Women were to be regarded as equals not only to fulfill the demand for individual rights and in order that they could survive in the public world of work, but also in order that women and men could form ethical relations of the highest order. Men and women alike had to "learn to cultivate their strongest sympathy with an equal in rights and in cultivation" (4: 236). Mill struggled, not always with total success, to talk about the quality of such association. For example, in *On Liberty*, Mill explicitly rejected von Humbolt's characterization of marriage as a contractual relationship which could be ended by "the declared will of either party to dissolve it." That kind of dissolution was appropriate when the benefits of partnership could be reduced to monetary terms. But marriage involved a person's expectations for the fulfillment of a "plan of life," and created "a new series of moral obligations . . . toward that person, which may possibly be overruled, but cannot be ignored."[31] Mill was convinced that difficult though it might be to shape the law to recognize the moral imperatives of such a relationship, there were ethical communities which transcended and were not reducible to their individual components.

At this juncture, however, the critical force of Mill's essay weakened, and a tension developed between his ideal and his prescriptions for his own society. For all his insight into the dynamics of domestic domination and subordination, the only specific means Mill in fact put forward for the fostering of this society of equals was providing equal opportunity to women in areas outside the family. Indeed, in *On Liberty* he wrote that "nothing more is needed for the complete removal of [the almost despotic power of husbands over wives] than that wives should have the same rights and should receive the same protection of law in the same manner, as all other persons."[32] In the same vein, Mill seemed to suggest that nothing more was needed for women to achieve equality than that "the present duties and protective bounties in favour of men should be recalled" (1: 154). Moreover, Mill did not attack the traditional assumption about men's and women's different responsibilities in an ongoing household, although he was usually careful to say that women "chose" their role or that it was the most "expedient" arrangement, not that it was theirs by "nature."

Mill by and large accepted the notion that once they marry, women should be solely responsible for the care of the household and children, men for providing the family income: "When the support of the family depends . . . on earnings, the common arrangement, by which the man earns the income and the wife superintends the domestic expenditure, seems to me in general the most suitable division of labour between the two persons" (2: 178). He did not regard it as "a desirable custom, that the wife should contribute by her labour to the income of the family" (2: 179). Mill indicated that women alone would care for any children of the marriage; repeatedly he called it the "care which . . . nobody else takes," the one vocation in which there is "nobody to compete with them," and the occupation which "cannot be fulfilled by others" (2: 178; 3: 183; 4: 241). Further, Mill seemed to shut the door on combining household duties and a public life: "like a man when he chooses a profession, so, when a woman marries, it may be in general understood that she makes a choice of the management of a household, and the bringing up of a family, as the first call upon her exertions . . . and that she renounces . . . all [other occupations] which are not consistent with the requirements of this" (1: 179).

Mill's acceptance of the traditional gender-based division of labor in the family has led some recent critics to fault Mill for supposing that legal equality of opportunity would solve the problem of women's subjection, even while leaving the sexual division of labor in the household intact. For example, Julia Annas, after praising Mill's theoretical arguments in support of equality, complains that Mill's suggestions for actual needed changes in sex roles are "timid and reformist at best. He assumes that most women will in fact want only to be wives and mothers."[33] Leslie Goldstein agrees that "the restraints which Mill believed should be imposed on married women constitute a major exception to his argument for equality of individual liberty between the sexes—an exception so enormous that it threatens to swallow up the entire argument."[34] But such arguments, while correctly identifying the limitations of antidiscrimination statutes as instruments for social change, incorrectly identify Mill's argument for equal opportunity as the conclusion of his discussion of male-female equality.[35] On the contrary, Mill's final prescription to end the subjection of women was not equal opportunity but spousal friendship; equal opportunity was a means whereby such friendship could be encouraged.

The theoretical force of Mill's condemnation of domestic hierarchy has not yet been sufficiently appreciated. Mill's commitment to equality in marriage was of a different theoretical order than his acceptance of a continued sexual division of labor. On the one hand, Mill's belief in the necessity of equality as a precondition to marital friendship was a profound theoretical tenet. It rested on the normative assumption that human relationships between equals were of a higher, more enriching order than those between unequals. Mill's belief that equality was more suitable to friendship than inequality was as unalterable as his conviction that democracy was a better system of government than despotism; the human spirit could not develop its fullest potential when living in absolute subordination to another human being or to government.[36] On the other hand, Mill's belief that friendship could be attained and sustained while women bore nearly exclusive responsibility for the home was a statement which might be modified or even abandoned if experience proved it to be wrong. In this sense it was like Mill's view that the question of whether socialism was preferable to capitalism could not be settled by verbal argument alone but must "work itself out on an experimental scale, by actual trial."[37] Mill believed that marital equality was a moral imperative; his view that such equality might exist where married men and women moved in different spheres of activity was a proposition subject to demonstration. Had Mill discovered that managing the household to the exclusion of most other activity created an impediment to the friendship of married women and men, *The Subjection of Women* suggests that he would have altered his view of practicable domestic arrangements, but not his commitment to the desirability of male-female friendship in marriage.

The most interesting shortcomings of Mill's analysis are thus not found in his belief in the efficacy of equal opportunity, but rather in his blindness to what other conditions might hinder or promote marital friendship. In his discussion of family life, for example, Mill seemed to forget his own warning that women could be imprisoned not only "by actual law" but also "by custom equivalent to law" (4: 241). Similarly, he overlooked his own cautionary observation that in any household "there will naturally be more potential voice on the side, whichever it is, that brings the means of support" (2: 170). And although he had brilliantly depicted the narrowness and petty concerns of contemporary women who were totally excluded from political participation, he implied that the mistresses of most households might content themselves simply with exercising the suffrage (were it to be granted), a view hardly consistent with his arguments in other works for maximizing the level of political discussion and participation whenever possible. More significantly, however, Mill ignored the potential barrier between husband and wife which such different adult life experiences might create, and the contribution of shared experience to building a common sensibility and strengthening the bonds of friendship.

Mill also never considered that men might take any role in the family other than providing the economic means of support. Perhaps Mill's greatest oversight in his paean of marital equality was his failure to entertain the possibilities that nurturing and caring for children might provide men with useful knowledge and experience, and that shared parenting would contribute to the friendship between spouses which he so ardently desired. Similarly, Mill had virtually nothing to say about the positive role which sex might play in marriage. The sharp language with which he condemned undesired sexual relations as the execution of "an animal function" was nowhere supplemented by an appreciation of the possible enhancement which sexuality might add to marital friendship. One of the striking features of Montaigne's lyrical praise of friendship was that it was devoid of sensuality, for Montaigne abhorred "the Grecian license," and he was adamant that women were incapable of the highest forms of friendship. Mill's notion of spousal friendship suggested the possibility of a friendship which partook of both a true union of minds and of a physical expression of the delight in one's companion, a friendship which involved all of the human faculties. It was an opportunity which (undoubtedly to the relief of those such as James Fitzjames Stephen) Mill himself was not disposed to use, but which was nonetheless implicit in his praise of spousal friendship.[38]

One cannot ask Mill or any other theorist to "jump over Rhodes" and address issues not put forward by conditions and concerns of his own society.[39] Nevertheless, even leaving aside an analysis of the oppression inherent in the class structure (an omission which would have to be rectified in a full analysis of liberation), time has made it clear that Mill's prescriptions alone will not destroy the master-slave relationship which he so detested. Women's aspirations for equality will not be met by insuring equal civic rights and equal access to jobs outside the home. To accomplish that end would require a transformation of economic and public structures which would allow wives and husbands to share those domestic tasks which Mill assigned exclusively to women. Some forms of publicly supported day-care, parental as well as maternity leaves, flexible work schedules, extensive and rapid public transportation, health and retirement benefits for part-time employment are among commonly proposed measures which would make the choice of Mill's ideal of marriage between equals possible. In their absence it is as foolish to talk about couples choosing the traditional division of labor in marriage as it was in Mill's day to talk about women choosing marriage: both are Hobson's choices, there are no suitable alternatives save at enormous costs to the individuals involved.

Mill's feminist vision, however, transcends his own immediate prescriptions for reform. The Subjection of Women is not only one of liberalism's most incisive arguments for equal opportunity, but it embodies as well a belief in the importance of friendship for human development and progress. The recognition of individual rights is important in Mill's view because it provides part of the groundwork for more important human relationships of trust, mutuality and reciprocity. Mill's plea for an end to the subjection of women is not made, as critics such as Gertrude Himmelfarb assert, in the name of "the absolute primacy of the individual," but in the name of the need of both men and women for community. Mill's essay is valuable both for its devastating critique of the corruption of marital inequality, and for its argument, however incomplete, that one of the aims of a liberal polity should be to promote the conditions which will allow friendship, in marriage and elsewhere, to take root and flourish.

Notes

1. Contemporary authors who criticize Mill's analysis of equal opportunity for women as not far-reaching enough are Julia Annas, "Mill and the Subjection of Women," *Philosophy* 52 (1977), 179–194; Leslie F. Goldstein, "Marx and Mill on the Equality of Women," paper presented at the Midwest Political Science Association Convention, Chicago, April 1978; Richard Krouse, "Patriarchal Liberalism and Beyond: From John Stuart Mill to Harriet Taylor," unpublished manuscript, Williamstown, MA; Susan Moller Okin, *Women in Western Political Thought* (Princeton: Princeton University Press, 1979). From a different perspective, Gertrude Himmelfarb, *On Liberty and Liberalism: the Case of John Stuart Mill* (New York: Alfred Knopf, 1974) criticizes Mill's doctrine of equality as being too absolute and particularly takes issue with modern feminist applications of his theory.
2. J. S. Mill, *The Subjection of Women* (1869) in Alice Rossi, ed., *Essays on Sex Equality* (Chicago: University of Chicago Press, 1970), ch. 2, p. 173. All references to *The Subjection of Women* will be to this edition and will be given in the body of the text using chapter and page, i.e., (2: 173).
3. Hansard, *Parliamentary Debates*, series 3, v. 189 (May 20, 1867), p. 820.
4. Letter to August Comte, October, 1843, *The Collected Works of John Stuart Mill* (hereafter *C. W.*). v. XIII, *The Earlier Letters*, ed. Francis C. Mineka (Toronto: University of Toronto Press, 1963), p. 609, my translation.
5. Mill's analysis of women's choice of marriage as a state of life reminds one of Hobbes' discussion of some defeated soldier giving his consent to the rule of a conquering sovereign. Women, it is true, could decide which among several men to marry, while Hobbes' defeated yeoman had no choice of master. But what could either do but join the only protective association available to each?
6. A brief account of the struggle to provide for women's higher education in England can be found in Ray Strachey, *The Cause* (London: G. Bell, 1928), pp. 124–165.
7. Hansard, v. 189 (May 20, 1867).
8. *Idem.* In the United States, one well-documented case in which a woman was prohibited from practicing law was Bradwell v. Illinois, 83 U.S. (16 Wall) 130 (1873).
9. *The Principles of Political Economy* (1848) in *C. W.*, II, p. 394 and III, pp. 765–766.
10. Tobias Hobson, a Cambridge carrier commemorated by Milton in two Epigraphs, would only hire out the horse nearest the door of his stable, even if a client wanted another. *Oxford English Dictionary*, II, p. 369.
11. William Blackstone, *Commentaries on the Laws of England* 4 vols. (Oxford: Clarendon Press, 1765–1769), Book I, ch. XV, p. 430. The consequences of the doctrine of spousal unity were various: a man could not make a contract with his wife since "to covenant with her would be to covenant with himself;" a wife could not sue without her husband's concurrence; a husband was bound to "provide his wife with necessaries . . . as much as himself"; a husband was responsible for certain criminal acts of his wife committed in his

presence; and, as a husband was responsible for his wife's acts, he "might give his wife moderate correction . . . in the same moderation that (he is) allowed to correct his apprentices or children."

12. The rich found ways around the common law's insistence that the management and use of any income belonged to a woman's husband, by setting up trusts which were governed by the laws and courts of equity. A succinct explanation of the law of property as it affected married women in the nineteenth century is found in Erna Reiss, *Rights and Duties of Englishwomen* (Manchester, 1934), pp. 20–34.

13. Hansard, v. 192 (June 10, 1867), p. 1371. Several Married Women's Property Bills, which would have given married women possession of their earnings were presented in Parliament beginning in 1857, but none was successful until 1870.

14. *Ibid.,* v. 189 (May 20, 1867), p. 826.

15. Mill's outrage at women's lack of recourse in the face of domestic violence is reminiscent of the protests in the United States during the civil rights movement at token sentences pronounced by white juries against whites accused of assaulting Blacks in Southern states, and of Susan Brownmiller's argument in *Against Our Will: Men, Women and Rape,* that the desultory prosecution of rapists is itself a manifestation of violence against women.

16. John Ruskin, "Of Queen's Gardens," in *Works,* ed. E. T. Cook and A.D.C. Wedderburn, 39 vols. (London: G. Allen, 1902–1912), XVIII, p. 122.

17. Walter E. Houghton, *The Victorian Frame of Mind* (New Haven: Yale University Press, 1957), p. 344.

18. James Fitzjames Stephen, *Liberty, Equality, Fraternity* (New York: Henry Holt, n. d.), p. 206.

19. On the relationship between John Stuart Mill and Harriet Taylor see F. A. Hayek, *John Stuart Mill and Harriet Taylor; their correspondence and subsequent marriage* (Chicago: University of Chicago Press, 1951); Michael St. John Packe, *The Life of John Stuart Mill* (New York: Macmillan, 1954); Alice Rossi, "Sentiment and Intellect" in *Essays on Sex Equality* (Chicago: University of Chicago Press, 1970); and Gertrude Himmelfarb, pp. 187–238.

20. The Matrimonial Causes Act of 1857, as the divorce measure was known, allowed men to divorce their wives for adultery, but women had to establish that their husbands were guilty of either cruelty or desertion in addition to adultery in order to obtain a separation. Mill was reluctant to say what he thought the terms of divorce should be in a rightly ordered society (see note 31), but he was adamant that the double standard was wrong in policy and unjust in principle.

   Mill also spoke out sharply against that sexual double standard in his testimony before the Commission studying the repeal of the Contagious Diseases Act, an act which allowed for the arrest and forced hospitalization of prostitutes with venereal disease, but made no provision for the arrest of their clients. "The Evidence of John Stuart Mill taken before the Royal Commission of 1870 on the Administration and Operation of the Contagious Diseases Acts of 1866 and 1869" (London, 1871).

21. For a discussion of Mill's views on equality generally, see Dennis Thompson, *John Stuart Mill and Representative Government* (Princeton: Princeton University Press, 1976), pp. 158–173.

22. See, for example, Dorothy Dinnerstein, *The Mermaid and the Minotaur: Sexual Arrangements and Human Malaise* (New York: Harper and Row, 1976); Nancy Chodorow, *The Reproduction of Mothering: Psychoanalysis and the Sociology of Gender* (Berkeley: University of California Press, 1978); and Philip Slater, *The Glory of Hera* (Boston: Beacon Press, 1971) and the references therein.

23. See also Mill's *Considerations on Representative Government* (1861) where he lambasted benevolent despotism because it encouraged "passivity" and "abdication of [one's] own energies," and his praise of the Athenian dicastry and ecclesia. *C. W.,* XIX, pp. 399–400, 411. During his speech on the Reform Bill of 1867, Mill argued that giving women the vote would provide "that stimulus to their faculties . . . which the suffrage seldom fails to produce." Hansard, v. 189 (May 20, 1867), 824.

24. Mill's insight was like that which Virginia Woolf used in *A Room of One's Own.* Woolf, trying to explain the source of men's anger at independent women, stated that such anger

could not be "merely the cry of wounded vanity"; it had to be "a protest against some in-fringement of his power to believe in himself." Women have served throughout history as "looking glasses possessing the magic and delicious power of reflecting the figure of a man at twice its natural size." Mill also argued that in order to create such a mirror, men had dis-torted women by education and had warped the reflection which women showed to men. Virginia Woolf, *A Room of One's Own* (New York: Harcourt Brace and World, 1929), p. 35.

25. G. W. F. Hegel, *The Phenomenology of Mind,* trans. J. B. Baillie (New York: Harper and Row, 1969). This paragraph is indebted to the excellent study of the *Phenomenology* by Judith N. Shklar, *Freedom and Independence* (Cambridge: Cambridge University Press, 1976), from which the quote is taken, p. 61. Mill's analysis also calls to mind Simone de Beauvoir's discussion of "the Other" and its role in human consciousness: in *The Second Sex,* trans. H. M. Parshley (New York: Random House, Vintage Books, 1974), pp. xix ff.

26. Mill argued in addition that men's injustices to women created habits which encouraged them to act unjustly towards others. In *The Subjection of Women* Mill asserted that the habits of domination are acquired in and fostered by the family, which is often, as respects its chief, "a school of wilfulness, overbearingness, unbounded self-indulgeance, and a double-dyed and idealized selfishness" (2: 165). Virtue, for Mill, was not simply action taken in accordance with a calculus of pleasure and pain, but was habitual behavior. In *Considerations on Representative Government,* he lamented the effects "fostered by the possession of power" by "a man, or a class of men" who "finding themselves worshipped by others . . . become worshipers of themselves." *C. W.,* XIX, p. 445.

27. For excellent studies of each of these authors views on women (except for Grotius) see Okin. Grotius' views can be found in his *De Juri Belli ac Pacis Libri Tres [On the Law of War and Peace.]* (1625), trans. Francis W. Kelsey (Oxford: Clarendon Press, 1925), Bk. II, ch. V, sec. i, p. 231.

28. Montaigne's essay, "Of Friendship" in *The Complete Works of Montaigne,* trans. Donald M. Frame (Stanford: Stanford University Press, 1948), pp. 135–144.

29. Letter to Thomas Carlyle, October 5, 1833, *C. W.,* XII, *Earlier Letters,* p. 184.

30. Letter to John Nichol, August 1869, *C. W.,* XVII, *The Later Letters,* ed. Francis C. Mineka and Dwight N. Lindley (Toronto: University of Toronto Press, 1972), p. 1834.

31. *C. W.,* XVIII, 300. Elsewhere Mill wrote, "My opinion on Divorce is that . . . nothing ought to be rested in, short of entire freedom on both sides to dissolve this like any other partnership." Letter to an unidentified correspondent, November 1855, *C. W.,* XIV, *Later Letters,* p. 500. But against this letter was the passage from *On Liberty,* and his letter to Henry Rusden of July 1870 in which he abjured making any final judgments about what a proper divorce law would be "until women have an equal voice in making it." He denied that he advocated that marriage should be dissolule "at the will of either party," and stated that no well-grounded opinion could be put forward until women first achieved equality under the laws and in married life. *C. W.,* XVII, *Later Letters,* pp. 1750–1751.

32. *C. W.,* XVIII, p. 301.

33. Annas, 189.

34. Goldstein, p. 8. Susan Okin makes a similar point, stating that "Mill never questioned or objected to the maintenance of traditional sex roles within the family, but, expressly considered them to be suitable and desirable" (Okin, p. 237). Okin's reading of Mill is basically sound and sympathetic, but does not recognize the theoretical priority of Mill's commitment to marital equality and friendship.

35. Of recent writers on Mill, only Richard Krouse seems sensitive to the inherent tension in Mill's thought about women in the household. Mill's own "ideal of a reformed family life, based upon a full nonpatriarchal marriage bond," Krouse points out, requires "on the logic of his own analysis . . . [the] rejection of the traditional division of labor between the sexes" (Krouse, p. 39).

36. *Considerations on Representative Government, C. W.,* XIX, pp. 399–403.

37. *Chapters on Socialism* (1879), *C. W.,* V, p. 736.

38. Throughout his writings Mill displayed a tendency to dismiss or deprecate the erotic dimension of life. In his *Autobiography* he wrote approvingly that his father looked forward

to an increase in freedom in relations between the sexes, freedom which would be devoid of any sensuality "either of a theoretical or of a practical kind." His own twenty-year friendship with Harriet Taylor before their marriage was "one of strong affection and confidential intimacy only." *Autobiography of John Stuart Mill* (New York: Columbia University Press, 1944), pp. 75, 161. In *The Principles of Political Economy* Mill remarked that in his own day "the animal instinct" occupied a "disproportionate preponderance in human life." *C. W.,* III, p. 766.

39. G. W. F. Hegel, *The Philosophy of Right,* ed. T. M. Knox (London: Oxford University Press, 1952), p. 11, quoted in Krouse, p. 40.

Friedrich Nietzsche

The name Friedrich Nietzsche calls to mind a vision of a man with a quirky and dark perspective on the human condition. Such a vision stems partly from his idiosyncratic manner of expression—short aphorisms punctuated by quotable phrases like "God is dead" or the "will to power," which often shocks or bewilders the first-time reader. Largely, however, that vision is the inevitable legacy of a writer who criticized all traditional moral values, who saw us as human beings stripped of all illusion. If we find the vision disconcerting, it may be because Nietzsche dares us to confront our innermost suspicions and insecurities with brutal honesty.

Nietzsche was born in Prussia in 1844. The son of a Lutheran pastor who died when he was four, Nietzsche was raised largely by his mother and other female relatives. An excellent student, in 1864 he began attending the University of Bonn where he studied philology and theology. A year later, he followed his favorite classics teacher, Friedrich Ritschl, to Liepzig. It was during this period that he discovered the work of Arthur Schopenhauer, whose pessimistic philosophy of blind will he found alluring. After a year of military service in 1867, he returned to Liepzig and befriended the German composer Richard Wagner.

In 1869, Nietzsche was made an associate professor of classical philology at the University of Basel; apparently because of Ritschl's influence, since Nietzsche had not yet completed his doctoral studies. Nietzsche's lectures and early works focused on Greek culture, thus setting the stage for his later views on the rebirth of culture in

Germany. In 1878, he gained a reputation as a social critic with the publication of *Human, All Too Human*. In 1879, Nietzsche retired from university teaching due to ill health, but he continued writing significant philosophical works for the rest of his life.

Throughout the 1880s, Nietzsche published a spate of now-classic works, including *The Gay Science, Beyond Good and Evil, The Genealogy of Morals,* and *Thus Spoke Zarathustra*. In these works, Nietzsche argued that morality is merely a tool used by the weak to restrain the strong and that, eventually, a superman or over-man (*Übermensch*) will emerge—the kind of person who will not be afraid to break with conventional morality and pursue new horizons through intense self-criticism and personal challenge.

As his repeated bouts with illness and poverty gave way to madness, Nietzsche spent his last days in an asylum. He finally died of a stroke in 1900. Several works were published posthumously, including *The Will to Power,* a compilation from the many scattered notes he left behind.

Among the many significant ideas Nietzsche advanced, the concept of a "will to power" is central. The term expresses the idea that all life, by its very presence, seeks to control its environment. This control can take various forms, from simple resource dominance among animal species, to self-confident assertions of mastery in more complex human interactions, such as intellectual argument or politics. Though this notion has been used to demonstrate his totalitarian tendencies, Nietzsche was more concerned with the will to power's artistic and philosophical aspects than with its political implications.

Nietzsche believed that Western civilization was in decline, largely because it had too long denied the elemental forces of human psychology and social life. Conventional morality, with such categories as sin, pity, and God, had submerged the will to power to an ethic of ascetic self-denial. At one time, moral viewpoints showed a capacity to elevate human horizons and to motivate noble action, but in modern times, morality has served only to perpetuate the control of the weak over the strong. This "slave morality" has outlived its usefulness and now stymies the opening of new intellectual and social horizons. With a fearless recognition that the old, illusory morality is obsolete (i.e., that God is dead), civilization's only hope for regeneration lies in a re-evaluation of all values, the development of a new moral code by the "man of the future"—the *Übermensch*.

The most obscure of Nietzsche's views concerns the concept of the "eternal recurrence." As a scientific doctrine, it refers to the perpetual recurrence of the same sequences of events; the same combinations of forces found in human life and history. Thus, we are destined to be reborn and live the same lives again in future worlds. As a philosophical myth, however, eternal recurrence indicates one's eagerness to embrace life by willing its infinite repetition. The point Nietzsche makes with this concept is essentially the point of his whole philosophy: one must live a life of meaningful self-assertion and mastery, rather than a life of complacent mediocrity and servility.

Since his political views are seldom explicitly stated, Nietzsche is sometimes overlooked by political philosophers. Yet, his social criticism and challenging psychology should force political theorists to reconsider their basic assumptions on a host of issues, from the nature of human beings to the moral basis of community. Nietzsche's influence has affected philosophers from Heidegger and Sartre to Derrida and Foucault, as well as schools of thought from existentialism to post-modernism.

Beyond Good and Evil and The Genealogy of Morals

The selections reprinted here illustrate Nietzsche's unique manner of expression, his genealogical method, and his central philosophical concerns. First published in 1886, *Beyond Good and Evil* contains 296 wide-ranging aphorisms, arranged in nine major sections, and linked by a concern to discuss the nature of morality. The central focus of the aphorisms included here is the nature of the will to power, especially as it relates to moral values. For example, aphorisms 257–260 and 263–264 suggest that one of the most important human characteristics is the drive to create new moral values—if we dare. Only through encouraging that creative energy can society overcome a corrupt civilization and achieve spiritual greatness.

The Genealogy of Morals, published in 1887, continues the discussion of morality—this time focusing on the important question of its origins. In this work, Nietzsche explores the linguistic origins and philosophic implications of such concepts as "good," "bad," "guilt," and "bad conscience." He believes that modern values may be traced to a conflict between a master morality of the strong, creatively affirming what is good, and a slave morality of the weak arising out of resentment and envy (ressentiment). The problem with Western civilization is that it has fallen victim to a pervasive sickness marked by philosophical illusion and ascetic self-denial—in short, a sickness brought about by the victory of slave morality.

Commentaries

In the first selection, Tracy Strong reviews Nietzsche's theory of the evolution of slave morality. What begins with the attempt by the weak to dictate terms of behavior to the strong, ends with the "ressentiment" that allocates to other people responsibility for the pain one suffers. Nietzsche traces the origin of slave morality to the philosophy of Socrates and the Stoics, and to the theology of Judaism and Christianity. In those worldviews, Nietzsche finds the kernel of a morality that used to be noble, but now needlessly corrupts society and limits human horizons.

Next, Mark Warren suggests that "neoaristocratic conservatism" is the proper label for Nietzsche's implicit political views. The term appropriately captures his fascination with social hierarchies and his organic view of culture. Despite this orientation, Warren finds that Nietzsche's views are still valuable. His remorseless critique of liberalism and other points of view may well provide the framework for a liberating political philosophy, a postmodern reconceptualization of politics.

Key Words

Will to power.   An elemental life force expressed, in social life, as the assertion of self over nature and over other people.

Superman, over-man, Übermensch.   The individual(s) of the future who will transcend the remnants of decaying Western culture by forging new horizons for the self and civilization.

Ressentiment.   A feeling of blame directed at those considered responsible for one's suffering; a characteristic of slave morality.

Pathos of distance. The feelings and values associated with society's division into ruling and servile, noble and base classes.

For Further Reading

Heidegger, M. 1979. *Nietzsche.* San Francisco: Harper & Row.

Love, N. 1986. *Marx, Nietzsche, and Modernity.* New York: Columbia University Press.

Megill, A. 1985. *Prophets of Extremity: Nietzsche, Heidegger, Foucault, Derrida.* Berkeley, Calif.: University of California Press.

Schutte, O. 1984. *Beyond Nihilism: Nietzsche Without Masks.* Chicago: University of Chicago Press.

Beyond Good and Evil

Part One
On the Prejudices of Philosophers

9

"According to nature" you want to *live?* O you noble Stoics, what deceptive words these are! Imagine a being like nature, wasteful beyond measure, indifferent beyond measure, without purposes and consideration, without mercy and justice, fertile and desolate and uncertain at the same time; imagine indifference itself as a power—how *could* you live according to this indifference? Living—is that not precisely wanting to be other than this nature? Is not living—estimating, preferring, being unjust, being limited, wanting to be different? And supposing your imperative "live according to nature" meant at bottom as much as "live according to life"—how could you *not* do that? Why make a principle of what you yourselves are and must be?

In truth, the matter is altogether different: while you pretend rapturously to read the canon of your law in nature, you want something opposite, you strange actors and self-deceivers! Your pride wants to impose your morality, your ideal, on nature—even on nature—and incorporate them in her; you demand that she should be nature "according to the Stoa," and you would like all existence to exist only after your own image—as an immense eternal glorification and generalization of Stoicism. For all your love of truth, you have forced yourselves so long, so persistently, so rigidly-hypnotically to see nature the wrong way, namely Stoically, that you are no longer able to see her differently. And some abysmal arrogance finally still inspires you with the insane hope that *because* you know how to tyrannize yourselves— Stoicism is self-tyranny—nature, too, lets herself be tyrannized: is not the Stoic—a *piece* of nature?

But this is an ancient, eternal story: what formerly happened with the Stoics still happens today, too, as soon as any philosophy begins to believe in itself. It always creates the world in its own image; it cannot do otherwise. Philosophy is this tyrannical drive itself, the most spiritual will to power, to the "creation of the world," to the *causa prima.* . . .

13

Physiologists should think before putting down the instinct of self-preservation as the cardinal instinct of an organic being. A living thing seeks above all to *discharge* its strength—life itself is *will to power;* self-preservation is only one of the indirect and most frequent *results.*

In short, here as everywhere else, let us beware of *superfluous* teleological principles—one of which is the instinct of self-preservation (we owe it to

Excerpts from Friedrich Nietzsche. [1966]. *Beyond Good and Evil: Prelude to the Philosophy of the Future* (translated and with commentary by Walter Kaufmann). New York: Vintage, pp. 15–16, 21, 25–32, 135–139, 174–177, 201–208, 212–214. Reprinted with the permission of Random House, Inc.

Spinoza's inconsistency).[1] Thus method, which must be essentially economy of principles, demands it. . . .

19

Philosophers are accustomed to speak of the will as if it were the best-known thing in the world; indeed, Schopenhauer has given us to understand that the will alone is really known to us, absolutely and completely known, without subtraction or addition. But again and again it seems to me that in this case, too, Schopenhauer only did what philosophers are in the habit of doing—he adopted a *popular prejudice* and exaggerated it. Willing seems to me to be above all something *complicated*, something that is a unit only as a word—and it is precisely in this one word that the popular prejudice lurks, which has defeated the always inadequate caution of philosophers. So let us for once be more cautious, let us be "unphilosophical": let us say that in all willing there is, first, a plurality of sensations, namely, the sensation of the state *"away from which,"* the sensation of the state *"towards which,"* the sensations of this *"from"* and *"towards"* themselves, and then also an accompanying muscular sensation, which, even without our putting into motion "arms and legs," begins its action by force of habit as soon as we "will" anything.

Therefore, just as sensations (and indeed many kinds of sensations) are to be recognized as ingredients of the will, so, secondly, should thinking also: in every act of the will there is a ruling thought—let us not imagine it possible to sever this thought from the "willing," as if any will would then remain over!

Third, the will is not only a complex of sensation and thinking, but it is above all an *affect*, and specifically the affect of the command. That which is termed "freedom of the will" is essentially the affect of superiority in relation to him who must obey: "I am free, 'he' must obey"—this conscious-ness is inherent in every will; and equally so the straining of the attention, the straight look that fixes itself exclusively on one aim, the unconditional evaluation that "this and nothing else is necessary now," the inward cer-tainty that obedience will be rendered—and whatever else belongs to the position of the commander. A man who *wills* commands something within himself that renders obedience, or that he believes renders obedience.

But now let us notice what is strangest about the will—this manifold thing for which the people have only one word: inasmuch as in the given circumstances we are at the same time the commanding *and* the obeying parties, and as the obeying party we know the sensations of constraint, impulsion, pressure, resistance, and motion, which usually begin immedi-ately after the act of will; inasmuch as, on the other hand, we are accus-tomed to disregard this duality, and to deceive ourselves about it by means of the synthetic concept "I," a whole series of erroneous conclusions, and consequently of false evaluations of the will itself, has become attached to the act of willing—to such a degree that he who wills believes sincerely that willing *suffices* for action. Since in the great majority of cases there has been exercise of will only when the effect of the command—that is, obedience;

---

1. Nietzsche admired Spinoza for, among other things, his critique of teleology.

that is, the action—was to be *expected*, the *appearance* has translated itself into the feeling, as if there were *a necessity of effect*. In short, he who wills believes with a fair amount of certainty that will and action are somehow one; he ascribes the success, the carrying out of the willing, to the will itself, and thereby enjoys an increase of the sensation of power which accompanies all success.

"Freedom of the will"—that is the expression for the complex state of delight of the person exercising volition, who commands and at the same time identifies himself with the executor of the order—who, as such, enjoys also the triumph over obstacles, but thinks within himself that it was really his will itself that overcame them. In this way the person exercising volition adds the feelings of delight of his successful executive instruments, the useful "under-wills" or under-souls—indeed, our body is but a social structure composed of many souls—to his feelings of delight as commander. *L'effet c'est moi*:[2]—what happens here is what happens in every well-constructed and happy commonwealth; namely, the governing class identifies itself with the successes of the commonwealth. In all willing it is absolutely a question of commanding and obeying, on the basis, as already said, of a social structure composed of many "souls." Hence a philosopher should claim the right to include willing as such within the sphere of morals—morals being understood as the doctrine of the relations of supremacy under which the phenomenon of "life" comes to be. . . .

21

The *causa sui* is the best self-contradiction that has been conceived so far, it is a sort of rape and perversion of logic; but the extravagant pride of man has managed to entangle itself profoundly and frightfully with just this nonsense. The desire for "freedom of the will" in the superlative metaphysical sense, which still holds sway, unfortunately, in the minds of the half-educated; the desire to bear the entire and ultimate responsibility for one's actions oneself, and to absolve God, the world, ancestors, chance, and society involves nothing less than to be precisely this *causa sui* and, with more than Münchhausen's audacity, to pull oneself up into existence by the hair, out of the swamps of nothingness. Suppose someone were thus to see through the boorish simplicity of this celebrated concept of "free will" and put it out of his head altogether, I beg of him to carry his "enlightenment" a step further, and also put out of his head the contrary of this monstrous conception of "free will": I mean "unfree will," which amounts to a misuse of cause and effect. One should not wrongly reify "cause" and "effect," as the natural scientists do (and whoever, like them, now "naturalizes" in his thinking), according to the prevailing mechanical doltishness which makes the cause press and push until it "effects" its end; one should use "cause" and "effect" only as pure concepts, that is to say, as conventional fictions for the purpose of designation and communication—*not* for explanation. In the "in-itself" there is nothing of "causal connections," of "necessity," or of "psychological non-freedom"; there the effect does *not* follow the cause, there is no rule of "law." It is *we* alone who have devised cause, sequence,

---

2. "*I* am the effect."

for-each-other, relativity, constraint, number, law, freedom, motive, and purpose; and when we project and mix this symbol world into things as if it existed "in itself," we act once more as we have always acted—*mythologically.* The "unfree will" is mythology; in real life it is only a matter of *strong* and *weak* wills.

It is almost always a symptom of what is lacking in himself when a thinker senses in every "causal connection" and "psychological necessity" something of constraint, need, compulsion to obey, pressure, and unfreedom; it is suspicious to have such feelings—the person betrays himself. And in general, if I have observed correctly, the "unfreedom of the will" is regarded as a problem from two entirely opposite standpoints, but always in a profoundly *personal* manner: some will not give up their "responsibility," their belief in *themselves,* the personal right to *their* merits at any price (the vain races belong to this class). Others, on the contrary, do not wish to be answerable for anything, or blamed for anything, and owing to an inward self-contempt, seek to *lay the blame for themselves somewhere else.* The latter, when they write books, are in the habit today of taking the side of criminals; a sort of socialist pity is their most attractive disguise. And as a matter of fact, the fatalism of the weak-willed embellishes itself surprisingly when it can pose as *"la religion de la souffrance humaine",*[3] that is *its* "good taste.". . .

23

All psychology so far has got stuck in moral prejudices and fears; it has not dared to descend into the depths. To understand it as morphology and *the doctrine of the development of the will to power,* as I do—nobody has yet come close to doing this even in thought—insofar as it is permissible to recognize in what has been written so far a symptom of what has so far been kept silent. The power of moral prejudices has penetrated deeply into the most spiritual world, which would seem to be the coldest and most devoid of presuppositions, and has obviously operated in an injurious, inhibiting, blinding, and distorting manner. A proper physio-psychology has to contend with unconscious resistance in the heart of the investigator, it has "the heart" against it: even a doctrine of the reciprocal dependence of the "good" and the "wicked" drives, causes (as refined immorality) distress and aversion in a still hale and hearty conscience—still more so, a doctrine of the derivation of all good impulses from wicked ones. If, however, a person should regard even the effects of hatred, envy, covetousness, and the lust to rule as conditions of life, as factors which, fundamentally and essentially, must be present in the general economy of life (and must, therefore, be further enhanced if life is to be further enhanced)—he will suffer from such a view of things as from seasickness. And yet even this hypothesis is far from being the strangest and most painful in this immense and almost new domain of dangerous insights; and there are in fact a hundred good reasons why everyone should keep away from it who—*can.*

On the other hand, if one has once drifted there with one's bark, well! all right! let us clench our teeth! let us open our eyes and keep our hand firm

---

3. "The religion of human suffering."

on the helm! We sail right *over* morality, we crush, we destroy perhaps the remains of our own morality by daring to make our voyage there—but what matter are *we!* Never yet did a *profounder* world of insight reveal itself to daring travelers and adventurers, and the psychologist who thus "makes a sacrifice"—it is *not* the *sacrifizio dell' intelletto,*[4] on the contrary!—will at least be entitled to demand in return that psychology shall be recognized again as the queen of the sciences, for whose service and preparation the other sciences exist. For psychology is now again the path to the fundamental problems. . . .

Part Six
We Scholars

211

I insist that people should finally stop confounding philosophical laborers, and scientific men generally, with philosophers; precisely at this point we should be strict about giving "each his due," and not far too much to those and far too little to these.

It may be necessary for the education of a genuine philosopher that he himself has also once stood on all these steps on which his servants, the scientific laborers of philosophy, remain standing—*have to* remain standing. Perhaps he himself must have been critic and skeptic and dogmatist and historian and also poet and collector and traveler and solver of riddles and moralist and seer and "free spirit" and almost everything in order to pass through the whole range of human values and value feelings and to be *able* to see with many different eyes and consciences, from a height and into every distance, from the depths into every height, from a nook into every expanse. But all these are merely preconditions of his task: this task itself demands something different—it demands that he *create values.*

Those philosophical laborers after the noble model of Kant and Hegel have to determine and press into formulas, whether in the realm of *logic* or *political* (moral) thought or *art*, some great data of valuations—that is, former *positings* of values, creations of value which have become dominant and are for a time called "truths." It is for these investigators to make everything that has happened and been esteemed so far easy to look over, easy to think over, intelligible and manageable, to abbreviate everything long, even "time," and to *overcome* the entire past—an enormous and wonderful task in whose service every subtle pride, every tough will can certainly find satisfaction. *Genuine philosophers, however, are commanders and legislators:* they say, *"thus* it *shall* be!" They first determine the Whither and For What of man, and in so doing have at their disposal the preliminary labor of all philosophical laborers, all who have overcome the past. With a creative hand they reach for the future, and all that is and has been becomes a means for them, an instrument, a hammer. Their "knowing" is *creating,* their creating is a legislation, their will to truth is—*will to power.*

Are there such philosophers today? Have there been such philosophers yet? *Must* there not be such philosophers?

---

4. Sacrifice of the intellect.

212

More and more it seems to me that the philosopher, being *of necessity* a man of tomorrow and the day after tomorrow, has always found himself, and *had* to find himself, in contradiction to his today: his enemy was ever the ideal of today. So far all these extraordinary furtherers of man whom one calls philosophers, though they themselves have rarely felt like friends of wisdom but rather like disagreeable fools and dangerous question marks, have found their task, their hard, unwanted, inescapable task, but eventually also the greatness of their task, in being the bad conscience of their time.

By applying the knife vivisectionally to the chest of the very *virtues of their time*, they betrayed what was their own secret: to know of a *new* greatness of man, of a new untrodden way to his enhancement. Every time they exposed how much hypocrisy, comfortableness, letting oneself go and letting oneself drop, how many lies lay hidden under the best honored type of their contemporary morality, how much virtue was *outlived*. Every time they said: "We must get there, that way, where *you* today are least at home."

Facing a world of "modern ideas" that would banish everybody into a corner and "specialty," a philosopher—if today there could be philosophers —would be compelled to find the greatness of man, the concept of "greatness," precisely in his range and multiplicity, in his wholeness in manifoldness. He would even determine value and rank in accordance with how much and how many things one could bear and take upon himself, how *far* one could extend his responsibility.

Today the taste of the time and the virtue of the time weakens and thins down the will; nothing is as timely as weakness of the will. In the philosopher's ideal, therefore, precisely strength of the will, hardness, and the capacity for long-range decisions must belong to the concept of "greatness"—with as much justification as the opposite doctrine and the ideal of a dumb, renunciatory, humble, selfless humanity was suitable for an opposite age, one that suffered, like the sixteenth century, from its accumulated energy of will and from the most savage floods and tidal waves of selfishness.

In the age of Socrates, among men of fatigued instincts, among the conservatives of ancient Athens who let themselves go—"toward happiness," as they said; toward pleasure, as they acted—and who all the while still mouthed the ancient pompous words to which their lives no longer gave them any right, *irony* may have been required for greatness of soul, that Socratic sarcastic assurance of the old physician and plebeian who cut ruthlessly into his own flesh, as he did into the flesh and heart of the "noble," with a look that said clearly enough: "Don't dissemble in front of me! Here—we are equal."

Today, conversely, when only the herd animal receives and dispenses honors in Europe, when "equality of rights" could all too easily be changed into equality in violating rights—I mean, into a common war on all that is rare, strange, privileged, the higher man, the higher soul, the higher duty, the higher responsibility, and the abundance of creative power and masterfulness—today the concept of greatness entails being noble, wanting to be by oneself, being able to be different, standing alone and having to live independently. And the philosopher will betray something of his own ideal when he posits: "He shall be greatest who can be loneliest, the most concealed, the most deviant, the human being beyond good and evil, the master of his virtues, he that is overrich in will. Precisely this shall be called *greatness:* being capable of being as manifold as whole, as ample as full." And to ask it once more: today—is greatness *possible?*...

Part Eight
Peoples and Fatherlands

241

We "good Europeans"—we, too, know hours when we permit ourselves some hearty fatherlandishness, a plop and relapse into old loves and narrownesses—I have just given a sample of that—hours of national agitations, patriotic palpitations, and various other sorts of archaizing sentimental inundations. More ponderous spirits than we are may require more time to get over what with us takes only hours and in a few hours has run its course: some require half a year, others half a life, depending on the speed and power of their digestion and metabolism. Indeed, I could imagine dull[5] and sluggish races who would require half a century even in our rapidly moving Europe to overcome such atavistic attacks of fatherlandishness and soil addiction and to return to reason, meaning "good Europeanism."

As I am digressing to this possibility, it so happens that I become an ear-witness of a conversation between two old "patriots": apparently both were hard of hearing and therefore spoke that much louder.

"*He* thinks and knows as much of philosophy as a peasant or a fraternity student," said one; "he is still innocent. But what does it matter today? This is the age of the masses: they grovel on their bellies before anything massive. In *politics,* too. A statesman who piles up for them another tower of Babel, a monster of empire and power, they call 'great'; what does it matter that we, more cautious and reserved, do not yet abandon the old faith that only a great thought can give a deed or cause greatness. Suppose a statesman put his people in a position requiring them to go in for 'great politics' from now on, though they were ill-disposed for that by nature and ill prepared as well, so that they would find it necessary to sacrifice their old and secure virtues for the sake of a novel and dubious mediocrity—suppose a statesman actually condemned his people to 'politicking' although so far they had had better things to do and think about, and deep down in their souls they had not got rid of a cautious disgust with the restlessness, emptiness, and noisy quarrelsomeness of peoples that really go in for politicking—suppose such a statesman goaded the slumbering passions and lusts of his people, turning their diffidence and delight in standing aside into a blot, their cosmopolitanism and secret infinity into a serious wrong, devaluating their most cordial inclinations, inverting their conscience, making their spirit narrow, their taste 'national'—what! a statesman who did all this, for whom his

---

5. *Dumpf* has no perfect equivalent in English. It can mean hollow or muted when applied to a sound, heavy and musty applied to air, dull applied to wits, and is a cousin of the English words, dumb and damp. Goethe still used it with a positive connotation when he wrote poetry about inarticulate feelings; Nietzsche uses the word often—with a strongly negative, anti-romantic connotation.

people would have to atone for all future time, if they have any future, such a statesman should be *great?*"

"Without a doubt!" the other patriot replied vehemently; "otherwise he would not have been *able* to do it. Perhaps it was insane to want such a thing? But perhaps everything great was merely insane when it started."

"An abuse of words!" his partner shouted back; "strong! strong! strong and insane! *Not* great!"

The old men had obviously become heated as they thus flung their truths into each other's faces; but I, in my happiness and beyond, considered how soon one stronger will become master over the strong; also that for the spiritual flattening[6] of a people there is a compensation, namely the deepening of another people.

242

Call that in which the distinction of the European is sought "civilization" or "humanization" or "progress," or call it simply—without praise or blame—using a political formula, Europe's *democratic* movement: behind all the moral and political foregrounds to which such formulas point, a tremendous *physiological* process is taking place and gaining momentum. The Europeans are becoming more similar to each other; they become more and more detached from the conditions under which races originate that are tied to some climate or class; they become increasingly independent of any *determinate* milieu that would like to inscribe itself for centuries in body and soul with the same demands. Thus an essentially supra-national and nomadic type of man is gradually coming up, a type that possesses, physiologically speaking, a maximum of the art and power of adaptation as its typical distinction.

The tempo of this process of the *"evolving European"* may be retarded by great relapses, but perhaps it will gain in vehemence and profundity and grow just on their account: the still raging storm and stress of "national feeling" belongs here, also that anarchism which is just now coming up. But this process will probably lead to results which would seem to be least expected by those who naïvely promote and praise it, the apostles of "modern ideas." The very same new conditions that will on the average lead to the leveling and mediocritization of man—to a useful, industrious, handy, multi-purpose herd animal—are likely in the highest degree to give birth to exceptional human beings of the most dangerous and attractive quality.

To be sure, that power of adaptation which keeps trying out changing conditions and begins some new work with every generation, almost with every decade, does not make possible the *powerfulness* of the type, and the over-all impression of such future Europeans will probably be that of manifold garrulous workers who will be poor in will, extremely employable, and as much in need of a master and commander as of their daily bread. But

---

6. *Verflachung* (becoming shallower) contrasted with *Vertiefung* (becoming more profound). The first people is, without a doubt, Germany; the statesman, Bismarck; and the second people probably France. Of course, the points made are also meant to apply more generally, but this evaluation of Bismarck at the zenith of his success and power certainly shows an amazing independence of spirit, and without grasping the full weight of the final sentence one cannot begin to understand Nietzsche's conceptions of the will to power or of "beyond good and evil."

while the democratization of Europe leads to the production of a type that is prepared for *slavery* in the subtlest sense, in single, exceptional cases the *strong* human being will have to turn out stronger and richer than perhaps ever before—thanks to the absence of prejudice from his training, thanks to the tremendous manifoldness of practice, art, and mask. I meant to say: the democratization of Europe is at the same time an involuntary arrangement for the cultivation of *tyrants*—taking that word in every sense, including the most spiritual. . . .

Part Nine
What Is Noble

257

Every enhancement of the type "man" has so far been the work of an aristocratic society—and it will be so again and again—a society that believes in the long ladder of an order of rank and differences in value between man and man, and that needs slavery in some sense or other. Without that *pathos of distance* which grows out of the ingrained difference between strata—when the ruling caste constantly looks afar and looks down upon subjects and instruments and just as constantly practices obedience and command, keeping down and keeping at a distance—that other, more mysterious pathos could not have grown up either—the craving for an ever new widening of distances within the soul itself, the development of ever higher, rarer, more remote, further-stretching, more comprehensive states —in brief, simply the enhancement of the type "man," the continual "self-overcoming of man," to use a moral formula in a supra-moral sense.

To be sure, one should not yield to humanitarian illusions about the origins of an aristocratic society (and thus of the presupposition of this enhancement of the type "man"): truth is hard. Let us admit to ourselves, without trying to be considerate, how every higher culture on earth so far has *begun.* Human beings whose nature was still natural, barbarians in every terrible sense of the word, men of prey who were still in possession of unbroken strength of will and lust for power, hurled themselves upon weaker, more civilized, more peaceful races, perhaps traders or cattle raisers, or upon mellow old cultures whose last vitality was even then flaring up in splendid fireworks of spirit and corruption. In the beginning, the noble caste was always the barbarian caste: their predominance did not lie mainly in physical strength but in strength of the soul—they were more *whole* human beings (which also means, at every level, "more whole beasts").

258

Corruption as the expression of a threatening anarchy among the instincts and of the fact that the foundation of the affects, which is called "life," has been shaken: corruption is something totally different depending on the organism in which it appears. When, for example, an aristocracy, like that of France at the beginning of the Revolution, throws away its privileges with a sublime disgust and sacrifices itself to an extravagance of its own moral feelings, that is corruption; it was really only the last act of that centuries-old corruption which had led them to surrender, step by step, their governmental prerogatives, demoting themselves to a mere *function* of the monarchy (finally even to a mere ornament and showpiece). The essential characteristic of a good and healthy aristocracy, however, is that it experiences itself *not* as a function (whether of the monarchy or the commonwealth) but as their *meaning* and highest justification—that it therefore accepts with a good conscience the sacrifice of untold human beings who, *for its sake,* must be reduced and lowered to incomplete human beings, to slaves, to instruments. Their fundamental faith simply has to be that society must *not* exist for society's sake but only as the foundation and scaffolding on which a choice type of being is able to raise itself to its higher task and to a higher state of *being*—comparable to those sun-seeking vines of Java—they are called *Sipo Matador*—that so long and so often enclasp an oak tree with their tendrils until eventually, high above it but supported by it, they can unfold their crowns in the open light and display their happiness.

259

Refraining mutually from injury, violence, and exploitation and placing one's will on a par with that of someone else—this may become, in a certain rough sense, good manners among individuals if the appropriate conditions are present (namely, if these men are actually similar in strength and value standards and belong together in *one* body). But as soon as this principle is extended, and possibly even accepted as the *fundamental principle of society,* it immediately proves to be what it really is—a will to the *denial* of life, a principle of disintegration and decay.

Here we must beware of superficiality and get to the bottom of the matter, resisting all sentimental weakness: life itself is *essentially* appropriation, injury, overpowering of what is alien and weaker; suppression, hardness, imposition of one's own forms, incorporation and at least, at its mildest, exploitation—but why should one always use those words in which a slanderous intent has been imprinted for ages?

Even the body within which individuals treat each other as equals, as suggested before—and this happens in every healthy aristocracy—if it is a living and not a dying body, has to do to other bodies what the individuals within it refrain from doing to each other: it will have to be an incarnate will to power, it will strive to grow, spread, seize, become predominant—not from any morality or immorality but because it is *living* and because life simply *is* will to power. But there is no point on which the ordinary consciousness of Europeans resists instruction as on this: everywhere people are now raving, even under scientific disguises, about coming conditions of society in which "the exploitative aspect" will be removed—which sounds to me as if they promised to invent a way of life that would dispense with all organic functions. "Exploitation" does not belong to a corrupt or imperfect and primitive society: it belongs to the *essence* of what lives, as a basic organic function; it is a consequence of the will to power, which is after all the will of life.

If this should be an innovation as a theory—as a reality it is the *primordial fact* of all history: people ought to be honest with themselves at least that far.

260

Wandering through the many subtler and coarser moralities which have so far been prevalent on earth, or still are prevalent, I found that certain features recurred regularly together and were closely associated—until I finally discovered two basic types and one basic difference.

There are *master morality* and *slave morality*—I add immediately that in all the higher and more mixed cultures there also appear attempts at mediation between these two moralities, and yet more often the interpenetration and mutual misunderstanding of both, and at times they occur directly alongside each other—even in the same human being, within a *single* soul. The moral discrimination of values has originated either among a ruling group whose consciousness of its difference from the ruled group was accompanied by delight—or among the ruled, the slaves and dependents of every degree.

In the first case, when the ruling group determines what is "good," the exalted, proud states of the soul are experienced as conferring distinction and determining the order of rank. The noble human being separates from himself those in whom the opposite of such exalted, proud states finds expression: he despises them. It should be noted immediately that in this first type of morality the opposition of "good" and "*bad*" means approximately the same as "noble" and "contemptible." (The opposition of "good" and "*evil*" has a different origin.) One feels contempt for the cowardly, the anxious, the petty, those intent on narrow utility; also for the suspicious with their unfree glances, those who humble themselves, the doglike people who allow themselves to be maltreated, the begging flatterers, above all the liars: it is part of the fundamental faith of all aristocrats that the common people lie. "We truthful ones"—thus the nobility of ancient Greece referred to itself.

It is obvious that moral designations were everywhere first applied to *human beings* and only later, derivatively, to actions. Therefore it is a gross mistake when historians of morality start from such questions as: why was the compassionate act praised? The noble type of man experiences *itself* as determining values; it does not need approval; it judges, "what is harmful to me is harmful in itself"; it knows itself to be that which first accords honor to things; it is *value-creating*. Everything it knows as part of itself it honors: such a morality is self-glorification. In the foreground there is the feeling of fullness, of power that seeks to overflow, the happiness of high tension, the consciousness of wealth that would give and bestow: the noble human being, too, helps the unfortunate, but not, or almost not, from pity, but prompted more by an urge begotten by excess of power. The noble human being honors himself as one who is powerful, also as one who has power over himself, who knows how to speak and be silent, who delights in being severe and hard with himself and respects all severity and hardness. "A hard heart Wotan put into my breast," says an old Scandinavian saga: a fitting poetic expression, seeing that it comes from the soul of a proud Viking. Such a type of man is actually proud of the fact that he is *not* made for pity, and the hero of the saga therefore adds as a warning: "If the heart is not hard in youth it will never harden." Noble and courageous human beings who think that way are furthest removed from that morality which finds the distinction of morality precisely in pity, or in acting for others, or in *désintéressement;* faith in oneself, pride in oneself, a fundamental hostility and irony against "selflessness" belong just as definitely to noble morality as does a slight disdain and caution regarding compassionate feelings and a "warm heart."

It is the powerful who *understand* how to honor; this is their art, their realm of invention. The profound reverence for age and tradition—all law rests on this double reverence—the faith and prejudice in favor of ancestors and disfavor of those yet to come are typical of the morality of the powerful; and when the men of "modern ideas," conversely, believe almost instinctively in "progress" and "the future" and more and more lack respect for age, this in itself would sufficiently betray the ignoble origin of these "ideas."

A morality of the ruling group, however, is most alien and embarrassing to the present taste in the severity of its principle that one has duties only to one's peers; that against beings of a lower rank, against everything alien, one may behave as one pleases or "as the heart desires," and in any case "beyond good and evil"—here pity and like feelings may find their place. The capacity for, and the duty of, long gratitude and long revenge—both only among one's peers—refinement in repaying, the sophisticated concept of friendship, a certain necessity for having enemies (as it were, as drainage ditches for the affects of envy, quarrelsomeness, exuberance—at bottom, in order to be capable of being good *friends*): all these are typical characteristics of noble morality which, as suggested, is not the morality of "modern ideas" and therefore is hard to empathize with today, also hard to dig up and uncover.

It is different with the second type of morality, *slave morality.* Suppose the violated, oppressed, suffering, unfree, who are uncertain of themselves and weary, moralize: what will their moral valuations have in common? Probably, a pessimistic suspicion about the whole condition of man will find expression, perhaps a condemnation of man along with his condition. The slave's eye is not favorable to the virtues of the powerful: he is skeptical and suspicious, *subtly* suspicious, of all the "good" that is honored there—he would like to persuade himself that even their happiness is not genuine. Conversely, those qualities are brought out and flooded with light which serve to ease existence for those who suffer: here pity, the complaisant and obliging hand, the warm heart, patience, industry, humility, and friendliness are honored—for here these are the most useful qualities and almost the only means for enduring the pressure of existence. Slave morality is essentially a morality of utility.

Here is the place for the origin of that famous opposition of "good" and "evil": into evil one's feelings project power and dangerousness, a certain terribleness, subtlety, and strength that does not permit contempt to develop. According to slave morality, those who are "evil" thus inspire fear; according to master morality it is precisely those who are "good" that inspire, and wish to inspire, fear, while the "bad" are felt to be contemptible.

The opposition reaches its climax when, as a logical consequence of slave morality, a touch of disdain is associated also with the "good" of this morality—this may be slight and benevolent—because the good human being has to be *undangerous* in the slaves' way of thinking: he is good-natured, easy to deceive, a little stupid perhaps, *un bonhomme.*[7] Wherever

---

7. Literally "a good human being," the term is used for precisely the type described here.

slave morality becomes preponderant, language tends to bring the words "good" and "stupid" closer together.

One last fundamental difference: the longing for *freedom*, the instinct for happiness and the subtleties of the feeling of freedom belong just as necessarily to slave morality and morals as artful and enthusiastic reverence and devotion are the regular symptom of an aristocratic way of thinking and evaluating.

This makes plain why love *as passion*—which is our European specialty—simply must be of noble origin: as is well known, its invention must be credited to the Provençal knight-poets, those magnificent and inventive human beings of the *"gai saber"*[8] to whom Europe owes so many things and almost owes itself. . . .

263

There is an *instinct for rank* which, more than anything else, is a sign of a *high* rank; there is a delight in the nuances of reverence that allows us to infer noble origin and habits. The refinement, graciousness, and height of a soul is tested dangerously when something of the first rank passes by without being as yet protected by the shudders of authority against obtrusive efforts and ineptitudes—something that goes its way unmarked, undiscovered, tempting, perhaps capriciously concealed and disguised, like a living touchstone. Anyone to whose task and practice it belongs to search out souls will employ this very art in many forms in order to determine the ultimate value of a soul and the unalterable, innate order of rank to which it belongs: he will test it for its *instinct of reverence.*

Différence engendre haine:[9] the baseness of some people suddenly spurts up like dirty water when some holy vessel, some precious thing from a locked shrine, some book with the marks of a great destiny, is carried past; and on the other hand there is a reflex of silence, a hesitation of the eye, a cessation of all gestures that express how a soul *feels* the proximity of the most venerable. The way in which reverence for the *Bible* has on the whole been maintained so far in Europe is perhaps the best bit of discipline and refinement of manners that Europe owes to Christianity: such books of profundity and ultimate significance require some external tyranny of authority for their protection in order to gain those millennia of *persistence* which are necessary to exhaust them and figure them out.

Much is gained once the feeling has finally been cultivated in the masses (among the shallow and in the high-speed intestines of every kind) that they are not to touch everything; that there are holy experiences before which they have to take off their shoes and keep away their unclean hands—this is almost their greatest advance toward humanity. Conversely, perhaps there is nothing about so-called educated people and believers in "modern ideas" that is as nauseous as their lack of modesty and the comfortable insolence of their eyes and hands with which they touch, lick, and finger everything;

---

8. "Gay science": in the early fourteenth century the term was used to designate the art of the troubadours, codified in *Leys d'amors.* Nietzsche subtitled his own *Fröhliche Wissenschaft* (1882), "*la gaya scienza,*". . .

9. Difference engenders hatred.

and it is possible that even among the common people, among the less educated, especially among peasants, one finds today more *relative* nobility of taste and tactful reverence than among the newspaper-reading *demi-monde* of the spirit, the educated.

264

One cannot erase from the soul of a human being what his ancestors liked most to do and did most constantly: whether they were, for example, assiduous savers and appurtenances of a desk and cash box, modest and bourgeois in their desires, modest also in their virtues; or whether they lived accustomed to commanding from dawn to dusk, fond of rough amusements and also perhaps of even rougher duties and responsibilities; or whether, finally, at some point they sacrificed ancient prerogatives of birth and possessions in order to live entirely for their faith—their "god"—as men of an inexorable and delicate conscience which blushes at every compromise. It is simply not possible that a human being should *not* have the qualities and preferences of his parents and ancestors in his body, whatever appearances may suggest to the contrary. This is the problem of race.[10]

If one knows something about the parents, an inference about the child is permissible: any disgusting incontinence, any nook envy, a clumsy insistence that one is always right—these three things together have always constituted the characteristic type of the plebeian—that sort of thing must as surely be transferred to the child as corrupted blood; and with the aid of the best education one will at best *deceive* with regard to such a heredity.

And what else is the aim of education and "culture" today? In our very popularity-minded—that is, plebeian—age, "education" and "culture" *have* to be essentially the art of deceiving—about one's origins, the inherited plebs in one's body and soul. An educator who today preached truthfulness above all and constantly challenged his students, "be true! be natural! do not pretend!"—even such a virtuous and guileless ass would learn after a while to reach for that *furca* of Horace to *naturam expellere:* with what success? "Plebs" *usque recurret.*[11] . . .

---

10. Here, as elsewhere, Nietzsche gives expression to his Lamarckian belief in the heredity of acquired characteristics, shared by Samuel Butler and Bernard Shaw but anathema to Nazi racists and almost universally rejected by geneticists. His Lamarckism is not just an odd fact about Nietzsche but symptomatic of his conception of body and spirit: he ridiculed belief in "pure" spirit but believed just as little in any "pure" body; he claimed that neither could be understood without the other. . . .

11. Horace's *Epistles*, I.10, 24: "Try with a pitchfork to drive out nature, she always returns."

The Genealogy of Morals

First Essay
"Good and Evil," "Good and Bad"

I

The English psychologists to whom we owe the only attempts that have thus far been made to write a genealogy of morals are no mean posers of riddles, but the riddles they pose are themselves, and being incarnate have one advantage over their books—they are interesting. What are these English psychologists really after? One finds them always, whether intentionally or not, engaged in the same task of pushing into the foreground the nasty part of the psyche, looking for the effective motive forces of human development in the very last place we would wish to have them found, e.g., in the inertia of habit, in forgetfulness, in the blind and fortuitous association of ideas: always in something that is purely passive, automatic, reflexive, molecular, and, moreover, profoundly stupid. What drives these psychologists forever in the same direction? A secret, malicious desire to belittle humanity, which they do not acknowledge even to themselves? A pessimistic distrust, the suspiciousness of the soured idealist? Some petty resentment of Christianity (and Plato) which does not rise above the threshold of consciousness? Or could it be a prurient taste for whatever is embarrassing, painfully paradoxical, dubious and absurd in existence? Or is it, perhaps, a kind of stew—a little meanness, a little bitterness, a bit of anti-Christianity, a touch of prurience and desire for condiments? . . . But, again, people tell me that these men are simply dull old frogs who hop and creep in and around man as in their own element—as though man were a bog. However, I am reluctant to listen to this, in fact I refuse to believe it; and if I may express a wish where I cannot express a conviction, I do wish wholeheartedly that things may be otherwise with these men—that these microscopic examiners of the soul may be really courageous, magnanimous, and proud animals, who know how to contain their emotions and have trained themselves to subordinate all wishful thinking to the truth—any truth, even a homespun, severe, ugly, obnoxious, un-Christian, unmoral truth. For such truths do exist.

II

All honor to the beneficent spirits that may motivate these historians of ethics! One thing is certain, however, they have been quite deserted by the true spirit of history. They all, to a man, think unhistorically, as is the age-old custom among philosophers. The amateurishness of their procedure is made plain from the very beginning, when it is a question of explaining the provenance of the concept and judgment *good*. "Originally," they decree, "altruistic actions were praised and approved by their recipients, that is, by those to whom they were useful. Later on, the origin of that praise having been forgotten, such actions were felt to be good simply because it was the habit to commend them." We notice at once that this first derivation has all the earmarks of the English psychologists' work. Here are the key ideas of utility, forgetfulness, habit, and, finally, error, seen as lying at the root of that value system which civilized man had hitherto regarded with pride as the prerogative of all men. This pride must now be humbled, these values devalued. Have the debunkers succeeded?

Now it is obvious to me, first of all, that their theory looks for the genesis of the concept *good* in the wrong place: the judgment *good* does not originate with those to whom the good has been done. Rather it was the "good" themselves, that is to say the noble, mighty, highly placed, and high-minded who decreed themselves and their actions to be good, i.e., belonging to the highest rank, in contradistinction to all that was base, low-minded and plebeian. It was only this *pathos of distance* that authorized them to create values and name them—what was utility to them? The notion of utility seems singularly inept to account for such a quick jetting forth of supreme value judgments. Here we come face to face with the exact opposite of that lukewarmness which every scheming prudence, every utilitarian calculus presupposes—and not for a time only, for the rare, exceptional hour, but permanently. The origin of the opposites *good* and *bad* is to be found in the pathos of nobility and distance, representing the dominant temper of a higher, ruling class in relation to a lower, dependent one. (The lordly right of bestowing names is such that one would almost be justified in seeing the origin of language itself as an expression of the rulers' power. They say, "This *is* that or that"; they seal off each thing and action with a sound and thereby take symbolic possession of it.) Such an origin would suggest that there is no *a priori* necessity for associating the word *good* with altruistic deeds, as those moral psychologists are fond of claiming. In fact, it is only after aristocratic values have begun to decline that the egotism-altruism dichotomy takes possession of the human conscience; to use my own terms, it is the herd instinct that now asserts itself. Yet it takes quite a while for this instinct to assume such sway that it can reduce all moral valuations to that dichotomy—as is currently happening throughout Europe, where the prejudice equating the terms *moral, altruistic,* and *disinterested* has assumed the obsessive force of an *idée fixe.* . . .

VI

Granting that political supremacy always gives rise to notions of spiritual supremacy, it at first creates no difficulties (though difficulties might arise later) if the ruling caste is also the priestly caste and elects to characterize itself by a term which reminds us of its priestly function. In this context we encounter for the first time concepts of *pure* and *impure* opposing each other as signs of class, and here, too, *good* and *bad* as terms no longer referring to class, develop before long. The reader should be cautioned, however, against taking pure and impure in too large or profound or symbolic a sense: all the ideas of ancient man were understood in a sense much more crude, narrow, superficial and non-symbolic than we are able to imagine today. The pure man was originally one who washed himself, who refused to eat certain foods entailing skin diseases, who did not sleep with the unwashed plebeian women, who held blood in abomination—hardly more than that. At the same time, given the peculiar nature of a priestly aristocracy, it becomes clear why the value opposites would early turn inward and become dangerously exacerbated; and in fact the tension between such opposites has opened abysses between man and man, over which not even an Achilles of free thought would leap without a shudder. There is from the very start something unwholesome about such priestly aristocracies, about their way of life, which is turned away from action and swings between brooding and emotional explosions: a way of life which may be seen as responsible for the morbidity and neurasthenia of priests of all periods. Yet are we not right in maintaining that the cures which they have developed for their morbidities have proved a hundred times more dangerous than the ills themselves? Humanity is still suffering from the after-effects of those priestly cures. Think, for example, of certain forms of diet (abstinence from meat), fasting, sexual continence, escape "into the desert"; think further of the whole anti-sensual metaphysics of the priests, conducive to inertia and false refinement; of the self-hypnosis encouraged by the example of fakirs and Brahmans, where a glass knob and an *idée fixe* take the place of the god. And at last, supervening on all this, comes utter satiety, together with its radical remedy, nothingness—or God, for the desire for a mystical union with God is nothing other than the Buddhist's desire to sink himself in nirvana. Among the priests everything becomes more dangerous, not cures and specifics alone but also arrogance, vindictiveness, acumen, profligacy, love, the desire for power, disease. In all fairness it should be added, however, that only on this soil, the precarious soil of priestly existence, has man been able to develop into an interesting creature; that only here has the human mind grown both profound and evil; and it is in these two respects, after all, that man has proved his superiority over the rest of creation.

VII

By now the reader will have got some notion how readily the priestly system of valuations can branch off from the aristocratic and develop into its opposite. An occasion for such a division is furnished whenever the priest caste and the warrior caste jealously clash with one another and find themselves unable to come to terms. The chivalrous and aristocratic valuations presuppose a strong physique, blooming, even exuberant health, together with all the conditions that guarantee its preservation: combat, adventure, the chase, the dance, war games, etc. The value system of the priestly aristocracy is founded on different presuppositions. So much the worse for them when it becomes a question of war! As we all know, priests are the most evil enemies to have—why should this be so? Because they are the most impotent. It is their impotence which makes their hate so violent and sinister, so cerebral and poisonous. The greatest haters in history—but also the most intelligent haters—have been priests. Beside the brilliance of priestly vengeance all other brilliance fades. Human history would be a dull and stupid thing without the intelligence furnished by its impotents. Let us begin with the most striking example. Whatever else has been done to damage the powerful and great of this earth seems trivial compared with what the Jews have done, that priestly people who succeeded in avenging themselves on their enemies and oppressors by radically inverting all their values, that is, by an act of the most spiritual vengeance. This was a strategy entirely appropriate to a priestly people in whom vindictiveness had gone most deeply underground. It was the Jew who, with frightening consistency, dared to invent the aristocratic value equations good/noble/powerful/beautiful/happy/favored-of-the-gods and maintain, with the furious hatred of the underprivileged and impotent, that "only the poor, the powerless, are good; only the suffering, sick, and ugly, truly blessed. But you noble and mighty ones of the earth will be, to all eternity, the evil, the cruel, the avaricious, the godless, and thus the cursed and damned!" . . . We know who has fallen heir to this Jewish inversion of values. . . . In reference to the grand and unspeakably disastrous initiative which the Jews have launched by this most radical of all declarations of war, I wish to repeat a statement I made in a different context (*Beyond Good and Evil*), to wit, that it was the Jews who started the slave revolt in morals; a revolt with two millennia of history behind it, which we have lost sight of today simply because it has triumphed so completely. . . .

Second Essay
"Guilt," "Bad Conscience," and Related Matters

XXII

By now the reader will have guessed what has really been happening behind all these façades. Man, with his need for self-torture, his sublimated cruelty resulting from the cooping up of his animal nature within a polity, invented bad conscience in order to hurt himself, after the blocking of the more natural outlet of his cruelty. Then this guilt-ridden man seized upon religion in order to exacerbate his self-torment to the utmost. The thought of being in God's debt became his new instrument of torture. He focused in God the last of the opposites he could find to his true and inveterate animal instincts, making these a sin against God (hostility, rebellion against the "Lord," the "Father," the "Creator"). He stretched himself upon the contradiction "God" and "Devil" as on a rack. He projected all his denials of self, nature, naturalness out of himself as affirmations, as true being, embodiment, reality, as God (the divine Judge and Executioner), as transcendence, as eternity, as endless torture, as hell, as the infinitude of guilt and punishment. In such psychological cruelty we see an insanity of the *will* that is without parallel: man's will to find himself guilty, and unredeemably so; his will to believe that he might be punished to all eternity without ever expunging his guilt; his will to poison the very foundation of things with the problem of guilt and punishment and thus to cut off once and for all his escape from this labyrinth of obsession; his will to erect an ideal (God's holiness) in order to assure himself of his own absolute unworthiness. What a mad, unhappy animal is man! What strange notions occur to him; what perversities, what paroxysms of nonsense, what bestialities of idea burst from him, the moment he is prevented ever so little from being a beast of action! . . . All this is exceedingly curious and interesting, but dyed with such a dark, somber, enervating sadness that one must resolutely tear away one's gaze. Here, no doubt, is sickness, the most terrible sickness that has wasted man thus far. And if one is still able to hear—but how few these days have ears to hear it!—in this night of torment and absurdity the cry *love* ring out, the cry of rapt longing, of redemption in love, he must turn away with a shudder of invincible horror. . . . Man harbors too much horror; the earth has been a lunatic asylum for too long. . . .

XXIV

It is clear that I am concluding this essay with three unanswered questions. It may occur to some reader to ask me, "Are you constructing an ideal or destroying one?" I would ask him, in turn, whether he ever reflected upon the price that had to be paid for the introduction of every new ideal on earth? On how much of reality, in each instance, had to be slandered and misconceived, how much of falsehood ennobled, how many consciences disturbed, how many gods sacrificed? For the raising of an altar requires the breaking of an altar: this is a law—let anyone who can prove me wrong. We moderns have a millennial heritage of conscience-vivisection and cruelty to the animals in our selves. This is our most ancient habit, our most consummate artistry perhaps, in any case our greatest refinement, our special fare. Man has looked for so long with an evil eye upon his natural inclinations that they have finally become inseparable from "bad conscience." A converse effort can be imagined, but who has the strength for it? It would consist of associating all the *unnatural* inclinations—the longing for what is unworldly, opposed to the senses, to instinct, to nature, to the animal in us, all the anti-biological and earth-calumniating ideals—with bad conscience. To whom, today, may such hopes and pretensions address themselves? The *good* men, in particular, would be on the other side; and of course all the comfortable, resigned, vain, moony, weary people. Does anything give greater offense and separate one more thoroughly from others than to betray something of the strictness and dignity with which one treats oneself? But how kind and accommodating the world becomes the moment we act like all the rest and let ourselves go! To accomplish that aim, different minds are needed than are likely to appear in this age of ours: minds strengthened by struggles and victories, for whom conquest, adventure, danger, even pain, have become second nature. Minds accustomed to the keen atmosphere of high altitudes, to wintry walks, to ice and mountains in every sense. Minds possessed of a sublime kind of malice, of that self-assured recklessness which is a sign of strong health. What is needed, in short, is just superb health. Is such health still possible today?

But at some future time, a time stronger than our effete, self-doubting present, the true Redeemer will come, whose surging creativity will not let him rest in any shelter or hiding place, whose solitude will be misinterpreted as a flight from reality, whereas it will in fact be a dwelling *on*, a dwelling *in* reality—so that when he comes forth into the light he may bring with him the redemption of that reality from the curse placed upon it by a lapsed ideal. This man of the future, who will deliver us both from a lapsed ideal and from all that this ideal has spawned—violent loathing, the will to extinction, nihilism—this great and decisive stroke of midday, who will make the will free once more and restore to the earth its aim, and to man his hope; this anti-Christ and anti-nihilist, conqueror of both God and Unbeing —*one day he must come....*

Third Essay
What Do Ascetic Ideals Mean?

XIII

But let us return to our argument. The kind of inner split we have found in the ascetic, who pits "life against life," is nonsense, not only in psychological terms, but also physiologically speaking. Such a split can only be *apparent;* it must be a kind of provisional expression, a formula, an adaptation, a psychological misunderstanding of something for which terms have been lacking to designate its true nature. A mere stopgap to fill a hiatus in human understanding. Let me state what I consider to be the actual situation. The ascetic ideal arises from the protective and curative instinct of a life that is degenerating and yet fighting tooth and nail for its preservation. It points to a partial physiological blocking and exhaustion, against which the deepest vital instincts, still intact, are battling doggedly and resourcefully. The ascetic ideal is one of their weapons. The situation, then, is exactly the opposite from what the worshipers of that ideal believe it to be. Life employs asceticism in its desperate struggle against death; the ascetic ideal is a dodge for the preservation of life. The ubiquitousness and power of that ideal, especially wherever men have adopted civilized forms of life, should impress upon us one great, palpable fact: the persistent morbidity of civilized man, his biological struggle against death, or to put it more exactly, against *taedium vitae,* exhaustion, the longing for "the end." The ascetic priest is an incarnation of the wish to be different, to be elsewhere; he *is* that wish, raised to its highest power, its most passionate intensity. And it is precisely the intensity of his wishing that forges the fetter binding him to this earth. At the same time he becomes an instrument for bettering the human condition, since by this intensity he is enabled to maintain in life the vast flock of defeated, disgruntled sufferers and self-tormentors, whom he leads instinctively like a shepherd. In other words, the ascetic priest, seemingly life's enemy and great negator, is in truth one of the major conserving and affirmative forces. . . . But what about the sources of man's morbidity? For certainly man is sicker, less secure, less stable, less firmly anchored than any other animal; he is the *sick* animal. But has he not also been more daring, more defiant, more inventive than all the other animals together? —man, the great experimenter on himself, eternally unsatisfied, vying with the gods, the beasts, and with nature for final supremacy; man, unconquered to this day, still unrealized, so agitated by his own teeming energy that his future digs like spurs into the flesh of every present moment. . . . How could such a brave and resourceful animal but be the most precarious, the most profoundly sick of all the sick beasts of the earth? There have been many times when man has clearly had enough; there have been whole epidemics of "fed-upness" (for example, around 1348, the time of the Dance of Death) but even this tedium, this weariness, this satiety breaks from him with such vehemence that at once it forges a new fetter to existence. As if by magic, his negations produce a wealth of tenderer affirmations. When this master of destruction, of self-destruction, wounds himself, it is that very wound that forces him to live.

XIV

The more regular morbidity becomes among the members of the human race, the more grateful we should be for the rare "windfalls"—men fortunate enough to combine a sound physical organization with intellectual authority. We should do our best to protect such men from the noxious air of the sickroom. It is the sick who are the greatest threat to the well; it is the weaklings, and not their own peers, who visit disaster upon the strong. But who, today, knows this, who acts on it? We try constantly to diminish man's fear of man; forgetting that it is the fear they inspire which forces the strong to be strong and, if need be, terrible. We should encourage that fear in every possible way, for it alone fosters a sound breed of men. The real danger lies in our loathing of man and our pity of him. If these two emotions should one day join forces, they would beget the most sinister thing ever witnessed on earth: man's *ultimate* will, his will to nothingness, nihilism. And indeed, preparations for that event are already well under way. One who smells not only with his nose but also with his eyes and ears will notice everywhere these days an air as of a lunatic asylum or sanatorium. (I am thinking of all the current cultural enterprises of man, of every kind of Europe now existing.) It is the diseased who imperil mankind, and not the "beasts of prey." It is the predestined failures and victims who undermine the social structure, who poison our faith in life and our fellow men. Is there anyone who has not encountered the veiled, shuttered gaze of the born misfit, that introverted gaze which saddens us and makes us imagine how such a man must speak to himself? "If only I could be someone else," the look seems to sigh, "but there's no hope of that. I am what I am; how could I get rid of myself? Nevertheless, I'm fed up." In the marshy soil of such self-contempt every poisonous plant will grow, yet all of it so paltry, so stealthy, so dishonest, so sickly-sweet! Here the worms of vindictiveness and *arrière-pensée* teem, the air stinks of secretiveness and pent-up emotion; here a perennial net of malicious conspiracy is woven—the conspiracy of the sufferers against the happy and successful; here victory is held in abomination. And what dissimulation, in order not to betray that this is hatred! What a display of grand attitudes and grandiose words! what an art of "honest calumny!" What noble eloquence flows from the lips of these ill-begotten creatures! What sugary, slimy, humble submissiveness swims in their eyes! What are they after, really? The ambition of these most abject invalids is to at least *mime* justice, love, wisdom, superiority. And how clever such an ambition makes them! For we cannot withhold a certain admiration for the counterfeiter's skill with which they imitate the coinage of virtue, even its golden ring. They have by now entirely monopolized virtue; "We alone," they say, "are the good, the just, we alone the Men of Good Will." They walk among us as warnings and reprimands incarnate, as though to say that health, soundness, strength, and pride are vicious things for which we shall one day pay dearly; and how eager they are, at bottom, to be the ones to make us pay!

How they long to be the executioners! Among them are vindictive characters aplenty, disguised as judges, who carry the word *justice* in their mouths like a poisonous spittle and go always with pursed lips, ready to spit on all who do not look discontent, on all who go cheerfully about their business. Nor are there lacking among them those most unspeakably vain and loathsome frauds who are bent on parading as innocents, those moral masturbators who bring their stunted sensuality to the market swathed in rhymes and other swaddling clothes and labeled "one hundred per cent pure." Is there any place today where the sick do not wish to exhibit some form of superiority and to exercise their tyranny over the strong? Especially the sick females, who have unrivaled resources for dominating, oppressing, tyrannizing. The sick woman spares nothing dead or alive; she digs up the longest-buried things. (The Abyssinian Bogos say "Woman is a hyena.") One look into the background of every family, every institution, every commonwealth is enough to convince us that the battle of the sick against the well is raging on all sides; for the most part a quiet battle, conducted with small doses of poison, with pinpricks, the insidious long-suffering look, but quite often too with the loud pharisaical gesture simulating noble indignation. The indignant barking of these sick dogs can be heard even in the sacred halls of science. (I need only remind the reader once more of that Prussian apostle of vindictiveness, Eugen Dühring, who today makes the most indecent and offensive use of moralistic claptrap. He stands out, even among his own crew of anti-Semites, by the vehemence of his moralistic drivel.) What would these men, so tireless in their masquerades, so insatiable in their thirst for vengeance, require in order to see themselves as triumphant? Nothing less than to succeed in implanting their own misery, and all misery, in the consciences of the happy, so as to make the happy one day say to one another, "It is a disgrace to be happy! *There is too much misery in the world!*" But no greater and more disastrous misunderstanding could be imagined than for the strong and happy to begin doubting their right to happiness. Let us have done with such topsy-turviness, with such dreadful emasculation of feeling! Our first rule on this earth should be that the sick must not contaminate the healthy. But this requires that the healthy be isolated from the sick, be spared even the sight of the sick, lest they mistake that foreign sickness for their own. Or is it their task, perhaps, to be medical attendants and doctors? There could be no worse way for them to misjudge their role. The higher must not be made an instrument of the lower; the "pathos of distance" must to all eternity keep separate tasks separate. The right to exist of the full-toned bell is a thousand times greater than that of the cracked, miscast one: it alone heralds in the future of all mankind. What the healthy can and should do must never be demanded of the sick, or placed within their power; but how should the former be able to do what they alone can do, and at the same time act the part of physicians, comforters, saviors of the sick? . . . Then let us have fresh air, and at any rate get far away from all lunatic asylums and nursing homes of culture! And let us have good company, our own company! Or solitude, if need be. But let us get far away, at any rate, from the evil vapor of internal corruption and dry rot. In order, my friends, that we may, at least for a while yet, guard ourselves against the two worst plagues which perhaps lie in store for us more than anyone—unrelieved loathing of man and unrelieved pity of him!

Friedrich Nietzsche and the Politics of Transfiguration
Tracy B. Strong

Masters and Slaves

Much has been said about these two categories in Nietzsche, and little of it is very favorable to the contemporary understanding. Master and slave have somewhat ominous resonance; memories of the Nazis and the racial contexts in which these terms were used by them leads easily to a conclusion that the categories have at best an emotive value, which is most happily distrusted.

This conclusion is, however, hasty, and on the surface of it, surprising. The notions of master and slave have an obvious apparent ancestry in Rousseau and Hegel; at the time Nietzsche is writing, Marx is developing an understanding of history as governed by the interaction of the oppressors and the oppressed. While a detailed consideration of the similarities and differences is not possible here, this is surely distinguished company; and, indeed, it should be, for Nietzsche is trying to deal with the same problem the others are. He must determine how the structure of action of one period comes to be replaced by that of another. When Hegel tries to uncover how one moves from the stage of the Enlightenment to that of absolute freedom and terror; or Marx, the transition from feudalism to capitalism; they, as well as Nietzsche, are trying to explain the transformation of the *pathe* of one period into that of another. The two principles meet, combine, interact, destroy each other, evolve, transform themselves.

The Genealogy of Morals is about the shift from one form of morality (master morality) to another (slave morality). It is a critical genealogical analysis of what Nietzsche believes to have been a development of the history of men's relations with each other. He seeks to show why the change came about, what its nature is, and to depict as its final consequence the development of men—the "last men"—who are no longer capable of generating new values, but merely of justifying their plight.

For Nietzsche, the development of the (moral) nature of the human-all-too-human has, as its result, the "last men." I take the term "last men" absolutely literally: Nietzsche means *last*; after them, no significant evolution is possible. The species has, so to speak, played itself out and can evolve no further. This serves to reemphasize the evolutionary nature of Nietzsche's view of morality. *The Genealogy of Morals* does not contrast master and slave morality; certainly it also does not seek a return to master morality, nor even advocate it. While there is little doubt that Nietzsche finds that men prey on themselves less in master morality, he also realizes, as had Rousseau before him, and Freud after, that it is in slave morality that much of Western culture has evolved. Unless one remembers that Nietzsche's book is designed to express the evolution and change of slave morality, and that the various notions of "bad conscience," "*ressentiment*," "guilt," the "ascetic priest," and so on are signal instances of the *pathos* for the will to power of slave morality, the book will remain as a collection of more or less well linked aphorisms. It is very important not to miss the scope of the book; it encompasses in outline both Freud's metapsychology of the West (*Civilization and Its Discontents*) and Max Weber's attempt at tracing the evolution of Western rationalism back to the problem of theodicy (*The Social Psychology of World Religions*).

In *Beyond Good and Evil*, Nietzsche gives a short summary of the conclusions he had reached a year earlier in *On the Genealogy of Morals*. "There are master and slave moralities—I add immediately that in all higher and more mixed cultures there also appear attempts at mediation between these two moralities . . . , at times they even occur within a single soul. The moral discrimination of values has originated either among a ruling group whose consciousness of its difference was accompanied by delight, or among slaves and dependents of every degree."[1] Even before any substantive consideration, three methodological points stand out. Firstly, the terms master morality and slave morality can be to some degree called ideal types. While a given historical period may be characterized more by one of them than by the other . . . , it is possible for them to be mingled, even in a single soul. Hence, as with ideal types, these are ways of looking at the world; they are not meant to correspond to something particular in the world, but rather to express the genealogical characteristics of a particular combination and logic of events. Secondly, a slavely moral individual is defined according to his or her "nature," not according to his behavior. Since these are not primarily sociological categories, and do not refer to empirical social data, there is no reason why someone who occupies the status of a president or king might not be slavely moral. One does not have slave morality in the same manner as one has social-economic status, or even in the manner in which one is a negro or Anglo-Saxon.

Master and slave morality may thus be found in some combination in anyone. There is no doubt, though, that Nietzsche sees the last twenty-three hundred years as increasingly dominated by slave morality. But the mere fact that one might happen to control the destinies of several million people is, in itself, no indication that one is a master. Conversely, a "slave" is not impotent, at least in the sense of lacking a will. What counts, in both cases, is the particular relationship between one's sense of self and one's sense of others.

In the passages in which Nietzsche describes the shift from master to slave morality,[2] a number of important observations stand out. The masters "do not know guilt, responsibility, or consideration"; they are "born organizers." The masters exteriorize their will on the environment around them; they almost, in fact, create it in their own image. The *direction* that their will to power assumes (the "whither?") is from inside out. Nietzsche thus sees their action as fundamentally characteristic of a "state," in which the masters "work" until the "raw material . . . [is] at last . . . formed."

These are obviously not slaves, but, as Nietzsche goes on to say, it is through their actions that slave morality becomes possible.

---

1. *Beyond Good and Evil.* In *Werke indrei Bänden.* Herausgegeben von Karl Schlechta. München: Carl Hanser Verlag, 1954, paragraph 260, Volume II, p. 730.

2. [Citations in this section] from *On the Genealogy of Morals* [In Schlecta] ii 17–18, II 826–829.

They are not they in whom bad conscience develops. . . . But it would not have developed without them, this ugly growth; it would be lacking if their artist violence had not with its hammer blows created a tremendous amount of freedom out of the world, at least out of that which was seen, and had made it, as it were, latent. This instinct of freedom which is forcibly made latent—we understand it already—this instinct of freedom which is pushed back, which has subsided, which is imprisoned within us, and, in the end, which is only let out and discharged against itself—this, and only this is what bad conscience is in its earliest beginnings.

As far as I can tell, Nietzsche is saying that the direction of the will had been turned outward in masters, that the slaves had taken the achievements of the masters and had turned them forcibly inward, thus giving rise to "bad conscience." Important immediately here is that the *direction* of willing seems to be the key difference. It is outward and expended in the masters, inward and "imposing a form upon oneself" in the slaves.

Aside from the matter of direction, to which I will return, Nietzsche also indicates that the practices of masters seem to give rise to the practices of slaves. In this section, master morality is tied to the early imposition of a state upon nomadic tribes by some early group of "blond beasts." It appears as deficient as Siegfried in the use of self-reflective consciousness (which would be turned inward). Indeed, to shift to bad conscience is "an illness, there is no doubt about that, but an illness as a pregnancy is an illness."[3] It seems that, for Nietzsche, the future is to the slaves, as it was in Hegel to the bondsman, and in Marx to the proletariat.

Why the Future Is to the Slaves

Nietzsche writes in *Beyond Good and Evil* that in the case of the master, "when the ruling group determines what is 'good,' the exalted proud states of the soul are experienced as conferring distinction and determining order of rank. . . . The noble type of man experiences itself as determining values; it knows itself to be value-creating."[4] Master morality is sufficient to itself and therefore lacks the sense of a time in which things might conceivably become better. Since such a person *is* his own standard, there can be no question of somehow moving closer to it in the future. Rather, the master seeks to behave in an honorable and unashamed fashion toward those who are his peers and his equals in that they too embody their own "morality." (It would seem that Nietzsche has in mind something like the assemblage of the Greek and Trojan heroes.) Much as in Hegel, there is a reciprocity of relationship. The master, for instance, does not "see the enemy as evil [*böse*]; he can requite [*vergelten*]. In Homer, both the Greeks and the Trojans are good. Not he who does us harm, but he who is contemptible is bad [*schlecht*]."[5] Evil (*böse*) and bad (*schlecht*) are technical terms introduced by Nietzsche to signify a difference in relation between master and slave as to whom they find morally "wrong." The Greek recognizes the Trojan as someone like him, even though this person seeks to kill him. The first recognition is sufficient for master morality.

---

3. *Genealogy of Morals* ii 19, II 829.

4. *Beyond Good and Evil* 260, II 730.

5. *Human, All too Human* [In Schlechta] i 45, I 483.

It is different with the slaves. Nietzsche continues:

> Suppose the vitiated, oppressed, suffering, and unfree who are uncertain of
> themselves and weary, moralize: what will their valuations have in common?
> Probably a pessimistic suspicion about the whole condition of mankind. . . .
> Slave morality is essentially a morality of utility. . . . According to slave mo-
> rality, those who are evil [*böse*] inspire fear; according to master morality, it is
> precisely those who are good that inspire and wish to inspire fear, while the
> bad [*schlechte*] man is found contemptible.[6]

When the master had judged those he found contemptible as bad (*schlecht*) he was
applying to them the same standard he applied to himself and his peers. It is not that
the "bad" men fail to live up to a standard, but rather that they do not have one.
The slave, on the other hand, makes his moral judgments on a quite different basis.
His initial premise is to set himself off from those who would do him harm, from the
evil ones (*bose*). The reciprocity of peers—whether enemies or friends—becomes
impossible.

Masters and Slaves: The Fable of the Lamb

How then does the evolution and change of morality take place? What is its *pathos*?
The distinction between master and slave morality can be formulated as the distinction between two paradigm statements. Characteristic of the master: "I am good,
therefore you are bad." Characteristic of the slave: "You oppress me, are thus evil; I,
therefore, am good." The important root of the difference lies in the sort of inter-
human relation implied in each case by the word "therefore." In the master's statement, the second part of the sentence is merely negative. There is no comparative
element. The master's sense of himself is not dependent on a calculated comparison with the outside. As Nietzsche says: "The bad of noble origin . . . [is] an after-
production, a side effect, a contrasting shade. . . ."[7] The premise of the statement is
positive and affirmative, as is the sort of man who perpetuates himself through this
stance. This is why Nietzsche says that no degeneration can come out of noble soil;
none could, for in itself it contains no seeds of corruption.

   The slave statement, "You oppress me, are thus evil; I, therefore, am good," is
signally different from that of the master. The moral sense of self and the identity of
the slave become in effect a negation of a negation, and consist of denying something
that affects one from without, and then asserting one's identity as the opposite of that
by which one is afflicted. As such, this notion of identity is not structurally different
from that which Hegel describes in the *Phenomenology,* where selfhood is arrived at
by progressively distinguishing oneself from nature and then from other people.
(Hegel, however, thought this to be the only form of knowledge and selfhood.) The
ultimate logical expression of this stance is found, as Nietzsche comes to realize, in
Schopenhauer. Schopenhauer*. . . thinks that release from the will is the only answer
to the problems of suffering. Here, too, identity does not consist of an active
component, but is reaction to something outside; action in itself, with its inevitable

---

6. *Beyond Good and Evil* 260, II 732.

7. *Genealogy of Morals* i 11, II 785.

* Arthur Schopenhauer, German Philosopher whose pessimistic philosophy influenced Nietzsche.

self-assertive qualities, must then become something evil, since it is identified with that against which one is reacting. The will to power of slave morality must constantly reassert that which gives definition to the slave: the pain he suffers by being in the world. Hence, any attempt to escape that pain will merely result in the reaffirmation of painful structures. As seen in the consideration of nihilism, already in the logic of (slave) moral ethics are those elements that lead to the ultimate triumph of nihilism.

The logic of slave morality leads men on; behind every moral statement lies a myriad of nihilistic imperatives. Nietzsche considers the sentence, "It was my fault."[8] The speaker must accept that morality rests on responsibility, which, in turn, rests first on the belief that matters could not have been otherwise given that I acted the way I did. This implies that my action must be understood as faulty, in terms of some standard that I must inevitably take from outside myself. The assumption, however, that there are moral standards outside of me to which I did not live up, and that my willed actions can be judged by those standards, is an assumption that my "true self" can be premised on that which is "not me." For Nietzsche, in such a perspective, negation is the very premise of the personality.

Furthermore, it would seem that in making such a statement about another person ("It was his fault"), or about oneself ("It was my fault"), one is guilty of treating not only the other person as an object, but also oneself—not, one might say, as one's own peer. Master morality, on the other hand, Nietzsche calls a "hard" morality. It insists that one demand both from oneself and others that one act and judge according to *his* will, and that the escape from self permitted by "It was my fault" simply not be allowed. Only if a person is bad (*schlecht*) can one recognize his insufficiency.

The essays of *On the Genealogy of Morals*, which Nietzsche refers to in his autobiography as "three decisive preliminary studies leading to a revaluation of all values," form the most coherent expression of the steps by which master morality is transmogrified into slave morality. Slave morality itself is the consequence of transvaluation of all values effectuated by Socrates and Christ. This constitutes a useful reminder: slave morality is not just master morality stood on its head, a simple reversal of the sociology of domination. It starts from different premises and arrives at *different,* not reverse, valuations. Nietzsche works out this process in an account of the lamb who became reflective.

It is not surprising that a lamb dislike a bird of prey. After all, for apparently no reason the eagle swoops down every now and then and carries off one of your companions; since they appear to have committed no fault, it is not impossible that one day the eagle may take *you.* The lamb, if he be somewhat of a rationalist, will seek to understand this process and try to stop it. Certainly he feels oppressed by the bird of prey, whom he calls evil; certainly thereby he would want to feel himself as good. However, no matter what protestations the lamb may raise, the bird keeps swooping down.

In effect, the lamb wishes that the eagle would not behave as an eagle. He wants the bird of prey to stop doing what he apparently does simply because he is an eagle. Yet this is problematic, for, as Nietzsche continues in the *Genealogy,* "to demand of strength that it not express itself as strength, that it not be a will to overcome, to cast down, to become master, a thirst after enemies, oppositions, and triumphs is just as absurd as to require strength to express itself as weakness."[9]

---

8. *Will to Power* [In Schlechta] 288 . . .

9. *Genealogy of Morals* i 13, II 790 . . .

The lamb thinks to himself something like this. "I have no reason to carry off lambs, but the eagle must have a reason for doing what he does." This implies that the eagle has the *choice* of carrying off the lamb and that the bird of prey sees the situation as presenting alternatives. If one is somehow *able* to produce an event, then the whole notion of an interior calculus becomes very important. And, "exploiting this belief for his own ends," the lamb will begin to think that the bird of prey may have acted other than as a bird of prey. It should be noted here that the lamb is attempting to account for its own suffering and can only do so by positing some general rule to which both he and the eagle should agree. If the lamb should come up with such a system, then, in terms of the system, the eagle would be evil (since he is not living by the rules), and the lamb would be good (since he is, though he can *do no other*). Such system of beliefs, though, is the product of the fact of his suffering.

The task of the lamb is clear: he must seek to force the eagle to think and reflect upon the sources and natures of his action in terms of a system that will stop him from carrying off lambs. If this can be achieved, the will of the master-eagles will be separable from their actions. The eagle is, however, set up for this process. It is the principle of his "morality" that it not be reflective. As with the Homeric heroes or with Siegfried, reflexive intelligence and knowledge are fatal curses. The slave will then seek to understand the outside world far better; indeed, such intellectual comprehension is, in fact, the very source of his identity. Generally speaking, therefore, intelligence and calculation ("what should one do when . . .") is characteristic of slave morality. The slave, Nietzsche writes, "honors cleverness to a far greater degree," for it is much more essential to him than "the perfect functioning of the regulating unconscious instincts." (I might add a reminder here that Socrates had, in Nietzsche's view, found the "unconscious"—*Unbewusst*—no longer an adequate basis for behavior.) And, in Nietzsche's interpretation, the slave-lamb proceeds to do just that. The masters are cunningly frustrated by the slaves through knavish dialectical tricks. And, when the hitherto unconscious will no longer results in successful action, the masters seek for a reasons, and with that comes their fall into slave morality.

This is a description of the process that Nietzsche sees at work in Socrates. There arise certain problems with unreflective unconscious action; even Homer becomes obsolete due to changes in the world situation. The glory of Aeschylus, in Nietzsche's eyes, is his near success at transforming the Homeric world to fit his times without causing a self-doubting break in the continuity of the polity. Socrates, on the other hand, thinks the "unconscious" to be so inaccessible (Nietzsche indicates that this was true of *him* and Euripides, but was not universal) that reflexive reason is the only resource left. Hence, Socrates constantly seeks to make people explain and justify their opinions and actions. This, however, is the very basis of slave morality: slave morality seeks to make the will to power (that which defines and makes a world) explicit and self-conscious, to force the eagle to think, and in the lamb's terms.

Until this point, I have been considering the process by which slave morality is set in motion, essentially the theme of the first essay of *The Genealogy of Morals*. The consequences of this beginning do not remain static but develop through a relentless internal logic. To this problem Nietzsche devotes much of the second and third essays in the *Genealogy*.

The Paths of *Ressentiment*

In considering the problems of the will in the chapter "On Redemption" in *Zarathustra*, Nietzsche notes that the attempt to deal with time often leads men to seek revenge on the past. In his consideration of slave morality in the *Genealogy*, Nietzsche links the pursuit of revenge with his notion of *ressentiment*. The term refers to the process of allocating responsibility and blame for the pain one suffers; in *ressentiment*, one takes the outside world seriously as a cause of the pain one suffers, and thereby assumes that if only one could deal with the outside world the pain would be alleviated. For Nietzsche, slave morality begins with "the *ressentiment* of natures that are denied the true reaction, that of deeds, and compensate themselves with an imaginary revenge. While every noble morality develops from a triumphant yes-saying to itself, slave morality says from the outset no to what is 'outside,' what is 'different,' what is 'not itself'; and *this* no is its creative deed. . . . This *need* to direct one's view outward instead of back to oneself is of the essence of *ressentiment*: in order to exist, slave morality always first needs an external hostile world; . . . its action is fundamentally reaction." [10]

Ressentiment, it would seem, occurs when men do not exteriorize their affect into action, or more precisely when the affect does not *necessarily* lead to action. Should *ressentiment* "appear in the noble man," it will, writes Nietzsche, "consummate and exhaust itself in immediate response, and therefore does not poison." The noble nature is able to get rid of what goes on inside, and thus is not permanently affected by reaction. Nietzsche proceeds to give an example of such a nature.

> To be incapable of taking one's enemies seriously, one's accidents, even one's misdeeds seriously for very long—that is the sign of strong full natures in whom there is *an excess of the power to form, to mold, to recuperate, and to forget* (a good example of this is Mirabeau, who had *no memory for* insults and vile actions done to him simply because he—forgot). Such a man shakes off with a *single* shrug much vermin that burrows into others; here alone genuine "love of one's enemies" is possible—supposing it to be possible at all on earth. How much reverence has a noble man for his enemies!—and such reverence is a bridge to love. [11]

Except for the word "single," the italics are mine: they serve to signal Nietzsche's notion that for the noble man, the past simply does not present itself as a problem; the will of the noble man is in no way trapped by what he has been. . . . For Nietzsche, the will to power characteristic of *ressentiment* assimilates experience into the person (makes it his past) in such a way that the man of *ressentiment* is always driven forward, unable to rest with the present. Since the will to power "functions in the assimilation of the new under the form of the old, the already experienced, that which still lives in memory," [12] it is the *manner* in which the new is assimilated which is first important, *not* the specifics that have been assimilated. As Nietzsche notes about the time of *The Dawn of Day*, "it is not . . . the presenting [*das Vorstellen*] of the goal, but rather the performance [*die Vorstellung*] of logical forms . . . in the form of

---

10. *Genealogy of Morals* i 10, II 782.

11. *Genealogy of Morals* i 10, II 784–785 (my italics).

12. Kröner. *Die Un Schuld des Werdens*. Herausgegeben von A. Bäumler. Kröner Verlag: Stuttgart, 1956, vol. II, pp. 68–69.

wishing. Thought must give the content."[13] Thought is opposed to will to power, which as *pathos* is the series of instances in which thought is manifest.

The past that will not let a man live in the present is the past of *ressentiment* and of slave morality. It seems to me here that Nietzsche in effect takes the behavior that Weber later diagnosed as characteristic of the Protestant and tries to show that its genealogical kernel is implicit in Western culture far before the time of the Reformation. The character that Weber imputed to Franklin is of a man constantly deferring gratification, always concerned with consequences, drawn by the future and pushed by the past, not toward fulfillment, but always and only onward. This process, which Weber sees as the structure of action of Protestantism, is, for Nietzsche, implicit in the attitude toward the past found in the men of slave morality. The only difference for Nietzsche is that by the time one gets to Protestantism and capitalism, the mnemonic principle has risen into consciousness itself, such that one is not only pushed by the structures of the mind, but actively encourages them.[14]

It is worth noting as an aside here that this account shows immediately why the notion that Nietzsche is a "Darwinian" is wrong. (One might have suspected as much, since Nietzsche is *also* castigated as a Lamarckian!) "Natural selection" is not what Nietzsche is ever talking about; not only does he believe that the mediocre win out instead of the most fit, but also, much more importantly, in a real sense he does not believe that there has been any social "progress" at all. For Nietzsche, the genealogical root of slave morality contains in bud all that it becomes. If the "new is apprehended under the form of old," then it makes little sense to speak of evolution as the survival of the fittest, or even of the mediocre. In this analysis, it is rather the operation of the unactualized internalized will that concerns Nietzsche.

Here Nietzsche's analysis seems to rejoin that of Freud. In *Totem and Taboo,* Freud works out a philosophico-anthropological account of the beginnings of human social existence. By his analysis, after many cycles of fruitlessly killing their father to gain access to women (their mothers), a primal band of brothers decides that, in certain areas of their life, no externalization of hostility and aggression will be allowed. A taboo is placed on such behavior and the figure from whom aggression is deflected back into the psyche of the primitives becomes a totem. From this, for Freud, repressed behavior, religion, society, and civilization itself are born. Nietzsche's account, as I have given it, resembles this, but is far more subtle. He sees a similar process not in some distant pseudo-anthropological past, but at some (admittedly dim) historical epoch, and sees the clash not in terms of tyranny versus self-repression, but in terms of two competing principles of morality and authority. But, for Freud and Nietzsche, the consequences are the same: the victory of *ressentiment* allows for a system of morality based on cleverness, on the rationalism required for teaching about tabooed areas, on a science of ethics, and on a class of people to teach such ethics. Both men understand subsequent civilization to represent the victory of the world of totems and taboos. Slave morality is to *ressentiment* what civilization is to neurosis.

So far, Nietzsche has tried to demonstrate that the existence of master morality necessarily generates conditions in which men are tempted toward *ressentiment.* Master morality always implies an oppressed class, but one that will inevitably win out, since it is more numerous and becomes much cleverer. *Ressentiment* seems to be characteristic of the first stage of slave morality; men who live in it attempt to

---

13. Kröner, II, p. 13.

14. Kröner, II, p. 68 . . .

account for their impotence by blaming the outside world and seeking ways in which to thwart their eternal enemies. Gradually, however, the victory is achieved. Men finally find themselves "enclosed within the walls of society and of peace." [15] They do not find peace through this achievement. To make his point as dramatically as possible, Nietzsche then compares the new situation of the slavely moral man to that of the animals who first came to be amphibians and then land-dwellers.

> The situation that faced sea animals when they were compelled to become land animals or perish was the same as that which faced these semi-animals, well adapted to the wilderness, to war, to prowling, to adventure: suddenly all their instincts were disvalued and "suspended." . . . They felt unable to cope with the simplest undertakings; in this new world, they no longer possessed their former guides, their regulating, unconscious, right-leading [*unbewusst-sicherführenden*] drives; they were reduced to thinking, concluding, calculating, coordinating cause and effect, . . . to their "consciousness," their weakest and most mistake-making [*Fehlgreifen*] organ.

Nietzsche proceeds to argue that the old instincts do not cease to exist simply because these men, for their own security, now live inside walls, be these political or psychic or, more properly, both. The old instincts can now no longer discharge themselves, and thus seek "subterranean gratification." The old instincts are forced "backward against man himself" by those bulwarks that make up the walls of the city and are required for its continuity, or on the psychic level of the metaphor, by those calculations necessary for slave morality. This turning inward marks the shift from *ressentiment* to the stage of bad conscience. "The man who, from lack of external enemies and resistances and forcibly confined to the oppressive narrowness and punctiliousness of custom, impatiently lacerated, persecuted, gnawed at, assaulted, and maltreated himself . . . , this yearning and desperate prisoner became the inventor of bad conscience." Whereas *ressentiment* had said "it is your fault," bad conscience now must say "it is my fault."

This is a key shift inside slave morality. In the *ressentiment* aspect of slave morality, man is driven by the inability to get rid of the memory of suffering. In the stage of bad conscience, man is driven by himself: for the first time a process is set in motion by which man himself will eventually be called into question. Man now perceives *himself* as the cause of his own suffering; to alleviate this suffering, he must find a way to redeem himself from himself. He begins to say in effect: "I cause my own suffering; to redeem myself, I must punish myself to expiate the fault for which I am suffering." (Nietzsche gives a lengthy account of the various forms of punishment.) From such a dialectical process, Nietzsche sees the development of the concept of original sin (as a "causa prima"), and Schopenhauerian notions of the worthlessness of existence. "The aim," he writes, "is now to turn back the concepts 'guilty' and 'duty' . . . against the 'debtor' . . . (where they spread) until the irredeemable debt gives rise to the conception of irredeemable penance." In the slavely moral perspective, even God does not escape this process, for "God sacrifices himself for the guilt of mankind, God makes payment to himself, God is the only being who can redeem man from that which has become irredeemable for man himself." [16]

In this account of slave morality, Nietzsche is attempting to show that the state of *ressentiment* leads physically and socially to bad conscience, which in turn sets in

---

15. *Genealogy of Morals* ii 16, II 824. All citations following are from this section. . . .

16. *Genealogy of Morals* ii 21, II 832 . . .

play dynamics that eventually force man himself into question. If man is seen to be the ultimate source of his own suffering, redemption from oneself can only be effectuated as it is in Christian morality, by the act of God becoming man and freely redeeming himself. There is a very strong clue here to why Nietzsche thinks that the announcement of the *fact* of the "death of God" breaks "history in two." The logic of slave morality had driven men to the point where the divinity was all that was holding the moral fabric together. After His death, men do not suddenly cease behaving along the moral lines to which they are accustomed; but, gradually, the horizon that had given human moral life some coherence becomes a pale husk. This is the "twilight of the idols"; what was once divine and sensuous is now empty and clanging. The end of this process cannot but call man himself into question.

An ultimate questioning of the "human-all-too-human" does not happen either immediately nor even, it would seem, necessarily. Humanity develops a whole set of ideals by which to ward off the awe-ful ultimate question of its own worth. These ideals are the subject of the last essay in the *Genealogy.* Nietzsche certainly thinks that the modern period marks the *end* of a long line of development. He does not think that the end will come of itself; it is too frightening not to be resisted. . . .

Nietzsche and Political Thought
Mark Warren

. . . Nietzsche provides a framework for a critically postmodern political philosophy, [but] it is no more than a preface, an incomplete beginning, a set of pregnant suggestions. We find the preface in his reconstruction of the capacities of agency presupposed by the modern rationalist values of freedom, responsibility, rational autonomy, and individuality. These values presuppose that human powers can be organized as an agency capable of acting in a historical and social world. Nietzsche tells us how, and under what conditions, this is possible. In so doing, he provides an account of the relation between subjectivity and historical practices that could not develop within modern rationalism because of its metaphysical assumptions about humans as agents. By going beyond the assumptions of the tradition, Nietzsche's philosophy could enable many of its progressive values. . . .

Characterizing Nietzsche's Politics

In contrast to his philosophy and critique of Western culture, there is little in Nietzsche's *political* philosophy that is novel or radical. Indeed, if Nietzsche's political philosophy is not easily placed, it is not because of its novelty, but because of its sketchy qualities. Still, something of a *prima facie* case can be made for characterizing Nietzsche's political philosophy as a *neoaristocratic conservatism*. On the face of it, Nietzsche's politics has more in common with a conservatism like Burke's or even Hegel's than with any other existing political philosophy. Despite his warning to conservatives that it is neither possible nor desirable to recapture the virtues of past eras,[1] his views on social and political matters are conservative in definitive respects. Like Burke, for example, Nietzsche emphasized that valuable traits of individuals, cultures, and societies grow slowly and organically. Radical changes result in chaos, and for this reason they are not intrinsically desirable even though they may often be unavoidable. Nietzsche also argued that societies can only be held together through evolved social custom and habit (what Burke called "just prejudice"). Rational agreement between individuals is an epiphenomenon of this underlying and arational unity of the cultural practices of a people. Nietzsche believed in ascriptive hierarchies of functions in society rather than in social and economic equality. And he thought that societies should be ruled by superior individuals rather than democratically.

In all these respects Nietzsche's ideas are traditionally conservative. It is true that Nietzsche's ideals of sovereign individuality are more akin to liberal than conservative ideals, but—unlike liberals—he did not think it either possible or desirable to universalize these ideals. Sovereign individuality is necessarily an attribute of the few, and possible only within an aristocratic society. In accordance with this, Nietzsche

Excerpts from Mark Warren. 1988. *Nietzsche and Political Thought.* Cambridge, Mass.: MIT Press, pp. 211–225. Used by permission of the publisher.

1. *Twilight of the Idols* (1888) Section 9, Aphorism 43 . . .

held that the ends of political community should be the production of a few culturally exceptional individuals rather than a universally satisfactory life. Moreover, he believed that these two possible ends must inevitably be in conflict, the demands of the many (who have neither the inclination nor capacity for cultural excellence) always endangering the cultural privileges of the few.

As a conservative Nietzsche was self-consciously political in the sense of desiring a hierarchical, ascriptive society in the future. Still, it is difficult to associate his politics with any contemporary political movement. For example, he certainly did not intend his politics as a defense of the monopoly capitalism developing in Germany in his day [as some have argued] . . . even though it may have had this effect. . . . Nietzsche was not a defender of the bourgeoisie, and—as I shall suggest—had little use for the economic ideals of market societies. It is also clear that his thought could not have led directly to fascism as . . . others have argued (although elements of his politics were undoubtedly consistent with fascism). He was antistatist, anti-*Reich*, and disgusted by anti-Semitism. Where we do find some positive political commitments in Nietzsche is in his nostalgia for the European nobility of a prebourgeois era, which he tended to see as a cultural rather than political or economic class . . . [suggesting an affinity between his] politics . . . and concerns of an increasingly marginalized landed aristocracy. . . . For these reasons, it seems most accurate to characterize Nietzsche's politics as a neoaristocratic conservatism—a conservatism looking back to the social orders that developed in Europe between the Renaissance and the emergence of bourgeois political orders, and forward to a time when similar cultural aristocracies might be established.

Nihilism and Liberal Democratic Culture

Nietzsche's assessment of the political situation of European cultures combines his neoaristocratic conservatism with an analysis of the political effects of nihilism. On the one hand, he held that Christian-moral culture had instilled political expectations for community, universal rights, and equality. Like other conservatives, he held that such expectations contravened the natural limits of the political universe, leading to a vulgar and trivialized politics. On the other hand, he thought that the contemporary cultural crisis had also determined the possible and probable course of liberal democratic political culture. One finds the continuity between Nietzsche's philosophy and his politics in the intersection of these perspectives.

Any attempt to interpret Nietzsche's criticisms of modern politics generally, and liberal democratic politics specifically, must be highly reconstructive, owing to the sketchy and fragmented nature of his comments. What follows in this section is *one* possible way of reading these comments, but they are so incomplete that it is undoubtedly not the *only* possible way. Many of Nietzsche's criticisms of liberal democracy seem simply to reflect his conservative assumptions, and would be interesting only if these assumptions were well-founded. Other criticisms are more interesting because they extend his analysis of nihilism to political culture.

Still, even in this latter case one needs to proceed with caution. The reason is that Nietzsche views liberal democratic political culture as little more than a secularized development of Christian culture. Nietzsche was either unaware of or chose to ignore essential differences, such as those having to do with the rise of market economies and the development of bureaucratic organizations. While these developments certainly have dimensions related to Christian-moral culture, they are not reducible to them—a problem to which I shall return. Thus while Nietzsche's approach may yield important insights, he cannot be said to be a critic of liberal democracy in any comprehensive sense, even though commentators often construe him in this way. The scope of his criticism should be viewed as being limited to those aspects in which Christian and liberal democratic culture are in fact continuous. Here, the important point is that if one takes these limitations into account, one finds that Nietzsche's views on the continuity of Christian and liberal democratic culture do reveal significant affinities. This suggests that in important respects he was justified in holding that liberal democracy was implicated in the crisis of European nihilism. The value of Nietzsche's criticisms of liberal democracy lies in these affinities, and they can be best appreciated if not overextended.

In what senses did Nietzsche see liberal democratic culture as developing out of Christian culture? Nietzsche seems to relate its *liberal* aspect to Christianity's conception of the individual, and its *democratic* aspect to Christianity's conceptions of community and social justice. The important difference between Christian and liberal democratic culture, Nietzsche seems to think, is only that the latter is an attempt to politicize the ideals of the former. Early liberal thinkers sought the foundations of a new political order in the Christian concept of the individual as an indestructible soul, although they revised the concept to make the individual into a subject of natural rights and inclinations. Democratic ideals, according to Nietzsche, consist primarily in the notion that the Christian promise of community can be realized in this world, combined with the view that (Christian-Platonic) ideals of justice can be politicized. But because liberal democracy relies on ideals that are part of a collapsing culture, it too is implicated in the crisis of nihilism.

Insofar as Nietzsche's criticisms of liberalism here have any plausibility at all, it can be found in his view that liberalism inherits the contradictions of Christian ideology that stem from its metaphysics of the subject. Christianity posited the existence of individual souls as unconditional, nonempirical, and irreducible beings. For this reason, the Christian individual remains nonactive and nonworldly; the self is displaced into a set of metaphysical identities that are divorced from practices. Liberalism inherited this metaphysical conception of the subject, while giving it a different content and putting it to different uses. Like the Christian concept of the individual, for example, the liberal concept is abstract in the sense of being unconditional. Similarly, it lends itself to reification from its material, social, and cultural conditions of possibility. The metaphysical formulation shows up clearly in the thought of liberal individualists beginning with Hobbes and extending at least through Bentham: the individual consists fundamentally of a set of natural inclinations, preferences, and rights that manifest themselves through social organizations (or least *ought* to do so: the concept of nature played both a normative and empirical role for early liberal thinkers). Society also becomes an abstraction: rather than a condition of individuation, society is seen as the result of individuals agreeing to enforce rules in terms of which they can maximize their desires and preferences. Similarly, liberal individuals become political beings by recognizing the need for, and assenting to, sovereign institutions that ensure orderly satisfaction of preexisting needs and desires.

By positing the individual as something that is prior to society in some metaphysical sense—as a locus of natural rights and inclinations, for example—liberal thinkers could justify political arrangements that preserve a private space for the individual. But they did so in an inherently unstable way. Because liberals put a metaphysical placeholder in the space of the individual, they failed to theorize this space. As a result, they justified liberal forms of the state in terms of a historically conditioned effect mistaken for a universal essence. This is why Nietzsche's understanding of nihilism in Western culture as the collapse of the individual *as agent* also implicates the individualistic metaphysics of liberalism. Extrapolating Nietzsche's logic, the criticism would be that in failing to theorize this space, liberalism unwittingly takes over the vacuous private space of the Christian soul, a private space that existed as promise and ideology but not as a reality. Building on this suggestion, one might say that if the private space of the Christian soul had served as an escape from social and political reality, liberalism turns this escape into a political foundation, for it represents the body politic as an aggregate of private spaces, socialized and politicized though contractual relations. Questions about the conditions of individuation become difficult to ask when the individual becomes a metaphysical foundation of society rather than—as in Nietzsche's philosophy—simply a value worthy of being realized. Early liberals confused norm and nature. As a result, even when the fragility of individuation is noticed by liberal thinkers like John Stuart Mill, their insights could not become a part of their social ontology. . . .

. . . One might capture Nietzsche's criticism of liberalism by analogy to his more comprehensively developed criticism of Christianity. Like Christian ideology, liberalism demands more of the individual than it can either conceptualize or provide for. Both ascribe responsibility to individuals for their fortunes in the world through the respective notions of sin and merit. And both deny individuals an understanding of the grounds on which they could actualize these ascriptions of responsibility. Both theorize individuality as a manifestation of human nature as such, as if it had no material, social, cultural, or self-reflective conditions of actualization. By disconnecting interior and exterior, they assert the unconditional value of the individual as soul and as a locus of rights, but fail to conceptualize these as historical possibilities. It is true that almost all liberal thinkers empirically recognize and always comment on the conditional nature of individuals. But they fail to articulate these insights theoretically. Because liberalism lacks a theory of power as agency, it also lacks the theory of individuation required by its own individualistic values. This is why the liberal defense of the individual is no guarantee against either politically enforced uniformity or social massification; this is why liberal political thinkers could often affirm social arrangements that undermine the individual as a reality. One sees this in Hobbes' authoritarian Sovereign, in Locke's view that labor activity and its products are the kinds of things that can and should be alienated from individuals on the market, in Bentham's affirmation of massive poverty produced by capitalism, and in Kant's moral argument for accepting prevailing political authoritarianism. Nietzsche, of course, does not draw these conclusions—his attacks on liberalism are usually no more than crude broadsides. But he *might* have developed his criticisms this way had he been as systematic here as in his critique of Christianity.

Nietzsche reserved most of his criticism of liberal democracy, however, for the democratic ideals that became wedded to liberalism, especially beginning with the French Revolution.[2] He held that the demand for equal rights had been formulated and legitimated within Christianity, insofar as Christianity had bestowed an equal dignity and worth upon each individual as a subject of God regardless of actual circumstance.[3] While the bulk of Nietzsche's opposition to the democratic movements of the nineteenth century can be explained by his opinion that only hier-

---

2. *Beyond Good and Evil* (1886) Aphorism 38. *On the Genealogy of Morals* (1887) Essay I, Section 16.

3. The AntiChrist (1845) Section 43. *Twilight of the Idols* Section 9, Aphorism 43.

archical, functionally delineated societies are desirable, here—as in his criticism of liberalism—an element of immanent critique exists from which democratic theory might benefit. To see this, one needs to remember that Nietzsche's thought does contain suggestions of what a positive political equality would involve . . . , assuming one is interested in this (Nietzsche is not). In order to satisfy Nietzsche's objections to egalitarian ideals, a positive political equality would have to be based on a *de facto* equality of the capacity to act and, inseparable from this, a political culture that sustains rights and duties by adjusting distributions of power in society. Reconstructing this strain in Nietzsche's thought suggests that his criticisms point toward the failure of many democratic ideologies to establish a relation between their ideals and the conditions under which they could be actualized. Without establishing such relations, Nietzsche thought, the ideals would literally demoralize themselves by appearing in retrograde form. Equality, which might be thought of as sustaining conditions of equal strength, becomes an "equality in violating rights" of those who are different,[4] a "certain factual increase in similarity," and a leveling to a universal mediocrity.[5] This inversion would hold true for other ideals of liberal democratic culture as well. Freedom—ideally understood as a capacity for responsible action —can turn into "*laisser aller.*"[6] Justice—ideally understood as impartial assessment of competing claims of power—can become an instrument of covetousness or revenge.[7] These considerations suggest that it is possible to give a generous reading of Nietzsche's opposition to liberal democracy, even if such a reading was clearly not his intention. Read generously, his critique calls for distinctions between the ideals of liberal democratic culture and their ideological effects when they are not an integral part of a self-reflective rationality.

Nihilism and the State

Nietzsche's own interest, however, was not in an immanent critique of liberal democracy, but rather in the political impact of European nihilism. His treatment of this issue can be construed in light of the following dilemma: liberal democratic society requires sovereign individuals in order to achieve a society within which individuals can protect themselves via a limited political sphere. But Nietzsche thought that Christian-moral culture had more or less permanently ruined the possibility of sovereign individuality for most people, even though its collapse increased possibilities for a few. The distinctive attributes of sovereign individuality—the capacities of memory and conscience, the senses of duty and obligation—are not, for most people, defining attributes of their self-identities. Rather, these behaviors remain dependent upon "herd" morality, the external commandments of social and religious *Sittlichkeit*. To the degree that sovereign individuals do not exist, liberal democracies remain dependent upon crumbling cultural supports.

The consequences of liberalism's unwitting reliance on a dying culture are not politically benign. They can be understood in terms of Nietzsche's suggestions that a symbiotic relation evolved during the Christian-moral period between the state's

---

4. *Beyond Good and Evil,* Aphorism 212.

5. *Twilight of the Idols,* Section 9, Aphorism 37.

6. *Twilight of The Idols,* Section 9, Aphorism 41.

7. *Human, All too Human,* Vol. 1, (1878) Aphorism 451. . .

construction of political experience and the church's rationalization of this experience.[8] By gaining its legitimacy through an attachment to Christianity, the state began to take upon itself demands (like those for community) that it could not fulfill without recourse to the Christian form of meaning. While institutionalized Christianity was intact, the state could claim to be the worldly form of community while deflecting the communal experiences that supported the claim back onto the church. With the breakdown of Christian-moral culture, however, the state is left with demands for meaning, but without the kind of culture that had once organized these demands and provided experiences of meaning, even if vicariously. The crisis . . . of the Christian-moral world view . . . has a political dimension insofar as the state loses its religious means of legitimation. Because the loss of Christian-moral culture occurs without the formation of a sovereign self, the opportunity exists for the state to provide its own legitimations by manipulating self-identities. In this way, the state assumes a role vacated by the church. Only in the modern period, then, does it become possible for the state to exploit reflexive needs directly by providing a vicarious identity for the self in relation to the community.

In these terms, one can understand Nietzsche's fear that the self might be regressively politicized in the wake of the vacuum left by Christian-moral culture. Although he implicitly shared this fear with liberals, he did not see the possibility of a resolution within the terms of liberal theory. Here again Nietzsche's comments are suggestive: liberals have always opposed the encroachment of institutionalized politics (if not institutionalized economics) into the "private" sphere of the self. They rightly fear totalitarianism in such instances. But liberals tend not to understand why totalitarianism is possible, because they do not understand the historically conditional nature of individual agency. They often make the fatal assumption that the individual provides a natural and unassailable cornerstone of private life, sustained by family, church, and work place. Yet central aspects of this system of identities dissolve in a cultural crisis. Nietzsche thought that for most the cultural crisis would lead to exposure of a "decadent" self, the "private person."[9] The "private person" coincides with what he later called the "last man."[10] The "last man" of the modern period is the result of a political culture that had mediated power relations between individuals through external identities, such as those of God and country. With the loss of external guidance in the modern cultural crisis, the last man's feeling of power is threatened. God is replaced by new kinds of religion, narcotic culture, and identity with national heroes and the state. The existence of "last men" leaves a fertile field for invasion of the self by the state or any other institutionalized power.

Nietzsche's sensitivity to this weakness of liberal democratic societies surely stemmed in part from the fact that liberal culture was never well established in Germany. For this reason, he was able to understand its contingent nature in ways that those in well-established liberal cultures could not. Even in Nietzsche's lifetime, processes of cultural breakdown coexisted with a rising German nationalism, a nationalism expressed in the Reich and anti-Semitism. Although Nietzsche welcomed in principle the growth of liberal institutions as a means for curbing state power, he took little comfort in their existence because he saw them as vehicles for the ideals of an

---

8. *Human, All too Human*, Vol. 1, Aphorism 472 . . .

9. . . . See *Human, All too Human*, Vol. 1, Aphorism 472.

10. *Thus Spoke Zarathustra*, Prologue.

increasingly massified society. Thus, reflecting the German situation of his time, Nietzsche emphasized not the pluralism of parliamentary processes but their relative ideological unity. "Parliamentarianism—that is, public permission to choose between five basic public opinions—flatters and wins the favor of all those who would like to *seem* independent and individual, as if they fought for their opinions. . . . Whoever deviates from the five public opinions and stands apart will always have the whole herd against him."[11] "Liberalism," Nietzsche writes elsewhere, is "herd-animalization."[12]

The plausibility of Nietzsche's polemics against the "herd" and its connections to liberal institutions can be found in his view—one already well-developed by de Tocqueville and John Stuart Mill—that parliamentary processes contain the danger of providing merely the formal appearance of pluralism while functioning to legitimate the state as a guarantor of mass values. Should parliament become the tool of the "herd"—and Nietzsche thought this imminent—it would surely use state power to impose "herd" values on everyone. "Liberal institutions," he generalizes, "cease to be liberal as soon as they are attained: later on, there are no worse and no more thorough injurers of freedom than liberal institutions."[13] He voiced similar concerns about leftist movements. Working at first through liberal institutions, the advocates of democracy on the left would wish to politicize "everything" by defining general standards of existence; they would dictate that "everyone should live and work according to such standards."[14] Foreshadowing the objections of later anarchists such as Emma Goldman against statist Marxists, Nietzsche believed that revolutionaries harbor a "reactionary" desire to reassert the power of the state over the individual.[15]

If Nietzsche was concerned about the growth of state power driven by the democratic aspirations of the left, he was equally concerned about the growth of state power fueled by the nationalist right.[16] The attempt of the state to step into the cultural vacuum left by the decay of Christian-moral culture was already occurring in Germany. Through his *Kulturkampf*—his attack on the Catholic Church—Bismarck clearly was attempting to draw the interpretive processes of society into the arena of the state. Nietzsche viewed Bismarck's *Kulturkampf* as a single instance of a more general trend for individual identities to be formed around secular institutions, a trend continuing and deepening the displacement of individual agency that had occurred under Christianity. "If one spends oneself for power," he explains in discussing the decline of German culture,

> for great politics, for economics, world trade, parliamentarianism, and military interests—if one spends in *this* direction the quantum of understanding, seriousness, will, and self-overcoming that one represents, then it will be lacking in the direction of culture. Culture and the state—one should not deceive oneself about this—are antagonists. . . . All great ages of culture are ages of political decline: what is great culturally has always been unpolitical, even *antipolitical*. . . . In the history of European culture the rise of the *"Reich"*

---

11. *The Gay Science* (1882). Aphorism 174 . . .

12. *Twilight of the Idols*, Section 9, Aphorism 38.

13. Ibid.

14. *Human, All too Human, Vol. 1*, Aphorism 438 . . .

15. *Human, All too Human, Vol. 1*, Aphorism 473 . . .

16. *Human, All too Human, Vol. 1*, Aphorism 475.

means one thing above all: *a displacement of the center of gravity* [*eine Verlegung des Schwergewichts*].[17]

Properly understood, Nietzsche's cultural ideal aimed at individual rather than institutional power. This is why even when writing on behalf of a rebirth of culture in Germany (which "matters most") he opposed Bismarck's incipiently fascist *Kultur-kampf* and attempt to establish a *Kultur-Staat*. A state-culture—as distinct from a culture that defines a "people"—was for Nietzsche a contradiction in terms.[18]

Nietzsche's fears that the state would move into the contemporary cultural vacuum are stated unequivocally in *Zarathustra*. He warns that the "new idol" (the state) lures the "all-too-many" to view it as a new god. The state attempts to identify itself with the cultural unity of entire peoples: "this lie crawls out of its mouth: 'I, the state, am the people.'"[19] The state hastens the destruction of peoples by usurping their social fabric of customs and rights (*Sitten und Rechten*), and by attempting to replace the lost culture. "'On earth there is nothing greater than I: the ordering finger of God am I' —thus roars the monster."[20] If European nihilism signifies the loss of self-identity for most people, the foremost political expression of nihilism would be an identity of political culture with the state. If connections are to be drawn between nihilism as Nietzsche understood it and the emergence of totalitarianism in the twentieth century—as they so often are—they should be drawn here.

Nietzsche's criticisms of the state provide some insight into the positive political values that are intrinsic to his philosophy. Most strikingly, Nietzsche's criticisms of the state are consistently antitotalitarian; they suggest the primacy of his concern with the way that different societies empower or subvert individual powers. The value implication, of course, is that societies that sustain individual powers are intrinsically more desirable than those that displace self-identities onto supraindividual institutions such as the state. Nietzsche's comments suggest that all politically sustained hierarchies ("for great politics, for economics, world trade, parliamentarianism, and military interests"[21]) are inconsistent with the intersubjective space of individuation. At least this much is implied in Nietzsche's critique of the state inasmuch as it is a critique on behalf of individuals as agents. Yet these observations only deepen the problem of interpreting Nietzsche's politics: why does Nietzsche fail to follow through on the immanent political logic of his philosophy, especially when he could draw out implications such as these?

Nihilism, Capitalism, and Class Conflict

It is only when one looks at a final arena of Nietzsche's criticism of modern society and politics that the limits of his political thinking begin to emerge. Through these limits one can begin to account for the politics he actually held, as opposed to other possibilities that are consistent with his philosophy of agency. . . . Nietzsche opposed not only the increasing tendency for the state to define cultural ideals, but also the increasing tendency for ideals to become economic in nature. Although little interested in the workings of contemporary economies, he resisted their increasing

---

17. *Twilight of the Idols,* Section 8, Aphorism 4.

18. Ibid . . .

19. *Thus Spoke Zarathustra.* On the New Idol.

20. Ibid.

21. *Twilight of the Idols,* Section 8, Aphorism 4.

dominion over everyday life. . . . . Nietzsche fits quite clearly the pattern that Lukács called "romantic anticapitalism," in spite of Lukács' own assessment.[22] For example, he viewed the capitalist work ethic as self-destructive: what his contemporaries referred to as the "blessing of work," Nietzsche saw as "mechanical activity," resulting in "absolute regularity, punctilious and unthinking obedience, a mode of life fixed once and for all, fully occupied time, a certain permission, indeed training [*Zucht*], for 'impersonality,' for self-forgetfulness, for *incuria sui* [lack of care for the self]."[23] Neither did it escape his attention that the experience of mechanized labor, coupled with contemporary economic ideals, aided and abetted the more general logic of nihilism. Thus Nietzsche set himself against the prevailing "economic optimism": "as if the increasing expenditure of everybody must necessarily involve the increasing welfare of everybody. The opposite seems to me to be the case: the expenditure of everybody amounts to a collective loss: man is diminished—so one no longer knows what *aim* this tremendous process has served."[24]

Nietzsche even registers occasional sympathy for the working classes. He suggests, for example, that Europe's workers possess a good deal more potential as powerful beings than Europe's bourgeoisie, and certainly more than their position in society could ever allow.[25] His concerns for the situation of Europe's laboring classes had narrow limits, however, because he believed class societies to be natural and inevitable. Thus he opposed the "forcible new distributions of property" proposed by socialists.[26] Instead, he could think only in terms of subjecting the working classes to a cultural aristocracy that could provide them with the kinds of vicarious goals lost with the Christian-moral world view.

The conflict between the possibilities of Nietzsche's philosophy and the goals dictated by his views on the limits of social organization produces our common and rather disconcerting experiences that there is both a "gentle" and a "bloody" Nietzsche. Both aspects of Nietzsche have inspired interpretive traditions. His "gentle" aspects belong to his philosophy and critique of culture. They show through in his claim that "I want to proceed as Raphael did and never paint another image of torture. There are enough sublime things so that one does not have to look for the sublime where it dwells in sisterly association with cruelty; and my ambition also could never find satisfaction if I became a sublime assistant at torture."[27] Although Nietzsche wished to see culture become a means of individuation rather than a means and reflection of oppression, he also believed that without a class of "slaves," no higher culture would be possible. . . . Nietzsche's politics, which contains the "bloody" aspects of his thought, follows in large part from this belief. . . .

The Uncritical Assumptions of Nietzsche's Politics

Criticism of Nietzsche's politics cannot concern the question of why he chooses as he does—for the choice follows clearly from the goal of his philosophy and the political alternatives as he sees them. Rather, we need to understand why Nietzsche structures

---

22. See Michael Löwy, *Georg Lukács: From Romanticism to Bolshevism* (London: New Left Books, 1979), pp. 25–26.

23. *On the Genealogy of Morals,* Essay III, Section 18.

24. *The Will to Power* (1901) Note 866 . . .

25. *The Will to Power,* Note 764.

26. *Human, All too Human, Vol. I,* Aphorism 452.

27. *The Gay Science,* Aphorism 313.

the political alternatives as he does. If Nietzsche conceives of all values in terms of a philosophy of power as agency, then it is axiomatic that the positive goal of politics would be to maintain conditions under which humans can fully develop and exert their powers as agents. Yet he holds this end to be possible only for a few individuals. Insofar as his politics is consistent with his philosophy of power, Nietzsche must hold that natural constraints to politics exist that make it impossible and undesirable to universalize these goals. The best *possible* situation would be a limited realization of these values within a hierarchy of political and economic domination that expresses these constraints. He makes four kinds of arguments that lead to this conclusion. First, he argues that political domination follows from the fact that life is will to power. Second, he argues that material conditions of economic scarcity require a hierarchical division of economic and cultural labor. Third, he argues that an unequal historical constitution of human natures both necessitates and makes desirable a hierarchy of political, cultural, and economic functions. And fourth, he holds that modern politics is overwhelmingly determined by a modern cultural crisis that is irreducibly cultural and not itself the effect of economic or political power relations. These assumptions lead Nietzsche to conclude that a cultural renewal from which a few "higher" individuals benefit ought to be the primary task of future politics.

. . . [T]he first argument is an unwarranted elaboration of the concept of will to power in Nietzsche's own terms. The other three arguments involve insupportable assumptions about the political, economic, and biological limits to social and political organization. Together, these assumptions account for the political elaboration Nietzsche chose to give his philosophy. Without these assumptions other political elaborations would have been possible. . . .

Hannah Arendt

In the 1950s, many scholars believed that political theory was dead. The tradition of philosophical efforts to develop a comprehensive view of political life apparently had ended in the latter part of the nineteenth century. Political and economic ideologies that once stirred popular passions and generated mass movements were similarly a thing of the past. The triumph of liberal democracy after two world wars, and the increasing sophistication of the social sciences, had ushered in an era in which the ideological debates about political ends had given way to technical disagreements about administrative means.

However, for Hannah Arendt and other thinkers, the postwar world—indeed, the modern world of the nineteenth and twentieth centuries—was not entirely worthy of celebration. The apparent death of political theory marked as well the end of politics as a meaningful activity. The end of ideology meant the success of bureaucratic rationality, the same unthinking processes that produced the totalitarian horrors characteristic of Nazism and Stalinism. Modernity had brought the sublimation of politics by administration and the replacement of political action by technical expertise.

Arendt's writings thus have an antimodernist character. She tends to lament the well-known evils of the modern age—totalitarian assaults on freedom; bureaucratic administration; politics affected by lying, violence, or absolute morality; and the end of the grand tradition of political theory. Although she discusses topics that now seem commonplace to us, her analyses of them often surprise us with unique approaches and sharp observations.

Born in Hanover, Germany, in 1906, Hannah Arendt made analyzing the meaning of modernity her life's work. A student of the phenomenology of both Martin Heidegger and Karl Jaspers, she became active in the Jewish opposition to the Nazis and fled Germany in 1933. Living in France until 1941, she emigrated to the United States where she entered a circle of New York intellectuals and writers. Arendt became famous with the publication of *The Origins of Totalitarianism* in 1951. Other noteworthy books soon followed. She held several college and university teaching posts and wrote a number of widely read essays on philosophy, culture, and the American political scene. Hannah Arendt died in 1975, and her last theoretical work, *The Life of the Mind,* was published posthumously in 1978.

For Arendt, the modern world carried with it a sense of strangeness or discontinuity, a sense of estrangement or alienation, and a sense of loss. One of the most important aspects of the past, which modernity had lost, was an understanding of the proper meaning of political action. Venerating the style of public life in the ancient Greek *polis,* Arendt believed that authentic politics can occur only through public deliberation over common purposes, not through blind partisan conflict or routine administration. Political action (rightly understood) reveals the best aspects of human beings; it involves people engaged in the process of making decisions as a community of equals. While the institutions of representative democracy brought us significant advances, such as civil liberties, they did not bring true freedom. Authentic freedom can come only from the noble words and great deeds of people engaged in political action. Arendt's stress on the will to act as essential to freedom and politics, and her preference for political institutions that permit extensive democratic participation, gave her many admirers among students of the New Left. She, in turn, gave them significant support and encouragement until their movement took an intolerant and violent turn.

The Human Condition

Arendt's classic work in political theory, *The Human Condition* (1958), is a study of the relationship between thinking and doing, between contemplation and action, between the *vita contemplativa* and the *vita activa.* For Arendt, the modern age has reversed the traditional priority given to contemplation over action; moreover, it has blurred the boundaries among three fundamental human activities: labor, work, and action. For Arendt, action (the speech and deeds of people engaged in public affairs) represents a more authentically human realm than either labor (toiling for survival, producing for necessity) or work (craftsmanship, making artifacts). Western civilization has long since deprived "action" of its original political meaning, and merging it with the concepts of labor and work, has made the *vita activa* synonymous with busy-ness and unquiet. Thus, despite her glorification of politics as the quintessential realm of action (moving speech and great deeds), Arendt closes the book with a quotation from Cato suggesting that the *vita contemplativa* may well be the most desirable life, after all.

Commentaries

Bhikhu Parekh locates Arendt's political philosophy within a phenomenological approach to political life, in which political institutions, experiences, and relationships are explored for their essential structures and significant meanings. After summarizing Arendt's views on the *vita activa,* Parekh discusses her political ideal of the participatory community. Finally, Parekh highlights and then criticizes Arendt's contributions to political theory, suggesting that her view of politics is incoherent, impractical, and paradoxical.

James T. Knauer considers the merit of criticisms that Arendt's concept of political action is devoid of motives and goals, of instrumental (means-ends) concerns. He claims that Arendt's critics have misread her position, overlooking the idea that political action is always about something (interests, motives, goals), even when it reveals a human meaning or expresses a person's unique identity. Though Arendt should be read as defending the expressive, human side of politics against excessive materialism and rationalism, she was not unaware of the strategic and instrumental elements in political life.

Key Words

Vita activa. The active life, whose aspects are labor, work, and (political) action; speaking, doing, making.
Vita contemplativa. The contemplative life, the solitary quest for truth; thinking.
Animal laborans. Human beings as laborers, toilers, consumers.
Homo faber. Human beings as makers of artifacts, as creators of an external world.
Phenomenology. An approach to social and political theory that aims to provide an understanding of the basic elements of human experience and consciousness.

For Further Reading

Canovan, M. 1974. *The Political Thought of Hannah Arendt.* New York: Harcourt Brace Jovanovich.

Hill, M., ed. 1979. *Hannah Arendt: The Recovery of the Public World.* New York: St. Martin's Press.

Kateb, G. 1983. *Hannah Arendt: Politics, Conscience, Evil.* Totowa, N.J.: Rowman and Allanheld.

Parekh, B. 1981. *Hannah Arendt and the Search for a New Political Theory.* Atlantic Highlands, N.J.: Humanities Press.

Young-Bruehl, E. 1982. *Hannah Arendt: For Love of the World.* New Haven, Conn.: Yale University Press.

The Human Condition

1
Vita Activa and the Human Condition

With the term *vita activa*, I propose to designate three fundamental human activities: labor, work, and action. They are fundamental because each corresponds to one of the basic conditions under which life on earth has been given to man.

Labor is the activity which corresponds to the biological process of the human body, whose spontaneous growth, metabolism, and eventual decay are bound to the vital necessities produced and fed into the life process by labor. The human condition of labor is life itself.

Work is the activity which corresponds to the unnaturalness of human existence, which is not imbedded in, and whose mortality is not compensated by, the species' ever-recurring life cycle. Work provides an "artificial" world of things, distinctly different from all natural surroundings. Within its borders each individual life is housed, while this world itself is meant to outlast and transcend them all. The human condition of work is worldliness.

Action, the only activity that goes on directly between men without the intermediary of things or matter, corresponds to the human condition of plurality, to the fact that men, not Man, live on the earth and inhabit the world. While all aspects of the human condition are somehow related to politics, this plurality is specifically *the* condition—not only the *conditio sine qua non*, but the *conditio per quam*—of all political life. Thus the language of the Romans, perhaps the most political people we have known, used the words "to live" and "to be among men" (*inter homines esse*) or "to die" and "to cease to be among men" (*inter homines esse desinere*) as synonyms. But in its most elementary form, the human condition of action is implicit even in Genesis ("Male and female created He *them*"), if we understand that this story of man's creation is distinguished in principle from the one according to which God originally created Man (*adam*), "him" and not "them," so that the multitude of human beings becomes the result of multiplication.[1] Action would be an unnecessary luxury, a capricious

---

1. In the analysis of postclassical political thought, it is often quite illuminating to find out which of the two biblical versions of the creation story is cited. Thus it is highly characteristic of the difference between the teaching of Jesus of Nazareth and of Paul that Jesus, discussing the relationship between man and wife, refers to Genesis 1:27: "Have ye not read, that he which made *them* at the beginning made them male and female" (Matt. 19:4), whereas Paul on a similar occasion insists that the woman was created "of the man" and hence "for the man," even though he then somewhat attenuates the dependence: "neither is the man without the woman, neither the woman without the man" (I Cor. 11:8–12). The difference indicates much more than a different attitude to the role of woman. For Jesus, faith was closely related to action (cf. § 33 below); for Paul, faith was primarily related to salvation. Especially interesting in this respect is Augustine (*De civitate Dei* xii. 21), who not only ignores Genesis 1:27 altogether but sees the difference between man and animal in that man was created *unum ac singulum*, whereas all animals were

interference with general laws of behavior, if men were endlessly reproducible repetitions of the same model, whose nature or essence was the same for all and as predictable as the nature or essence of any other thing. Plurality is the condition of human action because we are all the same, that is, human, in such a way that nobody is ever the same as anyone else who ever lived, lives, or will live.

All three activities and their corresponding conditions are intimately connected with the most general condition of human existence: birth and death, natality and mortality. Labor assures not only individual survival, but the life of the species. Work and its product, the human artifact, bestow a measure of permanence and durability upon the futility of mortal life and the fleeting character of human time. Action, in so far as it engages in founding and preserving political bodies, creates the condition for remembrance, that is, for history. Labor and work, as well as action, are also rooted in natality in so far as they have the task to provide and preserve the world for, to foresee and reckon with, the constant influx of newcomers who are born into the world as strangers. However, of the three, action has the closest connection with the human condition of natality; the new beginning inherent in birth can make itself felt in the world only because the newcomer possesses the capacity of beginning something anew, that is, of acting. In this sense of initiative, an element of action, and therefore of natality, is inherent in all human activities. Moreover, since action is the political activity par excellence, natality, and not mortality, may be the central category of political, as distinguished from metaphysical, thought.

The human condition comprehends more than the conditions under which life has been given to man. Men are conditioned beings because everything they come in contact with turns immediately into a condition of their existence. The world in which the *vita activa* spends itself consists of things produced by human activities; but the things that owe their existence exclusively to men nevertheless constantly condition their human makers. In addition to the conditions under which life is given to man on earth, and partly out of them, men constantly create their own, self-made conditions, which, their human origin and their variability notwithstanding, possess the same conditioning power as natural things. Whatever touches or enters into a sustained relationship with human life immediately assumes the character of a condition of human existence. This is why men, no matter what they do, are always conditioned beings. Whatever enters the human world of its own accord or is drawn into it by human effort becomes part of the human condition. The impact of the world's reality upon human existence is felt and received as a conditioning force. The objectivity of the world —its object- or thing-character—and the human condition supplement each other; because human existence is conditioned existence, it would be impossible without things, and things would be a heap of unrelated articles, a non-world, if they were not the conditioners of human existence.

To avoid misunderstanding: the human condition is not the same as human nature, and the sum total of human activities and capabilities which

---

ordered "to come into being several at once" (*plura simul iussit exsistere*). To Augustine, the creation story offers a welcome opportunity to stress the species character of animal life as distinguished from the singularity of human existence.

correspond to the human condition does not constitute anything like human nature. For neither those we discuss here nor those we leave out, like thought and reason, and not even the most meticulous enumeration of them all, constitute essential characteristics of human existence in the sense that without them this existence would no longer be human. The most radical change in the human condition we can imagine would be an emigration of men from the earth to some other planet. Such an event, no longer totally impossible, would imply that man would have to live under man-made conditions, radically different from those the earth offers him. Neither labor nor work nor action nor, indeed, thought as we know it would then make sense any longer. Yet even these hypothetical wanderers from the earth would still be human; but the only statement we could make regarding their "nature" is that they still are conditioned beings, even though their condition is now self-made to a considerable extent.

The problem of human nature, the Augustinian *quaestio mihi factus sum* ("a question have I become for myself"), seems unanswerable in both its individual psychological sense and its general philosophical sense. It is highly unlikely that we, who can know, determine, and define the natural essences of all things surrounding us, which we are not, should ever be able to do the same for ourselves—this would be like jumping over our own shadows. Moreover, nothing entitles us to assume that man has a nature or essence in the same sense as other things. In other words, if we have a nature or essence, then surely only a god could know and define it, and the first prerequisite would be that he be able to speak about a "who" as though it were a "what."[2] The perplexity is that the modes of human cognition applicable to things with "natural" qualities, including ourselves to the limited extent that we are specimens of the most highly developed species of organic life, fail us when we raise the question: And *who* are we? This is why attempts to define human nature almost invariably end with some construction of a deity, that is, with the god of the philosophers, who, since Plato, has revealed himself upon closer inspection to be a kind of Platonic idea of man. Of course, to demask such philosophic concepts of the divine as conceptualizations of human capabilities and qualities is not a demonstration of, not even an argument for, the non-existence of God; but the fact that attempts to define the nature of man lead so easily into an idea which definitely strikes us as "superhuman" and therefore is identified with the divine may cast suspicion upon the very concept of "human nature."

---

2. Augustine, who is usually credited with having been the first to raise the so-called anthropological question in philosophy, knew this quite well. He distinguishes between the questions of "Who am I?" and "What am I?" the first being directed by man at himself ("And I directed myself at myself and said to me: You, who are you? And I answered: A man"—*tu, quis es?* [*Confessiones* x. 6]) and the second being addressed to God ("What then am I, my God? What is my nature?"—*Quid ergo sum, Deus meus? Quae natura sum?* [x. 17]). For in the "great mystery," the *grande profundum*, which man is (iv. 14), there is "something of man [*aliquid hominis*] which the spirit of man which is in him itself knoweth not. But Thou, Lord, who has made him [*fecisti eum*] knowest everything of him [*eius omnia*]" (x. 5). Thus, the most familiar of these phrases which I quoted in the text, the *quaestio mihi factus sum*, is a question raised in the presence of God, "in whose eyes I have become a question for myself" (x. 33). In brief, the answer to the question "Who am I?" is simply: "You are a man—whatever that may be"; and the answer to the question "What am I?" can be given only by God who made man. The question about the nature of man is no less a theological question than the question about the nature of God; both can be settled only within the framework of a divinely revealed answer.

On the other hand, the conditions of human existence—life itself, natality and mortality, worldliness, plurality, and the earth—can never "explain" what we are or answer the question of who we are for the simple reason that they never condition us absolutely. This has always been the opinion of philosophy, in distinction from the sciences—anthropology, psychology, biology, etc.—which also concern themselves with man. But today we may almost say that we have demonstrated even scientifically that, though we live now, and probably always will, under the earth's conditions, we are not mere earth-bound creatures. Modern natural science owes its great triumphs to having looked upon and treated earth-bound nature from a truly universal viewpoint, that is, from an Archimedean standpoint taken, wilfully and explicitly, outside the earth.

2
The Term *Vita Activa*

The term *vita activa* is loaded and overloaded with tradition. It is as old as (but not older than) our tradition of political thought. And this tradition, far from comprehending and conceptualizing all the political experiences of Western mankind, grew out of a specific historical constellation: the trial of Socrates and the conflict between the philosopher and the *polis*. It eliminated many experiences of an earlier past that were irrelevant to its immediate political purposes and proceeded until its end, in the work of Karl Marx, in a highly selective manner. The term itself, in medieval philosophy the standard translation of the Aristotelian *bios politikos*, already occurs in Augustine, where, as *vita negotiosa* or *actuosa*, it still reflects its original meaning: a life devoted to public-political matters.[3]

Aristotle distinguished three ways of life (*bioi*) which men might choose in freedom, that is, in full independence of the necessities of life and the relationships they originated. This prerequisite of freedom ruled out all ways of life chiefly devoted to keeping one's self alive—not only labor, which was the way of life of the slave, who was coerced by the necessity to stay alive and by the rule of his master, but also the working life of the free craftsman and the acquisitive life of the merchant. In short, it excluded everybody who involuntarily or voluntarily, for his whole life or temporarily, had lost the free disposition of his movements and activities.[4] The remaining three

---

3. See Augustine *De civitate Dei* xix. 2, 19.

4. William L. Westermann ("Between Slavery and Freedom," *American Historical Review*, Vol. L [1945]) holds that the "statement of Aristotle . . . that craftsmen live in a condition of limited slavery meant that the artisan, when he made a work contract, disposed of two of the four elements of his free status [viz., of freedom of economic activity and right of unrestricted movement], but by his own volition and for a temporary period"; evidence quoted by Westermann shows that freedom was then understood to consist of "status, personal inviolability, freedom of economic activity, right of unrestricted movement," and slavery consequently "was the lack of these four attributes." Aristotle, in his enumeration of "ways of life" in the *Nicomachean Ethics* (i. 5) and the *Eudemian Ethics* (1215a35 ff.), does not even mention a craftsman's way of life; to him it is obvious that a *banausos* is not free (cf. *Politics* 1337b5). He mentions, however, "the life of money-making" and rejects it because it too is "undertaken under compulsion" (*Nic. Eth.* 1096a5). That the criterion is freedom is stressed in the *Eudemian Ethics:* he enumerates only those lives that are chosen *ep' exousian.*

ways of life have in common that they were concerned with the "beautiful," that is, with things neither necessary nor merely useful: the life of enjoying bodily pleasures in which the beautiful, as it is given, is consumed; the life devoted to the matters of the *polis*, in which excellence produces beautiful deeds; and the life of the philosopher devoted to inquiry into, and contemplation of, things eternal, whose everlasting beauty can neither be brought about through the producing interference of man nor be changed through his consumption of them.[5]

The chief difference between the Aristotelian and the later medieval use of the term is that the *bios politikos* denoted explicitly only the realm of human affairs, stressing the action, *praxis*, needed to establish and sustain it. Neither labor nor work was considered to possess sufficient dignity to constitute a *bios* at all, an autonomous and authentically human way of life; since they served and produced what was necessary and useful, they could not be free, independent of human needs and wants.[6] That the political way of life escaped this verdict is due to the Greek understanding of *polis* life, which to them denoted a very special and freely chosen form of political organization and by no means just any form of action necessary to keep men together in an orderly fashion. Not that the Greeks or Aristotle were ignorant of the fact that human life always demands some form of political organization and that ruling over subjects might constitute a distinct way of life; but the despot's way of life, because it was "merely" a necessity, could not be considered free and had no relationship with the *bios politikos*.[7]

With the disappearance of the ancient city-state—Augustine seems to have been the last to know at least what it once meant to be a citizen—the term *vita activa* lost its specifically political meaning and denoted all kinds of active engagement in the things of this world. To be sure, it does not follow that work and labor had risen in the hierarchy of human activities and were now equal in dignity with a life devoted to politics.[8] It was, rather, the other way round: action was now also reckoned among the necessities of earthly life, so that contemplation (the *bios theōrētikos*, translated into the *vita contemplativa*) was left as the only truly free way of life.[9]

However, the enormous superiority of contemplation over activity of any kind, action not excluded, is not Christian in origin. We find it in Plato's political philosophy, where the whole utopian reorganization of *polis* life is not only directed by the superior insight of the philosopher but has no aim other than to make possible the philosopher's way of life. Aristotle's very articulation of the different ways of life, in whose order the life of pleasure plays a minor role, is clearly guided by the ideal of contemplation (*theōria*).

---

5. For the opposition of the beautiful to the necessary and the useful see *Politics* 1333a30 ff., 1332b32.

6. For the opposition of the free to the necessary and the useful see *ibid.* 1332b2.

7. See *ibid.* 1277b8 for the distinction between despotic rule and politics. For the argument that the life of the despot is not equal to the life of a free man because the former is concerned with "necessary things," see *ibid.* 1325a24.

8. On the widespread opinion that the modern estimate of labor is Christian in origin, see below, § 44.

9. See Aquinas *Summa theologica* ii. 2. 179, esp. art. 2, where the *vita activa* arises out of the *necessitas vitae praesentis*, and *Expositio in Psalmos* 45.3, where the body politic is assigned the task of finding all that is necessary for life: *in civitate oportet invenire omnia necessaria ad vitam.*

To the ancient freedom from the necessities of life and from compulsion by others, the philosophers added freedom and surcease from political activity (*skholē*),[10] so that the later Christian claim to be free from entanglement in worldly affairs, from all the business of this world, was preceded by and originated in the philosophic *apolitia* of late antiquity. What had been demanded only by the few was now considered to be a right of all.

The term *vita activa*, comprehending all human activities and defined from the viewpoint of the absolute quiet of contemplation, therefore corresponds more closely to the Greek *askholia* ("unquiet"), with which Aristotle designated all activity, than to the Greek *bios politikos*. As early as Aristotle the distinction between quiet and unquiet, between an almost breathless abstention from external physical movement and activity of every kind, is more decisive than the distinction between the political and the theoretical way of life, because it can eventually be found within each of the three ways of life. It is like the distinction between war and peace: just as war takes place for the sake of peace, thus every kind of activity, even the processes of mere thought, must culminate in the absolute quiet of contemplation.[11] Every movement, the movements of body and soul as well as of speech and reasoning, must cease before truth. Truth, be it the ancient truth of Being or the Christian truth of the living God, can reveal itself only in complete human stillness.[12]

Traditionally and up to the beginning of the modern age, the term *vita activa* never lost its negative connotation of "un-quiet," *nec-otium, a-skholia*. As such it remained intimately related to the even more fundamental Greek distinction between things that are by themselves whatever they are and things which owe their existence to man, between things that are *physei* and things that are *nomō*. The primacy of contemplation over activity rests on the conviction that no work of human hands can equal in beauty and truth the physical *kosmos*, which swings in itself in changeless eternity without any interference or assistance from outside, from man or god. This eternity discloses itself to mortal eyes only when all human movements and activities are at perfect rest. Compared with this attitude of quiet, all distinctions and articulations within the *vita activa* disappear. Seen from the viewpoint of contemplation, it does not matter what disturbs the necessary quiet, as long as it is disturbed.

Traditionally, therefore, the term *vita activa* receives its meaning from the *vita contemplativa;* its very restricted dignity is bestowed upon it because it

---

10. The Greek word *skholē*, like the Latin *otium*, means primarily freedom from political activity and not simply leisure time, although both words are also used to indicate freedom from labor and life's necessities. In any event, they always indicate a condition free from worries and cares. An excellent description of the everyday life of an ordinary Athenian citizen, who enjoys full freedom from labor and work, can be found in Fustel de Coulanges, *The Ancient City* (Anchor ed. 1956), pp. 334–36; it will convince everybody how time-consuming political activity was under the conditions of the city-state. One can easily guess how full of worry this ordinary political life was if one remembers that Athenian law did not permit remaining neutral and punished those who did not want to take sides in factional strife with loss of citizenship.

11. See Aristotle *Politics* 1333a30–33. Aquinas defines contemplation as *quies ab exterioribus motibus* (*Summa theologica* ii. 2. 179. 1).

12. Aquinas stresses the stillness of the soul and recommends the *vita activa* because it exhausts and therefore "quietens interior passions" and prepares for contemplation (*Summa theologica* ii. 2. 182. 3).

serves the needs and wants of contemplation in a living body.[13] Christianity, with its belief in a hereafter whose joys announce themselves in the delights of contemplation,[14] conferred a religious sanction upon the abasement of the *vita activa* to its derivative, secondary position; but the determination of the order itself coincided with the very discovery of contemplation (*theōria*) as a human faculty, distinctly different from thought and reasoning, which occurred in the Socratic school and from then on has ruled metaphysical and political thought throughout our tradition.[15] It seems unnecessary to my present purpose to discuss the reasons for this tradition. Obviously they are deeper than the historical occasion which gave rise to the conflict between the *polis* and the philosopher and thereby, almost incidentally, also led to the discovery of contemplation as the philosopher's way of life. They must lie in an altogether different aspect of the human condition, whose diversity is not exhausted in the various articulations of the *vita activa* and, we may suspect, would not be exhausted even if thought and the movement of reasoning were included in it.

If, therefore, the use of the term *vita activa*, as I propose it here, is in manifest contradiction to the tradition, it is because I doubt not the validity of the experience underlying the distinction but rather the hierarchical order inherent in it from its inception. This does not mean that I wish to contest or even to discuss, for that matter, the traditional concept of truth as revelation and therefore something essentially given to man, or that I prefer the modern age's pragmatic assertion that man can know only what he makes himself. My contention is simply that the enormous weight of contemplation in the traditional hierarchy has blurred the distinctions and articulations within the *vita activa* itself and that, appearances notwithstanding, this condition has not been changed essentially by the modern break with the tradition and the eventual reversal of its hierarchical order in Marx and Nietzsche. It lies in the very nature of the famous "turning upside down" of philosophic systems or currently accepted values, that is, in the nature of the operation itself, that the conceptual framework is left more or less intact.

The modern reversal shares with the traditional hierarchy the assumption that the same central human preoccupation must prevail in all activities of men, since without one comprehensive principle no order could be established. This assumption is not a matter of course, and my use of the term *vita activa* presupposes that the concern underlying all its activities is not the same as and is neither superior or inferior to the central concern of the *vita contemplativa*. . . .

---

13. Aquinas is quite explicit on the connection between the *vita activa* and the wants and needs of the human body which men and animals have in common (*Summa theologica* ii. 2. 182. 1).

14. Augustine speaks of the "burden" (*sarcina*) of active life imposed by the duty of charity, which would be unbearable without the "sweetness" (*suavitas*) and the "delight of truth" given in contemplation (*De civitate Dei* xix. 19).

15. The time-honored resentment of the philosopher against the human condition of having a body is not identical with the ancient contempt for the necessities of life; to be subject to necessity was only one aspect of bodily existence, and the body, once freed of this necessity, was capable of that pure appearance the Greeks called beauty. The philosophers since Plato added to the resentment of being forced by bodily wants the resentment of movement of any kind. It is because the philosopher lives in complete quiet that it is only his body which, according to Plato, inhabits the city. Here lies also the origin of the early reproach of busy-bodiness (*polypragmosynē*) leveled against those who spent their lives in politics.

41
The Reversal of Contemplation and Action

Perhaps the most momentous of the spiritual consequences of the discoveries of the modern age and, at the same time, the only one that could not have been avoided, since it followed closely upon the discovery of the Archimedean point and the concomitant rise of Cartesian doubt, has been the reversal of the hierarchical order between the *vita contemplativa* and the *vita activa*.

In order to understand how compelling the motives for this reversal were, it is first of all necessary to rid ourselves of the current prejudice which ascribes the development of modern science, because of its applicability, to a pragmatic desire to improve conditions and better human life on earth. It is a matter of historical record that modern technology has its origins not in the evolution of those tools man had always devised for the twofold purpose of easing his labors and erecting the human artifice, but exclusively in an altogether non-practical search for useless knowledge. Thus, the watch, one of the first modern instruments, was not invented for purposes of practical life, but exclusively for the highly "theoretical" purpose of conducting certain experiments with nature. This invention, to be sure, once its practical usefulness became apparent, changed the whole rhythm and the very physiognomy of human life; but from the standpoint of the inventors, this was a mere incident. If we had to rely only on men's so-called practical instincts, there would never have been any technology to speak of, and although today the already existing technical inventions carry a certain momentum which will probably generate improvements up to a certain point, it is not likely that our technically conditioned world could survive, let alone develop further, if we ever succeeded in convincing ourselves that man is primarily a practical being.

However that may be, the fundamental experience behind the reversal of contemplation and action was precisely that man's thirst for knowledge could be assuaged only after he had put his trust into the ingenuity of his hands. The point was not that truth and knowledge were no longer important, but that they could be won only by "action" and not by contemplation. It was an instrument, the telescope, a work of man's hands, which finally forced nature, or rather the universe, to yield its secrets. The reasons for trusting *doing* and for distrusting *contemplation* or *observation* became even more cogent after the results of the first active inquiries. After being and appearance had parted company and truth was no longer supposed to appear, to reveal and disclose itself to the mental eye of a beholder, there arose a veritable necessity to hunt for truth behind deceptive appearances. Nothing indeed could be less trustworthy for acquiring knowledge and approaching truth than passive observation or mere contemplation. In order to be certain one had to *make sure*, and in order to know one had to do. Certainty of knowledge could be reached only under a twofold condition: first, that knowledge concerned only what one had done himself—so that its ideal became mathematical knowledge, where we deal only with self-made entities of the mind—and second, that knowledge was of such a nature that it could be tested only through more doing.

Since then, scientific and philosophic truth have parted company; scientific truth not only need not be eternal, it need not even be comprehensible or adequate to human reason. It took many generations of scientists before the human mind grew bold enough to fully face this implication of modernity. If nature and the universe are products of a divine maker, and if the human mind is incapable of understanding what man has not made himself, then man cannot possibly expect to learn anything about nature that he can understand. He may be able, through ingenuity, to find out and even to imitate the devices of natural processes, but that does not mean these devices will ever make sense to him—they do not have to be intelligible. As a matter of fact, no supposedly suprarational divine revelation and no supposedly abstruse philosophic truth has ever offended human reason so glaringly as certain results of modern science. One can indeed say with Whitehead: "Heaven knows what seeming nonsense may not to-morrow be demonstrated truth."[16]

Actually, the change that took place in the seventeenth century was more radical than what a simple reversal of the established traditional order between contemplation and doing is apt to indicate. The reversal, strictly speaking, concerned only the relationship between thinking and doing, whereas contemplation, in the original sense of beholding the truth, was altogether eliminated. For thought and contemplation are not the same. Traditionally, thought was conceived as the most direct and important way to lead to the contemplation of truth. Since Plato, and probably since Socrates, thinking was understood as the inner dialogue in which one speaks with himself (*eme emautō*, to recall the idiom current in Plato's dialogues); and although this dialogue lacks all outward manifestation and even requires a more or less complete cessation of all other activities, it constitutes in itself a highly active state. Its outward inactivity is clearly separated from the passivity, the complete stillness, in which truth is finally revealed to man. If medieval scholasticism looked upon philosophy as the handmaiden of theology, it could very well have appealed to Plato and Aristotle themselves; both, albeit in a very different context, considered this dialogical thought process to be the way to prepare the soul and lead the mind to a beholding of truth beyond thought and beyond speech—a truth that is *arrhēton*, incapable of being communicated through words, as Plato put it,[17] or beyond speech, as in Aristotle.[18]

The reversal of the modern age consisted then not in raising doing to the rank of contemplating as the highest state of which human beings are capable, as though henceforth doing was the ultimate meaning for the sake of which contemplation was to be performed, just as, up to that time, all activities of the *vita activa* had been judged and justified to the extent that they made the *vita contemplativa* possible. The reversal concerned only thinking, which from then on was the handmaiden of doing as it had been the *ancilla theologiae*, the handmaiden of contemplating divine truth in medieval

16. *Science and the Modern World*, p. 116.

17. In the *Seventh Letter* 341C: *rhēton gar oudamōs estin hōs alla mathēmata* ("for it is never to be expressed by words like other things we learn").

18. See esp. *Nicomachean Ethics* 1142a25 ff. and 1143a36 ff. The current English translation distorts the meaning because it renders *logos* as "reason" or "argument."

philosophy and the handmaiden of contemplating the truth of Being in ancient philosophy. Contemplation itself became altogether meaningless.

The radicality of this reversal is somehow obscured by another kind of reversal, with which it is frequently identified and which, since Plato, has dominated the history of Western thought. Whoever reads the Cave allegory in Plato's *Republic* in the light of Greek history will soon be aware that the *periagōgē*, the turning-about that Plato demands of the philosopher, actually amounts to a reversal of the Homeric world order. Not life after death, as in the Homeric Hades, but ordinary life on earth, is located in a "cave," in an underworld; the soul is not the shadow of the body, but the body the shadow of the soul; and the senseless, ghostlike motion ascribed by Homer to the lifeless existence of the soul after death in Hades is now ascribed to the senseless doings of men who do not leave the cave of human existence to behold the eternal ideas visible in the sky.[19]

In this context, I am concerned only with the fact that the Platonic tradition of philosophical as well as political thought started with a reversal, and that this original reversal determined to a large extent the thought patterns into which Western philosophy almost automatically fell wherever it was not animated by a great and original philosophical impetus. Academic philosophy, as a matter of fact, has ever since been dominated by the never-ending reversals of idealism and materialism, of transcendentalism and immanentism, of realism and nominalism, of hedonism and asceticism, and so on. What matters here is the reversibility of all these systems, that they can be turned "upside down" or "downside up" at any moment in history without requiring for such reversal either historical events or changes in the structural elements involved. The concepts themselves remain the same no matter where they are placed in the various systematic orders. Once Plato had succeeded in making these structural elements and concepts reversible, reversals within the course of intellectual history no longer needed more than purely intellectual experience, an experience within the framework of conceptual thinking itself. These reversals already began with the philosophical schools in late antiquity and have remained part of the Western tradition. It is still the same tradition, the same intellectual game with paired antitheses that rules, to an extent, the famous modern reversals of spiritual hierarchies, such as Marx's turning Hegelian dialectic upside down or Nietzsche's revaluation of the sensual and natural as against the supersensual and supernatural.

The reversal we deal with here, the spiritual consequence of Galileo's discoveries, although it has frequently been interpreted in terms of the traditional reversals and hence as integral to the Western history of ideas, is of an altogether different nature. The conviction that objective truth is not given to man but that he can know only what he makes himself is not the result of skepticism but of a demonstrable discovery, and therefore does not lead to resignation but either to redoubled activity or to despair. The world loss of modern philosophy, whose introspection discovered consciousness as the inner sense with which one senses his senses and found it to be the

---

19. It is particularly Plato's use of the words *eidōlon* and *skia* in the story of the Cave which makes the whole account read like a reversal of and a reply to Homer; for these are the key words in Homer's description of Hades in the *Odyssey*.

only guaranty of reality, is different not only in degree from the age-old suspicion of the philosophers toward the world and toward the others with whom they shared the world; the philosopher no longer turns from the world of deceptive perishability to another world of eternal truth, but turns away from both and withdraws into himself. What he discovers in the region of the inner self is, again, not an image whose permanence can be beheld and contemplated, but, on the contrary, the constant movement of sensual perceptions and the no less constantly moving activity of the mind. Since the seventeenth century, philosophy has produced the best and least disputed results when it has investigated, through a supreme effort of self-inspection, the processes of the senses and of the mind. In this aspect, most of modern philosophy is indeed theory of cognition and psychology, and in the few instances where the potentialities of the Cartesian method of introspection were fully realized by men like Pascal, Kierkegaard, and Nietzsche, one is tempted to say that philosophers have experimented with their own selves no less radically and perhaps even more fearlessly than the scientists experimented with nature.

Much as we may admire the courage and respect the extraordinary ingenuity of philosophers throughout the modern age, it can hardly be denied that their influence and importance decreased as never before. It was not in the Middle Ages but in modern thinking that philosophy came to play second and even third fiddle. After Descartes based his own philosophy upon the discoveries of Galileo, philosophy has seemed condemned to be always one step behind the scientists and their ever more amazing discoveries, whose principles it has strived arduously to discover *ex post facto* and to fit into some over-all interpretation of the nature of human knowledge. As such, however, philosophy was not needed by the scientists, who—up to our time, at least—believed that they had no use for a handmaiden, let alone one who would "carry the torch in front of her gracious lady" (Kant). The philosophers became either epistemologists, worrying about an over-all theory of science which the scientists did not need, or they became, indeed, what Hegel wanted them to be, the organs of the *Zeitgeist*, the mouthpieces in which the general mood of the time was expressed with conceptual clarity. In both instances, whether they looked upon nature or upon history, they tried to understand and come to terms with what happened without them. Obviously, philosophy suffered more from modernity than any other field of human endeavor; and it is difficult to say whether it suffered more from the almost automatic rise of activity to an altogether unexpected and unprecedented dignity or from the loss of traditional truth, that is, of the concept of truth underlying our whole tradition. . . .

45
The Victory of the *Animal Laborans*

The victory of the *animal laborans* would never have been complete had not the process of secularization, the modern loss of faith inevitably arising from Cartesian doubt, deprived individual life of its immortality, or at least of the certainty of immortality. Individual life again became mortal, as mortal as it had been in antiquity, and the world was even less stable, less permanent, and hence less to be relied upon than it had been during the Christian era. Modern man, when he lost the certainty of a world to come, was thrown back upon himself and not upon this world; far from believing that the world might be potentially immortal, he was not even sure that it was real. And in so far as he was to assume that it was real in the uncritical and apparently unbothered optimism of a steadily progressing science, he had removed himself from the earth to a much more distant point than any Christian otherworldliness had ever removed him. Whatever the word "secular" is meant to signify in current usage, historically it cannot possibly be equated with worldliness; modern man at any rate did not gain this world when he lost the other world, and he did not gain life, strictly speaking, either; he was thrust back upon it, thrown into the closed inwardness of introspection, where the highest he could experience were the empty processes of reckoning of the mind, its play with itself. The only contents left were appetites and desires, the senseless urges of his body which he mistook for passion and which he deemed to be "unreasonable" because he found he could not "reason," that is, not reckon with them. The only thing that could now be potentially immortal, as immortal as the body politic in antiquity and as individual life during the Middle Ages, was life itself, that is, the possibly everlasting life process of the species mankind.

We saw before that in the rise of society it was ultimately the life of the species which asserted itself. Theoretically, the turning point from the earlier modern age's insistence on the "egoistic" life of the individual to its later emphasis on "social" life and "socialized man" (Marx) came when Marx transformed the cruder notion of classical economy—that all men, in so far as they act at all, act for reasons of self-interest—into forces of interest which inform, move, and direct the classes of society, and through their conflicts direct society as a whole. Socialized mankind is that state of society where only one interest rules, and the subject of this interest is either classes or man-kind, but neither man nor men. The point is that now even the last trace of action in what men were doing, the motive implied in self-interest, disappeared. What was left was a "natural force," the force of the life process itself, to which all men and all human activities were equally submitted ("the thought process itself is a natural process")[20] and whose only aim, if it had an aim at all, was survival of the animal species man. None of the higher capacities of man was any longer necessary to connect individual life with the life of the species; individual life became part of the life process, and to labor, to assure the continuity of one's own life and the life of his family, was all that was needed. What was not needed, not necessitated by life's metabolism with nature, was either superfluous or could be justified only in terms of a peculiarity of human as distinguished from other animal life—so that Milton was considered to have written his *Paradise Lost* for the same reasons and out of similar urges that compel the silkworm to produce silk.

If we compare the modern world with that of the past, the loss of human experience involved in this development is extraordinarily striking. It is not only and not even primarily contemplation which has become an entirely

---

20. In a letter Marx wrote to Kugelmann in July, 1868.

meaningless experience. Thought itself, when it became "reckoning with consequences," became a function of the brain, with the result that electronic instruments are found to fulfil these functions much better than we ever could. Action was soon and still is almost exclusively understood in terms of making and fabricating, only that making, because of its worldliness and inherent indifference to life, was now regarded as but another form of laboring, a more complicated but not a more mysterious function of the life process.

Meanwhile, we have proved ingenious enough to find ways to ease the toil and trouble of living to the point where an elimination of laboring from the range of human activities can no longer be regarded as utopian. For even now, laboring is too lofty, too ambitious a word for what we are doing, or think we are doing, in the world we have come to live in. The last stage of the laboring society, the society of jobholders, demands of its members a sheer automatic functioning, as though individual life had actually been submerged in the over-all life process of the species and the only active decision still required of the individual were to let go, so to speak, to abandon his individuality, the still individually sensed pain and trouble of living, and acquiesce in a dazed, "tranquilized," functional type of behavior. The trouble with modern theories of behaviorism is not that they are wrong but that they could become true, that they actually are the best possible conceptualization of certain obvious trends in modern society. It is quite conceivable that the modern age—which began with such an unprecedented and promising outburst of human activity—may end in the deadliest, most sterile passivity history has ever known.

But there are other more serious danger signs that man may be willing and, indeed, is on the point of developing into that animal species from which, since Darwin, he imagines he has come. If, in concluding, we return once more to the discovery of the Archimedean point and apply it, as Kafka warned us not to do, to man himself and to what he is doing on this earth, it at once becomes manifest that all his activities, watched from a sufficiently removed vantage point in the universe, would appear not as activities of any kind but as processes, so that, as a scientist recently put it, modern motorization would appear like a process of biological mutation in which human bodies gradually begin to be covered by shells of steel. For the watcher from the universe, this mutation would be no more or less mysterious than the mutation which now goes on before our eyes in those small living organisms which we fought with antibiotics and which mysteriously have developed new strains to resist us. How deep-rooted this usage of the Archimedean point against ourselves is can be seen in the very metaphors which dominate scientific thought today. The reason why scientists can tell us about the "life" in the atom—where apparently every particle is "free" to behave as it wants and the laws ruling these movements are the same statistical laws which, according to the social scientists, rule human behavior and make the multitude behave as it must, no matter how "free" the individual particle may appear to be in its choices—the reason, in other words, why the behavior of the infinitely small particle is not only similar in pattern to the planetary system as it appears to us but resembles the life and behavior patterns in human society is, of course, that we look and live in this society as though we were as far removed from our own human existence as we are from the infinitely small and the immensely large which, even if they could be perceived by the finest instruments, are too far away from us to be experienced.

Needless to say, this does not mean that modern man has lost his capacities or is on the point of losing them. No matter what sociology, psychology, and anthropology will tell us about the "social animal," men persist in making, fabricating, and building, although these faculties are more and more restricted to the abilities of the artist, so that the concomitant experiences of worldliness escape more and more the range of ordinary human experience.[21]

Similarly, the capacity for action, at least in the sense of the releasing of processes, is still with us, although it has become the exclusive prerogative of the scientists, who have enlarged the realm of human affairs to the point of extinguishing the time-honored protective dividing line between nature and the human world. In view of such achievements, performed for centuries in the unseen quiet of the laboratories, it seems only proper that their deeds should eventually have turned out to have greater news value, to be of greater political significance, than the administrative and diplomatic doings of most so-called statesmen. It certainly is not without irony that those whom public opinion has persistently held to be the least practical and the least political members of society should have turned out to be the only ones left who still know how to act and how to act in concert. For their early organizations, which they founded in the seventeenth century for the conquest of nature and in which they developed their own moral standards and their own code of honor, have not only survived all vicissitudes of the modern age, but they have become one of the most potent power-generating groups in all history. But the action of the scientists, since it acts into nature from the standpoint of the universe and not into the web of human relationships, lacks the revelatory character of action as well as the ability to produce stories and become historical, which together form the very source from which meaningfulness springs into and illuminates human existence. In this existentially most important aspect, action, too, has become an experience for the privileged few, and these few who still know what it means to act may well be even fewer than the artists, their experience even rarer than the genuine experience of and love for the world.

Thought, finally—which we, following the premodern as well as the modern tradition, omitted from our reconsideration of the *vita activa*—is still possible, and no doubt actual, wherever men live under the conditions of political freedom. Unfortunately, and contrary to what is currently assumed about the proverbial ivory-tower independence of thinkers, no other human capacity is so vulnerable, and it is in fact far easier to act under conditions of tyranny than it is to think. As a living experience, thought has always been assumed, perhaps wrongly, to be known only to the

---

21. This inherent worldliness of the artist is of course not changed if a "non-objective art" replaces the representation of things; to mistake this "non-objectivity" for subjectivity, where the artist feels called upon to "express himself," his subjective feelings, is the mark of charlatans, not of artists. The artist, whether painter or sculptor or poet or musician, produces worldly objects, and his reification has nothing in common with the highly questionable and, at any rate, wholly unartistic practice of expression. Expressionist art, but not abstract art, is a contradiction in terms.

few. It may not be presumptuous to believe that these few have not become fewer in our time. This may be irrelevant, or of restricted relevance, for the future of the world; it is not irrelevant for the future of man. For if no other test but the experience of being active, no other measure but the extent of sheer activity were to be applied to the various activities within the *vita activa,* it might well be that thinking as such would surpass them all. Whoever has any experience in this matter will know how right Cato was when he said: *Numquam se plus agere quam nihil cum ageret, numquam minus solum esse quam cum solus esset—* "Never is he more active than when he does nothing, never is he less alone than when he is by himself."

Hannah Arendt
Bhikhu Parekh

Like Husserl, Heidegger, Jaspers, Sartre and others, Hannah Arendt contends that the Western tradition of philosophy, as it has developed since Plato, is inherently ill-equipped to study human affairs in general and politics in particular. In her view, philosophers were, from the very beginning, impressed and fascinated by the simplicity, vastness and regularity of the cosmos and repelled by the chaos, complexity and superficiality of human affairs. Accordingly, they took nature rather than man as their primary object of investigation. They devised appropriate bodies of questions, categories of thought, modes of reasoning and methods of inquiry and extended these to the study of man. They viewed man as a natural being, albeit more complex than, but fundamentally not very different from, other natural organisms and applied to him such distinctions as essence and appearance, the subject and the object, appearance and reality and Being and un-Being, that they had found useful in their study of nature. They also adopted a spectatorial approach to men, as if philosophers belonged to an entirely different species. Arendt argues that a tradition of philosophy whose entire conceptual framework is designed with nature in mind is inherently ill-equipped to study the human world, where many of its questions, distinctions and modes of inquiry simply do not apply, where man is both the subject and the object of investigation and cannot adopt a spectatorial and wholly neutral approach. Her basic concern is to develop a view of philosophy which does full justice to human affairs and sharply distinguishes it from other intellectual inquiries, especially science.

1

Men ask all kinds of questions about themselves and the world. In Arendt's view, most of these fall into two logically distinct categories. Some represent what she calls the 'pursuit of truth' and the others a 'quest for meaning'. For convenience I shall call them empirical and hermeneutic questions respectively. The terms are not entirely satisfactory, but no others capture Arendt's intended distinction as well as they do.

The empirical questions seek information about, or explanations for, some aspects of the sensually perceptible world. To ask the name of your neighbour or the capital of Ecuador, if your grandfather is live, the date when Caesar crossed the Rubicon, how a clock, a machine or an atom bomb works, or how cold weather, sexual frigidity, changes in temperature and earthquakes are caused is to ask empirical questions. Arendt argues that although these questions differ in their complexity and in the ease with which they can be answered, they all have several basic features in common. They relate to the sensually perceptible world, are amenable to empirical verification, yield an objective, public and impersonal body of knowledge, have a common origin in intellectual curiosity and a common *telos,* namely, the truth.

From *Contemporary Political Thinkers* by Bhikhu Parekh, pp. 1–21. Copyright © 1982 by Johns Hopkins University Press, Baltimore/London.

Hermeneutic questions are about meaning. Although the concept of meaning is central to her thought, Arendt nowhere clearly defines it, nor does she deal with some of the problems it raises. Sometimes she uses the term in the Hegelian sense of 'reconciliation with the world'; more often, however, she uses it in the Socratic sense of 'significance' or 'worth of things'. Again, sometimes she says that a meaning is conferred by a human agent, but more often that it is discovered by him. For Arendt, then, to ask to know the meaning of an activity, an object, an experience, an institution or a form of life is to ask to know about its significance or worth, that is, whether and why it is valuable and worth doing or supporting.

Arendt argues that, like empirical questions, hermeneutic questions can be asked at different levels and in different contexts. I may inquire into the meaning of a particular experience in my life or that of such organized activities and institutions as the pursuit of knowledge, education, art, the conquest of nature and the state. Going a step further, I may be perplexed about the meaning of a way of life geared to the accumulation of wealth and may wonder if other ways of life are nobler and more worthy of a human being. At the most basic level, I may ask if life itself has any meaning. Like worms and insects, men are born, live out their allotted spans of life and vanish without a trace. I may wonder if my life or human life in general has any point or meaning, whether it has any more worth than that of an insect, why I would be wrong to commit suicide, or why I am justified in killing a wasp but not a waspish neighbour. In Arendt's view, the quest for meaning is ultimately a desire to know what is worth doing or approving, what form of life is worth living, what kind of behaviour is worthy of a human being, and why. It owes its origin to the twofold fact that men cannot avoid making choices and that, as rational beings, they cannot help asking what choices are rational, and why.

Arendt argues that although hermeneutic questions differ greatly in their complexity, they share several basic features. First, they are non-empirical in nature. They do not ask if a thing exists, when it originated, how it works or is caused, but what its significance or worth is. Thus they cannot be answered on the basis of empirical knowledge of the world. No amount of empirical information can tell me why human life has greater worth than that of an insect, nor what behaviour is unworthy of a human being. Second, hermeneutic questions have their origin not in ignorance or curiosity about the world but in existential perplexity. Men undertake activities, undergo sufferings, encounter experiences and choose between forms of life whose point or significance is not obvious to them. As rational beings, they feel the 'need' to 'make sense' of, and give a 'satisfactory account' of, these in order that they can respond to them in an intelligent manner. Third, since hermeneutic questions are non-empirical in nature, the answers to them cannot be verified or falsified but only defended by arguments, and they cannot be judged true or false, only plausible or implausible, insightful or banal.

For Arendt, then to determine the meaning of something is to determine its significance. She is somewhat ambiguous about how its significance should be determined. Her general view seems to be that the significance of a thing is determined by its location within a larger relevant framework, the identification of its place in this framework and an assessment of its contribution. For example, if I wish to determine the meaning of a particular experience of mine, my life constitutes the relevant framework. I need to analyse the experience, relate it to my other experiences, locate it within my pattern of life and elucidate what it tells me about myself and how it affects my life. If I wish to determine the meaning of a particular historical event, I need to locate and analyse it within the context of the history of the nation concerned. If I wish to determine the meanings of culture, art, the pursuit of knowledge, forms of life and life itself, I need to locate them within the widest possible framework available to man. In Arendt's view, human existence constitutes such a framework. Accordingly, she argues that in order to determine the significance of such activities and institutions, one needs to develop a general perspective on human existence and assess their contributions to it.

For Arendt science and philosophy are paradigmatic expressions, respectively, of man's search for truth and meaning. As such, they are 'fundamentally different' modes of inquiry. Science inquires into 'what is', philosophy into 'what it means for it to be'. Science is motivated by a passionate love of truth, philosophy by an equally passionate love of wisdom. The 'basic goal' of science is 'to see and know the world as it is given to the senses'; the basic concern of philosophy is to 'make sense' of it. Science aims to provide a most systematic and comprehensive body of truth about the constitution and inner workings of nature; philosophy aims to provide an equally systematic and comprehensive theory of human existence and to determine in its light the meanings of human activities, institutions and forms of life. Following Kant, Arendt argues that science involves the exercise of *Verstand* (intellect) and philosophy that of *Vernunft* (reason). For her, as for Kant, *Verstand* is an analytical and investigative faculty and *Vernunft* a reflective and speculative one.

In the light of Arendt's views on the nature of philosophy outlined earlier, it is easy to see why she takes a somewhat unusual view of the nature and task of political philosophy. She nowhere clearly states it, but it underlies her entire work and determines both her questions and her manner of dealing with them.

As we have seen, philosophy for Arendt originates in the human search for significance, is sustained by the love of wisdom and aims to answer questions concerning meaning. In order to attain its hermeneutic objectives, philosophy develops an ontology of human existence by elucidating the constitutive and fundamental features of human experiences. To make use of jargon, philosophy is a hermeneutically orientated phenomenological ontology. For Arendt political philosophy is a similar inquiry but on a limited scale. Inspired by the love of political wisdom, it aims to answer hermeneutic questions about political life. And in order to answer them, it develops an ontology of politics by means of a phenomenological analysis of political experiences.

As in other areas of life, men are confronted in politics with such questions as how they should live as a community, choose between different forms of political life and government, respond to political events and institutions, decide whether or not to take an active part in the conduct of public affairs, obey or disobey a particular law, support a particular cause, movement, piece of legislation or government policy, and what objectives they should expect a government to realize. Accordingly, the political philosopher undertakes a phenomenological analysis of political life with a view to developing an ontology of it. He explores and articulates the structure of the political world and points out how its different aspects are internally related and constitute a coherent whole. He identifies and analyses its basic features, the fundamental forms of political relationship, the structures of political experiences, the forms of political consciousness and the modes of knowledge relevant to political life. He examines also the ways in which political actors define themselves, acquire public identity, recognize and respond to one another, the different capacities, aspirations, motivations, passions and emotions that underpin or undermine political life, and so on. Further, he examines the institutions by means of which citizens structure their political world, conduct their common affairs, evolve a collective identity, establish a system of authority and enact and enforce laws. By undertaking a rigorous and comprehensive analysis of these and other aspects of political life, a political philosopher constructs a coherent ontology of politics, which enables him to determine the 'hermeneutic place' of political institutions and practices on the map of political life.

Having determined the significance of political institutions and practices, the political philosopher goes on to determine the significance of political life itself. He aims to know what contribution it makes to human existence and how this compares with that of other human activities. Accordingly, he undertakes a full-scale ontological analysis of human existence along the lines sketched earlier, identifies the specific conditions of human existence that ontologically sustain political life and determines the character of its contribution.

Arendt argues that the political philosopher is primarily concerned to investigate political experiences rather than political concepts. For her concepts are conceptualizations of experiences, and hence their analysis is neither possible nor necessary, except in relation to the relevant experiences. Such concepts as liberty, equality and community articulate and derive their meanings from the relevant forms of human relationship and experience. They cannot, therefore, be analysed or defined in the abstract; in themselves, and taken in isolation, they are simply words which can be defined as one pleases. They become concepts when used to conceptualize specific experiences which determine their content and meaning. For a philosopher concepts have no intrinsic significance. He is concerned to explore the structure of human experience, and he needs concepts in order to articulate his analysis in systematic, theoretical language. In short, for Arendt political philosophy is concerned primarily not to analyse and define concepts but to decipher and interpret the text of political experience. To be sure, a political philosopher is interested not in the trivial details and infinite varieties but in the structures of political experiences and analyses them not from a psychological but from an ontological perspective.

For Arendt then the political philosopher develops a distinct perspective on human existence. He has a carefully worked out theory of the permanent features of the human condition and of man's basic capacities and needs, and a set of general principles by which to determine the relative worth of human activities, institutions and ways of life. In other words, the political philosopher possesses a measure of wisdom, his unique gift to his fellow men. Furthermore, he is a reflective person, possessing both the disposition and the capacity to examine critically and to assess the significance of the activities of his fellow men. In Arendt's view, the fact that the philosopher both loves and possesses some measure of wisdom and has a capacity for critical reflection enables him to play an important part in political life.

Although she does not herself put it this way, Arendt seems to think that the political philosopher's contribution to political life is fourfold.

First, he offers his fellow citizens the gift of self-knowledge. He provides insights into man's permanent needs as well as a set of general principles by which to determine the worth of human activities, institutions and forms of life. Although he cannot advise men about how to deal with specific situations, he can help them to make intelligent decisions by clarifying the nature, range and the likely consequences of the choices open to them.

Second, the philosopher is a social critic, a 'gadfly' who 'stings' his fellow citizens into critical self-examination. He exposes illusions, false promises and attractive but dangerous doctrines and in general acts as a watchdog for his community. Above all, by offering an example of a courageous thinker who is not afraid to swim against the currents of his time, he nourishes the spirit of dissent in his community and preserves the springs of intellectual criticism and creativity.

Third, Arendt argues that the philosopher is the custodian of the integrity of human existence. Unlike most of his fellow citizens, who are generally preoccupied with their material interests, the philosopher has a clear vision of human capacities and potentialities. He asserts the possibilities of human existence, recalls his contemporaries to their potentialities and awakens in them both guilt at what they are and pride in what they can become.

Finally, Arendt argues that the philosopher stands guard over the public realm and preserves its integrity. For her, political life, like human affairs in general, is a realm of opinion. There are no political truths which a political community can be expected to realize. Differently situated men view the world from their different perspectives and arrive at different opinions. As she puts it, a *doxa* is the 'formulation in speech of that *dokai moi*, what appears to me'. It represents my 'view' of the world from my distinct location in it. If a common and shared public world is to be created, different opinions must engage in a meaningful dialogue. In Arendt's view, the philosopher plays a vital role both in creating the necessary conditions for, and in sustaining, the dialogue. He critically examines conflicting opinions, points out their limitations and prevents them from hardening into dogmas. He elucidates also men's common assumptions, if any, highlights their insights, encourages a dialogue between them and helps them to arrive at a richer view of their common world. He might also demonstrate the restrictive character of the prevailing universe of discourse and help to loosen its constraints. In these and other ways the political philosopher exposes ideological rigidity and blindness, unclogs the channels of communication, increases mutual understanding among his fellow citizens and 'helps establish the common world'.

2

Arendt divides human activities into two broad categories, namely, the theoretical and the practical. Since the former is not relevant to our discussion, we shall ignore it.

For Arendt the world of practice—or what she calls the *vita activa*—consists of three fundamental human activities: labour, work and action. Her reasons for classifying them in this way and her principles of classification are to be found in her general conception of man. For Arendt man is distinguished from the rest of the natural world by his capacity for freedom or transcedence. All objects and organisms in the world have a nature, in the sense that they have a specific set of properties which are inherent in them and determine their behaviour. Hence we call them natural objects, or organisms, and the world they compose a natural world, or simply nature. To say that man has a nature is to imply that he is essentially like a stone or a tree, only more complex. For Arendt such a view reduces the difference between man and nature merely to one of degree and fails to appreciate his *qualitatively* distinct identity.

Man is unique in nature in possessing the capacity for freedom. By freedom Arendt means not a capacity for choice, which animals too possess and exercise, but a capacity to 'transcend' what is given and to 'begin' something new. Unlike other beings, which are constitutionally obliged to behave in specific ways, man is uniquely capable of interrupting natural and social processes and of starting new ones of his own. He is, therefore, the most 'unnatural' member of the natural world and enjoys an 'exceptional' status. No doubt, man has both a body and what Arendt, following Aristotle, calls a soul, or psyche. The human body is like any other natural object, in the sense that it too has a determinate nature and is governed by laws. Similarly, the human psyche, the 'inner life' of moods, passions, emotions and feelings, has its own nature, follows its own rhythm and is largely beyond human control. The moods and passions continually succeed and dissolve into one another and are, like bodily processes, governed by their own laws. Man is, however, not merely a body endowed with a psyche. He is a *human* being, a being endowed with a mind and capable of self-transcendence and freedom. *Qua* human, he not only has no nature but it is of his 'essence' not to have a nature. To the extent that he has a nature, he is not human; and to the extent that he is human, he has no nature. For Arendt the phrase 'human nature' is a contradiction in terms.

Taking nature as her point of reference, Arendt divides human activities into three categories: first, those in which man is lost in nature and indistinguishable from the animal; second, those in which he 'masters' and 'lords over' nature and creates a distinctively human world; and third, those in which he 'transcends' nature altogether and, like Kant's noumenal being, acts as a free and transcendent being. Arendt calls the three activities labour, work and action respectively.

For Arendt labour refers to all those activities whose essential purpose is to attend to life's needs. At the most basic level man must eat, drink, clothe himself, sleep, attend to basic biological functions and so on. He must earn his living, that is, take part in the collective process of material production and secure the means by which to meet his basic wants. He must also preserve the species and undertake such activities as raising children. He is tired at the end of the day's labour and needs relaxation and entertainment. In short, labour covers a wide range of activities which, although different in other respects, have one essential feature in common, namely, they have no other purpose but to serve life by sustaining, preserving, perpetuating or helping it periodically to recuperate its lost energies.

Arendt argues that since labour is required by the needs of the body, which is a natural organism, it has all the phenomenal characteristics of nature. It is necessary and cannot be avoided. It is cyclical and repetitive, in the sense that it follows the circular movement of our bodily functions and recurs with unerring regularity. It produces nothing permanent. Its results are used up by the life process the moment they are produced and must be continually generated afresh. They have no identity and independence of their own but derive their significance from their place in the life process. A loaf of bread, for example, has no other purpose than to assuage hunger. Its existence is entirely one-dimensional. It is made to be eaten, not to last a year, nor to embellish the world, nor to be contemplated with delight. In other words, labour's products are all consumer goods; it produces lasting objects 'only incidentally' and is primarily concerned with the means of its own reproduction. Although necessary, labour is also 'futile', in the sense that the expenditure of human energy involved in it is constantly used up and has nothing lasting to show for it. Its products do not and cannot create an 'objective' world capable of providing men with a permanent home on earth.

For Arendt work is qualitatively different from labour. Like the term 'labour', Arendt uses the term 'work' very widely and subsumes under it all those activities in which man exploits natural material to produce durable objects ranging from ordinary-use objects to everlasting works of art. For her the activities involved in producing chairs, tables, houses, tools and implements, writing a book, composing a poem or a piece of music and painting a picture are all forms of work. To be sure, thinking about what to write or imagining a scene to paint are not in themselves forms of work. Work is involved when a man writes down his thoughts or paints a picture and 'reifies' or gives a 'worldly expression' to his ideas and images.

The products of work constitute what Arendt calls the 'world'. The world is the ordered 'totality of man-made objects so organized that it can resist the consuming process of the people dwelling in it and thus outlast them'. With every durable object man creates a distinctively human world and increases the distance between himself and nature. The world is potentially immortal, and in any case less mortal than man. It stabilizes human existence by imposing a structure on the cyclical rhythm of nature. By creating a physical space between man and nature, it enables him to enclose himself within a man-made world and to acquire a sense of distinctively human identity. Further, the world creates a uniquely human concept of time and replaces nature's cyclical temporality by the distinctively human rectilinear one. Nature knows only the unending cycle of creation and destruction. By contrast, the world enables man to identify the appearance and disappearance of individual entities and makes it possible for him to talk of their birth and death.

Action is one of the most important categories in Arendt's political philosophy, yet the least clearly defined. For Arendt the birth of a human being marks the appearance of a unique being, a being unlike any other in the past, present and future, gifted with the capacity for freedom and self-transcendence. Action refers to that class of activities in which man 'fulfills the promise' inherent in his birth and 'actualizes' his capacity to begin something new. As Arendt puts it, to act 'in its most general sense means to take an initiative, to begin, to set something new into motion', to 'start new and spontaneous processes'. To act is to interrupt what is going on and to begin something new, to introduce an element of unpredictability in the world which can no longer go on as before and must take full account of the action and the agent involved.

Like labour and work, action covers a wide spectrum. In its most elementary form, a man acts when he makes an appearance before others by word or deed. No doubt, men appear to one another because of the very fact that they are embodied and visible beings. However, they remain inert and passive and do not 'count' unless they take the initiative and announce their presence by means of speech or action. By acting a man announces his presence, the presence of a being who is not a 'nobody but a somebody' and must be noticed and reckoned with by others. His presence is now a public event noticed and responded to by others. By making an appearance before others, a human being makes an impact on the world in however small a measure and makes it a 'little better or a little worse'.

For Arendt appearance by means of speech is the minimal form of action and represents one end of the spectrum. At the other end are acts in which an individual is not content to make a fleeting appearance but attempts to change the world, the established social order or specific institutions and practices. Jesus, Napoleon, Lenin, Mao, Gandhi and others acted in this maximal sense. An action can also take a wide variety of forms between the two extremes. Workers challenging the factory management, an academic pleading with his colleagues to change his university's structure and practices, students taking over a university building, civil rights demonstrators, Vietnam draft dodgers, a politician standing up to his bullying constituents and men undertaking acts of civil disobedience are all engaged in action.

Having classified practical activities into three categories, Arendt inquires where politics belongs. For her it cannot be a form of labour, as it would then have to be seen as a means of attending to the basic needs of life. In such a view, politics is reduced to simple administration; there is no scope for men to take part in the conduct of their common affairs; they are confined to the private realm, denied opportunities to appear in the public arena and to develop relevant capacities and treated not as free subjects but as mere objects of government's actions. Arendt argues that politics cannot be seen as a form of work either, as maintained by Plato, Aristotle, Machiavelli, St Simon, Marx and others, for we would then have to understand it as the activity of imposing a blueprint upon a group of men more or less in the way that a carpenter imposes the form of a table upon the wood. In such a view, men are treated as mere objects, denied the scope for freedom and action and deprived of the opportunity to live a fully human life.

For Arendt politics is best seen as a form of action. It is the activity of conducting the affairs of a community by means of speech. And the *polis,* or a political community, is a group of men united by their common commitment to a political way of life, one that implies that citizens actively participate in the conduct of their common affairs. It is not, however, identical with participation, for citizens may regularly turn up at public meetings and say nothing, or they may participate with a view to promoting their personal or group interests. The political way of life implies not participation *per se* but participation of a kind which springs from a commitment to the public way of being in the world and to all that it entails. Commitment to a public way of life implies that a citizen is concerned about the world, places communal well-being above his own, finds joy and happiness in debating and acting together with his peers, loves freedom, considers his dignity violated when decisions affecting him are made without his participation, takes a sustained interest in his community's affairs, has the courage to act when necessary and so on. Even as monks adopt a religious way of life—that is, make religion the organizing principle of their lives and judge everything in terms of it—citizens in a political community make politics their way of life and so organize other areas that they facilitate and promote the political way of life. Politics is their self-chosen mode of being in the world. Not every community sharing loyalty to a commonly acknowledged authority is a political community. A community owing allegiance to a common authority is a state; and if the state is governed not by arbitrary decrees but by laws, it is a legal community. Neither is a political community, for neither is *politically* constituted. Politics is not its organizing principle, and its members are not committed to 'living together . . . in the mode of acting and speaking'.

A political community, then, exists when its citizens are actively committed to a political way of life. Arendt argues that its existence is therefore entirely dependent upon what they say and do. Unlike a state or a legal community, a political community cannot be created once and for all, nor can its existence be guaranteed by the creation of a specific set of institutions. For her, representative assemblies, free elections, free speech, free press and so on are only the preconditions of politics and cannot by themselves create or sustain a political community. They do, no doubt, encourage people to appear in the public realm, exchange opinions, persuade one another and propose new ideas, but they do not guarantee political life. At best they can create a stable, 'civil' society characterized by civil liberties, civil rights, civil conduct and so forth, but not a public way of life. The latter exists only when most citizens, or at least a sizeable section of them, cherish public life, prize public matters more than their private interests and take an active and sustained part in the conduct of public affairs.

For Arendt the political community is the realm of action *par excellence.* Men act in all areas of life, but the political community is explicitly designed to encourage action. It provides a ready audience; it generally has a long and inspiring tradition of action; it offers countless occasions for action; and it guarantees 'immortal fame' for noble words and deeds. Arendt argues that because of all this the political community inspires and challenges men to 'dare the extraordinary', to stretch their resources, to 'bring forth what is great and radiant' and to leave behind inspiring stories. Like Plato's Ideas, which throw light on the otherwise dark world of the senses, such shining political deeds 'illuminate' and give meaning to the 'dark' and shadowy world of everyday life and raise the level of human existence.

3

Arendt argues that in the political community, as she defines it, the relation between the government and the citizens is radically different from the way in which it has been generally understood. The government is often conceived as a body of men ruling over its subjects and issuing laws or commands which the latter are obliged to obey. In a political community the government is not an external and superior agency but consists of men whom the people have 'empowered' to exercise the authority on their behalf and whom they are prepared to support. Arendt argues that it is therefore improper to say that the citizens are 'governed' or 'ruled' by the government. No doubt, the government has the final authority to make decisions binding on the community as a whole. However, since its decisions only crystallize and embody the consensus resulting from public discussion, the government's authority ultimately consists in little more than putting a final seal of authoritative approval upon what the vast majority of citizens wish to do anyway.

In Arendt's view, the fact that the government in a political community is not a ruler but an 'initiator' or 'leader' was clearly recognized in Classical Athens and Rome, the two most fully developed political communities known to Western mankind. For the Athenians every political action required the co-operation of other men and had two dimensions. It involved *archein,* meaning 'leading', 'initiating', 'beginning or setting into motion something new', and *prattein,* meaning 'carrying through', 'achieving' or 'finishing'. The Romans too used two separate but related words to describe action. *Agere* meant 'to lead', 'to set into motion'; *gerere* meant 'to bear', 'to carry through'. According to the self-understandings of both communities, a member of a political community initiated new ideas or proposals and persuaded his fellow citizens, upon whose support his initiatives depended, to co-operate with him in bringing them to fruition. An initiative could be made by a citizen or by the government. Like any ordinary citizen, the government proposed new policies, persuaded the citizens that these deserved their support and eventually enacted them as laws. To both the Greeks and the Romans governing meant initiating or leading and necessarily depended upon the support of the citizens. The government's initiative and popular support were two complementary and equally important stages in the single process of governing the country.

When political life in the two communities declined, the link between the two interdependent activities was severed. Initiating was equated with ruling or issuing commands, and popular support with obedience or the execution of commands. This is noticeable, says Arendt, in the ways in which *archein* and *agere* later came to mean 'ruling', and *prattein* and *gerere* to mean 'execution' or 'carrying out'. The interdependence of equals was replaced by a hierarchical structure in which the government, unwilling to 'woo' the support of its citizens, bypassed the process of persuasion and relied exclusively on command. In Arendt's view, Plato was the first to articulate this understanding of the relation between the government and the citizens. For him governing the country is not a public activity in which the government and the people co-operate as equal partners and for whose outcome they remain equally responsible. It is instead an activity in which the government possesses the monopoly of political initiative and *rules* over its passive subjects. For Arendt Plato's view of government as a ruler has had a decisive influence upon the Western tradition of political philosophy; hence it has been her lifelong concern to combat him.

Arendt proposes to revive the 'more accurate' classical conceptualization of the government's relations with its citizens. The conduct of political life requires that someone should take the initiative concerning what the community should do in a given situation and should 'woo' and 'win over' others' support. The initiative may be taken by a citizen or by the government. Since the government is explicitly charged with the conduct of public affairs, it has a greater responsibility to think about them and to propose new ideas. It is *primus inter pares,* and its job is to take the initiative, to guide and lead. It enters the public realm with specific proposals and invites comments and criticisms. After a full public debate, in which it participates as an equal, whatever proposal enjoys popular support is enacted as a law. The government and the people are interdependent. Without their support it is powerless, and without its initiative and guidance they lack a sense of direction. Arendt argues that both together govern the country, and hence the traditional distinction between government and governed or ruler and ruled is false and misleading.

Even as the government is essentially an initiator or leader and not a ruler, the laws are not commands or orders but directives. In Arendt's view, they direct human intercourse even as the rules of chess direct the game of chess and the 'laws' of logic direct thought. Like the latter, positive laws specify what may not be done, not what must be done, and lack the specificity and particularity of a command or an order. Further, although sanctions are attached to laws, they do not constitute their essence. Many ancient legal systems did not provide for sanctions, and even in modern legal systems several laws have no sanctions attached to them. It is possible to conceive a law without sanctions, but not one that does not regulate or direct human conduct. The direction of human behaviour and not the imposition of sanctions is the essence of law. In Arendt's view, laws can best be conceptualized not as commands, nor as descriptive statements of the way people behave, but rather as collective agreements. For example, a law requiring the payment of taxes can best be articulated not as 'Pay taxes', nor as 'Paying taxes is customary here', but rather as 'We have agreed to pay taxes here in this community'. The key word is 'agreed'. It implies that the law in question is no longer a mere proposal but an agreed and therefore authoritative directive; and second, that the citizens have consented to it, are willing parties to it and have given a 'pledge' to observe and to help enforce it.

Since a law is not a command, it cannot be obeyed, only supported. In Arendt's view, the language of obedience and disobedience is derived from the 'age-old notion . . . that tells us—since Plato and Aristotle—that every body politic is constituted of rulers and ruled, and that the former give commands and the latter obey orders'. Only a child or a slave obeys; a citizen freely decides whether or not a law deserves his support. Further 'obedience' to a law cannot be detached from the general approval or disapproval of a government, for by obeying laws the citizens sustain a government in existence. To obey a law is necessarily to support the government and to help it stay in power. By obeying the laws in the Nazi Germany ordinary law-abiding citizens helped to maintain the totalitarian apparatus of terror. Obedi-ence to a law is, therefore, never mere obedience but a form of support for the government and involves a measure of responsibility for its deeds. As an adult responsible for his actions, a citizen cannot blindly obey a law; he needs to decide if the government deserves his general support and whether he should extend it to the law in question. 'Much would be gained', Arendt argues, 'if we could eliminate this pernicious word "obedience" from our vocabulary or moral and political thought.'

For Arendt, then, a political community is by definition a participatory commu-nity. It provides formal and informal forums in which its citizens meet, exchange opinions, persuade one another to action and distinguish themselves. As a partici-patory community, it is constructed from the bottom upwards rather than from the top downwards, as is the case with all modern states, including the liberal democratic states. In Arendt's view, the political community properly so-called is a 'council state', a 'new power structure' based on a 'federal principle' and composed of 'elementary republics' representing the 'direct regeneration of democracy'. Its basic outlines are broadly similar to those proposed by such other advocates of participatory democracy as Proudhon, Bakunin, Marx and early Lenin. The neighbourhood and ward councils or, where towns are small, town hall meetings constitute its basic units. The councils are not 'local' bodies discussing merely local matters but are concerned with national issues. The citizens meet here not as members of political parties but as individuals expressing their well considered opinions, which they are willing to change in the light of the public debate. The councils elect representatives to meet their counter-parts from other wards or towns; these in turn elect representatives to meet their counterparts from other regions, and so on, until the national assembly is constituted. Arendt calls the council state a 'people's Utopia'. She argues that in every revolu-tionary situation the people involved have spontaneously created and fought for this, although the organized political parties have invariably dismantled it and replaced it by a centralized state. She hopes that although this has been the historical pattern so far, the 'next revolution' will perhaps produce different results.

4

In the previous sections we outlined Arendt's political theory. Parts of it are illuminating; the rest is not persuasive.

Although Arendt's discussion of the *vita activa* contains many useful insights, her trichotomous classification is the source of many of her difficulties. First, the three activities, labour, work and action, do not exhaust the *vita activa,* for many activities, such as making love, humanitarian work and religion, fall outside them. Second, since Arendt defines each activity in terms of the relevant human condition, she is led to define it so broadly that the activities subsumed under it have little in common. For example, as earning one's living serves life, so do eating, sleeping and relaxing. And one can earn one's living in several different ways, such as by working in a factory, teaching in a university and owning a shop. Arendt calls all these activities labour and is unable to specify the characteristics they have in common except the vague and vacuous one of 'serving life'. Third, the three activities are not mutually exclusive. For example, an artist painting a picture to earn his living would seem to be engaged not only in labour but also in work and, if his picture has a political message, action as well. It is not clear how his activity should be categorized. Arendt runs into similar difficulties on many an occasion, and her categorization in each case seems rather arbitrary and dogmatic. She says, for example, that a carpenter making a table is engaged in work, but that if he made many tables in order to earn his living, he would be engaged in labour. Apart from its other obvious difficulties, this form of categorization makes the subjective reason for undertaking an activity, not its objective structure, the locus of its identity, which contradicts Arendt's basic thesis.

As for Arendt's theory of politics, its central insight consists in integrating politics with our general conception of culture. Over the centuries the philosophers have regarded politics as a rather crude and ultimately trivial activity, to be avoided by a man of refined sensibility. In their view a man is deficient if he shows no regard for his fellow men or lacks the ability to appreciate the artistic, literary and other cultural achievements of the human spirit, but not if he lacks active political interest. Arendt questions this view. For her, like morality and culture, politics forms an integral part of human existence. Even as we expect a man to possess aesthetic, moral and other sensitivities, we must expect him to take active interest in the state of the world at large. Like culture, politics springs from an active interest in, and concern for, the state of the world; hence if a man lacking in cultural interests is incomplete, so is one who is politically apathetic. Similarly, just as morality springs from regard for one's fellow men, so does politics. Politics is the vehicle of morality, for political decisions affect the lives of millions; and therefore a man who is politically apathetic is as blameworthy as one who is amoral. Politics is not a 'brutish' and coercive activity, but a cultural and moral activity which has in its charge the custody of a civilization. Almost like Nietzsche, Arendt argues for the transvaluation of traditional values. She pleads for nothing less than that we should include among the cardinal human virtues an active concern for the community and the world and should consider it an essential factor in our overall judgement of a man.

Arendt's analysis of the nature of politics is refreshingly original and perceptive. Her view that the government can best be viewed as the initiator and governing as a co-operative activity in which both the government and the citizens participate is novel and provocative. Further, she explores whole new areas of political life that have rarely been discussed—for example, the structures of political experiences, political emotions, virtues and sentiments, political action and the nature of the shared public world. She shows that in addition to the coercive, the political life has heroic, expressivist, inspirational and other dimensions as well, and that it is concerned not merely with the maintenance of order but also with action, the development of character, public freedom, public happiness, the collective assertion of human dignity and the humanization of the world. As she so ably shows, political life calls into play not merely the much discussed human hunger for power but also such noble passions as justice, honour, public recognition, historical immortality and self-revelation. Hardly any political philosopher in history has given as much attention to the phenomenology of political life as she has.

Although Arendt's view of politics is original and offers rich and brilliant insights, it is defective in several crucial respects. She holds two different conceptions of politics and never manages to integrate them. In *Human Condition,* in which she first fully develops her political theory, she advances what she calls an agonal and individualistic view of politics. She argues that politics is an activity in which one strives to excel by doing extraordinary deeds. One is motivated by a 'passionate drive to show one's self in measuring up against others', prove that one is the best of all, become 'apparent' and 'transparent' to others and attain historical immortality. She conceives of political life almost as a sports tournament, a competitive contest in which each tries to break his rivals' or his own previous records. Not surprisingly,

Arendt takes as the paradigm of political speech the heroic and defiant polemic rather than persuasion, pays little attention to political institutions and bases political life almost entirely on freely given promises.

In her later writings she takes a more realistic, participatory view of politics. She argues that politics is concerned with the conduct of public affairs and involves co-operation rather than contest, and that a 'politically minded' citizen is motivated by *amor mundi* rather than by a desire to attain glory. She justifies political participation and the political way of life in terms not of glory and historical immortality, but of public freedom and happiness. Not surprisingly, she takes persuasion to be the paradigmatic form of political speech, emphasizes the 'relativity' of opinion, insists on the importance of compromise and consensus and explores new institutions upon which a participatory community could be constructed.

Since Arendt was not aware of the shift in her thought or of the fact that she subscribed to two different conceptions of politics, she capitalized on ambiguity and ascribed to participatory politics a degree of importance attributable only to agonal politics. It makes sense to say that Pericles, de Gaulle, Churchill, Lenin, Gandhi and Mao lived the highest type of active life possible for man and raised the level of human existence. It sounds odd, even false, to say this of an active citizen, a party activist or even a Member of Parliament. Again, it makes perfect sense to say of the great men mentioned above that they left behind inspiring stories and attained historical immortality, but the same cannot be said of active citizens and ordinary Members of Parliament. In other words the type of politics which Arendt glorifies is not a daily occurrence; conversely, ordinary participatory politics does not merit her grandiose description.

Further, Arendt's view of politics is highly spatial and prevents her from giving an adequate account of political life. As she imagines it, the political community consists of unique citizens each of whom occupies a distinct 'location' in the world and forms his own distinct opinions based on his unique 'view' of the world. They have little in common save their concern for the world and common allegiance to the constitution. It is difficult to see how such men can debate and resolve their differences, especially as Arendt insists that no 'common measurement or denominator' can be devised for reconciling the views of differently situated men. She also rules out objective principles and standards and lacks a clearly worked out notion of public interest. *Amor mundi* is too indeterminate to reconcile conflicting views. And since she stresses space and not time as the central category of politics, she is unable to appreciate the importance of traditions in political life. Her citizens exist in a historical vacuum, are not heirs to a common political tradition and do not share an agreed body of values.

Arendt's view of politics contains an area of incoherence and generates a paradox. For her, politics involves great words and deeds. Now great words and deeds require great and noble objectives. One utters inspiring words when one feels passionately about issues involving questions of principle and interest. Since Arendt generally excludes economic, moral and other questions from politics, and since her political epistemology rules out principles and strong convictions, it is not easy to see what issues can inspire men to utter great words. One cannot make a moving speech about the location of a public park or the design of a public monument. Again, it is difficult to see how a man can stake his life on his views and defiantly demand, 'This shall happen or I shall fall for it,' if the issue is not sufficiently noble or if he is firmly convinced that his opinion is necessarily partial and no better than anyone else's. In Arendt's society politics is likely to become a theatrical rather than a dramatic activity, involving a good deal of style, elegant self-presentation and virtuosity but not much clash of powerful passions and principles. Paradoxically the kind of politics she greatly admires is unlikely to occur in her type of society. Her political community is predicated on the assumption that there are no great conflicts of interests, ideologies and moral principles, and that each citizen, not being passionately committed to his beliefs and opinions, disinterestedly canvasses and examines his own and others' opinions and aims to arrive at a generally acceptable consensus. Political discussion here is almost like a leisurely academic seminar. Plato abolished politics; Arendt comes too close to doing so. The reversal of Platonism has the same basic consequences as Platonism itself.

Arendt's phenomenological method is a source of some of her valuable insights. The virtues of her method are obvious. Thanks to it, she focuses her attention on structures rather than on formal features and analyses human activities and experiences as integral wholes. Further, she pays close attention to the differences between activities and appreciates their distinctive character, thereby avoiding positivist reductionism. Again, she does not analyse concepts in the abstract but locates them in their experimental contexts and uncovers the structures of underlying experiences. Despite all their limitations, her analyses of totalitarianism, politics and revolution bring these phenomena to life, uncover the passions and aspirations inspiring and sustaining them and give perceptive accounts of the structures of experiences of those living in a totalitarian society, participating in the conduct of public affairs and engaging in a revolution.

Arendt's phenomenological method is also, however, a source of many of her difficulties. First, like other phenomenologists, she is sensitive to the qualitative diversity of phenomena but not to their relations. She is so concerned to emphasize the autonomous nature of each activity and form of experience that she loses sight of their internal connections. As we saw, her world is a neatly constructed architectonic structure in which each activity is assigned a specific place and required to be conducted in a specific manner. For her labour, work and action are all very different types of activity and totally unrelated. And, similarly, the realms of necessity and freedom, knowing and thinking, truth and meaning are all totally different and entirely unrelated. Her obsession with autonomy prevents her from noticing that economic forces condition political life, that class structure shapes and distorts the language of political discourse, that meaning not based on 'truth' becomes arbitrary, and that action is not 'supernatural' but rooted in, and conditioned by, the natural and social order.

Further, like several other phenomenologists Arendt advocates an untentable form of essentialism and even determinism. Since she treats each activity or form of experience as autonomous and self-contained, she obviously cannot explain its development in terms of its relations with other activities. She has no alternative but to locate its source of movement within itself and to explain it in terms of its own inner logic. Accordingly, she unwittingly equates the structure of an activity with its essence and argues that since an activity has a specific structure, it *must* develop in a specific manner and take specific forms in specific social and historical context. For example, she says that once a totalitarian form of government was introduced into Germany in the 1930s, it had to lead, as a matter of inner necessity, to concentration camps and to plans for global conquest. Once the French launched a revolution to attain economic objectives, it was bound to lead to a reign of terror. Once the activity of labour emerged from the shadowy private realm into the public realm, it had to be subjected to the minute division of labour, for it is in the very nature of the public realm to organize an activity by dividing it into manageable parts. Paradoxically, the method that was intended to enhance our appreciation of diversity and contingency in human affairs leads, in Arendt's hands, to reductionist oversimplification, essentialism and determinism, all of which she so vehemently and rightly criticizes in Hegel and others.

Motive and Goal in Hannah Arendt's Concept of Political Action

James T. Knauer

The seminal thinking of the late Hannah Arendt will, I suspect, come to be seen as one of the major twentieth-century contributions to the history of political thought. The importance of Arendt's work lies primarily in the categories of thought she originates, especially her concept of political action. One indication of the power of her concept of politics is its potential for illuminating our political present as well as some possible paths from that present into a better political future. But unfortunately a serious misinterpretation of her position obscures the light which her thinking can shed on questions of political strategy. Indeed, her work is frequently criticized for being irrelevant to, or incapable of comprehending, strategic concerns. This criticism is based, I believe, on a misreading of her discussions of one crucial facet of politics: the relationship of specific motives and goals to political action. It has been argued that Arendt insists on a radical split between politics and all instrumental activity, that she defines politics as devoid of instrumental concerns. Thus she is seen as proposing an understanding of politics that is divorced from the cares and concerns of the real world. Closely related to this point is the contention that she insists on an absolute split between politics and economics so that true political activity must be free from all economic interests. In fact, the belief that Arendt conceived true politics as devoid of strategic and economic concerns appears to be widely accepted. I will argue that this interpretation arises from a misreading of the relevant texts and, furthermore, that it obscures one of the most powerful and subtle of her insights: her account of the relationship between instrumentality and meaning in politics.

The structure of my argument is as follows. In the first section I present a preliminary and partial explication of Arendt's understanding of politics which reveals those aspects of her conception that the critics have focused on and the basis, insofar as there is one, for their charge that she sees true politics as devoid of motives and goals. The second section introduces three examples of criticisms of Arendt on this point as they have been advanced by Kirk Thompson, Jürgen Habermas, and Martin Jay. Part 3 is devoted to a more thorough analysis of Arendt's texts on this issue, presenting what I take to be a correct reading of Arendt on the relationship between instrumentality and meaning in action. This detailed textual explication reveals the subtlety and power of Arendt's conception of the role of motive and goal in political action and provides the basis for an evaluation of her critics. In the fourth section I proceed to an evaluation of the critiques advanced by Thompson, Habermas, and Jay. And finally, in the fifth section, I discuss some of the strengths and weaknesses of Arendt's position and the relevance of her conception of action to questions of political strategy.

James T. Knauer. "Motive and Goal in Hannah Arendt's Concept of Political Action." *American Political Science Review,* 74, (September 1980): 721–729, 732–733. Reprinted by permission of the author and the American Political Science Association.

Arendt's Concept of Politics: A First Look

Hannah Arendt's political thought is both eclectic and original. By her own account she employs a simple method: "What I propose, therefore, is very simple: it is nothing more than to think what we are doing" (1958, p. 5). This method leads her to focus on the meaning of the human experience of "living-together" for those involved, and by focusing on the historical forms of human living-together she develops a set of fundamental categories in terms of which one can understand human history. The human world of meaning is created out of the natural world by acts of human freedom, and Arendt's concept of freedom is based on an existentialist understanding of man. Man is a self-determining or self-creating being; there is no given and immutable human nature. But human freedom is political for Arendt in that it is never a purely individual or private affair. Freedom is a matter of human association, and while some associations foster freedom, others destroy it. Freedom is not guaranteed man by nature.

The Greek city-state, in particular Periclean Athens, represents for Arendt the first historical appearance of the political association, which is to say that the *polis* marks the beginning of the Western tradition of politics. The rise of the *polis* gave to the Greeks a political life sharply distinguished from their private lives; it added a realm of common concerns to the pre-existing private concerns of the household (1958, p. 24). For Arendt the city-state is the original instance of the "right-ordering" of the life of action; the life of the city-state is based on a correct understanding of the relationships among the three categories of human activity: labor, work, and politics. This understanding finds its expression in the distinction the Greeks drew between the life of the household (the realm of natural necessity) and the life of the city (the realm of freedom).[1]

In developing her own conception of political action, Arendt identifies it as one of the fundamental modes of human activity. The *vita activa* comprises three basic activities which correspond to three fundamental conditions of human life. *Labor* corresponds to the condition of biological life itself. Man as laborer, or *animal laborans,* is submerged in the biological life process. Since laboring is essential to sustain biological life, *animal laborans* operates in the realm of necessity.

Work corresponds to the condition of worldliness, to the unnaturalness of human existence. While not unrelated to the biological life process, work is not embedded in it. *Homo faber* rescues *animal laborans* from the endless flow of biological life and transcends his own subjectivity by constructing a durable world of his own which stands apart from both the maker and the natural world. But "during the work process, everything is judged in terms of suitability and usefulness for the desired end, and for nothing else" (1958, p. 153). *Homo faber* degrades the world by instrumentalizing it, thus depriving it of any intrinsic value.

Animal laborans and *homo faber* are participants in the *vita activa,* but the only uniquely human activity is that of acting and speaking, or simply, *action.* "A life without speech and without action . . . is literally dead to the world; it has ceased to be a human life because it is no longer lived among men" (1958, p. 176). The condition of action is plurality, and plurality is unique to man. Plurality, as Arendt conceives it, combines the sameness of the species and the diversity of individuals. This plurality is a potential given by the fact of natality, the birth of new human individuals, but it

---

1. The reader will notice that the account which follows parallels Aristotle in many respects; see *Politics,* Book 1.

can be realized only through political association. It is in their acting and speaking together that unique individuals emerge out of the sameness and eternal recurrence of the species. And it is only when living together as acting beings in political association that human beings encounter other human beings, that plurality is realized. While in ordinary usage we often distinguish between action and speech, Arendt's category of action combines speaking and doing. In fact, action would be impossible without speech, for "speech is what makes man a political being" (1958, p. 3). Speaking as a persuasive public act is prototypical of action. Thus Arendt distinguishes action both from behavior, which is the predictable and automatic obedience to norms, and from purely instrumental activity, which is merely putting into practice a preconceived plan.

Arendt's distinction between political action and instrumental activity is further developed in her discussion of the identity-revealing quality of action and in her emphasis on the uniqueness and novelty of that which is revealed. "In acting and speaking, men show who they are, reveal actively their unique personal identities and thus make their appearance in the human world, while their physical identities appear without any activity of their own in the unique shape of the body and sound of the voice." This unique identity which is revealed in action is not the objectified essence of the individual, not simply a composite of "his qualities, gifts, talents, and shortcomings" (1958, p. 179). It is the uniqueness of the individual as subject, as acting human being, which can be revealed to others only through action: the acting individual creates his or her own human identity.

To act is to introduce into the public realm something which, though intangible, is perfectly real and has consequences of its own. Every action is a new beginning and thus unexpected. This unexpectedness is the appearance of freedom, not freedom of the will or freedom of choice, but "the freedom to call something into being which did not exist before." Thus free action, while not unrelated to motives and goals, is never determined by them and is free only "to the extent that it is able to transcend them" (1968, p. 151). Free action always makes a new beginning, a beginning that is new even to the motives and goals of the actor. To put the same point differently, the meaning of action cannot be comprehended solely by reference to its motives and goals, and beginning has its source in action itself, not in the thinking about or planning of action. Action as beginning is "not bound into a reliable chain of cause and effect . . . it is as though the beginner had abolished the sequence of temporality itself" (1963, p. 207).

One final perspective can be gained on Arendt's contrast between politics and instrumental concerns by looking at her reading of Plato's political philosophy. Plato began the Western tradition of political thought, Arendt argues, by turning away from the life of the *polis* to the life of the philosopher, and this turning finds its best expression in the allegory of the cave which poses a direct challenge to the world order of the *polis*. Plato's fundamental error consisted in the perversion of philosophic truths that are beyond language into standards for the governance of human affairs. The result of this Platonic misconception was the substitution of making for acting in the realm of human affairs. In Plato's philosophy the city is divided into expert and non-expert, ruler and ruled. His authoritative interpretation is based on a set of categories that preclude the conceptualization of the truly political at all. By conceptualizing the political on the analogy of fabrication, Plato destroyed action in the realm of thought.

To summarize briefly the points in Arendt's treatment that concern us here: the historical emergence of politics in the *polis* was based on a separation between the economic affairs of the household and the speaking and acting of citizens in the *agora;* political action is to be sharply distinguished from the instrumental activity of *homo faber;* action as the disclosure of individual identity and the introduction of that which is genuinely novel into the world must transcend all motives and goals of the individual actor; and finally, Plato, developing categories that became authoritative for the Western tradition, destroyed politics in the realm of thought by conceiving it in instrumental or craft terms. Certainly there is sufficient basis here for the contention that Arendt proposes a conception of politics devoid of instrumental concerns and divorced from economics. Let us turn now to the specifics of that contention.

Three Criticisms of Arendt

Three separate critiques of Arendt must be considered here. They advance three different but related criticisms of Arendt's position, and taken together they constitute an interpretation that is widely accepted in the growing secondary literature (see also Schwartz, 1970; O'Sullivan, 1973).

Kirk Thompson's brief but important critique of Arendt occurs in the context of what is in part a very Arendtian argument, the contention that modern constitutional theory is fundamentally deficient because "it does not contain a concept of political action" (1969, p. 655). Arendt's account is inadequate, he contends, because she conceives of politics as nonpurposive; she "maintains that action, to be free, must be free from motive, aim, or goal, and that it cannot be understood in a means-end framework. Action thus seems to fade away into an existential life-process and lose all clarity of purpose" (1969, p. 659). If Arendt's conception of political action is to have any value, Thompson argues, it must be altered to include a clear specification of the instrumental nature of political action.

In an article that, like Thompson's, combines praise and criticism, Jürgen Habermas focuses his attention on what he takes to be a serious deficiency in Arendt's concept of political action, a deficiency that he links to her rigid separation of praxis from work, labor, and thinking, and her tracing of political power exclusively to praxis:

> This narrowing of the political to the practical permits illuminating contrasts to the presently palpable elimination of essentially practical contents from the political process. But for this Arendt pays a certain price: (a) she screens all strategic elements, as force, out of politics; (b) she removes politics from its relations to the economic and social environment in which it is embedded through the administrative system; and (c) she is unable to grasp structural violence (1977, p. 16).

Thus Habermas, like Thompson, focuses on the sharp separation Arendt imposes between politics and instrumental action.

In a very recent piece, Martin Jay continues this critical theme in a manner which further elucidates the connection between the different views on this issue advanced by Thompson and Habermas. Jay places Arendt in the political existentialist tradition of the 1920s and sees her as asserting the primacy of the political realm in contrast to the nineteenth-century tendency to see politics as a function of socioeconomic forces. In her effort to establish the "utmost possible autonomy," Jay continues, Arendt "saw politics not merely as irreducible to socioeconomic forces, but also as unhampered by all normative or instrumental constraints as well . . ." (Jay, 1978, pp. 352–53).

Presenting a thoroughly critical reading of Arendt, Jay, unlike either Thompson or Habermas, goes on to suggest that Arendt's conception of politics has totalitarian implications because of the absolute separation she imposes between political and instrumental action, between politics and socioeconomic factors. Continuing but radicalizing the line of criticism developed by Thompson and Habermas, Jay condemns Arendt's vision of politics as pure unconstrained expressive action with no purposes and no criteria for judgment beyond itself.

Motive and Goal: A Closer Look

The criticisms advanced by Thompson, Habermas, and Jay may indeed suggest some important deficiencies in Arendt's political thought generally, as I will discuss later, but all three critics claim to find a fundamental flaw specifically in Arendt's notion of political action. This claim is based on a misreading of Arendt's position. To demonstrate the lack of textual basis for this critique requires taking a closer look at those portions of Arendt's exposition that concern the role of motives and goals in action. We have already seen how action, for Arendt, involves the revelation of the unique identity of the actor and the introduction of something genuinely new into the world; action is always disclosure and beginning. Because action is beginning, it is unpredictable, lying outside any chains of cause and effect. This unpredictability of action makes it appear arbitrary, but only when one attempts to explain its occurrence as one object in a world of objects. This seeming arbitrariness disappears once the true character of action is recognized. As she writes in *On Revolution*:

> What saves the act of beginning from its own arbitrariness is that it carries its own principle within itself, or, to be more precise, that beginning and principle, *principium* and principle, are not only related to each other, but are coeval. The absolute from which the beginning is to derive its own validity and which must save it, as it were, from its inherent arbitrariness is the principle which, together with it, makes its appearance in the world (1963, p. 214).

What otherwise might appear to be totally unrelated to anything, and thus to be a matter of sheer chance, is in fact grounded in an absolute, the principle which manifests itself along with the action. In the human world as opposed to the world of the physicist, one is not forced to choose between the predictability of determined events and the meaninglessness of random occurrences. The free actions of human beings acquire meaning through their inherent relationship with principles. In fact, strictly speaking, action is not merely some occurrence in the physical world, some behavioral event; it *is* its meaning. And the principles which inspire actions and in terms of which they have their meaning must not be mistaken for eternal truths, for principles have their existence only through action. Action and principle are coeval.

Thus, for Arendt, the manifestation of principle, the disclosure of "who," and the revelation of meaning, are three fundamental aspects of action. In order to elucidate these relationships we may begin by taking a closer look at the relation of principle to action:

> Action insofar as it is free is neither under the guidance of the intellect nor under the dictate of the will—although it needs both for the execution of any particular goal—but springs from something altogether different which . . . I shall call a principle. Principles do not operate from within the self as motives

do . . . but inspire, as it were, from without: and they are much too general to prescribe goals, although every particular aim can be judged in the light of its principle once the act has been started. For unlike the judgment of the intellect which precedes action, and unlike the command of the will which initiates it, the inspiring principle becomes fully manifest only in the performing act itself. . . . In distinction from its goal, the principle of an action can be repeated time and again, it is inexhaustible, and in distinction from its motive, the validity of a principle is universal, it is not bound to any particular person or to any particular group. However, the manifestation of principles comes about only through action, they are manifest in the world as long as the action lasts, but no longer (1968, p. 152).

This passage is an important test for those who interpret Arendt as insisting that action be entirely free from motive and goal. It at once provides the basis for and belies that interpretation. Certainly Arendt says that insofar as action is free, it is determined by neither intellect nor will. But she also writes that action "needs both for the execution of any particular goal." In other words, action does, or more accurately *may*, involve the achievement of specific goals. What is only suggested here, and what will be verified shortly, is that the *meaning* of the action is not prefigured either by the intellect or by the will; rather, it is tied up with the principle manifested in that action.

Thus while Arendt might agree with the contention that some human activity is caused by motives and intentions, she insists that free action is related in a special noncausal manner to principles which may be understood as "inspiring" the action. "Such principles are honor or glory, love of equality, . . . or distinction or excellence, . . . but also fear or distrust or hatred" (1968, p. 152). These principles are universally valid and thus too general to prescribe (or cause) any particular goal (or act); on the other hand, it is in terms of a principle that an individual act can have meaning and be judged. Thus action combines the universality of thought with the particularity of human activity. What the critics fail to understand is that action is a *combination* of the particular, e.g., goals, and the universal, principles of human association. Arendt's point is not that action must have no goals but that it cannot be defined in terms of them. The particular ends of action are always transcended by the general principles which give them significance and meaning. Insofar as a universal principle is manifested in a particular act, it becomes possible to judge that act in terms of what Arendt calls the "greatness" of the act, that is, the greatness of the manifestation of principle. Thus we might say, for example, that a certain action was a great manifestation of the love of equality. In *The Human Condition* Arendt writes:

Motives and aims, no matter how pure or how grandiose, are never unique; like psychological qualities, they are typical, characteristic of different types of persons. Greatness, therefore, or the specific meaning of each deed, can lie only in the performance itself and neither in its motivation nor in its achievement (1958, p. 206).

Because action is free and "neither under the guidance of the intellect nor under the dictate of the will," its *meaning* cannot be explained in terms of motives or aims, but only in terms of the greatness of its manifestation of the absolute which inspires it. In fact, it is the greatness of this manifestation which is "the specific meaning of each deed."

The meaning of action is also interpreted by Arendt to refer to the disclosure of the actor as subject, and it is in this connection that Arendt emphasizes the inescapable intangibility of meaning:

> The manifestation of who the speaker and doer unexchangeably is, though it is plainly visible, retains a curious intangibility that confounds all efforts toward unequivocal verbal expression. The moment we want to say *who* somebody is, our very vocabulary leads us astray into saying *what* he is; we get entangled in a description of qualities he necessarily shares with others like him; we begin to describe a type or a "character" in the old meaning of the word, with the result that his specific uniqueness escapes us. . . . The impossibility, as it were, to solidify in words the living essence of the person as it shows itself in the flux of action and speech, has great bearing upon the whole realm of human affairs, where we exist primarily as acting and speaking beings. It excludes in principle our ever being able to handle these affairs as we handle things whose nature is at our disposal because we can name them. The point is that the manifestation of the "who" comes to pass in the same manner as the notoriously unreliable manifestations of ancient oracles, which, according to Heraclitus, "neither reveal nor hide in words, but give manifest signs" (1958, pp. 181–82, emphasis in original).

Insofar as the meaning of action is the disclosure of the acting subject, that meaning is only revealed in the form of signs and must be comprehended, we might say, indirectly. This is why Arendt argues, with obvious reference to Plato's treatment of politics in the *Republic,* we can never "handle" human affairs. The disclosure of unique identity is something which transcends any "objective" description of the action. To describe the action as an object is necessarily to omit that aspect of it which reveals the actor as subject, as a free being standing up in public for the sake of some principle of human association. It is by virtue of this free staking-of-oneself that the "who" is disclosed. By showing what one stands for, one reveals who one is.

Perhaps the complexities of this account of meaning, principle, and disclosure can be further elucidated using terms Arendt would have been unlikely to have used herself. A particular action may be described most generally as S doing A in order to achieve G for the sake of P. Here S is the actor revealed as the unique author of this action (A), which is also to say that S is revealed as an individual taking a public stand by attempting to achieve some goal (G) for the sake of a particular political principle (P). Several comments are in order here. While all action is likely to involve an element of purposiveness, it is not in virtue of that purposiveness that it is action in Arendt's special sense. In fact, A is action properly so-called only insofar as by manifesting P, the meaning of A transcends the pursuit of G. And the principle emerges directly from the action itself. Even when S does A consciously for the sake of P, as may sometimes be the case, the principle which emerges from the act can be considered neither a motive nor a goal of the action, since principles are too general to prescribe specific actions or goals. This is why Arendt emphasizes the courage involved in action, because the actor can never know in advance either *who* he reveals or what or how great a principle will emerge from his action (1958, pp. 36, 186–87). Thus it is worth observing, although Arendt does not make this point, that any action involving a conscious commitment to principle contains an element of faith. To stand up for a principle is always fundamentally risky, since neither the implications of that principle nor its relationship to this particular act can be fully comprehended in advance.

Up to this point our investigation of the role of motives and goals in action has been one-sided because we have discussed action primarily in relation to the individual actor. But action, for Arendt, is not merely individuals doing certain things. It is a specific mode of human being-together. Not only can action take place only where there is political community; it is action itself that constitutes that community. Politics is done in public, in what Arendt calls "the common world":

> The term "public" signifies the world itself, in so far as it is common to all of us and distinguished from our privately owned place in it. This world, however, is not identical with the earth or with nature, as the limited space for the movement of men and the general condition of organic life. It is related, rather, to the human artifact, the fabrication of human hands, as well as to affairs which go on among those who inhabit the man-made world together. To live together in the world means essentially that a world of things is between those who have it in common, as a table is located between those who sit around it; the world, like every in-between, relates and separates men at the same time (1958, p. 52).

The common world, Arendt is saying, exists in two aspects, the world of human artifice and the world of human affairs, and the latter can arise only when men are related by that artifice. The human artifice is composed of those durable products of man the maker, *homo faber,* and it is not to be confused with articles made for consumption by *animal laborans* in the endless biological cycle of laboring and consuming. It is *homo faber* who alone can create that objective aspect of the common world within which human action becomes a possibility. The *natural* condition of man is as a member of the species, a condition with no individuality and utter subjectivity. It is only the creation of *artificial* conditions, artifice and affairs, which permits individuals to stand apart. The world of artifice permits individuals to retain a sense of their own identity through time and to realize their sameness, or equality, with each other. Obviously, this objectivity of the world of things and the resulting sense of sameness are necessary preconditions to action, which relies for its very creation on the possibility of human communication and for its endurance on the capacity for recollection.

If the common world in its aspect of human artifice is a precondition for sameness or equality, then the common world in its aspect of human affairs is the precondition for diversity or uniqueness. Human plurality (combining equality and uniqueness) can only be realized in public, and this realization requires the combined aspects of the common world as artifice and affairs. The precise nature of these relations which permit plurality to be realized in public can be elucidated by a consideration of what Arendt terms the "web of human relationships." This web is simply the common world of human affairs looked at as the context for human action. The passage in which Arendt discusses the web of human relationships is crucial here because in it Arendt explicitly contradicts the interpretation of her advanced by her critics:

> Action and speech go on between men, as they are directed toward them, and they retain their agent-revealing capacity even if their content is exclusively "objective," concerned with the matters of the world of things in which men move, which physically lies between them and out of which arise their specific, objective, worldly interests. These interests constitute, in the word's most literal significance, something which *inter-est,* which lies between people and therefore can relate and bind them together. Most action and speech is con-

cerned with this in-between, which varies with each group of people, so that most words and deeds are *about* some worldly objective reality in addition to being a disclosure of the acting and speaking agent. Since this disclosure of the subject is an integral part of all, even the most "objective" intercourse, the physical, worldly in-between along with its interests is overlaid and, as it were, overgrown with an altogether different in-between which consists of deeds and words and owes its origin exclusively to men's acting and speaking directly *to* one another. This second, subjective in-between is not tangible, since there are no tangible objects into which it could solidify; the process of acting and speaking can leave behind no such results and end products. But for all its intangibility, this in-between is no less real than the world of things we visibly have in common. We call this reality the "web" of human relationships, indicating by the metaphor its somewhat intangible quality (1958, pp. 182–83, emphasis in original).

Here Arendt quite clearly states what her critics interpret her as denying, that most action is concerned with interests. Indeed, that may be its "exclusive" concern! That is, action typically involves the pursuit of particular goals; it is based on certain motives and intentions. But where action is involved, this structure of interests, motives, and goals is "overlaid" with a subjective meaning which, as we have already seen, is constituted when individuals take a public stand for the sake of some principle of human association, thus revealing who they are. Such stands are made in the context of conflict and cooperation concerning objective interests, but in their world-constituting power they transcend those mere interests which they are about (see also Isaak and Hummel, 1975). In other words, there is a distinction within the process of speaking and acting which parallels that between the human artifice and the web of relationships. Most often action and speech are *about* some objective reality (things or interests) at the same time that they *disclose* the uniqueness of the individual actor. The web of relationships produced by this disclosure is "subjective" precisely because it constitutes the realization of men as subjects, as actors.

In this crucial passage Arendt also clarifies the relationship between the two aspects of the common world, the objective and the subjective, artifice and web. She begins by qualifying her statement quoted earlier that the world of things "relates and separates men." It now appears more precise to say that this relating and separating is a result of the "specific, objective, worldly interests" which arise out of this world of things as men live in it. The human experience of the world of things generates objective (recallable and communicable) interests which relate and bind men together. But it also creates the possibility for diversity by *placing* men in an objective world, that is, by giving them a location, a perspective, and this unique perspective is what gives meaning to action. "Being seen and being heard by others derive their significance from the fact that everybody sees and hears from a different position" (1958, p. 57). In turn, of course, this possibility of diversity can only be realized in the realm of human affairs. It is because of this relationship between the human artifice and the possibility of diversity that Arendt can say, "The human artifice, . . . unless it is the scene of action and speech, of the web of human affairs and relationships and the stories engendered by them, lacks its ultimate *raison d'être*" (1958, p. 204). The products of *homo faber* find their ultimate justification in their function as a setting for human action.

Arendt's concept of plurality is not merely formal but substantive and normative. As we have already seen, Arendt specified plurality, combining sameness and diversity, as the fundamental condition of human existence corresponding to action. But plurality is not a natural fact, except as a human possibility; plurality can only be realized in action. And most importantly, not all forms of association involve plurality.

When Arendt is attending to the explicitly substantive, as opposed to the merely formal, meaning of "public" as it hinges on her conception of plurality, she often uses the phrase, "the space of appearance," by which she refers to that stage provided for political action whenever a group of people are together as actors:

> The space of appearance comes into being wherever men are together in the manner of speech and action, and therefore predates and precedes all formal constitution of the public realm and the various forms of government, that is, the various forms in which the public realm can be organized. Its peculiarity is that, unlike the spaces which are the work of our hands, it does not survive the actuality of the movement which brought it into being, but disappears not only with the dispersal of men . . . but with the disappearance or arrest of the activities themselves (1958, p. 199).

Arendt identifies power as the public characteristic which maintains the space of appearance. She is careful to distinguish power from strength, force, and violence:

> Power is what keeps the public realm, the potential space of appearance between acting and speaking men, in existence. . . . Power is always, as we would say, a power potential and not an unchangeable, measurable, and reliable entity like force or strength. While strength is the natural quality of an individual seen in isolation, power springs up between men when they act together and vanishes the moment they disperse. . . . What keeps people together after the fleeting moment of action has passed . . . and what, at the same time, they keep alive through remaining together is power (1958, pp. 200–01; also see 1972, pp. 142–55).

Power, then, might be called a public capacity or virtue. Like the virtue of the individual as actor, power is only actualized when the body politic is acting, but it is power as the potential of that body to act, so long as it retains its identity, which maintains the space of appearance. Power is the public virtue of a political association; it is the political virtue par excellence.

Power can only be realized in certain settings, however, only when men are together in a particular way. "Power is actualized only where word and deed have not parted company, where words are not empty and deeds not brutal, where words are not used to veil intentions but to disclose realities, and deeds are not used to violate and destroy but to establish relations and create new realities" (1958, p. 200). The power of the body politic will be dissipated by systematic hypocrisy and by any *use* of the space of appearance merely to accomplish goals without assuming the risks inherent in disclosure. To use the political realm as a means to nonpolitical ends will lead to the destruction of that realm:

> This revelatory quality of speech and action comes to the fore where people are *with* others and neither for nor against them—that is, in sheer human togetherness. Although nobody knows whom he reveals when he discloses himself in deed or word, he must be willing to risk the disclosure, and this neither the doer of good works, who must be without self and preserve complete anonymity, nor the criminal, who must hide himself from the others, can take upon themselves. . . . Because of its inherent tendency to disclose the

agent together with the act, action needs for its full appearance the shining brightness we once called glory, and which is possible only in the public realm.

Without the disclosure of the agent in the act, action loses its specific character and becomes one form of achievement among others. It is then indeed no less a means to an end than making is a means to produce an object (1958, p. 180, emphasis in original).

Looked at in terms of motives and intentions, political action transcends concern either for or against individuals. Any activity which can be completely explained as an effort to do something for or against another individual is not action but merely achievement, which can be understood in terms of the craft model of action. As we have already seen, only activity which involves a public commitment to principle, regardless of whether that commitment is consciously intended, can reveal the acting subject. Arendt's notion of "sheer human togetherness" might best be thought of as the associational analogue of this commitment to principle. To act for the sake of principle is to be together in the mode of sheer human togetherness; it is to be together as subjects not objects. Action degenerates into achievement "whenever human togetherness is lost."

Arendt develops another perspective on this aspect of action in her analysis of understanding, that mental activity through which we came to make sense of the human world (1953, pp. 377–92). The activity of understanding directs itself toward questions of meaning, meaning as revealed in political action. Thus understanding is in an important sense a political ability, and it appeared historically, Arendt argues, only with the experience of life in the *polis*. As a result of speaking and acting in public, the Greek citizen acquired the ability to experience the common world as others experienced it, and to acquire this ability, Arendt suggests, is precisely what we mean by developing understanding.

In fact, Arendt's political conception of understanding and her notion of "sheer human togetherness" are closely related. The political experience depends on the ability of the citizens to exchange perspectives, to experience the common world as citizens, that is, as actors. Thus I can only understand the other's viewpoint so long as I view him as an actor, as a subject, rather than as an object. It is this characteristic of political association which I believe Arendt had in mind when she says that citizens must be neither for nor against each other. Citizens are in a relationship of "sheer human togetherness" when they experience each other as the creators of meaning through speech and action in the public realm. "Sheer human togetherness" becomes both a condition for and a description of political association, in which men are engaged in acting and understanding. And thus it is only when associated as political equals that the unique human identities of individuals can emerge into the objective world.

Now we can see more clearly the nature of the relationship between the meaning of action and the motives and goals of the actor. Any given instance of action will involve an actor with motives and goals, but insofar as it is political action, its meaning will transcend those motives and goals and can never be comprehended by an account of them. Insofar as it is an action, it is constituted by the revelation of meaning, and thus can only be judged in terms of greatness. This transcendent quality of action depends, as we have seen, on the existence of a political association, which is to say, it requires the realization of plurality. The character of political association is an important key to Arendt's theory of action.

When examining action from the perspective of the individual, we saw that action transcends motive and intention and is inspired, but not determined, by the principle which it manifests. Now we see that action transcends the individual in another sense, in that action can only occur where people are assembled in a state of sheer human togetherness. Strictly speaking, however, we are not concerned here with two types of transcendence but with a single transcendence viewed from two perspectives. The transcendence of motive and intention *is* self-transcendence just as political action *is* a mode of human being-together. The acting *is* the being-together. It is only in the context of an association based on the mutual recognition of each other as subjects that human beings are able to act—to manifest principles, to disclose themselves as political agents, and to reveal the meaning of unique deeds.

One of Arendt's great insights, as revealed in the preceding explication of the relevant texts, is her subtle and powerful conception of the role of motives and goals in political action. . . .

Conclusions and Comments

Hannah Arendt's writing on politics illuminates aspects of political action that have been little explored: politics as the expression of individual identity and political principle, politics as the creation of an intersubjectively shared life-world, politics as the creation of a uniquely human mode of being-together, political community as praxis. She directed much of her attention to the examination and elucidation of these widely ignored qualities of political action and to their public discussion within an intellectual climate largely hostile and blind to them. She was deeply troubled by the course of modern history as well as by such efforts to come to terms with that history as materialist Marxism and utilitarian liberalism. What she saw in these events and intellectual traditions was the loss of humanity. Her writing must be understood as a response to and reaction against that situation. As Leon Botstein has put it, "Her ambitions were to act through speech within historical events, to speak with impact to a broad thinking readership" (1978, p. 369). To understand and appreciate her work requires that it be read in light of these concerns.

But if her emphasis was on these largely ignored characteristics of politics, she displayed no lack of awareness of those other, more widely recognized, aspects of political action: politics as purposive action with motives and goals, politics motivated by socioeconomic interests, politics as the struggle for power. Nor did she try to purify politics by defining it to exclude these elements. What she did was choose language, focus, and emphasis as part of an effort to act against history. Why should she emphasize the instrumental aspect of all politics when her aim was to overcome its instrumentalization and trivialization? Why should she elaborate the strategic aspects of politics when her goal was to recommend politics as an activity transcending the mere struggle for power? And this is not to say that the value of her thought is limited to its illumination of those ignored aspects of politics. As I have argued above, she provides us with a powerful insight into the complex and subtle relationship between politics as instrumental and strategic action and politics as expression and praxis.

Arendt's work does, however, suffer from a deficiency that is related to the line of criticism examined here in the work of Thompson, Habermas, and Jay. This deficiency lies not in Arendt's concept of political action but in her rather one-dimensional treatment of economic activity. Perhaps because of her reliance on the household economics model of the *polis*, she gives insufficient consideration to the great variety of possible modes of economic organization and to their different political implications. In focusing on the negative impact of economic concerns on the political realm, she overlooks the possible positive effects of certain modes of economic organization as well as the potential humanizing of economic relations that could arise out of political association. Just as the motives and goals involved in action must ultimately be evaluated in terms of political principles, so various modes of economic organization must be evaluated in terms of their implications for the political life of the community as Arendt conceived it. The clear implication of Arendt's work for the economic realm, I would argue, is that the realization of political freedom requires movement in the direction of a decentralized and democratic socialism with extensive worker and community control of economic enterprise (see also Knauer, 1976, pp. 303–34). And the starting point for an investigation of the relevance of Arendt's work to these matters is an appreciation of her insight into the relationship between politics as instrumental and strategic activity and politics as expression and praxis.

References

Arendt, Hannah (1953). "Understanding and Politics." *Partisan Review* 20: 377–92.
—— (1958). *The Human Condition.* Chicago: University of Chicago Press.
—— (1963). *On Revolution.* New York: Viking Press.
—— (1968). *Between Past and Future: Eight Exercises in Political Thought.* New York: Viking Press.
—— (1972). *Crises of the Republic.* New York: Harcourt Brace Jovanovich.
Aristotle (1946). *Politics.* Edited and translated by Ernest Barker. Oxford: Oxford University Press.
Botstein, Leon (1978). "Hannah Arendt: Opposing Views." *Partisan Review* 45: 368–80.
Habermas, Jürgen (1970a). "On Systematically Distorted Communication." *Inquiry* 13: 205–18.
—— (1970b). "Towards a Theory of Communicative Competence." *Inquiry* 13: 360–75.
—— (1977). "Hannah Arendt's Communications Concept of Power." *Social Research* 44: 3–24.
Isaak, Robert A., and Ralph P. Hummel (1975). *Politics for Human Beings.* North Scituate, Mass.: Duxbury Press.
Jay, Martin (1978). "Hannah Arendt: Opposing Views." *Partisan Review* 45: 348–67.
Knauer, James T (1976). "Hannah Arendt and the Reassertion of the Political: Toward a New Democratic Theory." Ph.D. dissertation, State University of New York, Binghamton.
O'Sullivan, N. K. (1973). "Politics, Totalitarianism and Freedom: The Political Thought of Hannah Arendt." *Political Studies* 21: 183–98.
Schwartz, Benjamin I. (1970). "The Religion of Politics." *Dissent* 17: 144–61.
Thompson, Kirk (1969). "Constitutional Theory and Political Action." *Journal of Politics* 31: 655–81.

John Rawls

How do we know when a contemporary work in political theory has achieved the classic status? One answer must surely be: when nearly every major contemporary theorist has felt compelled to read and comment upon it. Upon its publication in 1971, *A Theory of Justice* quickly became such a work. This significant book by John Rawls (born in Baltimore in 1921, a professor of philosophy at Harvard since the 1950s) was the culmination of more than a decade of essays on the topic of social justice. By the mid-1970s, a veritable Rawls industry had developed among theorists in political science, philosophy, sociology, and the law. Liberals hailed the book as a long-awaited solution to the dilemmas posed by liberty and equality; conservatives viewed it as a pernicious justification for activist government; and radicals saw it as a poorly disguised justification for the American liberal welfare state. No matter what perspective was taken, though, the book was never regarded as just another volume of uninspiring academic philosophy.

As a result, Rawls's book quickly attained the status of a modern classic. The steady stream of books, articles, and symposia responding to or commenting upon Rawls's published works continues today. Appearing at a time when political theory was considered moribund or even dead, *A Theory of Justice* has often been credited with reviving long-dormant traditions in Anglo-American philosophy. At the very least, it renewed theoretical concern with the substance (as opposed to the language) of such concepts as justice, liberty, and equality.

A rather simple thought experiment forms the premise for Rawls's book; the kind of thought experiment characteristic of the social contract tradition in political theory.

Imagine that a group of rational people, knowing nothing about their own positions in society or their eventual fates, meet to discuss what principles of justice should govern their community. Given the conditions under which they meet, Rawls believes that two principles of justice would emerge out of this hypothetical "original position." These principles not only would have everyone's consent, but they also would fit with our well-considered intuitions about the nature of social justice.

After discussing the nature of the choice facing individuals in the original position, Rawls states (in several different formulations) the two principles of justice. One such principle is that each person would have the same basic liberty as anyone else. The other is that social and economic inequalities would be permitted, so long as they would provide some benefit to the least advantaged members of society. Acceptance of these principles would mean that the just society is one in which "primary social goods" (e.g., liberties, opportunities, economic resources, offices, and self-esteem) are distributed in ways that provide individuals with equal respect, equal liberty, and equal opportunity. In part because of this essential stress on equality (and partly because of the method by which the principles of justice are derived), Rawls summarizes his theory as a theory of "justice as fairness."

The remainder of Rawls's book involves applying the two principles of justice to such questions as property rights, civil disobedience, and the constitutional obligations of elected officials. Since the appearance of his book, however, Rawls has not tended to apply his theory to other contemporary political issues. Generally, his more recent work has responded to the legion of interpreters and critics the book and subsequent articles have attracted. While clarifying and modestly amending his earlier views, Rawls has begun discussing other important philosophical and political concepts associated with the theory of justice.

A *Theory of Justice* and "Justice as Fairness"

In the selections from *A Theory of Justice* that follow, Rawls first observes that successful theorizing about justice is essential to the operation of a "well-ordered society," one that agrees upon certain principles for assigning rights and duties, as well as on distributing benefits and burdens across society. He then offers a preliminary discussion of his key concepts: the basic structure; justice as fairness; the original position with its veil of ignorance; the principle of liberty; and the difference principle.

In a more recent essay, Rawls clarifies his views on justice as fairness. He argues that it is not a generalized moral or metaphysical conception, applicable to all times and places, but rather a political conception, falling clearly within the liberal democratic tradition. Specifically, it attempts to reconcile a libertarian version of liberalism (originating with Locke) with an egalitarian version (originating with Rousseau).

Commentaries

Amy Gutmann offers a useful overview of Rawls's work and its importance for political theory. She notes as well the central place Rawls's work has occupied for both socialist and communitarian critics of liberalism. Above all, she views Rawls's book as having a profound impact upon political theory and upon public debates about a wide variety of policy issues.

William Galston presents a detailed examination of Rawls's clarifications and modifications of the theory of justice. In particular, he analyzes Rawls's more recent thinking on the notion of moral personality, the nature of the good, and the political context of his theory of justice. Galston concludes that, though Rawls has correctly posed the question of how we can generate agreement on basic principles, Rawls's own view of the nature of political philosophy does not lead to an acceptable answer.

Key Words

Basic structure.   The major institutions and arrangements by which society distributes rights, duties, benefits, burdens, opportunities, and conditions among its members.

The original position.   The hypothetical situation in which rational parties operating under a "veil of ignorance" (i.e., unaware of their eventual position in society) choose principles of justice to govern their society.

The difference principle.   The second principle of justice which accepts inequalities of condition only if they provide some benefit to the least advantaged in society.

Justice as fairness.   Rawls's summary term for his general theory of justice; the idea that, since the original position embodies fairness, any principles of justice chosen by people in that situation would also be fair.

For Further Reading

Daniels, N., ed. 1975. *Reading Rawls*. Oxford: Basil Blackwell.

Neal, P. 1990. "Justice as Fairness: Political or Metaphysical?" *Political Theory* 18: 24–50.

Okin, S. M. 1989. *Justice, Gender, and the Family.* New York: Basic Books.

Ryan, A. 1985. "John Rawls." In *The Return of Grand Theory in the Human Sciences,* ed. Q. Skinner, pp. 101–119. Cambridge: Cambridge University Press.

Sandel, M. 1982. *Liberalism and the Limits of Justice.* Cambridge, Mass.: Harvard University Press.

Wolff, R. P. 1977. *Understanding Rawls: A Reconstruction and Critique of "A Theory of Justice".* Princeton, N.J.: Princeton University Press.

A Theory of Justice

Chapter I
Justice as Fairness

In this introductory chapter I sketch some of the main ideas of the theory of justice I wish to develop. The exposition is informal and intended to prepare the way for the more detailed arguments that follow. Unavoidably there is some overlap between this and later discussions. I begin by describing the role of justice in social cooperation and with a brief account of the primary subject of justice, the basic structure of society. I then present the main idea of justice as fairness, a theory of justice that generalizes and carries to a higher level of abstraction the traditional conception of the social contract. The compact of society is replaced by an initial situation that incorporates certain procedural constraints on arguments designed to lead to an original agreement on principles of justice. I also take up, for purposes of clarification and contrast, the classical utilitarian and intuitionist conceptions of justice and consider some of the differences between these views and justice as fairness. My guiding aim is to work out a theory of justice that is a viable alternative to these doctrines which have long dominated our philosophical tradition.

1. The Role of Justice

Justice is the first virtue of social institutions, as truth is of systems of thought. A theory however elegant and economical must be rejected or revised if it is untrue; likewise laws and institutions no matter how efficient and well-arranged must be reformed or abolished if they are unjust. Each person possesses an inviolability founded on justice that even the welfare of society as a whole cannot override. For this reason justice denies that the loss of freedom for some is made right by a greater good shared by others. It does not allow that the sacrifices imposed on a few are outweighed by the larger sum of advantages enjoyed by many. Therefore in a just society the liberties of equal citizenship are taken as settled; the rights secured by justice are not subject to political bargaining or to the calculus of social interests. The only thing that permits us to acquiesce in an erroneous theory is the lack of a better one; analogously, an injustice is tolerable only when it is necessary to avoid an even greater injustice. Being first virtues of human activities, truth and justice are uncompromising.

These propositions seem to express our intuitive conviction of the primacy of justice. No doubt they are expressed too strongly. In any event I wish to inquire whether these contentions or others similar to them are sound, and if so how they can be accounted for. To this end it is necessary to work out a theory of justice in the light of which these assertions can be interpreted and assessed. I shall begin by considering the role of the principles of justice. Let us assume, to fix ideas, that a society is a more or less self-sufficient association of persons who in their relations to one another recognize certain rules of conduct as binding and who for the most part act in accordance with them. Suppose further that these rules specify a system of cooperation designed to advance the good of those taking part in it. Then, although a society is a cooperative venture for mutual advantage, it is typically marked by a conflict as well as by an identity of interests. There is an identity of interests since social cooperation makes possible a better life for all than any would have if each were to live solely by his own efforts. There is a conflict of interests since persons are not indifferent as to how the greater benefits produced by their collaboration are distributed, for in order to pursue their ends they each prefer a larger to a lesser share. A set of principles is required for choosing among the various social arrangements which determine this division of advantages and for underwriting an agreement on the proper distributive shares. These principles are the principles of social justice: they provide a way of assigning rights and duties in the basic institutions of society and they define the appropriate distribution of the benefits and burdens of social cooperation.

Now let us say that a society is well-ordered when it is not only designed to advance the good of its members but when it is also effectively regulated by a public conception of justice. That is, it is a society in which (1) everyone accepts and knows that the others accept the same principles of justice, and (2) the basic social institutions generally satisfy and are generally known to satisfy these principles. In this case while men may put forth excessive demands on one another, they nevertheless acknowledge a common point of view from which their claims may be adjudicated. If men's inclination to self-interest makes their vigilance against one another necessary, their public sense of justice makes their secure association together possible. Among individuals with disparate aims and purposes a shared conception of justice establishes the bonds of civic friendship; the general desire for justice limits the pursuit of other ends. One may think of a public conception of justice as constituting the fundamental charter of a well-ordered human association.

Existing societies are of course seldom well-ordered in this sense, for what is just and unjust is usually in dispute. Men disagree about which principles should define the basic terms of their association. Yet we may still say, despite this disagreement, that they each have a conception of justice. That is, they understand the need for, and they are prepared to affirm, a characteristic set of principles for assigning basic rights and duties and for determining what they take to be the proper distribution of the benefits and burdens of social cooperation. Thus it seems natural to think of the concept of justice as distinct from the various conceptions of justice and as being specified by the role which these different sets of principles, these different conceptions, have in common. Those who hold different conceptions of justice can, then, still agree that institutions are just when no arbitrary distinctions are made between persons in the assigning of basic rights and duties and when the rules determine a proper balance between competing claims to the advantages of social life. Men can agree to this description of just institutions since the notions of an arbitrary distinction and of a proper balance, which are included in the concept of justice, are left open for each to interpret according to the principles of justice that he accepts. These principles single out which similarities and differences among persons are relevant in determining rights and duties and they specify which division of advantages is appropriate. Clearly this distinction between the concept and the various conceptions of justice settles no important questions. It simply helps to identify the role of the principles of social justice.

Some measure of agreement in conceptions of justice is, however, not the only prerequisite for a viable human community. There are other fundamental social problems, in particular those of coordination, efficiency, and stability. Thus the plans of individuals need to be fitted together so that their activities are compatible with one another and they can all be carried through without anyone's legitimate expectations being severely disappointed. Moreover, the execution of these plans should lead to the achievement of social ends in ways that are efficient and consistent with justice. And finally, the scheme of social cooperation must be stable: it must be more or less regularly complied with and its basic rules willingly acted upon; and when infractions occur, stabilizing forces should exist that prevent further violations and tend to restore the arrangement. Now it is evident that these three problems are connected with that of justice. In the absence of a certain measure of agreement on what is just and unjust, it is clearly more difficult for individuals to coordinate their plans efficiently in order to insure that mutually beneficial arrangements are maintained. Distrust and resentment corrode the ties of civility, and suspicion and hostility tempt men to act in ways they would otherwise avoid. So while the distinctive role of conceptions of justice is to specify basic rights and duties and to determine the appropriate distributive shares, the way in which a conception does this is bound to affect the problems of efficiency, coordination, and stability. We cannot, in general, assess a conception of justice by its distributive role alone, however useful this role may be in identifying the concept of justice. We must take into account its wider connections; for even though justice has a certain priority, being the most important virtue of institutions, it is still true that, other things equal, one conception of justice is preferable to another when its broader consequences are more desirable.

2. The Subject of Justice

Many different kinds of things are said to be just and unjust: not only laws, institutions, and social systems, but also particular actions of many kinds, including decisions, judgments, and imputations. We also call the attitudes and dispositions of persons, and persons themselves, just and unjust. Our topic, however, is that of social justice. For us the primary subject of justice is the basic structure of society, or more exactly, the way in which the major social institutions distribute fundamental rights and duties and determine the division of advantages from social cooperation. By major institutions I understand the political constitution and the principal economic and social arrangements. Thus the legal protection of freedom of thought and liberty of conscience, competitive markets, private property in the means of production, and the monogamous family are examples of major social institutions. Taken together as one scheme, the major institutions define men's rights and duties and influence their life-prospects, what they can expect to be and how well they can hope to do. The basic structure is the primary subject of justice because its effects are so profound and present from the start. The intuitive notion here is that this structure contains various social positions and that men born into different positions have different expectations of life determined, in part, by the political system as well as by economic and social circumstances. In this way the institutions of society favor certain starting places over others. These are especially deep inequalities. Not only are they pervasive, but they affect men's initial chances in life; yet they cannot possibly be justified by an appeal to the notions of merit or desert. It is these inequalities, presumably inevitable in the basic structure of any society, to which the principles of social justice must in the first instance apply. These principles, then, regulate the choice of a political constitution and the main elements of the economic and social system. The justice of a social scheme depends essentially on how fundamental rights and duties are assigned and on the economic opportunities and social conditions in the various sectors of society.

The scope of our inquiry is limited in two ways. First of all, I am concerned with a special case of the problem of justice. I shall not consider the justice of institutions and social practices generally, nor except in passing the justice of the law of nations and of relations between states (§58). Therefore, if one supposes that the concept of justice applies whenever there is an allotment of something rationally regarded as advantageous or disadvantageous, then we are interested in only one instance of its application. There is no reason to suppose ahead of time that the principles satisfactory for the basic structure hold for all cases. These principles may not work for the rules and practices of private associations or for those of less comprehensive social groups. They may be irrelevant for the various informal conventions and customs of everyday life; they may not elucidate the justice, or perhaps better, the fairness of voluntary cooperative arrangements or procedures for making contractual agreements. The conditions for the law of nations may require different principles arrived at in a somewhat different way. I shall be satisfied if it is possible to formulate a reasonable conception of justice for the basic structure of society conceived for the time being as a closed system isolated from other societies. The significance of this special case is obvious and needs no explanation. It is natural to conjecture that once we have a sound theory for this case, the remaining problems of justice will prove more tractable in the light of it. With suitable modifications such a theory should provide the key for some of these other questions.

The other limitation on our discussion is that for the most part I examine the principles of justice that would regulate a well-ordered society. Everyone is presumed to act justly and to do his part in upholding just institutions. Though justice may be, as Hume remarked, the cautious, jealous virtue, we can still ask what a perfectly just society would be like. Thus I consider primarily what I call strict compliance as opposed to partial compliance theory (§§25, 39). The latter studies the principles that govern how we are to deal with injustice. It comprises such topics as the theory of punishment, the doctrine of just war, and the justification of the various ways of opposing unjust regimes, ranging from civil disobedience and militant resistance to revolution and rebellion. Also included here are questions of compensatory justice and of weighing one form of institutional injustice against another. Obviously the problems of partial compliance theory are the pressing and urgent matters. These are the things that we are faced with in everyday life. The reason for beginning with ideal theory is that it provides, I believe, the only basis for the systematic grasp of these more pressing problems. The discussion of civil disobedience, for example, depends upon it (§§ 55–59). At least, I shall assume that a deeper understanding can be gained in no other way, and that the nature and aims of a perfectly just society is the fundamental part of the theory of justice.

Now admittedly the concept of the basic structure is somewhat vague. It is not always clear which institutions or features thereof should be included. But it would be premature to worry about this matter here. I shall proceed by discussing principles which do apply to what is certainly a part of the basic structure as intuitively understood; I shall then try to extend the application of these principles so that they cover what would appear to be the main elements of this structure. Perhaps these principles will turn out to be perfectly general, although this is unlikely. It is sufficient that they apply to the most important cases of social justice. The point to keep in mind is that a conception of justice for the basic structure is worth having for its own sake. It should not be dismissed because its principles are not everywhere satisfactory.

A conception of social justice, then, is to be regarded as providing in the first instance a standard whereby the distributive aspects of the basic structure of society are to be assessed. This standard, however, is not to be confused with the principles defining the other virtues, for the basic structure, and social arrangements generally, may be efficient or inefficient, liberal or illiberal, and many other things, as well as just or unjust. A complete conception defining principles for all the virtues of the basic structure, together with their respective weights when they conflict, is more than a conception of justice; it is a social ideal. The principles of justice are but a part, although perhaps the most important part, of such a conception. A social ideal in turn is connected with a conception of society, a vision of the way in which the aims and purposes of social cooperation are to be understood. The various conceptions of justice are the outgrowth of different notions of society against the background of opposing views of the natural necessities and opportunities of human life. Fully to understand a conception of justice we must make explicit the conception of social cooperation from which it derives. But in doing this we should not lose sight of the special role of the principles of justice or of the primary subject to which they apply.

In these preliminary remarks I have distinguished the concept of justice as meaning a proper balance between competing claims from a conception of justice as a set of related principles for identifying the relevant considerations which determine this balance. I have also characterized justice as but one part of a social ideal, although the theory I shall propose no doubt extends its everyday sense. This theory is not offered as a description of ordinary meanings but as an account of certain distributive principles for the basic structure of society. I assume that any reasonably complete ethical theory must include principles for this fundamental problem and that these principles, whatever they are, constitute its doctrine of justice. The concept of justice I take to be defined, then, by the role of its principles in assigning rights and duties and in defining the appropriate division of social advantages. A conception of justice is an interpretation of this role.

Now this approach may not seem to tally with tradition. I believe, though, that it does. The more specific sense that Aristotle gives to justice, and from which the most familiar formulations derive, is that of refraining from *pleonexia*, that is, from gaining some advantage for oneself by seizing what belongs to another, his property, his reward, his office, and the like, or by denying a person that which is due to him, the fulfillment of a promise, the repayment of a debt, the showing of proper respect, and so on. It is evident that this definition is framed to apply to actions, and persons are thought to be just insofar as they have, as one of the permanent elements of their character, a steady and effective desire to act justly. Aristotle's definition clearly presupposes, however, an account of what properly belongs to a person and of what is due to him. Now such entitlements are, I believe, very often derived from social institutions and the legitimate expectations to which they give rise. There is no reason to think that Aristotle would disagree with this, and certainly he has a conception of social justice to account for these claims. The definition I adopt is designed to apply directly to the most important case, the justice of the basic structure. There is no conflict with the traditional notion.

3. The Main Idea of the Theory of Justice

My aim is to present a conception of justice which generalizes and carries to a higher level of abstraction the familiar theory of the social contract as found, say, in Locke, Rousseau, and Kant. In order to do this we are not to think of the original contract as one to enter a particular society or to set up a particular form of government. Rather, the guiding idea is that the principles of justice for the basic structure of society are the object of the original agreement. They are the principles that free and rational persons concerned to further their own interests would accept in an initial position of equality as defining the fundamental terms of their association. These principles are to regulate all further agreements; they specify the kinds of social cooperation that can be entered into and the forms of government that can be established. This way of regarding the principles of justice I shall call justice as fairness.

Thus we are to imagine that those who engage in social cooperation choose together, in one joint act, the principles which are to assign basic rights and duties and to determine the division of social benefits. Men are to decide in advance how they are to regulate their claims against one another and what is to be the foundation charter of their society. Just as each person must decide by rational reflection what constitutes his good, that is, the system of ends which it is rational for him to pursue, so a group of persons must decide once and for all what is to count among them as just and unjust. The choice which rational men would make in this hypothetical situation of equal liberty, assuming for the present that this choice problem has a solution, determines the principles of justice.

In justice as fairness the original position of equality corresponds to the state of nature in the traditional theory of the social contract. This original position is not, of course, thought of as an actual historical state of affairs, much less as a primitive condition of culture. It is understood as a purely hypothetical situation characterized so as to lead to a certain conception of justice. Among the essential features of this situation is that no one knows his place in society, his class position or social status, nor does any one know his fortune in the distribution of natural assets and abilities, his intelligence, strength, and the like. I shall even assume that the parties do not know their conceptions of the good or their special psychological propensities. The principles of justice are chosen behind a veil of ignorance. This ensures that no one is advantaged or disadvantaged in the choice of principles by the outcome of natural chance or the contingency of social circumstances. Since all are similarly situated and no one is able to design principles to favor his particular condition, the principles of justice are the result of a fair agreement or bargain. For given the circumstances of the original position, the symmetry of everyone's relations to each other, this initial situation is fair between individuals as moral persons, that is, as rational beings with their own ends and capable, I shall assume, of a sense of justice. The original position is, one might say, the appropriate initial status quo, and thus the fundamental agreements reached in it are fair. This explains the propriety of the name "justice as fairness": it conveys the idea that the principles of justice are agreed to in an initial situation that is fair. The name does not mean that the concepts of justice and fairness are the same, any more than the phrase "poetry as metaphor" means that the concepts of poetry and metaphor are the same.

Justice as fairness begins, as I have said, with one of the most general of all choices which persons might make together, namely, with the choice of the first principles of a conception of justice which is to regulate all subsequent criticism and reform of institutions. Then, having chosen a conception of justice, we can suppose that they are to choose a constitution and a legislature to enact laws, and so on, all in accordance with the principles of justice initially agreed upon. Our social situation is just if it is such that by this sequence of hypothetical agreements we would have contracted into the general system of rules which defines it. Moreover, assuming that the original position does determine a set of principles (that is, that a particular conception of justice would be chosen), it will then be true that whenever social institutions satisfy these principles those engaged in them can say to one another that they are cooperating on terms to which they would agree if they were free and equal persons whose relations with respect to one another were fair. They could all view their arrangements as meeting the stipulations which they would acknowledge in an initial situation that embodies widely accepted and reasonable constraints on the choice of principles. The general recognition of this fact would provide the basis for a public acceptance of the corresponding principles of justice. No society can, of course, be a scheme of cooperation which men enter voluntarily in a literal sense; each person finds himself placed at birth in some particular position in some particular society, and the nature of this position materially affects his life prospects. Yet a society satisfying the principles of justice as fairness comes as close as a society can to being a voluntary scheme, for it meets the principles which free and equal persons would assent to under circumstances that are fair. In this sense its members are autonomous and the obligations they recognize self-imposed.

One feature of justice as fairness is to think of the parties in the initial situation as rational and mutually disinterested. This does not mean that the parties are egoists, that is, individuals with only certain kinds of interests, say in wealth, prestige, and domination. But they are conceived as not taking an interest in one another's interests. They are to presume that even their spiritual aims may be opposed, in the way that the aims of those of different religions may be opposed. Moreover, the concept of rationality must be interpreted as far as possible in the narrow sense, standard in economic theory, of taking the most effective means to given ends. I shall modify this concept to some extent, as explained later (§25), but one must try to avoid introducing into it any controversial ethical elements. The initial situation must be characterized by stipulations that are widely accepted.

In working out the conception of justice as fairness one main task clearly is to determine which principles of justice would be chosen in the original position. To do this we must describe this situation in some detail and formulate with care the problem of choice which it presents. These matters I shall take up in the immediately succeeding chapters. It may be observed, however, that once the principles of justice are thought of as arising from an original agreement in a situation of equality, it is an open question whether the principle of utility would be acknowledged. Offhand it hardly seems likely that persons who view themselves as equals, entitled to press their claims upon one another, would agree to a principle which may require lesser life prospects for some simply for the sake of a greater sum of advantages enjoyed by others. Since each desires to protect his interests, his capacity to advance his conception of the good, no one has a reason to acquiesce in an enduring loss for himself in order to bring about a greater net balance of satisfaction. In the absence of strong and lasting benevolent impulses, a rational man would not accept a basic structure merely because it maximized the algebraic sum of advantages irrespective of its permanent effects on his own basic rights and interests. Thus it seems that the principle of utility is incompatible with the conception of social cooperation among equals for mutual advantage. It appears to be inconsistent with the idea of reciprocity implicit in the notion of a well-ordered society. Or, at any rate, so I shall argue.

I shall maintain instead that the persons in the initial situation would choose two rather different principles: the first requires equality in the assignment of basic rights and duties, while the second holds that social and economic inequalities, for example inequalities of wealth and authority, are just only if they result in compensating benefits for everyone, and in particular for the least advantaged members of society. These principles rule out justifying institutions on the grounds that the hardships of some are offset by a greater good in the aggregate. It may be expedient but it is not just that some should have less in order that others may prosper. But there is no injustice in the greater benefits earned by a few provided that the situation of persons not so fortunate is thereby improved. The intuitive idea is that since everyone's well-being depends upon a scheme of cooperation without which no one could have a satisfactory life, the division of advantages should be such as to draw forth the willing cooperation of everyone taking part in it, including those less well situated. Yet this can be expected only if reasonable terms are proposed. The two principles mentioned seem to be a fair agreement on the basis of which those better endowed, or more fortunate in their social position, neither of which we can be said to deserve, could expect the willing cooperation of others when some workable scheme is a necessary condition of the welfare of all. Once we decide to look for a conception of justice that nullifies the accidents of natural endowment and the contingencies of social circumstance as counters in quest for political and economic advantage, we are led to these principles. They express the result of leaving aside those aspects of the social world that seem arbitrary from a moral point of view.

The problem of the choice of principles, however, is extremely difficult. I do not expect the answer I shall suggest to be convincing to everyone. It is, therefore, worth noting from the outset that justice as fairness, like other contract views, consists of two parts: (1) an interpretation of the initial situation and of the problem of choice posed there, and (2) a set of principles which, it is argued, would be agreed to. One may accept the first part of the theory (or some variant thereof), but not the other, and conversely. The concept of the initial contractual situation may seem reasonable although the particular principles proposed are rejected. To be sure, I want to maintain that the most appropriate conception of this situation does lead to principles of justice contrary to utilitarianism and perfectionism, and therefore that the contract doctrine provides an alternative to these views. Still, one may dispute this contention even though one grants that the contractarian method is a useful way of studying ethical theories and of setting forth their underlying assumptions.

Justice as fairness is an example of what I have called a contract theory. Now there may be an objection to the term "contract" and related expressions, but I think it will serve reasonably well. Many words have misleading connotations which at first are likely to confuse. The terms "utility" and "utilitarianism" are surely no exception. They too have unfortunate suggestions which hostile critics have been willing to exploit; yet they are clear enough for those prepared to study utilitarian doctrine. The same should be true of the term "contract" applied to moral theories. As I have mentioned, to understand it one has to keep in mind that it implies a certain level of abstraction. In particular, the content of the relevant agreement is not to enter a given society or to adopt a given form of government, but to accept certain moral principles. Moreover, the undertakings referred to are purely hypothetical: a contract view holds that certain principles would be accepted in a well-defined initial situation.

The merit of the contract terminology is that it conveys the idea that principles of justice may be conceived as principles that would be chosen by rational persons, and that in this way conceptions of justice may be explained and justified. The theory of justice is a part, perhaps the most significant part, of the theory of rational choice. Furthermore, principles of justice deal with conflicting claims upon the advantages won by social cooperation, they apply to the relations among several persons or groups. The word "contract" suggests this plurality as well as the condition that the appropriate division of advantages must be in accordance with principles acceptable to all parties. The condition of publicity for principles of justice is also connoted by the contract phraseology. Thus, if these principles are the outcome of an agreement, citizens have a knowledge of the principles that others follow. It is characteristic of contract theories to stress the public nature of political principles. Finally there is the long tradition of the contract doctrine. Expressing the tie with this line of thought helps to define ideas and accords with natural piety. There are then several advantages in the use of the term "contract." With due precautions taken, it should not be misleading.

A final remark. Justice as fairness is not a complete contract theory. For it is clear that the contractarian idea can be extended to the choice of more or less an entire ethical system, that is, to a system including principles for all the virtues and not only for justice. Now for the most part I shall consider only principles of justice and others closely related to them; I make no attempt to discuss the virtues in a systematic way. Obviously if justice as fairness succeeds reasonably well, a next step would be to study the more general view suggested by the name "rightness as fairness." But even this wider theory fails to embrace all moral relationships, since it would seem to include only our relations with other persons and to leave out of account how we are to conduct ourselves toward animals and the rest of nature. I do not contend that the contract notion offers a way to approach these questions which are certainly of the first importance; and I shall have to put them aside. We must recognize the limited scope of justice as fairness and of the general type of view that it exemplifies. How far its conclusions must be revised once these other matters are understood cannot be decided in advance.

4. The Original Position and Justification

I have said that the original position is the appropriate initial status quo which insures that the fundamental agreements reached in it are fair. This fact yields the name "justice as fairness." It is clear, then, that I want to say that one conception of justice is more reasonable than another, or justifiable with respect to it, if rational persons in the initial situation would choose its principles over those of the other for the role of justice. Conceptions of justice are to be ranked by their acceptability to persons so circumstanced. Understood in this way the question of justification is settled by working out a problem of deliberation: we have to ascertain which principles it would be rational to adopt given the contractual situation. This connects the theory of justice with the theory of rational choice.

If this view of the problem of justification is to succeed, we must, of course, describe in some detail the nature of this choice problem. A problem of rational decision has a definite answer only if we know the beliefs and interests of the parties, their relations with respect to one another, the alternatives between which they are to choose, the procedure whereby they make up their minds, and so on. As the circumstances are presented in different ways, correspondingly different principles are accepted. The concept of the original position, as I shall refer to it, is that of the most philosophically favored interpretation of this initial choice situation for the purposes of a theory of justice.

But how are we to decide what is the most favored interpretation? I assume, for one thing, that there is a broad measure of agreement that principles of justice should be chosen under certain conditions. To justify a particular description of the initial situation one shows that it incorporates these commonly shared presumptions. One argues from widely accepted but weak premises to more specific conclusions. Each of the presumptions should by itself be natural and plausible; some of them may seem innocuous or even trivial. The aim of the contract approach is to establish that taken together they impose significant bounds on acceptable principles of justice. The ideal outcome would be that these conditions determine a unique set of principles; but I shall be satisfied if they suffice to rank the main traditional conceptions of social justice.

One should not be misled, then, by the somewhat unusual conditions which characterize the original position. The idea here is simply to make vivid to ourselves the restrictions that it seems reasonable to impose on arguments for principles of justice, and therefore on these principles themselves. Thus it seems reasonable and generally acceptable that no one should be advantaged or disadvantaged by natural fortune or social circumstances in the choice of principles. It also seems widely agreed that it should be impossible to tailor principles to the circumstances of one's own case. We should insure further that particular inclinations and aspirations, and persons' conceptions of their good do not affect the principles adopted. The aim is to rule out those principles that it would be rational to propose for acceptance, however little the chance of success, only if one knew certain things that are irrelevant from the standpoint of justice. For example, if a man knew that he was wealthy, he might find it rational to advance the principle that various taxes for welfare measures be counted unjust; if he knew that he was poor, he would most likely propose the contrary principle. To represent the desired restrictions one imagines a situation in which everyone is deprived of this sort of information. One excludes the knowledge of those contingencies which sets men at odds and allows them to be guided by their prejudices. In this manner the veil of ignorance is arrived at in a natural way. This concept should cause no difficulty if we keep in mind the constraints on arguments that it is meant to express. At any time we can enter the original position, so to speak, simply by following a certain procedure, namely, by arguing for principles of justice in accordance with these restrictions.

It seems reasonable to suppose that the parties in the original position are equal. That is, all have the same rights in the procedure for choosing principles; each can make proposals, submit reasons for their acceptance, and so on. Obviously the purpose of these conditions is to represent equality between human beings as moral persons, as creatures having a conception of their good and capable of a sense of justice. The basis of equality is taken to be similarity in these two respects. Systems of ends are not ranked in value; and each man is presumed to have the requisite ability to understand and to act upon whatever principles are adopted. Together with the veil of ignorance, these conditions define the principles of justice as those which rational persons concerned to advance their interests would consent to as equals when none are known to be advantaged or disadvantaged by social and natural contingencies.

There is, however, another side to justifying a particular description of the original position. This is to see if the principles which would be chosen match our considered convictions of justice or extend them in an acceptable way. We can note whether applying these principles would lead us to make the same judgments about the basic structure of society which we now make intuitively and in which we have the greatest confidence; or whether, in cases where our present judgments are in doubt and given with hesitation, these principles offer a resolution which we can affirm on reflection. There are questions which we feel sure must be answered in a certain way. For example, we are confident that religious intolerance and racial discrimination are unjust. We think that we have examined these things with care and have reached what we believe is an impartial judgment not likely to be distorted by an excessive attention to our own interests. These convictions are provisional fixed points which we presume any conception of justice must fit. But we have much less assurance as to what is the correct distribution of wealth and authority. Here we may be looking for a way to remove our doubts. We can check an interpretation of the initial situation, then, by the capacity of its principles to accommodate our firmest convictions and to provide guidance where guidance is needed.

In searching for the most favored description of this situation we work from both ends. We begin by describing it so that it represents generally shared and preferably weak conditions. We then see if these conditions are strong enough to yield a significant set of principles. If not, we look for further premises equally reasonable. But if so, and these principles match our considered convictions of justice, then so far well and good. But presumably there will be discrepancies. In this case we have a choice. We can either modify the account of the initial situation or we can revise our existing judgments, for even the judgments we take provisionally as fixed points are liable to revision. By going back and forth, sometimes altering the conditions of the contractual circumstances, at others withdrawing our judgments and conforming them to principle, I assume that eventually we shall find a description of the initial situation that both expresses reasonable conditions and yields principles which match our considered judgments duly pruned and adjusted. This state of affairs I refer to as reflective equilibrium. It is an equilibrium because at last our principles and judgments coincide; and it is reflective since we know to what principles our judgments conform and the premises of their derivation. At the moment everything is in order. But this equilibrium is not necessarily stable. It is liable to be upset by further examination of the conditions which should be imposed on the contractual situation and by particular cases which may lead us to revise our judgments. Yet for the time being we have done what we can to render coherent and to justify our convictions of social justice. We have reached a conception of the original position.

I shall not, of course, actually work through this process. Still, we may think of the interpretation of the original position that I shall present as the result of such a hypothetical course of reflection. It represents the attempt to accommodate within one scheme both reasonable philosophical conditions on principles as well as our considered judgments of justice. In arriving at the favored interpretation of the initial situation there is no point at which an appeal is made to self-evidence in the traditional sense either of general conceptions or particular convictions. I do not claim for the principles of justice proposed that they are necessary truths or derivable from such truths. A conception of justice cannot be deduced from self-evident premises or conditions on principles; instead, its justification is a matter of the mutual support of many considerations, of everything fitting together into one coherent view.

A final comment. We shall want to say that certain principles of justice are justified because they would be agreed to in an initial situation of equality. I have emphasized that this original position is purely hypothetical. It is natural to ask why, if this agreement is never actually entered into, we should take any interest in these principles, moral or otherwise. The answer is that the conditions embodied in the description of the original position are ones that we do in fact accept. Or if we do not, then perhaps we can be persuaded to do so by philosophical reflection. Each aspect of the contractual situation can be given supporting grounds. Thus what we shall do is to collect together into one conception a number of conditions on principles that we are ready upon due consideration to recognize as reasonable. These constraints express what we are prepared to regard as limits on fair terms of social cooperation. One way to look at the idea of the original position, therefore, is to see it as an expository device which sums up the meaning of these conditions and helps us to extract their consequences. On the other hand, this conception is also an intuitive notion that suggests its own elaboration, so that led on by it we are drawn to define more clearly the standpoint from which we can best interpret moral relationships. We need a conception that enables us to envision our objective from afar: the intuitive notion of the original position is to do this for us. . . .

11. Two Principles of Justice

I shall now state in a provisional form the two principles of justice that I believe would be chosen in the original position. In this section I wish to make only the most general comments, and therefore the first formulation of these principles is tentative. As we go on I shall run through several formulations and approximate step by step the final statement to be given much later. I believe that doing this allows the exposition to proceed in a natural way.

The first statement of the two principles reads as follows.

> First: each person is to have an equal right to the most extensive basic liberty compatible with a similar liberty for others.
>
> Second: social and economic inequalities are to be arranged so that they are both (a) reasonably expected to be to everyone's advantage, and (b) attached to positions and offices open to all.

There are two ambiguous phrases in the second principle, namely "everyone's advantage" and "open to all." Determining their sense more exactly will lead to a second formulation of the principle in § 13. The final version of the two principles is given in § 46; § 39 considers the rendering of the first principle.

By way of general comment, these principles primarily apply, as I have said, to the basic structure of society. They are to govern the assignment of rights and duties and to regulate the distribution of social and economic advantages. As their formulation suggests, these principles presuppose that the social structure can be divided into two more or less distinct parts, the first principle applying to the one, the second to the other. They distinguish between those aspects of the social system that define and secure the equal liberties of citizenship and those that specify and establish social and economic inequalities. The basic liberties of citizens are, roughly speaking, political liberty (the right to vote and to be eligible for public office) together with freedom of speech and assembly; liberty of conscience and freedom of thought; freedom of the person along with the right to hold (personal) property; and freedom from arbitrary arrest and seizure as defined by the concept of the rule of law. These liberties are all required to be equal by the first principle, since citizens of a just society are to have the same basic rights.

The second principle applies, in the first approximation, to the distribution of income and wealth and to the design of organizations that make use of differences in authority and responsibility, or chains of command. While the distribution of wealth and income need not be equal, it must be to everyone's advantage, and at the same time, positions of authority and offices of command must be accessible to all. One applies the second principle by holding positions open, and then, subject to this constraint, arranges social and economic inequalities so that everyone benefits.

These principles are to be arranged in a serial order with the first principle prior to the second. This ordering means that a departure from the institutions of equal liberty required by the first principle cannot be justified by, or compensated for, by greater social and economic advantages. The distribution of wealth and income, and the hierarchies of authority, must be consistent with both the liberties of equal citizenship and equality of opportunity.

It is clear that these principles are rather specific in their content, and their acceptance rests on certain assumptions that I must eventually try to explain and justify. A theory of justice depends upon a theory of society in ways that will become evident as we proceed. For the present, it should be observed that the two principles (and this holds for all formulations) are a special case of a more general conception of justice that can be expressed as follows.

> All social values—liberty and opportunity, income and wealth, and the bases of self-respect—are to be distributed equally unless an unequal distribution of any, or all, of these values is to everyone's advantage.

Injustice, then, is simply inequalities that are not to the benefit of all. Of course, this conception is extremely vague and requires interpretation.

As a first step, suppose that the basic structure of society distributes certain primary goods, that is, things that every rational man is presumed to want. These goods normally have a use whatever a person's rational plan of life. For simplicity, assume that the chief primary goods at the disposition of society are rights and liberties, powers and opportunities, income and wealth. (Later on in Part Three the primary good of self-respect has a central place.) These are the social primary goods. Other primary goods such as health and vigor, intelligence and imagination, are natural goods; although their possession is influenced by the basic structure, they are not so directly under its control. Imagine, then, a hypothetical initial arrangement in which all the social primary goods are equally distributed: everyone has similar rights and duties, and income and wealth are evenly shared. This state of affairs provides a benchmark for judging improvements. If certain inequalities of wealth and organizational powers would make everyone better off than in this hypothetical starting situation, then they accord with the general conception.

Now it is possible, at least theoretically, that by giving up some of their fundamental liberties men are sufficiently compensated by the resulting social and economic gains. The general conception of justice imposes no restrictions on what sort of inequalities are permissible; it only requires that everyone's position be improved. We need not suppose anything so drastic as consenting to a condition of slavery. Imagine instead that men forego certain political rights when the economic returns are significant and their capacity to influence the course of policy by the exercise of these rights would be marginal in any case. It is this kind of exchange which the two principles as stated rule out; being arranged in serial order they do not permit exchanges between basic liberties and economic and social gains. The serial ordering of principles expresses an underlying preference among primary social goods. When this preference is rational so likewise is the choice of these principles in this order.

In developing justice as fairness I shall, for the most part, leave aside the general conception of justice and examine instead the special case of the two principles in serial order. The advantage of this procedure is that from the first the matter of priorities is recognized and an effort made to find principles to deal with it. One is led to attend throughout to the conditions under which the acknowledgment of the absolute weight of liberty with respect to social and economic advantages, as defined by the lexical order of the two principles, would be reasonable. Offhand, this ranking appears extreme and too special a case to be of much interest; but there is more justification for it than would appear at first sight. Or at any rate, so I shall maintain (§ 82). Furthermore, the distinction between fundamental rights and liberties and economic and social benefits marks a difference among primary social goods that one should try to exploit. It suggests an important division in the social system. Of course, the distinctions drawn and the ordering proposed are bound to be at best only approximations. There are surely circumstances in which they fail. But it is essential to depict clearly the main lines of a reasonable conception of justice; and under many conditions anyway, the two principles in serial order may serve well enough. When necessary we can fall back on the more general conception.

The fact that the two principles apply to institutions has certain consequences. Several points illustrate this. First of all, the rights and liberties referred to by these principles are those which are defined by the public rules of the basic structure. Whether men are free is determined by the rights and duties established by the major institutions of society. Liberty is a certain pattern of social forms. The first principle simply requires that certain sorts of rules, those defining basic liberties, apply to everyone equally and that they allow the most extensive liberty compatible with a like liberty for all. The only reason for circumscribing the rights defining liberty and making men's freedom less extensive than it might otherwise be is that these equal rights as institutionally defined would interfere with one another.

Another thing to bear in mind is that when principles mention persons, or require that everyone gain from an inequality, the reference is to representative persons holding the various social positions, or offices, or whatever, established by the basic structure. Thus in applying the second principle I assume that it is possible to assign an expectation of well-being to representative individuals holding these positions. This expectation indicates their life prospects as viewed from their social station. In general, the expectations of representative persons depend upon the distribution of rights and duties throughout the basic structure. When this changes, expectations change. I assume, then, that expectations are connected: by raising the prospects of the representative man in one position we presumably increase or decrease the prospects of representative men in other positions. Since it applies to institutional forms, the second principle (or rather the first part of it) refers to the expectations of representative individuals. As I shall discuss below, neither principle applies to distributions of particular goods to particular individuals who may be identified by their proper names. The situation where someone is considering how to allocate certain commodities to needy persons who are known to him is not within the scope of the principles. They are meant to regulate basic institutional arrangements. We must not assume that there is much similarity from the standpoint of justice between an administrative allotment of goods to specific persons and the appropriate design of society. Our common sense intuitions for the former may be a poor guide to the latter.

Now the second principle insists that each person benefit from permissible inequalities in the basic structure. This means that it must be reasonable for each relevant representative man defined by this structure, when he views it as a going concern, to prefer his prospects with the inequality to his prospects without it. One is not allowed to justify differences in income or organizational powers on the ground that the disadvantages of those in one position are outweighed by the greater advantages of those in another. Much less can infringements of liberty be counterbalanced in this way. Applied to the basic structure, the principle of utility would have us maximize the sum of expectations of representative men (weighted by the number of persons they represent, on the classical view); and this would permit us to compensate for the losses of some by the gains of others. Instead, the two principles require that everyone benefit from economic and social inequalities. It is obvious, however, that there are indefinitely many ways in which all may be advantaged when the initial arrangement of equality is taken as a benchmark. How then are we to choose among these possibilities? The principles must be specified so that they yield a determinate conclusion. I now turn to this problem. . . .

"Justice as Fairness: Political, Not Metaphysical"

In this discussion I shall make some general remarks about how I now understand the conception of justice that I have called "justice as fairness" (presented in my book *A Theory of Justice*). I do this because it may seem that this conception depends on philosophical claims I should like to avoid, for example, claims to universal truth, or claims about the essential nature and identity of persons. My aim is to explain why it does not. I shall first discuss what I regard as the task of political philosophy at the present time and then briefly survey how the basic intuitive ideas drawn upon in justice as fairness are combined into a political conception of justice for a constitutional democracy. Doing this will bring out how and why this conception of justice avoids certain philosophical and metaphysical claims. Briefly, the idea is that in a constitutional democracy the public conception of justice should be, so far as possible, independent of controversial philosophical and religious doctrines. Thus, to formulate such a conception, we apply the principle of toleration to philosophy itself: the public conception of justice is to be political, not metaphysical. Hence the title.

I want to put aside the question whether the text of *A Theory of Justice* supports different readings than the one I sketch here. Certainly on a number of points I have changed my views, and there are no doubt others on which my views have changed in ways that I am unaware of.[1] I recognize further that certain faults of exposition as well as obscure and ambiguous passages in *A Theory of Justice* invite misunderstanding; but I think these matters need not concern us and I shan't pursue them beyond a few footnote indications. For our purposes here, it suffices first, to show how a conception of justice with the structure and content of justice as fairness can be understood as political and not metaphysical, and second, to explain why we should look for such a conception of justice in a democratic society.

I

One thing I failed to say in *A Theory of Justice*, or failed to stress sufficiently, is that justice as fairness is intended as a political conception of justice. While a political conception of justice is, of course, a moral conception, it is a moral conception worked out for a specific kind of subject, namely, for political, social, and economic institutions. In particular, justice as fairness is framed to apply to what I have called the "basic structure" of a modern

John Rawls, "Justice as Fairness: Political not Metaphysical," *Philosophy and Public Affairs*, Vol. 14, no. 3 (Summer 1985). Copyright © 1985 Princeton University Press, pp. 223–231, 234–239, 245–248. Reprinted by permission of Princeton University Press.

1. A number of these changes, or shifts of emphasis, are evident in three lectures entitled "Kantian Constructivism in Moral Theory," *Journal of Philosophy* 77 (September 1980). . . .

constitutional democracy. (I shall use "constitutional democracy" and "democratic regime," and similar phrases interchangeably.) By this structure I mean such a society's main political, social, and economic institutions, and how they fit together into one unified system of social cooperation. Whether justice as fairness can be extended to a general political conception for different kinds of societies existing under different historical and social conditions, or whether it can be extended to a general moral conception, or a significant part thereof, are altogether separate questions. I avoid prejudging these larger questions one way or the other.

It should also be stressed that justice as fairness is not intended as the application of a general moral conception to the basic structure of society, as if this structure were simply another case to which that general moral conception is applied. In this respect justice as fairness differs from traditional moral doctrines, for these are widely regarded as such general conceptions. Utilitarianism is a familiar example, since the principle of utility, however it is formulated, is usually said to hold for all kinds of subjects ranging from the actions of individuals to the law of nations. The essential point is this: as a practical political matter no general moral conception can provide a publicly recognized basis for a conception of justice in a modern democratic state. The social and historical conditions of such a state have their origins in the Wars of Religion following the Reformation and the subsequent development of the principle of toleration, and in the growth of constitutional government and the institutions of large industrial market economies. These conditions profoundly affect the requirements of a workable conception of political justice: such a conception must allow for a diversity of doctrines and the plurality of conflicting, and indeed incommensurable, conceptions of the good affirmed by the members of existing democratic societies.

Finally, to conclude these introductory remarks, since justice as fairness is intended as a political conception of justice for a democratic society, it tries to draw solely upon basic intuitive ideas that are embedded in the political institutions of a constitutional democratic regime and the public traditions of their interpretation. Justice as fairness is a political conception in part because it starts from within a certain political tradition. We hope that this political conception of justice may at least be supported by what we may call an "overlapping consensus," that is, by a consensus that includes all the opposing philosophical and religious doctrines likely to persist and to gain adherents in a more or less just constitutional democratic society.

II

There are, of course, many ways in which political philosophy may be understood, and writers at different times, faced with different political and social circumstances, understand their work differently. Justice as fairness I would now understand as a reasonably systematic and practicable conception of justice for a constitutional democracy, a conception that offers an alternative to the dominant utilitarianism of our tradition of political thought. Its first task is to provide a more secure and acceptable basis for constitutional principles and basic rights and liberties than utilitarianism seems to allow. The need for such a political conception arises in the following way.

There are periods, sometimes long periods, in the history of any society during which certain fundamental questions give rise to sharp and divisive political controversy, and it seems difficult, if not impossible, to find any shared basis of political agreement. Indeed, certain questions may prove intractable and may never be fully settled. One task of political philosophy in a democratic society is to focus on such questions and to examine whether some underlying basis of agreement can be uncovered and a mutually acceptable way of resolving these questions publicly established. Or if these questions cannot be fully settled, as may well be the case, perhaps the divergence of opinion can be narrowed sufficiently so that political cooperation on a basis of mutual respect can still be maintained.

The course of democratic thought over the past two centuries or so makes plain that there is no agreement on the way basic institutions of a constitutional democracy should be arranged if they are to specify and secure the basic rights and liberties of citizens and answer to the claims of democratic equality when citizens are conceived as free and equal persons (as explained in the last three paragraphs of Section III). A deep disagreement exists as to how the values of liberty and equality are best realized in the basic structure of society. To simplify, we may think of this disagreement as a conflict within the tradition of democratic thought itself, between the tradition associated with Locke, which gives greater weight to what Constant called "the liberties of the moderns," freedom of thought and conscience, certain basic rights of the person and of property, and the rule of law, and the tradition associated with Rousseau, which gives greater weight to what Constant called "the liberties of the ancients," the equal political liberties and the values of public life. This is a stylized contrast and historically inaccurate, but it serves to fix ideas.

Justice as fairness tries to adjudicate between these contending traditions first, by proposing two principles of justice to serve as guidelines for how basic institutions are to realize the values of liberty and equality, and second, by specifying a point of view from which these principles can be seen as more appropriate than other familiar principles of justice to the nature of democratic citizens viewed as free and equal persons. What it means to view citizens as free and equal persons is, of course, a fundamental question and is discussed in the following sections. What must be shown is that a certain arrangement of the basic structure, certain institutional forms, are more appropriate for realizing the values of liberty and equality when citizens are conceived as such persons, that is (very briefly), as having the requisite powers of moral personality that enable them to participate in society viewed as a system of fair cooperation for mutual advantage. So to continue, the two principles of justice (mentioned above) read as follows:

1. Each person has an equal right to a fully adequate scheme of equal basic rights and liberties, which scheme is compatible with a similar scheme for all.

2. Social and economic inequalities are to satisfy two conditions: first, they must be attached to offices and positions open to all under

conditions of fair equality of opportunity; and second, they must be to the greatest benefit of the least advantaged members of society.

Each of these principles applies to a different part of the basic structure; and both are concerned not only with basic rights, liberties, and opportunities, but also with the claims of equality; while the second part of the second principle underwrites the worth of these institutional guarantees.[2] The two principles together, when the first is given priority over the second, regulate the basic institutions which realize these values. But these details, although important, are not our concern here.

We must now ask: how might political philosophy find a shared basis for settling such a fundamental question as that of the most appropriate institutional forms for liberty and equality? Of course, it is likely that the most that can be done is to narrow the range of public disagreement. Yet even firmly held convictions gradually change: religious toleration is now accepted, and arguments for persecution are no longer openly professed; similarly, slavery is rejected as inherently unjust, and however much the aftermath of slavery may persist in social practices and unavowed attitudes, no one is willing to defend it. We collect such settled convictions as the belief in religious toleration and the rejection of slavery and try to organize the basic ideas and principles implicit in these convictions into a coherent conception of justice. We can regard these convictions as provisional fixed points which any conception of justice must account for if it is to be reasonable for us. We look, then, to our public political culture itself, including its main institutions and the historical traditions of their interpretation, as the shared fund of implicitly recognized basic ideas and principles. The hope is that these ideas and principles can be formulated clearly enough to be combined into a conception of political justice congenial to our most firmly held convictions. We express this by saying that a political conception of justice, to be acceptable, must be in accordance with our considered convictions, at all levels of generality, on due reflection (or in what I have called "reflective equilibrium").

The public political culture may be of two minds even at a very deep level. Indeed, this must be so with such an enduring controversy as that concerning the most appropriate institutional forms to realize the values of liberty and equality. This suggests that if we are to succeed in finding a basis of public agreement, we must find a new way of organizing familiar ideas and principles into a conception of political justice so that the claims in conflict, as previously understood, are seen in another light. A political conception need not be an original creation but may only articulate familiar intuitive ideas and principles so that they can be recognized as fitting together in a somewhat different way than before. Such a conception may, however, go further than this: it may organize these familiar ideas and principles by means of a more fundamental intuitive idea within the complex structure of

---

2. The statement of these principles differs from that given in *Theory* and follows the statement in "The Basic Liberties and Their Priority," *Tanner Lectures on Human Values*, Vol. III (Salt Lake City: University of Utah Press, 1982), p. 5. The reasons for the changes are discussed at pp. 46–55 of that lecture. They are important for the revisions made in the account of the basic liberties found in *Theory* in the attempt to answer the objections of H.L.A. Hart; but they need not concern us here.

which the other familiar intuitive ideas are then systematically connected and related. In justice as fairness, as we shall see in the next section, this more fundamental idea is that of society as a system of fair social cooperation between free and equal persons. The concern of this section is how we might find a public basis of political agreement. The point is that a conception of justice will only be able to achieve this aim if it provides a reasonable way of shaping into one coherent view the deeper bases of agreement embedded in the public political culture of a constitutional regime and acceptable to its most firmly held considered convictions.

Now suppose justice as fairness were to achieve its aim and a publicly acceptable political conception of justice is found. Then this conception provides a publicly recognized point of view from which all citizens can examine before one another whether or not their political and social institutions are just. It enables them to do this by citing what are recognized among them as valid and sufficient reasons singled out by that conception itself. Society's main institutions and how they fit together into one scheme of social cooperation can be examined on the same basis by each citizen, whatever that citizen's social position or more particular interests. It should be observed that, on this view, justification is not regarded simply as valid argument from listed premises, even should these premises be true. Rather, justification is addressed to others who disagree with us, and therefore it must always proceed from some consensus, that is, from premises that we and others publicly recognize as true; or better, publicly recognize as acceptable to us for the purpose of establishing a working agreement on the fundamental questions of political justice. It goes without saying that this agreement must be informed and uncoerced, and reached by citizens in ways consistent with their being viewed as free and equal persons.

Thus, the aim of justice as fairness as a political conception is practical, and not metaphysical or epistemological. That is, it presents itself not as a conception of justice that is true, but one that can serve as a basis of informed and willing political agreement between citizens viewed as free and equal persons. This agreement when securely founded in public political and social attitudes sustains the goods of all persons and associations within a just democratic regime. To secure this agreement we try, so far as we can, to avoid disputed philosophical, as well as disputed moral and religious, questions. We do this not because these questions are unimportant or regarded with indifference, but because we think them too important and recognize that there is no way to resolve them politically. The only alternative to a principle of toleration is the autocratic use of state power. Thus, justice as fairness deliberately stays on the surface, philosophically speaking. Given the profound differences in belief and conceptions of the good at least since the Reformation, we must recognize that, just as on questions of religious and moral doctrine, public agreement on the basic questions of philosophy cannot be obtained without the state's infringement of basic liberties. Philosophy as the search for truth about an independent metaphysical and moral order cannot, I believe, provide a workable and shared basis for a political conception of justice in a democratic society.

We try, then, to leave aside philosophical controversies whenever possible, and look for ways to avoid philosophy's longstanding problems. Thus, in what I have called "Kantian constructivism," we try to avoid the problem of truth and the controversy between realism and subjectivism about the status of moral and political values. This form of constructivism neither asserts nor denies these doctrines. Rather, it recasts ideas from the tradition of the social contract to achieve a practicable conception of objectivity and justification founded on public agreement in judgment on due reflection. The aim is free agreement, reconciliation through public reason. And similarly, as we shall see (in Section V), a conception of the person in a political view, for example, the conception of citizens as free and equal persons, need not involve, so I believe, questions of philosophical psychology or a metaphysical doctrine of the nature of the self. No political view that depends on these deep and unresolved matters can serve as a public conception of justice in a constitutional democratic state. As I have said, we must apply the principle of toleration to philosophy itself. The hope is that, by this method of avoidance, as we might call it, existing differences between contending political views can at least be moderated, even if not entirely removed, so that social cooperation on the basis of mutual respect can be maintained. Or if this is expecting too much, this method may enable us to conceive how, given a desire for free and uncoerced agreement, a public understanding could arise consistent with the historical conditions and constraints of our social world. Until we bring ourselves to conceive how this could happen, it can't happen. . . .

IV

I now take up the idea of the original position. This idea is introduced in order to work out which traditional conception of justice, or which variant of one of those conceptions, specifies the most appropriate principles for realizing liberty and equality once society is viewed as a system of cooperation between free and equal persons. Assuming we had this purpose in mind, let's see why we would introduce the idea of the original position and how it serves its purpose.

Consider again the idea of social cooperation. Let's ask: how are the fair terms of cooperation to be determined? Are they simply laid down by some outside agency distinct from the persons cooperating? Are they, for example, laid down by God's law? Or are these terms to be recognized by these persons as fair by reference to their knowledge of a prior and independent moral order? For example, are they regarded as required by natural law, or by a realm of values known by rational intuition? Or are these terms to be established by an undertaking among these persons themselves in the light of what they regard as their mutual advantage? Depending on which answer we give, we get a different conception of cooperation.

Since justice as fairness recasts the doctrine of the social contract, it adopts a form of the last answer: the fair terms of social cooperation are conceived as agreed to by those engaged in it, that is, by free and equal persons as citizens who are born into the society in which they lead their lives. But their agreement, like any other valid agreement, must be entered into under appropriate conditions. In particular, these conditions must situate free and equal persons fairly and must not allow some persons greater bargaining advantages than others. Further, threats of force and coercion, deception and fraud, and so on, must be excluded.

So far so good. The foregoing considerations are familiar from everyday life. But agreements in everyday life are made in some more or less clearly specified situation embedded within the background institutions of the basic structure. Our task, however, is to extend the idea of agreement to this background framework itself. Here we face a difficulty for any political conception of justice that uses the idea of a contract, whether social or otherwise. The difficulty is this: we must find some point of view, removed from and not distorted by the particular features and circumstances of the all-encompassing background framework, from which a fair agreement between free and equal persons can be reached. The original position, with the feature I have called "the veil of ignorance," is this point of view. And the reason why the original position must abstract from and not be affected by the contingencies of the social world is that the conditions for a fair agreement on the principles of political justice between free and equal persons must eliminate the bargaining advantages which inevitably arise within background institutions of any society as the result of cumulative social, historical, and natural tendencies. These contingent advantages and accidental influences from the past should not influence an agreement on the principles which are to regulate the institutions of the basic structure itself from the present into the future.

Here we seem to face a second difficulty, which is, however, only apparent. To explain: from what we have just said it is clear that the original position is to be seen as a device of representation and hence any agreement reached by the parties must be regarded as both hypothetical and nonhistorical. But if so, since hypothetical agreements cannot bind, what is the significance of the original position? The answer is implicit in what has already been said: it is given by the role of the various features of the original position as a device of representation. Thus, that the parties are symmetrically situated is required if they are to be seen as representatives of free and equal citizens who are to reach an agreement under conditions that are fair. Moreover, one of our considered convictions, I assume, is this: the fact that we occupy a particular social position is not a good reason for us to accept, or to expect others to accept, a conception of justice that favors those in this position. To model this conviction in the original position the parties are not allowed to know their social position; and the same idea is extended to other cases. This is expressed figuratively by saying that the parties are behind a veil of ignorance. In sum, the original position is simply a device of representation: it describes the parties, each of whom are responsible for the essential interests of a free and equal person, as fairly situated and as reaching an agreement subject to appropriate restrictions on what are to count as good reasons.

Both of the above mentioned difficulties, then, are overcome by viewing the original position as a device of representation: that is, this position models what we regard as fair conditions under which the representatives of free and equal persons are to specify the terms of social cooperation in the case of the basic structure of society; and since it also models what, for this case, we regard as acceptable restrictions on reasons available to the parties for favoring one agreement rather than another, the conception of justice the parties would adopt identifies the conception we regard—*here and now*—as fair and supported by the best reasons. We try to model restrictions on reasons in such a way that it is perfectly evident which agreement would be made by the parties in the original position as citizens' representatives. Even if there should be, as surely there will be, reasons for and against each conception of justice available, there may be an overall balance of reasons plainly favoring one conception over the rest. As a device of representation the idea of the original position serves as a means of public reflection and self-clarification. We can use it to help us work out what we now think, once we are able to take a clear and uncluttered view of what justice requires when society is conceived as a scheme of cooperation between free and equal persons over time from one generation to the next. The original position serves as a unifying idea by which our considered convictions at all levels of generality are brought to bear on one another so as to achieve greater mutual agreement and self-understanding.

To conclude: we introduce an idea like that of the original position because there is no better way to elaborate a political conception of justice for the basic structure from the fundamental intuitive idea of society as a fair system of cooperation between citizens as free and equal persons. There are, however, certain hazards. As a device of representation the original position is likely to seem somewhat abstract and hence open to misunderstanding. The description of the parties may seem to presuppose some metaphysical conception of the person, for example, that the essential nature of persons is independent of and prior to their contingent attributes, including their final ends and attachments, and indeed, their character as a whole. But this is an illusion caused by not seeing the original position as a device of representation. The veil of ignorance, to mention one prominent feature of that position, has no metaphysical implications concerning the nature of the self; it does not imply that the self is ontologically prior to the facts about persons that the parties are excluded from knowing. We can, as it were, enter this position any time simply by reasoning for principles of justice in accordance with the enumerated restrictions. When, in this way, we simulate being in this position, our reasoning no more commits us to a metaphysical doctrine about the nature of the self than our playing a game like Monopoly commits us to thinking that we are landlords engaged in a desperate rivalry, winner take all. We must keep in mind that we are trying to show how the idea of society as a fair system of social cooperation can be unfolded so as to specify the most appropriate principles for realizing the institutions of liberty and equality when citizens are regarded as free and equal persons. . . .

VI

I now take up a point essential to thinking of justice as fairness as a liberal view. Although this conception is a moral conception, it is not, as I have said, intended as a comprehensive moral doctrine. The conception of the citizen as a free and equal person is not a moral ideal to govern all of life, but is rather an ideal belonging to a conception of political justice which is to apply to the basic structure. I emphasize this point because to think otherwise would be incompatible with liberalism as a political doctrine. Recall that as such a doctrine, liberalism assumes that in a constitutional democratic state under modern conditions there are bound to exist conflicting and incommensurable conceptions of the good. This feature characterizes modern culture since the Reformation. Any viable political conception of justice that is not to rely on the autocratic use of state power must recognize this fundamental social fact. This does not mean, of course, that such a conception cannot impose constraints on individuals and associations, but that when it does so, these constraints are accounted for, directly or indirectly, by the requirements of political justice for the basic structure.[3]

Given this fact, we adopt a conception of the person framed as part of, and restricted to, an explicitly political conception of justice. In this sense, the conception of the person is a political one. As I stressed in the previous section, persons can accept this conception of themselves as citizens and use it when discussing questions of political justice without being committed in other parts of their life to comprehensive moral ideals often associated with liberalism, for example, the ideals of autonomy and individuality. The absence of commitment to these ideals, and indeed to any particular comprehensive ideal, is essential to liberalism as a political doctrine. The reason is that any such ideal, when pursued as a comprehensive ideal, is incompatible with other conceptions of the good, with forms of personal, moral, and religious life consistent with justice and which, therefore, have a proper place in a democratic society. As comprehensive moral ideals, autonomy and individuality are unsuited for a political conception of justice. As found in Kant and J. S. Mill, these comprehensive ideals, despite their very great importance in liberal thought, are extended too far when presented as the only appropriate foundation for a constitutional regime. So understood, liberalism becomes but another sectarian doctrine.

This conclusion requires comment: it does not mean, of course, that the liberalisms of Kant and Mill are not appropriate moral conceptions from which we can be led to affirm democratic institutions. But they are only two such conceptions among others, and so but two of the philosophical doctrines likely to persist and gain adherents in a reasonably just democratic regime. In such a regime the comprehensive moral views which support its basic institutions may include the liberalisms of individuality and autonomy; and possibly these liberalisms are among the more prominent doctrines in an overlapping consensus, that is, in a consensus in which, as noted earlier, different and even conflicting doctrines affirm the publicly shared basis of politial arrangements. The liberalisms of Kant and Mill have a certain historical preeminence as among the first and most important philosophical views to espouse modern constitutional democracy and to develop its underlying ideas in an influential way; and it may even turn out that societies in which the ideals of autonomy and individuality are widely accepted are among the most well-governed and harmonious.

By contrast with liberalism as a comprehensive moral doctrine, justice as fairness tries to present a conception of political justice rooted in the basic

---

3. For example, churches are constrained by the principle of equal liberty of conscience and must conform to the principle of toleration, universities by what may be required to maintain fair equality of opportunity, and the rights of parents by what is necessary to maintain their childrens' physical well-being and to assure the adequate development of their intellectual and moral powers. Because churches, universities, and parents exercise their authority within the basic structure, they are to recognize the requirements this structure imposes to maintain background justice.

intuitive ideas found in the public culture of a constitutional democracy. We conjecture that these ideas are likely to be affirmed by each of the opposing comprehensive moral doctrines influential in a reasonably just democratic society. Thus justice as fairness seeks to identify the kernel of an overlapping consensus, that is, the shared intuitive ideas which when worked up into a political conception of justice turn out to be sufficient to underwrite a just constitutional regime. This is the most we can expect, nor do we need more. We must note, however, that when justice as fairness is fully realized in a well-ordered society, the value of full autonomy is likewise realized. In this way justice as fairness is indeed similar to the liberalisms of Kant and Mill; but in contrast with them, the value of full autonomy is here specified by a political conception of justice, and not by a comprehensive moral doctrine.

It may appear that, so understood, the public acceptance of justice as fairness is no more than prudential; that is, that those who affirm this conception do so simply as a *modus vivendi* which allows the groups in the overlapping consensus to pursue their own good subject to certain constraints which each thinks to be for its advantage given existing circumstances. The idea of an overlapping consensus may seem essentially Hobbesian. But against this, two remarks: first, justice as fairness is a moral conception: it has conceptions of person and society, and concepts of right and fairness, as well as principles of justice with their complement of the virtues through which those principles are embodied in human character and regulate political and social life. This conception of justice provides an account of the cooperative virtues suitable for a political doctrine in view of the conditions and requirements of a constitutional regime. It is no less a moral conception because it is restricted to the basic structure of society, since this restriction is what enables it to serve as a political conception of justice given our present circumstances. Thus, in an overlapping consensus (as understood here), the conception of justice as fairness is not regarded merely as a *modus vivendi*.

Second, in such a consensus each of the comprehensive philosophical, religious, and moral doctrines accepts justice as fairness in its own way; that is, each comprehensive doctrine, from within its own point of view, is led to accept the public reasons of justice specified by justice as fairness. We might say that they recognize its concepts, principles, and virtues as theorems, as it were, at which their several views coincide. But this does not make these points of coincidence any less moral or reduce them to mere means. For, in general, these concepts, principles, and virtues are accepted by each as belonging to a more comprehensive philosophical, religious, or moral doctrine. Some may even affirm justice as fairness as a natural moral conception that can stand on its own feet. They accept this conception of justice as a reasonable basis for political and social cooperation, and hold that it is as natural and fundamental as the concepts and principles of honesty and mutual trust, and the virtues of cooperation in everyday life. The doctrines in an overlapping consensus differ in how far they maintain a further foundation is necessary and on what that further foundation should be. These differences, however, are compatible with a consensus on justice as fairness as a political conception of justice. . . .

The Central Role of Rawls's Theory
Amy Gutmann

When John Rawls began writing *A Theory of Justice* in the 1950s, philosophers were busy lamenting the death of political philosophy. Grand political theories, Bernard Crick observed, were treated like "corpses for students to practice dissection upon." Some philosophers, calling themselves "emotivists," elaborated versions of the view that morality is just a matter of opinion. If any systematic view could claim adherents in the academy, it was utilitarianism, which asserted the seemingly simple principle, "maximize social welfare." Utilitarianism was also extremely influential outside the academy. It seemed to provide a straightforward and rigorous method by which public officials could solve hard political problems: for every policy alternative, add up the social benefits, subtract the social costs, and implement the alternative that maximizes net benefits.

The common intuition that the rights of individuals should not be sacrificed for the sake of social welfare somehow persisted alongside the academic ascendancy of utilitarianism—a testimony, perhaps, to the tenacity of our moral intuitions. But believers in rights lacked systematic philosophical arguments against the opposing Benthamite intuition that rights are nothing more than "nonsense on stilts." Rights advocates also lacked a convincing response to the enduring Marxist critique of rights as—not nonsense—but the common sense of capitalism, confusing the class interests of the bourgeoisie with the universal interests of humanity.

Political thinking in the academy has changed since the 1950s and early 1960s in at least three significant ways. First, most rights advocates now embrace part of the Marxist critique and defend not only the traditional list of civil and political liberties but also more equal distributions of income, wealth, education, job opportunities, health care, and other goods essential to secure the welfare and dignity of the disadvantaged. Second, most prominent political philosophers are now rights theorists. Utilitarianism is everywhere on the defensive. Third, grand political theory is once again alive in the academy.

All three of these changes are attributable to the influence of *A Theory of Justice*. Of course, reading Rawls did not suddenly convert utility maximizers and "emotivists" into rights theorists. Some scholars were already searching for a systematic alternative to utilitarianism and emotivism. Many students read Rawls in their philosophically formative years and grew up, as it were, with strong Rawlsian sympathies. Still other, more established scholars first criticized *A Theory of Justice* and then constructed systematic theories to replace it. Most of these (like Ronald Dworkin's theory of equality) resemble Rawls's theory in significant ways, but even those that are radically different would not have been conceived, as Michael Walzer acknowledges in *Spheres of Justice*, without Rawls's work. Rawls's critics pay the greatest tribute to *A Theory of Justice* by affirming Henry James's view that "to criticize is to appreciate, to appropriate, to take intellectual possession, to establish in fine a relation with the

Ms. Gutmann's article originally appeared in *DISSENT,* A Quarterly Publication of the Foundation for the Study of Independent Social Ideas, Inc. Summer 1989, pp. 338–342.

criticized thing and to make it one's own." Among twentieth-century philosophical works Rawls's theory may be our most common possession.

Joining Socialist Criticism and Liberal Theory

To appreciate the political substance of Rawls's theory, it is best to begin with the first and most specific change that Rawls has wrought: the integration of socialist criticism into liberal theory. *A Theory of Justice* offers no philosophical rationalizations for the interests of any dominant class or group. The first principle of Rawlsian justice—the equal liberty principle—gives priority to securing basic liberal freedoms: freedom of thought, conscience, speech, assembly, universal suffrage, freedom from arbitrary arrest and seizure, the right to hold public office and personal property. Conspicuously absent from these basic liberties are capitalist market freedoms: to own commercial property, to appropriate what one has produced, to inherit or to pass on one's possessions. The absence of these freedoms from the list of basic liberties is no oversight or inconsistency on Rawls's part. Unlike the parties to Locke's social contract, Rawlsian "contractors" must choose distributive principles without knowing their relative wealth or their social class. Unaware of whether they are capitalists or workers, they will care more about securing a decent life for themselves and their children than about protecting the profits of property owners.

The second principle of Rawlsian justice has two parts. The first (and most famous) part—the "difference principle"—justifies only those social and economic inequalities that maximize benefits to the least advantaged citizens. The second part requires "fair equality of opportunity" for all, equalizing not only job opportunities but life chances. People with "similar abilities and skills should have similar life chances . . . irrespective of the income class into which they are born."

This is a liberalism for the least advantaged, a liberalism that pays a moral tribute to the socialist critique. The "difference principle" prevents the poor from falling (even into a safety net) so long as it is possible to raise their life prospects higher. Nothing short of securing their highest practicable life prospects will satisfy Rawlsian demands. Similarly, fair equality of opportunity goes far beyond the classical liberal ideal of careers open to talents. It also requires compensatory education and limits on economic inequalities so that "in all sectors of society there should be roughly equal prospects of culture and achievement for everyone similarly motivated and endowed."

Liberals can consistently support the theory's egalitarian economic implications because the first principle, the liberal core of Rawls's theory, rejects equalization at the expense of the basic liberties of any citizen. The income of the least advantaged may not be maximized, for example, by denying freedom of association to professionals or freedom of speech to neoconservatives. Socialists can consistently support the liberalism of the first principle because the second principle (the socialist core of Rawlsian justice) renders liberal freedoms far more than mere formalities for the disadvantaged.

This integration of liberal and socialist principle explains the appeal of Rawlsian principles to left-liberals. Although they find flaws and suggest revisions in the Rawlsian framework, most consider the principles a stimulus to their own thinking about justice. It also explains why *other* liberals and socialists have been more critical of Rawls's theory. Liberals who believe in distribution according to the market or individual desert (or both) have criticized Rawls for not counting the freedom to appropriate the fruits of one's own labor as among the basic liberties. Socialists who believe capitalist ownership of large-scale enterprises to be a postfeudal form of private government have criticized Rawls for leaving the choice between private and collective ownership of large-scale industry open to empirical argument rather than settling it on moral grounds.

Why both libertarians (like Robert Nozick) and democratic socialists (like Walzer) would criticize Rawls's theory is clear enough. Harder to justify are the rejections of Rawls based upon contradictory misrepresentations of Rawlsian principles. Many liberal critics have followed Robert Nisbet's reading of Rawls's theory as a radically egalitarian rejection of liberal freedom (reminiscent of Rousseau), while many socialist scholars have followed Norman Daniel's first reading of the theory as yet another liberal rationalization of large-scale inequalities in income, wealth, and power between classes (reminiscent of Locke). It is curious that both sets of critics misrepresent the substance of Rawls's theory in a direction opposite to their own political sympathies. The result has been to stir up old ideological debates between partisans of liberty and equality, individual and community, equality of opportunity and equality of results.

Communitarian Critique

The most recent misrepresentation of Rawls is the communitarian critique. Michael Sandel's *Liberalism and the Limits of Justice* and Alasdair MacIntyre's *After Virtue* suggest that we must choose between a Rawlsian politics of individual rights, in which atomistic individuals languish without a shared morality, and an Aristotelian politics of the common good, in which solidaristic citizens fare well without the protection of individual rights. It is doubtful that our political alternatives are, or ever were, so stark or simple.

Were Rawls the first philosopher to suggest a way of narrowing the gap between classical liberalism and socialism, the misinterpretation of Rawlsian principles would be less surprising. But he follows a long line of liberal philosophers—John Stuart Mill, Henry Sidgwick, T.H. Green, L.T. Hobhouse, R.H. Tawney, John Dewey, among others—who defend a politics explicitly more egalitarian than Lockeanism and explicitly more libertarian than Marxism. The reluctance to accept the political meaning of Rawlsian principles is even harder to explain because on a wide range of political issues—such as compensatory education, equal pay for equal work, national health insurance, antitrust, and plant-closing legislation—many of Rawls's critics support positions that are both politically liberal and economically egalitarian. Ideological divisions of the past die harder in academic discourse than in actual politics.

Yet new philosophical ideas also catch on faster in the academy than in the real world. The Rawlsian idea that was accepted most readily is the "original position," a hypothetical situation in which a "veil of ignorance" deprives us of all knowledge of our natural talents, moral views, and place in the social order so that we can rationally choose principles of justice that are not biased in our own favor. Not knowing my own religion, I will choose a principle of religious toleration to govern society. Not knowing my social class, I will choose principles that guarantee fair equality of opportunity and maximize my life prospects if I turn out to be among the least advantaged citizens. And so will you and so will every other rational person, because in the "original position" there is nothing to distinguish us from each other. There we are all rational choosers. Here (in everyday social life) we are all "free and equal moral persons," led by our sense of "justice as fairness" to accept the "original position" as the fairest way to agree about political principles, to forge a new social contract.

Rawls's revival (and revision) of contract theory gave rise to the second significant change in political thinking in the academy: the ascendancy of rights over utility. Rawls's conception of justice as fairness challenged the dominant utilitarian understanding of how to treat people as equals. Thomas Nagel, T.M. Scanlon, Bernard Williams, and (most recently) Will Kymlicka have elaborated the challenge. Although utilitarians and social-contract theorists are both committed to equality, their commitments differ dramatically. For utilitarians, treating people as equals means counting each person's interests equally in calculations of social welfare. For social contract theorists, it means securing each person's basic interests *against* routine calculations of welfare. Philosophers still contend over which understanding is morally correct, but utilitarianism is now on the defensive against Rawls's argument that contract theory is a better *public* philosophy for a democratic society governed by a bill of rights. Many of our constitutionally guaranteed rights—free speech, religion, press, suffrage, and so on—are among those that would be chosen by people in the "original position."

But what about the large bundle of rights necessary to secure fair equality of opportunity and the "difference principle"? Where are these rights to be found in our Constitution? The enormous interest in *A Theory of Justice* among legal scholars has been plausibly attributed to the opportunity it seems to offer American courts to expand the domain of individual rights. Democratic critics point out that such an expansion carries serious moral costs and reveals a significant tension within Rawls's theory: to the extent that courts read more rights into the Constitution, they narrow the domain of democratic decision making created by the fundamental political rights of citizens (to vote, to hold office, to influence public policy, and so on). If Rawls's theory requires such an expansive reading of our rights, the courts could put Congress into receivership. Judges would decide cases in the name of hypothetical rather than actual people.

Scholars allied with the critical legal studies movement carry this challenge one step further. Mark Tushnet and others question whether abstract rights derived from the "original position" (or any other philosophical position) can be translated into something as specific as a legally enforceable right to health care, housing, or a minimum income in the United States today. How much health care, housing, and guaranteed income would satisfy the presumed Rawlsian right? Whom would the courts hold responsible for providing the necessary goods and services? These are not questions that Rawls ever claims to answer. He recognizes, as some of his admirers do not, the intellectual gap that exists between an ideal theory of justice and a theory applicable to any nonideal society.

What, then, is the relevance of justice as fairness for American politics? Does the duty to further Rawlsian principles apply in some special way to judges? Since judges have more political power than the rest of us but less accountability than legislators, a Rawlsian philosopher (concerned to preserve the priority of equal political liberty) might discourage them from recognizing new welfare rights against legislative will. If this is a practical implication of Rawls's theory, then it is more compatible with democratic decision making than its critics suggest. But it is also a less critical conception, at least in its legal implications, than some admirers of Rawls's theory hope.

Or, it may be that Rawlsian judges should be more "activist" and read a defense of welfare rights into the equal protection clause of the Constitution. On this view, the greater power of judges brings with it a greater responsibility than that of ordinary citizens to act on behalf of relatively powerless and poor citizens, especially when legislators fail to fulfill their responsibility to the least advantaged. The legal theorist Frank Michelman concludes that it is quite unclear what Rawlsian judges should do. Michelman's inconclusive conclusion seems correct. The absolute priority of liberty holds only for the ideal world. In our nonideal world, where inadequate education, housing, health care, and income may deprive the disadvantaged of their self-respect (a "primary good" to which Rawls also gives the highest priority), Rawlsian judges face a hard choice between deferring to legislative will (for the sake of equal political liberty) and enforcing welfare rights (for the sake of self-respect, the difference principle, fair equality of opportunity, and the fair value of liberty).

Although Rawls says little about the obligations of judges, legislators, or ordinary citizens in our society, his silence has stimulated scholars in many disciplines—law, philosophy, political science, economics, education, and medicine among others—to delve into issues of practical ethics in the spirit of Rawls's goal "to guide the course of social reform." To be sure, scholars stimulated by Rawls's theory have not singlehandedly (or together) guided the course of social reform. But they have broadly influenced public debates on a wide variety of controversial issues, among them affirmative action for minorities and women, legalization of abortion, distribution of health care and education, prevention of international famine, conscientious objection, civil disobedience, nuclear deterrence and foreign aid, and qualifications for appointments to the Supreme Court. Their forays into practical ethics invoke moral considerations similar to Rawls's—what it means to treat people as equals, what kinds of claims can legitimately count as moral arguments in a public forum, whether individual rights or only matters of public policy are at stake, whether a policy endangers the self-respect of citizens—but they rarely reach their conclusions in specific cases without generating new moral distinctions and priority rules, distinctions and rules tailored to the case at hand rather than derivable from an ideal theory of justice, Rawls's or even their own.

A Theory of Justice is still a triumph within the tradition of grand political theory. The triumph rests on more than the philosophical richness, originality, and wisdom that Rawls's work manifests to a degree not seen since John Stuart Mill. It rests on more than its influence in renewing philosophical defenses of human rights. Rawls's most distinctive contribution to the tradition of grand theory is his defense of a method of justification, which he calls "reflective equilibrium."

Grand theorists as different as Plato, Hobbes, and Mill wrote as if their conceptions of justice were justified for all people at all times. They searched for a set of eternal forms, a self-evident truth, or a very simple first principle from which to derive all practical moral imperatives. In defending the method of "reflective equilibrium," Rawls is the most modest, and in this respect wisest, of the grand philosophers. He argues that we have no better way of justifying principles that meet the minimum standards of moral reason (logical consistency, generality, and so on) than by translating the principles into social practices and judging whether the practices are consistent with our moral convictions. If a practice derived from the principles conflicts with a conviction, then we must either reformulate the principle or change our conviction. To decide which course to take, we must use our practical judgment to weigh a variety of considerations (the firmness and consistency of our convictions, the certainty of the principles and of the evidence underlying the practice, and so on). When philosophers sidestep this process of approaching reflective equilibrium, they act on faith rather than reason.

Most philosophers today accept some version of Rawls's method of "reflective equilibrium," but few—including Rawls himself—actually practice it, at least in public. In *A Theory of Justice* and subsequent writings, Rawls stops short of translating his two principles into specific social practices and judging the principles in light of common convictions concerning the practices, even though this step is essential to the method of justification that he defends. The most distinctive principle of Rawls's theory, the "difference principle," is also the most counterintuitive. Is a society unjust if it falls short of *maximizing* benefits to the least advantaged? Outside the "original position," it seems more reasonable to call a society unjust if it fails to provide everyone with decent life prospects (adequate not optimal health care, housing, education, and income) and with the freedoms necessary to participate as an equal citizen in influencing the remaining distributions. The "difference principle" seems not to leave enough moral room for democratic decision making, or for distributions according to desert—not even for Nobel Prizes or Most Valuable Player awards (unless they can be shown to maximize the life prospects of the least advantaged).

But to invoke my intuitions, or anyone else's, against Rawls's does not constitute a devastating criticism of his theory—not only because his intuitions may be morally better, but more important because the method of "reflective equilibrium" welcomes just this kind of criticism. It challenges every critic to offer constructive revisions of justice as fairness, to defend another systematic theory whose premises and conclusions are more intuitively compelling, or to justify something other than a systematic theory (such as a plurality of principles refined and balanced by our practical judgment of particular cases). This is a formidable but fair challenge. An extraordinary number of philosophers, political scientists, economists, and constitutional lawyers have accepted it.

Pluralism and Social Unity
William A. Galston

In the nearly two decades since the publication of *A Theory of Justice,* John Rawls has not significantly altered the content of the principles the denizens of the original position are said to embrace. But many other aspects of his theory have changed. Four shifts strike me as being of particular importance. First, Rawls has placed an expanded notion of "moral personality" at the center of his argument and has revised several aspects of his theory (in particular, the accounts of primary goods and of individual rationality) accordingly. Second, he has fleshed out his views on the good and on the role that a conception of the good can play within the priority of the right. Third, he now characterizes the overall theory as "political"—that is, as drawn in part from basic political facts that constitute practical constraints and as detached from broader philosophical or metaphysical considerations. Finally, he has come to view his theory of justice not as developed *sub specie aeternitatis* but, rather, as drawn from (and addressed to) the public culture of democratic societies.

Underlying these shifts, I believe, is a core concern that has become increasingly prominent in Rawls's thought. Modern liberal-democratic societies are characterized by an irreversible pluralism, that is, by conflicting and incommensurable conceptions of the human good (and, Rawls now stresses, of metaphysical and religious conceptions as well). The grounds of social unity are not hard to specify in homogeneous communities. But where are they to be found in societies whose members disagree so fundamentally? The answer, Rawls believes, lies in the lessons liberal-democratic societies have slowly learned in the modern era. Alongside the "fact of pluralism" is a kind of rough agreement on certain basics: the treatment of all individuals as free and equal; the understanding of society as a system of uncoerced cooperation; the right of each individual to claim a fair share of the fruits of that cooperation; and the duty of all citizens to support and uphold institutions that embody a shared conception of fair principles. Once we devise a strategy for excluding from public discourse the matters on which we fundamentally disagree and for reflecting collectively on the beliefs we share, we can be led to workable agreements on the content of just principles and institutions.

I believe that in focusing his recent thought on the problem of forging unity amid diversity, Rawls has posed exactly the right question. I am less sure that he has arrived at the right answer. In addressing the fact of pluralism, I would argue, Rawls goes both too far and not far enough: too far, because in trying to avoid all deep differences of metaphysics and religion and to set questions of truth to one side, he deprives social philosophy (including his own) of resources essential to its success; not far enough, because the grounds of agreement he professes to find latent in our public culture would be rejected by many individuals and groups who form important elements of that culture. The alternative, I would suggest, is to recognize that social philosophy, liberalism included, cannot wholly rest its case on social agree-

William A. Galston, 1989. "Pluralism and Social Unity," *Ethics* 99, pp. 711–726. Reprinted by the permission of the University of Chicago Press.

ment and must ultimately advert to truth-claims that are bound to prove controversial. This is a problem for liberalism only if the concept of individual freedom central to liberalism is construed so broadly as to trump the force of such truth-claims. But there are no sufficient reasons to understand liberal freedom so expansively, and many compelling reasons not to.[1]

I

Let me begin with Rawls's revised notion of moral personality. Moral persons are, Rawls tells us, "characterized by two moral powers and by two corresponding highest-order interests in realizing and exercising these powers. The first power is the capacity for an effective sense of justice, that is, the capacity to understand, to apply and to act from (and not merely in accordance with) the principles of justice. The second moral power is the capacity to form, to revise, and rationally to pursue a conception of the good."[2]

As members of a democratic society, we agree not only on the content of this conception but also on the capacity of all (normal) members of our society to fulfill it. Rawls's account of moral personality thus lays the foundation for what might be called a democratic teleology. Individuals choosing principles of justice will seek, first and foremost, to create circumstances in which they can realize and express their moral powers. In addition, we as observers will appraise social institutions in light of their propensity to promote the realization and facilitate the expression of these powers. From the standpoint of both participants and observers, moreover, these goals will take priority over other concerns—in particular, over the realization of the specific conceptions of the good that individuals may embrace. (That is what it means to identify the moral powers as our "highest-order" interests.)

This expanded conception of moral personality places, if not a "thick" theory, at least a greater than thin theory, of the good at the very foundation of Rawls's conception of justice. An indication—and consequence—of this shift is a dramatically revised account of primary goods. In *A Theory of Justice,* these goods were defined relative to the undefined objectives of rational calculators. They were, Rawls specified, a class of goods "that are normally wanted as parts of rational plans of life which may include the most varied sorts of ends," and the specification of these goods depends on psychological premises.[3] In the wake of the new account of moral personality, by contrast, "primary goods are singled out by asking which things are generally necessary as social conditions and all-purpose means to enable human beings to realize and exercise their moral powers . . . the conception of moral persons as having certain specified highest-order interests selects what is to count as primary goods. . . . Thus these goods are not to be understood as general means essential for achieving whatever final ends a comprehensive empirical or historical survey might show people usually or normally have in common under all social conditions."[4]

---

1. In defending these contentions I have drawn on three of my previously published articles: "Liberalism and Public Morality," in *Liberals on Liberalism,* ed. Alphonso J. Damico (Totowa, N.J.: Rowman & Littlefield, 1986), "Moral Personality and Liberal Theory: John Rawls's 'Dewey Lectures,'" *Political Theory* 10 (1982): 492–519, and "Defending Liberalism," *American Political Science Review* 76 (1982): 621–29.

2. John Rawls, "Kantian Constructivism in Moral Theory: The Dewey Lectures 1980." *Journal of Philosophy* 77 (1980): 525 (hereafter cited as "Dewey Lectures").

3. John Rawls, *A Theory of Justice* (Cambridge, Mass.: Harvard University Press, 1971), p. 260.

4. Rawls, "Dewey Lectures," pp. 526–27.

I have discussed elsewhere, at length, the implications of Rawls's expanded conception of moral personality. Let me raise just two problems here.

First, Rawls asserts that for an ideal conception of personality to be acceptable, "it must be possible for people to honor it sufficiently closely." Hence, "the feasible ideals of the person are limited by the capacities of human nature."[5] In his view, nothing we now know, or are likely to learn, about human nature suggests that his own conception is beyond our capacities.[6] But that view is at least controversial. One may wonder, for example, whether the men who drafted the U.S. Constitution would have embraced it. There is much evidence to suggest that they did not, that in their view the dominance of both passion and interest was such as to make an effective sense of justice the exception rather than the rule. While they did not wholly denigrate the social role of individual virtue, they felt compelled to rely heavily on what they called "auxiliary precautions"—that is, on institutions whose workings did not depend on the just motives of officeholders or of ordinary citizens. At the very least, I would suggest, the question of the feasibility of Rawls's ideal deserves much more than the cursory, almost dismissive, treatment he provides.

Second, while Rawls's conception of moral personality may strike some as unattainable, it may strike others as unacceptable. Rawls says that he hopes to "invoke a conception of the person implicitly affirmed in [our] culture, or else one that would prove acceptable to citizens once it was properly presented and explained."[7] But I wonder whether, for example, religious fundamentalists would regard the capacity to form and revise a conception of the good as a good at all, let alone a highest-order interest of human beings. They might well declare that the best human life requires the capacity to receive an external good (God's truth) rather than to form a conception of the good for oneself, and to hold fast to that truth once received rather than to revise it. Rawls's Kantian conception would strike them as a sophisticated, and therefore dangerous, brand of secular humanism. Nor would they be impressed with the suggestion that whatever may be true of their nonpublic identity, their public personality should be understood in Rawls's fashion. From their perspective, the disjunction between the public and nonpublic realms represents an injunction to set aside God's word, the only source of salvation, in determining the principles of our public order. I would argue, in short, that Rawls's conception of moral personality will appeal only to those individuals who have accepted a particular understanding of the liberal political community and that our public culture is at present characterized not by consensus but, rather, by acute conflict over the adequacy of that understanding.

II

The expanded account of moral personality is a part, but by no means the totality, of the second major shift in Rawls's position—the expanded account of the good and its enhanced role in the overall theory.

In 1982 I published an article in which I argued that every contemporary liberal theory relies, explicitly or tacitly, on the same triadic theory of the good, which asserts the worth of human existence, the value of the fulfillment of human purposes, and the

---

5. Ibid., p. 534.

6. Ibid., p. 566.

7. Ibid., p. 518.

commitment to rationality as the chief guide to both individual purposiveness and collective undertakings. This is, to be sure, a restricted theory of the good, but it is by no means a trivial one, for it is possible to identify approaches to social morality that deny one or more of its elements.[8]

In a recent paper, in part an explicit rejoinder to my argument, Rawls acknowledges the presence of these elements of the good in his theory. He writes that any workable conception of justice "must count human life and the fulfillment of basic human needs and purposes as in general good, and endorse rationality as a basic principle of political and social organization. A political doctrine for a democratic society may safely assume, then, that all participants in political discussions of right and justice accept these values, when understood in a suitably general way. Indeed, if the members of society did not do so, the problems of political justice, in the form with which we are familiar with them, would seem not to arise."[9]

Nor is this the totality of the liberal theory of the good as Rawls now understands it. In another recent paper, he develops the notion of a workable political conception of justice for a modern democratic society as resting on the fact of pluralism, that is, on the existence of diverse and irreconcilable conceptions of the good. This "fact" does not, however, have the status of an unchangeable law of nature but is relative to specific institutions and policies. Rawls acknowledges that a public agreement on a single conception of the good can indeed be established and maintained, but "only by the oppressive use of state power."[10] The empirical fact of pluralism, then, rests on the normative commitment to noncoercion and to the achievement of "free and willing agreement."[11]

This commitment to noncoercion goes very deep. It might be thought, for example, that pluralism makes sense only if no conception of the good can be known to be rationally preferable to any other. Rawls denies this: "The view that philosophy in the classical sense as the search for truth about a prior and independent moral order cannot provide the shared basis for a political conception of justice . . . does not presuppose the controversial metaphysical claim that there is no such order."[12] Even if there were such an order and it could be rationally specified, it could not properly serve as the basis for a political order unless it happened to be generally accepted by the citizenry, which would be highly unlikely in the absence of a coercive or at least tutelary state. In short, the claims of noncoercion—of individual freedom—trump even claims based on comprehensive philosophical truths. The freedom to choose one's own conception of the good is among the highest-order goods.

Finally, Rawls's expanded conception of the human good offers an account of justice itself as a key element of that good. Citizens of a just society "share one very basic political end, and one that has high priority: namely, the end of supporting just institutions and of giving one another justice accordingly." This is the case in large measure because "the exercise of the two moral powers [the basic elements of moral personality] is experienced as good."[13] Not only, then, is justice a highest-order

---

8. Galston, "Defending Liberalism," pp. 625–26.

9. John Rawls, "The Priority of Right and Ideas of the Good," *Philosophy and Public Affairs* 17 (1988): 254 (hereafter cited as "Priority of Right").

10. John Rawls, "The Idea of an Overlapping Consensus," *Oxford Journal of Legal Studies* 7 (1987): 4 (hereafter cited as "Overlapping Consensus").

11. Ibid., p. 5.

12. Ibid., p. 13n.

13. Rawls, "Priority of Right," pp. 269–70.

moral power and interest, but also there is an intrinsic impulse to develop and employ it in society.

Yet Rawls hesitates to embrace this argument in its full rigor. In the very article in which he most decisively links justice to moral personality as an end in itself, he also asserts that justice must be compatible with the comprehensive conceptions of the good held by individuals: "Just institutions and the political virtues expected of citizens would serve no purpose—would have no point—unless those institutions and virtues not only permitted but also sustained ways of life that citizens can affirm as worthy of their full allegiance. A conception of political justice must contain within itself sufficient space, as it were, for ways of life that can gain devoted support. In a phrase: justice draws the limit, the good shows the point."[14]

This assertion raises two very different kinds of issues. The first is conceptual: if doing justice is truly one of the two highest-order interests of moral personality, an end in itself, then why does it need a "point" outside itself? If individuals genuinely accept that justice is "supremely regulative as well as effective"[15] and that citizens' desires to pursue ends that transgress the limits of justice "have no weight,"[16] then, to be sure, adequate space for conceptions of the good lends added support for just institutions but it cannot be vital to their acceptability. Conversely, if space for ways of life is indeed critical, then a purportedly just regime that is systematically biased against certain kinds of lives cannot expect wholehearted support from individuals who cherish those lives.

This brings me to the second issue raised by Rawls's revised account of the relation between just institutions and individual ways of life. In his earlier account, Rawls had already conceded that certain ways of life were systematically likely to lose out in liberal society. But that did not imply (so he then argued) that this bias in any sense represented a morally relevant loss: "A well-ordered society defines a fair background within which ways of life have a reasonable opportunity to establish themselves. If a conception of the good is unable to endure and gain adherents under institutions of equal freedom and mutual toleration, one must question whether it is a viable conception of the good, and whether its passing is to be regretted."[17] The bias of liberalism, then, poses no special difficulty because the sorts of lives it tends to screen out are in themselves questionable from the standpoint of justice.

In Rawls's more recent account, however, the bias of liberalism becomes much more problematic. He now repudiates the view that only unworthy ways of life lose out in a just constitutional regime. "That optimistic view," he states flatly, "is mistaken." In its place, he endorses the view of Isaiah Berlin that "there is no social world without loss—that is, no social world that does not exclude some ways of life that realize in special ways certain fundamental values."[18] In particular, a society constructed in accordance with the conception of justice as fairness will ask certain individuals and groups to give up for themselves their ways of life or to surrender any real chance of passing their most cherished values on to children. Moreover, what Rawls calls "the facts of common-sense political sociology" tell us which ways of life are most likely to lose out—to wit, those that presuppose more control over the immediate cultural environment than is feasible within liberal societies.

---

14. Ibid., pp. 251–52.

15. Rawls, "Dewey Lectures," p. 525.

16. Rawls, "Priority of Right," p. 251.

17. John Rawls, "Fairness to Goodness," *Philosophical Review* 84 (1975): 549.

18. Rawls, "Priority of Right," p. 265.

This new position, it seems to me, poses a deep difficulty for justice as fairness. If I know that the principles adopted in the original position may impair my ability to exercise, or even require me altogether to surrender, the values that give my life its core meaning and purpose, then how can I agree in advance to accept those principles as binding—any more than I could subscribe to a procedure that might result in my enslavement as the outcome of a utilitarian calculus? Freedom is a great good, but is one's moral identity a lesser good? If it is unimaginable to risk losing the former, how can it make sense to embrace a decision procedure that risks losing the latter?

Rawls's answer is that there is no alternative, once justice is cast as a fair system of cooperation among free and equal persons within the fact of pluralism: if the oppressive use of state power is ruled out, justice as fairness—with its characteristic bias—is the necessary outcome. It is not, however, adequate to depict adherents of endangered ways of life as facing a choice between becoming victims or oppressors. There is a third alternative—retreat or exit from pluralistic societies into communities marked by a greater degree of moral, religious, or cultural homogeneity. And this is likely to be the preferred option for groups that see themselves as the probable victims of liberal bias.

This line of argument amounts to the proposition that, for some, the costs of treating pluralism as a "fact" are prohibitive, for it is a pluralism that excludes them. We reach a similar conclusion, starting with the observation that Rawls takes for granted the existence of a demarcated society whose members already accept the necessity of living together under common rules. From his perspective, the question is not whether I will seek grounds of cooperation with the other members of my society but, rather, what form that cooperation will take. But it is perfectly possible to treat as problematic precisely what Rawls takes for granted. The costs of cooperation under common rules with individuals who differ radically from me may appear prohibitive, especially if those rules are to be drafted under procedures that require free and willing consent. It might well be rational for me to prefer a multiplicity of separate homogeneous communities, one of which is my natural home, to a single pluralistic community in which I fear I may have no real place.

A similar difficulty may be reached via another line of argument. In his recent work, Rawls has focused increasingly on the possibility of conflict between individual conceptions of the good on the one hand and the demands of social cooperation on the other. He has sought to reduce the probability—and severity—of this conflict in two ways: by emphasizing the respects in which justice as fairness both promotes its own political vision of the good and allows for the pursuit of many (though not all) individual conceptions of the good; and by indicating how justice as fairness can be seen as the focus of an "overlapping consensus" among differing religious and comprehensive philosophical views.

As the role of the political good in Rawls's theory has expanded, the theory has become noticeably more teleological. Not only have existence, purposiveness, and social rationality received explicit recognition as intrinsic goods, but also the account of moral personality has provided the foundation for the recognition of freedom and justice as ends in themselves—that is, as essential aspects of our human good. In the process, justice as fairness has verged on a kind of democratic perfectionism.

We may then ask: if the teleological component of Rawls's theory is so enhanced, then what of the much-discussed priority of the right over the good? The answer, I think, is that the priority of the right is subtly reinterpreted as the priority of the public over the nonpublic. That is, permissible conceptions of the good are delimited by the determination to give priority to social cooperation. Over and over again in his recent writings, Rawls repeats his hope that, taking as his point of departure the core concept of a fair system of cooperation, he can arrive at an expression of political values that "normally outweigh whatever other values may oppose them."[19]

Yet matters are not so simple. Rawls never really addresses the charge, leveled by Bernard Williams, among others, that the public understanding of moral personality comports poorly with our nonpublic aims and attachments and that no basis for the unification of these two dimensions of our character is offered in the revised account of justice as fairness. The possibility therefore looms that giving priority to the requirements of social cooperation will compel individuals to make sacrifices of their core commitments and of aspects of their character they regard as basic to their identity and integrity.[20]

In the end, Rawls recognizes this. He concedes that the priority of the public is always provisional, always threatened: "Political good, no matter how important, can never in general outweigh the transcendent values—certain religious, philosophical, and moral values—that may possibly come into conflict with it."[21] And because a liberal society cannot be equally hospitable to all conceptions of the good, the social basis for such conflict is always likely to exist. From the standpoint of social stability, the best that can be hoped for is that the overwhelming majority of individuals and groups will find sufficient space within liberal society for the expression of their distinctive conceptions of the good. But for those who are left out, it is hard to see how liberalism can be experienced as anything other than an assault. Resistance is therefore to be expected, and it is far from clear on what basis it is to be condemned.

III

Of all the distinctive claims of Rawls's more recent work, the one he presses most forcefully and develops most fully is the assertion that justice as fairness is a *political* conception. In Rawls's hand, this adjective takes on manifold meanings. A political conception of justice is directed toward the basic structure of society rather than toward the full range of moral conduct, and it is therefore prepared to accept sharp differences between public and nonpublic principles. It is nevertheless a moral notion in the sense that it rests on the possibility of conscientious public action from, and not merely in accordance with, principles of public right; that is, it rejects as inadequate the pure "Hobbesian" appeal to rational self-interest. A political conception is based on the facts of political history and sociology. It is constrained by the requirements of practicality; indeed, these requirements are said to enter into the construction of first principles and not merely their application. It must meet the criterion of publicity; no principles that depend on secrecy or misrepresentation can be deemed acceptable. A political conception is both drawn from and addressed to a specific public culture, and its justification lies in its fidelity to the shared understandings of that culture rather than its correspondence to some universe of

19. Rawls, "Overlapping Consensus," pp. 9, 17, 21–22. See also his "Priority of Right," pp. 252–53, 274–75, and "Dewey Lectures," pp. 552–53.

20. Bernard Williams, "Persons, Character, and Morality," in The Identities of Persons, ed. Amelie Oksenberg Rorty (Berkeley: University of California Press, 1976), pp. 210, 215.

21. Rawls, "Priority of Right," p. 275.

moral facts. Finally, it is (so far as possible) detached from, independent of, and neutral with respect to broader and inherently controversial philosophical, metaphysical, and religious commitments.

I have discussed many of these theses elsewhere, and the final section of this article will examine the notion of political philosophy as cultural interpretation. In this section, I want to focus on what I take to be Rawls's key—and highly controversial—contention that principles of justice can be independent of broader commitments.

Contemporary communitarians offer a searching critique of what they take to be the metaphysical conception of individuality peculiar—and necessary—to Rawlsian liberalism: a conception of the self as freely chosen and self-created; as separable from its aims and attachments; as detached from, critical of, unencumbered by, its history and circumstances. This critique is most closely identified with Michael Sandel, and I cannot improve on his summary:

> Can we view ourselves as independent selves, independent in the sense that our identity is never attached to our aims and attachments? I do not think we can, at least not without cost to those loyalties and convictions whose moral force consists partly in the fact that living by them is inseparable from understanding ourselves as the particular persons we are—as members of this family or community or nation or people, as bearers of that history, as citizens of this republic. . . . To imagine a person incapable of constitutive attachments such as these is not to conceive an ideally free and rational agent, but to imagine a person wholly without character, without moral depth. For to have character is to know that I move in a history I neither summon nor command, which carries consequences nonetheless for my choices and conduct.[22]

Any sensible response to this argument must begin by accepting one of its essential premises. There are aims and allegiances that are not in the first instance chosen, that arise out of our history and circumstances, and that to some considerable extent constitute our individual identities. No one chooses to be the child of these particular parents, a relationship that nonetheless creates not only special duties to those parents but also the special identity of that child. Analogous relationships exist between citizens and the communities into which they are born. To reject these facts would not only impoverish individual identity but also deny the obvious.

Once this point is granted, defenders of liberalism must choose between two strategies. The first, espoused most directly by Rawls, is to draw a sharp line between those constitutive relations and the conception of the person required by the political conception of liberal justice—that is, to deny that liberalism rests on any specific conception of individuality. Properly understood, liberalism is "political not metaphysical." The original position within which the various alternative principles of social cooperation are to be examined is simply a "device of representation." That is, it embodies the distinction between considerations that are held to be relevant in choosing principles of justice and those thought not to be relevant. The veil of ignorance, therefore, has "no metaphysical implications concerning the nature of the self; it does not imply that the self is ontologically prior to the facts about persons that the parties are excluded from knowing." We enter the original position not by denying our unique selfhood but, rather, by screening out, for purposes of moral justi-

---

22. Michael Sandel, "The Procedural Republic and the Unencumbered Self," *Political Theory* 12 (1984): 90–91.

fication, knowledge of social position and other individual contingencies held to be morally arbitrary.[23]

Rawls's argument is exposed to several objections. To begin, as Amy Gutmann has argued, it is one thing to say that liberalism does not presuppose a single metaphysical view of the individual, but quite another to say that liberalism is compatible with all such views. Rawls depends on the latter—stronger—claim, which cannot be sustained. There are some conceptions of the individual (understood, e.g., as "radically situated") that liberalism simply cannot accommodate.[24]

The second objection to Rawls's argument is that conflict within liberal societies may force metaphysical issues onto the public agenda. Consider abortion. Many individuals who share an understanding of moral personality disagree fundamentally on who is to be considered a moral person, so understood. Opponents of abortion insist that fetuses must be taken to be persons; proponents of unrestricted abortion must at a minimum deny this proposition. Each position raises deep metaphysical issues, and the fact that the contending parties must live together under common rules means that—tacitly if not in its declaratory doctrine—the state must incline toward one or the other metaphysical view.

At this juncture, some liberals may retort that to the extent that the state neither commands nor prohibits, but merely permits, abortion, it is not inclining toward one or the other view but rather is refraining from offering an authoritative judgment. Yet this claim too is bound to be controversial. No one denies that the state should prohibit murder. To permit abortion is therefore to determine (at least implicitly) that abortion is not murder. But this is precisely the point at issue.

From the opponents' perspective, abortion is like slavery—an issue that raises the question of who is to be treated as an equal member of the moral community, an issue that deeply divides the public culture but about which one side is right and the other wrong. The thesis underlying state permissiveness on abortion is thus parallel to the position that Judge Douglas upheld in his debates with Abraham Lincoln—and just as mistaken. We violate no one's rights by using public authority to defend equal rights for all moral persons. Yes, doing this in circumstances of deep moral disagreement risks discord and even violence. But how many Americans believe that the Civil War was too high a price to pay for the abolition of slavery?

Rawls eventually acknowledges the force of this objection. In affirming a political conception of justice, he concedes, "We may eventually have to assert at least certain aspects of our own comprehensive . . . religious or philosophical doctrine. This happens whenever someone insists, for example, that certain questions are so fundamental that to ensure their being rightly settled justifies civil strife. . . . At this point we may have no alternative but to deny this, and to assert the kind of thing we had hoped to avoid."[25] I should note that while Rawls speaks only of rejecting the necessity of strife, the example of slavery suggests that we may sometimes be compelled to accept it.

There is yet a third objection to the sharp separation between the political conception of justice and broader commitments. It is that Rawls's argument manifestly depends on a specific affirmative conception of individuality. Persons must be

---

23. John Rawls, "Justice as Fairness: Political not Metaphysical," *Philosophy and Public Affairs* 14 (1985): 237–39 (hereafter cited as "Political not Metaphysical").

24. Amy Gutmann, "Communitarian Critics of Liberalism," *Philosophy and Public Affairs* 14 (1985): 319. See also Rawls's own qualifications in "Political not Metaphysical," p. 240n.

25. Rawls, "Overlapping Consensus," p. 14.

emotionally, intellectually, and ontologically capable of drawing an effective line between their public and nonpublic identities and of setting aside their particular commitments, at least to the extent needed to enter the original position and to reason in a manner consistent with its constraints.

In reflecting on this fact and on the course of the preceding arguments, I am led to the conclusion that liberalism does indeed presuppose a conception of individuality. Liberalism, I suggest, rests not on the unencumbered self (which Sandel rightly criticizes) but rather on the *divided* self. On the one side stands the individual's personal and social history, with all the aims and attachments it may imply. On the other side stands the possibility of critical reflection on—even revolt against—these very commitments. Crucial to the liberal self is the potentiality for such critical distance from one's inheritance and the possibility that the exercise of critical faculties may in important respects modify that inheritance.

At the heart of the liberal vision is the conviction that individuality is not only shaped but also threatened by the community, that concentrations of social and political power can serve as vehicles for repressing as well as expressing individual identity. Liberalism endeavors to give due weight to both sides of this complex equation. On the theoretical level, this understanding requires that individuals be endowed both with the capacity for critical reflection on the institutions and presuppositions of their society and with the capacity for noncoerced choice essential to moral action. Properly understood, liberalism's Archimedean point is neither Cartesian nor Kantian but, rather, Socratic. To have the capacity to become aware of the inner contradictions of one's own society is precisely the kind of reflective distance required by the liberal conception of individuality. Rawls must, I think, concede no less; liberal theory needs no more; and the communitarian critics of liberalism cannot in the last analysis deny its possibility.

IV

I turn, finally, to Rawls's new conception of political philosophy as both drawn from and addressed to a specific public culture.

Liberalism in its classic form saw itself as the product of a decisive break with opinion, tradition, and myth. It claimed for its key premises the status of universal knowledge, independent of time and place, and it maintained that these premises could be used to judge all existing regimes.

In this self-understanding, at least, liberalism was simply a continuation of the tradition of political philosophy pioneered by Plato and Aristotle and taken over by medieval thinkers of different faiths. The highest task of political philosophy, so understood, was the comparative evaluation of regimes. To this end, philosophers developed idealized accounts of desirable political orders, in the form either of discursive principles or of concrete utopias. On this account, it should be noted, the discovery of truth is an activity quite distinct from argument within a public consensus. The former is the task of political philosophy, while the latter is the province of rhetoric.

The "death" of political philosophy proclaimed a generation ago was the loss of confidence in the possibility of transcultural, truth-based political evaluation. *A Theory of Justice* was greeted with excitement in part because it was seen as restoring the legitimacy of political evaluation so conceived. Rawls's "ideal theory," abstracted from the empirical contingencies that differentiate existing political orders, was designed to judge and (when possible) to improve them. And, he contended, his theory was neither produced by specific historical and social circumstances nor intended to defend any existing order. The theory was rather "impartial," for it was constructed *sub specie aeternitatis,* regarding the human situation "not only from all social but also from all temporal points of view."[26]

In the Dewey lectures and subsequently, however, Rawls abandons this effort. Political philosophy, he now contends, is always addressed to a specific "public culture." It either appeals to the principles latent in the common sense of that culture or proposes principles "congenial to its most essential convictions and historical traditions." In particular, justice as fairness addresses the public culture of a democratic society. It tries "to draw solely upon basic intuitive ideas that are embedded in the political institutions of constitutional democratic regimes and the public traditions of their interpretation." Justice as fairness "starts from within a certain political tradition" and (we may add) it remains there.[27] The question of truth or falsity is thus irrelevant. Justice as fairness presents itself "not as a conception of justice that is true, but one that can serve as a basis of informed and willing political agreement. . . . Philosophy as the search for truth about an independent metaphysical and moral order cannot, I believe, provide a workable and shared basis for a political conception of justice in a democratic society."[28] As a consequence, the classic distinction between political philosophy and rhetoric collapses: "On this view, justification is not regarded simply as valid argument from listed premises, even should these premises be true. Rather justification is addressed to others who disagree with us, and therefore it must always proceed from some consensus, that is, from premises that we and others publicly recognize as true; or better, publicly recognize as acceptable to us for the purpose of establishing a working agreement on the fundamental questions of political justice."[29]

In the Dewey lectures and subsequently, Rawls sets aside the central concern of traditional political philosophy and puts in its place a new set of questions, to which justice as fairness purports to provide the answer. How are "we"—reflective citizens of a liberal democracy—to understand freedom and equality, the ideals to which we are (or so we say) individually and collectively committed? How are we to resolve the recurrent conflict between these ideals? Which principles of justice are most consistent with them, and how are we to transform these principles into workable institutions?

These questions are well worth asking. But they raise three difficulties that Rawls does not appear to me to have adequately addressed.

To begin with, it is unlikely (to say the least) that the interpretation of a public culture will be less controversial than the interpretation of a literary creation. Thus, for example, Rawls's core notion of free and equal moral personality, allegedly derived from an inspection of our traditions, excludes knowledge of differing conceptions of the good from the original position and rules out individual desert as a core element of our collective self-understanding that should help structure the principles of justice we adopt. I and others have argued that this account of moral personality does violence not only to a reasonable account of the "moral point of view" but also to the

---

26. Rawls, *A Theory of Justice,* p. 587.

27. Rawls, "Dewey Lectures," p. 518, and "Political not Metaphysical," p. 225.

28. Rawls, "Political not Metaphysical," p. 230.

29. Ibid., p. 229.

most plausible description of the shared understanding of our public culture. Now is not the occasion to join this issue or other comparable controversies. The point is rather that cultural interpretation is far more likely to recapitulate than (as Rawls supposes) to resolve the deep disputes that now divide our political order.

The second difficulty with Rawls's account of political philosophy is that it leaves no basis for the comparative assessment of regimes. When we are faced with evils like Hitlerism, Stalinism, and apartheid, it is not enough to say that these practices violate our shared understandings. The point is that we insist on the right to apply our principles to communities that reject them. Indeed, these evils challenge the very validity of these principles, which therefore require a defense that transcends interpretation.

If principles of political right do not apply across the boundaries of public cultures, then many practices we take for granted would have to be abandoned. No American president could go to Moscow and criticize Soviet restraints on freedom of speech and expression—restraints that more nearly reflect than repudiate the tradition of Russia's public culture. Organizations such as Amnesty International could not rightly apply a common standard of decency to all nations. And forceful, even coercive, efforts to foster liberal democracy would be ruled out. In the wake of World War II, for example, the United States undertook to reconstruct not just the political institutions but also the public culture of its defeated enemies. Authoritarian social and economic groupings were dismantled; textbooks were purged; democratic doctrines were aggressively purveyed to bolster the viability of the democratic practices we had imposed. In virtually every respect, we overrode the preferred self-understandings of our adversaries. It was a perfect example of what political theory understood solely as cultural interpretation would preclude. But it was not wrong.

Now it is open to Rawls to reply (as indeed he does) that he does not wish to deny the possibility that certain normative principles may apply across cultural boundaries. Rather, he begins from the special case of the closed, self-sufficient community. The extent to which conclusions reached within this domain may be extended farther "cannot be foreseen in advance." Moreover, methods of moral argument, such as the appeal to independent and preexisting moral facts, ruled out in the construction principles of justice for a single society, may conceivably be used for the elucidation of principles governing relations among societies.[30]

Indeed, it may be argued that Rawls's entire argument tacitly proceeds in two steps. The first is the premise—supported perhaps by moral philosophy—that liberal democracy in its broad outlines is clearly superior to alternative forms of political organization, while the second step is the effort—to which Rawls devotes nearly all his attention—to arrive at the most plausible interpretation of what the core commitments of liberal democracy entail. The former step employs strategies of moral validation that cannot be reduced to (deep) consensus, while the latter can only appeal to what we believe, or can be led to believe, on due reflection.[31]

This reply raises, in turn, the following question: if there can be public principles whose validity rests on truth rather than agreement, then why can't such principles apply within liberal democratic communities? Rawls's answer is that, within such communities, the freedom of moral persons is not to be violated, not even in the name of truth. But is the absolute priority of freedom over truth really the polestar of liberal-democratic public culture? And how is that alleged priority to be squared with a public culture that begins by declaring, "We hold these truths to be self-evident"?

---

30. Rawls, "Dewey Lectures," pp. 524, 561–62.

31. I am indebted to Richard Arneson for this suggestion.

   This question leads me to the third and final objection to Rawls's account of political philosophy: by asking us to separate general truth-claims from the elucidation of our shared understandings, it distorts the deepest meaning of those understandings. When Americans say that all human beings are created equal and endowed with certain unalienable rights, we intend this not as a description of our local convictions but, rather, as universal truths, valid everywhere and binding on all. Indeed, that claim is at the heart of their normative force. If our principles are valid for us only because we (happen to) believe them, then they are not binding even for us.

   The reason is straightforward. If someone argues that we ought to do something because it corresponds to the best interpretation of the shared understandings that constitute our culture, it is always open to me to ask why I should consider myself bound by those understandings. That simple question launches the philosophic quest for grounds of action and belief beyond the sheer facticity of culture—a quest that cannot be set aside without doing violence to the profoundest of all human longings. There may in the end be no viable grounds of transcultural justification, in which case we will be faced after all with Nietzsche's choice between life-denying openness and life-affirming horizons. But to set aside in advance the quest for truth, to insist as Rawls does that the principle of religious toleration must for political purposes be extended to philosophy itself, is to demand something that no self-respecting individual or public culture can reasonably grant.

Jürgen Habermas

Jürgen Habermas, one of today's most prolific social theorists, has uniquely synthesized an extensive literature in Anglo-American and Continental philosophy, linguistics, and the social sciences. Attentive both to academic debates (in which he has frequently engaged) and to contemporary political events, his own writings have been the subject of an almost equally extensive set of interpretative and critical essays across a wide range of disciplines. His grounding in the esoteric tradition of German social theory, along with a ponderously academic writing style, has made reading Habermas's works (let alone the innumerable commentaries) a challenging labor. However, despite the fear and loathing many students (and even some political theorists) may have for Habermas, his works can be profitably read once the basic concerns and motivations underlying his thought are understood.

Now a professor of philosophy at the University of Frankfurt, Habermas was born in 1929. Growing up under the Nazi regime, listening as a teenager to radio broadcasts of the Nuremberg trials of Nazi war criminals, and coming of age in a democratic and prosperous Germany, have all left a mark on his intellectual development. His university studies in the 1950s (especially his work at the reestablished Institute for Social Research in Frankfurt) gave Habermas a thorough background in the grand tradition German philosophy and social theory. Since then, Habermas has pursued his own path of both criticizing and continuing the work of the Frankfurt School and other traditions in recent social and political thought.

The Frankfurt School's founders and early associates (Theodor Adorno, Max Horkheimer, Herbert Marcuse, and Erich Fromm, among others) were concerned with developing an alternative approach (labelled "critical theory") to social science and philosophy. Under the influence of Hegel and Marx, critical theorists tried to overcome the epistemological problems and political conservatism of traditional theory; theory as used in the natural and social sciences. Critical theory aims to use philosophy and the empirical sciences to criticize the existing social order (not simply reproduce or justify it), and thereby, to improve the human condition. What sociologist Michael Pusey says of Habermas can just as easily be said of the Frankfurt School: "The single purpose of the work is to anticipate and to justify a *better* world society—one that affords greater opportunities for happiness, peace, and community. [Moreover], the *better society is the more rational society,* in short, a society that is geared to collective needs rather than to arbitrary power." [1]

Habermas has spent his intellectual career exposing the questionable assumptions of traditional social theory. Because he engages in debate with many different theoretical traditions and political activists, Habermas seeks not merely to lay the groundwork for an authentic critical theory, but he also aims to assess the possibilities for social transformation in advanced capitalist countries. In his magnum opus, *The Theory of Communicative Action* (1984), Habermas pulls together the various themes of his lifelong work to restructure social theory on the foundation of a concept of communicative action; to analyze the root causes of various social pathologies endemic in modern society (e.g., a loss of meaning in social life, the rise of instrumental reason and the fall of practical reason); and to consider again the potential for constructing a truly critical theory of society.

Knowledge and Human Interests and *Legitimation Crisis*

The selections presented below come from two of Habermas's early works.[2] First, in *Knowledge and Human Interests* (1971), Habermas produces a history of ideas to show how the critical component in philosophy was lost as the natural and social sciences developed. Aiming to recapture that spirit, Habermas argues that science cannot be seen as the only legitimate or objective path to knowledge. Instead, the objects, categories, and procedures of all knowledge are constituted (created, shaped, and made meaningful) by certain attitudes or orientations, called "cognitive interests" or "knowledge-constitutive interests." Each type of interest (technical, practical, and emancipatory) corresponds to a dimension of social life (work or labor, interaction, and power) and to a set of scientific disciplines (empirical-analytic sciences, historical-hermeneutic disciplines, and critical theory).

Second, *Legitimation Crisis* (1975) offers an analysis of the stresses and strains faced by contemporary polities in the advanced industrial world. Habermas uses a mix of systems theory, Marxist economic and political theory, and Weberian sociology to support his argument that advanced capitalism will continue to encounter unique legitimation and motivation crises. These crises have emerged as a result of increasing state management and regulation of the economy, the rise of the welfare

1. Michael Pusey, *Jurgen Habermas* (London: Tavistock Publications, 1987), p. 14.

2. Since *The Theory of Communicative Action* is more abstract and turgid than some of Habermas's other work, and since its concerns are more with sociological than political theory, we have chosen not to reprint it here. However, there are some informative and helpful commentaries that provide summaries of the central ideas of this very significant work.

state, the depoliticization of public life, and the increasingly controversial nature of once-accepted aspects of government and policy. In the absence of any legitimizing myths (other than those promoted by a discredited state regime), social integration and personal identity begin to break down, and conflicts between system and lifeworld become more difficult to resolve.

Commentaries

Richard J. Bernstein's essay summarizes and criticizes the arguments in *Knowledge and Human Interests.* Bernstein believes that, in that work, Habermas provided an ambiguous and insufficient basis for the development of a critical analysis of society. However, he sees Habermas's more recent work as a sustained effort (using the concept of communicative action) to remedy the central flaws of the earlier attempt to secure a foundation for critical theory.

David Held's essay similarly presents a summary and critique of Habermas's views. This time, though, the focus is on the various crises Habermas finds possible or likely in advanced capitalist societies. Held acknowledges that this typology has some validity and utility, but he believes that Habermas's views on the specific nature of the crisis tendencies (as well as their interrelationships) are ultimately unsatisfactory.

Key Words

Knowledge-constitutive (cognitive) interests. The orientations or attitudes taken toward the objects, concepts, procedures, and aims of philosophical or scientific inquiry.

Legitimation and motivation crises. The inability of a society to ensure popular acceptance of and participation in its political, economic, and cultural systems.

Communicative action. Human action oriented toward achieving mutual understanding. Its nature is best seen in an "ideal speech situation," wherein disagreements regarding "validity claims" (claims about the truth, rightness, and sincerity of what is said) are resolved through reason rather than coercion.

System. The political and economic structures, as well as the bureaucratic and market processes, which permit a society to survive through successful integration and adaptation.

Lifeworld. The shared values or taken-for-granted views of the world that give meaning and direction to human action and social life.

For Further Reading

Fraser, N. 1987. "What's Critical About Critical Theory?: The Case of Habermas and Gender." In *Feminism as Critique: On the Politics of Gender,* ed. S. Benhabib and D. Cornell, pp. 31–56. Minneapolis, Minn.: University of Minnesota Press.

Giddens, A. 1985. "Jurgen Habermas." In *The Return of Grand Theory in the Human Sciences,* ed. Q. Skinner, pp. 121–139. Cambridge: Cambridge University Press.

Ingram, D. 1987. *Habermas and the Dialectic of Reason.* New Haven, Conn.: Yale University Press.

McCarthy, T. 1978. *The Critical Theory of Jurgen Habermas.* Cambridge, Mass.: MIT Press.

Schroyer, T. 1973. *The Critique of Domination: The Origin and Development of Critical Theory.* Boston: Beacon Press.

White, S.K. 1989. *The Recent Work of Jurgen Habermas: Reason, Justice, and Modernity.* Cambridge: Cambridge University Press.

Knowledge and Human Interests

Appendix

I

In 1802, during the summer semester at Jena, Schelling gave his Lectures on the Method of Academic Study. In the language of German Idealism he emphatically renewed the concept of theory that has defined the tradition of great philosophy since its beginnings.

> The fear of speculation, the ostensible rush from the theoretical to the practical, brings about the same shallowness in action that it does in knowledge. It is by studying a strictly theoretical philosophy that we become most immediately acquainted with Ideas, and only Ideas provide action with energy and ethical significance.[1]

The *only* knowledge that can truly orient action is knowledge that frees itself from mere human interests and is based on Ideas—in other words, knowledge that has taken a theoretical attitude.

The word "theory" has religious origins. The *theoros* was the representative sent by Greek cities to public celebrations. Through *theoria*, that is through looking on, he abandoned himself to the sacred events. In philosophical language, *theoria* was transferred to contemplation of the cosmos. In this form, theory already presupposed the demarcation between Being and time that is the foundation of ontology. This separation is first found in the poem of Parmenides and returns in Plato's *Timaeus*. It reserves to *logos* a realm of Being purged of inconstancy and uncertainty and leaves to *doxa* the realm of the mutable and perishable. When the philosopher views the immortal order, he cannot help bringing himself into accord with the proportions of the cosmos and reproducing them internally. He manifests these proportions, which he sees in the motions of nature and the harmonic series of music, within himself; he forms himself through mimesis. Through the soul's likening itself to the ordered motion of the cosmos, theory enters the conduct of life. In *ethos* theory molds life to its form and is reflected in the conduct of those who subject themselves to its discipline.

This concept of theory and of life in theory has defined philosophy since its beginnings. The distinction between theory in this traditional sense and theory in the sense of critique was the object of one of Max Horkheimer's most important studies. Today, a generation later, I should like to reexamine this theme,[2] starting with Husserl's *The Crisis of the European Sciences*, which appeared at about the same time as Horkheimer's. Husserl used as his frame of reference the very concept of theory that Horkheimer was countering with that of critical theory. Husserl was concerned with crisis: not with crises in the sciences, but with their crisis as science. For "in our vital state of need this science has nothing to say to us." Like almost all philosophers before him, Husserl, without second thought, took as the norm of his critique an idea of knowledge that preserves the Platonic connection of pure theory with the conduct of life. What ultimately produces a scientific culture is not the information content of theories but the formation among theorists themselves of a thoughtful and enlightened mode of life. The evolution of the European mind seemed to be aiming at the creation of a scientific culture of this sort. After 1933, however, Husserl saw this historical tendency endangered. He was convinced that the danger was threatening not from without but from within. He attributed the crisis to the circumstance that the most advanced disciplines, especially physics, had degenerated from the status of true theory.

II

Let us consider this thesis. There is a real connection between the positivistic self-understanding of the sciences and traditional ontology. The *empirical-analytic* sciences develop their theories in a self-understanding that automatically generates continuity with the beginnings of philosophical thought. For both are committed to a theoretical attitude that frees those who take it from dogmatic association with the natural interest of life and their irritating influence; and both share the cosmological intention of describing the universe theoretically in its lawlike order, just as it is. In contrast, the *historical-hermeneutic* sciences, which are concerned with the sphere of transitory things and mere opinion, cannot be linked up so smoothly with this tradition—they have nothing to do with cosmology. But they, too, comprise a *scientistic consciousness*, based on the model of science. For even the symbolic meanings of tradition seem capable of being brought together in a cosmos of facts in ideal simultaneity. Much as the cultural sciences may comprehend their facts through understanding and little though they may be concerned with discovering general laws, they nevertheless share with the empirical-analytic sciences the methodological consciousness of describing a structured reality within the horizon of the theoretical attitude. Historicism has become the positivism of the cultural and social sciences.

Positivism has also permeated the self-understanding of the *social sciences*, whether they obey the methodological demands of an empirical-analytic behavioral science or orient themselves to the pattern of normative-analytic sciences, based on presuppositions about maxims of action. In this field of inquiry, which is so close to practice, the concept of value-freedom (or ethical neutrality) has simply reaffirmed the ethos that modern science owes to the beginnings of theoretical thought in Greek philosophy: psychologically an unconditional commitment to theory and epistemologically the severance of knowledge from interest. This is represented in logic by the distinction between descriptive and prescriptive statements, which makes grammatically obligatory the filtering out of merely emotive from cognitive contents.

Yet the very term "value freedom" reminds us that the postulates associated with it no longer correspond to the classical meaning of theory. To dissociate values from facts means counterposing an abstract Ought to pure

Being. Values are the nominalistic by-products of a centuries-long critique of the emphatic concept of Being to which theory was once exclusively oriented. The very term "values," which neo-Kantianism brought into philosophical currency, and in relation to which science is supposed to preserve neutrality, renounces the connection between the two that theory originally intended.

Thus, although the sciences share the concept of theory with the major tradition of philosophy, they destroy its classical claim. They borrow two elements from the philosophical heritage: the methodological meaning of the theoretical attitude and the basic ontological assumption of a structure of the world independent of the knower. On the other hand, however, they have abandoned the connection of *theoria* and *kosmos*, of *mimesis* and *bios theoretikos* that was assumed from Plato through Husserl. What was once supposed to comprise the practical efficacy of theory has now fallen prey to methodological prohibitions. The conception of theory as a process of cultivation of the person has become apocryphal. Today it appears to us that the mimetic conformity of the soul to the proportions of the universe, which seemed accessible to contemplation, had only taken theoretical knowledge into the service of the internalization of norms and thus estranged it from its legitimate task. . . .

IV

In the Greek tradition, the same forces that philosophy reduces to powers of the soul still appeared as gods and superhuman powers. Philosophy domesticated them and banished them to the realm of the soul as internalized demons. If from this point of view we regard the drives and affects that enmesh man in the empirical interests of his inconstant and contingent activity, then the attitude of pure theory, which promises *purification* from these very affects, takes on a new meaning: disinterested contemplation then obviously signifies emancipation. The release of knowledge from interest was not supposed to purify theory from the obfuscations of subjectivity but inversely to provide the subject with an ecstatic purification from the passions. What indicates the new stage of emancipation is that catharsis is now no longer attained through mystery cults but established in the will of individuals themselves by means of theory. In the communication structure of the polis, individuation has progressed to the point where the identity of the individual ego as a stable entity can only be developed through identification with abstract laws of cosmic order. Consciousness, emancipated from archaic powers, now anchors itself in the unity of a stable cosmos and the identity of immutable Being.

Thus it was only by means of ontological distinctions that theory originally could take cognizance of a self-subsistent world purged of demons. At the same time, the illusion of pure theory served as a protection against regression to an earlier stage that had been surpassed. Had it been possible to detect that the identity of pure Being was an objectivistic illusion, ego identity would not have been able to take shape on its basis. The repression of interest appertained to this interest itself.

If this interpretation is valid, then the two most influential aspects of the Greek tradition, the theoretical attitude and the basic ontological assumption of a structured, self-subsistent world, appear in a connection that they explicitly prohibit: the connection of knowledge with human interests. Hence we return to Husserl's critique of the objectivism of the sciences. But this connection turns *against* Husserl. Our reason for suspecting the presence of an unacknowledged connection between knowledge and interest is not that the sciences have abandoned the classical concept of theory, but that they have not completely abandoned it. The suspicion of objectivism exists because of the *ontological illusion of pure theory* that the sciences still deceptively share with the philosophical tradition *after casting off its practical content.*

With Husserl we shall designate as objectivistic an attitude that naively correlates theoretical propositions with matters of fact. This attitude presumes that the relations between empirical variables represented in theoretical propositions are self-existent. At the same time, it suppresses the transcendental framework that is the precondition of the meaning of the validity of such propositions. As soon as these statements are understood in relation to the prior frame of reference to which they are affixed, the objectivist illusion dissolves and makes visible a knowledge-constitutive interest.

There are three categories of processes of inquiry for which a specific connection between logical-methodological rules and knowledge-constitutive interests can be demonstrated. This demonstration is the task of a critical philosophy of science that escapes the snares of positivism. The approach of the empirical-analytic sciences incorporates a *technical* cognitive interest; that of the historical-hermeneutic sciences incorporates a *practical* one: and the approach of critically oriented sciences incorporates the *emancipatory* cognitive interest that, as we saw, was at the root of traditional theories. I should like to clarify this thesis by means of a few examples.

V

In the *empirical-analytic sciences* the frame of reference that prejudges the meaning of possible statements establishes rules both for the construction of theories and for their critical testing. Theories comprise hypothetico-deductive connections of propositions, which permit the deduction of law-like hypotheses with empirical content. The latter can be interpreted as statements about the covariance of observable events; given a set of initial conditions, they make predictions possible. Empirical-analytic knowledge is thus possible predictive knowledge. However, the *meaning* of such predictions, that is their technical exploitability, is established only by the rules according to which we apply theories to reality.

In controlled observation, which often takes the form of an experiment, we generate initial conditions and measure the results of operations carried out under these conditions. Empiricism attempts to ground the objectivist illusion in observations expressed in basic statements. These observations are supposed to be reliable in providing immediate evidence without the admixture of subjectivity. In reality basic statements are not simple representations of facts in themselves, but express the success or failure of our operations. We can say that facts and the relations between them are apprehended descriptively. But this way of talking must not conceal that as such the facts relevant to the empirical sciences are first constituted through an a priori organization of our experience in the behavioral system of instrumental action.

Taken together, these two factors, that is the logical structure of admissible systems of propositions and the type of conditions for corroboration suggest that theories of the empirical sciences disclose reality subject to the constitutive interest in the possible securing and expansion, through information, of feedback-monitored action. This is the cognitive interest in technical control over objectified processes.

The *historical-hermeneutic sciences* gain knowledge in a different methodological framework. Here the meaning of the validity of propositions is not constituted in the frame of reference of technical control. The levels of formalized language and objectified experience have not yet been divorced. For theories are not constructed deductively and experience is not organized with regard to the success of operations. Access to the facts is provided by the understanding of meaning, not observation. The verification of lawlike hypotheses in the empirical-analytic sciences has its counterpart here in the interpretation of texts. Thus the rules of hermeneutics determine the possible meaning of the validity of statements of the cultural sciences.

Historicism has taken the understanding of meaning, in which mental facts are supposed to be given in direct evidence, and grafted onto it the objectivist illusion of pure theory. It appears as though the interpreter transposes himself into the horizon of the world or language from which a text derives its meaning. But here, too, the facts are first constituted in relation to the standards that establish them. Just as positivist self-understanding does not take into account explicitly the connection between measurement operations and feedback control, so it eliminates from consideration the interpreter's pre-understanding. Hermeneutic knowledge is always mediated through this pre-understanding, which is derived from the interpreter's initial situation. The world of traditional meaning discloses itself to the interpreter only to the extent that his own world becomes clarified at the same time. The subject of understanding establishes communication between both worlds. He comprehends the substantive content of tradition by *applying* tradition to himself and his situation.

If, however, methodological rules unite interpretation and application in this way, then this suggests that hermeneutic inquiry discloses reality subject to a constitutive interest in the preservation and expansion of the intersubjectivity of possible action-orienting mutual understanding. The understanding of meaning is directed in its very structure toward the attainment of possible consensus among actors in the framework of a self-understanding derived from tradition. This we shall call the *practical* cognitive interest, in contrast to the technical.

The systematic *sciences of social action*, that is economics, sociology, and political science, have the goal, as do the empirical-analytic sciences, of producing nomological knowledge. A critical social science, however, will not remain satisfied with this. It is concerned with going beyond this goal to determine when theoretical statements grasp invariant regularities of social action as such and when they express ideologically frozen relations of dependence that can in principle be transformed. To the extent that this is the case, the *critique of ideology*, as well, moreover, as *psychoanalysis*, take into account that information about lawlike connections sets off a process of reflection in the consciousness of those whom the laws are about. Thus the level of unreflected consciousness, which is one of the initial conditions of such laws, can be transformed. Of course, to this end a critically mediated knowledge of laws cannot through reflection alone render a law itself inoperative, but it can render it inapplicable.

The methodological framework that determines the meaning of the validity of critical propositions of this category is established by the concept of *self-reflection*. The latter releases the subject from dependence on hypostatized powers. Self-reflection is determined by an emancipatory cognitive interest. Critically oriented sciences share this interest with philosophy.

However, as long as philosophy remains caught in ontology, it is itself subject to an objectivism that disguises the connection of its knowledge with the human interest in autonomy and responsibility (*Mündigkeit*). There is only one way in which it can acquire the power that it vainly claims for itself in virtue of its seeming freedom from presuppositions: by acknowledging its dependence on this interest and turning against its own illusion of pure theory the critique it directs at the objectivism of the sciences.

VI

The concept of knowledge-constitutive human interests already conjoins the two elements whose relation still has to be explained: knowledge and interest. From everyday experience we know that ideas serve often enough to furnish our actions with justifying motives in place of the real ones. What is called rationalization at this level is called ideology at the level of collective action. In both cases the manifest content of statements is falsified by consciousness' unreflected tie to interests, despite its illusion of autonomy. The discipline of trained thought thus correctly aims at excluding such interests. In all the sciences routines have been developed that guard against the subjectivity of opinion, and a new discipline, the sociology of knowledge, has emerged to counter the uncontrolled influence of interests on a deeper level, which derive less from the individual than from the objective situation of social groups. But this accounts for only one side of the problem. Because science must secure the objectivity of its statements against the pressure and seduction of particular interests, it deludes itself about the fundamental interests to which it owes not only its impetus but *the conditions of possible objectivity* themselves.

Orientation toward technical control, toward mutual understanding in the conduct of life, and toward emancipation from seemingly "natural" constraint establish the specific viewpoints from which we can apprehend reality as such in any way whatsoever. By becoming aware of the impossibility of getting beyond these transcendental limits, a part of nature acquires, through us, autonomy in nature. If knowledge could ever outwit its innate human interest, it would be by comprehending that the mediation of subject and object that philosophical consciousness attributes exclusively to *its own* synthesis is produced originally by interests. The mind can become aware of this natural basis reflexively. Nevertheless, its power extends into the very logic of inquiry.

Representations and descriptions are never independent of standards. And the choice of these standards is based on attitudes that require critical consideration by means of arguments, because they cannot be either logically deduced or empirically demonstrated. Fundamental methodological decisions, for example such basic distinctions as those between categorial and noncategorial being, between analytic and synthetic statements, or between descriptive and emotive meaning, have the singular character of being neither arbitrary nor compelling. They prove appropriate or inappropriate. For their criterion is the metalogical necessity of interests that we can neither prescribe nor represent, but with which we must instead *come to terms.* Therefore my first thesis is this: *The achievements of the transcendental subject have their basis in the natural history of the human species.*

Taken by itself this thesis could lead to the misunderstanding that reason is an organ of adaptation for men just as claws and teeth are for animals. True, it does serve this function. But the human interests that have emerged in man's natural history, to which we have traced back the three knowledge-constitutive interests, derive both from nature and *from the cultural break* with nature. Along with the tendency to realize natural drives they have incorporated the tendency toward release from the constraint of nature. Even the interest in self-preservation, natural as it seems, is represented by a social system that compensates for the lacks in man's organic equipment and secures his historical existence *against* the force of nature threatening from without. But society is not only a system of self-preservation. An enticing natural force, present in the individual as libido, has detached itself from the behavioral system of self-preservation and urges toward utopian fulfillment. These individual demands, which do not initially accord with the requirement of collective self-preservation, are also absorbed by the social system. That is why the cognitive processes to which social life is indissolubly linked function not only as means to the reproduction of life; for in equal measure they themselves determine the definitions of this life. What may appear as naked survival is always in its roots a historical phenomenon. For it is subject to the criterion of what a society intends for itself as *the good life.* My *second thesis* is thus that *knowledge equally serves as an instrument and transcends mere self-preservation.*

The specific viewpoints from which, with transcendental necessity, we apprehend reality ground three categories of possible knowledge: information that expands our power of technical control; interpretations that make possible the orientation of action within common traditions; and analyses that free consciousness from its dependence on hypostatized powers. These viewpoints originate in the interest structure of a species that is linked in its roots to definite means of social organization: work, language, and power. The human species secures its existence in systems of social labor and self-assertion through violence, through tradition-bound social life in ordinary-language communication, and with the aid of ego identities that at every level of individuation reconsolidate the consciousness of the individual in relation to the norms of the group. Accordingly the interests constitutive of knowledge are linked to the functions of an ego that adapts itself to its external conditions through learning processes, is initiated into the communication system of a social life-world by means of self-formative processes, and constructs an identity in the conflict between instinctual aims and social constraints. In turn these achievements become part of the productive forces accumulated by a society, the cultural tradition through which a society interprets itself, and the legitimations that a society accepts or criticizes. My *third thesis* is thus that *knowledge-constitutive interests take form in the medium of work, language, and power.*

However, the configuration of knowledge and interest is not the same in all categories. It is true that at this level it is always illusory to suppose an autonomy, free of presuppositions, in which knowing first grasps reality theoretically, only to be taken subsequently into the service of interests alien to it. But the mind can always reflect back upon the interest structure that joins subject and object a priori: this is reserved to self-reflection. If the latter cannot cancel out interest, it can to a certain extent make up for it.

It is no accident that the standards of self-reflection are exempted from the singular state of suspension in which those of all other cognitive processes require critical evaluation. They possess theoretical certainty. The human interest in autonomy and responsibility is not mere fancy, for it can be apprehended a priori. What raises us out of nature is the only thing whose nature we can know: *language.* Through its structure, autonomy and responsibility are posited for us. Our first sentence expresses unequivocally the intention of universal and unconstrained consensus. Taken together, autonomy and responsibility constitute the only Idea the we possess a priori in the sense of the philosophical tradition. Perhaps that is why the language of German Idealism, according to which "reason" contains both will and consciousness as its elements, is not quite obsolete. Reason also means the will to reason. In self-reflection knowledge for the sake of knowledge attains congruence with the interest in autonomy and responsibility. The emancipatory cognitive interest aims at the pursuit of reflection as such. My *fourth thesis* is thus that *in the power of self-reflection, knowledge and interest are one.*

However, only in an emancipated society, whose members' autonomy and responsibility had been realized, would communication have developed into the non-authoritarian and universally practiced dialogue from which both our model of reciprocally constituted ego identity and our idea of true consensus are always implicitly derived. To this extent the truth of statements is based on anticipating the realization of the good life. The ontological illusion of pure theory behind which knowledge-constitutive interests become invisible promotes the fiction that Socratic dialogue is possible everywhere and at any time. From the beginning philosophy has presumed that the autonomy and responsibility posited with the structure of language are not only anticipated but real. It is pure theory, wanting to derive everything from itself, that succumbs to unacknowledged external conditions and becomes ideological. Only when philosophy discovers in the dialectical course of history the traces of violence that deform repeated attempts at dialogue and recurrently close off the path to unconstrained communication does it further the process whose suspension it otherwise legitimates: mankind's evolution toward autonomy and responsibility. My *fifth thesis* is thus that *the unity of knowledge and interest proves itself in a dialectic that takes the historical traces of suppressed dialogue and reconstructs what has been suppressed....*

Notes

1. Friedrich W. J. von Schelling, *Werke*, edited by Manfred Schröter (Munich: Beck, 1958–59), 3:299.
2. The appendix was the basis of my inaugural lecture at the University of Frankfurt am Main on June 28, 1965. Bibliographical notes are restricted to a few references. [here omitted]

Legitimation Crisis

Part II
Crisis Tendencies in Advanced Capitalism

I must neglect here the very complex transition from liberal to organized capitalism, which took place in interesting national variations, and limit myself to a *model* of the most important structural features of organized capitalism (Chapter 1) in order to derive from them the possible classes of crisis tendencies that *can* arise in this social formation (Chapters 2 and 3). It is not easy to determine empirically the probability of boundary conditions under which the *possible* crisis tendencies *actually* set in and prevail. The empirical indicators we have at our disposal are as yet inadequate. I will therefore limit myself to a presentation of important arguments and counterarguments (Chapters 4–7). It goes without saying that this argumentation sketch cannot replace empirical investigations, but can at best guide them.

Chapter 1
A Descriptive Model of Advanced Capitalism

The expression "organized or state-regulated capitalism" refers to two classes of phenomena, both of which can be attributed to the advanced stage of the accumulation process. It refers, on the one hand, to the process of economic concentration—the rise of national and, subsequently, of multinational corporations—and to the organization of markets for goods, capital, and labor. On the other hand, it refers to the fact that the state intervenes in the market as functional gaps develop. The spread of oligopolistic market structures certainly means the end of *competitive capitalism*. But however much companies broaden their temporal perspectives and expand control over their environments, the steering mechanism of the market remains in force as long as investment decisions are made according to criteria of company profits. Similarly, the supplementation and partial replacement of the market mechanism by state intervention marks the end of *liberal capitalism*. Nonetheless, no matter how much the scope of the private autonomous commerce of commodity owners is administratively restricted, political planning of the allocation of scarce resources does not occur as long as the priorities of the society as a whole develop in an unplanned, nature-like manner—that is, as secondary effects of the strategies of private enterprise. In advanced-capitalist societies the economic, the administrative, and the legitimation systems can be characterized, approximately and at a very general level, as follows.

The Economic System. During the sixties, various authors, using the United States as an example, developed a three-sector model based on the distinction between the private and the public sectors. According to the model, private production is market-oriented, one sub-sector still being regulated by competition while the other is determined by the market strategies of oligopolies that tolerate a "competitive fringe." By contrast, in the public sector, especially in the armaments and space-travel industries, huge concerns have arisen whose investment decisions can be made almost without regard for the market. These concerns are either enterprises directly controlled by the state or private firms living on government contracts. In the monopolistic and the public sectors, capital-intensive industries predominate; in the competitive sector, labor-intensive industries predominate. In the monopolistic and public sectors, companies are faced with strong unions. In the competitive sector workers are less well organized, and wage levels are correspondingly different. In the monopolistic sector, we can observe relatively rapid advances in production. In the public sector, companies do not need to be rationalized to the same extent. In the competitive sector, they cannot be.

The Administrative System.   The state apparatus carries out numerous imperatives of the economic system. These can be ordered from two perspectives: by means of global planning, it regulates the economic cycle as a whole; and it creates and improves conditions for utilizing excess accumulated capital. Global planning is limited by the private autonomous disposition of the means of production (for the investment freedom of private enterprises cannot be restricted) and positively by the avoidance of instabilities. To this extent, the fiscal and financial regulation of the business cycle, as well as individual measures intended to regulate investment and overall demand—credits, price guarantees, subsidies, loans, secondary redistribution of income, government contracts guided by business-cycle policy, indirect labor-market policy, etc.—have the reactive character of avoidance strategies within the framework of a system of goals. This system is determined by a formulistically [*leerformelhaft*] demanded adjustment between competing imperatives of steady growth, stability of the currency, full employment, and balance of foreign trade.

While global planning manipulates the boundary conditions of decisions made by private enterprise in order to correct the market mechanism with respect to dysfunctional secondary effects the state actually *replaces* the market mechanism whenever it creates and improves conditions for the realization of capital:

> —through "strengthening the competitive capability of the nation" by organizing supranational economic blocks, securing international stratification by imperalist means, etc.;
> —through unproductive government consumption (for example, armaments and space exploration);
> —through guiding, in accord with structural policy, the flow of capital into sectors neglected by an autonomous market;
> —through improvement of the material infrastructure (transportation, education, health, recreation, urban and regional planning, housing construction, etc.);
> —through improvement of the immaterial infrastructure (general promotion of science, investments in research and development, provision of patents, etc.);

—through heightening the productivity of human labor (general system of education, vocational schools, programs for training and re-education, etc.);

—through relieving the social and material costs resulting from private production (unemployment compensation, welfare, repair of ecological damage).

Improving the nation's position in the international market, government demand for unproductive commodities, and measures for guiding the flow of capital, open up or improve chances for capital investment. With all but the last of the remaining measures this is indeed a concomitant phenomenon; but the goal is to increase the productivity of labor and thereby the "use value" of capital (through provision of collective commodities and through qualification of labor power).

The Legitimation System.   With the appearance of functional weaknesses in the market and dysfunctional side effects of the steering mechanism, the basic bourgeois ideology of fair exchange collapses. Re-coupling the economic system to the political—which in a way repoliticizes the relations of production—creates an increased need for legitimation. The state apparatus no longer, as in liberal capitalism, merely secures the general conditions of production (in the sense of the prerequisites for the continued existence of the reproduction process), but is now actively engaged in it. It must, therefore—like the pre-capitalist state—be legitimated, although it can no longer rely on residues of tradition that have been undermined and worn out during the development of capitalism. Moreover, through the universalistic value-systems of bourgeois ideology, civil rights—including the right to participate in political elections—have become established; and legitimation can be disassociated from the mechanism of elections only temporarily and under extraordinary conditions. This problem is resolved through a system of formal democracy. Genuine participation of citizens in the processes of political will-formation . . . that is, substantive democracy, would bring to consciousness the contradiction between administratively socialized production and the continued private appropriation and use of surplus value. In order to keep this contradiction from being thematized, then the administrative system must be sufficiently independent of legitimating will-formation.

The arrangement of formal democratic institutions and procedures permits administrative decisions to be made largely independently of specific motives of the citizens. This takes place through a legitimation process that elicits generalized motives—that is, diffuse mass loyalty—but avoids participation. This structural alteration of the bourgeois public realm . . . provides for application of institutions and procedures that are democratic in form, while the citizenry, in the midst of an objectively . . . political society, enjoy the status of passive citizens with only the right to withhold acclamation. Private autonomous investment decisions thus have their necessary complement in the civic privatism of the civil public.

In the structurally depoliticized public realm, the need for legitimation is reduced to two residual requirements: The first, civic privatism—that is, political abstinence combined with an orientation to career, leisure, and consumption . . . promotes the expectation of suitable rewards within the system (money, leisure time, and security). This privatism is taken into account by a welfare-state substitute program, which also incorporates elements of an achievement ideology transferred to the educational system. Secondly, the structural depoliticization itself requires justification, which is supplied either by democratic elite theories (which go back to Schumpeter and Max Weber) or by technocratic systems theories (which go back to the institutionalism of the twenties). In the history of bourgeois social science, these theories today have a function similar to that of the classical doctrine of political economy. In earlier phases of capitalist development, the latter doctrine suggested the "naturalness" of the capitalist economic society.

Class Structure. While the political form of the relations of production in traditional societies permitted easy identification of ruling groups, in liberal capitalism manifest domination was replaced by the politically anonymous power of civil subjects. (Of course, during economically induced social crises these anonymous powers again assumed the identifiable form of a political adversary, as can be seen in the fronts of the European labor movement.) But, while in organized capitalism the relations of production are indeed repoliticized to a certain extent, the political form of the class relationship is not thereby restored. Instead, the political anonymity of class domination is superseded by social anonymity. That is, the structures of advanced capitalism can be understood as reaction formations to endemic crisis. To ward off system crisis, advanced-capitalist societies focus all forces of social integration at the point of the structurally most probable conflict—in order all the more effectively to keep it latent. At the same time, in doing so they satisfy the political demands of reformist labor parties.

In this connection, the quasi-political wage structure, which depends on negotiations between companies and unions, plays a historically epochmaking role. "Price setting" [*Machtpreisbildung*, W. Hofmann], which replaces price competition in the oligopolistic markets, has its counterpart in the labor market. Just as the great concerns quasi-administratively control price movements in their markets, so too, on the other side, they obtain quasi-political compromises with union adversaries on wage movements. In those branches of industry belonging to the monopolistic and the public sectors, which are central to economic development, the commodity called labor power receives a "political price." The "wage-scale partners" . . . find a broad zone of compromise, since increased labor costs can be passed on through prices and since there is a convergence of the middle-range demands of both sides on the state—demands that aim at increasing productivity, qualifying labor power, and improving the social situation of the workers. The monopolistic sector can, as it were, externalize class conflict.

The consequences of this immunization of the original conflict zone are: (*a*) disparate wage developments and/or a sharpening of wage disputes in the public service sector; (*b*) permanent inflation, with corresponding temporary redistribution of income to the disadvantage of unorganized workers and other marginal groups; (*c*) permanent crisis in government finances, together with public poverty (that is, impoverishment of public transportation, education, housing and health care); and (*d*) an inadequate adjustment of disproportional economic developments, sectoral (agriculture) as well as regional (marginal areas).

In the decades since World War II the most advanced capitalist countries have succeeded (the May 1968 events in Paris notwithstanding) in keeping class conflict latent in its decisive areas; in extending the business cycle and transforming periodic phases of capital devaluation into a permanent inflationary crisis with milder business fluctuations; and in broadly filtering the dysfunctional secondary effects of the averted economic crisis and scattering them over quasi-groups (such as consumers, schoolchildren and their parents, transportation users, the sick, the elderly, etc.) or over natural groups with little organization. In this way the social identity of classes breaks down and class consciousness is fragmented. The class compromise that has become part of the structure of advanced capitalism makes (almost) everyone at the same time both a participant and a victim. Of course, with the clearly (and increasingly) unequal distribution of wealth and power, it is important to distinguish between those belonging more to one than the other category.

The question whether, and if so how, the class structure and the principle of organization that developed in liberal capitalism have been altered through class compromise cannot be examined from the point of view of what role the principle of scarcity and the mechanism of money play at the level of the social system. For the monetization of landed property and of labor, and the "progressive monetization of use values and areas of life that were heretofore closed off to the money form," do not indicate conclusively that exchange has remained the dominant medium of control over social relations. Politically advanced claims to use values shed the commodity form, even if they are met with monetary rewards. What is decisive for class structure is whether the real income of the dependent worker is still based on an exchange relation, or whether production and appropriation of surplus value are limited and modified by relations of political power instead of depending on the market mechanism alone.

A theory of advanced capitalism must attempt to clarify the following questions. First:

> —do the structures of advanced capitalism provide space for an evolutionary self-transformation . . . of the contradiction of socialized production for non-generalizable goals?
> —if so, what developmental dynamic leads in this direction?
> —if not, in what crisis tendencies does the temporarily suppressed, but unresolved class antagonism express itself?

Then:

> —do the structures of advanced capitalism suffice to ward off economic crisis permanently?
> —if not, does economic crisis lead, as Marx expected, through social crisis to political crisis; in other words, can there be a revolutionary struggle on a world scale?
> —if not, whither is economic crisis displaced?

Finally:

> —does the displaced crisis retain the form of a system crisis, or must we reckon with different crisis tendencies that work together?

> —if the latter is the case, which crisis tendencies are transformed
> into deviant behavior, and in which social groups?
> —does the expected anomic potential permit directed political
> action, or does it lead rather to undirected dysfunctionalization
> of subsystems?

At the moment I can see no possibility of cogently deciding the question about the chances for a self-transformation of advanced capitalism. But I do not exclude the possibility that economic crisis can be permanently averted, although only in such a way that contradictory steering imperatives that assert themselves in the pressure for capital realization would produce a series of other crisis tendencies. The continuing tendency toward disturbance of capitalist growth can be administratively processed and transferred, by stages, through the political and into the socio-cultural system. I am of the opinion that the contradiction of socialized production for particular ends thereby directly takes on again a political form—naturally not that of political class warfare. Because in advanced capitalism politics takes place on the basis of a processed and repressed system crisis, there are constant disputes (among shifting coalitions and with fragmented class consciousness) that can alter the terms of class compromise. Thus, whether, and to what extent, the class structure is softened and the contradiction grounded in the capitalist principle of organization itself is affected, depends on the actual constellations of power.

I shall draw up next an abstract classification of the crisis tendencies that are *possible* in advanced capitalism. . . .

Chapter 3
A Classification of Possible Crisis Tendencies

We shall leave aside the global dangers that are *consequences of capitalist growth* and limit ourselves to *crisis tendencies specific to the system.* Crises can arise at different points; and the forms in which a crisis tendency manifests itself up to the point of its political eruption—that is, the point at which the existing political system is delegitimized—are just as diverse. I see four *possible* crisis tendencies, which are listed in the following table.

Point of Origin	*System Crisis*	*Identity Crisis*
Economic System	Economic Crisis	—
Political System	Rationality Crisis	Legitimation Crisis
Socio-Cultural System	—	Motivation Crisis

Economic Crisis Tendencies. The economic system requires an input of work and capital. The output consists in consumable values, which are distributed over time according to quantity and type among social strata. A crisis that derives from inadequate input is atypical of the capitalist mode of production. The disturbances of liberal capitalism were output crises. The crisis cycle again and again placed in question the distribution of values in conformity with the system. ("In conformity with the system" here means all patterns of distribution of burdens and rewards permissible within the range of variation of the legitimating value system.) If economic crisis tendencies persist in advanced capitalism, this indicates that government actions intervening in the realization process obey, no less than exchange processes, spontaneously working economic laws. Consequently, they are subject to the logic of the economic crisis as expressed in the law of the tendential fall of the rate of profit. According to this thesis, the state pursues the continuation of the politics of capital by other means. The altered forms of appearance (such as crises in government finances, permanent inflation, growing disparities between public poverty and private wealth, etc.) are explained by the fact that self-regulation of the realization process now also operates through legitimate power as a medium of control. But since the crisis tendency is still determined by the law of value—that is, the structurally necessary asymmetry in the exchange of wage labor for capital—the activity of the state cannot compensate for the tendency of the falling rate of profit. It can at best mediate it, that is, itself consummate it by political means. Thus, economic crisis tendency will also assert itself as a social crisis and lead to political struggles in which class opposition between owners of capital and masses dependent on wages again becomes manifest. According to another version, the state apparatus does not obey the logic of the law of value in an unplanned, nature-like manner, but consciously looks after the interests of united monopoly capitalists. This agency theory, tailored to advanced capitalism, conceives of the state, not as a blind organ of the realization process, but as a potent collective capitalist . . . who makes the accumulation of capital the substance of political planning.

Political Crisis Tendencies.   The political system requires an input of mass loyalty that is as diffuse as possible. The output consists in sovereignly executed administrative decisions. Output crises have the form of a *rationality crisis* in which the administrative system does not succeed in reconciling and fulfilling the imperatives received from the economic system. Input crises have the form of a *legitimation crisis*; the legitimizing system does not succeed in maintaining the requisite level of mass loyalty while the steering imperatives taken over from the economic system are carried through. Although both crisis tendencies arise in the political system, they differ in their form of appearance. The rationality crisis is a displaced systemic crisis which, like economic crisis, expresses the contradiction between socialized production for non-generalizable interests and steering imperatives. This crisis tendency is converted into the withdrawal of legitimation by way of a disorganization of the state apparatus. The legitimation crisis, by contrast, is directly an identity crisis. It does not proceed by way of endangering system integration, but results from the fact that the fulfillment of governmental planning tasks places in question the structure of the depoliticized public realm and, thereby, the formally democratic securing of the private autonomous disposition of the means of production.

We can speak of a rationality crisis in the strict sense only if it takes the place of economic crisis. In this case, the logic of problems of capital realization is not merely reflected in another steering medium, that of legitimate power; rather, the crisis logic is itself altered by the displacement of the contradictory steering imperatives from market commerce into the administrative system. This assertion is advanced in two versions. One version starts with the familiar thesis of the anarchy of commodity production that is built into market commerce. On the one hand, in advanced capitalism the need for administrative planning to secure the realization of capital grows. On the other hand, the private autonomous disposition of the means of production demands a limitation to state intervention and prohibits planned coordination of the contradictory interests of individual capitalists. Another version has been developed by Offe. While the state compensates for the weaknesses of a self-blocking economic system and takes over tasks complementary to the market, it is forced by the logic of its means of control to admit more and more foreign elements into the system. The problems of an economic system controlled by imperatives of capital realization cannot be taken over into the administratively controlled domain, and processed there, without the spread of orientations alien to the structure.

A rationality deficit in public administration means that the state apparatus cannot, under given boundary conditions, adequately steer the economic system. A legitimation deficit means that it is not possible by administrative means to maintain or establish effective normative structures to the extent required. During the course of capitalist development, the political system shifts its boundaries not only into the economic system but also into the socio-cultural system. While organizational rationality spreads, cultural traditions are undermined and weakened. The residue of tradition must, however, escape the administrative grasp, for traditions important for legitimation cannot be regenerated administratively. Furthermore, administrative manipulation of cultural matters has the unintended side effect of causing meanings and norms previously fixed by tradition and belonging to the *boundary* conditions of the political system to be publicly thematized. In this way, the scope of discursive will-formation expands—a process that shakes the structures of the depoliticized public realm so important for the continued existence of the system.

Socio-Cultural Crisis Tendencies. The socio-cultural system receives its input from the economic and political systems in the form of purchasable and collectively demandable goods and services, legal and administrative acts, public and social security, etc. Output crises in both of the other systems are also input disturbances in the socio-cultural system and translate into withdrawal of legitimation. The aforementioned crisis tendencies can break out only through the socio-cultural system. For the social integration of a society is dependent on the output of this system—directly on the motivations it supplies to the political system in the form of legitimation and indirectly on the motivations to perform it supplies to the educational and occupational systems. Since the socio-cultural system does not, in contrast to the economic system, organize its own input, there can be no socio-culturally produced input crisis. Crises that arise at this point are always output crises. We have to reckon with cultural crisis tendencies when the normative structures change, according to their inherent logic, in such a way that the complementarity between the requirements of the state apparatus and the occupational system, on the one hand, and the interpreted needs and legitimate expectations of members of society, on the other, is disturbed. Legitimation crises result from a need for legitimation that arises from changes in the political system (even when normative structures remain unchanged) and that cannot be met by the existing supply of legitimation. Motivational crises, on the other hand, are a result of changes in the socio-cultural system itself.

In advanced capitalism such tendencies are becoming apparent at the level of cultural tradition (moral systems, world-views) as well as at the level of structural change in the system of childrearing (school and family, mass media). In this way, the residue of tradition off which the state and the system of social labor lived in liberal capitalism is eaten away (stripping away traditionalistic padding), and core components of the bourgeois ideology become questionable (endangering civil and familial-professional privatism). On the other hand, the remains of bourgeois ideologies (belief in science, post-auratic art, and universalistic value systems) form a normative framework that is dysfunctional. Advanced capitalism creates "new" needs it cannot satisfy.

Our abstract survey of *possible* crisis tendencies in advanced capitalism has served an analytic purpose. I maintain that advanced-capitalist societies, assuming that they have not altogether overcome the susceptibility to crisis intrinsic to capitalism, are in danger from at least one of these possible crisis tendencies. It is a consequence of the fundamental contradiction of the capitalist system that, other factors being equal, either

- —the economic system does not produce the requisite quantity of consumable values, or;
- —the administrative system does not produce the requisite quantity of rational decisions, or;
- —the legitimation system does not provide the requisite quantity of generalized motivations, or;
- —the socio-cultural system does not generate the requisite quantity of action-motivating meaning.

The expression "the requisite quantity" refers to the extent, quality, and temporal dimension of the respective system performances (value, administrative decision, legitimation and meaning). Substitution relations between different system performances themselves are not excluded. Whether performances of the subsystems can be adequately operationalized and isolated and the critical need for system performances adequately specified is another question. This task may be difficult to solve for pragmatic reasons. But it is insoluble, in principle, only if levels of development of a social system—and in this way identity-guaranteeing limits of variation of its goal states—cannot be determined within the framework of a theory of social evolution.

Of course, the same macrophenomena may be an expression of different crisis tendencies. Each individual crisis argument, if it proves correct, is a sufficient explanation of a possible case of crisis. But in the explanation of actual cases of crisis, several arguments can supplement one another. I assert analytical completeness only for the crisis tendencies and not, of course, for the list of explanatory arguments, which I would like to discuss briefly below.

Crisis Tendencies	*Proposed Explanations*
Economic Crisis	a) the state apparatus acts as unconscious, nature-like executive organ of the law of value;

	b) the state apparatus acts as planning agent of united "monopoly capital."
Rationality Crisis	destruction of administrative rationality occurs through
	c) opposed interests of individual capitalists;
	d) the production (necessary for continued existence) of structures foreign to the system.
Legitimation Crisis	*e)* systematic limits;
	f) unintended side effects (politicization) of administrative interventions in the cultural tradition;
Motivation Crisis	*g)* erosion of traditions important for continued existence;
	h) overloading through universalistic value-systems ("new" needs).

Habermas and Modernity
Richard J. Bernstein

II

In *Knowledge and Human Interests* the outlines of Habermas's *first* systematic synthesis began to become clear. His major theses were succinctly summarized in the inaugural address he gave at Frankfurt University (published as an appendix to the book). He distinguished three non-reducible "quasi-transcendental" cognitive interests: the technical, the practical, and the emancipatory. These knowledge-constitutive interests served as the basis for three different forms of knowledge and three different types of discipline—each with its own distinctive methodological approach, object domain, and aims. Each of these cognitive interests is itself rooted in a dimension of human social existence: work, symbolic interaction, and power. "The approach to the empirical-analytic sciences incorporates a *technical* cognitive interest; that of the historical-hermeneutic sciences incorporates a *practical* one; and the approach of critically oriented sciences incorporates the *emancipatory* cognitive interest."[1]

By a technical cognitive interest, Habermas did *not* mean to suggest that the empirical-analytic sciences are to be understood as technical applied disciplines. Rather he stressed the *form* of these inquiries which require the isolation (constitution) of objects and events into dependent and independent variables, and the investigation of nomological regularities. This type of inquiry is based upon a model of negative feedback where prediction plays a central role, and where there are established procedures for the confirmation and falsification of empirical hypotheses and theories. It is because empirical-analytic science has this form that it lends itself to powerful technical application. There is a sense in which the pursuit of such science can be pure and disinterested. But the character of this disinterested pursuit of pure scientific research is itself determined by a "quasi-transcendental" technical cognitive interest. This is the type of scientific knowledge that logical positivists, logical empiricists, and philosophers of science in the analytic tradition were primarily interested in analyzing. Habermas was not denigrating or criticizing this form of knowledge. His point is that it is only *one* type of knowledge; it is not to be taken as the canonical standard for all forms of knowledge. This is why Habermas challenged positivistically minded philosophers of science who explicitly or implicitly presupposed that the empirical-analytical sciences provide *the* model for all legitimate knowledge, and dismissed all other claims to knowledge as pseudo-knowledge. This is also why Habermas was so sympathetic with philosophers (such as Gadamer) and social scientists influenced by the hermeneutical tradition of the *Geisteswissenschaften* who exposed the false "objectivism" and "scientism" of those who claimed that the empirical-analytic sciences are the proper measure and standard for all legitimate scientific inquiry.

Excerpts from Richard J. Bernstein. 1985. "Introduction" in *Habermas and Modernity,* Cambridge, MA: The MIT Press, pp. 8–25. Copyright © 1985 by Polity Press. Used by permission of the publisher.

The historical-hermeneutic disciplines are governed by a practical interest of furthering understanding (*Verstehen*).

> The *historical-hermeneutic* sciences gain knowledge in a different methodological framework. Here the meaning of the validity of propositions is not constituted in the frame of reference of technical control . . . Access to the facts is provided by the understanding of meaning . . . The verification of lawlike hypotheses in the empirical-analytic sciences has its counterpart in the interpretation of texts. Thus the rules of hermeneutics determine the possible meaning of the validity of statements of the cultural sciences.[2]

In using the expressions "technical" and "practical" to identify the first two cognitive interests, Habermas was self-consciously drawing upon the insights of the contemporary appropriation of Aristotle's distinction of *techne* and *praxis* (as in the works of Gadamer and Arendt). *Techne* names the type of purposive action exhibited in making or fabricating (*poesis*), while *praxis*—which for Aristotle is closely associated with *lexis* (speech)—names the distinctive form of human interaction exhibited in intersubjective communication.

Although Habermas has appropriated the insights of the hermeneutic tradition, especially insofar as it illuminates the distinctive character of understanding, interpretation, and communicative symbolic interaction, he has been sharply critical of its implicit historicism—its own hidden form of positivism. This hidden positivism becomes evident in hermeneutical and interpretative approaches to social phenomena when it is mistakenly claimed that we can understand and interpret forms of life and *bracket* critical rational evaluation of these forms of life. One of Habermas's most basic and challenging theses is that we cannot even make sense of the concepts of meaning, understanding, and interpretation unless we rationally evaluate the validity claims that are made by participants in these forms of life. We must be able to discriminate what participants themselves count as reasons for their actions, and this requires a performative attitude on our part where we assess what "they" count as good reasons for action with reference to "our" standards of rationality. . . . We are always in danger of being ethnocentric, but we never escape the horizon of rationality. It is a fiction to think that we can leap out of such a horizon and bracket all judgments of the validity claims made by participants in a form of life.

So, while Habermas does think that positivistically oriented philosophers of science have enabled us to grasp the important features of the empirical-analytic sciences, and hermeneutically oriented thinkers have illuminated the methodological framework of the historical-hermeneutical disciplines, both camps have been guilty of a false universalism. Implicitly or explicitly they valorize a distinctive form of knowledge as if it were the *only* or the most fundamental type of knowledge.

A critical social science is a dialectical synthesis of the empirical-analytic and the historical-hermeneutical disciplines. It incorporates the study of nomological regularities and the interpretation of the meaning of symbolic interaction. But, at the same time, it goes beyond both of these one-sided approaches. Habermas's synthesis comes into clear focus when we turn to the third type of cognitive interest: the emancipatory interest. This interest is at once derivative and the most fundamental cognitive interest. If we reflect upon the forms of knowledge and the disciplines guided by the technical and practical interests, we realize that they contain an internal demand for open, free, non-coercive communication. The validity of knowledge claims in empirical-analytic sciences and the historical-hermeneutical disciplines always allows of further testing, challenge, and rational reevaluation. This is the "truth" contained in Popper's call for constant and vigilant criticism, and it is paralleled by Gadamer's insistence that ongoing dialogue can never reach *final* closure. We can "derive" the emancipatory interest from what is presupposed by the technical and practical interests. But an emancipatory interest is basic in the sense that the interest of reason is in furthering the conditions for its full development; the demand for non-distorted communication becomes fully explicit. Furthermore, we can begin to grasp the practical implications of disciplines that are governed by an emancipatory interest. Non-distorted, reciprocal communication cannot exist unless we realize and institute the material social conditions that are required for mutual communication.

A critical social science which is at once empirical and interpretive has as its goal (as do the empirical-analytic sciences) the discovery of nomological knowledge. However

> A critical social science will not remain satisfied with this. It is concerned with going beyond this goal to determine when theoretical statements grasp invariant regularities of social action as such and when they express ideologically frozen relations of dependence that can in principle be transformed . . . Thus the level of [non-reflective] consciousness which is one of the initial conditions of such laws, can be transformed. Of course, to this end, a critically mediated knowledge of laws cannot through reflection alone render a law itself inoperative but can render it inapplicable.
>
> The methodological framework that determines the meaning of the validity of critical propositions of this category is established by the concept of *self-reflection.* The latter releases the subject from dependence on hypostatized powers. Self-reflection is determined by an emancipatory cognitive interest.[3]

III

When *Knowledge and Human Interests* was published it immediately attracted an enormous amount of critical attention. Habermas had touched upon fundamental issues that preoccupied thinkers in a variety of fields. He had advanced a provocative interpretation of a movement of thought that encompassed Kant, Fichte, Hegel, Marx, Dilthey, Peirce, Nietzsche, Comte, and Freud. He had integrated his narrative account with a systematic examination of the basic cognitive interests and the different forms of knowledge that they govern; and he explored the relation of these cognitive interests to the dimensions of social existence and action. Against positivists and historicists, he argued for a critical social science that redeems the "forgotten" experience of emancipatory self-reflection. One of the many reasons why Habermas's work attracted so much attention is that he not only argued for the contemporary relevance and validity of a major motif of the German idealistic tradition, but he sought to vindicate and revitalize a theme that has also been central for western philosophy. This theme is exemplified in the Platonic portrait of Socrates. Socrates in his words and deeds embodies the basic conviction that there is a type of self-reflection that can free us from the tyranny and bondage of false opinion (*doxa*). Habermas is also in the Socratic tradition in linking self-reflection with dialogue. For it is only in and through dialogue that one can achieve self-understanding. If dialogue is not to be an empty impotent ideal, then a transformation and reconstruction of the social institutions and practices in which dialogic communication is embedded becomes a practical imperative.

However, Habermas soon came to realize that the systematic program sketched in *Knowledge and Human Interests* was seriously flawed. I want to indicate four major flaws or inadequacies, and how Habermas has addressed these in his writings during the past fifteen years—culminating with the publication of *The Theory of Communicative Action*. In this book, and in the writings leading up to it, one can discern a new systematic synthesis—which preserves Habermas's earlier insights, corrects its inadequacies, and points to new directions for research.

The most glaring flaw, which Habermas himself recognized almost as soon as he completed *Knowledge and Human Interests,* goes to the heart of his analysis. There is a radical ambiguity in the basic concepts of reflection and self-reflection. There are at least two logically distinct concepts of reflection which needed to be carefully distinguished (and which Habermas had fused together). The first concept derives from the Kantian sense of the self-reflection of reason upon the conditions of its employment. This is the core of Kant's own understanding of *Critique*—where reason can self-reflexively come to grasp the universal and necessary conditions for the very possibility of theoretical knowledge, practical reason, and teleological and aesthetic judgment. But the second concept of self-reflection is one that aims at freeing a subject from dependence on hypostatized powers—"from ideological frozen forms of dependence that can in principle be transformed." This is the emphatic emancipatory sense of self-reflection. We can also find this concept in Kant, especially in his understanding of "What is Enlightenment." This concept of emancipatory self-reflection is subtly transformed in Hegel and Marx. Although these two concepts of self-reflection are logically distinct, they are intimately related. Emancipatory self-reflection is dependent on giving a rational reconstruction of the universal conditions for reason. To use the Kantian analogy, only when we understand the nature and limits of theoretical and practical reason does it become intelligible to specify what must be done to achieve autonomy and enlightenment.

Habermas fails not only to make this crucial distinction fully explicit in *Knowledge and Human Interests,* he slides from one pole to the other. Thus when he proposes that Marx's critique of ideology and Freud's therapeutic psychoanalysis are models of critical sciences based upon self-reflection, he emphasizes the second sense of emancipatory self-reflection—without however fully explaining its normative foundations; without adequately elucidating the dialogical character of communicative rationality that is presupposed by them.

The second major flaw is closely related to the first one. When Habermas classified the knowledge-constitutive interests as "quasi-transcendental" he was really identifying a tangled problem, not offering a solution. These cognitive interests are not merely contingent or accidental. They are basic and unavoidable, rooted in what we are as human beings. Consequently, they approximate the epistemological status of transcendental claims. But for Kant—and for the tradition of transcendental philosophy he helped to initiate—transcendental claims are *a priori* and must be distinguished from what is *a posteriori* and empirical. For Kant, we cannot justify the universality and necessity of synthetic *a priori* judgments unless we "purify" them of empirical content.

Habermas has always been sympathetic with the idea that we can identify basic structures, rules, and categories that are presupposed by reason and communicative action. But he has also been extremely skeptical that such an inquiry can be carried out by pure transcendental philosophy. A critical social science, which develops genuine scientific empirical hypotheses, demands a break with this legacy of pure *a priori* transcendental philosophy. But in *Knowledge and Human Interests* Habermas had not yet shown us how we can at once justify the claim that there are unavoidable necessary universal conditions of communicative action and rationality, and maintain that these can be discovered and warranted in a scientific manner.

We can approach the basic issue here from a slightly different perspective. In Habermas's reply to his critics (included in this volume) he begins by sketching two extreme responses to the modern experience of radical pluralism: pure historicism and pure transcendentalism. He indicates the difficulties of both extremes—how they lead us to a "double bind." In *Knowledge and Human Interests* he was already aware of this "double bind," and it was clear he was seeking to escape from it. But he did not adequately show how this is to be accomplished. Yet without showing a "third way," his systematic interplay of philosophy and social science was in danger of foundering.

The third flaw radicalizes the first two difficulties. For Habermas, this is the most basic inadequacy of his first systematic synthesis. It is the key for understanding what has been called his "linguistic turn"—a shift required not because of contemporary fashions but necessitated in order to justify his most fundamental intuitions. The methodological approach in *Knowledge and Human Interests* was oriented by epistemological concerns. But an epistemological orientation is itself dependent of what Habermas now calls "the philosophy of consciousness" and "the philosophy of the subject." It has its modern roots in the Cartesian turn to subjectivity. In German idealism and Husserl's phenomenology, "consciousness" and the "subject" still have primary status. Habermas came to realize that this orientation—even as modified in *Knowledge and Human Interests*—obscures and even blocks the way to grasping the intrinsic intersubjective and dialogical character of communicative action. Even the expression "intersubjectivity" carries the burden of the philosophy of the subject, insofar as it suggests that the main problem is to understand how self-sufficient subjects can be interrelated, rather than focusing attention on how subjects are constituted and formed in and through their social interactions. Habermas became acutely aware of how even in Hegel and Marx (and in his own early writings) there was an unresolved tension between the philosophy of consciousness and the philosophy of the subject on the one hand, and the need to do full justice to the integrity of the intersubjectivity of communicative action which always involves a genuine *plurality* of actors.

The fourth shortcoming in *Knowledge and Human Interests* can be seen as a "promissory note" which had not yet been redeemed. When Habermas adumbrated the physiognomy of a critical social science, he directed his attention primarily to the idea or the possibility (in the Kantian sense) of such a science, not to its *substantive* development. The use he made of Marx's critique of ideology and his interpretation of Freudian psychoanalysis highlighted the methodological character of a critical social science. Considering the intellectual climate of the time, we can sympathetically understand the rationale for this emphasis. Not only had the legacies of positivism and historicism called into question the very possibility of a critical social science, but as we noted earlier, the older generation of critical theorists were also voicing their skepticism about the real historical possibility of a critical social science. One needed to establish a clearing for, to show the conceptual possibility of, a critical social science in the face of these multifaceted challenges. Here, too, a formal analogy with Kant may be helpful. When Kant began his critical project and took up the question of metaphysics, he realized that one first needed to ask whether such a "science" is possible and how it is possible. So Habermas's first task was to show the viability of a critical social science. But he had promised much more. Even if one were persuaded that such a scientific research program is feasible, one might remain skeptical about its substantive realization. There were suggestions about how such a research program might be developed but he had not yet made much progress in its systematic articulation. *Knowledge and Human Interests* was a prolegomenon to a future critical scientific analysis of society.

IV

Habermas's self-criticism is the mark of a genuine dialectical thinker. When difficulties have been pointed out by his critics, or when he has come to appreciate deficiencies of his analyses, he has confronted them directly. He does this in a spirit of *rejecting* what is no longer defensible, *preserving* what he still deems valid, and *moving beyond* earlier formulations to new frontiers. This is why one can detect continuities and discontinuities throughout his intellectual journey. Habermas's work during the past fifteen years can be viewed from the perspective of addressing the four flaws that I have outlined of his first systematic synthesis. *The Theory of Communicative Action* draws together the many strands of his thinking into a new, more detailed, and much more persuasively argued systematic whole. I want to indicate some of the major aspects of his current position by showing how he meets the difficulties that I have outlined. This will enable a reader to understand the context for the current discussions of Habermas on modernity and postmodernity.

Because the first two problems are so closely intertwined, I will discuss them together. In discriminating the two concepts of self-reflection, I indicated (as does Habermas himself) that emancipatory self-reflection is dependent upon giving a rational reconstruction of the universal conditions of reason. Habermas has argued that the legacy of what is sound in the Kantian project of transcendental philosophy is to be found in what he now calls the "reconstructive sciences." These are sciences that elucidate the depth, grammar, and rules of "pre-theoretical" knowledge. These reconstructive sciences must be carefully distinguished from empirical-analytic sciences typified by contemporary natural sciences. Chomsky's generative grammar, Piaget's theory of cognitive development, and Kohlberg's theory of moral development are *examples* of reconstructive sciences. In each case—to use Ryle's distinction between "knowing-how" and "knowing-that"—the aim is to provide explicit theoretical knowledge ("knowing-that") of implicit pre-theoretical "knowing-how." These sciences study a symbolically structured social reality. The rational reconstructions advanced by these sciences are directed toward making explicit universal species competences (e.g., the competence to speak and understand a language). Like all scientific disciplines the hypotheses they advance are fallible. But the hypothetical quality of such reconstructive sciences is not incompatible with the aim of discovering the universal conditions presupposed by and required to perform the relevant competence. The most important methodological point, however, is that reconstructive sciences are *empirical* (not disguised forms of transcendental philosophy). They are themselves subject to appropriate canons of confirmation and falsification. They are to be critically evaluated by their empirical success in substantiating their claims to identify species competences and to account for the rules and conditions that these competences presuppose. Unlike the empirical-analytic sciences that seek to *replace* "pretheoretical knowledge" with a more adequate scientific explanation of the world, reconstructive sciences explain and clarify the basic grammar and rules of our "pretheoretical knowledge." The theory of communicative action and rationality is a reconstructive science. But it has a more universal thrust than linguistics and current theories of psychological and moral development. It seeks to isolate, identify, and clarify the conditions required for human communication. This reconstructive science, which Habermas also calls "universal pragmatics," enables us to specify the contributions and limitations of reconstructive sciences that have more restricted domains. All human symbolic competences presuppose the universal species competence of communication.

We can now see how this new methodological analysis of the character of reconstructive sciences addresses the first two flaws described above. Habermas does want to preserve what he takes to be sound in the Kantian program of transcendental philosophy—in the program of reason reflecting on the universal conditions required for its employment. Yet he also wants to break with the notion that such an enquiry is *a priori*. Such an inquiry is hypothetical, fallible, empirical—in short, it is scientific and must satisfy the procedures for the acceptance and rejection of scientific hypotheses. The reconstructive science of a universal pragmatics enables us to understand the foundation or ground for emancipatory critique (the second concept of self-reflection). For it shows that emancipatory critique does not rest upon arbitrary norms which we "choose"; rather it is grounded in the very structures of intersubjective communicative competences. One reason why many critics, even sympathetic critics, of Habermas have been perplexed by his "linguistic turn" is because during the past fifteen years he has been more concerned with elaborating, justifying, and working out the details of this ambitious research program of a theory of communicative action or universal pragmatics than with engaging in the practice of emancipatory critique. But the rationale for this emphasis should now be clear. The very intelligibility of emancipatory critique—if it is to escape the charge of being arbitrary and relativistic—requires a clarification and justification of its normative foundations. This is what the theory of communicative action seeks to establish.

Habermas no longer speaks of "quasi-transcendental" cognitive interests. This has led some to think that he has simply abandoned the major systematic theses of *Knowledge and Human Interests.* It is true he has sought to purge his thinking of the vestiges of the philosophy of consciousness and the philosophy of the subject. But the insights contained in his original trichotomy of human interests are conceptually transformed in a new register within the context of his theory of communicative action. The distinction between the technical interest on the one hand, and the practical and the emancipatory interests on the other hand, is itself based upon a categorial distinction of purposive-rational action and communicative (symbolic) action. This distinction is not abandoned in Habermas's universal pragmatics. On the contrary, it is refined and developed in far more detail than in his earlier work. Furthermore, from the perspective of the theory of communicative action, we gain a clearer understanding of the conceptual space and foundations for what Habermas called the practical and emancipatory cognitive interests.

I have already anticipated how Habermas meets the third difficulty. The theory of communicative action is no longer wedded to the philosophy of consciousness and the philosophy of a self-sufficient subject. Its primary source of inspiration is the philosophy of language, specifically speech act theory (which Habermas significantly modifies and refines). Habermas fully realizes that the range of communicative interactions is broader than that of explicit speech acts. Nevertheless, by approaching communication from the perspective of speech we can gain an understanding of the distinctive features of communication. One primary reason—perhaps *the* primary reason—for "the linguistic turn" is that it no longer entraps us in the *monological* perspective of the philosophy of the subject. Communicative action is intrinsically *dialogical.* The starting point for an analysis of the pragmatics of speech is the situation of a speaker *and* a hearer who are oriented to *mutual* reciprocal understanding; a speaker and a hearer who have the capacity to take an affirmative or negative stance when a validity claim is challenged.

Although the details of Habermas's theory of communicative action are subtle, complex, and controversial, we can sketch some of its leading ideas. (Most of the articles included in this volume touch on various aspects of it.) Communicative action is a distinctive type of social interaction—the type of action oriented to mutual understanding. It must be distinguished from other types of social action and non-social action which are oriented to "success," to the efficient achievement of ends. These latter action-types exhibit the form of purposive-rational action where we seek to achieve an end or goal by appropriate means.

However "the goal of coming to an understanding [*Verständigung*] is to bring about an agreement [*Einverständis*] that terminates in the intersubjective mutuality of reciprocal understanding, shared knowledge, mutual trust, and accord with one another. Agreement is based on recognition of the corresponding validity claims of comprehensibility, truth, truthfulness and rightness."[4] All communicative action takes place against a background consensus. But this consensus can break down or be challenged by one of the participants in the communicative context. Habermas argues that anyone acting communicatively *must,* in performing a speech action, raise universal validity claims and suppose that such claims can be vindicated or redeemed. As indicated in the above quotation there are four types of validity claims: comprehensibility, truth, truthfulness (sincerity), and normative rightness. These are not always thematic but they are implicit in every speech act. In most empirical situations we resolve our conflicts and disagreements by a variety of strategies and techniques. But to resolve a breakdown in communication, we can move to a level of *discourse* and argumentation where we explicitly seek to warrant the validity claims that have been called into question. Ideally, the only force that should prevail in such a discourse is the "force of the better argument." Habermas, of course, is aware that he is describing an "ideal type," that in many empirical contexts we do not engage in such uncoerced argumentation. We break off communication, or seek strategically to manipulate others. But his major point is that however we in fact resolve disputes and breakdowns in communication, universal validity claims "are set in the general structures of possible communication," in "the intersubjective structures of social reproduction." This is true not only in our everyday "pretheoretical" communicative interactions, but also in our theoretical, practical, and aesthetic discourses.

The point that Habermas is making has long been recognized in the realm of scientific discourse. When there are serious conflicts between competing scientific theories and hypotheses, research programs, or paradigms, we are committed to resolving such differences through nonmanipulative and noncoercive argumentation. As Habermas interprets recent work in the philosophy of science, he does not believe that it significantly challenges this ideal. Rather it teaches us that there may be no algorithms for resolving scientific disputes, that even what constitutes "the better argument" may itself be open to rational dispute. The novel feature of his theory of communicative action is that he claims that the same appeal to redeeming validity claims through appropriate types of argumentation is implicit in practical (moral and legal) disputes as well as in disputes about aesthetic judgments. In this sense, Habermas defends a strong "cognitivist" thesis. No dispute about a validity claim is beyond rational argumentation by the participants involved. But what is most fundamental for Habermas—the basic intuition which he seeks to develop systematically—is that this anticipation and presupposition of noncoercive and nondistortive argumentation is "built into" our everyday, pretheoretical communicative interactions.

There is a danger that, with a social theorist whose thought is as complex and as textured as is Habermas's, we can lose sight of his overall vision when pursuing details. Habermas has been extremely eloquent in expressing the vision that informs his detailed analyses. Speaking of practical discourse, he tells us:

> In practical discourse we thematize one of the validity claims that underlie speech as its *validity basis.* In action oriented to reaching understanding validity claims are "always already" implicitly raised. These universal claims (to the comprehensibility of the symbolic expression, the truth of the propositional content, the truthfulness of the intentional expression, and the rightness of the speech act with respect to existing norms and values) are set in the general structures of possible communication. In these validity claims communication theory can locate a gentle, but obstinate, a never silent although seldom redeemed claim to reason, a claim that must be recognized de facto whenever and wherever there is to be consensual action.[5]

In a similar spirit, he writes:

> Again and again this claim [to reason] is silenced, and yet in fantasies and deeds it develops a stubbornly transcending power, because it is renewed with each act of unconstrained understanding, with each moment of living together in solidarity, of successful individuation, and of saving emancipation.[6]

These passages point to what I earlier called the diachronic dimension of communicative rationality. Thus far I have concentrated on the synchronic dimension of the theory of communicative action and rationality, on what is presupposed and anticipated in communication, on what is "always already" implicit in this type of interaction. But the theory would be radically incomplete if we did not grasp how different types of action and rationality are embedded in historical social institutions and practices, how they change and develop in historical time. This is what Habermas calls "rationalization" processes. The expression in English can be misleading because we frequently think of "rationalization" as an activity that disguises or conceals underlying motives and intentions. This common use of "rationalization" has been influenced by the legacy of the "hermeneutics of suspicion." But by "rationalization" Habermas means increasing the rationality or reasonableness of a form of social action. Nevertheless the meanings of the rationalization of purposive-rational actions and communicative actions are categorically distinct.

> *Purposive-rational actions* can be regarded under two different aspects—the empirical efficiency of technical means and the consistency of choice between suitable means. Actions and action systems can be rationalized in both respects. The rationality of means requires technically utilizable, empirical knowledge. The rationality of decisions requires the explication and inner consistency of value systems and decision maxims, as well as the correct derivation of acts of choice.[7]

These rationalization processes closely approximate what Weber meant by *Zweckrationalität*—the form of rationalization process which he took to be basic to modernization. In the twentieth century the advance of the empirical-analytic sciences and the explosive development of decision and game theory have increased our understanding of this form of rationalization.

But the rationalization of communicative action is radically and categorically different.

> Rationalization here means extirpating those relations of force that are inconspicuously set in the very structures of communication and that prevent conscious settlement of conflicts, and consensual regulation of conflicts by means of interpsychic as well as interpersonal communication. Rationalization means overcoming such systematically distorted communication in which the action-supporting consensus concerning the reciprocally raised validity claims —especially consensus concerning the truthfulness of intentional expressions and the rightness of underlying norms—can be sustained in appearance only, that is counterfactually.[8]

When we grasp the import of Habermas's theory of communicative action, and especially the way in which he categorically distinguishes the two different types of rationalization processes, we can discern how he rectifies the fourth deficiency, how he substantively develops a research program for a critical social science. Here too the details are enormously complex, but I want to indicate briefly some of the major strands that he weaves together.

At the most fundamental level, Habermas argues that a theory of communicative action and an adequate sociological theory that can explain the dynamics of social processes are *not* two independent endeavors. They are conceptually and inextricably related to each other. One of the major goals of *The Theory of Communicative Action* is to explain and demonstrate this. The "rationality debates" that have so preoccupied contemporary philosophers lead us to develop a sociological theory where we can discriminate the different forms of rationalization processes. And no adequate sociological theory can escape confronting the question of rationality. Once again, but in a far more detailed and penetrating manner than previously, Habermas argues against the bias that we can "simply" describe, explain, and understand social forms of life without explicitly or implicitly evaluating the rationality of social action and action systems.

This dialectical mediation reflects Habermas's long-standing conviction that critical theory must fuse together both philosophical and scientific-empirical dimensions of analysis. In *The Theory of Communicative Action* he supports this basic thesis by showing how Marx, Weber, Durkheim, Mead, Lukács, Horkheimer, Adorno, and Parsons can all be seen as making contributions to (or are blinded from aspects of) a comprehensive sociological theory grounded in a full understanding of rationality and rationalization processes.

Given this basic approach, Habermas explores the concepts of system and life-world. Retrospectively we can see how much of the sociological tradition has gravitated to these two competing orientations. There have always been social scientists who have argued that the proper study of society is one that studies society as a complex system, where there are underlying interacting structures, systematic imperatives, and dynamic forms of systemic integration and/or breakdown. In its extreme form a systems theory approach diminishes the significance of the role of social actors. They are seen as "place-holders" within a total system. But the other pole in sociological analyses gives primacy to the creative role of social actors, and the ways in which they construct, negotiate, and reconstruct the social meanings of their world. In its extreme form, advocates of this orientation claim that the very concepts of system and structure are reified fictions.

In *The Theory of Communicative Action* Habermas forges a dialectical synthesis of these "competing" orientations. He wants to do justice to the integrity of the life-world and social systems, and to show how each presupposes the other. We cannot understand the character of the life-world unless we understand the social systems that shape it, and we cannot understand social systems unless we see how they arise out of activities of social agents. The synthesis of system and life-world orientations is integrated with Habermas's delineation of different forms of rationality and rationalization: systems rationality is a type of purposive-rational rationality, life-world rationality is communicative rationality. Furthermore, Habermas's diagnosis of the dominating trends in the recent history of industrialized societies enables him to formulate what Wellmer calls "the paradox of rationalization" in a new way. As Wellmer succinctly phrases it:

> The *paradox* of rationalization [is] that a rationalization of the life-world [is] the *precondition* and the *starting point* for a process of systemic rationalization and differentiation, which then [becomes] more and more autonomous vis-à-vis the normative constraints embodied in the life-world, until in the end the systematic imperatives begin to instrumentalize the life-world and threaten to destroy it (see p. 56).

In Habermas's telling phrase, we are threatened today by the "colonization of the life-world" by systemic rationalization processes.

This brings us to the real "pay off" of Habermas's careful and elaborate reconstruction of a sociological orientation grounded in a theory of rationality. Strictly speaking, "the paradox of rationalization" is *not* a paradox. There is no logical, conceptual, or historical *necessity* that systemic imperatives *must* destroy the life-world. The dialectic of Enlightenment *does* highlight what is characteristic of contemporary industrialized societies—the real threats they pose to the communicative integrity of the life-world. What has happened in modern society (and continues to happen at an alarming rate) is a *selective* process of rationalization—where purposive-rational rationalization prevails, encroaches upon, and deforms the life-world of everyday life. As Wellmer tells us:

> Against Weber and Horkheimer/Adorno . . . Habermas objects that this paradox of rationalization does *not* express an internal *logic* (or dialectic) of modern rationalization processes; it is strictly speaking, not a paradox of *rationalization,* if we use this term in the broad sense of a post-traditional conception of rationality which, as Habermas shows, we have to substitute for Weber's restricted conception of rationality. From the perspective of an action theory in Weber's sense, then, there would neither be a paradox of rationalization nor a "dialectic of enlightenment"; rather it would be more adequate to speak of a "selective" process of rationalization, where the selective character of this process may be *explained* by the peculiar restrictions put upon communicative rationalization by the boundary conditions and the dynamics of a capitalist process of production (p. 56).

This thesis about the *selectivity* of rationalization processes is Habermas's most important substantive sociological claim. To speak of "selectivity" entails that there are alternative possibilities. All of the lines of Habermas's reflections on modernity lead to, and are intended to clarify and support, this thesis. We can appreciate anew

Habermas's fusing of the theory of communicative action and rationality and his sociological perspective on modernity. It is only when we grasp the different forms of action and rationality that we can clarify and justify the claim that rationalization processes can take a variety of historical forms. We can see through and critically evaluate claims that there is an *inevitable* logic of modernization. Furthermore we can explain why there has been a "colonization of the life-world" by analyzing the causes and dynamics of systemic rationalization and differentiation. We can not only explain, but also diagnose the "pathologies of modernity." But what is most crucial is that this explanatory-diagnostic function of Habermas's theoretical perspective also helps to illuminate our future prospects—not in the sense of predicting the future, but rather by conceptually highlighting the need to further the communicative rationality of the life-world and achieving a proper balance between the legitimate demands of systemic rationalization and the communicative rationalization of the life world.

We can even approach the study of new social movements from this communicative-theoretical perspective: movements such as the ecological, antinuclear, women's, and liberation movements—and even neoconservative movements so dominant today. They can be seen (even when misguided) as defensive reactions to preserve the integrity of the communicative structures of the life-world against the impingements and distortions imposed upon it by the processes of systemic rationalization.

Habermas does think that Weber (building on an insight of Kant) was right in distinguishing the *differentiation* of three cultural spheres: science, morality (including law), and art. He is deeply suspicious of those romantic and neoromantic tendencies which lead us to believe that it is still possible to imagine a "new" organic wholeness where all differentiations are overcome (*Aufgehoben*), where human beings are not only reconciled with each other, but also with nature. But he also seeks to root out the bias that cultural differentiation *must* inevitably result in unresolved alienation and reification. There is a logic to social evolution *in the sense* that once social learning processes are achieved we cannot forget them unless we consciously or unconsciously repress them. For Habermas it is an achievement of modernity to differentiate the cultural spheres or worlds of science, morality, and art. But we can accept this differentiation and still seek new ways to integrate and harmonize our everyday lives. We can still seek to restore a proper balance between the legitimate demands of social systems and the life-world. The prospect of furthering the communicative rationalization of our everyday life-world is still a real historical possibility.

Habermas categorically rejects a utopianism that tempts us to think there is a dialectical necessity which inevitably leads to the "good society." He also rejects the mirror image of this conception which calls for a total break with history, or which "places" utopian aspirations in a Never Never Land of fantasy. The utopian aspirations of Marxism and critical theory are transformed. There are rational grounds for social hope. This has nothing to do with either optimism or pessimism about our future prospects. There is no guarantee that what is still possible will be actualized. But against all the varieties of "totalizing critique" which seduce us into despair and defeatism, Habermas takes seriously the role of the philosopher as a "guardian of reason." He is a strong and powerful voice reminding us that the practical need to embody and nurture communicative rationality in our everyday social practices has "a stubbornly transcending power, because it is renewed with each act of unconstrained understanding, with each moment of living together in solidarity, of successful individuation, and of saving emancipation." As he tells us, "Communicative reason operates in history as an avenging force."[9]. . .

Notes

1. *Knowledge and Human Interests,* p. 308.
2. Ibid., p. 307.
3. Ibid., p. 310.
4. Jürgen Habermas, "What is Universal Pragmatics?" in *Communication and the Evolution of Society* (Boston, 1974), p. 3.
5. Jürgen Habermas, "Historical Materialism and the Development of Normative Structures," in *Communication and the Evolution of Society* (Boston, 1979), p. 97.
6. Jürgen Habermas, "A Reply to my Critics," in *Habermas: Critical Debates,* ed. John B. Thompson and David Held (London, 1982), p. 221.
7. Jürgen Habermas, "Historical Materialism," p. 117.
8. Ibid., pp. 119–120.
9. "A Reply to my Critics," loc. cit., p. 227.

Crisis Tendencies, Legitimation and the State
David Held

Habermas's writings on advanced capitalist societies represent an important contribution to social theory. In conjunction with his colleagues he has helped to direct our understanding of the organisational principles of society away from old dogmas—dogmas asserting, for instance, that the state is merely 'a system of coercion to support the dominant class' or that it is 'a coalition balancing all legitimate interests'. Since the advantages of Habermas's work over less sophisticated approaches have been succinctly emphasised elsewhere, I shall focus this essay, first, on a brief account of his work and, second, on a number of problems which, I think, weaken its utility and scope.

In *Strukturwandel der Öffentlichkeit* (1962) and *Toward a Rational Society* (a selection of essays written in the latter half of the 1960s but not published in English until 1970), Habermas documents the growth of large-scale economic and commercial organisations, the increasing interdependence of science, technology and industry, the increasing interdependence of state and society, and the extension of instrumental reason (a concern with the adequacy of means to pre-given goals) to ever more areas of life. These developments, he argues, have created a new constellation of economics and politics: 'politics is no longer *only* a phenomenon of the superstructure'.[1] The expansion of the state—symptomatic of the crisis tendencies of capitalist society—leads to an ever greater involvement of administrators and technicians in social and economic affairs. It also leads, in conjunction with the fusion of science, technology and industry, to the emergence of a new form of ideology: ideology is no longer simply based on notions of just exchange but also on a technocratic justification of the social order. A perspective emerges in which political decisions *seem*, as Habermas puts it, 'to be determined by the logic of scientific-technical progress'.[2] Practical issues, underpinned by particular historical class interests, are defined as technical problems: politics becomes the sphere for the technical elimination of dysfunctions and the avoidance of risks that threaten 'the system'.

In his more recent works, *Legitimation Crisis* (1973) and *Communication and the Evolution of Society* (1979), Habermas seeks to analyse in greater detail changes in contemporary society. He does so in the context of the development of a theory of social evolution. Part of this project involves the identification of (a) the 'possibility spaces', i.e. the potential avenues of development, which a society's 'core structures' create; and (b) the crisis tendencies to which such structures are vulnerable. Although Habermas is concerned to investigate pre-civilisation (primitive communities) and traditional societies, his main focus hitherto has been on modern capitalism. He explores, in particular, the way 'advanced' (or, as he sometimes calls it, 'late' or 'organised') capitalism is susceptible to 'legitimation crisis'—the withdrawal from the existing order of the support or loyalty of the mass of the population as their motivational commitment to its normative basis is broken. It is his contention that the seeds of a new evolutionary development—the overcoming of capitalism's underlying class contradiction—can be uncovered in this and other related crisis tendencies.[3]

Habermas first provides an analysis of liberal capitalism which follows Marx closely. He explicates the organisational principle of this type of society—the principle which circumscribes the 'possibility spaces' of the system—as the *relationship of wage labour and capital*. The fundamental contradiction of capitalism is formulated as that between social production and private appropriation, i.e. social production for the enhancement of particular interests. But, as Habermas stresses, a number of questions have to be posed about the contemporary significance of Marx's views. Have events in the last hundred years altered the mode in which the fundamental contradiction of capitalism affects society's dynamic? Has the logic of crisis changed from the path of crisis growth, unstable accumulation, to something fundamentally different? If so, are there consequences for patterns of social struggle? These questions informed Habermas's early writings. However, the way he addresses them from *Legitimation Crisis* onwards represents a marked elaboration of his earlier views.

The model of advanced capitalism Habermas uses follows many well-known recent studies.[4] He begins by delineating three basic sub-systems, the economic, the political-administrative and the socio-cultural. The economic sub-system is itself understood in terms of three sectors: a public sector and two distinct types of private sector. The public sector, i.e. industries such as armaments, is orientated towards state production and consumption. Within the private sector a distinction is made between a sector which is still orientated towards market competition and an oligopolistic sector which is much freer of market constraints. Advanced capitalism, it is claimed, is characterised by capital concentration and the spread of oligopolistic structures.

Habermas contends that crises specific to the current development of capitalism can arise at different points. These he lists as follows:

Point of origin (sub-systems)	System crisis	Identity crisis
Economic	Economic crisis	—
Political	Rationality crisis	Legitimation crisis
Socio-cultural	—	Motivation crisis

His argument is that late-capitalist societies are endangered from at least one of four possible crisis tendencies. It is a consequence of the fundamental contradiction of capitalist society (social production versus private appropriation) that, other factors being equal, there is either: an economic crisis because the 'requisite quantity' of consumable values is not produced; or a rationality crisis because the 'requisite quantity' of rational decisions is not forthcoming; or a legitimation crisis because the 'requisite quantity' of 'generalised motivations' is not generated; or a motivational crisis because the 'requisite quantity' of 'action-motivating meaning' is not created. The expression 'the requisite quantity' refers to the extent and quality of the respective sub-system's products: 'value, administrative decision, legitimation and meaning'.[5]

The reconstruction of developmental tendencies in capitalism is pursued in each of these dimensions of possible crisis. For each sphere, theorems concerning the nature of crisis are discussed, theories which purport to explain crisis are evaluated, and possible strategies of crisis avoidance are considered. 'Each individual crisis argument, if it proves correct, is a sufficient explanation of a possible case of crisis.' But in the explanation of actual cases of crises, Habermas stresses, 'several arguments can supplement one another'.[6]

At the moment, in Habermas's opinion, there is no way of cogently deciding questions about the chances of the transformation of advanced capitalism. He does not exclude the possibility that economic crises can be permanently averted; if such is the case, however, contradictory steering imperatives, which assert themselves in the pressure of capital utilisation, produce a series of other crisis tendencies. That is not to say economic crises will be avoided, but that there is, as Habermas puts it, no 'logically necessary' reason why the system cannot mitigate the crisis effects as they manifest themselves in one sub-system. The consequences of controlling crises in one sub-system are achieved only at the expense of *displacing and transforming* the contradictions into another. What is presented is a typology of crisis tendencies, a logic of their development and, ultimately, a postulation that the system's identity can only be preserved at the cost of individual autonomy, i.e. with the coming of a totally administered world in which dissent is successfully repressed and crises are defused. Since Habermas regards legitimation and motivation crises as the distinctive or central types of crisis facing advanced capitalist societies, I should like to give a brief *résumé of them.*

Increased state activity in economic and other social realms is one of the major characteristics of contemporary capitalism. In the interests of avoiding economic crisis, government and the state shoulder an increasing share of the costs of production. But the state's decisions are not based merely on economic considerations. While on the one hand, the state has the task of sustaining the accumulation process, on the other it must maintain a certain level of 'mass loyalty'. In order for the system to function, there must be a general compliance with the laws, rules, etc. Although this compliance can be secured to a limited extent by coercion, societies claiming to operate according to the principles of bourgeois democracy depend more on the existence of a widespread belief that the system adheres to the principles of equality, justice and freedom. Thus the capitalist state must act to support the accumulation process and at the same time act, if it is to protect its image as fair and just, to conceal what it is doing. If mass loyalty is threatened, a tendency towards a legitimation crisis is established.

As the administrative system expands in late capitalism into areas traditionally assigned to the private sphere, there is a progressive demystification of the nature-like process of social fate. The state's very intervention in the economy, education, etc., draws attention to issues of choice, planning and control. The 'hand of the state' is more visible and intelligible than 'the invisible hand' of liberal capitalism. More and more areas of life are seen by the general population as politicised, i.e. as falling within its (via the government's) potential control. This development, in turn, stimulates ever greater demands on the state, for example for participation and consultation over decisions. If the administrative system cannot fulfil these demands within the potentially legitimisable alternatives available to it, while at the same time avoiding economic crisis, that is, 'if governmental crisis management fails . . . the penalty . . . is withdrawal of legitimation'.[7] The underlying cause of the legitimation crisis is, Habermas states rather bluntly, the contradiction between class interests: 'in the final analysis . . . *class structure* is the source of the legitimation deficit'.[8] The state must secure the loyalty of one class while systematically acting to the advantage of another. As the state's activity expands and its role in controlling social reality becomes more transparent, there is a greater danger that this asymmetrical relation will be exposed. Such exposure would only increase the demands on the system. The state can ignore these demands only at the peril of further demonstrating its non-democratic nature.

So far the argument establishes only that the advanced capitalist state might experience legitimation problems. Is there any reason to expect that it will be confronted by a legitimation crisis? It can be maintained that since the Second World War, Western capitalism has been able to buy its way out of its legitimation difficulties (through fiscal policy, the provision of services, etc.). While demand upon the state may outstrip its ability to deliver the goods, thus creating a crisis, it is not necessary that this occurs. In order to complete his argument, therefore, and to show—as he seeks to—that 'social identity' crises are the central form of crises confronting advanced capitalism, Habermas must demonstrate that needs and expectations are being produced (on the part of at least a section of the population) which will 'tax the state's legitimizing mechanisms beyond their capacity'.

Habermas's position, in essence, is that the general development of late capitalism, and in particular the increasing incursion of the state into formerly private realms, has significantly altered the patterns of motivation formation. The continuation of this tendency will lead, he contends, to a dislocation of existing demands and commitments. Habermas analyses these issues, not under the heading 'legitimation crisis' (a point I shall come back to later), but under the heading 'motivation crisis'. 'I speak of a motivation crisis when the socio-cultural system changes in such a way that its output becomes dysfunctional for the state and for the system of social labor.'[9] This crisis will result in demands that the state cannot meet.

The discussion of the motivation crisis is complex. The two major patterns of motivation generated by the socio-cultural system in late capitalist societies are, according to Habermas, civil and familial-vocational privatism. Civil privatism engenders in the individual an interest in the output of the political system (steering and maintenance performances) but at a level demanding little participation. Familial-vocational privatism promotes a family-orientated behavioural pattern centred on leisure and consumption on the one hand, and a career interest orientated towards status competition on the other. Both patterns are necessary for the maintenance of the system under its present institutions. Habermas argues that these motivational bases are being systematically eroded in such a way that crisis tendencies can be discerned. This argument involves two theses: (1) that the traditions which produce these motivations are being eroded; and (2) that the logic of development of normative structures prevents a functionally equivalent replacement of eroded structures.

The motivational patterns of late capitalism are produced, Habermas suggests, by a mixture of traditional pre-capitalist elements (e.g. the old civic ethic, religious tradition) and bourgeois elements (e.g. possessive individualism and utilitarianism). Given this overlay of traditions, thesis (1) can itself by analysed into two parts: (a) that the pre-bourgeois components of motivational patterns are being eroded; and (b) that the core aspects of bourgeois ideology are likewise being undermined by social developments. Habermas acknowledges that these theses can only be offered tentatively.

The process of erosion of traditional (pre-bourgeois) world-views is argued to be an effect of the general process of rationalisation. This process results in, among other things, a loss of an interpretation of the totality of life and the increasing subjectivising and relativising of morality. With regard to thesis (1b), that the core elements of bourgeois ideology are being undermined, Habermas examines three phenomena:

achievement ideology, possessive individualism, and the orientation towards exchange value. The idea of endless competitiveness and achievement-seeking is being destroyed gradually as people lose faith in the market's capacity to distribute scarce values fairly—as the state's very intervention brings issues of distribution to the fore and, for example, the increasing level of education arouses aspirations that cannot be co-ordinated with occupational opportunity. Possessive individualism, the belief that collective goals can only be realised by private individuals acting in competitive isolation, is being undermined as the development of the state, with its contradictory functions, is (ever more) forced into socialising the costs and goals of urban life. Additionally, the orientation to exchange value is weakening as larger segments of the population—for instance, welfare clients, students, the criminal and sick, the unemployable—no longer reproduce their lives through labour for exchange value (wages), thus 'weakening the socialization effects of the market'.

The second thesis—that the logic of development of normative structures prevents a functionally equivalent replacement of eroded traditions—also has two parts. They are (a) that the remaining residues of tradition in bourgeois ideology cannot generate elements to replace those of destroyed privatism, but (b) that the remaining structures of bourgeois ideology are still relevant for motivation formation. With regard to (a), Habermas looks at three elements of the contemporary dominant cultural formation: scientism, post-auratic or post-representational art, and universalistic morality. He contends that in each of these areas the logic of development is such that the normative structures no longer promote the reproduction of privatism and that they could only do so again at the cost of a regression in social development, i.e. increased authoritarianism which suppresses conflict. In each of these areas the changing normative structures embody marked concerns with universality and critique. It is these developing concerns which undermine privatism and which are potentially threatening to the inequalities of the economic and political system.

But the undermining of privatism does not necessitate that there will be a motivation crisis. If the motivations being generated by the emerging structures are dysfunctional for the economic and political systems, one way of avoiding a crisis would be to 'uncouple' (an obscure notion in Habermas's writings) the socio-cultural system from the political-economic system so that the latter (apparently) would no longer be dependent on the former. To complete his argument Habermas must make plausible the contention that the uncoupling process has not occurred and that the remaining structures are still relevant for some type of motivation formation, i.e. thesis (2b). His claim is that evidence from studies of adolescent socialisation patterns (from Kenniston and others) and such phenomena as the students' and women's movements indicate that a new level of consciousness involving a universalistic (communicative) ethic is emerging as a functional element in motivation formation. On this basis he argues that individuals will increasingly be produced whose motivational norms will be such as to demand a rational justification of social realities. If such a justification cannot be provided by the system's legitimising mechanisms on the one hand, or bought off via distribution of value on the other, a motivation crisis is the likely outcome—the system will not find sufficient motivation for its maintenance.

Habermas's conclusion, then, is that, given its logic of crisis tendencies, organised capitalism cannot maintain its present form. If Habermas's argument is correct, then capitalism will either evolve into a kind of 'Brave New World' or it will have to overcome its underlying class contradiction. To do the latter would mean the adoption of a new principle of organisation. Such a principle would involve a universalistic morality embedded in a system of participatory democracy, i.e. an opportunity for discursive will-formation. What exact institutional form the new social formation might take Habermas does not say; nor does he say, in any detail, how the new social formation might evolve.

In the remainder of this essay, I should like to indicate a number of areas in which Habermas's formulations lead to difficulties. The areas of concern I want to single out particularly are: the relation between legitimation and motivation crises; the analysis of components of culture and social order; the boundary conditions of crisis tendencies; and questions relating to political transformation and the role of critical theory. My critical remarks have, it should be stressed, a tentative status, for Habermas's thought in each of these areas is still in the process of development.

Legitimation and motivation crises

The novelty of Habermas's conception of crisis theory lies both in his emphasis on different types of crisis tendencies and on his formulation of the idea of crisis displacement. I do not wish to question that these notions constitute a significant contribution to the understanding of social crises: the disclosure of the relation between economic, political and socio-cultural phenomena is a vital step in overcoming the limitations of economistic theories of crisis, and of theories that place a disproportionate emphasis on the role of ideas in social change. Nevertheless, I do not think that Habermas's focus on legitimation and motivation crises is satisfactory.

In the first instance, difficulties arise because the distinction between legitimation and motivation crises is, at best, obscure. Habermas's formulation of these crisis tendencies oscillates between seeing them as distinct and conceiving of them as a single set of events. The latter position is consistent with the absence of a clear differentiation between the scarce resources to which the two types of crisis are, respectively, linked—'generalised motivations' and 'action-motivating meaning'. As he elaborates them, legitimation and motivation crises are thoroughly enmeshed: a legitimation crisis is a crisis of 'generalised motivations', a crisis which depends on the undermining of traditional 'action-motivating meaning'; a motivation crisis is a crisis that issues in the collapse of mass loyalty. I believe the source of this ambiguity lies in an inadequate conception of the way societies cohere—that is, in a problematic emphasis on the centrality of shared norms and values in social integration and on the importance of 'internalisation' in the genesis of individual identity and social order.

For Habermas, social integration refers to 'the system of institutions in which speaking and acting subjects are socially related'. Social systems are conceived here as '*life-worlds* that are symbolically structured'. From this perspective one can 'thematize the normative structures (values and institutions) of a society'.[10] Events and states can be analysed from 'the point of view of their dependency on functions of social integration (in Parsons's vocabulary, integration and pattern maintenance)'.[11] A society's capacity for reproduction is directly connected, Habermas contends, to successful social integration. Disturbances of a society endanger its existence only if social integration is threatened; that is, 'when the *consensual foundations* of normative structures are so much impaired that the society becomes *anomic*'.[12] Although Habermas acknowledges the difference between dominant cultural value systems and meaning structures generated by individuals in their everyday lives when he criticises Parsons for not distinguishing 'institutional values' and 'motivational forces', he himself fails to utilise these distinctions adequately in his substantive analysis of capitalism.

It is crucial to preserve at all levels of social theory the distinction between dominant normative prescriptions—those involved in procuring legitimation—and the 'frames of meaning' and motives of people in society. Any theory that blurs the boundaries between these, as does Habermas's crisis theory, needs to be regarded with scepticism. For, as I argue below, social integration, when tied to the generation of a shared sense of 'the worthiness of a political order to be recognised' (legitimacy), is not a necessary condition for every relatively stable society. Clearly, some groups have to be normatively integrated into the governing political culture to ensure a society's reproduction. But what matters most is not the moral approval of the majority of a society's members—although this will sometimes be forthcoming, for instance during wars—but the approval of the dominant groups. Among the latter, it is the politically powerful and mobilised, including the state's personnel, that are particularly important for the continued existence of a social system. Habermas does acknowledge this on some occasions, but he does not pursue its many implications. His failure to do so can be explained, I think, by his use of 'unreconstructed' systems concepts and assumptions. Many ideas and assumptions from systems theory—in combination with concepts from action theory, structuralism and genetic structuralism—are intermingled in his work in a manner which is often unsatisfactory and difficult to disentangle. These notions do not provide a suitable framework for the analysis of social cohesion and legitimation: for theories concerned with social stability must be developed without ties to the 'internalised value-norm-moral consensus theorem' and its residues. What is required here is a more adequate theory of the production and reproduction of action.

Components of culture and social order

The notion of legitimation crisis presupposes that the motivation of the mass of the population was at one time constituted to a significant extent by the normative structures established by powerful groups.[13] But Habermas, in my view, overestimates the degree to which one may consider the individual as having been integrated into society, as well as the degree to which bourgeois ideology has been eroded and the extent to which contemporary society is threatened by a 'legitimation/motivation' crisis.

If one examines the substantial number of studies debating the nature of the social cohesion of capitalist societies, one thing emerges with clarity: patterns of consciousness, especially class consciousness, vary across and within specific cultures and countries. To the extent that generalisations can be made, they must take account of 'the lack of consensus' about norms, values and beliefs (excepting perhaps a general adherence to nationalism). Moreover, they must recognise that a 'dual consciousness' is often expressed in communities and work-places. This implies a quite radical interpretation of many everyday events—often linking dissatisfactions with divisions between the 'rich and poor', the 'rulers and ruled'—and a relatively 'conservative' (defined below), privatistic interest in dominant political parties and processes. Many institutions and processes are perceived and hypostatised as 'natural', 'the way things have been and always will be'; but the language used to express and account for immediate needs and their frustration often reveals a marked penetration of ideology or dominant interpretative systems.

Although there is evidence of dissensus and various levels of class-consciousness, it is clear, none the less, that this rarely constitutes revolutionary consciousness. There is a fairly widespread 'conservatism' about conventional political processes; that is, seeming compliance to dominant ideas, a high interest in the system's output combined with low interest in political input (participation), and no coherent conception of an alternative to the existing order. The question is: What does this 'conservatism' mean? What does it entail? Does it reflect normative integration, depoliticisation, a combination of these, or something different again?

While Habermas argues that the legitimacy of the political order of capitalist society is related to 'the social-integrative preservation of a normatively determined social identity', I would argue that stability is related to the 'decentring' or fragmentation of culture, the atomisation of people's experiences of the social world. Fragmentation acts as a barrier to a coherent conception of the social totality—the structure of social practices and possibilities. The political order is acknowledged not because it is regarded as 'worthy' but because of the adoption of an instrumental attitude towards it; compliance most often comprises pragmatic acquiescence to the status quo. In certain places in his writings Habermas appears to recognise the importance of these points, but he does not accommodate them adequately.[14] By presupposing that the cultural system once generated a large stock of unquestioned values and norms—values which are now regarded as threatened by increased state intervention—his analysis detracts from a systematic appraisal of the process of 'atomisation' and of 'pragmatic' adaptation. I should like to discuss briefly the importance of the latter phenomena by indicating the significance of precisely those things that are least considered by Habermas—they include the social and technical division of labour (social and occupational hierarchies, the splits between unskilled and skilled and physical and mental labour), the organisation of work relations (relations between trade unions, management and state), and the 'culture industry' (the creation of a system of pseudo-gratifications).

Working-class consciousness, along with the consciousness of other social classes and groups, is impregnated by the work process. Analyses by Marcuse, as early as 1941, and more recently by Braverman, point to the significance of understanding the way in which the rationalisation and standardisation of production fragments tasks.[15] As tasks become increasingly mechanised, there are fewer and fewer chances for mental and reflective labour. Work experiences are increasingly differentiated. Knowledge of the total work process is hard to come by and rarely available, particularly for those on the shop floor. The majority of occupations (despite the possibility of a greater exchange of functions) tend to become atomised, isolated units, which *seem* to require for their cohesion 'co-ordination and management from above'. With the development of the capitalist division of labour, knowledge and control of the whole work process are ever more absent from daily work situations. Centralised control mechanisms and private and public bureaucracies then appear as agencies which are necessary for, and guarantee, 'a rational course and order'.[16] With the fragmentation of tasks and knowledge, the identity of social classes is threatened. The social relations which condition these processes are reified: they become ever harder to grasp.

A number of factors, have, furthermore, conjoined to reduce the receptivity of many people to critical thinking. Aronowitz has pointed to the way the debilitating impact of the technical division of labour is compounded not only by social divisions based on ethnicity, race and sex, but also by 'the credential routes to higher occupations, the seniority system as a basis for promotion, the classification of jobs grounded in arbitrary distinctions which have no basis in job content or skill level'.[17] Social and occupational hierarchies threaten attempts to create solidarity. Moreover, organised opposition is all too often ineffective because the representatives of these forces—although they have not lost the 'title of opposition'—are vulnerable to incorporation. This has been the fate of the trade-union movement in many countries. Its organisations have been transformed into mass organisations with highly bureaucratised leadership structures, concentrating on 'economistic' issues and acting as barriers to the expression of rank-and-file protest about, among other things, lack of control of the work process. Although the exact effects of these processes constitute an empirical question, there are strong reasons to believe that they further remove from the mass of people a chance to understand and affect the institutions that impinge upon their lives.

Factors such as differentiated wage structures, permanent inflation, crisis in government finances and uneven economic development—factors which disperse the effects of economic crisis, as Habermas points out, on to 'quasi-groups', consumers, the elderly, the sick, schoolchildren—are all part of a complex series which combine to make the fronts of class opposition repeatedly fragmented, less comprehensible. The 'culture industry', furthermore, reinforces this state of affairs. The Frankfurt School's analysis indicates the potency of the system of pseudo-gratifications—diversions and distractions—which the culture industry generates. As Adorno showed in study after study, while the culture industry offers a temporary escape from the responsibilities and drudgery of everyday life, it reinforces the structure of the world people seek to avoid: it strengthens the belief that misfortunes and deprivations are due to natural causes or chance, thus promoting a sense of fatalism and dependence.[18]

The analysis above is, of course, incomplete and, in many ways, partial and one-sided. The point, however, is to stress the significance of a complex of institutions and developments which seemingly fragment society and people's comprehension of it. Reference to these processes explains, I believe, the research findings which indicate that many people do not have a very coherent set of beliefs, norms and values, as well as the 'conservative' component of dual consciousness. The structural conditions of work and of many other activities atomises individuals' experience and 'draws off', and/or fails to allow access to, knowledge of the work process as a whole and of the organisational principles of society. This constitutes a crucial barrier to knowledge of dominant trends in the social totality on the one hand, and to potential solidarity on the other. The 'conservative' aspects of dual consciousness comprise in many cases a mixture of pragmatic acquiescence to existing institutions and false consciousness. Pragmatic acquiescence is involved because all men and women, who seek the maintenance of their own lives, have to act 'rationally'; that is, they have to act 'according to the standards which insure the functioning of the apparatus'.[19] Few alternatives to the status quo are perceived, and it is recognised that participation in the status quo is necessary for comfort and security. False consciousness is involved (as Habermas recognises) because the asymmetrical distribution of power ('transformative capacity') in contemporary society is mobilised (albeit often unintentionally) to prevent working people from properly understanding the reality they experience. Frames of meaning often utilised to articulate needs and account for everyday life frequently diverge from the interpretative schemes employed to make sense of traditional political institutions.

Modern capitalist society's stability is linked, I believe, to this state of affairs—to what has been aptly referred to as the 'lack of consensus' in the crucial intersection of concrete daily experiences and the often confused values and interpretative schemes articulated in relation to dominant institutions. Stability is dependent on the atomisation or 'decentring' of knowledge of work and politics. I suspect that modern society has never been legitimated by the mass of the population. This does not mean, of course, that the political and economic order is permanently vulnerable to disintegration or revolution. The reasons for this should be apparent; the order does not depend for its reproduction on strongly shared normative ideals.

It is because of considerations such as these that I do not find convincing Habermas's view that civil and familial privatism are dependent for their efficacy on pre-capitalist traditions. A preoccupation with one's own 'lot in life', with the fulfilment of one's own needs, is both a product of, and an adaptive mechanism to, contemporary society. The social and technical division of labour, in a society orientated towards the maximisation of profit, is, it seems, a sufficient condition for atomisation, isolation and privatism. It is for these reasons also that I do not find convincing Habermas's belief that the forces undermining achievement ideology, the orientation to exchange, etc., have further delegitimising effects. A more plausible position is that, in the context of an atomised society, changes of this kind enhance an already widespread scepticism about the virtue of existing political institutions, a cynicism and a pragmatic/instrumental orientation. Furthermore, at the empirical level there is no ready evidence to support Habermas's contention of the potentially imminent realisation of a communicative ethics—the highest stage of the human being's 'inner cognitive logic'. Contemporary changes in normative structures have, at best, a very ambiguous relationship to discursive will-formation, universality and critique. On the available evidence (and in light of there being no substantial evidence in his own work), there does not seem to be a sufficient basis to locate the emergence of a principle of organisation of a 'post-modern' society.

But to disagree with Habermas's conception of the vulnerability of contemporary Western society is not to deny, of course, that the system is faced with severe challenges—challenges to the basis on which rights and obligations are structured. The question to ask, however, is not under what conditions will there be a legitimation crisis (although, it must be added, this question remains relevant to the state's personnel and to dominant groups generally), but under what conditions can the 'cognitive penetration' of the order be radically extended? Or, to put the question in the terminology used hitherto, under what conditions can pragmatic, dual, fragmented consciousness be overcome and a grasp of the social totality (the organisational principles determining the allocation of 'value' and 'meaning' and alternatives to them) be rendered possible? Answers to this question depend less, I believe, on factors affecting social identity and more on economic and political crisis tendencies in capitalism. The issues discussed below are only some of those that require analysis; they are *not* intended as a direct response to the question just raised.

The boundary conditions of system crises

System crises (economic and rationality) can, on Habermas's account, be potentially contained (although it does not follow that they will be). Containment occurs, however, only at the cost of increasing legitimation pressures on the state: the state is the interface at which the tensions of both system integration and social integration meet. Habermas's argument rests, of course, on the claim that organised capitalism can control its potential system crises. Can this claim be supported?

Most of Habermas's remarks on system crises centre upon considerations of the nation-state; that is, the focus is on the changing relation between the state and economy within an ideal-typical capitalist country. His discussion of past and present economic tendencies pays little, if any, attention to developments of international capitalism. He raises important considerations in connection with the law of value; but the referent and context is usually that of the nation-state. It is crucially important to explore the development of capitalism in one country in the context of international political economy. The capitalist world was created in dependence on an international market and is ever more dependent on international trade. Before one can conclude that economic crises can be contained (on either a national or an international level), the relationship between economic crises in the nation-state and crisis tendencies in the international market must be better analysed and explained. These issues deserve a much more substantial treatment than Habermas gives them. Without an analysis of them, Habermas's conception of the logic of crisis development can be questioned, for the political-economic constraints on capitalist development appear much less open to control and manipulation than Habermas suggests.

In his recent work on the development of the modern state, Poggi has emphasised the significance of 'the highly contingent, inherently dangerous' nature of the international system of nation-states.[20] Wallerstein's analysis of the 'European world economy' indicates the importance of comprehending economic interconnections between nation-states which are beyond the control of any one such state.[21] Disproportionate economic development and uneven development generally within and between advanced industrial societies and Third World countries have serious implications for any conception of the logic or dynamic of crisis—implications which should centre attention on the primacy of struggles over who is on the centre and periphery, who controls what resources, and over a host of other basic differences in material interests.

Furthermore, although Habermas recognises the significance of analysing different types of state activity, the nature of crisis management, and the organisational logic (rationality) of the administrative apparatus, he does not, as far as I know, stress the need for a differentiated analysis of state forms, party structures and the relation of government and party structures to socio-economic structure. This also has consequences for an analysis of crisis tendencies; for it is precisely these things, analysed in the context of international conditions and pressures, that have been shown to be crucial determinants in key cases of political and 'social-revolutionary' crisis. No analytic account of crisis tendencies can claim completeness without examining these phenomena.

Political transformation and critical theory

One of the most distinctive features of the Marxist tradition—a tradition with which Habermas closely identifies—is a concern to draw from an examination of 'what exists' an account of 'what exists in possibility'. Inquiry into historical conditions and processes is linked to a desire to reveal political potentialities. In the third and final part of *Legitimation Crisis,* Habermas focuses directly on the problem of analysing potentiality. He argues that a critique of ideology, concerned both with the existing pattern of distorted communication and with how things could be otherwise, must take as its starting-point the 'model of the suppression of generalizable interests'.[22] The model permits a comparison of the normative structures of a society with those which hypothetically would be the case if norms were arrived at, *ceteris paribus,* discursively. Linked to a number of assumptions about the conditions under which conflict breaks out, the model establishes the basis for what Habermas calls 'the advocacy role' of critical theory.

The advocacy role consists in 'ascertaining generalizable, though nevertheless suppressed, interests in a representatively simulated discourse between groups that are differentiated . . . from one another by an articulated, or at least virtual, opposition of interests'.[23] Using such indicators of potential conflict as discrepancies between claims and demands, and politically permitted levels of satisfaction, one can, Habermas maintains, indicate the nature of ideological repression and the level of generalisable interests possible at a given historical point. In the final analysis 'the theory serves to enlighten its addressees about the position which they occupy in an antagonistic social system and about the interests of which they could become conscious as objectively their own'.[24]

The following questions—frequently put to those in the tradition of critical theory—are pertinent: To whom is critical theory addressed? How, in any concrete situation, can critical theory be applied? Who is to be the instigator or promoter of enlightenment? It is clear that a discussion of these issues is important if Habermas is to argue successfully that the organisation of enlightenment at the social level can be fashioned after critical theory. Yet, as these issues are only discussed in Habermas's writings at a most abstract level, it is difficult to draw any specific political conclusions from his advocacy model and crisis argument. Within the terms of reference of his work on modern capitalist societies we remain very much in the dark as to political processes and events. The practical implications of his theory are left undeveloped.

Habermas might reply to this charge by saying that at the present time it is extremely difficult to draw any definite political conclusions from the state of contemporary advanced capitalist countries. He might say, moreover, that while aspects of his analysis undermine the traditional faith of orthodox Marxists, other aspects suggest the importance of social struggles over gender, race, ecology and bureaucracy, as well as over the nature and quantity of state goods and services and over economistic issues. With both of these points I would agree. However, in the context of what seems to be widespread scepticism (or cynicism) about politics—understood as traditional party politics—and the success of 'cold war' attitudes (and, of course, Stalinism itself) in discrediting socialist ideals, this does not seem enough. There is a need, greater than ever I believe, to establish the credibility of socialism, to develop concrete proposals for alternative ways of organising society and to show how these can be connected to wants and demands that crystallise in people's experience of dominant social relations. In a fascinating interview for *Rinascita*, the weekly journal of the Italian Communist Party, Habermas himself appears to express sympathy for this enterprise. But it is hard to see how his own investigations of advanced capitalism connect in a direct way with this project.

Notes

1. *TRS,* p. 101.
2. Ibid, p. 105.
3. See *LC,* part II.
4. Cf., for example, James O'Connor, *The Fiscal Crisis of the State* (New York: St. Martin's Press, 1973): Andrew Schonfield, *Modern Capitalism* (London: Oxford University Press, 1965); and the work of Claus Offe on the capitalist state, e.g. 'Political Authority and Class Structure', in *Critical Sociology,* ed. P. Connerton (Harmondsworth: Penguin, 1976) pp. 388–421.
5. *LC,* p. 49.

6. Ibid, pp. 49–50.
7. Ibid, p. 69.
8. Ibid, p. 73.
9. Ibid, p. 75.
10. Ibid, p. 4. By contrast, Habermas speaks of system integration 'with a view to the specific steering-performances of a self-regulated *system*. Social systems are considered here from the point of view of their capacity to maintain their boundaries and their continued existence by mastering the complexity of an inconstant environment' (ibid, p. 4). Both perspectives, 'life-world' and 'system' are, Habermas stresses, important.
11. Ibid, pp. 4–5.
12. Ibid, p. 3 (my emphasis).
13. Habermas argues that with the development of the liberal-capitalist social formation the economic sub-system took over certain socially integrative tasks, i.e. integration was accomplished in part through exchange relations. But although he emphasises the importance of understanding the ways in which social integration achieved through norms and values is replaced with a system integration operating through exchange (and the ideology of the exchange of equivalents), he also emphasises how the loyalty and support of the proletariat to the political order is dependent upon pre-capitalist traditions. See *LC*, pp. 20–6; and 'Legitimation Problems in the Modern State', in *CES*, p. 190.
14. See Habermas's early work, especially *Toward A Rational Society* and *Strukturwandel der Öffentlichkeit*, for important analyses of the expansion of instrumental reason into everyday life. *Toward a Rational Society* is a considerable aid to understanding the impersonal nature of domination.
15. Cf. Herbert Marcuse, 'Some Social Implications of Modern Technology', *Studies in Philosophy and Social Science*, 9 (1941); and Harry Braverman, *Labor and Monopoly Capital: the Degradation of Work in the Twentieth Century* (New York: Monthly Review Press, 1974).
16. Marcuse, 'Some Social Implications of Modern Technology', pp. 430–1.
17. Stanley Aronowitz, *False Promises: the Shaping of American Working Class Consciousness* (New York: McGraw-Hill, 1973) p. 408. Although Aronowitz focuses on factors that have affected the American working class, his analysis has more general implications.
18. For a more detailed analysis of Adorno's views see my *Introduction to Critical Theory: Horkheimer to Habermas* (London: Hutchinson, 1980) ch. 3.
19. Marcuse, 'Some Social Implications of Modern Technology'. p. 424.
20. Gianfranco Poggi. *The Development of the Modern State: A Sociological Introduction* (London: Hutchinson, 1978) ch. 5.
21. Immanuel Wallerstein, *The Modern World-System* (New York: Academic Press, 1974). Habermas recognises the importance of this issue for understanding 'the *external aspect* of the new [modern] state structures', but he does not explicate their relevance for the logic of crisis tendencies.
22. See *LC*, pp. 111–17.
23. Ibid, p. 117.
24. *TP*, p. 32 (translation modified).

Index